Autodesk Fusion 360 For Beginners (November 2025)

Tutorial Books

For resource files contact us at

Online.books999@gmail.com

Table of Contents

Introduction

Welcome to *Autodesk Fusion 360 For Beginners* book. This book is written to assist students, designers, and engineering professionals in designing 3D models. It covers the essential features and functionalities of Autodesk Fusion 360 using relevant examples and exercises.

This book is written for new users, who can use it as a self-study resource to learn Autodesk Fusion 360. In addition, experienced users can also use it as a reference. The focus of this book is part modelling, assemblies, and drawings.

Topics covered in this Book

- Chapter 1, "Getting Started with Autodesk Fusion 360," gives an introduction to Autodesk Fusion. The user interface and terminology are discussed in this chapter.
- Chapter 2, "Sketch Techniques," explores the sketching commands in Autodesk Fusion. You will learn to create parametric sketches.
- Chapter 3, "Extrude and Revolve features," teaches you to create basic 3D geometry using the Extrude and Revolve commands.
- Chapter 4, "Placed Features," covers the features which can be created without using sketches.
- Chapter 5, "Patterned Geometry," explores the commands to create patterned and mirrored geometry.
- Chapter 6, "Sweep Features," covers the commands to create swept and helical features.
- Chapter 7, "Loft Features," covers the Loft command and its core features.
- Chapter 8, "Additional Features and Multibody Parts," covers additional commands to create complex geometry. In addition, the multibody parts are also covered.
- Chapter 9, "Modifying Parts," explores the commands and techniques to modify the part geometry.
- Chapter 10, "Assemblies," explains you to create assemblies using the bottom-up and top-down design approaches.
- Chapter 11, "Drawings," covers how to create 2D drawings from 3D parts and assemblies

Chapter 1: Getting Started with Autodesk Fusion 360

Introduction to Autodesk Fusion 360

Autodesk Fusion 360 is a cloud-based CAD application. It is a parametric and feature-based system that allows you to create 3D parts, assemblies, and 2D drawings. In addition to that, you can perform engineering analysis and simulate manufacturing operations. The design process in Autodesk Fusion 360 is shown below.

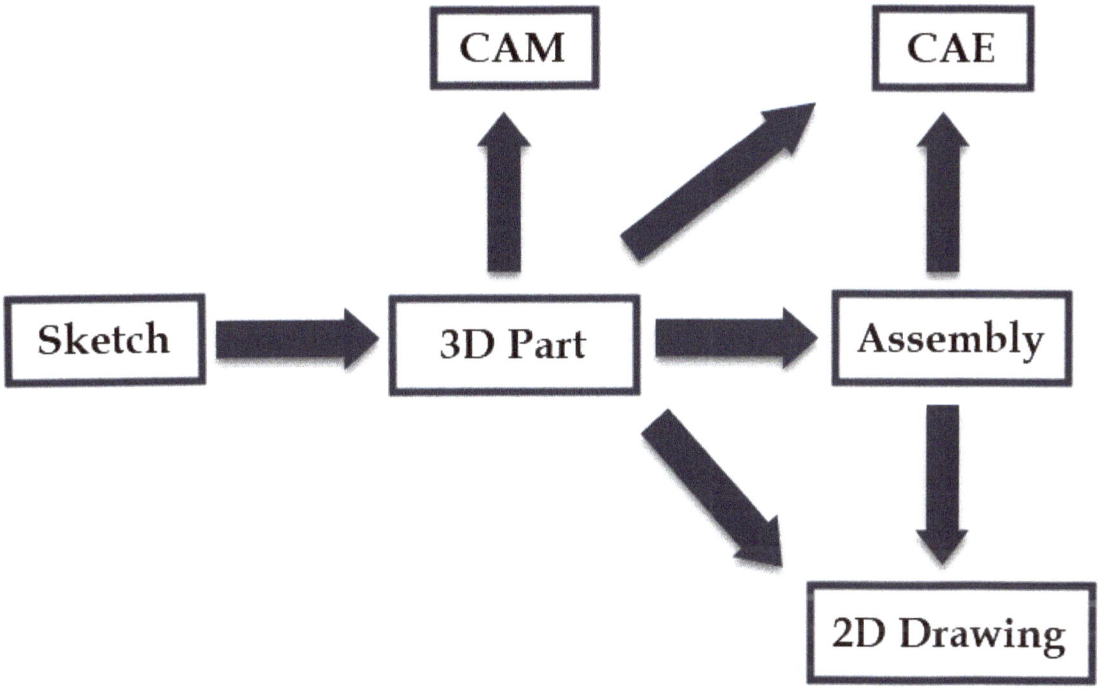

In Autodesk Fusion 360, everything is controlled by parameters, dimensions, or constraints. For example, if you want to change the position of the hole shown in the figure, you need to change the dimension or relation that controls its position.

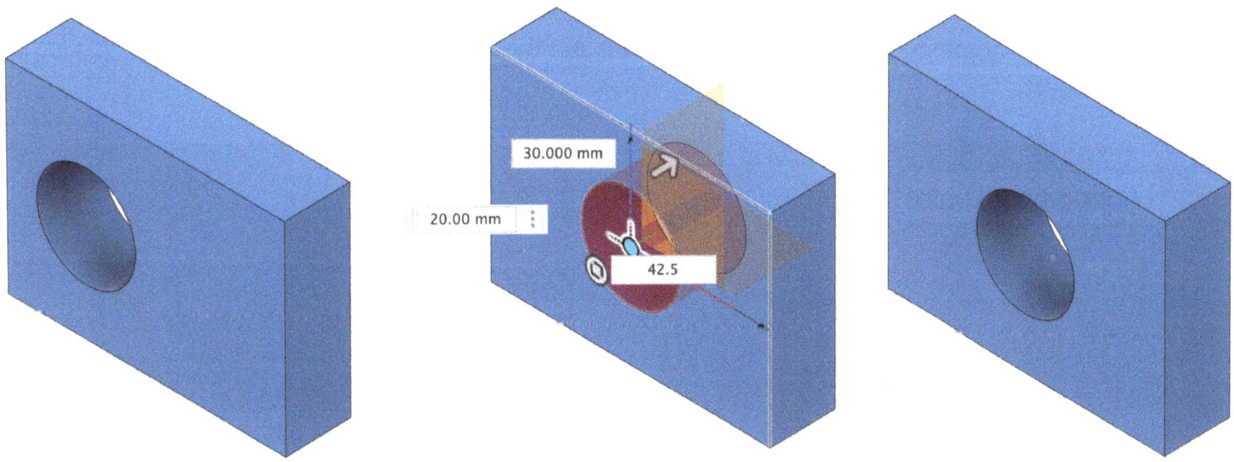

The parameters and constraints that you set up allow you to have control over the design intent. The design intent describes the way your 3D model will behave when you apply dimensions and constraints to it. For example, if you want to position the hole at the center of the block, one way is to add dimensions between the hole and the adjacent edges. However, when you change the size of the block, the hole will not be at the center.

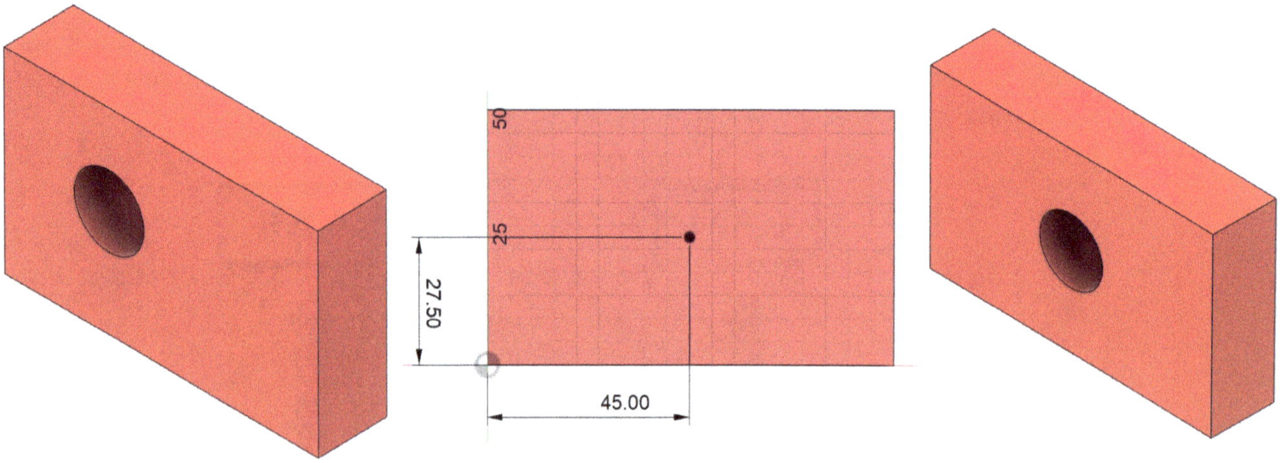

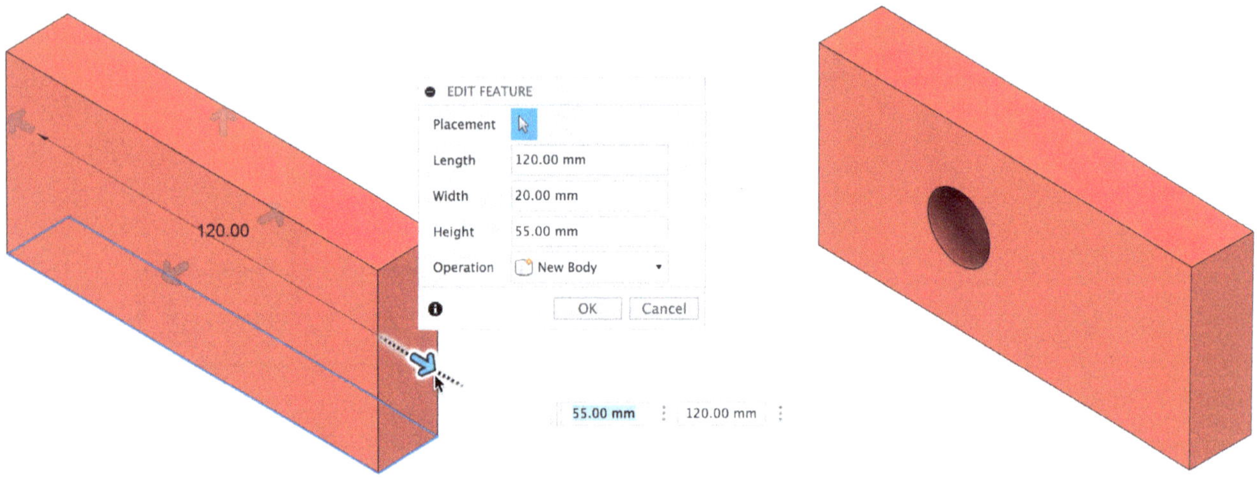

You can make the hole to be at the center, even if the size of the block changes. To do this, right click on the sketch used to create the hole and select **Edit Sketch**. Next, delete the dimensions and create a diagonal construction line. Apply the Midpoint constraint between the hole point and the diagonal construction line. Next, click **Finish Sketch** on the toolbar.

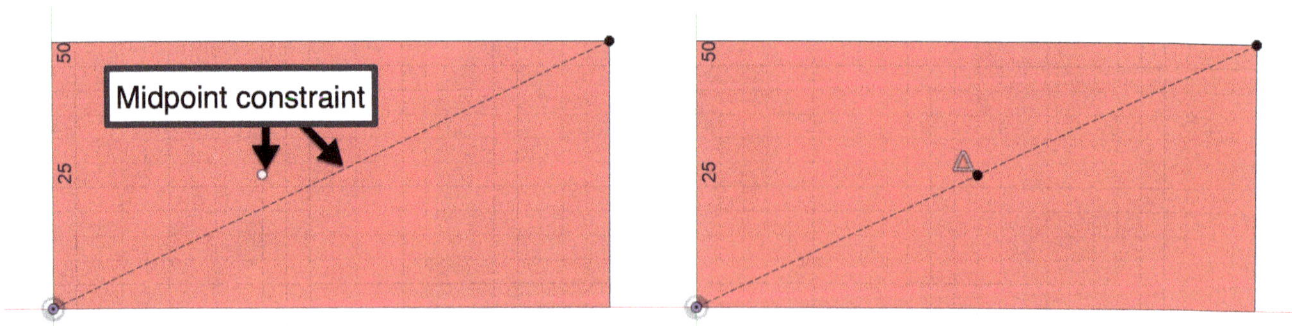

Now, even if you change the size of the block, the hole will always remain at the center.

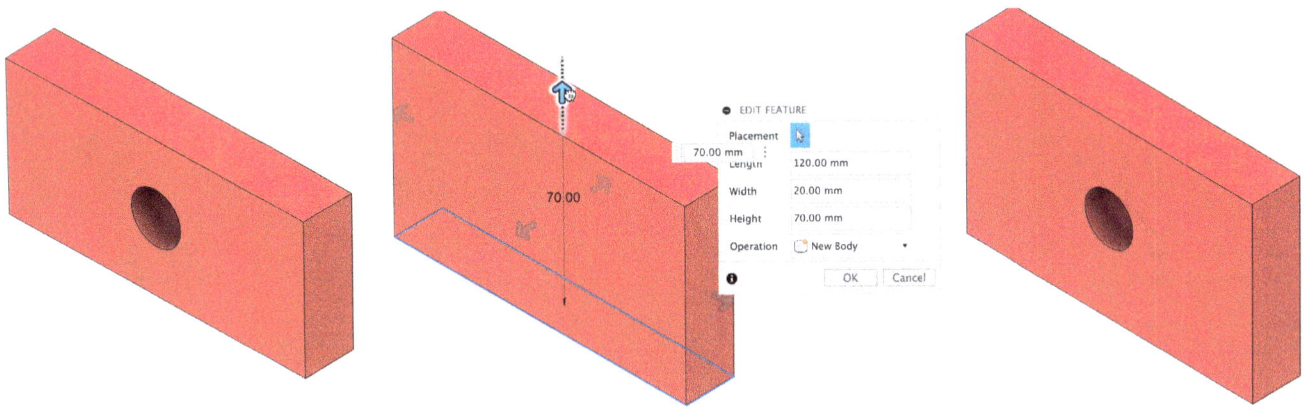

Starting Autodesk Fusion 360

To start **Autodesk Fusion 360**, click the **Autodesk Fusion 360** icon on your computer screen. An untitled design file will appear on the screen. You can change the working units of the file. To do this, expand the **Document Settings** in the **Browser window**, and place the cursor on the **Change Active Units** icon. Click the **Change Active Units** icon and select **Unit Type** and click **OK**.

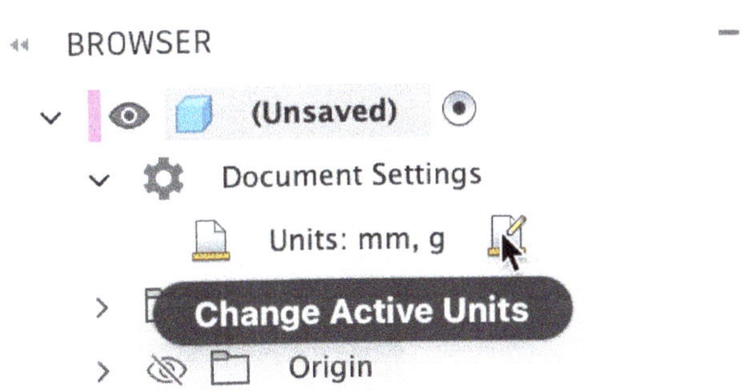

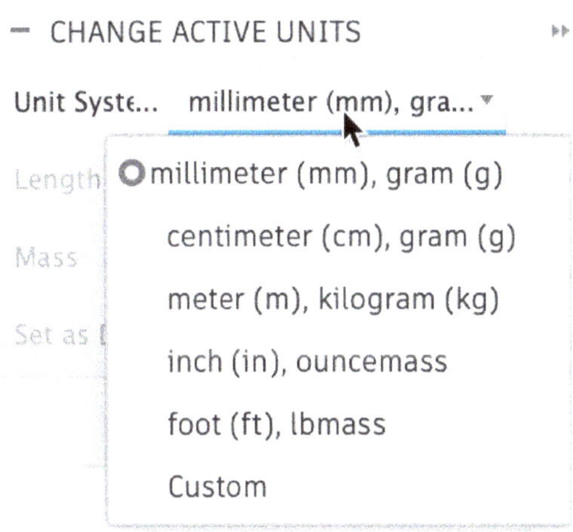

User Interface

The following image shows the **Autodesk Fusion 360** application window.

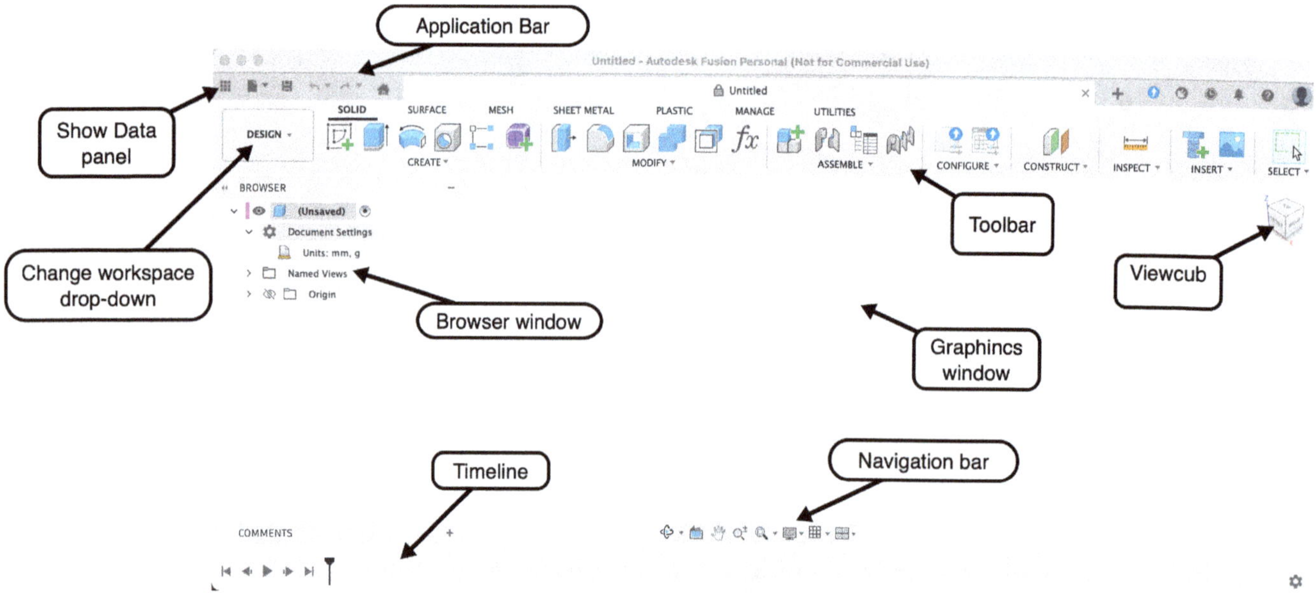

Workspaces in Autodesk Fusion 360

There are seven main workspaces available in Autodesk Fusion: **Design**, **Generative Design**, **Render**, **Animation**, **Simulation**, **Manufacturing**, and **Drawing**.

Design Workspace

This workspace has all the commands to create 3D part models and assemblies. In this workspace, the Timeline stores every feature or sketch that you create. You can always go back and edit the feature or sketch. It has the toolbar located at the top of the screen. The toolbar has tabs. The tabs such as **Solid**, **Surface**, **Sheet Metal,** and **Utilities** consist of commands, which are grouped based on their usage.

The **Solid** tab has all the commands to create solid models.

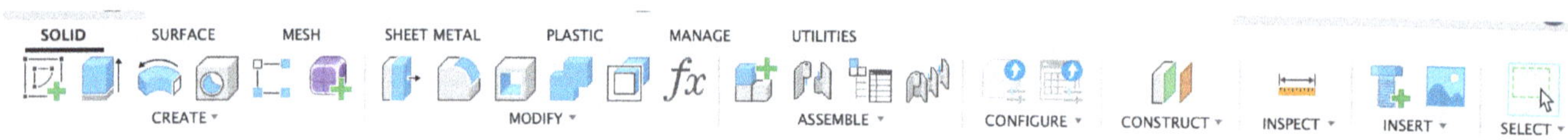

The **Surface** tab has all the commands to create surfaces.

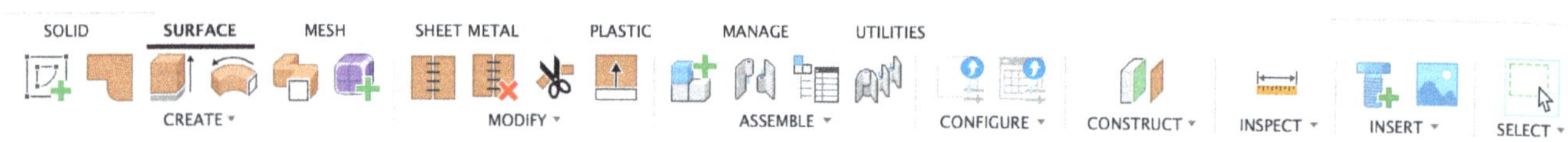

The **Sheet Metal** tab has to create sheet metal parts.

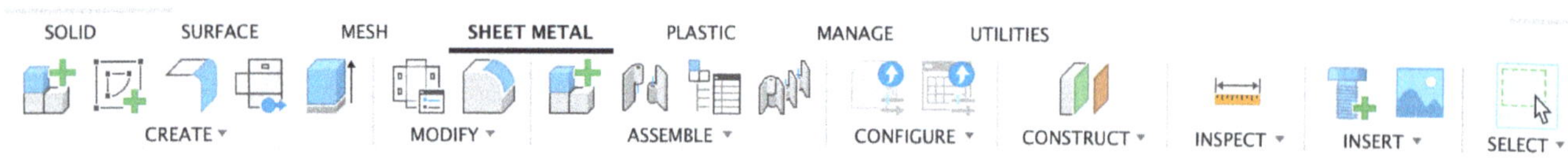

The **Utilities** tab has some advanced commands, which will help you to 3D print, automate processes, add external apps, and inspect the model.

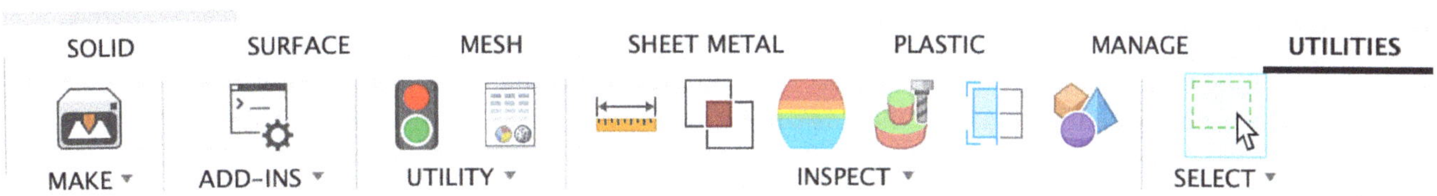

Render Workspace

This workspace is used to apply colors, materials, scenes, and lighting to model, and then create a photorealistic image.

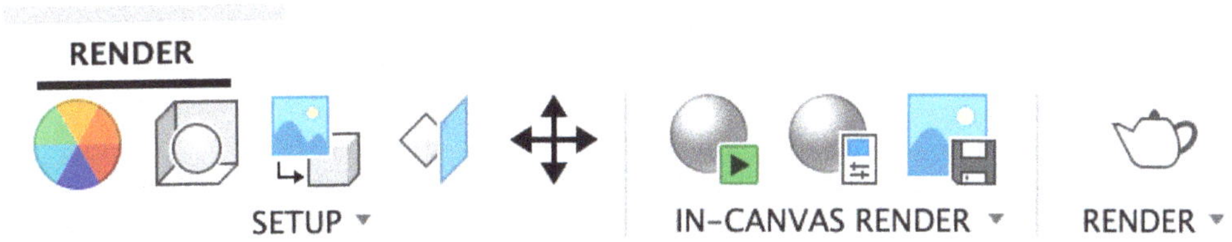

Drawing Workspace

This workspace has all the commands to generate 2D drawings of parts and assemblies.

Animation Workspace

This workspace has all the commands to create an animation of the design file.

Manufacturing Workspace

This workspace has commands to simulate the manufacturing operations, and then generate the tool paths.

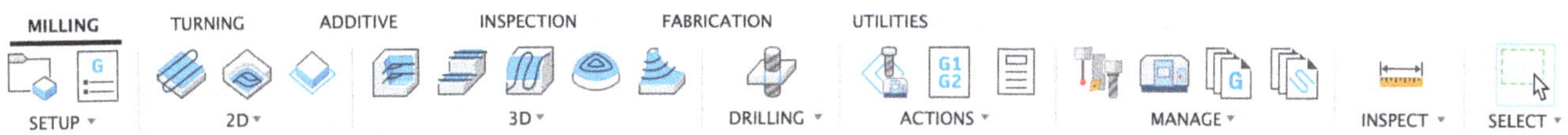

Simulation Workspace

This workspace has commands to perform various types of engineering analysis on the model.

The other components of the user interface are discussed next.

Application bar

This is located at the top of the window. It consists of commonly used commands such as **New**, **Save**, **Open**, and so on. You can select these commands from the **File** drop-down.

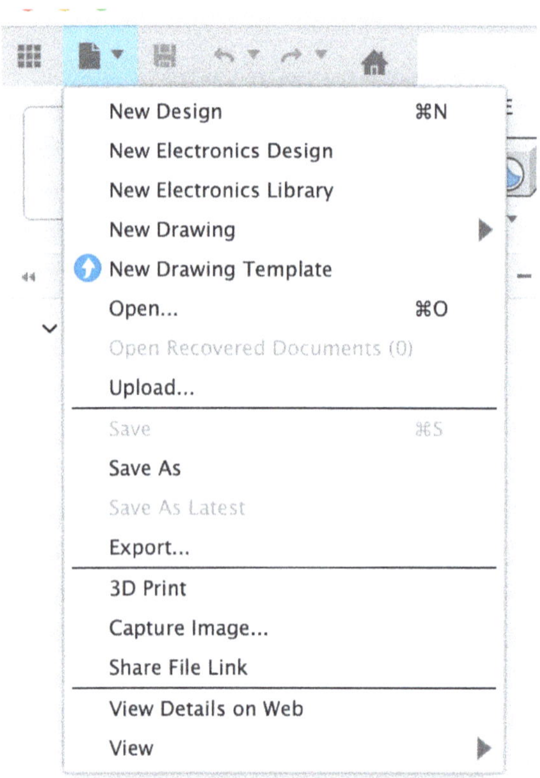

Graphics Window

The graphics window is the blank space located below the toolbar. You can draw sketches and create 3D geometry in the Graphics window. The left corner of the graphics window has a **Browser window**. Using the **Browser window**, you can turn ON/OFF the bodies, planes, and sketches of the 3D model.

Timeline

The timeline is located at the bottom of the **Autodesk Fusion 360** window. It captures the design history of the model. You can edit the sketches and features of the model using the timeline. In addition to that, you can play the sequence in which the features are created.

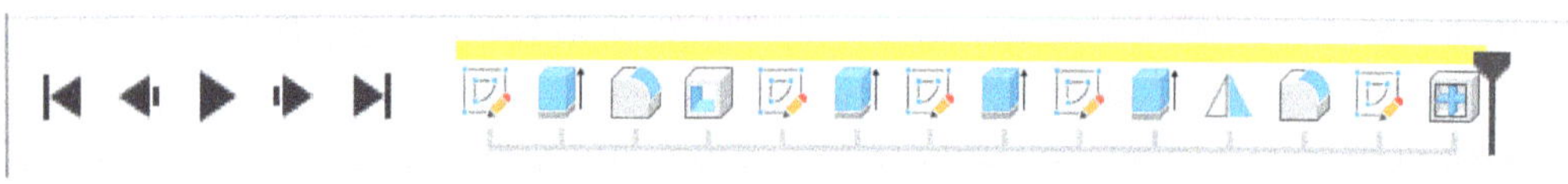

If you do not want to capture the design history, click the gear icon located at the right side of the Timeline and select the **Change to Direct Modeling** option. Next, click **Delete Parametric History**; the Timeline is hidden. However, if you want to capture the design history, right click on the **Document Settings** option and select **Change to Parametric Modeling.**

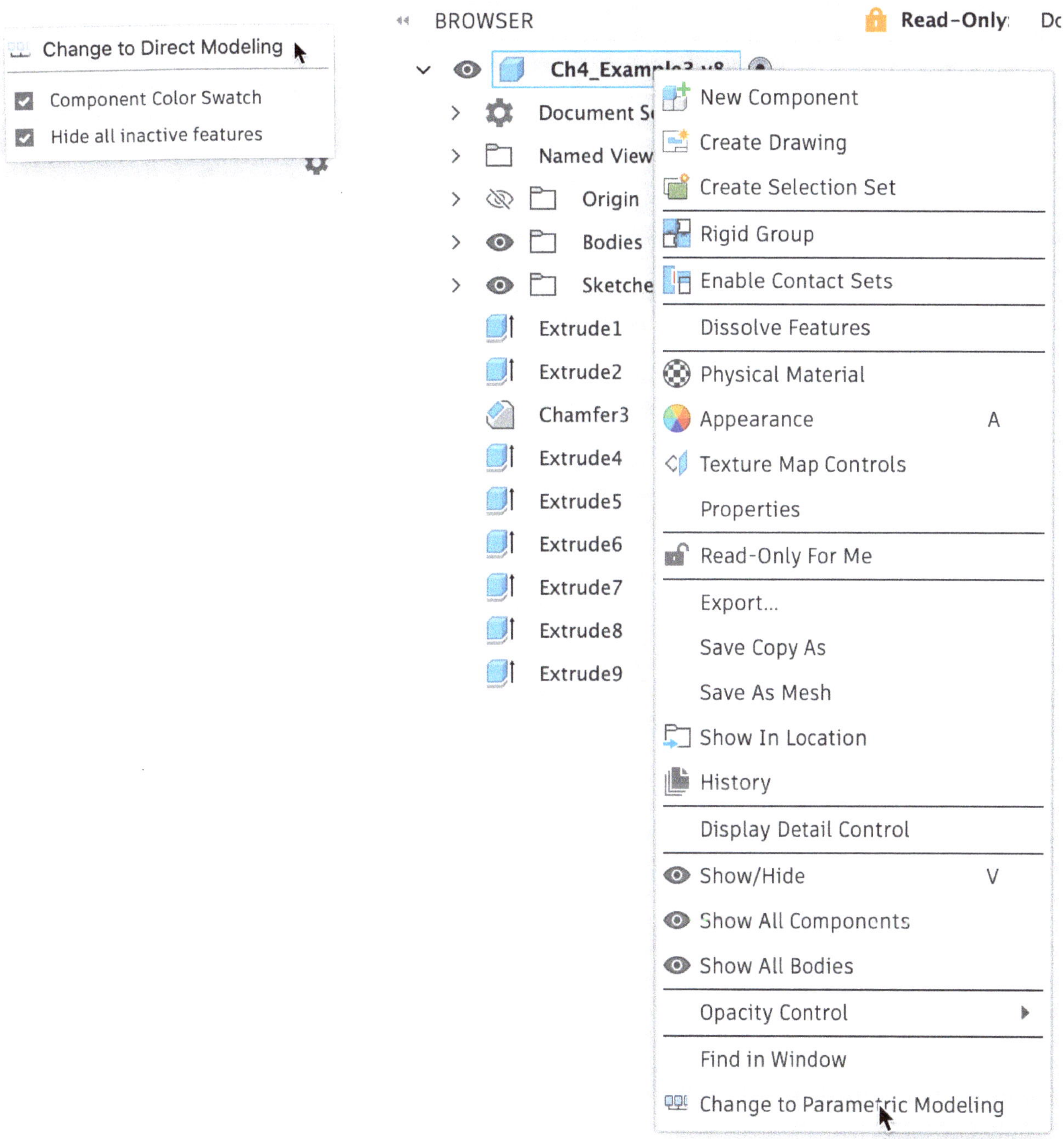

Comments pane

The **Comments** pane is located at the bottom left corner of the window and is used to add comments to the design. Click the **Plus** icon to expand it. Notice the three options on the **Comments** pane: **Capture an image**, **Comment on an Object,** and **Comment on a point**. You can add comments to the design by using any one of these options.

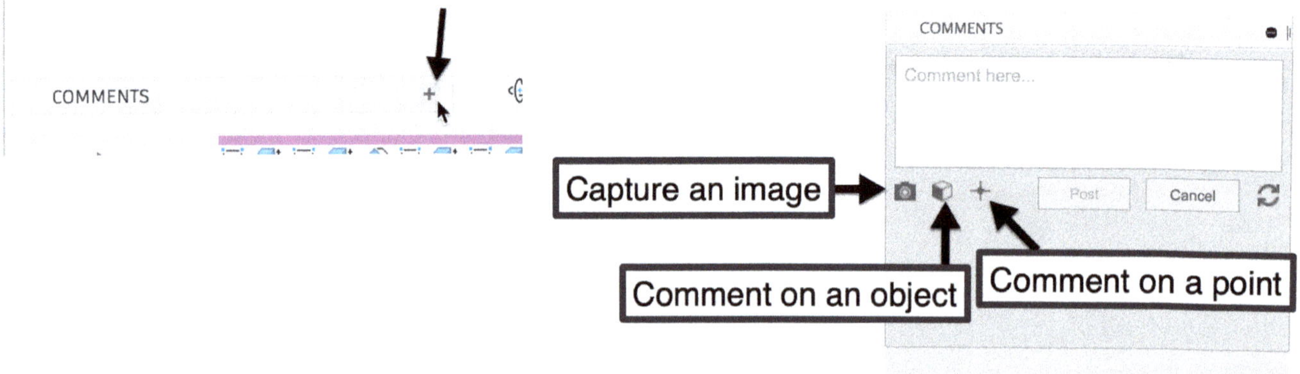

Navigation Bar

This is located at the bottom of the window. It contains the tools to zoom, orbit, pan, or look at the face of the model. It also has display settings, grid and snap, and viewports options.

View Cube

It is located at the top right corner of the graphics window and is used to set the view orientation of the model.

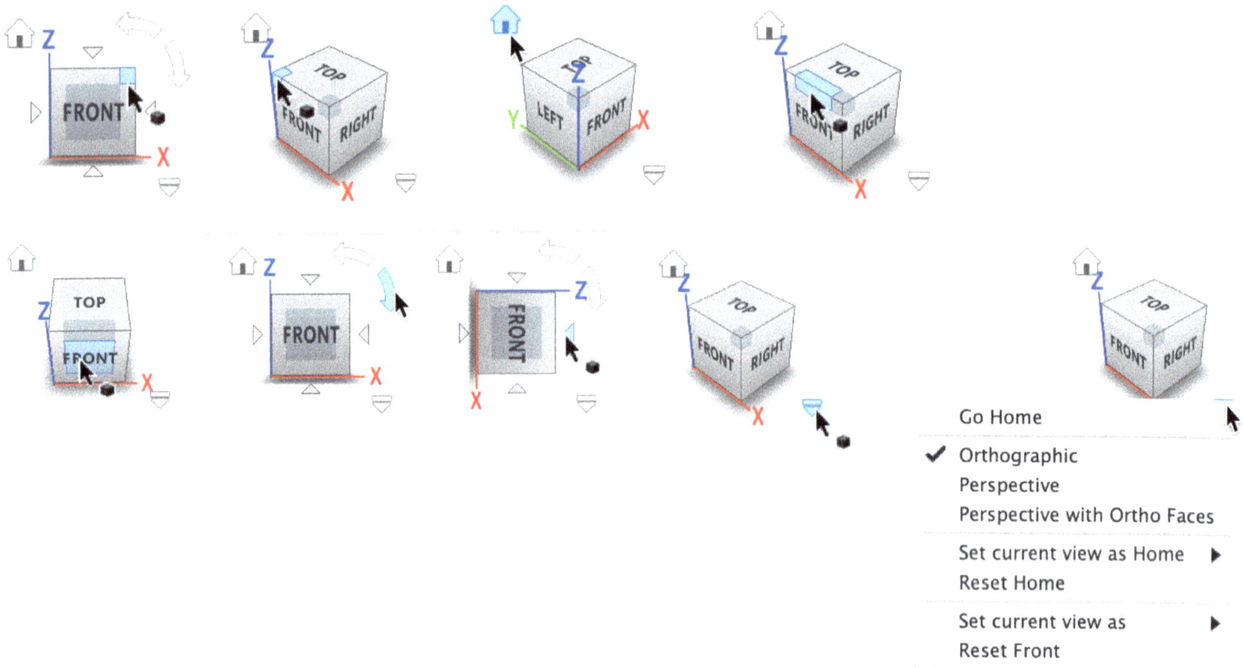

Dialogs

Dialogs are part of the Autodesk Fusion 360 user interface. Using a dialog, you can easily specify many settings and options. Various components of a dialog are shown below.

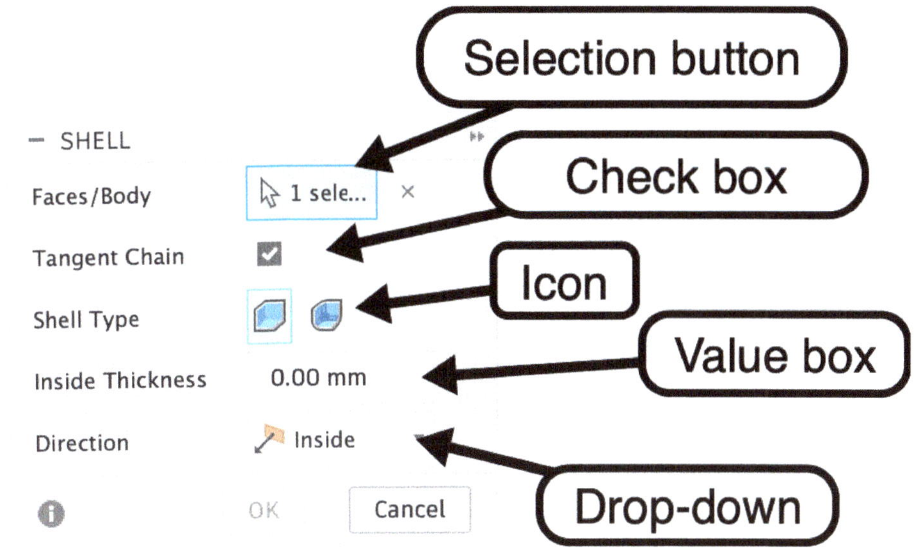

Shortcut and Marking Menus

Shortcut Menus are displayed when you right-click on the graphics window. Autodesk Fusion 360 provides various shortcut menus in order to help you access some options very easily and quickly. The options in shortcut menus vary based on the workspace. Marking Menu provides you with another way of activating commands. You can display Marking Menu by clicking the right mouse button. A Marking Menu has various commands arranged in a radial manner.

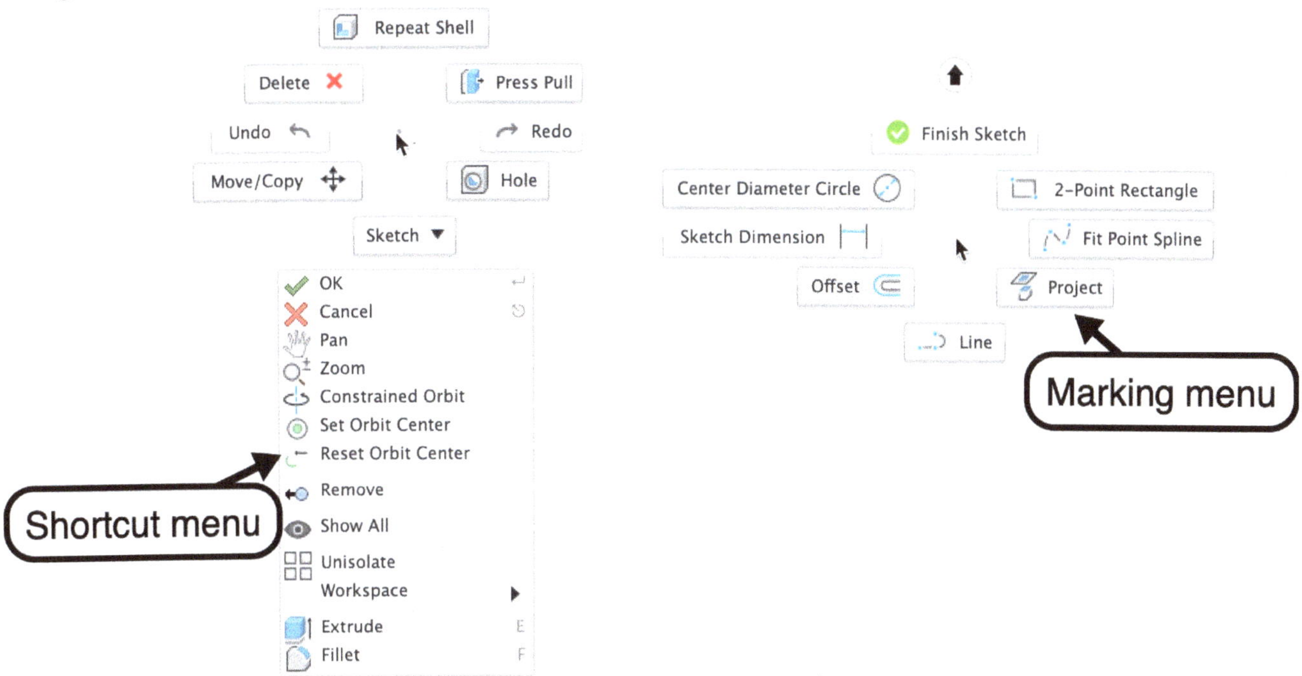

Autodesk Fusion Help

Autodesk Fusion offers you the help system that goes beyond basic command definition. You can access Autodesk Fusion help by clicking on the **Help** icon on the right side of the window.

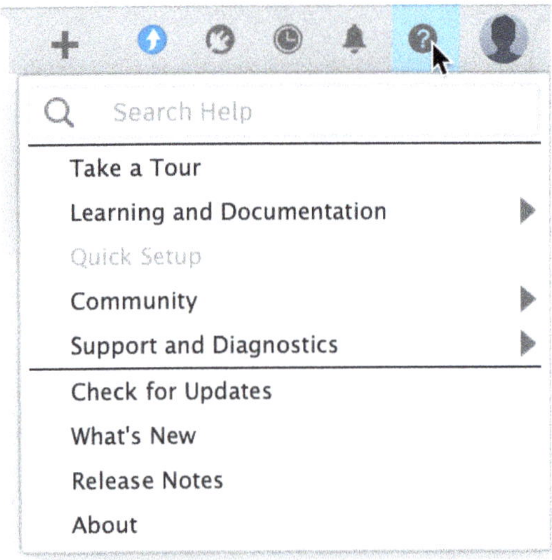

Data Panel

The **Data** panel is an essential feature of Autodesk Fusion 360. It is used to store, organize, and share the project and design data. By default, the **Data** panel is hidden, and you can display it by clicking the **Show Data Panel** icon located at the top left corner of the window. It displays a list of projects created by you. By default, the **Demo Project** is displayed. You can create a new project using the **New Project** button. After creating the project, double-click on it to view the data details. You can upload already existing files using the **Upload** button.

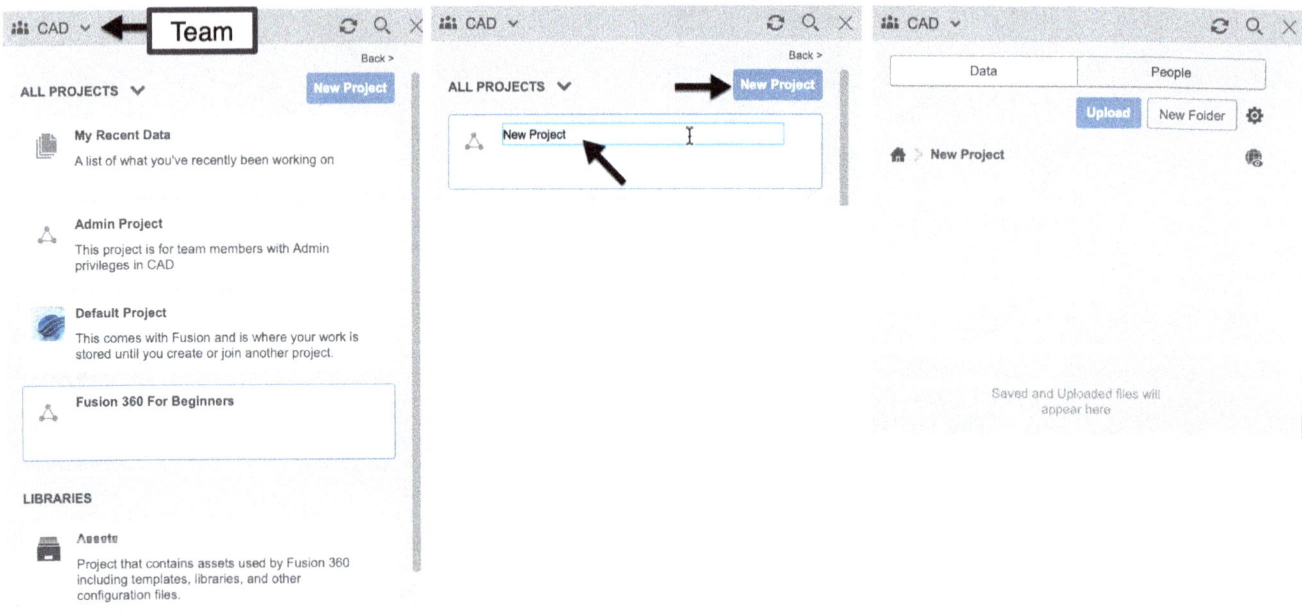

Questions

1. Explain how to set the default units of the design.
2. Give one example of where you would establish a relationship between a part's features.
3. How to activate the Marking Menu?
4. How is Autodesk Fusion a parametric modeling application?

Chapter 2: Sketch techniques

This chapter covers the methods and commands to create sketches in Autodesk Fusion 360. In Autodesk Fusion 360, you create a rough sketch, and then apply dimensions and constraints that define its shape and size. The dimensions define the length, size, and angle of a sketch element, whereas constraints define the relations between sketch elements.

In this chapter, you will:

- Create sketches
- Use constraints and dimensions to control the shape and size of a sketch
- Learn sketching commands
- Learn commands and options that help you to create sketches easily

Creating Sketches

Autodesk Fusion 360 allows you to create sketches directly in the graphics window. To create sketches, click **Create** panel > **Create Sketch** on the toolbar. Next, click on any of the planes displayed at the center of the graphics window. On the **Sketch** contextual tab of the toolbar, you can find different sketch commands. You can use these commands and start drawing the sketch on the selected plane. After creating the sketch, click **Finish Sketch** on the toolbar to finish the sketch.

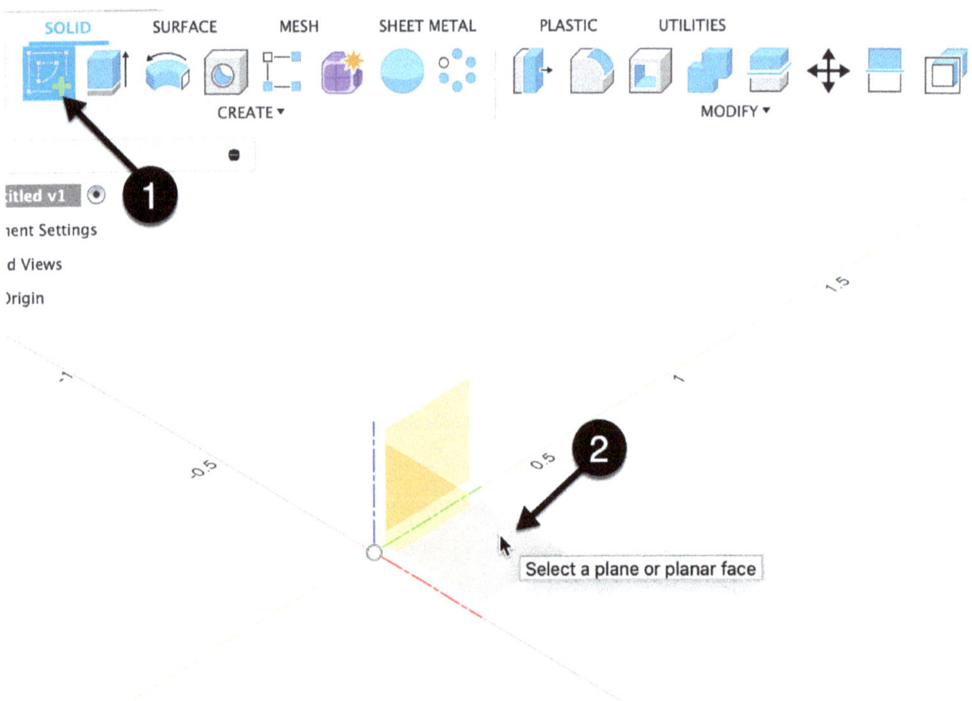

Sketch Commands

Autodesk Fusion 360 provides you with a set of commands to create sketches. These commands are available on **Create** panel of the **Sketch** contextual tab of the toolbar.

Sketch techniques

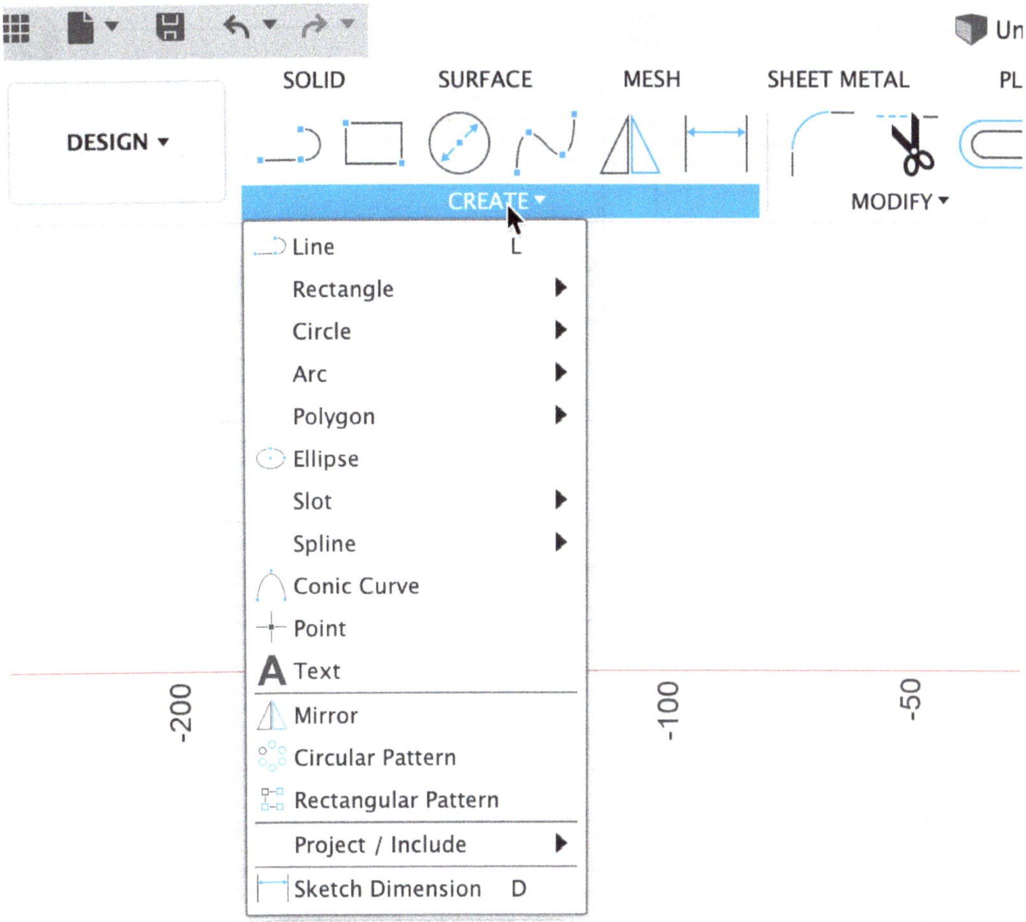

The Line command

This is the most commonly used command while creating a sketch. To activate this command, click **Sketch** contextual tab > **Create** panel > **Line** on the toolbar. To create a line, click on the graphics window, move the pointer and click again. After clicking for the second time, you can see that an endpoint is added, and another line segment is started. This is a convenient way to create a chain of lines. Continue to click to add more line segments. You can right-click on the graphics window and click **OK** if you want to deactivate the **Line** command.

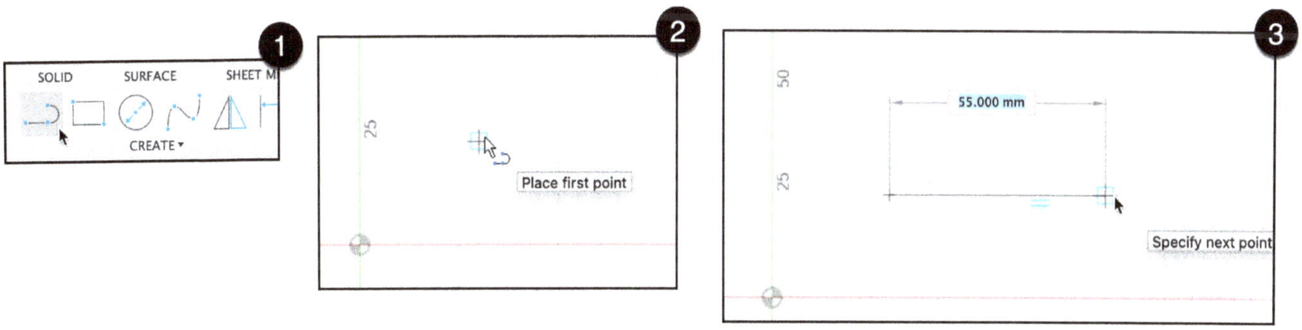

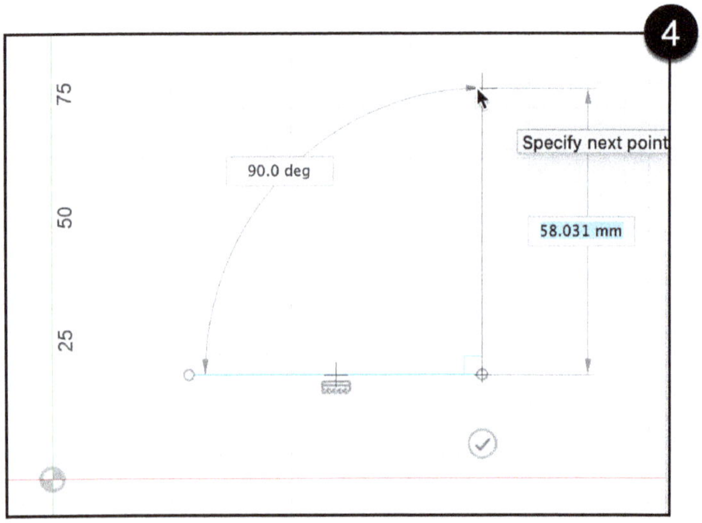

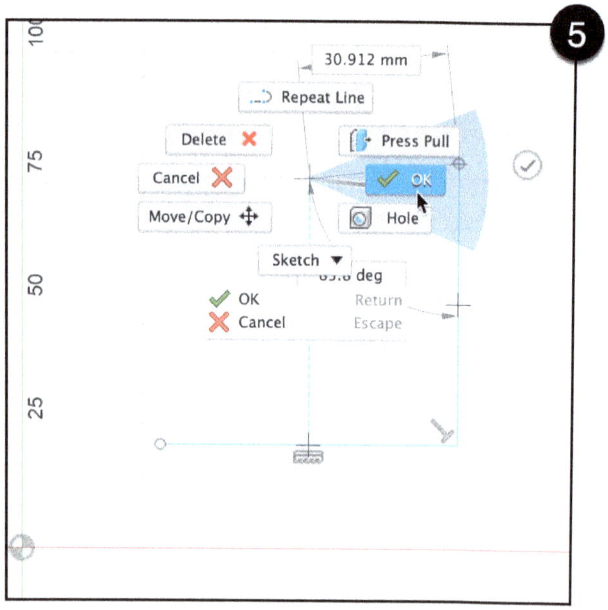

Tip: *To create a horizontal line, specify the start point of the line and move the pointer horizontally; the Horizontal constraint glyph appears below the line. Click to create a horizontal line with the Horizontal constraint applied to it. You will learn about constraints later in this chapter. Likewise, you can create a vertical line by moving the pointer vertically and clicking.*

Creating Arcs

An arc is a smooth curve joining two endpoints. It a portion of a circle. Autodesk Fusion 360 allows you to create arcs using three commands: **3-Point Arc, Center Point Arc**, and **Tangent Arc**.

The 3-Point Arc command

This command creates an arc by defining its start, end, and radius. Activate the **3-Point Arc** command (On the **Sketch** contextual panel of the toolbar, expand the **Create** panel and click **Arc > 3-Point Arc**). In the graphics window, click to define the start point of the arc. Next, move the pointer and click again to define the endpoint of the arc. After defining the start and end of the arc, you need to define the size and position of the arc. To do this, move the pointer and click to define the radius and position of the arc.

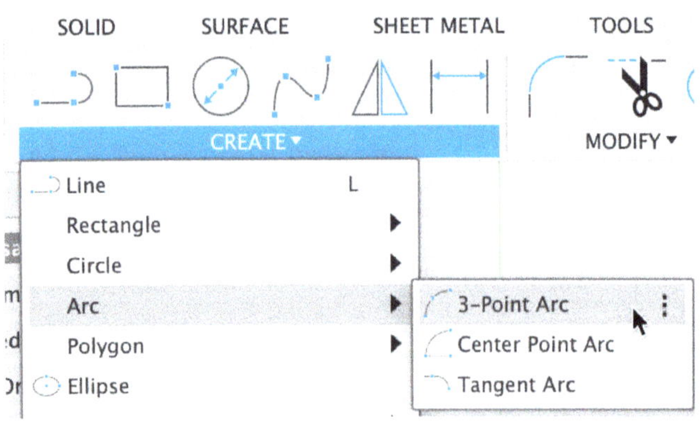

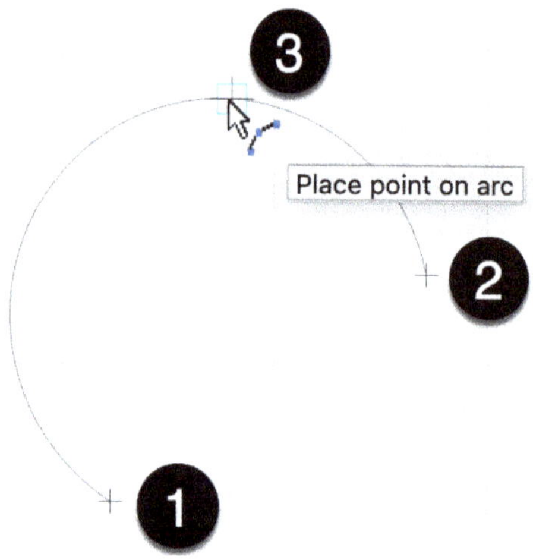

The Tangent Arc Command

This command creates an arc tangent to the connecting sketch entity. To activate this command, expand the **Create** panel and click **Arc > Tangent Arc** on the **Sketch** contextual panel of the toolbar. Click on the endpoint of an entity to start the arc. Next, move the pointer and click to define the radius and position of the arc.

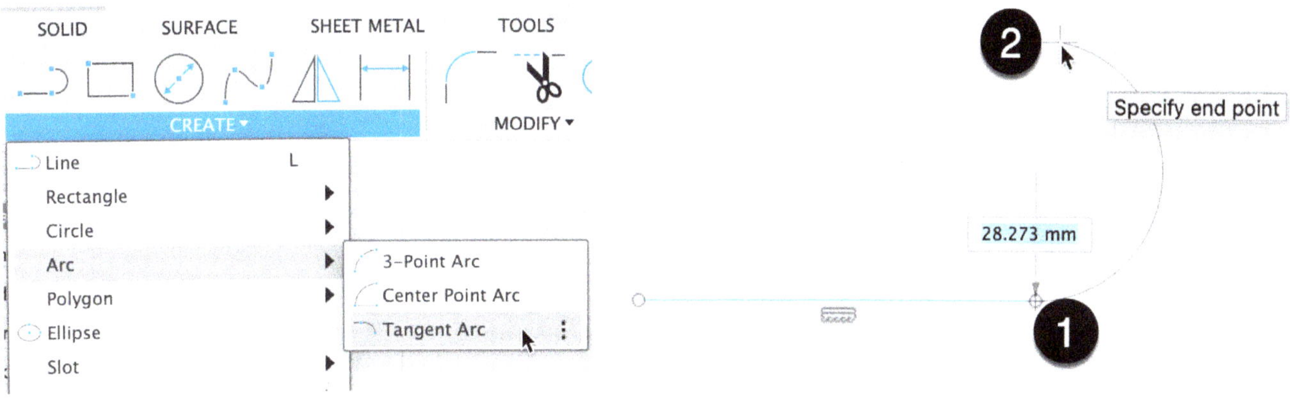

Autodesk Fusion 360 allows you to create an arc tangent to the line without activating the **Tangent Arc** command. To do this, activate the **Line** command and create a line. Next, move the pointer away, and then take it back to the endpoint of the line. Now, press and hold the left mouse button and drag the pointer up to the required distance. Next, release the left mouse button to specify the endpoint of the arc.

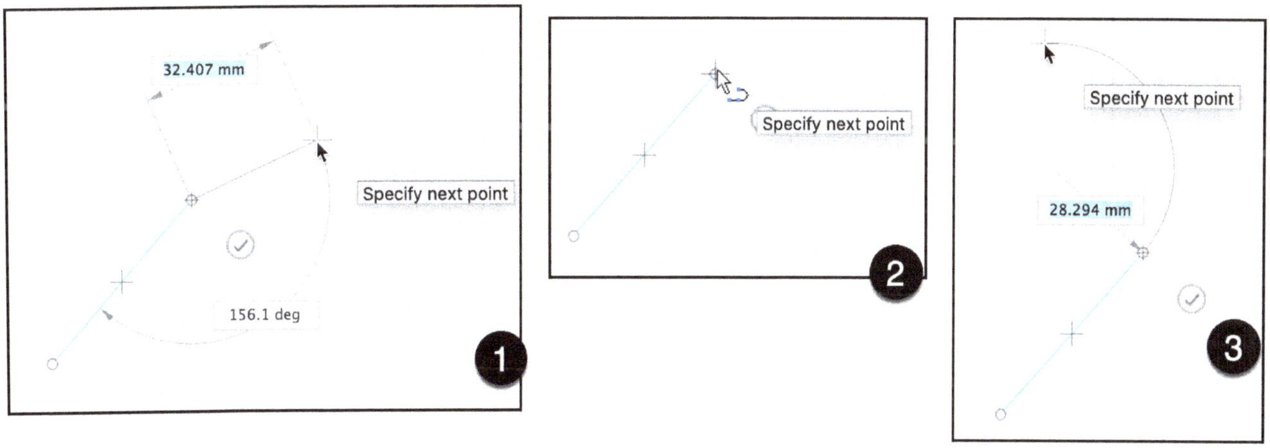

The Center Point Arc command

This command creates an arc by defining its center, start, and end. Activate the **Center Point Arc** command (On the **Sketch** contextual panel of the toolbar, expand the **Create** panel and click **Arc > Center Point Arc** on the toolbar). Click to define the center point. Next, move the pointer and click to define the start point of the arc. Move the pointer and notice that an arc is drawn from the start point. Once the arc appears the way you want, click to define its endpoint.

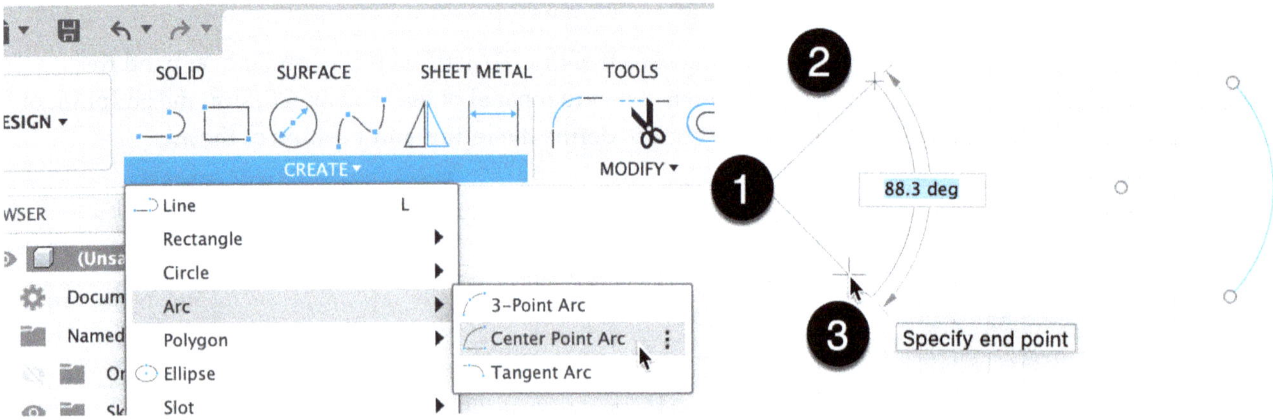

Creating Circles

A circle is a round shape without any corners. Autodesk Fusion 360 allows you to create circles using five commands: **Center Diameter Circle, 2-Point Circle, 3-Point Circle, 2-Tangent Circle**, and **3-Tangent Circle.**

Center Diameter Circle

This is the most common way to draw a circle. Activate the **Center Diameter Circle** command (click the **Center Diameter Circle** icon on the **Create** panel of the **Sketch** contextual tab on the toolbar). Click to define the center point of the circle. Drag the pointer, and then click again to define the diameter of the circle.

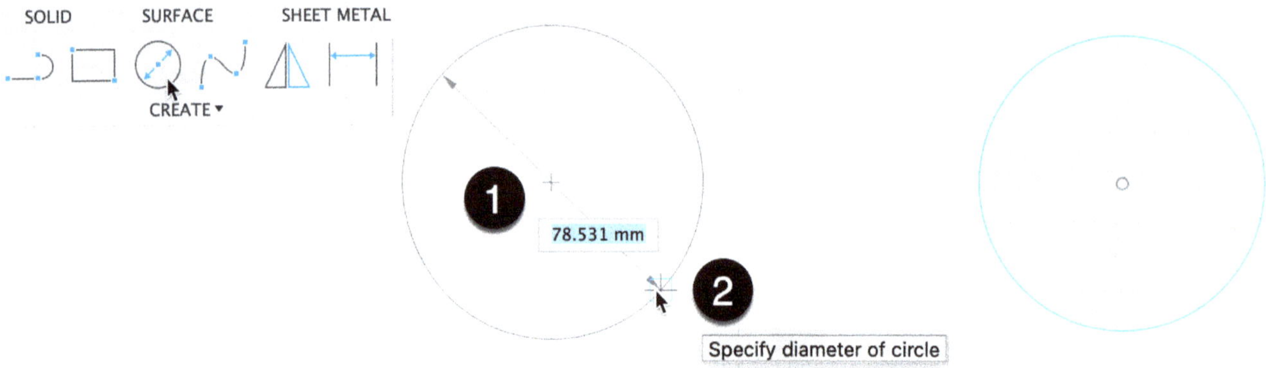

2-Point Circle

You can create this type of circle by specifying two points or by selecting two existing points. To do this, activate the **2-Point Circle** command (On the **Sketch** contextual tab of the toolbar, expand the **Create** panel and click **Circle > 2-Point Circle**). Click to define the first point of the circle. Drag the pointer, and then click again to define the diameter of the circle.

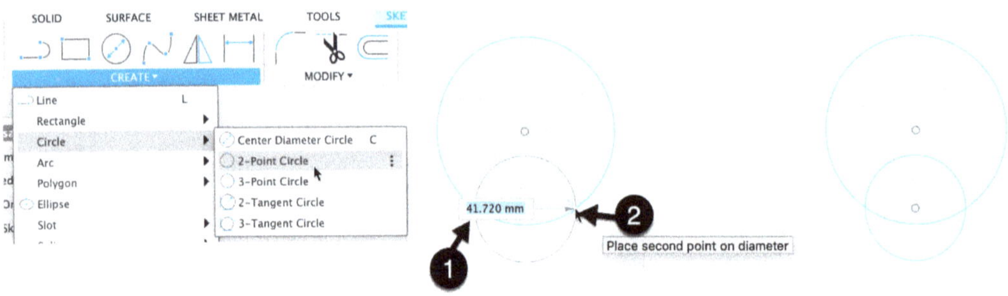

3-Point Circle

You can create this type of circle by specifying three points or by selecting three existing points. Activate the **3-Point Circle** command (On the **Sketch** contextual tab of the toolbar, expand the **Create** panel and click **Circle > 3-Point Circle**). Next, specify the three points of the circle, as shown.

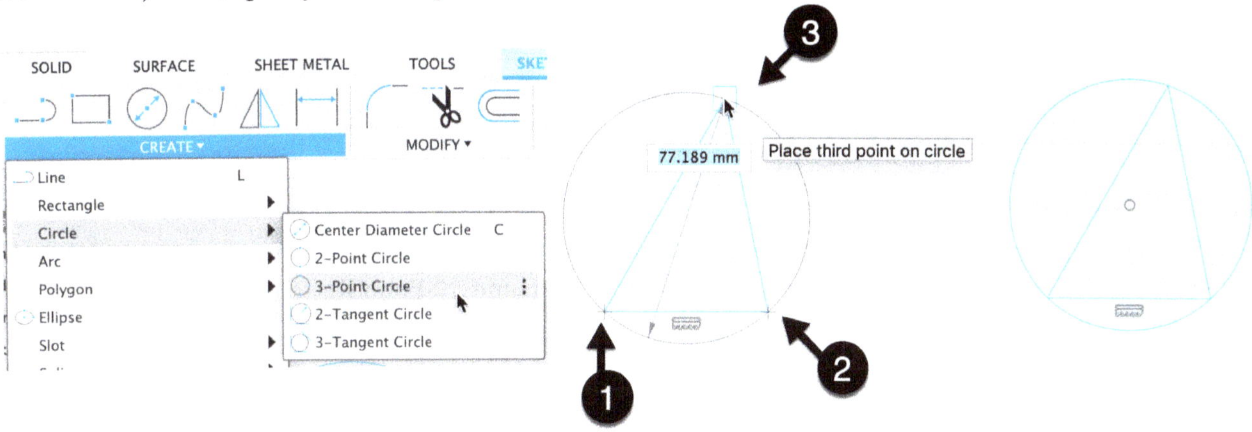

2-Tangent Circle

This command creates a circle tangent to two lines. Activate this command (expand the **Create** panel and click **Circle > 2-Tangent Circle** on the toolbar). Next, select two lines from the model geometry. Move the pointer and click to specify the radius of the circle (or) type the radius in the radius box and press ENTER; a circle is created tangent to the selected lines.

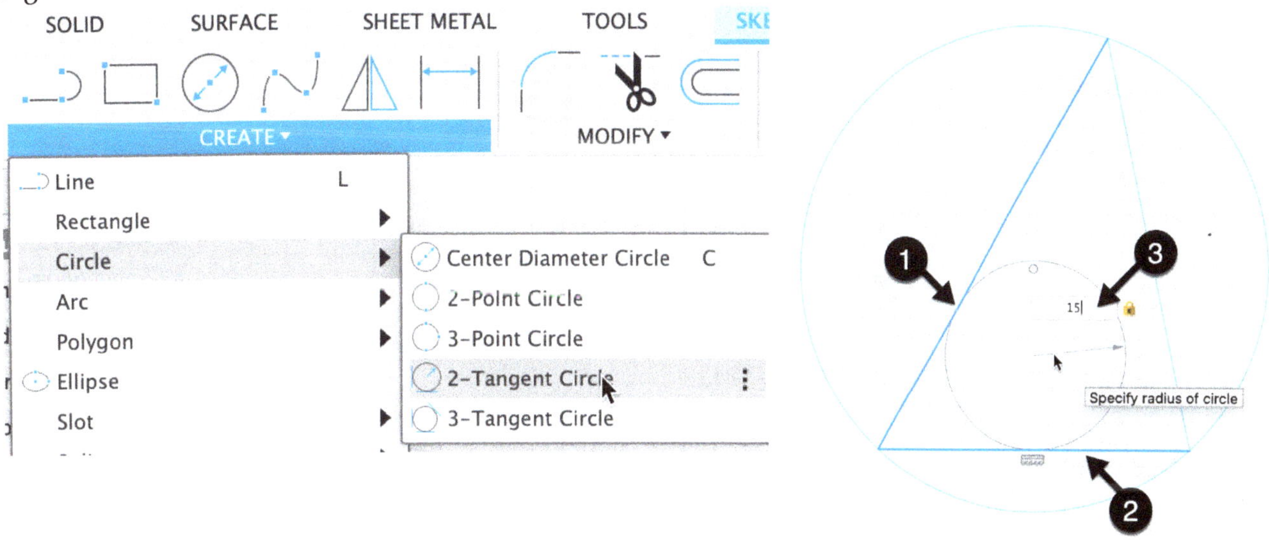

3-Tangent Circle

This command creates a circle tangent to three lines. Activate this command (expand the **Create** panel and click **Circle > 3-Tangent Circle** on the toolbar). Select three lines from the model geometry; a circle is created tangent to the selected lines.

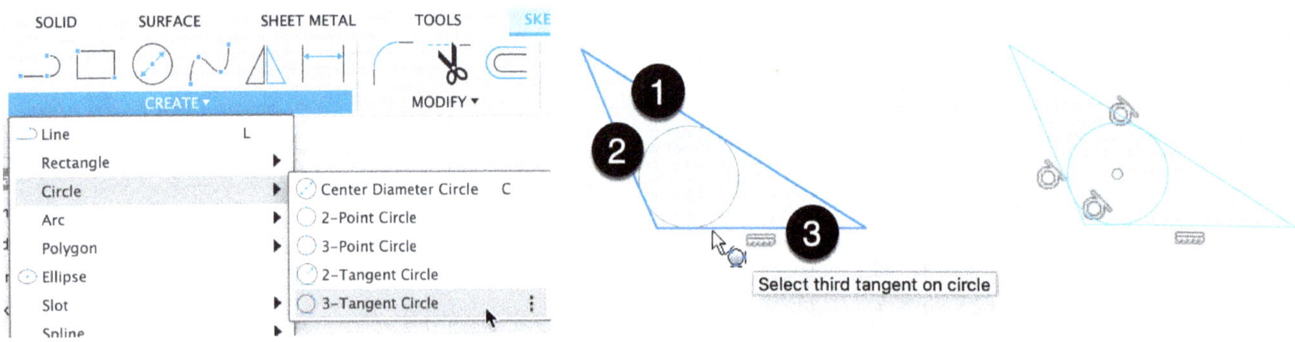

Creating Rectangles

A rectangle is a two-dimensional shape in which the opposite sides are equal and parallel to each other. Autodesk Fusion 360 allows you to create rectangles using three different commands: **2-Point Rectangle, 3-Point Rectangle,** and **Center Rectangle.**

2-Point Rectangle

This command creates a rectangle by defining its diagonal corners. Activate the **2-Point Rectangle** command (click the **2-Point Rectangle** icon on the **Create** panel of the **Sketch** contextual tab of the toolbar). Click on the graphics window to define the first corner of the rectangle. Move the pointer and click to define the second corner. You can also type-in values in the length and width boxes attached to the rectangle. To do this, specify the first corner of the rectangle. Type-in the length of the first side press the TAB. Next, type-in the length value of the next side and press ENTER.

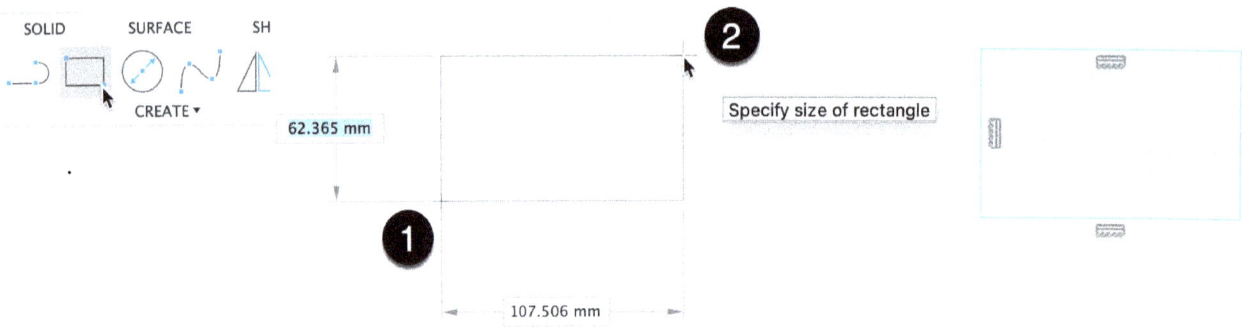

3-Point Rectangle

This command allows you to create an inclined rectangle. Activate the **3-Point Rectangle** command (On the **Sketch** contextual tab of the toolbar, expand the **Create** panel, and click **Rectangle** > **3-Point Rectangle**). Specify the first two points to define the width and inclination angle of the rectangle. You can also enter the width value in the value box displayed in the graphics window. Next, specify the third point to define the height of the rectangle.

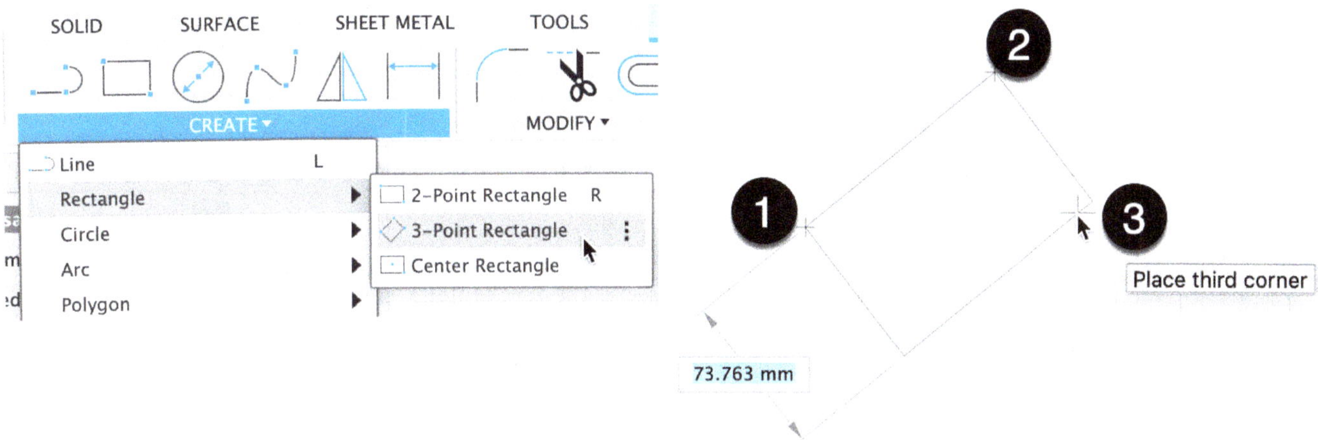

Center Rectangle

This command creates a rectangle using two points: center and corner points. Activate the **Center Rectangle** command (On the **Sketch** contextual tab of the toolbar, expand the **Create** panel, and click **Rectangle** > **Center Rectangle**). Click on the graphics window to define the center of the rectangle. Next, specify the corner point to define the width and height of the rectangle. You can also type-in values in the value boxes displayed in the graphics window. Use the TAB key to switch between the value boxes.

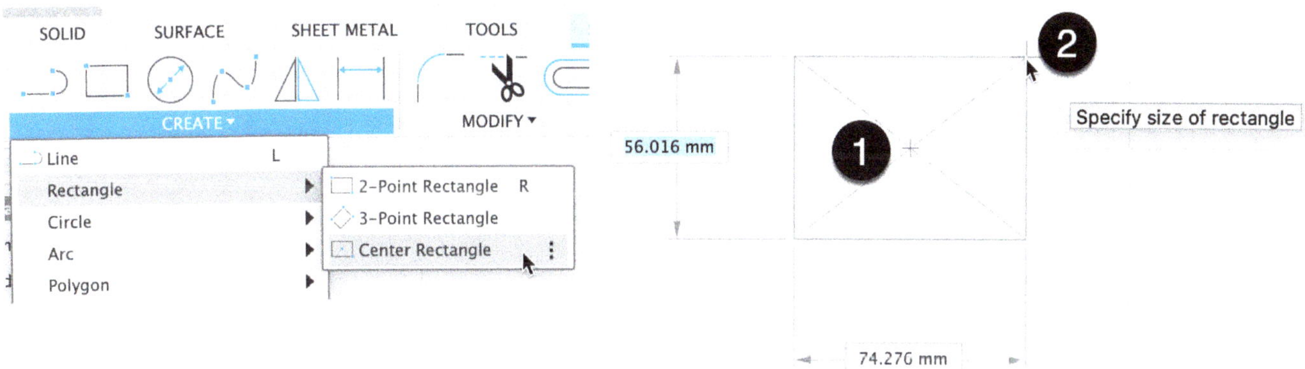

Creating Slots

A slot is a long narrow opening or hole. In Autodesk Fusion 360, you can create straight and arc slots using five different commands: **Center to Center Slot**, **Overall Slot**, **Center Point Slot**, **Three Point Arc Slot**, **Center Point Arc Slot**.

Center to Center Slot

This command allows you to create a straight slot by specifying the centers of the slot endcaps and the slot width. Activate this command (On the **Sketch** contextual tab of the toolbar, expand the **Create** panel and click **Slot > Center to Center Slot**). Click to specify the start point of the slot. Next, move the pointer and click to specify the endpoint; the length and orientation of the slot are defined. Now, move the pointer outward and click to define the slot width.

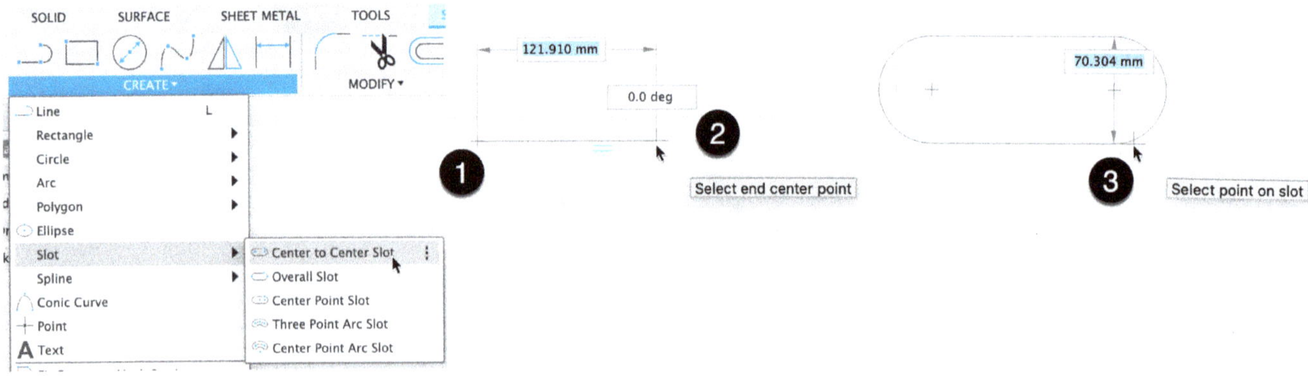

Overall Slot

This command creates a straight slot by defining its start, end, and width. Activate this command (On the **Sketch** contextual tab of the toolbar, expand the **Create** panel and click **Slot > Overall Slot**). Specify the start and endpoints of the slot. Next, move the pointer outward and click to specify the slot width.

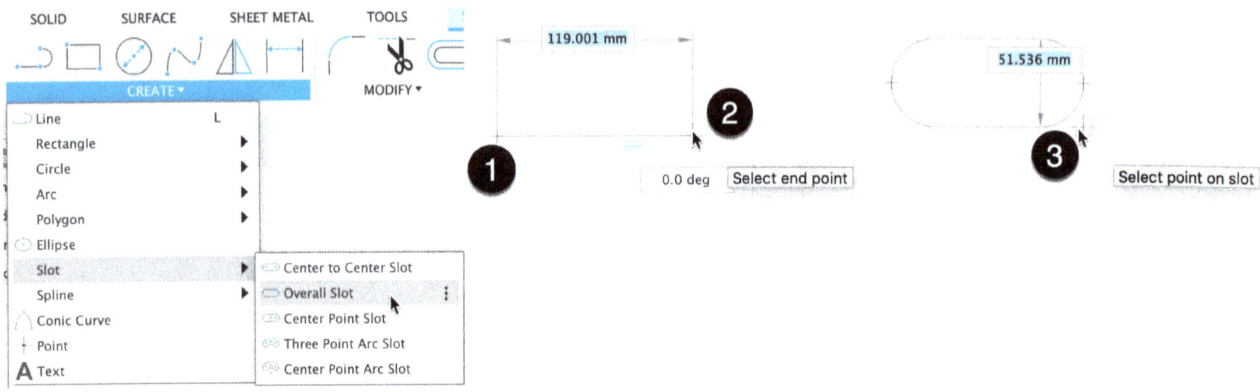

Center Point Slot

This command creates a straight slot by defining its centerpoint, endpoint, and width. Activate this command (On the **Sketch** contextual tab of the toolbar, expand the **Create** panel and click **Slot > Center Point Slot**) and click to specify the centerpoint of the slot. Next, move the pointer and click to specify the centerpoint of the endcap; this defines the length and orientation of the slot. Now, move the pointer outward and click to define the slot width.

Three Point Arc Slot

This command is similar to the **3-Point Arc** command. Activate this command (On the **Sketch** contextual tab of the toolbar, expand the **Create** panel and click **Slot > Three Point Arc Slot**) and specify the start and endpoints of the center arc of the slot. Next, you need to specify the third point of the center arc; this defines its radius. Now, move the pointer outward and click to define the slot width.

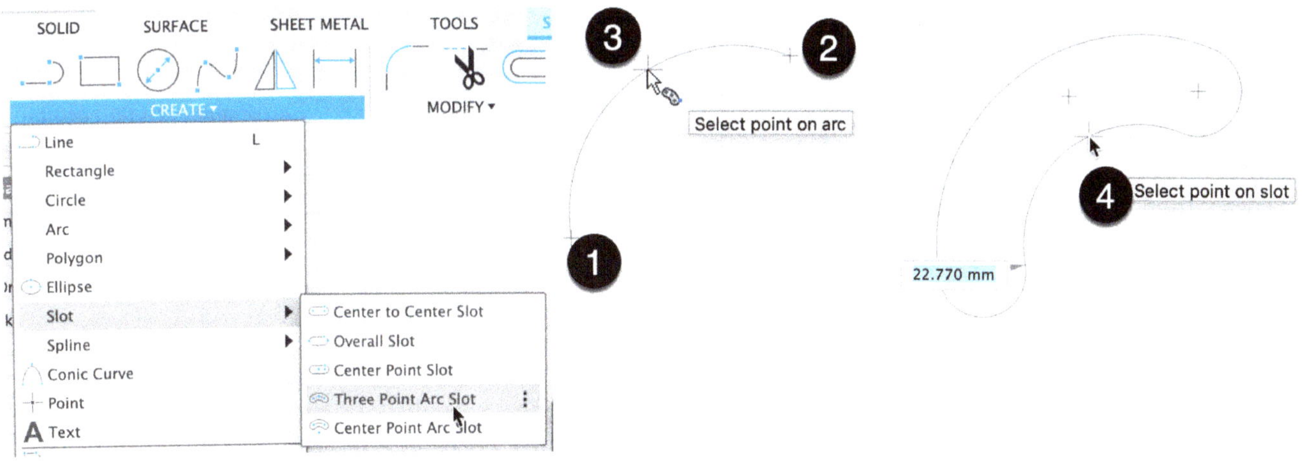

Center Point Arc Slot

This command works on the same principle as that of the **Center Point Arc** command. Activate this command (On the **Sketch** contextual tab of the toolbar, expand the **Create** panel and click **Slot > Center Point Arc Slot**) and specify the center of the arc slot. Next, specify the start and endpoints of the center arc. Now, move the pointer outward and click to define the slot width.

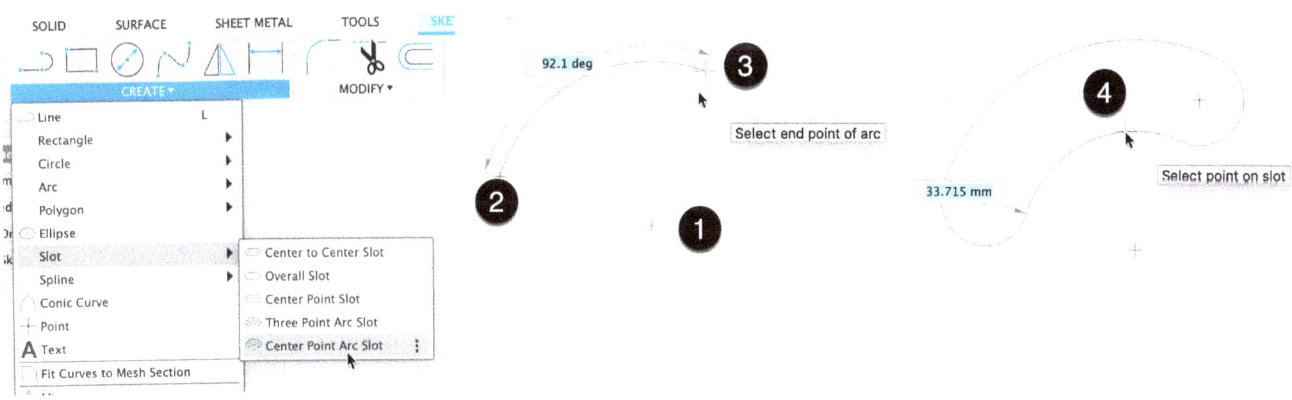

Creating Polygons

A Polygon is a closed two-dimensional shape formed by straight edges. In Autodesk Fusion 360, you can create a polygon using three different commands: **Circumscribed Polygon**, **Inscribed Polygon**, and **Edge Polygon**.

Circumscribed Polygon

This command provides a simple way to create a polygon with any number of sides. Activate this command (On the **Sketch** contextual tab of the toolbar, expand the **Create** panel and click **Polygon > Circumscribed Polygon**) and click on the graphics window to define the center of the polygon. Next, press the TAB key and type the number of sides of the polygon in the box displayed in the graphics window. Notice that a circle is displayed touching the flat sides of the polygon. Now, move the pointer outward and click to specify the radius of the circle (or) type the radius of the circle in the value box; the polygon is created with its sides touching the circle.

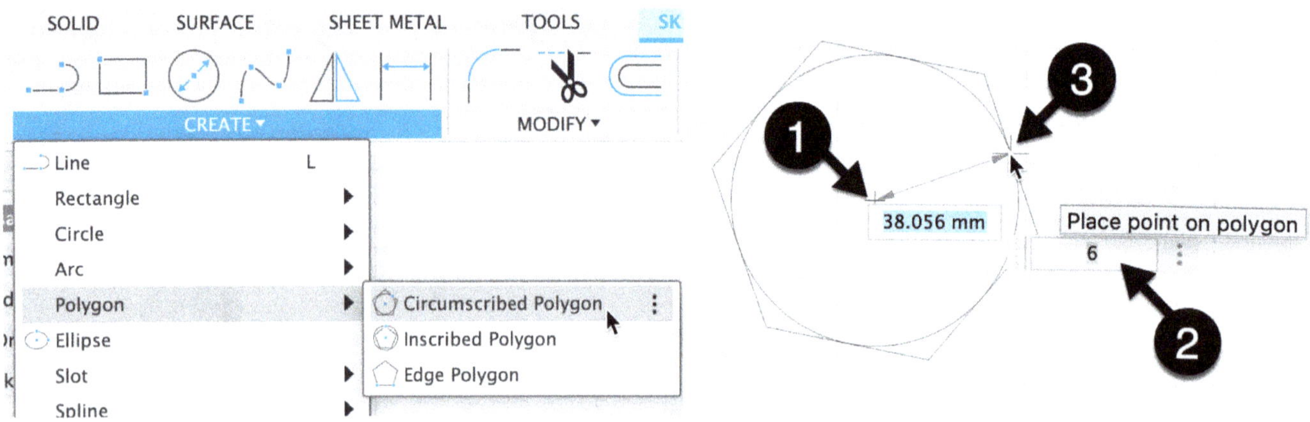

Inscribed Polygon

This command creates a polygon with its vertices touching the imaginary circle. Activate this command (On the **Sketch** contextual tab of the toolbar, expand the **Create** panel and click **Polygon > Inscribed Polygon**) and click on the graphics window to define the center of the polygon. Next, specify the number of sides of the polygon. Notice that a circle is displayed touching the vertices of the polygon. Move the pointer outward and click to specify the radius of the circle; the polygon is created with its vertices touching the circle.

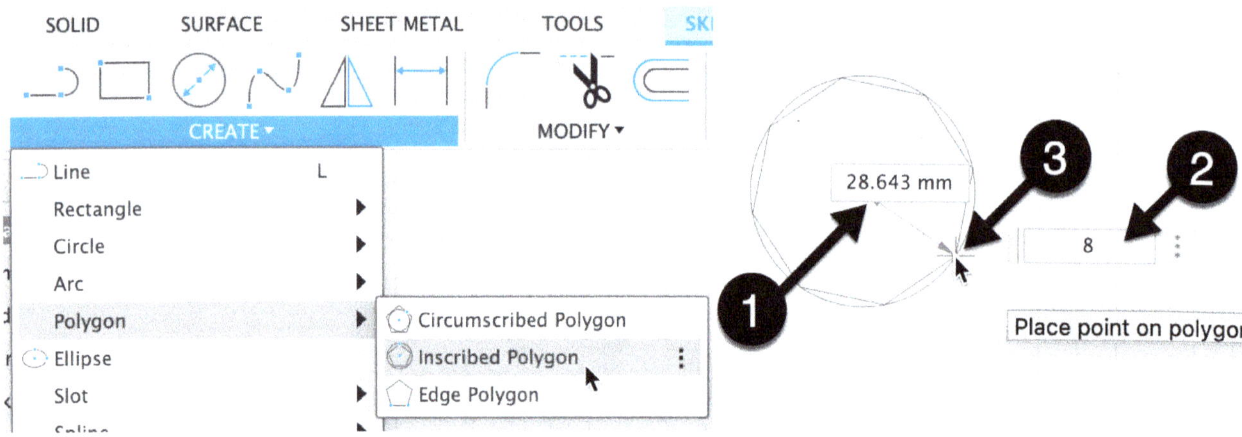

Edge Polygon

This command allows you to create a polygon by specifying the length and angle of one of its sides. Activate this command (On the **Sketch** contextual tab of the toolbar, expand the **Create** panel and click **Polygon > Edge Polygon**) and click on the graphics window to define the first point of a side. Move the pointer and click to specify the length and angle of the side. Next, specify the number of sides of the polygon. Next, move the pointer and click to specify the side of the polygon. Press **Esc** on the keyboard to deactivate the command.

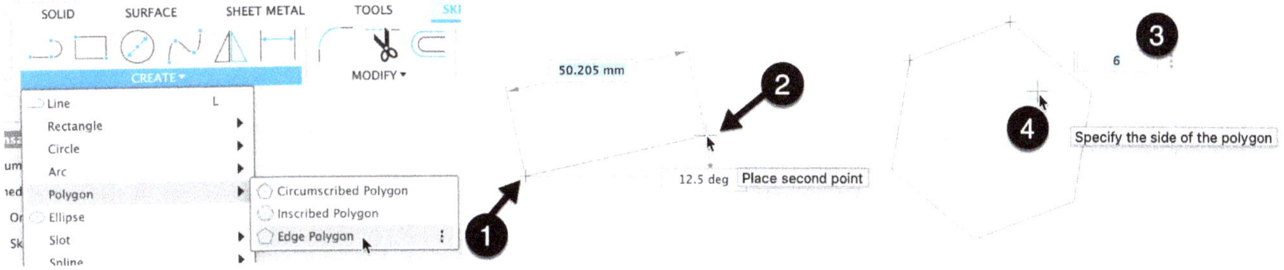

The Ellipse command

This command creates an ellipse using a center point, and major and minor axes. Activate this command (On the **Sketch** contextual tab of the toolbar, expand the **Create** panel and click **Ellipse**). In the graphics window, click to define the center point of the ellipse. Move the pointer away from the center point and click to define the distance and orientation of the first axis. Next, move the pointer in the direction perpendicular to the first axis and click; the ellipse is created.

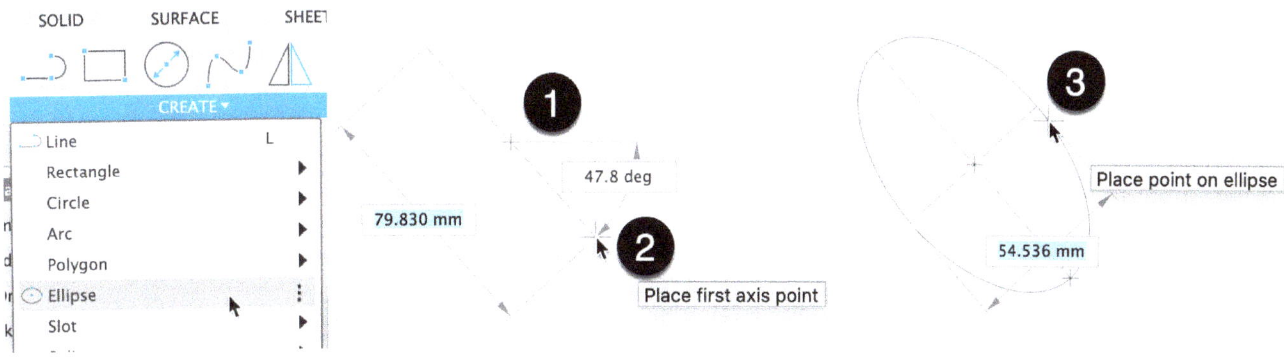

The Sketch Dimension command

It is generally considered a good practice to ensure that every sketch you create is fully constrained before creating solid features. The term 'fully-constrained' means that the sketch has a definite shape and size. You can fully-constrain a sketch by using dimensions and constraints. You can add dimensions to a sketch by using the **Sketch Dimension** command. You can use this command to add all types of dimensions, such as length, angle, and diameter, and so on. This command creates a dimension based on the geometry you select. For instance, to dimension a circle, activate the **Sketch Dimension** command (Click the **Sketch Dimension**  icon on the **Create** panel of the **Sketch** contextual tab) and then select the circle. Next, move the pointer and click again to position the dimension; the Dimension box pops up. Type-in a value in this box, and then press Enter to update the dimension.

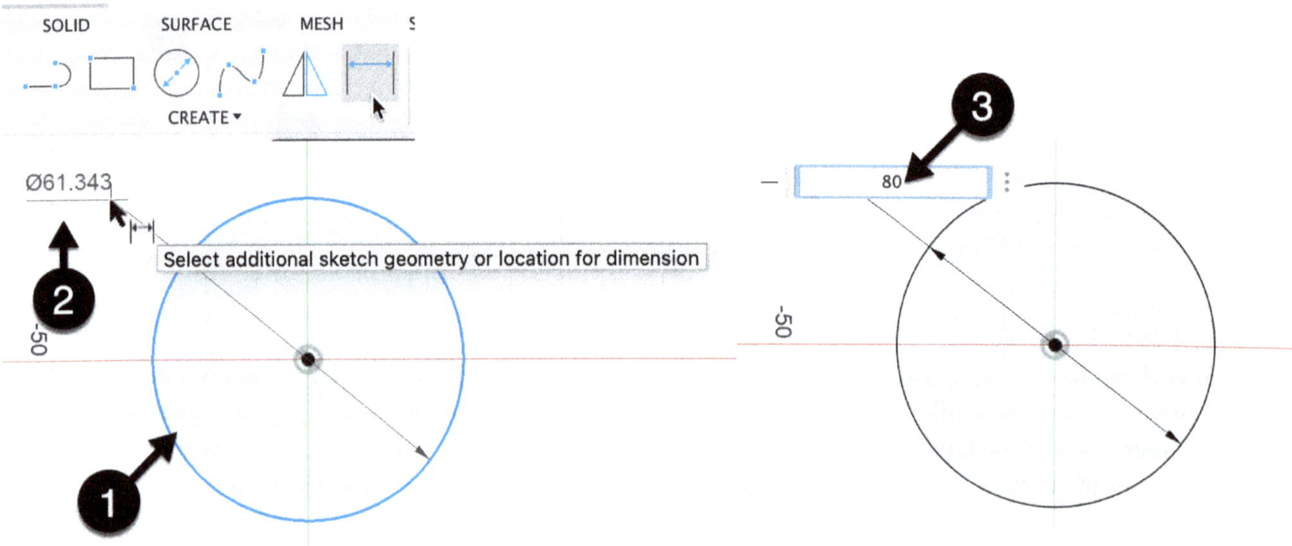

Linear Dimensions

To add dimension to a line, activate the **Sketch Dimension** command, and select the line. Next, move the pointer in the vertical direction (or) right-click and select **Horizontal** from the menu; the horizontal dimension is created. Click to position the dimension.

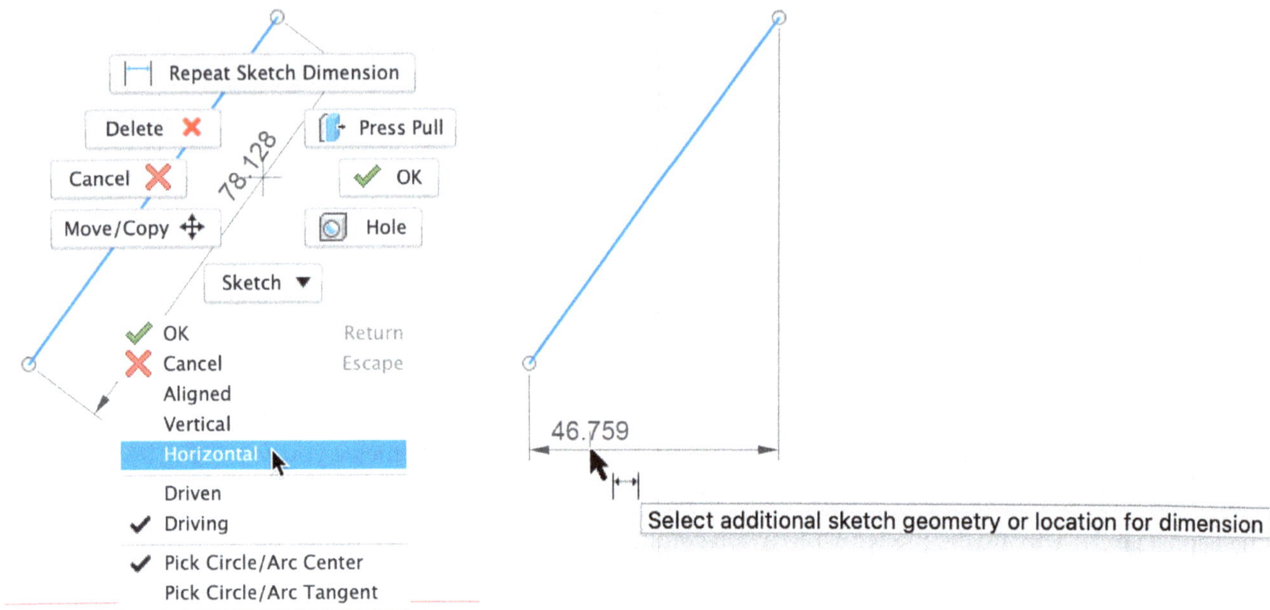

To create a vertical dimension, activate the **Sketch Dimension** command and select a line. Move the pointer in the horizontal direction (or) right-click and select **Vertical** from the shortcut menu; the vertical dimension is created. Click to position the dimension.

Sketch techniques

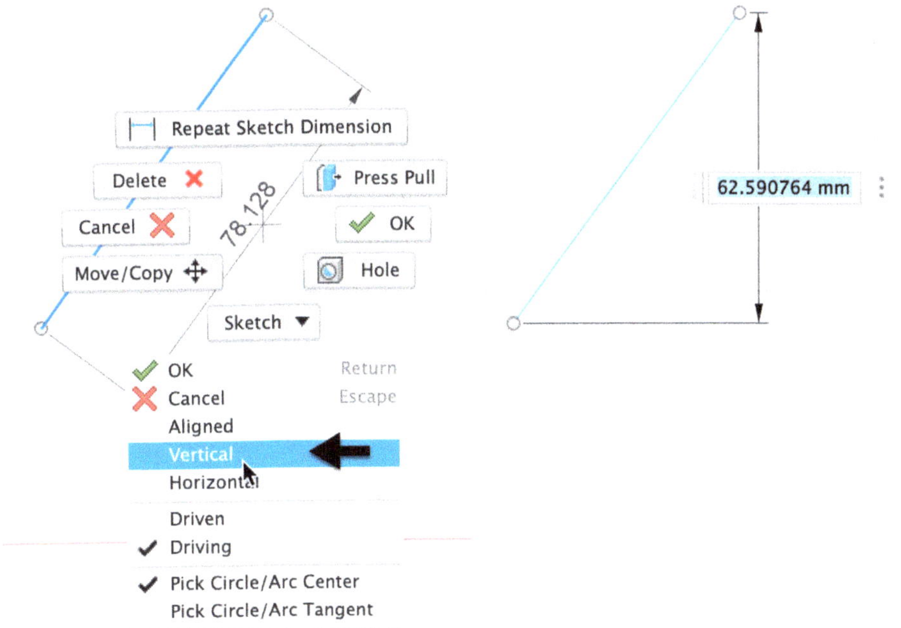

To create a dimension aligned to the selected line, right click and select **Aligned** from the shortcut menu. Next, position the dimension and edit its value.

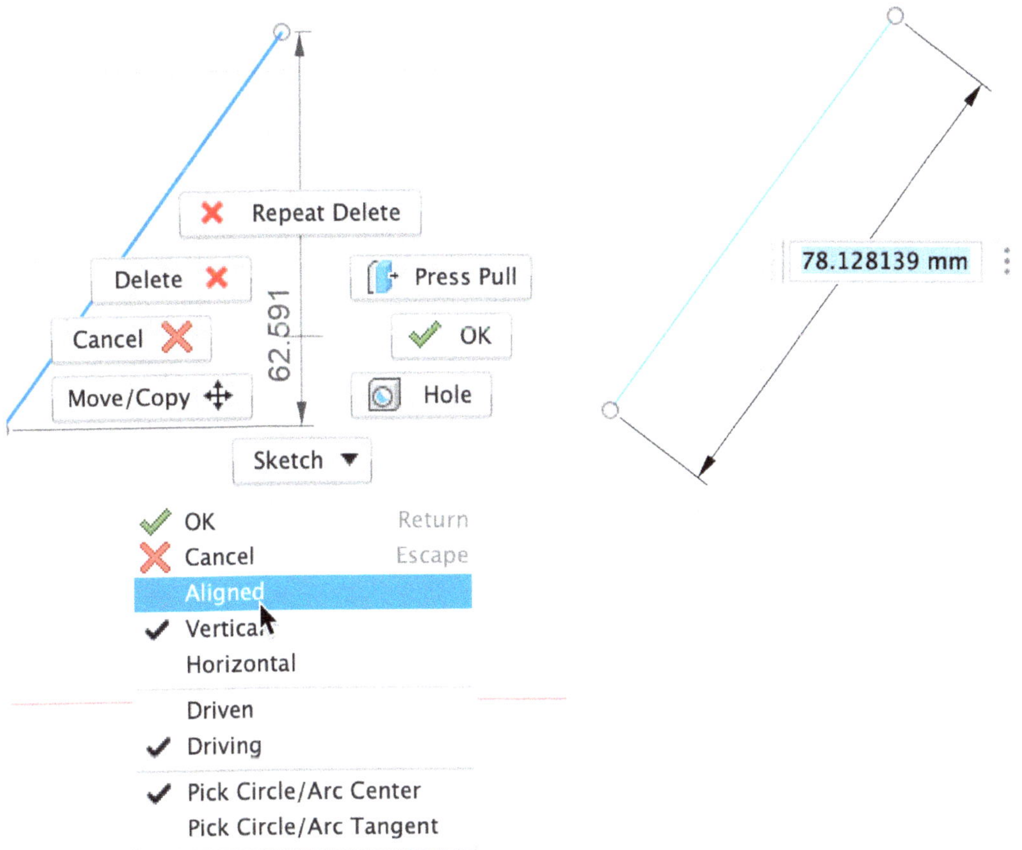

Angular Dimensions

Click the **Sketch Dimension** command on the **Create** panel. Next, select two lines that are positioned at an angle to each other. Move the pointer between the selected lines and click to position the dimension. Next, type in a value, right-click, and then select the **OK** button.

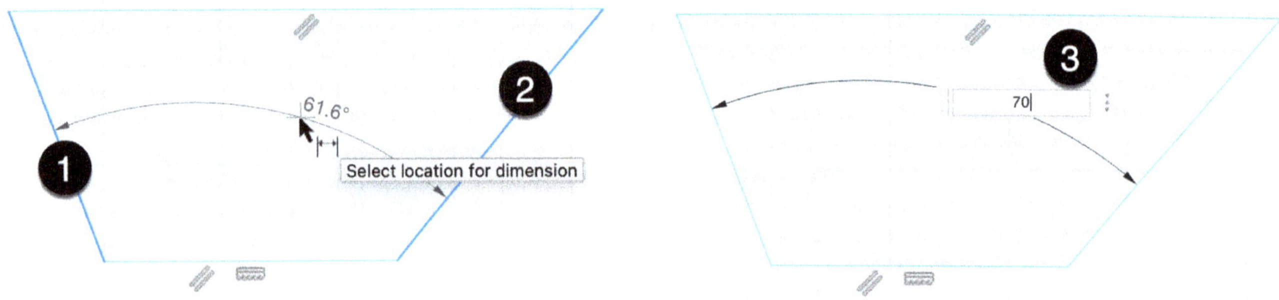

Adding Dimensions to an Arc

Autodesk Fusion 360 allows you to add five types of dimensions to an arc: Radius, Diameter, Arc Length, Arc angle, and Linear dimension.

Adding a Radius or Diameter dimension

To add a radius or diameter or arc length dimension to an arc, activate the **Sketch Dimension** command and select the arc. Next, right click and select **Radius** or **Diameter**. Position the dimension and edit the dimension value.

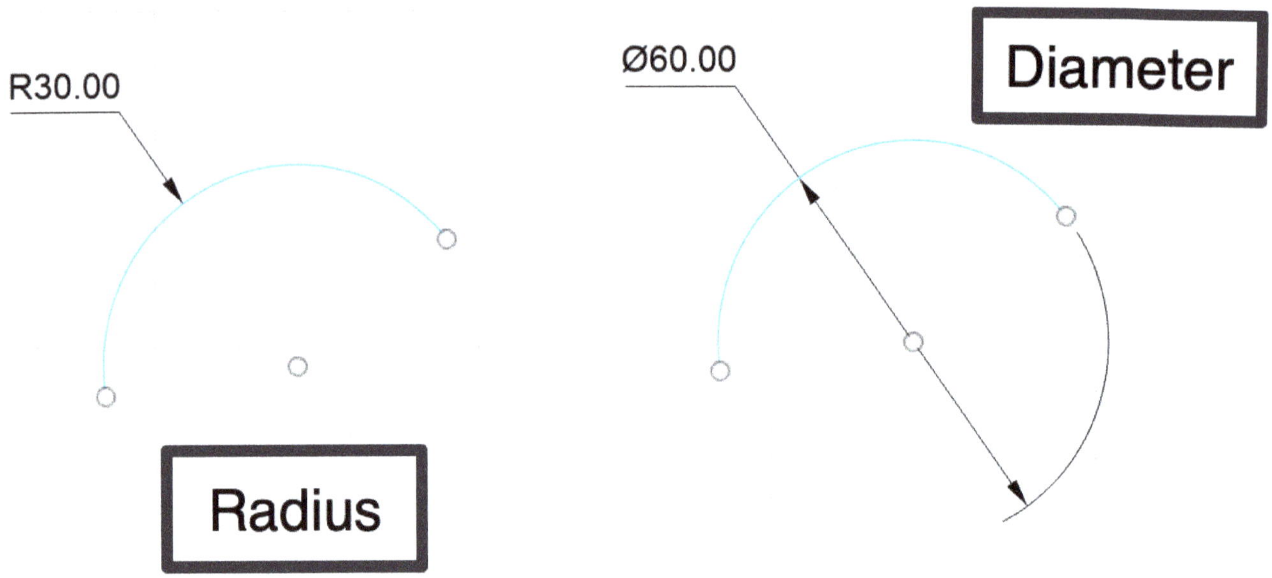

Adding a Linear dimension to the Arc

To add a linear dimension to an arc, activate the **Sketch Dimension** command and select its endpoints. Move the pointer and position the linear dimension.

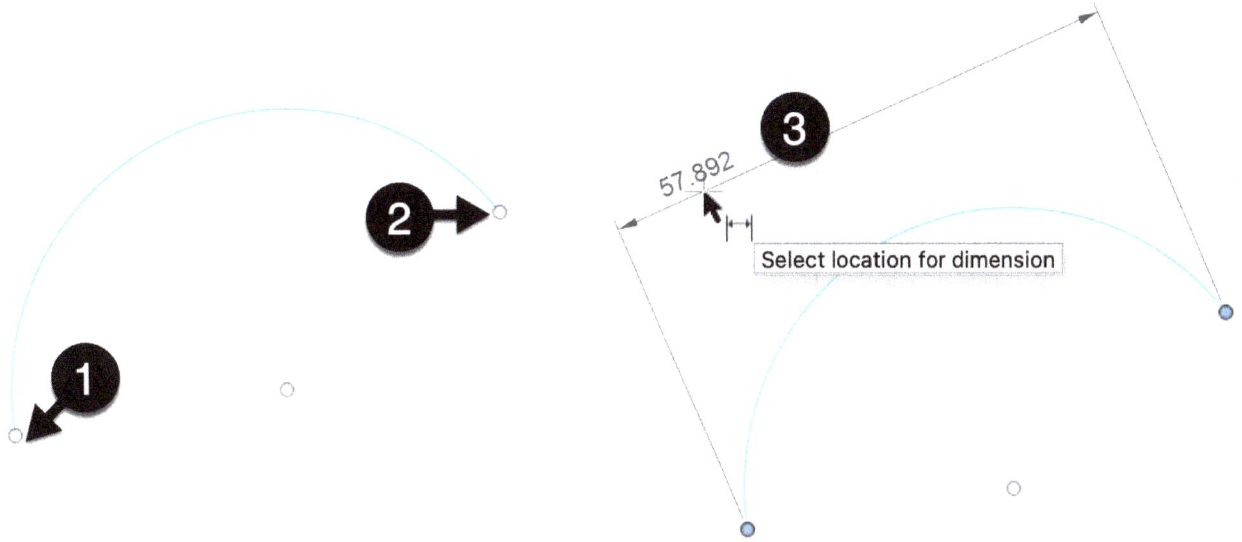

Adding an Angular dimension to an Arc

To add an angular dimension to an arc, activate the **Sketch Dimension** command and select an endpoint of the arc. Next, select the centerpoint of the arc, and then the other endpoint. Move the pointer between the endpoints of the arc and click to place the angular dimension.

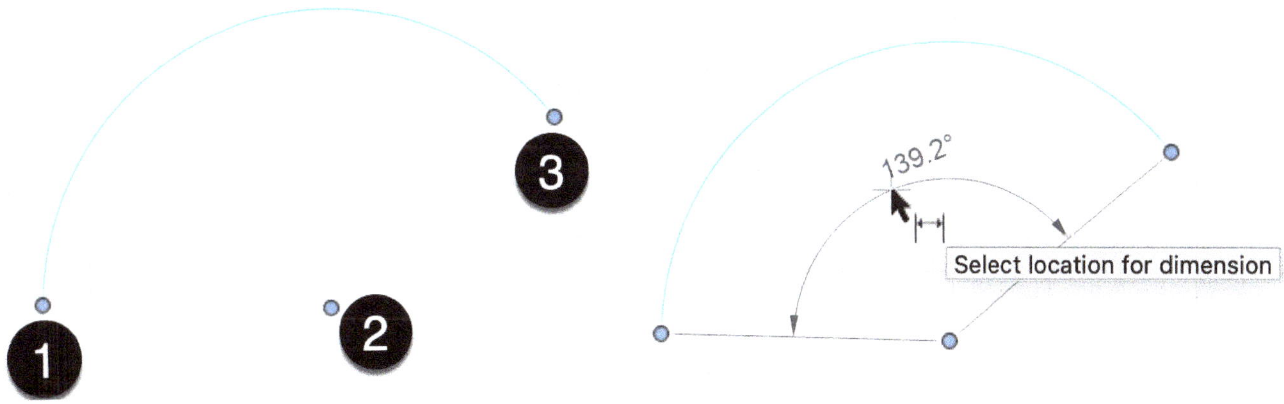

Over-constrained Sketch

When creating sketches for solid or surface features, Autodesk Fusion 360 will not allow you to over-constrain the geometry. The term 'over-constrain' means adding more dimensions than required. The following figure shows a fully constrained sketch. If you add another dimension to this sketch (e.g., diagonal dimension), the **Over-constrained sketch** message pops up. It shows that the dimension would over-constrain the sketch. If you click **Create Driven**, then the new dimension will be displayed in brackets. The dimension displayed in the brackets is called a driven dimension. The value of a driven dimension changes when you modify the driving dimensions.

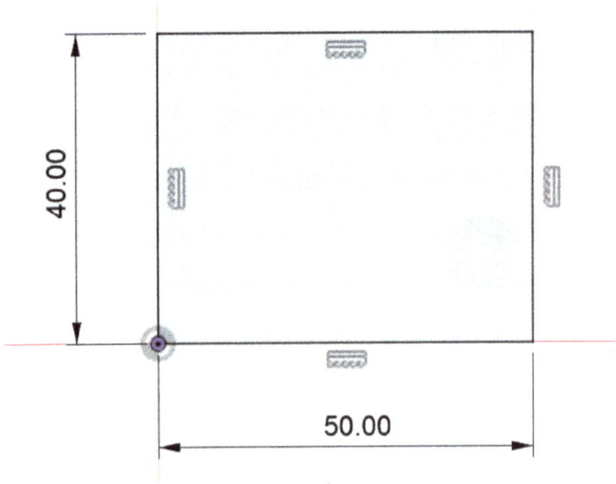

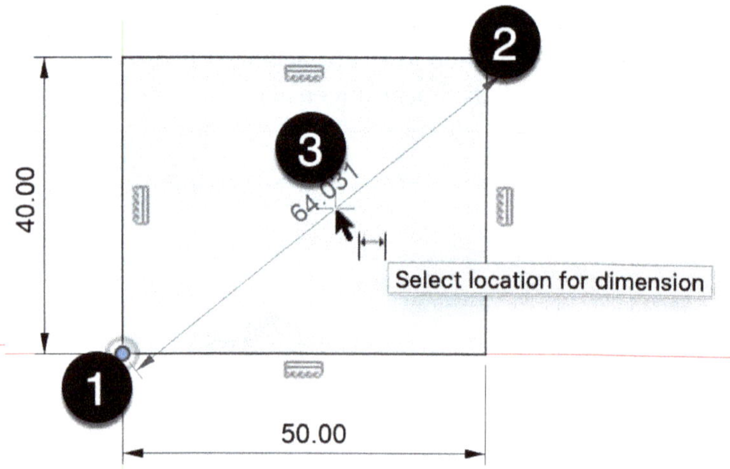

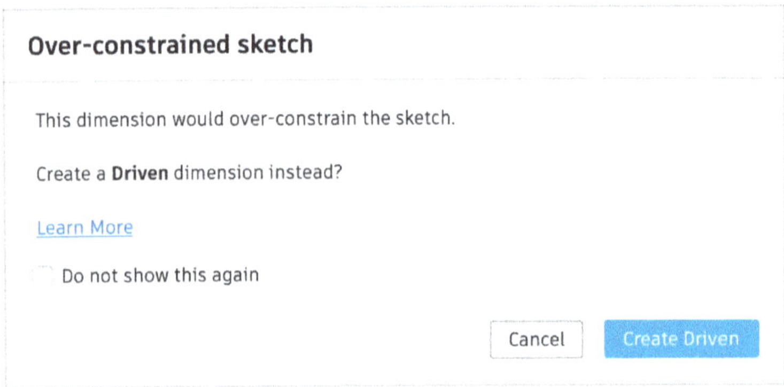

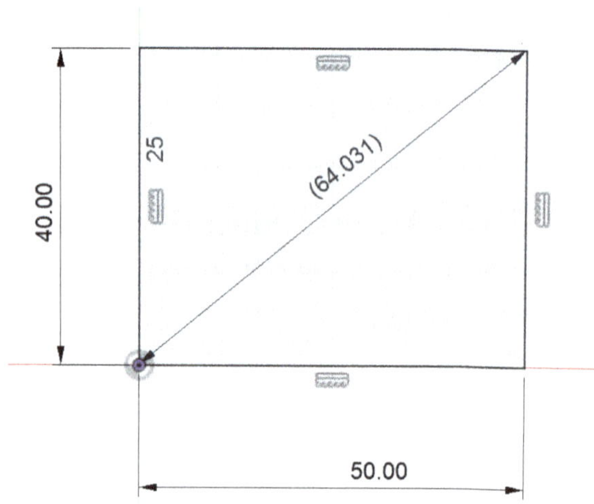

Constraints

The constraints are used to control the shape of a drawing by establishing relationships between the sketch elements. You can apply constraints to a sketch using the commands displayed on the **Constraints** panel of the **Sketch** contextual tab.

Coincident Constraint

This constraint connects a point with another point. On the **Sketch** contextual tab of the toolbar, click **Constraints > Coincident** and select the points to be made coincident to each other. The selected points will be connected.

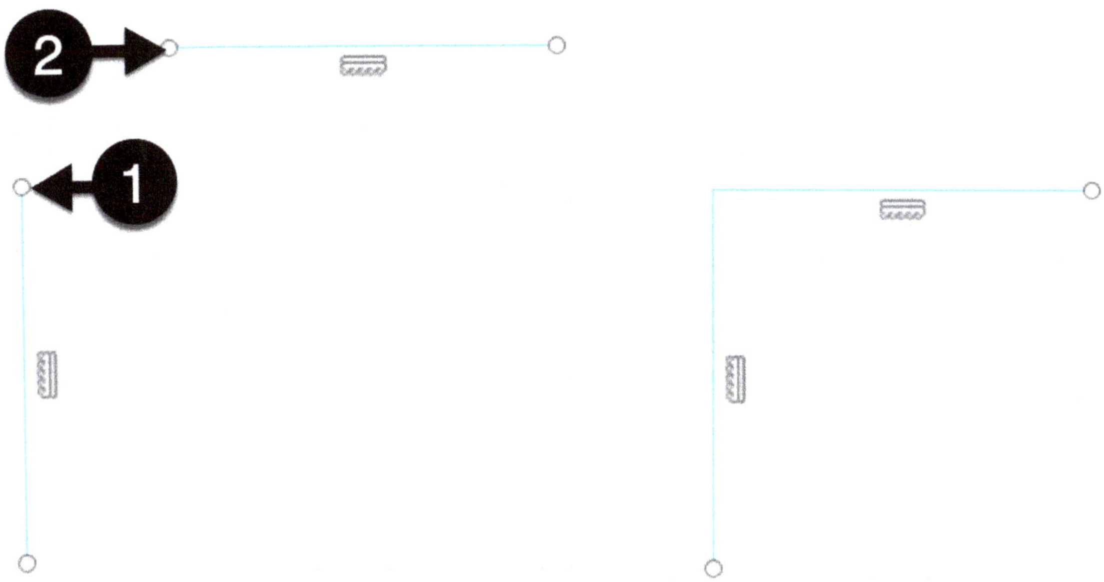

In addition to that, this constraint makes a vertex or a point to be on a line, curve, arc, or circle. Click the **Coincident** button on the **Constraints** panel and select a line, circle, arc, or curve. Next, select the point to be made coincident. The point will lie on the selected entity or its extension.

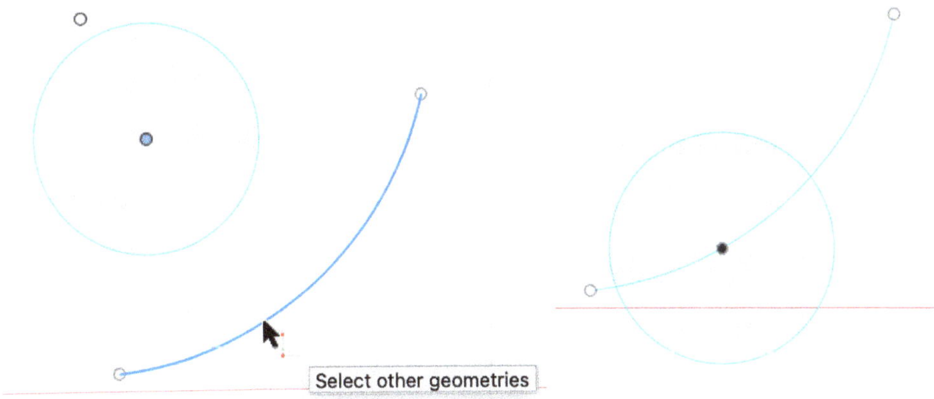

Midpoint Constraint

The **Midpoint** constraint forces a point or vertex to be aligned with the midpoint of a line. On the **Sketch** contextual tab of the toolbar, click **Constraints > Midpoint** and click on a point or vertex. Next, click on a line; the point will coincide with the midpoint of the line.

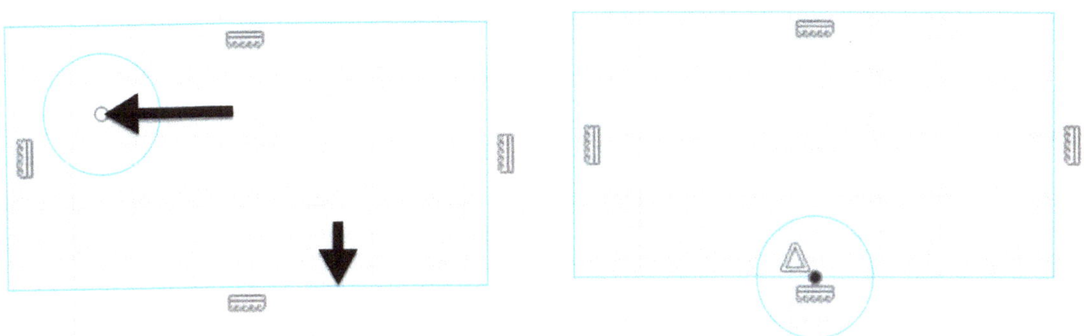

Horizontal/Vertical Constraint

This constraint makes a line horizontal or vertical based on its position. Click the **Horizontal/Vertical Constraint** icon on the **Constraints** panel and select a line positioned at an angle below 45-degrees from the horizontal axis of the sketch; the line is made horizontal.

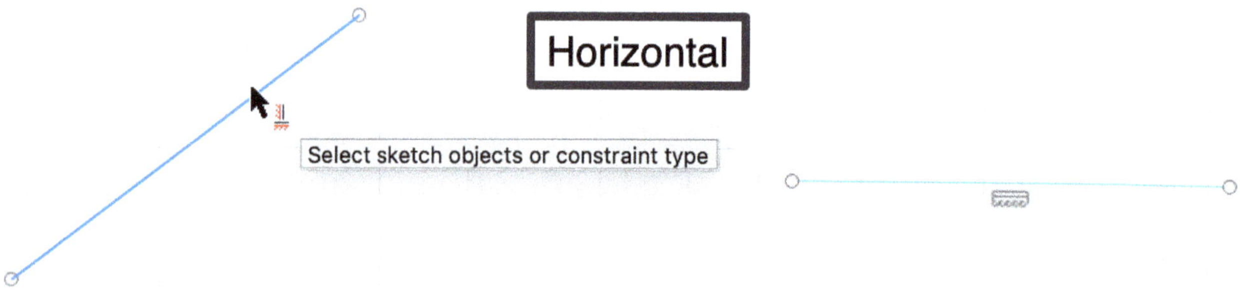

This constraint also makes a line vertical. Click the **Horizontal/Vertical Constraint** button on the **Constraints** panel and select a line positioned at 45-degrees or more from the horizontal axis of the sketch; the line is made vertical.

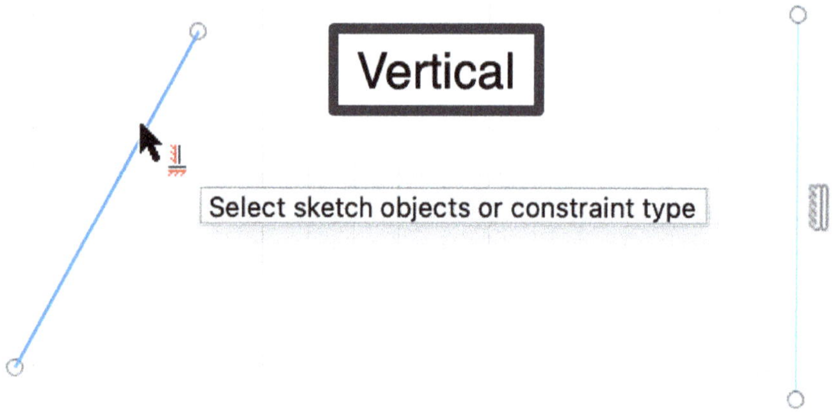

The **Horizontal/Vertical Constraint** also aligns the two selected points horizontally or vertically depending on the position to each other. Click the **Horizontal/Vertical Constraint** button on the **Constraints** panel and then select the points to align them horizontally or vertically.

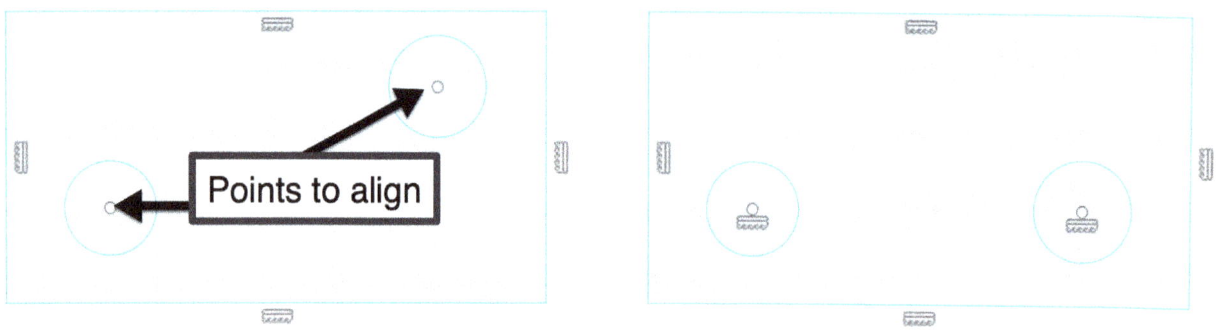

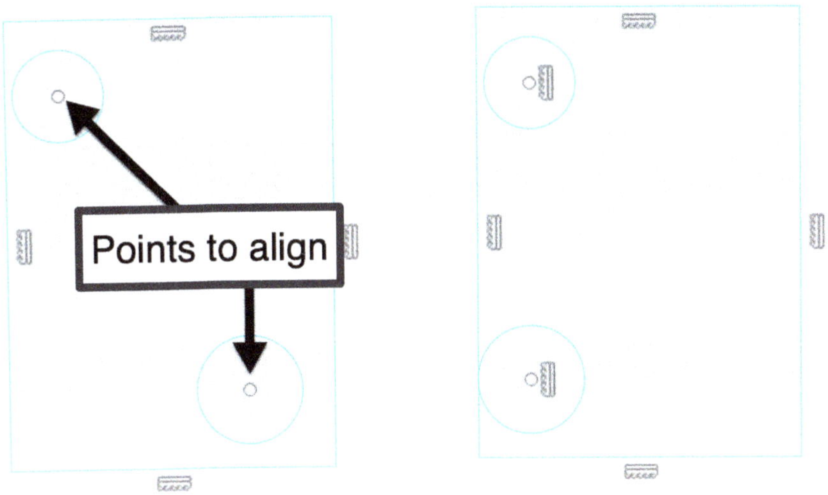

Concentric Constraint

This constraint makes the center points of two arcs, circles, or ellipses coincident with each other. Click the **Concentric** button on the **Constraints** panel and select a circle or arc from the sketch. Select another circle or arc. The circles/arcs will be concentric to each other.

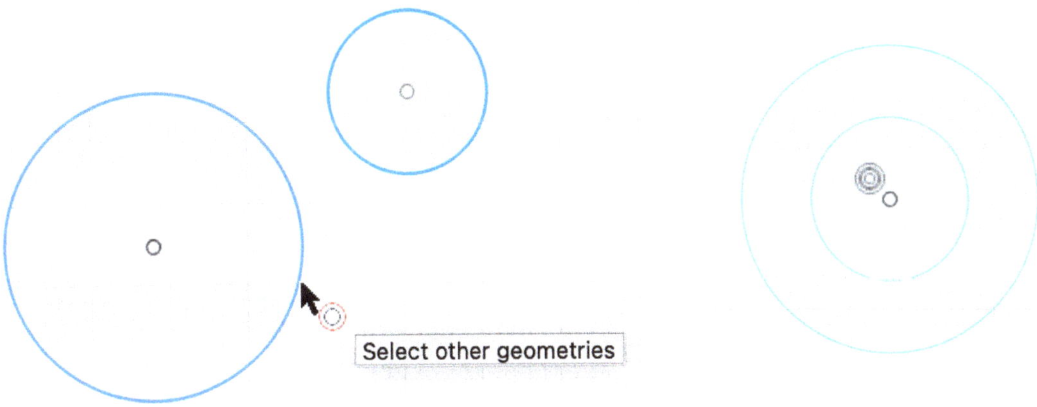

Equal

The **Equal** constraint makes two lines equal in length.

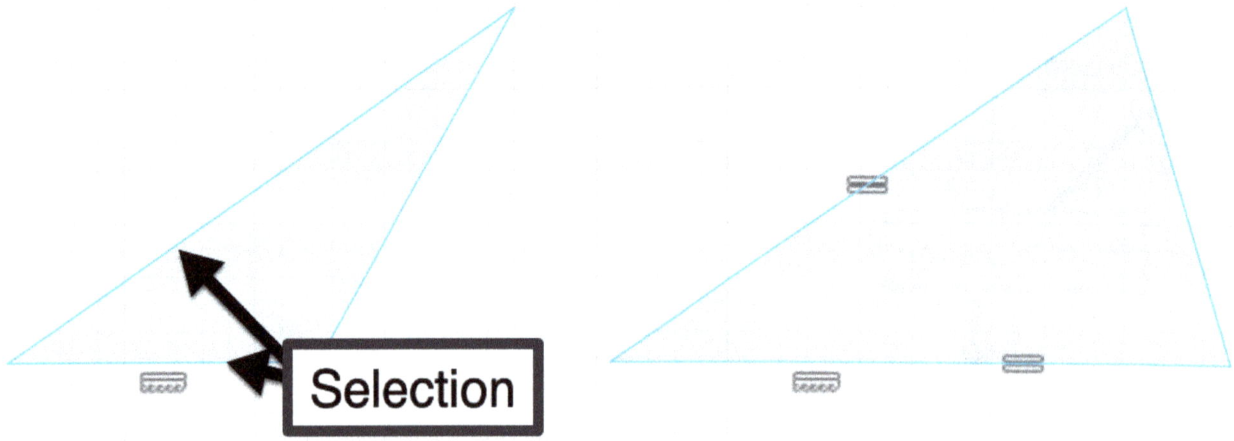

In addition to that, this constraint makes two circles or arcs equal in size.

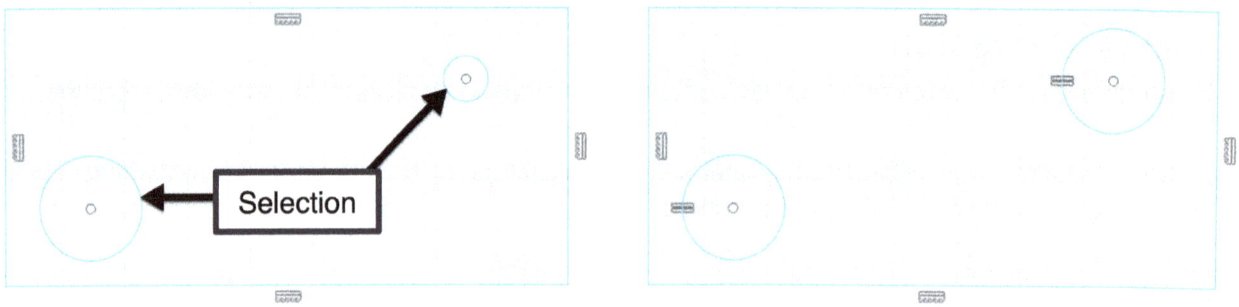

Collinear Constraint

This constraint forces a line to be collinear to another line. The lines are not required to touch each other. On the **Sketch** contextual tab of the toolbar, click **Constraints > Collinear**. Select the two lines, as shown. The second line will be collinear to the first line.

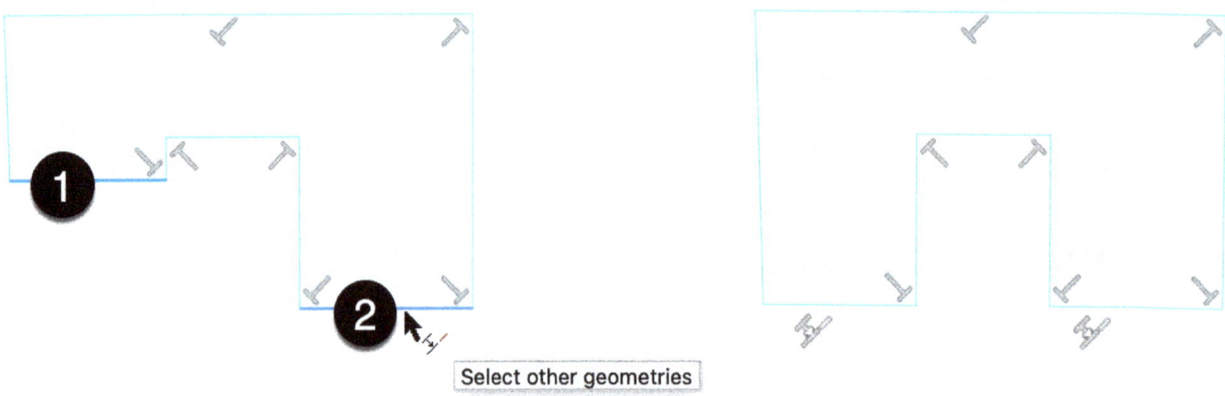

Tangent

This constraint makes an arc, circle, or line tangent to another arc or circle. On the **Sketch** contextual tab of the toolbar, click the **Tangent** button and select a circle, arc, or line. Select another circle, arc, or line; both the elements become tangent to each other.

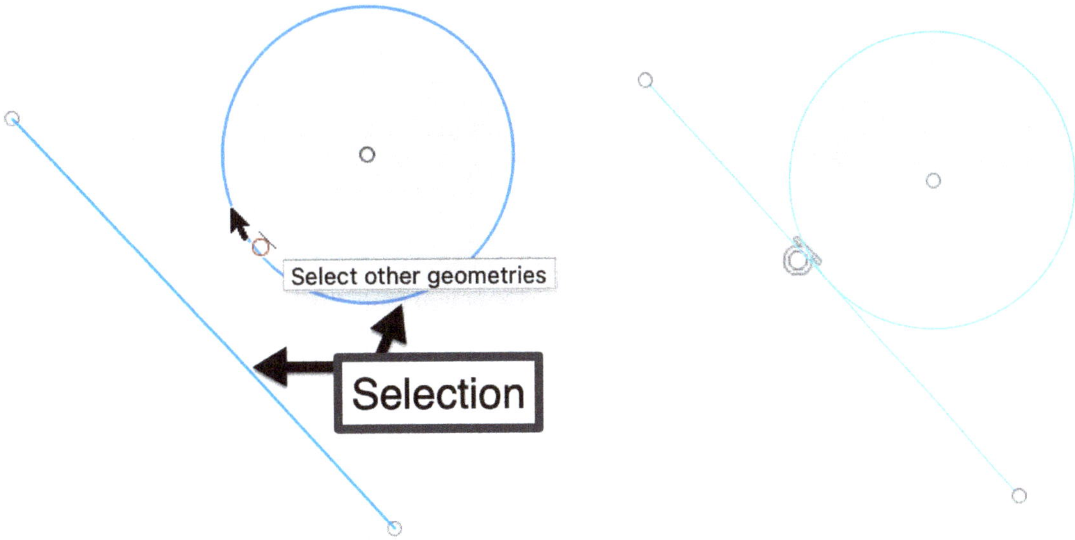

Parallel Constraint

This constraint makes two lines parallel to each other. Click the **Parallel** button on the **Constraints** panel and select two lines from the sketch. The under-constrained line is made parallel to the constrained line. For example, if you select a line with the **Horizontal/Vertical** constraint and a free to move line, the free-to-move line becomes parallel to the horizontal/vertical line.

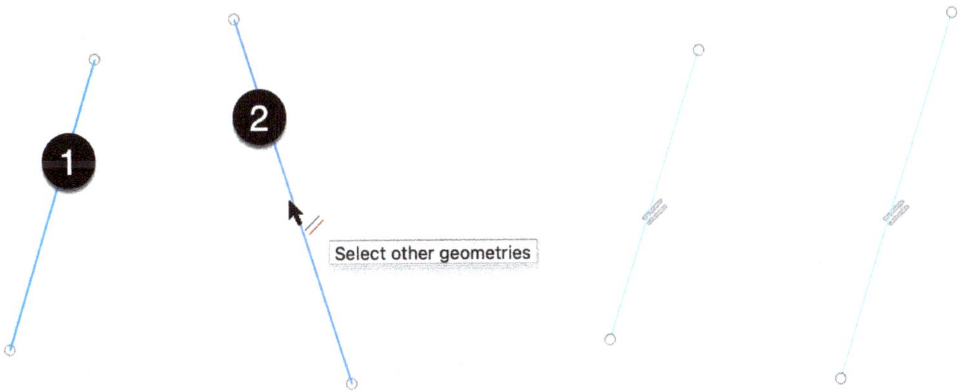

Perpendicular Constraint

This constraint makes two lines perpendicular to each other. Click the **Perpendicular** icon on the **Constraints** panel and select two lines from the sketch. The two lines will be made perpendicular to each other.

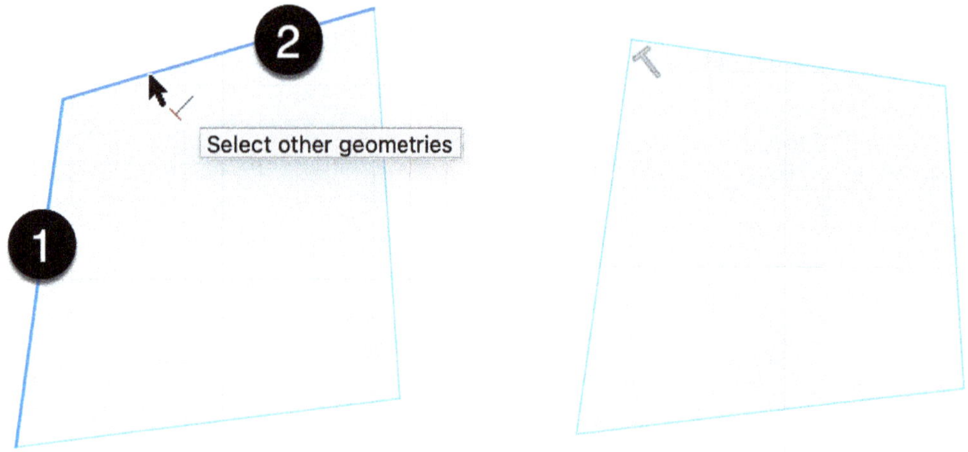

Symmetry Constraint

This constraint makes two objects symmetric about a line. The objects will have the same size, position, and orientation about the symmetry line. Activate this command (on the **Sketch** contextual tab of the toolbar, click **Constraints > Symmetry**), and click on the first object. Next, click on the second object, and then select the symmetry line. The two objects will be made symmetric about the symmetry line.

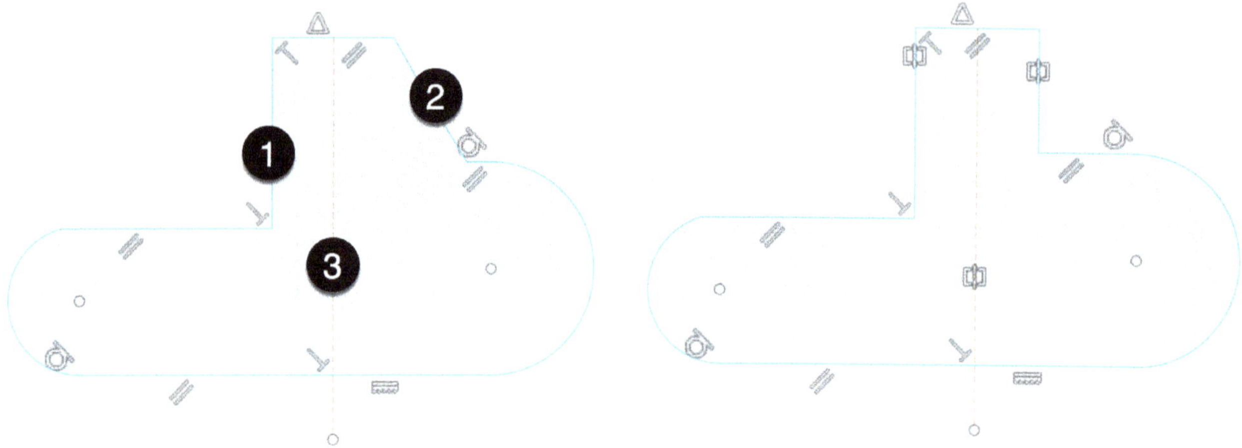

Fix/Unfix Constraint

This constraint fixes the selected objects at their current location. On the **Sketch** contextual tab, click **Constraints > Fix/Unfix** . Next, select single or multiple objects from the graphics window. Right-click and select **OK**. Now, click on the fixed objects and try to drag them; the objects are unmovable.

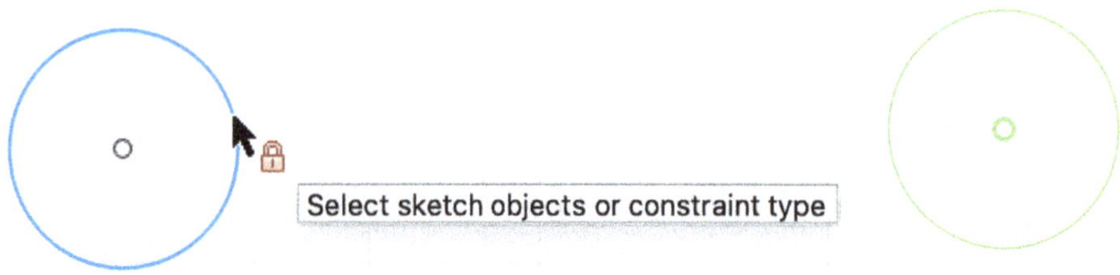

You can unfix the fixed objects by clicking the **Fix/Unfix** icon on the **Constraints** panel and selecting them.

Sketch Palette

Sketch Palette has options that will make it easy for you to work with sketches. You can check or uncheck these options. These options are explained next:

Construction

This option converts a sketch element into a construction element. The construction elements support you in creating a sketch of the desired shape and size. To convert a sketch element to a construction element, select it and click **Linetype > Construction**  on the **Sketch Palette**. You can also convert it back to a sketch element by selecting it and deactivating the **Construction** button on the **Sketch Palette**.

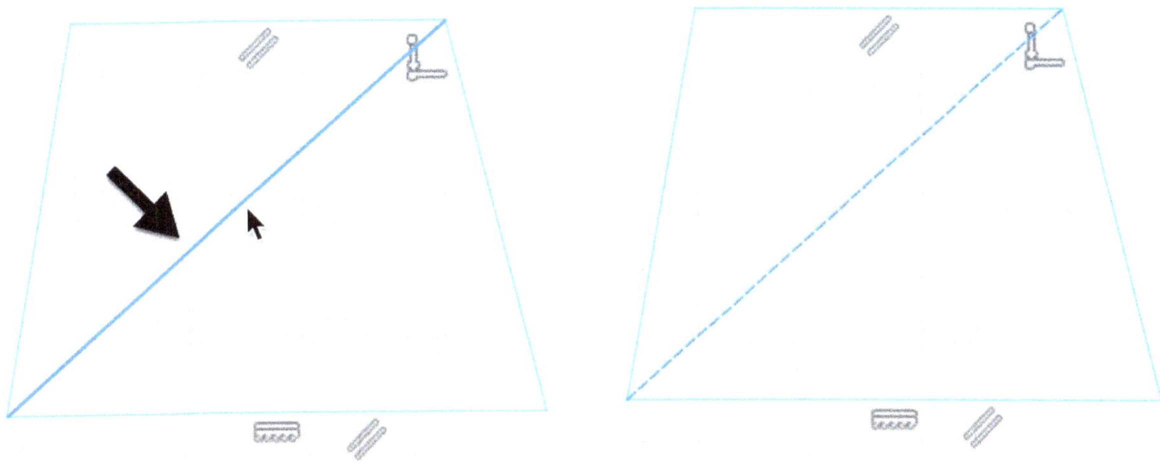

Constraints

As constraints are created, you can display or hide them using the **Constraints** option. To view all the constraints of a sketch, check the **Constraints** option under the **Options** section of the **Sketch Palette**. When dealing with complicated sketches involving numerous constraints, you can turn off all the constraints. To do this, uncheck the **Constraints** option on the **Sketch Palette**.

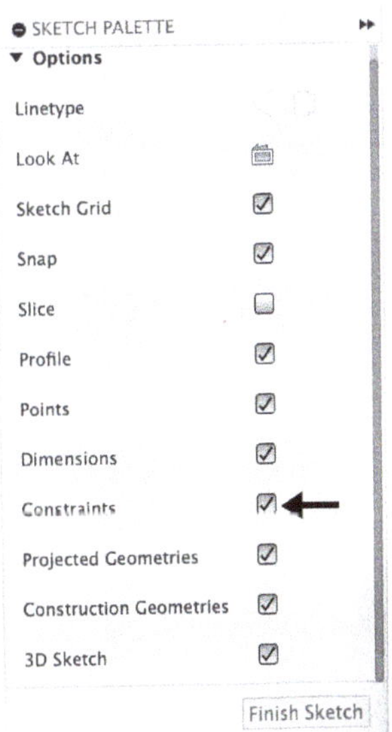

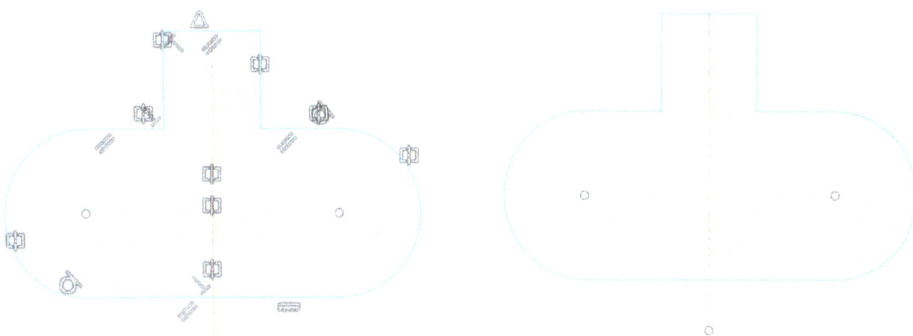

Constraints ON **Constraints OFF**

Sketch Grid

The **Sketch Grid** displays the grid lines in the graphics window. This option is available in the **Sketch Palette** under the **Options** section. By default, the **Sketch Grid** option is checked. Uncheck this option if you want to turn off the grid lines. The grid lines will be not visible in the graphics window.

Sketch Grid ON

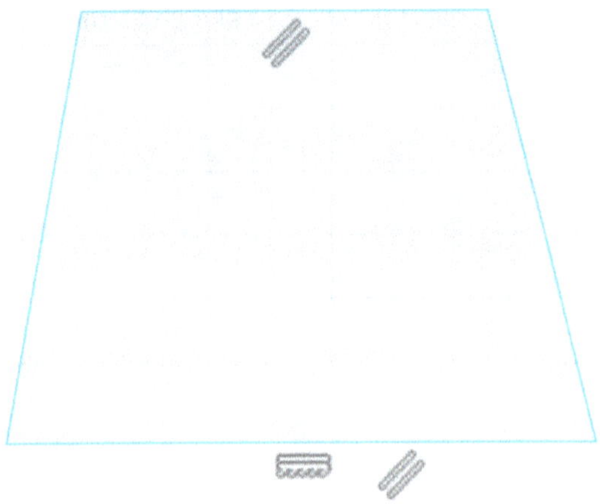

Sketch Grid OFF

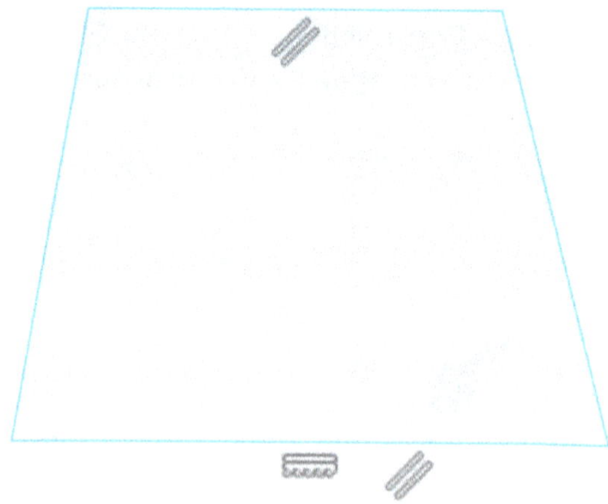

Points

The **Points** option is used to turn ON or OFF the sketch points in the graphics window. By default, the **Points** option is checked. As a result, the sketch points are visible on the screen. You can uncheck this option if you do not want to view the sketch points.

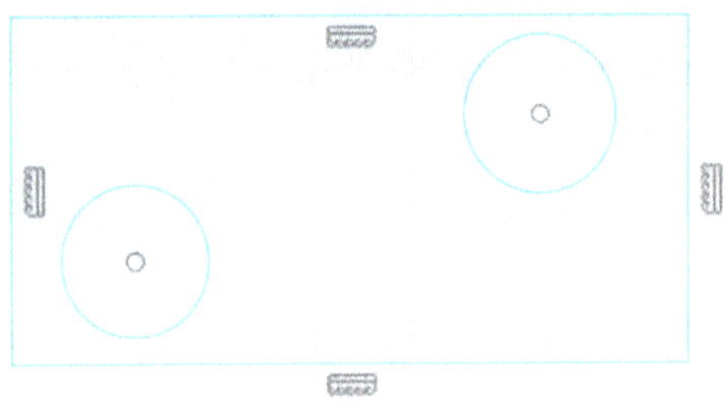

Points ON

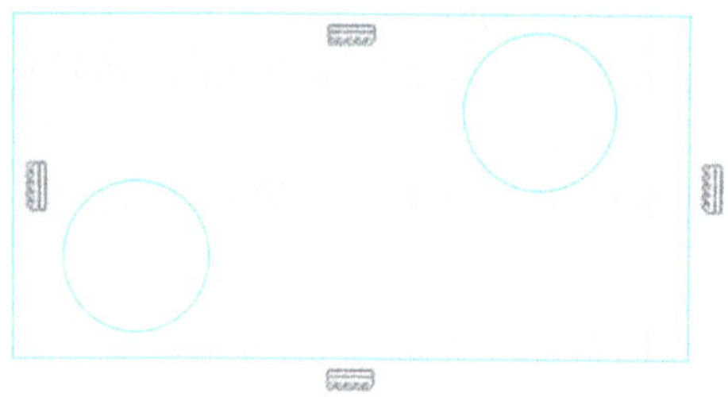

Points OFF

Profile

The **Profile** option displays the closed sketch as shaded.

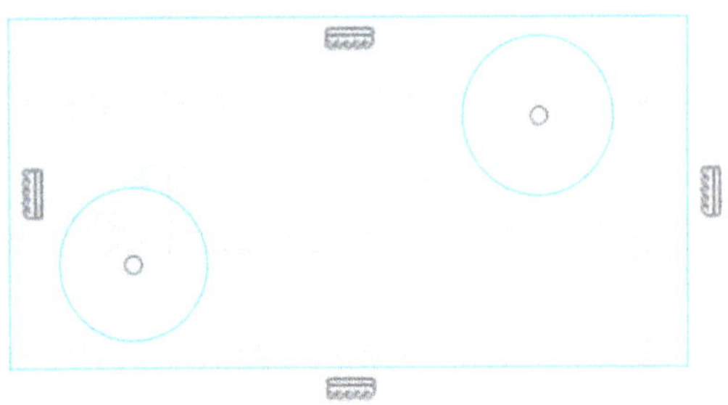

Profile ON

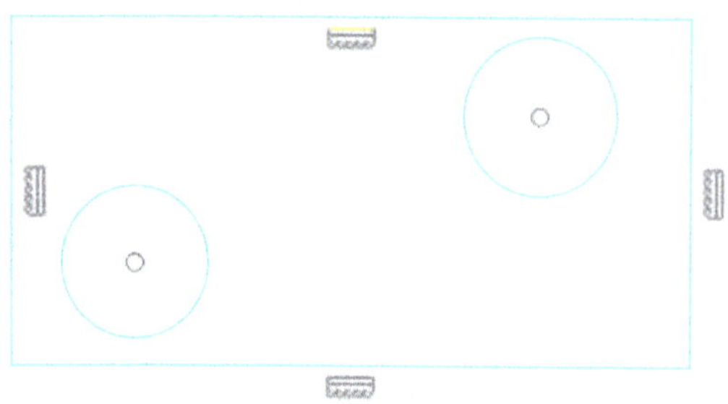

Profile OFF

Snap

The **Snap** option allows you to snap to the grid points. This will make it easy for you to create sketches accurately. To turn ON the snap mode, check the **Snap** option in the **Options** section of the **Sketch Palette**. Next, activate a sketch command and notice a blue square attached to the pointer. The blue square snaps to the grid points as you move the pointer. Next, click on the graphics window and notice that a grid point is selected. Likewise, continue to draw the sketch by selecting other grid points.

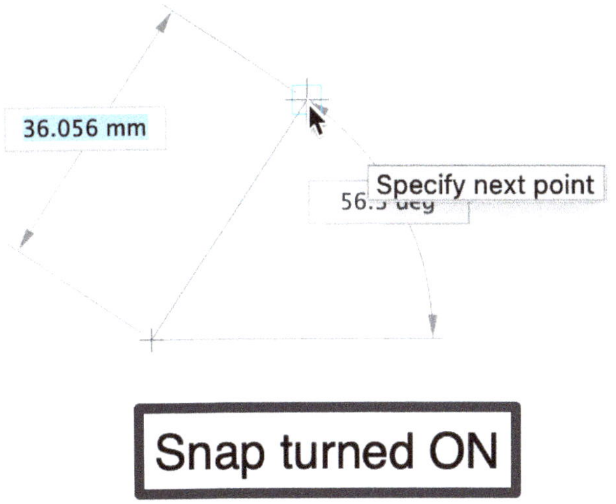

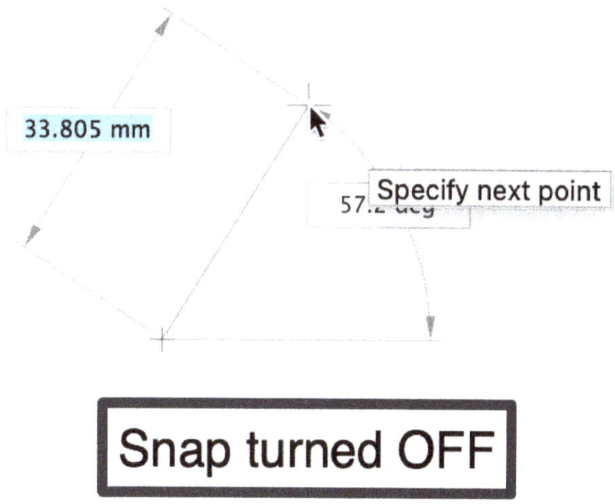

Slice

The **Slice** option is used to cut objects using the sketch plane. This option is used only for display, and it will not change the geometry. It helps you to view the sketch clearly when the sketch plane is located inside the model. This option is available in the **Options** section of the **Sketch Palette**.

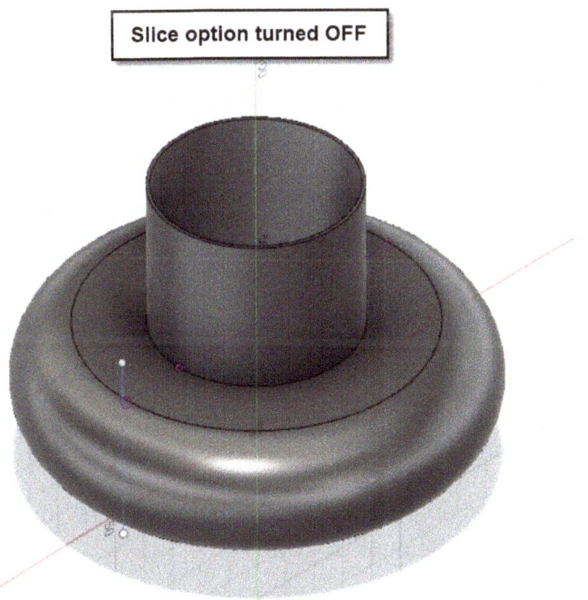

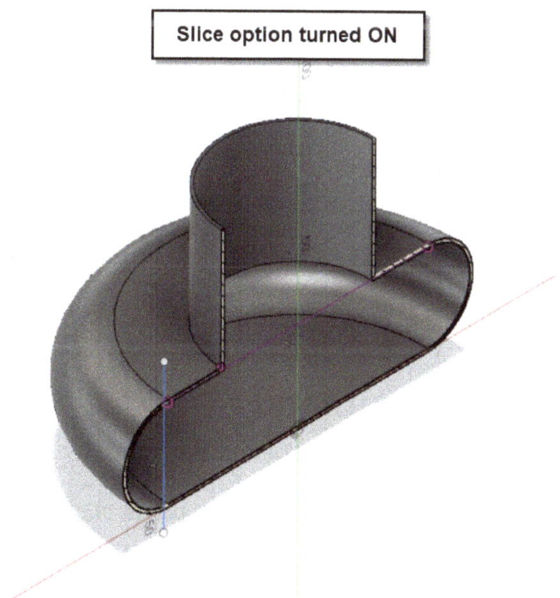

The Fillet command

This command rounds a sharp corner created by the intersection of two lines, arcs, circles, and rectangle. Activate this command (On the **Sketch** contextual tab of the toolbar, click the **Fillet** icon on the **Modify** panel), and select the elements to be filleted. Enter the radius value in the **Fillet radius** box to create the fillet. The elements to be filleted are not required to touch each other. Keep on selecting the elements of the sketch; the fillets are added at the corners at which two selected elements intersect. Also, notice that the fillets are created with an equal radius, and a dimension is added to every fillet.

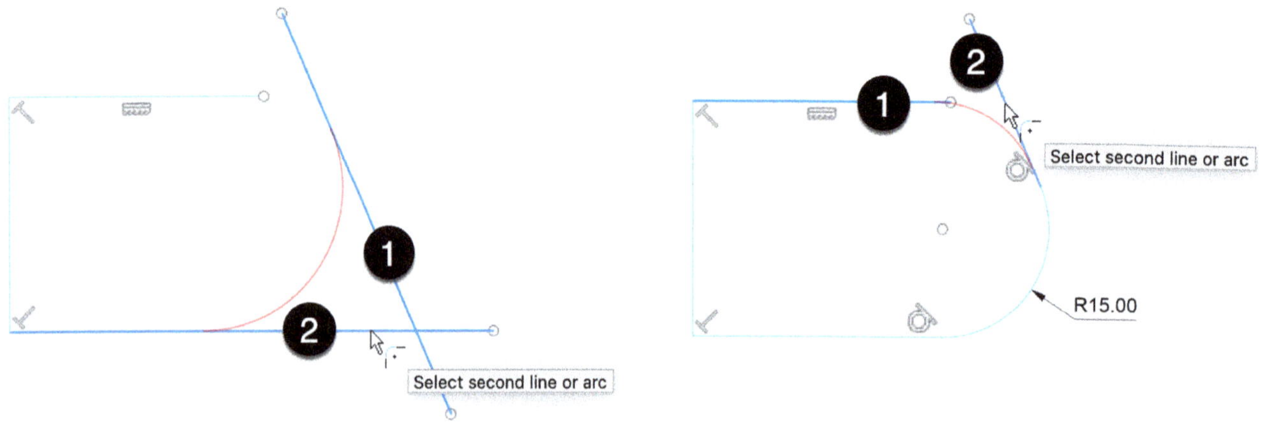

If you want to create a fillet with a different radius, then you need to create them as separate instances.

The Extend command

This command extends elements such as lines, arcs, and curves until they touch another element called the boundary edge. Activate this command (On the **Sketch** contextual tab of the toolbar, expand the **Modify** panel and click **Extend**), and click on the element to extend. It will extend up to the next element.

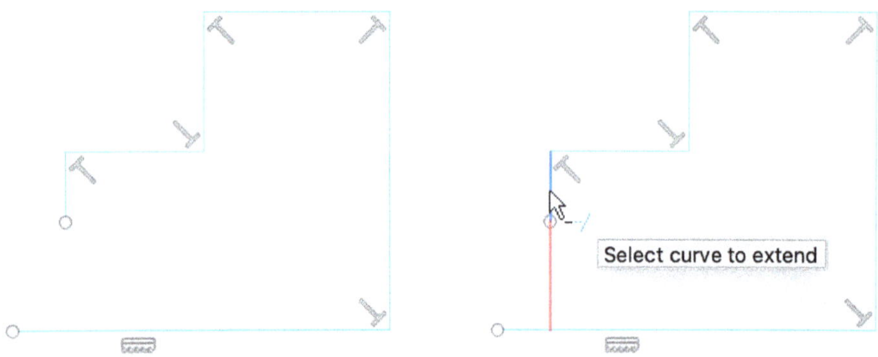

The Trim command

This command trims the end of an element back to the intersection of another element. Activate this command (On the **Sketch** contextual tab of the toolbar, click the **Trim** icon on the **Modify** panel) and click on the element or elements to trim. You can also drag the pointer across the elements to trim.

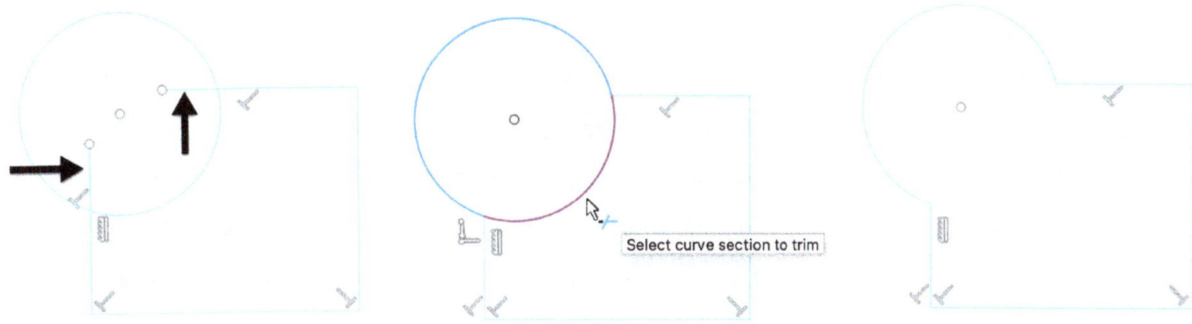

The Offset command

This command creates a parallel copy of a selected element or chain of elements. Activate this command (On the **Sketch** contextual tab of the toolbar, click the **Offset** icon on the **Modify** panel), and select an element or chain of elements to offset. Make sure that the **Chain Selection** option is checked to select a chain of element. After selecting the element(s), select an option from the Direction drop-down: **One Side**, **Two Sides**, or **Symmetric**. The **One Side** option allows you to create the offset on one side of the selected sketch element. If you select this option, you should type-in a value in the Distance box to specify the offset distance. Next, you can flip the side on which the offset is created by clicking the Flip button. The Two Sides option allows you to create the offset on both the side of the selected sketch element. You need to type-in values in the Distance 1 and Distance 2 boxes. Make sure that you type a negative value in one these boxes and positive value in the other. Next, click the Flip button, if you need to reverse the sides. The **Symmetric** option allows you to create the offset with same distance on both sides of the selected element. After specifying the required settings, click the **OK** button; the parallel copy of the elements will be created.

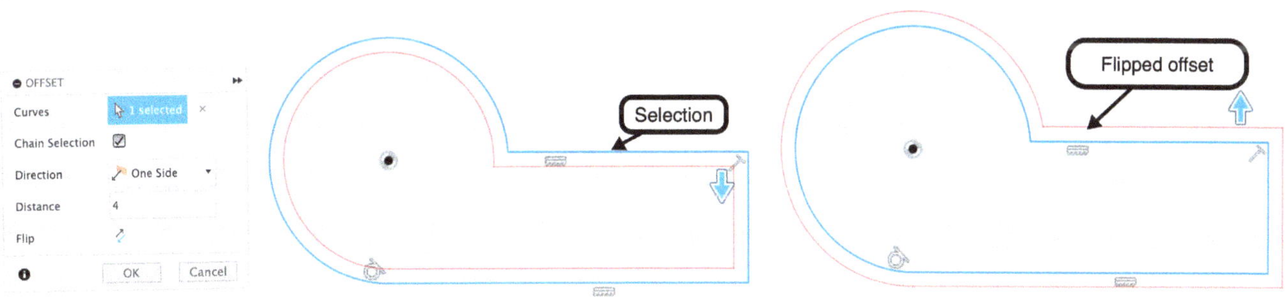

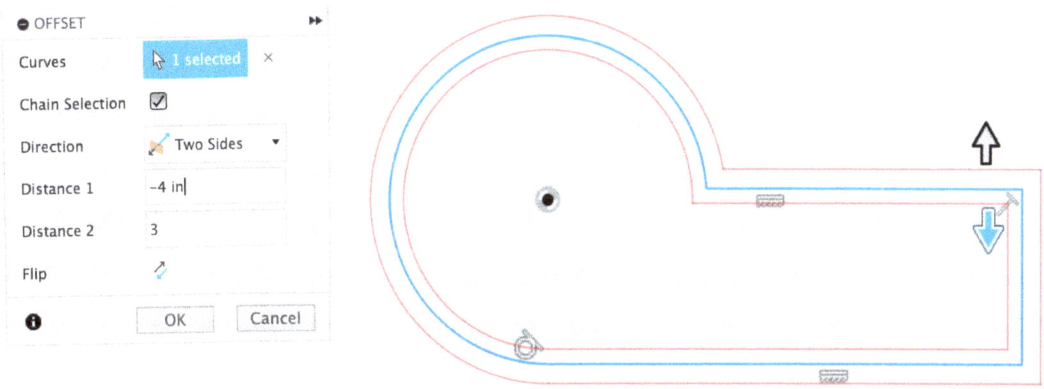

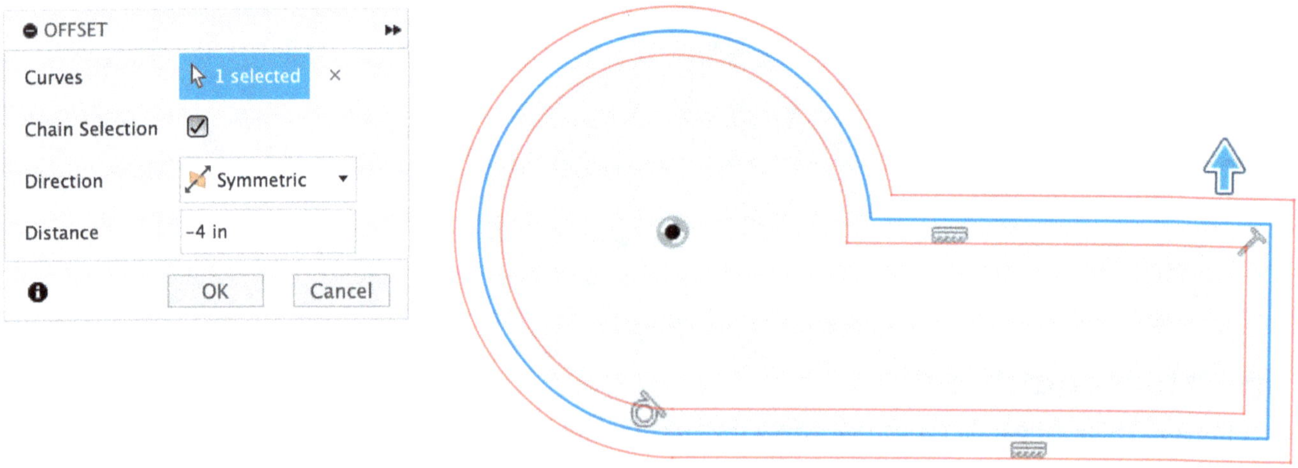

The Sketch Scale command

This command increases or decreases the size of elements in a sketch. Activate this command (On the **Sketch** contextual tab of the toolbar, expand the **Modify** panel and click **Sketch Scale**) and then click the **Entities** selection button and select the elements to scale. After selecting the elements, click the **Point** button and select a base point. Next, click and drag the arrow displayed in the graphics window (or) enter a scale factor value in the **Scale Factor** box on the **Sketch Scale** dialog. Click **OK** on the **Sketch Scale** dialog to scale the sketch elements.

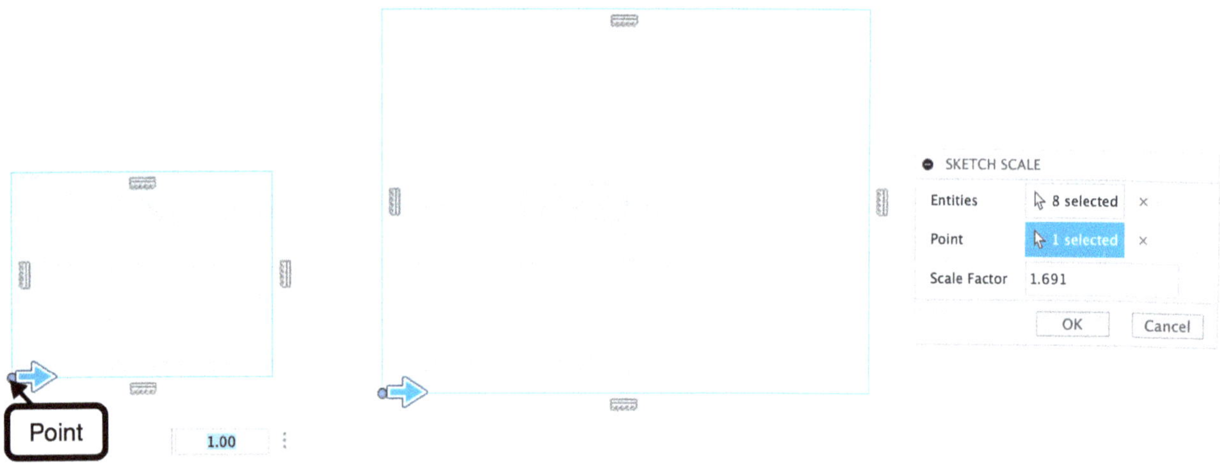

Circular Sketch Pattern

This command creates a circular pattern of the selected sketch elements. Activate the **Circular Pattern** command (On the **Sketch** contextual tab of the toolbar, expand the **Create** panel, and click **Circular Pattern**), and select the objects to be patterned. On the **Circular Pattern** dialog, click the **Center Point** selection button and select a point around which the sketch elements will be patterned. Next, type-in a value in the **Quantity** box to define the instance count of the pattern. Next, specify the type of pattern from the **Angular Spacing** drop-down. There are three options in this drop-down: **Full**, **Partial**, and **Symmetric**. The **Full** option creates a full 360-degree circular pattern.

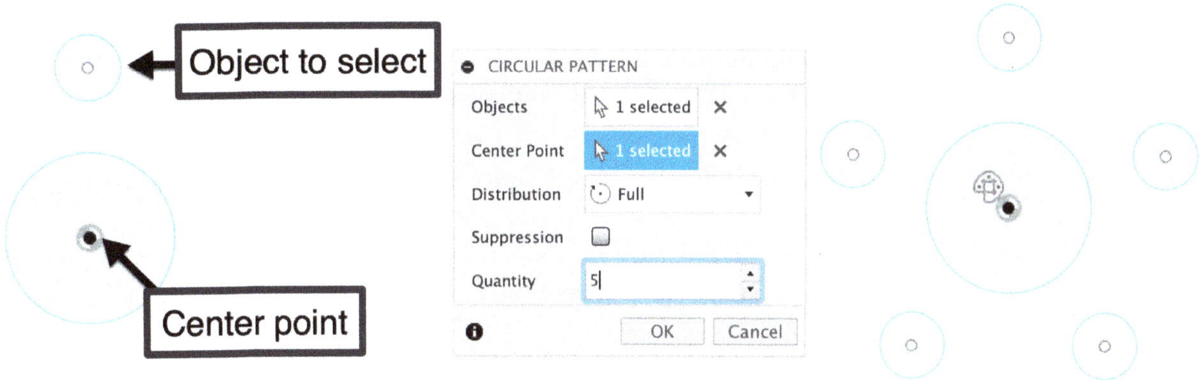

If you select the **Partial** option, then you need to specify the total angle in the **Angle** box. The occurrences will be placed equally within the specified total angle value.

If you select the **Symmetric** option, then a circular pattern will be created with an equal number of occurrences on both sides of the base point. Also, you need to specify the total angle in the **Angle** box.

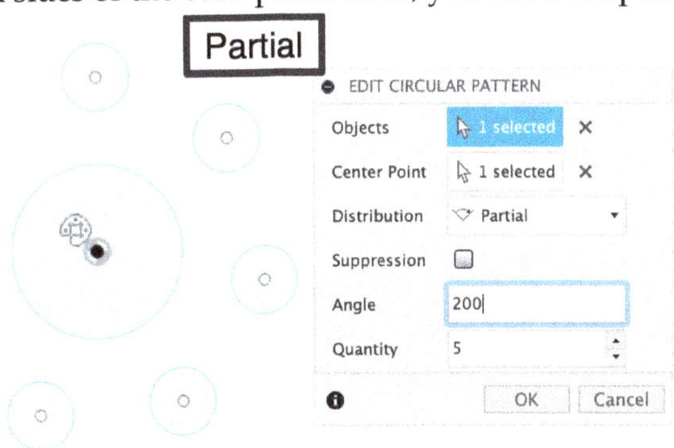

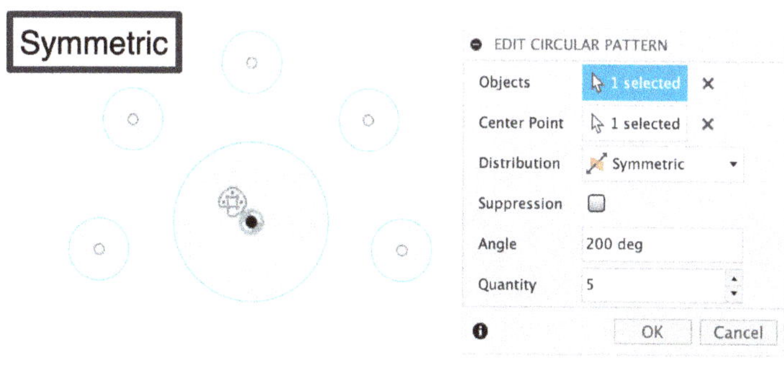

Check the **Suppression** option to display the checkboxes on individual occurrences. You can uncheck the checkboxes if you want to suppress the occurrences. Click **OK** to create a circular sketch pattern.

To edit an existing circular pattern, double-click on the Circular Pattern symbol displayed at the center of the circular pattern; the **Edit Circular Pattern** dialog pops up on the screen. Modify the values on this dialog and click **OK**.

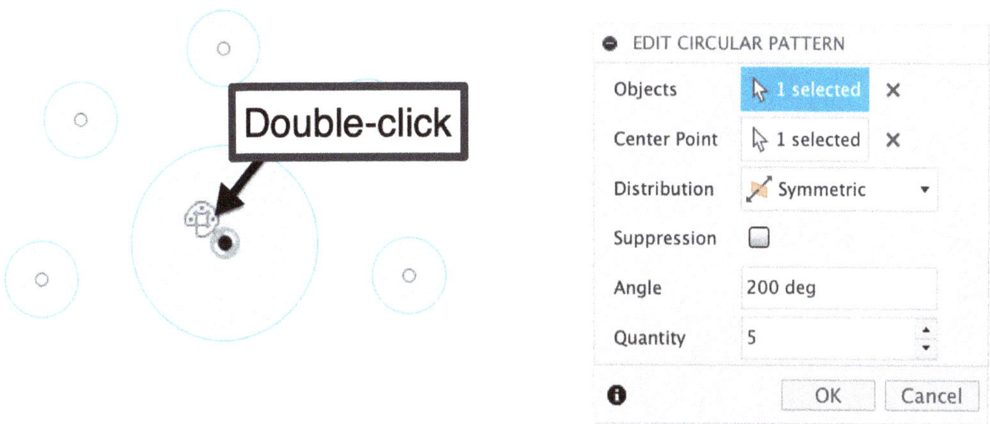

Rectangular Sketch Pattern

This command creates a rectangular pattern of the selected sketch elements. Activate the **Rectangular Pattern** command (On the **Sketch** contextual tab of the toolbar, expand the **Create** panel, and click **Rectangle Pattern** 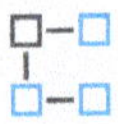), and select the objects to pattern. Next, you need to specify the orientation of the rectangular pattern. By default, the rectangular pattern is created along the X and Y axes of the sketch. However, you can orient the rectangular pattern along an inclined edge. To do this, click the **Direction/s** selection button on the **Rectangular Pattern** dialog and select a line to define the first direction. Next, type-in values in the **Quantity** and **Distance** boxes.

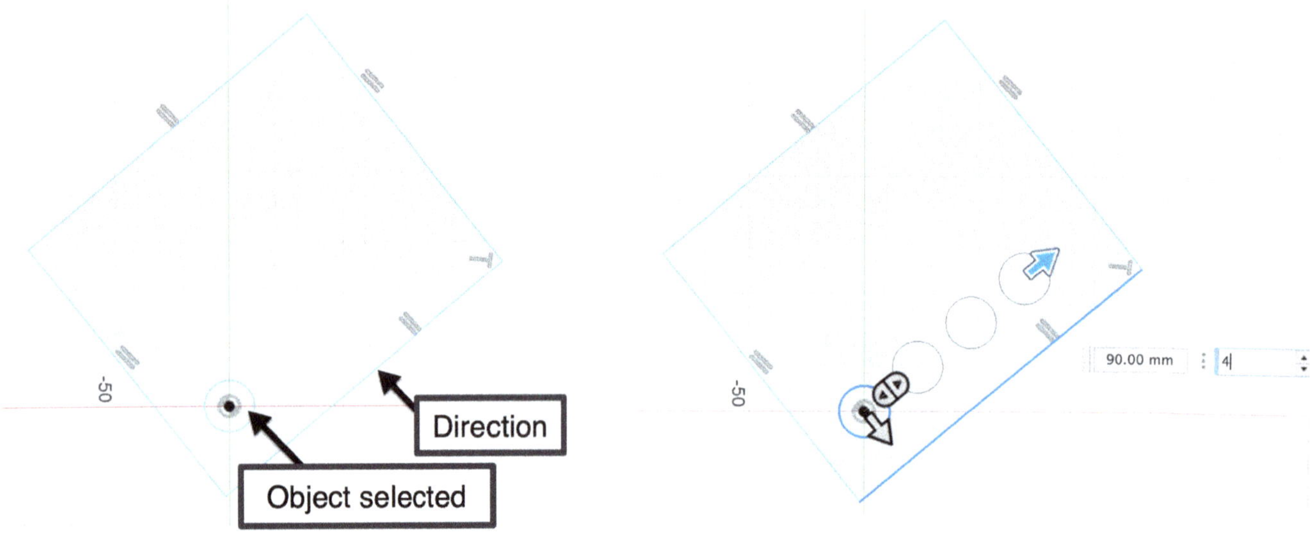

Select an option from the **Distribution** drop-down (**Extent** or **Spacing**). The **Extent** option equally places the occurrences of the pattern in the specified **Distance** value. The **Spacing** option allows you to specify the specify the spacing between the individual occurrences of the pattern in the **Distance** box.

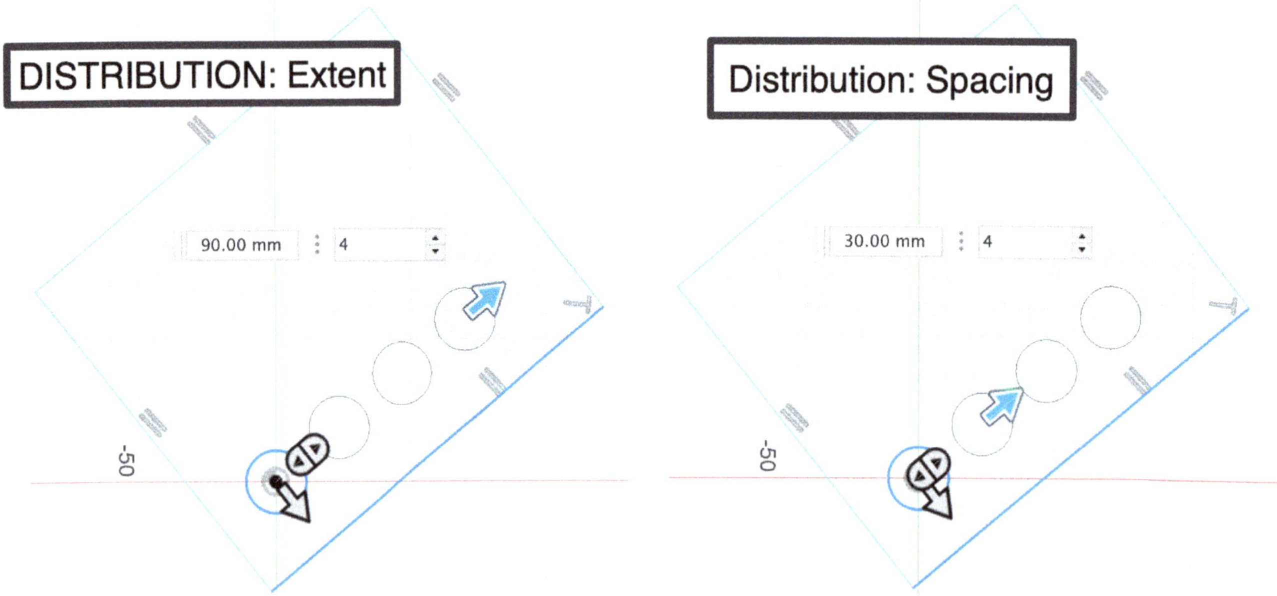

Click **Direction > One Direction**. You can also select the Symmetric option from the **Direction** drop-down. It places the instances equally on both sides of the base object.

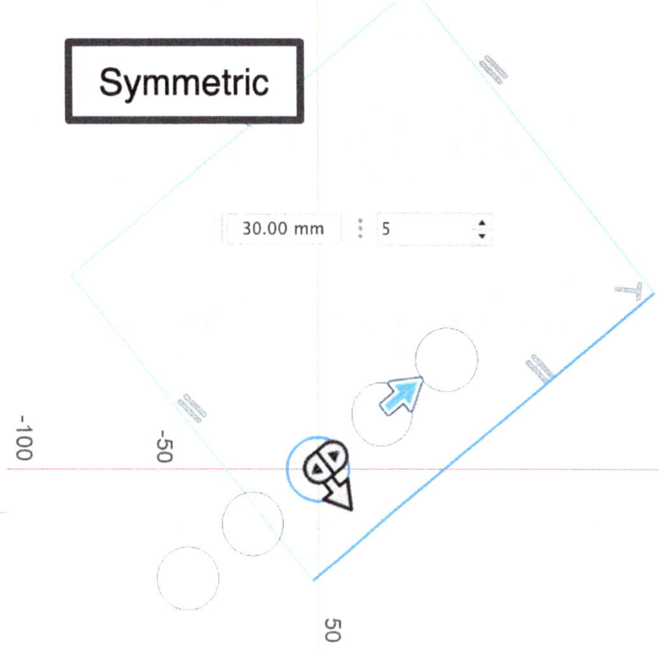

Likewise, specify the **Quantity**, **Distance**, and **Direction** values at the bottom of the dialog. You can reverse the direction by entering a negative value in the **Distance** box. Click **OK** to complete the rectangular pattern.

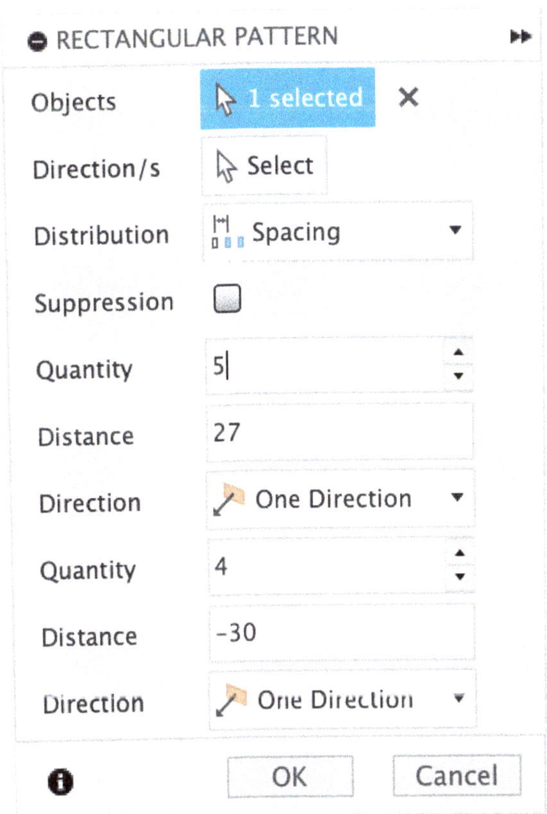

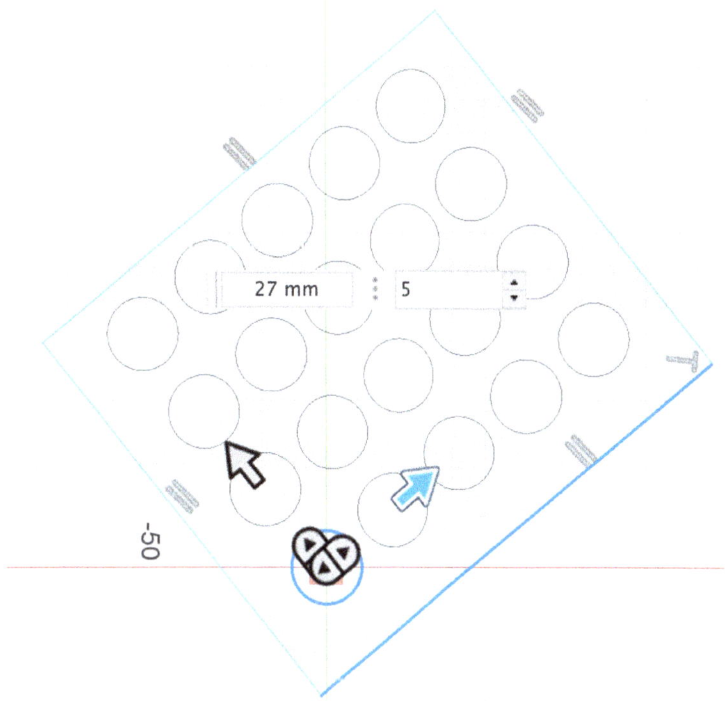

The Mirror command

This command creates a mirror copy of the selected elements. It also creates the **Symmetry** constraint between the original and mirrored elements. Activate this command (On the **Sketch** contextual tab of the toolbar, expand the **Create** panel and click **Mirror** ) and then select the objects to mirror. Next, click the **Mirror Line** selection button and select a line to define the mirror-line. Click **OK** on the **Mirror** dialog to mirror the objects.

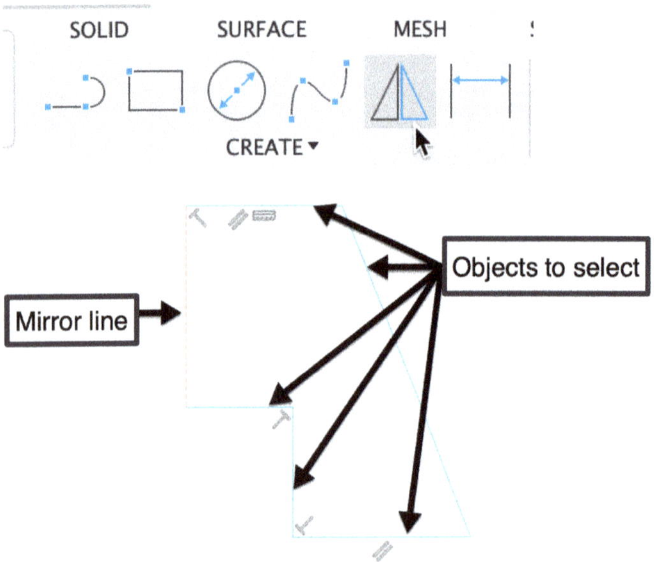

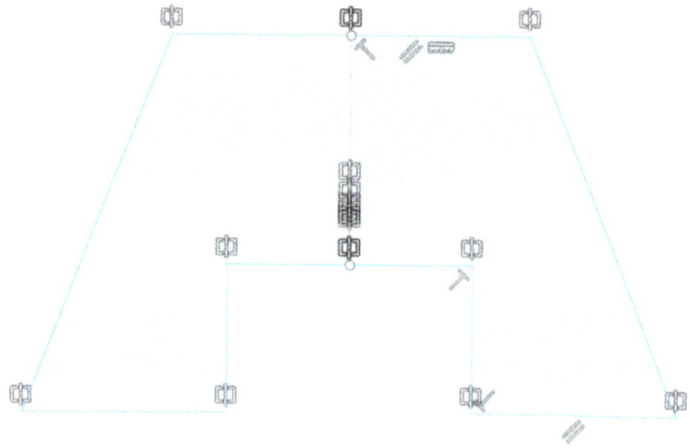

Creating Splines

Splines are non-uniform curves, which are used to create smooth shapes. In Autodesk Fusion 360, you can create a smooth spline curve using two commands: **Control Point Spline** and **Fit Point Spline**.

Control Point Spline

The **Control Point Spline** command helps you to create a spline by defining various points called as control points. Activate this command (On the **Sketch** contextual tab of the toolbar, expand the **Create** panel and click **Spline > Control Point Spline**). In the graphics window, click to specify the first control point. Move the pointer and specify the second point. Likewise, specify the other control points. As you define the control points, the dotted lines are created connecting them. Also, the spline will be created. Right-click and click **OK** to complete the spline. You can control the shape of the spline using the control points. Indeed, you can add dimensions and constraints to the control point.

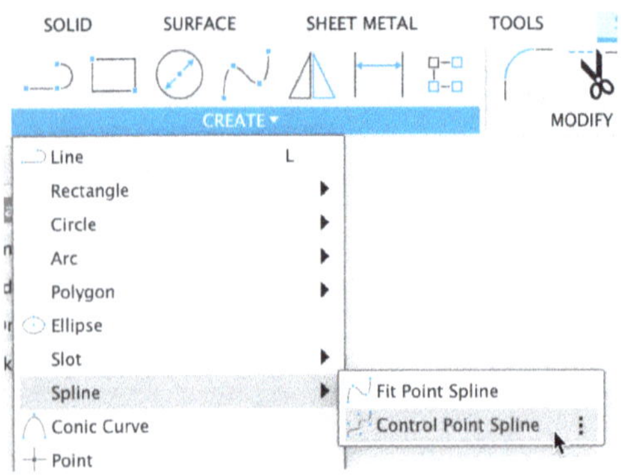

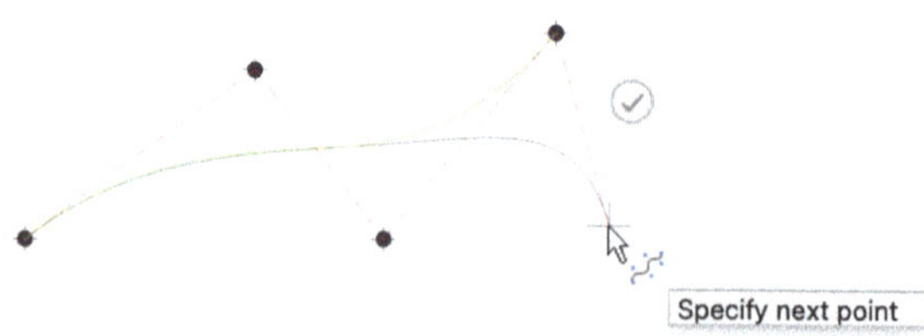

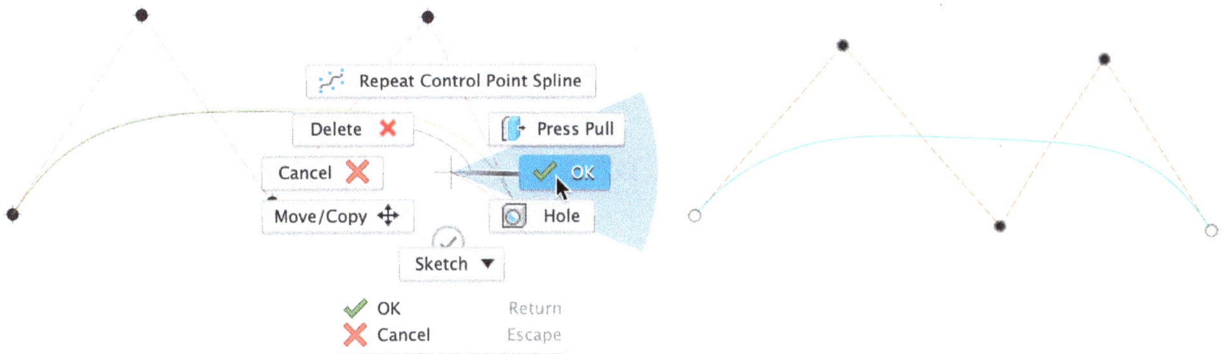

Fit Point Spline

The **Fit Point Spline** command creates a smooth spline passing through a series of points called fit points. Activate this command (On the **Sketch** contextual tab of the toolbar, click the **Fit Point Spline** on the **Create** panel). In the graphics window, click to specify the first point of the spline. Move the pointer and specify the second point of the spline. Likewise, specify the other points of the spline, and then right-click and click **OK** to create the spline. The endpoints are in white color, whereas the fit points along the curve are in black color. You can change the shape of the spline by dragging the fit points.

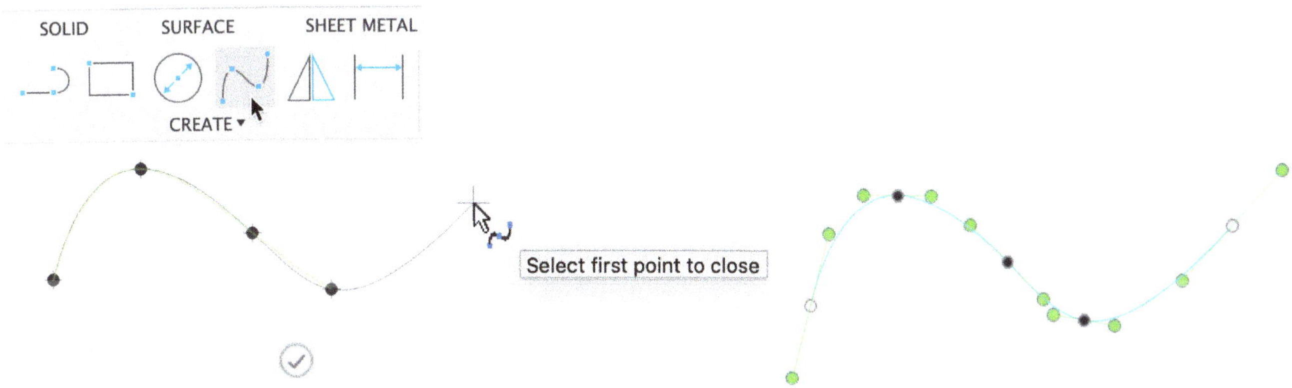

Curvature Constraint

This constraint matches the curvatures of two connected splines. On the **Sketch** contextual tab, click **Constraints > Curvature** . Next, select the two connected splines; the curvature of the first spline matches the second one.

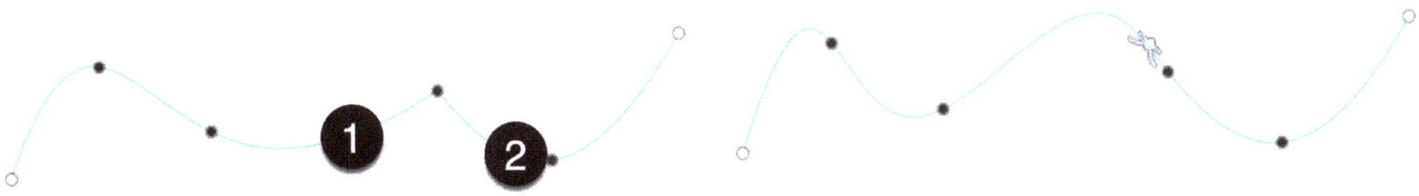

Examples

Example 1 (Millimeters)

In this tutorial, you will draw the sketch shown below.

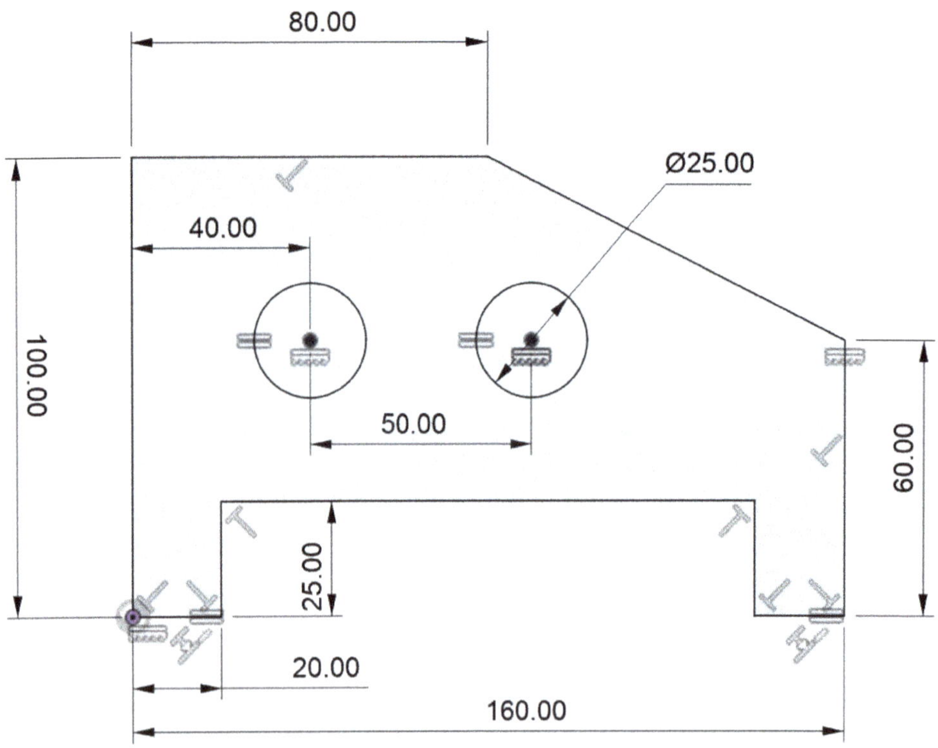

1. Start **Autodesk Fusion 360** by double-clicking the **Autodesk Fusion 360** icon on your desktop; the new design file is opened.
2. In the Browser bar, expand the **Document Settings** node and place the pointer on the **Units** option; the **Change Active Units** icon appears.
3. Click the **Change Active Units** icon, and then select the **millimeter (mm), gram (g)** option from the **Unit Type** drop-down. Next, click **OK** to set the units to millimeters.

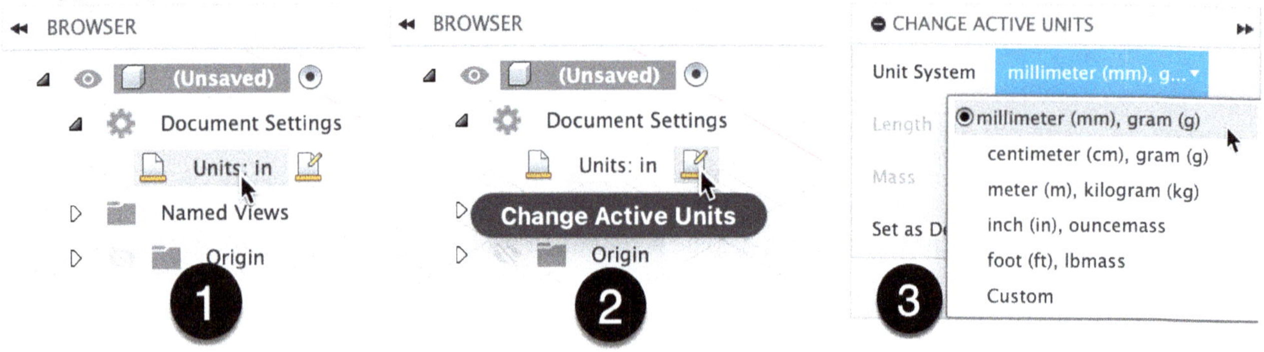

4. To start a sketch, click the **Create Sketch** icon on the **Create** panel of the **Solid** tab. Click on the XY plane. The sketch starts.
5. Click the **Line** button on the **Create** panel of the **Sketch** contextual tab. Click on the origin point to define the first point of the line.

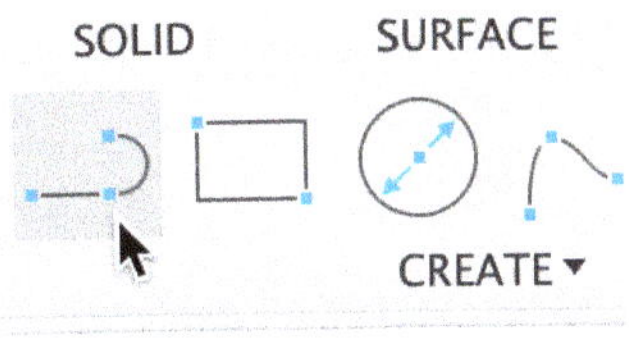

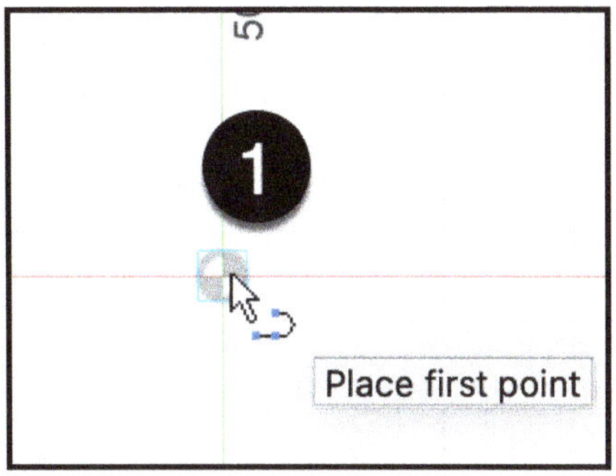

6. Move the pointer along the horizontal axis (red axis) and toward the right.
7. Click to define the endpoint of the line.
8. Move the pointer vertically upwards. Click to create the second line.

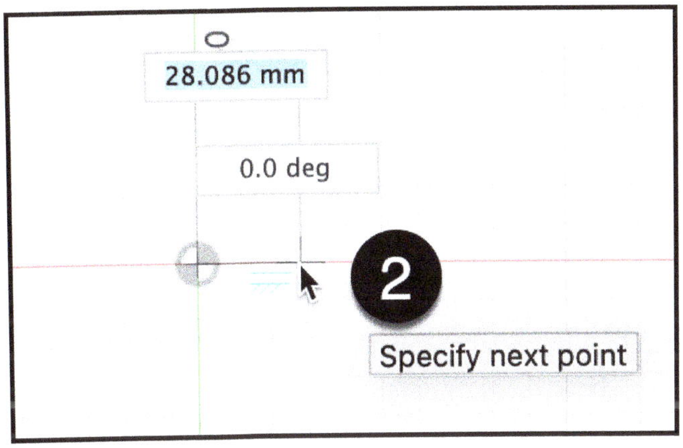

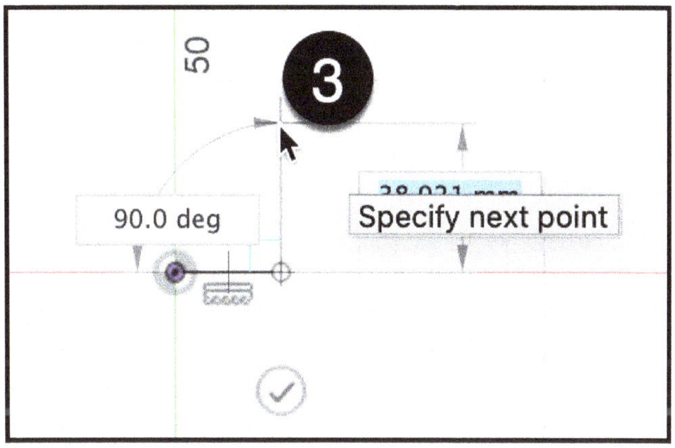

9. Create a closed-loop by selecting points in the sequence, as shown below.

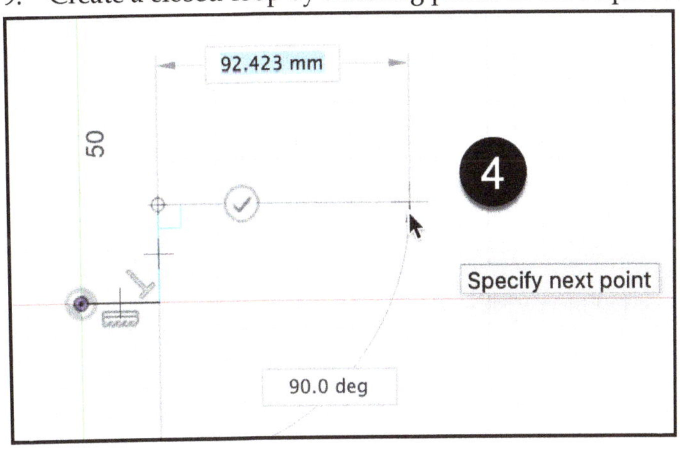

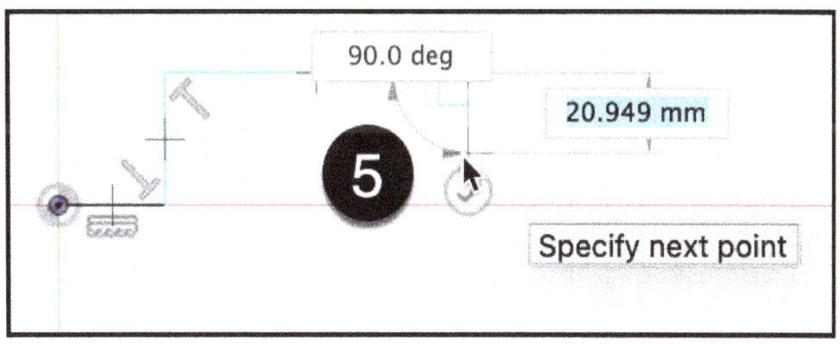

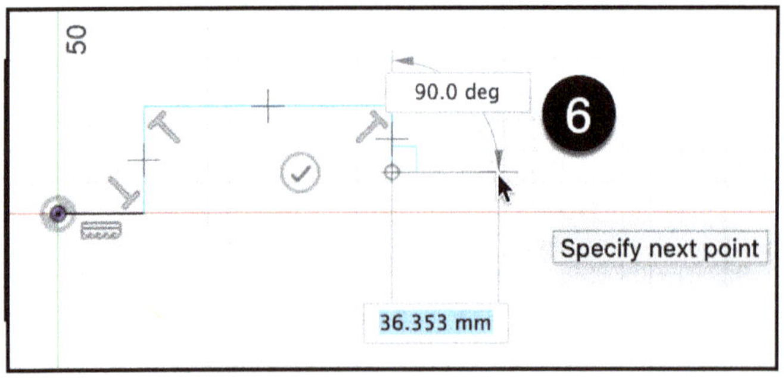
50
90.0 deg
6
Specify next point
36.353 mm

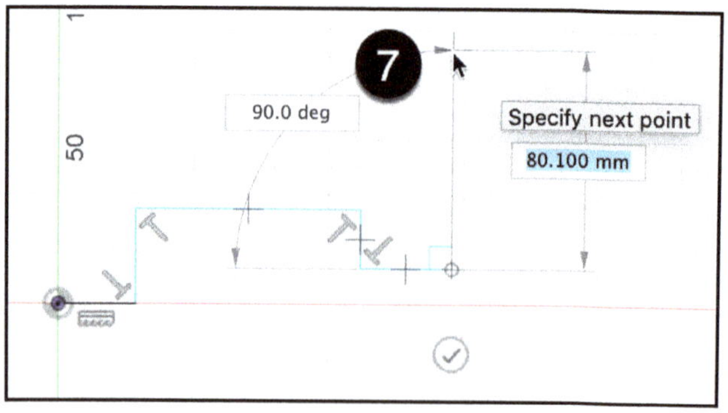
50
90.0 deg
7
Specify next point
80.100 mm

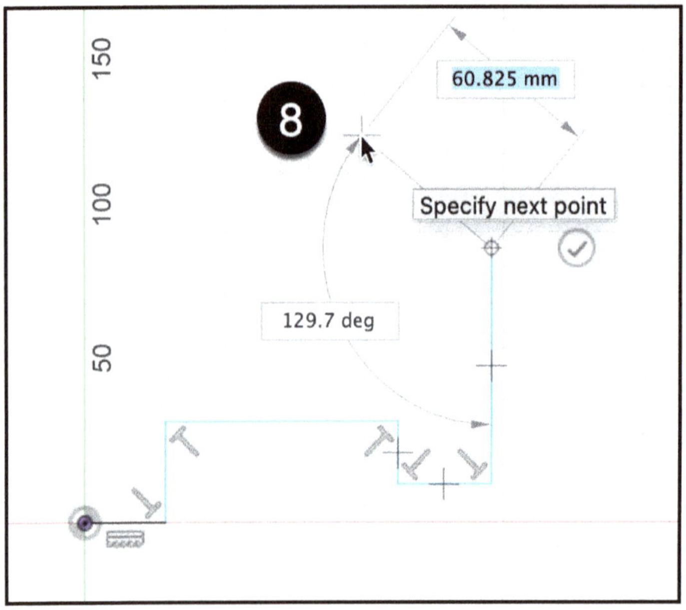
150
100
50
8
60.825 mm
Specify next point
129.7 deg

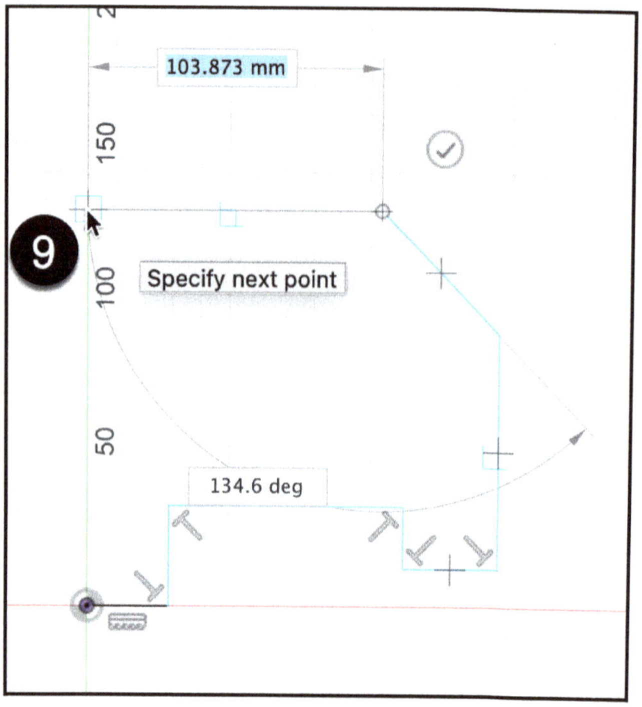
103.873 mm
150
100
50
9
Specify next point
134.6 deg

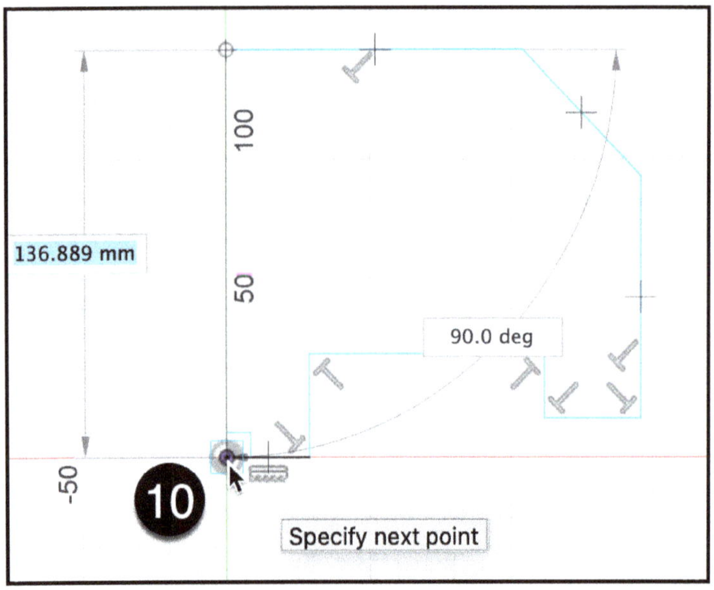
100
50
-50
136.889 mm
90.0 deg
10
Specify next point

Adding Constraints

1. Click **Constraints > Collinear** on the **Sketch** contextual tab of the toolbar, and then click on the two horizontal lines at the bottom; they become collinear.

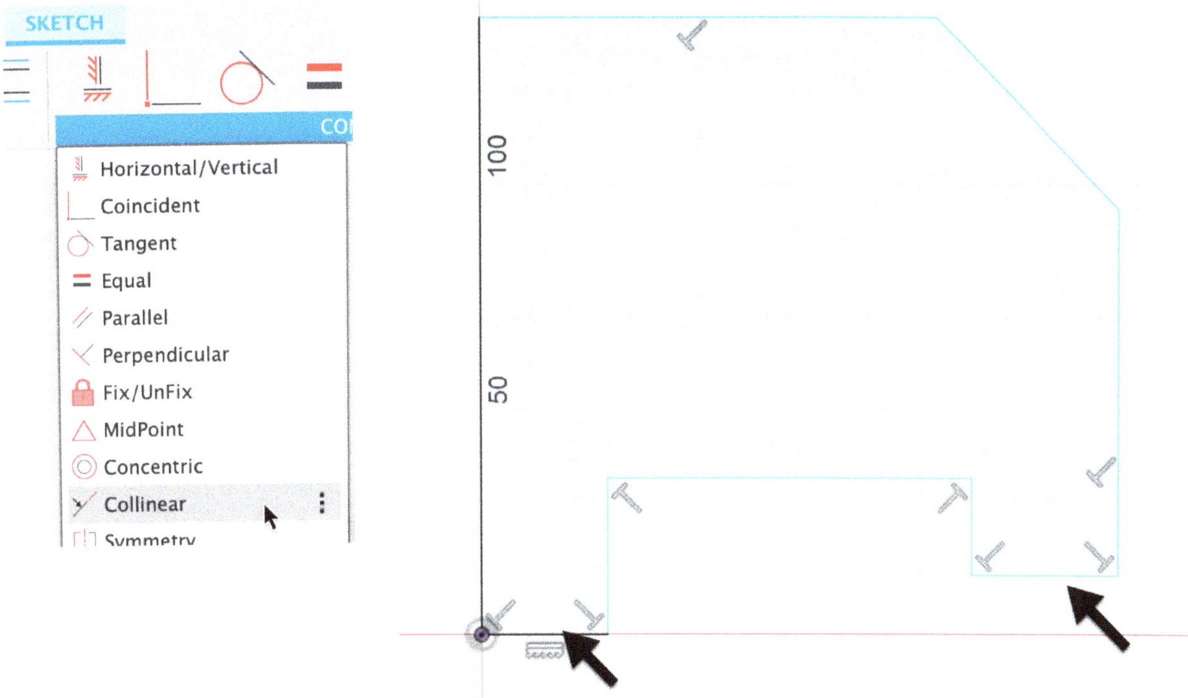

2. Click **Constraints > Equal** on the **Sketch** contextual tab of the toolbar and click on the two horizontal lines at the bottom; they become equal in length.

Adding Dimensions

1. On the **Sketch** contextual tab of the toolbar, click the **Sketch Dimension**  button on the **Create** panel.
2. Click on the left and right vertical lines. Move the mouse pointer downward and click to locate the dimension.
3. Type-in **160** in the **Edit dimension** box and press Enter.

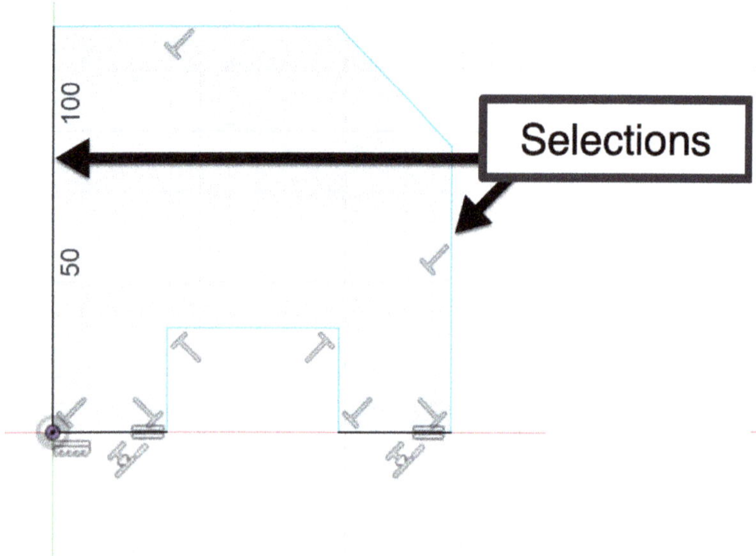

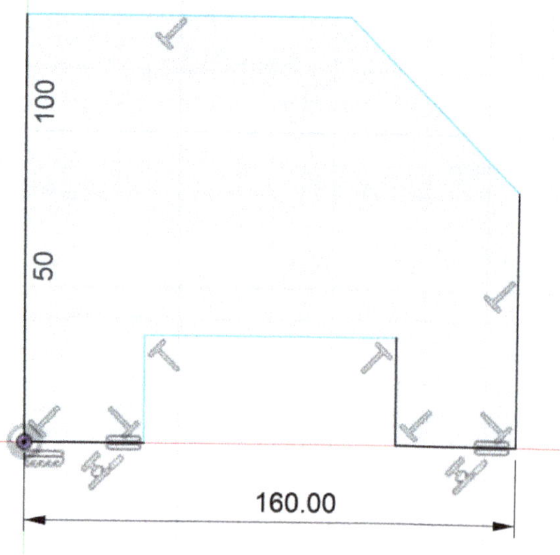

4. On the **Navigation Bar**, click **Zoom > Fit**; the sketch is fit in the graphics window.

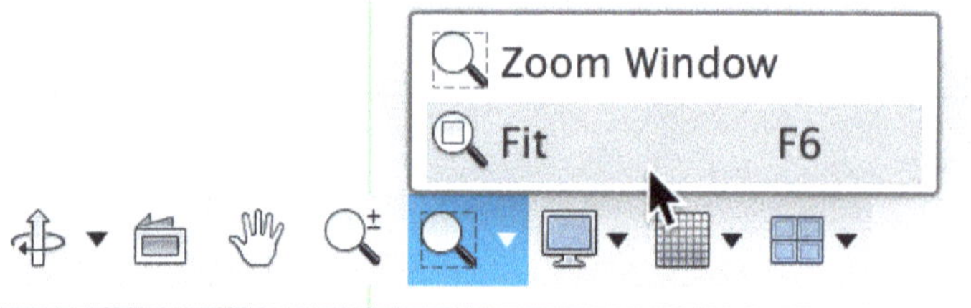

5. Click on the lower-left horizontal line. Move the mouse pointer downward and click to locate the dimension.
6. Type-in **20** in the dimension box and press Enter.

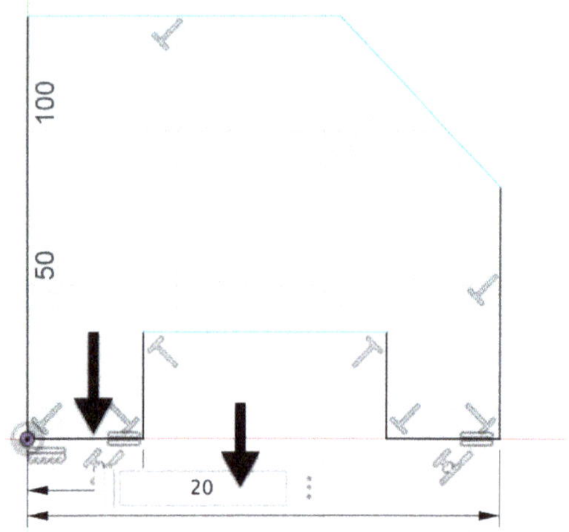

7. Click on the small vertical line located at the left side. Move the mouse pointer towards the right and click to position the dimension.
8. Type-in **25** in the dimension box and press Enter.

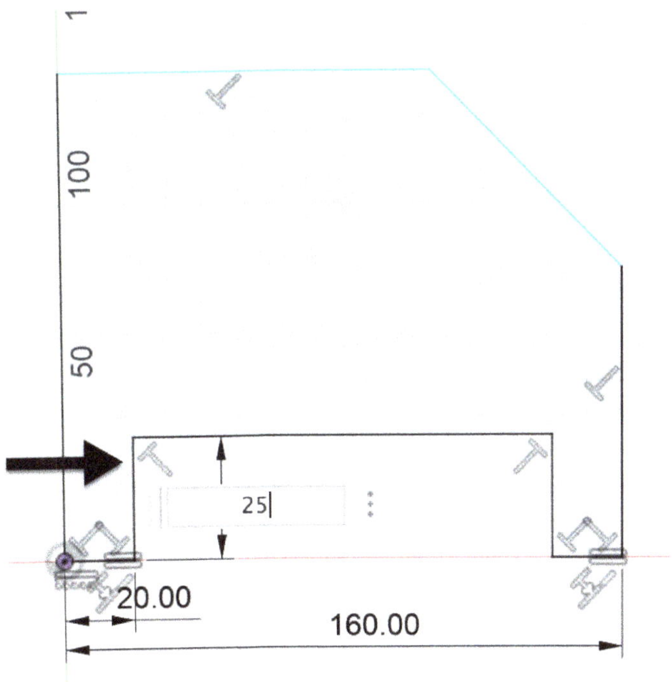

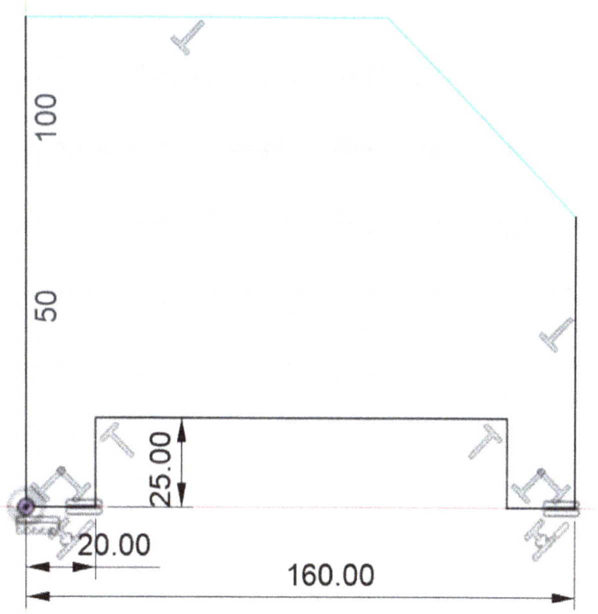

9. Create other dimensions in the sequence, as shown below. Press Esc to deactivate the **Sketch Dimension** command.

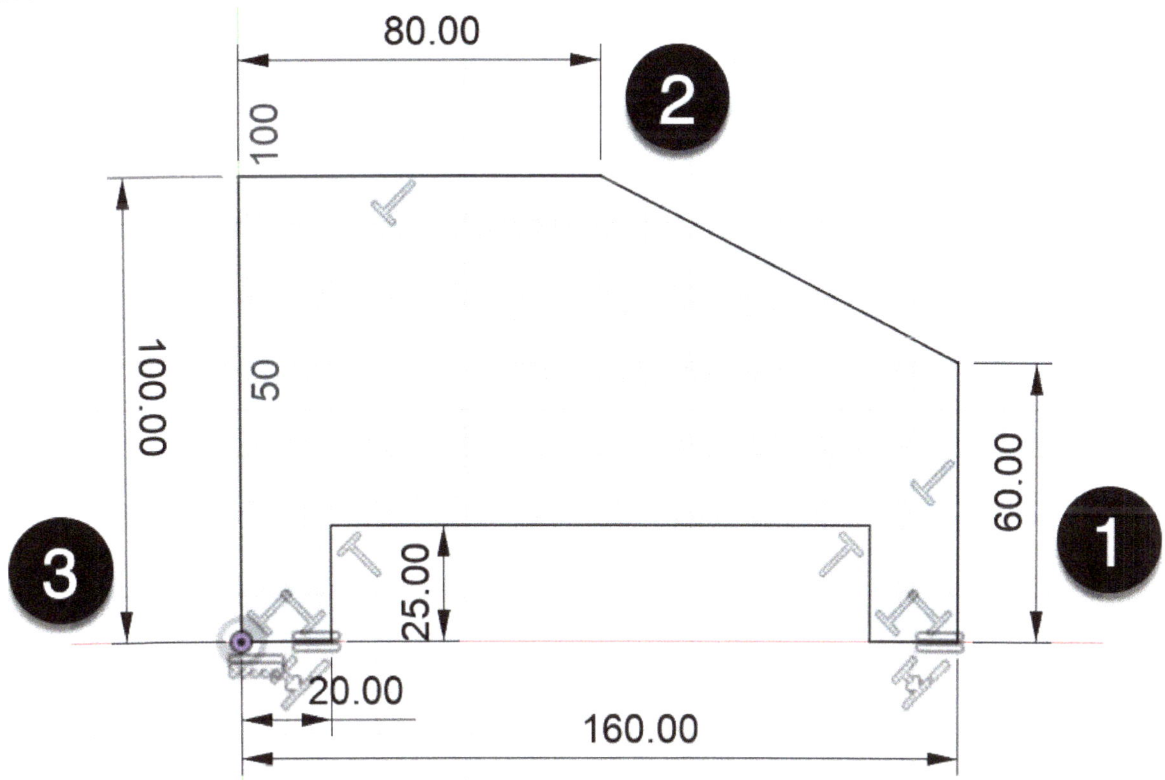

10. On the **Sketch** contextual tab of the toolbar, expand the **Create** panel and click **Circle > Center Diameter Circle** . Next, click inside the sketch region to define the center point of the circle. Move the mouse pointer and click to define the diameter. Likewise, create another circle.

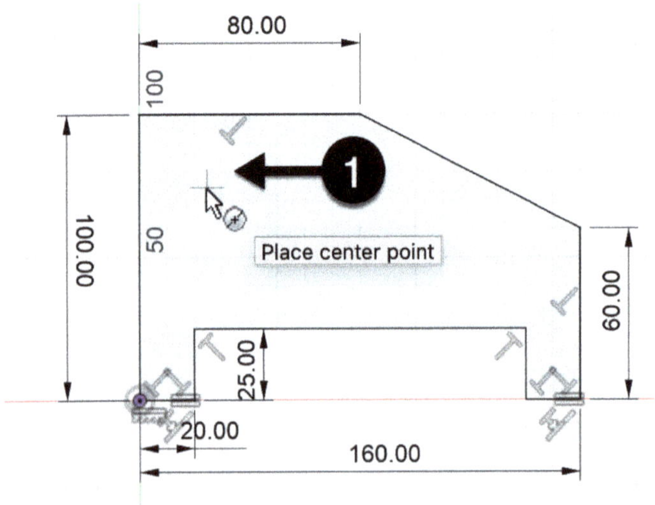

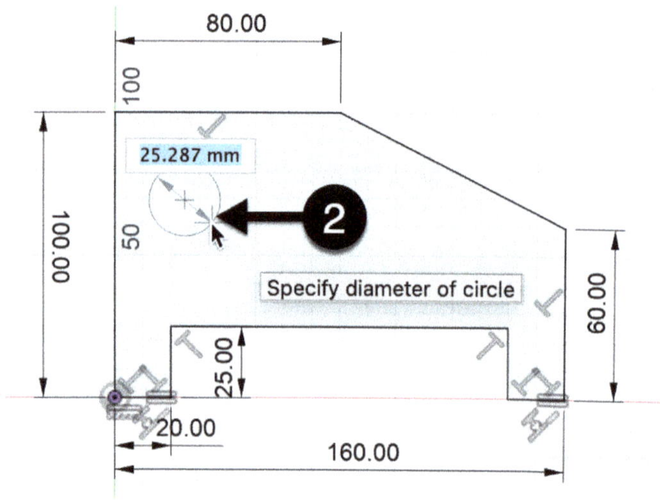

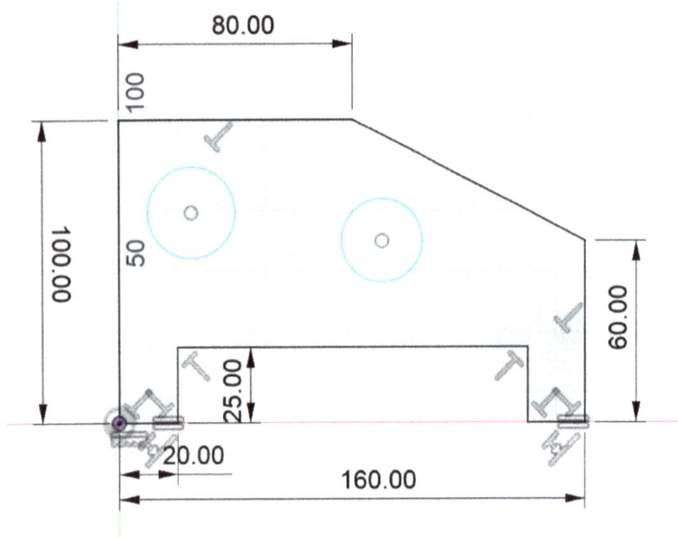

11. Click **Constraints > Horizontal/Vertical** on the **Sketch** contextual tab of the toolbar. Click on the center points of the two circles to make them horizontally aligned.

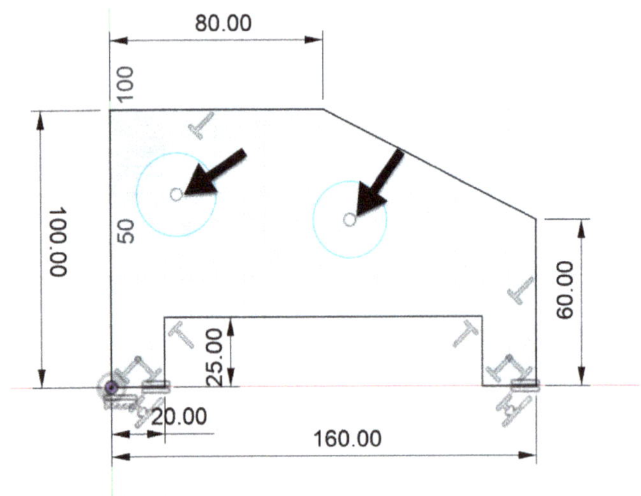

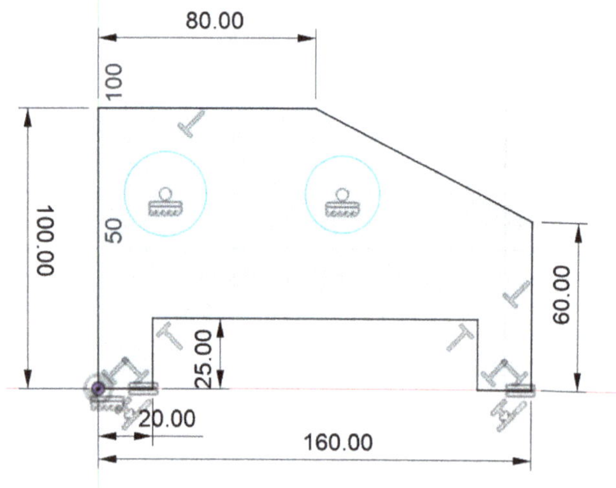

12. Select the center point of any one of the circles and the corner point, as shown. The circles are aligned horizontally with the corner point.

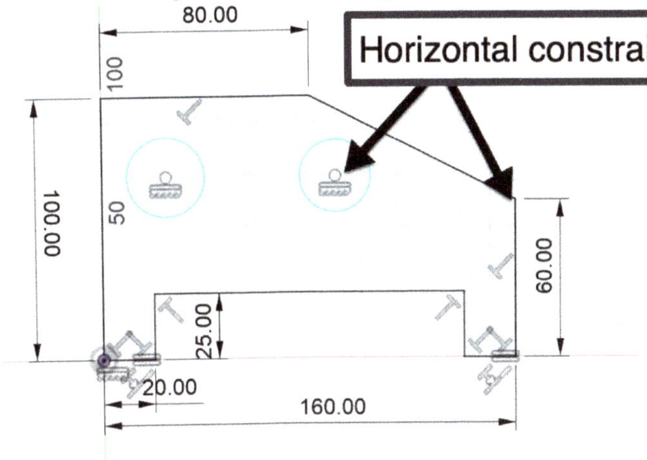

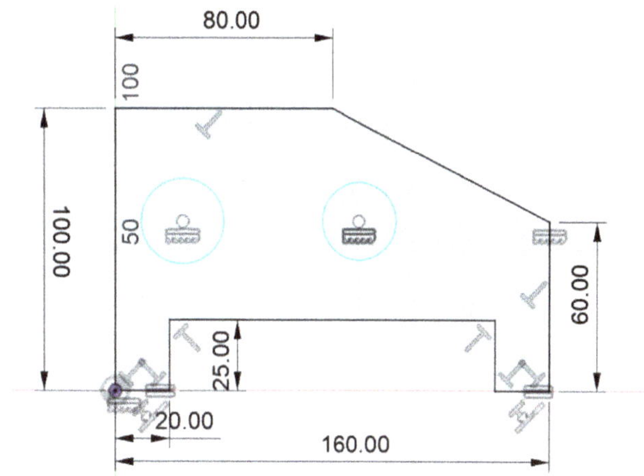

13. Click **Constraints > Equal** on the **Sketch** contextual tab of the toolbar, and then click on the two circles. The diameters of the circles will become equal.

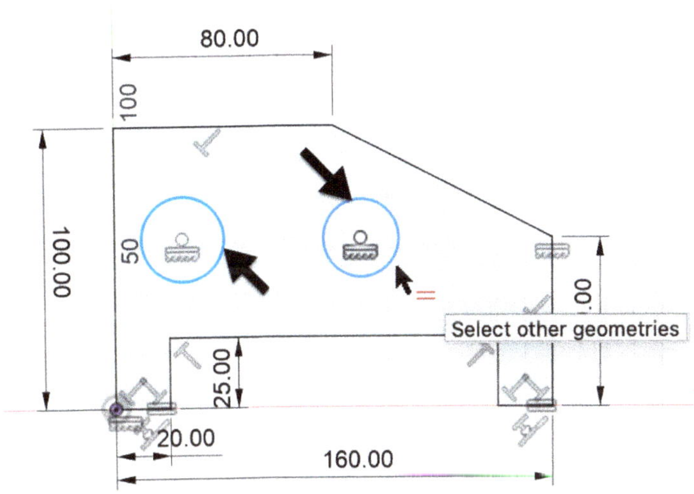

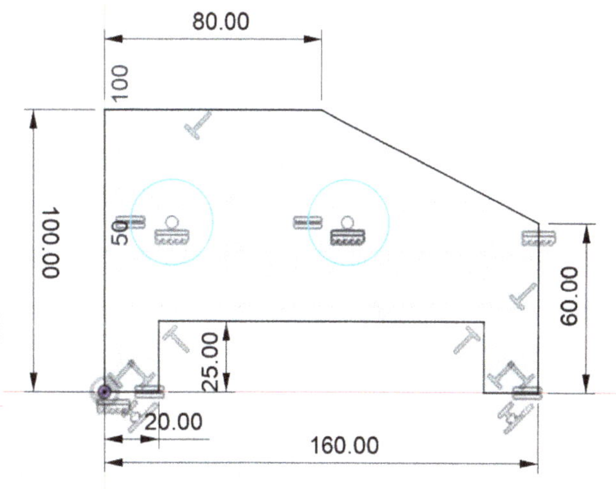

14. Activate the **Sketch Dimension** command and click on any one of the circles. Move the mouse pointer and click to position the dimension. Type 25 in the dimension box and press Enter.
15. Click on the left circle and the left vertical line. Place the dimension and type 40 in the dimension box – next, press Enter.
16. Select the two circles and move the pointer downward and click. Type 50 in the dimension box and press Enter.

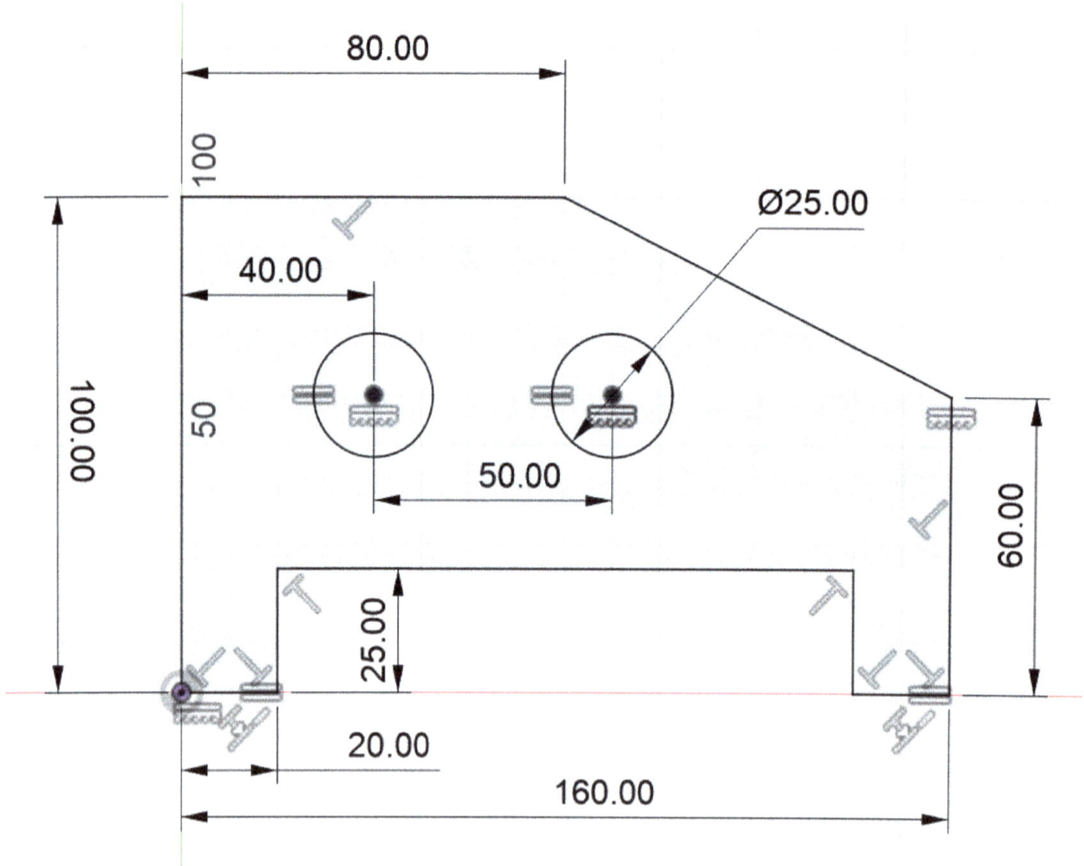

Finishing the Sketch and Saving it

1. On the toolbar, click **Finish Sketch** to complete the sketch.

2. Click the **Save** icon on the **Application bar**; the **Save** dialog pops-up on the screen.

3. On the **Save** dialog, click the down-arrow  button next to the **Location** box; the dialog is expanded. Next, click the **New Project** button located at the bottom left corner of the **Save** dialog.
4. Type **Fusion 360 For Beginners** and press Enter. Next, select the newly created project, and then click the **New Folder** button.
5. Type **Chapter 2** and press Enter. Next, double-click on the **Chapter 2** folder to open it.
6. Type **Example 1** in the **Name** box located at the top of the **Save** dialog, and then click the **Save** button.

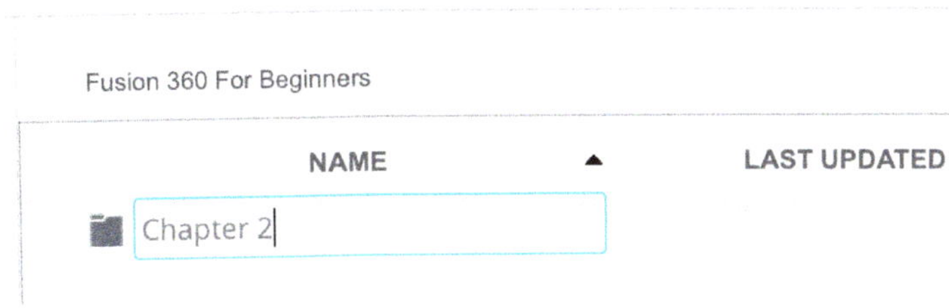

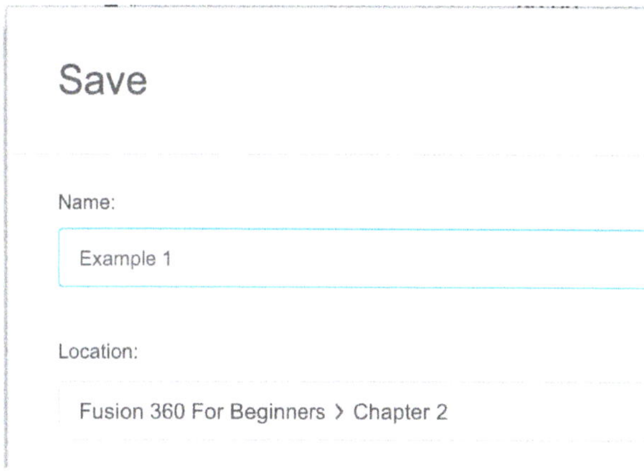

7. Click **Close** on the **File** tab to close the part file.

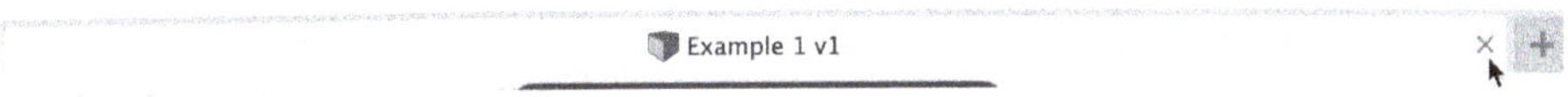

Example 2 (Inches)

In this tutorial, you will draw the sketch shown next.

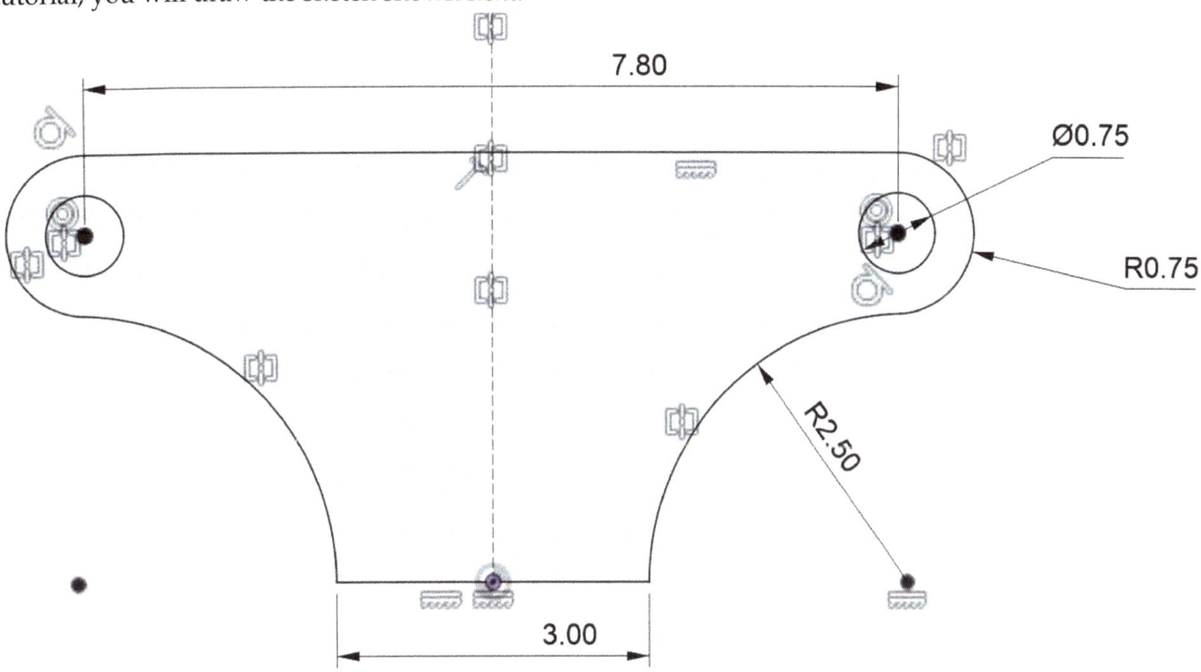

1. Start **Autodesk Fusion 360** by double-clicking the **Autodesk Fusion 360** icon on your desktop.
2. To start a new design file, click the **File** drop-down **> New Design** on the Application bar.
3. On the **Browser window**, expand **Document Settings** and place the cursor on **Units**; the **Change Active Units** icon appears.
4. Click on the **Change Active Units** icon to change the units; the **Change Active Units** dialog appears.
5. On this dialog, select **Unit Type** drop-down > **inch (in), ouncemass** and click **OK**.

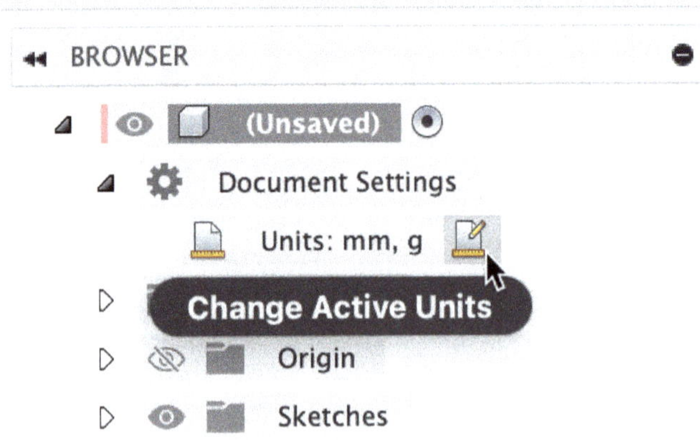

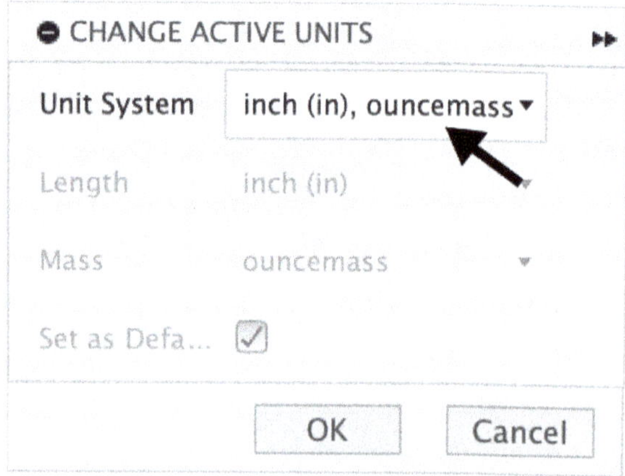

Starting a Sketch

1. To start a sketch, click **Solid** tab > **Create** panel **> Create Sketch** on the toolbar. Select the XY plane to start the sketch.
2. Activate the **Line** command (On the **Sketch** contextual tab of the toolbar, click **Create** panel **> Line)**.
3. Click on the second quadrant of the coordinate system to define the start point of the profile. Drag the pointer horizontally and click to define the endpoint.

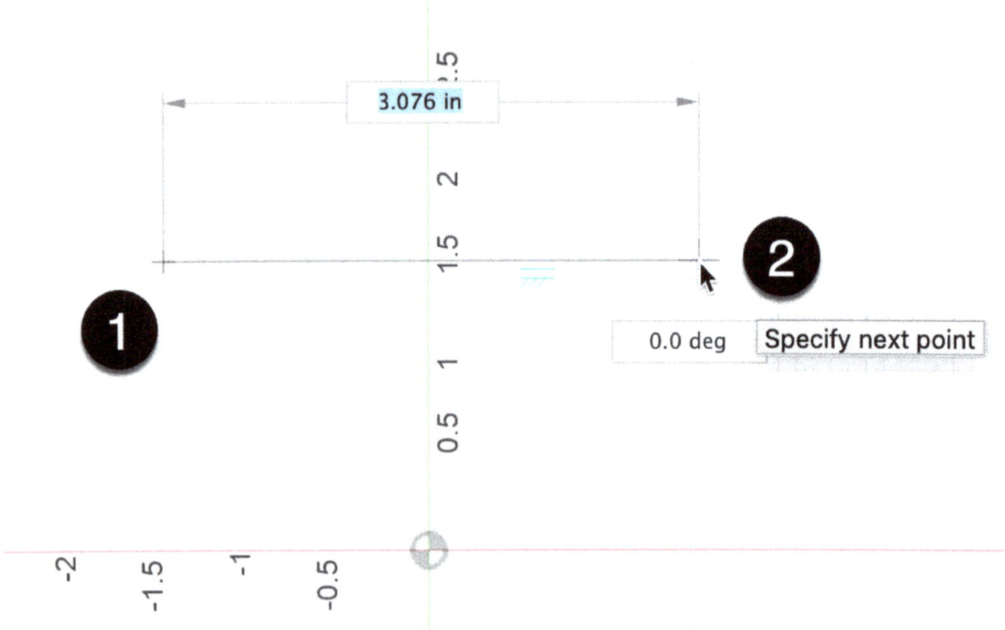

4. On the **Sketch** contextual tab of the toolbar, expand the **Create** panel and click **Arc > 3-Point Arc**.
5. Select the right endpoint of the line to define the first point of the arc. Next, move the pointer in the upward right direction and click to define the second point of the arc.
6. Move the pointer and click to define the third point of the arc, as shown.

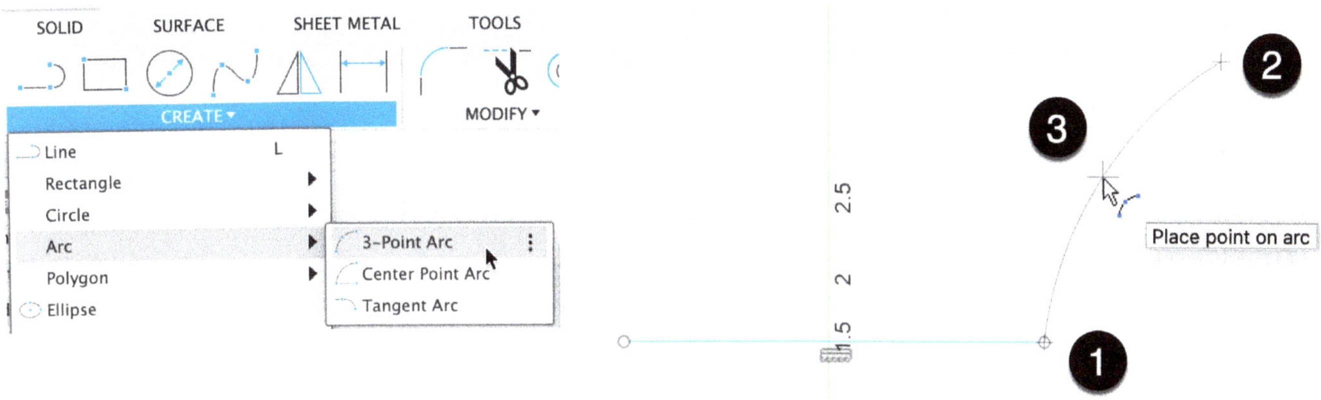

7. On the **Sketch** contextual tab of the toolbar, click **Create** panel > **Arc > Tangent Arc.** Next, select the endpoint of the arc.
8. Move the pointer upwards and click to create a tangent arc, as shown.

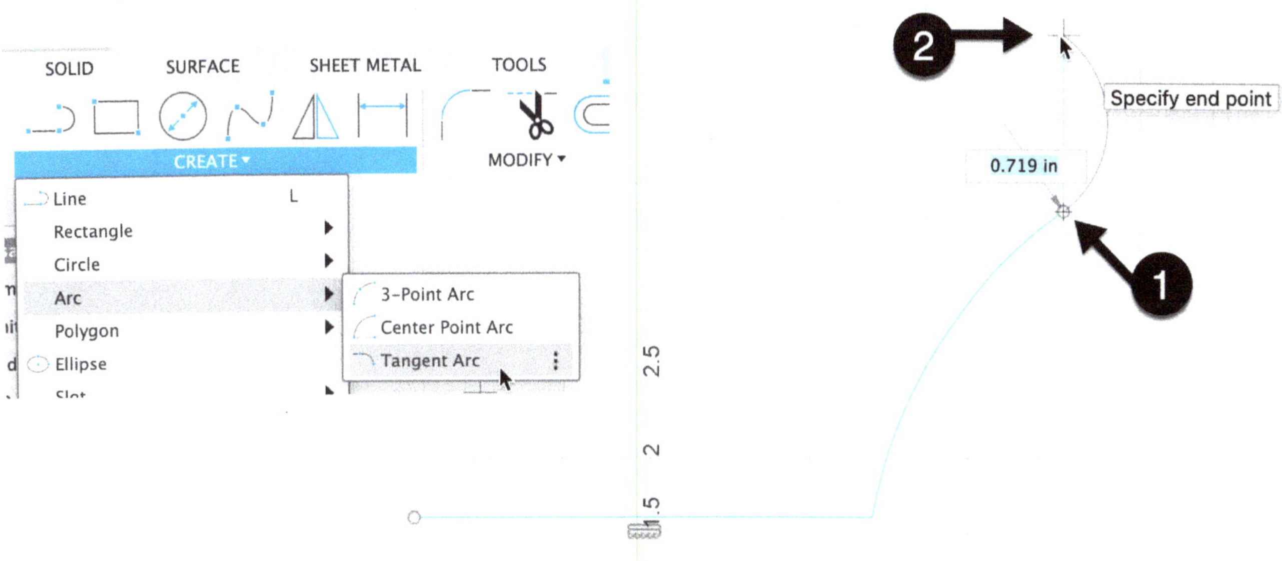

9. Click the **Line** tool on the **Create** panel. Next, move the pointer toward the left and click to create a horizontal line.

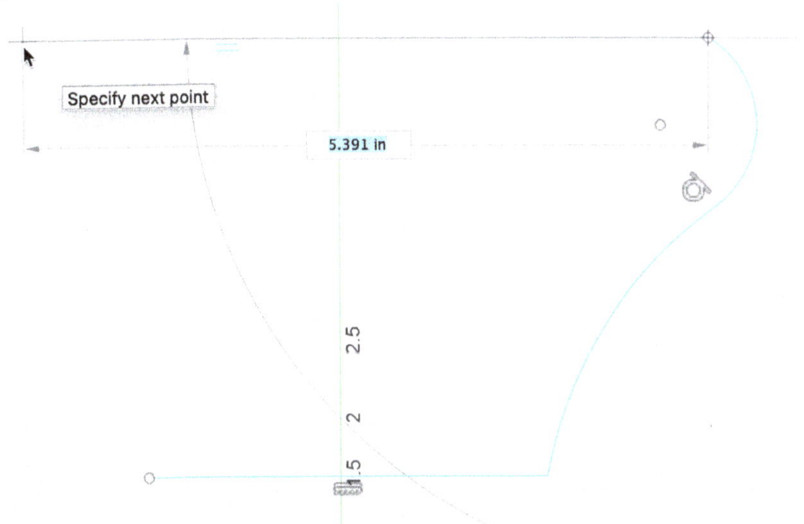

10. Make sure that the **Line** command is active. Place the pointer on the endpoint of the line. Next, press and hold the left mouse button and drag it towards left, and then downwards. Click to create a tangent arc, as shown.

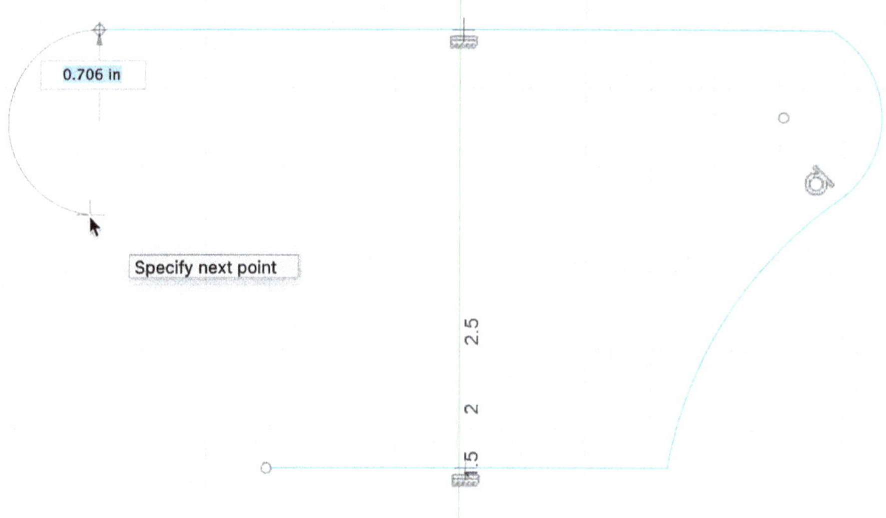

11. On the **Sketch** contextual tab of the toolbar, expand the **Create** panel and click **Arc > 3-Point Arc**.
12. Select the endpoint of the last arc to define the first point of the arc. Next, select the start point of the lower horizontal line to define the second point of the arc.
13. Move the pointer and click to define the third point of the arc, as shown.

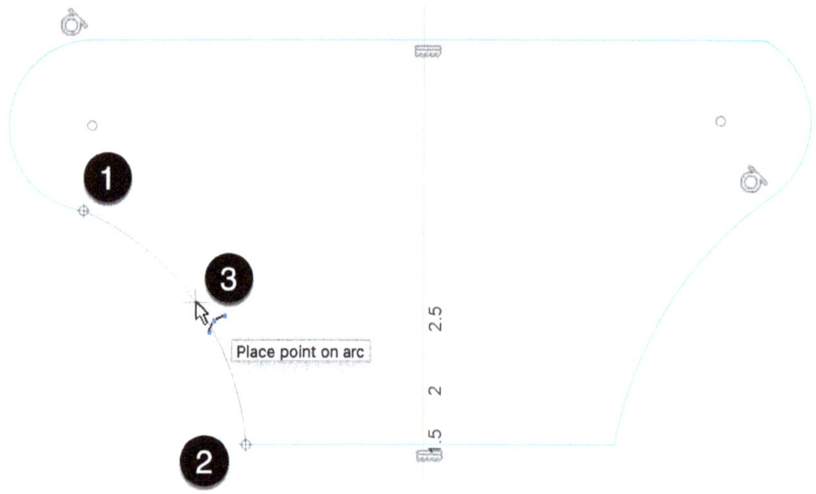

14. On the **Sketch** contextual tab of the toolbar, click the **Center Diameter Circle** tool on the **Create** panel. Draw a circle inside the closed sketch, as shown.

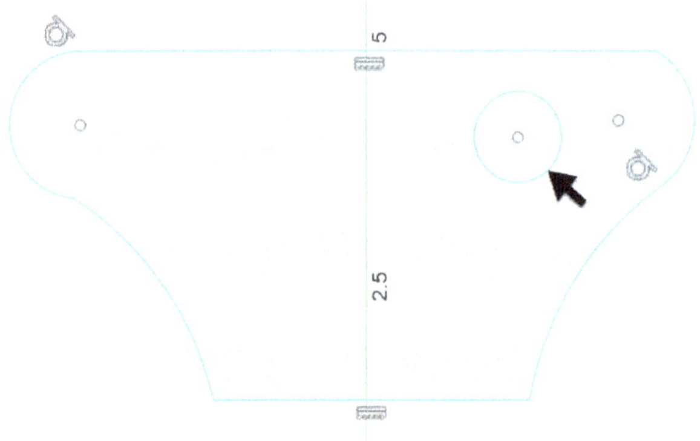

15. On the **Sketch** contextual tab of the toolbar, click **Constraints > Concentric** .

16. Click on the circle and small arc on the upper right side. The circle and arc are made concentric.

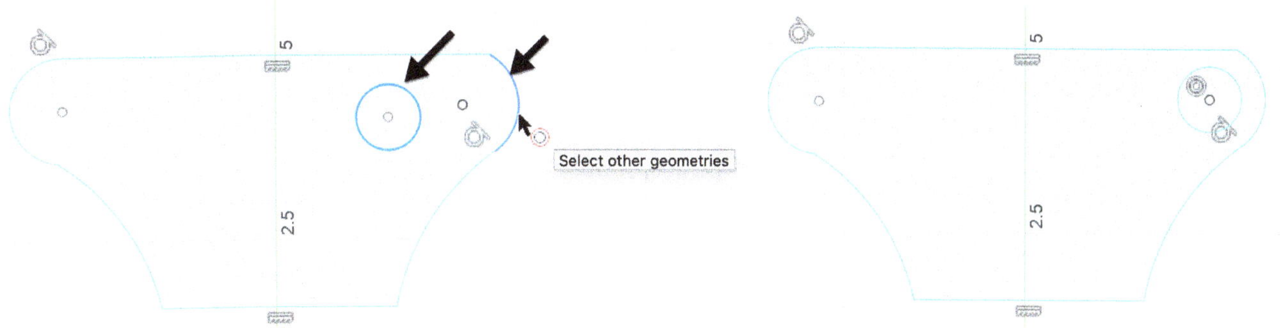

17. Likewise, create another circle concentric to the small arc located on the left side.

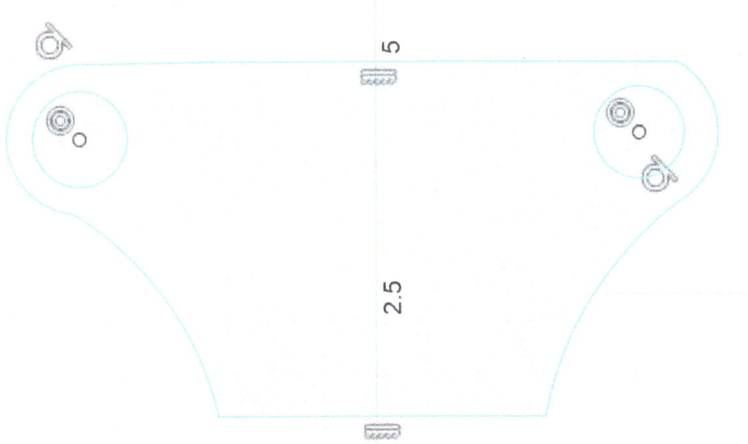

18. Activate the **Line** command and click **Linetype > Construction** in the **Options** section of the **Sketch Palette**.

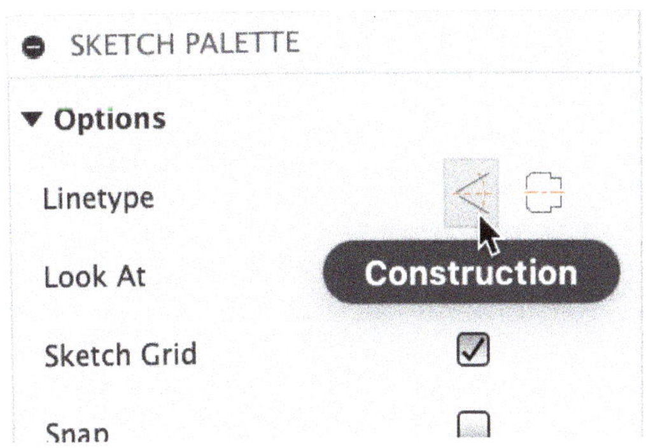

19. Select the sketch origin and move the pointer vertically upward. Next, click to create a construction line, as shown. Right-click and select **OK**.

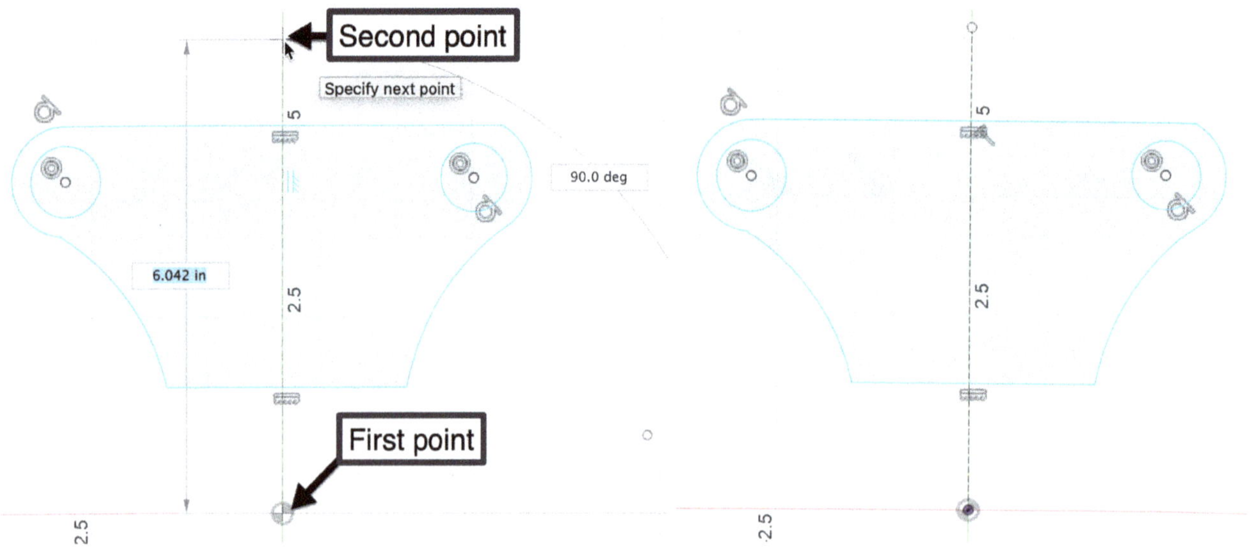

20. On the **Sketch** contextual tab of the toolbar, click **Constraints > Symmetry** .
21. Click on the large arcs on both sides of the centerline. Next, select the centerline; arcs are made symmetric about the centerline.
22. Deactivate the **Construction** icon on the **Sketch Palette**.
23. Likewise, make the small arcs and circles symmetric about the centerline.

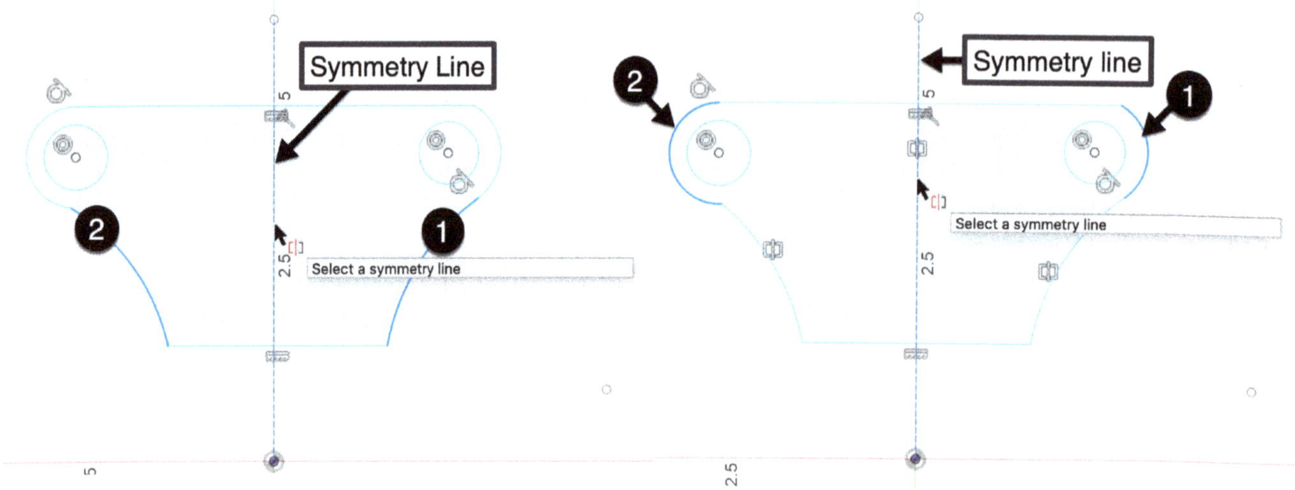

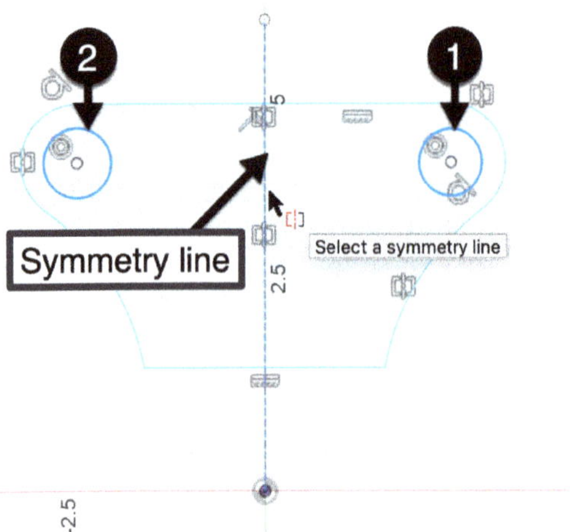

24. On the **Sketch** contextual tab of the toolbar, click **Constraints > Coincident**. Next, select the bottom horizontal line and the sketch origin.

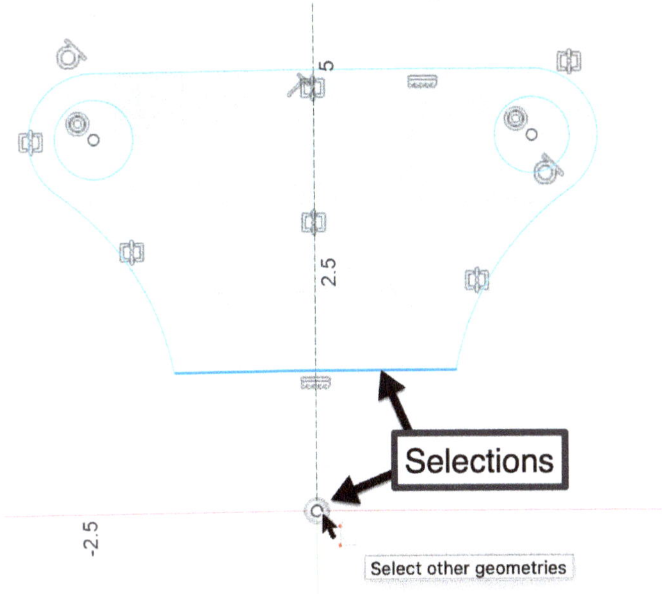

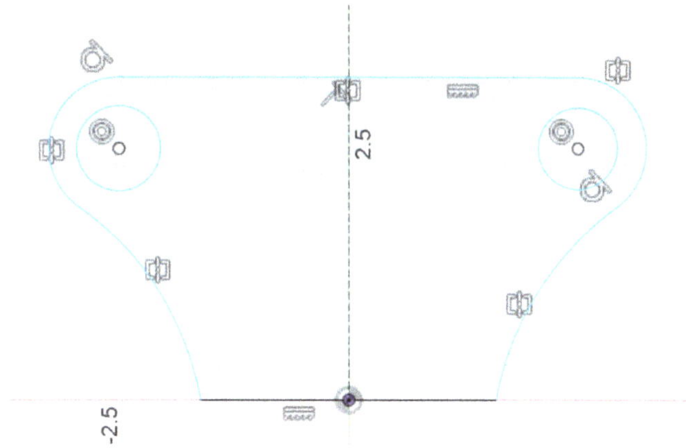

25. On the **Sketch** contextual tab of the toolbar, click **Constraints > Horizontal/Vertical** .

26. Select the sketch origin and the centerpoint of any one of the large arcs; the two points are aligned horizontally.

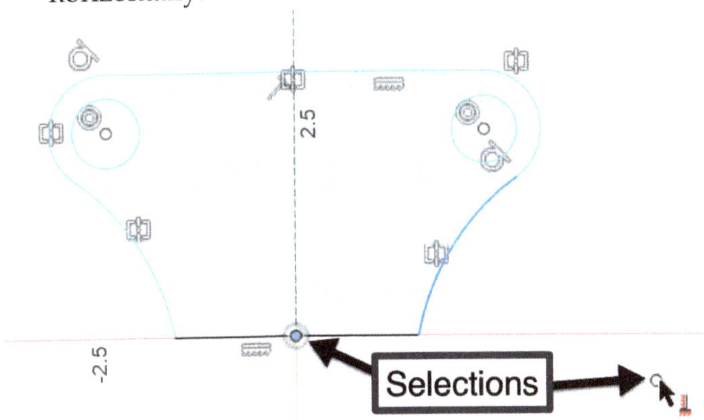

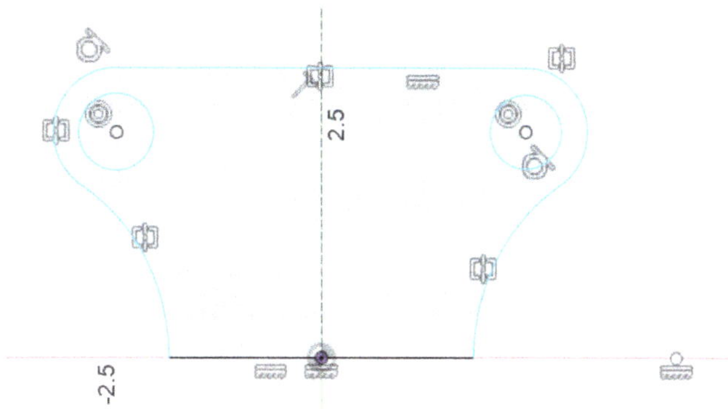

27. Activate the **Sketch Dimension** command and select the right circle. Next, move the pointer and click to position the dimension.
28. Type 0.75 and press ENTER.
29. Select the small right arc, move the pointer and click to position the dimension. Type 0.75 and press ENTER.
30. Select the large right arc, move the pointer and click to position the dimension. Type 2.5 and press ENTER.
31. Select the upper horizontal line, move the pointer and click to position the dimension. Type 7.8 and press ENTER.
32. Select the lower horizontal line, move the pointer and click to position the dimension. Type 3 and press ENTER.

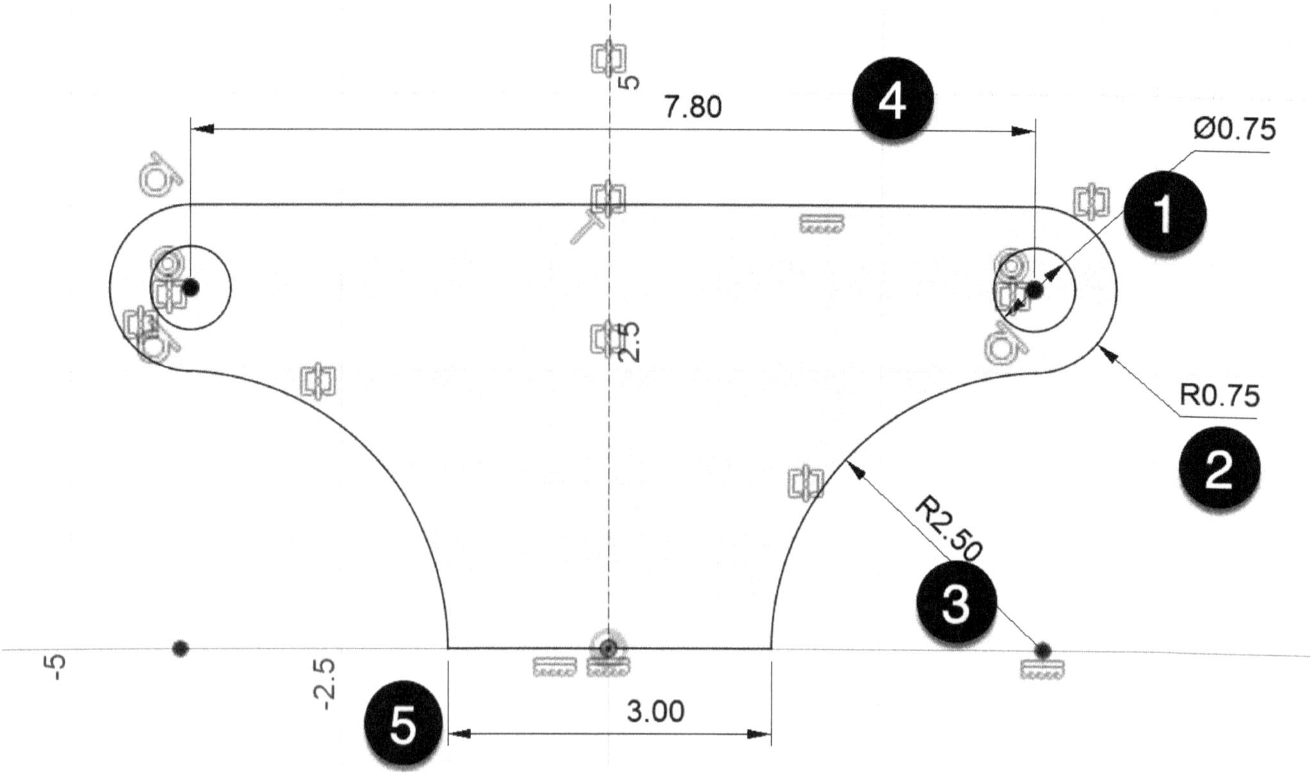

The sketch is fully constrained, and all the sketch elements are displayed in black color.

33. Click **Finish Sketch** on the toolbar to complete the sketch.
34. To save the file, click **Save** on the Application bar.
35. On the **Save** dialog, type-in **Example2** in the **Name** box and click the **Save** button.
36. To close the file, click **Close** on the File tab.

Questions

1. What is the procedure to create sketches in Autodesk Fusion 360?
2. List any two sketch *Constraints* in Autodesk Fusion 360.
3. Which command allows you to apply dimensions to a sketch?
4. Describe two methods to create circles.
5. How to define the shape and size of a sketch?
6. How to create a tangent arc using the **Line** command?
7. Which command is used to apply multiple types of dimensions to a sketch?
8. List the commands to create arcs?
9. List the commands to create slots?
10. List the options of Sketch Palette?

Exercises

Exercise 1

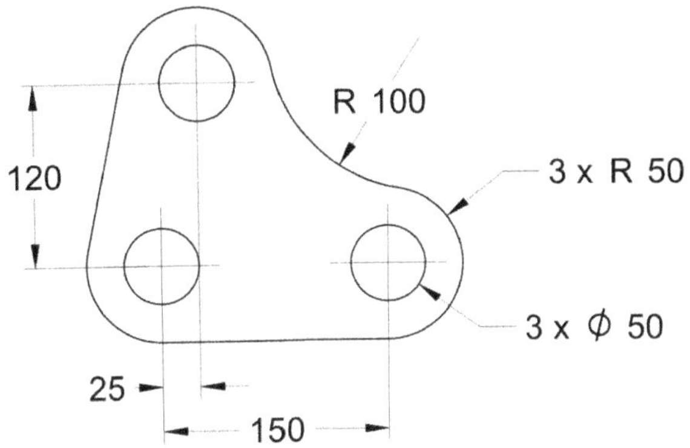

Exercise 2

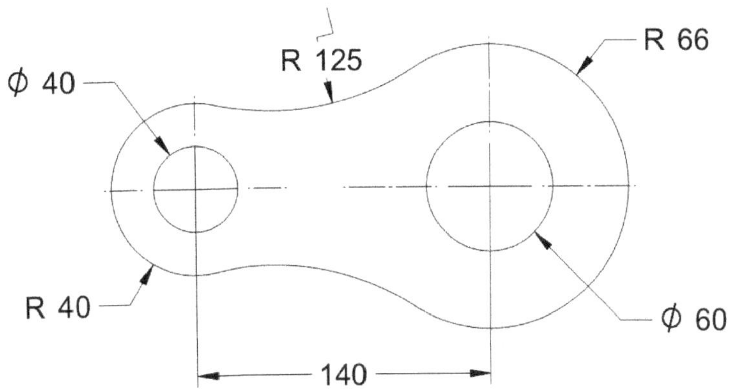

Exercise 3

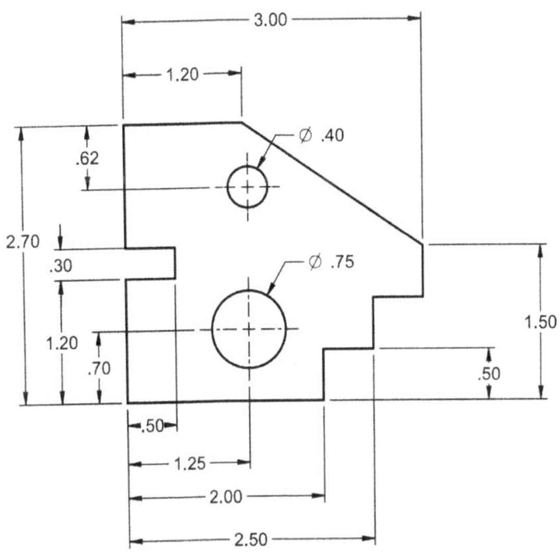

Chapter 3: Extrude and Revolve Features

Extrude and revolve features are used to create basic and simple parts. Most of the time, they form the base for complex parts, as well. These features are easy to create and require a single sketch. Now, you will learn the commands to create these features.

In this chapter, you will learn to:

- Create the *Extrude* and *Revolve* features
- Create Construction Planes
- Work with additional options in the *Extrude* and *Revolve* commands

Extruded Features

Extruding is the process of taking a two-dimensional profile and converting it into a 3D model by giving it some thickness. A simple example of this would be taking a circle and converting it into a cylinder. Once you have created a sketch profile or profiles you want to *Extrude*, activate the **Extrude** command (On the **Solid** tab of the toolbar, click **Create** panel > **Extrude**); the sketch is selected automatically. Click and drag the arrow that appears on the selected sketch (or) Type-in a value in the **Distance** box to specify the extrude distance.

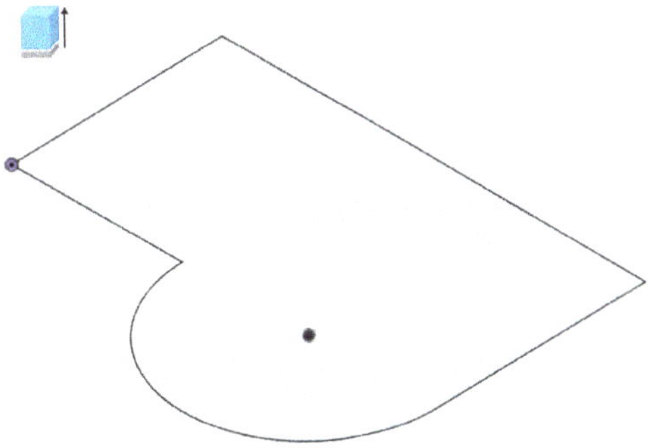

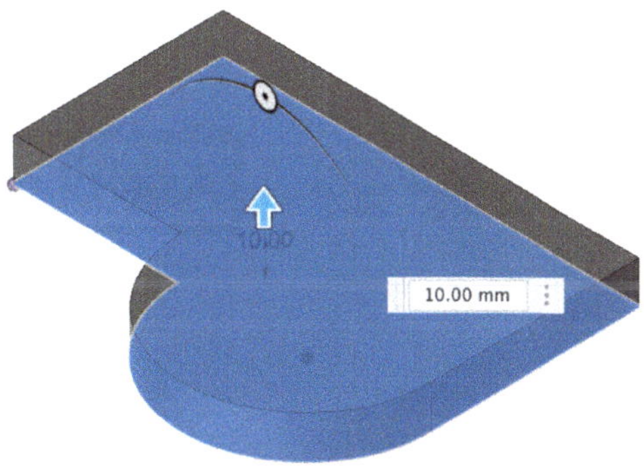

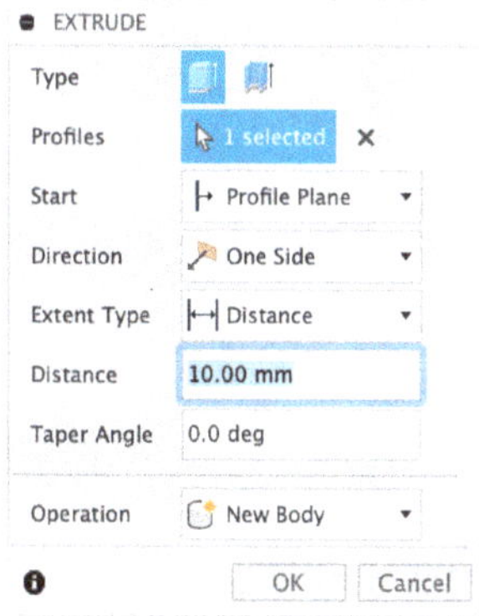

You can select **Direction > Symmetric** on the dialog to extrude the sketch symmetrically about the sketch plane.

Click the **Measurement** > **Half Length** icon to add the specified extrude distance on both sides of the sketch.

Click the **Measurement > Whole Length** icon to divide the specified extrude distance equally on both sides of the sketch.

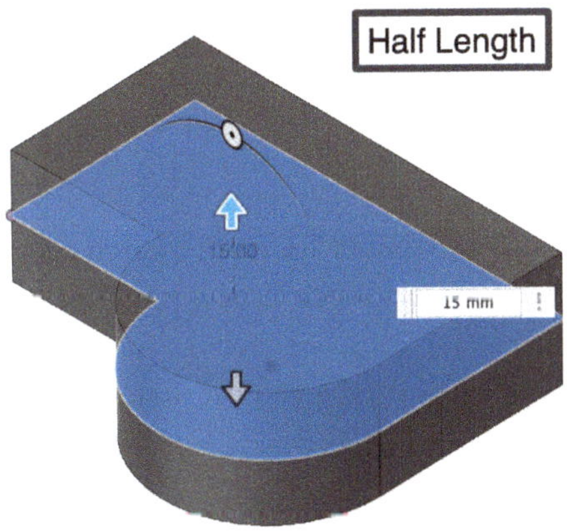

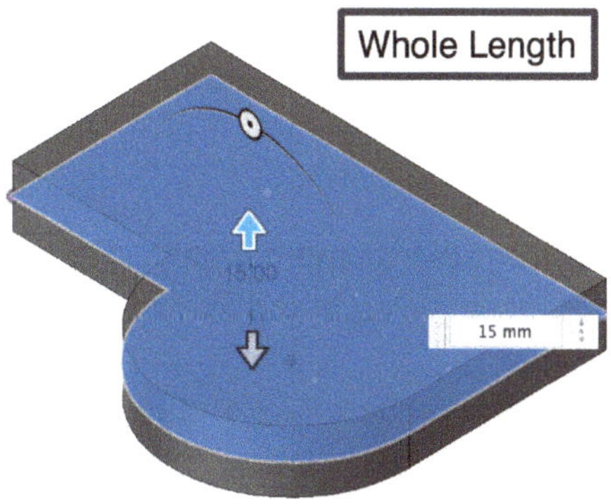

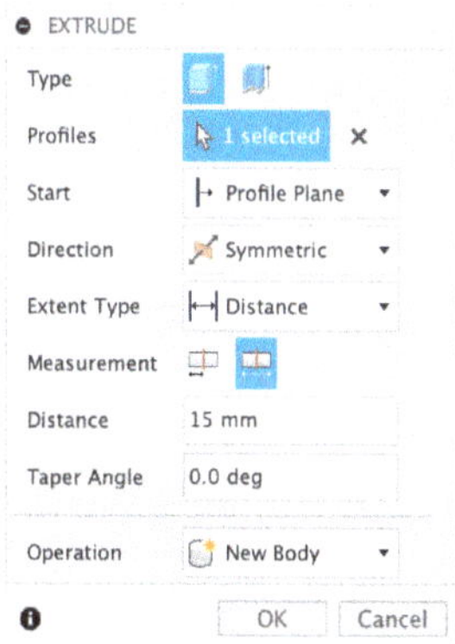

On the dialog, click **OK** to complete the *Extruded* feature.

Revolved Features

Revolving is the process of taking a two-dimensional profile and revolving it about a centerline to create a 3D geometry (shapes that are axially symmetric). While creating a sketch for the *Revolved* feature, it is vital to think about the cross-sectional shape that will define the 3D geometry once it is revolved around an axis. For instance, the following geometry has a hole in the center. This could be created with a separate *Extruded Cut* or *Hole* feature. But in order to make that hole part of the *Revolved* feature, you need to sketch the axis of revolution so that it leaves a space between the profile and the axis.

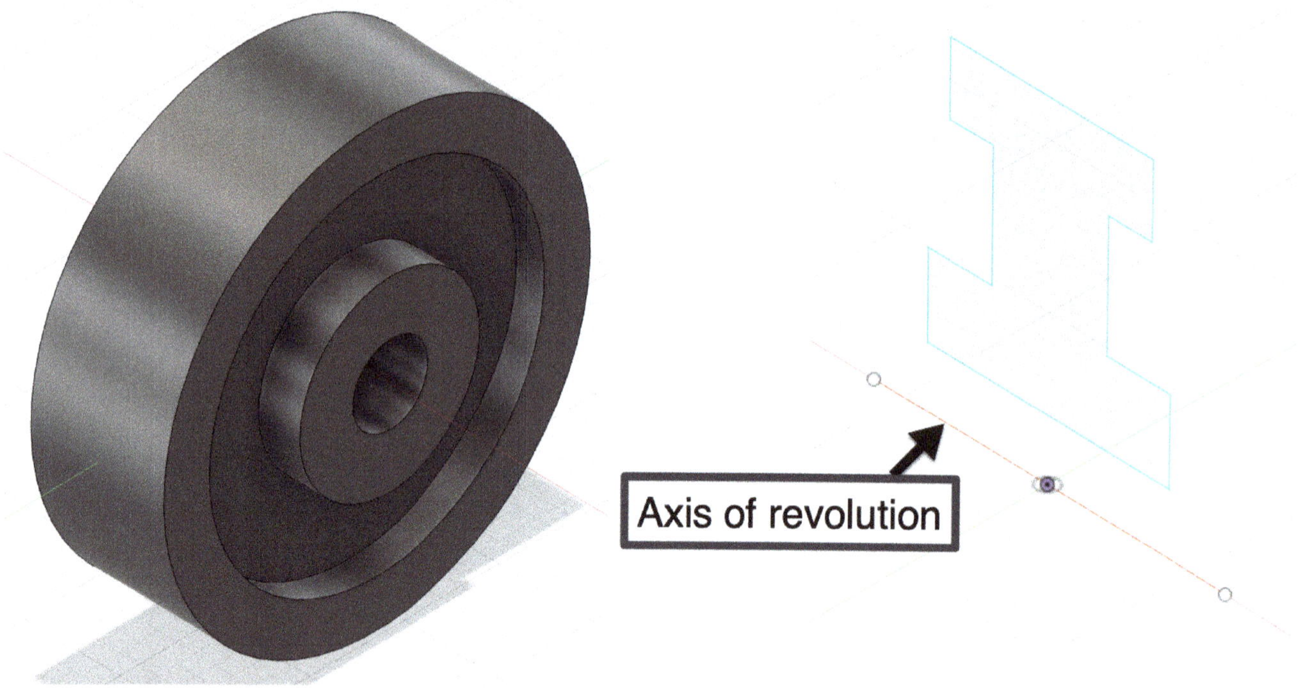

After completing the sketch, activate the **Revolve** command (On the **Solid** tab of the toolbar, click **Create > Revolve** ); the sketch profile is selected automatically. Next, you have to select the axis of revolution. You need to click the **Axis** selection button on the dialog and select the axis.

On the **Revolve** dialog, select **Full** from the **Type** drop-down; the sketch will be revolved by full 360 degrees. If you select **Partial** from the **Type** drop-down, you need to type-in a value in the **Angle** box. In addition to that, you need to specify the revolution direction using the direction options: **One Side**, **Two Sides**, and **Symmetric**. On the dialog, click **OK** to complete the *Revolved* feature.

Project Geometry

This command projects the edges of a 3D geometry onto a sketch plane. Click **Create** panel > **Create Sketch** on the toolbar and select a plane or model face. On the **Sketch** contextual tab of the toolbar, click **Create** panel > **Project/Include > Project** . Click on the edges of the model geometry. Click **OK** on the **Project** dialog to project the edge on to the sketch plane.

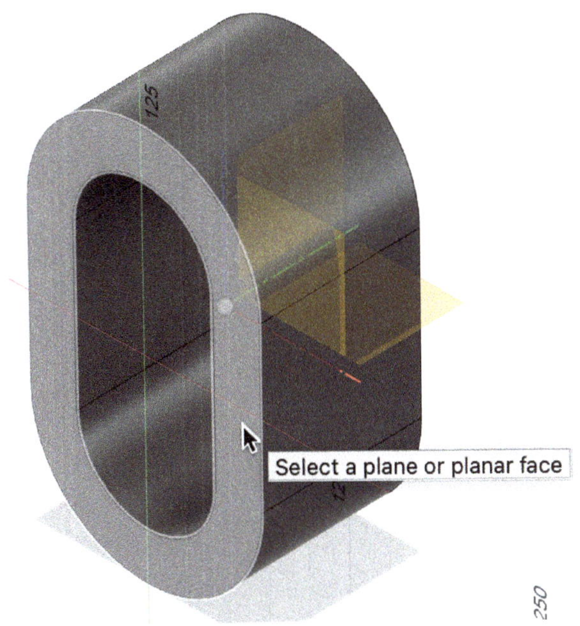

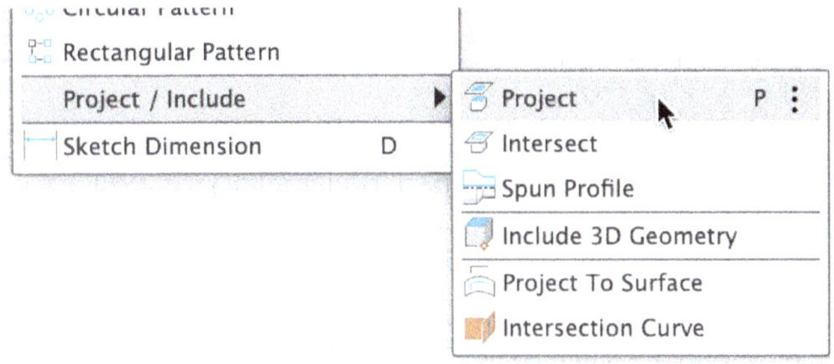

The projected element will be violet in color and fully constrained. If you want to convert it into a typical sketch element, then right click on it and select **Break Link**.

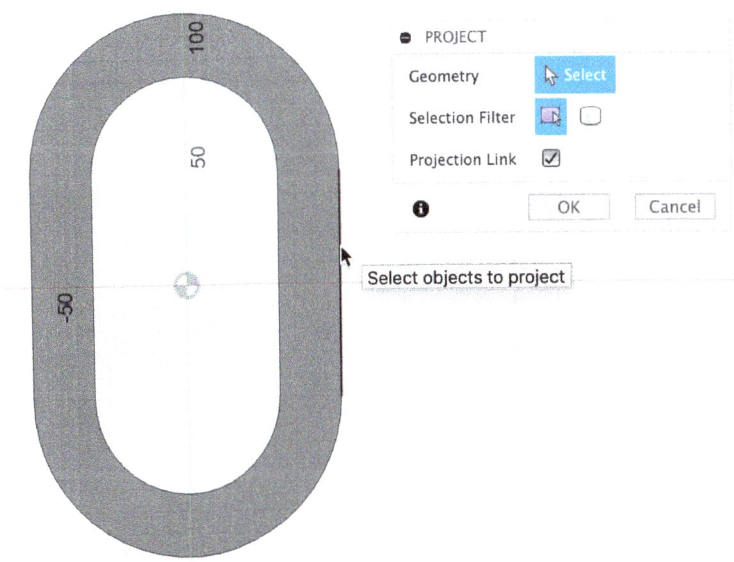

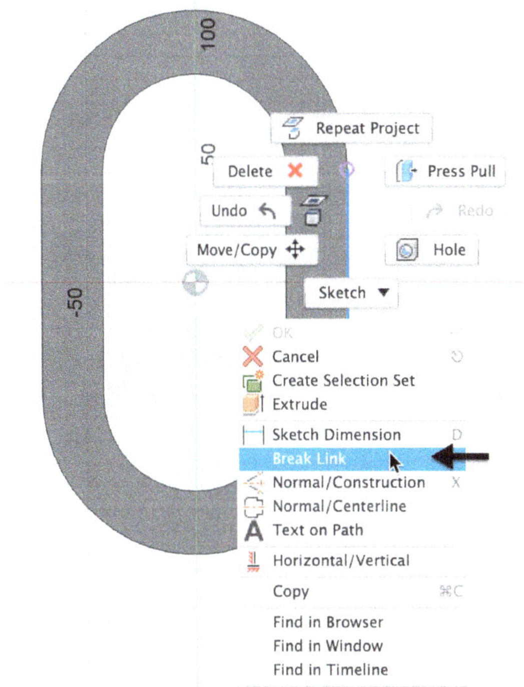

Planes

Planes are a specific type of element in Autodesk Fusion 360, known as Construction Features. These features act as supports to your 3D geometry. Each time you start a new part file, Autodesk Fusion 360 automatically creates default planes (XY, YZ, and XZ planes). Until now, you have learned to create sketches on any of the default planes. If you want to create sketches and geometry at locations other than default planes, you can create new planes manually. You can do this by using the commands available on the **Construct** panel.

Offset Plane

This command creates a plane, which will be parallel to a face or another plane. Activate the **Offset Plane** command (click **Construct** panel > **Offset Plane** on the **Solid** tab of the toolbar). Click on a flat face and drag the arrow that appears on the plane (or) type-in a value in the **Distance** box on the **Offset Plane** dialog.

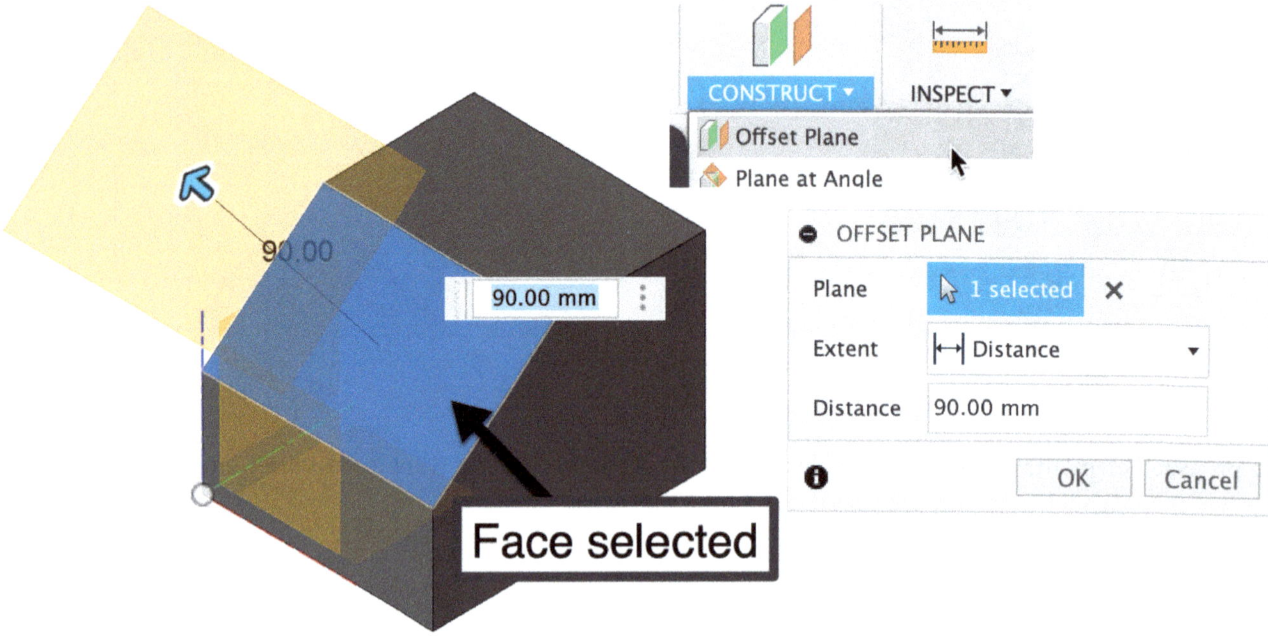

Click **OK** on the dialog to create the offset plane from a plane.

Plane at Angle

This command creates a plane, which will be positioned at an angle to a face. Activate the **Plane at Angle** command (click **Construct** drop-down > **Plane at Angle** on the toolbar). Click on an edge or line of the part geometry and type-in a value in the **Angle** box and click **OK** to create the plane.

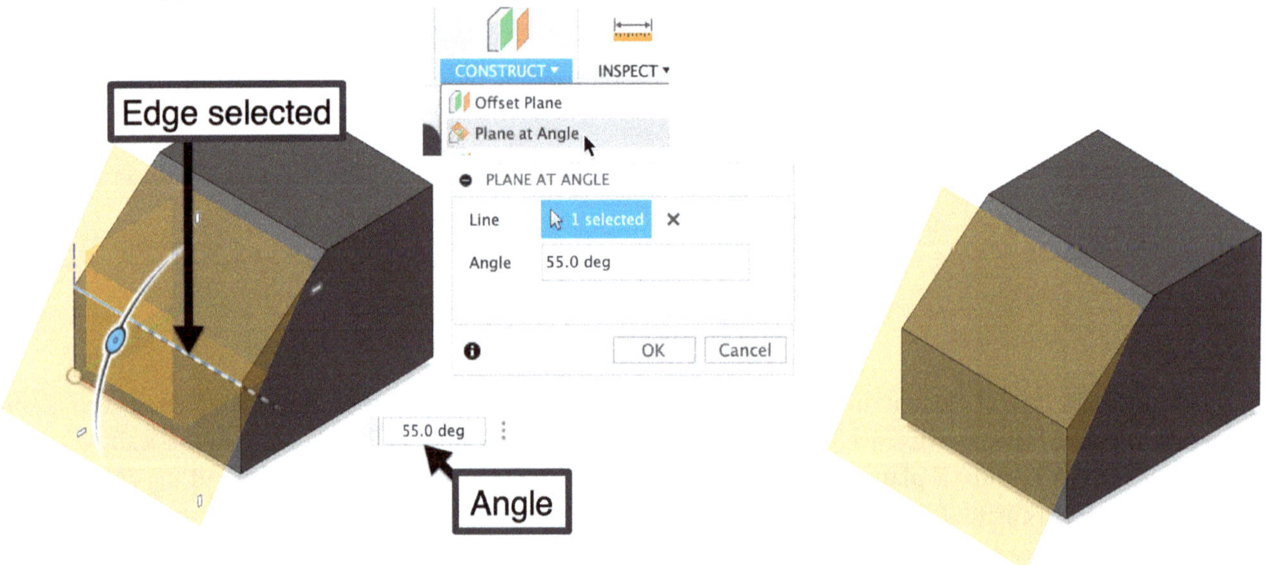

Tangent Plane

This command creates a plane tangent to a curved face. Activate this command (click **Construct** drop-down > **Tangent Plane** on the toolbar) and select a curved face. Next, select a planar face as the reference plane; the preview of the new plane appears parallel to the selected face. Type-in the angle value in the **Angle** box; the plane will be positioned at the specified angle to the reference face. Next, click **OK** on the **Tangent Plane** dialog.

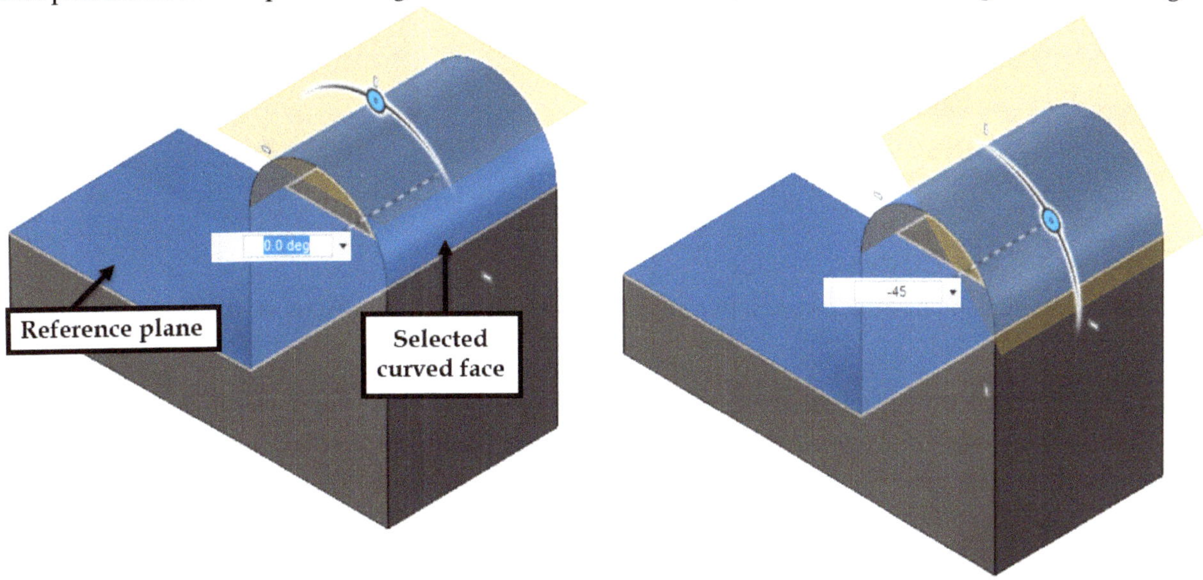

Midplane

This command creates a plane, which lies at the midway between two selected planes. You can also create a plane passing through the intersection point of the two selected faces. Activate the **Midplane** command (click **Construct** panel > **Midplane** on the toolbar) and click on the two faces of the model geometry. Click **OK** to create the Midplane.

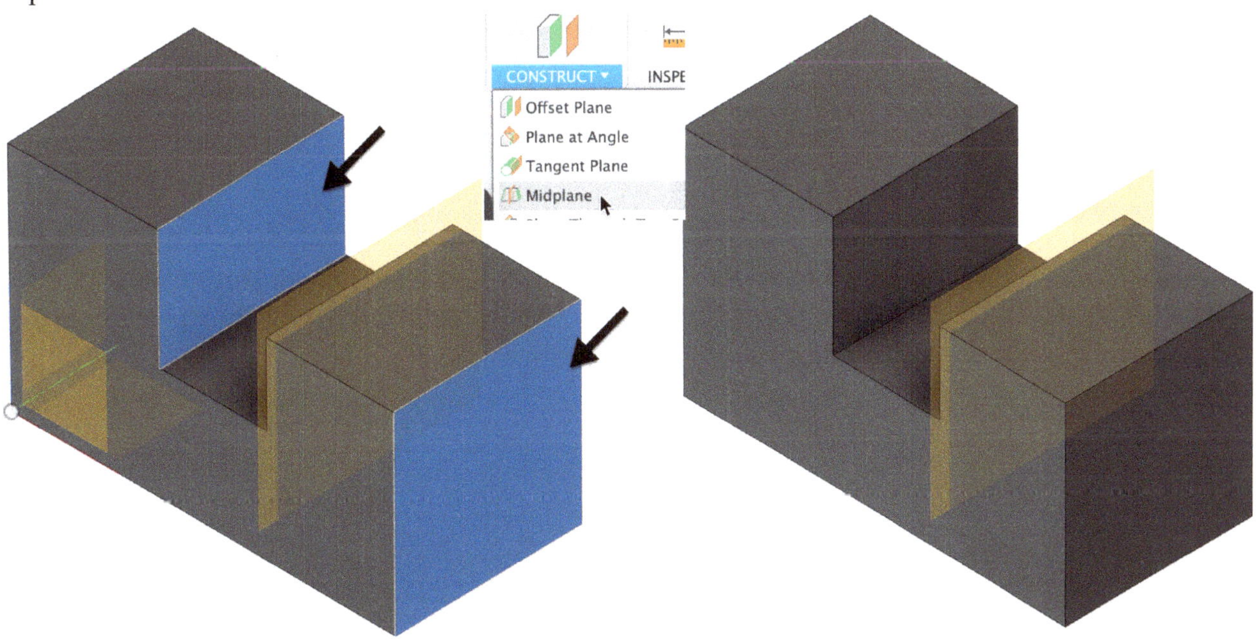

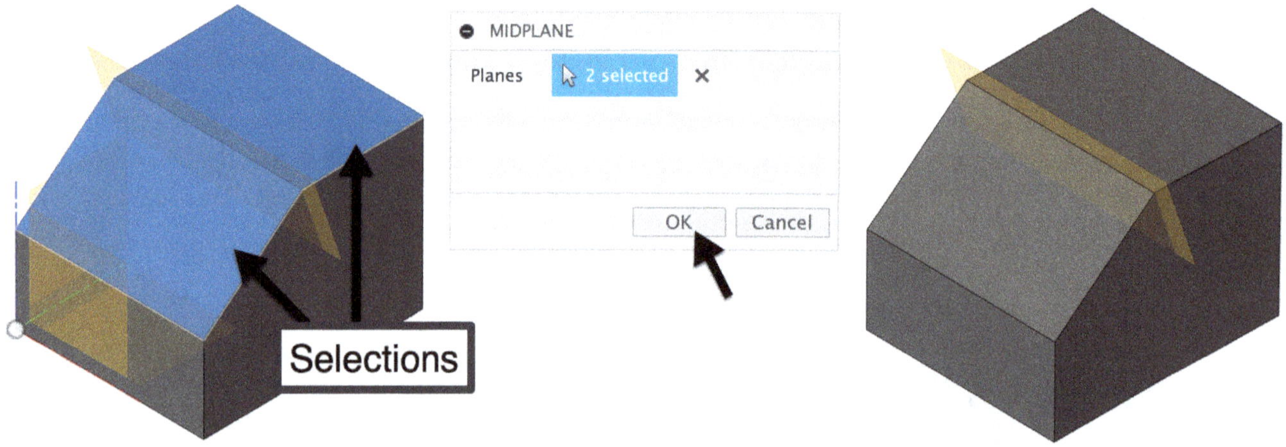

Plane Through Two Edges

This command creates a plane passing through two coplanar axes, edges or lines. Activate the **Plane Through Two Edges** command (click **Construct** panel > **Plane through Two Edges**  on the toolbar) and select the first edge. Next, click on the second edge and click **OK** on the **Plane Through Two Planes** dialog.

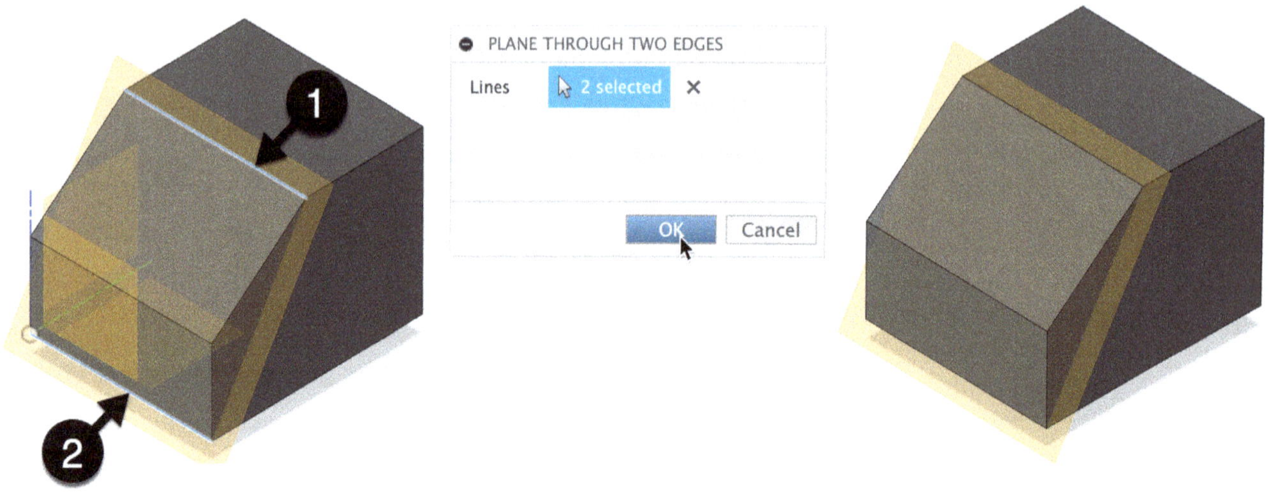

Plane Through Three Points

This command creates a plane passing through three points. Activate the **Plane Through Three Points**  command (click **Construct** panel **> Plane Through Three Points** on the toolbar) and select three points from the model geometry. A plane will be created, passing through the selected points.

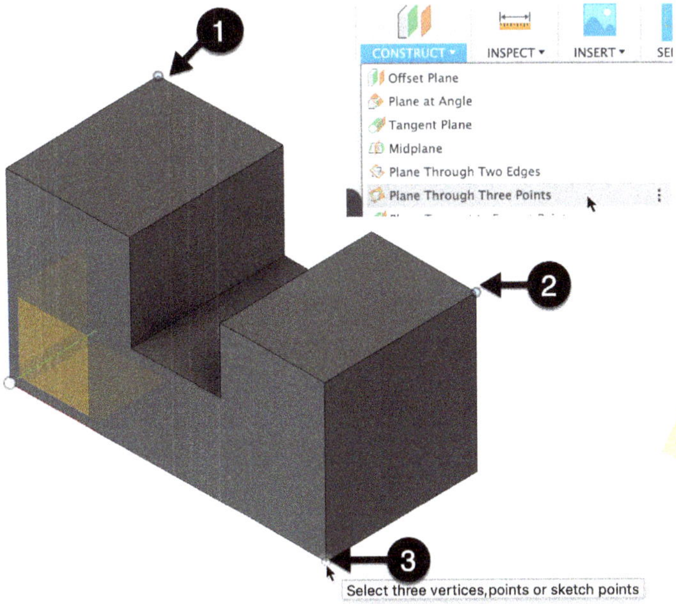

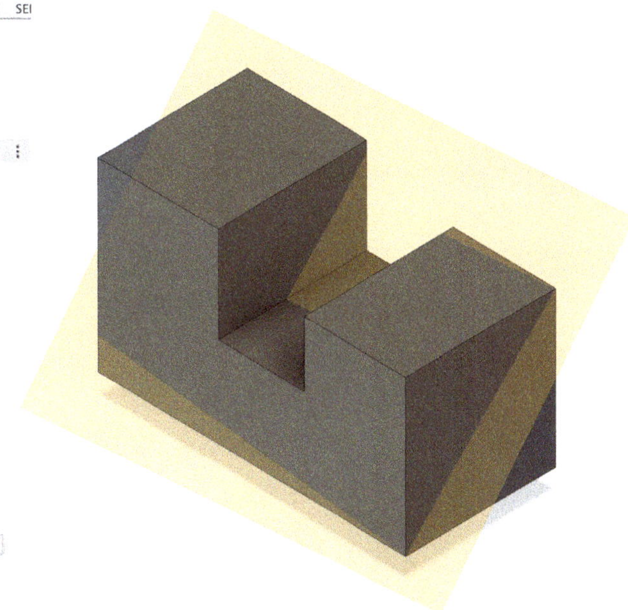

Plane Tangent to Face at Point

This command creates a plane passing through a point and tangent to a curved face. Activate this command (click **Construct** panel **> Plane Tangent to Face at Point** on the toolbar) and select a curved face and a point. Click **OK** on the **Plane Tangent to Face at Point** dialog. A plane tangent to the curved face passing through a point will be created.

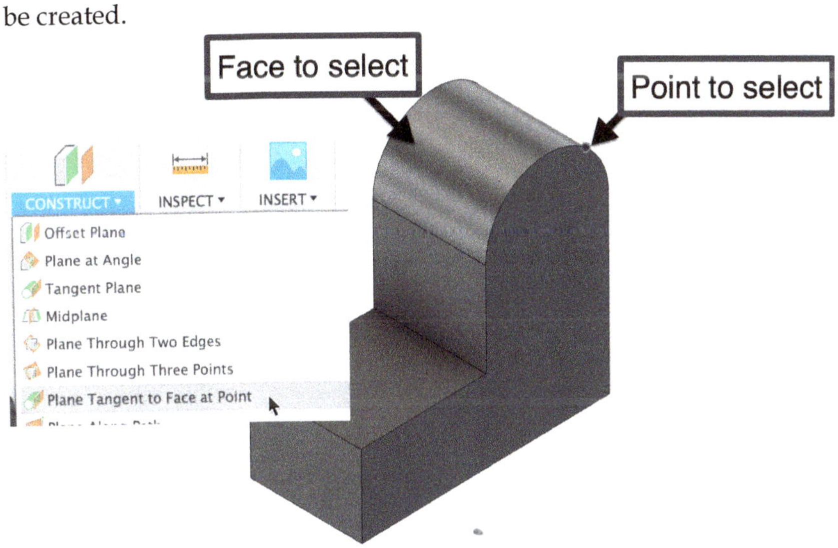

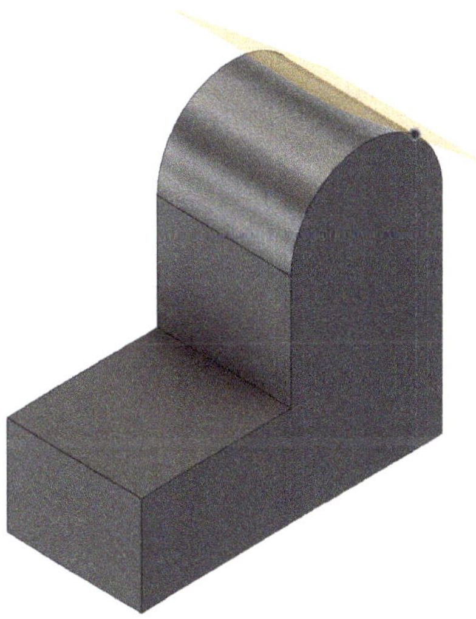

Plane Along Path

This command creates a plane, which will be normal to a line, curve, or edge. Activate the command **Plane Along Path** command (click **Construct** panel **> Plane Along Path** on the toolbar) and select an edge, line, curve, arc, or circle. Next, you need to specify the location of the plane on the selected path. To do this, select an option from the **Distance Type** drop-down. The **Proportional** option allows you to specify the location of the plane by entering a value between 0 and 1. The **Physical** option allows you to specify the location of the plane by entering its exact distance. Click **OK** on the **Plane Along Path** dialog. A plane normal to the path will be created.

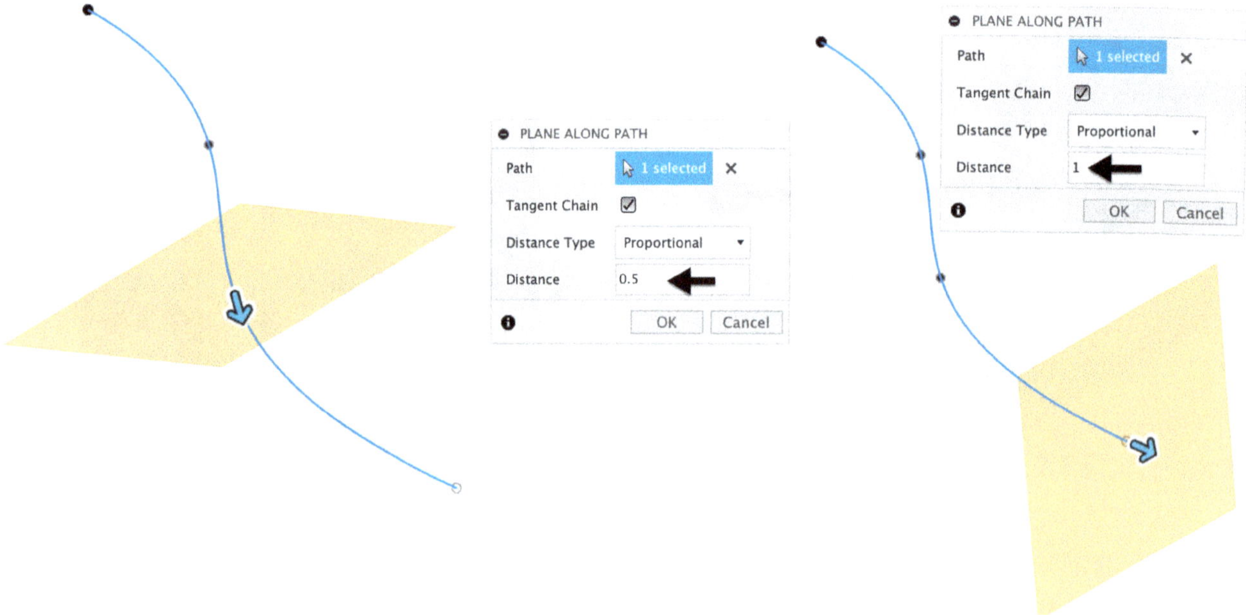

Axis

An axis is another type of construction element that helps you in building a 3D model. For example, you can use an axis to create a revolved feature. You can create various types of axes in Autodesk Fusion 360. They are discussed next.

Axis Through Cylinder/Cone/Torus

This command creates an axis through a cylinder or cone or torus. Activate the **Axis Through Cylinder/Cone/Torus** command (click **Construct** drop-down **> Axis Through Cylinder/Cone/Torus**  on the toolbar) and select a round face, cone, or torus to create an axis.

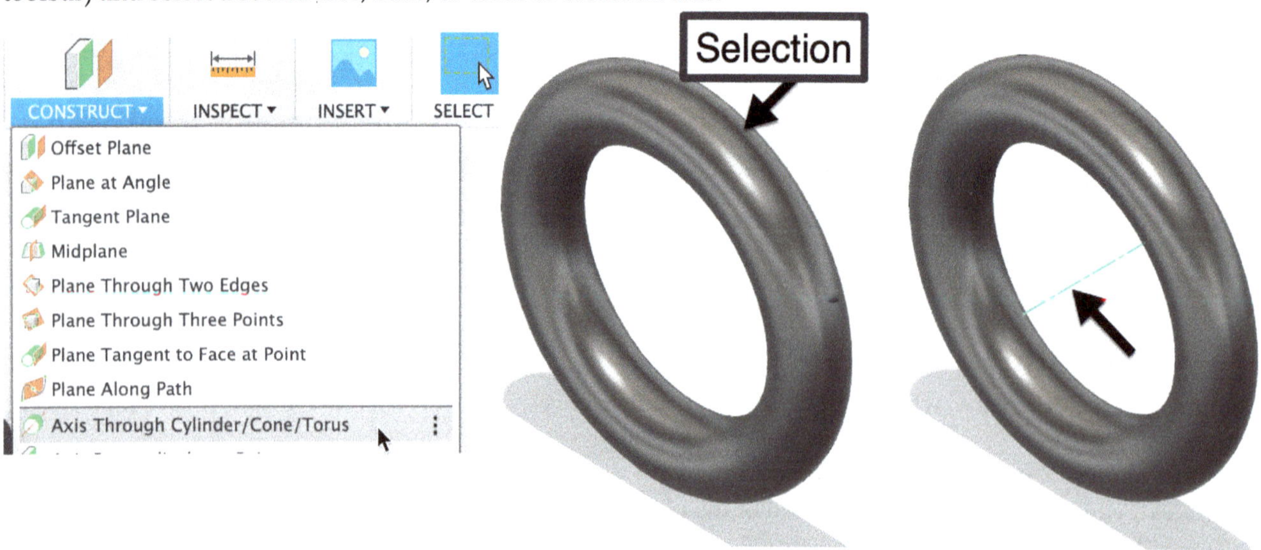

Axis Perpendicular at Point

This command creates an axis, which will be perpendicular to a face at the point of selection. Activate this command (click **Construct** panel **> Axis Perpendicular at Point** on the toolbar) and select a flat face. Next, click **OK** to create an axis perpendicular to the selected face.

Axis Through Two Planes

This command creates an axis at the intersection of two planes or two faces. Activate this command (click **Construct** panel > **Axis Through Two Planes** on the toolbar) and select the two planes or two faces that intersect with each other. Click **OK** on the **Axis Through Two Planes** dialog.

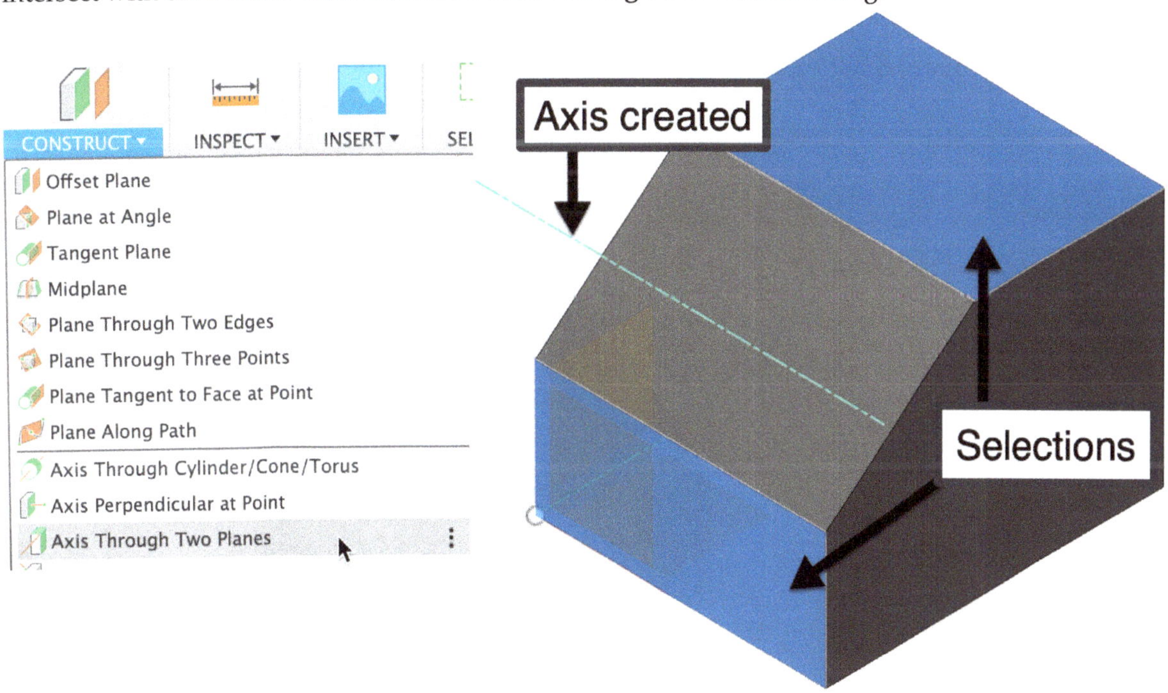

Axis Through Two Points

This command creates an axis passing through two selected points. Activate this command (click **Construct** panel **> Axis Through Two Points** on the toolbar) and select two points. Click **OK** on the **Axis Through Two Points** dialog.

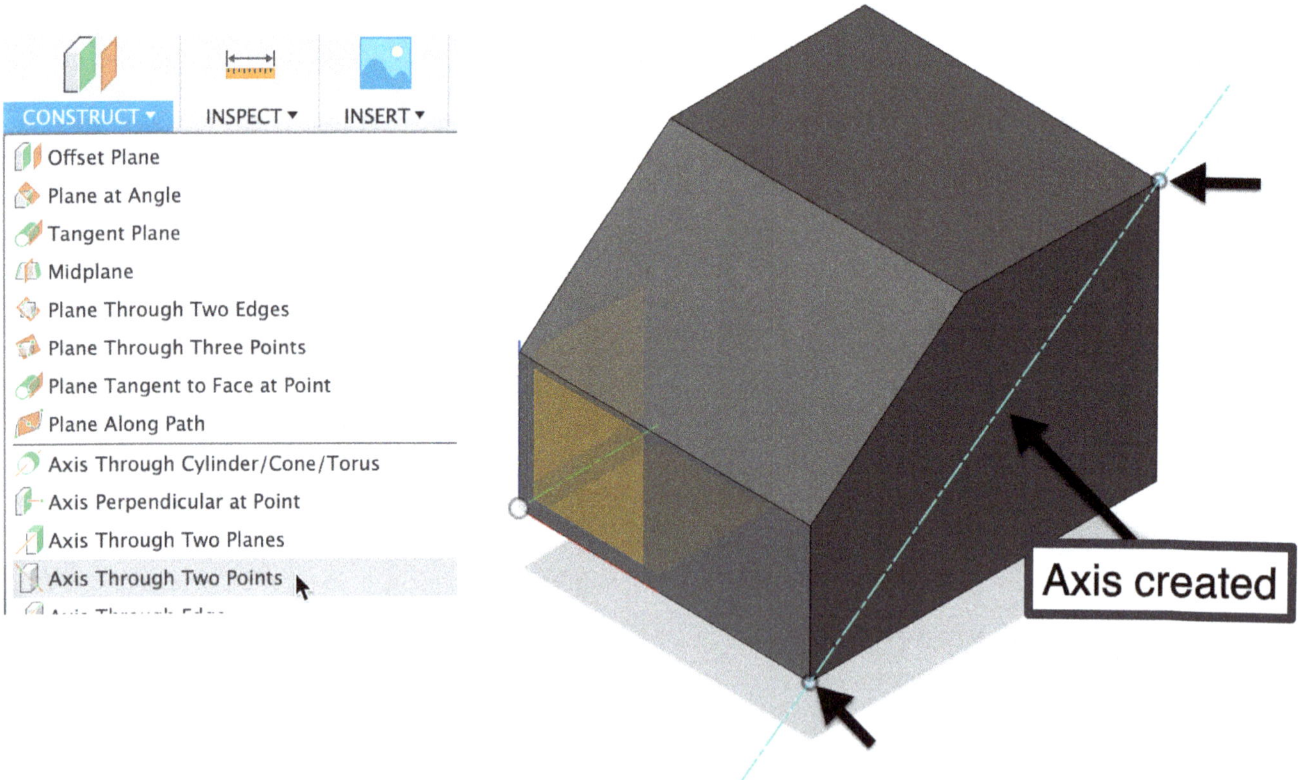

Axis Through Edge

This command creates an axis passing through the selected edge. Activate this command (click **Construct > Axis Through Edge** on the toolbar) and select an edge. Click **OK** on the **Axis Through Edge** dialog.

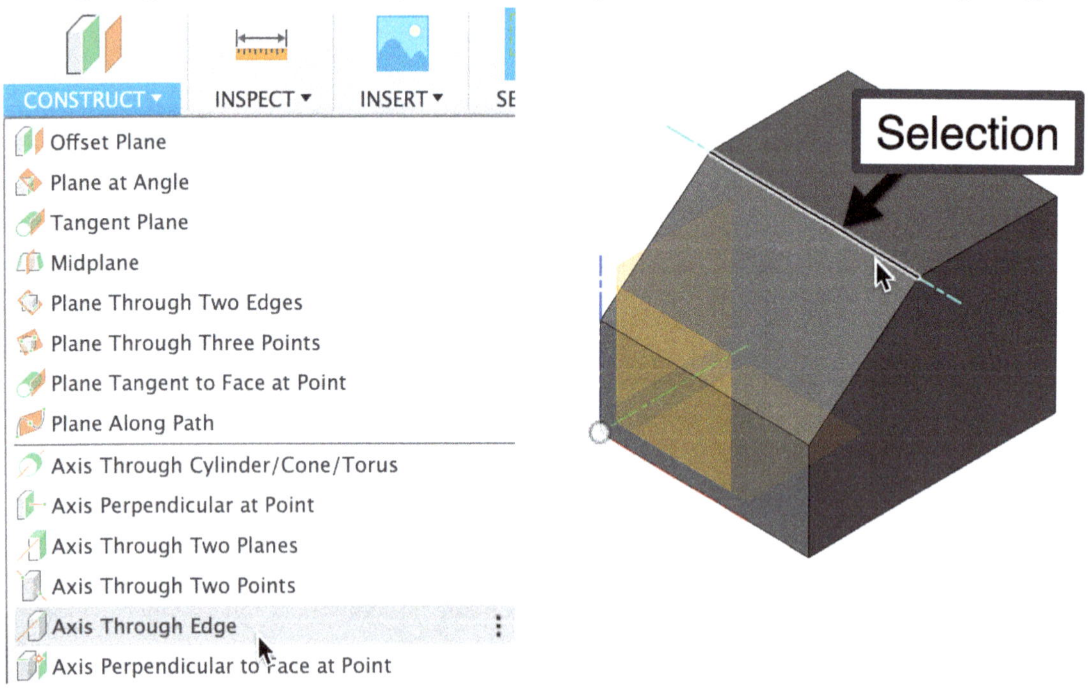

Axis Perpendicular to Face at Point

This command creates an axis, which will be perpendicular to a face and point. Activate this command (click **Construct** panel **> Axis Perpendicular to Face at Point** on the toolbar) and select a face. Next, click on a point to define the location of the axis. Click **OK** on the **Axis Perpendicular to Face at Point** dialog.

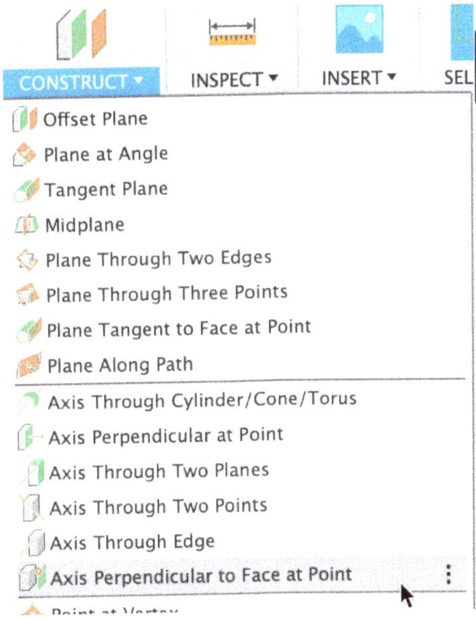

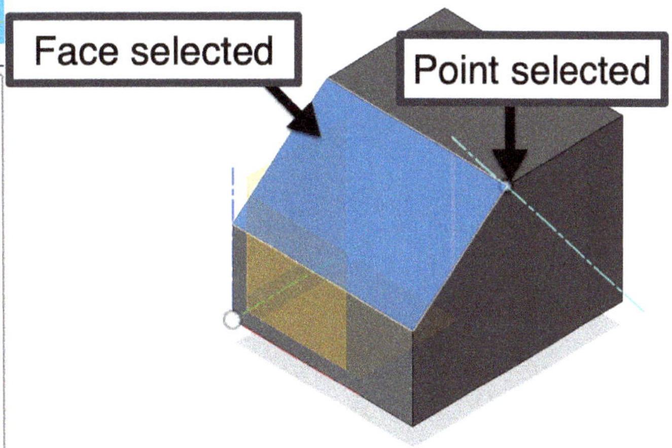

Point

Points are another type of construction element in addition to planes and axes. The commands to create construction points are explained next.

Point at Center of Circle/Sphere/Torus

This command creates a construction point at the center of a circle or sphere or torus. Activate the **Point at Center of Circle/Sphere/Torus** command (click **Construct** panel **> Point at Center of Circle/Sphere/Torus** on the toolbar) and select a circle, sphere, or torus. Next, click **OK** to create the construction point.

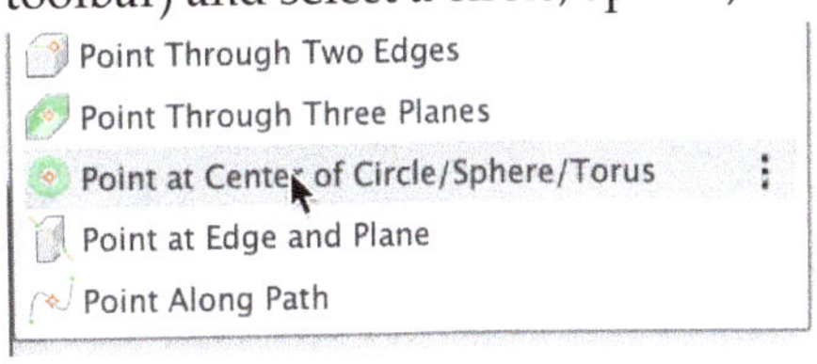

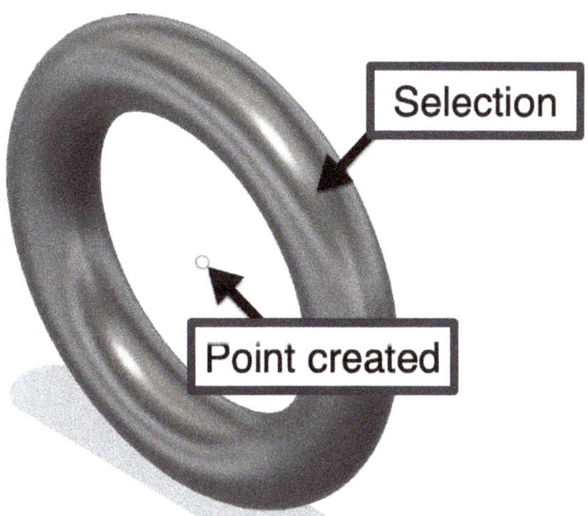

Point at Vertex

This command creates a construction point at a selected point or vertex. Activate the **Point at Vertex** command (click **Construct** panel **> Point at Vertex** on the toolbar) and select a point or vertex of the model. Next, click **OK** to create the point.

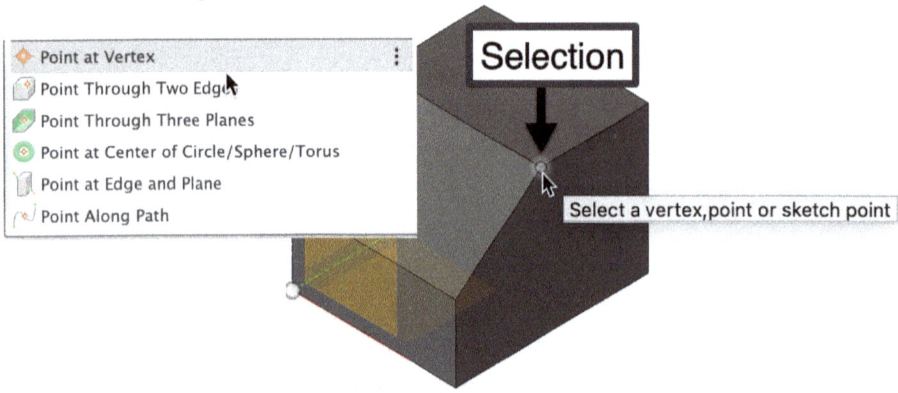

Point through Two Edges

This command creates a construction point at an intersection of two selected edges or sketch lines. Activate the **Point Through Two Edges** command (click **Construct** panel **> Point Through Two Edges** on the toolbar) and select two edges. Next, click **OK** to create the point.

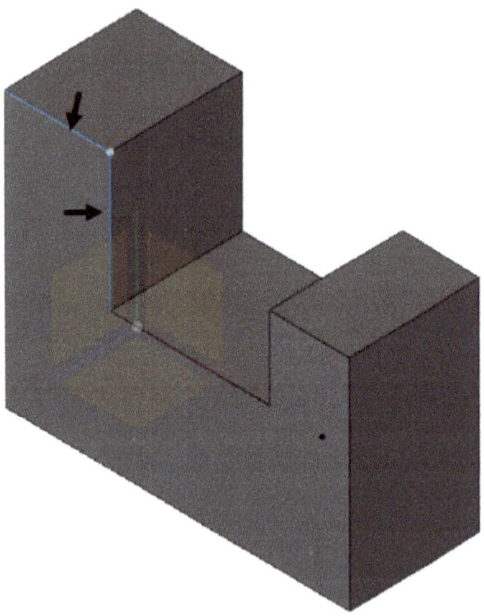

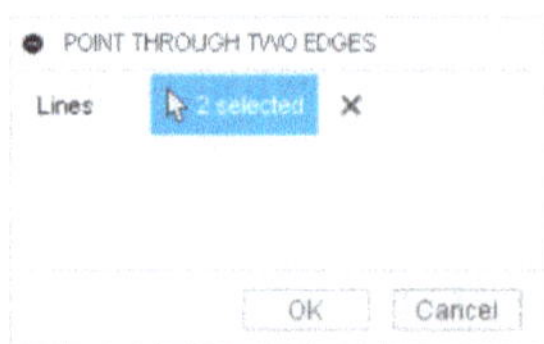

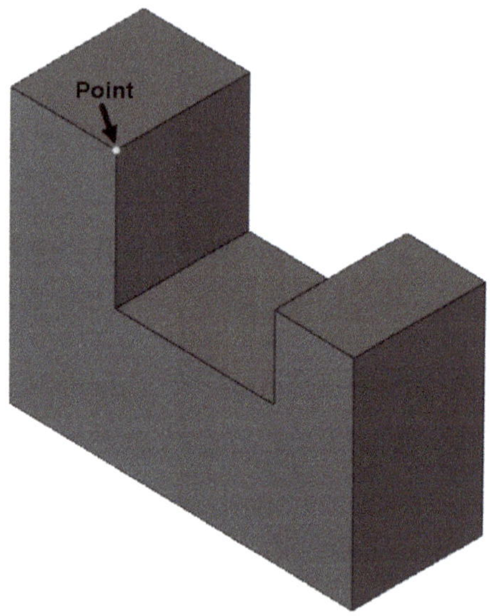

Point Through Three Planes

This command creates a construction point at the intersection of three planes or planar faces. Activate the **Point Through Three Planes** command (click **Construct** panel **> Point Through Three Planes** on the toolbar) and select the three planes or three planar faces. Next, click **OK** to create the point.

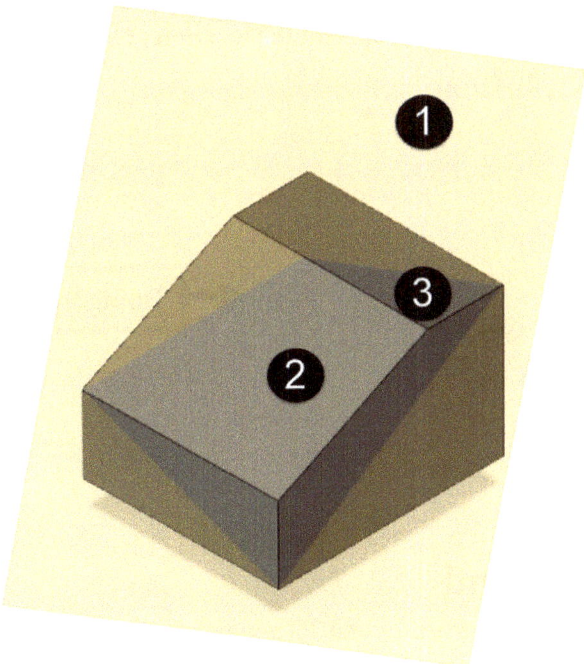

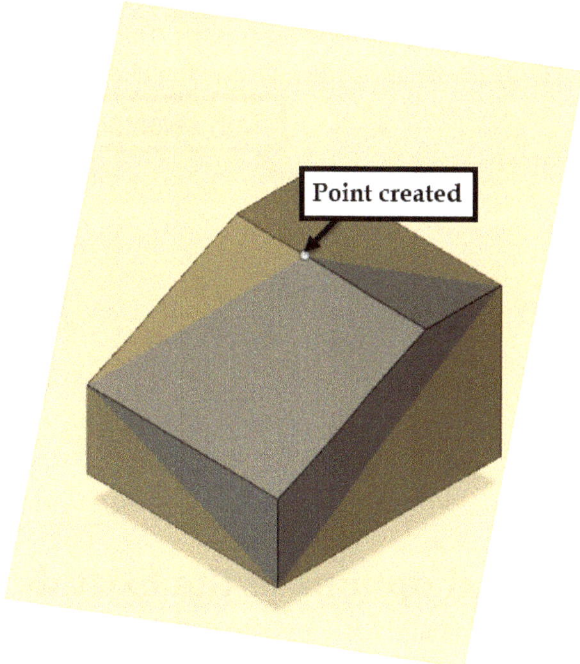

Point at Edge and Plane

This command creates a construction point at an intersection of a construction plane and an axis or sketch line or edge. Activate the **Point at Edge and Plane** command (click **Construct** drop-down > **Point at Edge and Plane** on the toolbar) and select a sketch plane and an edge. Next, click **OK** to create the point.

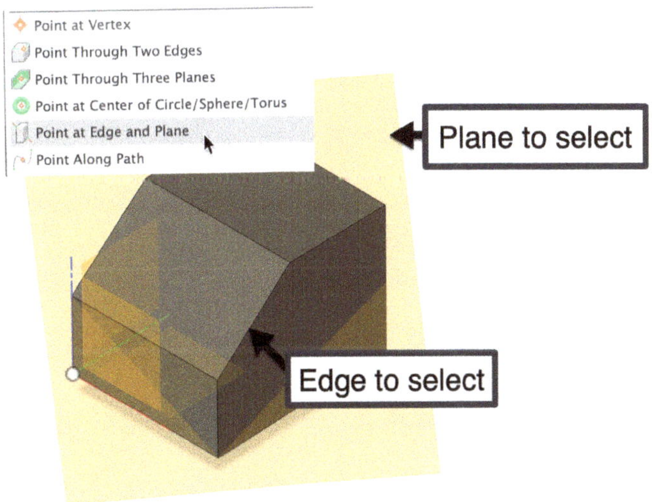

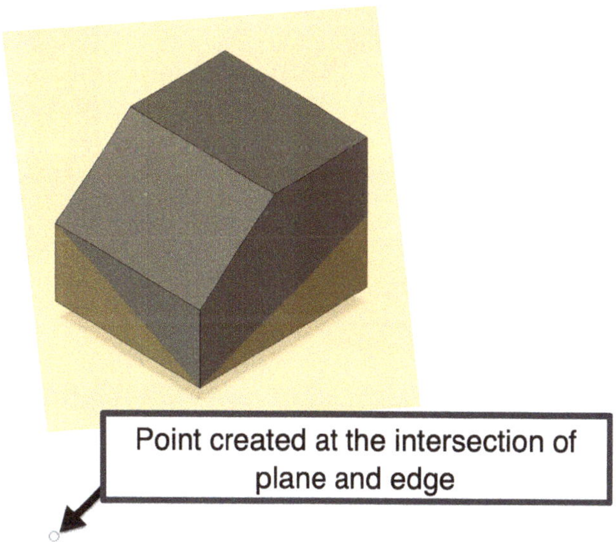

Point along Path

This command creates a construction point along a curve, line, edge, arc, or circle. Activate the command **Point Along Path** command (click **Construct** panel > **Point Along Path** on the toolbar) and select an edge, line, curve, arc, or circle. Next, you need to specify the location of the point on the selected path. To do this, select an option from the **Distance Type** drop-down. The **Proportional** option allows you to specify the location of the point by entering a value between 0 and 1. The **Physical** option allows you to specify the location of the plane by entering its exact distance. Click **OK** on the **Plane Along Path** dialog.

Additional options of the Extrude command

The **Extrude** command has some additional options to create complex features of a 3D geometry.

Thin Extrude

The **Thin Extrude**  option is used to create a thin extruded feature using a closed or open sketch.

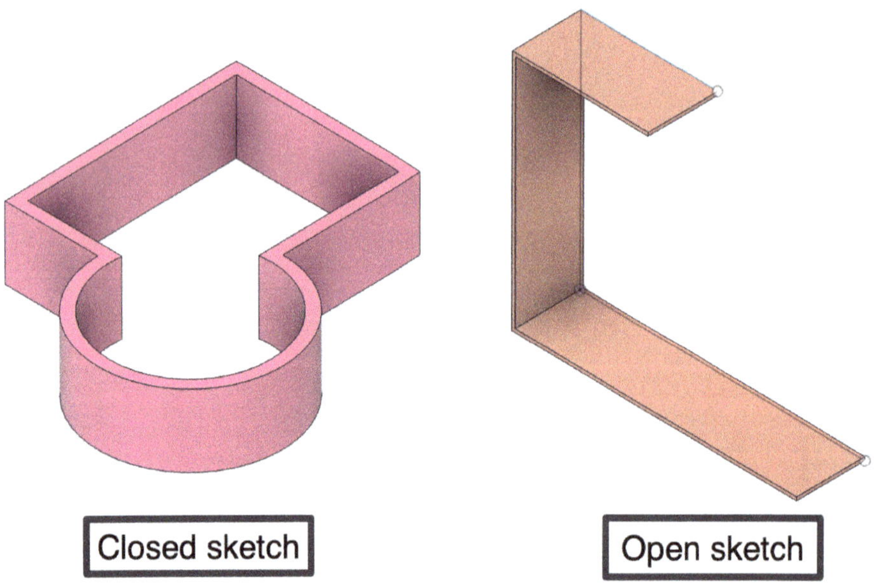

Select **Type > Thin Extrude** from the **Extrude** dialog. Next, select the open or closed sketch. Check the **Chaining** option if you want to select the chain of elements.

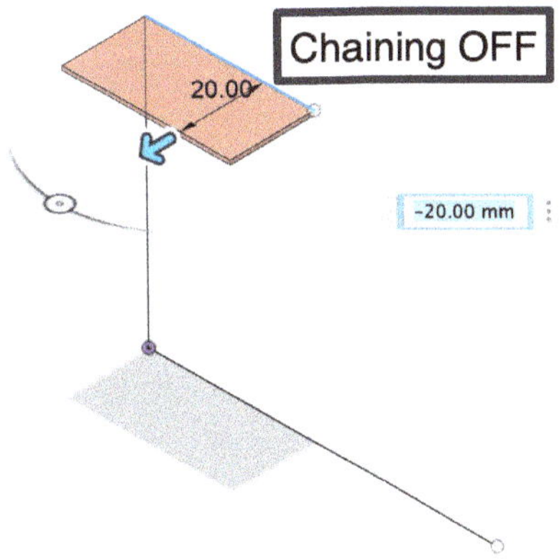

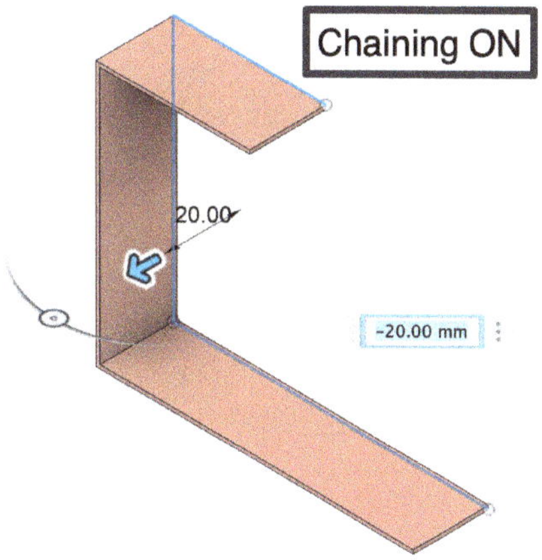

Enter a value in the **Wall Thickness** box. Next, use the **Wall Location** drop-down to control how the thickness is applied relative to the sketch profile. The **Side 1** option creates the feature on the inside of the sketch, while **Side 2** creates it on the outside. Alternatively, selecting **Center** distributes the thickness evenly on both sides of the sketch, positioning the sketch line along the center of the resulting wall.

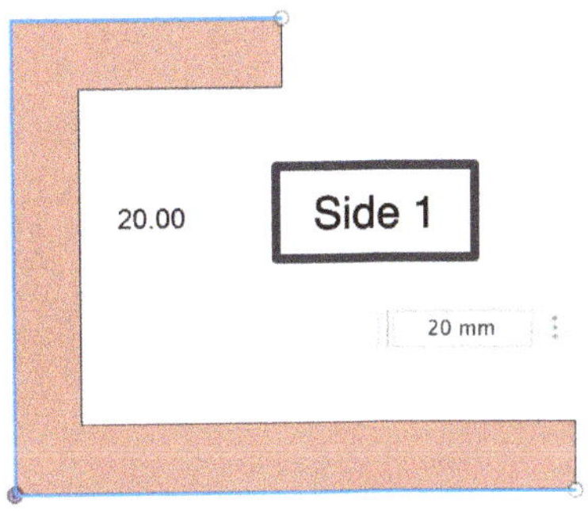

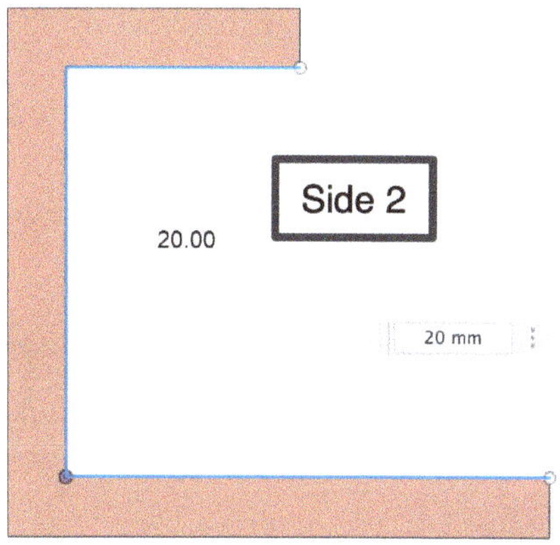

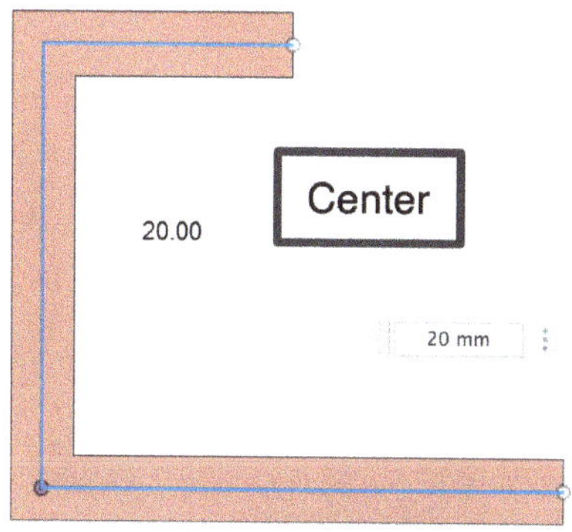

Operation

When you extrude a sketch that interacts with existing geometry, the **Operation** drop-down allows you to define how the new feature will relate to the existing solid body. This drop-down controls whether you add material, remove material, or create a new body based on the intersecting volumes.

Join

The **Join**  option merges the extruded volume with the existing solid body it contacts. As shown in the image, extruding the circular sketch with the **Join** operation adds a cylindrical feature to the block.

Cut

The **Cut** option subtracts the extruded volume from any solid body it passes through. In the example, selecting **Cut** removes a semi-circular section from the block, creating a recess or hole.

Intersect

The **Intersect** option creates a new solid that consists only of the volume shared between the extruded feature and the existing body. The result is a solid that represents the overlapping geometry of the two. As illustrated, the intersect operation leaves only the semi-circular volume where the extruded cylinder and the block overlapped..

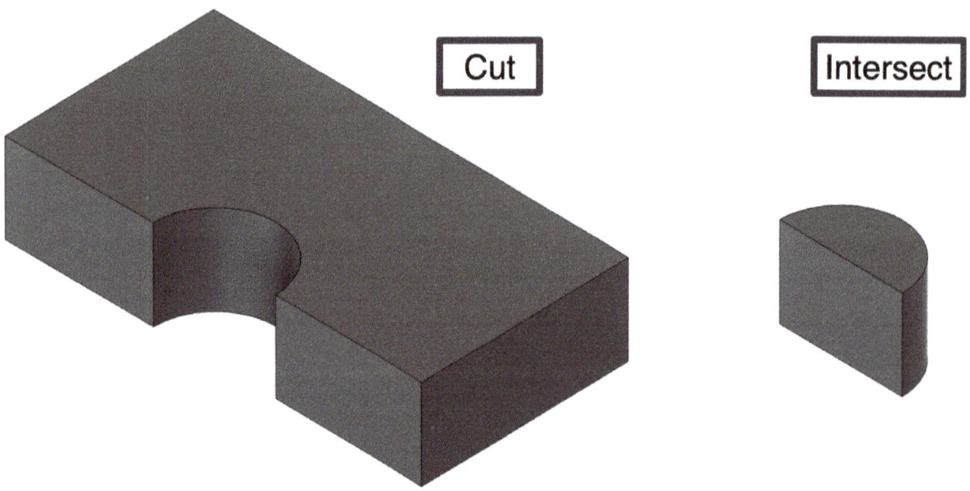

New Body

The **New Body** option creates a new, independent solid body from your extruded sketch. Unlike the **Join** operation, which would merge the new feature with any existing geometry it touches, **New Body** ensures the result is a distinct and separate object within the same part file.

This **option** is essential for multi-body part design. As shown in your image, after extruding the circular sketch using the **New Body** option, the Browser window on the left lists two separate solids: **Body1** (the original block) and **Body2** (the new cylinder). Even though the two bodies are in contact, they are not merged and can be manipulated, modified, or moved independently.

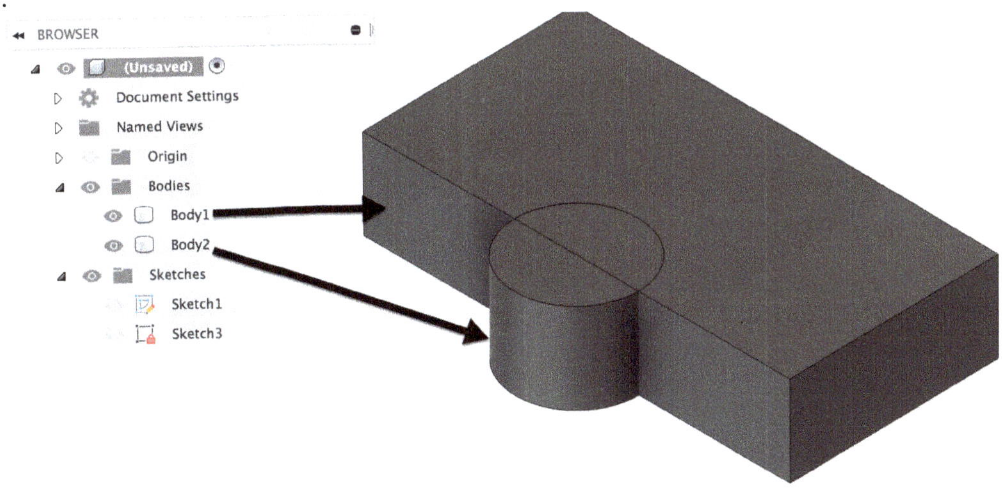

New Component

The **New Component** option creates an entirely new and independent component from your extruded sketch. This is essential for top-down assembly design, where you build multiple parts within a single file. Unlike **New Body**, this option elevates the new solid to a full component, complete with its own origin and browser entry (**Component1** in the image). This allows you to define joints and motion between it and other components, which is crucial for building and simulating assemblies.

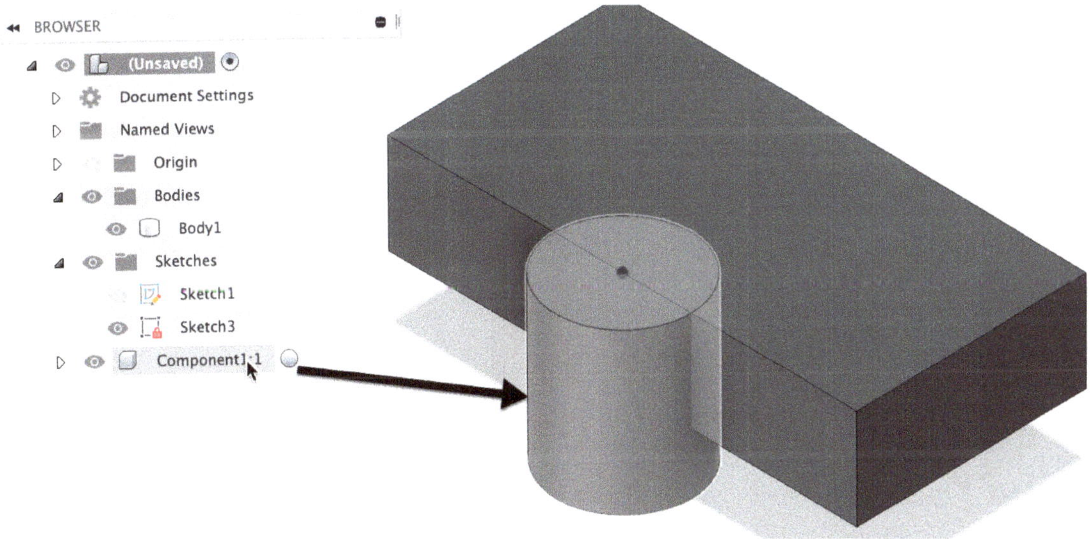

Start

The **Start** drop-down available on the **Extrude** dialog helps you to define the starting limit of the Extruded feature.

The **Profile Plane** option defines the starting limit of the Extruded feature from the plane on which the sketch is created.

The **Offset** option extrudes the sketch from a plane offset to the sketch plane. You can define the location of the offset plane by entering a value in the **Offset** box available on the **Extrude** dialog.

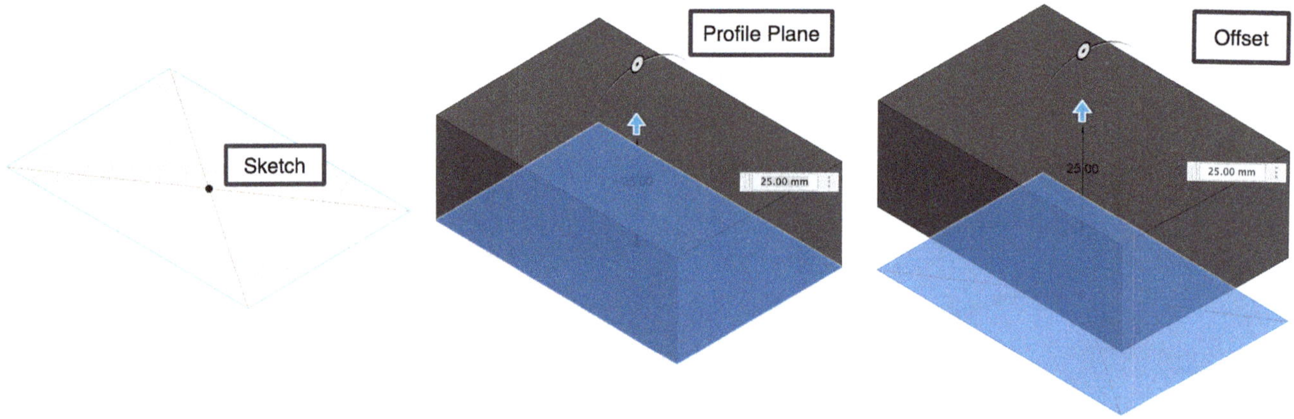

The **Object** option extrudes the sketch from the selected face up to the specified distance. First, select the sketch to be extruded. Next, select **Object** from the **Start** drop-down. Click on the **Object** selection button displayed below the **Start** drop-down and select the starting face. Next, specify the distance in the **Distance** box. The base of the new feature will conform to the shape of the selected starting surface, as shown in the image where the cylinder's base matches the angled plane.

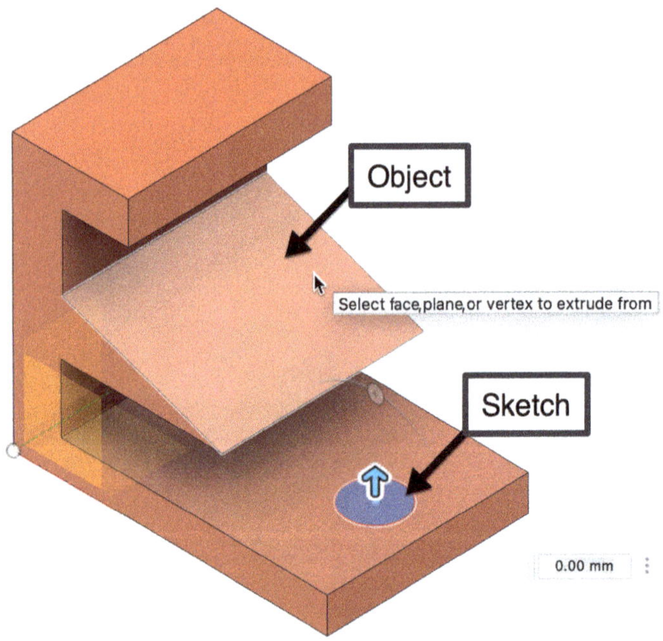

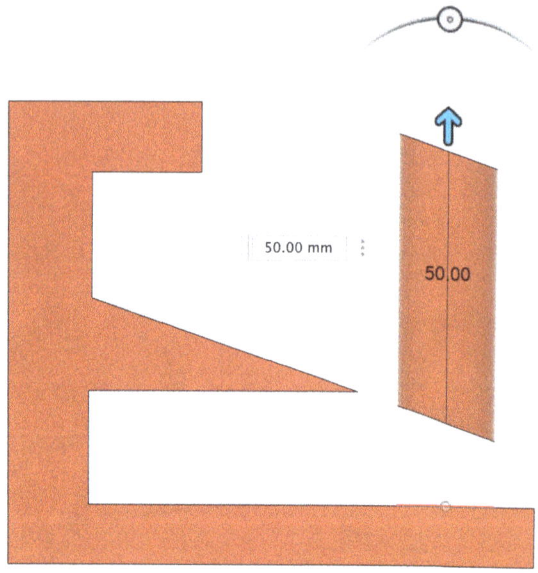

Extent Type

On the **Extrude** dialog, the **Extent Type** drop-down has three options to define the end limit of the *Extrude* feature. These options are **Distance**, **To Object**, and **All**.

The **Distance** option extrudes the sketch up to the specified distance. On the **Extrude** dialog, select **Distance** from the **Extent** drop-down. Next, specify the distance in the **Distance** box and select the required option from the **Direction** drop-down. There are three options in the **Direction** drop-down: *One Side*, *Two Sides*, and *Symmetric* icons.

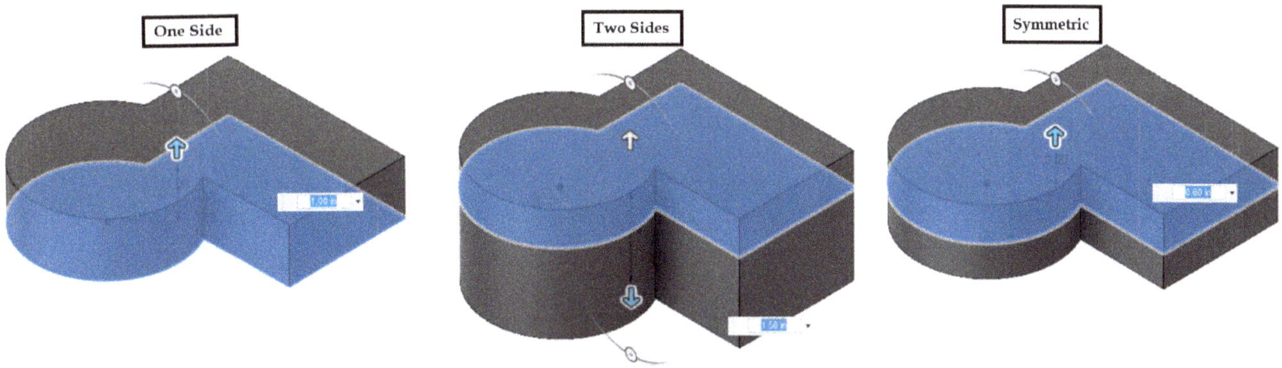

The **To Object** option defines the termination point of an extrusion by using an existing surface, plane, or body as its boundary. Instead of specifying a fixed distance, you select a target object, and Autodesk Fusion 360 automatically calculates the required length to make the new feature meet that object precisely. On the **Extrude** dialog, select **Operation** > **Join** to add material to the part and select **To Object** from the **Extent** drop-down. Next, select the face or plane; the sketch will be extruded up to the selected face or plane. The behaviour of this option can be modified using the **Chain Faces** options.

Click **Chain Faces > Extend Faces** on the **Extrude** dialog to treats the target face as an infinite plane. This ensures the extrusion stops at the intended boundary, even if the selected face does not completely cover the sketch profile.

Click **Chain Faces > Chain Faces** on the **Extrude** dialog to extrude the sketch up to the chain of faces connected to the selected face.

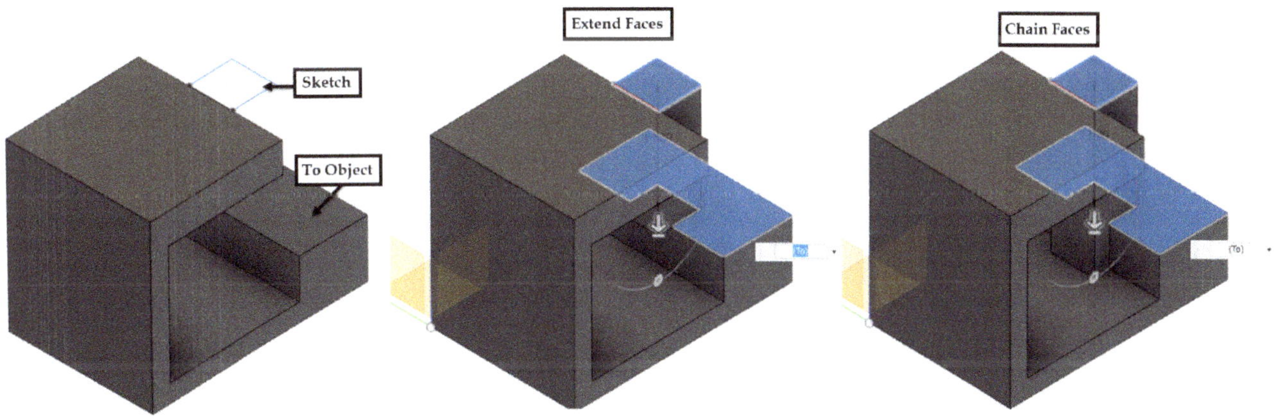

The **All** option extrudes the sketch throughout the 3D geometry. On the **Extrude** dialog, select **All** from the **Extent** drop-down. Select any one of the options from the **Direction** drop-down to specify the direction. Click the **Flip** icon to reverse the direction.

Adding Taper to the Extruded Feature

The **Taper** option will help you to apply taper to the extrusion. On the **Extrude** dialog, type-in the angle value in the **Taper** box. After specifying the taper angle, click the **Direction** drop-down and select anyone of the direction icons.

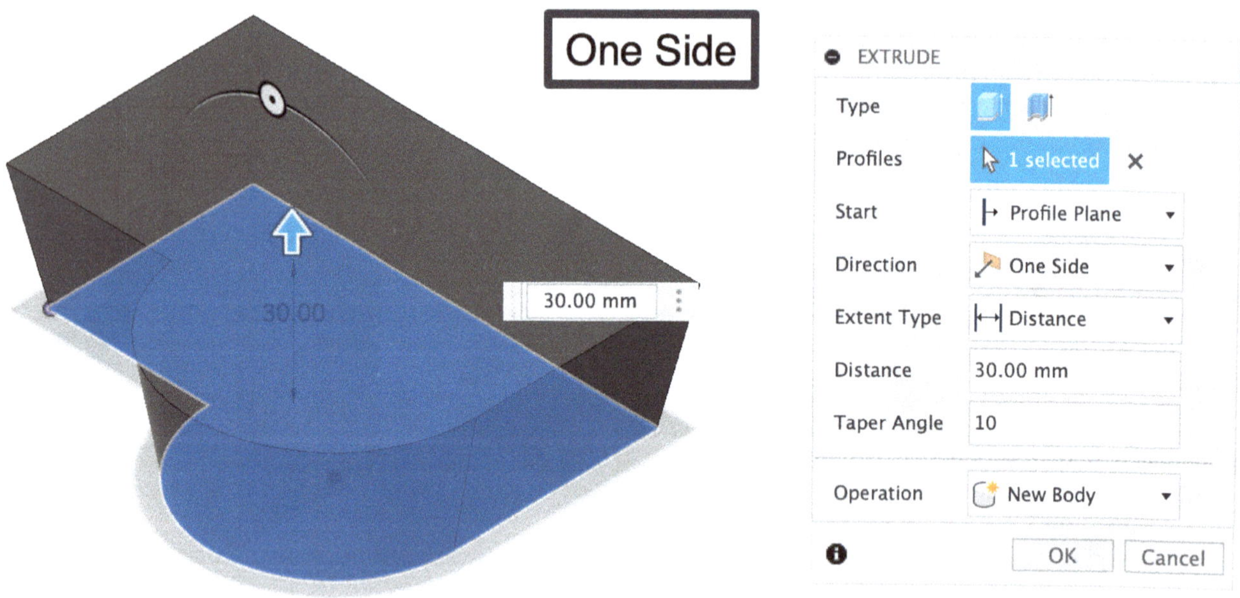

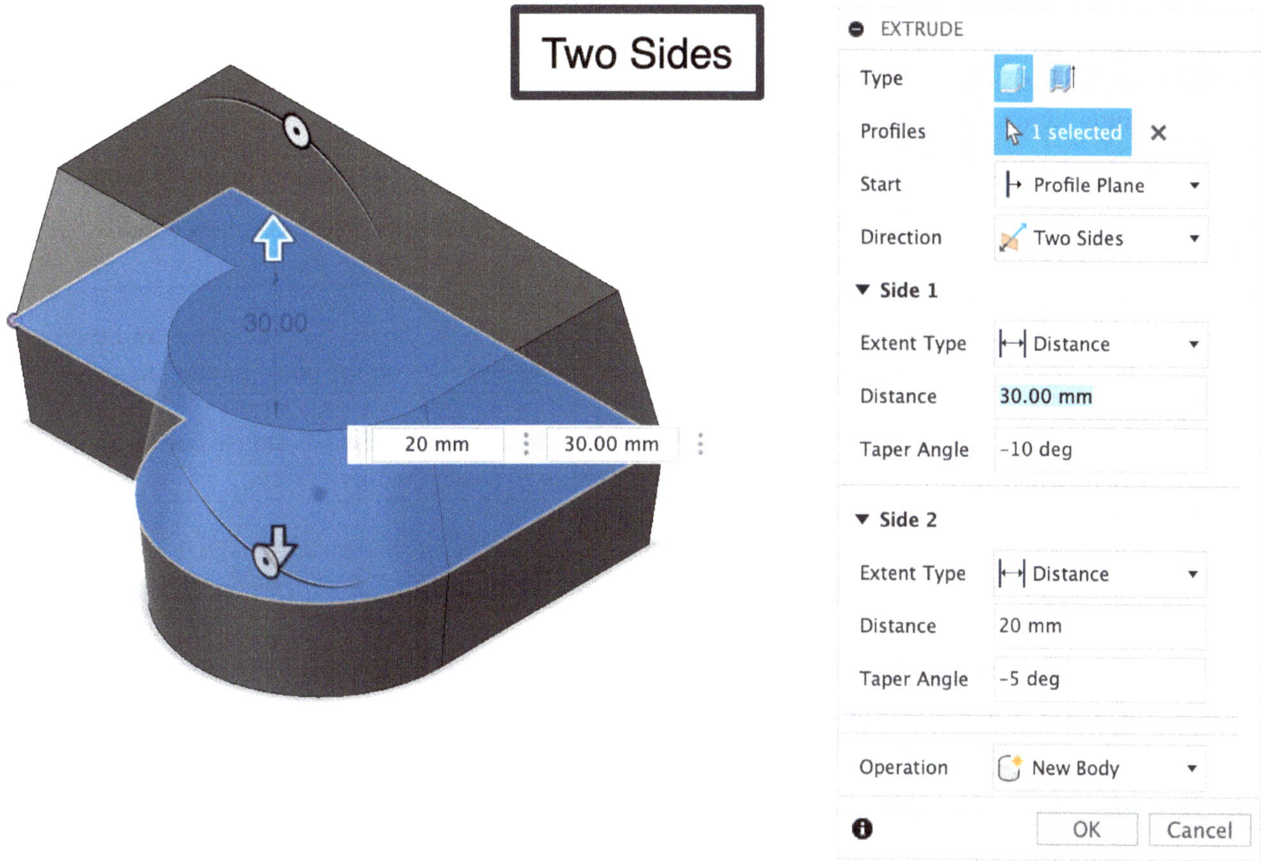

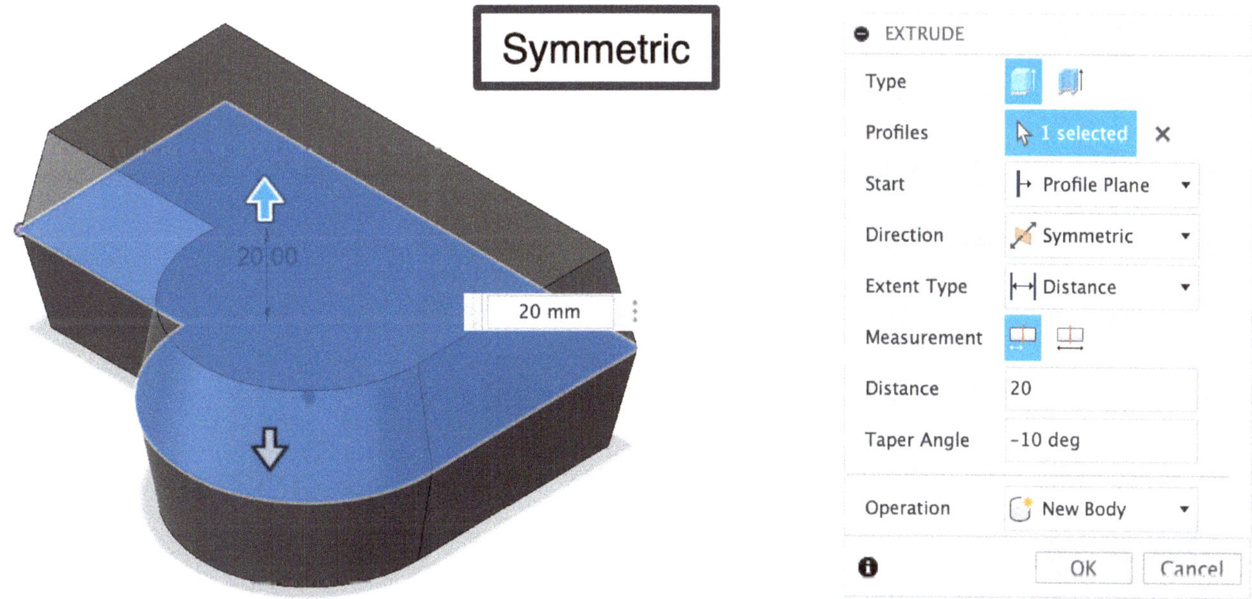

Click **OK** to complete the Extruded Feature.

View Modification commands

The model displayed in the graphics window can be changed using various view modification commands. These commands can be accessed from the **Navigation bar** in the graphics window. The following are some of the main view modification commands:

	Fit	This option fits the model in the current size of the graphics window so that it will be visible completely.
	Pan	Activate this command, press and hold the left mouse button, and then drag the pointer to move the model view on the plane parallel to screen.
	Free Orbit	Activate this command and press and hold the left mouse button on the model. Next, drag the pointer to rotate the model view.
	Zoom	Activate this command and press the left mouse button. Drag the mouse to vary the size of the objects accordingly.
	Look At	This command positions a selected planar face parallel to the screen.
	Zoom window	Activate this command and drag a rectangle. The contents inside the rectangle will be zoomed.
	Constrained Orbit	Activate this command and notice a light grey circle with quadrant partitions. Place the pointer on anyone of the quadrant partitions. Next, press and hold the left mouse button and drag the pointer; the model is rotated about the quadrant partition. 

	**Display Settings**	This drop-down has many display settings such as *Visual Style, Mesh Display, Environment, Effects, Object Visibility,Camera and Ground Plane Offset,* and *Enter Full Screen.*	
Visual Style	**Shaded with Visible Edges only**	This represents the model with shades along with visible edges.	
	Shaded	This represents the model with shades without visible edges.	

	Shaded with Hidden Edges	This represents the model with shades with hidden edges. The hidden edges are displayed in dashed lines.	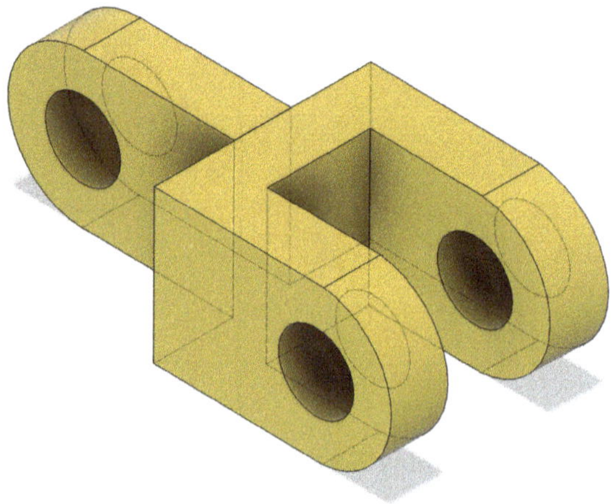
	Wireframe	This represents the model in wireframe along with the hidden edges	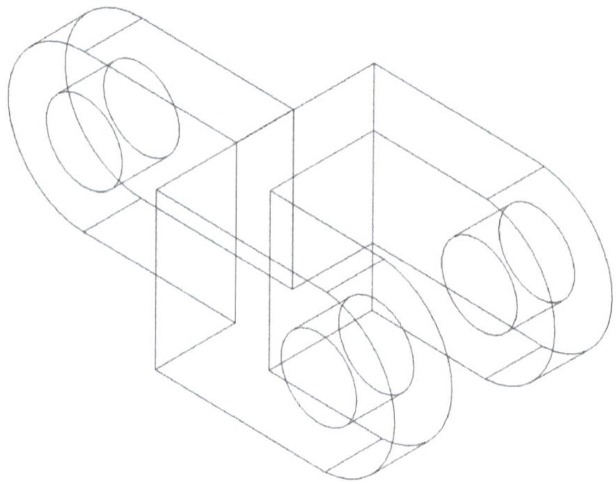
	Wireframe with hidden edges	This represents the model in wireframe. The hidden edges are displayed in dashed lines.	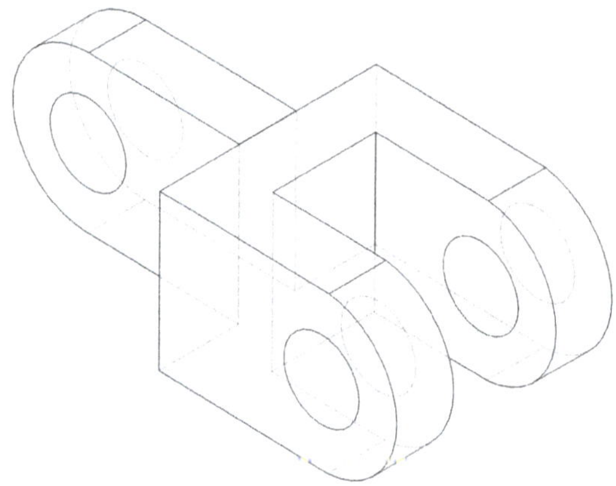

	Wireframe with Visible edges only	This represents the model in wireframe. The hidden edges are not shown.	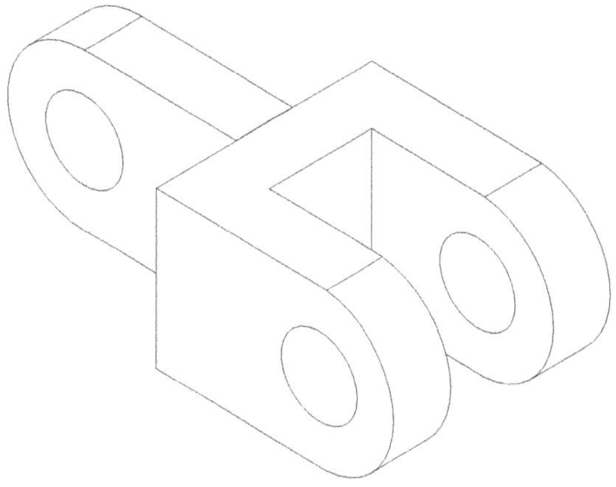

Examples

Example 1 (Millimeters)

In this example, you will create the part shown below.

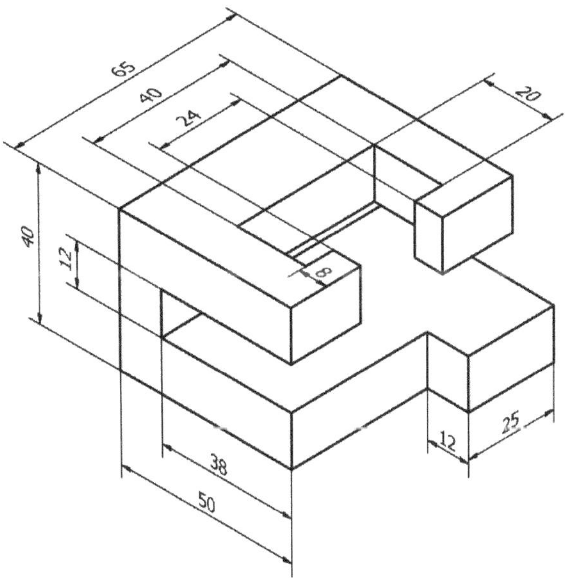

Creating the Base Feature

1. Start **Autodesk Fusion 360** by double-clicking the **Autodesk Fusion 360** icon on your desktop.
2. On the **Browser window**, expand **Document Settings** and place the cursor on **Units**; the **Change Active Units** icon appears.
3. Click on the **Change Active Units** icon to change the units; the **Change Active Units** dialog appears.
4. On this dialog, select **Unit Type > millimeter (mm), gram (g)** from the drop-down and click **OK**.
5. To start a sketch, click **Create > Create Sketch** on the toolbar. Click on the XZ plane. The sketch starts.

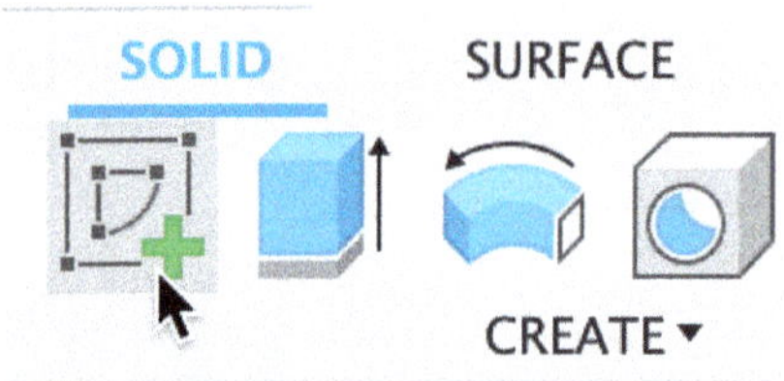

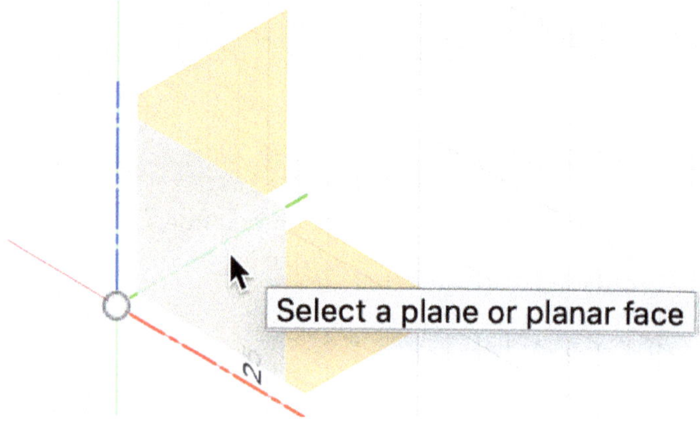

6. Click **Create** panel > **2-Point Rectangle** on the **Sketch** contextual tab of the toolbar. Click the origin point to define the first corner of the rectangle. Next, move the pointer toward the top right corner and click to define the second corner.
7. Click **Create** panel **> Sketch Dimension** on the **Sketch** contextual tab of the toolbar.
8. Select the horizontal line of the rectangle, move the pointer vertically, and then click.
9. Type 50 in the **Dimension** box and press Enter.
10. Select the vertical line of the rectangle, move the pointer horizontally, and then click to position the dimension.
11. Type 40 in the **Dimension** box and press Enter.
12. Press **Esc** to deactivate the **Sketch Dimension** command.
13. On the **Sketch** contextual tab of the toolbar, click **Finish Sketch**.
14. Click the **Home** icon next to the ViewCube.

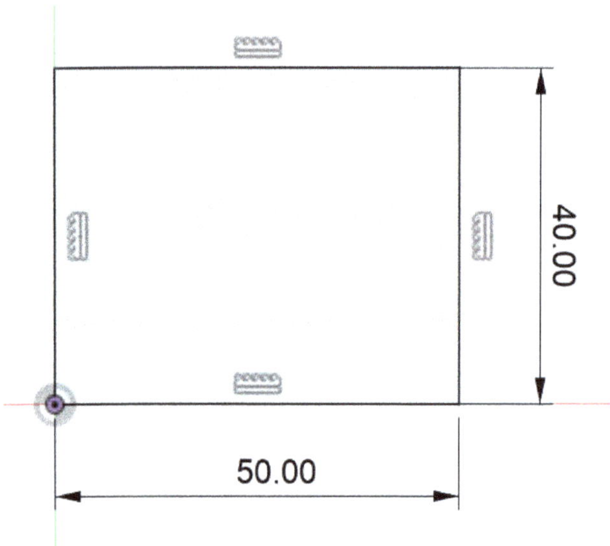

15. On the **Solid** tab of the toolbar, click **Create > Extrude** . Next, click in the sketch region.
16. Select **Type > Extrude** on the **Extrude** dialog.
17. On the **Extrude** dialog, click the **Extent Type** drop-down and select **Distance**.
18. Type-in **32.5** in the **Distance** box.
19. Click the **Direction** drop-down and select **Symmetric**.

20. Click the **Measurement > Half Length** icon.
21. Click **OK** on the **Extrude** dialog to complete the *Extrude* feature.

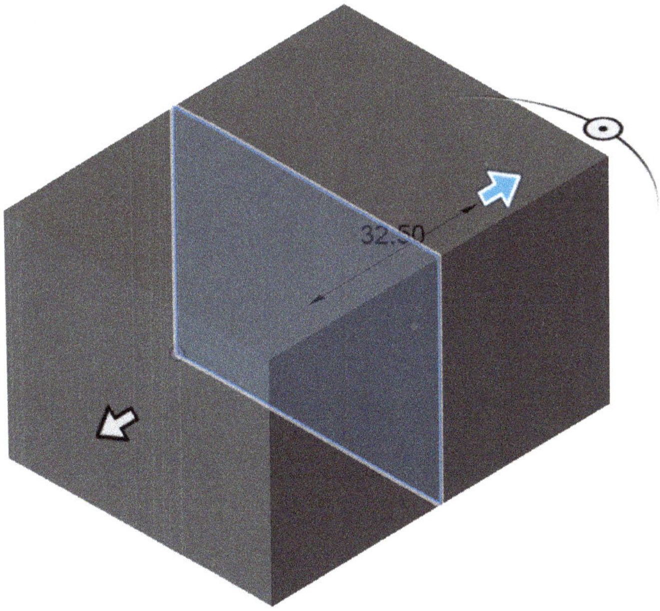

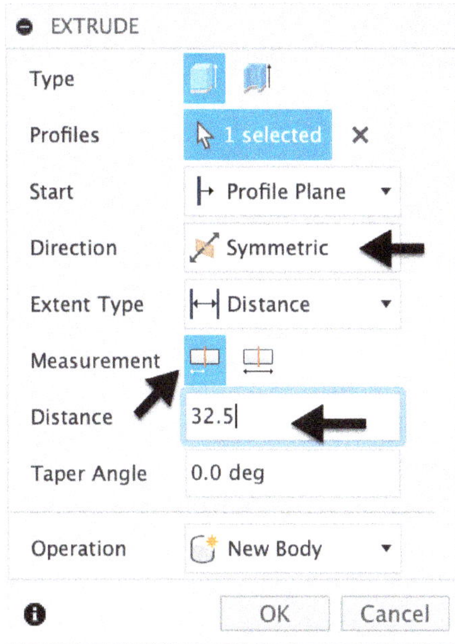

Creating the Extrude Cut throughout the Part model

1. To start a sketch, click **Create** panel > **Create Sketch** on the toolbar.
2. Click on the front face of the part geometry.
3. Click **Create** panel **> 2-Point Rectangle** on the **Sketch** contextual tab of the toolbar.
4. Click near the top right corner to define the first corner of the rectangle.
5. Move the pointer diagonally toward the bottom-left corner, and then click.

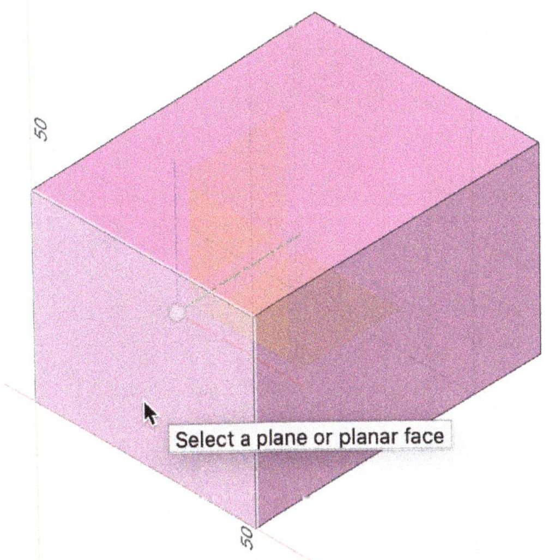

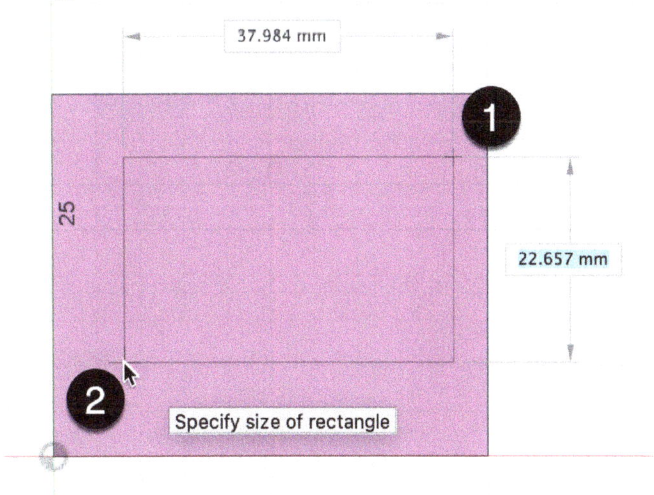

6. On the **Sketch** contextual tab of the toolbar, click **Constraints** panel > **Midpoint**, and then select the right vertical line of the rectangle. Next, select the right vertical edge of the model; the midpoints of the two selected entities are made coincident to each other.

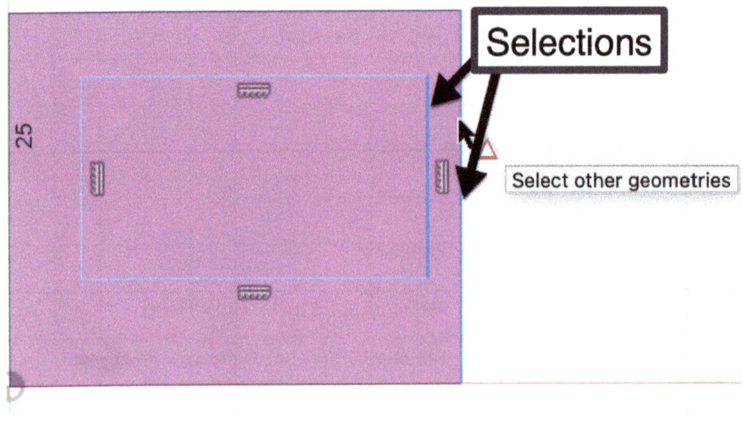

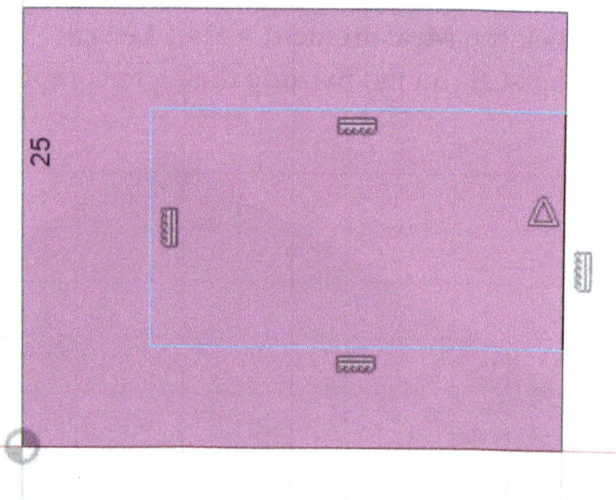

7. On the **Sketch** contextual tab of the toolbar, click **Create** panel > **Sketch Dimension** .
8. Select the horizontal line of the sketch, move the pointer vertically downward, and click to position the dimension.
9. Type **38** in the Dimension box and press Enter.
10. Select the vertical line of the sketch, move the pointer horizontally, and click to position the dimension.
11. Type **12** in the Dimension box and press Enter. Press **Esc** to deactivate the **Sketch Dimension** command.
12. Click **Finish Sketch** on the **Sketch** contextual tab of the toolbar. Click the **Home** icon next to the ViewCube.

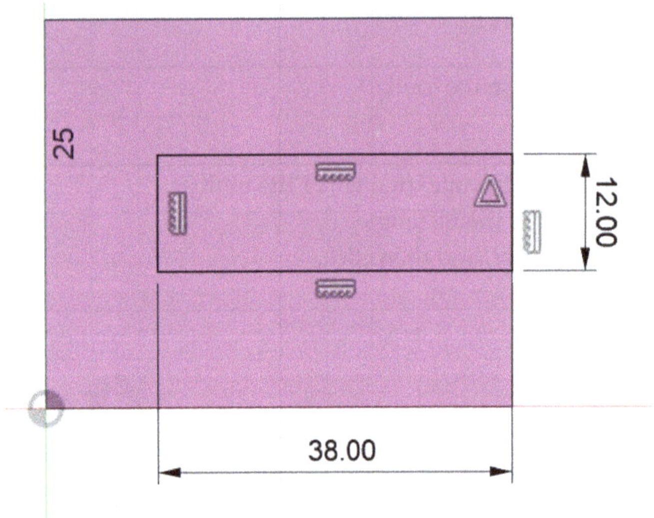

13. On the **Solid** tab of the toolbar, click **Create** panel > **Extrude** . Next, click on the region enclosed by the sketch.
14. On the **Extrude** dialog, click **Direction > One Side**. Next, click the **Extent Type** drop-down and select **All**.
15. Click the **Flip** icon to reverse the extrusion direction.
16. Select the **Cut** option from the **Operation** drop-down.

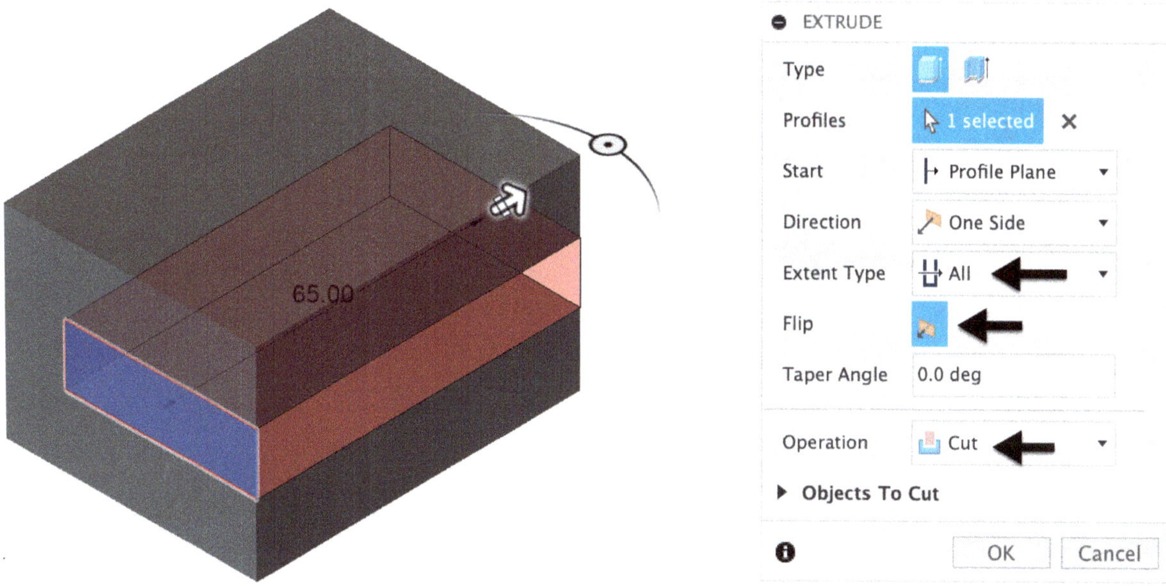

17. Click **OK** to create the extruded cut throughout the part model.

Creating the Extruded Cut up to the surface next to the sketch plane

1. Click **Create > Create Sketch** on the toolbar and click on the top face of the part model, as shown.

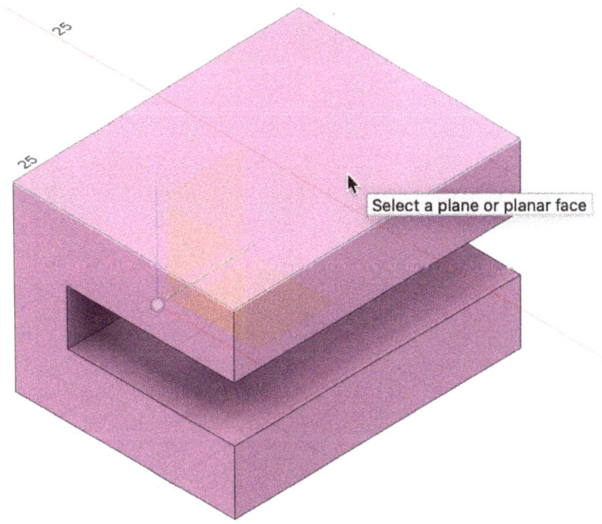

2. Activate the **Center Rectangle** command (click **Create > Rectangle > Center Rectangle** on **Sketch** contextual tab of the toolbar).
3. Click on the mode face and move the pointer outward. Next, type 40 and press the TAB key.
4. Type **20** and press ENTER.
5. On the toolbar, click **2-Point Rectangle** on the **Create** panel of the **Sketch** contextual tab.
6. Click on the right vertical edge of the rectangle. Type **24** and press the TAB key.
7. Type **8** in the width box. Next, move the pointer toward right and click to create the rectangle.

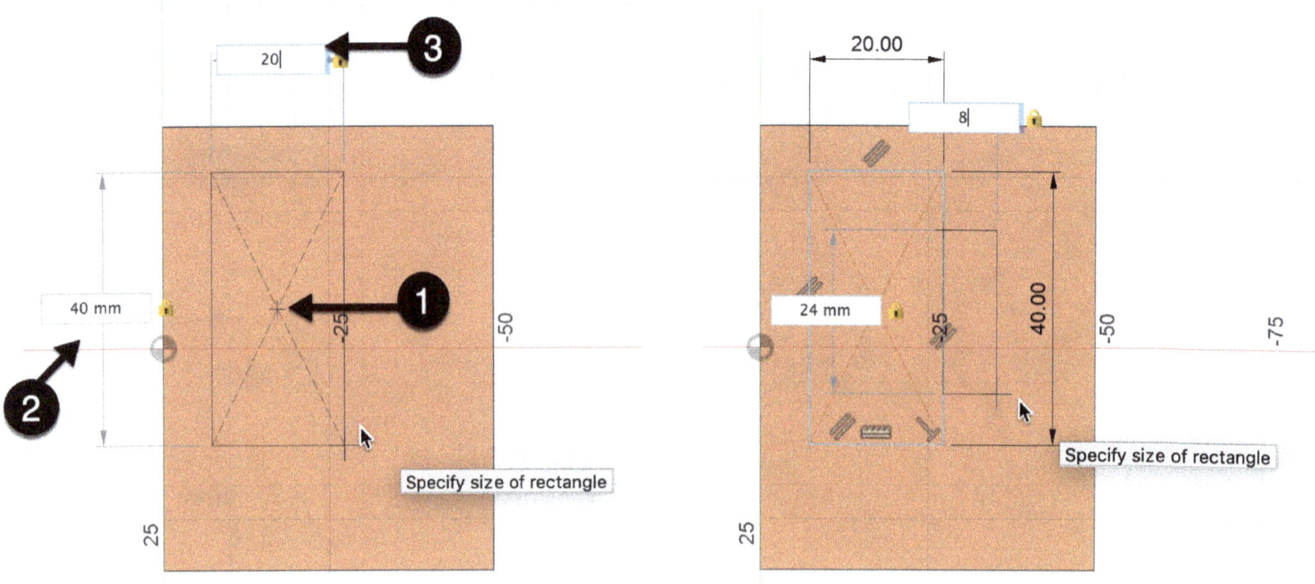

8. On the toolbar, click the **Trim** icon on the **Modify** panel of the **Sketch** tab. Next, click twice on the inner vertical line, as shown. The two overlapping vertical lines are trimmed.

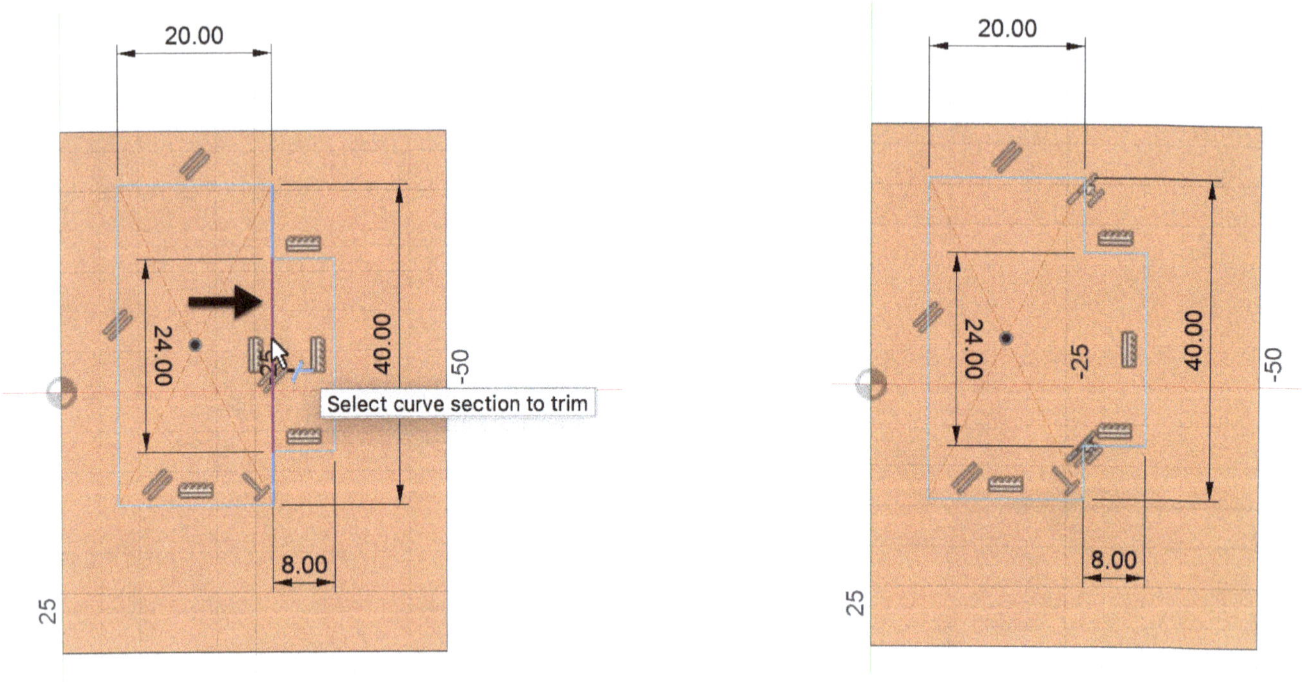

9. Click **Constraints > Equal** on **Sketch** contextual tab of the toolbar.
10. Select the lower and upper vertical lines, as shown.
11. Click **Constraints > Midpoint** on **Sketch** contextual tab of the toolbar.
12. Select the right vertical line of the rectangle and the right vertical edge of the model; the midpoints of the selected lines are made coincident to each other.

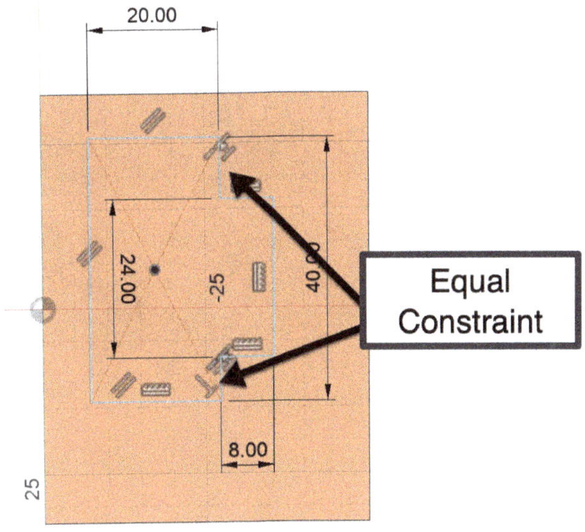

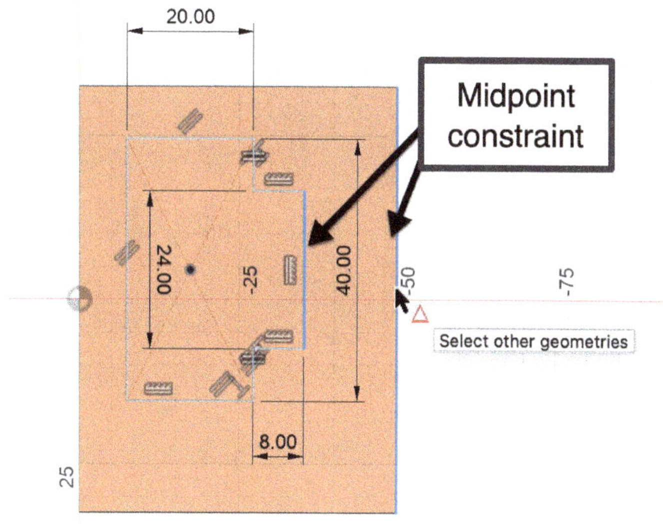

The sketch is fully constrained and the sketch elements are turned black in color.

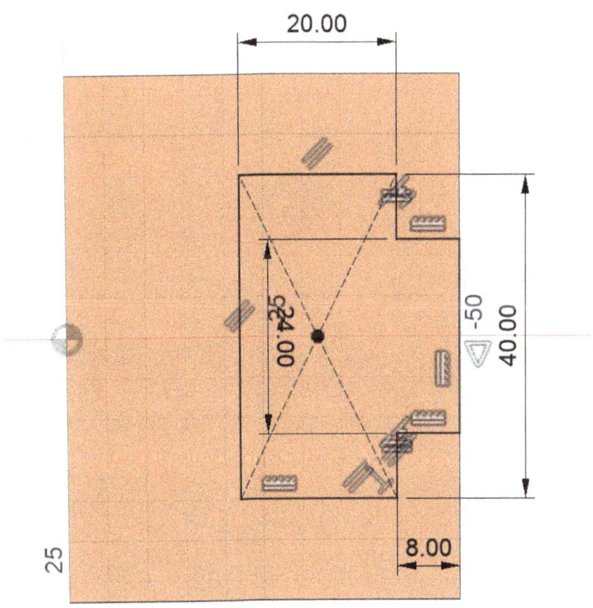

13. On the **Sketch** contextual tab of the toolbar, click **Finish Sketch**. Click the **Home** icon next to the ViewCube.
14. On the **Solid** tab of the toolbar, click **Create** panel > **Extrude** and select the sketch.
15. On the **Extrude** dialog, click **Operation > Cut**.
16. Select **To Object** from the **Extent Type** drop-down.
17. Select the vertex of the model, as shown.

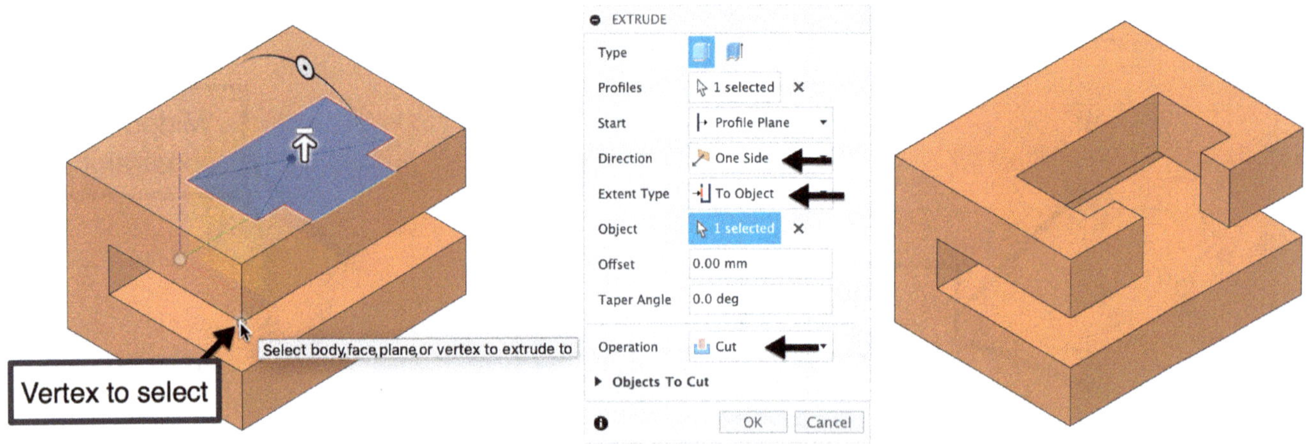

18. Click **OK** to create the *Extruded Cut* feature up to the selected surface.

Extruding the sketch up to a Surface

1. On the toolbar, click **Create > Create Sketch** command.
2. Expand the **Origin** folder in the Browser and select the XY Plane.

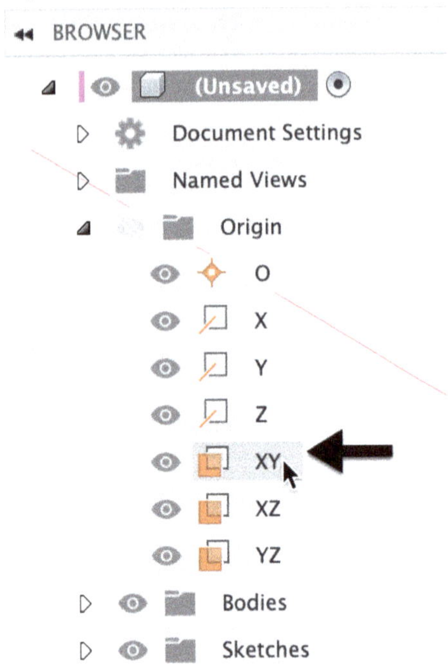

3. Draw a rectangle. Apply the **Coincident** constraint between the top left corner of the rectangle and the top right corner of the model. Add dimensions and click **Finish Sketch** on the toolbar.

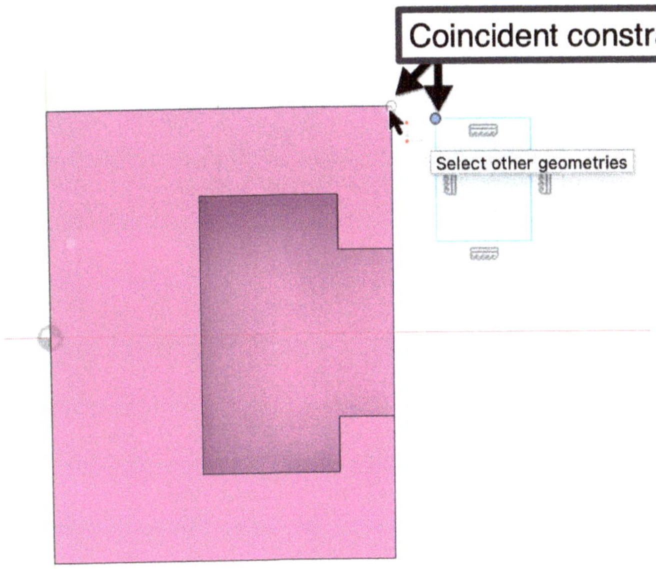

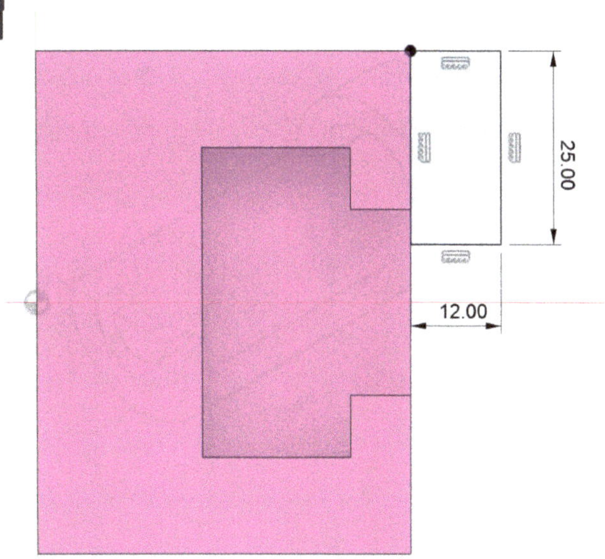

4. Click the **Home** icon next to the ViewCube.
5. On the **Solid** tab of the toolbar, click **Create** panel > **Extrude**  .
6. On the **Extrude** dialog, select **To Object** from the **Extent Type** drop-down.
7. Select the horizontal face of the extruded cut, as shown.
8. Select **Operation** drop-down > **Join**.

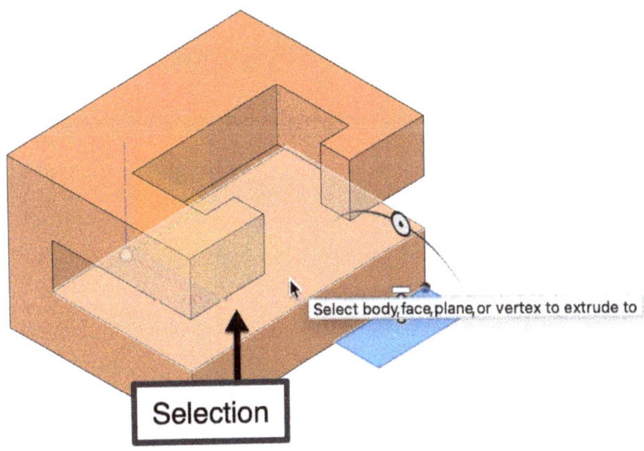

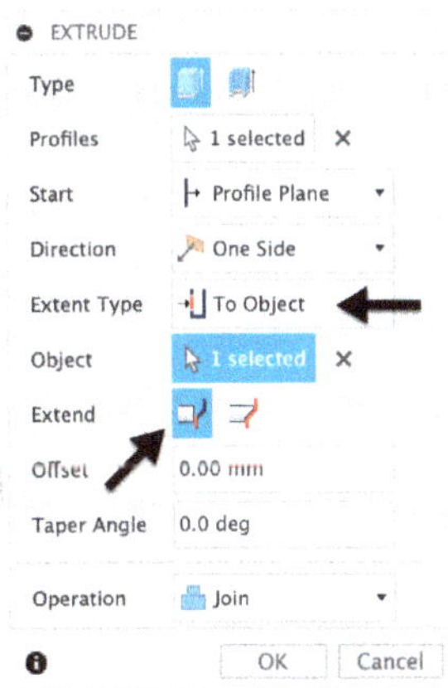

9. Click **OK** to complete the part model.
10. Save and close the file.

Example 2 (Inches)

In this example, you will create the part shown below.

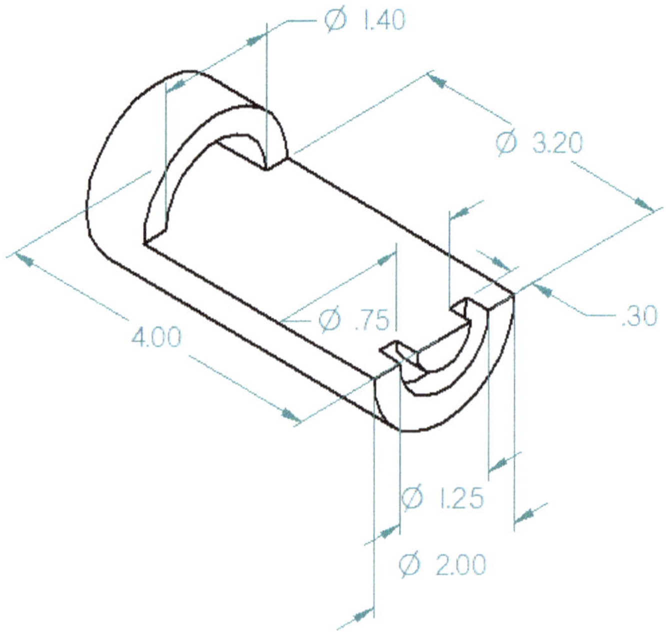

Creating the Revolved Solid Feature

1. Start **Autodesk Fusion 360** by double-clicking the **Autodesk Fusion 360** icon on your desktop.
2. On the **Browser window**, expand **Document Setting** and place the cursor on **Units**; the **Change Active Units** icon appears.
3. Click on the **Change Active Units** icon; the **Change Active Units** dialog appears.
4. On this dialog, select **inch (in), ouncemass** from the **Unit Type** drop-down and click **OK**.
5. To start the sketch, click **Create > Create Sketch** on the toolbar. Click on the **XY** plane.
6. On the **Sketch** contextual tab of the toolbar, expand the **Create** panel and click **Rectangle > Center Rectangle** and specify the two points of the rectangle, as shown. Press **Esc** to deactivate the **Center Rectangle** command.

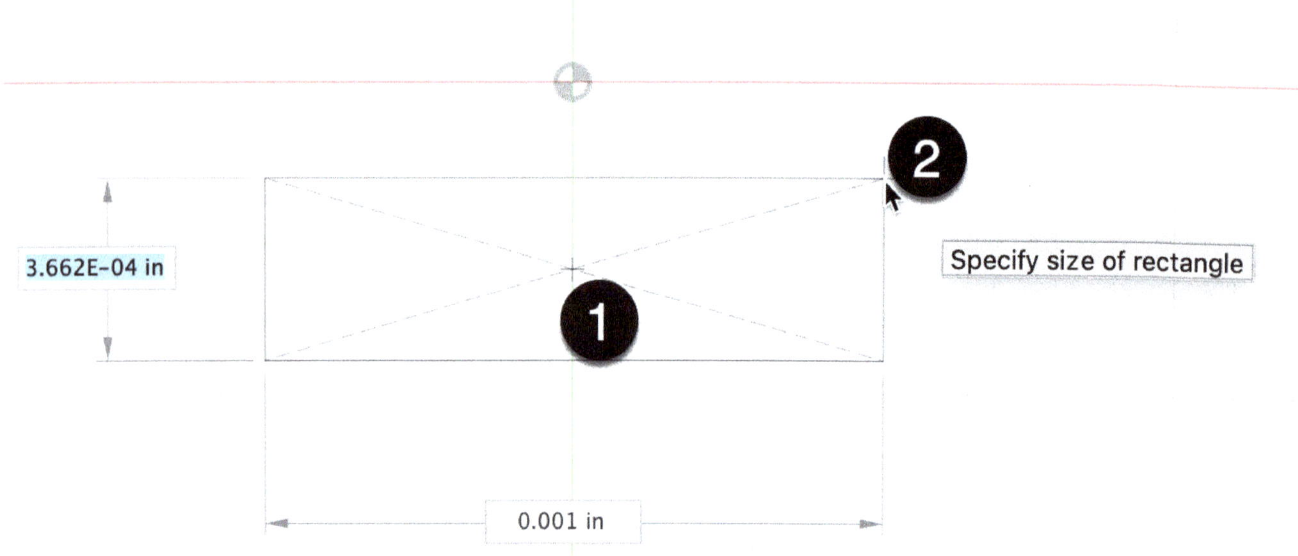

7. Click **Create** panel > **Sketch Dimension** on the **Sketch** contextual tab of the toolbar and apply dimensions, as shown.

8. On the **Sketch** contextual tab of the toolbar, click **Constraints** panel > **Midpoint**, and then select the top horizontal line and the sketch origin.

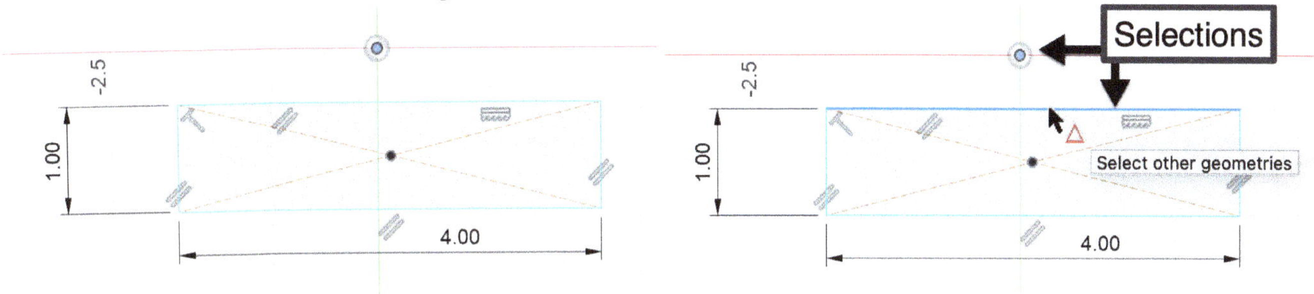

11. Click **Finish Sketch** on the toolbar. Next, click the **Home** icon next to the ViewCube.

9. Activate the **Revolve** command (click the **Create** panel > **Revolve** on the **Solid** tab of the toolbar); the sketch is selected automatically.
10. On the **Revolve** dialog, click the **Axis** selection button and select the axis line, as shown.
11. Select the **Partial** option from the **Type** drop-down and enter **-180** in the **Angle** box.
12. Click **Direction > One Side** and click **OK** to create the *Revolve* feature.

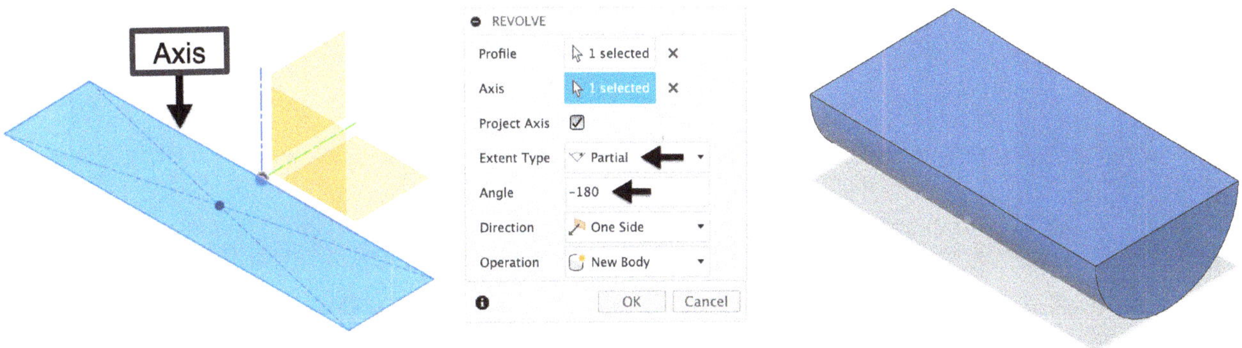

Creating the Revolved Cut

1. On the toolbar, click **Create** panel > **Create Sketch**. Click on the top face of the part model, as shown.

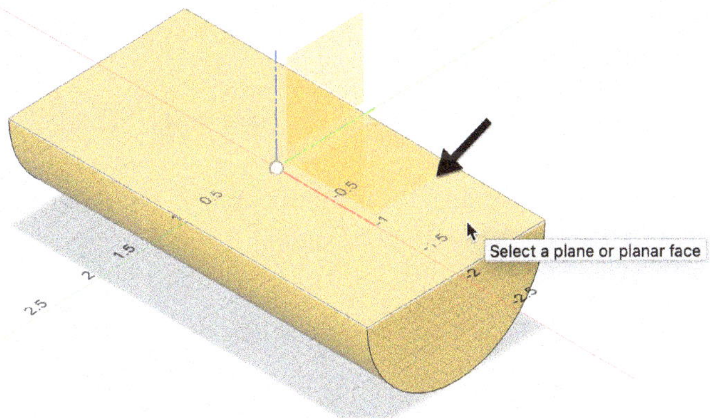

2. On the toolbar, click **Create** panel > **2-Point Rectangle**. Click to specify the first corner of the rectangle.
3. Move the pointer upward. Type .25 and press the TAB key. Next, type .3 and press ENTER.
4. On the toolbar, click **Create** panel > **Sketch Dimension**.
5. Select the right vertical line of the rectangle and the lower right corner point of the model face, as shown.
6. Move the pointer toward right and click. Type 0.375 and press ENTER.

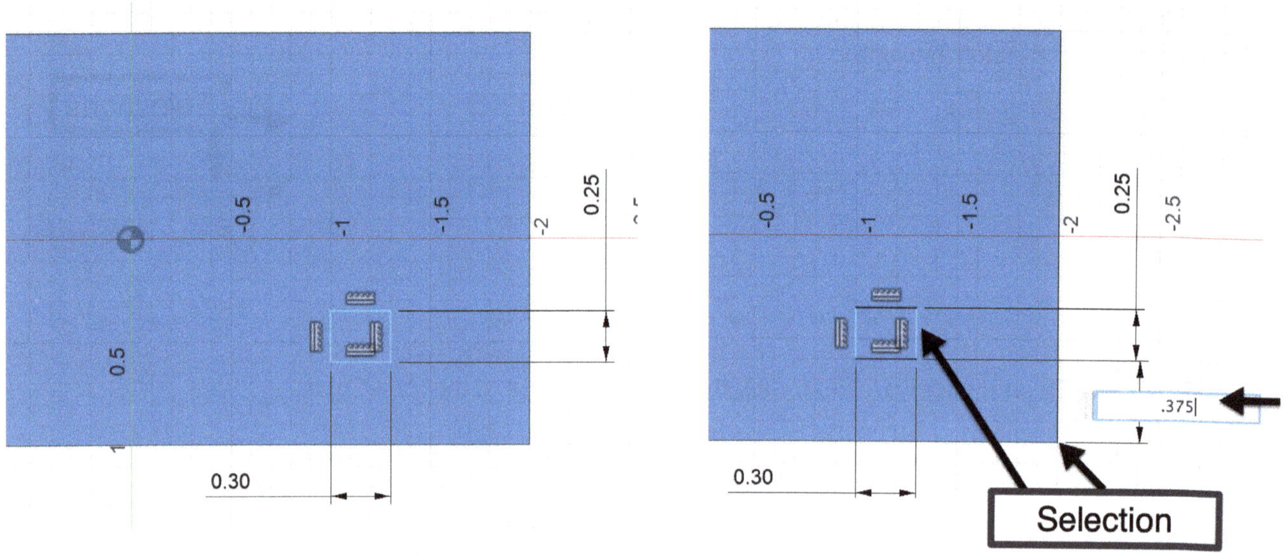

7. Click **Constraints > Collinear** on the **Sketch** contextual tab of the toolbar and select the left vertical line of the rectangle. Next, select the left vertical edge of the model. Click **Finish Sketch**.

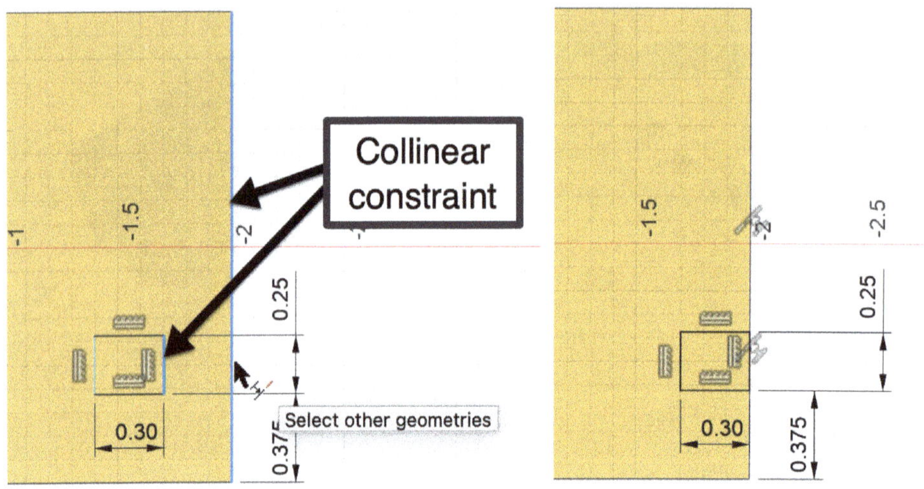

8. Activate the **Revolve** command and click in the region of the sketch, as shown.
9. On the **Revolve** dialog, click the **Axis** selection button and select the cylindrical face of the model; the axis of the cylindrical face is selected as the axis of the new revolved feature.
10. On the **Revolve** dialog, select the **Partial** option from the **Type** drop-down and enter -180 in the **Angle** box.
11. Select **Direction > One Side** and select **Operation > Cut** from the **Revolve** dialog.

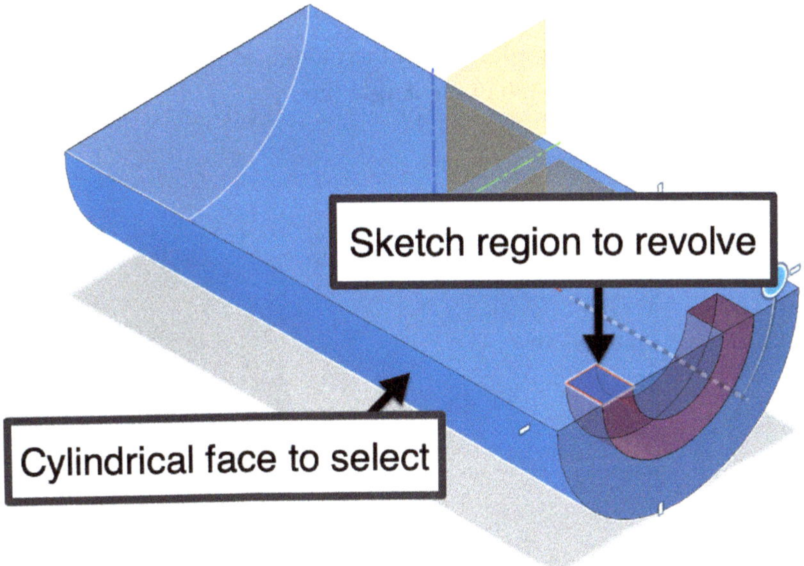

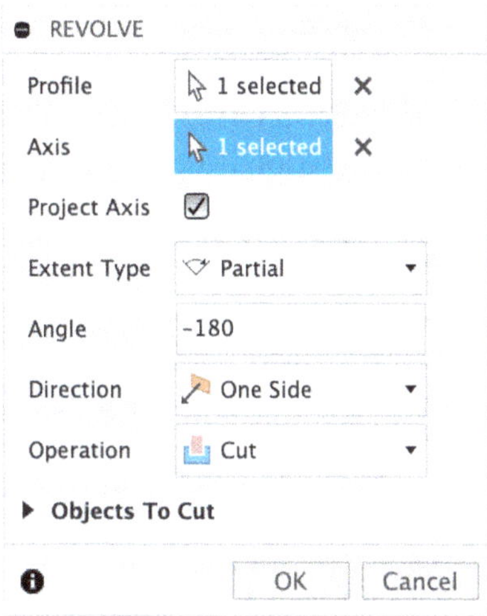

12. Click **OK** to create the *Revolved Cut* feature.

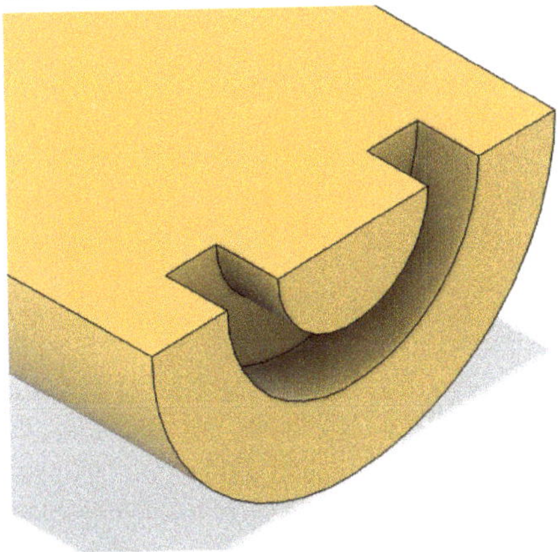

Adding a Revolved Feature to the model

1. Activate the **Create Sketch** command and click on the top face of the part model.
2. On the toolbar, click **Create** panel **> 2-Point Rectangle**. Click to specify the first corner of the rectangle.
3. Move the pointer upward. Type .3 and press the TAB key. Next, type .8 and press ENTER.
4. On the Sketch tab of the toolbar, click Constrtaints > Coincident.
5. Draw the sketch and apply dimensions and constraints, as shown. Click **Finish Sketch**.

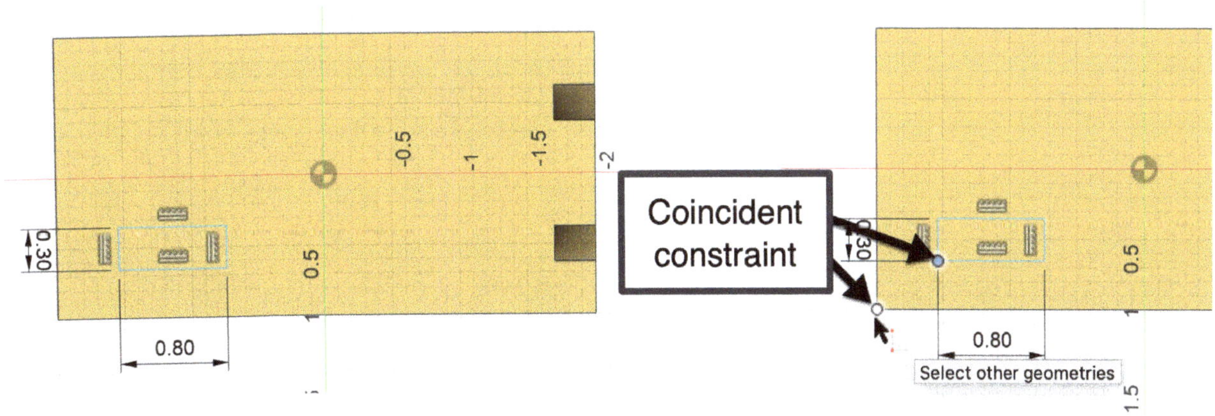

6. Click the **Home** icon next to the ViewCube.
7. Activate the **Revolve** command and select the sketch from the part model.
8. On the **Revolve** dialog, click the **Axis** selection button and circular face of the model, as shown.
9. Select the **Angle** option from the **Type** drop-down and enter 180 in the **Angle** box.
10. Click **Direction** drop-down **>** **One Side**.
11. Click **Operation** drop-down > **Join**.

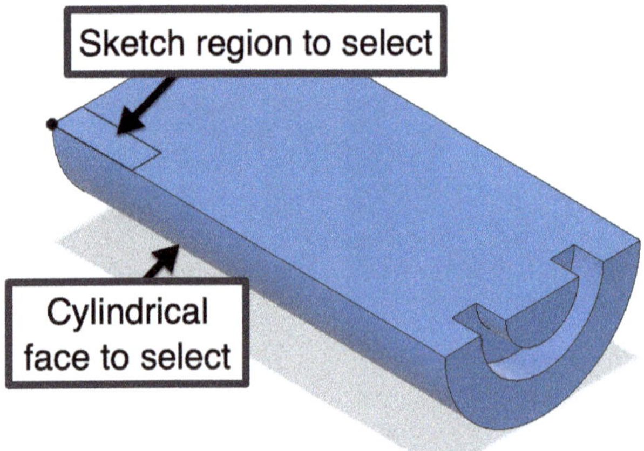

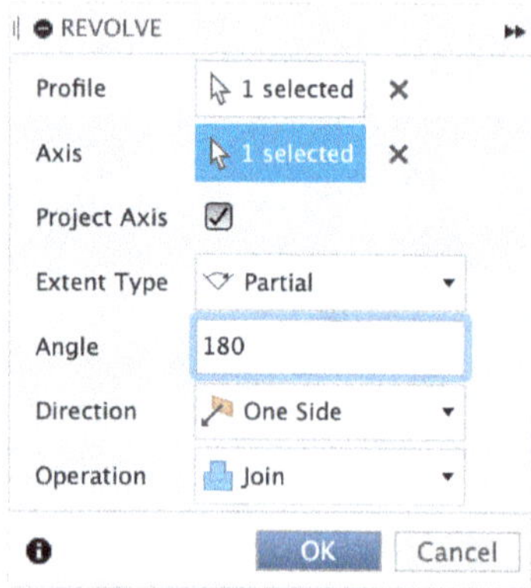

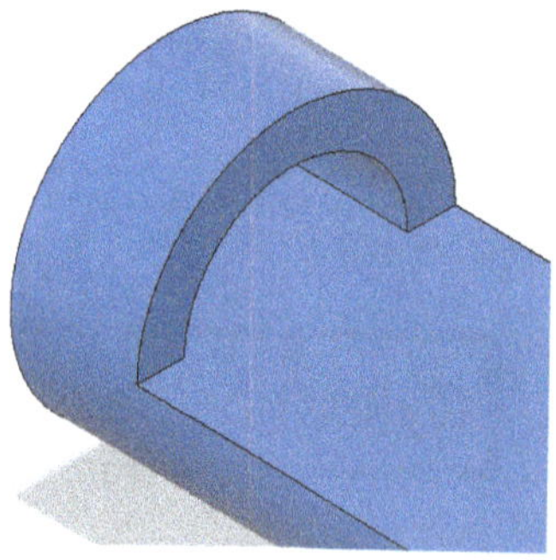

12. Click **OK** to add the *Revolved* feature to the part model.
13. Save and close the file.

Questions

1. How to create parallel planes in Autodesk Fusion 360?
2. What are the **Direction** options available on the **Extrude** dialog?
3. List the **Extent types** available on the **Extrude** dialog.
4. List the options available in the **Type** drop-down of the **Revolve** dialog.
5. List the operations available on the **Extrude** dialog.
6. How to create angled planes in Autodesk Fusion 360?
7. List the commands to create axes.
8. List the commands to points.
9. How to make the projected geometry independent?
10. What are the visual styles available in Autodesk Fusion 360?

Exercises

Exercise 1 (Inches)

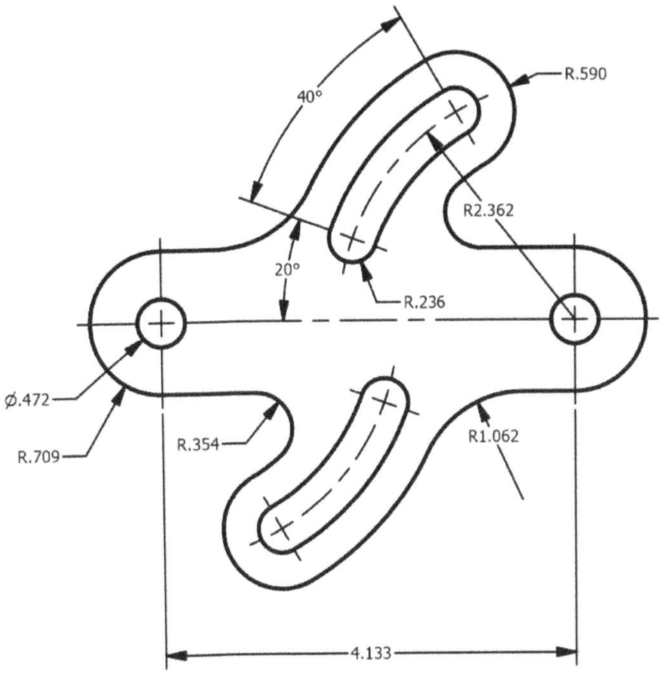

Exercise 2 (Millimetres)

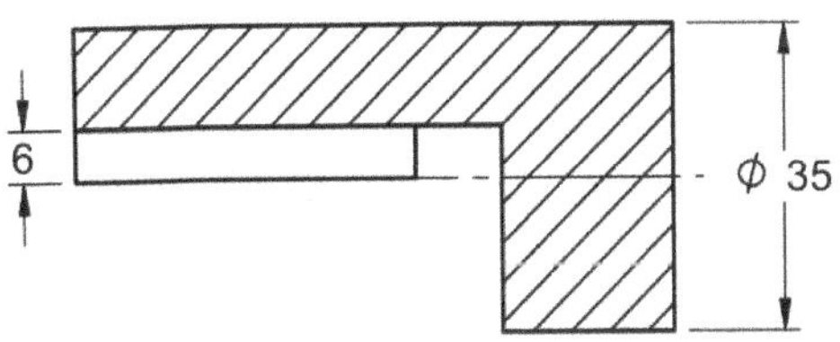

SECTION A-A

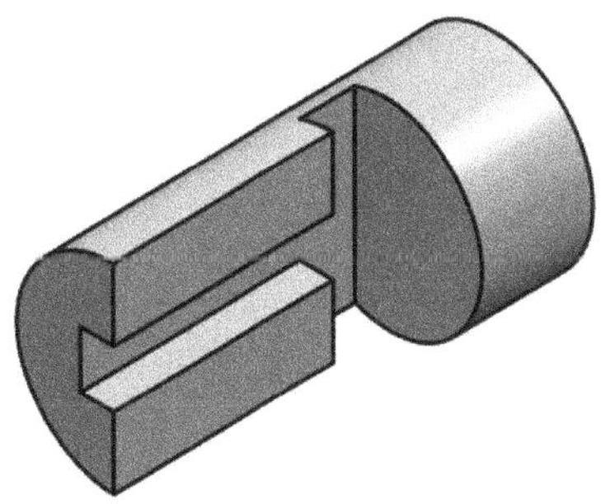

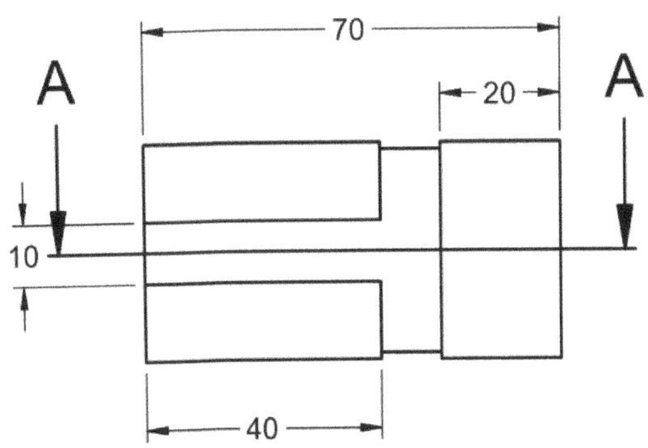

Exercise 3 (Millimetres)

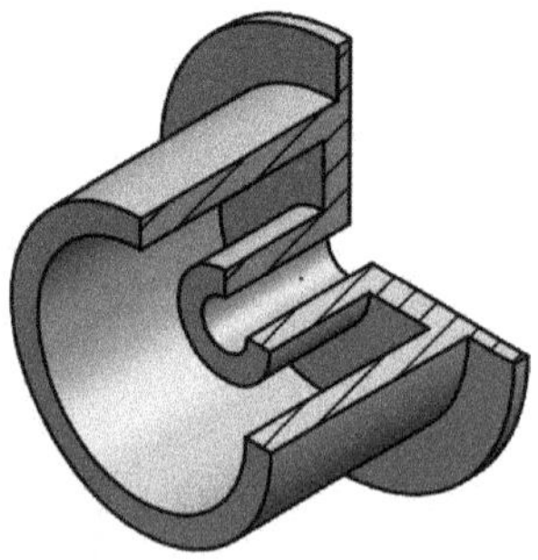

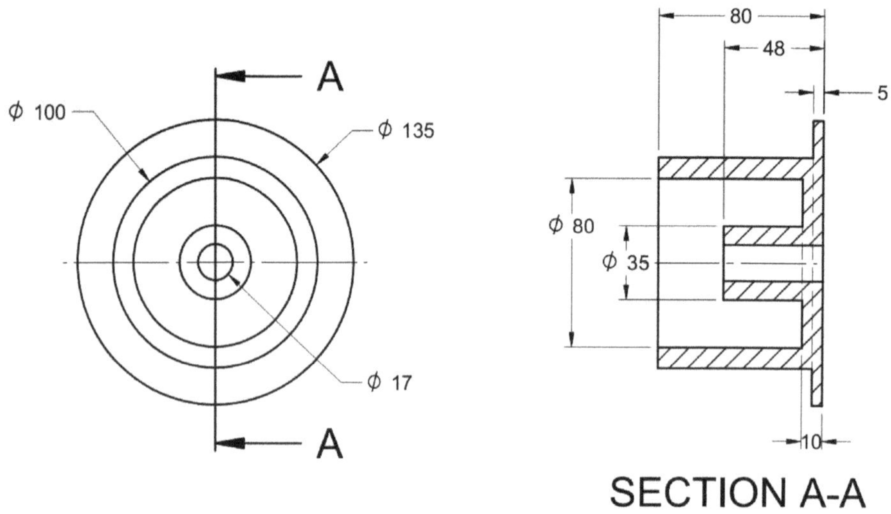

Exercise 4 (Inches)

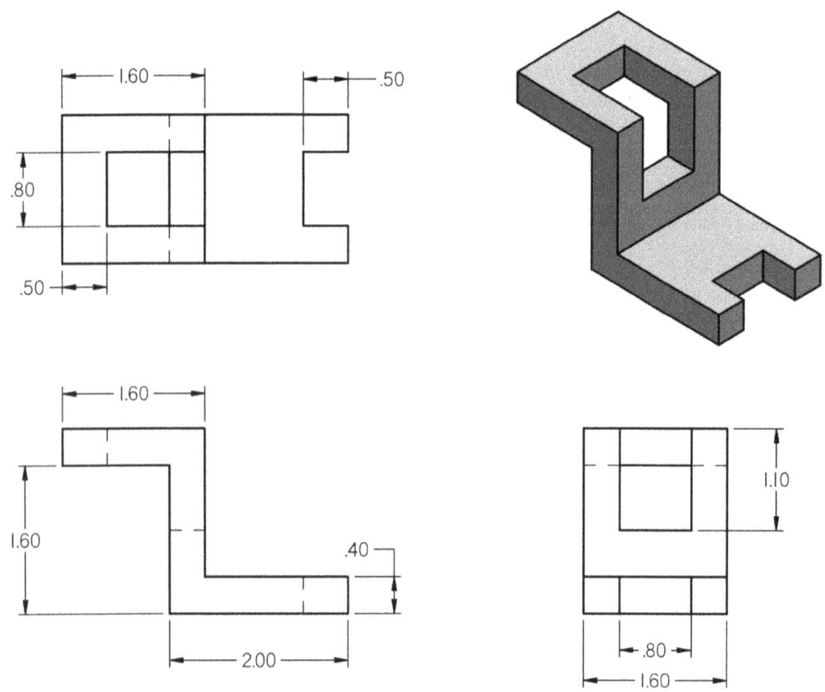

Chapter 4: Placed Features

So far, all of the features that were covered in the previous chapter were based on two-dimensional sketches. However, there are certain features in Autodesk Fusion 360 that do not require a sketch at all. Features that do not require a sketch are called placed features. You can simply place them on your models. However, to do so, you must have some existing geometry. Unlike a sketch-based feature, you cannot use a placed feature for the first feature of a model. For example, to create a *Fillet* feature, you must have an already existing edge. In this chapter, you will learn how to add placed features to your design.

The topics covered in this chapter are:

- *Holes*
- *Threads*
- *Fillets*
- *Chamfers*
- *Drafts*
- *Shells*

Hole

As you know, it is possible to use the *Extrude* command to create cuts and remove material. But, if you want to drill holes that are of standard sizes, the **Hole** command is a better way to do this. The reason for this is it has many hole types already predefined for you. All you have to do is choose the correct hole type and size. The other benefit is when you are going to create a 2D drawing, Fusion can place the correct hole annotation automatically.

Activate this command (Click **Create** panel > **Hole**  on the **Solid** tab of the toolbar), and you will notice that the **Hole** dialog appears on the screen. There are options on this dialog that make it easy to create different types of holes.

Simple Hole

To create a simple hole feature, select **Hole Type > Simple** under the **Shape Settings** section of the **Hole** dialog. Also, select **Hole Tap Type > Simple.** Next, you need to specify the exact location of the hole by using the **Placement** methods. There are two **Placement** methods: **At Point (Single Hole)**  and **From Sketch (Multiple Holes)** .

At Point (Single Hole)

Click **Placement > At Point (Single Hole)** on the **Hole** dialog. Next, click on a face to place the hole. Select any one of the boundary edges of the placement face; a value box appears between the selected edge and the centerpoint of the hole. Type-in the distance value in the value box. Next, select an edge perpendicular to the previously selected edge. Type-in the dimension in the value box.

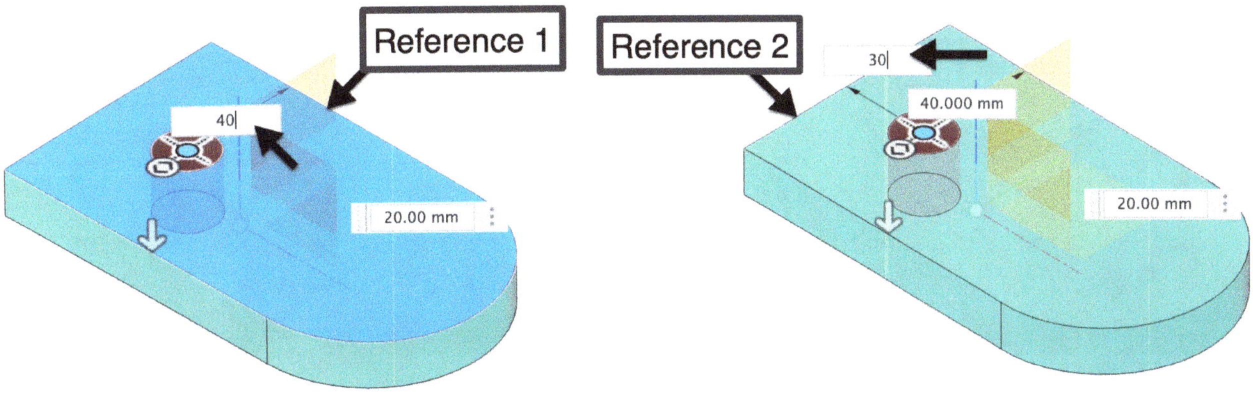

If you want to create a hole concentric to a circular edge, click on the circular edge. The hole will be concentric to the circular edge.

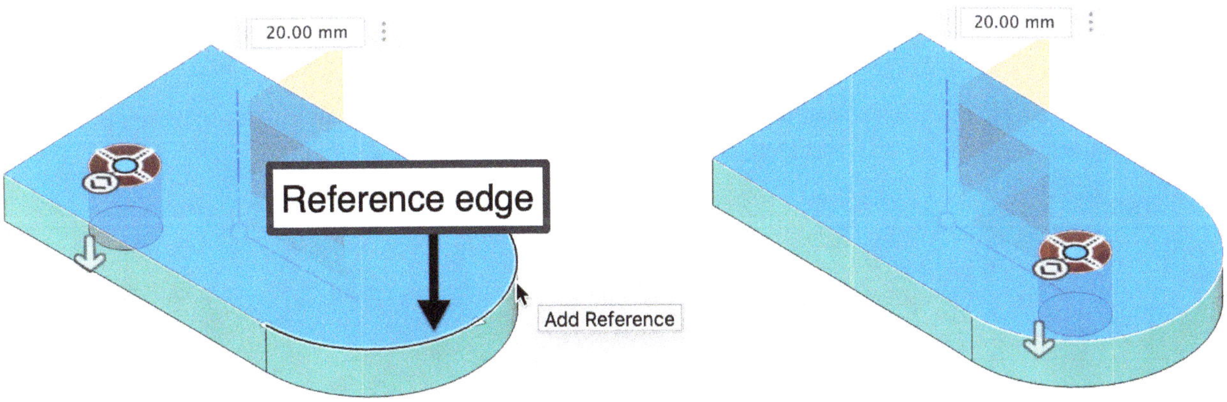

From Sketch (Multiple Holes)

In this method, first click **Create** panel > **Create Sketch** on the toolbar, and then click on the placement face. Next, place one or more sketch points, and then add dimensions and constraints to them. Click **Finish Sketch**, and then activate the **Hole** command and click **Placement > From Sketch (Multiple Holes)**  on the **Hole** dialog. Next, select the sketch points from the graphics window.

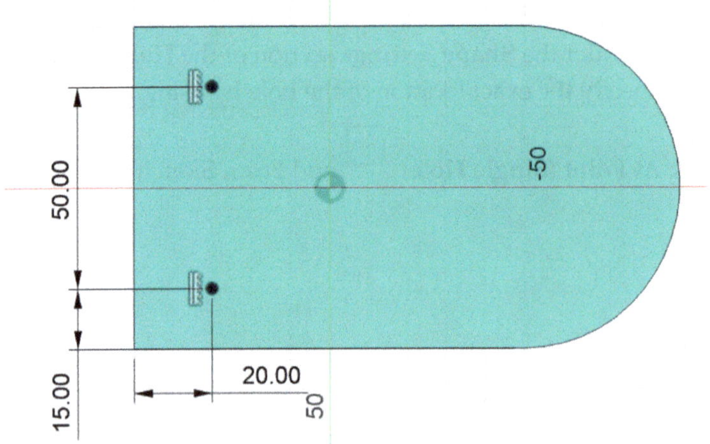

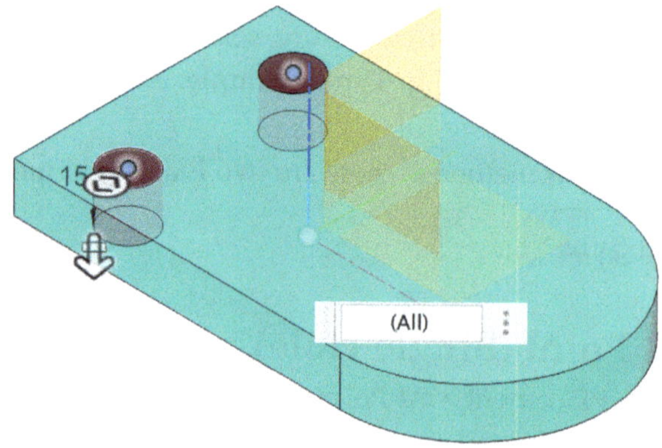

Next, select the **Extents** type. If you want a through-hole, select **Extents > All**. If you want the hole only up to some depth, then select **Extents > Distance**, and then type-in a value in the **Hole Depth** box attached to the hole image.

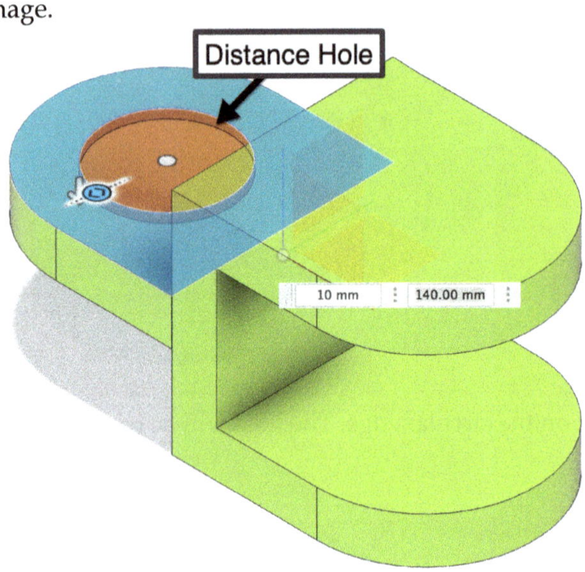

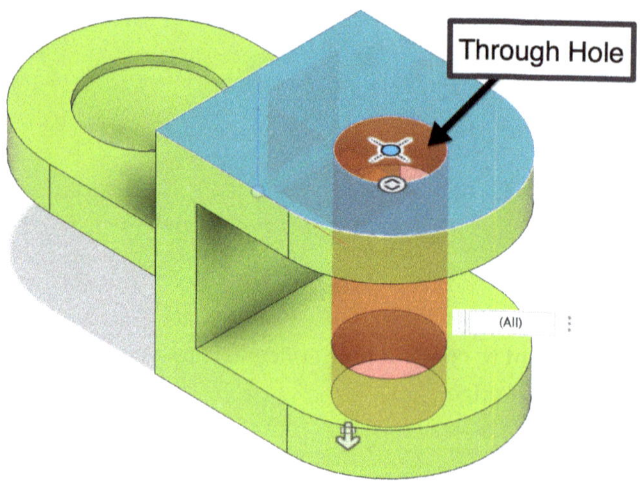

If you want the hole only up to a surface, then select **Extents > To** and select a face, surface, or vertex point from the graphics window; the hole will be created up to the selected entity.

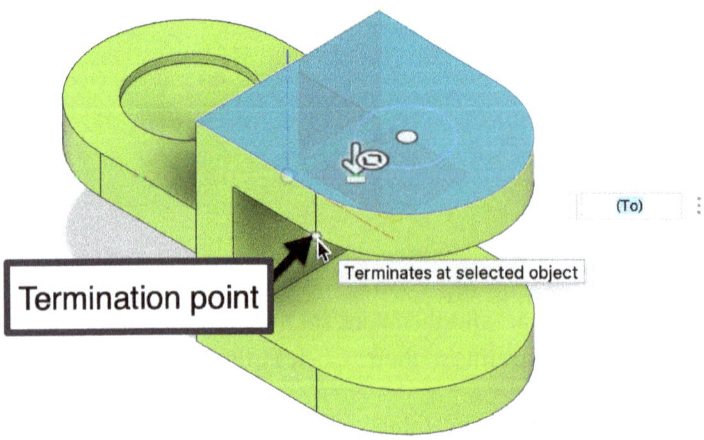

The **Drill Point** section has two options to define the depth of the hole: **Flat** and **Angle**. The **Flat** option creates a hole with a flat bottom. The **Angle** option creates a hole with an angled bottom. The **Drill Point Angle** box defines the angle of the cone tip at the bottom.

Next, specify the size setting of the hole and click **OK** to complete the hole feature.

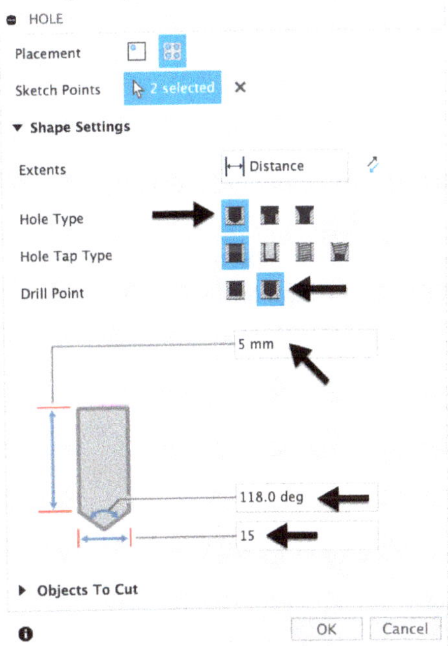

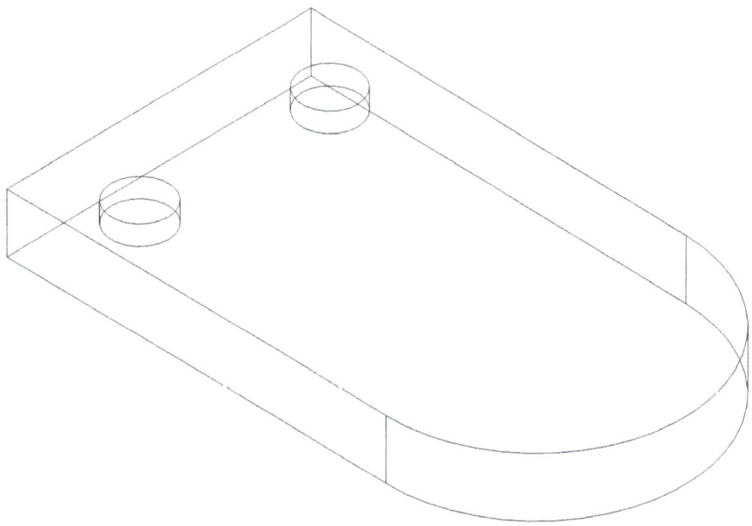

Counterbored Hole

A counterbore hole is a large diameter hole added at the opening of another hole. It is used to accommodate a fastener below the level of the workpiece surface. To create a counterbore hole, select **Hole Type > Counterbore** . Next, specify the Hole Depth, Counterbore Diameter, and Counterbore Depth. Next, specify the desired **Drill Point** option (**Flat** or **Angle**). If you click the **Angle** option, then specify the **Hole Diameter** and **Tip Angle** value.

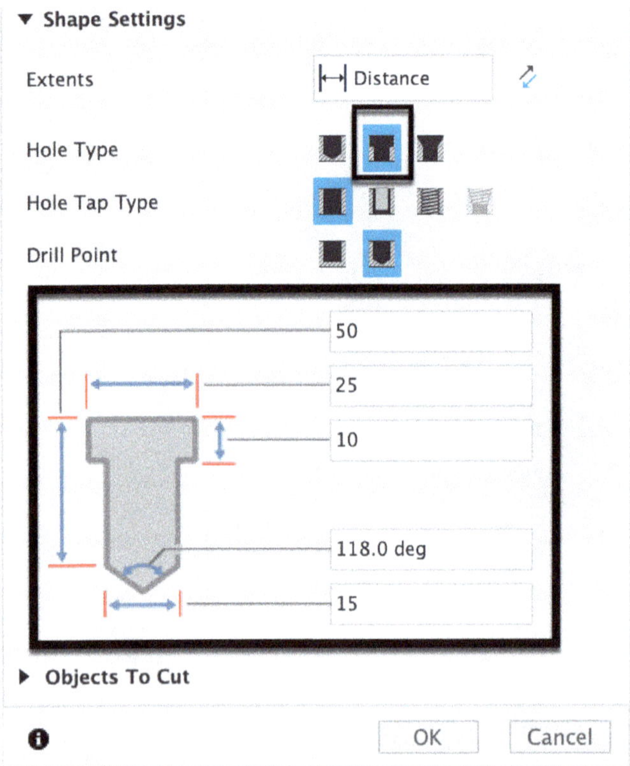

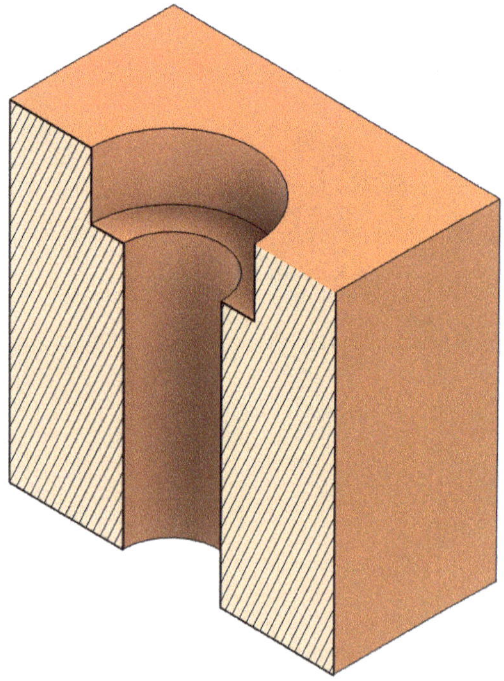

Countersink Hole

A countersunk hole has an enlarged V-shaped opening to accommodate the fastener below the level of the workpiece surface. To create a countersink hole, select **Hole Type > Countersink** . Type-in values in the **Hole Diameter**, **Countersink Diameter,** and **Countersink Angle** boxes. Set the hole diameter and drill point.

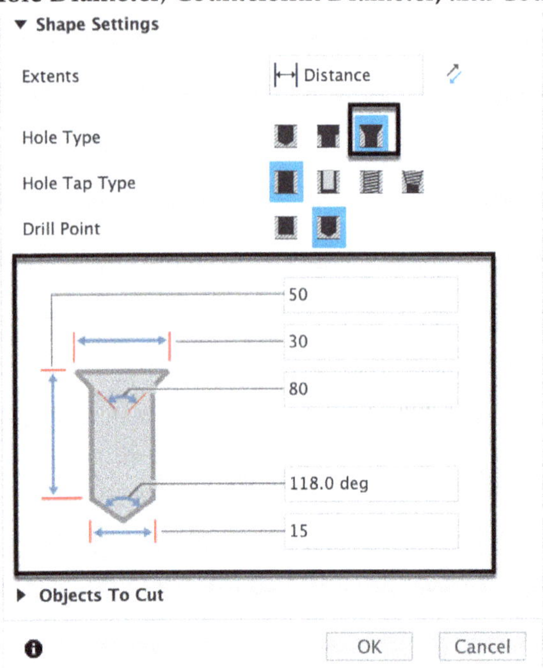

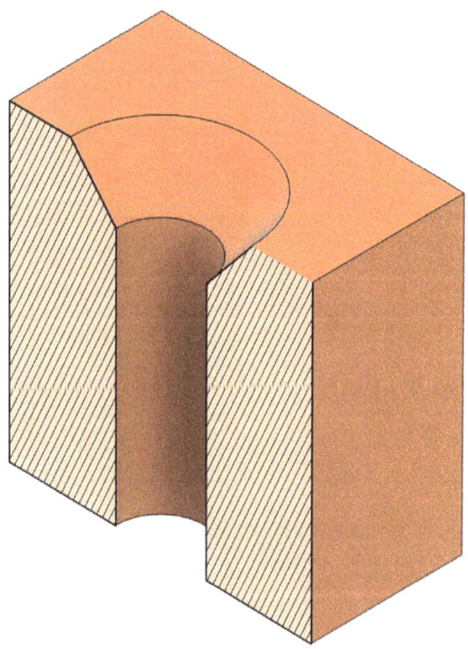

Tapped Hole

To create a tapped hole feature, select **Hole Type > Simple** and **Hole Tap Type > Tapped Hole**. Select **Thread Offset > Full** to create a thread to the full depth of the hole. If you select the **Thread Offset > Offset** option, then you need to specify the thread depth in the **Thread Depth** box. Select the thread standard from **Thread Type** drop-down. Also, specify the **Size, Designation**, **Class**, and **Direction**. Specify the remaining hole options that are similar to the simple hole feature. Click **OK** to create the Tapped Hole.

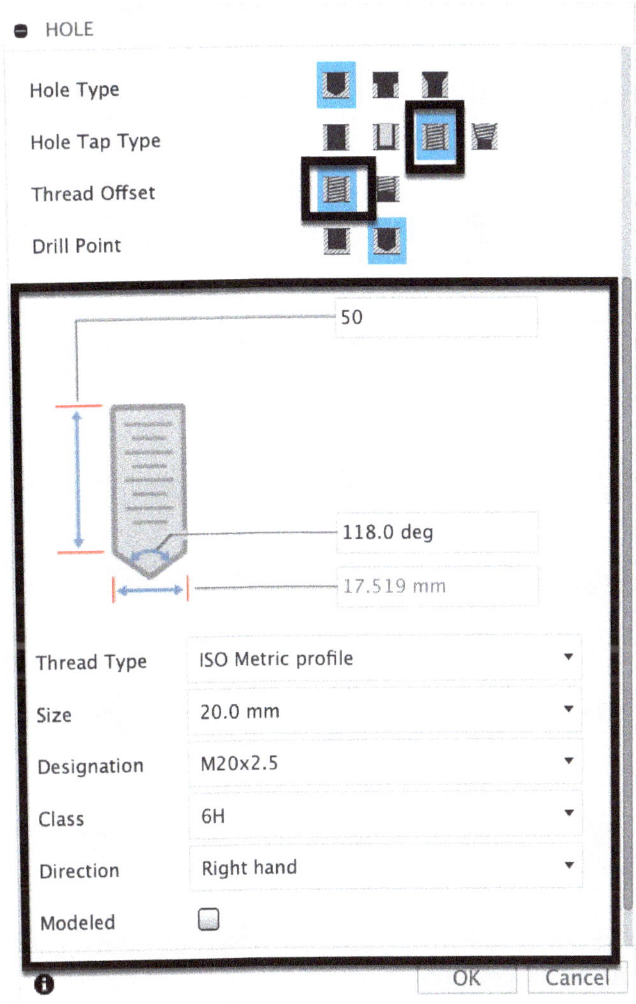

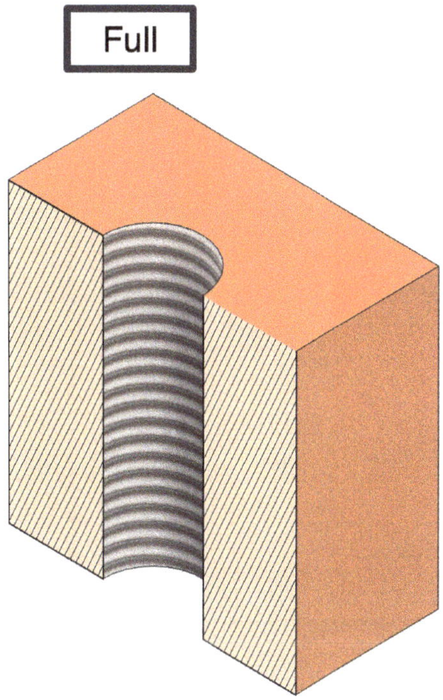

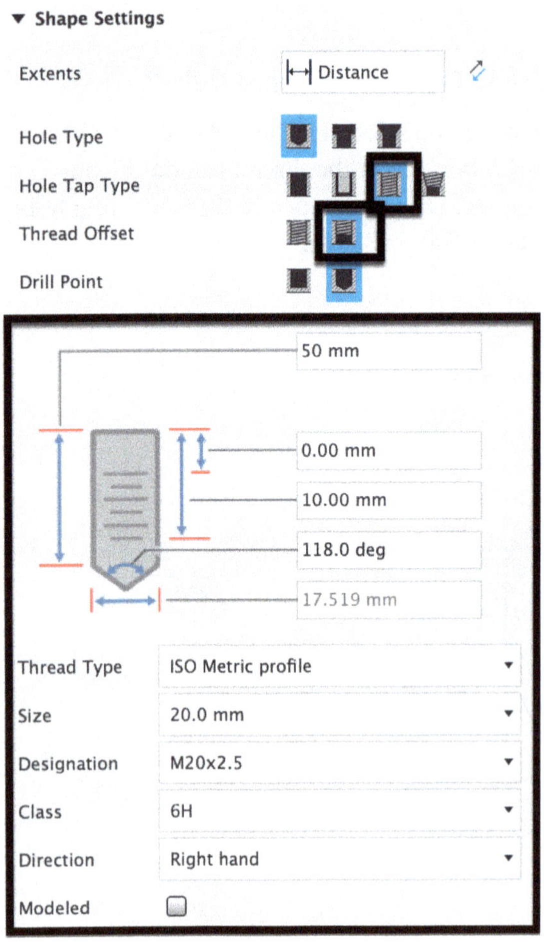

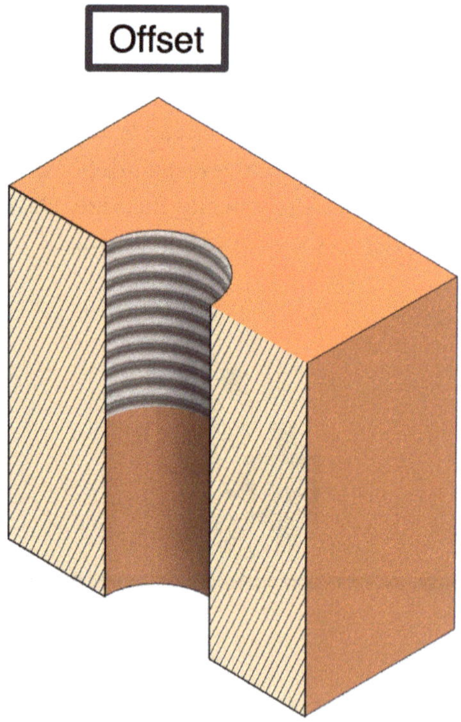

Thread

This command adds a thread feature to a round face. If you add a thread feature to a 3D geometry, Autodesk Fusion 360 can automatically place the correct thread annotation in the 2D drawing. Activate this command (click **Create** panel > **Thread** 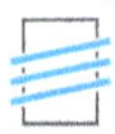 on the **Solid** tab of the toolbar) and select the cylindrical face of the part geometry. Next, specify the **Thread Type**. The **Size** is automatically selected as per the size of the cylindrical face of the part geometry. However, you can select the thread size from the **Size** drop-down. In doing so, the size of the circular face is adjusted automatically. Next, specify the **Designation** and **Class** values. Also, select the thread direction (**Right hand** or **Left hand**).

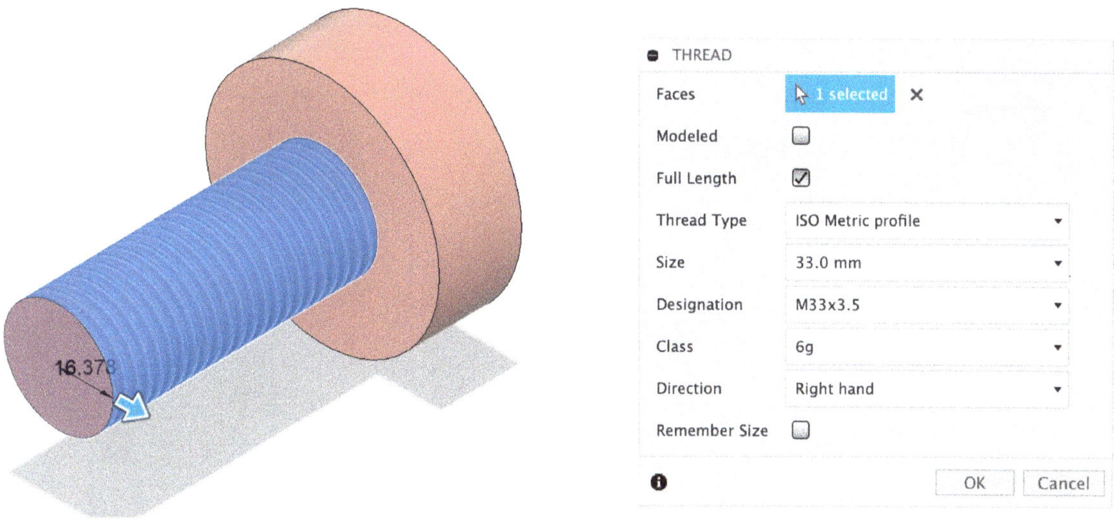

Notice that the **Full Length** option is selected by default. It creates the thread up to the entire length of the cylindrical face. Uncheck this option if you want to specify the length of the thread in the **Length** box. Next, enter a value in the **Offset** box, if you want to create a thread at a distance from the start face of the cylinder.

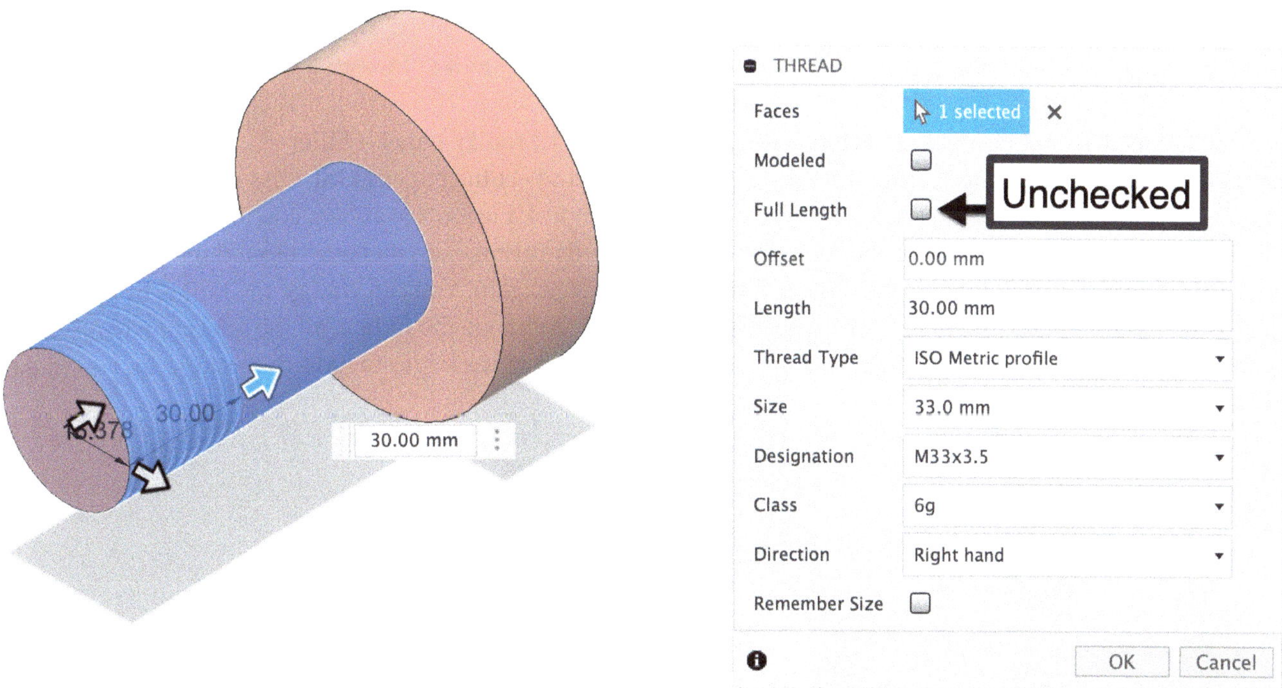

Select the **Modeled** option to view the 3D thread in the part geometry. Note that if you deselect this option, the image of the thread will be displayed on the part geometry. Click **OK** to complete the thread feature.

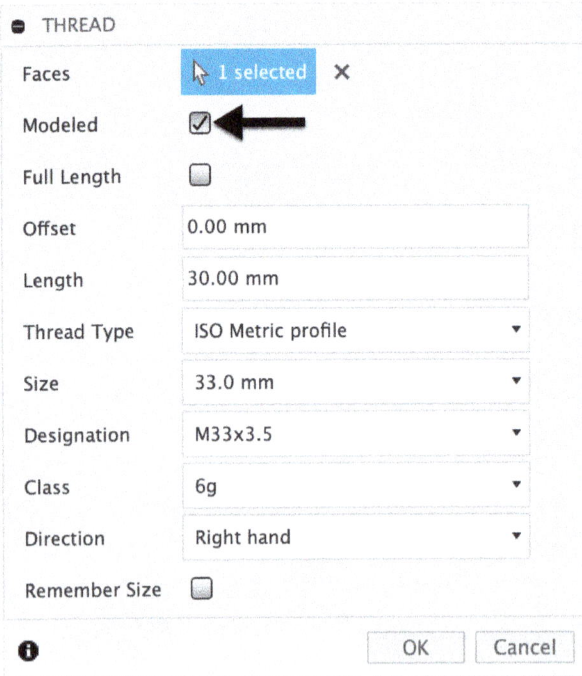

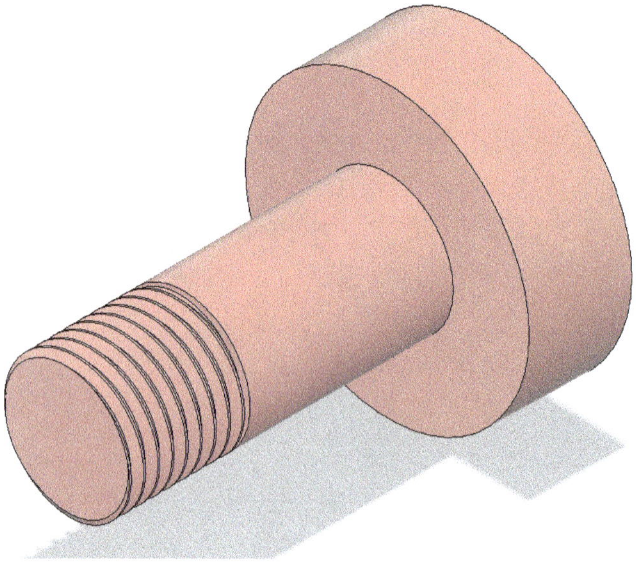

Fillet

This command breaks the sharp edges of a model and blends them. You do not need a sketch to create a fillet. All you need to have is model edges. To activate this command, click **Modify** panel > **Fillet**  on the **Solid** tab of the toolbar. Next, select **Type > Fillet** from the **Fillet** dialog and select the edges to fillet. As you start selecting edges, you will see that the edges are highlighted in blue. Autodesk Fusion 360 allows you to select the edges, which are located at the back of the model without rotating it. By mistake, if you have selected the wrong edge, you can deselect it by holding the Shift key and selecting the edge again. You can change the radius by typing a value in the **Radius** box displayed near the selected edge. As you change the radius, all the selected edges will be updated. This is because they are all part of one instance. If you want the edges to have different radii, you must create fillets in separate instances.

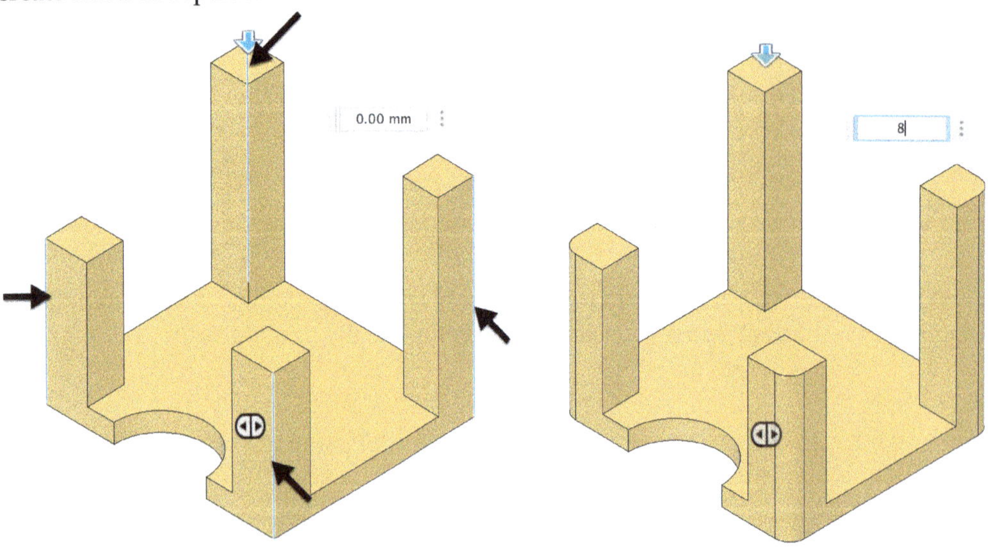

Select the **Tangent (G1)** from the **Continuity** drop-down to create fillets that are tangent to the adjacent faces. Select the required number of edges and click **OK** to complete the fillet feature. The *Fillet* feature will be listed in the **Timeline**.

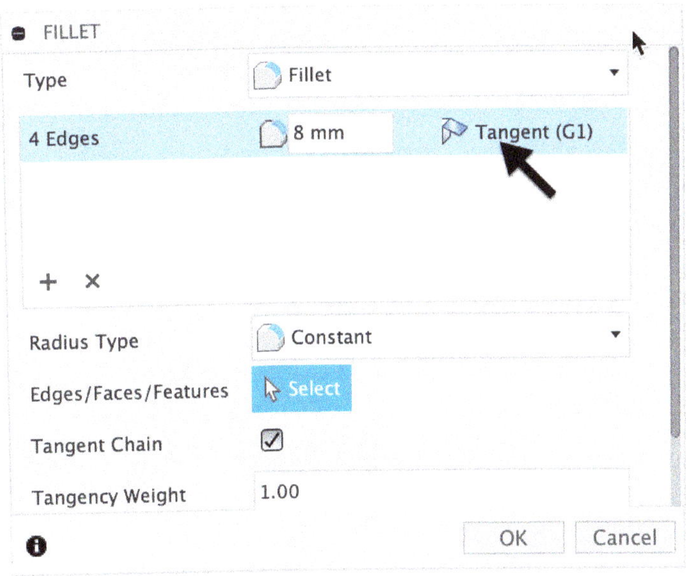

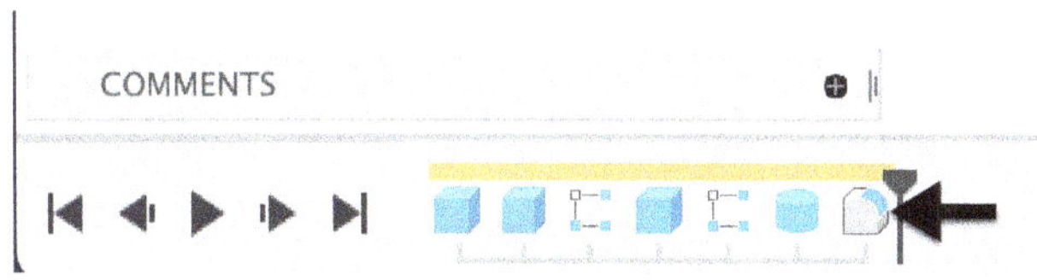

Selection Modes

The **Fillet** command allows you to select the edges to be filleted using three selection modes: **Edges**, **Faces**, and **Features**.

You can select individual edges just by clicking on them.

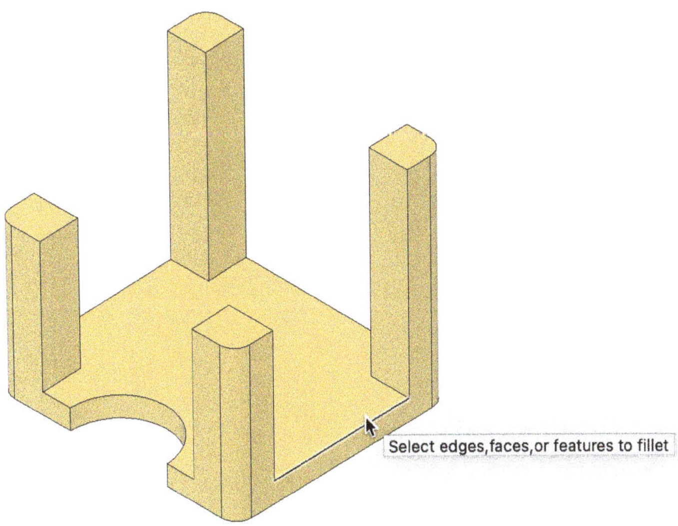

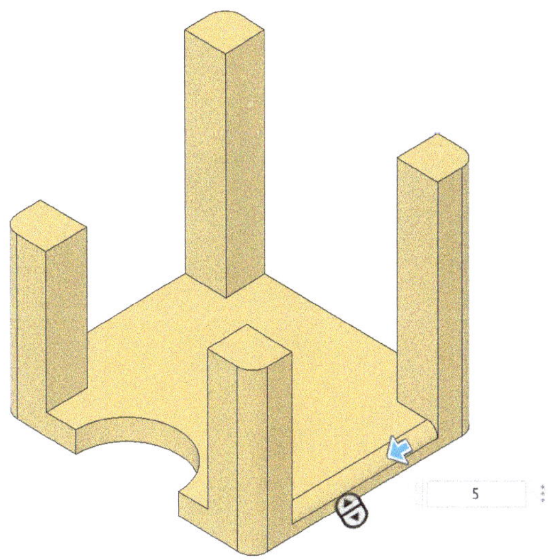

You can select all the edges of a face by merely clicking on it.

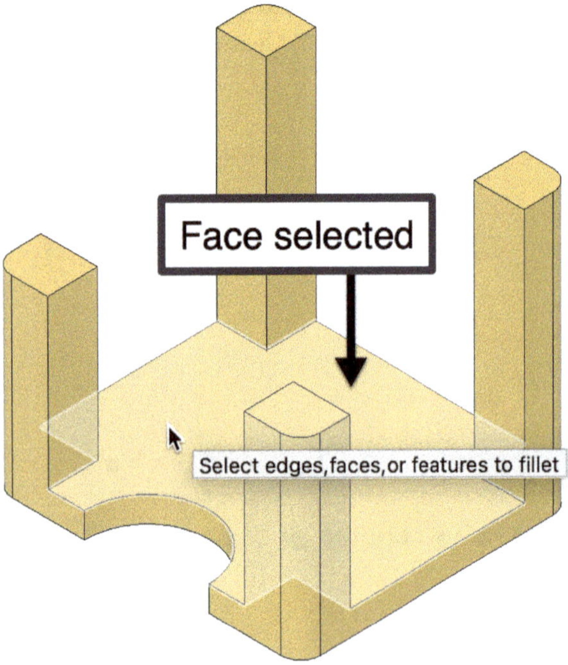

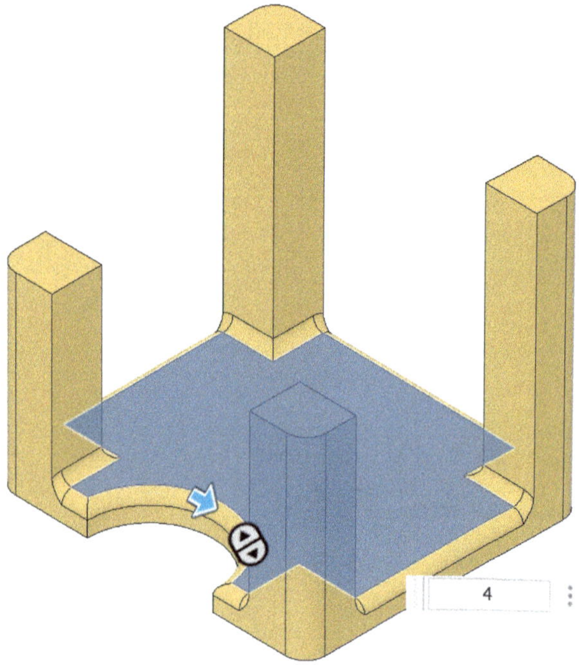

You can select the entire feature to be filleted from the timeline.

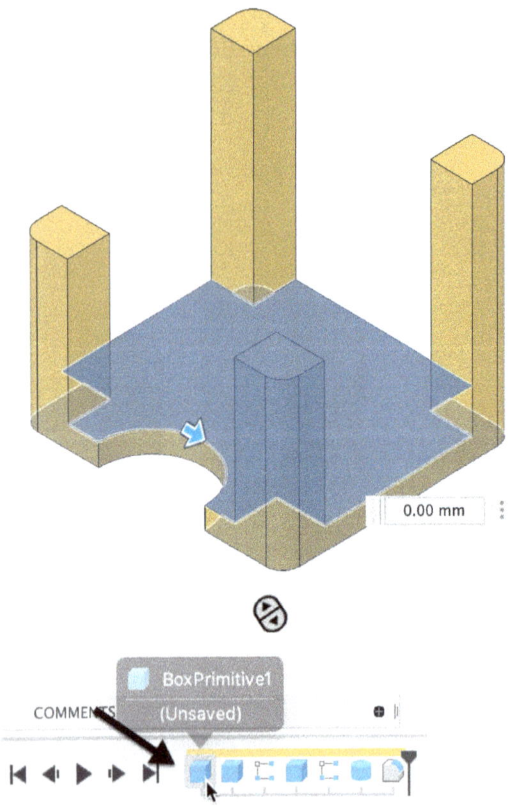

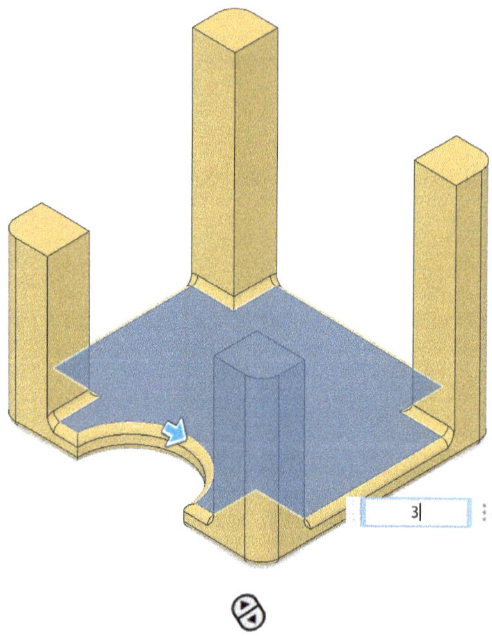

Tangent Chain

This option is used to select the edges that are connected tangently in a single click. If you uncheck this option, you can select individual edges from tangently connected edges.

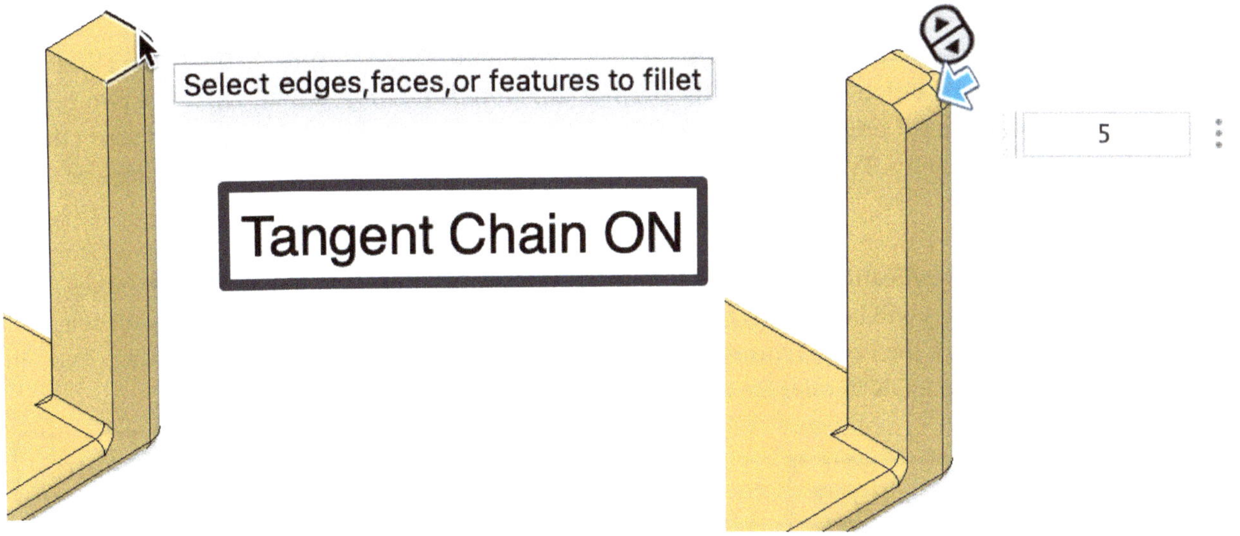

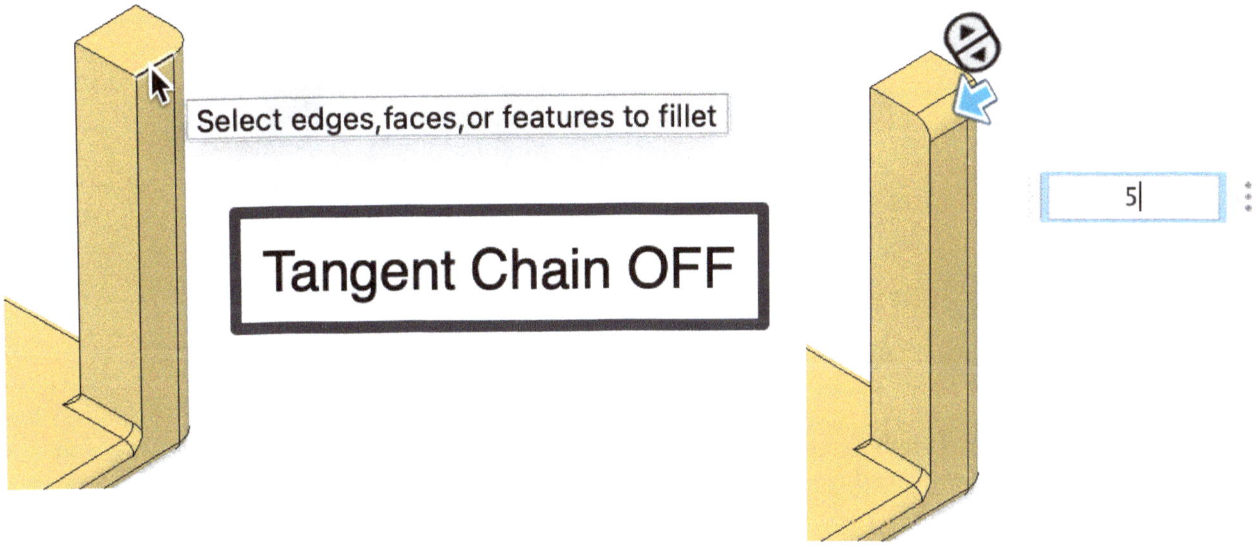

Curvature G2 Continuity

By default, the edge fillets are tangent to the adjacent faces. However, if you want to create a smooth fillet that is curvature continuous with the adjacent faces, then select the **Curvature G2** option from the **Continuity** drop-down on the **Fillet** dialog. Next, type-in a value in the **Radius** box. The following figure displays the Curvature comb of the Curvature (G2) and Tangent (G1) continuity. You can display the curvature combs by clicking **Tools > Inspect > Curvature Comb Analysis** on the toolbar, and selecting the edge of the fillet face.

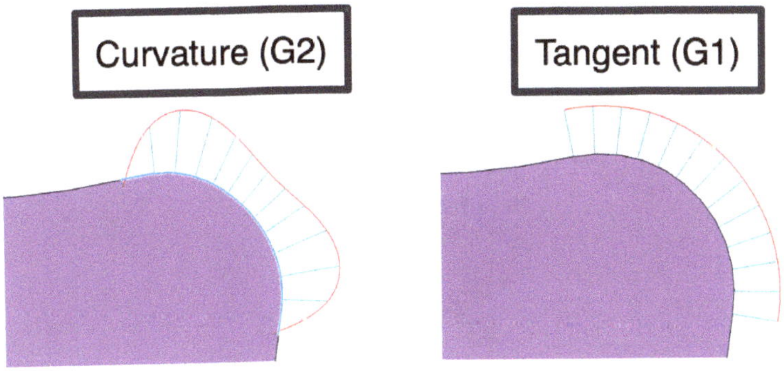

Rule Fillet

The rule fillet adds fillets to edges of the model geometry, depending on the specified rule. Activate the **Fillet** command and select **Type > Rule Fillet**. Next, select the desired rule from **Rule** drop-down. There are two rules available in the **Rule** drop-down: **All Edges** and **Between Face/Features**. Select **Rule > All Edges** and select the face or feature of the model geometry. Type-in a value in the **Radius** box; all the edges of the selected face or feature will be filleted.

If you select **Rule > Between Faces/Features**, you need to select two face/features from the model; the edges between the selected face/features will be filleted. To do this, click the **Faces/Features 1** select button and select the first face or feature. Next, click the **Faces/Features 2** select button and select the second face or feature. Type-in a value in the **Radius** box and click **OK** to fillet the edge between the selected faces/features.

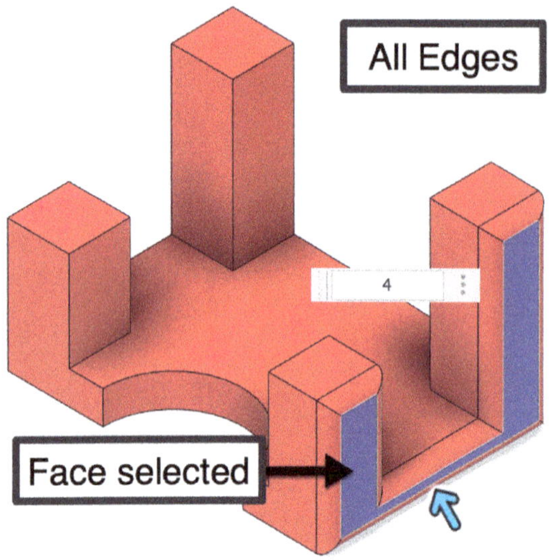

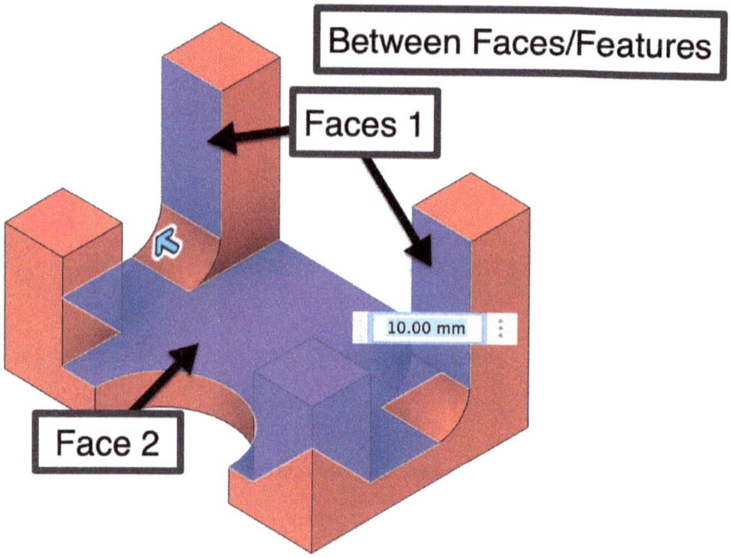

Next, select an option from the **Topology** drop-down. It has three options *Rounds and Fillets, Rounds Only,* and *Fillets Only*. These options are explained next.

Rounds and Fillets

If you select the **Rounds and Fillets** option, then it blends the inner and outer edges of the model. The following figure shows the rounds and fillets added to the inner and outer edges of the selected face.

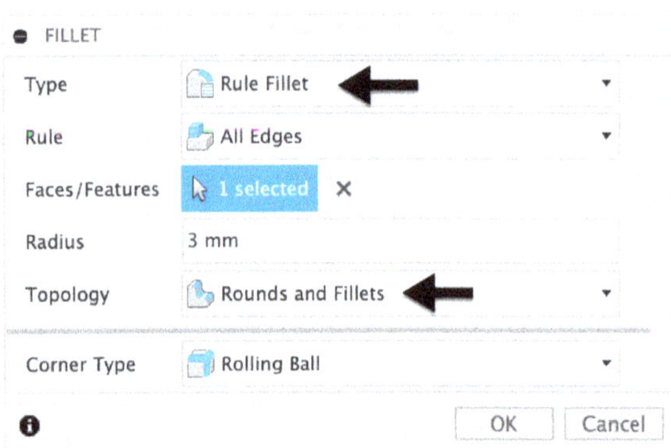

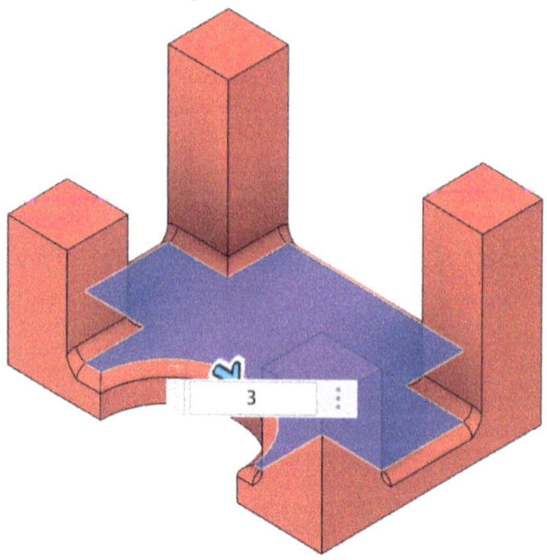

Rounds Only

If you select the **Rounds Only** option, then it blends only the exterior edges of the model. The following figure shows the rounds added only to the exterior edges of the model.

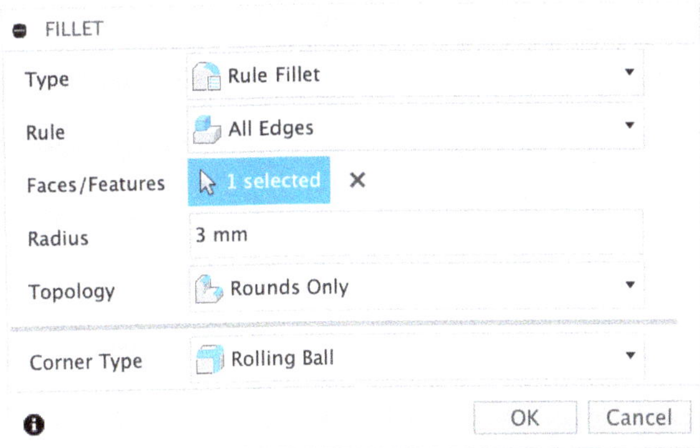

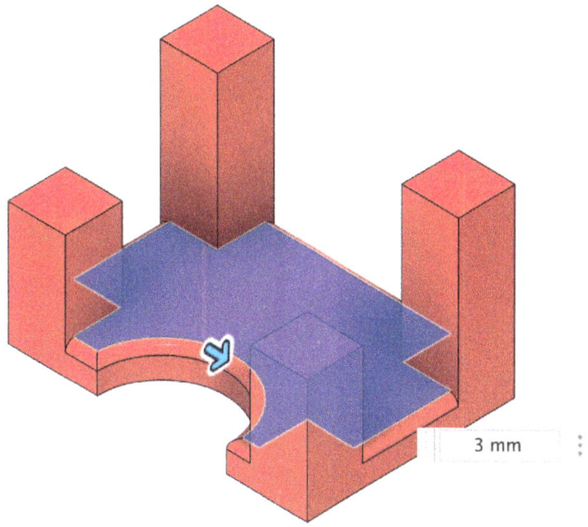

Fillets Only

If you select the **Fillets Only** option, then it creates fillets only on the interior edges of the model. The following figure shows the fillets added only to the interior edges of the model.

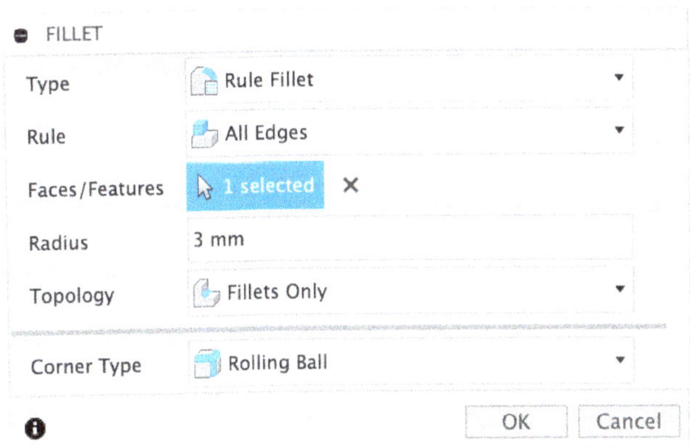

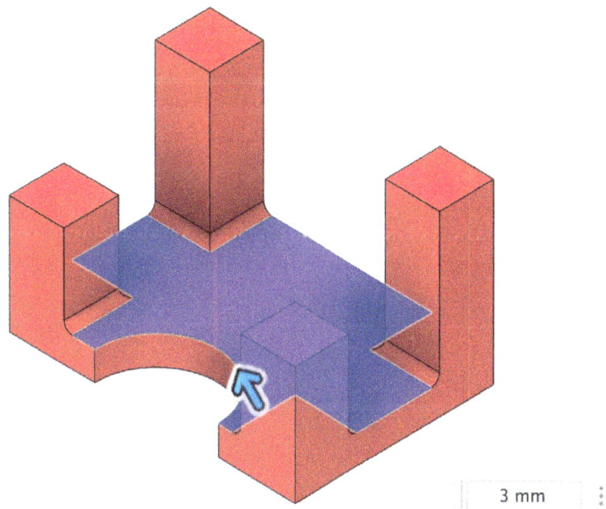

Full Round Fillet

This option creates a fillet between three faces. It replaces the center face with a fillet. Select **Type > Full Round Fillet**. Place the pointer on the face to be replaced; the side faces are highlighted. Move the pointer of the face to be replaced and notice that a different set of the side faces highlighted. Click when the desired set of side faces are highlighted; the selected face is replaced with a fillet.

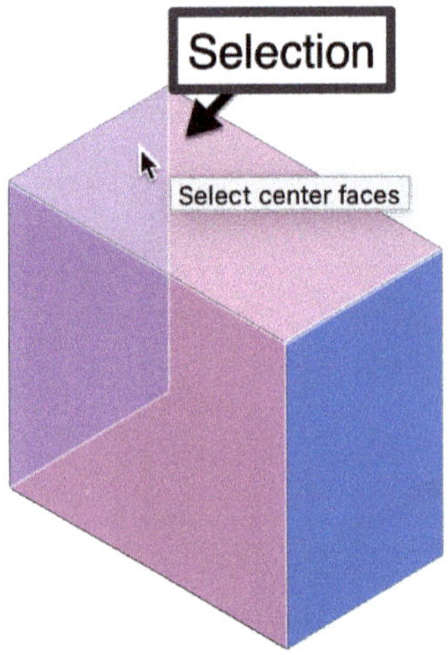

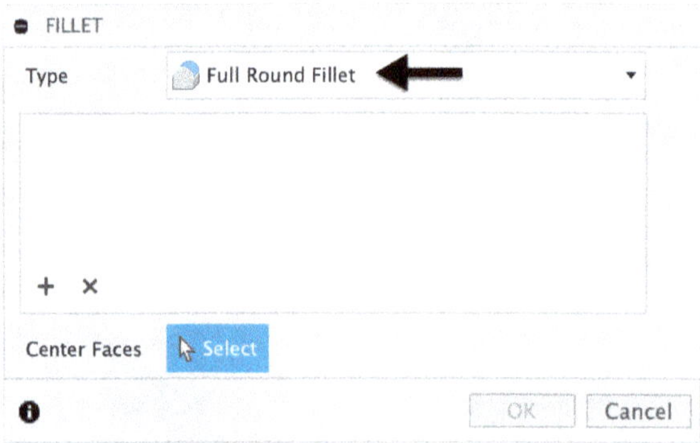

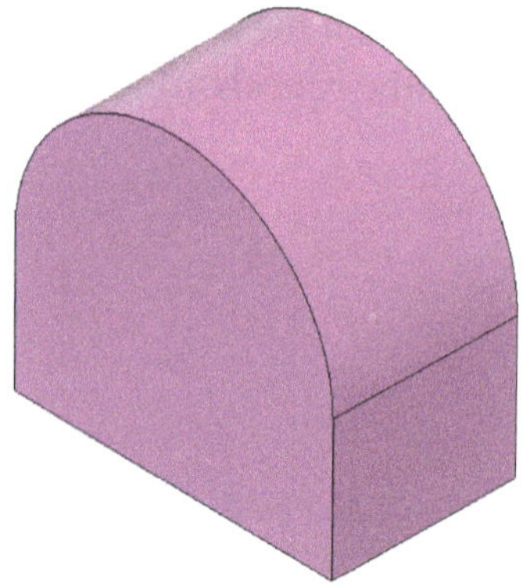

Variable Radius

Autodesk Fusion 360 allows you to create a fillet with a varying radius along the selected edge. Activate the **Fillet** command to create a variable fillet. On the **Fillet** dialog, select **Radius Type > Variable Radius**, and then select the edge to add a fillet. Specify the variable radius points on the selected edge. Drag the arrows to change the radius value at each location. You can also change the radius values of each point on the **Fillet** dialog box. Click **OK** to create the variable radius fillet.

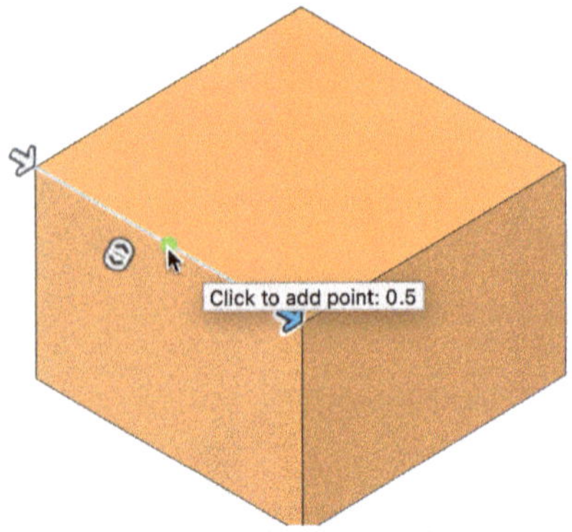

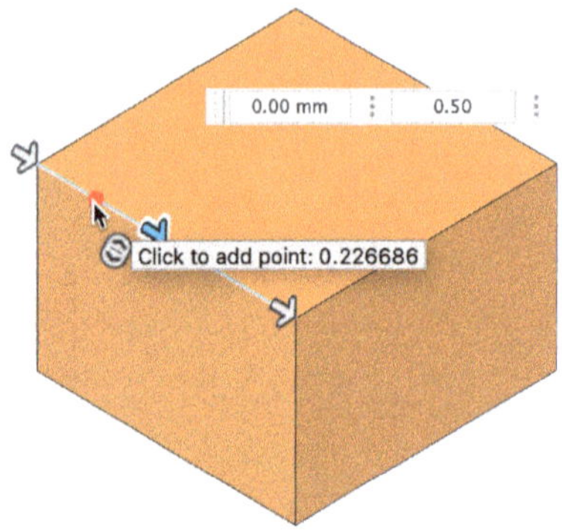

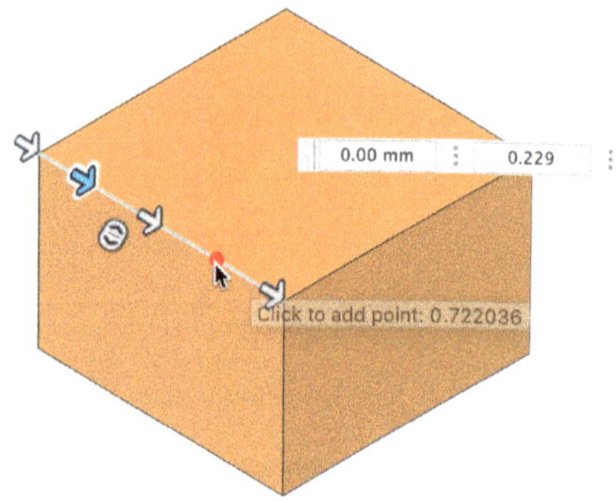

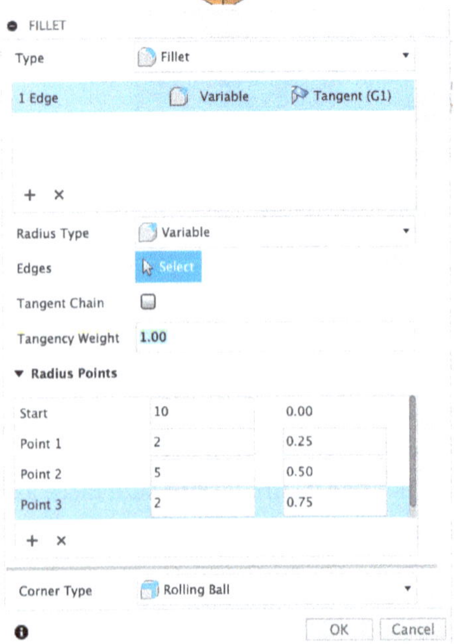

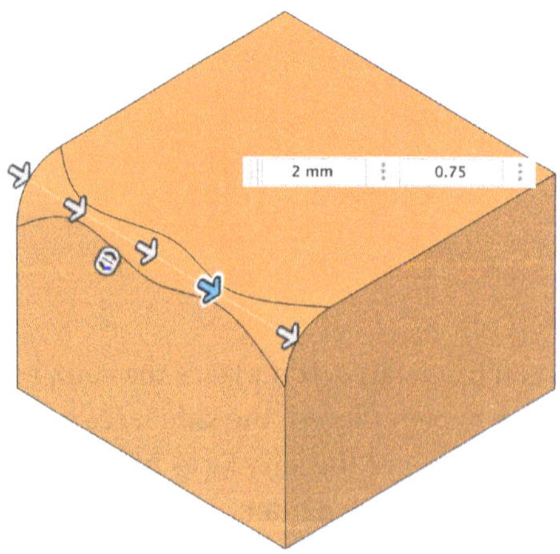

Chordal Fillet

This option helps you to create a fillet by specifying its chord length instead of a radius. The chord length is the distance between the endpoints of the fillet profile.

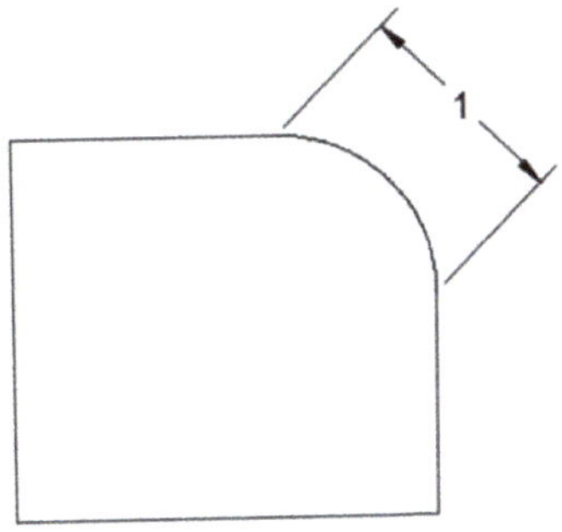

The **Chord Fillet** option helps you to create fillets at some locations where the **Constant** option fails to give desired results. For example, create a fillet at the edge between the horizontal face and the inclined face using the **Constant** option. Notice that a thin fillet is created at the given location.

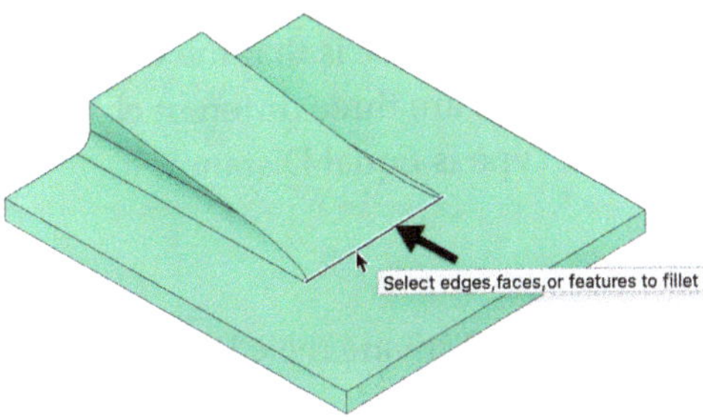

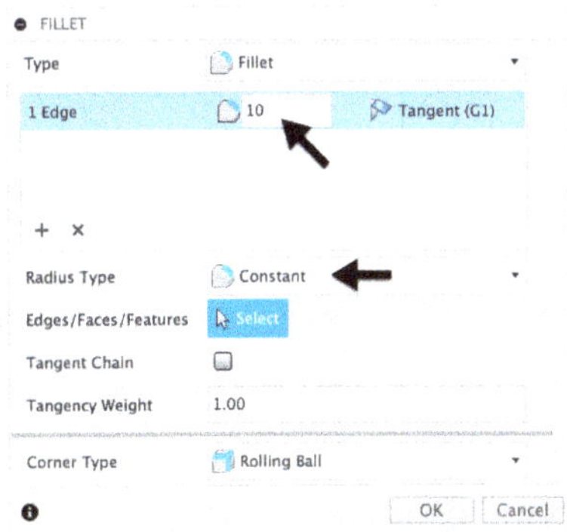

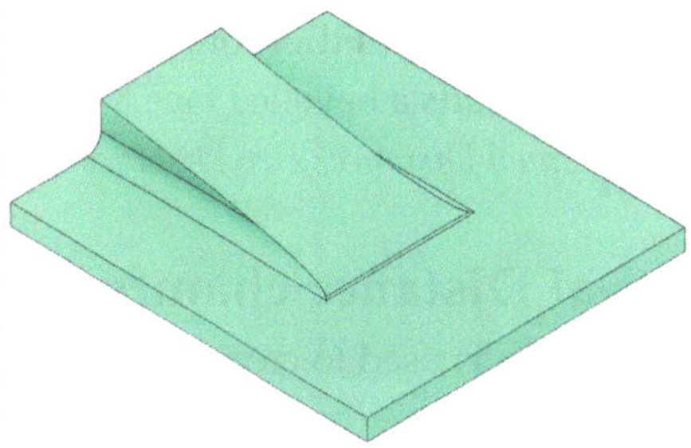

Delete the fillet and activate the **Fillet** command. Next, select **Type > Fillet** from the **Fillet** dialog. Select **Radius Type > Chord Length** and select the edge to fillet. Type-in a value in the **Chord Length** box click **OK** to create the chord length fillet.

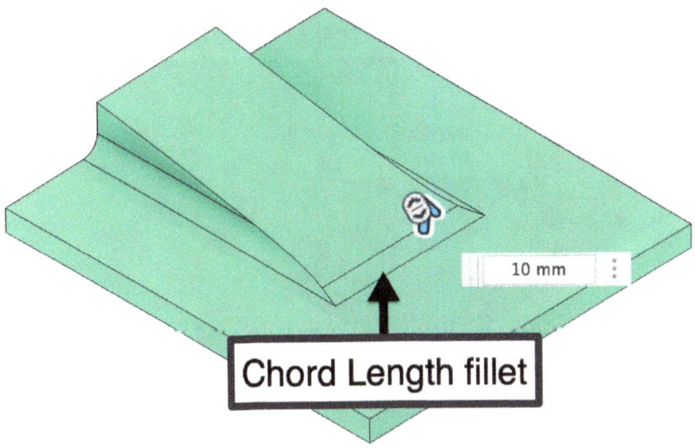

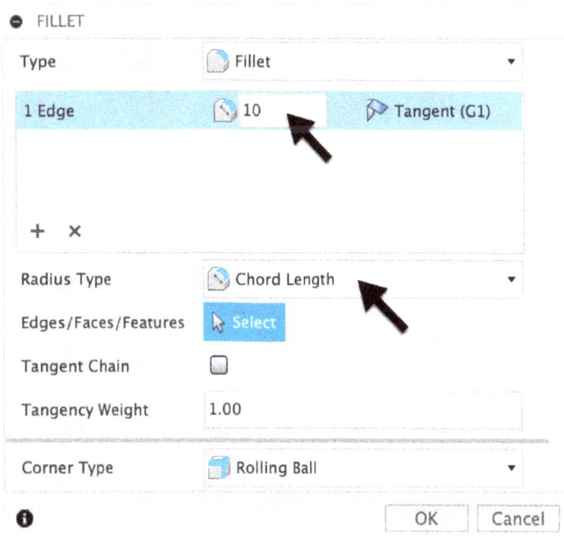

Corner Setback

If you create fillets on three edges that come together at a corner, you have the option to control how these three fillets are blended together. Activate the **Fillet** command and select the three edges that meet together at a corner. Next, select the **Setback** option from the **Corner Type** drop-down on the **Fillet** dialog. Select the **Rolling Ball** option from the **Corner Type** drop-down, if you do not want to apply the setback.

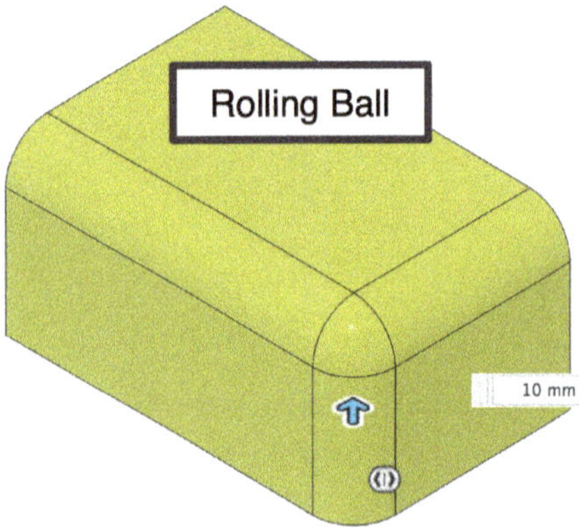

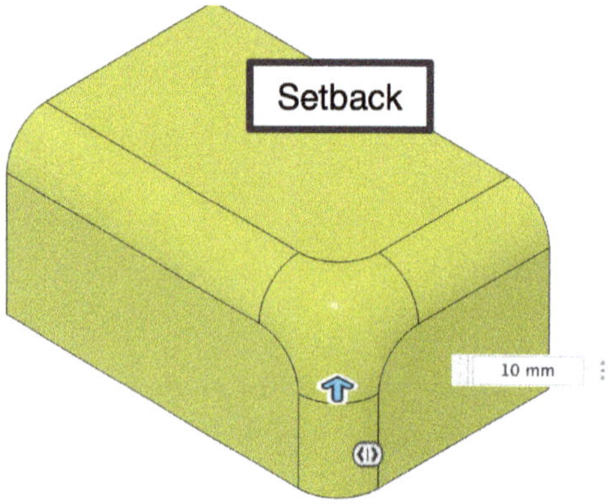

Chamfer

The **Chamfer** and **Fillet** commands are commonly used to break sharp edges. The difference is that the **Chamfer** command adds a bevelled face to the model. A chamfer is also a placed feature. There are three different chamfer types: *Equal Distance, Two Distances* and *Distance and Angle*. The default Chamfer Type is Equal Distance.

Equal Distance chamfer

This option is used to create a chamfer with equal distance on both sides of the edge. Activate the **Chamfer** command (click **Modify** panel > **Chamfer**  on the **Solid** tab of the toolbar) and select the edge to chamfer. On the **Chamfer** dialog, select **Type > Equal Distance**. Next, type-in a value in the **Distance** box. Click **OK** to complete the chamfer.

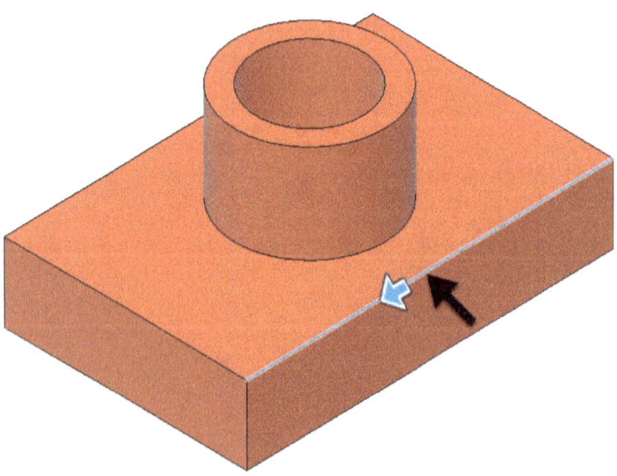

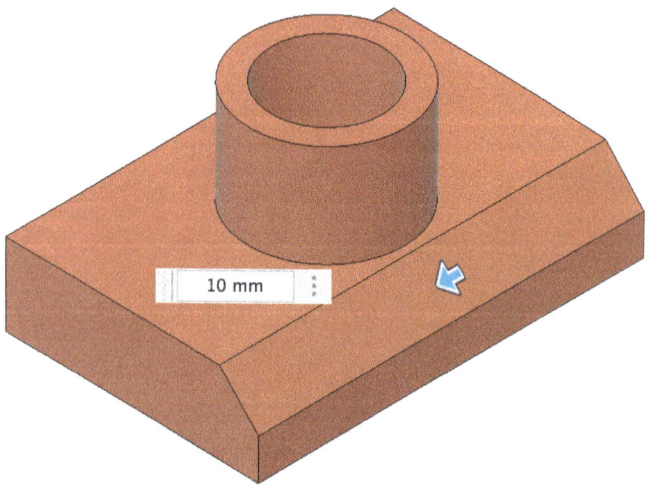

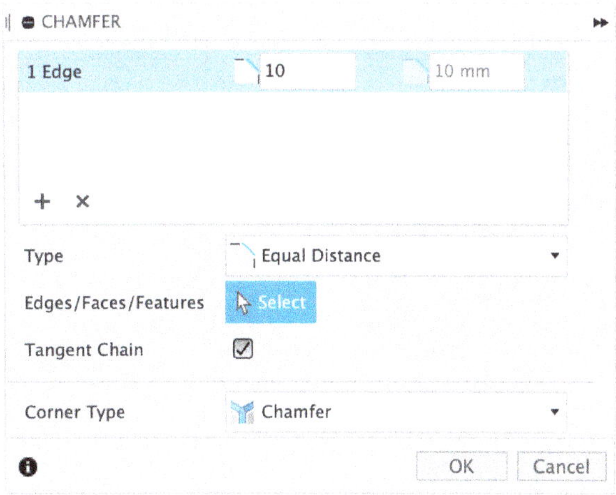

Distance and Angle chamfer

This option lets you create a chamfer by defining its distance and angle values. On the **Chamfer** dialog, select **Chamfer Type > Distance and Angle.** Next, select the edge to chamfer. Type-in values in the **Distance** and **Angle** boxes; the distance and angle values are measured from the vertical and horizontal faces, respectively. Click **OK** to complete the feature.

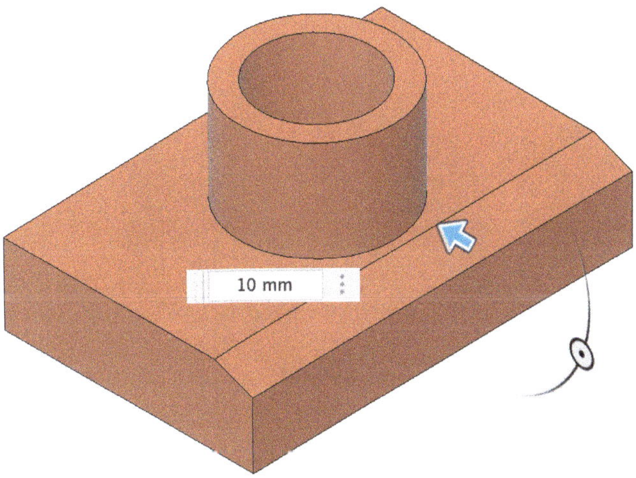

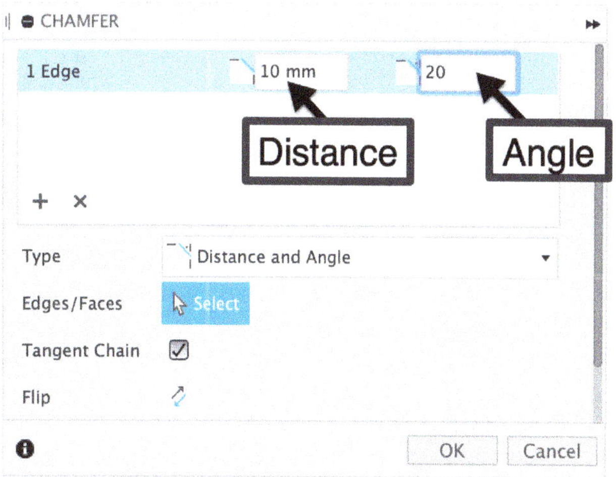

Two Distance chamfer

If you want a chamfer to have different setbacks on both sides of the edge, then select **Chamfer Type > Two Distance** option on the **Chamfer** dialog. Next, select the edge to chamfer. Type-in values in the first **Distance** and the second **Distance** boxes on the dialog. Click **OK** to complete the feature.

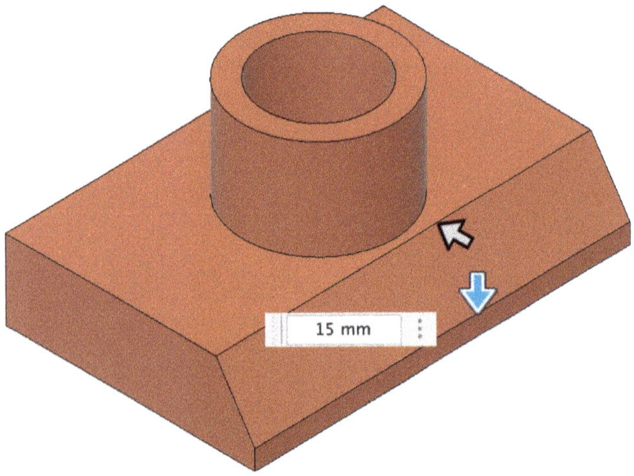

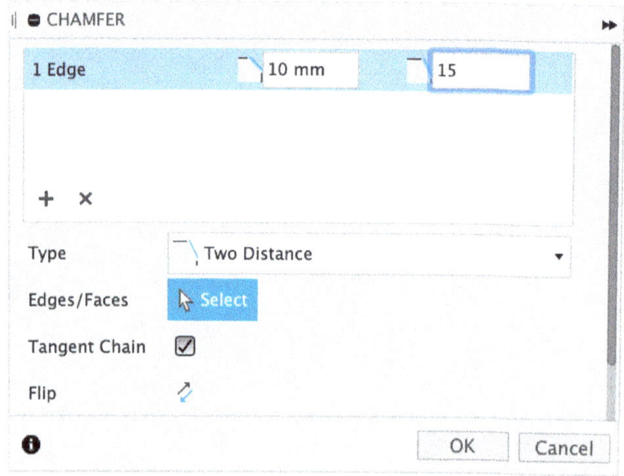

Corner Type

If you create chamfers on three edges that come together at a corner, you have the option to control how these three fillets are blended together. The **Corner Type** drop-down provides you with three options: **Chamfer**, **Miter**, and **Blend**.

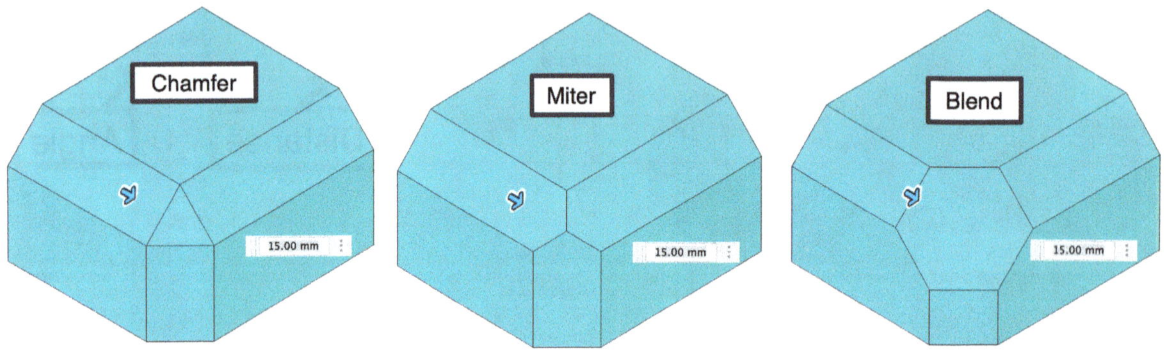

The Draft command

When creating cast or plastic parts, you are often required to add a draft on them so that they can be molded easily. A draft is an angle or taper applied to the faces of components so that they can be removed from the mold easily without any damage. The following illustration shows a molded part with and without a draft.

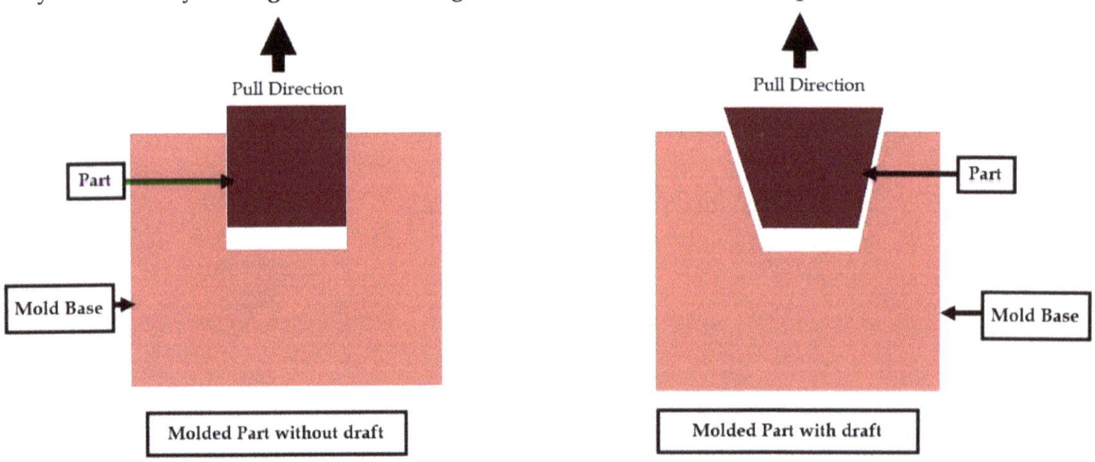

The **Draft** command will help you to apply a draft to the model geometry. To activate this command, click **Modify** panel > **Draft**  on the **Solid** tab of the toolbar. The **Draft** dialog pops up on the screen. Select the plane or face to define the pull direction. On the **Draft** dialog, click the **Faces** selection button and select the face to be drafted. Type-in a value in the **Angle** box or use the manipulator to specify the angle. Next, you need to specify the **Draft side** of the draft. You can specify the **Draft side using three options:** *One Side, Two Sides,* and *Symmetric*. These options are explained next.

One Side

If you select the **One Side** option, the face selected will be drafted in a single direction irrespective of the location of the reference plane. Click the **Flip Direction** icon to reverse the direction of the draft. Click **OK** to create the draft feature.

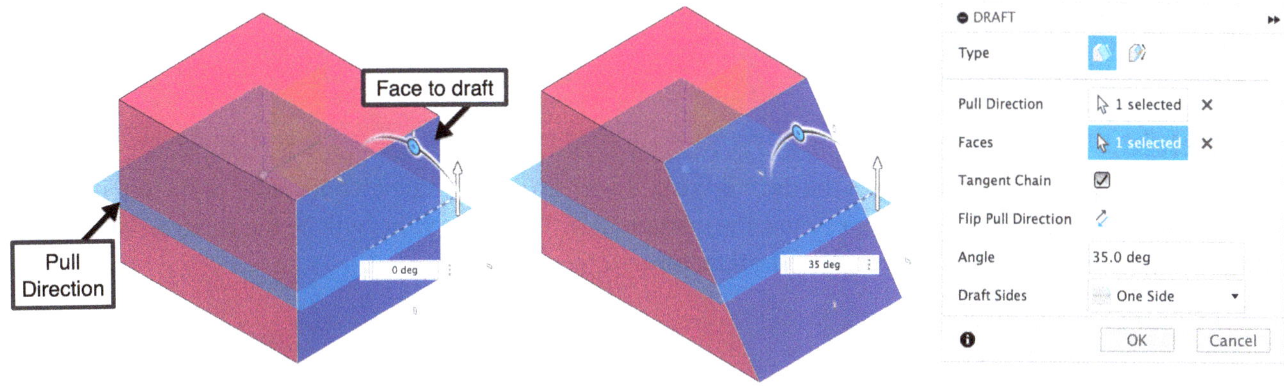

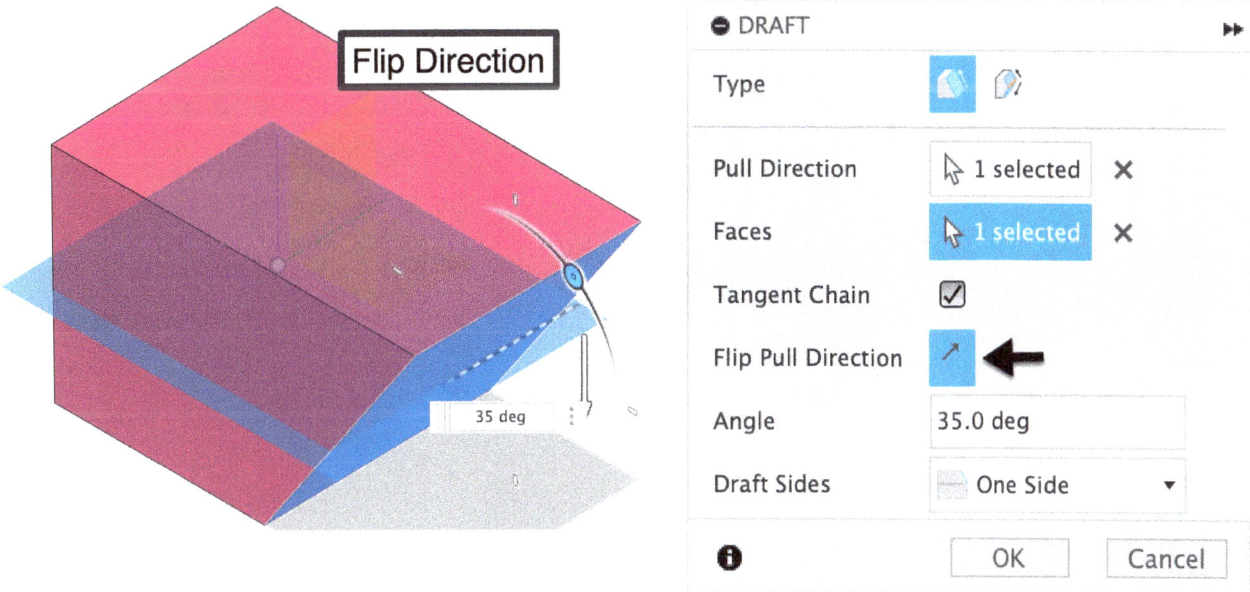

Two Sides

If you select the **Two Side** option, then the draft is created on both sides of the reference plane. Specify the angle in the **Angle** boxes for both sides or use the manipulator to specify the angle values. You can enter different angle values. Click **OK** to create the draft feature.

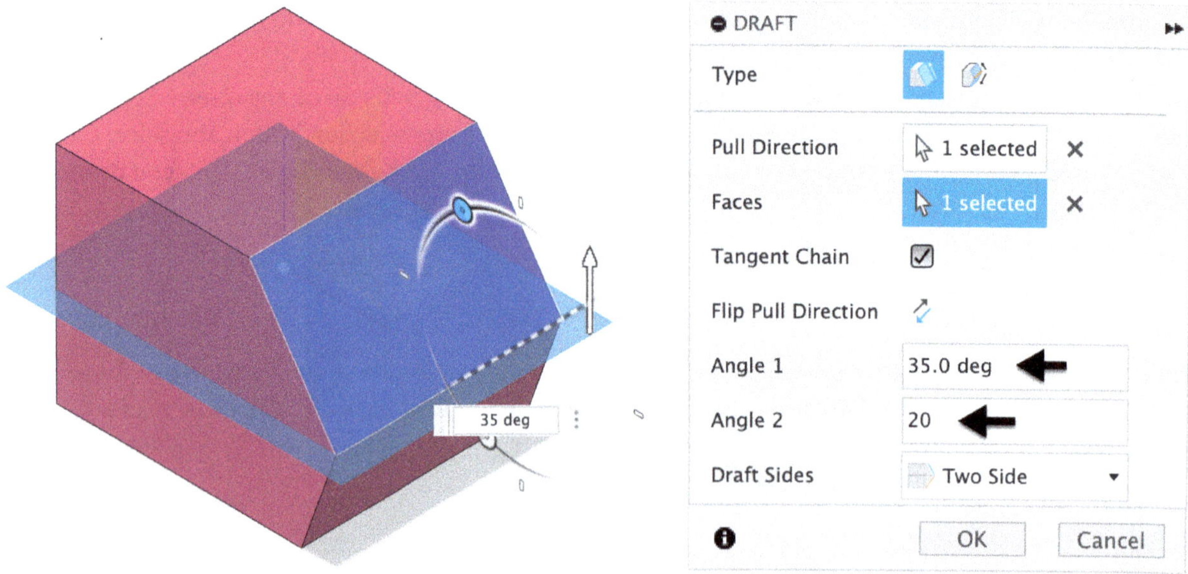

Symmetric

If you select the **Symmetric** option, then the draft is created with an equal angle on both sides of the reference plane. Specify the angle in the **Angle** box or use the manipulator. The angle value will be the same on both sides of the reference plane. Click **OK** to create the draft feature.

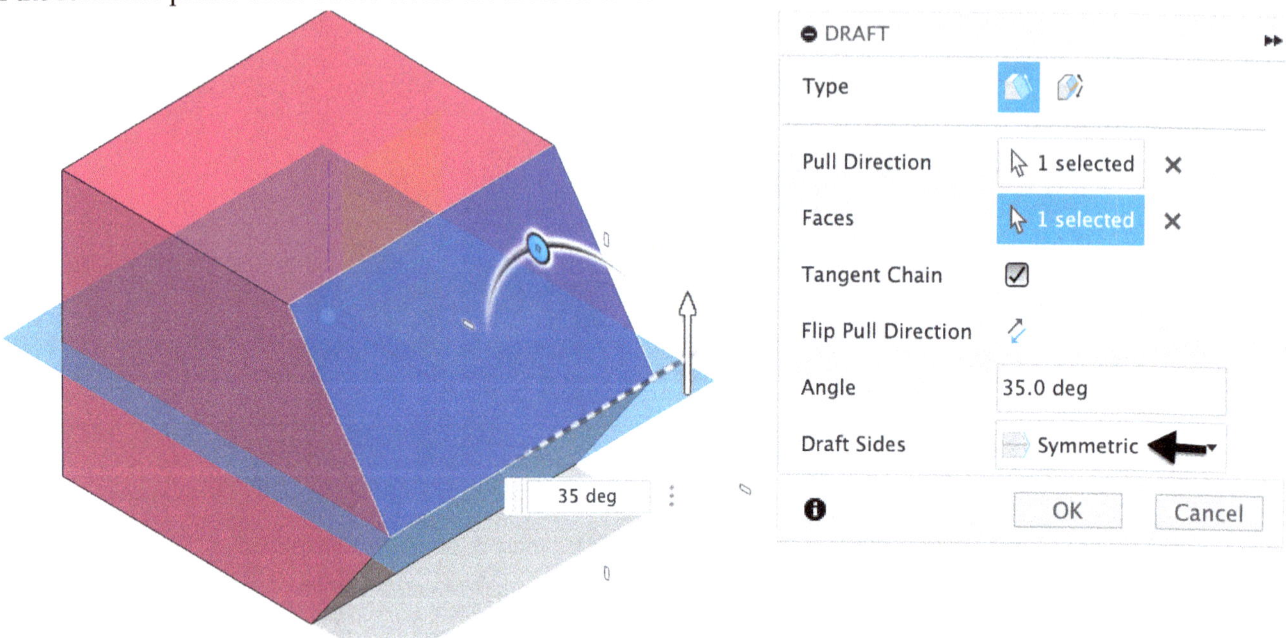

Tangent Chain

The **Tangent Chain** option allows you to select tangentially connected faces by clicking anyone of them.

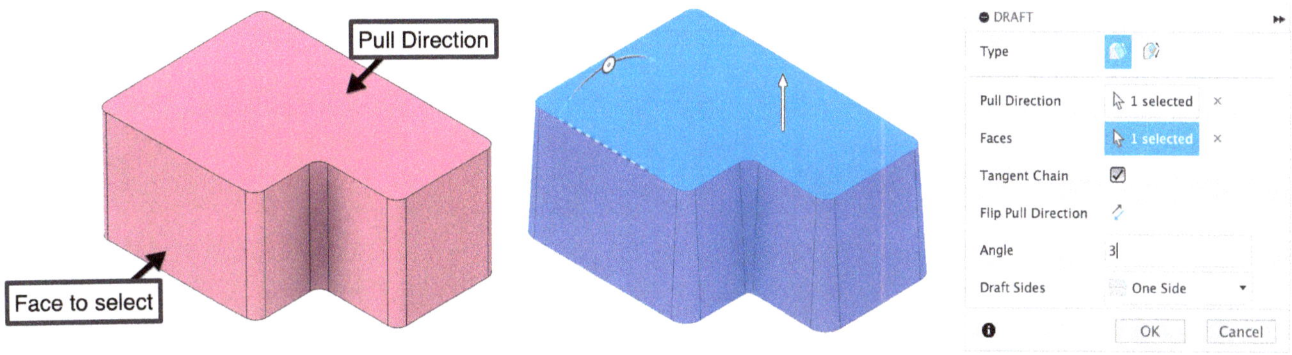

If you uncheck the **Tangent Chain** option, then only the selected face will be drafted.

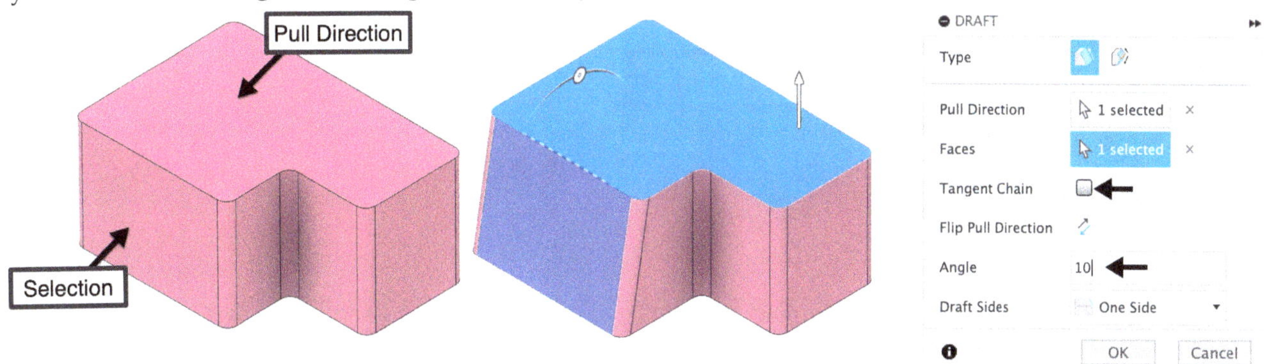

Note that it is a best practice to apply fillets at the end of the model. You may get some undesired geometry if you apply fillets before the draft feature. If you already have an existing fillet, you need to drag the timeline marker to the left side of the fillet. Next, apply the draft to the geometry, and then drag the timeline marker to the right-side of the fillet.

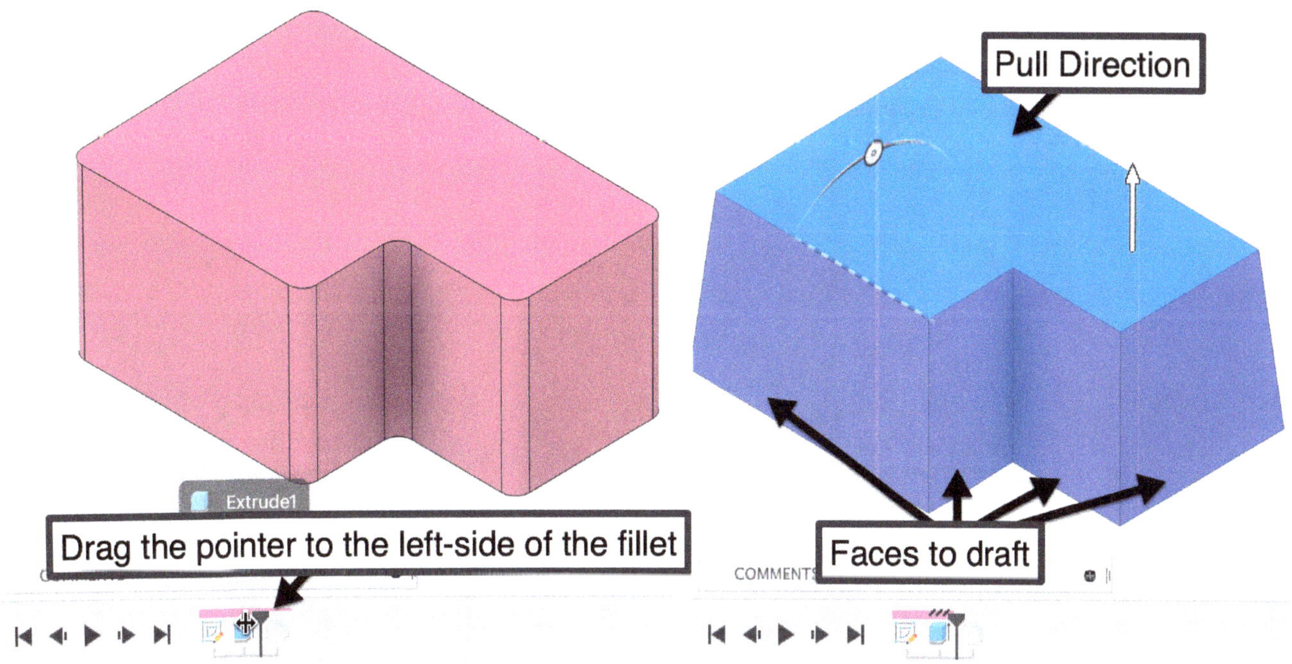

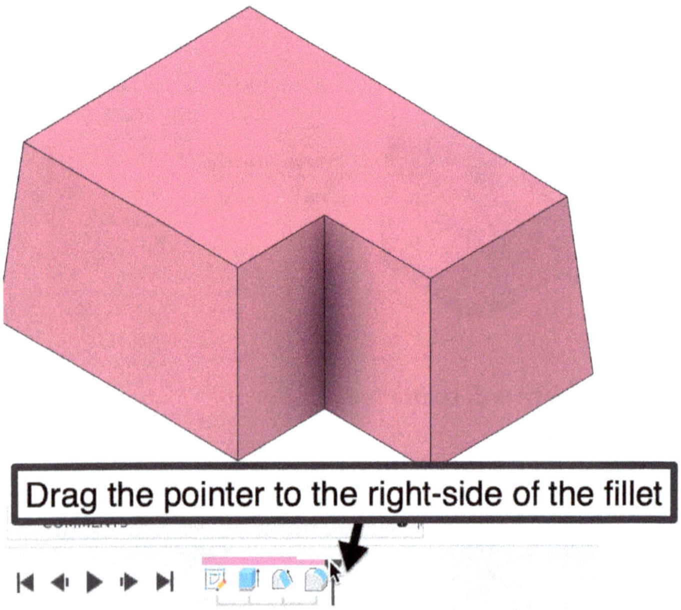

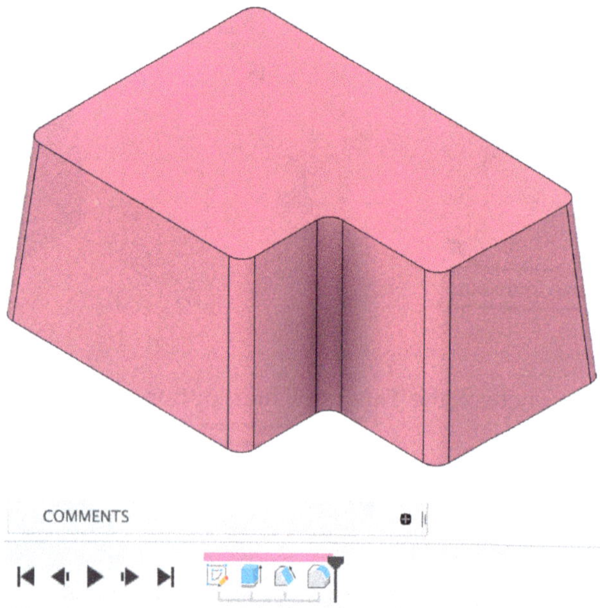

Shell

The **Shell** command is another useful command that can be applied directly to a solid model. It allows you to take a solid geometry and make it hollow. This can be a powerful and timesaving technique when designing parts that call for thin walls such as bottles, tanks, and containers. This command is easy to use. You should have a solid part to use this command. Activate this command (On the **Solid** tab of the toolbar, click **Modify** panel > **Shell**) and select the faces to remove.

Under **Shell Type**, you can choose between **Sharp Shell** and **Round Shell**. The **Sharp Shell** option creates hollowed parts with sharp, defined edges, preserving the original sharpness of the model edges. The **Round Shell** option rounds off the edges, producing smooth, filleted transitions.

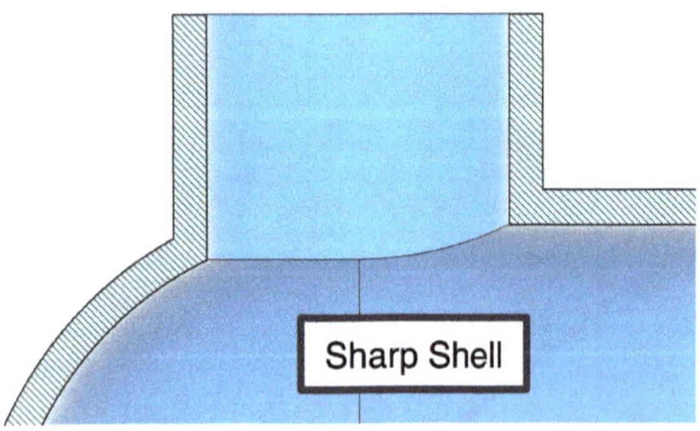

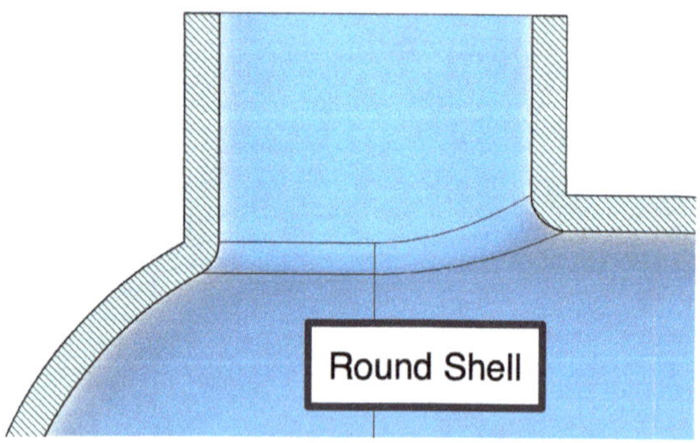

Type-in the wall thickness in the **Inside thickness** box. Note that there are three different types of thickness. They are Inside, Outside, and Both. Click **Direction** drop-down and select **Inside** or **Outside** or **Both** options to specify whether the thickness is added inside or outside or both sides of the model. You can deselect the **Tangent Chain** option to unselect the tangentially connected faces. Click **OK** to create the Shell feature.

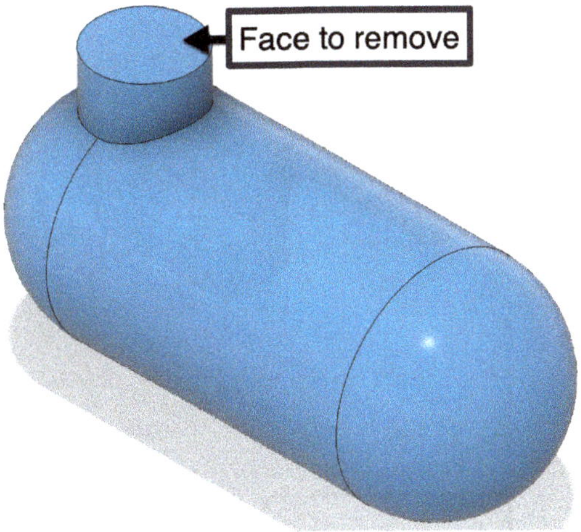

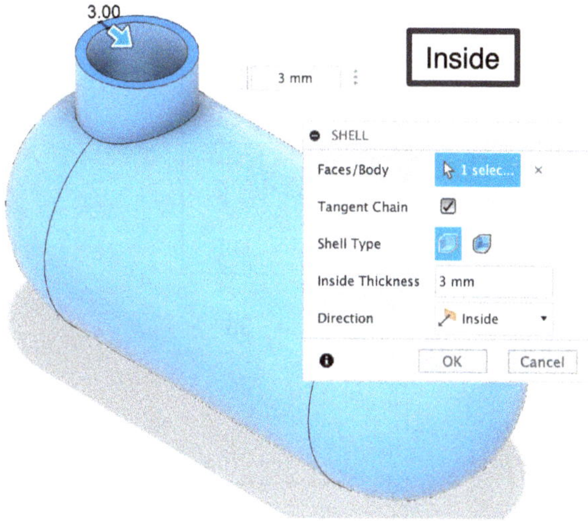

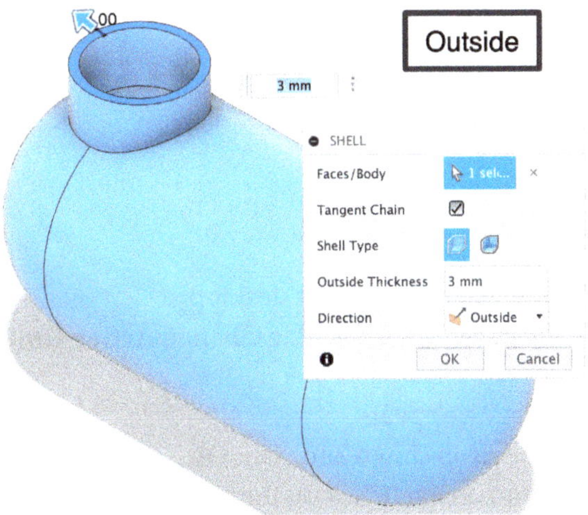

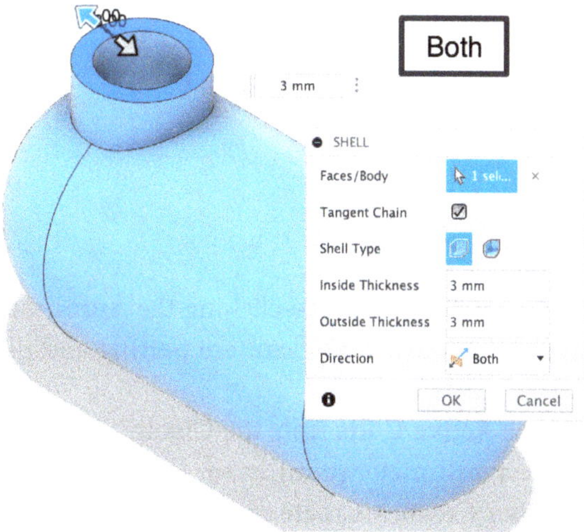

Examples

Example 1 (Millimeters)

In this example, you will create the part shown below.

Placed Features

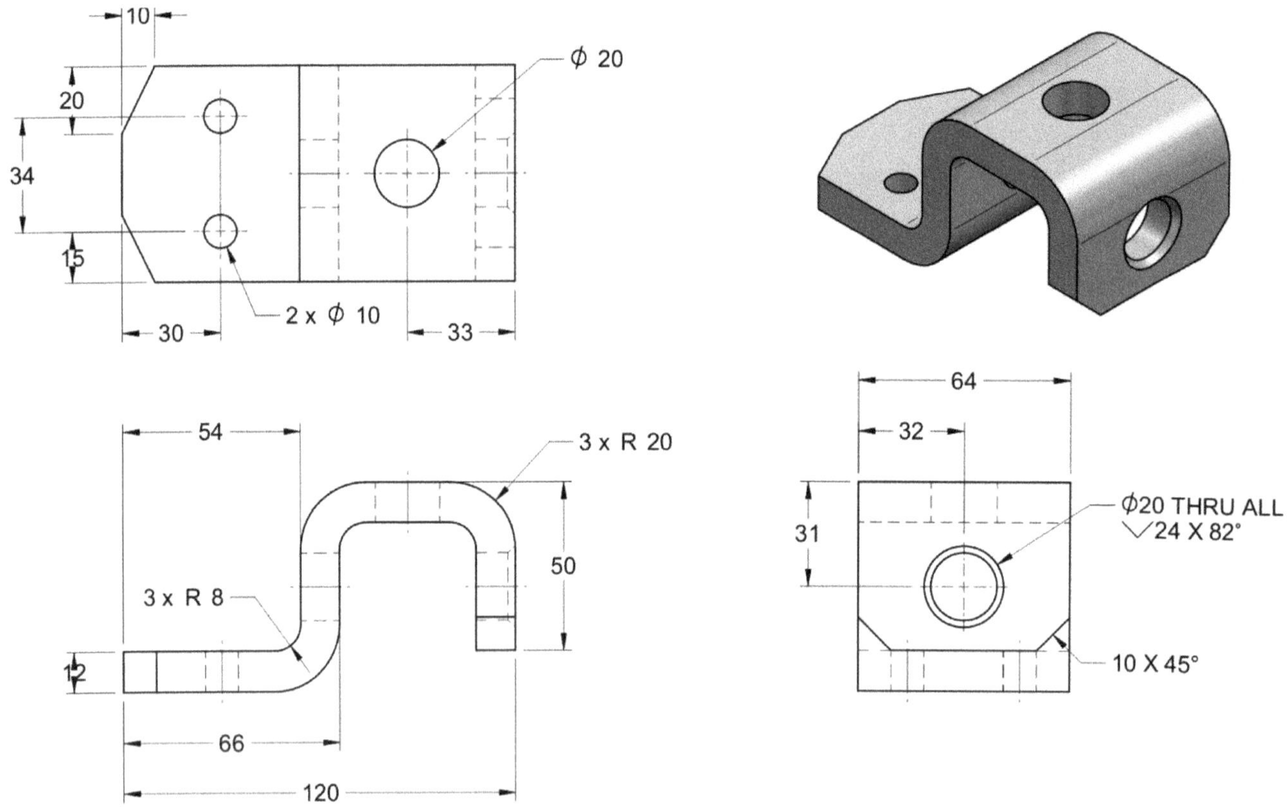

1. Start **Autodesk Fusion 360** by double-clicking the **Autodesk Fusion 360** icon on your desktop.
2. On the **Browser window**, expand **Document Setting** and place the cursor on **Units**; the **Change Active Units** icon appears.
3. Click on the **Change Active Units** icon; the **Change Active Units** dialog appears.
4. On this dialog, select **millimeter (mm), gram (g)** from the **Unit Type** drop-down and click **OK**.
5. To start a sketch, click **Create > Create Sketch** on the **Solid** tab of the toolbar. Click on the **XZ** plane.
6. Click **Create > Line**, on the **Sketch** contextual tab of the toolbar.
7. Select the sketch origin located at the center. Next, move the pointer horizontally toward right and click on the horizontal axis of the sketch.
8. Move the pointer vertically upward and click. Next, move the pointer horizontally toward right and click.
9. Move the pointer vertically downward and click.
10. On the **Sketch** contextual tab of the toolbar, click the **Sketch Dimension** icon on the **Create** panel.
11. Select the lower horizontal line, move the pointer downward and click. Type 66 and press ENTER.
12. Likewise, add dimensions to other lines, as shown. Next. click **Finish Sketch** on the toolbar.

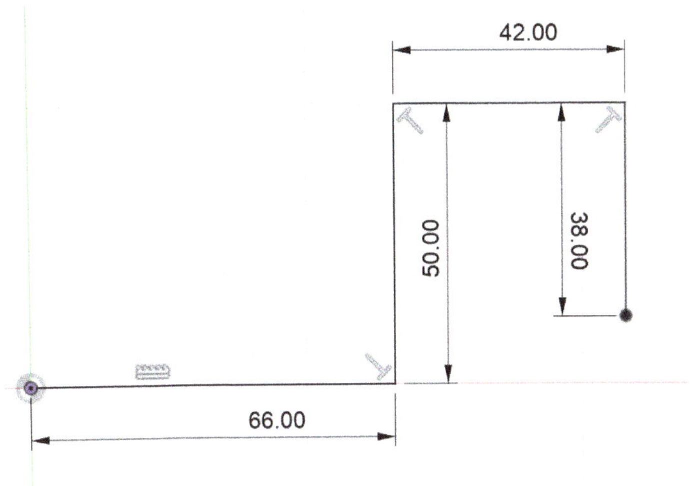

13. Activate the **Extrude** command (on the **Solid** tab of the toolbar, click **Create > Extrude**).

14. On the **Extrude** dialog, select **Type > Thin Extrude** .
15. On the **Extrude** dialog, type **64** in the **Distance** box. Next, select **Direction > Symmetric**.
16. Click the **Measurement > Whole Length** icon.
17. Type **12** in the **Wall Thickness** box.
18. Select **Wall Location > Side 1**. Next, click **OK**.

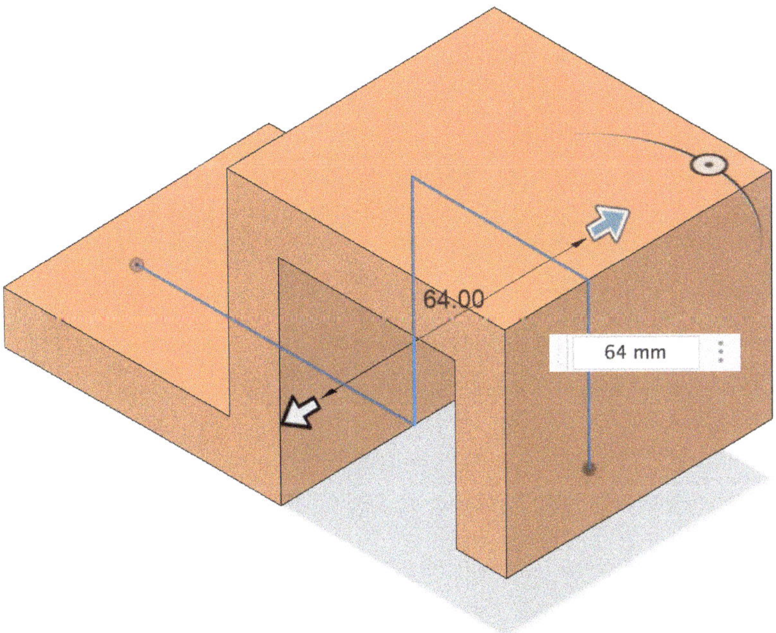

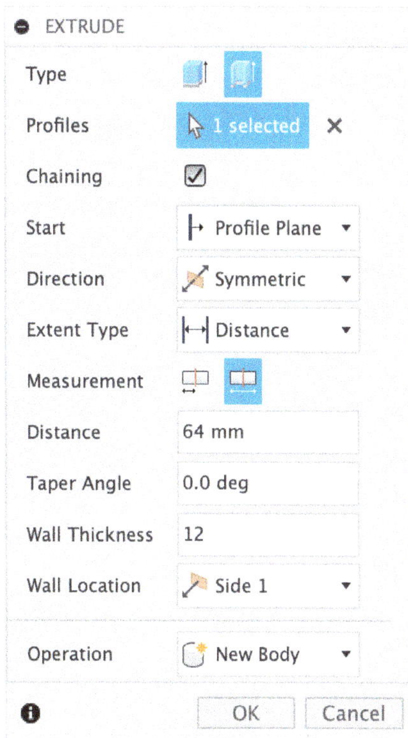

19. On the **Solid** tab of the toolbar, click **Create > Hole** . Click on the right-side face of the model, as shown.

20. On the **Hole** dialog, click **Hole Type > Countersink** . Also, select **Hole Tap Type > Simple** .
21. Under the **Shape Settings** section, select **Extents > All**. Also, set the **Countersink Diameter** and **Countersink Angle** values to **24** and **82**, respectively. Set the **Diameter** value to **20** mm.

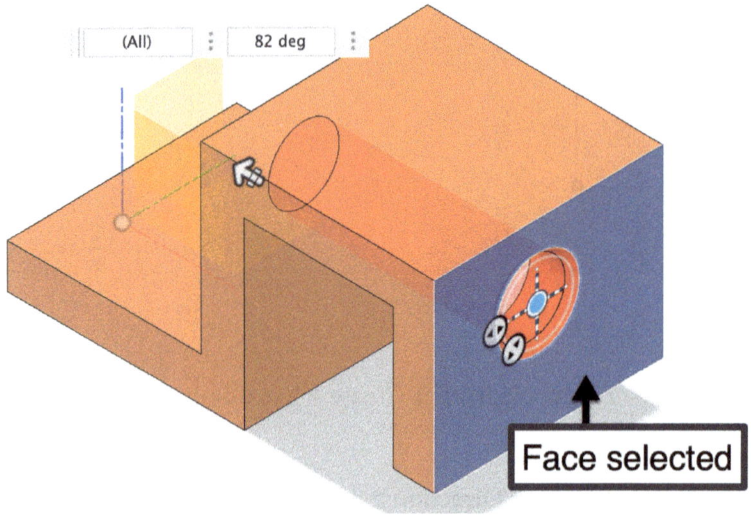

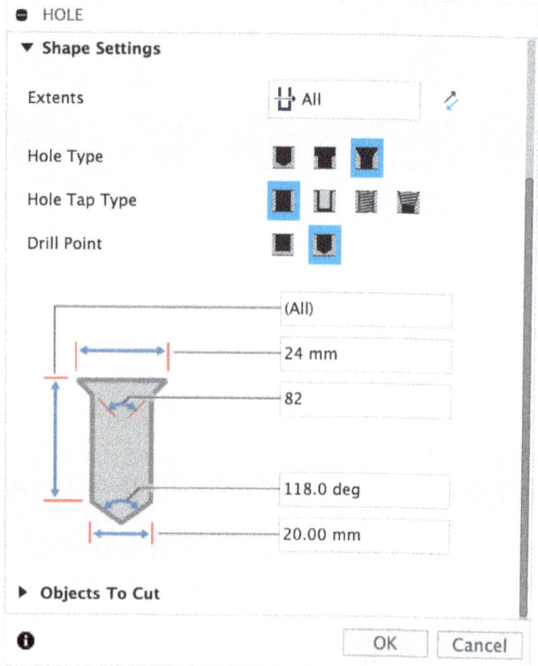

22. Click on the **Reference** Select button.
23. Place the pointer on the top edge of the right-face, and click when **Add Reference** appears.
24. Enter **31** in the distance box. Likewise, select the right vertical edge and enter **32** in the distance box.

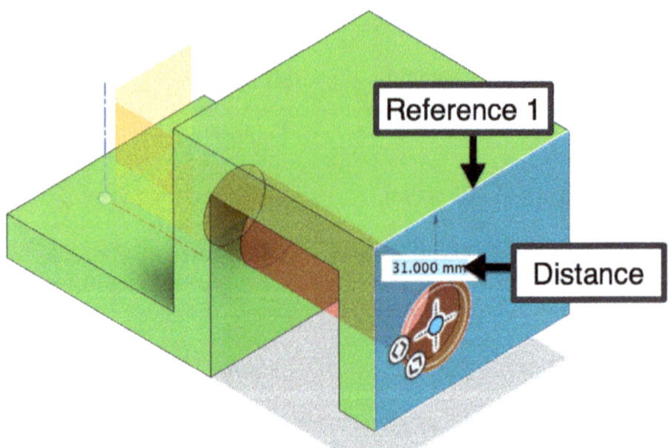

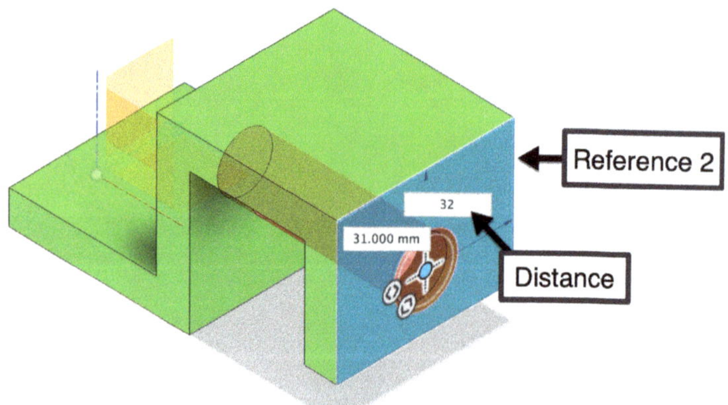

25. On the **Hole** dialog, you can view the reference values in the **Distance** boxes. Click **OK** to complete the hole feature.

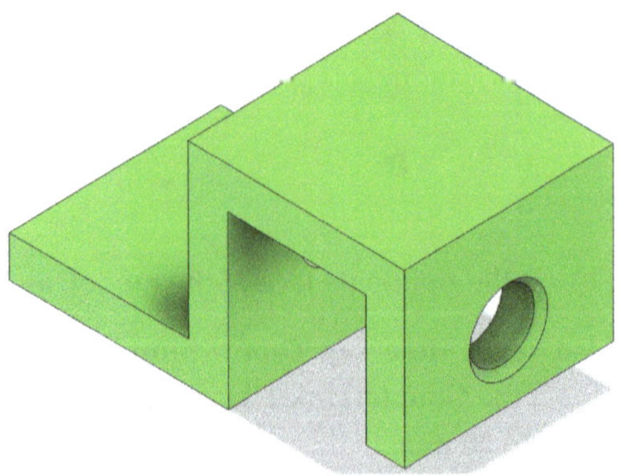

26. Activate the **Hole** command and click on the top face of the part model.
27. On the **Hole** dialog, select **Extents** drop-down **> All**; last used values will appear automatically.
28. Next, select **Hole Type > Simple** . Also, select **Hole Tap Type > Simple** .
29. Set the **Diameter** value to 20 mm.
30. Next, place the pointer on the front edge of the top-face, and click when the **Add Reference** appears.
31. Enter **33** in the distance box. Likewise, select the left edge and enter **32** in the distance box.

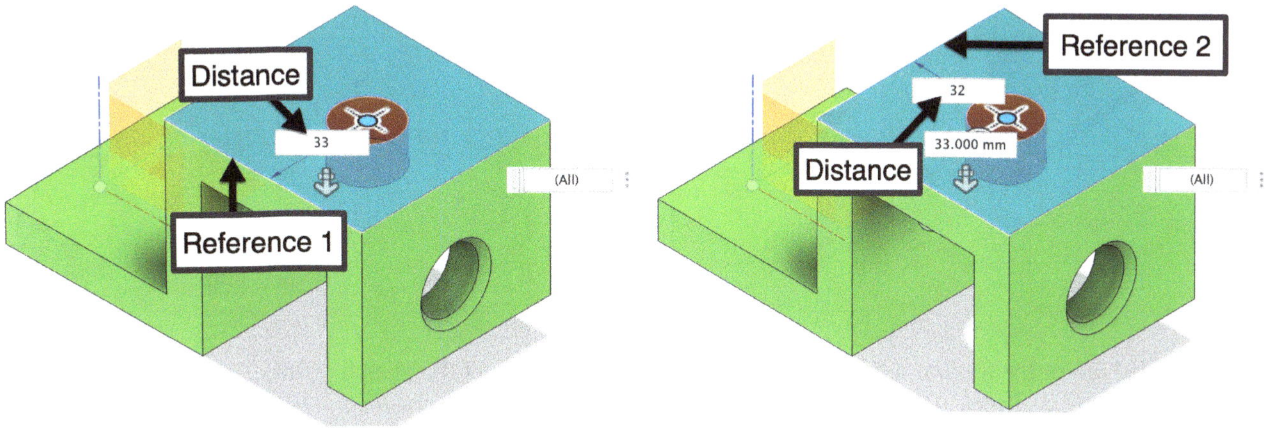

32. Click **OK** on the **Hole** dialog to complete the hole feature.
33. Click the top-left corner point of the ViewCube, as shown; the view orientation of the model is changed.

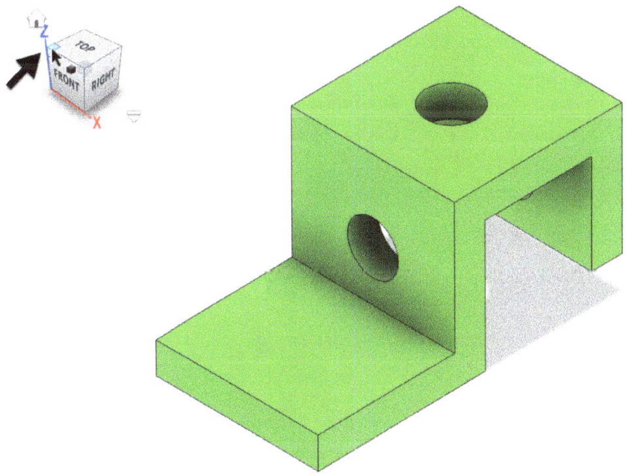

34. Activate the **Create Sketch** command and click on the lower top face of the model.
35. On the **Sketch** contextual tab of the toolbar, expand the **Create** panel, and click the **Point** button. Next, Place two points and add dimensions and Vertical constraint between the points, as shown. Click **Finish Sketch** on the toolbar.

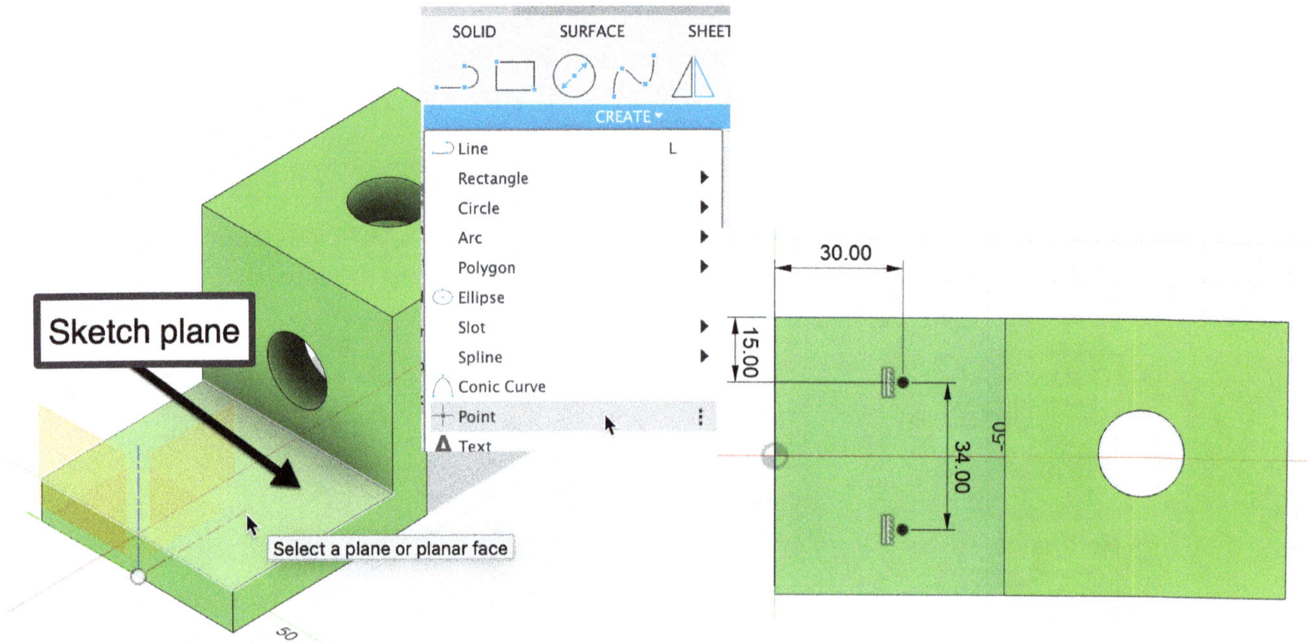

36. On the **Solid** tab of the toolbar, click **Create** panel **> Hole**. Next, select the sketch points.

37. On the **Hole** dialog, select **Hole Type > Simple** .

38. Select **Hole Tap Type > Simple** .

39. Set the **Diameter** value to 10 mm. Next, select **Extents > All**.

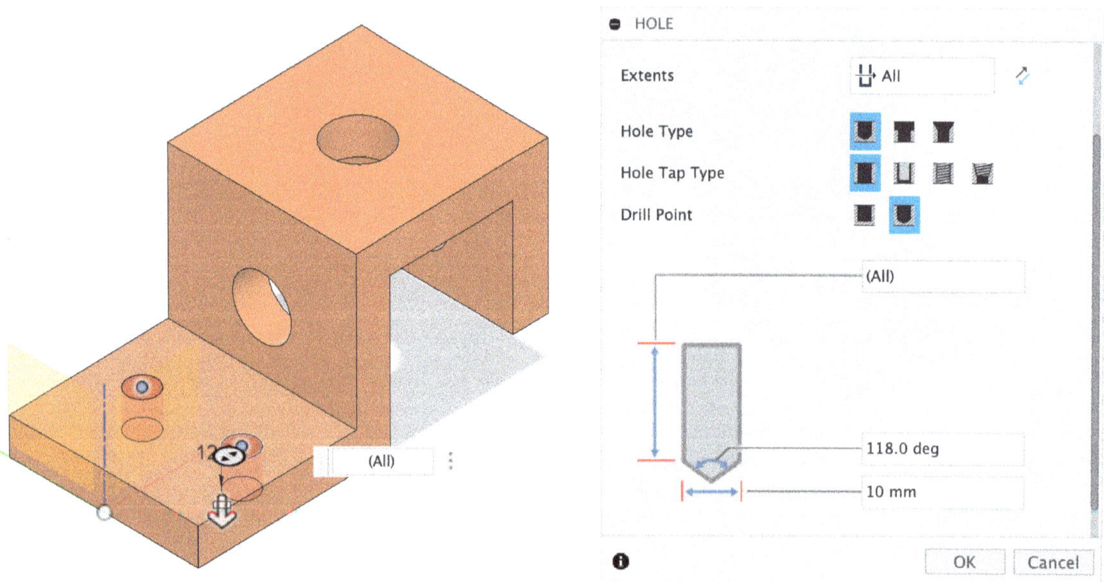

40. Click **OK** to complete the hole feature.

41. Click **Modify** panel > **Chamfer** on the **Solid** tab of the toolbar. Click on the corner edge, as shown in the figure.

42. On the **Chamfer** dialog, click **Type > Two Distance**. Enter **10** and **20** in the two **Distance** boxes, respectively.

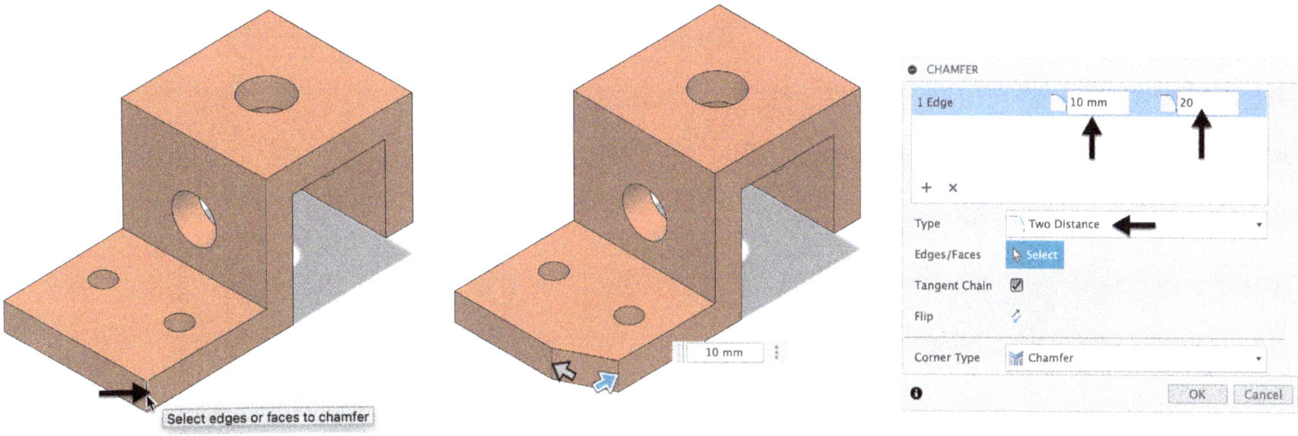

43. Click the **Add Selection set** + icon on the **Chamfer** dialog.
44. Type 20 and 10 in the two Distance boxes. Next, click **OK** to create the chamfers.

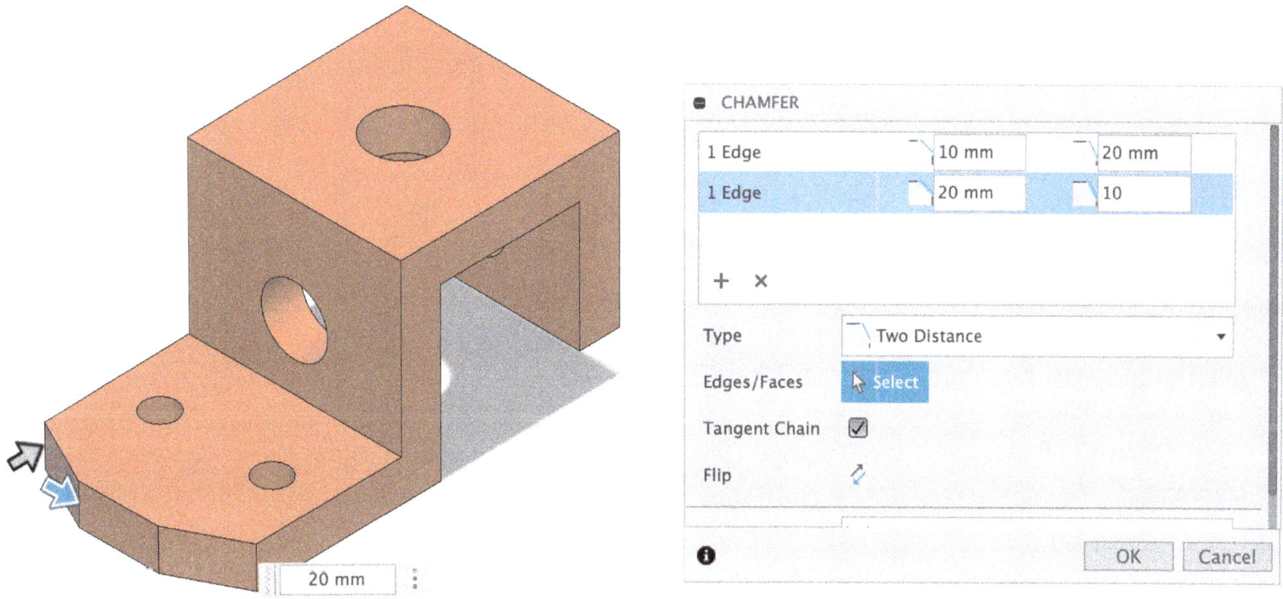

45. Click **Modify** panel > **Fillet** on the **Solid** tab of the toolbar.
46. Click on the horizontal edges of the model, as shown below. Type **8** in the radius box and click **OK** on the dialog

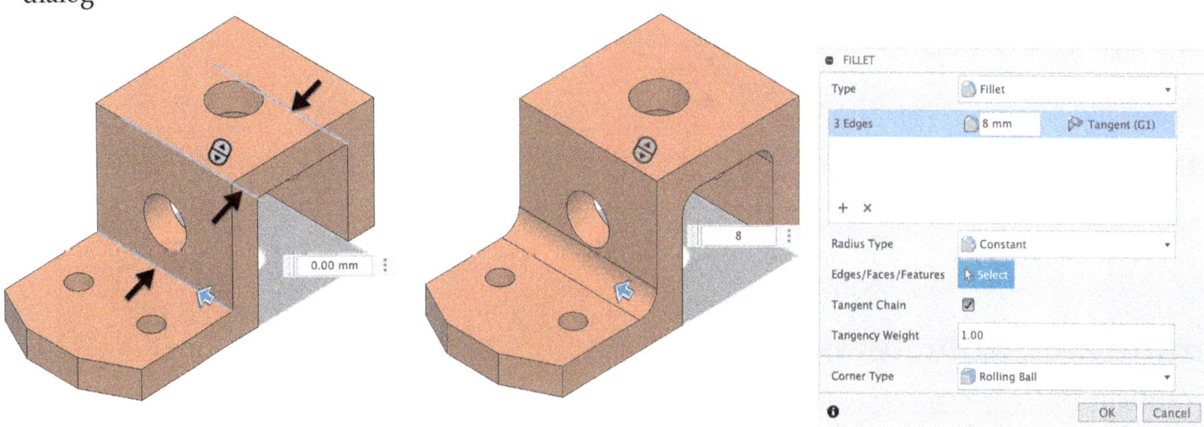

47. Click **Modify** panel **>** **Fillet** on the **Solid** tab of the toolbar.
48. Click on the outer edges of the part model, as shown below – Type-In 20 mm in the **Radius** box.
49. Click **OK** to complete the fillet feature.

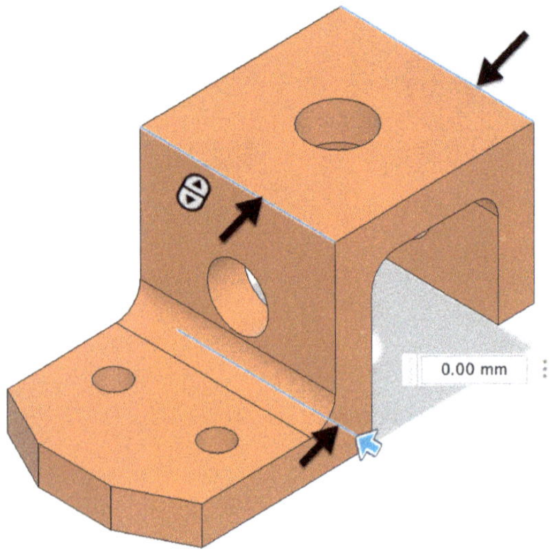

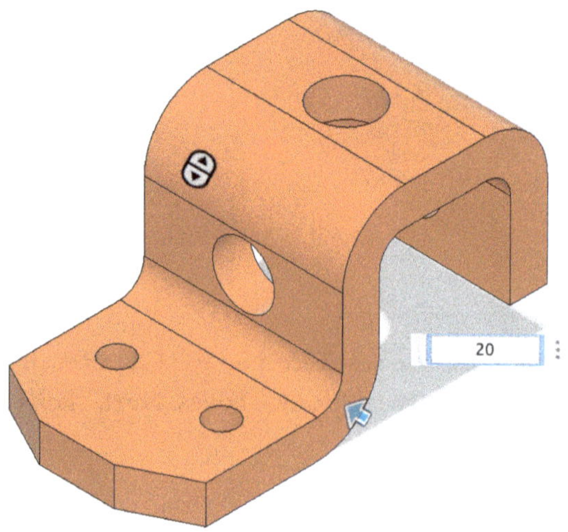

50. Click on the **Home** icon located at the top left corner of the ViewCube.

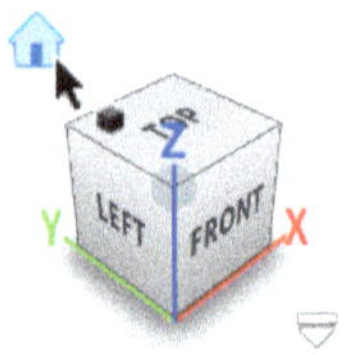

51. On the **Solid** tab of the toolbar, click **Modify** panel **>** **Chamfer** and click on the lower corner edges of the model, as shown.
52. On the **Chamfer** dialog, click **Type > Equal Distance** and type-in 10 in the **Distance** box. Click **OK** to chamfer the edges.

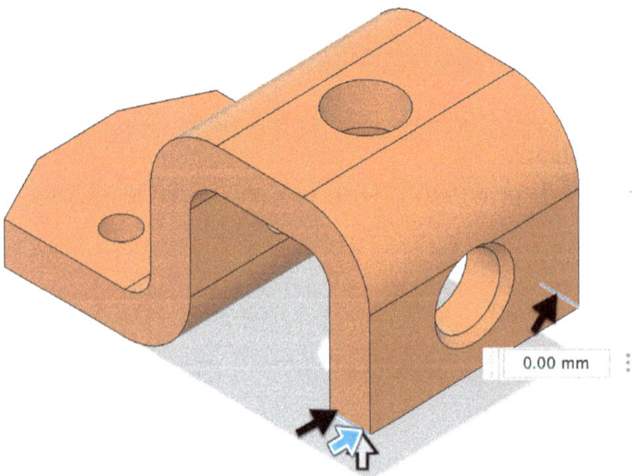

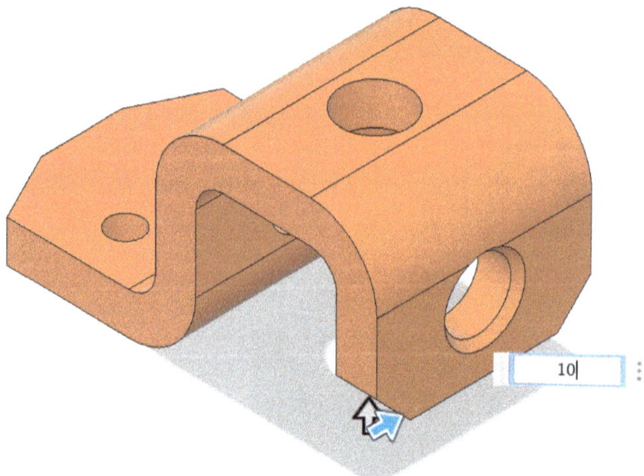

53. Save and close the file.

Example 2 (Millimeters)

In this example, you create the part shown next.

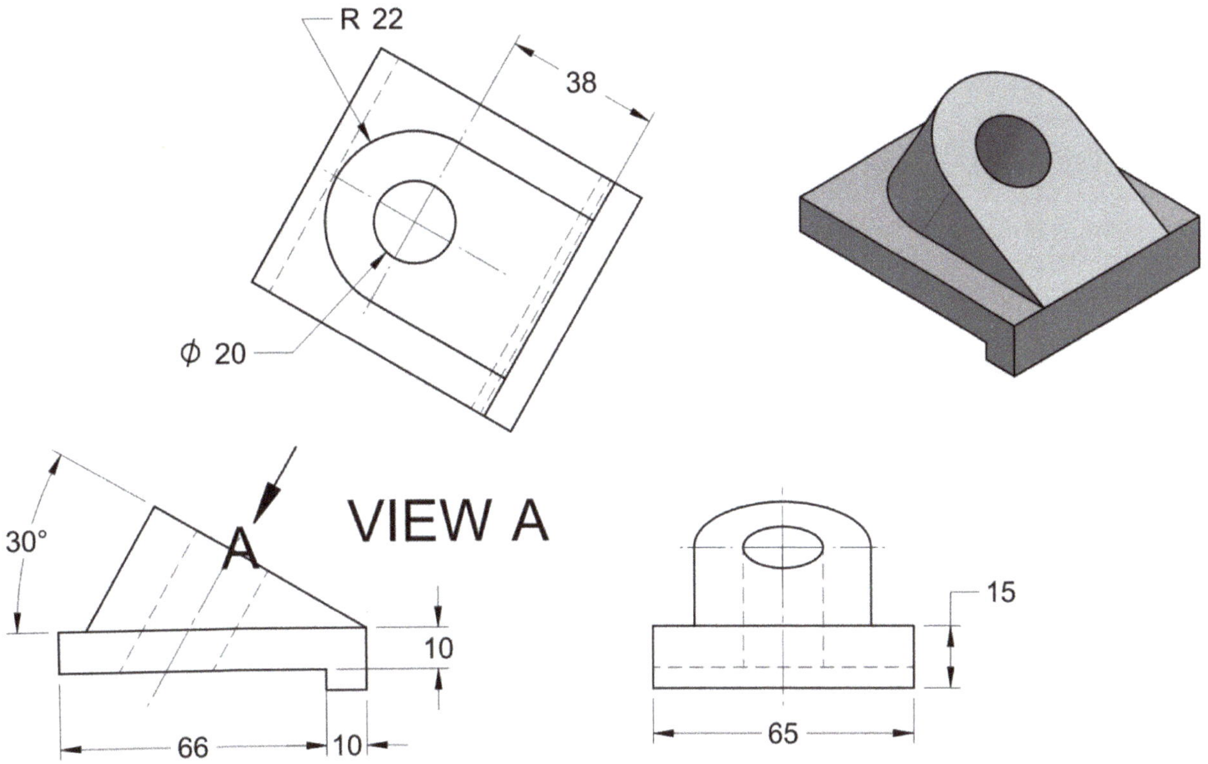

Creating a New document

1. Click **Autodesk Fusion 360** on the desktop to start the application.
2. On the **Browser window**, expand **Document Settings** and place the cursor on **Units**; the **Change Active Units** icon appears.
3. Click on the **Change Active Units** icon to change the units; the **Change Active Units** dialog appears.
4. On this dialog, select **Unit Type > millimeter (mm), gram (g)** from the drop-down and click **OK**.

Creating the Pad features

1. Click the **Create Sketch** icon on the **Create** panel and select the XZ_plane. Next, click **OK**.
2. Create the closed sketch and dimensions and geometric constraints, as shown.

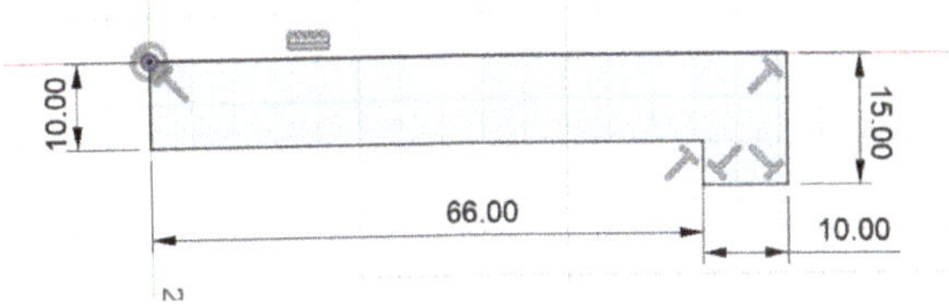

3. Click **Finish Sketch**.
4. Click the **Extrude** icon on the **Create** panel.
5. On the **Extrude** dialog, select Extent **Type > Distance** and enter **65** in the **Distance** box.
6. Select **Direction > Symmetric**.
7. Select **Measurement > Whole Length**.
8. Click **OK** to create the *Extrude* feature.

Creating the Angled Plane

1. On the toolbar, click **Solid** tab > **Construct** panel > **Plane at angle**.

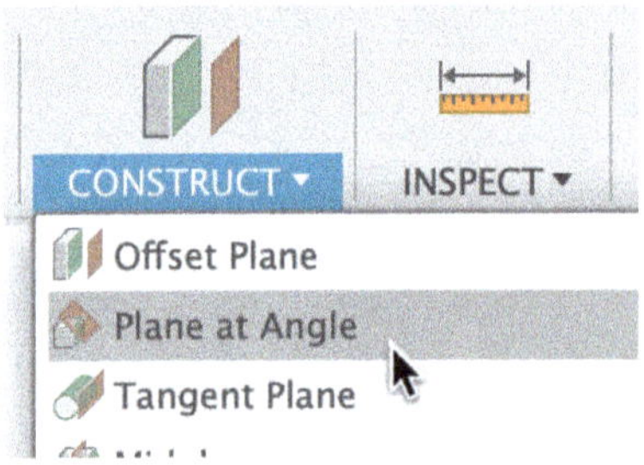

2. Select the horizontal edge of the model, as shown.
3. Type -30 in the **Radius** box. Next, click **OK**.

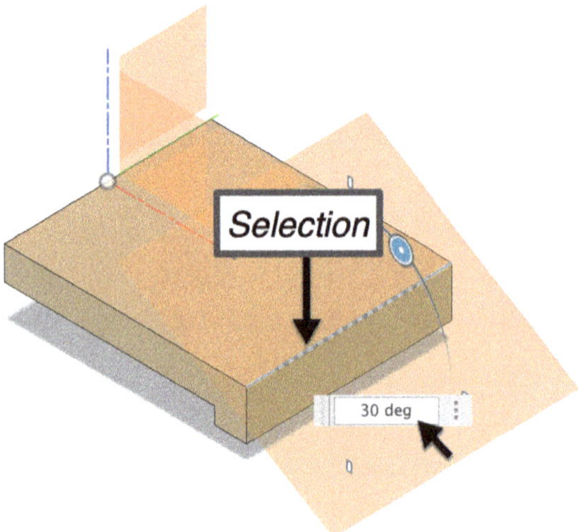

Creating the Pad feature

1. Click the **Create Sketch** icon on the **Create** panel and select the newly created plane.
2. On the toolbar, click **Create** panel > **Slot** > **Center to Center Slot**.
3. Select sketch origin.
4. Move the pointer upward and click.
5. Move the pointer outward and click.

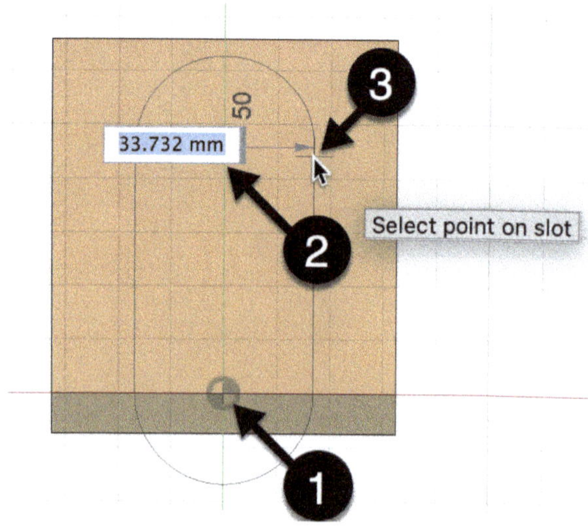

6. Click the **Line** icon on the **Create** panel.
7. Select the lower endpoints of the vertical lines of the slot, as shown.
8. Click the **Trim** icon on the **Modify** panel.
9. Select the lower arc of the slot.
10. Add dimensions and constraints, as shown.

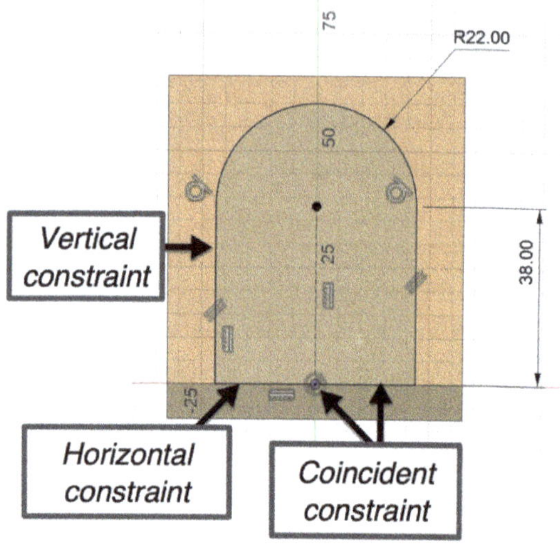

11. Click the **Finish Sketch** button on the **Sketch Palette**.
12. On the **Create** panel, click the **Extrude** command.
13. Select **Extent Type > To Object** from the **Extrude** dialog.
14. Select the horizontal face of the model, as shown. Next, click **OK**.

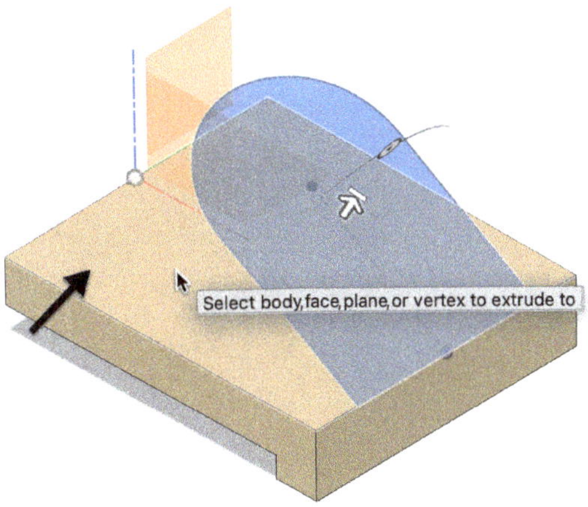

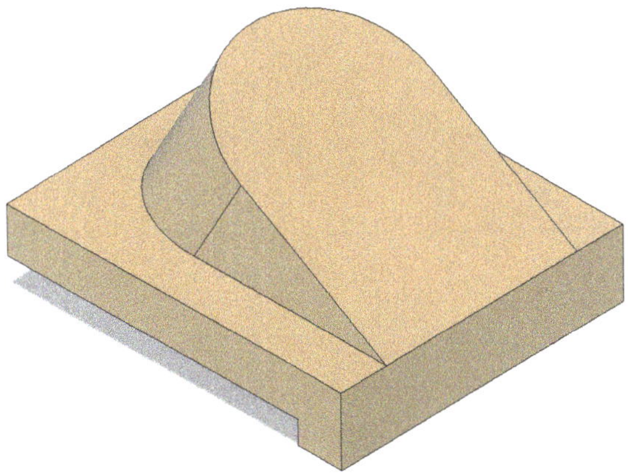

Creating the Hole feature

1. Click the **Hole** icon on the **Create** panel.
2. Select the inclined face of the model.
3. Select the circular edge of the model; the hole is made concentric to the circular edge.

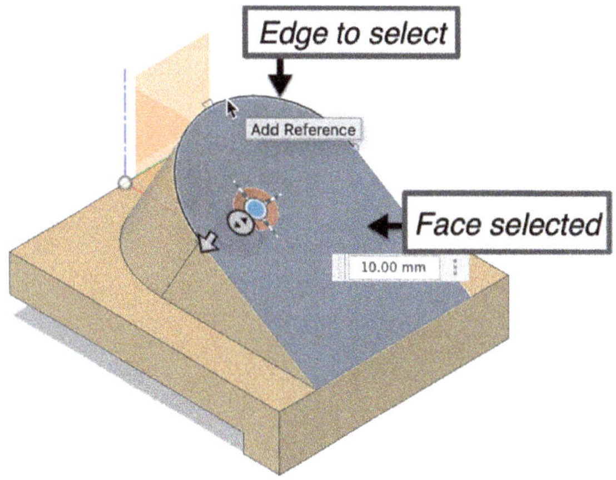

4. On the **Hole** dialog, select **Extents > All**.
5. Select **Hole Type > Simple**.
6. Select **Hole Tape Type > Simple**.
7. Type **20** in the **Diameter** box.
8. Click **OK** to create the hole.

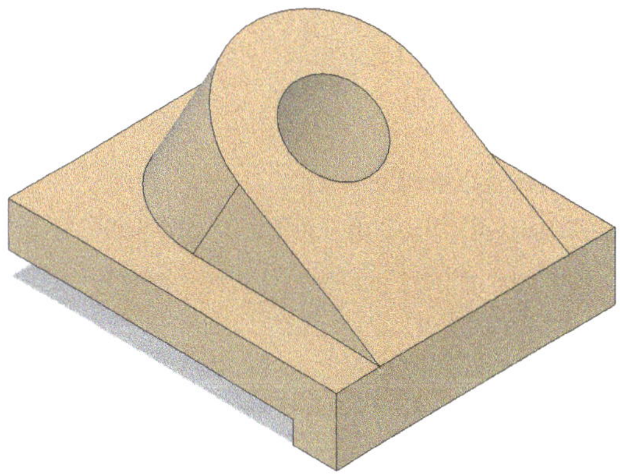

9. Save and close the file.

Example 3

In this example, you will create the model given below:

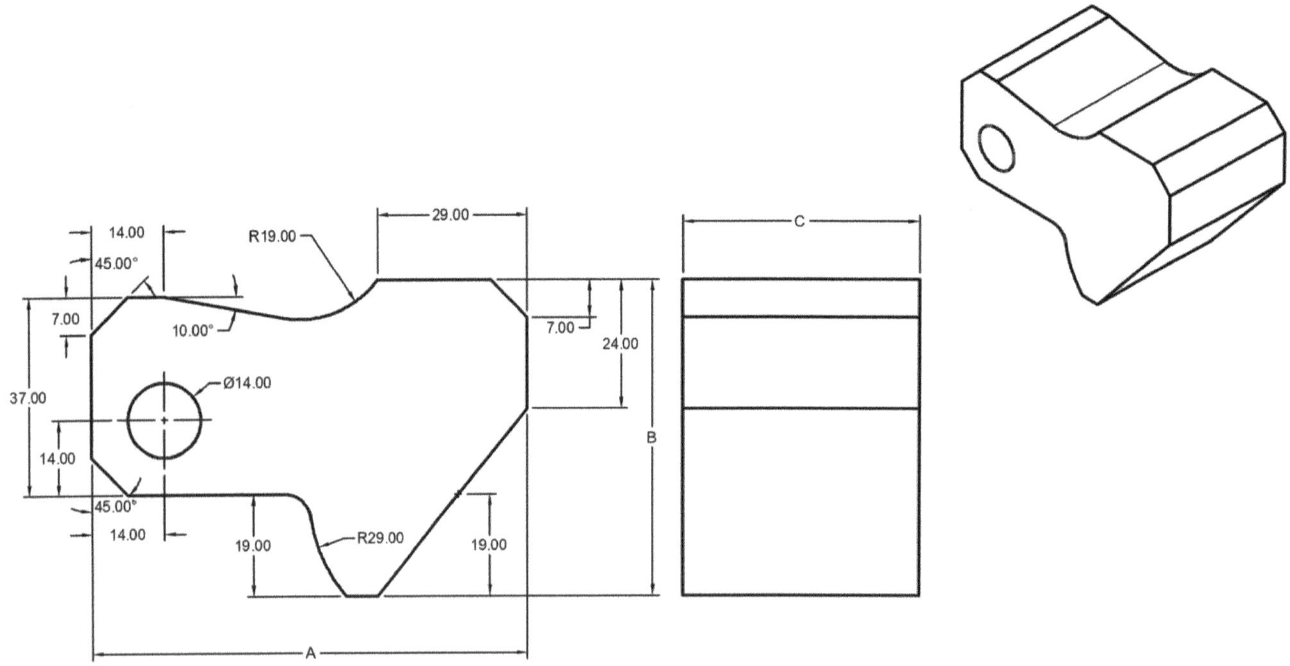

Creating the Base Feature

1. Start **Autodesk Fusion 360** by double-clicking the **Autodesk Fusion 360** icon on your desktop.
2. On the **Browser window**, expand **Document Settings** and place the cursor on **Units**; the **Change Active Units** icon appears.
3. Click on the **Change Active Units** icon to change the units; the **Change Active Units** dialog appears.
4. On this dialog, select **Unit Type > millimeter (mm), gram (g)** from the drop-down and click **OK**.
5. On the toolbar, click **Solid > Modify > Change Parameters** *fx*.
6. On the **Parameters** dialog, click the **Add User Parameter** button; the Add User Parameter dialog appears.
7. On the **Add User Parameter** dialog, type **A1** in the **Name** box. Select **Unit > mm**, type **81** in the **Expression** box. Click **OK** on the **Add User Parameter** dialog.

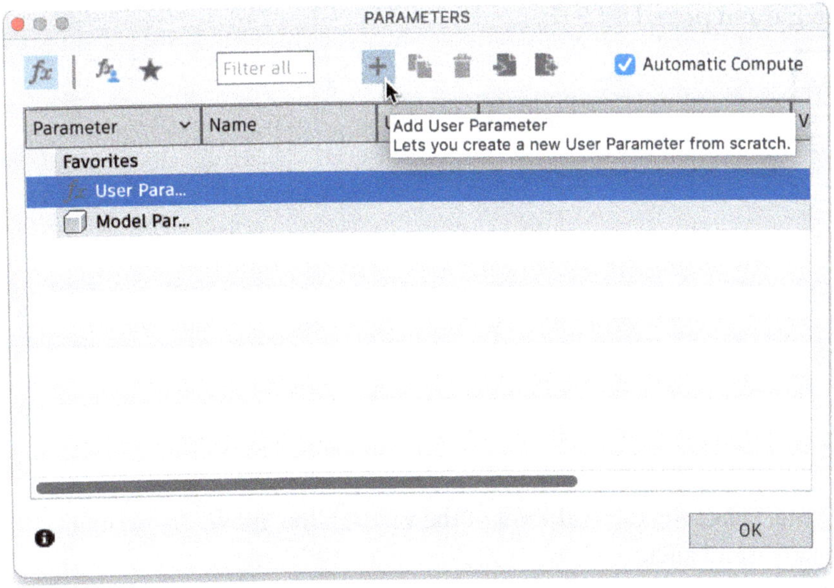

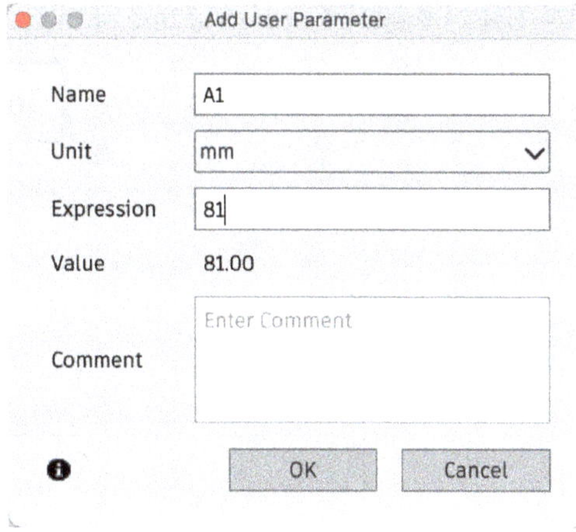

User parameters are user-defined names assigned to numeric values that allow you to create adaptive and easily modifiable designs. For instance, if you are designing a box, you could create user parameters for its length, width, and height. By applying these parameters in your sketch dimensions, the entire model becomes linked to their values. If you later decide to change the box's size, you simply need to update the parameter values, and the model will automatically adjust. This makes user parameters a powerful tool for creating flexible and easily adjustable designs.

8. Likewise, create other user parameters with the values, as shown. Next, click **OK**.

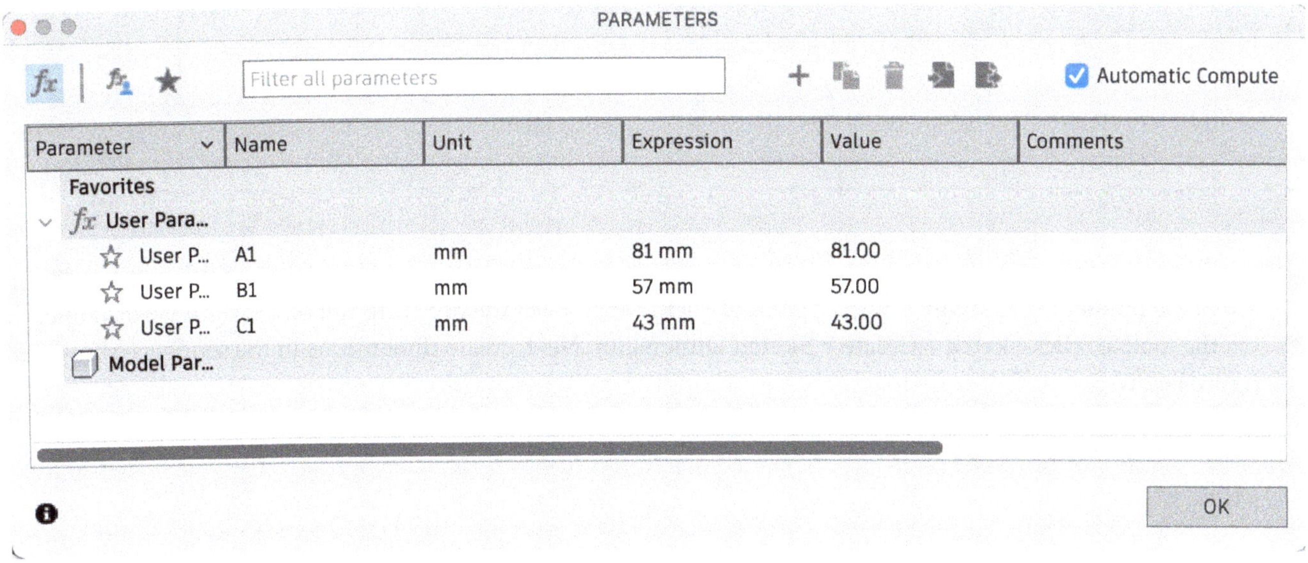

9. To start a sketch, click **Create > Create Sketch** on the toolbar. Click on the XZ plane. The sketch starts.
10. On the toolbar, click **Sketch > Create > Rectangle > 2-Point Rectangle**.
11. Select the origin point of the sketch. Next, move the pointer toward top-right corner.
12. Type **30** in the Width box of the rectangle and press TAB.
13. Type **A1** in the Length box and select the **A1 81.00 mm** parameter. Next, move the pointer upward and click to create the rectangle.

14. Select the top horizontal line of the rectangle and press DELETE.

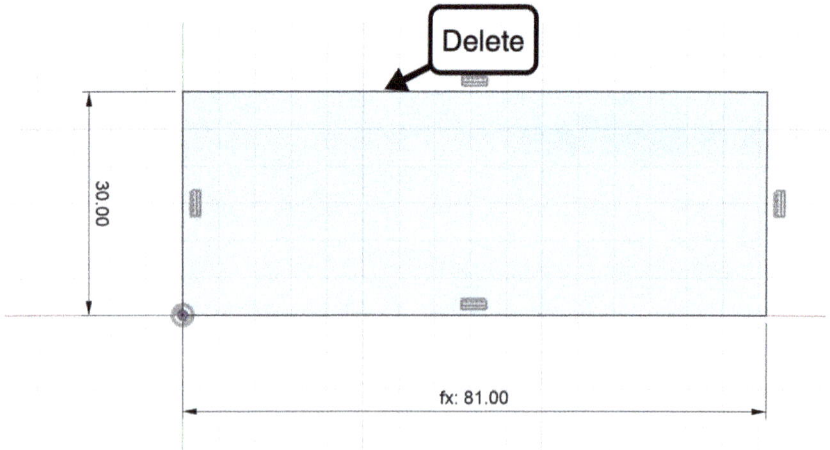

15. On the toolbar, click **Sketch > Create > Line**. Select the top endpoint of the vertical line, move the pointer toward top-right corner up to a small distance and click.
16. Move the pointer horizontally toward right and click.
17. Move the pointer toward bottom right corner up to a small distance and click.
18. Move the pointer and place it on endpoint of the inclined line.
19. Press and hold the left mouse button and drag the pointer away from the endpoint toward down.
20. Move the pointer toward top-right corner up to a small distance and release the pointer; an arc is created tangent to the inclined line.

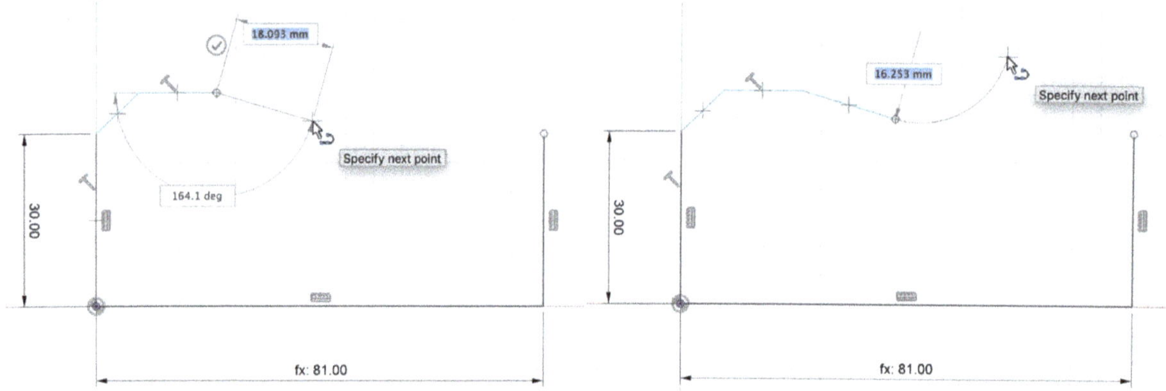

21. Move the pointer horizontally toward right and click. Next, select the top endpoint of the right vertical line.
22. On the toolbar, click **Sketch > Create > Sketch Dimension**. Next, create dimensions in the sequence shown in figure below.

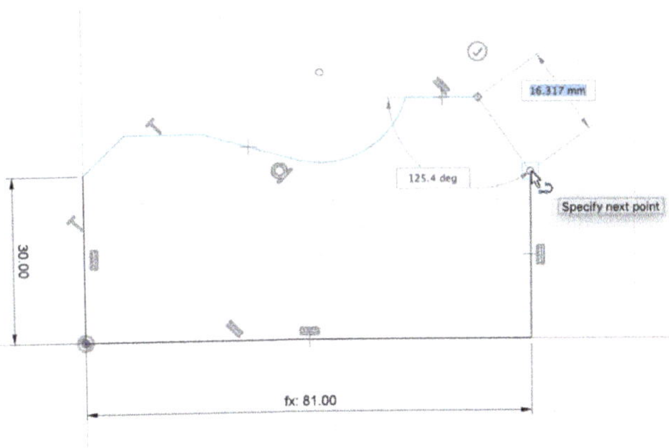

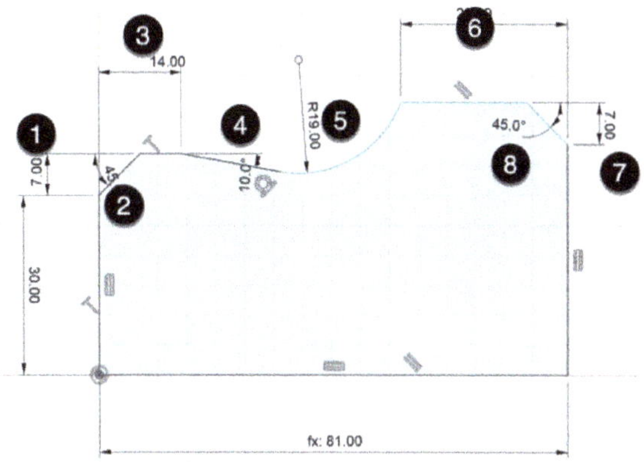

23. On the toolbar, click **Sketch > Create > Arc drop-down > Center Point Arc**.
24. Specify the centerpoint of the arc on the bottom horizontal line of the rectangle, as shown.
25. Move the pointer toward left and specify the start point of the arc on the bottom horizontal line of the rectangle.
26. Move pointer downward and click to specify the end point of the arc.
27. On the toolbar, click **Sketch > Create > Line**. Next, select the endpoint of the arc.
28. Move the pointer horizontally toward right up to a small distance and click.

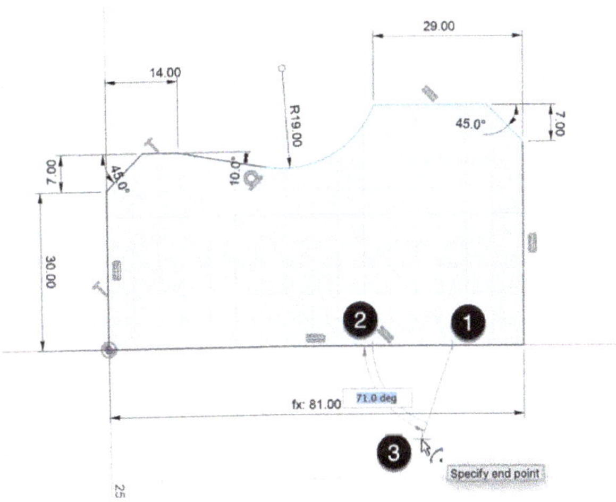

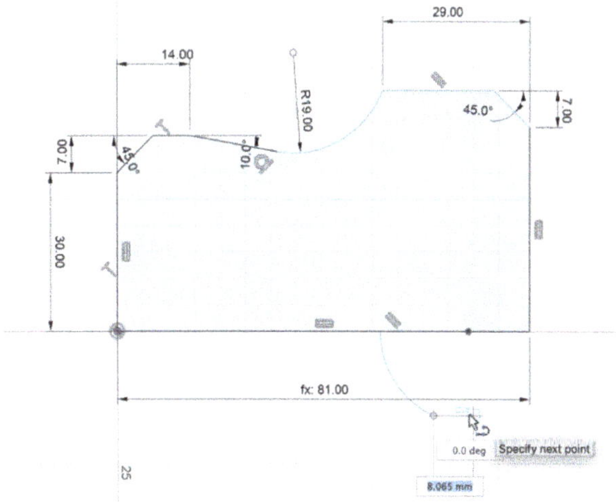

29. Move the pointer and click on the right vertical line to create an inclined line.
30. On the toolbar, click **Sketch > Modify > Trim**. Next, trim the portions of the rectangle, as shown.

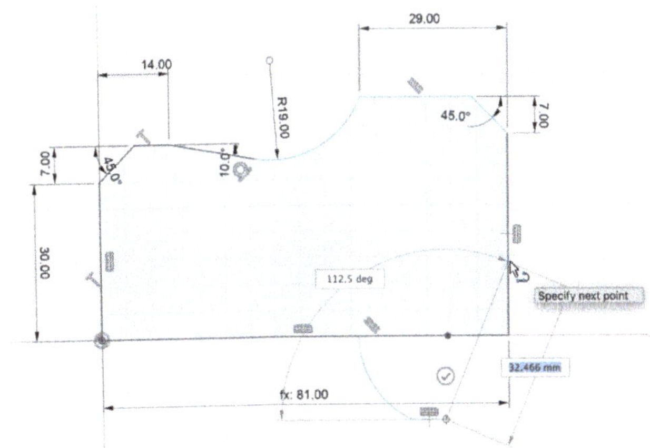

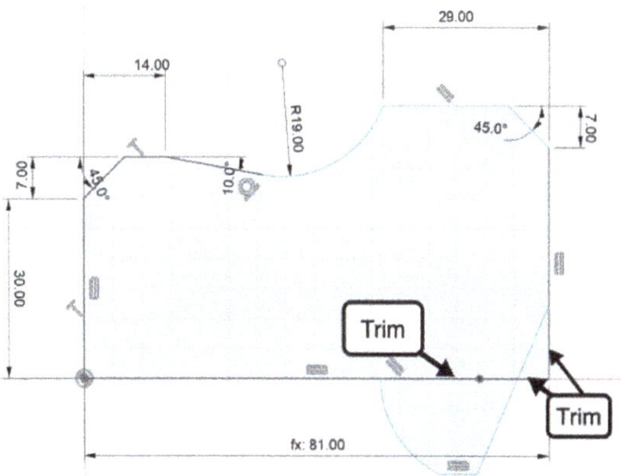

31. On the toolbar, click **Sketch > Modify > Fillet**. Next, select the vertex between the horizontal line and the arc.

32. Type **5** in the **Change Radius** box and press ENTER.
33. On the toolbar, click **Sketch > Create > Sketch Dimension**. Next, create dimensions in the sequence shown in figure below.
34. On the toolbar, click **Sketch > Constraints > Coincident**. Next, select the centerpoint of the arc and the inclined line, as shown.

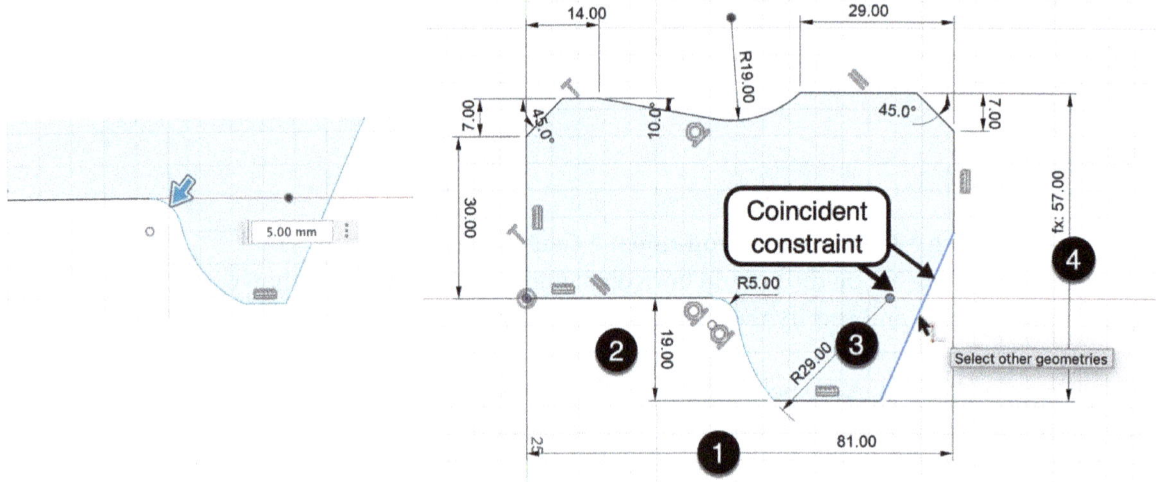

35. On the toolbar, click **Sketch > Create > Sketch Dimension**. Next, create dimensions in the sequence shown in figure below.

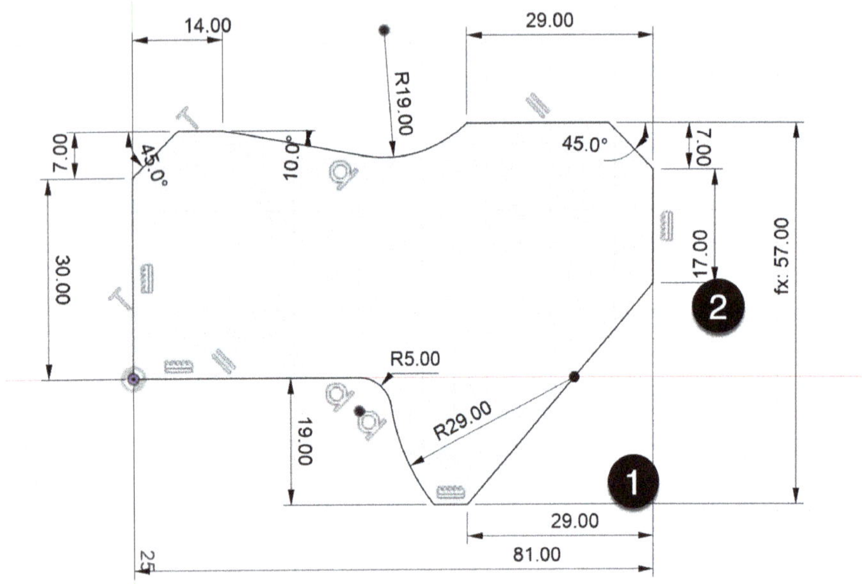

36. Click **Finish Sketch** on the Toolbar.

Extruding the Sketch

1. Click the **Create > Extrude** on the **Solid** tab of the toolbar. Next, select the sketch.
2. Select **Type > Extrude** on the **Extrude** dialog.
3. On the **Extrude** dialog, click the **Extent Type** drop-down and select **Distance**.
4. Type **C1** in the **Distance** box and select the C1 user parameter.
5. Click the **Direction** drop-down and select **Symmetric**.
6. Click the **Measurement > Whole Length** icon.

7. Click **OK** on the **Extrude** dialog to complete the *Extrude* feature.

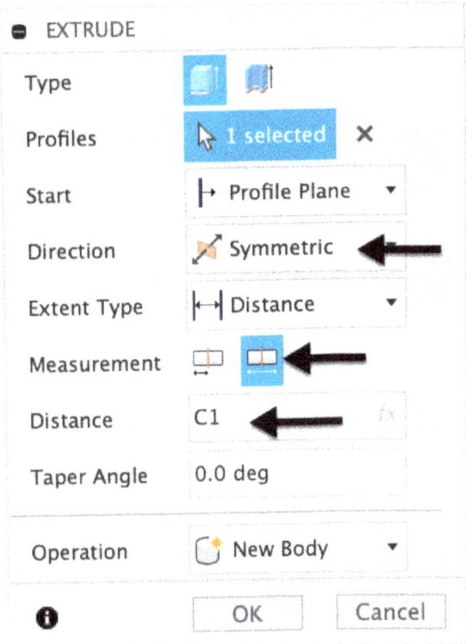

8. On the toolbar, click **Solid** tab > **Create** > **Create Sketch**.
9. Click on the front face of the model. Next, create a circle and add dimensions to it, as shown.

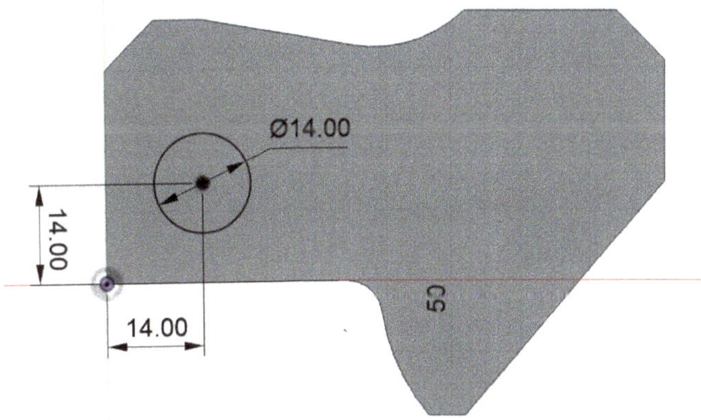

10. Click **Finish Sketch** on the toolbar.
11. Click the **Create** > **Extrude** on the **Solid** tab of the toolbar. Next, click in the region enclosed by the circle.
12. On the **Extrude** dialog, click the **Extent Type** drop-down and select **All**.
13. Click the **Flip** button and make sure that the **Cut** option is select from the **Operation** drop-down.
14. Click **OK**.

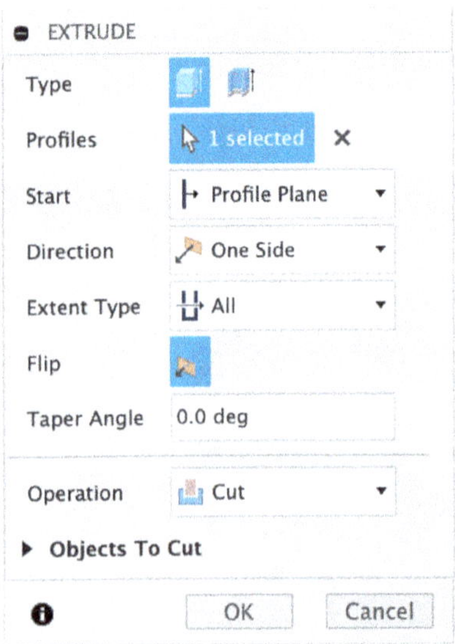

15. On the toolbar, click **Solid** tab > **Modify** > **Chamfer**.
16. Select **Type** > **Distance and Angle** from the **Chamfer** dialog.
17. Select the lower right edge of the model, as shown.
18. Type 7 and **45** in the **Distance** and **Angle** boxes, respectively. Click **OK** on the **Chamfer** dialog.

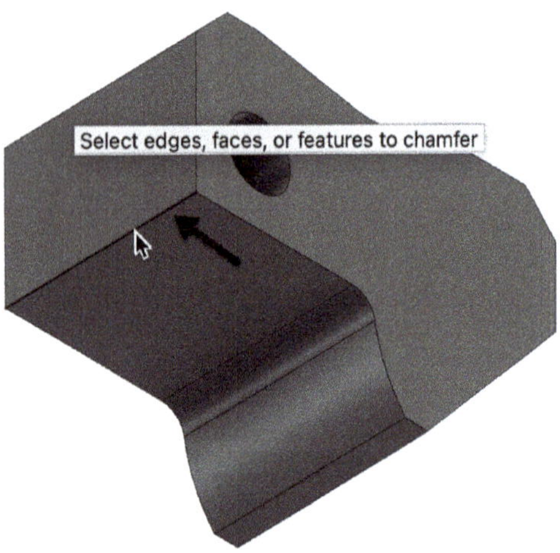

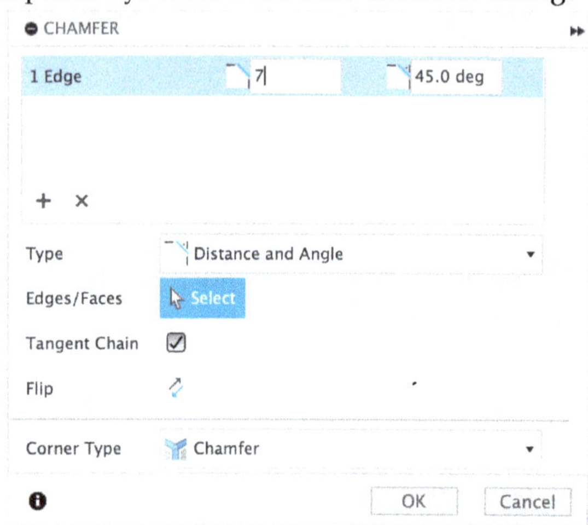

19. In the model Browser, right-click on the part name and select **Physical Material**.
20. On the **Physical Material** dialog, expand the **Metal** folder and select the **Aluminum** material. Next, press and hold left mouse button, drag it and release the **Aluminum** material into the **In This Design** section.

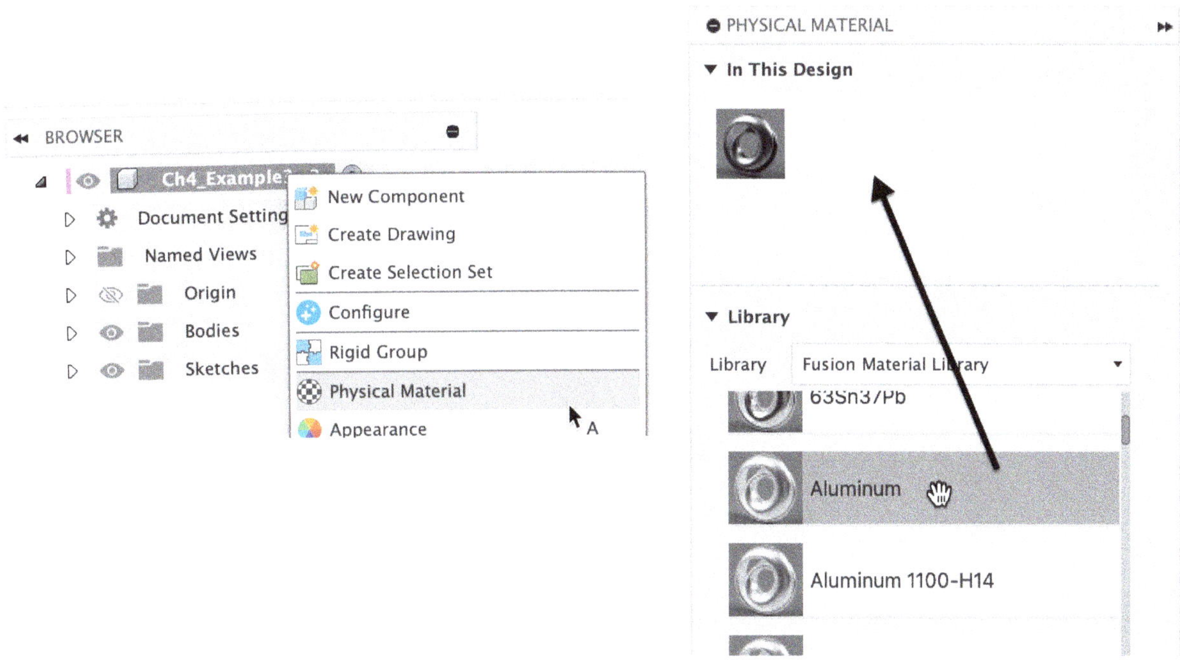

21. Click and drag the **Aluminum** material from the **In This Design** section, and then release it on the model.

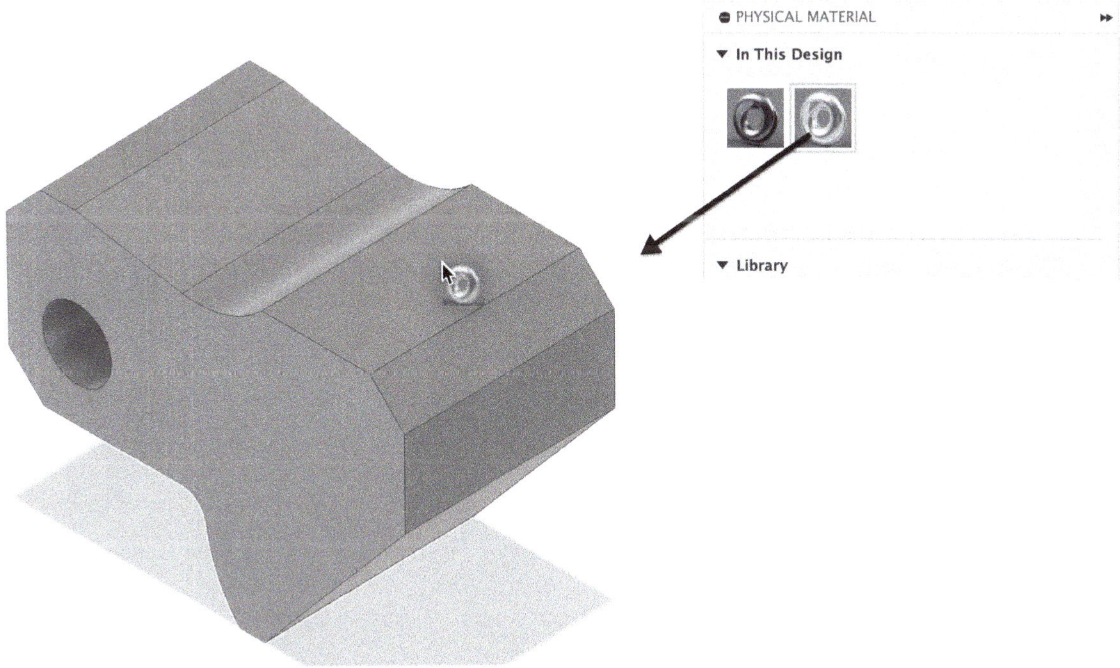

22. Click **Close** on the **Physical Material** dialog.
23. On the Model Browser, right-click on the part name and select **Properties**; on the **Properties** dialog, the **Mass** is displayed as **345.866 g**.

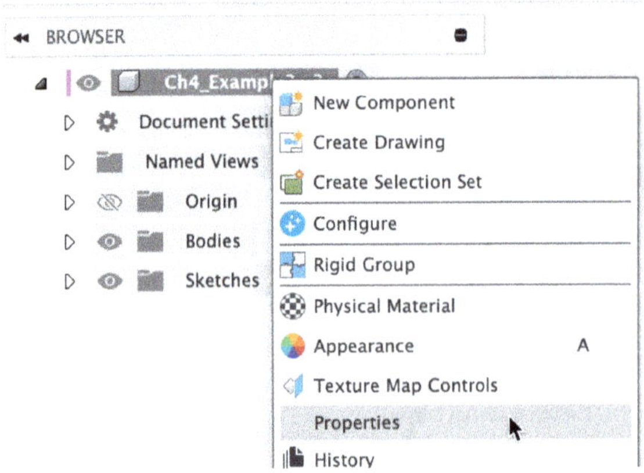

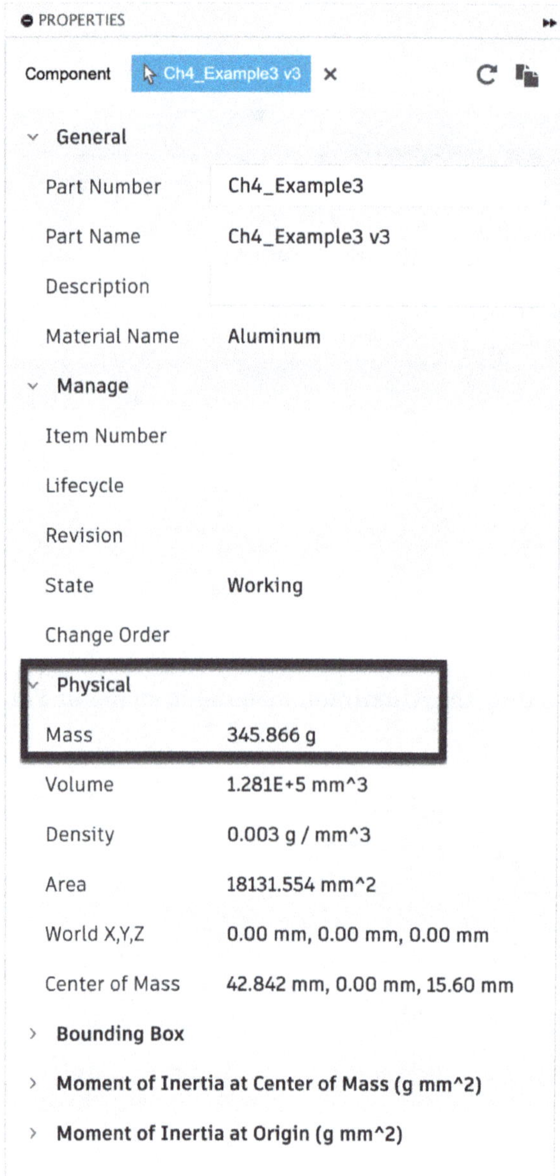

24. Close the **Properties** dialog.
25. Click **Save** on the Quick Access Toolbar.
26. Type **C4_Tutorial3** in the **Name** box and click **Save**.

Modifying the User Parameters

1. On the toolbar, click **Solid > Modify > Change Parameters**.
2. On the **Parameters** dialog, click in the **Expression** box of the **A1** user parameter. Next, type **84**.
3. Likewise, change the **B1** and **C1** values to **59** and **45** respectively.

PARAMETERS

Parameter	Name	Unit	Expression	Value
Favorites				
User Parameters				
User Parameter	A1	mm	84 mm	84.00
User Parameter	B1	mm	59 mm	59.00
User Parameter	C1	mm	45 mm	45.00

4. Click **OK**; the model is updated.

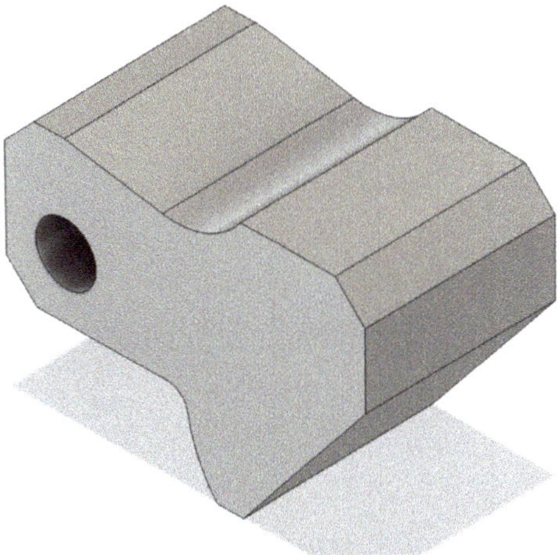

5. On the Model Browser, right-click on the part name and select **Properties**; on the **Properties** dialog, the **Mass** is displayed as **369.384 g**.
6. Close the **Properties** dialog.
7. Save the file.

Example 4

In this example, you will add some Extruded Cut features to the part file created in Example 3.

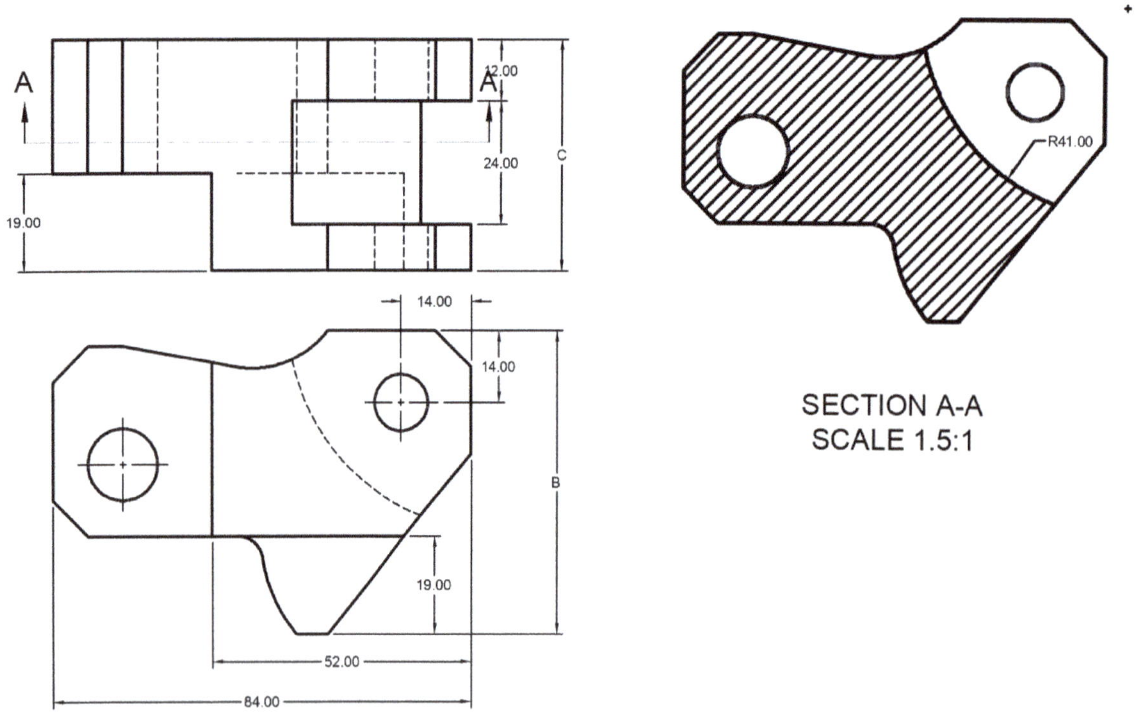

Creating the Extruded Cuts

1. On the toolbar, click **Solid** tab > **Create** > **Create Sketch**. Select the bottom face of the model, as shown.
2. On the toolbar, click **Sketch > Create > Project/Include > Project**. Select the top-right corner vertex of the model. Next, click **OK** on the **Project** dialog.

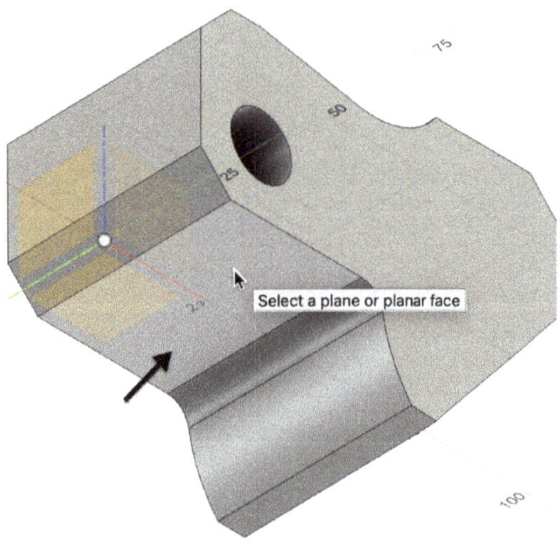

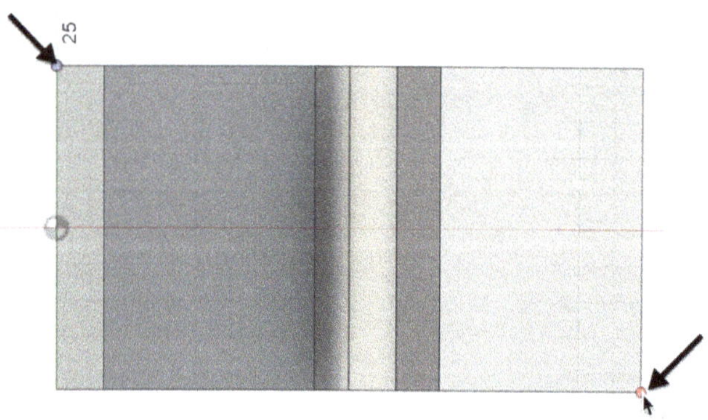

3. On the toolbar, click **Sketch > Create > 2-Point Rectangle**.
4. Select the top right corner vertex of the model. Move the pointer toward right and click.
5. Add dimensions to the rectangle using the **Smart Dimension** command, as shown.
6. Click **Finish Sketch** on the toolbar. Next, click the **Home** icon next to the ViewCube.
7. Click the **Create** > **Extrude** on the **Solid** tab of the toolbar. Next, click in the regions enclosed by the rectangle.

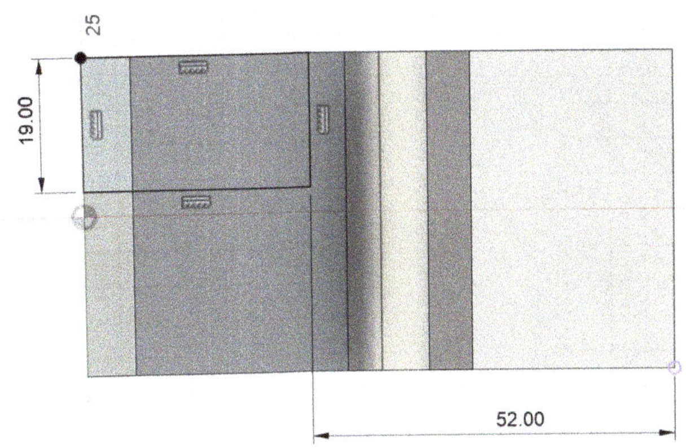

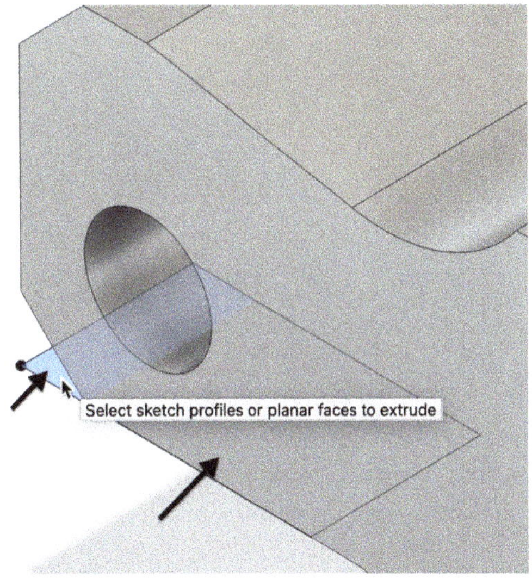

8. On the **Extrude** dialog, click the **Extent Type** drop-down and select **All**.
9. Click the **Flip** button and make sure that the **Cut** option is select from the **Operation** drop-down.

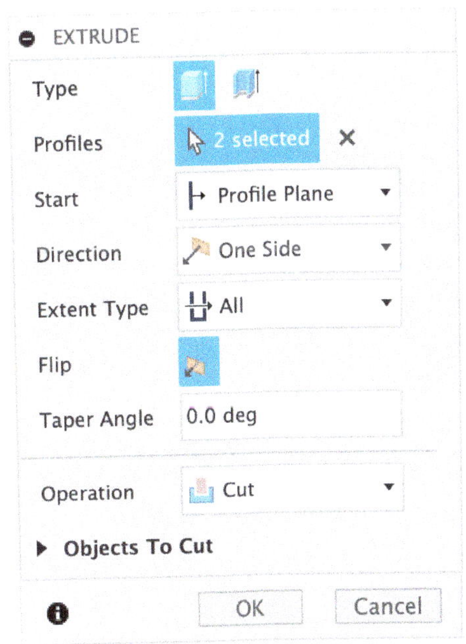

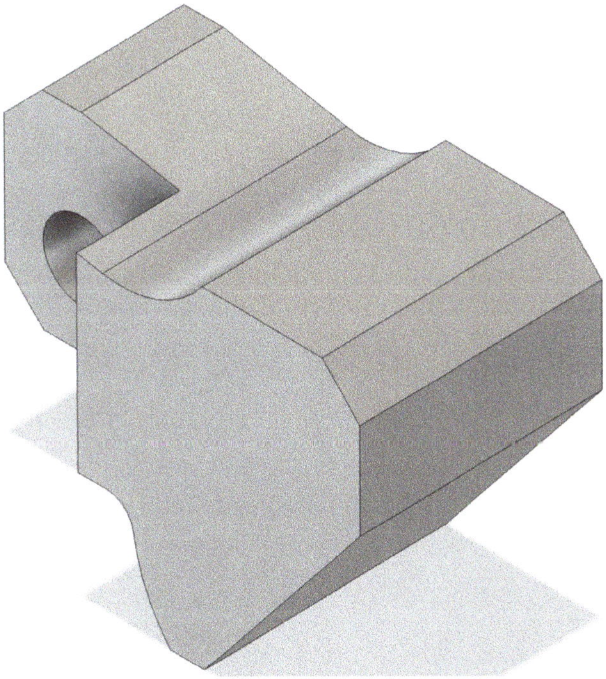

10. On the toolbar, click **Solid** tab > **Create** > **Create Sketch**. Select the vertical face of the model revealed after creating the extruded cut, as shown.

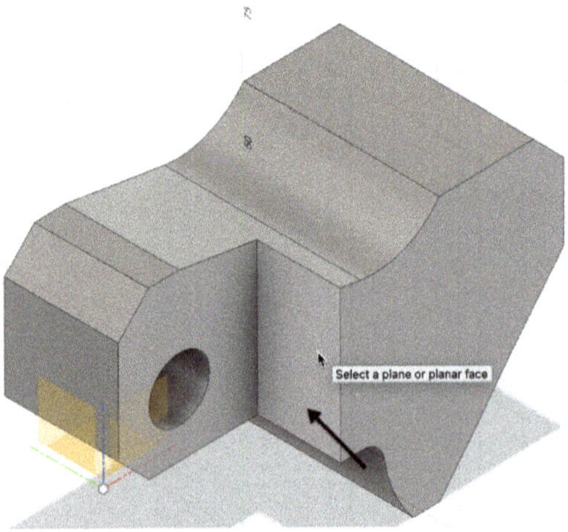

11. On the toolbar, click **Sketch > Create > Rectangle** drop-down **> 3-Point Rectangle**.
12. Select the two vertices, as shown. Next, move the pointer downward and click.

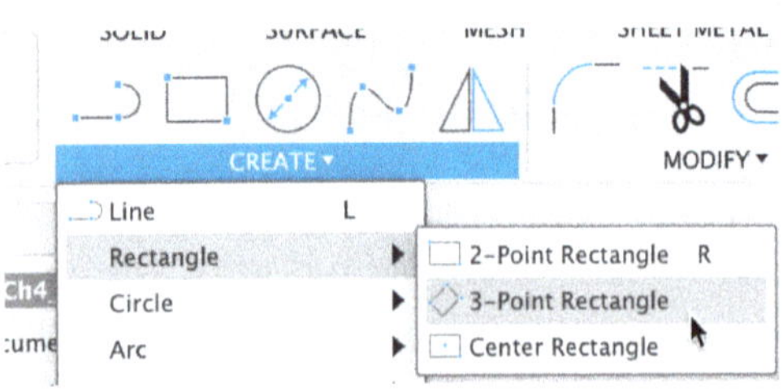

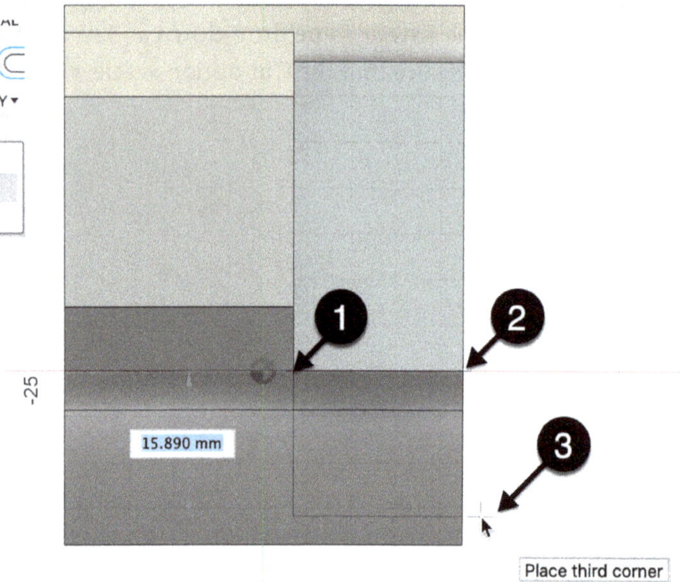

13. On the toolbar, click **Sketch > Constraints > Coincident**.
14. Select the bottom-right corner of the rectangle and the bottom-right vertex of the model, as shown.

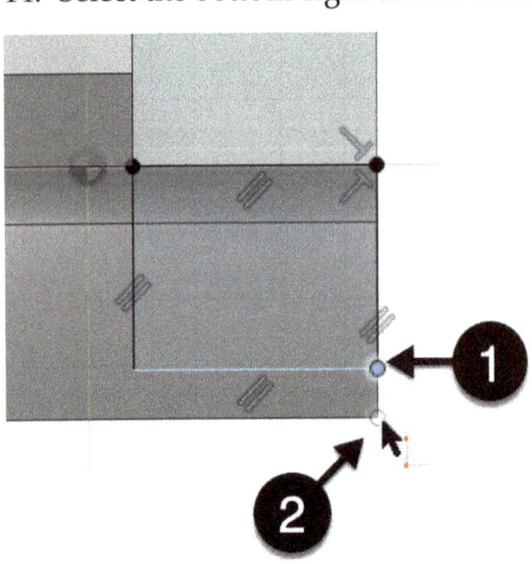

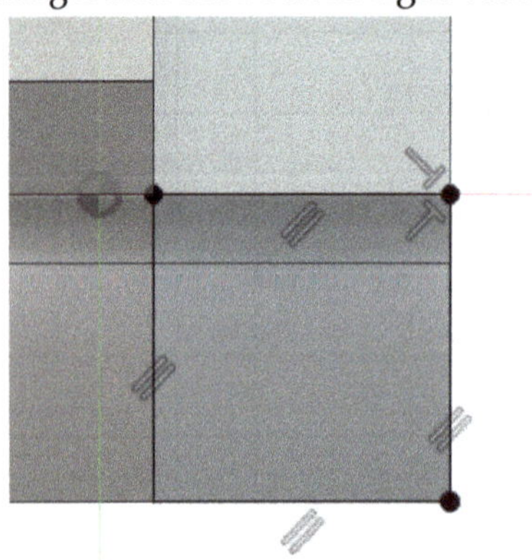

15. Click **Finish Sketch** on the toolbar.

16. On the toolbar, click **Solid > Create > Extrude**.
17. On the **Extrude** dialog, click the **Extent Type** drop-down and select **All**. Next, click **OK**.

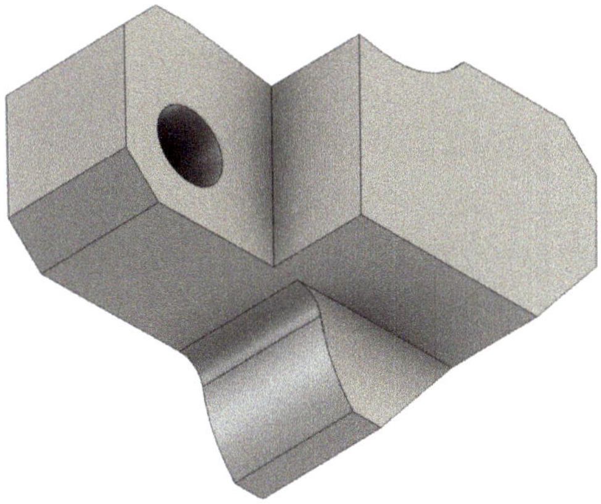

18. On the toolbar, click **Solid** tab > **Create** > **Create Sketch**. In the graphics window, rotate the model and select the back face of the model, as shown.

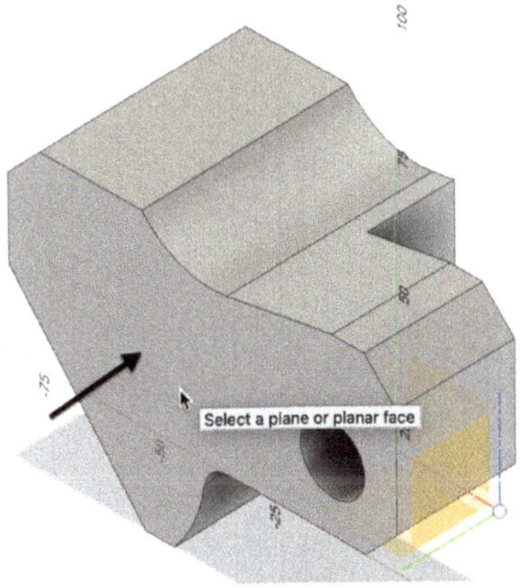

19. On the Toolbar, click **Arc** drop-down > **Center Point arc**.
20. Click on the region outside the model, close to the upper-right corner.
21. Move the pointer toward left and click on the curved edge in the top portion of the model.
22. Activate the **Line** tool and select the endpoint of the arc, as shown.
23. Move the pointer vertically upward and click. Move the pointer horizontally toward right and click
24. Move the pointer vertically downward and click. Move the pointer toward left and select the lower endpoint of the arc.

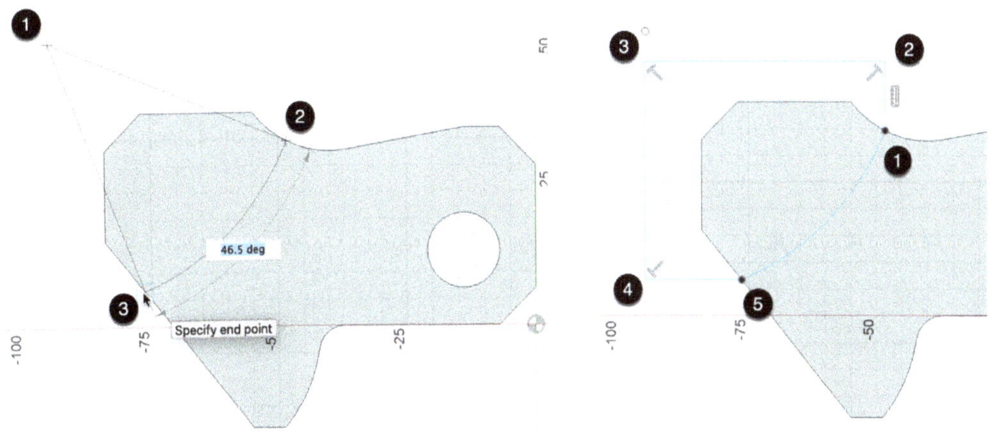

25. On the toolbar, click **Sketch > Constraints > Collinear**. Next, select the horizontal line and the top horizontal edge, as shown.
26. Select the right vertical line and the vertical edge.
27. Apply equal constraints between the two lines of the sketch. Add dimensions to sketch, as shown.

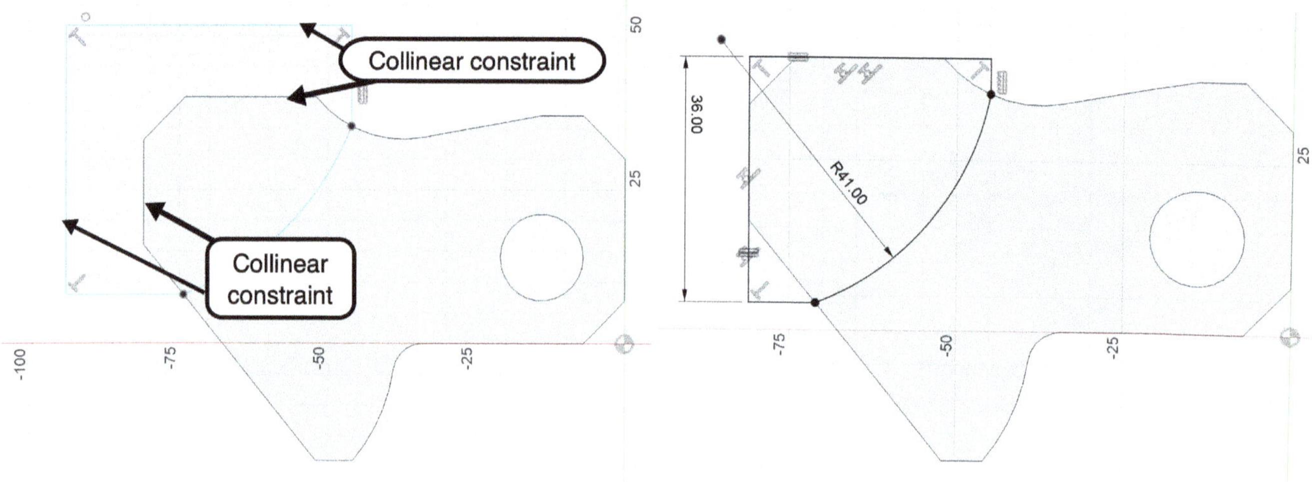

28. Click **Finish Sketch** on the Toolbar.
29. On the toolbar, click **Solid > Create > Extrude**. Next, select the regions enclosed by the sketch.

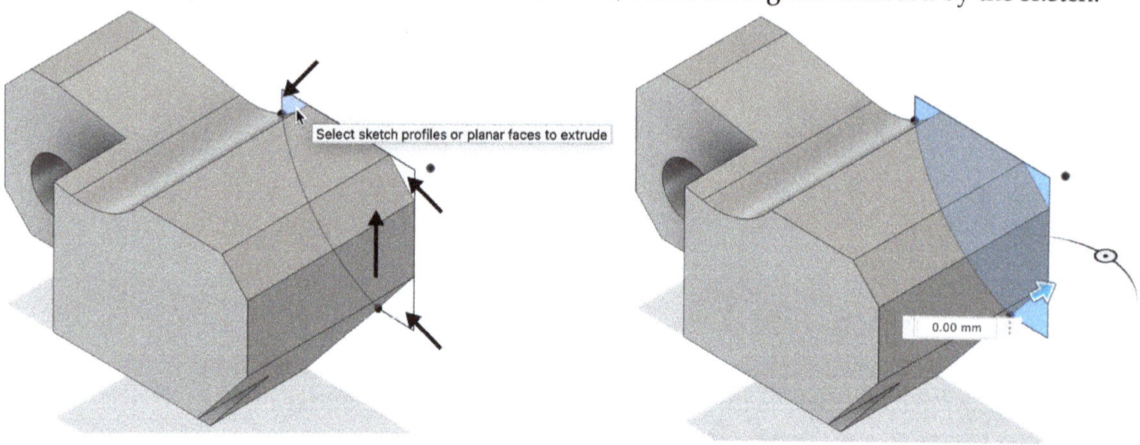

30. On the **Extrude** dialog, select **Offset** from the **Start** drop-down. Type **-12** in the **Offset** box.
31. Select **Distance** from the **Extent Type** drop-down. Type **-24** in the **Distance** box.
32. Select **Operation > Cut**. Click **OK**.

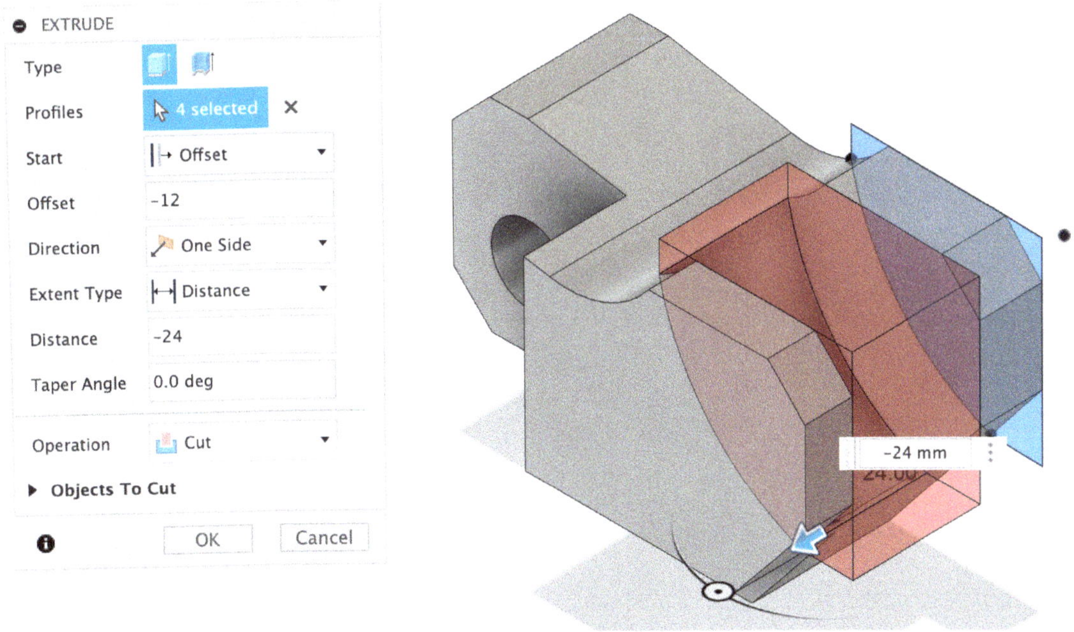

33. On the toolbar, click **Solid** tab > **Create** > **Create Sketch**.
34. Click on the front face of the model. Next, create a circle and add dimensions to it, as shown.

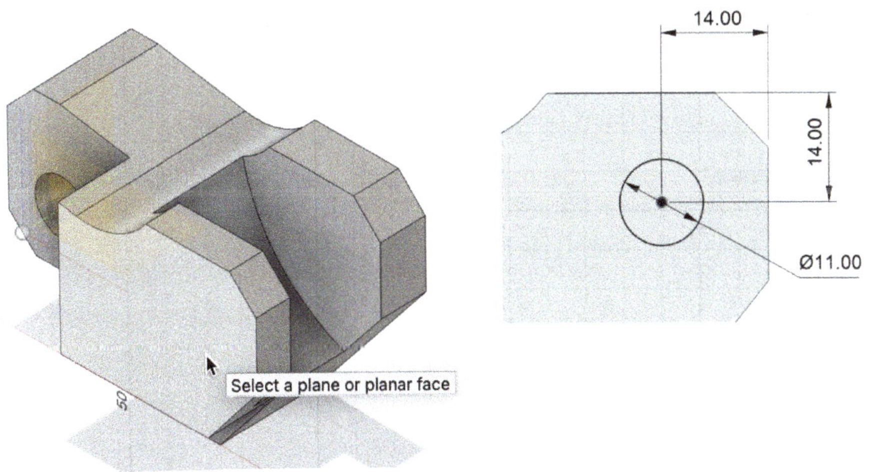

35. Click **Finish Sketch** on the toolbar.
36. Click the **Create** > **Extrude** on the **Solid** tab of the toolbar. Next, click in the region enclosed by the circle.
37. On the **Extrude** dialog, click the **Extent Type** drop-down and select **All**.
38. Click the **Flip** button and make sure that the **Cut** option is select from the **Operation** drop-down.
39. Click **OK**.

40. On the Model Browser, right-click on the part name and select **Properties**; on the **Properties** dialog, the **Mass** is displayed as **241.219 g**. Close the **Properties** dialog.

Example 5

In this example, you will add some Extruded Cut features to the part file created in Example 4.

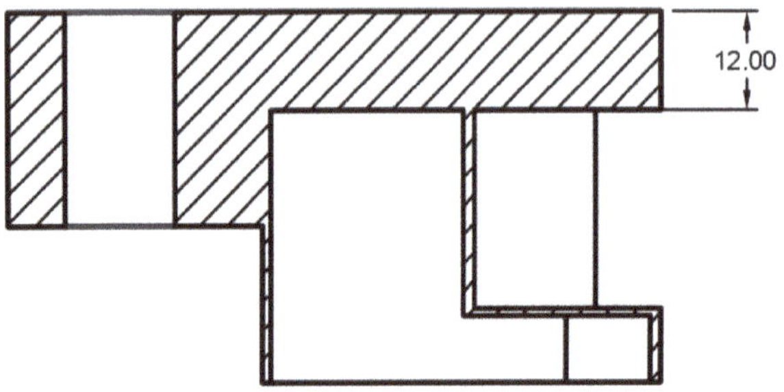

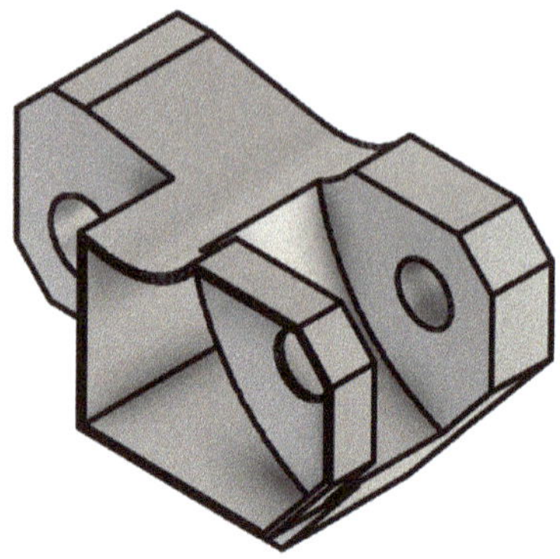

SECTION A-A
SCALE 1.3:1

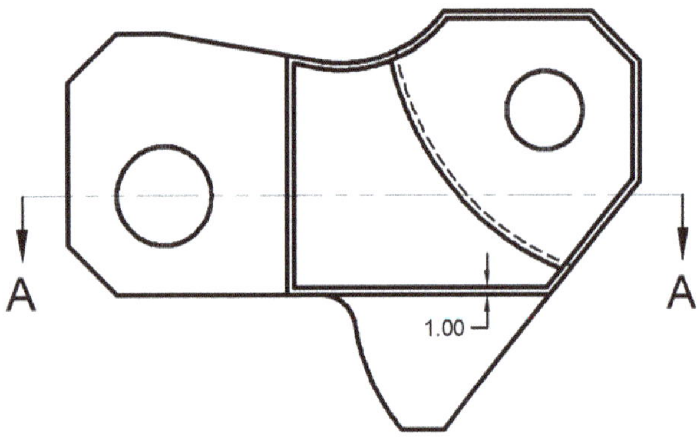

1. On the toolbar, click **Solid** tab > **Create** > **Create Sketch**. Click on the front face of the model.
2. On the toolbar, click **Sketch > Modify > Offset** . Make sure that the **Chain Selection** option is checked.
3. Select the edge chain of the face selected to start the sketch. Type **1** in the **Offset position** box.
4. Click the **Flip** button and click **OK**.

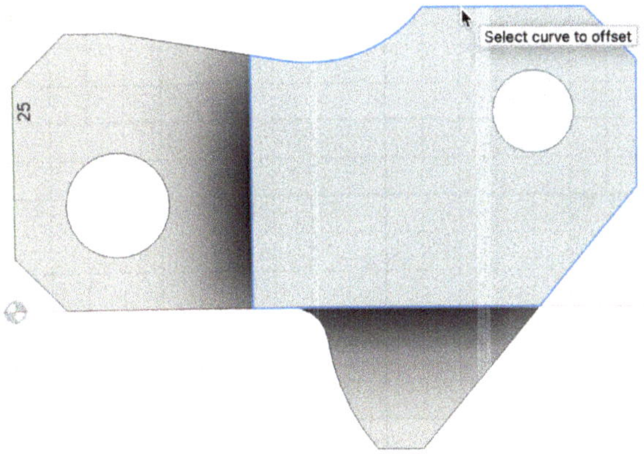

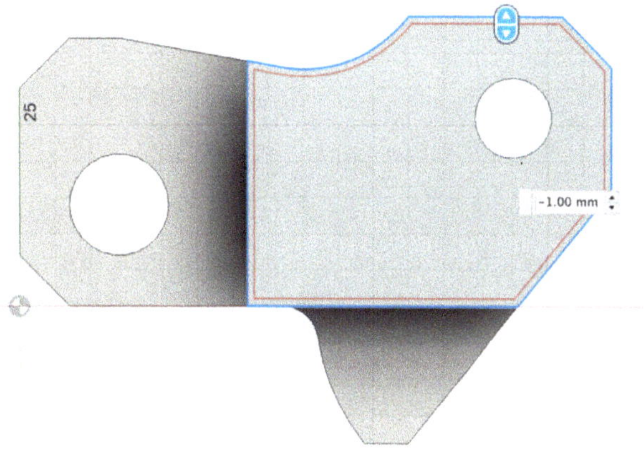

5. Click **Finish Sketch** on the toolbar.
6. Click the **Create** > **Extrude** on the **Solid** tab of the toolbar. Next, click in the region enclosed by the sketch.
7. On the **Extrude** dialog, click the **Start** drop-down and select **Object**.
8. Rotate the model and select the inner face of the extruded cut feature, as shown.
9. Type **-1** in **Offset Distance** box. Next, select **Extent Type > All**.
10. Select **Operation > Cut** and click **OK**.

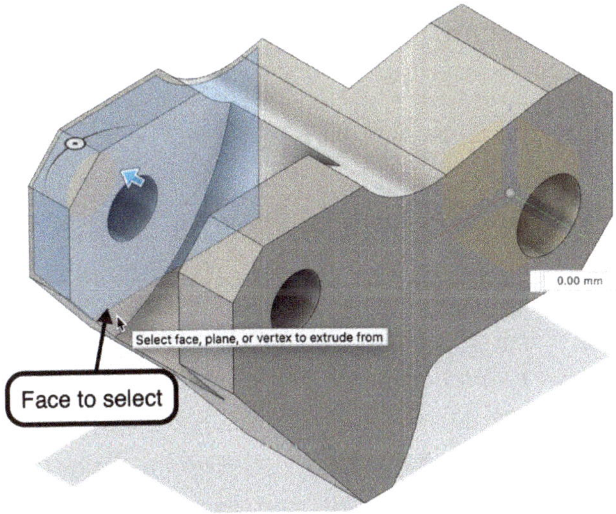

11. On the toolbar, click **Solid** tab > **Create** > **Create Sketch**.
12. Click on the face revealed after creating the previous extruded cut feature.
13. On the Toolbar, click **Sketch > Create > Project/Include > Project**.
14. Select the edges of the model, as shown.

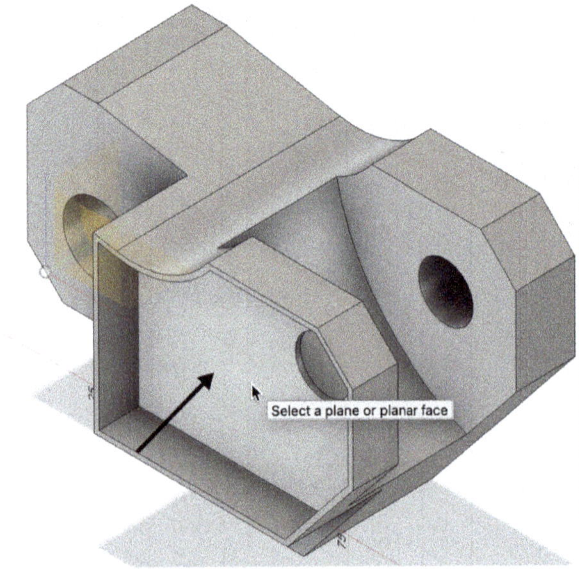

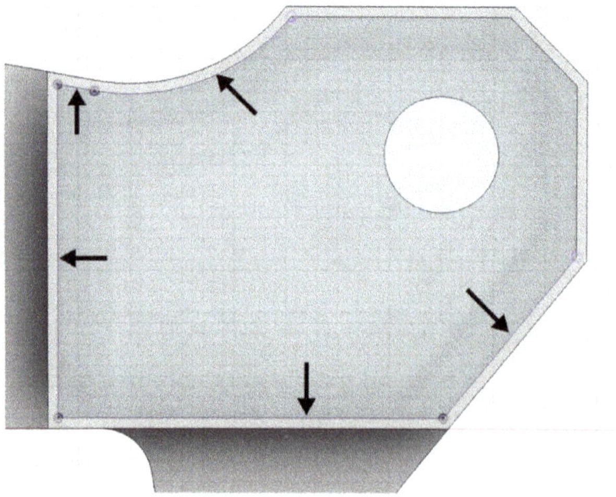

15. Click **OK** on the **Project** dialog.
16. On the **View** toolbar, click **Display Settings > Visual Style > Wireframe**.
17. On the Toolbar, click **Sketch > Create > Arc** drop-down **> 3-Point Arc**.
18. Click on the curved edge to specify the first point of the arc.
19. Click on the inclined edge to specify the second point of the arc.
20. Move the pointer and click to specify the third point of the arc.

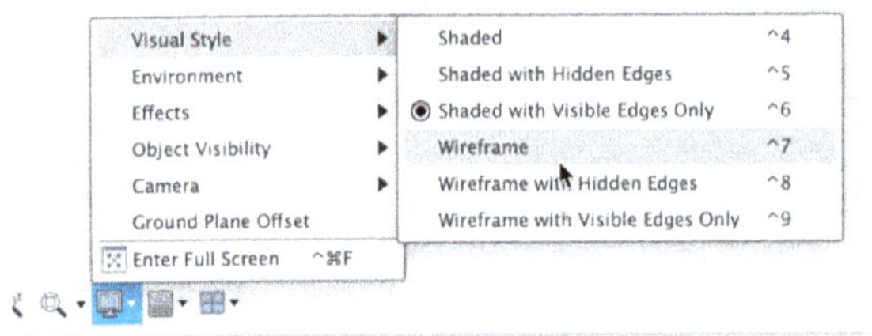

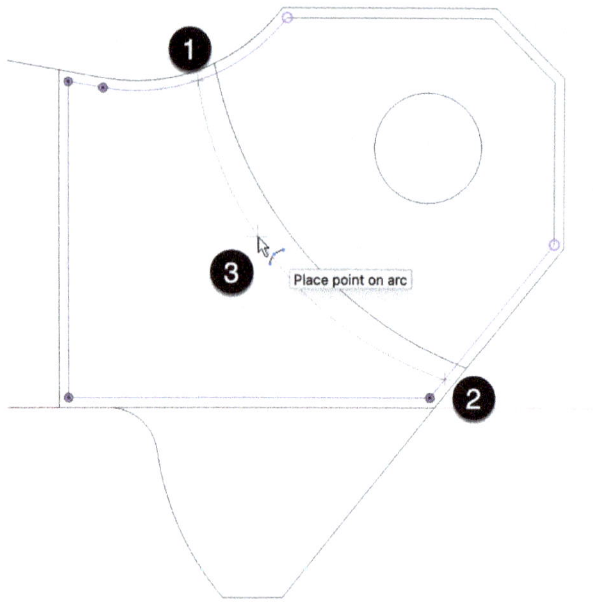

21. On the toolbar, click **Sketch > Constraints > Concentric**. Next, select the arc and the curved edge.
22. On the toolbar, click **Sketch > Create > Sketch Dimension**. Next, select the arc and the curved edge. Next, move the pointer and click to place the dimension.
23. Type **1** in the **Dimension Value** box and press ENTER.

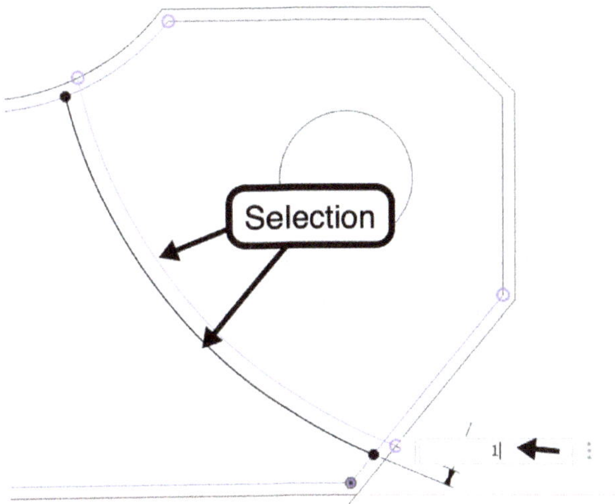

24. Click **Finish Sketch** on the Toolbar.
25. On the **View** toolbar, select **Display Settings > Visual Style > Shaded with Visible Edges Only**.
26. On the toolbar, click **Solid > Create > Extrude**. Next, click in the region enclosed by the sketch.
27. On the **Extrude** dialog, select **To Object** from the **Extent Type** drop-down.
28. Rotate the model and select the back face of the model, as shown.

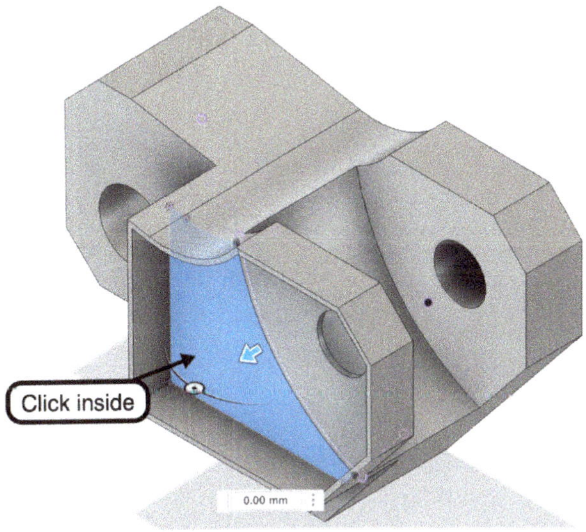

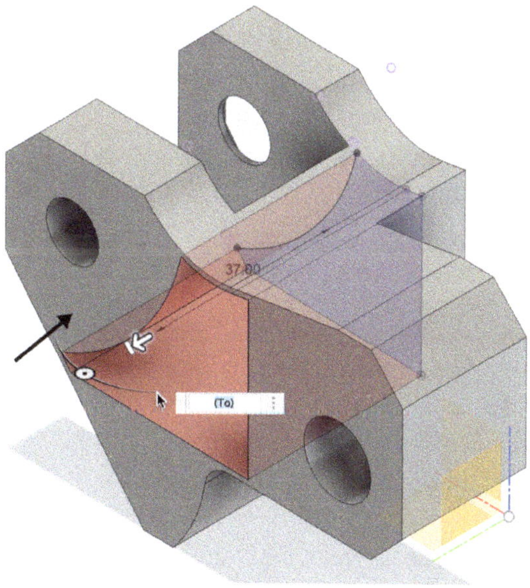

29. Type **-12** in **Offset** box and click **OK**.

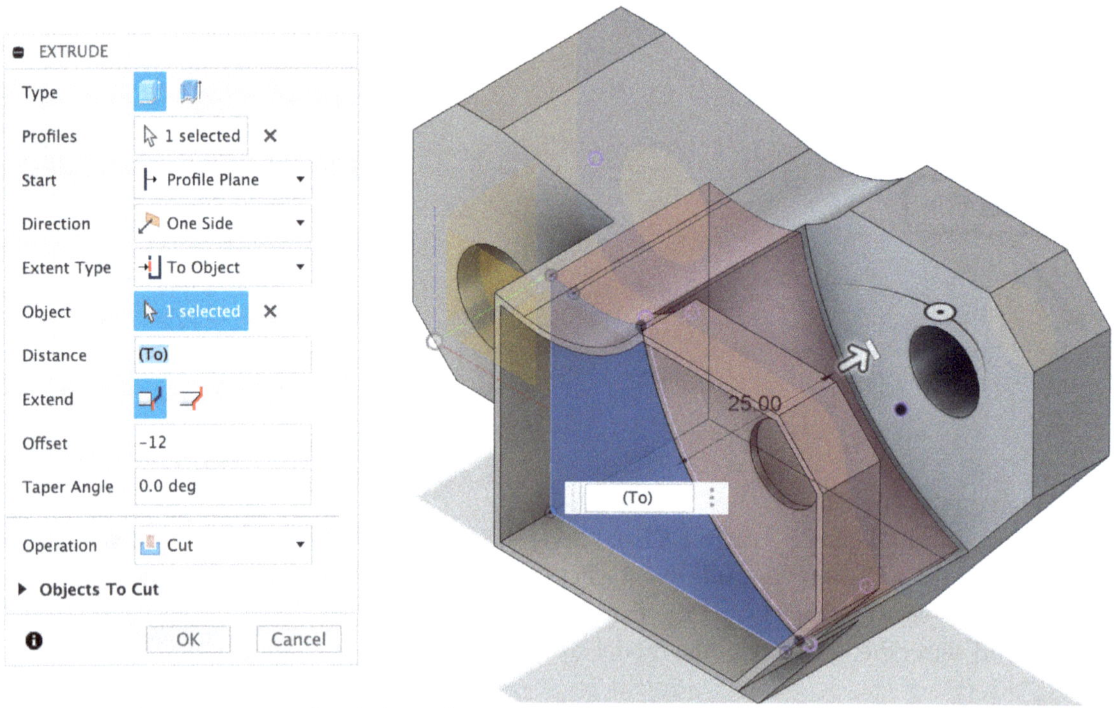

30. On the Model Browser, right-click on the part name and select **Properties**; on the **Properties** dialog, the **Mass** is displayed as **156.029 g**.
31. Close the **Properties** dialog.
32. Save and close the file as C4_Example_5.

Questions

1. What are the placed features?
2. How to create a counterbored hole?
3. Which option allows you to create chamfer with unequal distances?
4. Which option allows you to create a variable radius fillet?
5. How to create an external thread?
6. How to specify the **Curvature (G2)** continuity?
7. What is the difference between the **One Side** and **Two Sides** option in the **Draft** command?
8. What is the difference between the Countersink and Counterbored Holes?

Exercises

Exercise 1 (Inches)

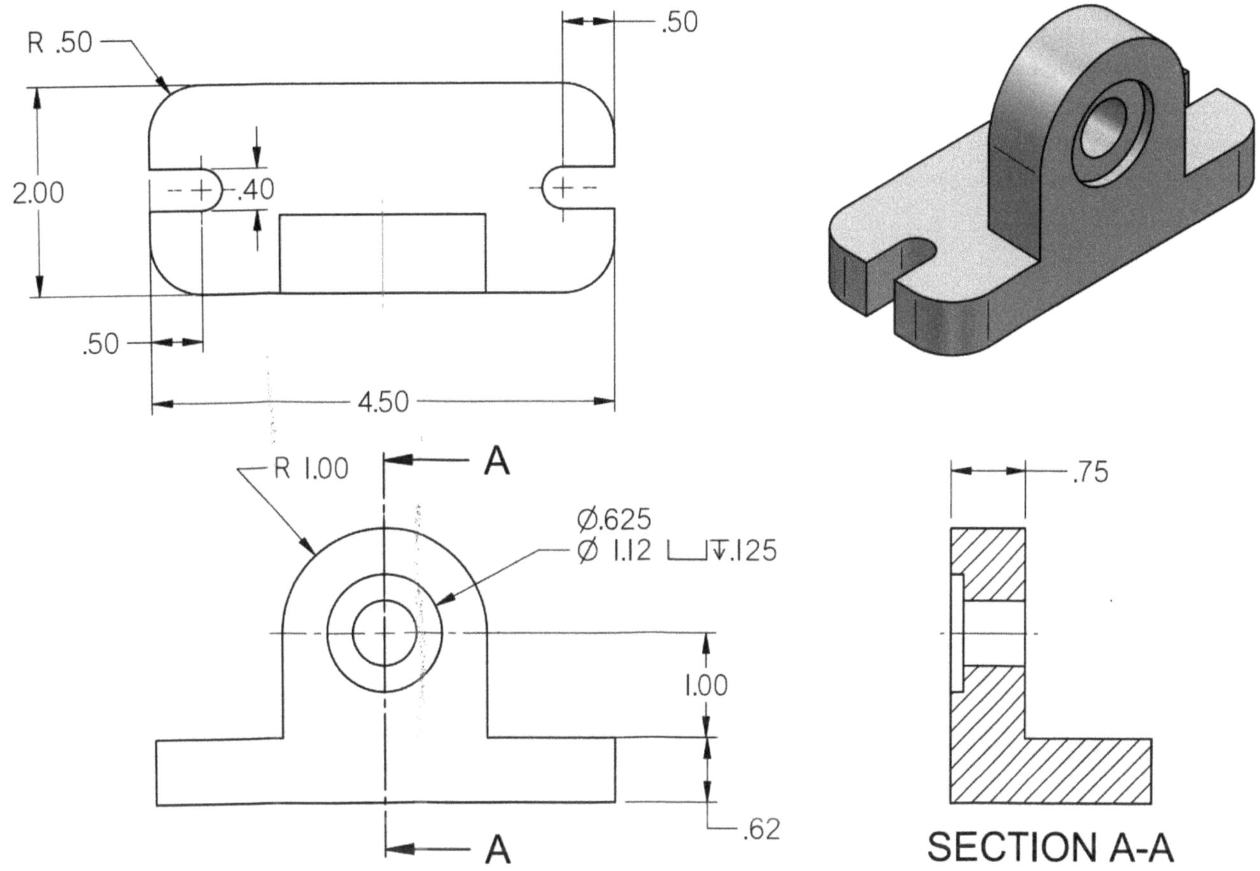

Chapter 5: Patterned Geometry

When designing a part geometry, most of the time, there are elements of symmetry in each part, or there are at least a few features that are repeated multiple times. In these situations, Autodesk Fusion 360 offers some commands that save you time. For example, you can use mirror features to design symmetric parts, which makes designing the part quicker. This is because you only have to design a portion of the part and use the mirror feature to create the remaining geometry.

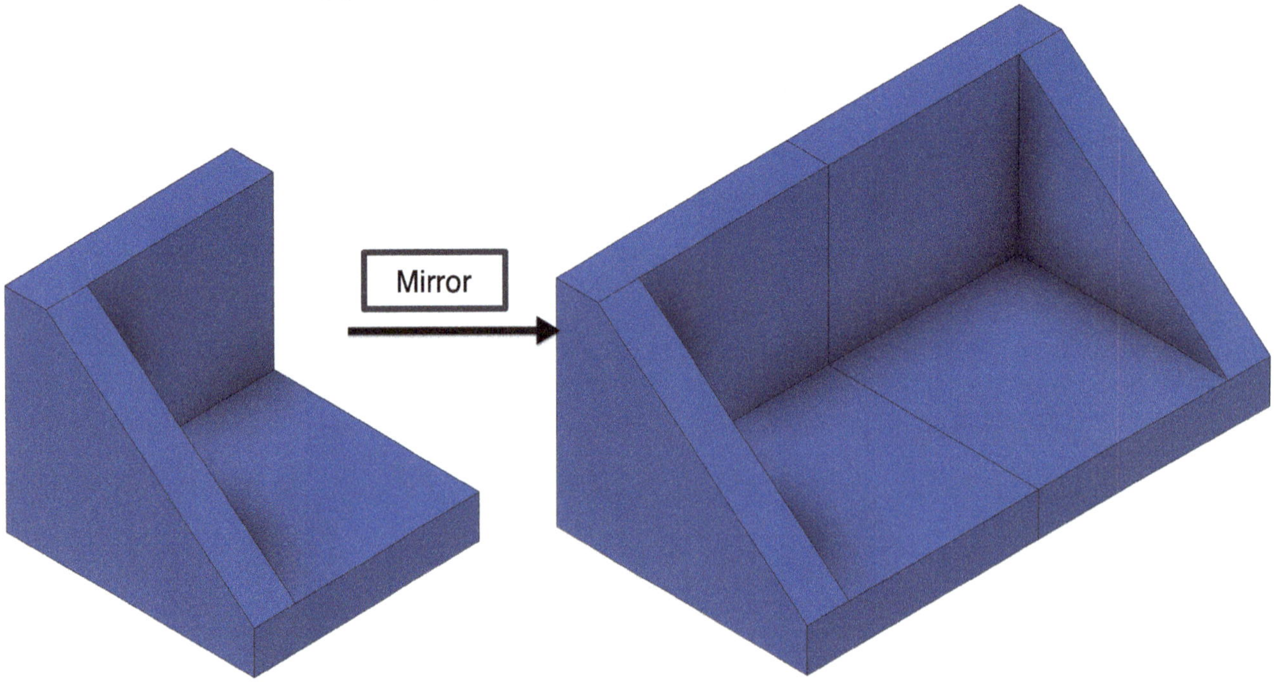

In addition, there are some pattern commands to replicate a feature throughout a part quickly. They save you time from creating additional features individually and help you modify the design easily. If the design changes, you only need to change the first feature; the rest of the pattern features will update automatically. In this chapter, you will learn to create mirrored and pattern geometries using the commands available in Fusion.

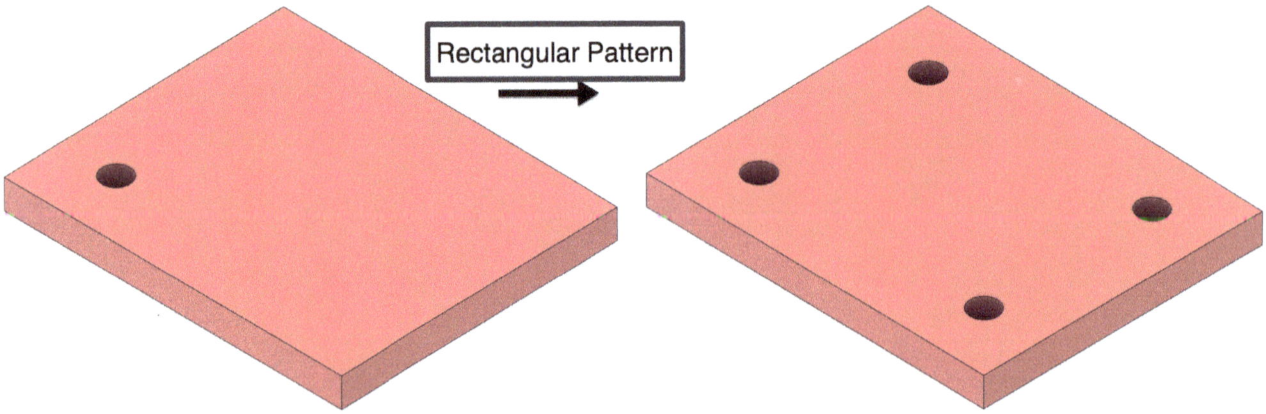

The topics covered in this chapter are:

- *Mirror* features
- *Rectangular Patterns*
- *Circular Patterns*
- *Pattern on Path*

Mirror

If you are designing a part that is symmetric, you can save time by using the **Mirror** command. Using this command, you can replicate the individual features of the entire body. To mirror features (3D geometry), you need to have a face or plane to use as a reference. You can use a model face, default plane, or create a new plane if it does not exist where it is needed.

Mirror Features

Activate the **Mirror** command (click **Create** panel > **Mirror** on the **Solid** tab of the toolbar). On the **Mirror** dialog, select **Type > Features** and select the features to mirror the model geometry or timeline. Next, click on the **Mirror Plane** selection button and select the reference plane about which the features are to be mirrored. Click **OK** to mirror the selected features.

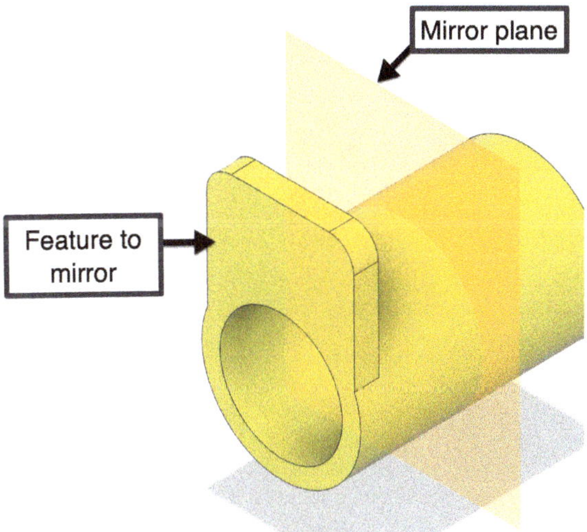

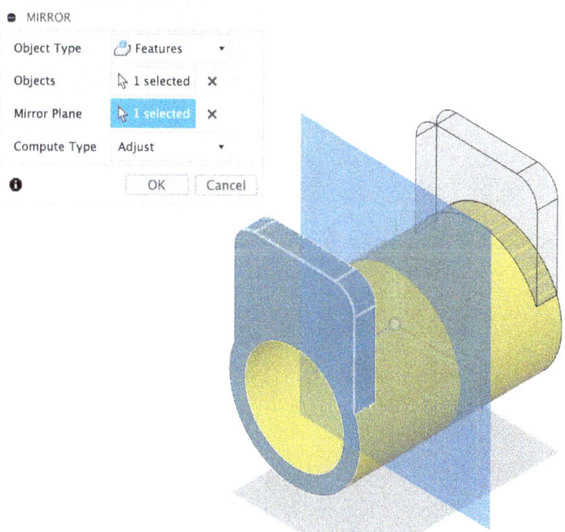

Now, if you make changes to the original feature, the mirrored feature will be updated automatically.

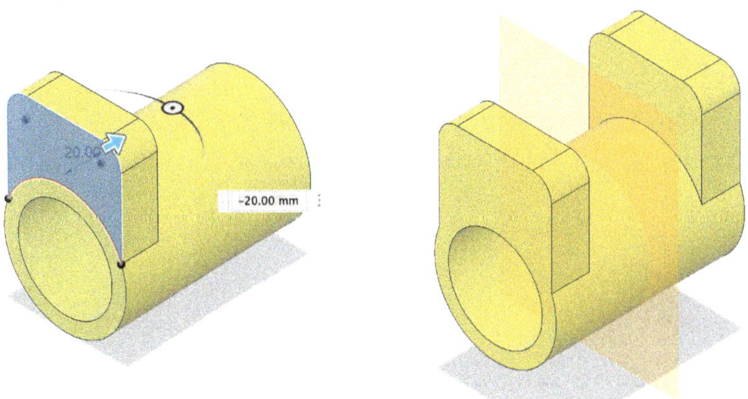

Mirror Bodies

If the part you are creating is entirely symmetric, you can save more time by creating half of it and mirroring the entire geometry rather than individual features. Activate the **Mirror** command (On the **Solid** tab of the toolbar, click **Create** panel **> Mirror**) and select **Type > Bodies** from the **Mirror** dialog. Select the solid body from the model geometry. On the **Mirror** dialog, click the **Mirror Plane** selection button and select the face about which the geometry is to be mirrored. Next, select **Operation > Join** to merge the mirrored body with the original. Click **OK** to complete the mirror geometry.

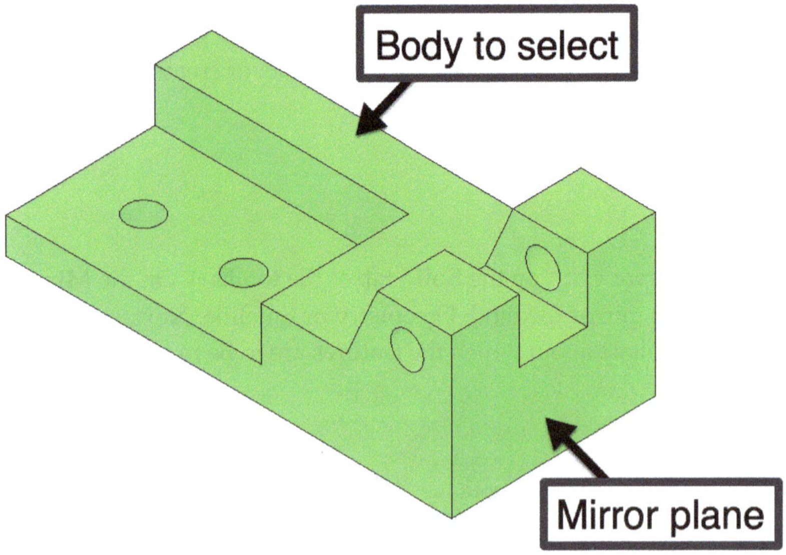

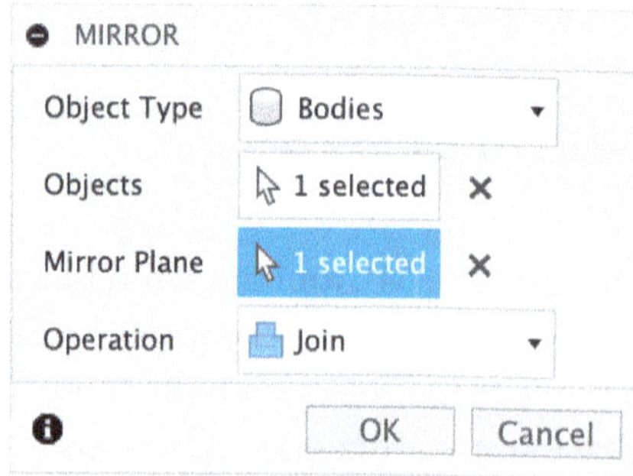

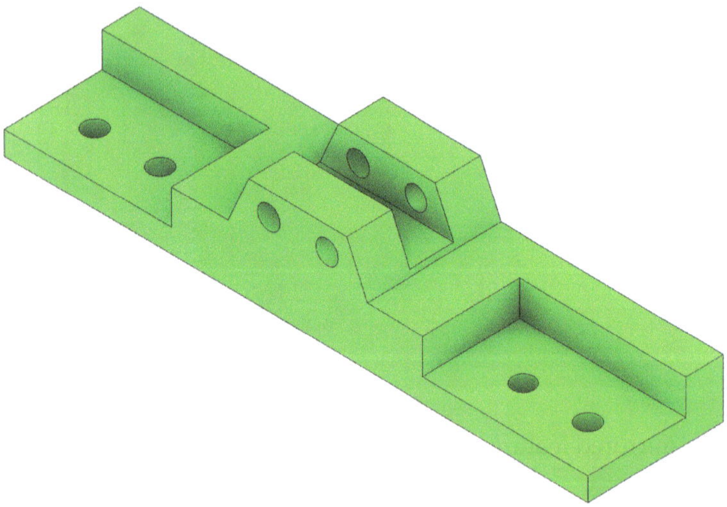

Create Patterns

Autodesk Fusion 360 allows you to replicate a feature using the pattern commands: **Rectangular Pattern**, **Circular Pattern**, and **Pattern on Path**. The following sections explain the different patterns that can be created using the three pattern commands.

Rectangular Pattern

To create a pattern in a rectangular fashion, you must first activate the **Rectangular Pattern** command (On the **Solid** tab of the toolbar, click **Create** panel **> Pattern > Rectangular Pattern**). On the **Rectangular Pattern** dialog, click **Type > Rectangular Pattern**. Next, select **Object Type > Features**, and then select the feature to pattern from the model geometry. Click the **Axes** selection button and select an edge or axis to define the first axis of the pattern.

Next, select an option from the **Distribution** drop-down (**Extent** or **Spacing**). Select **Extent** from the **Distribution** drop-down, and then type-in values in the **Quantity** and **Distance** boxes available in the **Axis 1** section; the value entered in the **Distance** box defines the total length of the pattern. If you select the **Spacing** option from the **Distribution** drop-down, the value entered in the **Distance** box defines the spacing between the pattern occurrences.

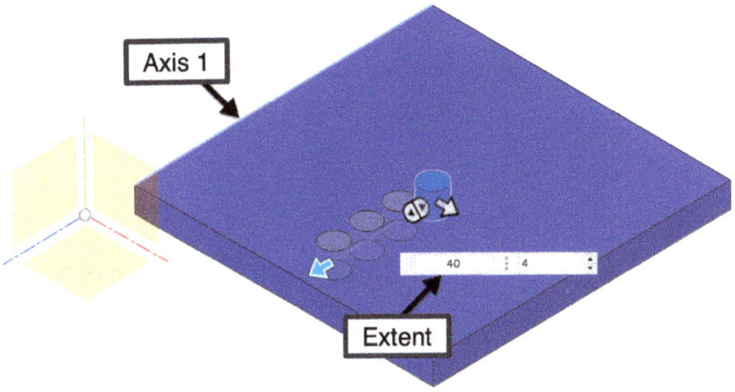

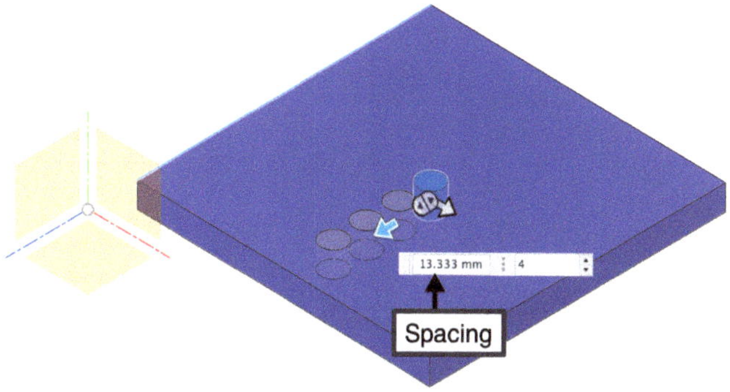

Next, select an option from the **Direction** drop-down (**One Direction** or **Symmetric**). The **One Direction** option creates the pattern on one side of the source feature. The **Symmetric** option places the occurrences equally on both sides of the source feature.

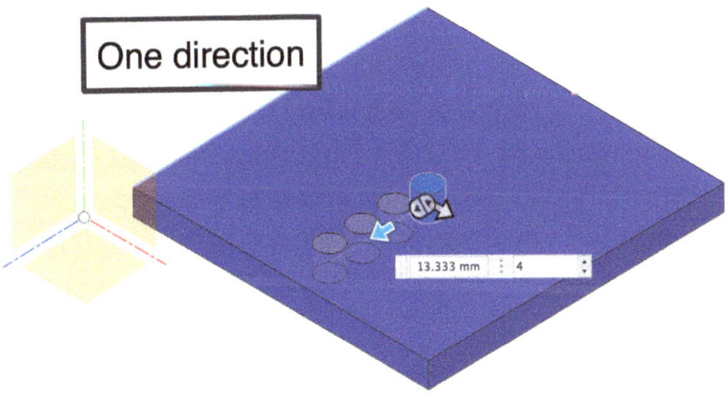

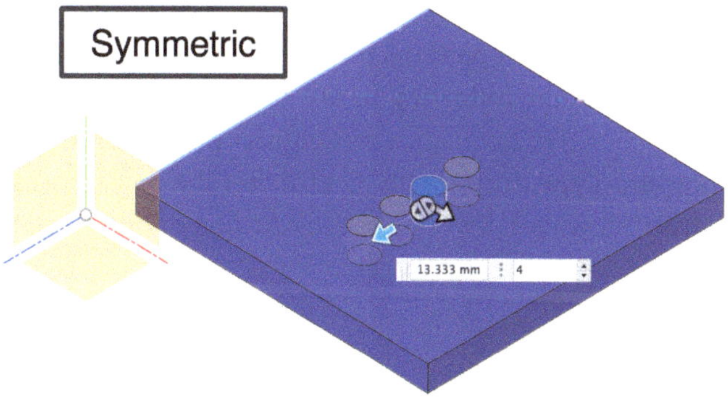

Enter values in the **Quantity** and **Distance** boxes available in the **Axis 2** section; the quantity and distance along the second direction are defined. Also, specify the **Direction Type** in the second direction. Next, click **OK** to complete the pattern.

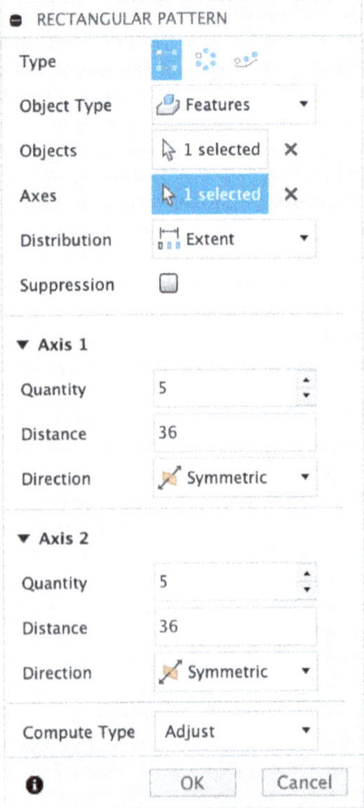

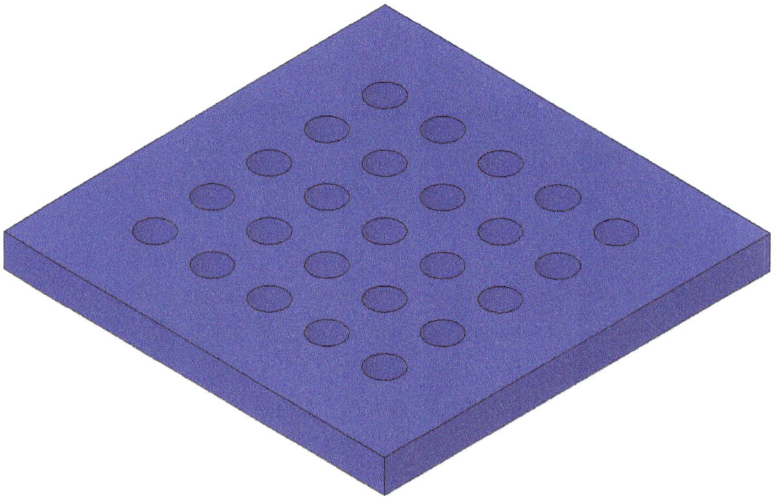

Using the Compute options

The **Compute Type** drop-down has three options: **Optimized**, **Identical**, and **Adjust**.

The **Optimized** option is used to create a pattern with a high number of occurrences.

The **Identical** option creates the exact copies of the feature.

The **Adjust** option patterns the selected feature by calculating the extents of individual instances. For example, the following figure shows an Extruded feature which is created by extruding a circle up to the curved face. Try to create a rectangular pattern of the extruded feature with the **Identical** option selected from the **Compute Type** drop-down. Notice that the occurrences of the rectangular pattern are identical to the original feature. However, if you select the **Adjust** option from the **Compute Type** drop-down, the occurrences will be extruded up to the curved face.

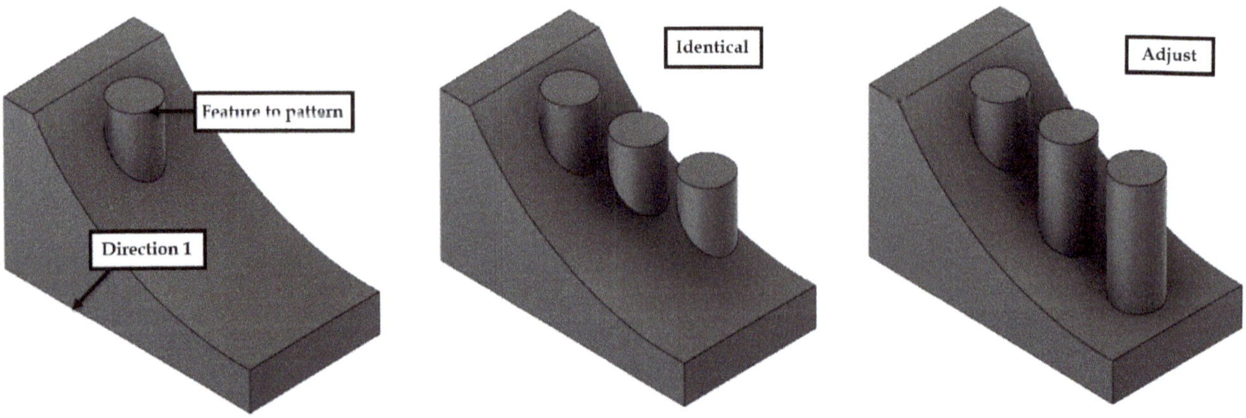

Suppressing Occurrences

If you want to suppress an occurrence of the pattern, then click the right mouse button on the **Rectangular Pattern** feature on the **Timeline** and then select **Edit Feature** from the list. Check the **Suppression** option on the dialog. Next, uncheck the checkboxes available on the occurrences. Click **OK** on the **Edit Feature** dialog.

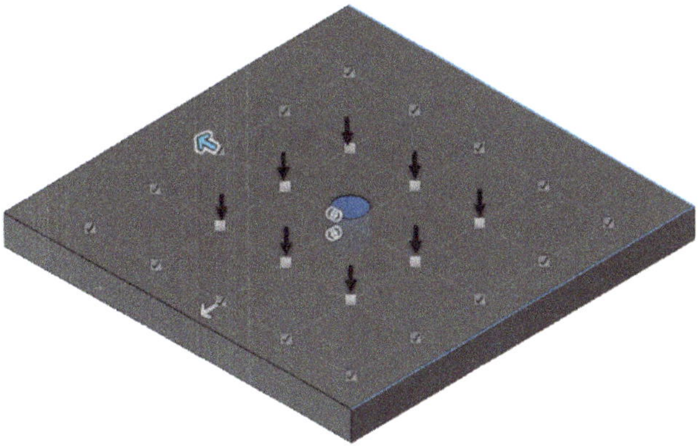

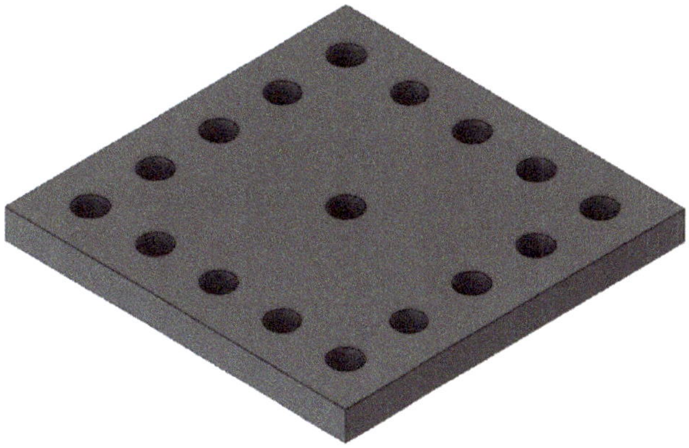

Patterning the entire geometry

The **Bodies** option allows you to pattern the entire part geometry. Activate the **Rectangular Pattern** command and select the **Bodies** option from the **Object Type** drop-down. Next, select the body from the graphics window, and then define the axes, quantity, and distance.

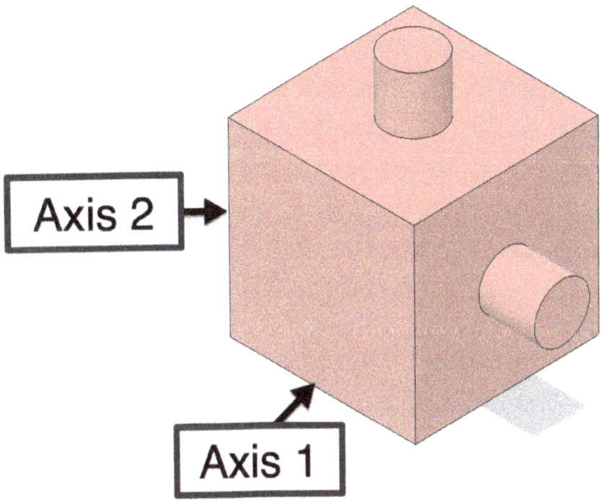

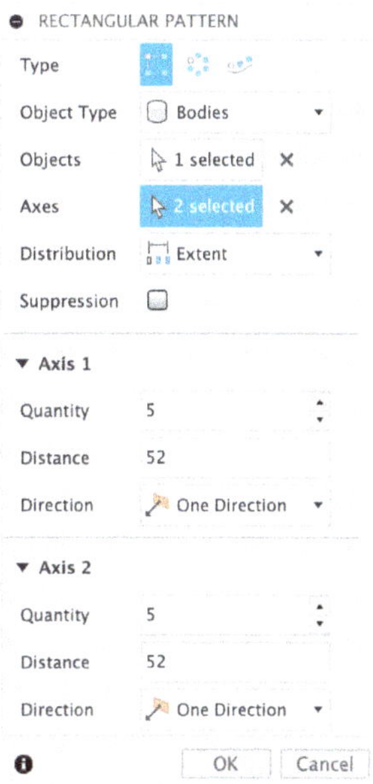

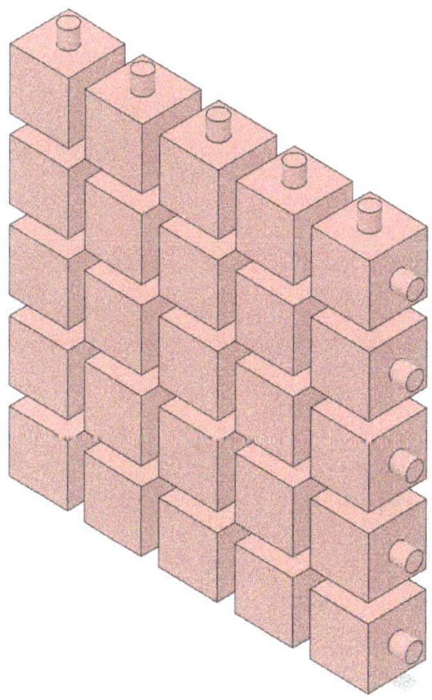

Pattern on Path

You can create a pattern along a selected curve or edge using the **Pattern on Path** command. Activate the **Pattern on Path** command (click **Create** panel > **Pattern > Pattern on Path** on the **Solid** tab of the toolbar) and click **Type > Pattern on Path** icon. On the **Pattern on Path** dialog, click **Object Type > Features** and select the feature to pattern. Click the **Path** selection button and select a curve, edge, or sketched path.

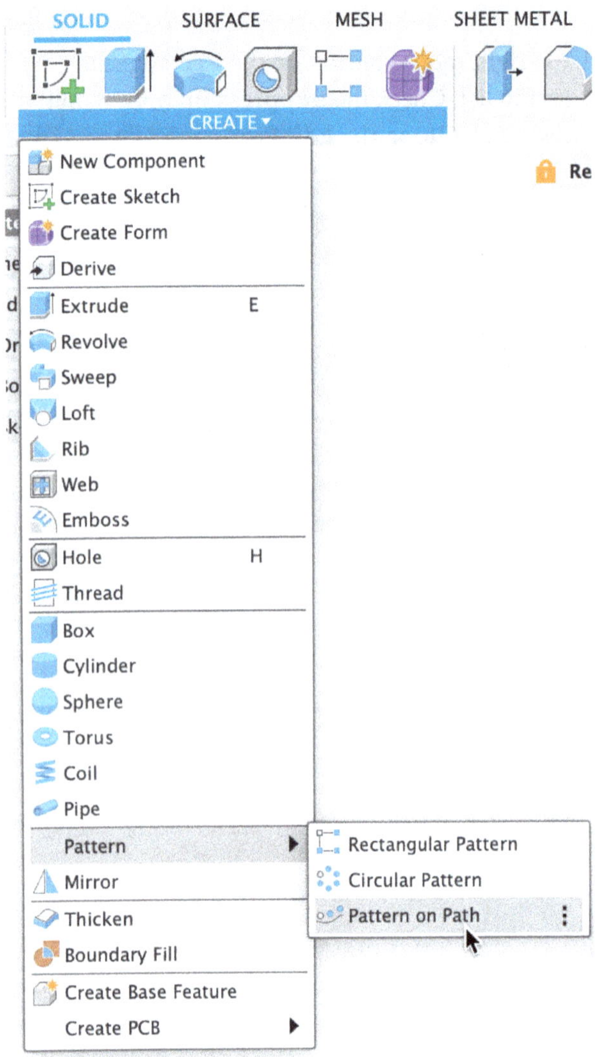

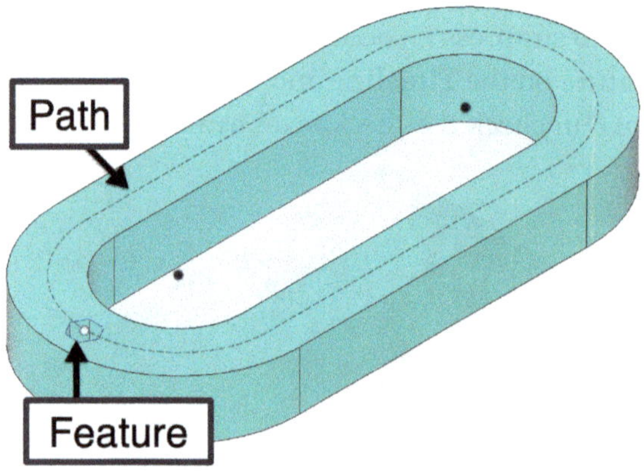

On the **Pattern on Path** dialog, select an option (**Extent** or **Spacing**) from the **Distribution** drop-down. The **Extent** option allows to specify the total extent up to which the pattern will be created. The **Spacing** option allows you to specify the spacing between the individual occurrences of the pattern along path. You can specify Extent or Spacing value in the **Distance** box. Next, specify the number of occurrences in the **Quantity** value.

Next, specify the direction from the **Direction** drop-down (*One Direction* or *Symmetric*). The One Direction option creates the pattern on one side of the original feature. The Symmetric option creates the pattern on both sides of the original feature.

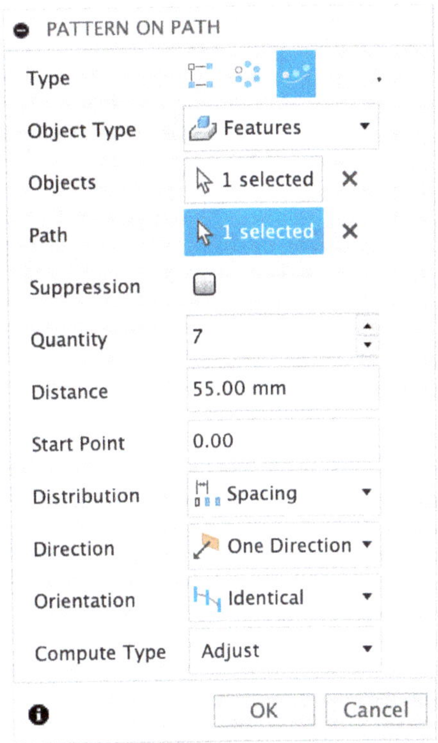

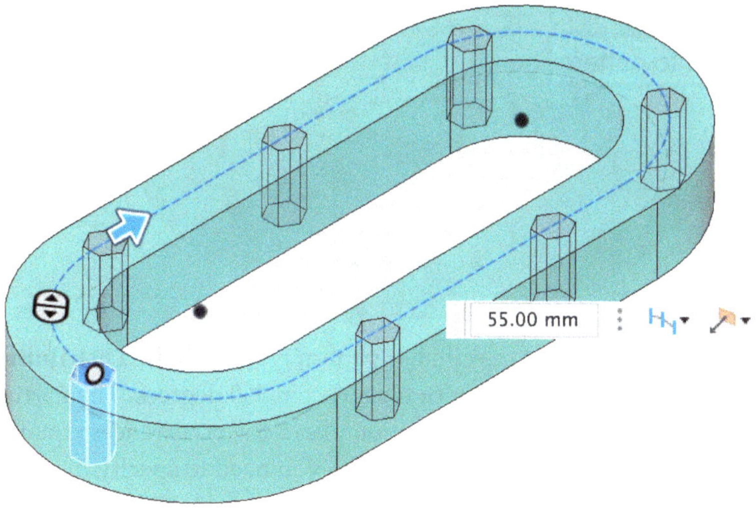

Specify the orientation using the **Orientation** drop-down: **Identical** and **Path Direction**. The **Identical** option keeps the orientation of the pattern occurrences identical to the origin feature. The **Path Direction** option changes the orientation of the occurrences to align with the path.

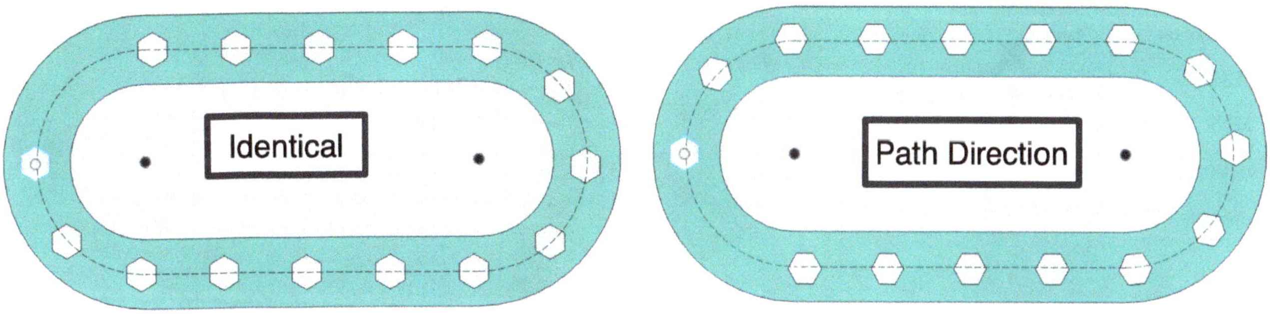

Select an option from the **Compute Type** drop-down. The options in this drop-down are discussed earlier. Click **OK** to create the pattern along the path.

Circular Pattern

The circular pattern is used to pattern the selected features in a circular fashion. Activate the **Circular Pattern** command (click **Create** panel **> Pattern > Circular Pattern**  on the **Solid** tab of the toolbar) and select **Type > Features**. Next, select **Object Type > Features**, and then select the feature to pattern from the model geometry. Click on the **Axis** selection button and select the axis from the model geometry or click on a round face; the axis of the rotation is defined.

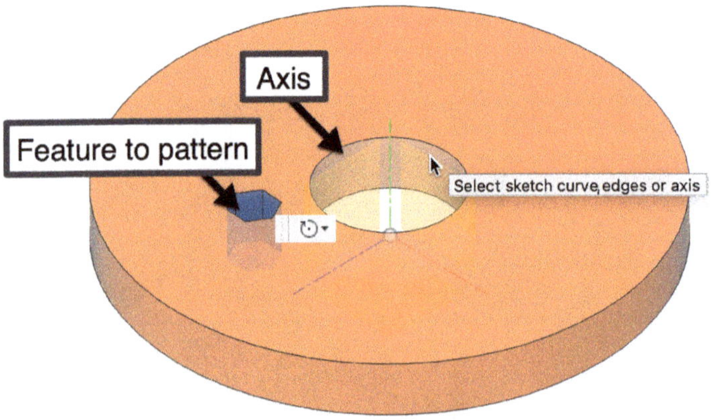

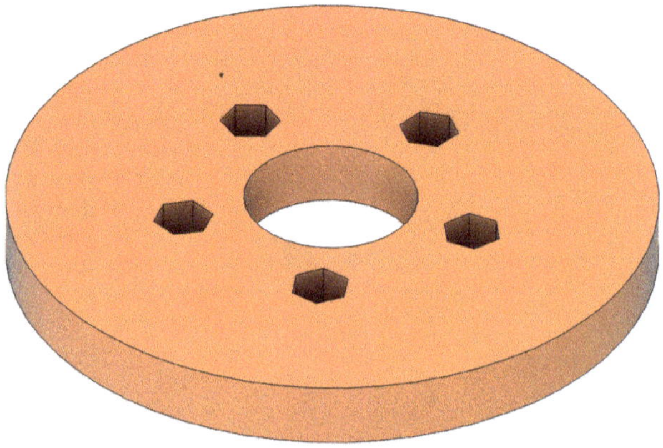

Next, you have to select the circular pattern type from the **Distribution** drop-down (*Full, Partial,* and *Symmetric*). the **Full** option is used to pattern the object in 360 degrees. The **Partial** option patterns the object up to the specified angle. The **Symmetric** option places the occurrences equally on both sides of the source object. If you select **Partial** or **Symmetric** options, then you need to specify the angle and number of occurrences values in the **Angle** and **Quantity** boxes, respectively. Next, select the required **Compute Type** and click **OK** to create a circular pattern.

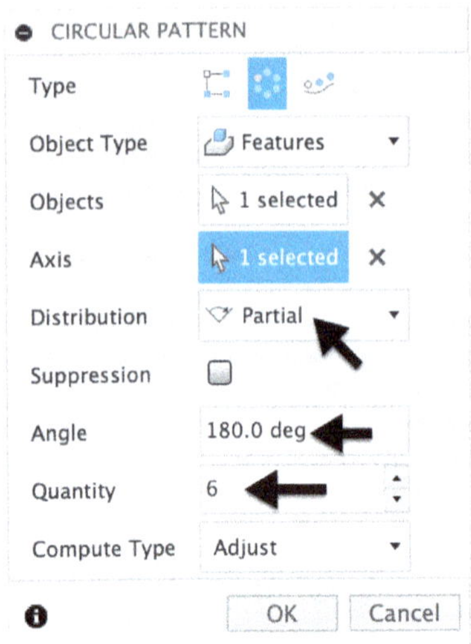

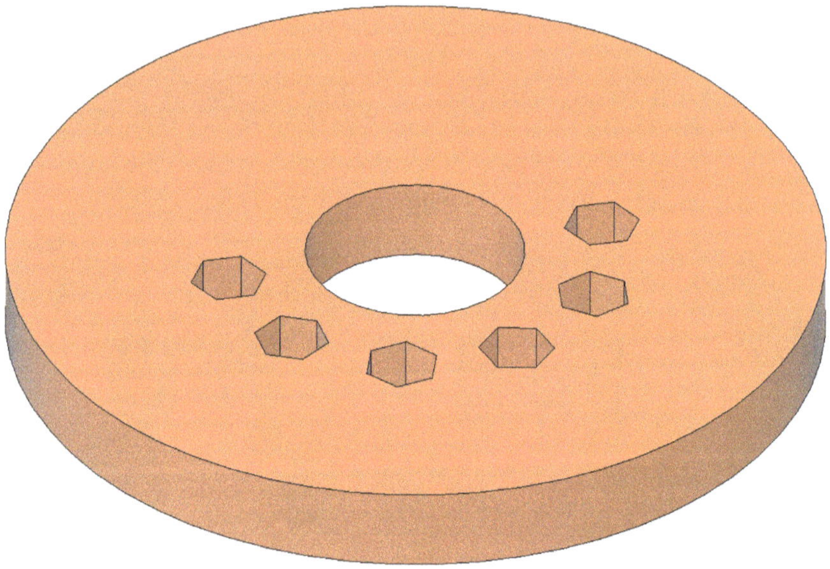

Examples

Example 1 (Millimeters)

In this example, you will create the part shown below.

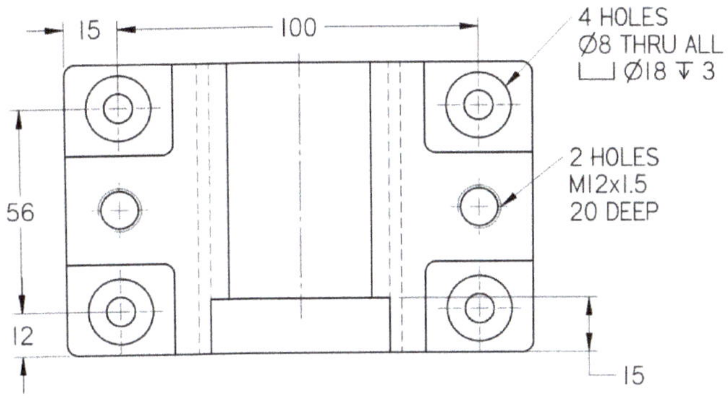

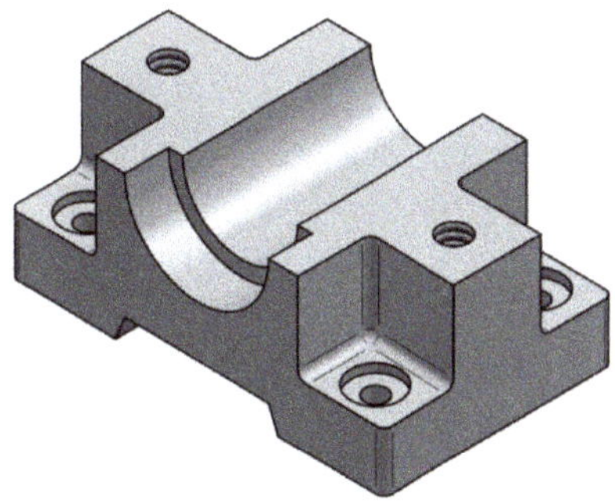

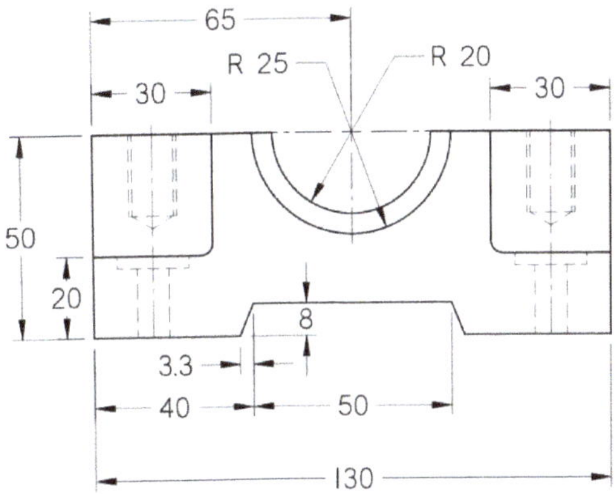

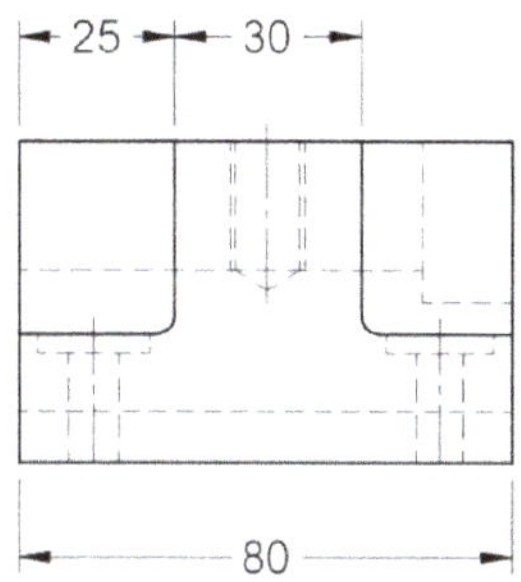

1. Start **Autodesk Fusion 360.**
2. In the Browser window, expand **Document Settings** and place the cursor on **Units** and click the **Change Active Units** icon.
3. On the **Change Active Units** dialog, click **Unit Type > millimeter (mm), gram (g)** and click **OK**.
4. To start a sketch, click **Sketch > Create Sketch** on the toolbar. Click on the **XZ** plane.
5. Create a rectangular sketch, add dimensions as shown, and click **Finish Sketch** on the toolbar.
6. Activate the **Extrude** command (on the **Solid** tab of the toolbar, click **Create** panel > **Extrude**).
7. On the **Extrude** dialog, select **Distance** from the **Extent Type** drop-down and type-in 80 in the **Distance** box. Click **Direction > Symmetric** and click the **Measurement > Whole Length** icon.

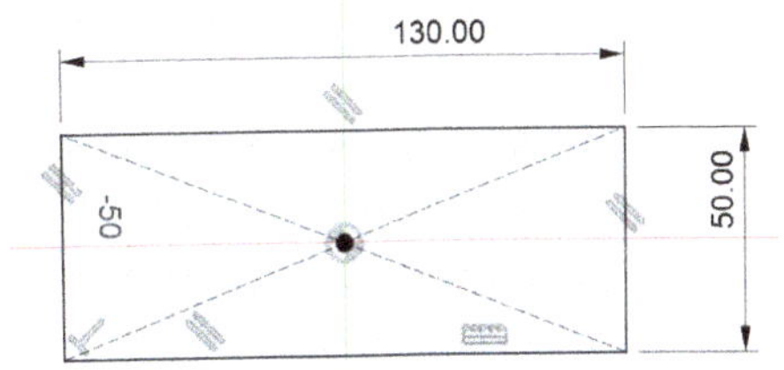

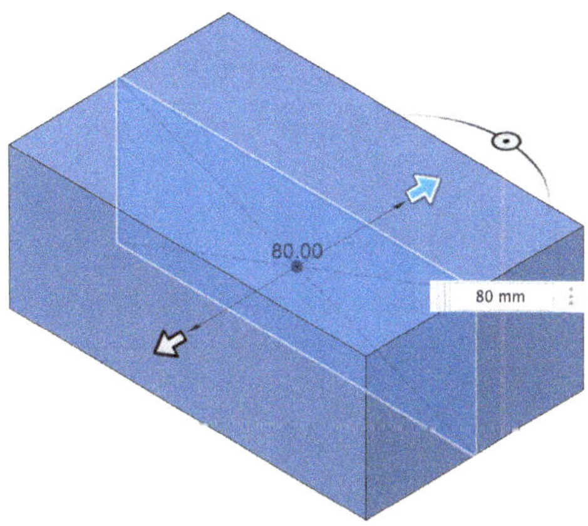

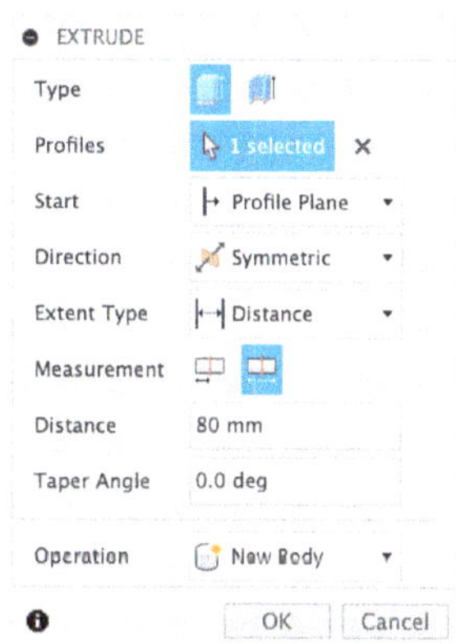

8. Click **OK** to complete the *Extrude* feature.
9. Click **Create** panel > **Create Sketch**, on the **Solid** tab of the toolbar.

10. Click on the top face of the part model, as shown in the figure. Next, draw the sketch, as shown. Click **Finish Sketch** on the toolbar.

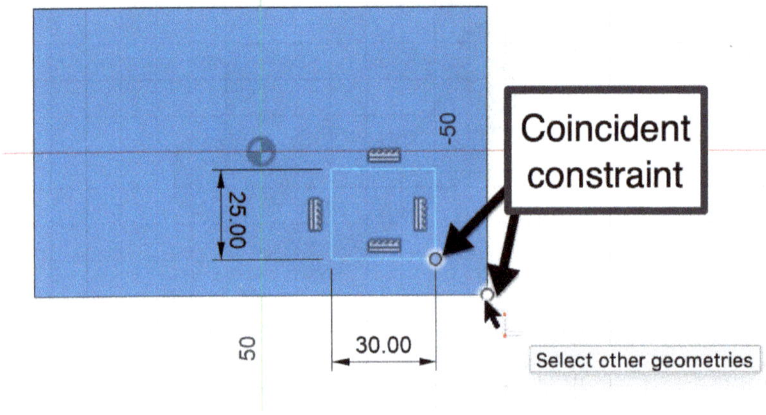

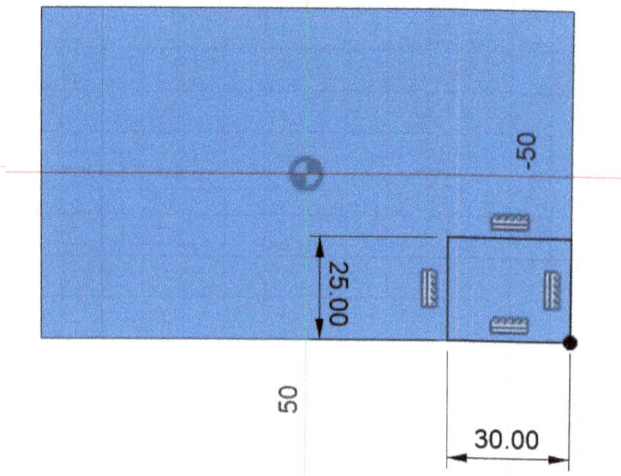

11. Activate the **Extrude** command (on the **Solid** tab of the toolbar, click **Create** panel > **Extrude**). Next, click on the region enclosed by the sketch.
12. On the **Extrude** dialog, click **Operation > Cut** and select **Extent Type > Distance**. Type-in -30 in the **Distance** box and click **OK** to create the *Cut* feature.

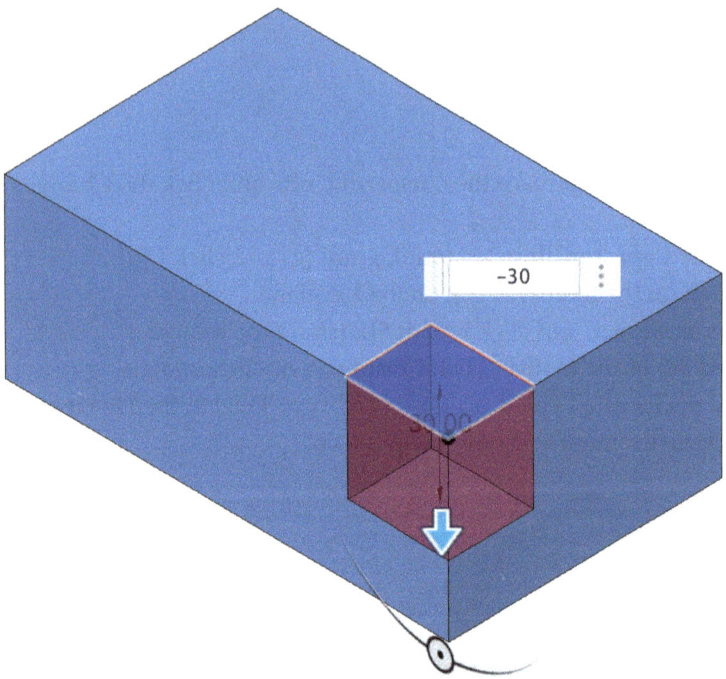

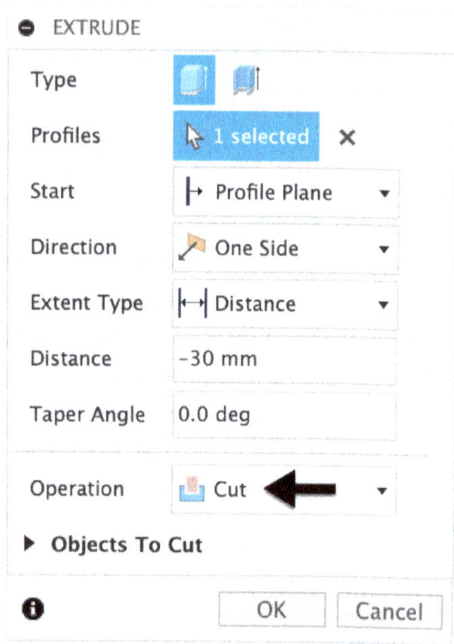

13. Activate the **Create Sketch** command and click on the top face of the *Cut* feature.
14. Click **Create** panel **> Point** on the **Sketch** contextual tab of the toolbar and place the point and add dimensions, as shown.

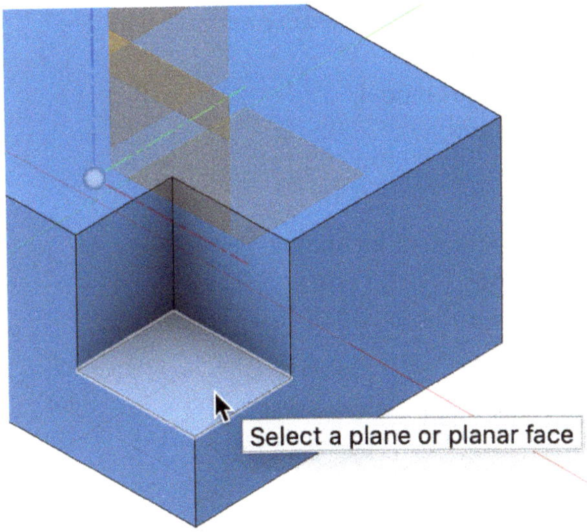

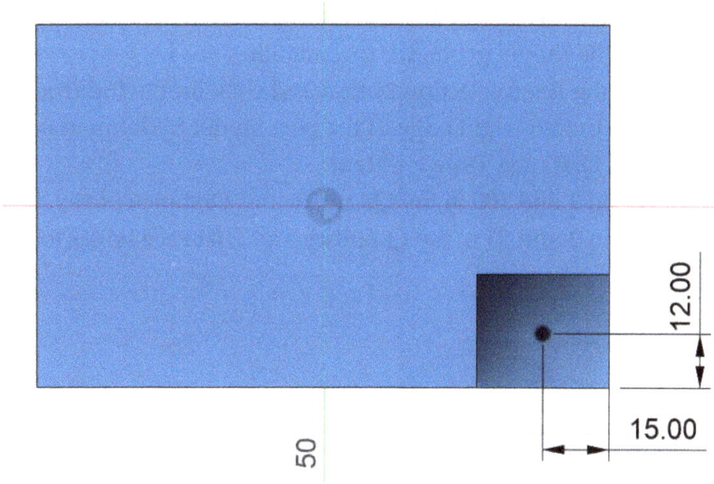

15. Click **Finish Sketch** on the toolbar.
16. Activate the **Hole** command and select the sketch point. Next, click **Hole Type > Counterbore**.
17. Select **Extents > All**. Next, select **Hole Tap Type > Simple**.
18. Specify the dimension of the counterbore hole, as shown. Next, click **OK**.

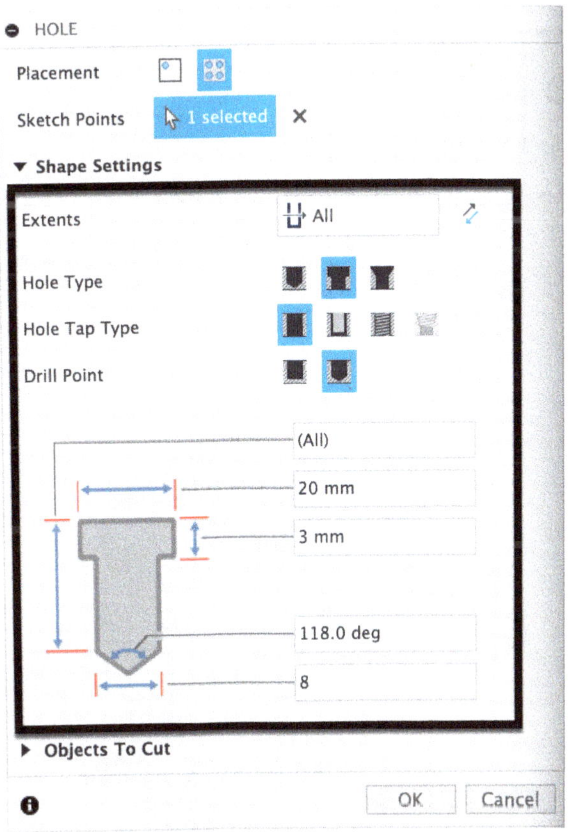

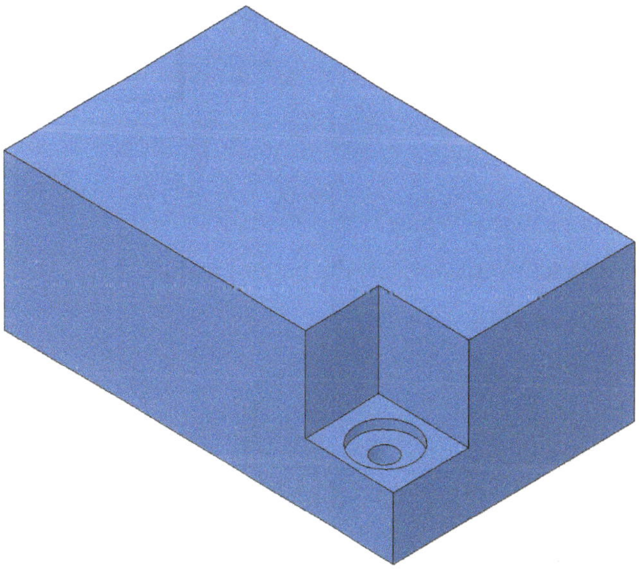

19. Click **Create** panel > **Rectangular Pattern** 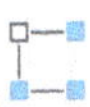 , on the **Solid** tab of the toolbar.
20. On the **Rectangular Pattern** dialog, select **Object Type > Features**.

21. On the **Rectangular Pattern** dialog, click the **Objects** selection button and select the *Hole* and *Cut* features from the model geometry or Timeline.
22. Click the **Axes** selection button and click on the top front edge of the part model.
23. Select the top-right edge of the part model to define the second direction.
24. Select **Distance Type > Extent**.
25. Type in **2** and **100** in the **Quantity** and **Distance** boxes, respectively.
26. Type in **2** and **55** in the **Quantity** and **Distance** boxes located at the bottom of the dialog, respectively.

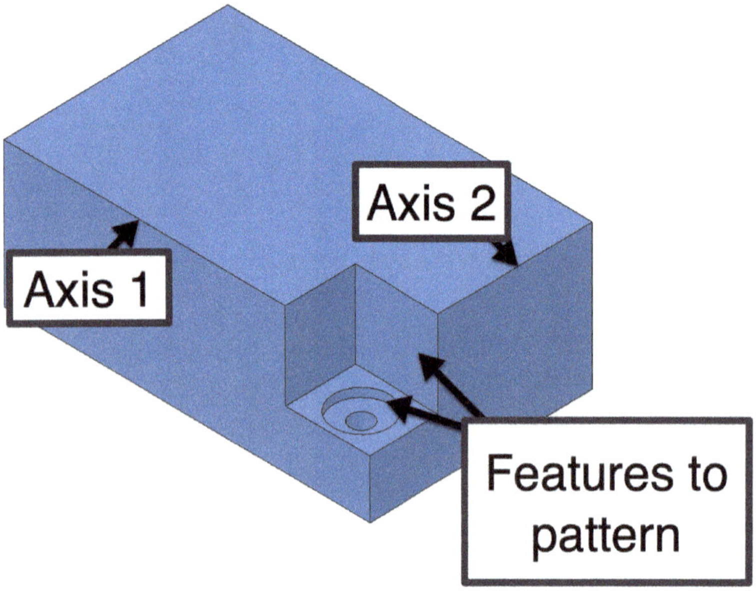

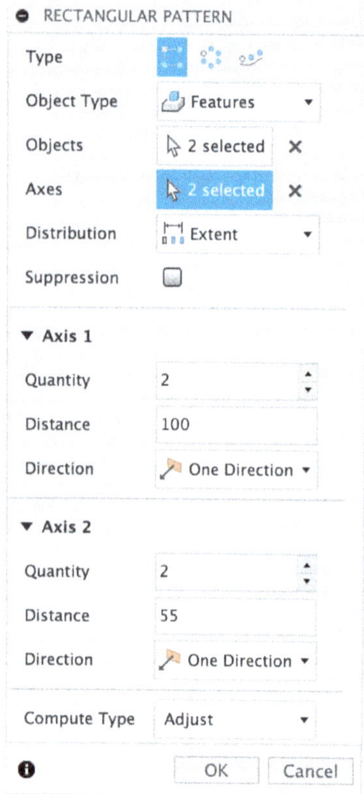

27. Click **OK** to complete the pattern feature.

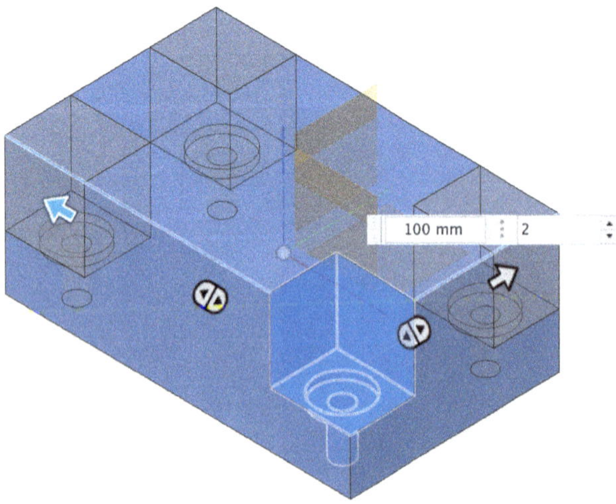

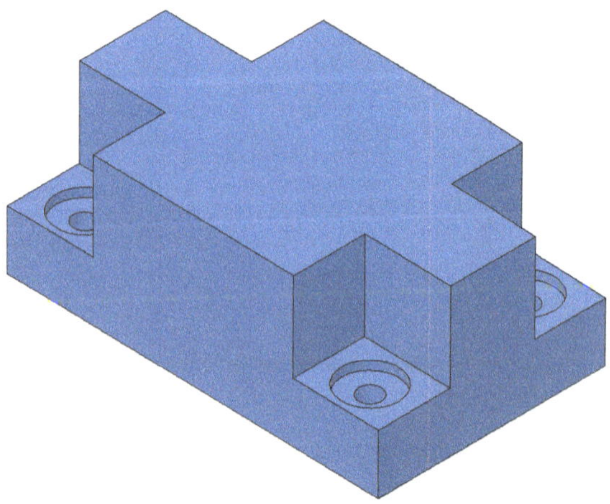

28. Click **Create** panel **> Create Sketch**, on the toolbar. Click on the front face of the part model.

29. Click **Create** panel **> Point** , on the **Sketch** contextual tab of the toolbar. Place the pointer on the midpoint of the top edge, as shown.
30. Click when the Midpoint constraint glyph is displayed; the Midpoint constraint is created between the point and the top edge. Click **Finish Sketch** on the toolbar.

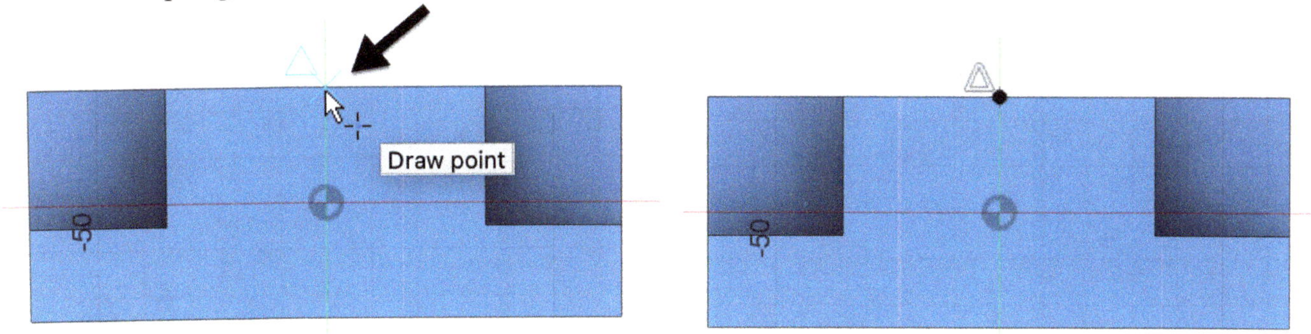

31. Click **Create** panel > **Hole**, on the **Solid** tab of the toolbar. Next, select the sketch point.
32. On the **Hole** dialog, click **Hole Type > Counterbore**.
33. Click **Hole Tap Type > Simple** and click **Drill Point > Flat** on the **Hole** dialog.
34. Select **All** from the **Extents** drop-down.
35. Type-in **50** and **15** mm in the **Counterbore Diameter** and **Counterbore Depth** boxes, respectively.
36. Set the **Diameter** value to **40** mm and click **OK** to create the counterbore hole.

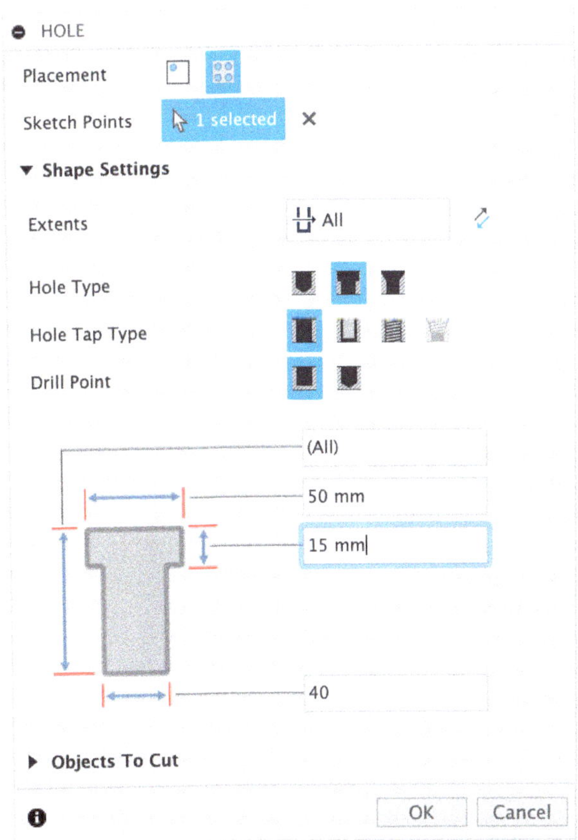

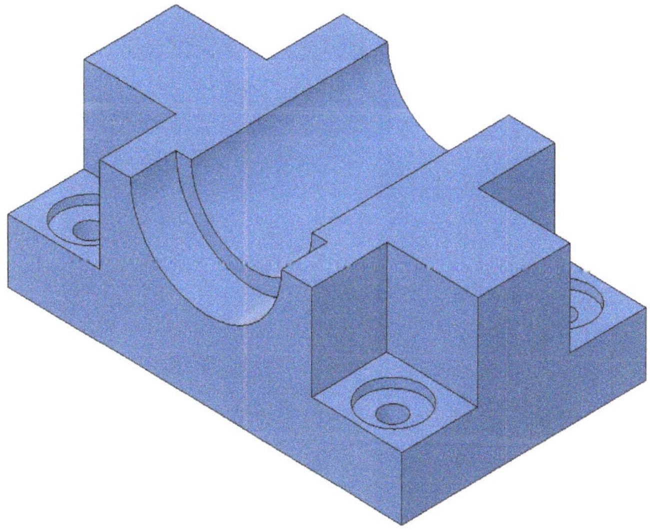

37. Click **Create** panel **> Hole** on the **Solid** tab of the toolbar, and click on the top face of the part model, as shown.

38. On the **Hole** dialog, click **Extents > Distance.**
39. Select **Hole Type > Simple** and **Hole Tap Type > Tapped**.
40. Select **Drill Point > Angle**.
41. Specify the thread parameters at the bottom of the **Hole** dialog, as shown.

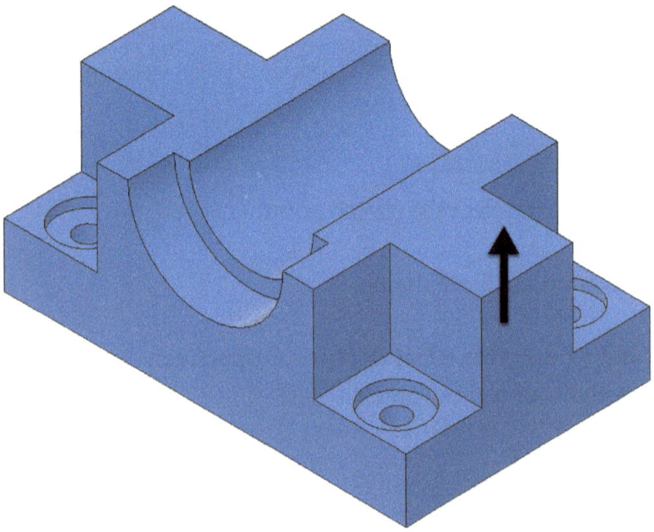

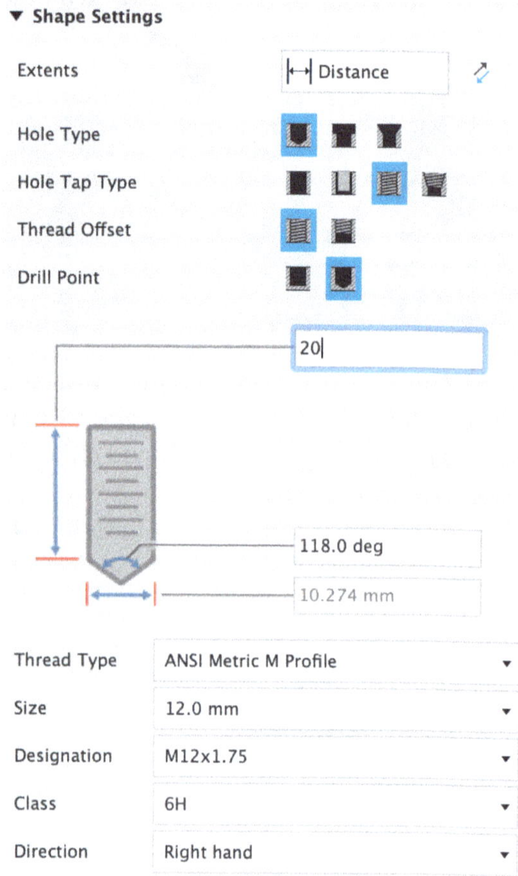

42. Place the pointer on the top-right edge, as shown. Click when the **Add Reference** appears and enter **15** in the distance box. Likewise, add another reference by clicking on the back edge and entering **15** in the distance box, as shown in the figure.

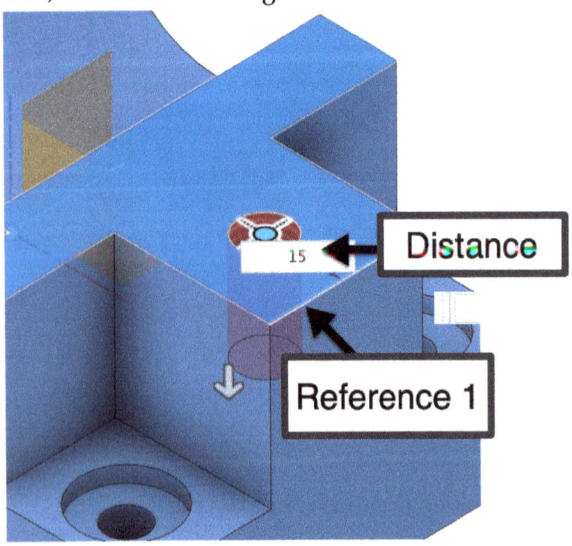

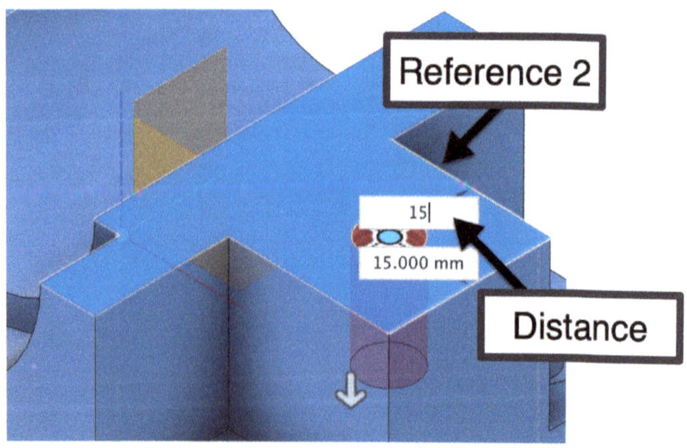

43. Click **OK** to create the *Hole* feature.

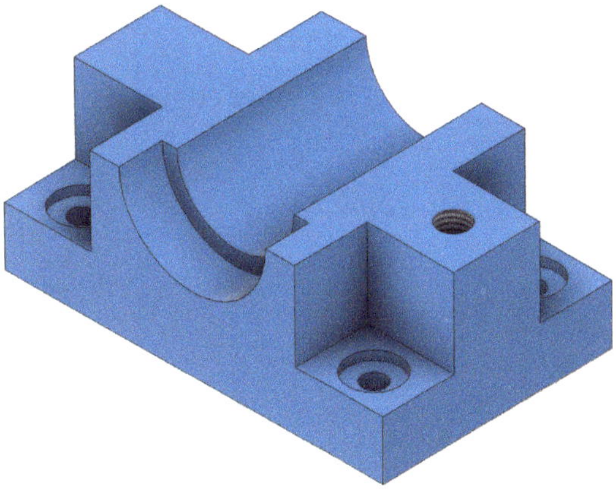

44. On the **Solid** tab of the toolbar, click **Create** panel **>** **Mirror** . Next, select **Object Type > Features**.
45. On the **Mirror** dialog, click the **Objects** button and select the threaded hole feature from the part model.
46. Click the **Mirror Plane** button and select the **YZ** plane, as shown. Click **OK** to complete the *Mirror* feature.

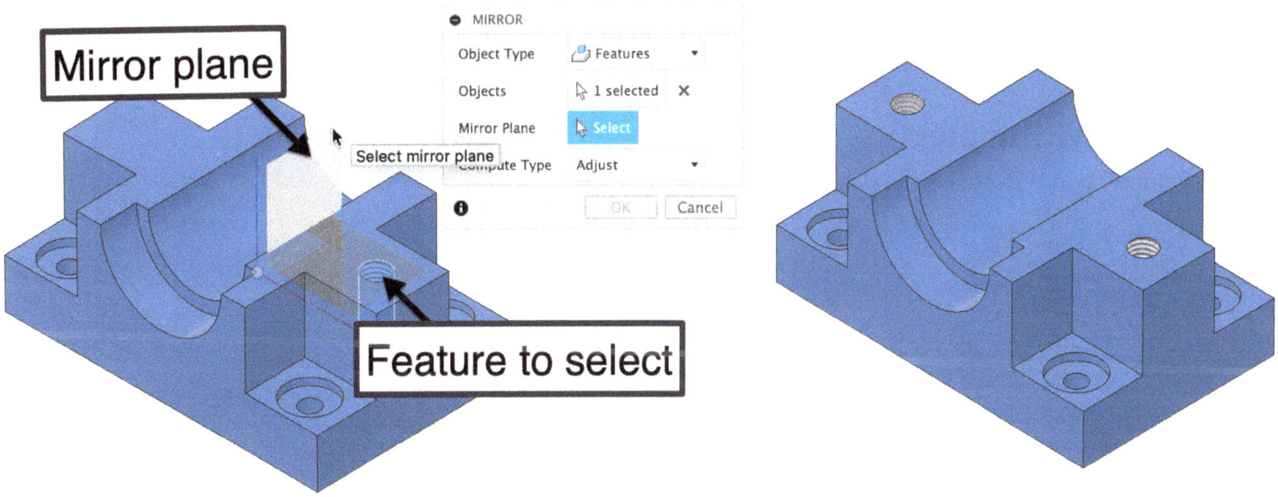

47. Activate the **Create Sketch** command and click on the front face of the part model.
48. Draw the sketch and add dimensions to it, as shown in the figure. Note that you should apply the **Symmetric** constraint between the two inclined lines. Click **Finish Sketch** on the toolbar.
49. Create a *Cut* throughout the part model, as shown.

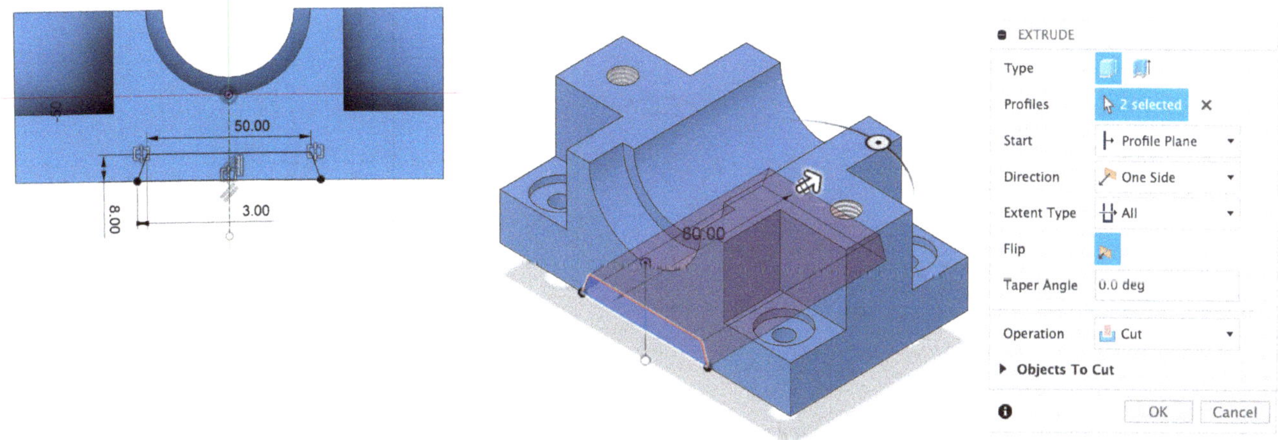

50. On the **Solid** tab of the toolbar, click **Modify** panel **> Fillet**.
51. On the **Fillet** dialog, click the **Edges/Faces/Features** selection button and then select the inner edges of the cut feature. Type 2 in the **Radius** box available on the **Fillet** dialog.

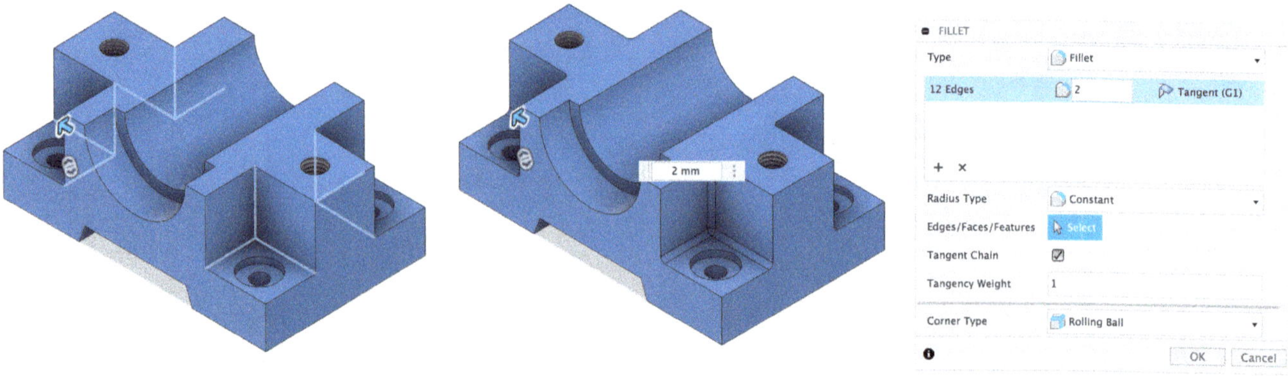

52. Click **OK** to create the fillet.
53. Save and close the part file.

Example 2 (Millimeters)

In this example, you will create the part shown below.

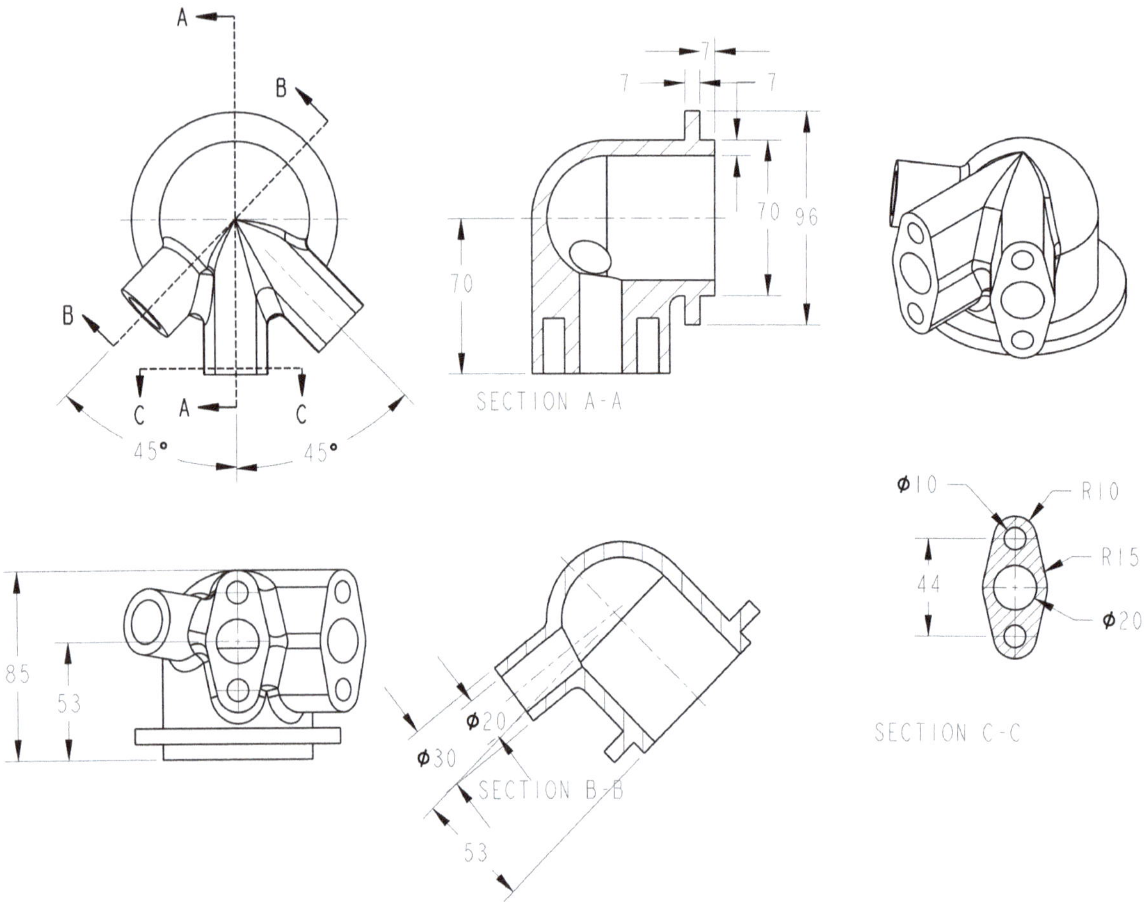

Creating the First Feature

1. Start **Autodesk Fusion 360**.
2. On the **Browser window**, expand **Document Settings** and place the cursor on **Units**; the **Change Active Units** icon appears.
3. Click on the **Change Active Units** icon to change the units; the **Change Active Units** dialog appears.
4. On this dialog, select **Unit Type > millimeter (mm), gram (g)** from the drop-down and click **OK**.
5. To start a sketch, click **Create > Create Sketch** on the toolbar. Click on the XZ plane. The sketch starts.
6. On the toolbar, click **Sketch** tab > **Create** panel > **Line**.
7. Specify the start point of the line on the vertical reference.
8. Click on the origin point to define the second point.
9. Move the pointer horizontally toward right and click on the horizontal reference.
10. Move the pointer vertically up to a small distance and click.
11. Move the pointer horizontally toward right up to a small distance and click.
12. Move the pointer vertically up to a small distance and click.
13. Move the pointer horizontally toward left up to a small distance and click.
14. Move the pointer vertically upward and click.

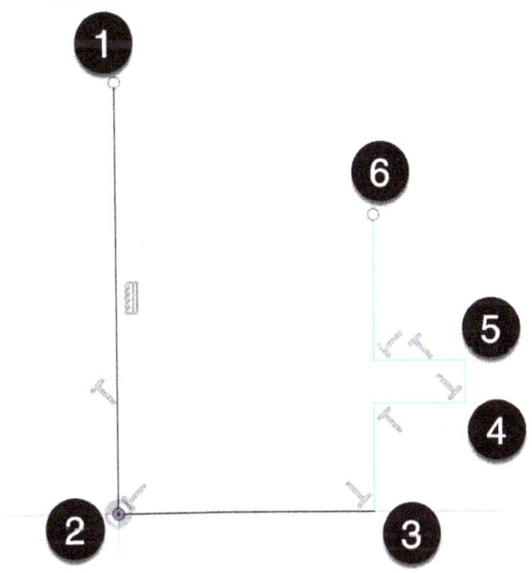

15. On the toolbar, click **Sketch** tab > **Create** panel > **Arc** drop-down > **Tangent End**.

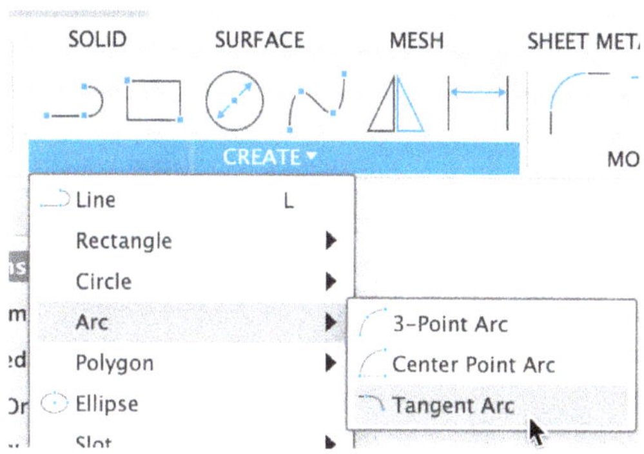

16. Select the endpoint of the right vertical line.
17. Select the endpoint of the left vertical line.

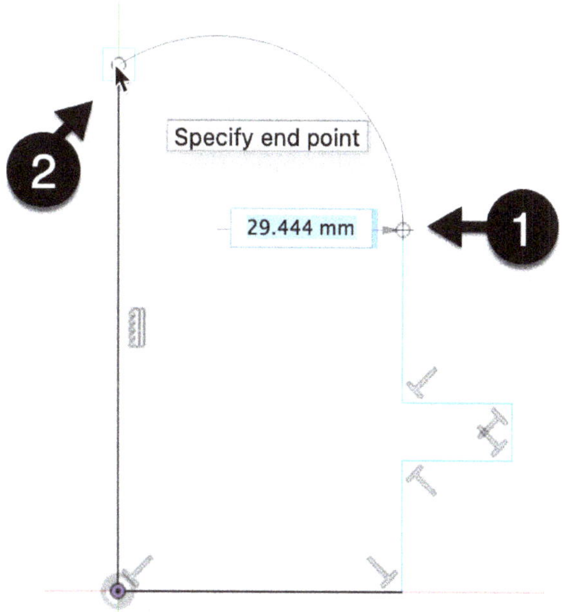

18. Apply the **Coincident** constraint between the centerpoint of the arc and the left vertical line.

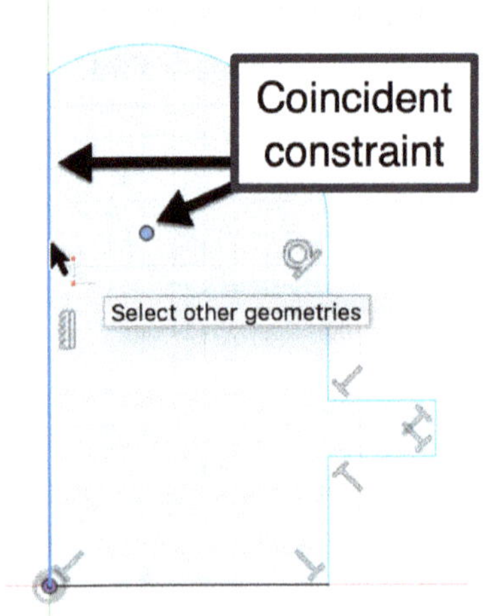

19. Add dimensions to the sketch, as shown.

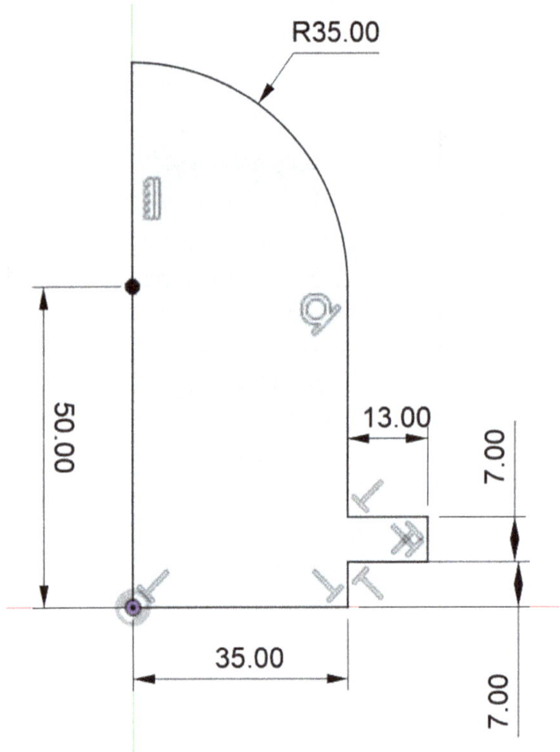

20. On the toolbar, click **Finish Sketch**.
21. On the toolbar, click **Solid** tab > **Create** panel > **Revolve**.
22. Select the vertical line passing through the origin to define the axis of revolution.

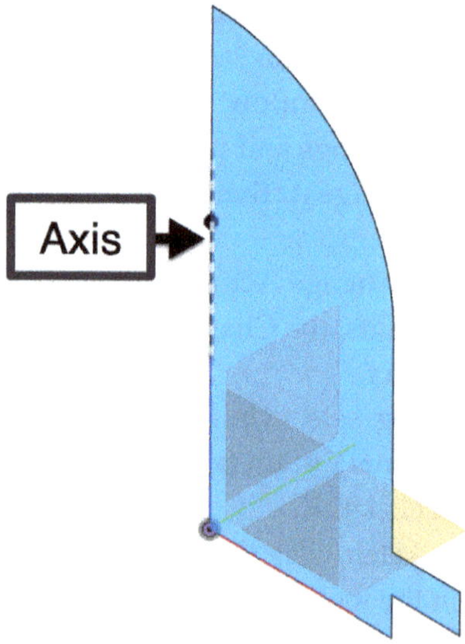

23. On the **Revolve** dialog, select **Extent Type** > **Full**.
24. Click **OK** to create the *Revolved* feature.

Creating the Second Feature

1. On the toolbar, click **Solid** tab > **Datum** panel > **Sketch**.
2. Click on the XZ plane.
3. Create three circles, as shown.
4. Apply the **Equal** constraint between the two circles, as shown.

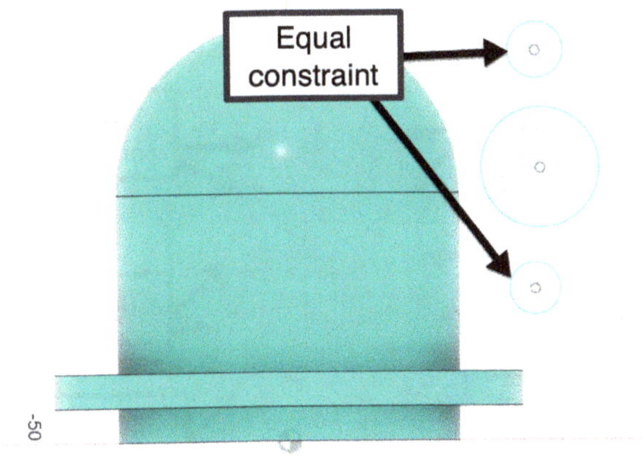

5. Apply the **Vertical** constraint between the center points of the circles.

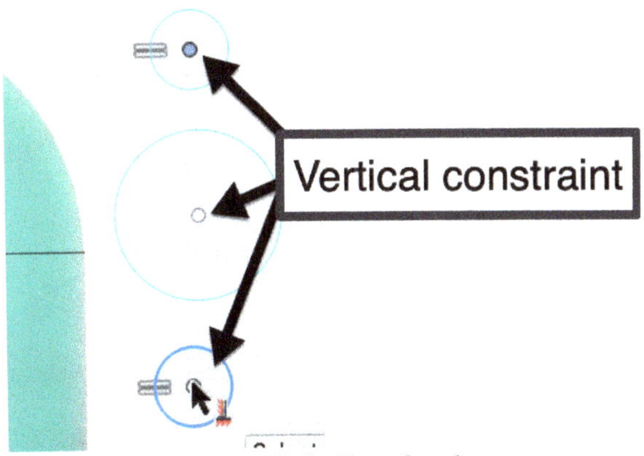

6. On the toolbar, click **Sketch** tab > **Constraints** panel > **Horizontal/Vertical**.
7. Select the centerpoint of anyone of the circles.
8. Select the sketch origin.

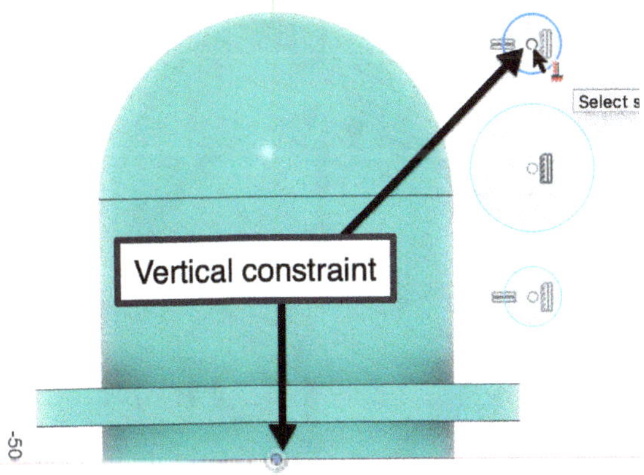

9. Check the **Slice** option on the **Sketch Palette**.
10. On the toolbar, click **Sketch** tab > **Create** panel > **Project/Include > Intersect**.

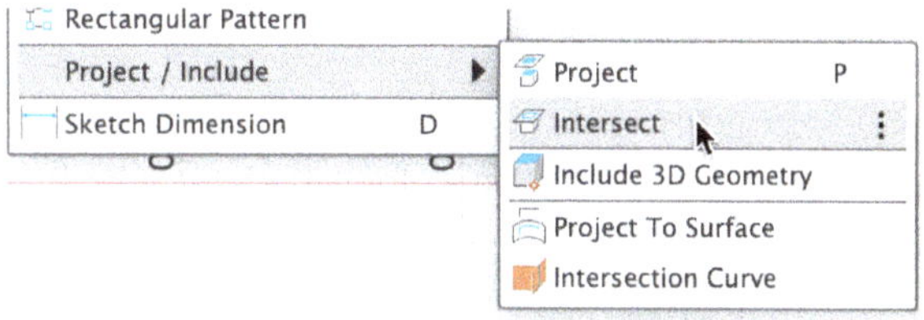

11. Select the curved edge and click **OK**.

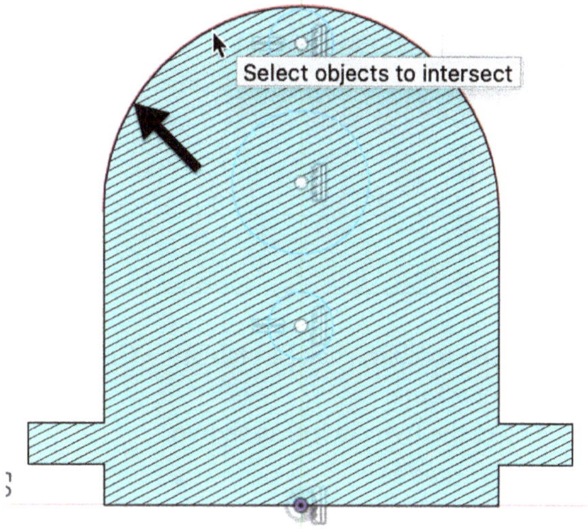

12. Click and drag the upper circle inside the model geometry.
13. On the toolbar, click **Sketch** tab > **Constraints** panel > **Tangent**.
14. Select the circle and the intersection edge, as shown.

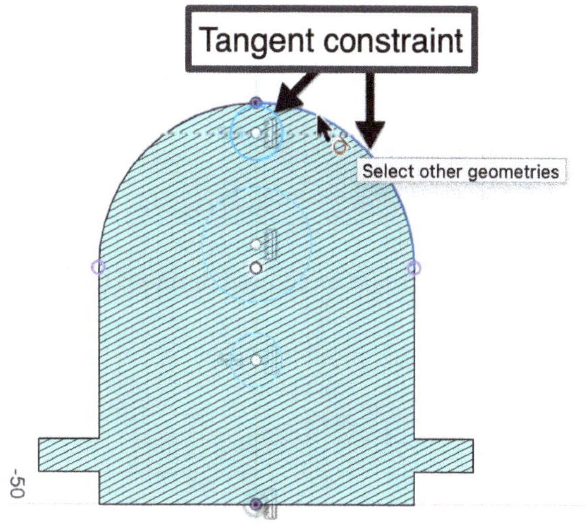

15. On the toolbar, click **Sketch** tab > **Dimension** panel > **Dimension**.
16. Create the dimensions, as shown.

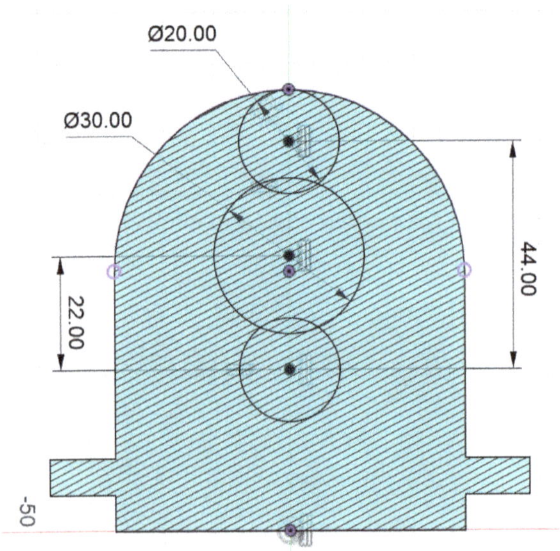

17. On the toolbar, click **Sketch** tab > **Create** panel > **Line**.
18. Select the two circles, as shown.

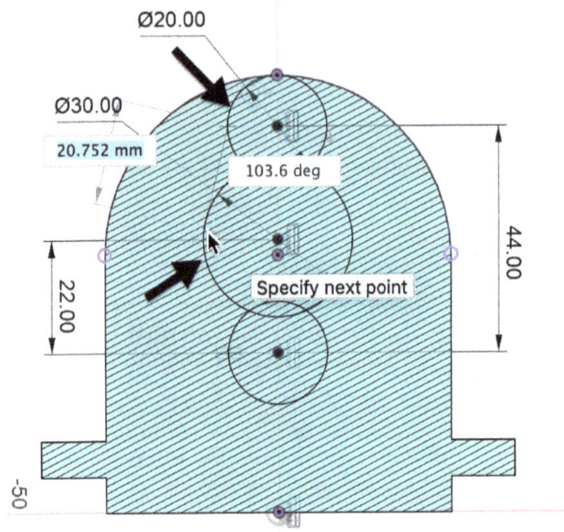

19. Likewise, create three more tangent lines, as shown.

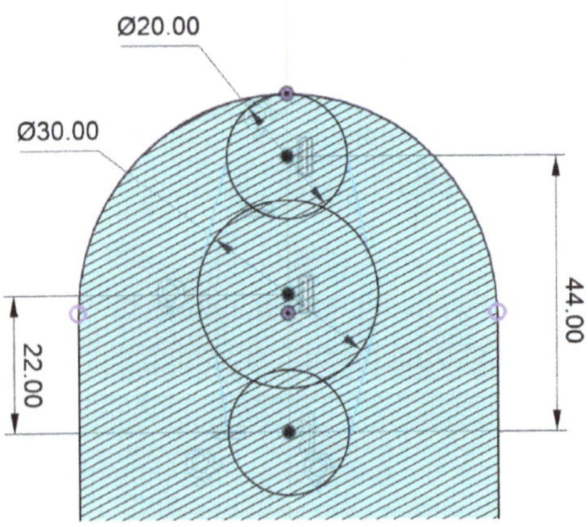

20. Apply the **Tangent** constraint between the circles and the lines.

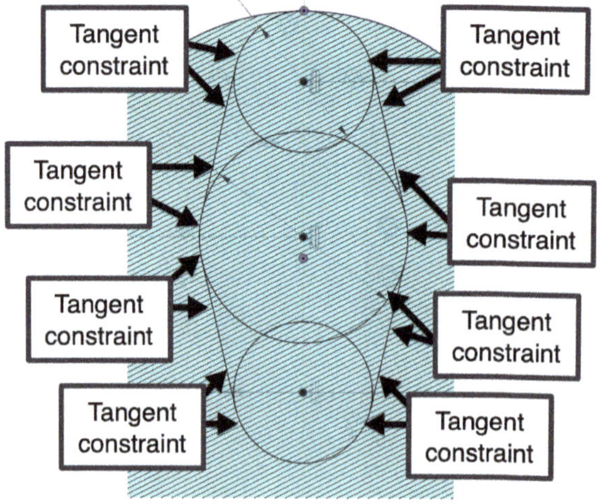

21. On the toolbar, click **Sketch** tab > **Modify** panel > **Trim**.
22. Select the inner segments of the circles, as shown.

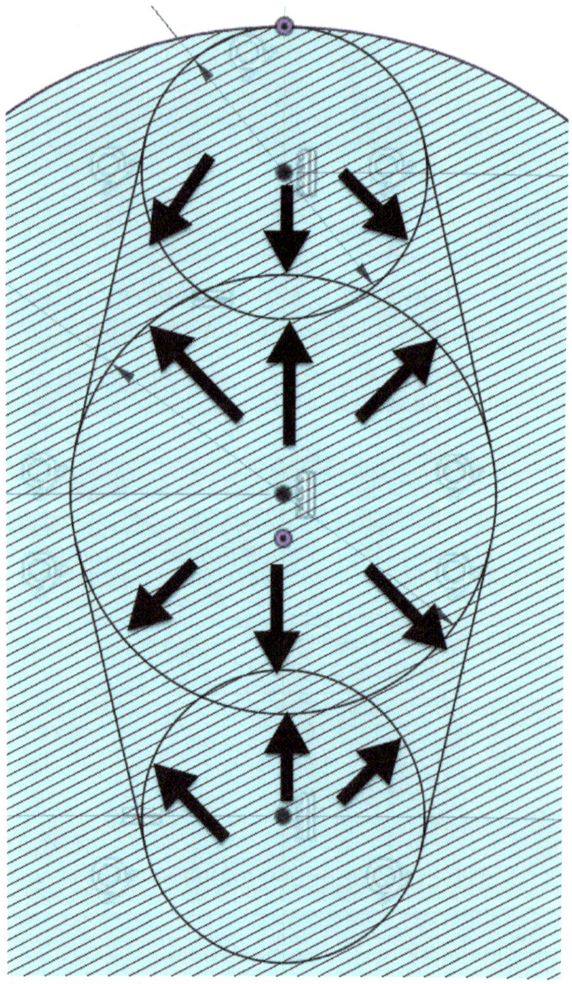

23. Click **Finish Sketch** on the toolbar.

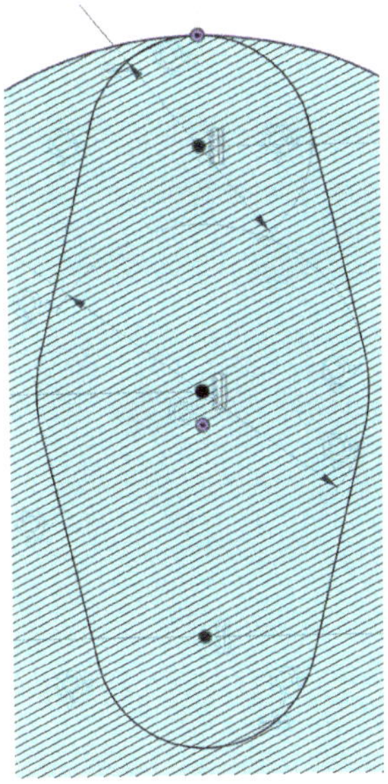

24. On the toolbar, click **Solid** tab > **Create** panel > **Extrude**  .
25. On the **Extrude** Dialog, type **-70** in the **Distance** box.
26. Select **Operation > Join.**

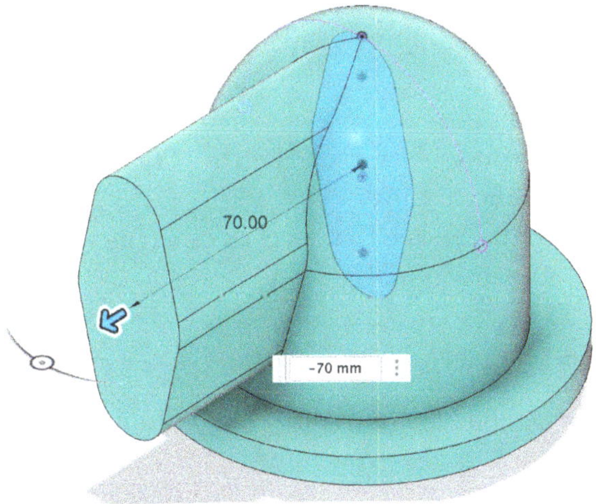

27. Click **OK** on the **Extrude** Dialog.

Creating the Circular Pattern

1. Select the **Extrude** feature timeline.
2. On the toolbar, click **Sketch** tab > **Create** panel > **Pattern** drop-down > **Circular Pattern.**
3. On the **Pattern** Dialog, click the **Axis** selection button.
4. Select the cylindrical face of the model.

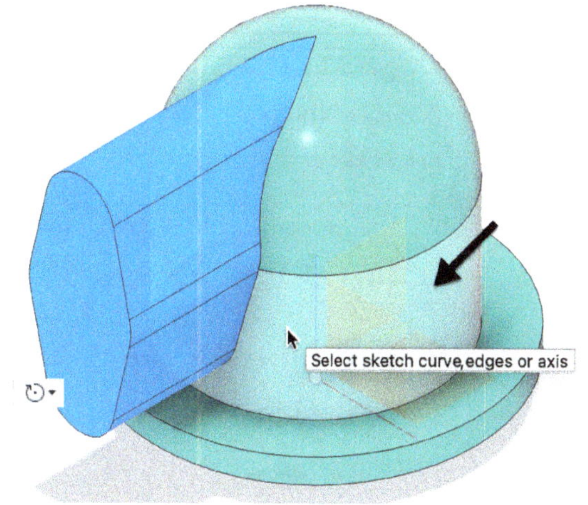

5. Select **Distribution > Partial.**
6. Type **2** in the **Quantity** box.
7. Type **45** in the **Angle** box.
8. Click **OK.**

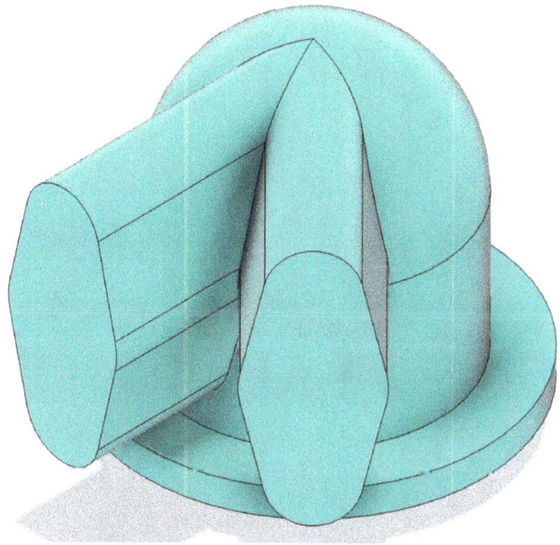

Creating the Inclined Boss

1. On the toolbar, click **Solid > Construct > Midplane.**

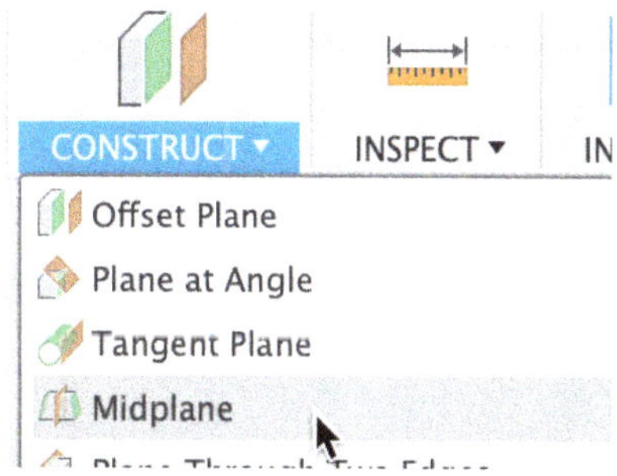

2. Select the XZ and YZ planes.

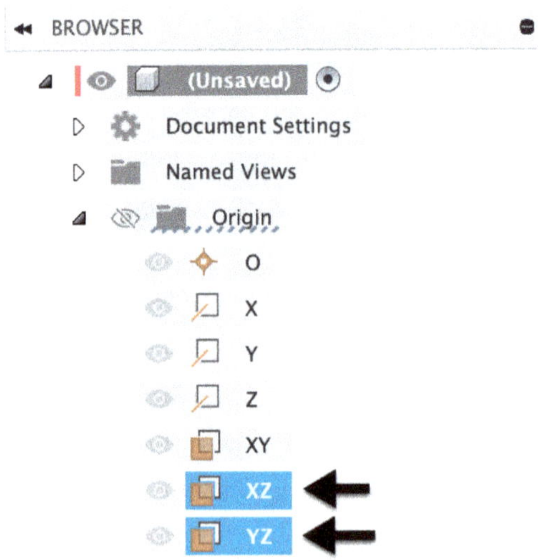

3. Click **OK**.

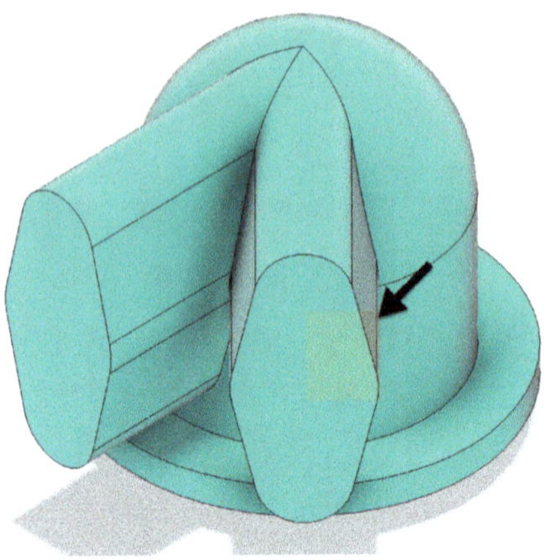

4. Select the newly created plane from the Timeline.

5. On the toolbar, click **Solid > Create > Create Sketch**.
6. Check the **Slice** option on the **Sketch Palette**.
7. On the toolbar, click **Sketch > Create > Rectangle** drop-down > **3-Point Rectangle**.

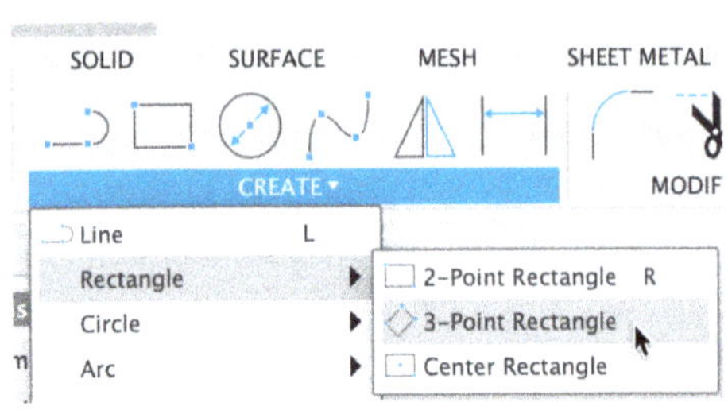

8. Select the two points, as shown.
9. Move the pointer upward and click.

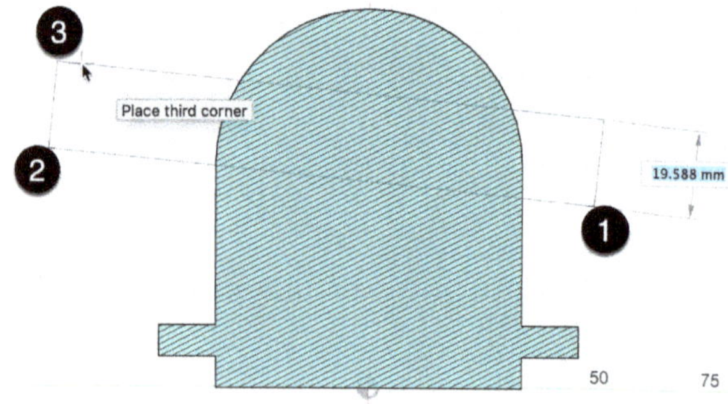

10. On the toolbar, click **Sketch** > **Create** panel > **Project/Include** > **Intersect**.
11. Select the horizontal edge and click **OK**.

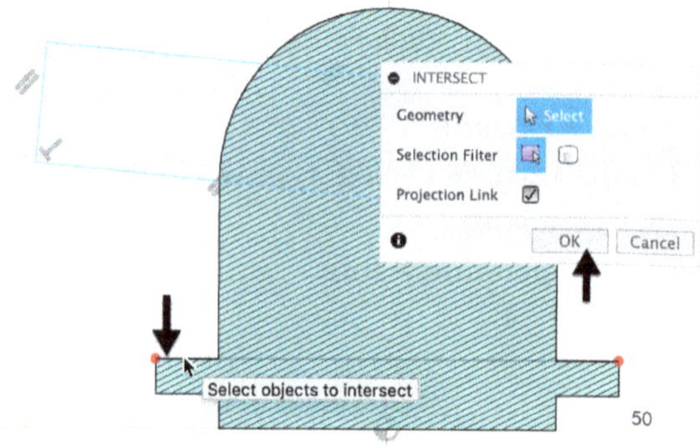

12. On the toolbar, click **Sketch** > **Create** panel > **Line**.
13. On the Sketch Palette, click **Linetype > Construction**.

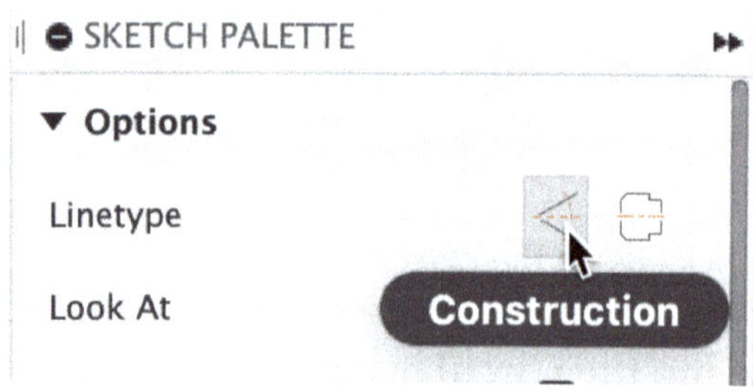

14. Select the left endpoint of the intersected edge.
15. Move the pointer horizontally toward left and click to create a horizontal construction line.

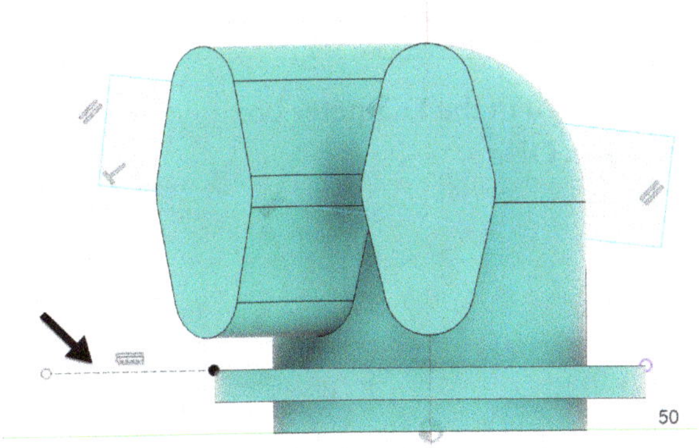

16. Add dimensions to the sketch, as shown.

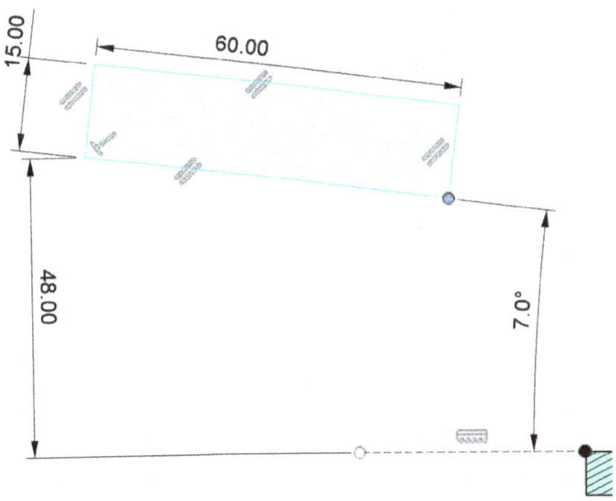

17. On the toolbar, click **Sketch** tab > **Constraints** panel > **Horizontal/Vertical**.
18. Select the lower right corner of the rectangle.
19. Select the sketch origin.

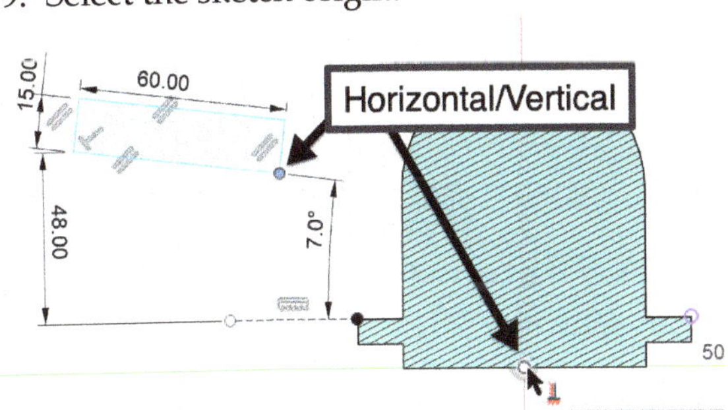

20. Click **Finish Sketch** on the toolbar.
21. On the toolbar, click **Solid > Create > Revolve**.
22. Select the newly created sketch.
23. Select the lower inclined line to define the axis.
24. Select **Operation > Join**.
25. Click **OK**.

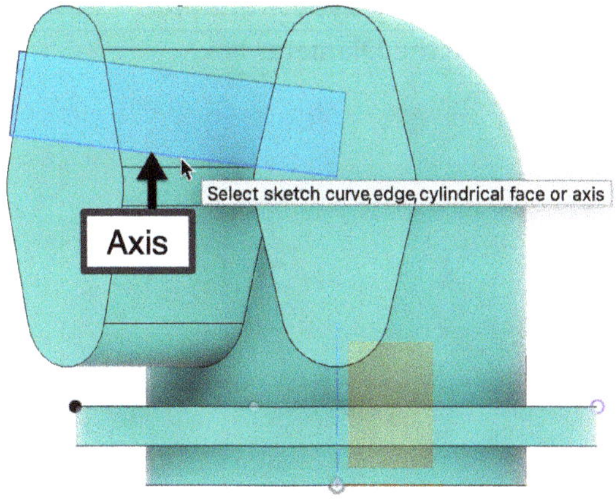

26. On the toolbar, click **Solid** tab > **Create** panel > **Hole** .
27. Click on the flat face of the inclined boss.

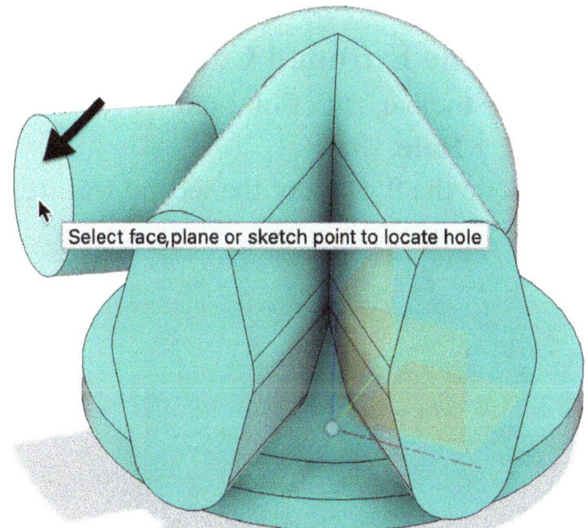

28. Select the circular edge of the inclined boss.

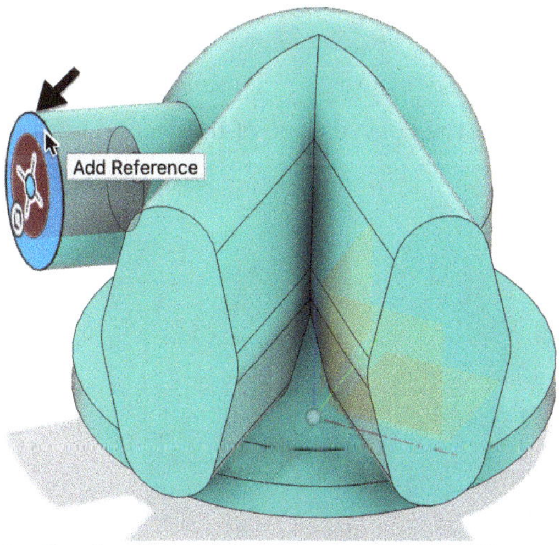

29. On the **Hole** dialog, type **60** in the **Distance** box.

30. Select **Hole Tap Type > Simple**.
31. Type **20** in the **Diameter** box.
32. Click **OK**.

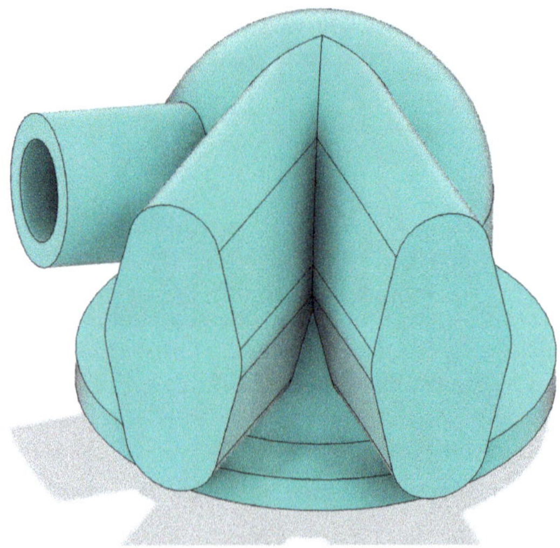

33. On the **Hole** dialog, type **70** in the **Distance** box.
34. Type **20** in the **Diameter** box.
35. Click **OK**.

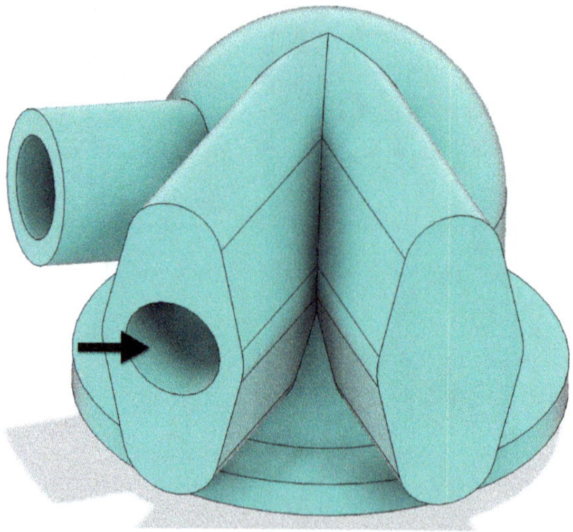

Creating the Extruded Cut Features

1. On the toolbar, click **Solid** tab > **Create** panel > **Hole**.
2. Click on the flat face of the second feature.

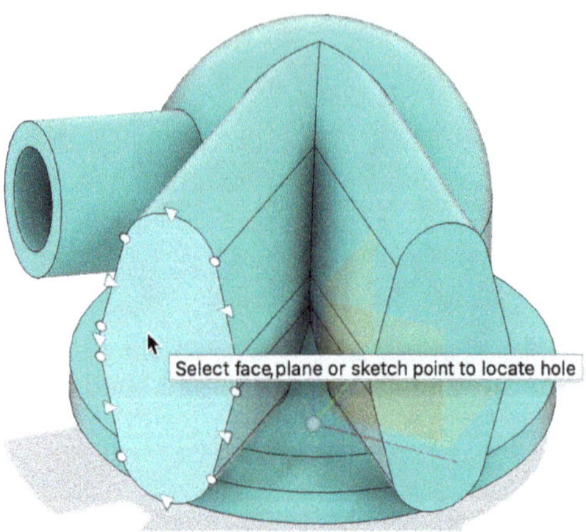

3. Select the curved edge of the second feature.

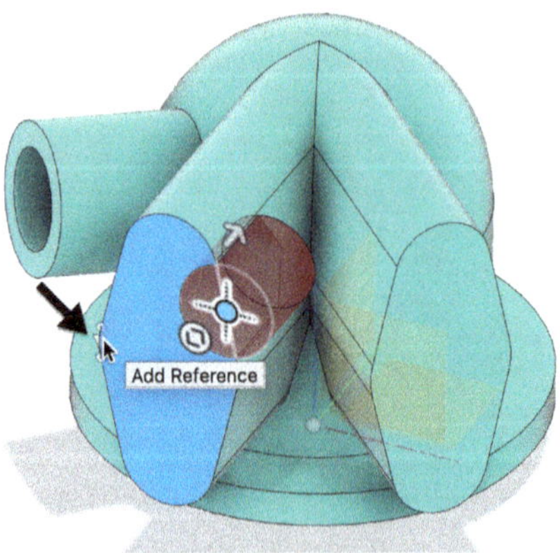

4. On the toolbar, click **Solid** tab > **Create** panel > **Hole**.
5. Click on the flat face of the second feature.

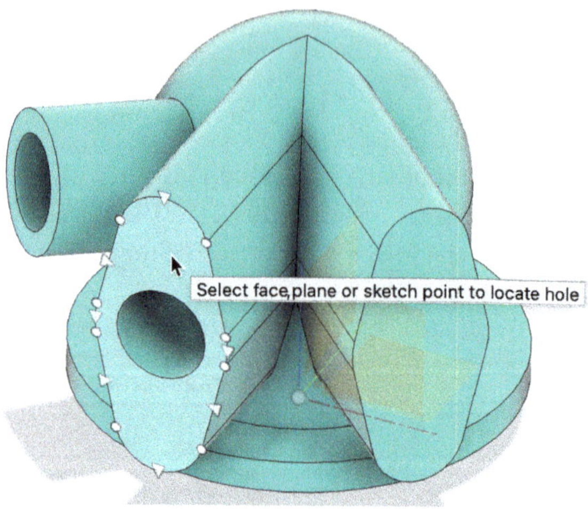

6. Select the curved edge of the second feature, as shown.

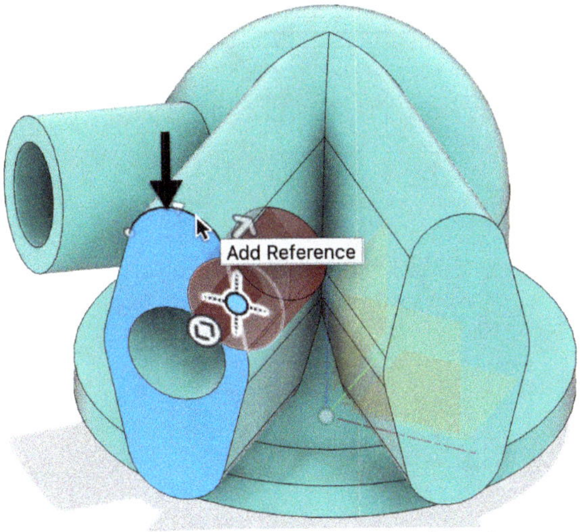

36. On the **Hole** Dialog, type **25** in the **Distance** box.
37. Type **10** in the **Diameter** box.
38. Click **OK**.

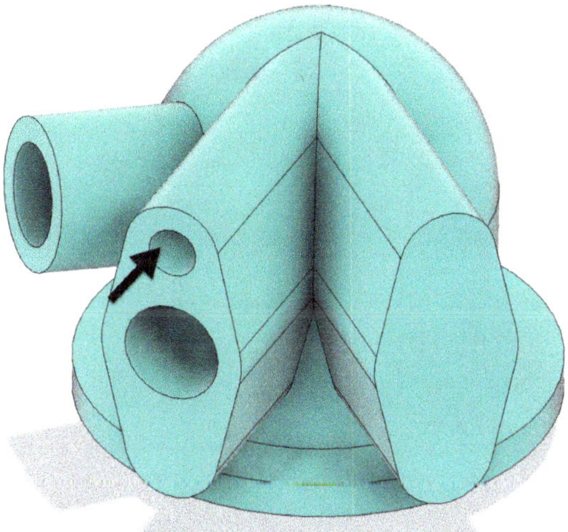

39. Likewise, create another 10 mm diameter hole, as shown.

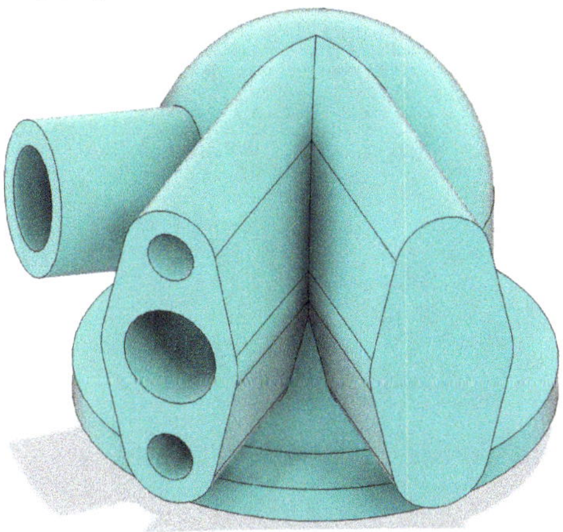

40. Create the circular patterns of the holes (refer to the **Creating Circular Pattern** section of this Example).

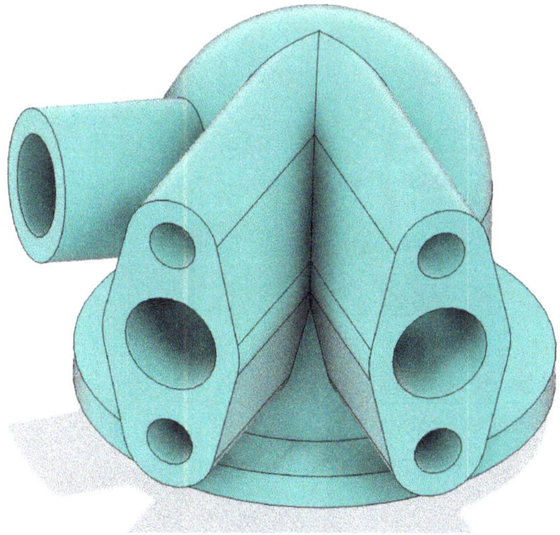

Creating the Revolved Cut Feature

1. On the toolbar, click **Solid > Create > Create Sketch**.
2. Select the XZ plane.
3. Check the **Slice** option on the **Sketch Palette**.
4. Create the sketch, as shown.

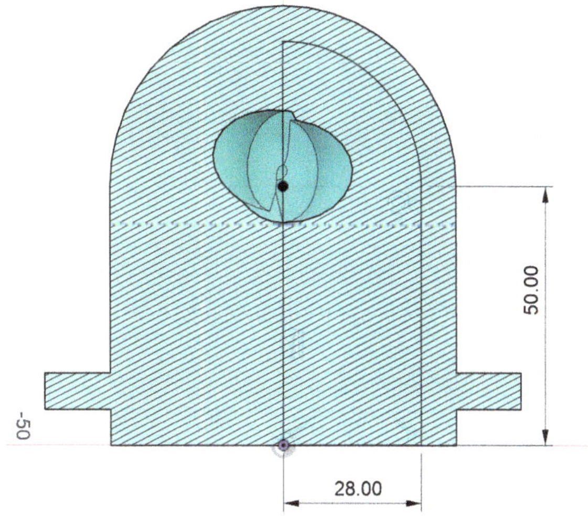

5. Click **Finish Sketch** on the toolbar.
6. On the toolbar, click **Solid > Create > Create Revolve**.
7. Select the vertical line passing through the origin to define the axis of revolution.

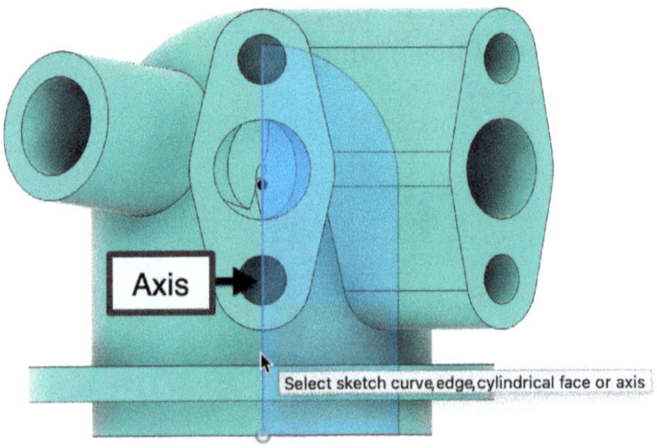

8. Select **Extent Type > Full**.
9. Select **Operation > Cut**.
10. Click **OK** on the **Revolve** Dialog.

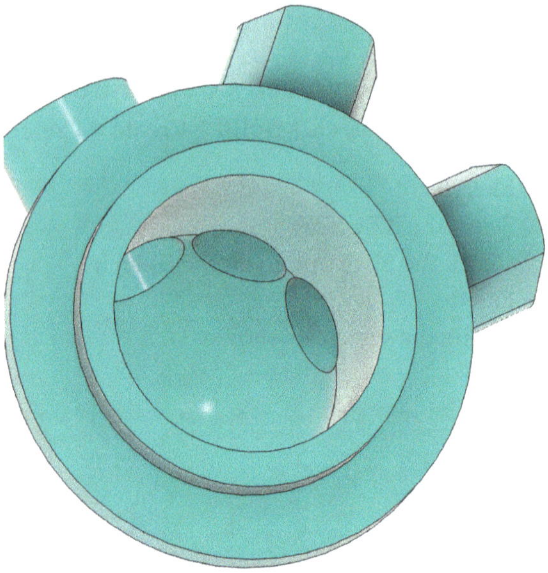

Creating the Rounds

1. On the toolbar, click **Solid > Modify > Fillet** .
2. Select the edges between the second and the third features.

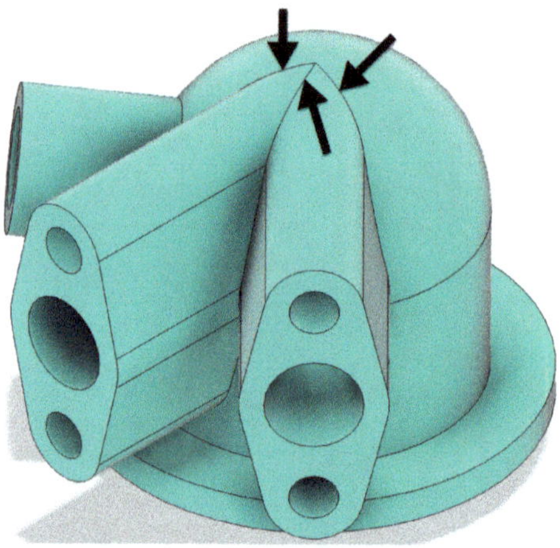

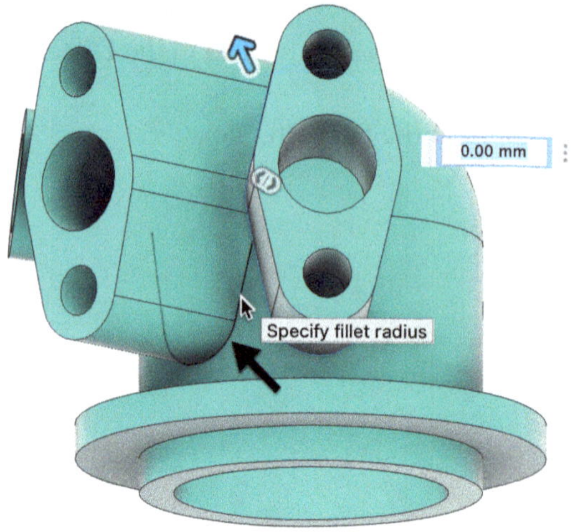

3. On the **Fillet** dialog, type **5** in the **Radius** box.
4. Click **OK**.

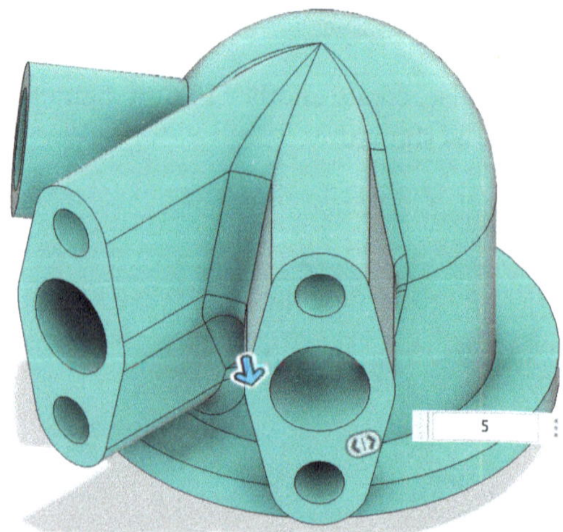

5. On the toolbar, click **Solid > Modify > Fillet**.
6. Select the edge between the main body and the revolved feature, as shown.

7. Type **5** in **Radius** box.

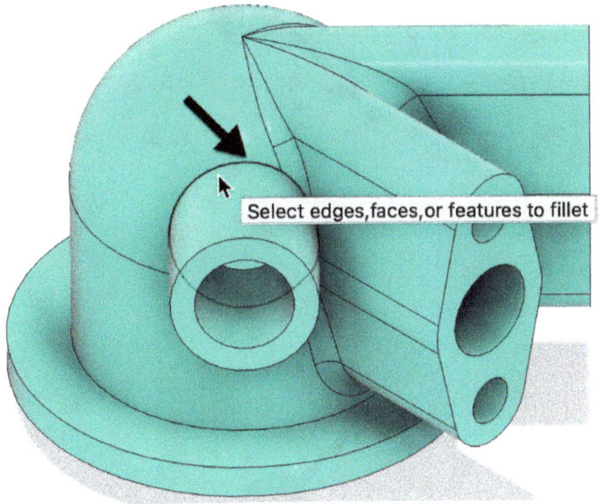

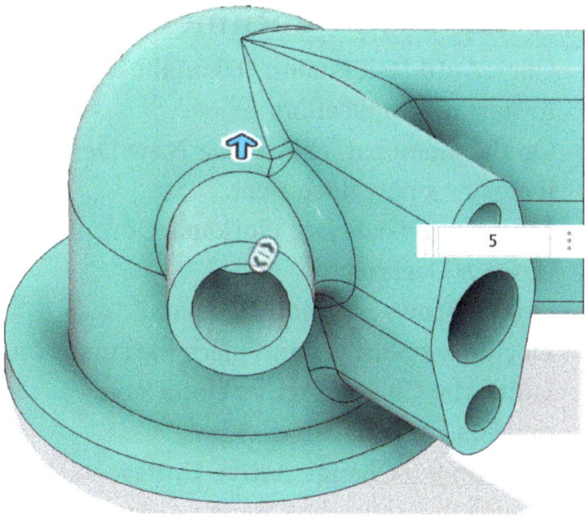

8. Click **OK**.
9. Save and close the file.

Example 3 (Millimeters)

In this example, you create the part shown next.

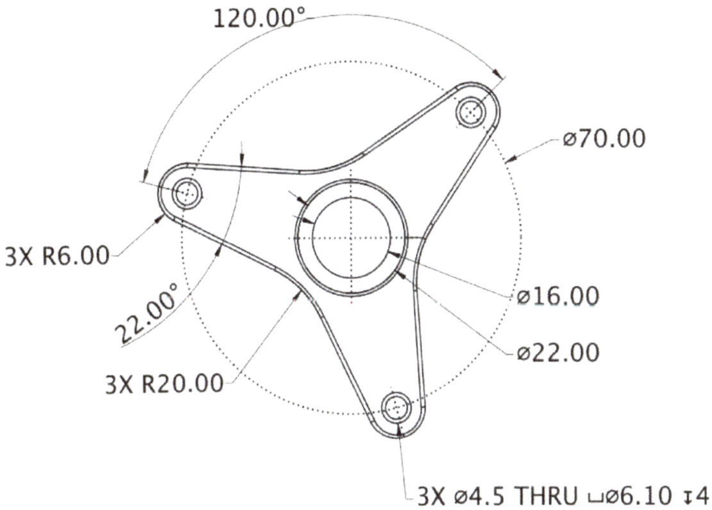

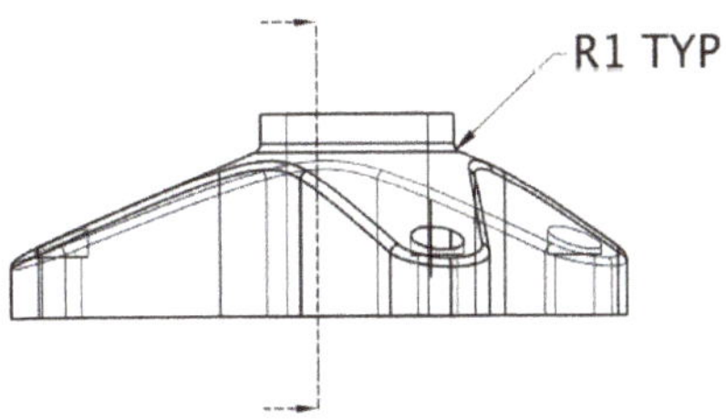

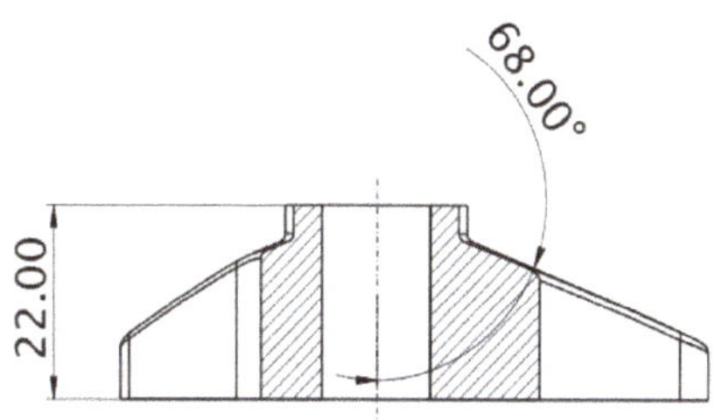

Creating a New document

1. Click **Autodesk Fusion 360** on the desktop to start the application.
2. On the menu bar, click **File > New Design**; it creates a new document.
3. On the toolbar, select **Workspace** drop-down **> Design**.
4. On the **Browser window**, expand **Document Settings** and place the cursor on **Units**; the **Change Active Units** icon appears.
5. Click on the **Change Active Units** icon to change the units; the **Change Active Units** dialog appears.
6. On this dialog, select **Unit Type > millimeter (mm), gram (g)** from the drop-down and click **OK**.

Creating the Extruded feature

1. To start a sketch, click **Create > Create Sketch** on the toolbar. Click on the XY plane. The sketch starts.
2. On the **Sketch** contextual tab of the toolbar, click **Create** panel **> Slot > Center to Center Slot**.

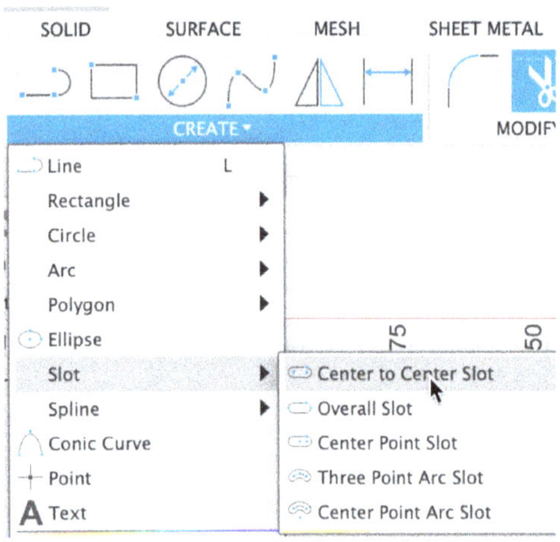

3. Select the origin point of the sketch, move the pointer downward and click on the vertical axis of the sketch.

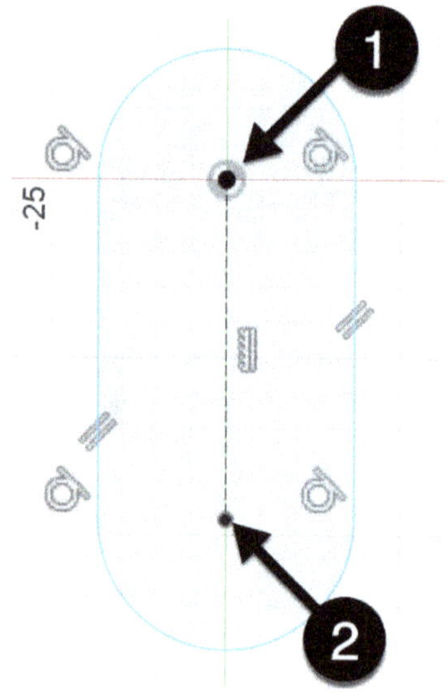

4. Click the **Line** icon on the **Create** panel and select the upper endpoints of the two vertical lines of the slot.

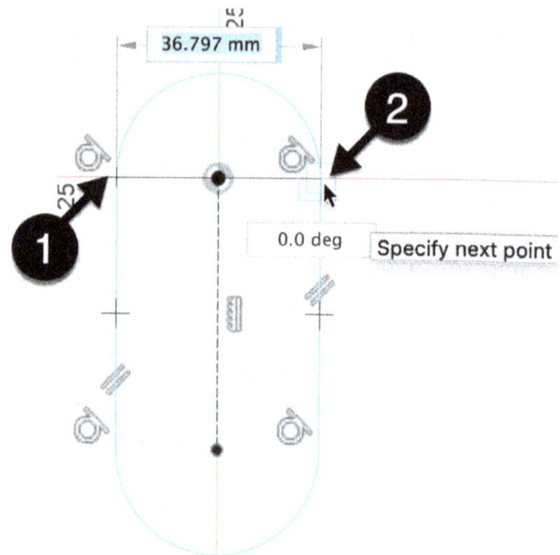

5. Click the **Trim** icon on the **Modify** panel and select the top arc of the slot.

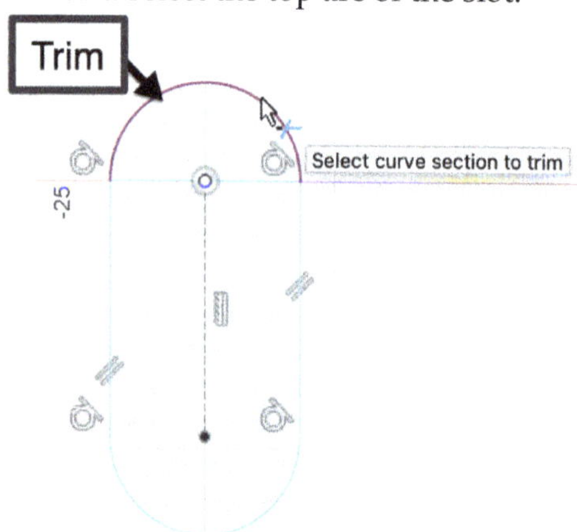

6. Press ESC.
7. Select the **Parallel Constraint** glyph and press DELETE.
8. Click the **Symmetry** icon on the **Constraints** panel and select the right vertical line.
9. Select the left vertical line.
10. Select the centerline.

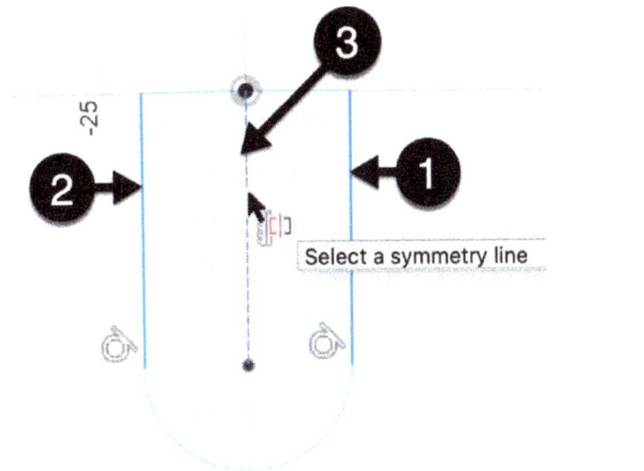

11. Click the **Coincident Constraint** icon on the **Constraints** panel and select the horizontal line.
12. Select the sketch origin.

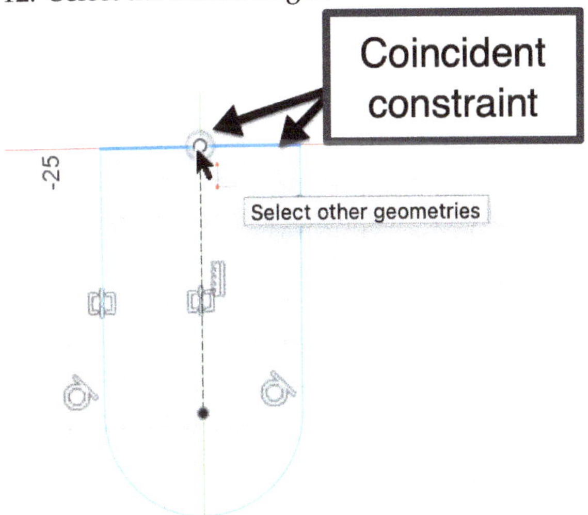

13. Click the **Horizontal/Vertical** icon on the Constraints panel.
14. Select the line coinciding with the sketch origin.
15. Click the **Sketch Dimension** icon on the **Create** panel and select the arc.
16. Type **6** in the **Dimension Value** box and press ENTER.
17. Select the two inclined lines.
18. Move the pointer and click.
19. Type 22 and press ENTER.
20. Select the sketch origin and the center point of the arc.
21. Move the pointer toward left and click.
22. Type 35 in the **Dimension Value** box and press ENTER.

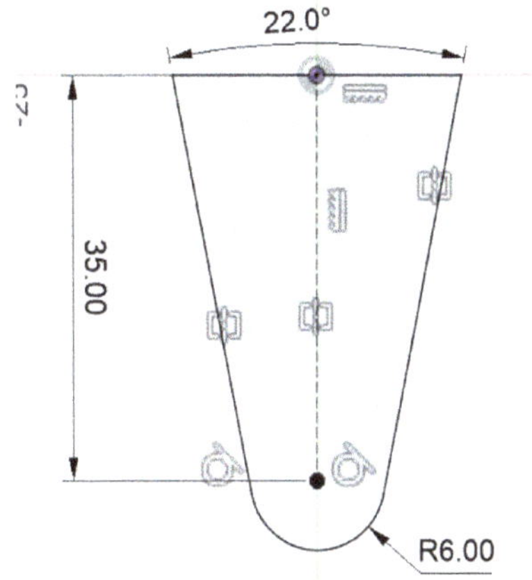

23. Click the **Finish Sketch** on the **Sketch Palette**.
24. Click the **Extrude** command on the **Create** panel.
25. On the **Extrude** dialog, select **Extent Type > Distance** and enter **22** in the **Distance** box. Next, click **OK** to create the *Extrude* feature.

Creating the Counterbore Hole

1. Select the horizontal face of the *Extrude* feature and click the **Hole** tool on the **Create** panel.
2. Click the **Reference** selection button on the **Hole** dialog and select the circular edge of the model, as shown.

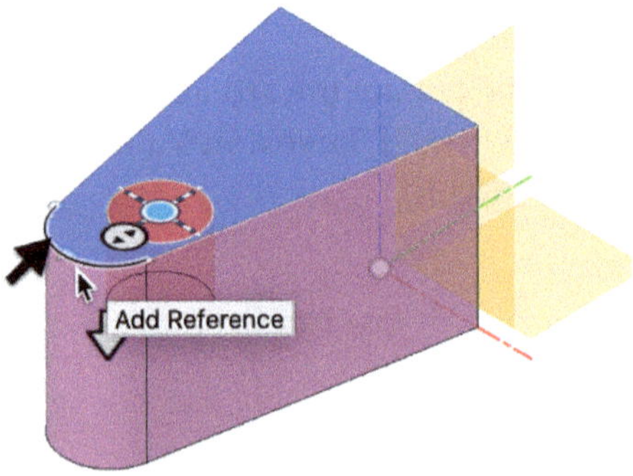

3. Select **Extents > All**.
4. Click **Hole Type > Counterbore**.
5. Click **Hole Tap Type > Tapped**.
6. Click **Thread Offset > Full**.
7. Select **Thread Type > ISO metric profile**.
8. Select **Size > 4.0 mm**.
9. Select **Designation > M4x0.7**.
10. Type-in **6.10** and **17** in the **Counterbore Diameter** and **Counterbore Depth** boxes, respectively.

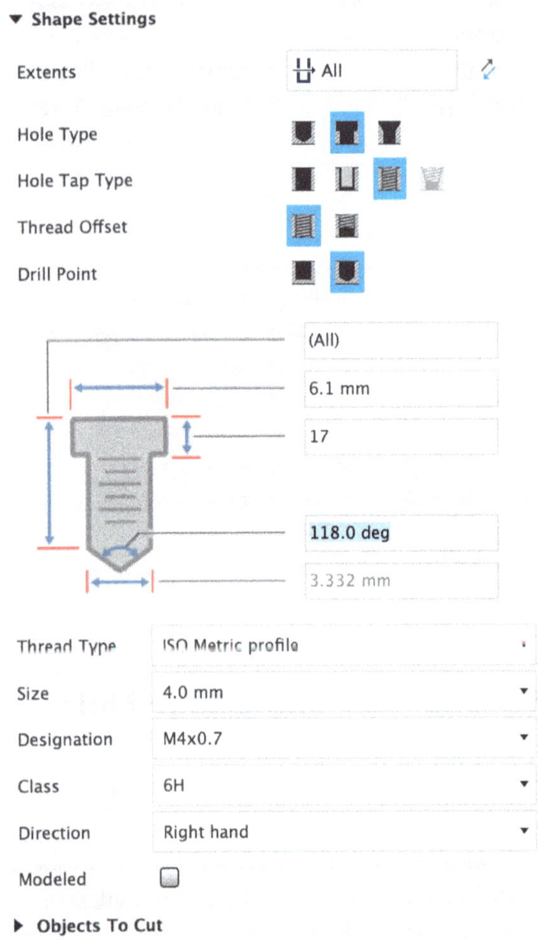

11. Click **OK**; the counterbore hole is created.

Creating the Circular Pattern

1. Click **Solid** tab > **Create** panel > **Pattern** > **Circular Pattern** on the toolbar.
2. Select **Object Type > Features**.
3. Press and hold the CTRL key and select the **Hole** and **Extrude** features from the **Timeline**.
4. Click the **Axis** selection button on the **Circular Pattern** dialog.
5. Select the **Origin > Z-axis** from the Browser.

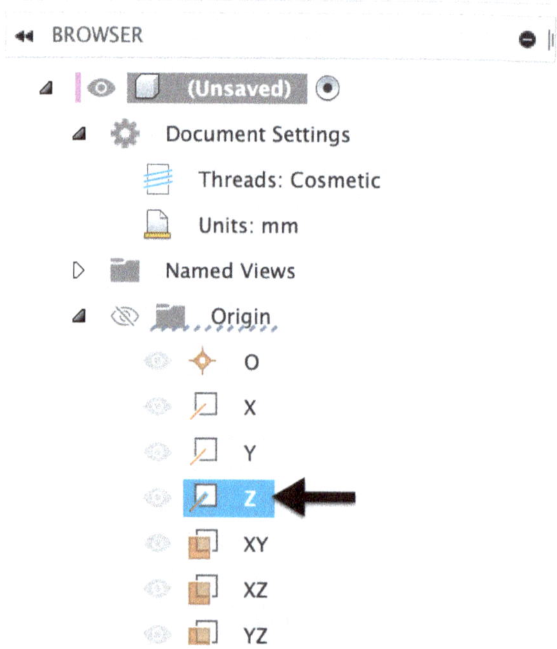

6. Select **Distribution > Full**.

7. Type **3** in the **Quantity** box.
8. Click **OK** to create the pattern.

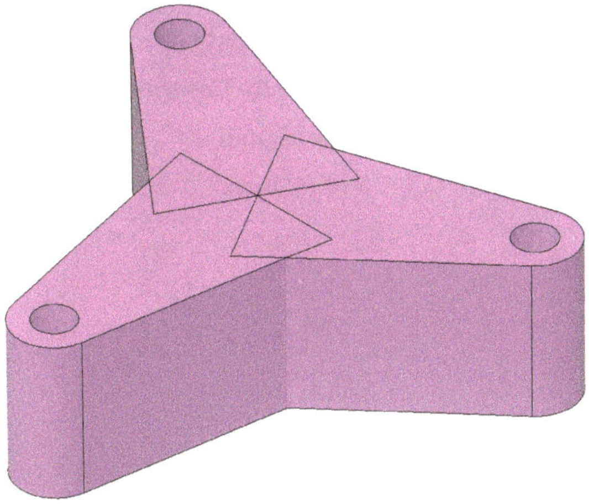

Creating Revolved Intersection

1. To start a sketch, click **Create > Create Sketch** on the toolbar. Click on the YZ plane. The sketch starts.
2. Check the **Slice** option on the Sketch Palette.
3. On the **Create** panel, click the **Line** icon.
4. Select the origin point of the sketch, move the pointer upward and click on the vertical axis of the sketch.
5. Move the pointer toward left and downward. Next, click to create the inclined line.
6. Move the pointer vertically downward and click of the horizontal axis to create the vertical line.
7. Move the pointer horizontally toward right and click on the sketch origin.

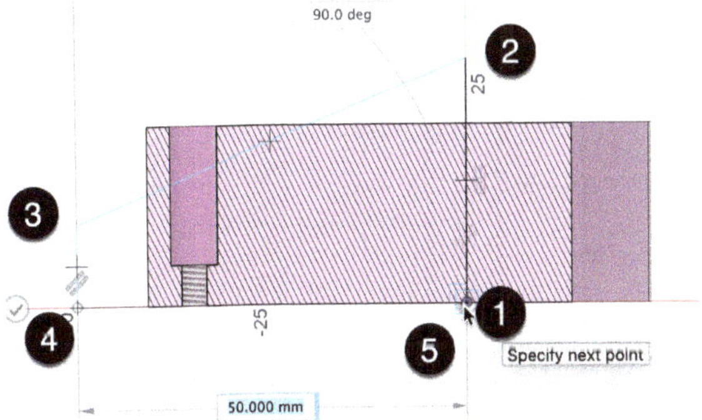

8. Apply constraints and dimensions to the sketch and click **Finish Sketch**.

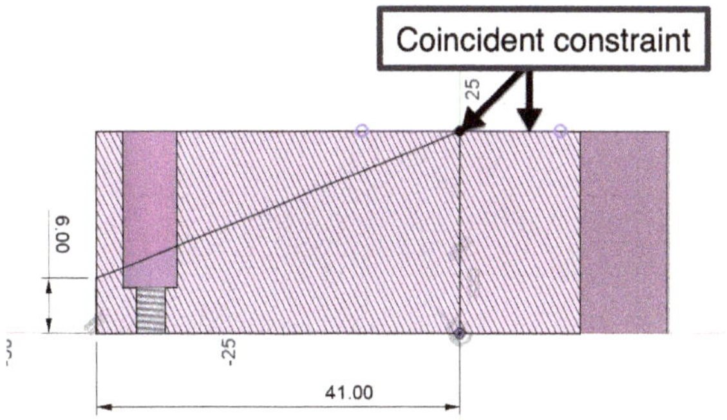

9. Click the **Revolve** 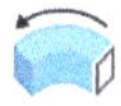 icon on the **Create** panel; the sketch profile is selected automatically.
10. Select the vertical line passing through the sketch origin.

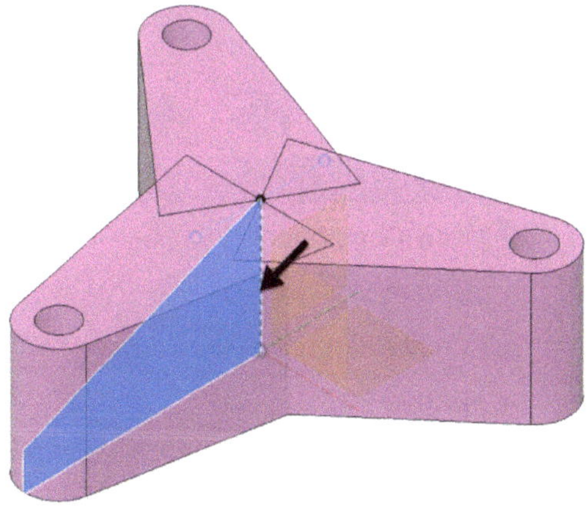

11. Select **Operation > Intersect** on the Revolve dialog.

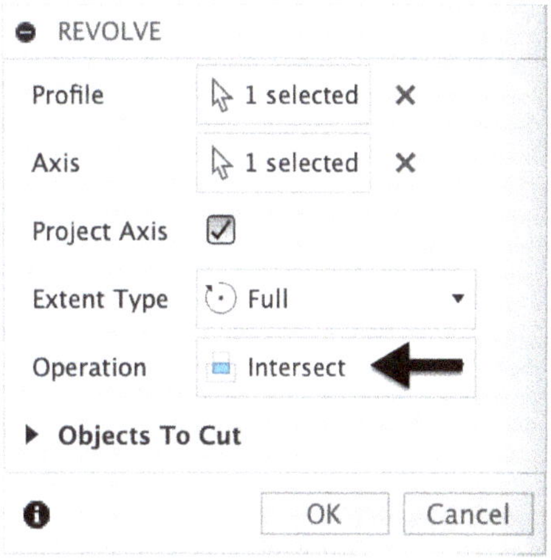

12. Select **Extent Type > Full**. Next, click **OK**.

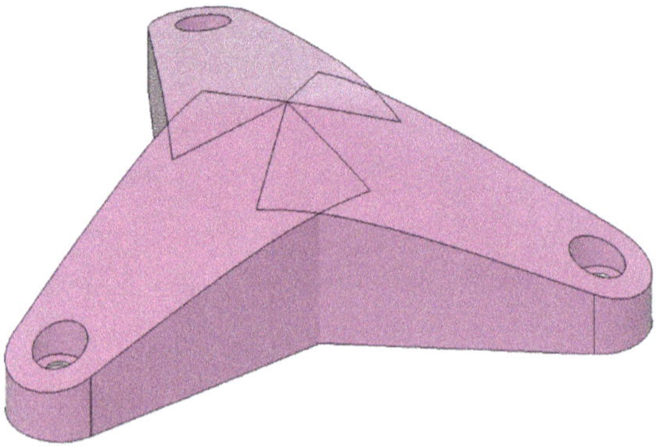

Creating the Cylindrical Feature and Hole at the center

1. On the toolbar, click **Solid** tab > **Create** panel > **Cylinder**.

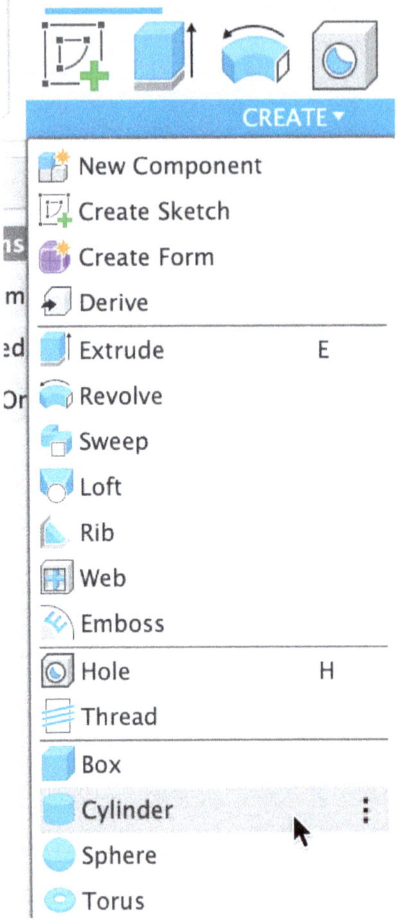

2. Select the XY plane from the **Origin** folder in the Browser.

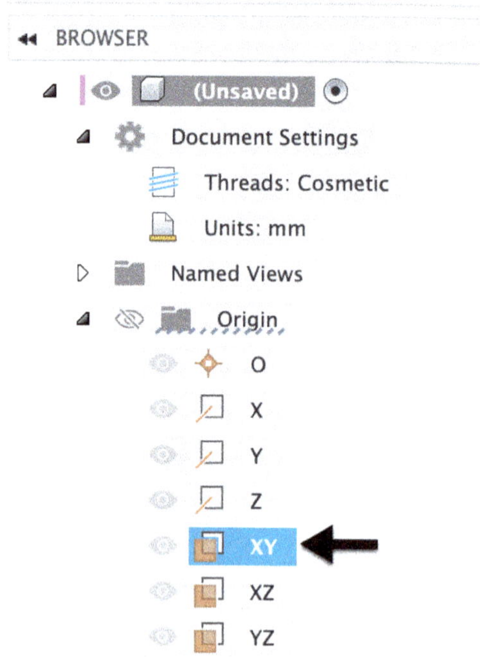

3. Select the origin point of the sketch, move the pointer outward and click.

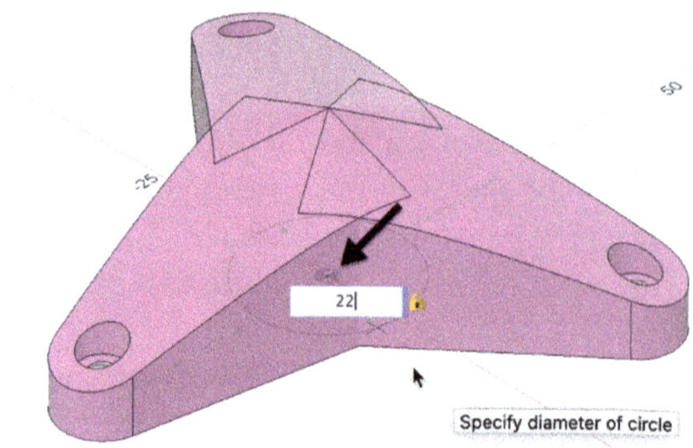

4. Type **22** in the **Diameter** and **Height** boxes on the **Cylinder** dialog.
5. Select **Operation > Join**.

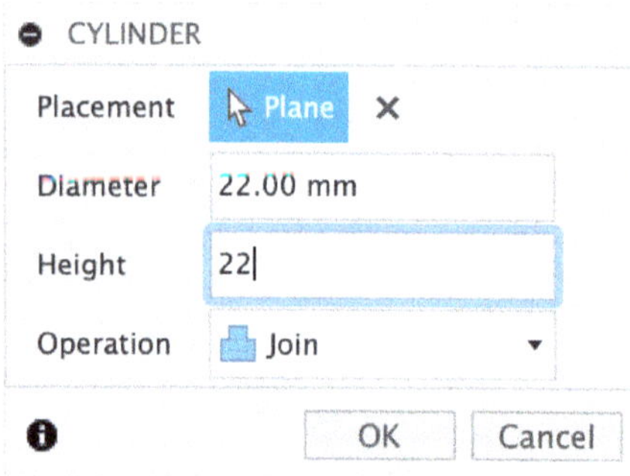

6. Click **OK** to create the cylinder.

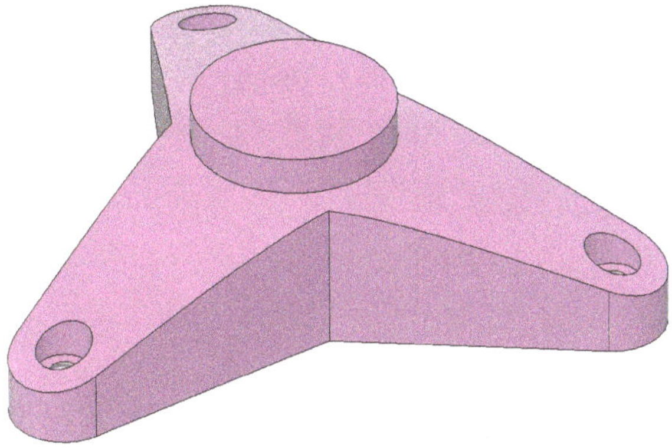

7. Click the **Hole** tool on the **Create** panel.
8. Click on the top face of the cylindrical feature.
9. Select the circular edge of the model, as shown.

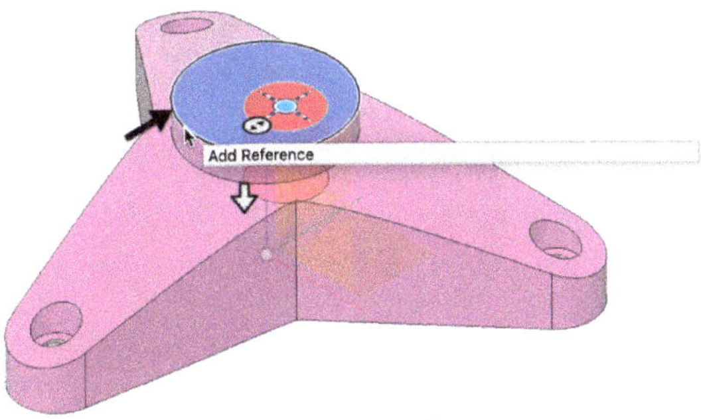

10. Select **Hole Type > Simple**. Next, type **16** in the **Diameter** box.
11. Select **Hole Tap Type > Simple**.
12. Select **Extents > All**. Next, click **OK**; the hole is created.

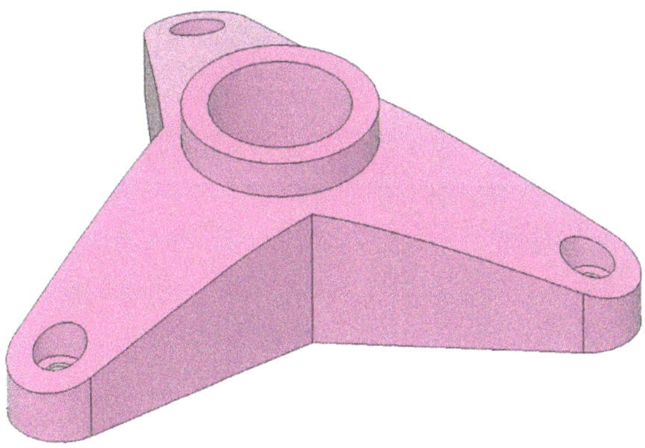

Creating Fillets

1. Click the **Fillet** icon on the **Modify** panel.
2. Select the edges, as shown.

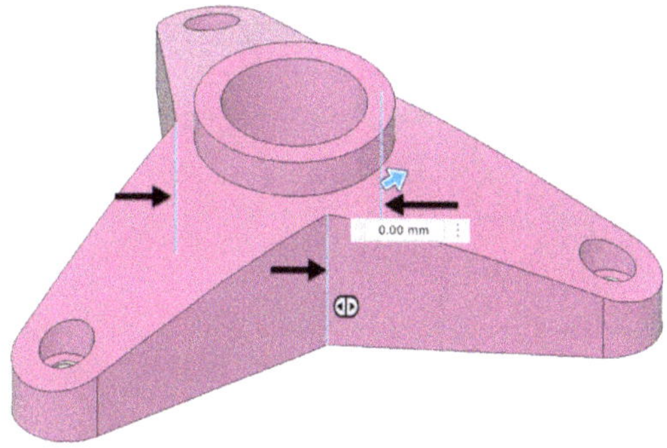

3. Type **20** in the **Specify radius value** box and click **OK**.

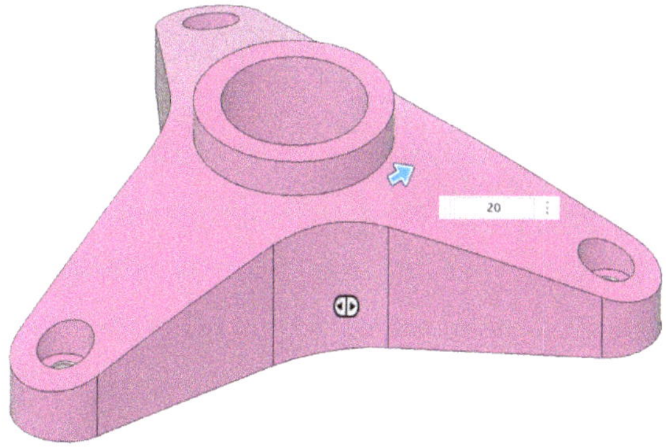

4. Click the **Fillet** icon on the **Modify** panel.
5. Select the edges of the model, as shown.

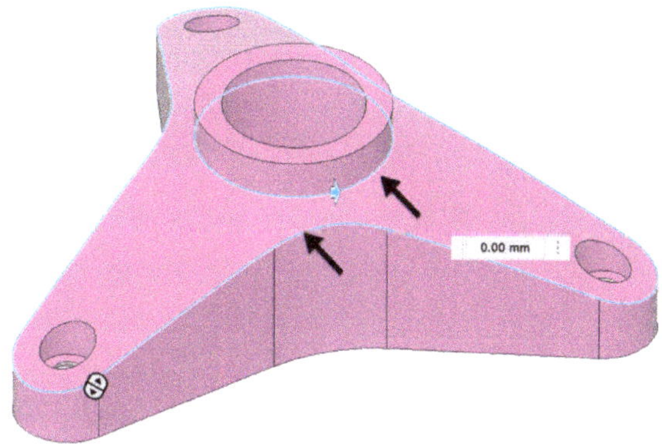

6. Type **1** in the **Specify radius value** box and click **OK**.

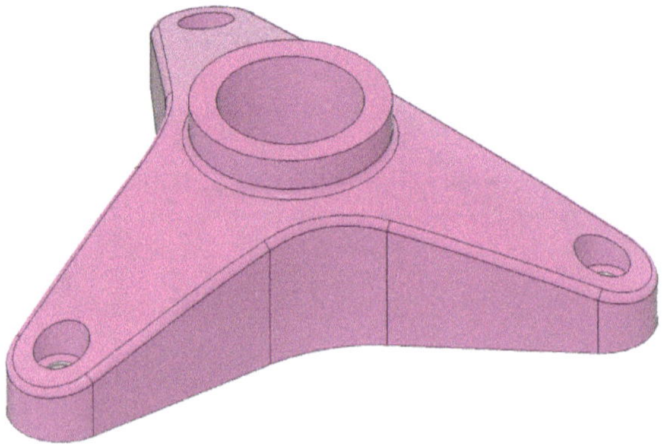

7. Save and close the design file.

Example 4 (Millimeters)

In this example, you create the part shown next.

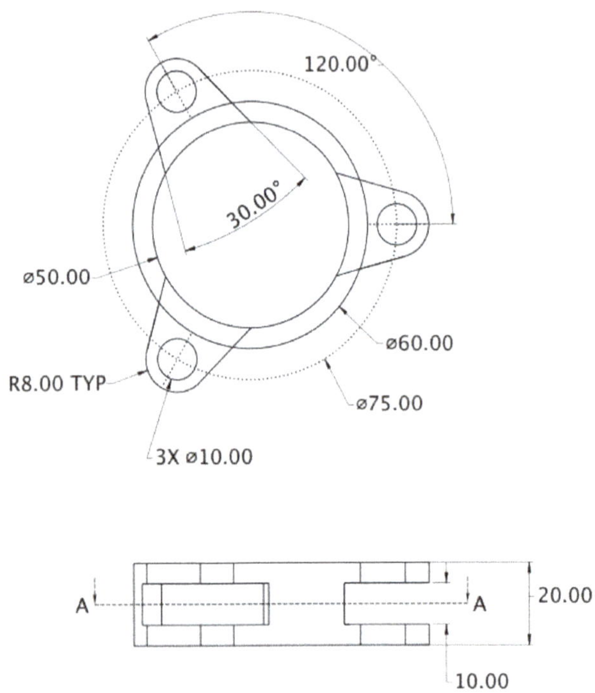

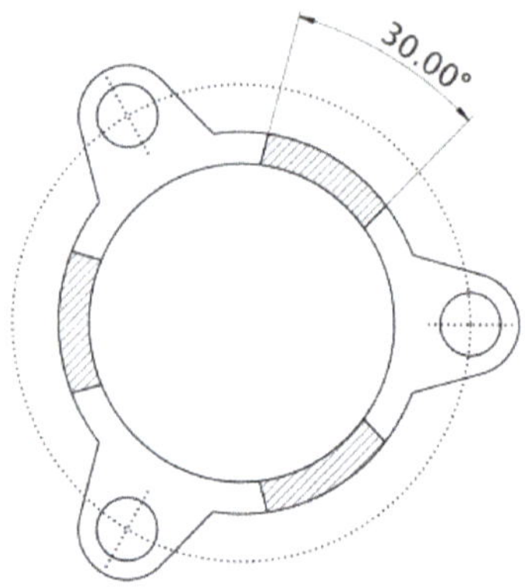

Creating a New document

1. Click **Autodesk Fusion 360** on the desktop to start the application.
2. On the menu bar, click **File > New Design**; it creates a new document.
3. On the toolbar, select **Workspace** drop-down > **Design**.
4. On the **Browser window**, expand **Document Settings** and place the cursor on **Units**; the **Change Active Units** icon appears.
5. Click on the **Change Active Units** icon to change the units; the **Change Active Units** dialog appears.
6. On this dialog, select **Unit Type > millimeter (mm), gram (g)** from the drop-down and click **OK**.

Creating the Cylindrical feature

1. On the toolbar, click **Solid** tab > **Create** panel > **Cylinder** .
2. Select the XY plane.
3. Select the origin point of the sketch, move the pointer outward and click.

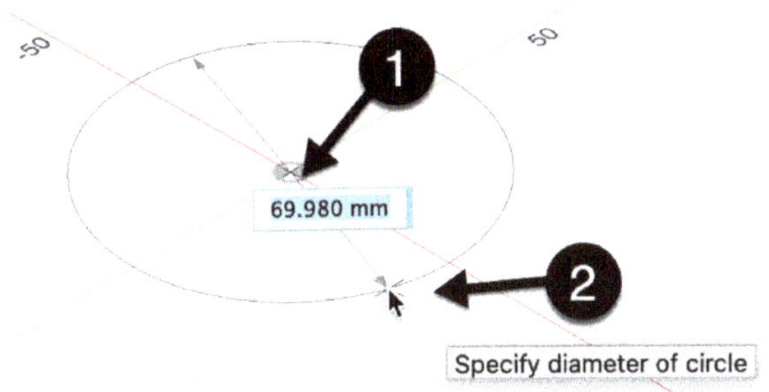

4. Type **60** and **20** in the **Diameter** and **Height** boxes, respectively on the **Cylinder** dialog.
5. Click **OK** to create the cylinder.

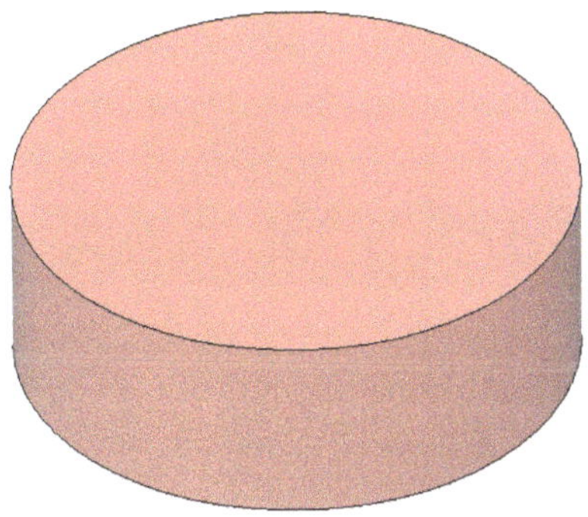

Adding the Extruded feature

1. To start a sketch, click **Create > Create Sketch** on the toolbar. Click on the XY plane. The sketch starts.
2. Check the **Slice** option on the Sketch Palette.
3. On the **Sketch** toolbar, click **Create** panel > **Polygon** > **Edge Polygon**.

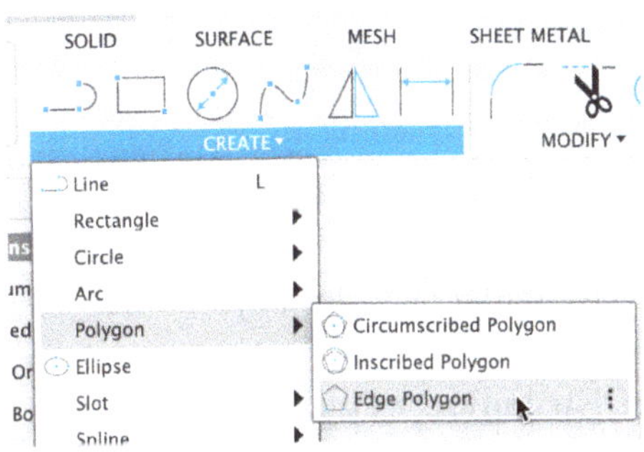

4. Click in the top-left quadrant of the sketch.
5. Move the pointer vertically downward and click to define the edge of the polygon.

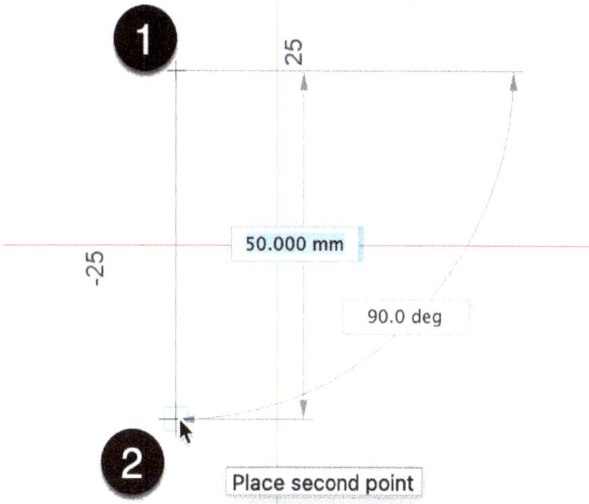

6. Move the pointer toward left.
7. Type 3 in the **Edge Number** box and press ENTER.

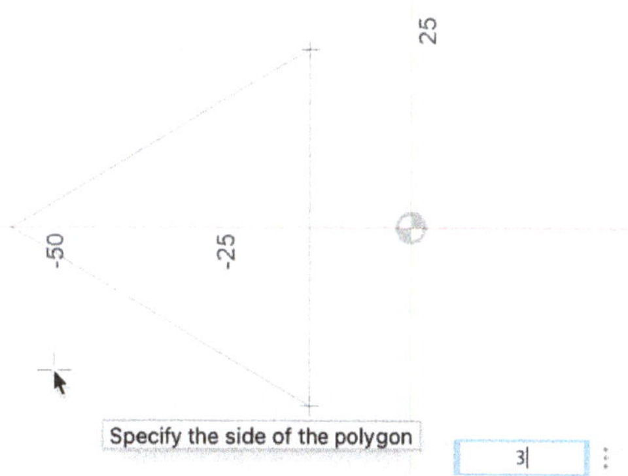

8. Click the **Fillet** icon on the **Modify** panel.
9. Select the left vertex point of the polygon, as shown.

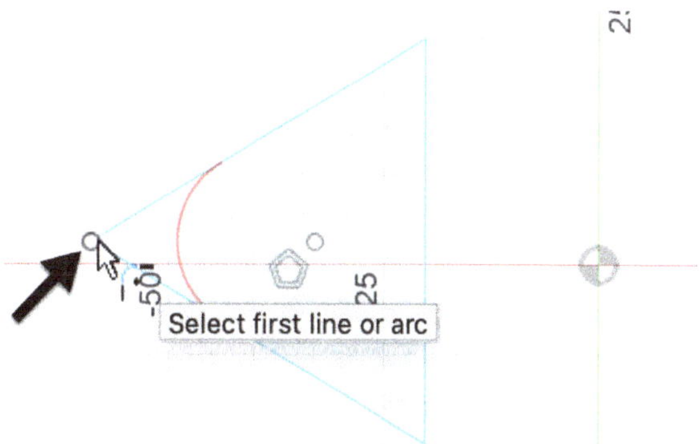

10. Type 8 in the **Fillet radius** box and press ENTER.

11. Click the Horizontal/Vertical icon on the Constraints panel.
12. Select the centerpoint of the arc and the sketch origin.
13. Select the vertical line of the sketch.

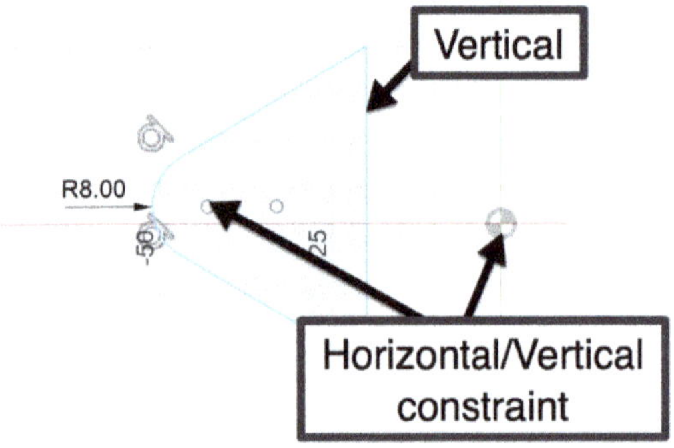

14. Add the **Equal Constraint** between the two inclined lines.
15. Add dimensions to the sketch.

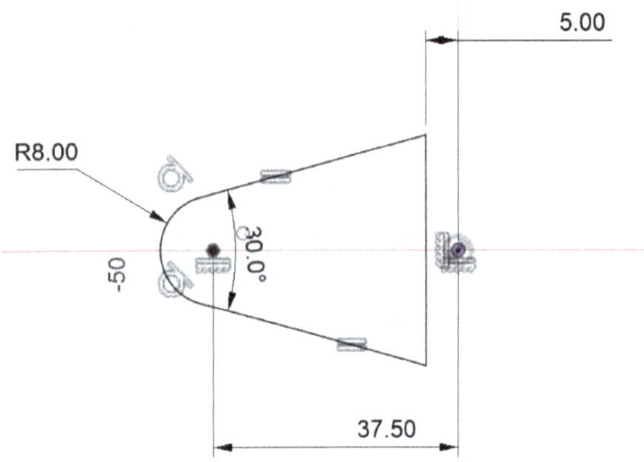

16. Create a circle concentric to the center point of the arc. Next, add a dimension to it.

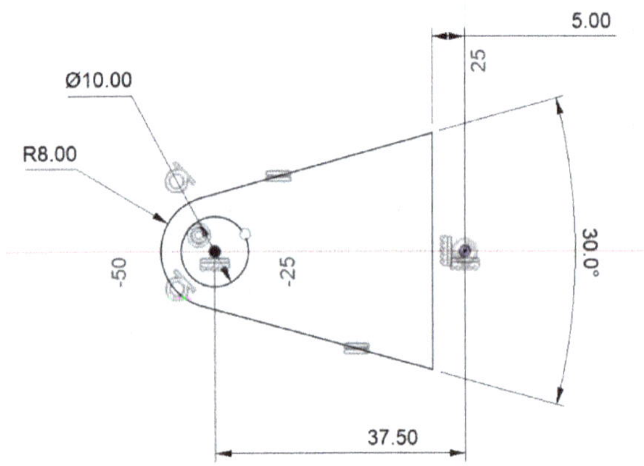

17. Click the **Finish Sketch** button on the toolbar.
18. On the toolbar, click **Solid** tab > **Create** panel > **Extrude**.
19. Click in the sketch region, as shown.

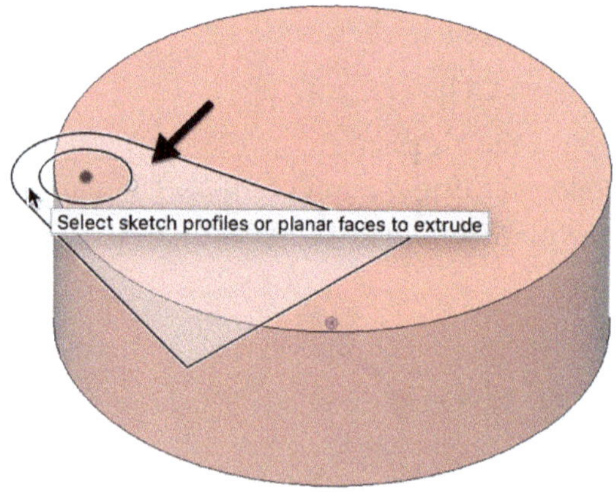

20. Enter **20** in the **Distance** box. Next, select **Operation > Join** and click **OK** to create the *Extrude* feature.

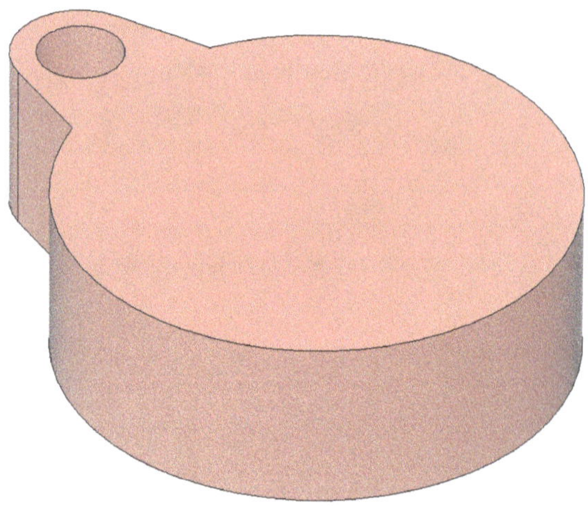

Creating the Circular Pattern

1. Click the **Rectangular Pattern** command on the **Create** panel.
2. Select **Type > Circular Pattern** on the dialog.

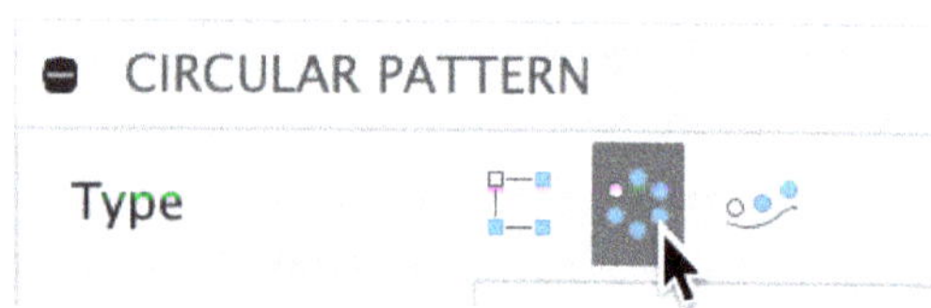

3. Select **Object Type > Features**.
4. Select the **Extrude** feature from the Timeline.
5. Select the circular face of the cylindrical feature.
6. Select **Distribution > Full**.
7. Type-in **3** in the **Quantity** box.

8. Click **OK** to create the pattern.

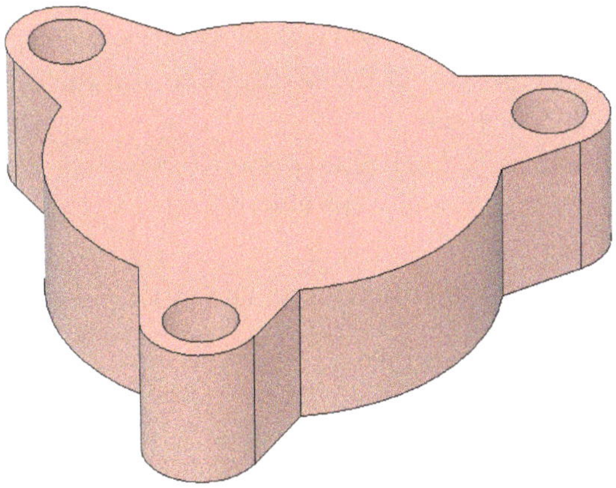

Creating the Cut Features

1. Click on the top face of the model and click the **Create Sketch** command on the **Create** panel.
2. On the **Sketcher geometries** toolbar, click the **Center Diameter Circle** icon. Next, select the origin point of the sketch, move the pointer outward and click.
3. Apply the dimension to the circle and click **Finish Sketch**.

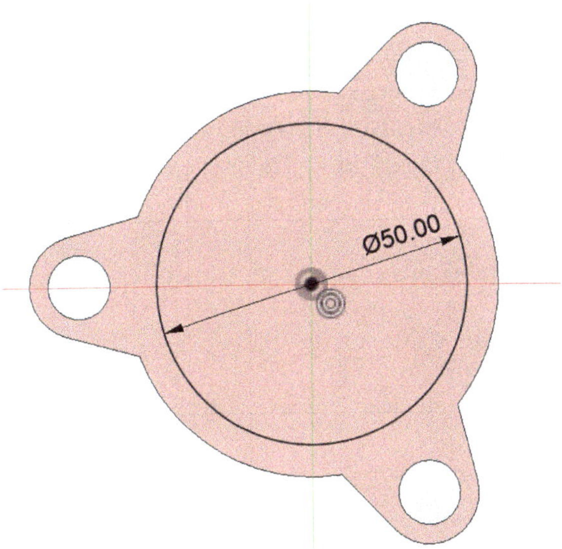

4. Click the **Extrude** icon on the **Create** panel.
5. Click in the sketch region.
6. Select **Extent Type > All**.
7. Select **Operation > Cut**.
8. Click the **Flip** icon to reverse the direction of extrusion. Next, click **OK**.

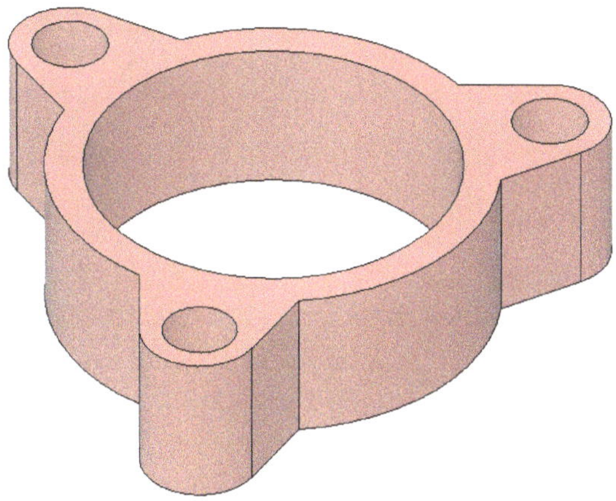

9. On the toolbar, click **Solid** tab > **Construct** panel > **Midplane**.

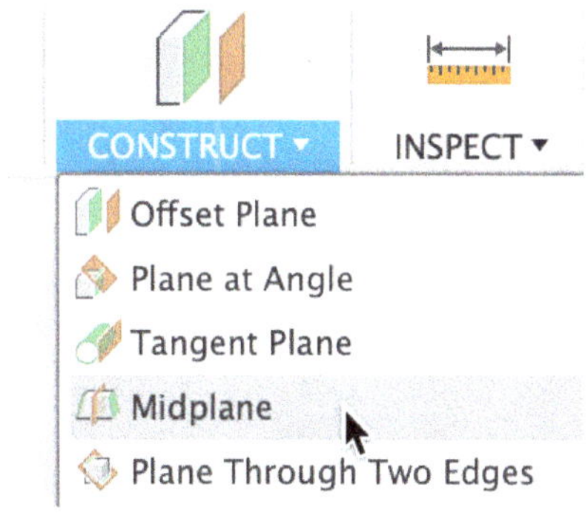

10. Select the top and bottom faces of the model.

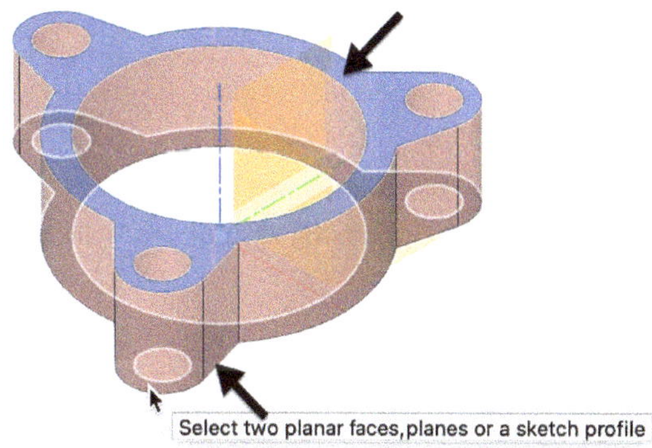

11. Click **OK**.
12. Click the **Create Sketch** command on the **Create** panel. Next, select the newly created plane from the graphics window.

13. On the **Sketch** toolbar, click **Create > Line** icon. Next, click on the horizontal axis of the sketch, move the pointer to top-left corner and click.
14. Move the pointer vertically downward and click to create a vertical line.
15. Move the pointer and select the start point of the sketch.

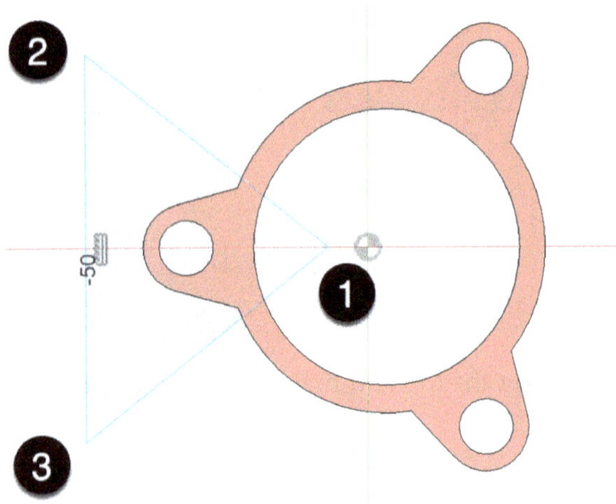

16. Apply the **Equal** constraint between the two inclined lines.
17. Apply the **Horizontal/Vertical** constraint between the right vertex point of the sketch and sketch origin.

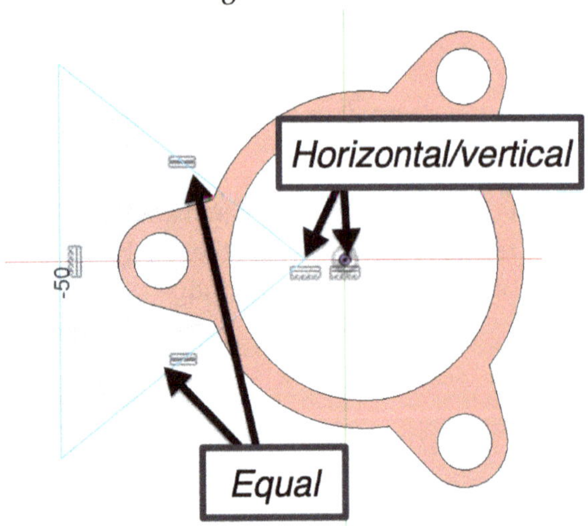

18. Apply the Angle dimension between the two inclined lines.
19. Apply the horizontal dimension between the endpoint of the vertical line and the sketch origin.
20. Apply the horizontal dimension between the start point of the sketch and the sketch origin.
21. Click **Finish Sketch** on the toolbar.

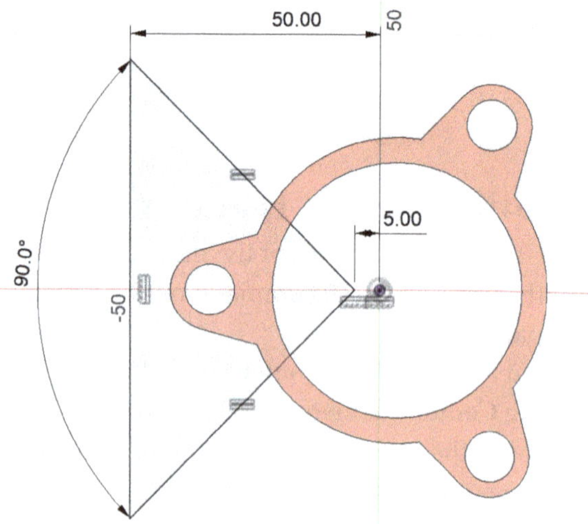

22. Click the **Extrude** icon on the **Create** panel.
23. On the **Extrude** dialog, select Extent **Type > Distance** and enter **10** in the **Distance** box.
24. Select **Direction > Symmetric**.
25. Select **Measurement > Whole Length**.
26. Select **Operation > Cut** and click **OK** to create the *Cut* feature.

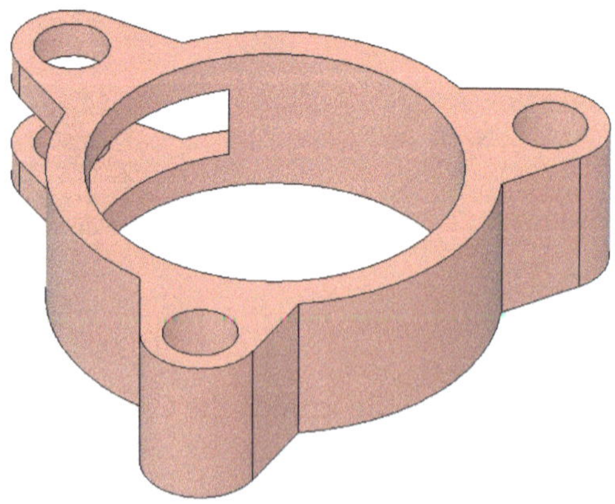

Creating a Full Round Fillet

1. Click the **Orbit** icon on the **Navigation Bar** located at the bottom of the graphics

window.

2. Press and hold the left mouse button and drag the pointer such that the cut feature is displayed.

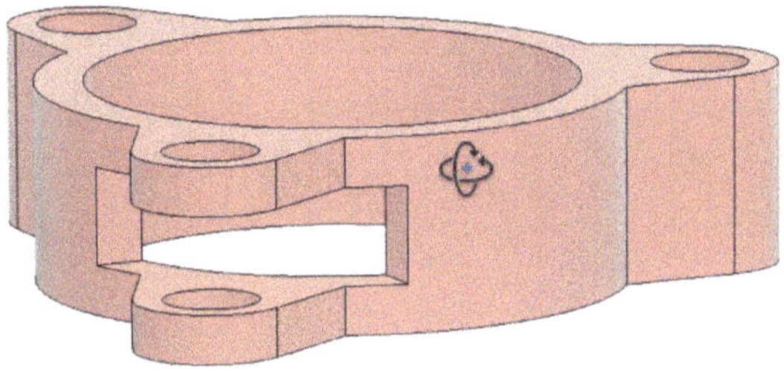

3. Right-click and select **OK**.
4. Click the **Fillet** icon on the **Modify** panel.
5. On the **Fillet** dialog, select **Full Round Fillet** from the **Type** drop-down.
6. Select the vertical face of the cut feature as the Center Face.
7. Click the **Side 1** selection button.
8. Select the lower bottom face of the cut feature to define the Side 1.

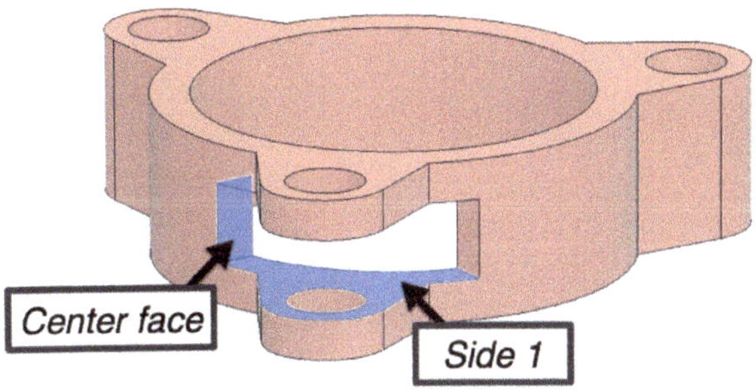

9. Click the **Orbit** icon on the **Navigation Bar** located at the bottom of the graphics window.
10. Press an hold the left mouse button and drag the pointer upward.
11. Click the **Side 2** selection button and select the top inner face, as shown.

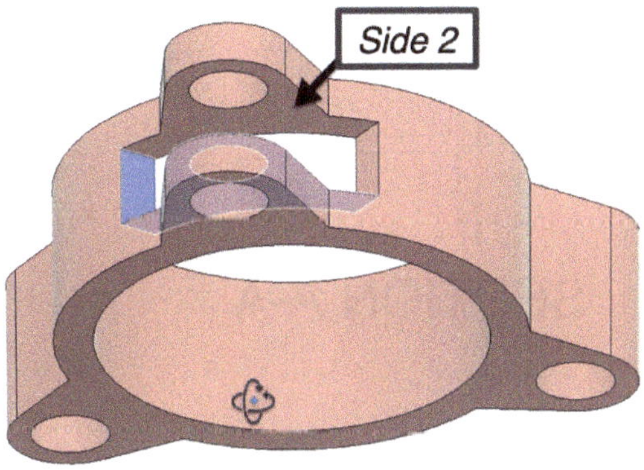

12. Right-click and select **OK**.
13. Click **OK** to create the full round fillet.

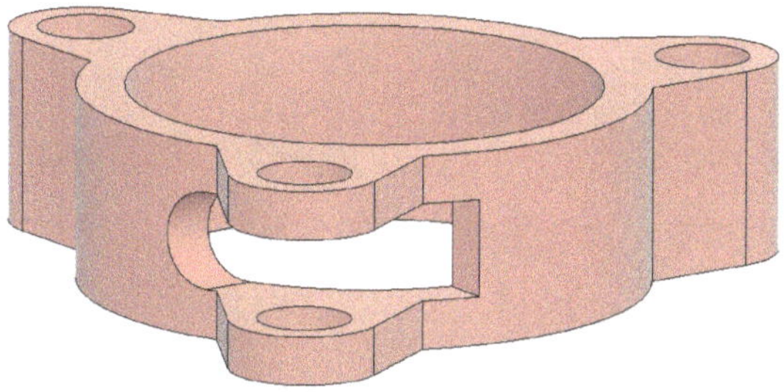

14. Likewise, create another full round fillet, as shown.

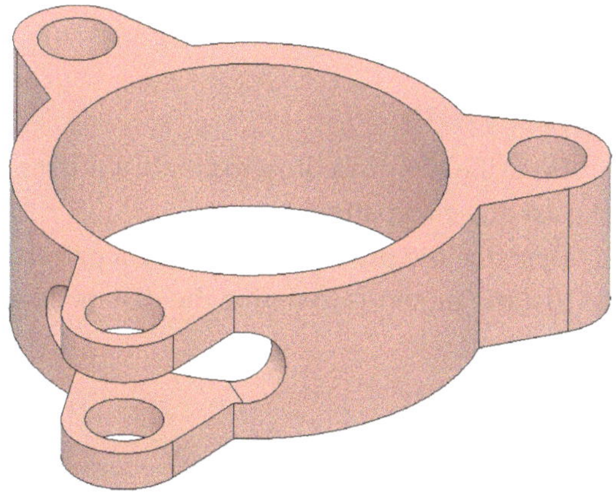

Creating a Circular Pattern

1. Click the **Rectangular Pattern** command on the **Create** panel.
2. Select **Type > Circular Pattern** on the dialog.

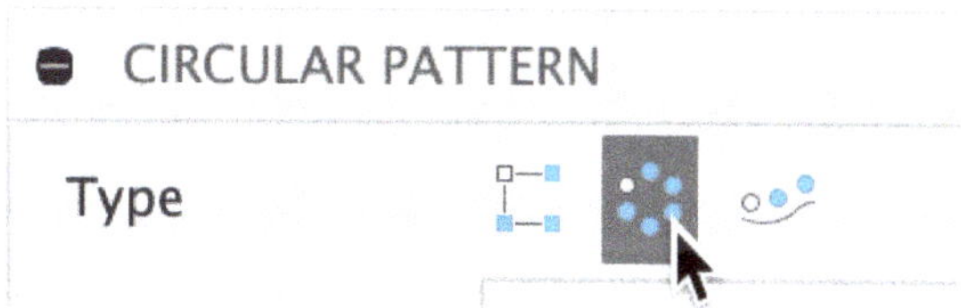

3. Select **Object Type > Features**.
4. Select the **Extrude** and **Fillet** features from the Timeline.

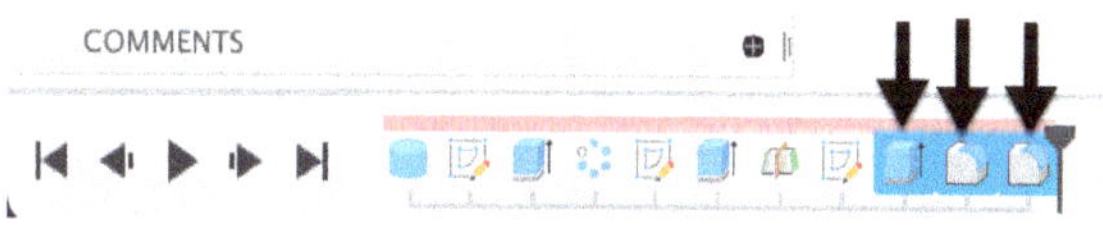

5. Click the **Axis** selection button.
6. Select the circular face of the cylindrical feature.
7. Select **Distribution > Full**.

8. Type-in **3** in the **Quantity** box.
9. Click **OK** to create the pattern.
10. Save and close the design file.

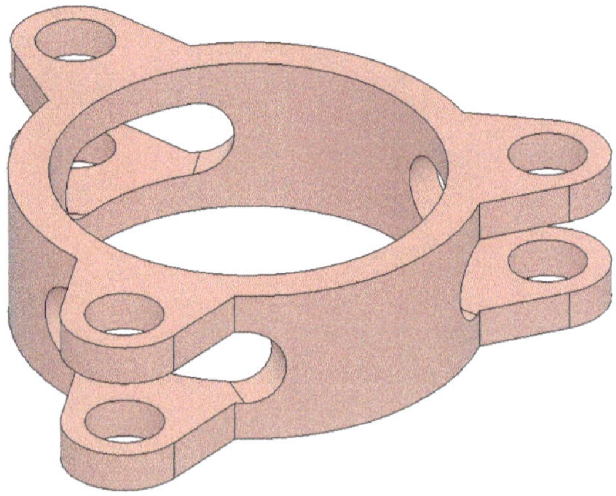

Questions

1. Describe the procedure to create a mirror feature.
2. List any two pattern types.
3. Describe the procedure to create a pattern along a curve.
4. List the methods to define the distance between occurrences in a Rectangular pattern.

Exercises

Exercise 1 (Millimetres)

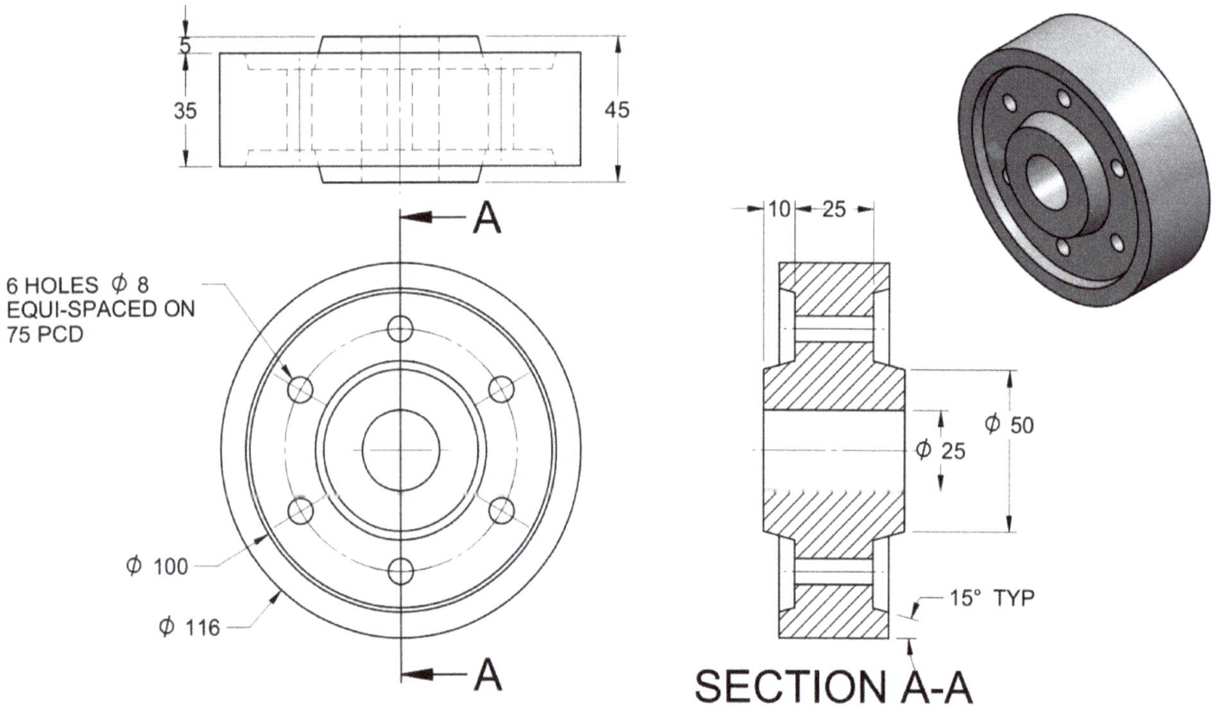

Chapter 6: Sweep Features

The **Sweep** command is one of the basic commands available in Autodesk Fusion 360 that allow you to generate solid geometry. It can be used to create simple geometry as well as complex shapes. A sweep is composed of two items: a profile and a path. The profile controls the shape of the sweep while the path controls its direction. For example, take a look at the angled cylinder shown in the figure. This is created using a simple sweep with the circle as the profile and an angled line as the path.

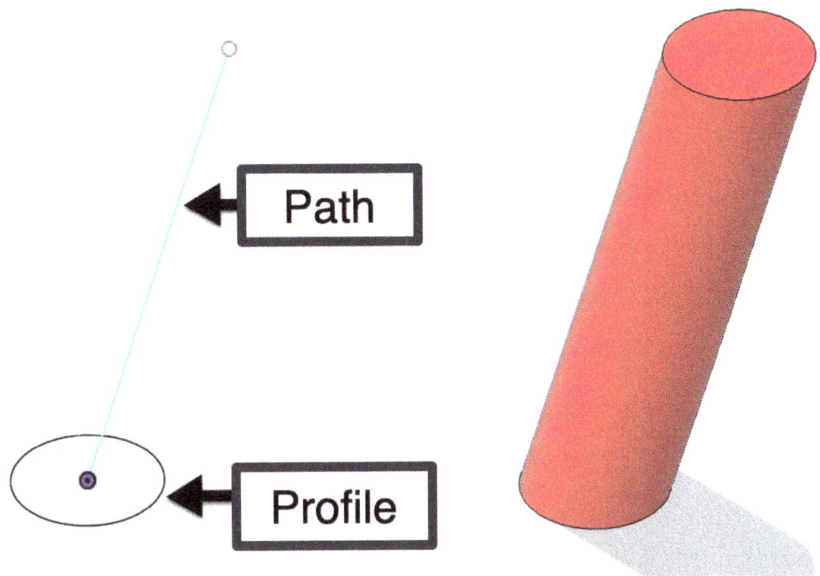

By making the path a bit more complex, you can see that a sweep allows you to create shapes you would not be able to create using commands such as **Extrude** or **Revolve**.

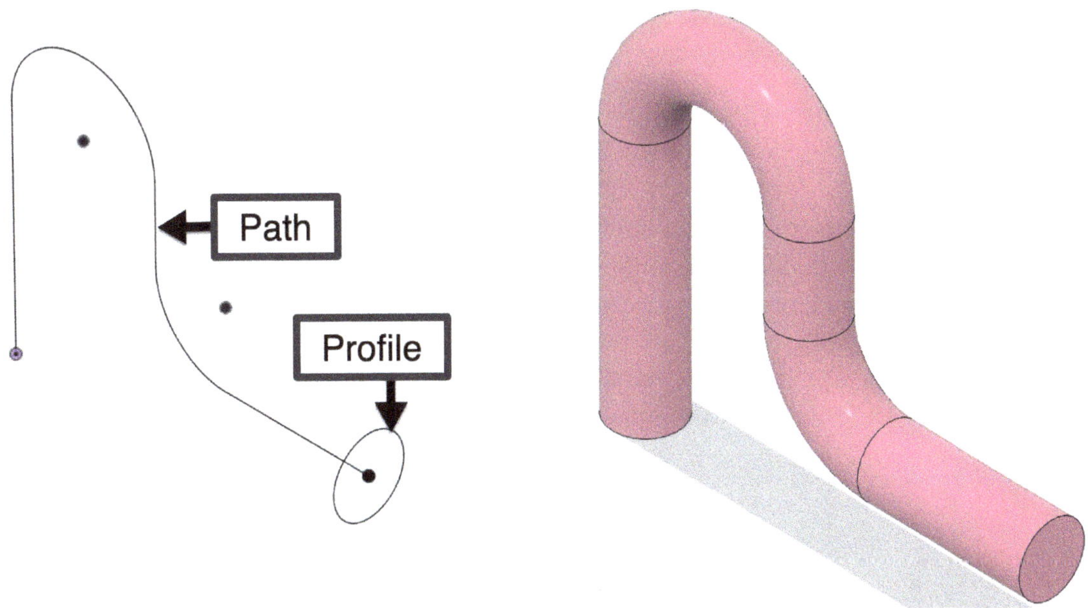

To take the sweep feature to the next level of complexity, you can add guide rails and guide surface. By doing so, the shape of the geometry is controlled by guide rails or guide surfaces. For example, the circular profile in the figure varies in size along the path because a guide rail controls it.

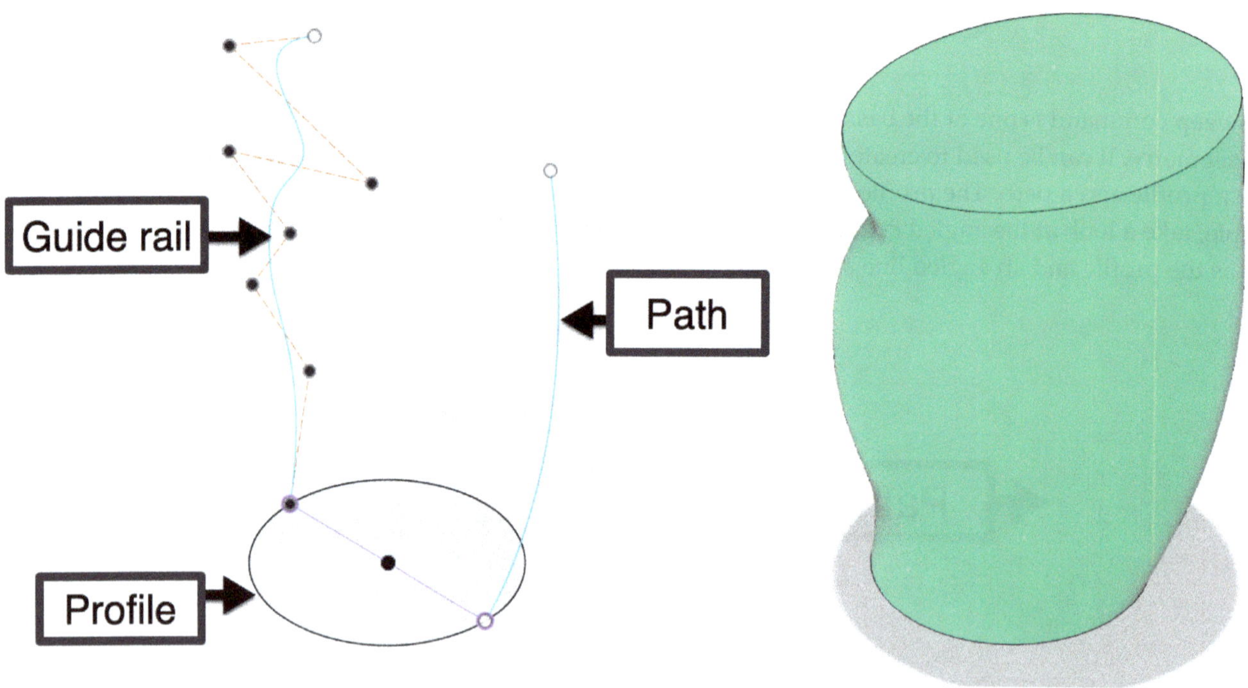

The topics covered in this chapter are:

- *Path sweeps*
- *Path and Guide rail sweeps*
- *Path and Guide Surface sweeps*
- *Scaling the profile along the path*
- *Swept Cutouts*
- *Coils*
- *Pipes*

Single Path sweeps

This type of sweep requires two elements: a path and profile. The profile defines the shape of the sweep along the path. A path is used to control the direction of the profile. A path can be a sketch or an edge. To create a sweep, you must first create a path and a profile. Create a path by drawing a sketch. It can be an open or closed sketch.

Next, click **Construct** panel > **Plane Along Path**  on the **Solid** tab of the toolbar, and then create a plane normal to the path. Sketch the profile on the plane normal to the path.

Sweep Features

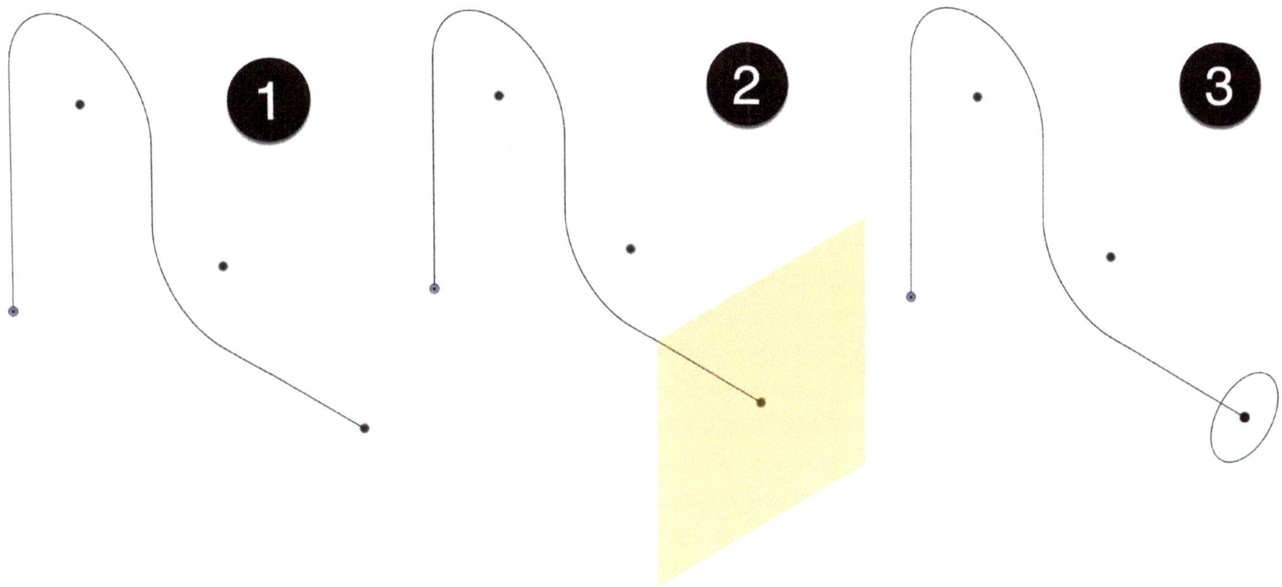

Activate the **Sweep** command (click **Create** panel **>** **Sweep** on the **Solid** tab of the toolbar). As you activate this command, a dialog appears showing different options to create the sweep. Select the **Single Path** option from the **Type** drop-down on the dialog. Select the profile from the graphics window. Next, click the **Path** selection button and select the path. Click **OK** to create the sweep.

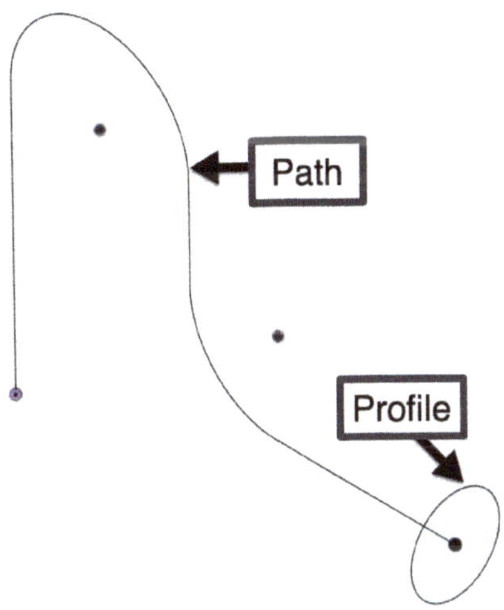

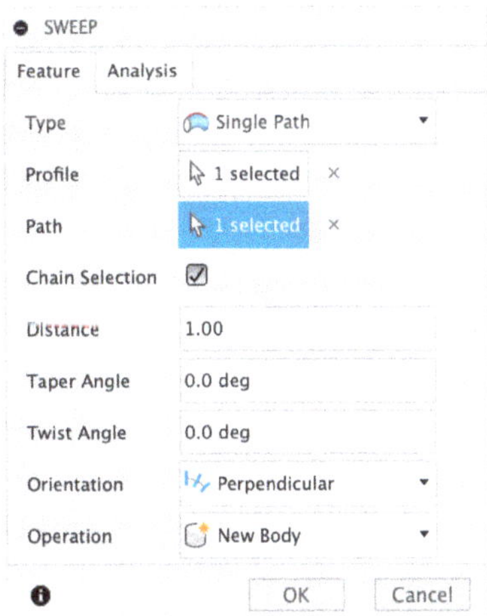

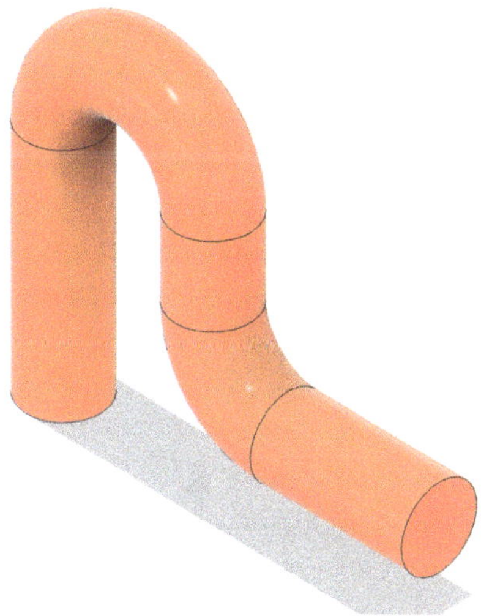

Fusion 360 will not allow the sweep to result in a self-intersecting geometry. As the profile is swept along a path, it cannot come back and cross itself. For example, if the profile of the sweep is larger than the curves on the path, the resulting geometry will intersect, and the sweep will fail.

Sweep Features

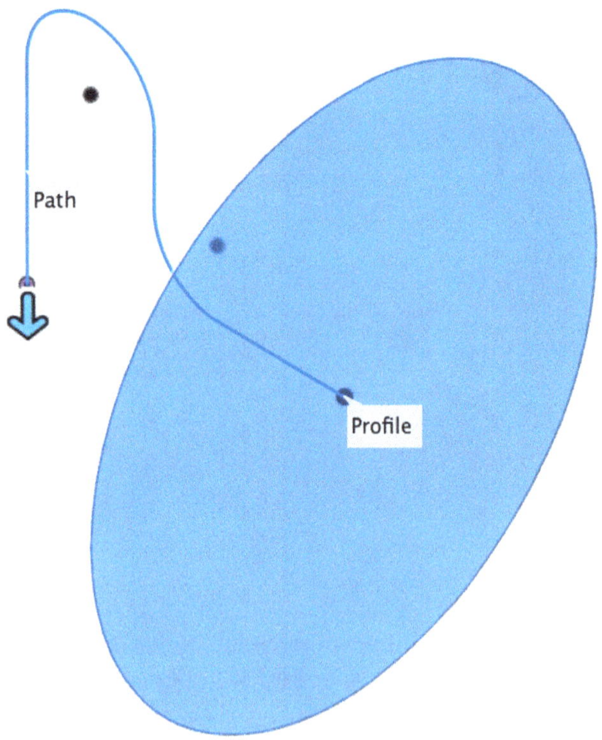

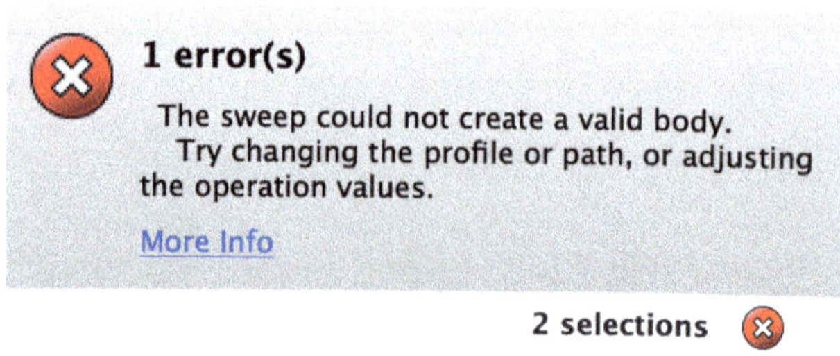

A sweeping profile must be created as a sketch. However, a path can be a sketch or an edge. The following illustrations show various types of paths and resultant sweep features.

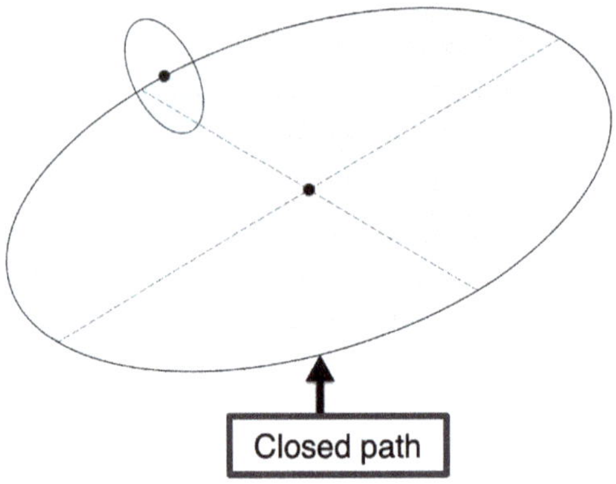

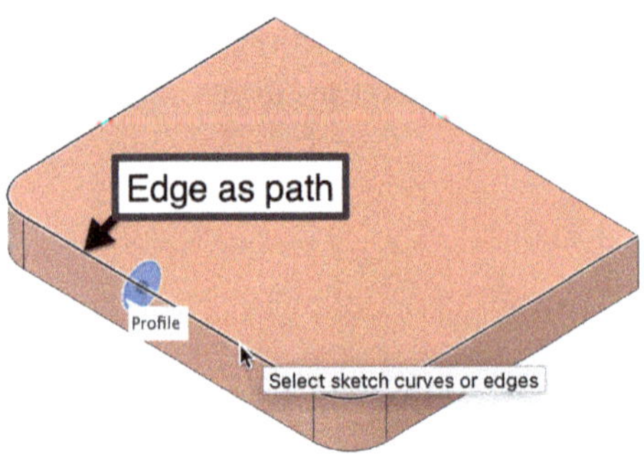

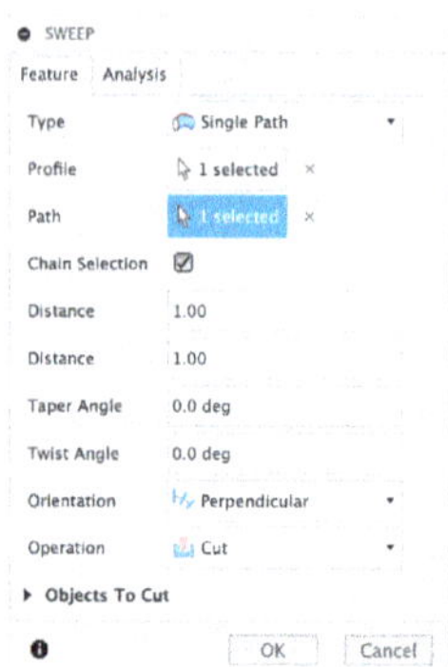

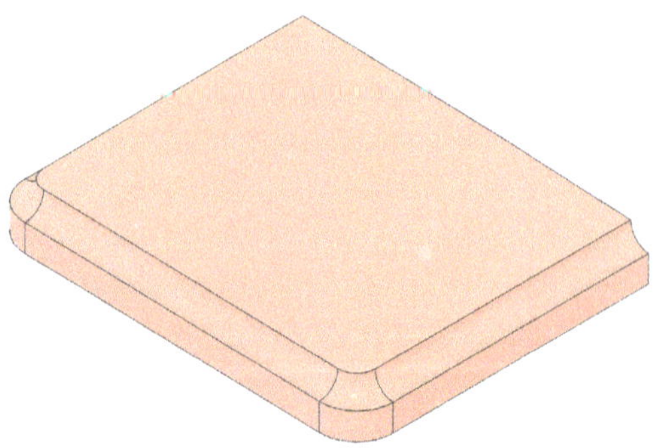

Profile Orientation

The **Orientation** options define the orientation of the resulting geometry. The **Perpendicular** option sweeps the cross-section in the direction perpendicular to the path. The **Parallel** option sweeps the cross-section in the direction parallel to itself.

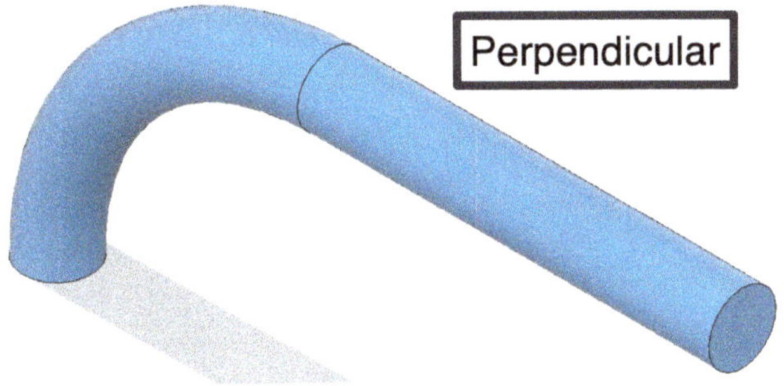

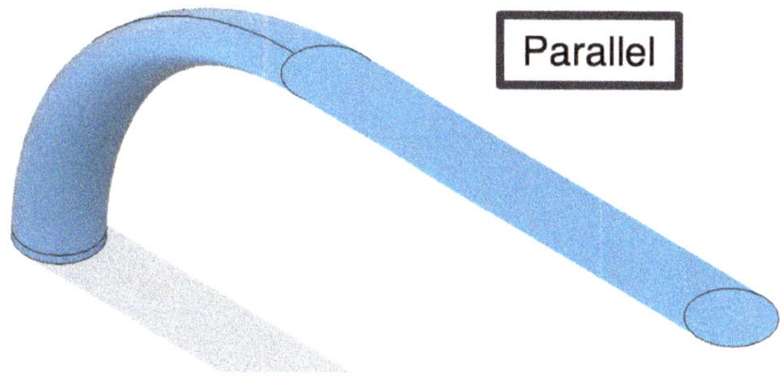

Taper Angle

Autodesk Fusion 360 allows you to taper the sweep along the path. Select the profile and the path, and then type in a value in the **Taper Angle** box. Click **OK** to create the tapered sweep feature.

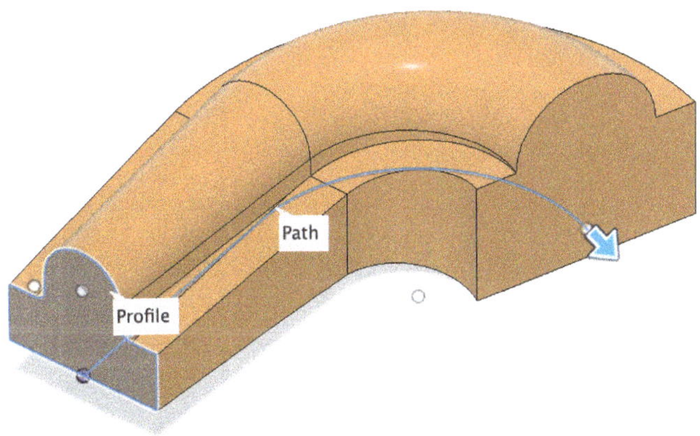

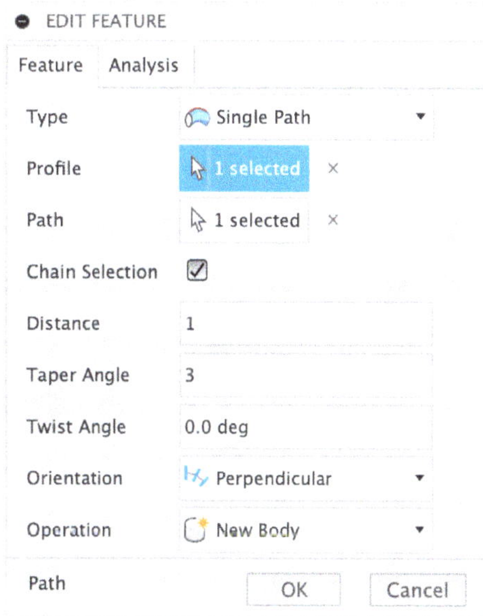

Twist Angle

Autodesk Fusion 360 allows you to twist the profile along the path. Define the profile and path, and then type-in the twist angle in the **Twist Angle** box; the twist is applied to the profile.

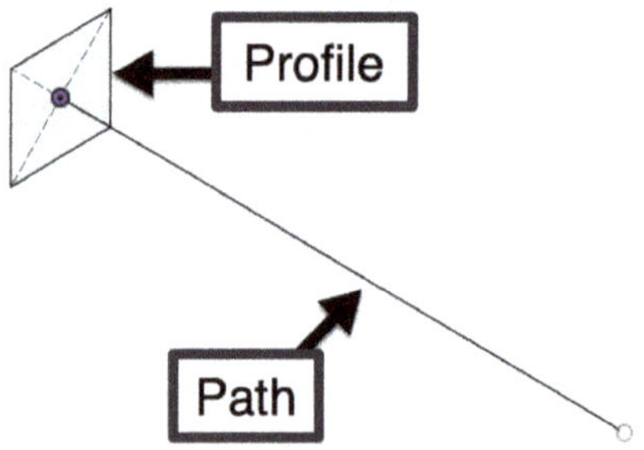

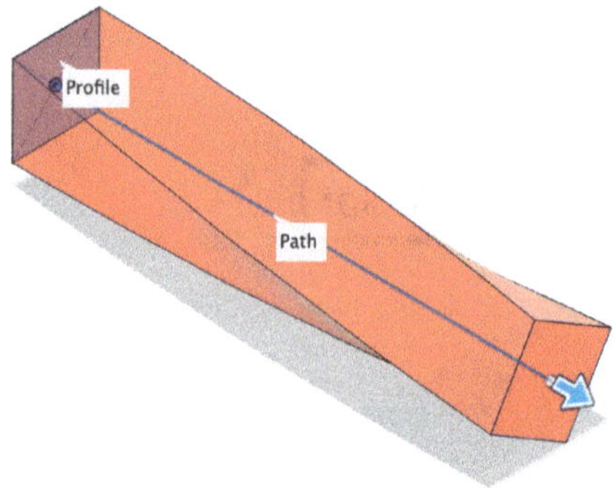

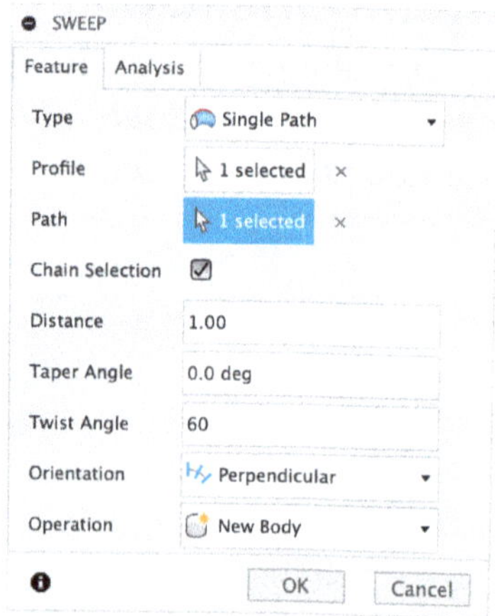

Path and Guide Rail Sweeps

Autodesk Fusion 360 allows you to create sweep features with path and guide rails. This can be useful while creating complex geometry and shapes. To create this type of sweep feature, first, create a path. Next, create a profile and guide rail, as shown in the figure. Activate the **Sweep** command and select **Type > Path + Guide Rail** from the **Sweep** dialog. Next, select the profile.

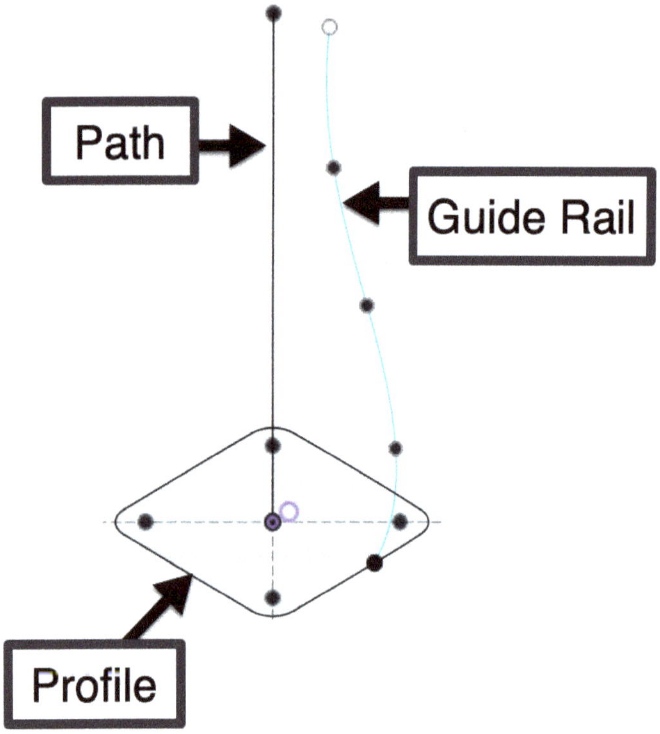

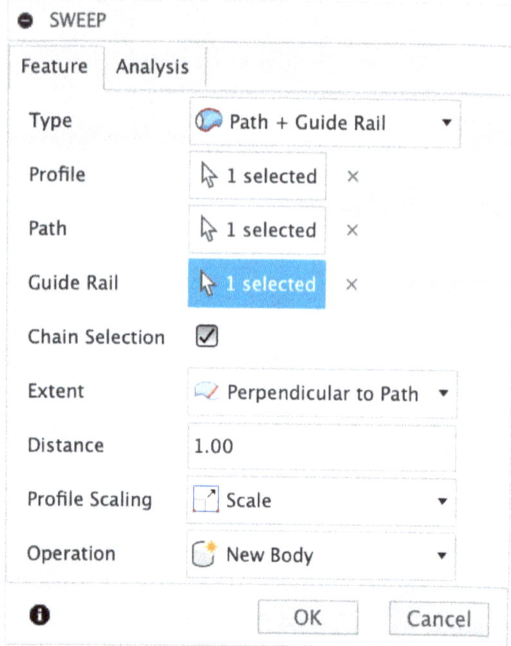

Click the **Path** selection button and select the path. Next, click the **Guide Rail** selection button and select the guide rail. The preview of the geometry will appear. Select an option from the **Profile scaling** section. The **Scale** option scales the geometry uniformly along the guide rail. The **Stretch** option scales the geometry on the side of the guide rail. The **None** option just sweeps the profile along the path without considering the guide rail. Click **OK** to complete the feature.

Profile Scaling: Scale **Profile Scaling: Stretch** **Profile Scaling: None**

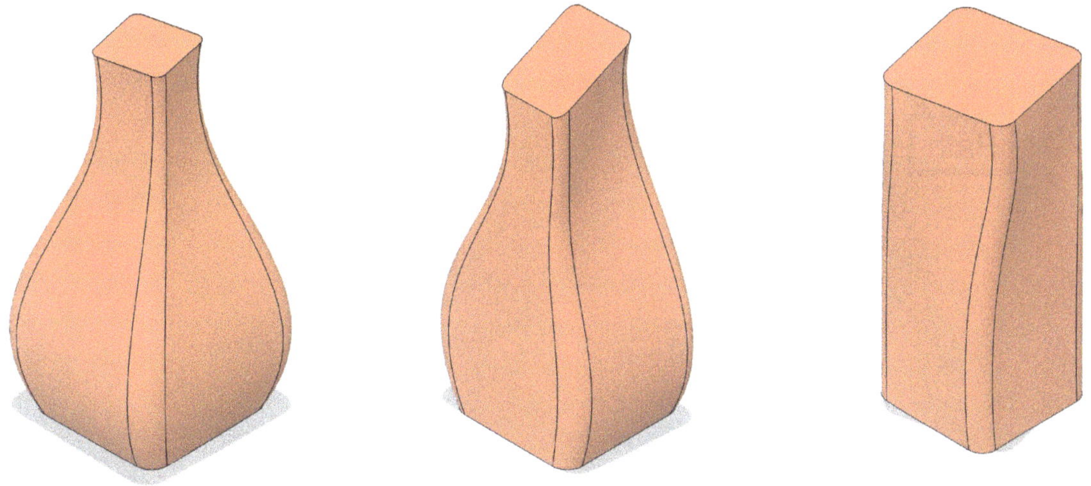

The **Extent** drop-down has options to control the extent of the profile. The **Perpendicular to Path** option sweeps the profile until the profile remains perpendicular to the path. The **Full Extents** option sweeps the profile up to full extents of the path and guide rail.

Perpendicular to Path **Full Extents**

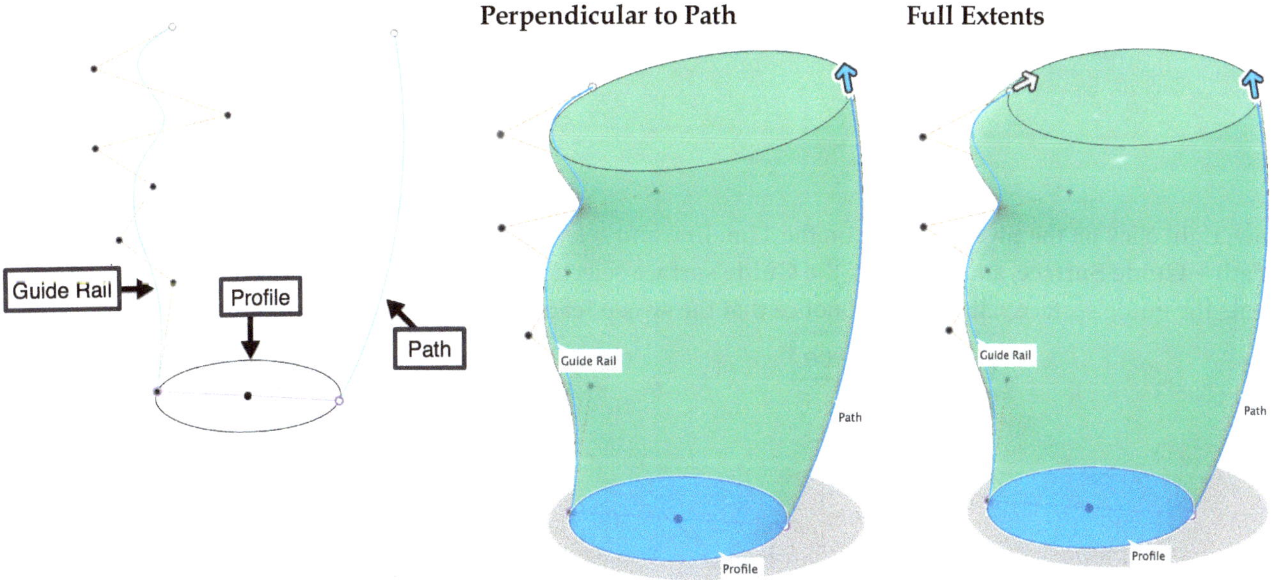

Path and Guide Surface Sweeps

The **Path + Guide Surface** option on the **Sweep** dialog will be useful while sweeping a profile along a non-planar path. For example, create a path and profile similar to the one shown in the figure. Next, create a sweep feature using the **Single Path** option; the sweep is not attached to the cylindrical surface.

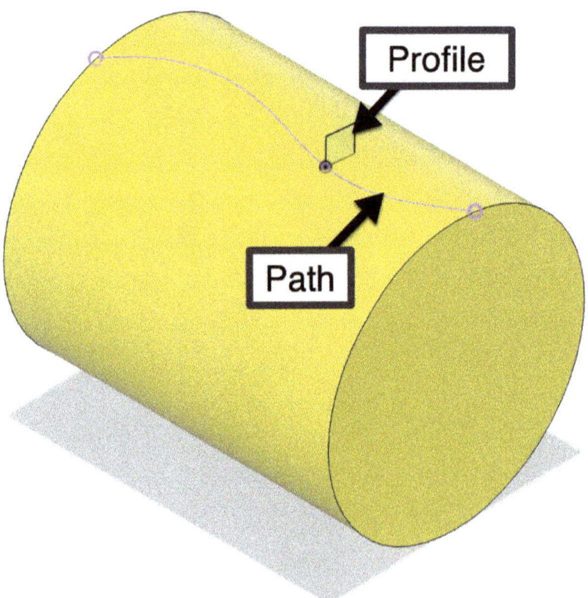

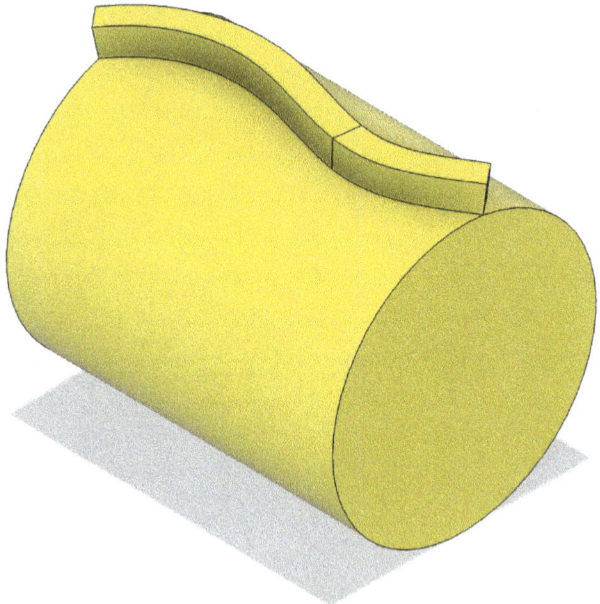

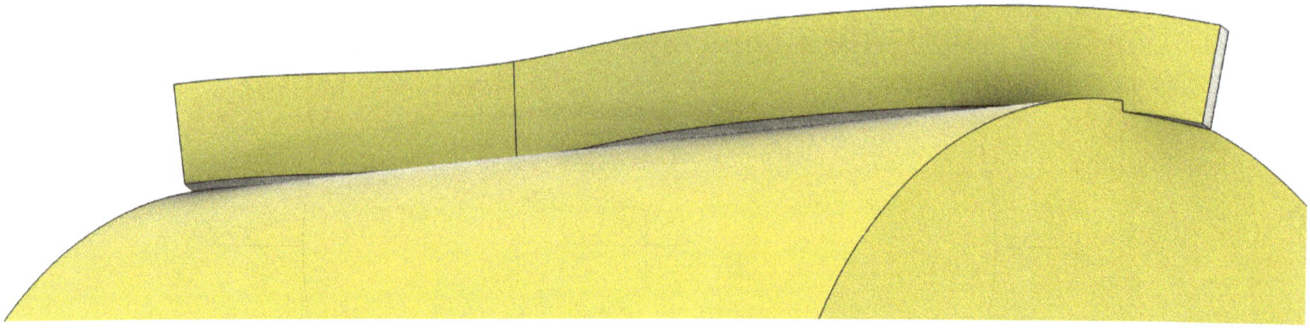

Now, right click on the **Sweep** feature on the **Timeline** and select **Edit Feature**. On the **Sweep** dialog, select **Type > Path + Guide Surface**, and then click the **Guide surface** selection button. Next, select the cylindrical surface to define the guide surface. Click **OK** and notice that the sweep feature is attached to the cylindrical surface.

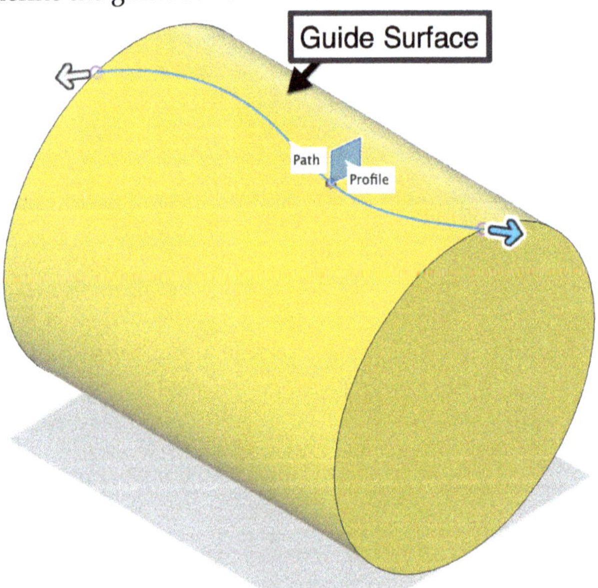

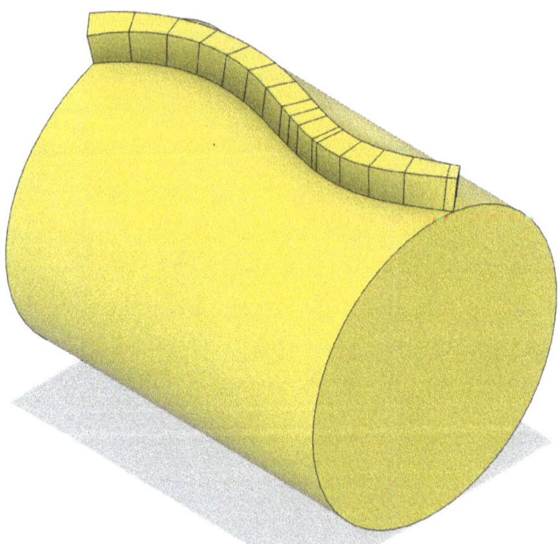

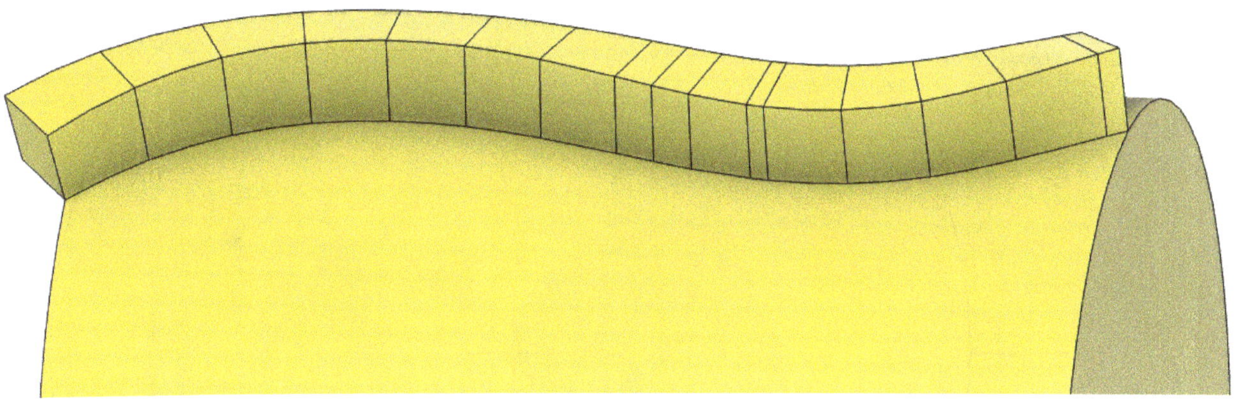

Analysis tab

The **Analysis** tab has the options to get the information and check the quality of the surfaces of the swept feature. They include **Zebra**, **Curvature map**, and **Isocurve**.

Zebra

The zebra stripes recreate the reflection of long strips of light on the smooth faces of the geometry. This can help you to detect wrinkles or defects in a surface that may not be visible with a standard shaded display. Additionally, by using this option, you can confirm that two adjacent faces are in contact, are tangent, or have continuous curvature.

Click the **Analysis** tab and select **Analysis Type > Zebra**; the faces of the swept feature is displayed with zebra stripes. Next, specify the **Direction** of the zebra stripes. You can select the **Vertical** or **Horizontal** option to define the direction. Specify the number of stripes using the **Repeats** slider or entering a value in the **Repeats** box. You can also change the opacity of the zebra stripes using the **Opacity** slider.

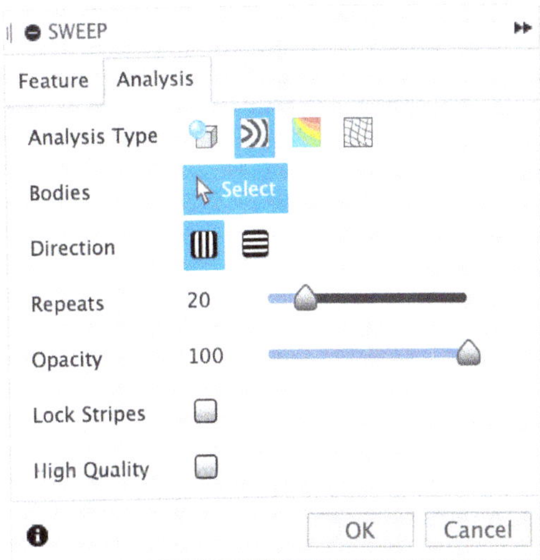

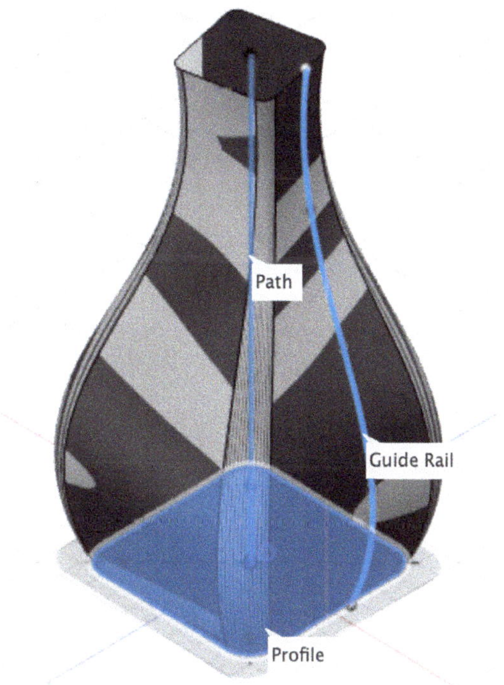

Click the **Orbit** icon on the **Navigation Bar** and rotate the model; the pattern of the zebra stripes changes. Right-click and select **OK** to exit the **Orbit** tool.

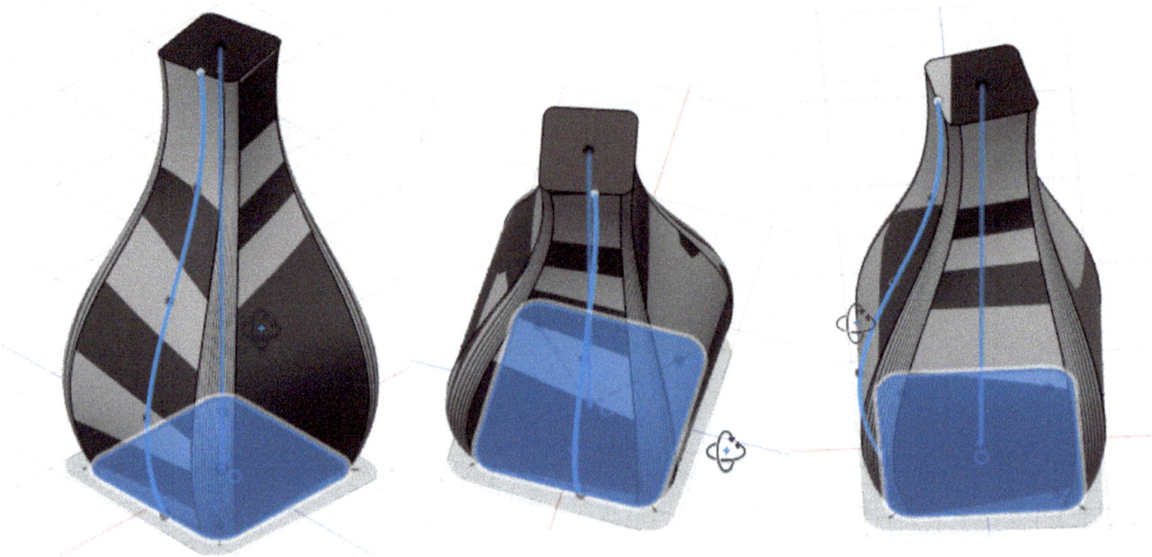

On the **Sweep** dialog, check the **Lock Stripes** option. Next, click the **Orbit** icon on the **Navigation Bar** and rotate the model; notice that the zebra stripes are locked to the faces of the geometry.

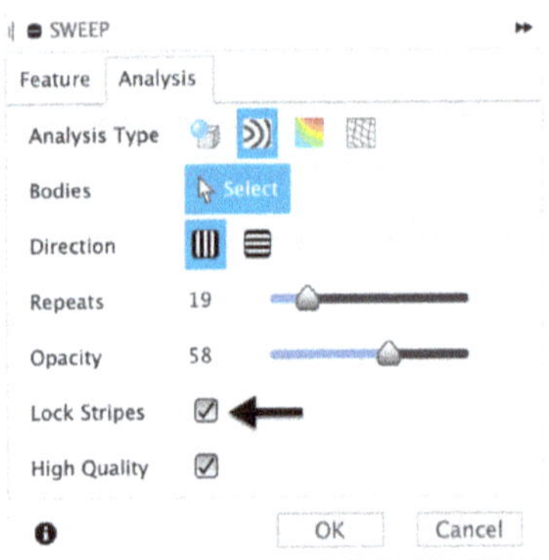

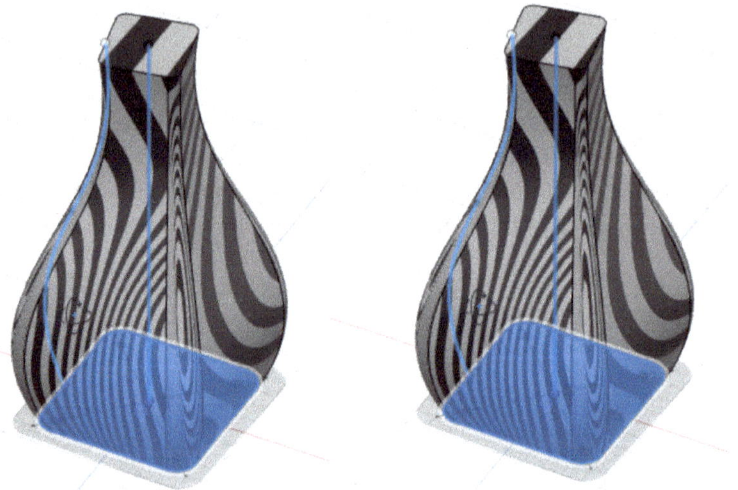

You can use the Zebra stripes to identify the Tangent faces, Curvature Continuous faces, and faces that are Contact with each other.

Tangent Faces: When two faces are tangent to each other, the zebra stripes of the two faces match each other but there is sudden change in their direction.

Curvature Continuous faces: The zebra stripes continue smoothly between the two curvature continuous faces.

Contact faces: The zebra stripes do not match each other when two faces are in contact with each other without any continuity.

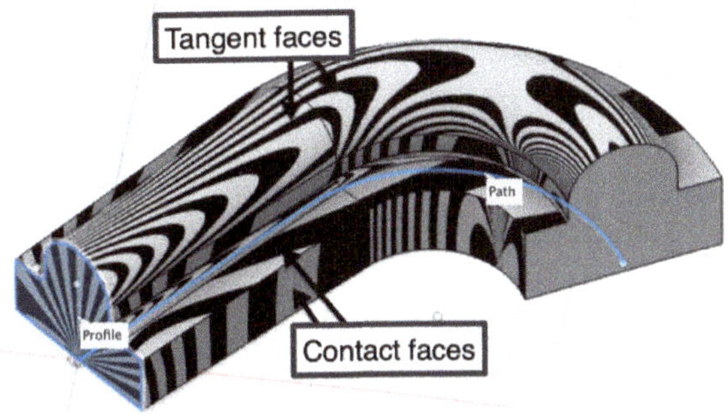

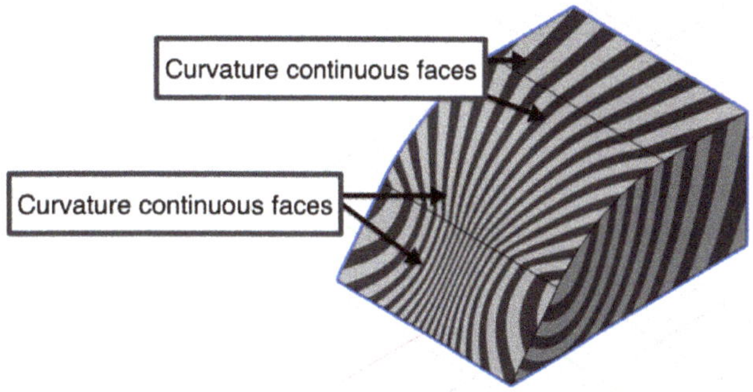

Curvature map

The **Curvature map** option displays color gradients of the face based of the curvature. Select **Analysis Type > Curvature map** on the **Analysis** tab of the **Sweep** dialog. Next, select curvature map type from the **Type** section. There are three Type options: **Gaussian, Principal Minimum, Principal Maximum.**

Gaussian: This options visualizes the surface's curvature by applying a color gradient based on the Gaussian curvature formula. The Gaussian curvature is determined by multiplying the two principal curvatures, which represent the curvature in the U and V directions.

Principal Minimum: This option highlights areas of low curvature with a combination of green and red colors. You can adjust the minimum limit of the curvature to identify the low curvature areas using the **Minimum Limit** slider or the **Minimum Limit** box.

Principal Maximum: This option highlights areas of high curvature with a combination of green and red colors. You can adjust the maximum limit of the curvature to identify the high curvature areas using the **Maximum Limit** slider or the **Maximum Limit** box.

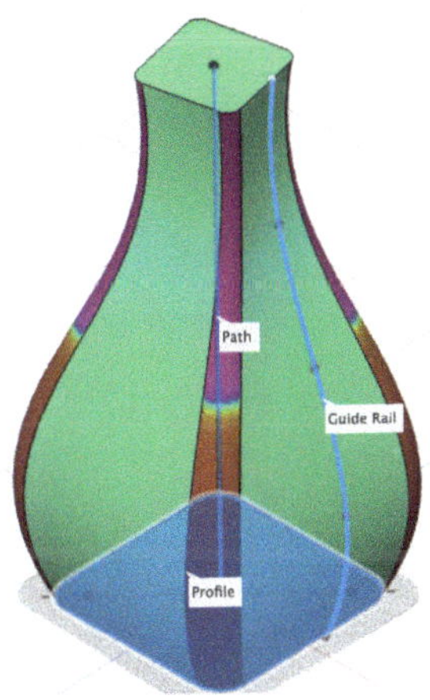

Gaussian

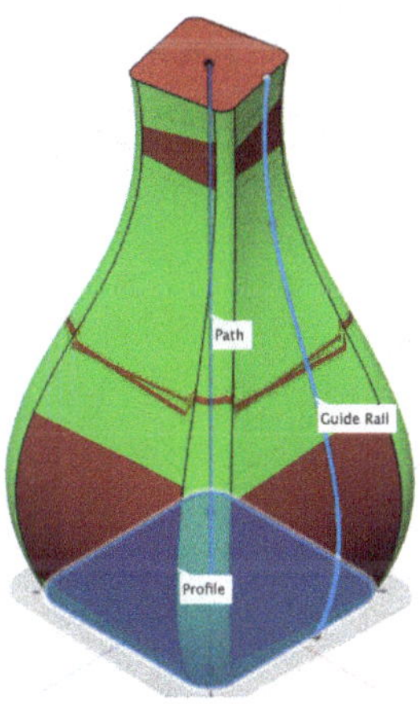

Principal Minimum

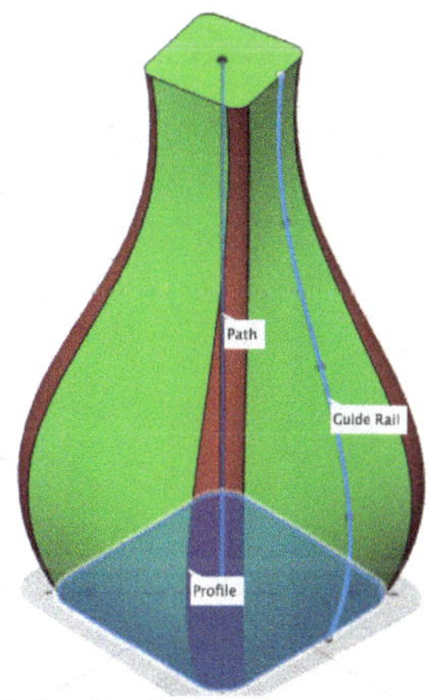

Principal Maximum

Isocurve

This option displays isoparametric curves along the **U** and **V** directions of the surface. Select **Analysis Type > Isocurve**. Select **Type > U** and **V** to display the isocurves in the **U** and **V** directions. Select **Type > U** to display the isocurves in the U direction. Likewise, select **Type > V** to display the isocurves in the V direction. Next, specify the number of isocurves using the **Isocurves** slider.

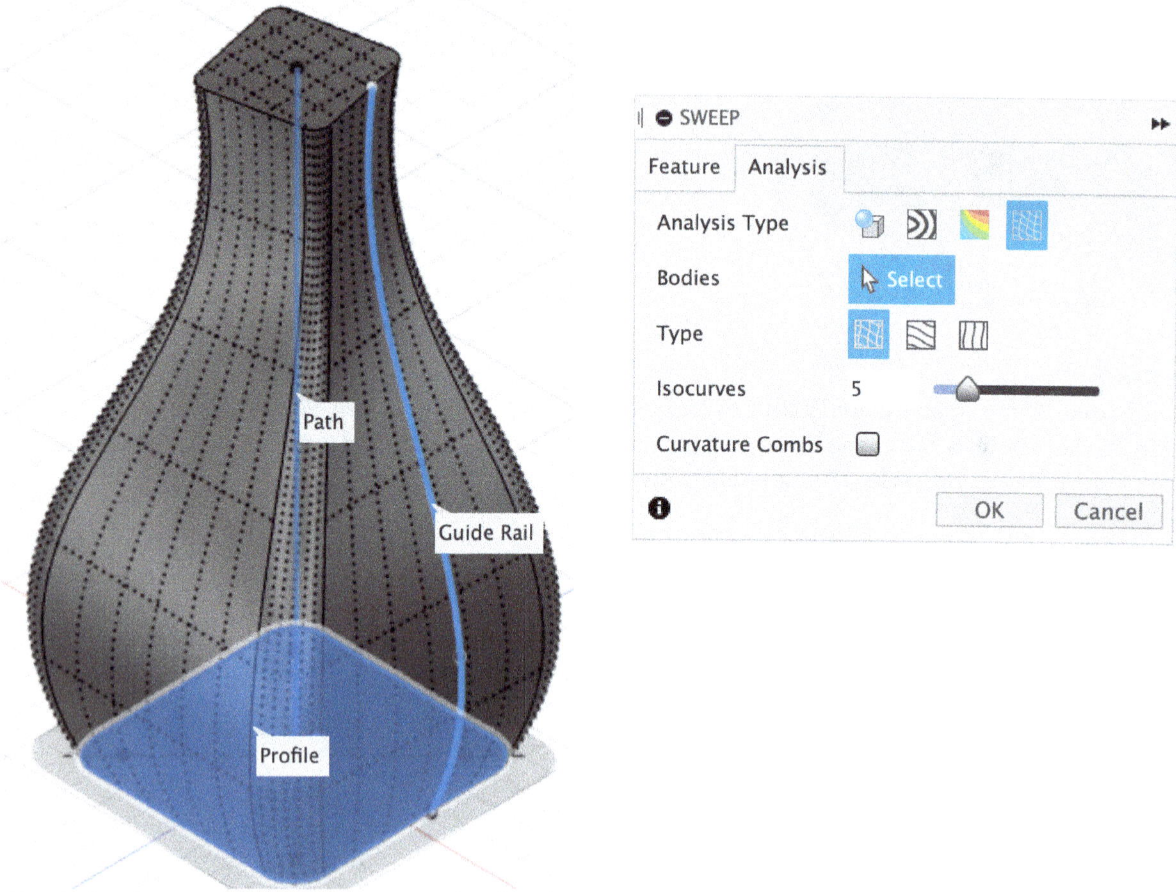

Check the **Curvature Combs** option to display the curvature combs along the isocurves. You can change the Density and Scale of the curvature combs using the **Density** and **Scale** sliders.

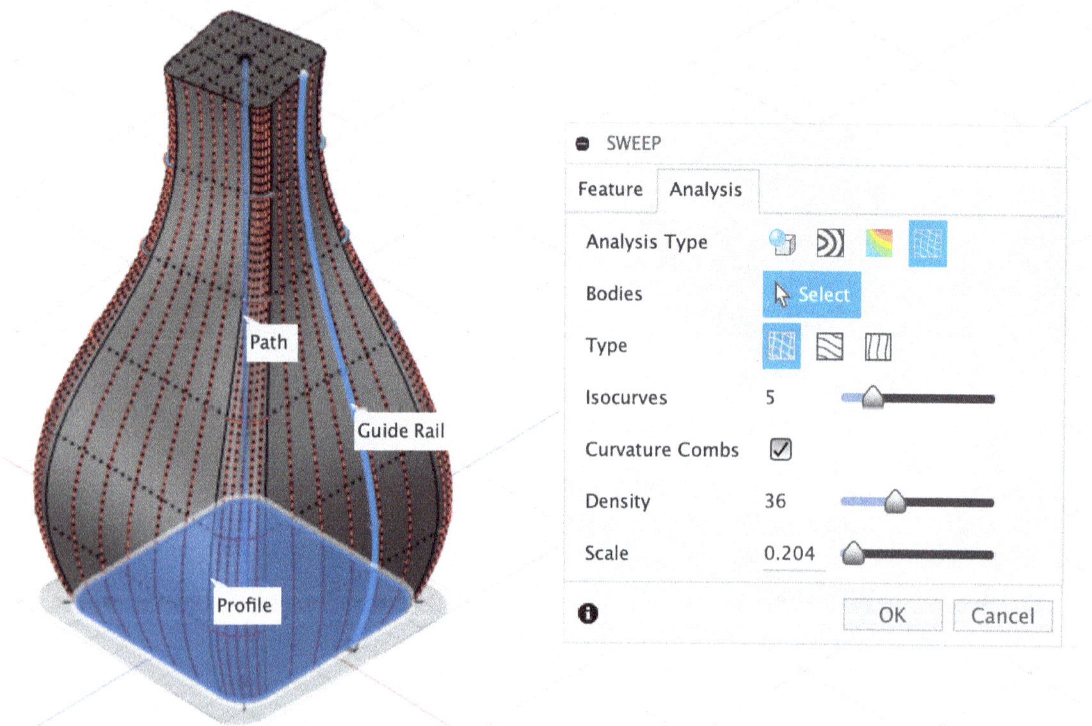

Swept Cutout

In addition to adding swept features, Autodesk Fusion 360 allows you to remove geometry using the **Sweep** command. Activate this command (click **Create** panel **> Sweep** on the **Solid** tab of the toolbar) and select the profile. Click the **Path** selection button and select the path. Select **Operation** > **Cut** from the dialog. Click **OK** to create the swept cutout.

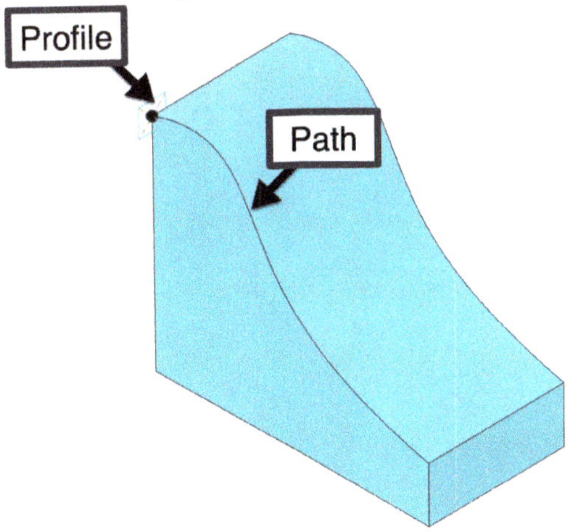

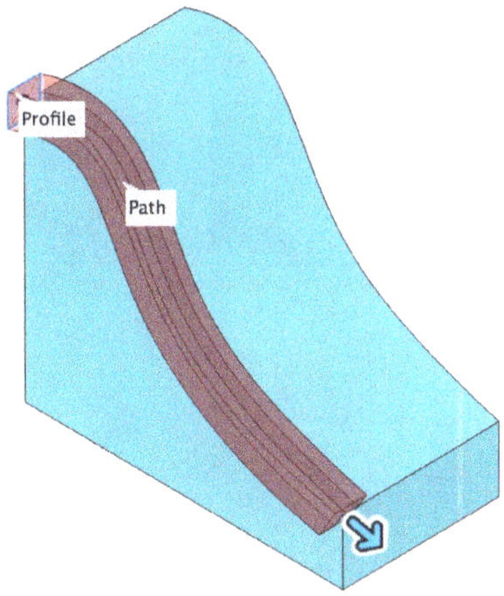

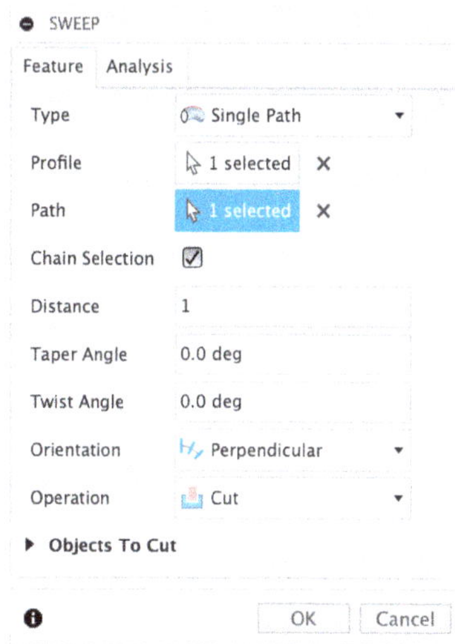

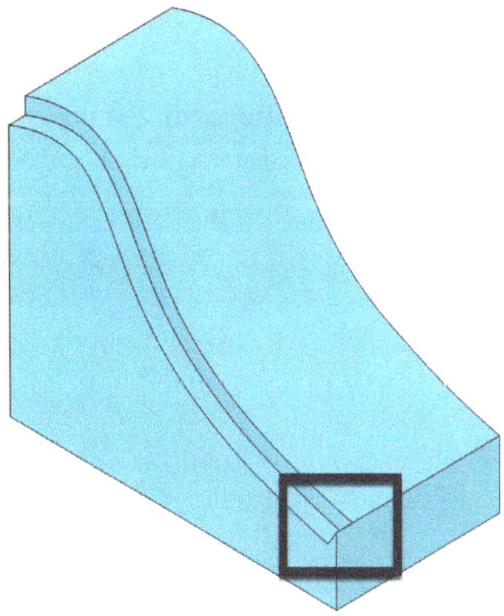

You will notice that the swept cutout is not created throughout the geometry. This is because the profile is swept only up to the endpoints of the path. In this case, you need to change the orientation of the profile. To do this, right click on the **Sweep** feature on the **Timeline** and select **Edit Feature**. Next, select **Orientation > Parallel** from the **Sweep** dialog. Click **OK** to complete the feature. The resultant swept cutout will be throughout the geometry.

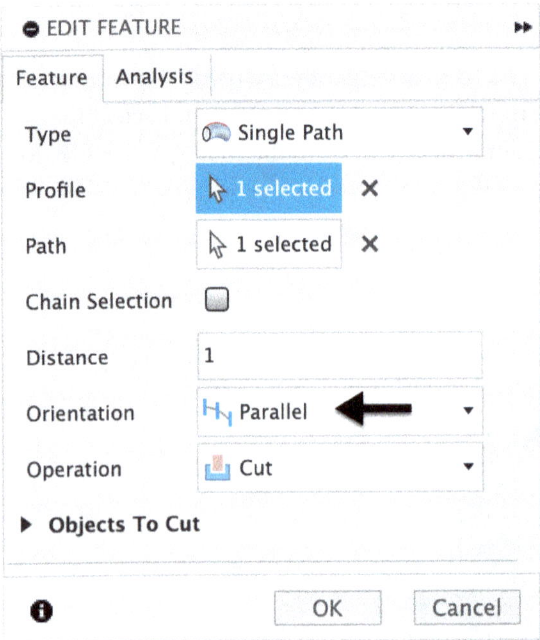

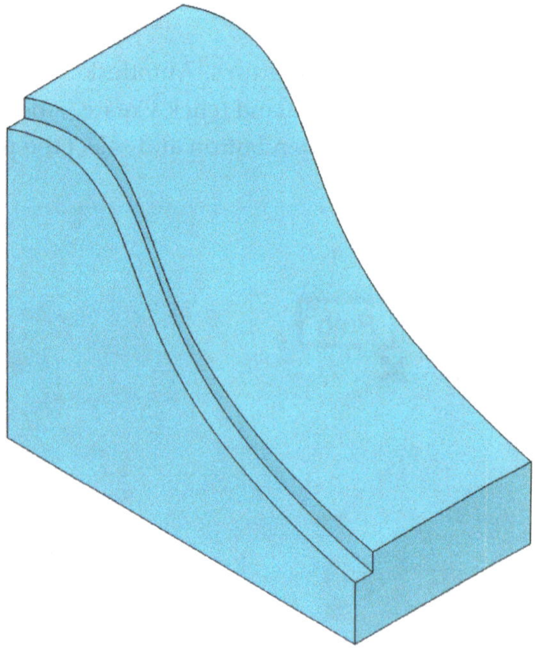

Coil

This command creates a spring or spiral-shaped feature. To create this type of feature, you must first activate the **Coil** command (click **Create** panel > **Coil** on the **Solid** tab of the toolbar) and then select a plane. Next, specify the center point of the circle, move the pointer outward and click. Next, specify the diameter of the coil in the **Diameter** box available on the **Coil** dialog.

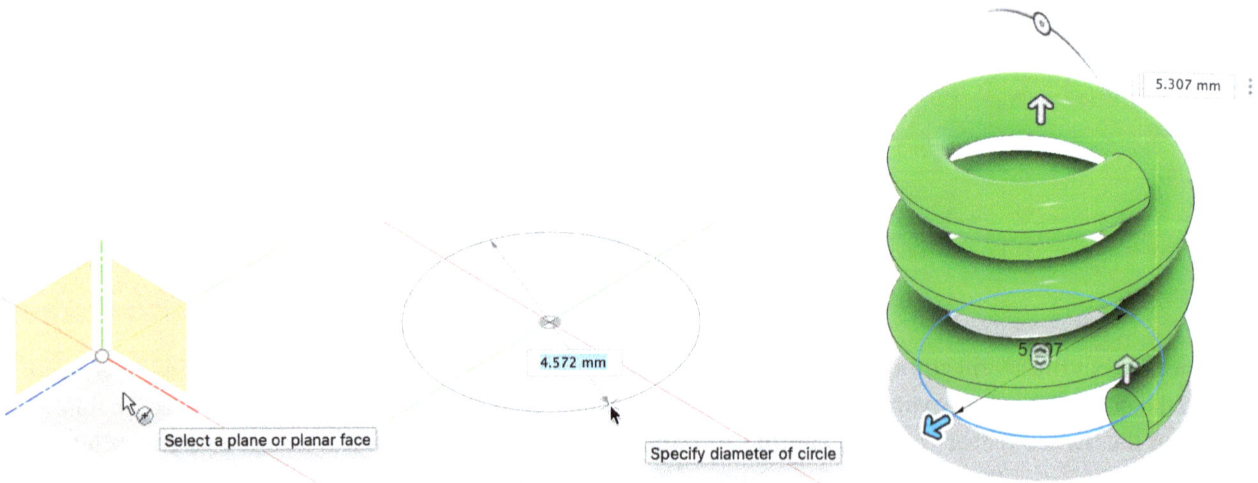

Next, select the method to define the size of the coil from the **Type** drop-down available on the **Coil** dialog. It has four options: **Revolution and Height**, **Revolution and Pitch**, **Height and Pitch**, and **Spiral**.

The **Revolution and Height** option allows you to create a coil by entering its height and number of revolutions in the **Height** and **Revolutions** boxes, respectively.

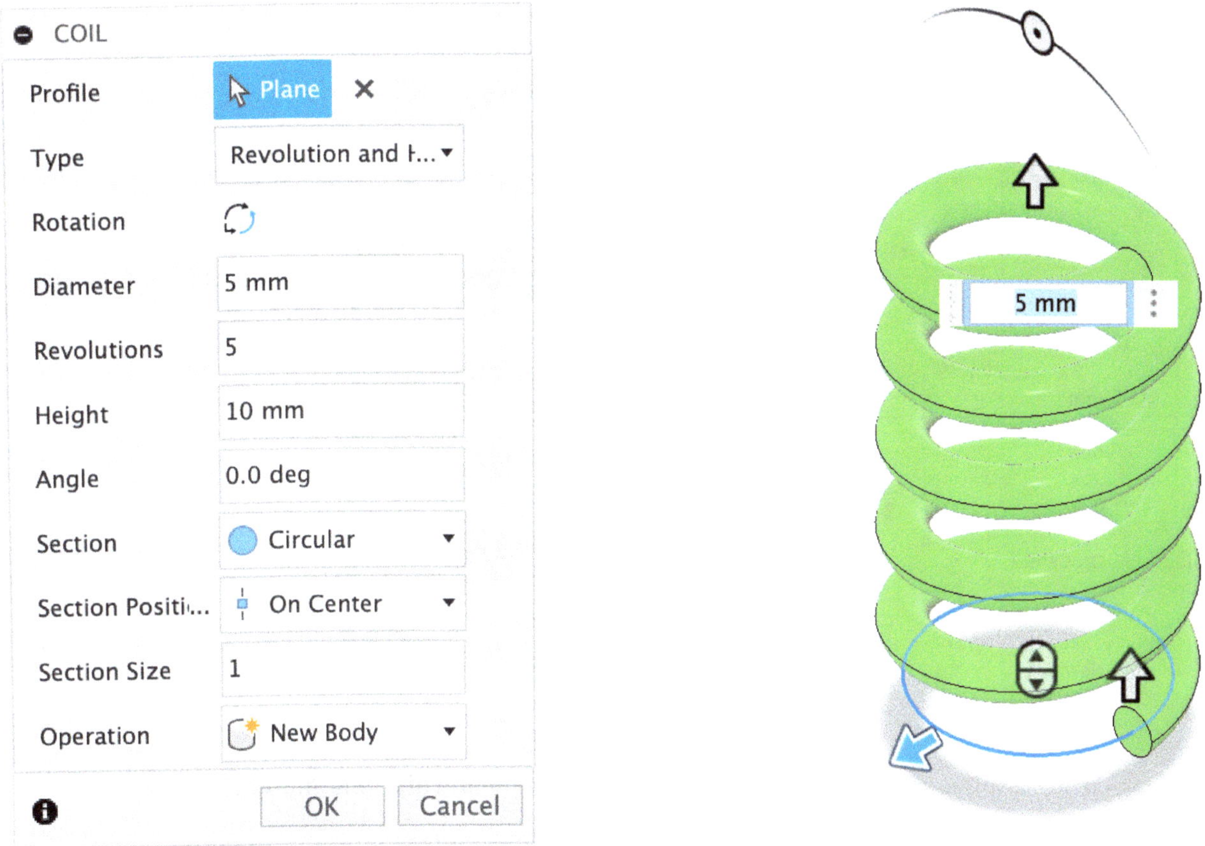

The **Revolution and Pitch** option allows you to create a coil by entering the number of revolutions and the distance between the revolutions in the **Revolutions** and **Pitch** boxes, respectively.

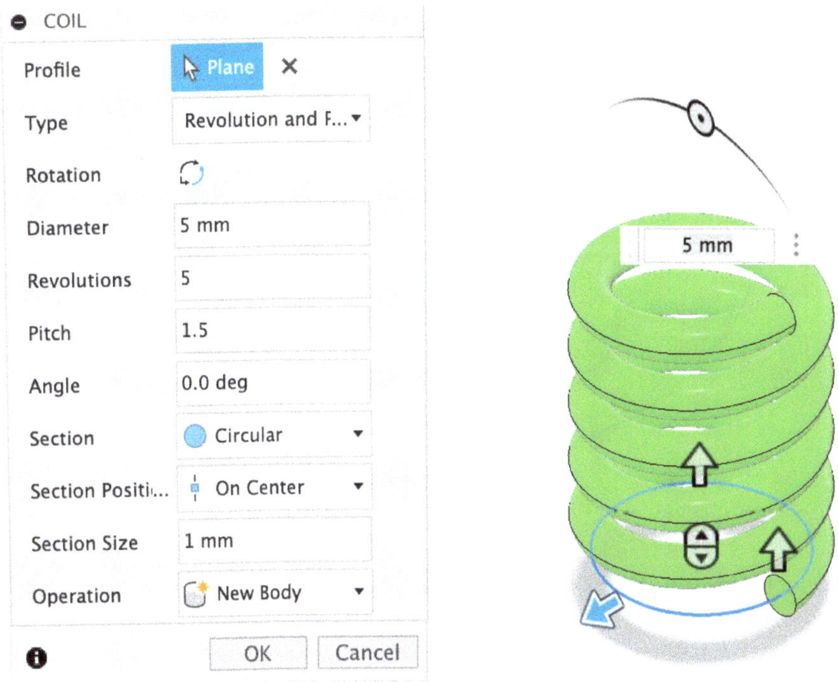

The **Height and Pitch** option allows you to create a coil by entering its height and the distance between the revolutions in the **Height** and **Pitch** boxes, respectively.

The **Spiral** option creates a spiral-shaped feature. You need to specify the **Revolutions** and **Pitch** values.

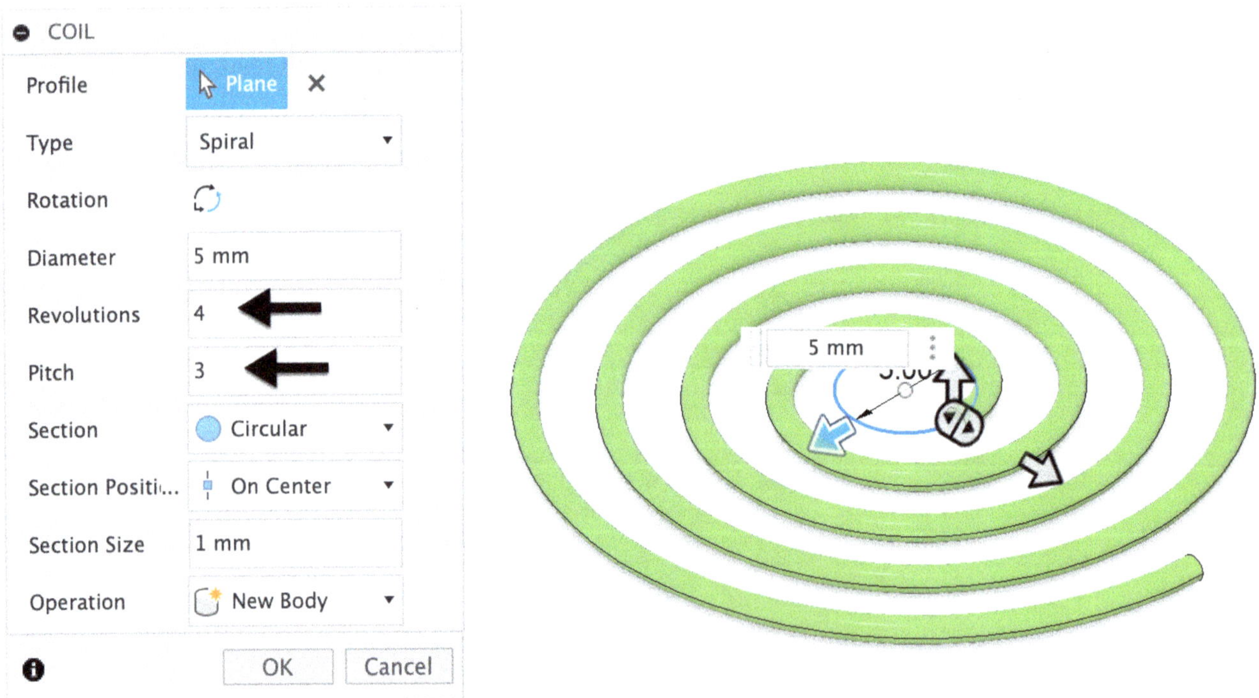

The default rotation direction of the coil is clockwise (i.e., Right-hand side). To change the rotation direction, click on the **Rotation** icon.

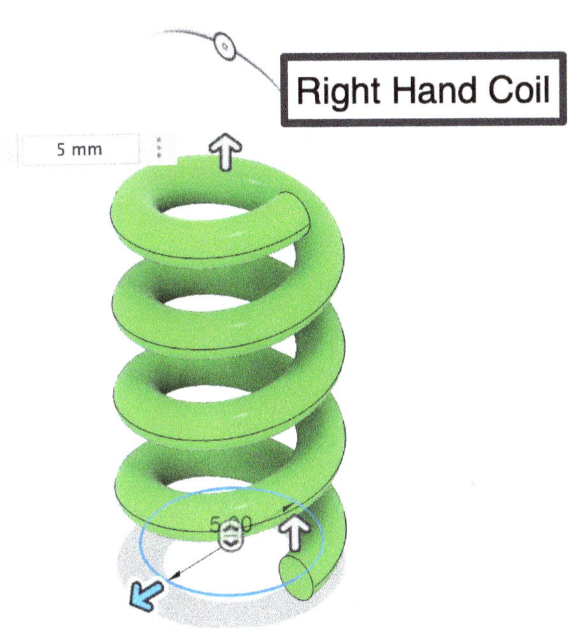

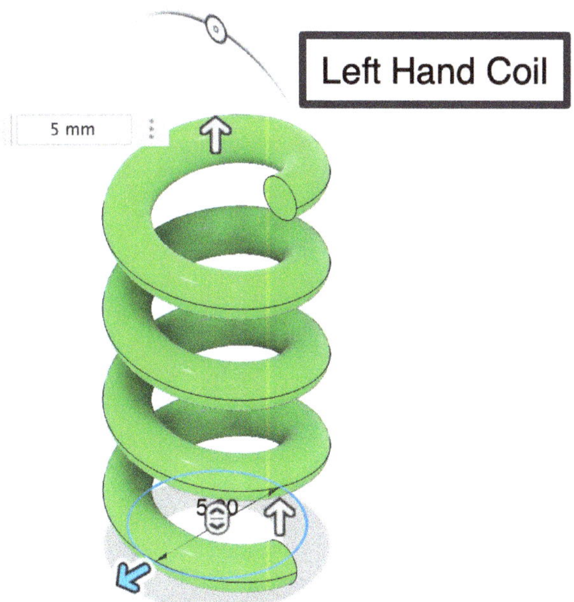

The **Angle** box on the **Coil** dialog helps you to apply taper to the coil. You can apply taper to the coil by entering a value in the **Angle** box. The negative angle reverses the taper direction.

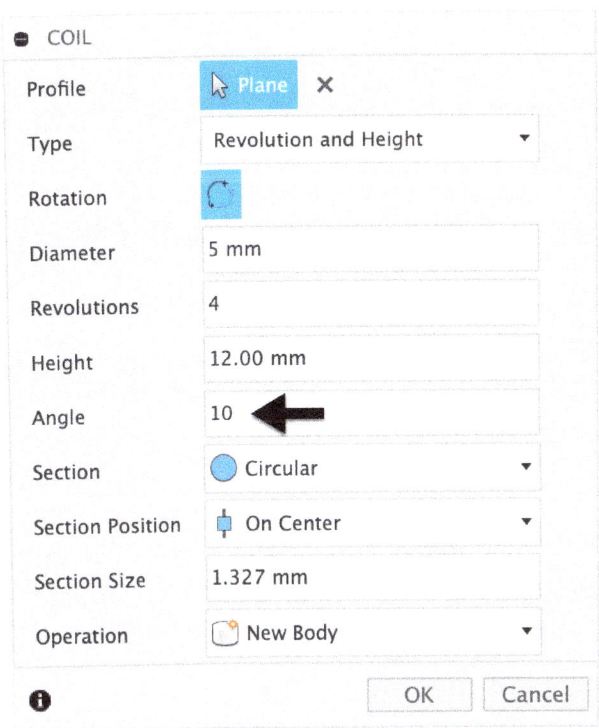

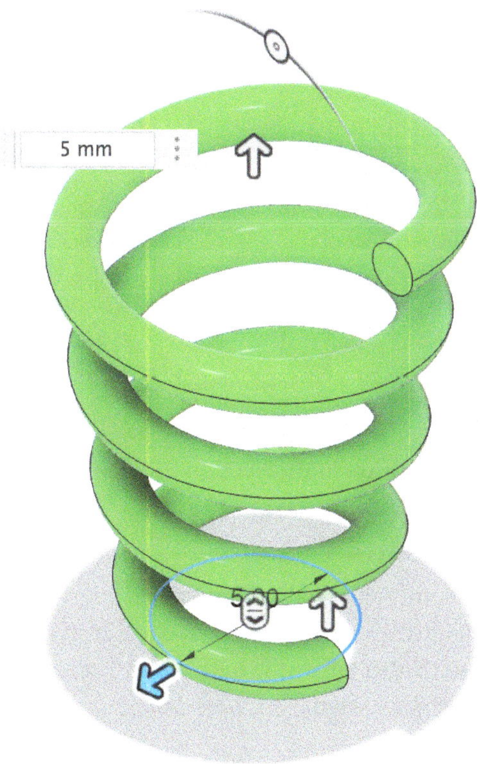

The **Section** drop-down has four options: **Circular, Square, Triangle (External)**, and **Triangle (Internal)**.

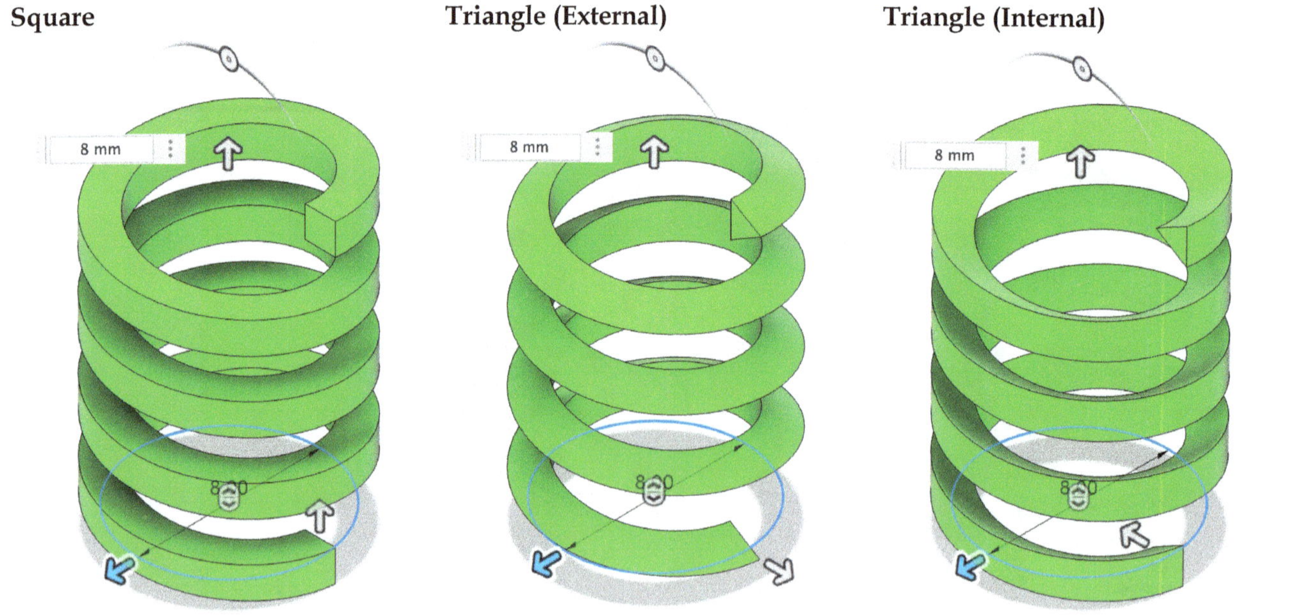

The **Section position** drop-down is used to specify the position of the section on the circle drawn to create the coil. It has three options: **Inside, On Center,** and **Outside**. **Inside.** The **Inside** option positions the section inside the circle. The **On Center** option positions the center of the section on the circle. The **Outside** option positions the section outside the circle.

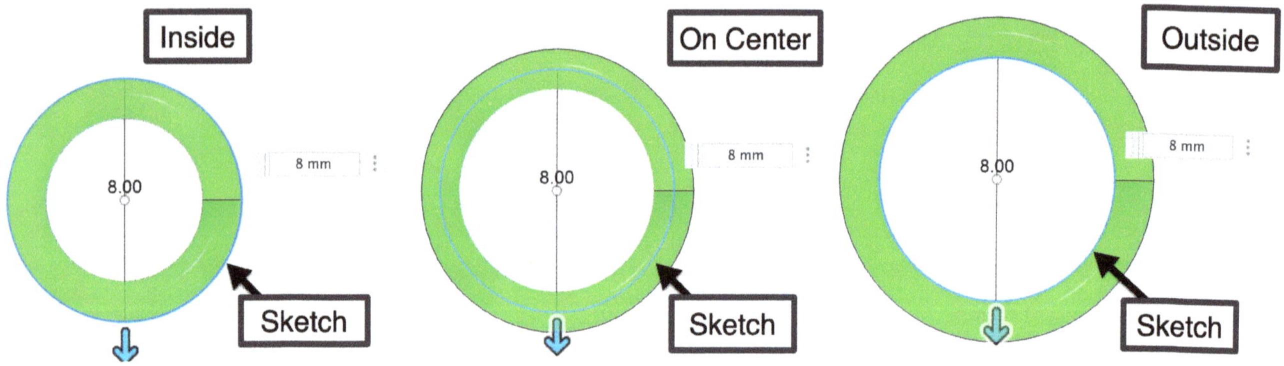

Next, enter a value in the **Section Size** box and click **OK** on the **Coil** dialog.

Helical Cutout

The **Coil** command can also be used to remove material from the part geometry by creating a helical feature. To create this feature, first, you must have an existing geometry. Activate the **Coil** command (click **Create** panel > **Coil** on the **Solid** tab of the toolbar) and select the plane to create a sketch. Next, draw a circle; the **Coil** dialog pops up on the screen.

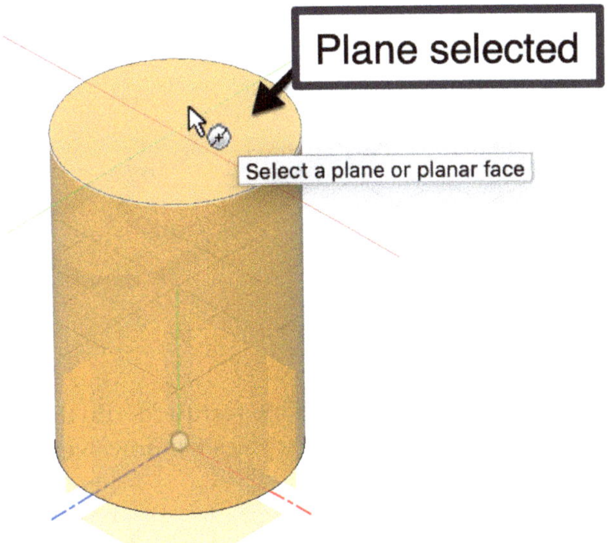

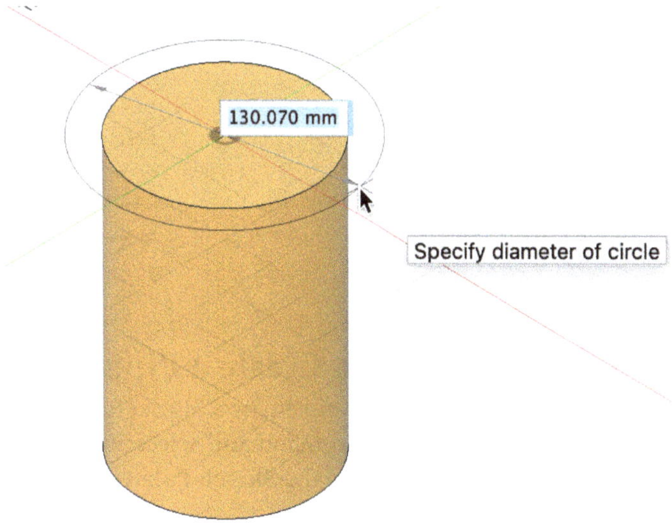

Select the helix method from the **Type** drop-down and specify the values such as Height, Revolutions, and/or Pitch. Next, select **Operation > Cut** and click **OK** to create the helical cutout.

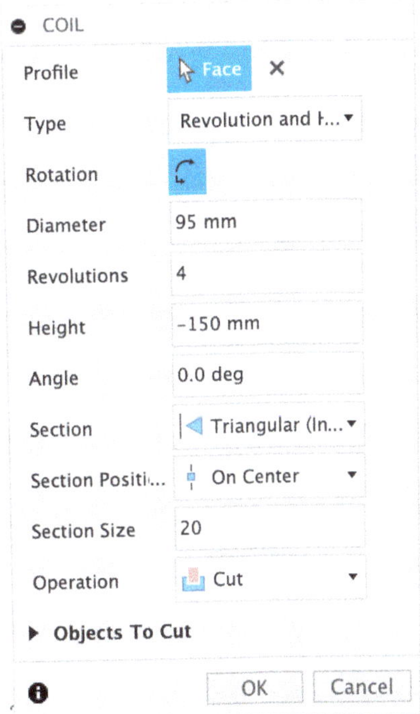

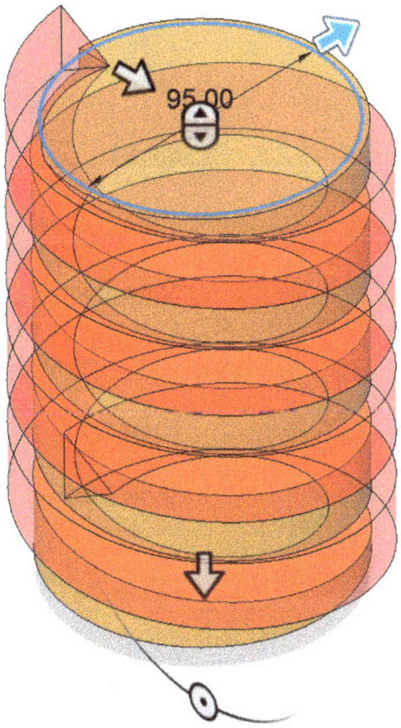

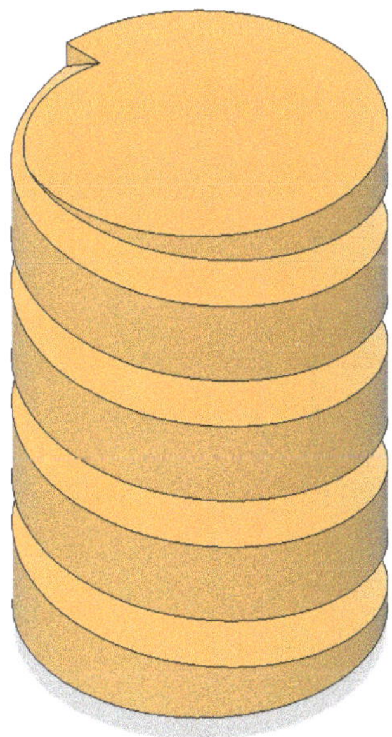

Pipe

The **Pipe** command sweeps a predefined profile along the selected path. To do this, first, you need to have a path. A path can be a sketch or edge. Next, activate the **Pipe** command (on the **Solid** tab of the toolbar, click **Create** panel > **Pipe** ) and select the path. On the **Pipe** dialog, select an option from the **Section** drop-down. Next, enter a value in the **Section Size** box. Check the **Hollow** option if you want to create a hollow pipe.

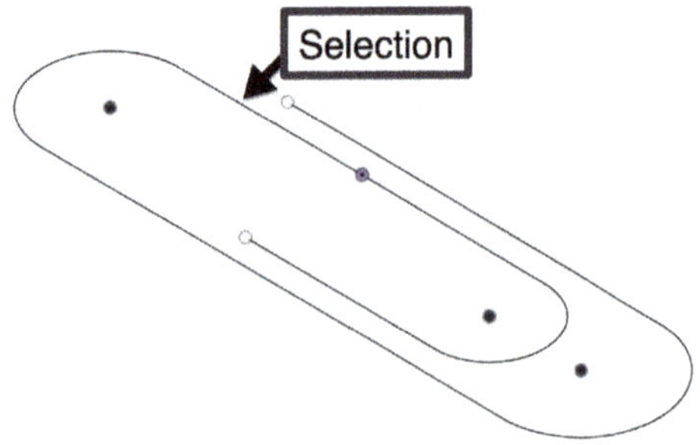

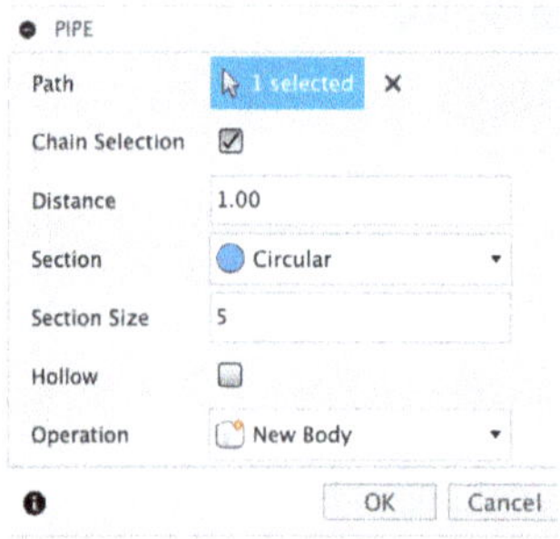

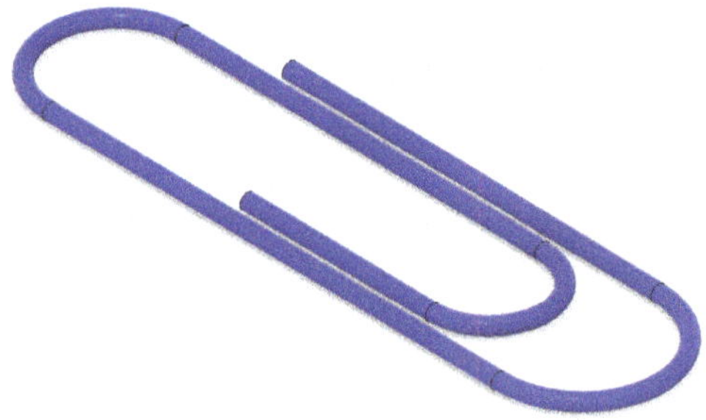

Using a 3D Sketch to Create a Pipe Feature

In Autodesk Fusion 360, you can create a 3D Sketch that can be used to create a swept or Pipe feature. To do this, activate the **Create Sketch** command and select anyone of the reference planes from the graphics window. Next, check the **3D Sketch** option on the **Sketch Palette** dialog.

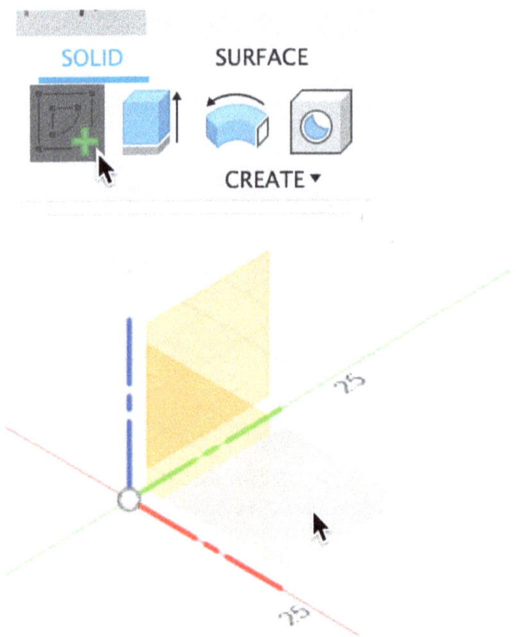

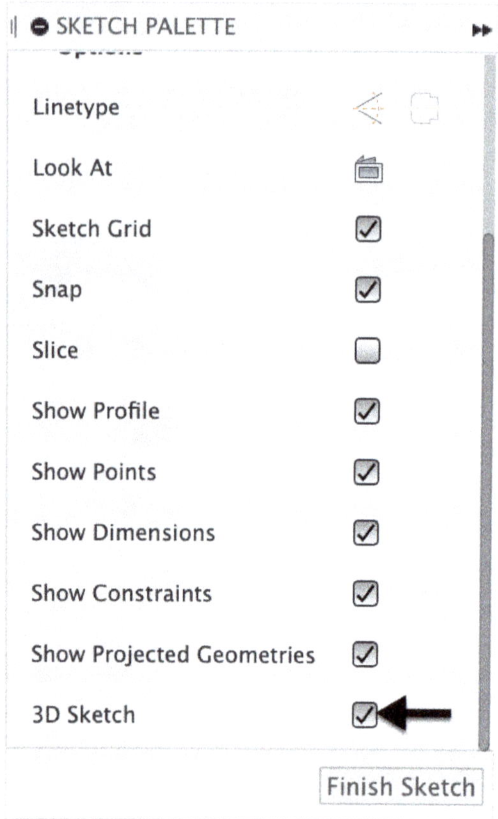

Next, you can create the sketch elements on three reference planes. For example, first create a line, as shown. Click the **Home** icon located next to the ViewCube.

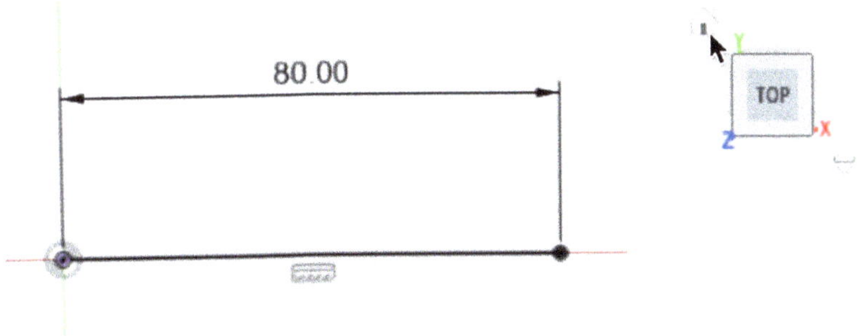

Activate the **Line** command and select the XZ plane from the triad. Click on the left endpoint of the rectangle. Move the pointer toward left and click; an inclined line is created.

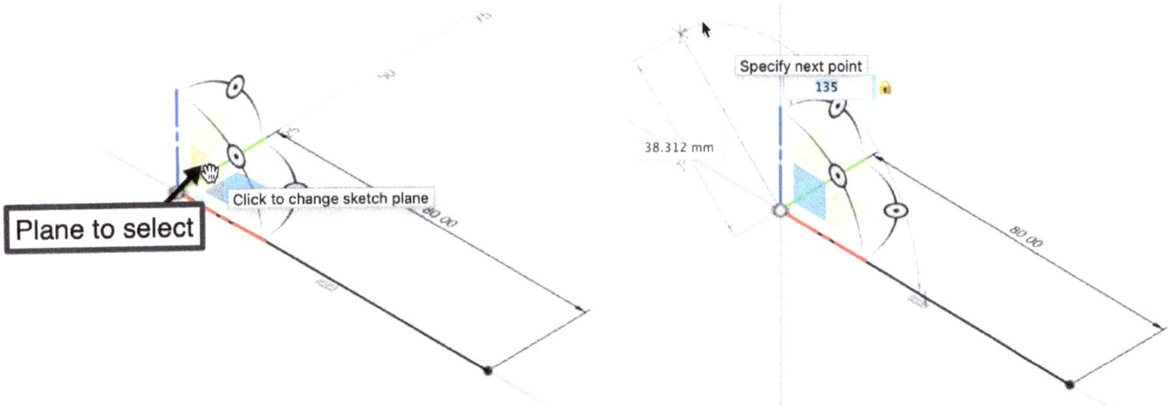

Next, move the pointer along the Y-axis of the triad and notice that the Parallel constraint glyph is displayed on the new line. Type **25** and press ENTER to create a horizontal line. Create two lines connected to the endpoints of the inclined, as shown.

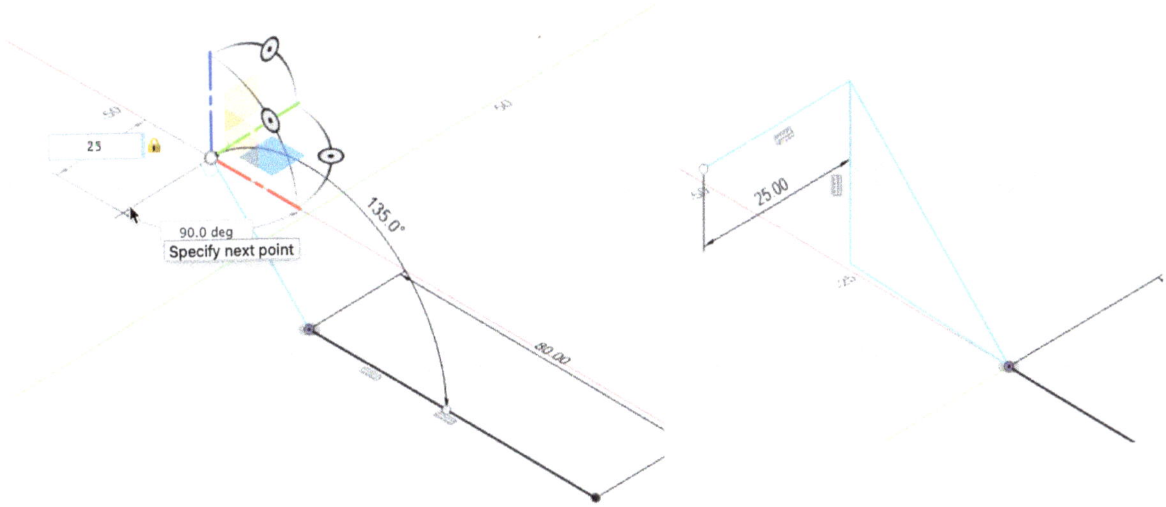

Select the two newly created lines and click **Linetype > Construction** on the Sketch Palette. Apply the the **Horizontal/Vertical** constraint to the lines, as shown. Add dimensions to the construction lines.

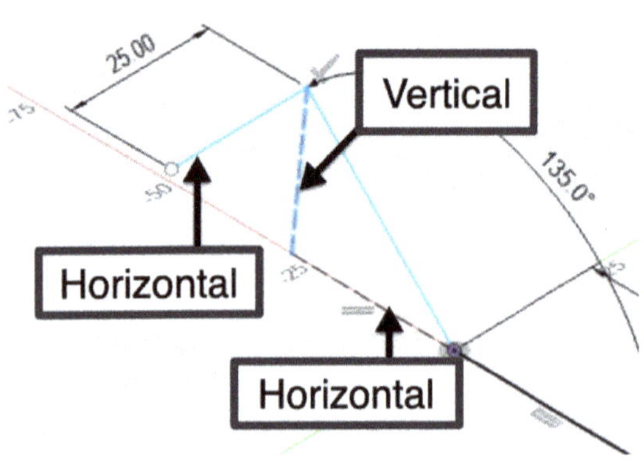

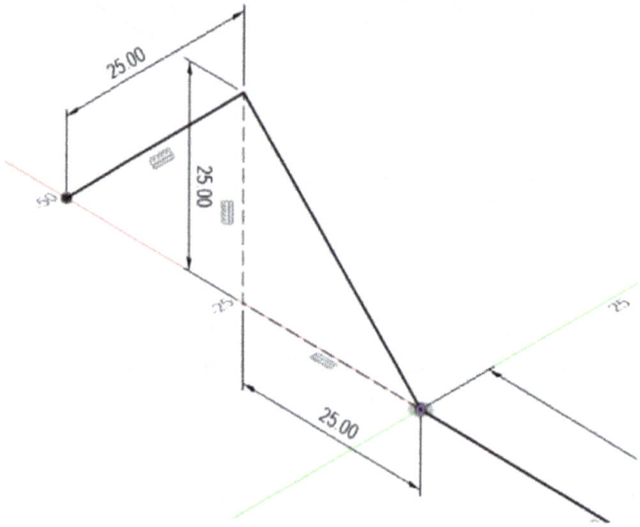

Click **Sketch > Modify > Fillet** on the toolbar and create three fillets, as shown. Next, add the angle dimension between the inclined line and the horizontal construction line. Click **Finish Sketch**.

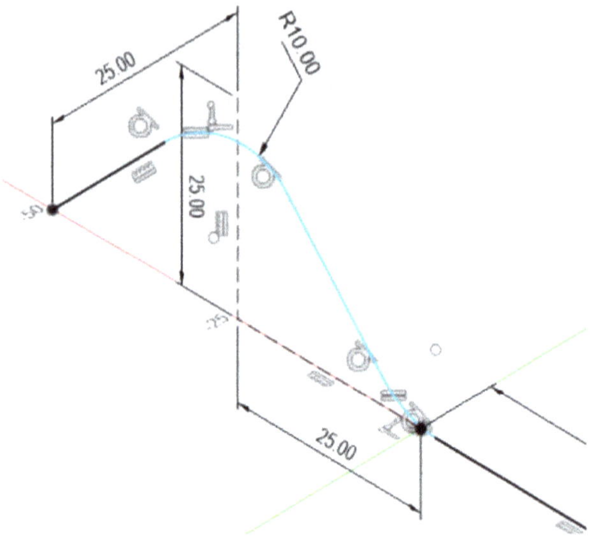

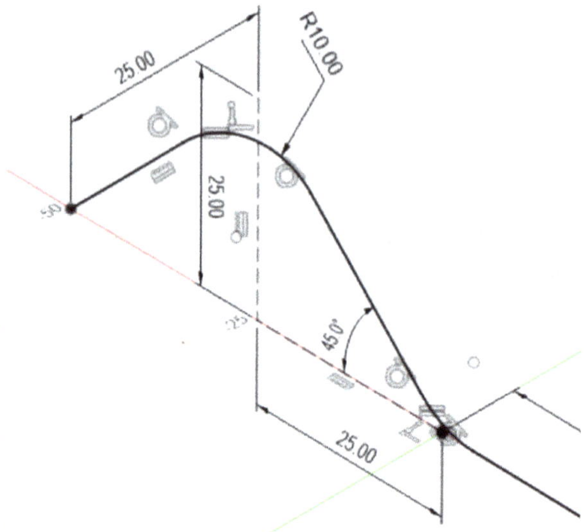

Activate the **Pipe** command (on the toolbar, click **Solid > Create > Pipe**) and select the 3D sketch. On the **Pipe** dialog, select **Section > Circular** and type **3** in the **Section Size** box. Next, check the **Hollow** option and type **0.5** in the **Section Thickness** box. Click **OK** to create the pipe feature.

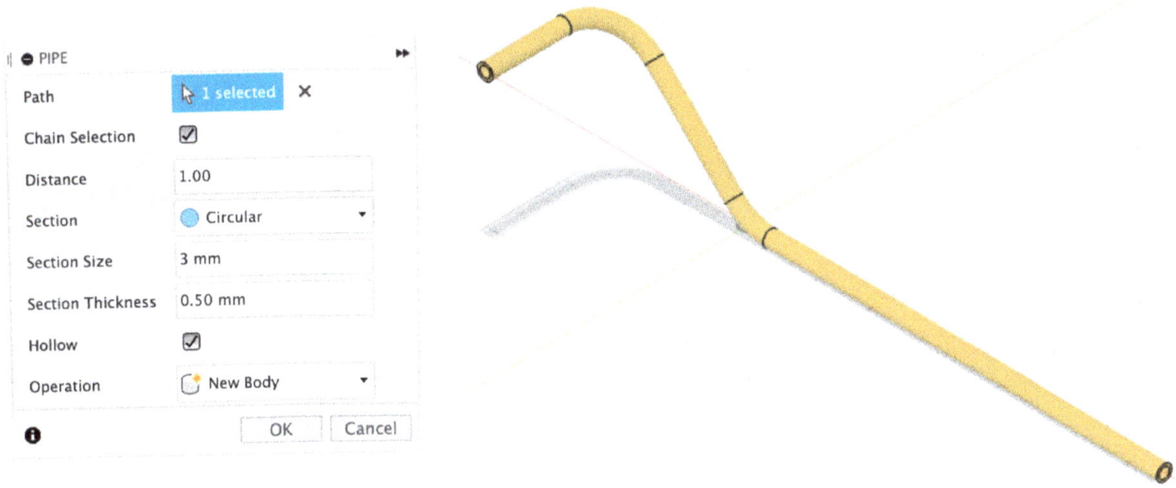

On the toolbar, click **Solid > Create > Mirror** and select the pipe feature. Next, click the **Mirror Plane** selection button and select the end face of the pipe feature, as shown. Click **OK** on the **Mirror** dialog.

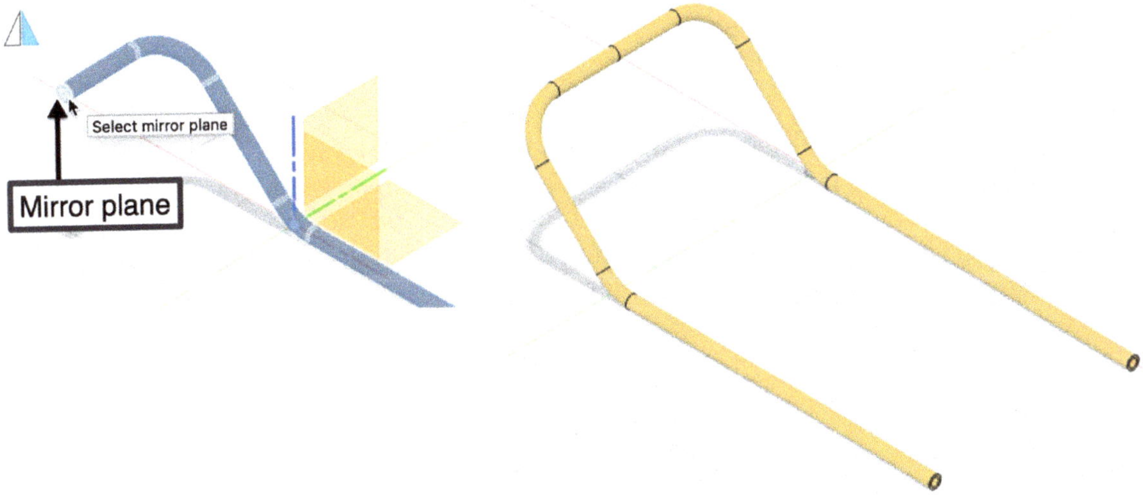

Examples

Example 1 (Inches)

In this example, you will create the part shown below.

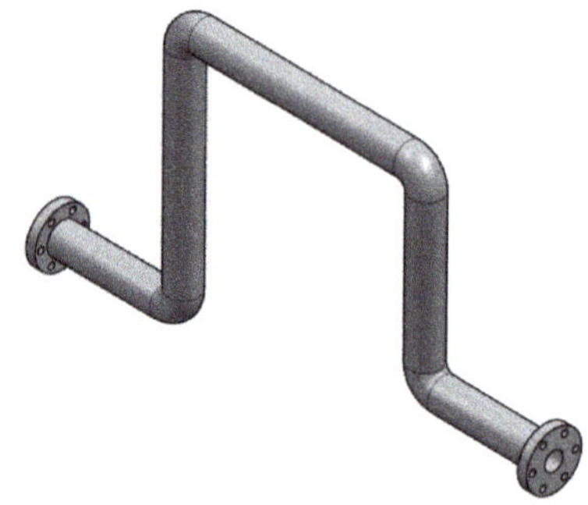

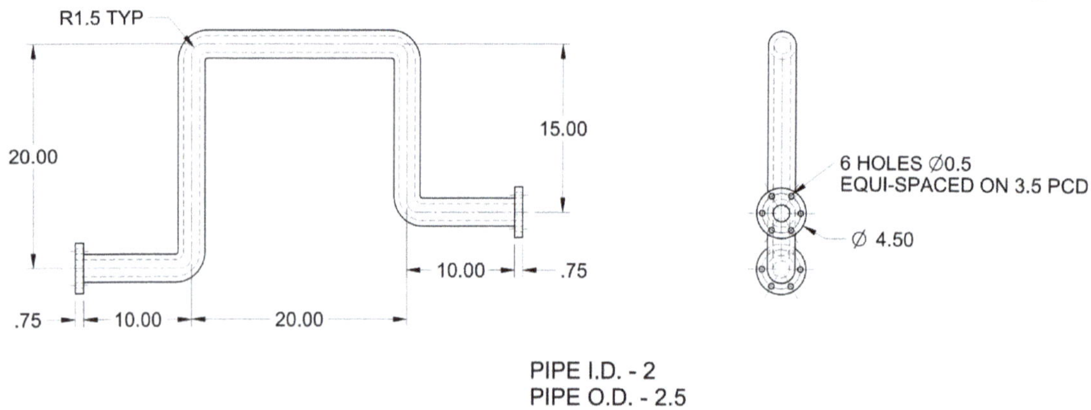

1. Start **Autodesk Fusion 360**.
2. On the **Application bar**, click **File > New Design**; the **New Design File** is created.
3. In the Browser window, expand **Document Settings** and place the cursor on **Units** and click **Change Active Units** icon.
4. On the **Change Active Units** dialog, click **Unit Type** drop-down > **inch (in), ouncemass** and click **OK**.
5. On the toolbar, click **Create** panel > **Create Sketch** and draw the sketch on the XZ plane, as shown below.

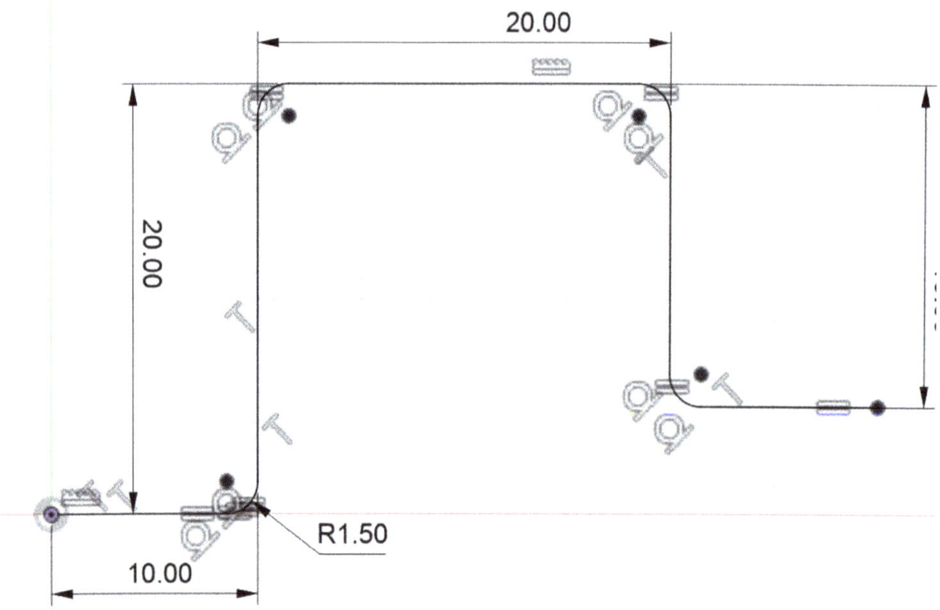

6. Click **Finish Sketch** on the toolbar.

7. On the **Solid** tab of the toolbar, click **Construct** panel **> Plane Along Path** and click on the lower horizontal line.
8. Click and drag the arrow on to the endpoint of the line, as shown. Next, click **OK** to create the plane along the selected path.

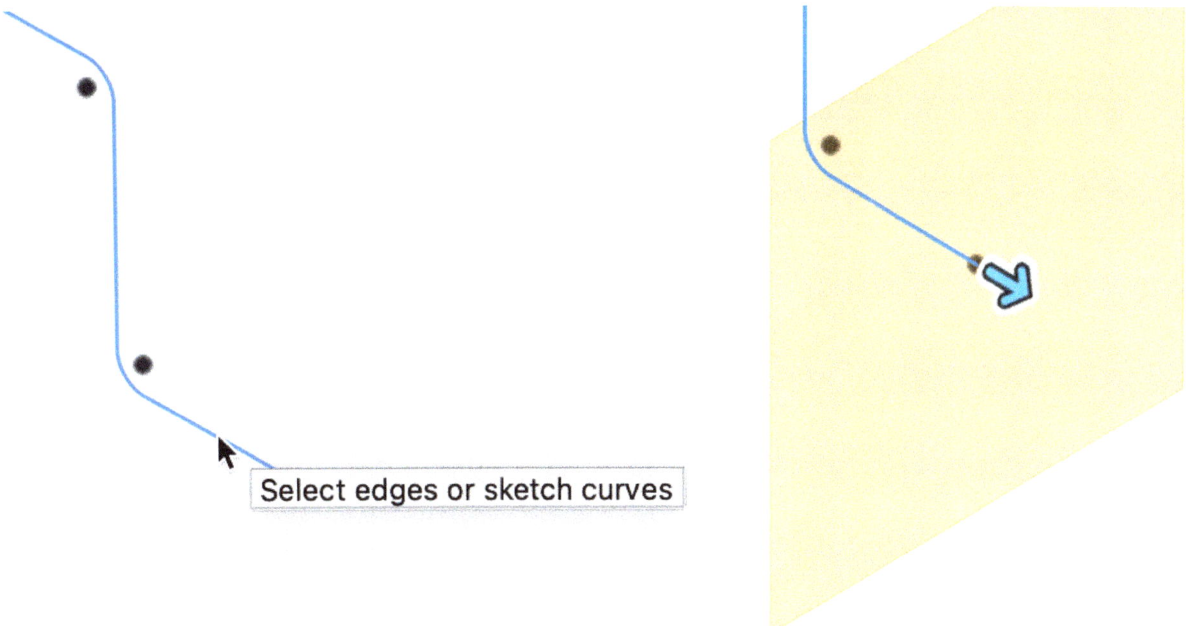

9. On the toolbar, click **Create** panel **> Create Sketch**, and then select the plane normal to the curve.
10. On the **Sketch** contextual tab of the toolbar, click **Create** panel > **Center Diameter Circle** and draw a circle of 2.5-inch diameter. Click **Finish Sketch**.

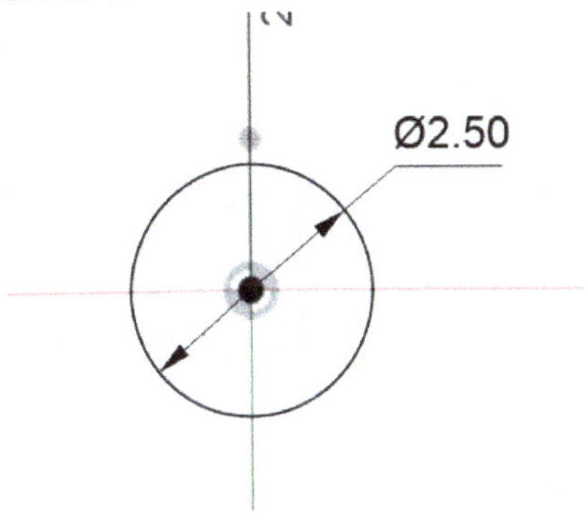

11. On the **Solid** tab of the toolbar, click **Create** panel > **Sweep** ; the **Sweep** dialog pops up. On this dialog, select **Type > Single Path**.
12. Click the **Profile** selection button and click on the circle to define the profile of the *Sweep* feature.
13. Click the **Path** selection button, and then click on the first sketch to define the path of the *Sweep* feature. Click **OK** to complete the *Sweep* feature.

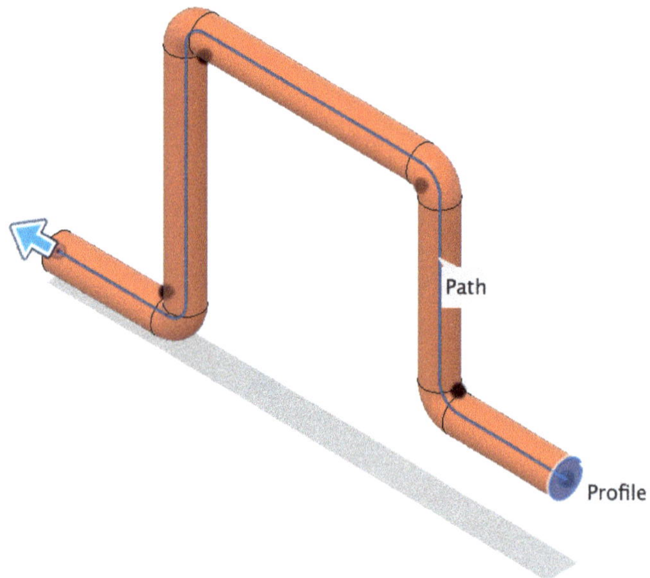

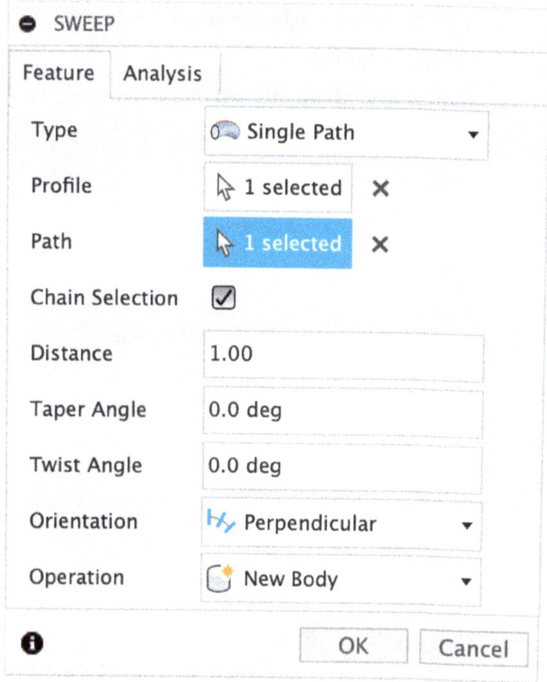

14. On the **Solid** tab of the toolbar, click **Modify** panel **> Shell**. Click on the end face of the *Sweep* feature.
15. Rotate the part geometry and click on the end face on the other side.

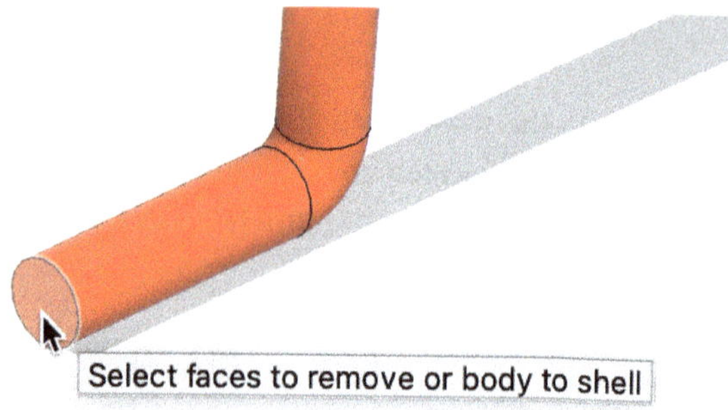

16. Type-in **0.5** in the **Inside Thickness** box. Next
17. Click **OK** to shell the *Sweep* feature.

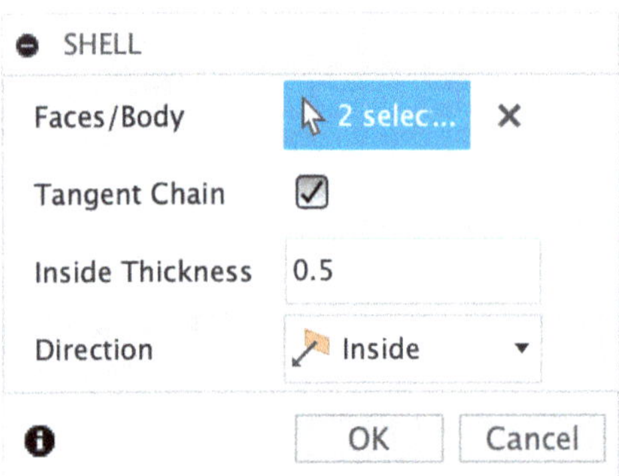

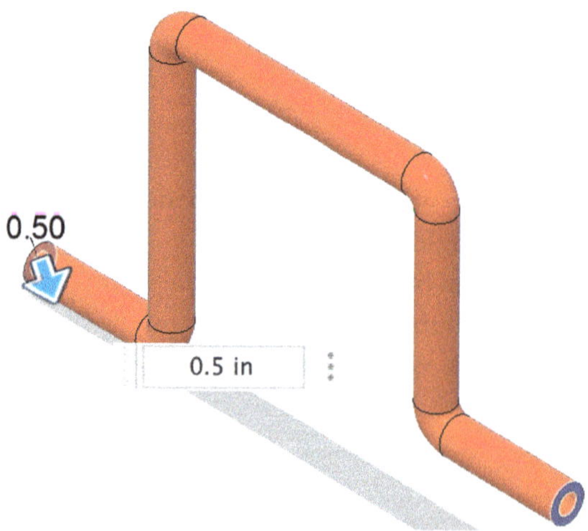

18. On the toolbar, click **Create** panel > **Create Sketch** and click on the front end face.

19. On the **Sketch** contextual tab of the toolbar, click **Create** panel > **Project / Include** > **Project**. Click on the inner edge of the end face to project it.

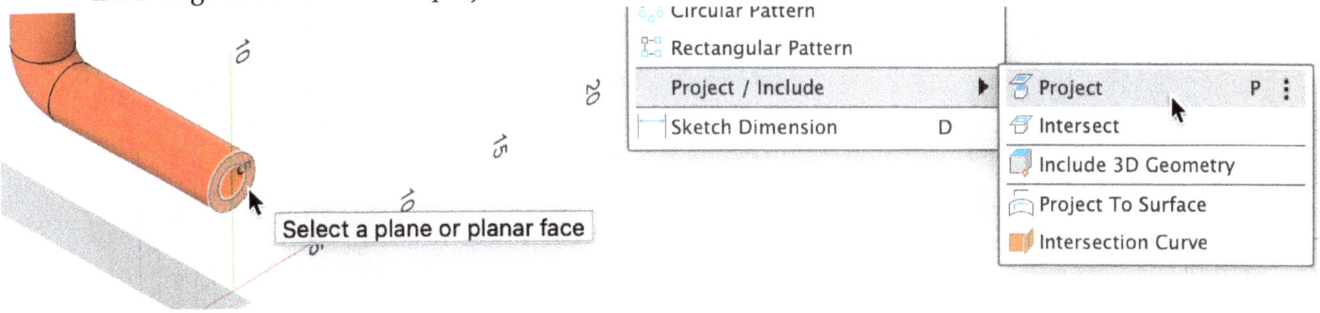

20. Draw a circle of 4.5 in diameter. Click **Finish Sketch** on the toolbar.

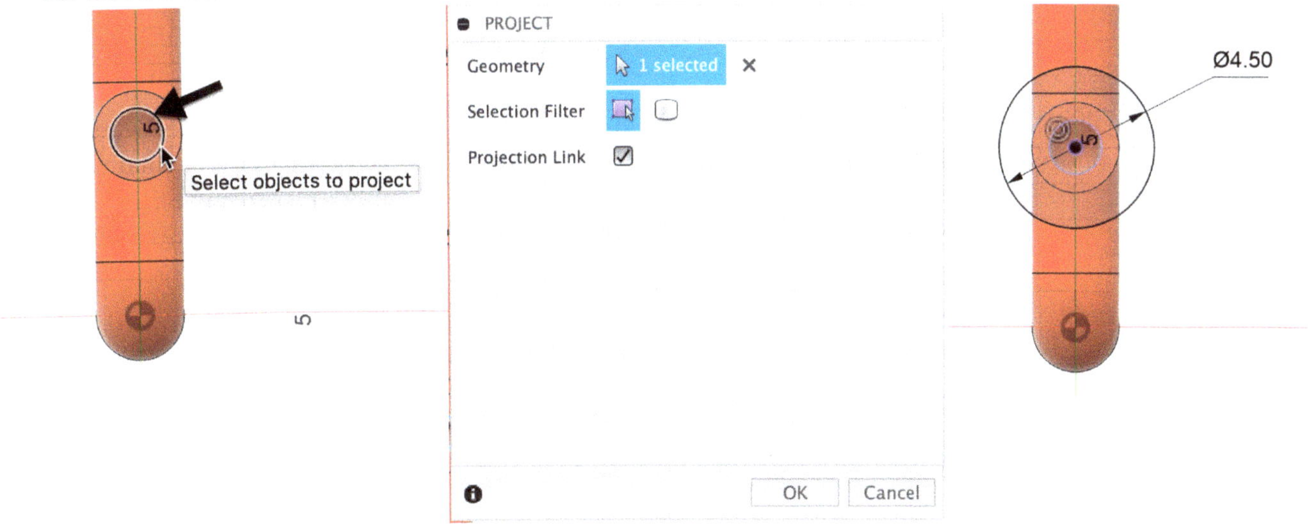

21. Click on the **Home** icon located at the top left corner of the ViewCube.

22. Activate the **Extrude** command and click inside the sketch regions, as shown.

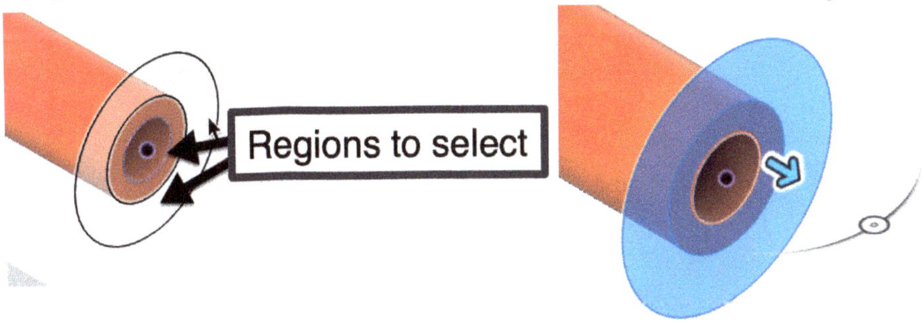

23. Type-in 0.75 in the **Distance** box. Click **Operation** > **Join** and click **OK** to create the flange.

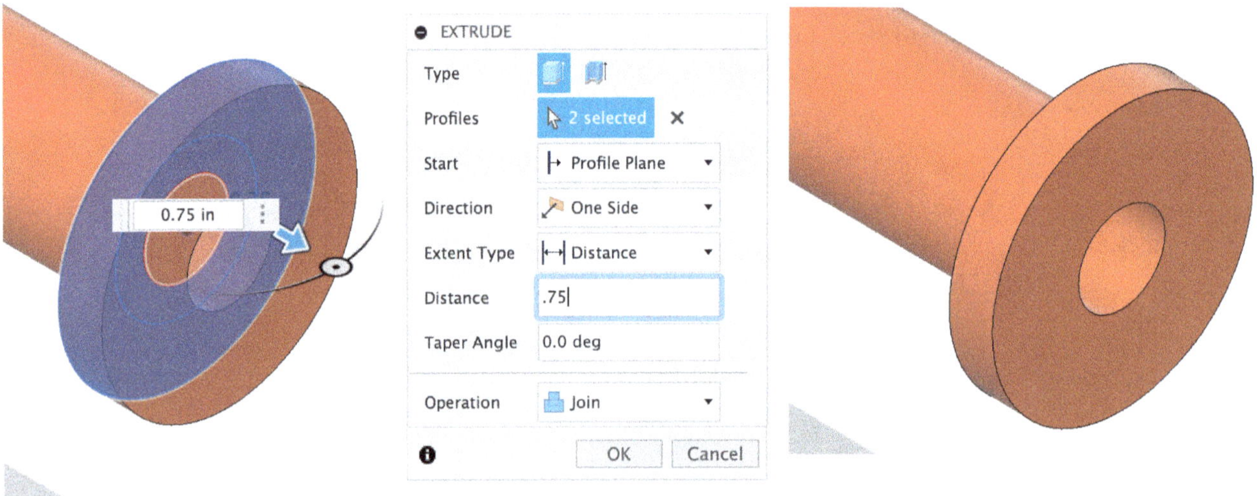

24. On the toolbar, click **Create** panel > **Create Sketch** and click on the front face of the extruded feature.
25. Place a point and add the **Horizontal/Vertical** constraint between the centerpoint of the circular edge and the point.

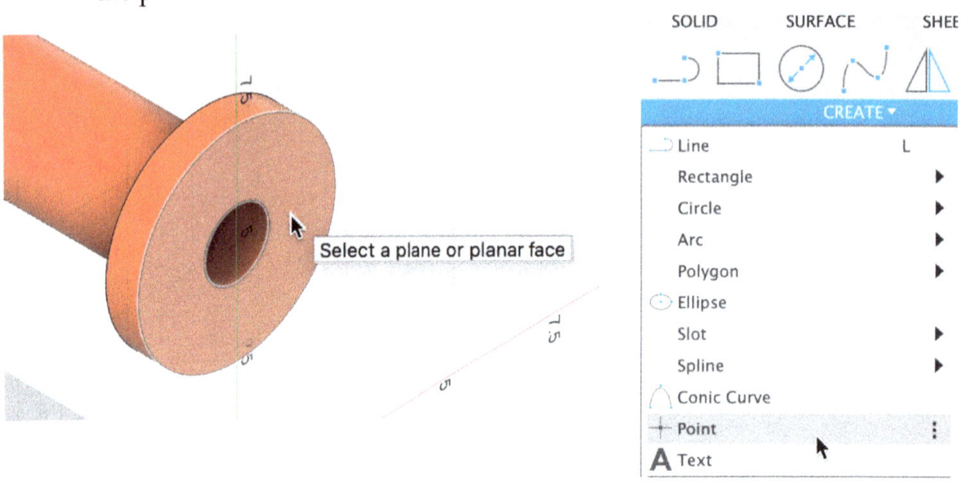

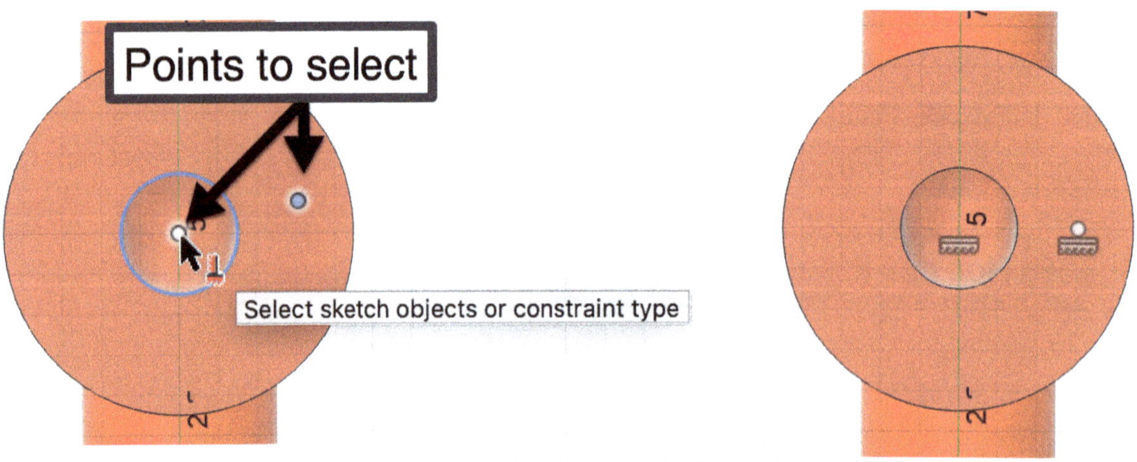

26. Activate the **Sketch Dimension** command and create the linear dimension between the two points, as shown. Click **Finish Sketch** on the toolbar.

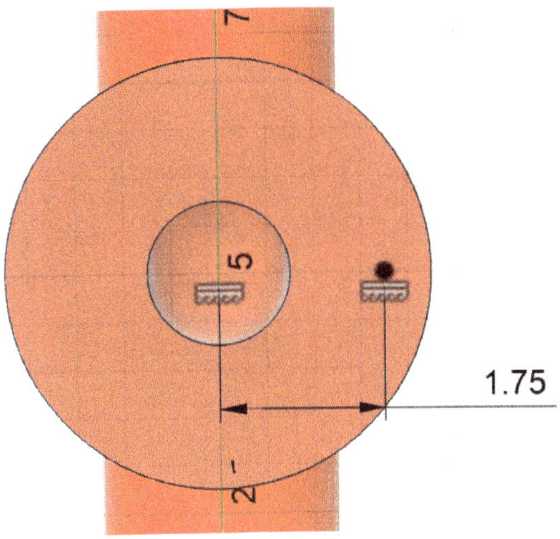

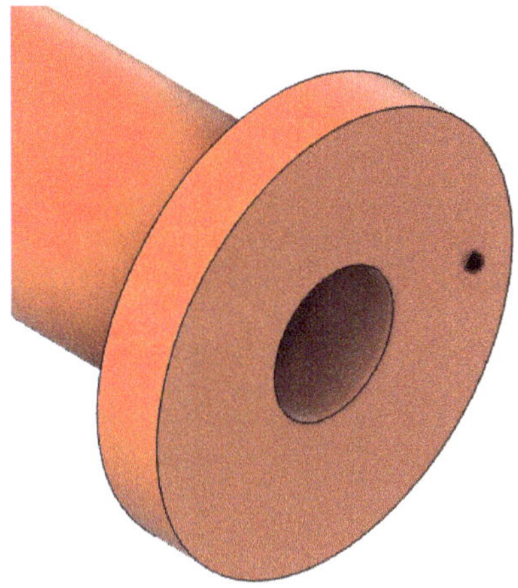

27. Create a simple hole of a 0.5-inch diameter on the extruded feature.

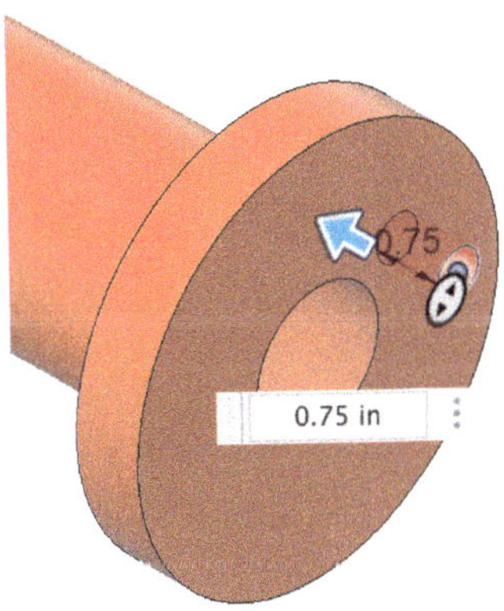

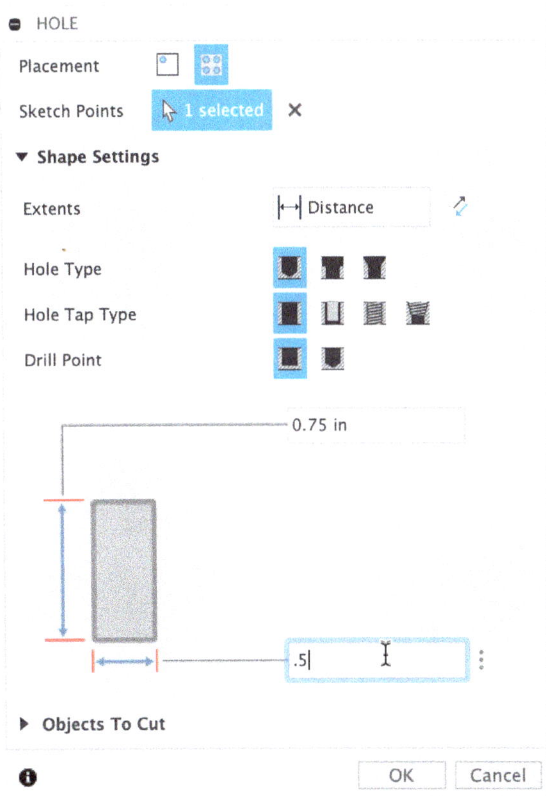

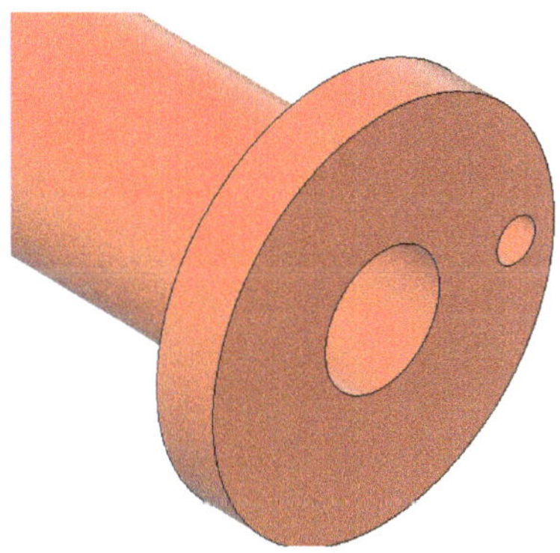

28. On the **Solid** tab of the toolbar, click **Create** panel **> Pattern > Circular Pattern**. Next, select **Object Type > Features**.
29. Click the **Objects** selection button and select the hole feature from the geometry. Now, you have to define the axis of the circular pattern.
30. Click the **Axis** selection button and select the cylindrical face of the extruded feature; the pattern axis is defined.
31. Type-in **6** in the **Quantity** box and click **OK** on the dialog. The hole is patterned in a circular fashion.

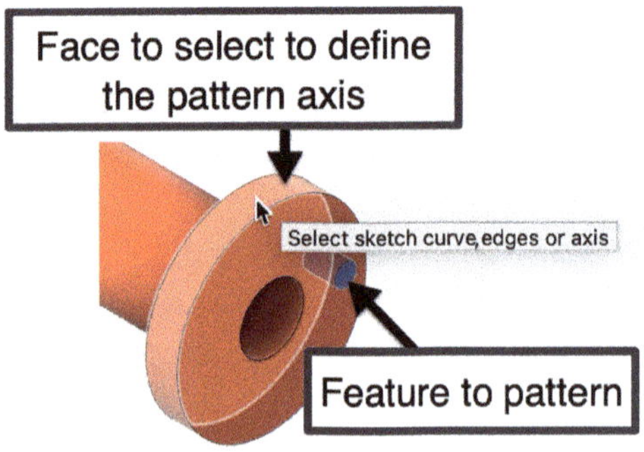

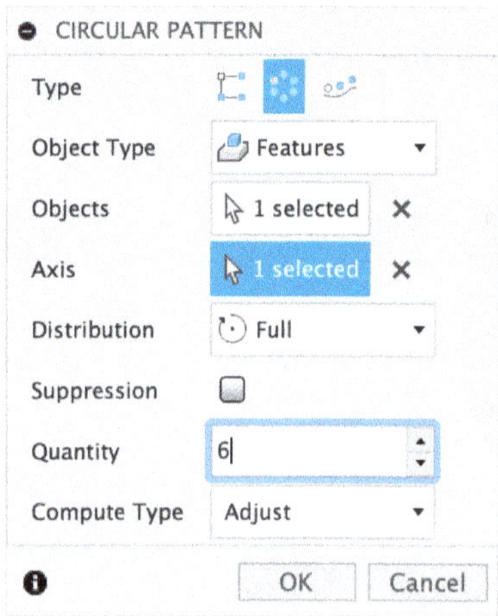

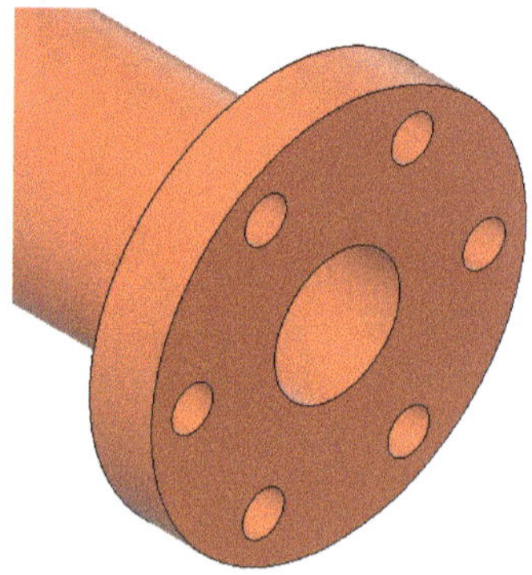

32. Likewise, create another flange on the other end.

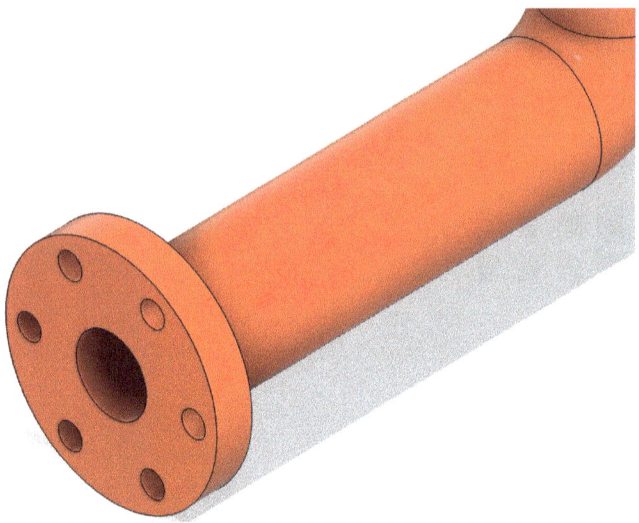

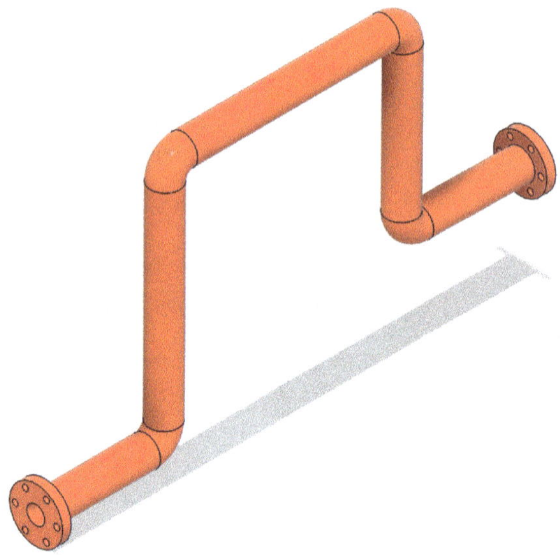

33. Save and close the part file.

Questions

1. List the methods to create the *Sweep* features.
2. How to apply twists and turns to *Sweep* features?
3. How is the **Path and Guide Surface** option useful?
4. List any two options to define the size of the coil features.

Exercises

Exercise 1

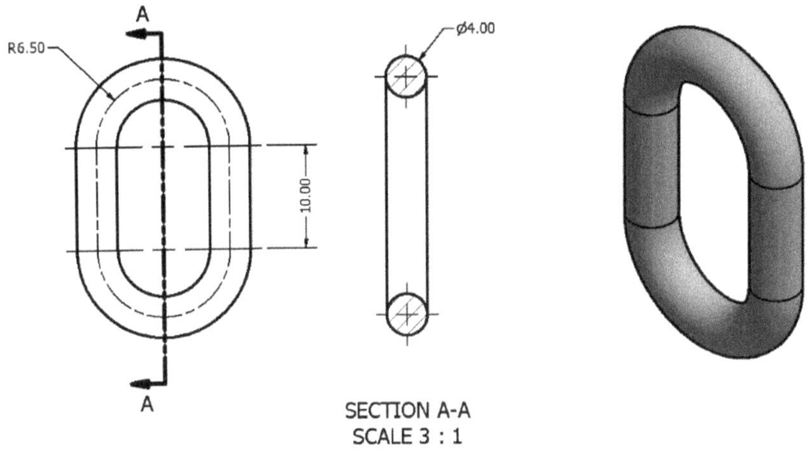

Exercise 2

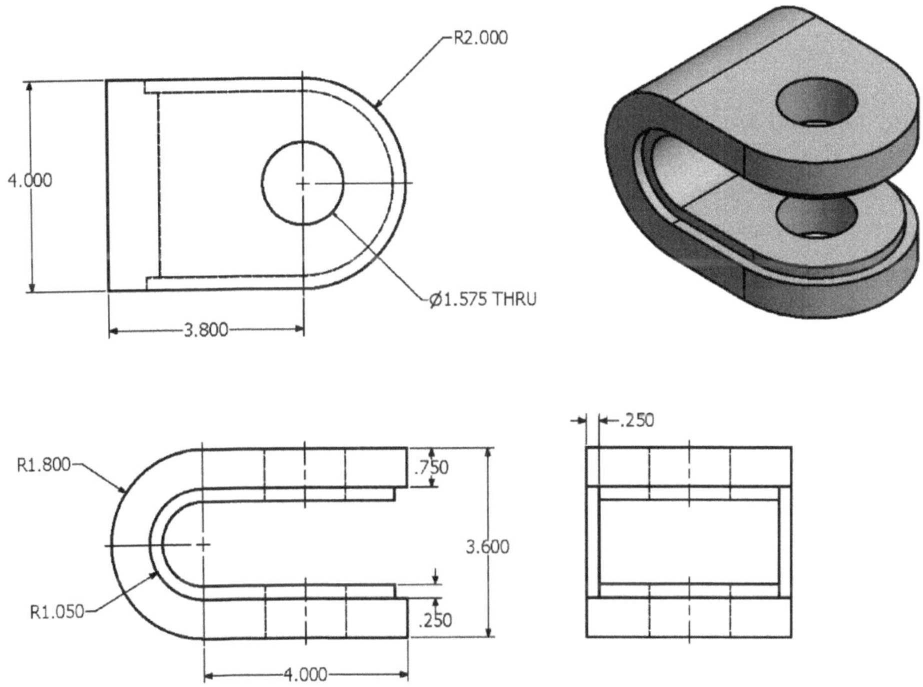

Chapter 7: Loft Features

The **Loft** command is one of the advanced commands available in Autodesk Fusion 360 that allows you to create simple as well as complex shapes. A basic loft is created by defining two profiles and joining them together. For example, if you create a loft feature between a circle and a square, you can easily change the cross-sectional shape of the solid. This ability is what separates the loft feature from the sweep feature.

The topics covered in this chapter are:

- *Basic Lofts*
- *Loft sections*
- *Conditions*
- *Rails*
- *Closed Loop*
- *Center Line Loft*
- *Area Loft*
- *Loft Cutouts*

Loft

This command creates a loft feature between different profiles. To create a loft, first, create two or more profiles on different planes. The planes can be parallel or perpendicular to each other. Activate the **Loft** command (click **Create > Loft**  on the toolbar); the **Loft** dialog appears. Now, you need to select two or more profiles that will define the loft. Select the profiles from the graphics window and click **OK** to create the loft.

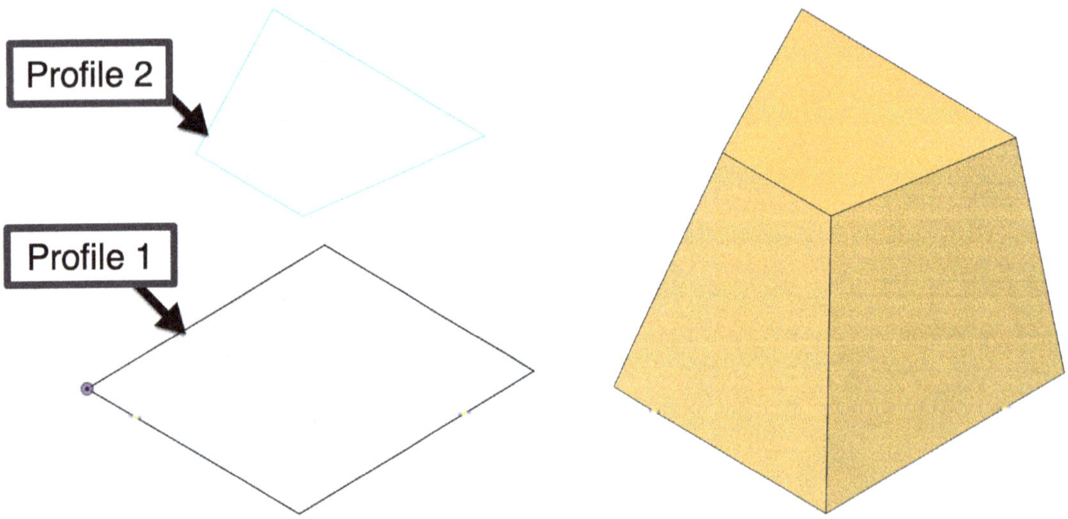

Loft sections

In addition to 2D sketches, you can also define loft profiles by using different element types. For instance, you can use existing model faces, surfaces, and points. The only restriction is that the points can be used at the beginning or end of a loft.

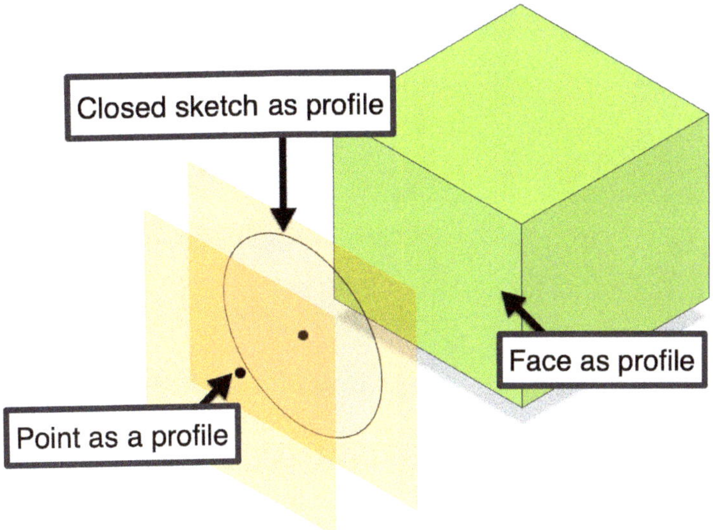

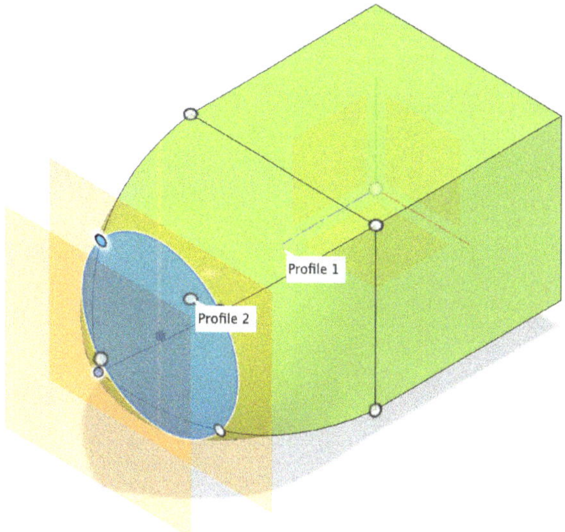

Conditions

The shape of a simple loft is controlled by the profiles and the plane location. However, the **Conditions** drop-down options can control the behavior of the side faces.

Direction Condition

Click the **Condition** drop-down and select **Direction** from the drop-down located next to the first profile. Next, enter 10 in the **Takeoff Angle** box; the preview of the loft feature updates. You can also use the Angle Manipulator. You can control how much influence the angle will have by adjusting the parameter in the **Takeoff Weight** box. A lower value will have a lesser effect on the feature. As you increase the **Takeoff Weight** value, the more noticeable the effect will be, eventually. If you increase the number higher, the direction angle will lead to self-intersecting results.

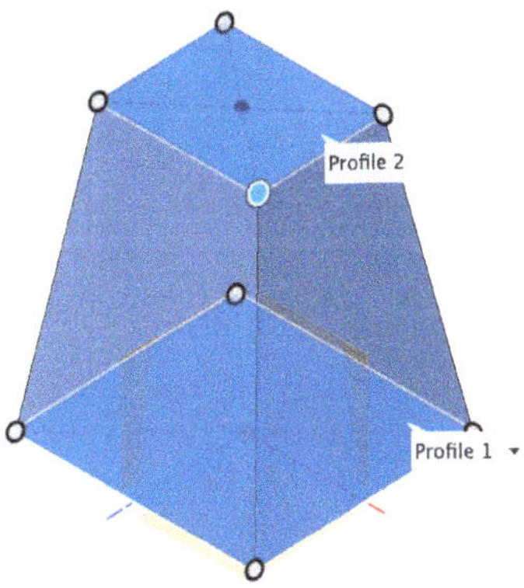

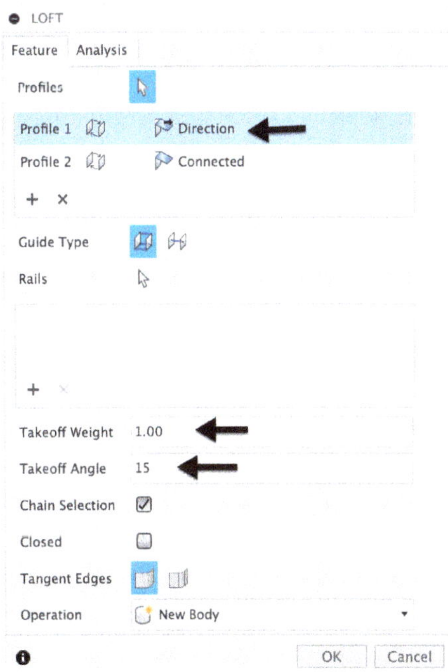

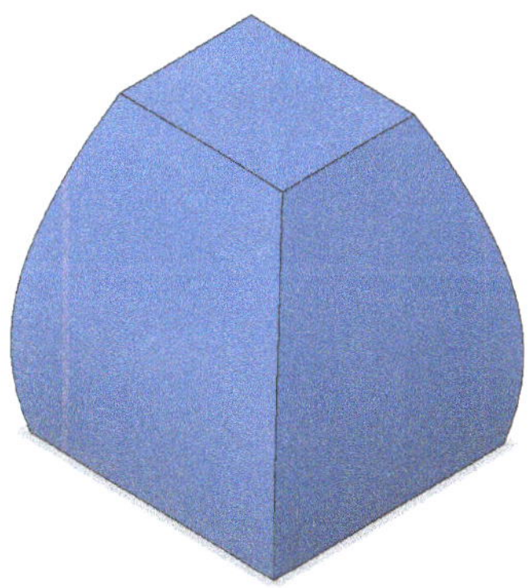

Likewise, you can also apply the **Direction** condition to the second profile of the loft.

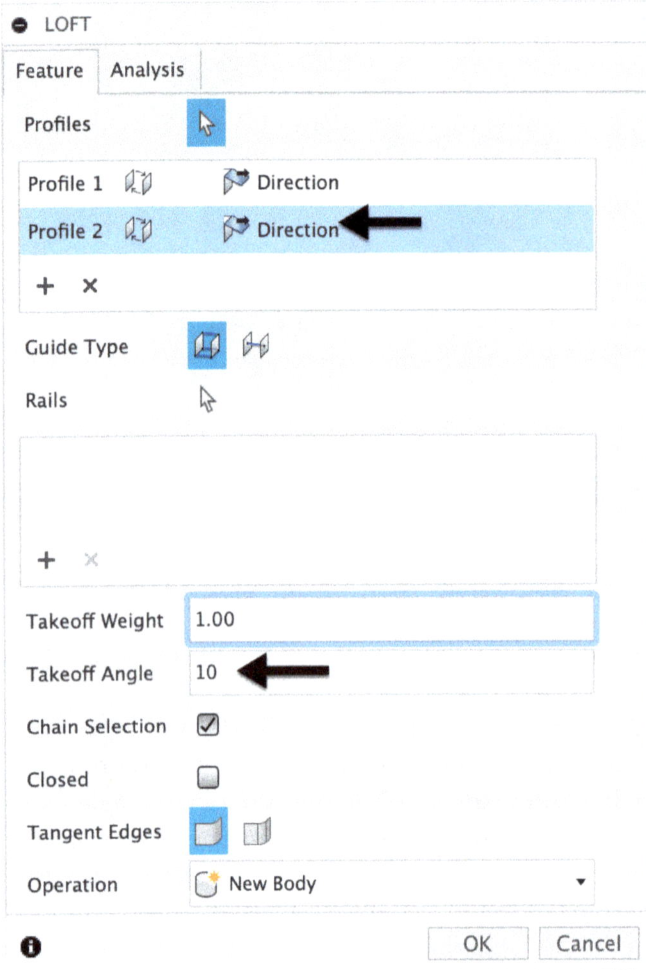

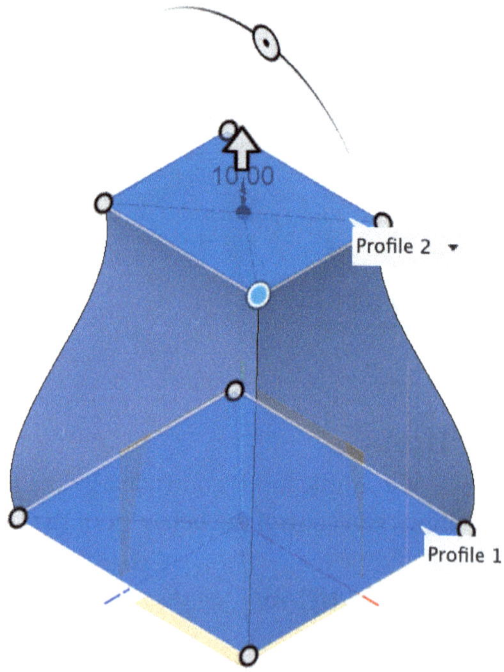

Tangent (G1) Condition

The **Tangent (G1)** option is available when you select a sketch and an existing face as the profiles. This option makes the side faces of the loft feature tangent to the side faces of the existing geometry.

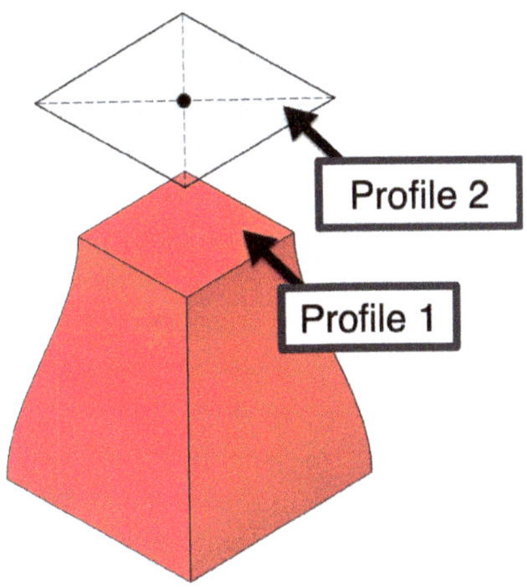

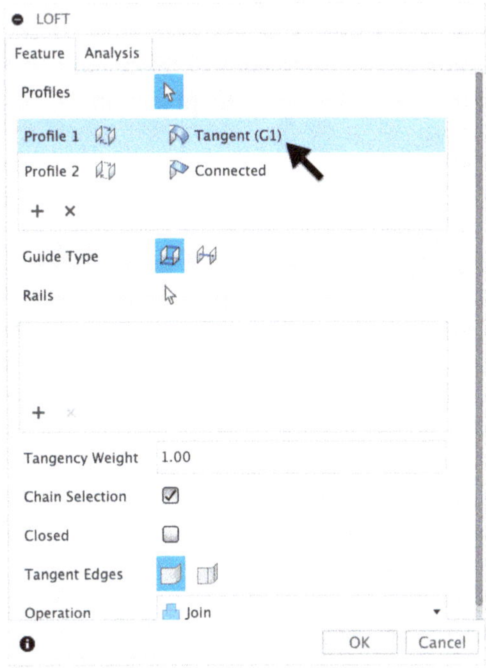

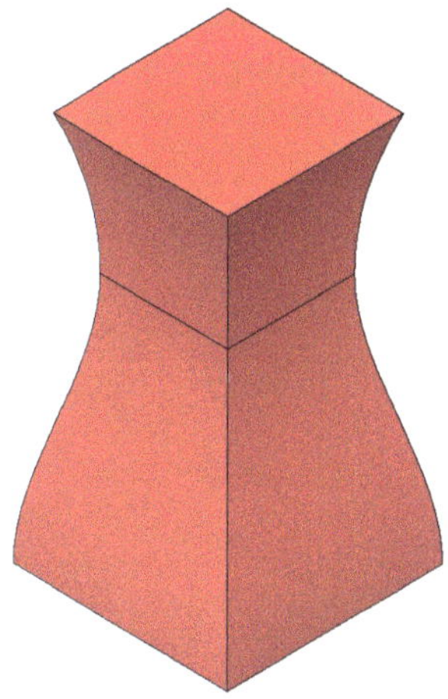

Curvature (G2) Condition

The **Curvature (G2)** option is available when you select an existing face loop as one of the cross-sections. This option makes the side faces of the loft feature curvature continuous with the side faces of the existing geometry.

Sharp Condition

The **Sharp** option is available when you select a point as one of the cross-sections. This option keeps the end of the loft sharp.

Point Tangent

The **Point Tangent** option is available when you select a point as one of the cross-sections. This option makes the side faces of the loft feature tangent to the point selected.

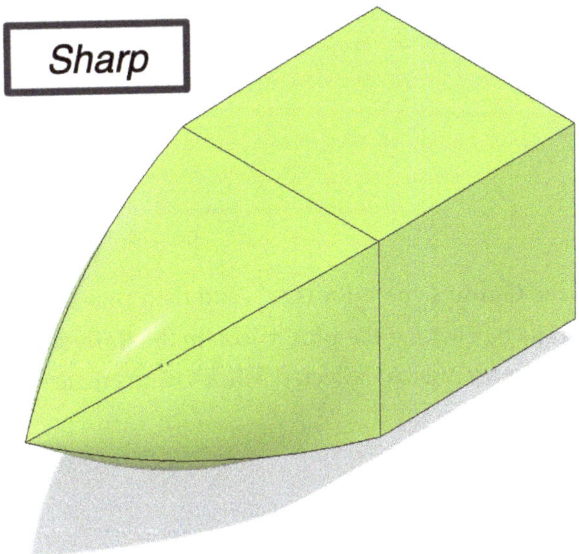

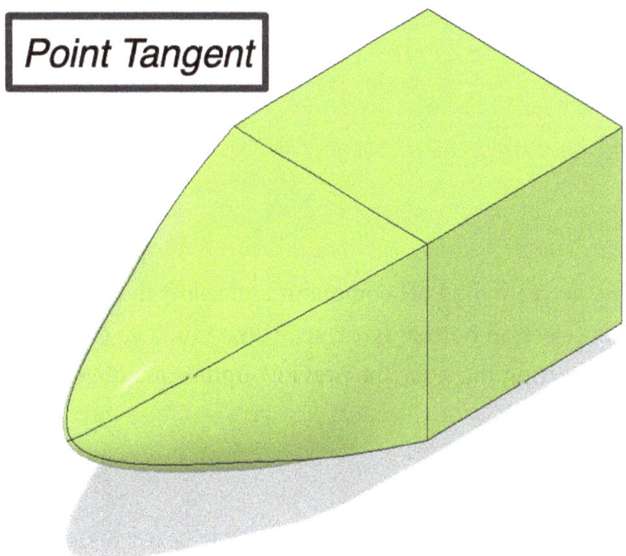

Rails

Similar to the **Condition** options, rails allow you to control the behavior of a loft between profiles. You can create rails by using sketches. For example, start a sketch on the plane intersecting with the profiles, and then create a spline, as shown.

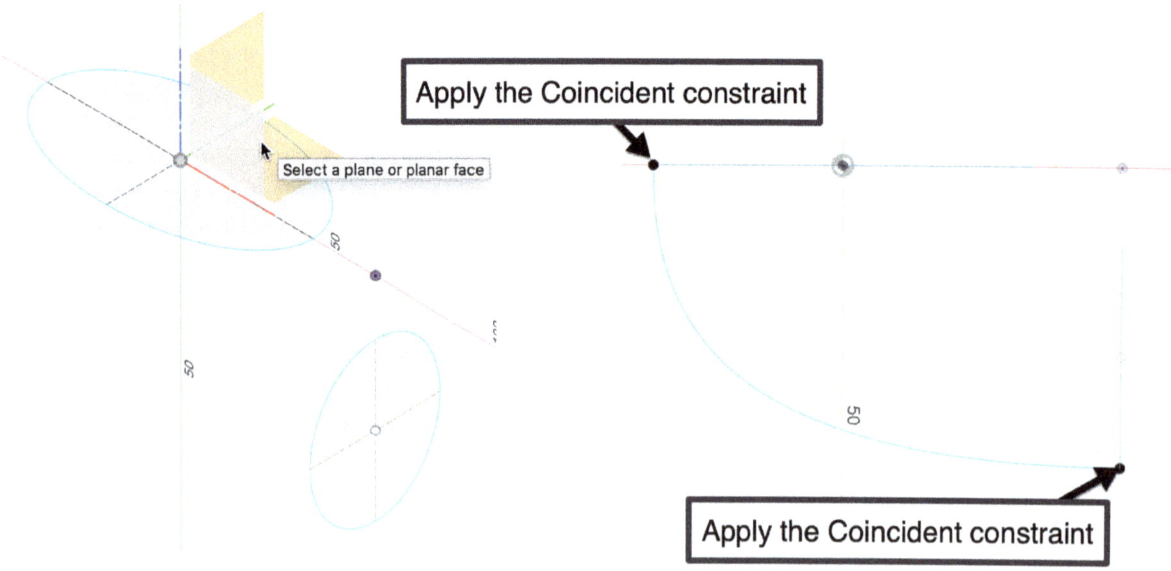

Next, you need to connect the endpoints of the spline with the profiles. Click **Constraints** panel > **Coincident** on the **Sketch** tab of the toolbar. Next, make the endpoints of the spline coincident with the profiles. Click **Finish Sketch** on the toolbar.

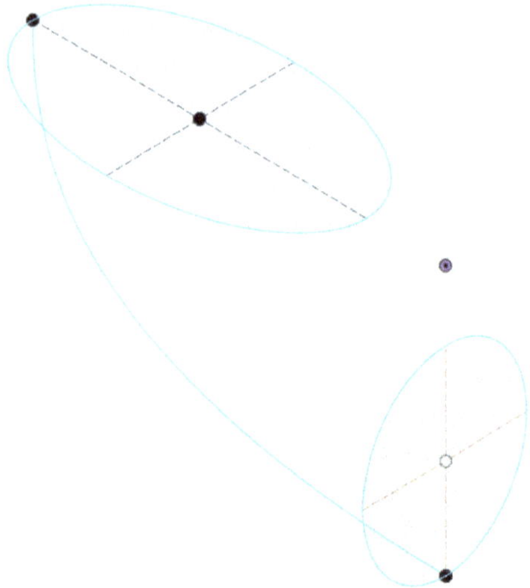

Next, activate the **Loft** command and select the profiles. Click the **Guide Type > Rails** , and then click the **Rails** selection button. Next, select the rail. You can add more rails by clicking the plus + icon in the **Rails** section and selecting the rails; the preview updates. Notice that the edges with rails are affected. Click **OK** to create rails.

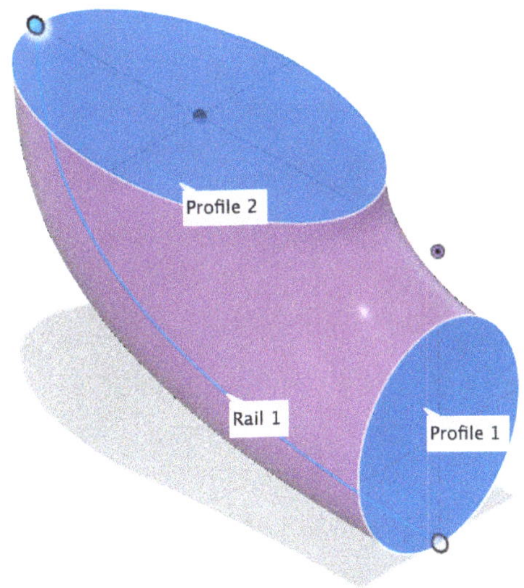

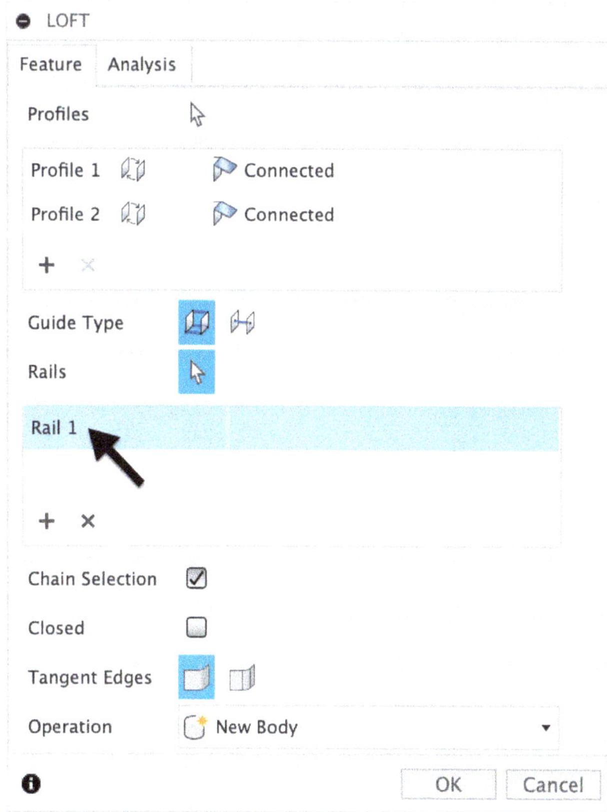

Closed

Autodesk Fusion 360 allows you to create a loft that closes on itself. For example, to create a model that lofts between each of the shapes, you must select four sketches as shown in the figure, and then check the **Closed** option on the dialog. Next, click **OK**; this will give you a closed loft.

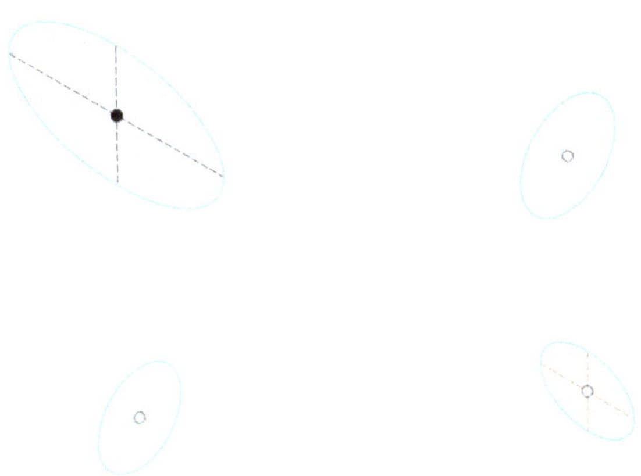

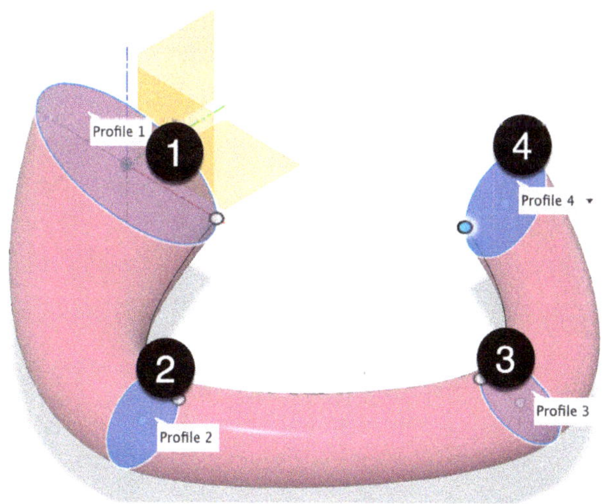

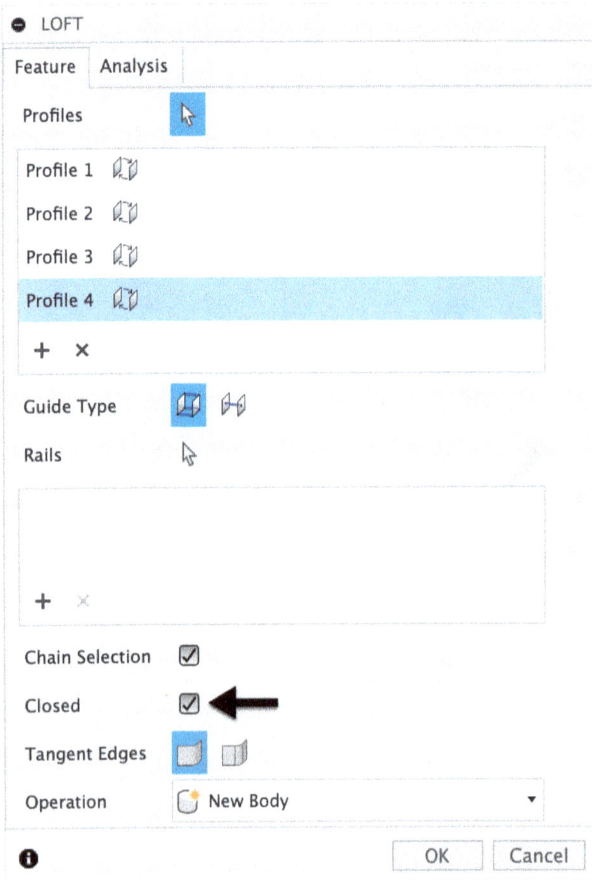

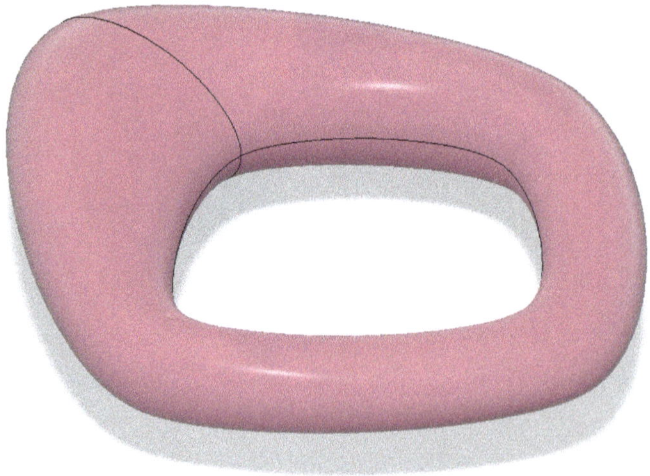

Center Line Loft

In the previous section, you have created a closed loft using four sections. However, the transition between the sections was not smooth. The **Centerline** option helps you to create a smooth transition between the sections. First, create a centerline passing through all the sections, as shown. Next, activate the **Loft** command and select loft profiles. Next, select **Guide Type > Centerline** and select the centerline; the preview of the loft appears. Check the **Closed Loop** option, if you want to create a closed-loop, and then click **OK**.

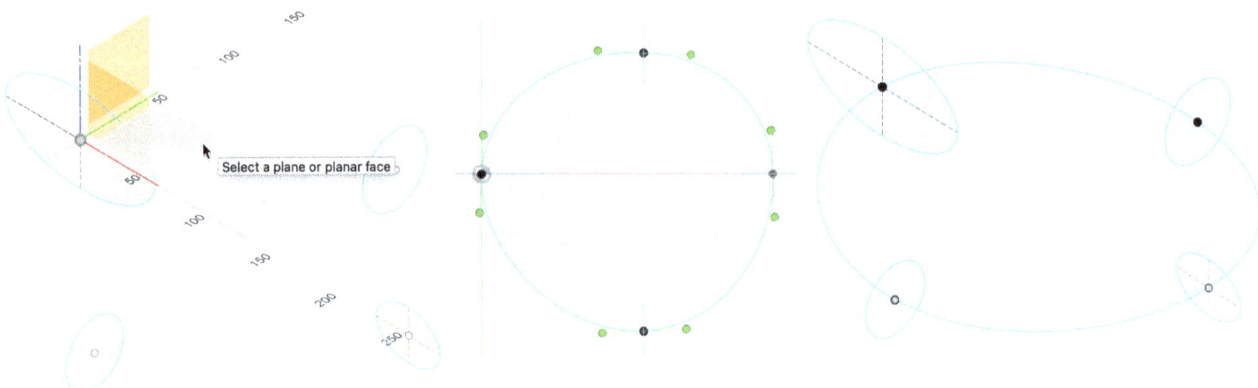

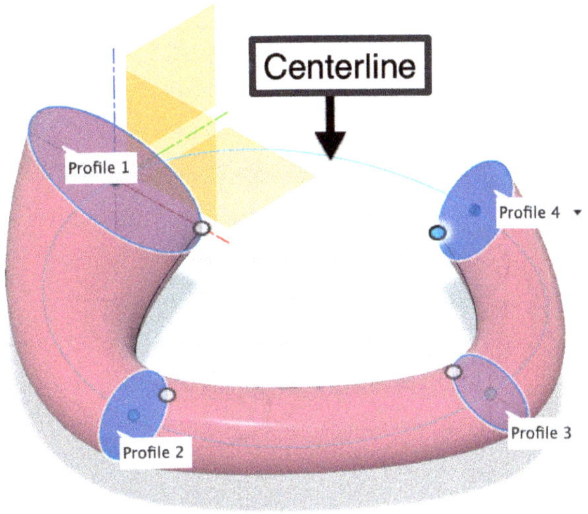

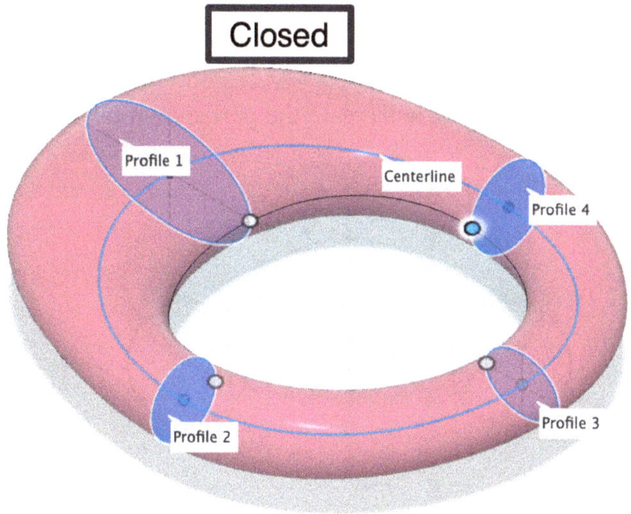

Loft Cutout

Like other standard features such as extrude, revolve and sweep, the loft feature can be used to add or remove material. You can remove material by using the **Loft** command. Activate this command (click **Create** panel **> Loft** on the **Solid** tab of the toolbar) and select the profiles. Click **Operation > Cut** and **OK** to create the loft cutout.

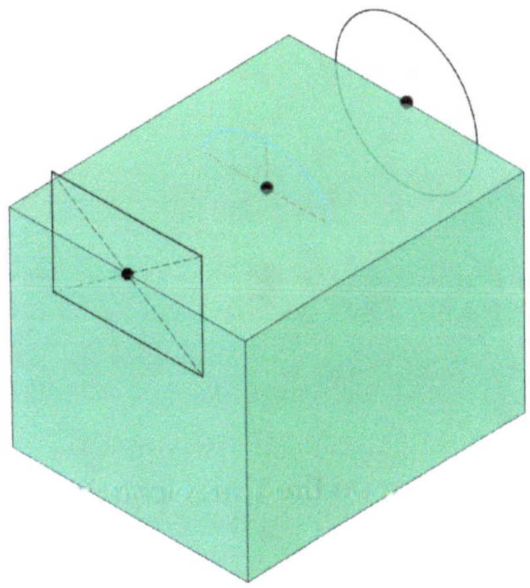

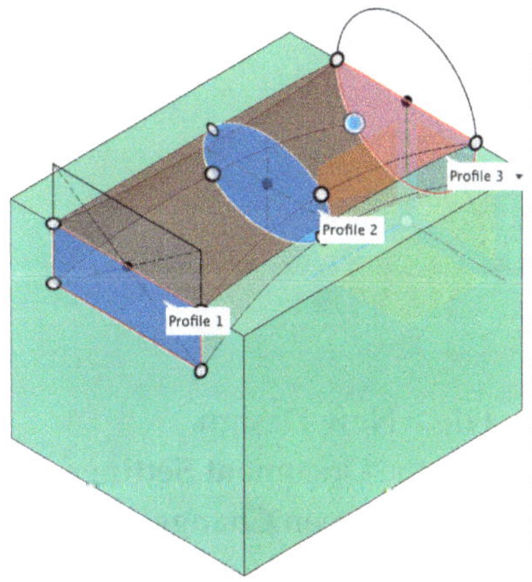

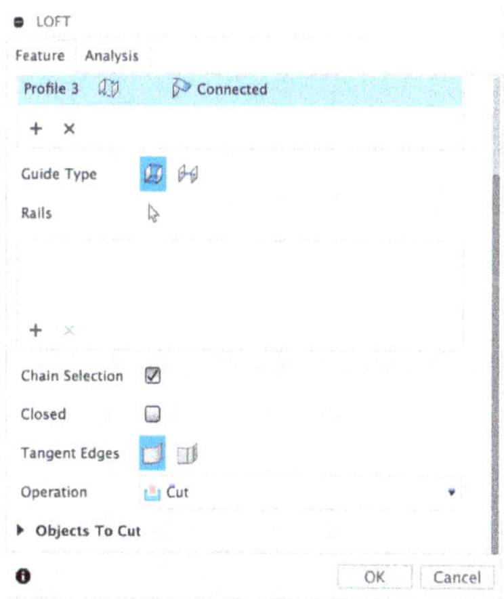

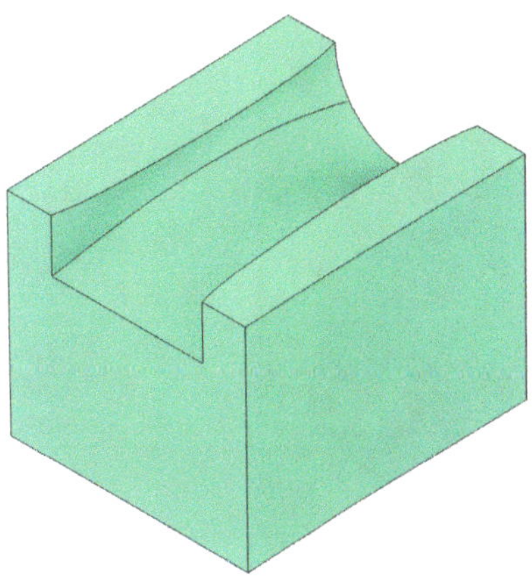

Examples

Example 1 (Millimetres)

In this example, you will create the part shown below.

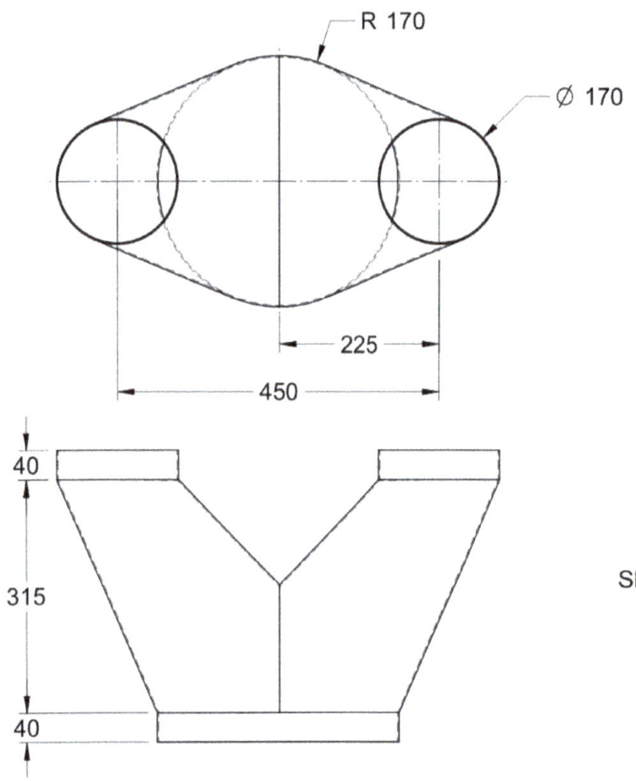

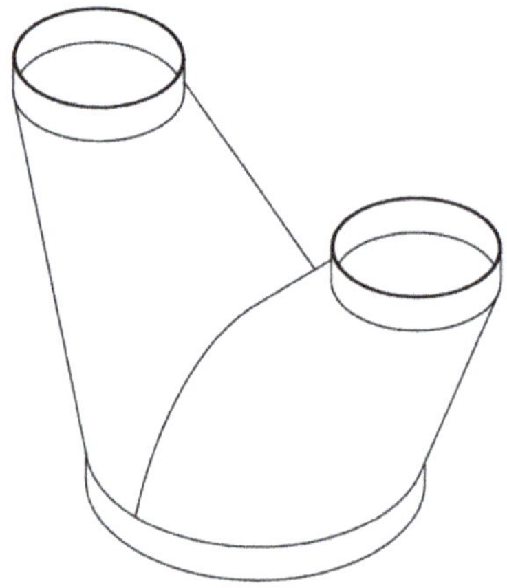

SHELL INSIDE TO 2 mm

1. Start **Autodesk Fusion 360**.
2. On the Application bar, click **File > New Design.**
3. On the Browser window, expand the **Document Settings** and place the pointer on the **Units** icon. Next, click the **Change Active Units** icon to open **Change Active Units** dialog.
4. Click **Unite Type > millimeter (mm), gram (g)** and click **OK**.
5. To start a new sketch, click **Create** panel **> Create Sketch** on the toolbar.
6. Select the XY Plane and draw a circle of 340 mm in diameter. Click **Finish Sketch** on the toolbar.
7. Create the *Extrude* feature with a 40 mm thickness.

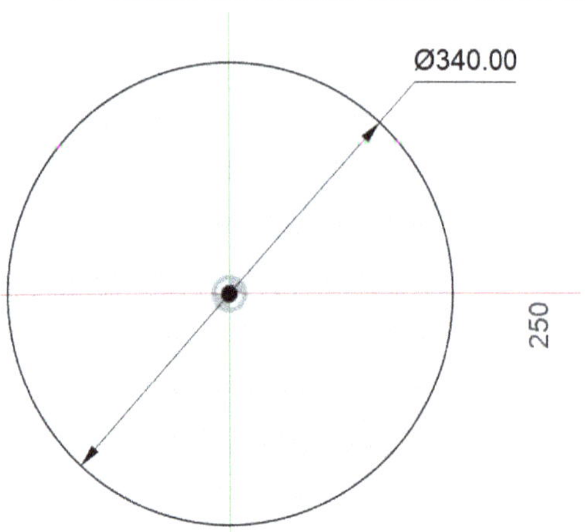

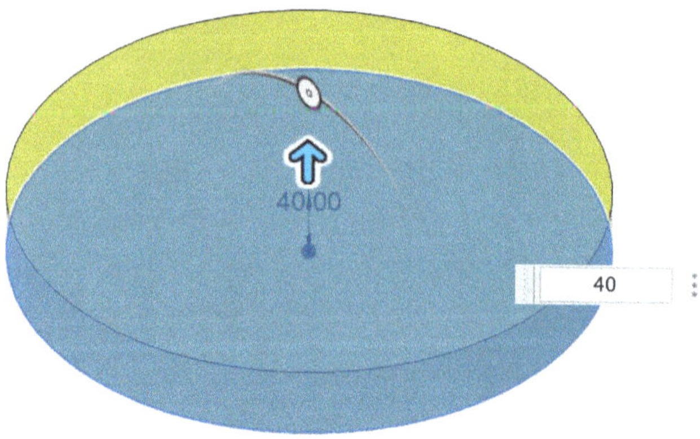

8. On the **Solid** tab of the toolbar, click **Construct > Offset Plane**.
9. Click on the top face of the geometry. Type-in **315** mm in the **Distance** box and click **OK**.
10. On the toolbar, click **Create** panel **> Create Sketch**, and then select the newly created plane.
11. Activate the **Center Diameter Circle** command and draw a circle of **170** mm in diameter. Also, add dimensions and constraints to the circle, as shown. Click **Finish Sketch** on the toolbar.

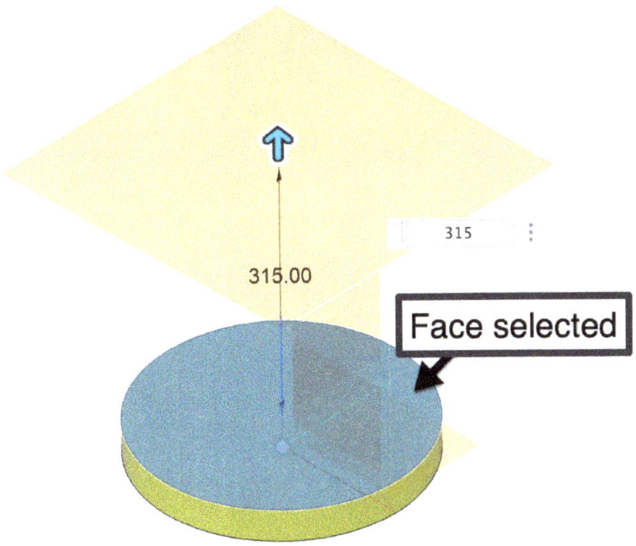

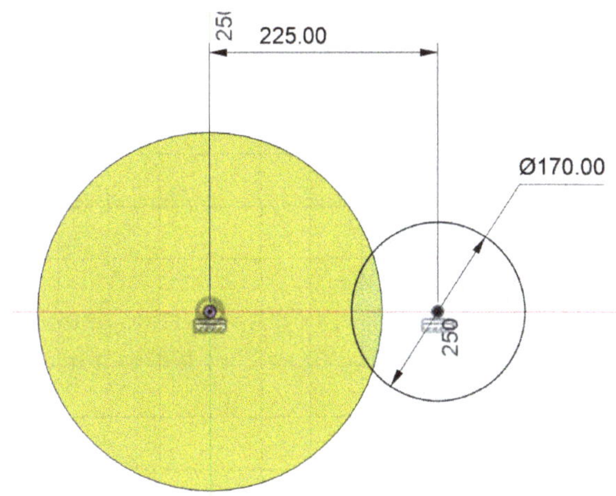

12. On the **Solid** tab of the toolbar, click **Create** panel **> Loft**.
13. Click on the circle and the top circular edge of the *Extrude* feature. Click **OK** to complete the *Loft* feature.

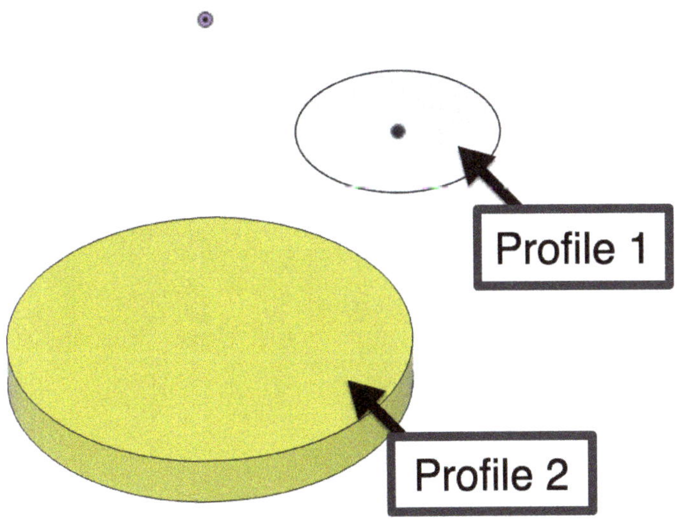

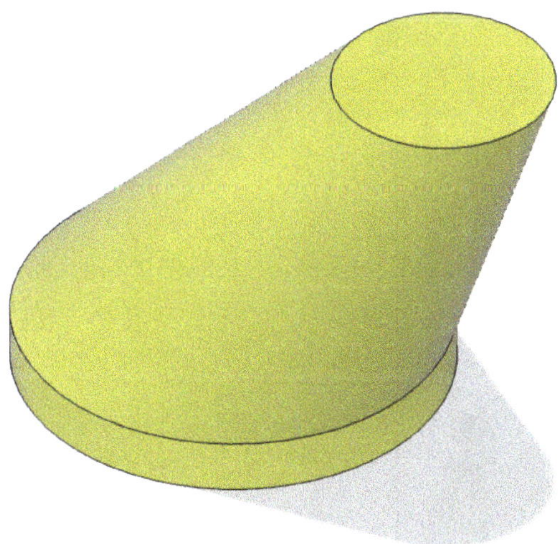

14. Activate the **Extrude** command and click on the top face of the loft feature.
15. Type **40** in the **Distance** box. Click **OK**.

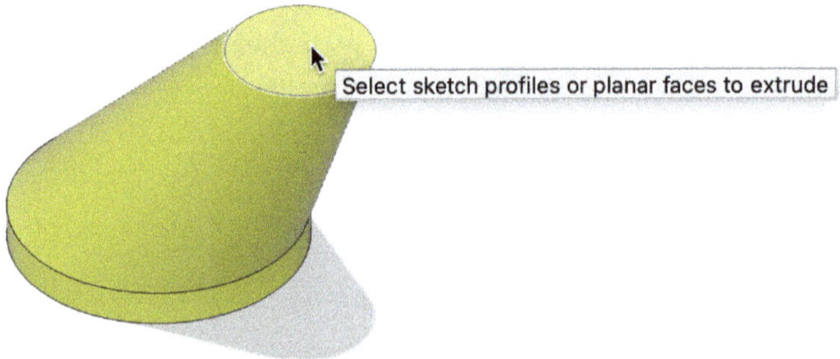

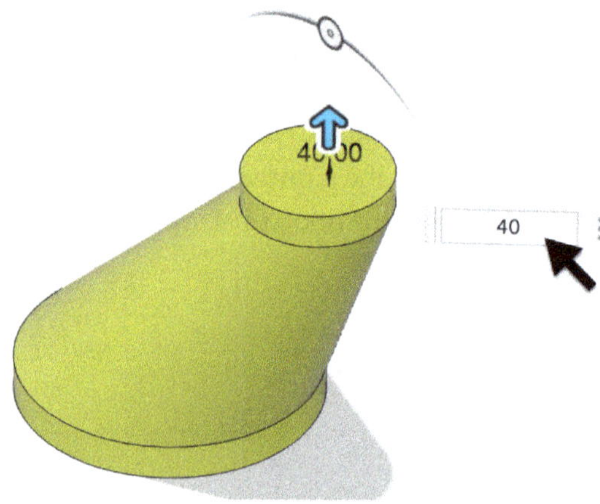

16. On the **Solid** tab of the toolbar, click **Create** panel > **Mirror**. On the **Mirror** dialog, select **Pattern Type** > **Features**.
17. Click the **Object** selection button and select the loft feature and the extruded feature on top of it.
18. Click the **Mirror Plane** selection button on the **Mirror** dialog.
19. Select the YZ Plane. Click **OK** to mirror the selected features.

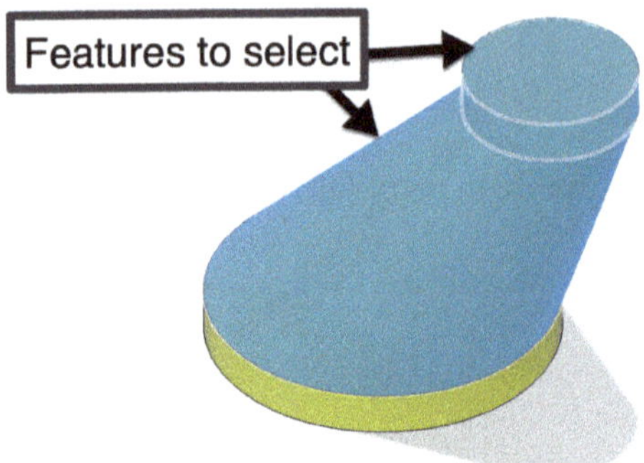

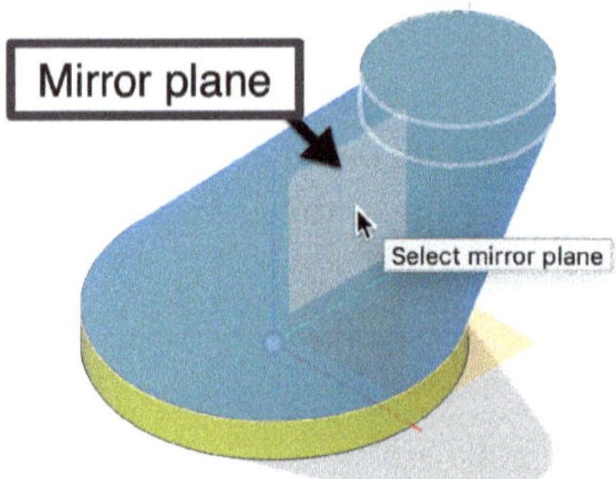

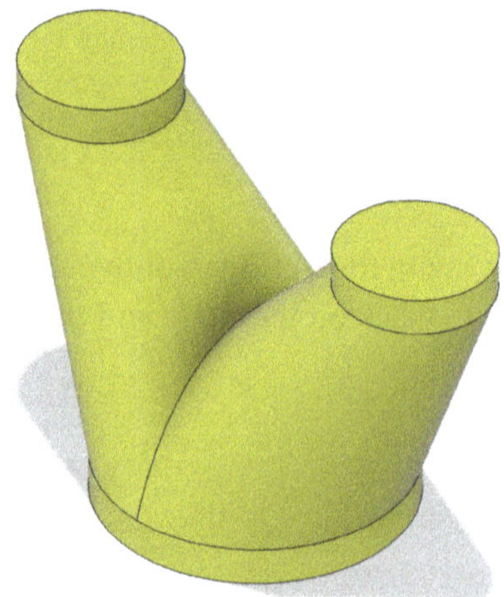

20. On the **Solid** tab of the toolbar, click **Modify** panel > **Shell** and click on the flat faces of the part geometry. Next, select **Shell Type** > **Sharp Shell**.
21. Type **2** in the **Inside Thickness** box and click **OK**. The part geometry is shelled.

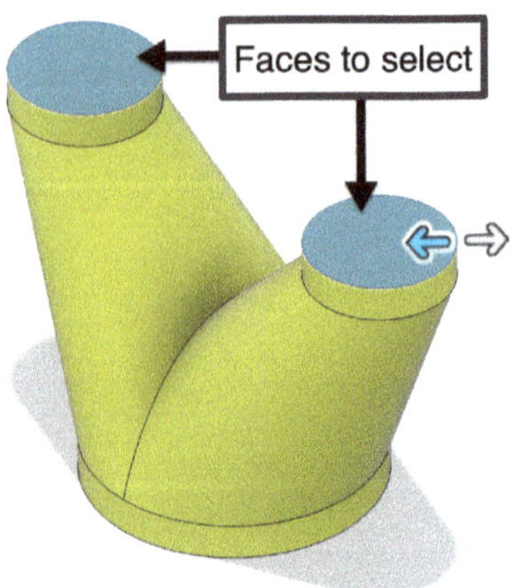

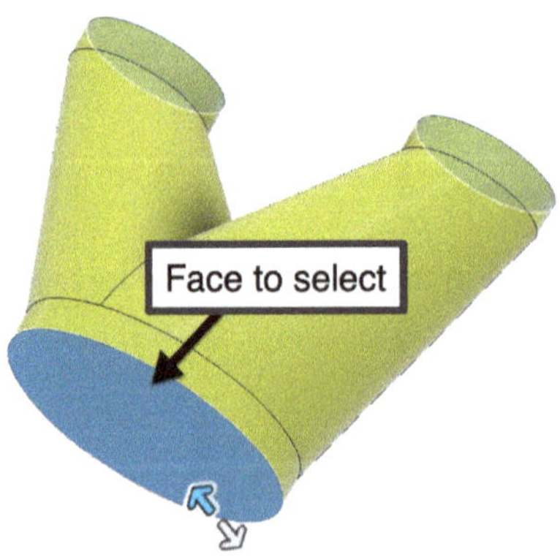

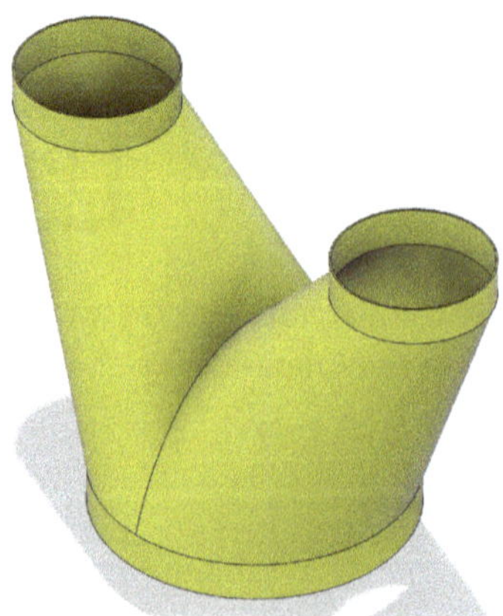

22. Save and close the part file.

Example 2 (Inches)

In this example, you will create the part shown below.

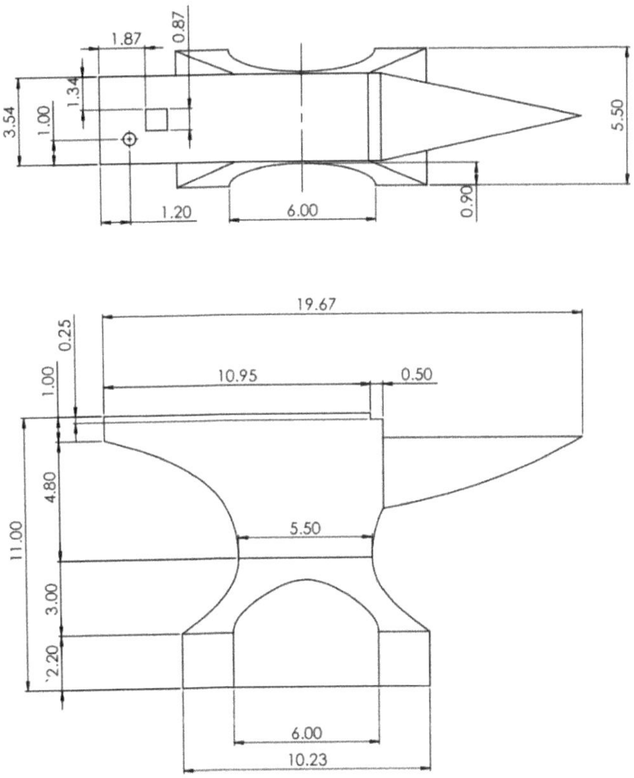

Creating an Extruded Feature

1. Start **Autodesk Fusion 360**.
2. On the Application bar, click **File > New Design**.
3. In the **Browser Window**, expand the **Document Settings** and place the cursor on the **Units** icon. Next, click the **Change Active Units** icon.
4. Select **Unit Type drop-down > inch (in), ouncemass** on the **Change Active Units** dialog and then click **OK**. (leave the third and fourth steps if Inch is set as the Default units)
5. To start a new sketch, click **Create** panel > **Create Sketch** on the toolbar. Click on the XY plane.
6. Click **Create** panel **> Rectangle > Center Rectangle** on the **Sketch** contextual tab of the toolbar.
7. Click on the origin point to define the center point of the rectangle. Move the mouse pointer upward and click to draw a rectangle.
8. Activate the **Sketch Dimension** command and apply dimensions to the sketch, as shown below.
9. Click **Finish Sketch** on the toolbar.
10. Click the **Home** icon located at the bottom left corner of the ViewCube.
11. Click **Create** panel **> Extrude** on the **Solid** tab of the toolbar, and then select the sketch.
12. On the **Extrude** dialog, select **Extents > Distance** and type-in 2.2 in the **Distance** box.
13. Click **OK** to create the *Extrude* feature.

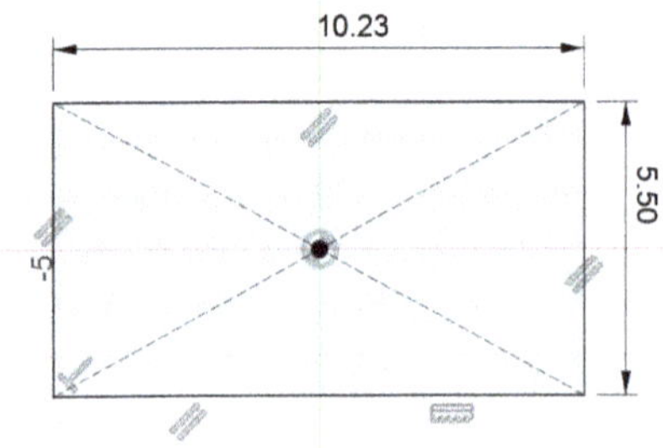

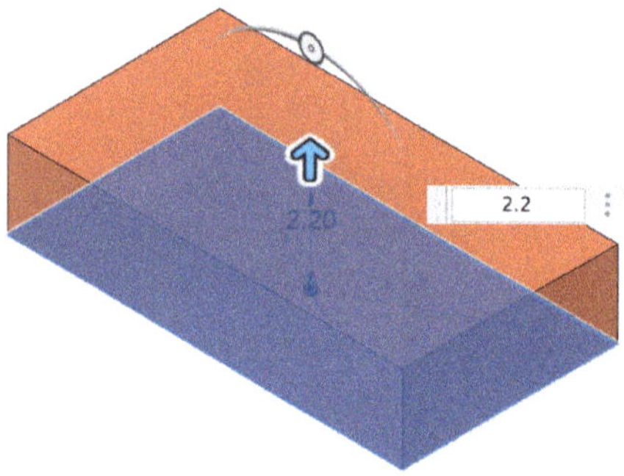

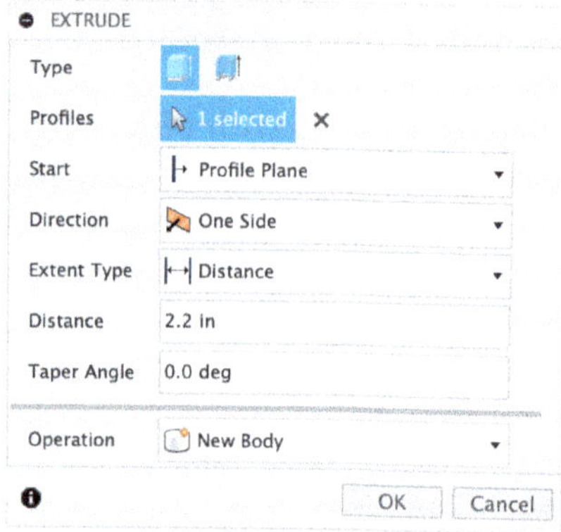

Creating a Simple Loft Feature

1. Click **Construct** panel > **Offset Plane** on the **Solid** tab toolbar and click on the top face of the model.
2. On the **Offset Plane** dialog, type-in 3 in the **Distance** box and click **OK** to create an offset plane.

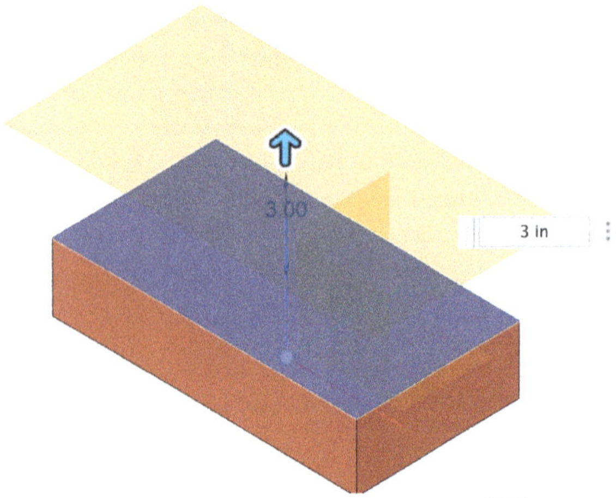

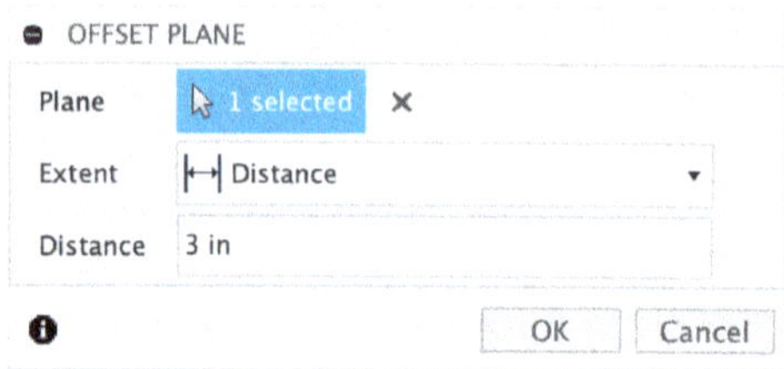

3. Click **Create** panel **> Create Sketch** on the toolbar and click on the newly created plane.
4. Click **Create** panel **> Rectangle > Center Rectangle** on the **Sketch** contextual tab of the toolbar.
5. Click on the origin point to define the center point of the rectangle. Move the mouse pointer upward and click to draw a rectangle.
6. Activate the **Sketch Dimension** command and apply dimensions to the sketch.
7. Click **Finish Sketch** on the toolbar.

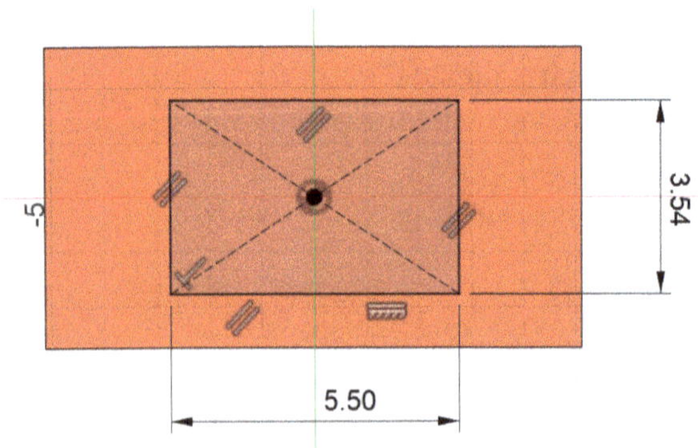

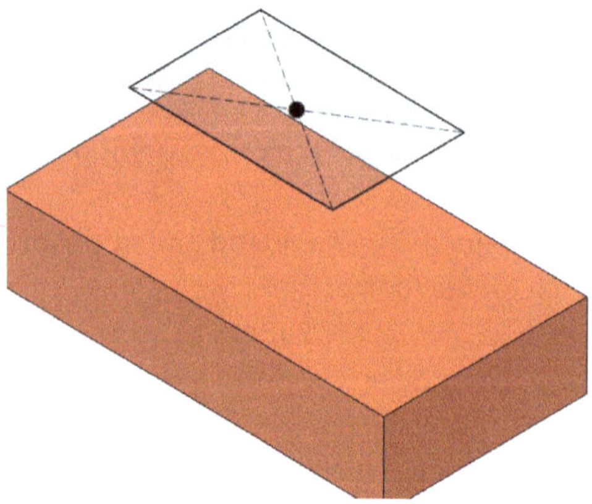

8. Click **Create** panel **> Loft** on the **Solid** tab toolbar; the **Loft** dialog appears on the screen.
9. Click the top face of the first feature and then click the rectangular sketch.
10. On the **Loft** dialog, click **Profile 2 > Condition** drop-down **> Direction**.
11. Make sure that the **Takeoff Weight** is 1 and **Takeoff Angle** is 0 deg.
12. Click **Operation > Join** and click **OK** to create the **Loft** feature.

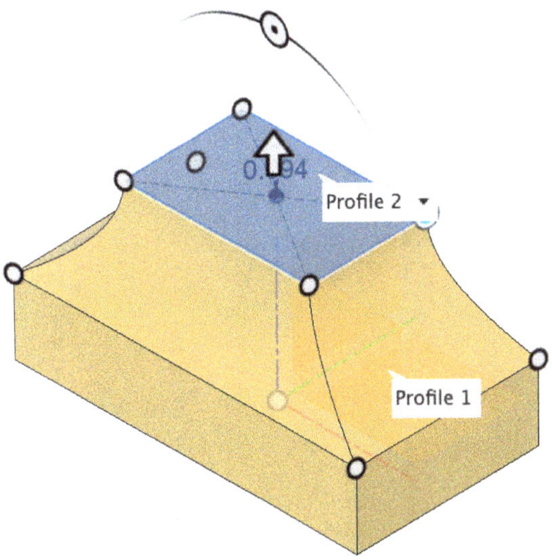

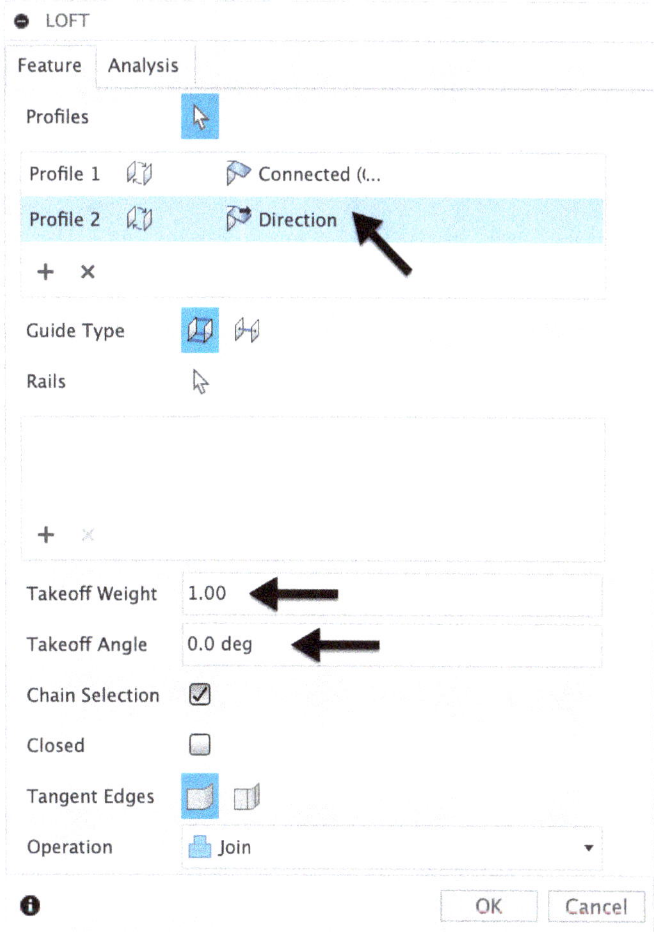

Creating the Extruded Cut Feature

1. On the toolbar, click **Create** panel > **Create Sketch** . Next, select the top face of the loft feature.
2. Click **Create** panel **> Ellipse** on the **Sketch** contextual tab of the toolbar.
3. Specify the center point of the ellipse. Move the mouse pointer vertically and click to specify the first axis. Next, move the pointer horizontally and click to create the second axis of the ellipse.

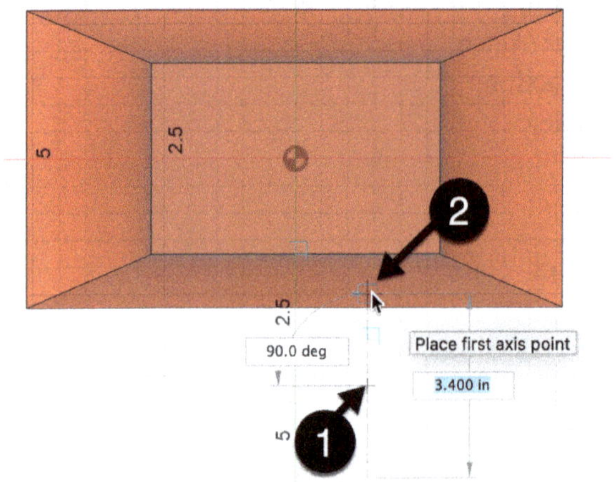

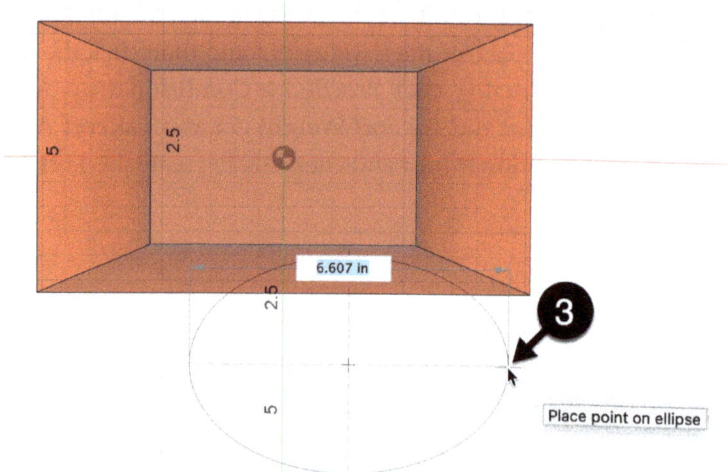

4. On the **Sketch** contextual tab of the toolbar, click **Constraints** panel > **Midpoint**.
5. Select the centerpoint of the ellipse and the horizontal edge of the model, as shown.

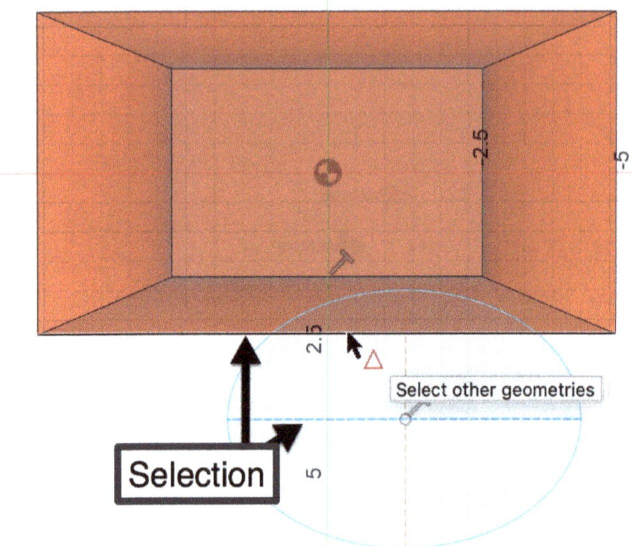

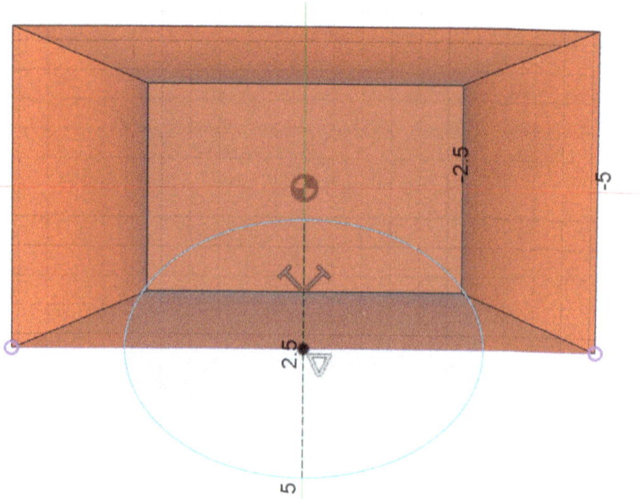

6. Click **Create** panel **> Sketch Dimension** on the **Sketch** contextual tab of the toolbar and select the two horizontal quadrant points of the ellipse, as shown. Place the dimension, type 6 in the dimension box, and press Enter.

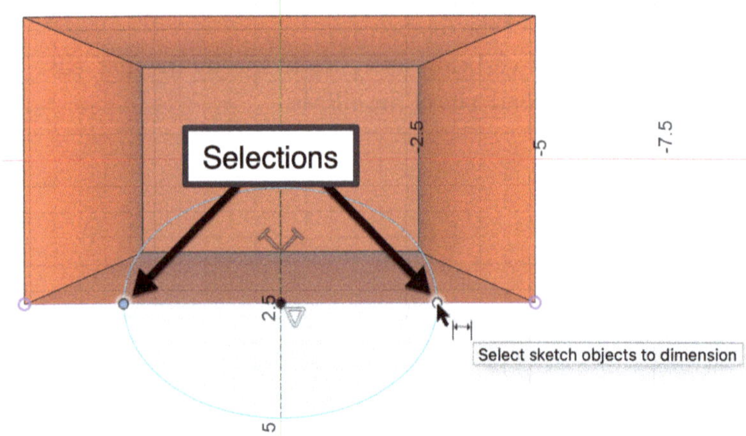

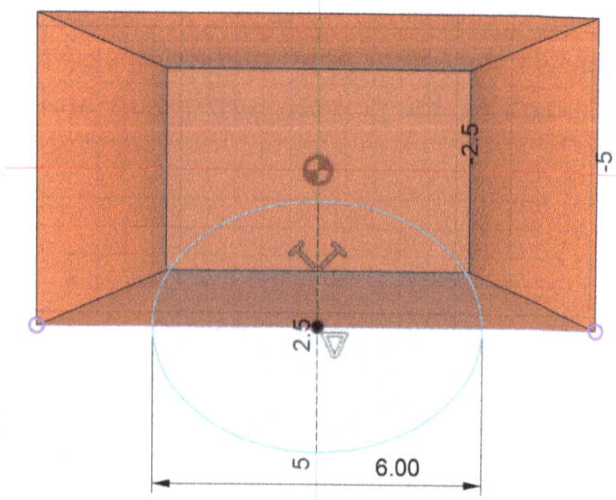

7. Select the two vertical quadrant points and place the dimension. Type 1.8 in the dimension box and press Enter.

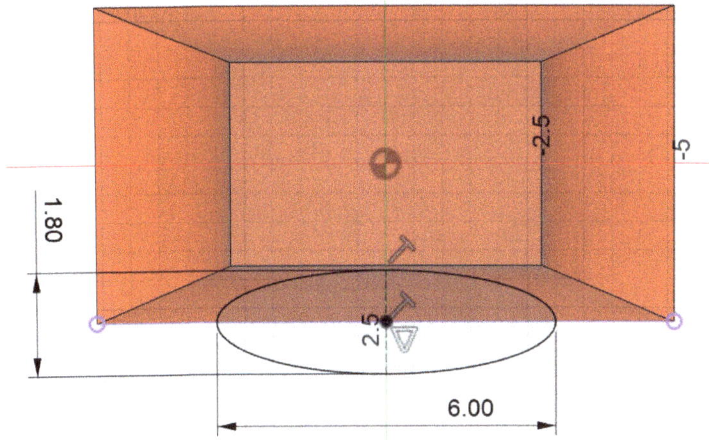

8. Click **Finish Sketch** on the toolbar.
9. Click **Create** panel > **Extrude** on the **Solid** tab of the toolbar and click on the region enclosed by the sketch, as shown.
10. On the **Extrude** dialog, click **Extent Type > All** and click the **Flip** icon to reverse the direction.
11. Click **Operation > Cut** and click **OK** to create the extruded cut.

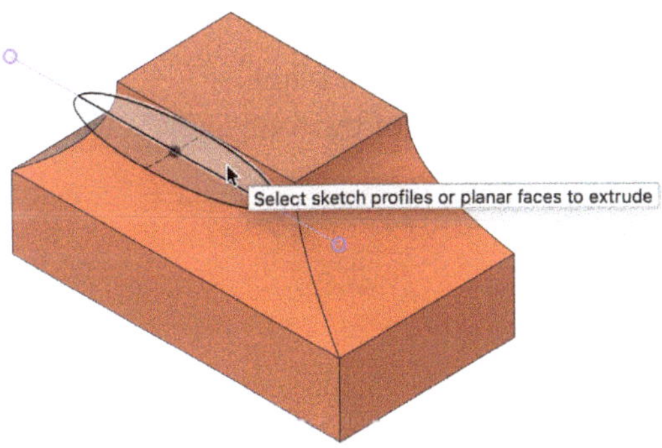

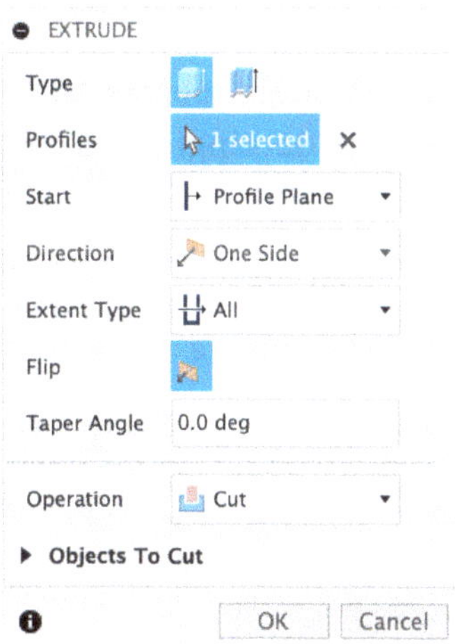

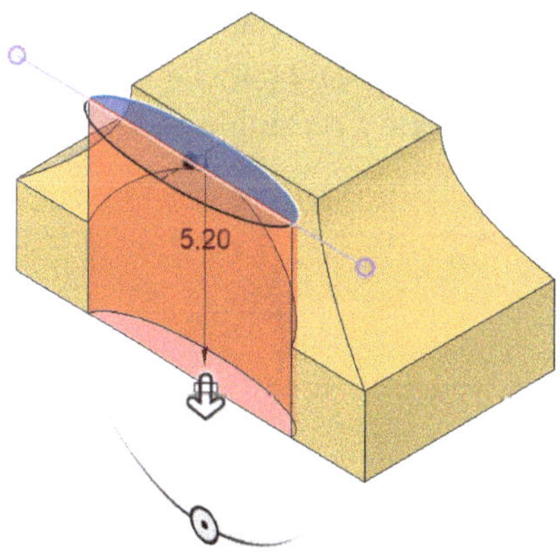

12. On the Solid tab of the toolbar, click **Create** panel > **Mirror**. Next, select **Object Type > Features**.
13. Select the newly created cut feature. Next, click the Mirror Plane selection button and select the XZ plane.

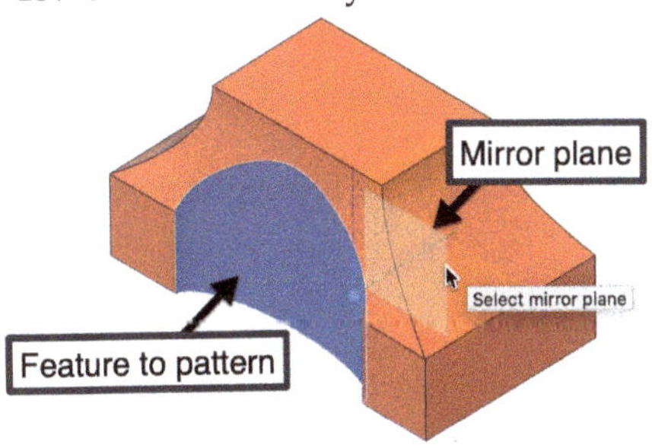

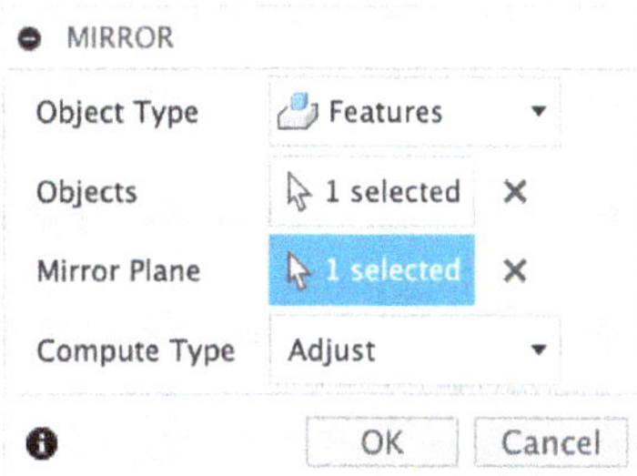

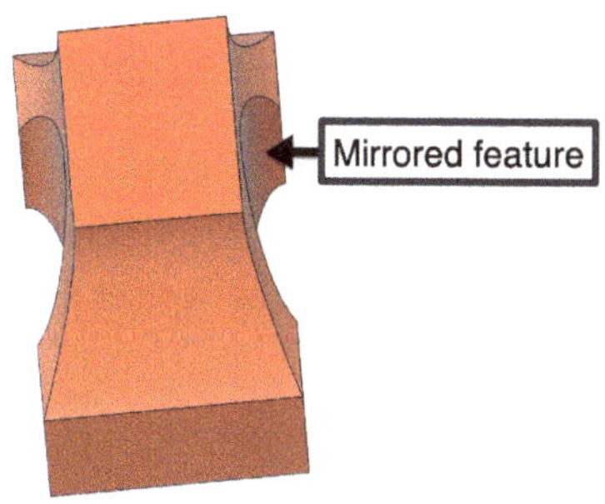

14. Click **Construct** panel **> Offset Plane** on the toolbar. Next, click on the top face of the loft feature. Enter 4.8 in the **Distance** box and click **OK**.

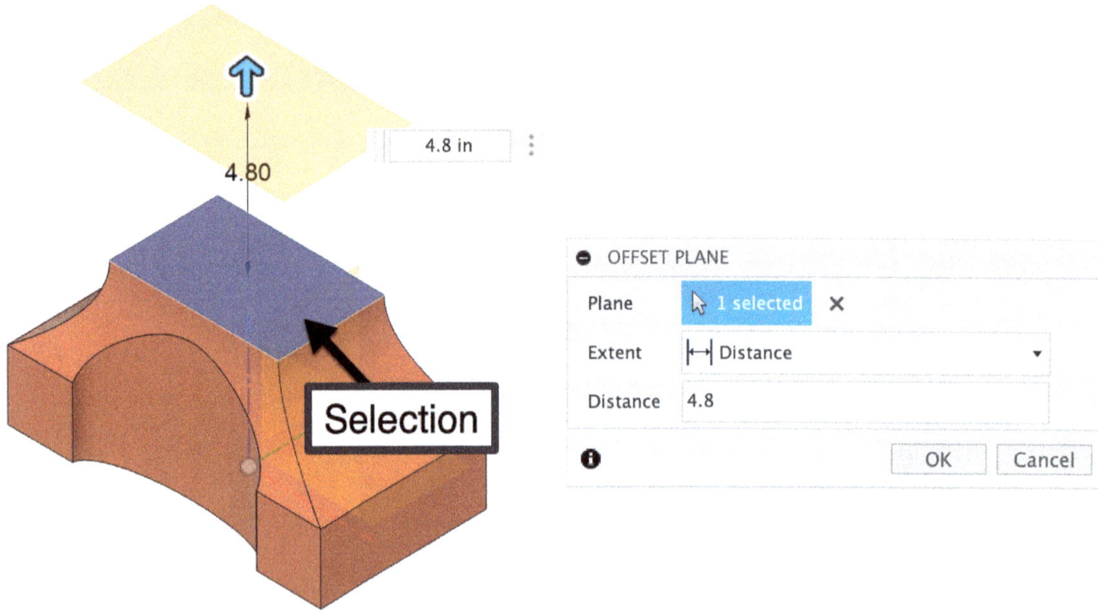

Creating the Loft Feature using Sections and Rails

1. Click **Create** panel > **Create Sketch** on the toolbar. Next, select the newly created plane.
2. Click **Create** panel **> Rectangle > Center Rectangle** on the **Sketch** contextual tab of the toolbar.
3. Create a rectangle and add dimensions, as shown.

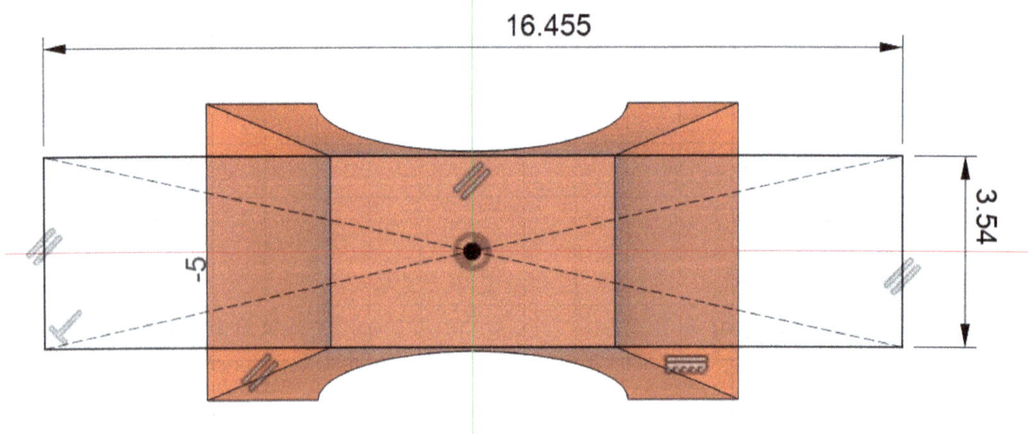

4. Click **Finish Sketch** on the toolbar.
5. Click **Construct** panel > **Offset Plane** on the toolbar. Select the **XZ** plane and click on the top-right vertex of the loft feature, as shown. Click **OK** to create the plane.
6. Likewise, create another offset plane in the back face of the loft feature.

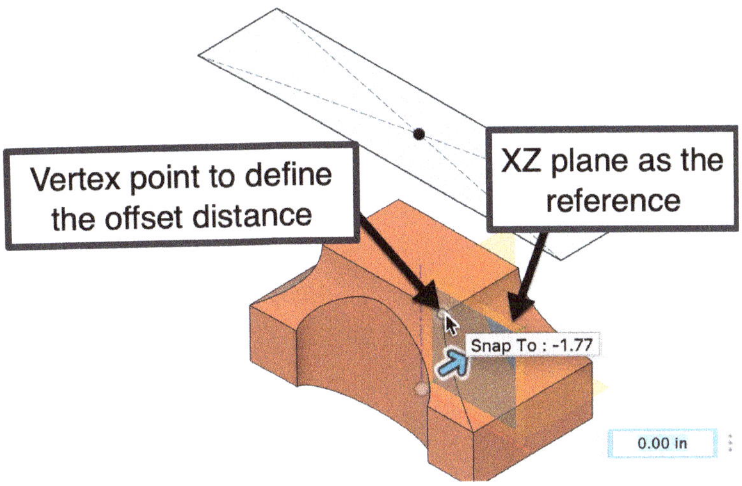

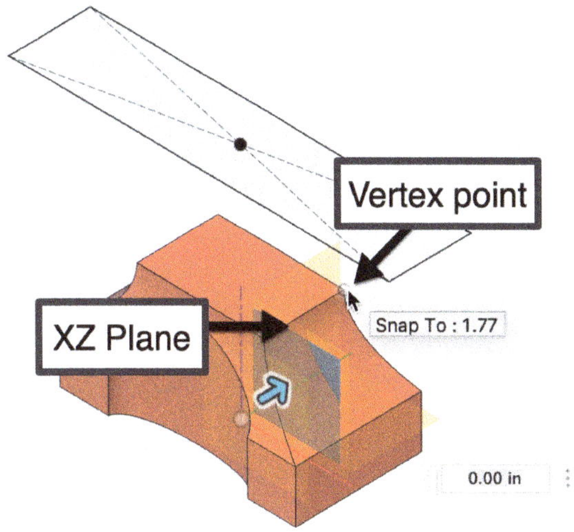

7. Click **Create** panel > **Create Sketch** on the toolbar and select the offset plane on the front side.

8. Click **Create** panel > **Project / Include** > **Project** on the **Sketch** contextual tab of the toolbar and click the edge, as shown. Next, click **OK** to project the edge.

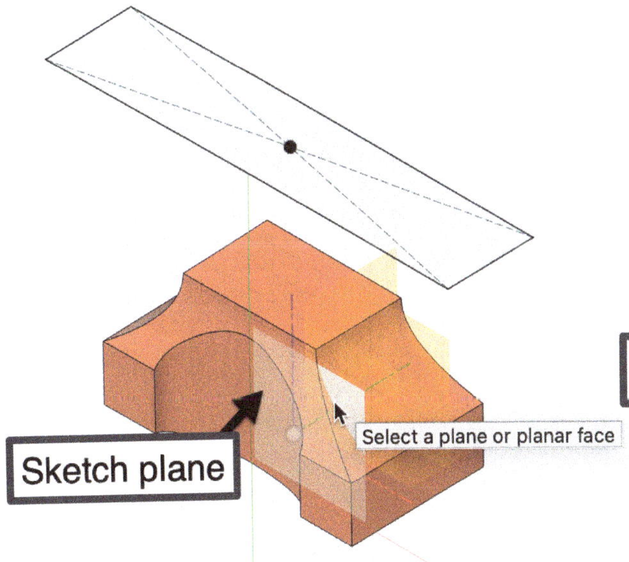

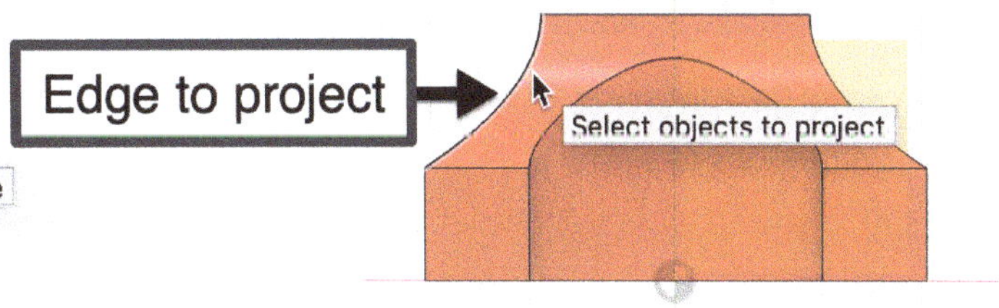

9. Click **Create** panel **> Fit Point Spline** on the **Sketch** contextual tab of the toolbar and draw a spline, as shown.

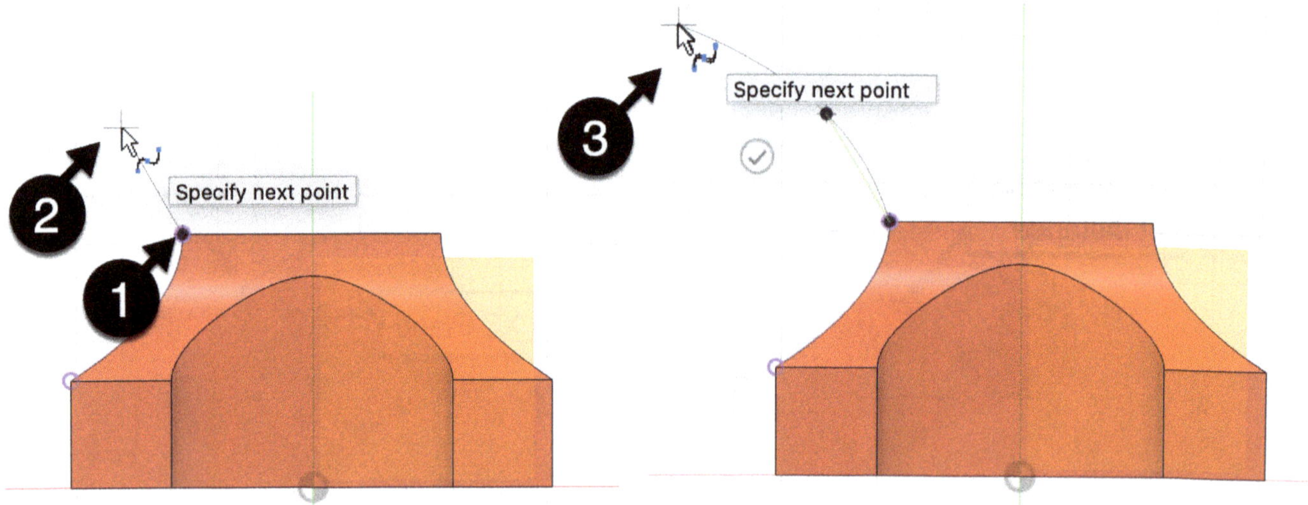

10. Click **Constraints** panel > **Tangent** on the **Sketch** contextual tab of the toolbar and click on the projected curve and the spline; the spline will become tangent to the projected sketch.

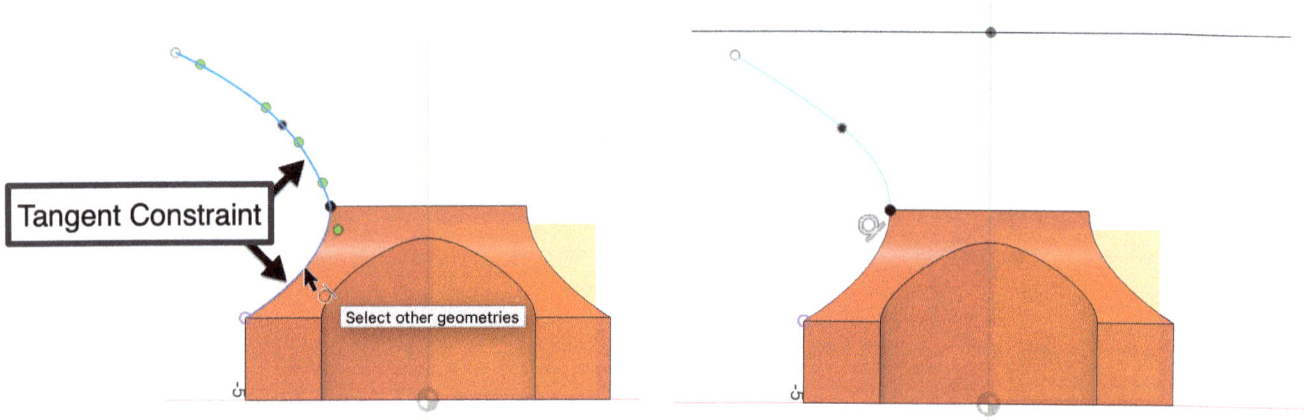

11. Click the **Home** icon on the top left corner of the ViewCube; the orientation of the model is changed.
12. Click **Constraints** panel **>** **Coincident** on the **Sketch** contextual tab of the toolbar.
13. Select the endpoint of the spline and the corner point of the rectangular sketch, as shown. The endpoint of the spline is made coincident with the corner point of the rectangular sketch.

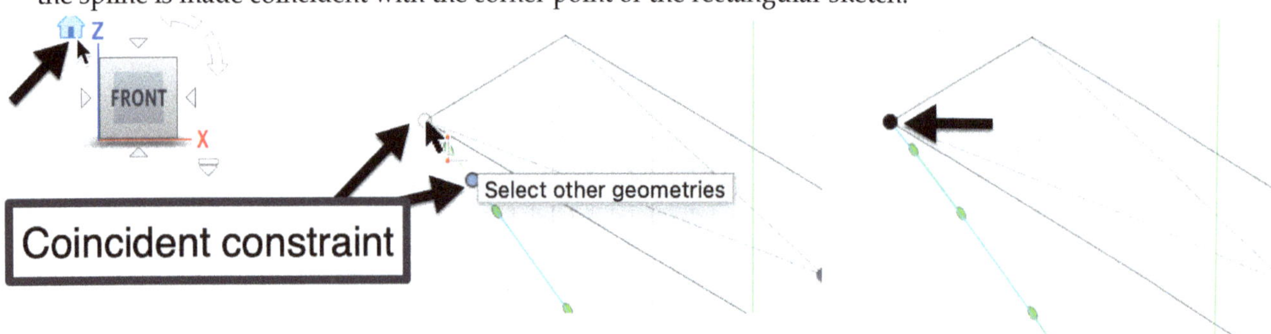

14. Click on the front face of the ViewCube; the orientation of the model is changed.
15. On the **Sketch** contextual tab of the toolbar, click **Create** panel **>** **Sketch Dimension** and then apply the linear dimensions to the middle point of the spline, as shown.

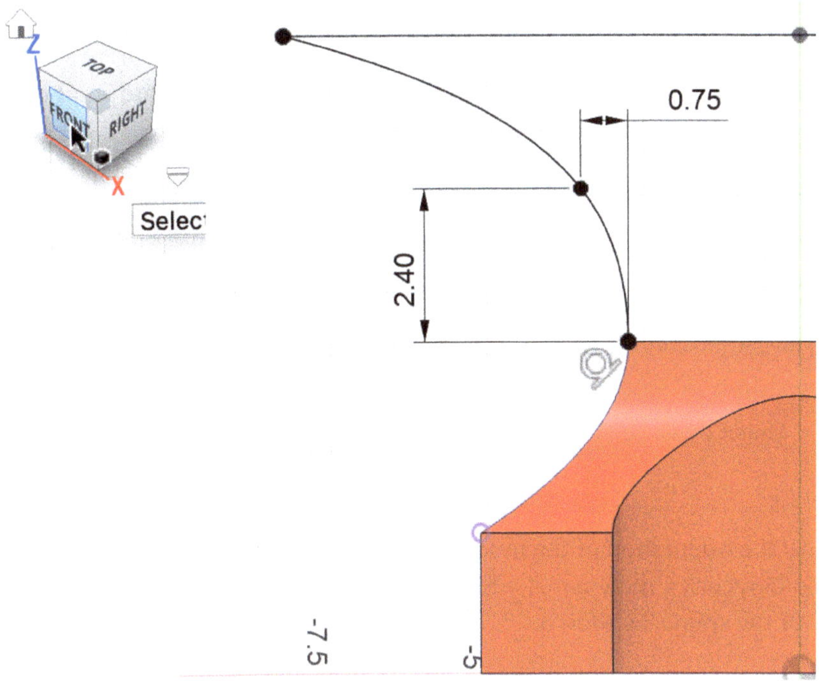

16. Click **Finish Sketch** on the toolbar.
17. In the Browser Window, expand the **Construction** folder and turn ON the display of the plane used to create the last sketch.
18. Click **Create** panel **> Create Sketch** on the toolbar and select the plane created on the front side.
19. Likewise, project the right edge, and then draw a spline connected to it.

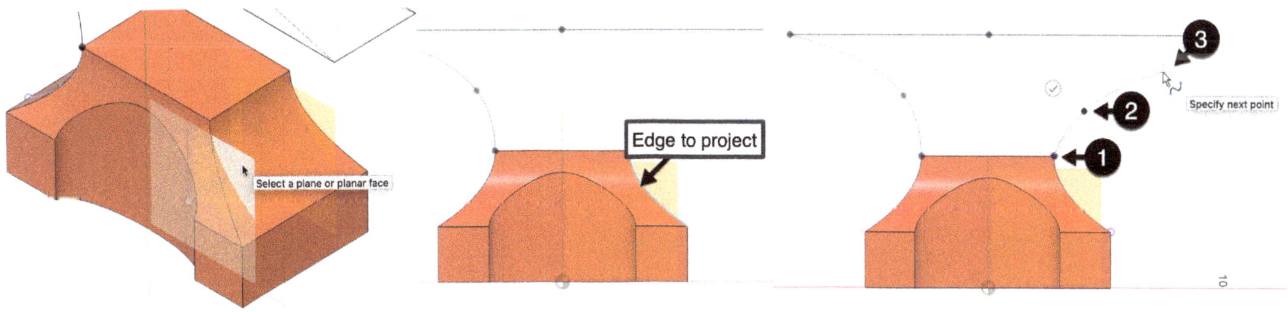

20. Apply the **Tangent** constraint between the projected sketch and spline.

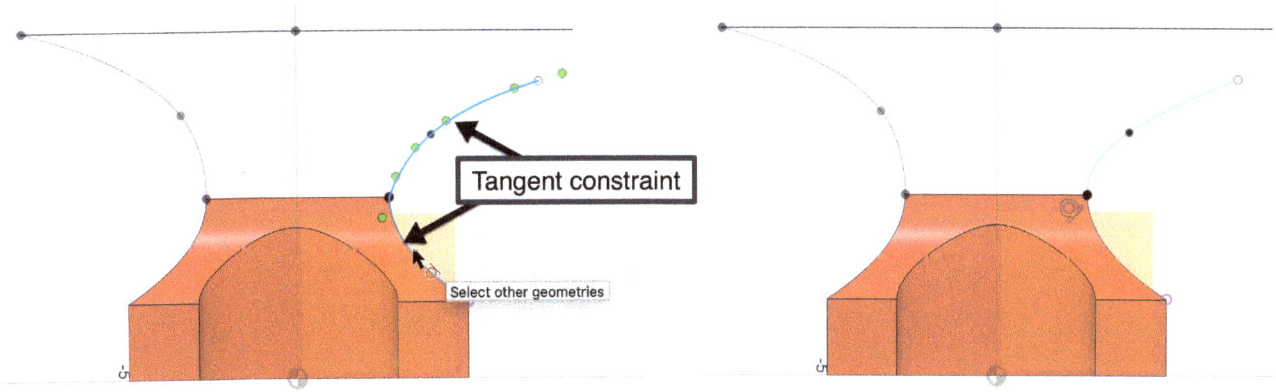

21. Click the **Home** icon on the top left corner of the ViewCube; the orientation of the model is changed.
22. Click **Constraints** panel > **Coincident** on the **Sketch** contextual tab of the toolbar.
23. Select the endpoint of the spline and the corner point of the rectangular sketch, as shown. The endpoint of the spline is made coincident with the corner point of the rectangular sketch.

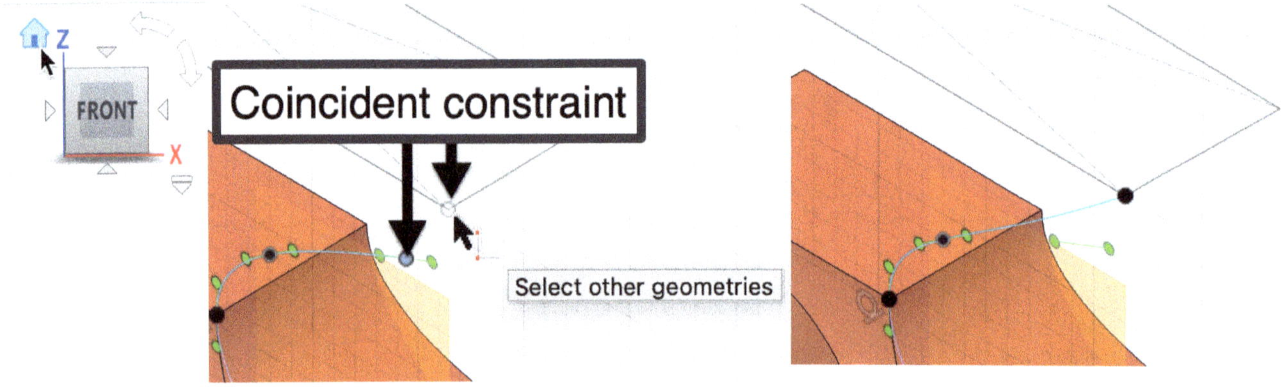

24. Click on the front face of the ViewCube; the orientation of the model is changed.
25. On the **Sketch** contextual tab of the toolbar, click **Create** panel > **Sketch Dimension** and then apply the linear dimensions to the middle point of the spline, as shown.

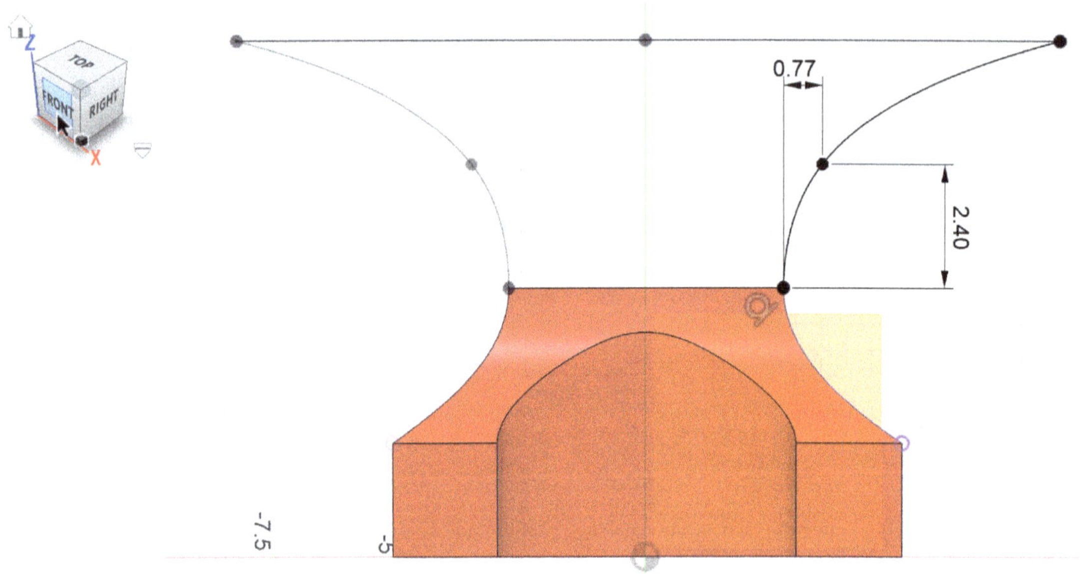

26. Click **Finish Sketch** on the toolbar.
27. Click **Create** panel > **Create Sketch** on the toolbar and select the plane on the backside.
28. Click **Create** panel > **Project / Include** > **Project** on the **Sketch** contextual tab of the toolbar. Next, select the left spline, as shown. Click **OK** to project the spline.

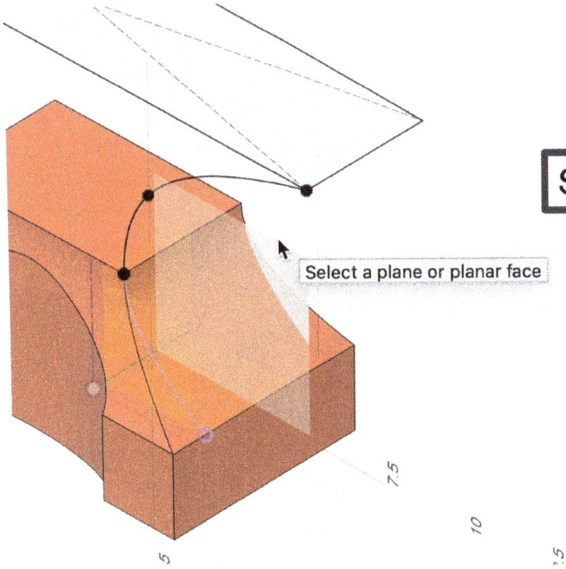

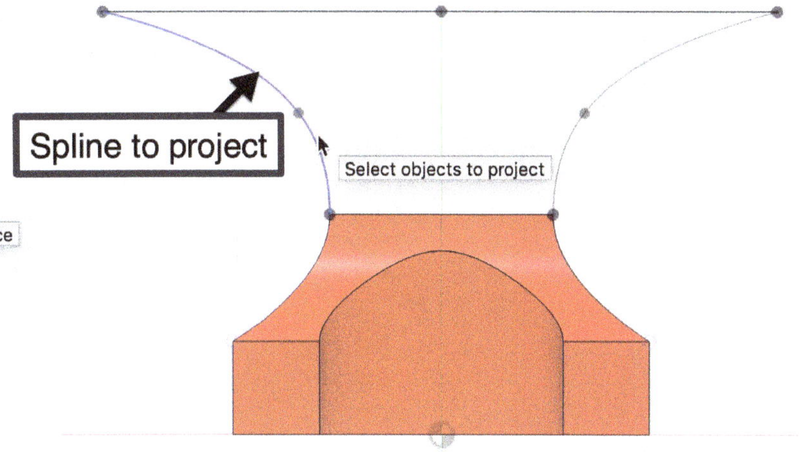

29. Click **Finish Sketch** on the toolbar.
30. In the Browser Window, expand the **Construction** folder and turn ON the display of the plane used to create the last sketch.

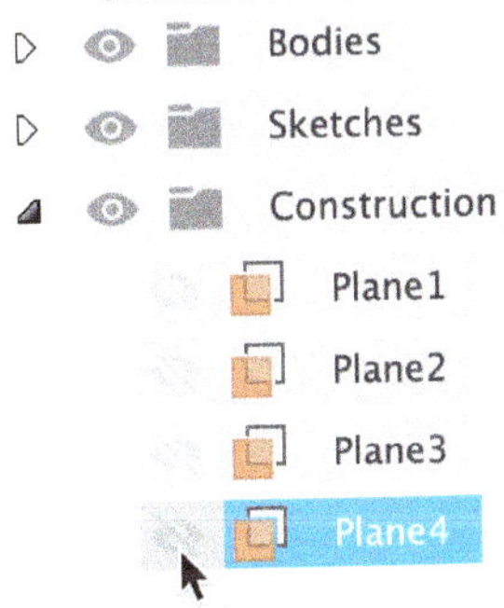

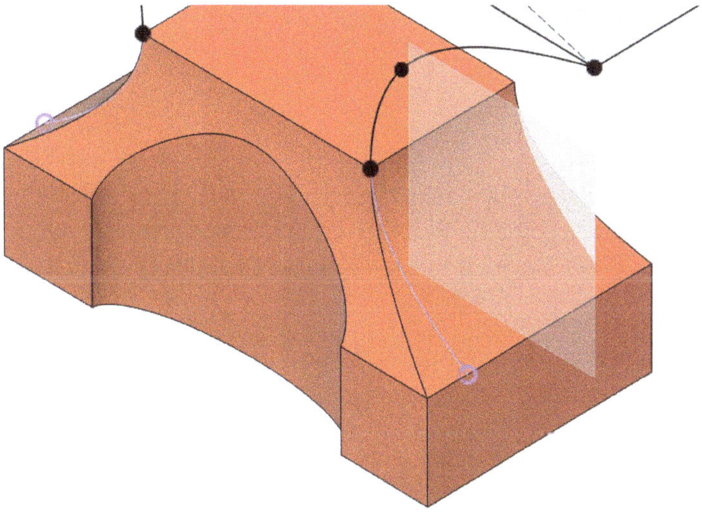

31. Click **Create** panel > **Create Sketch** on the toolbar and select the plane created on the backside.
32. Project the right spline, and then click **Finish Sketch** on the toolbar.

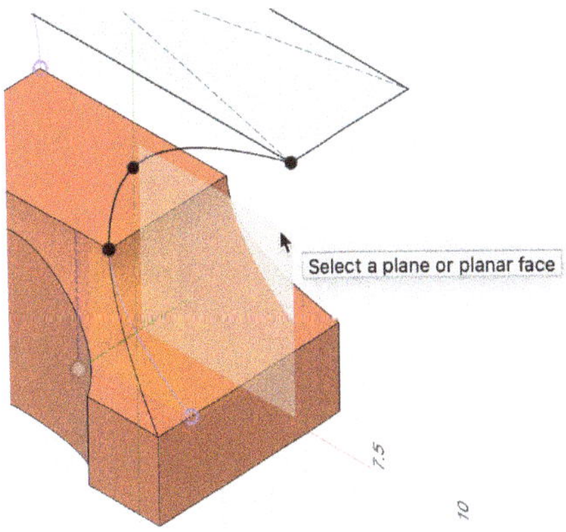

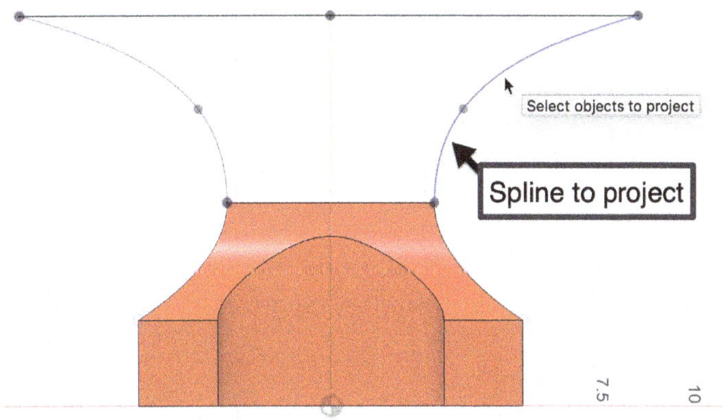

33. Click **Create** panel **> Loft** on the **Solid** tab of the toolbar; the **Loft** dialog appears on the screen.
34. Click on the top face of the first loft feature. Next, select the rectangular sketch.

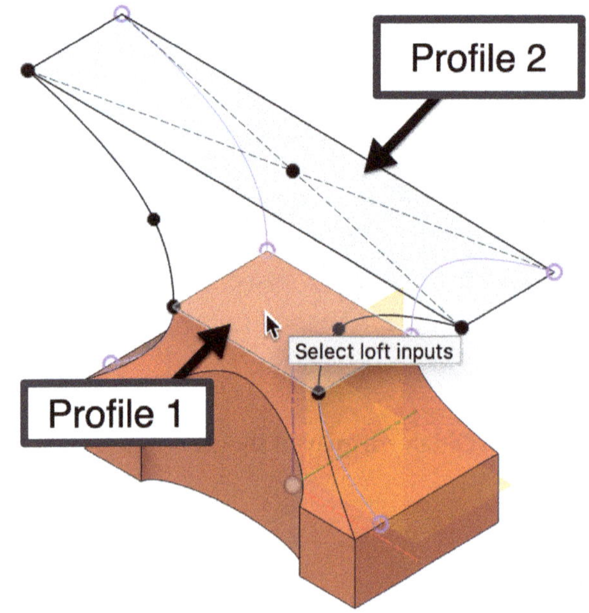

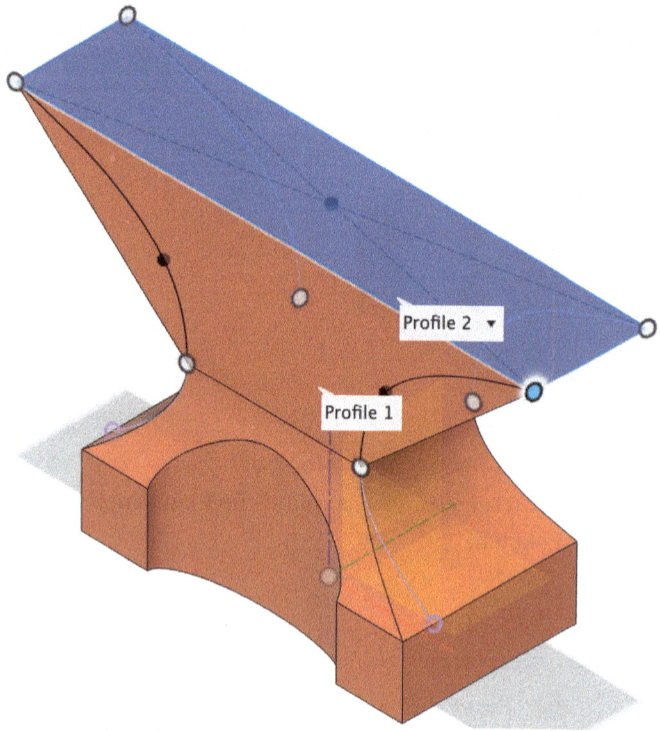

35. On the **Loft** dialog, click the **Rails** selection button and select the first spline.
36. Click the **Plus** icon in the **Rails** selection box and select the second spline.
37. Likewise, select the other two splines and click **OK** to create the loft.

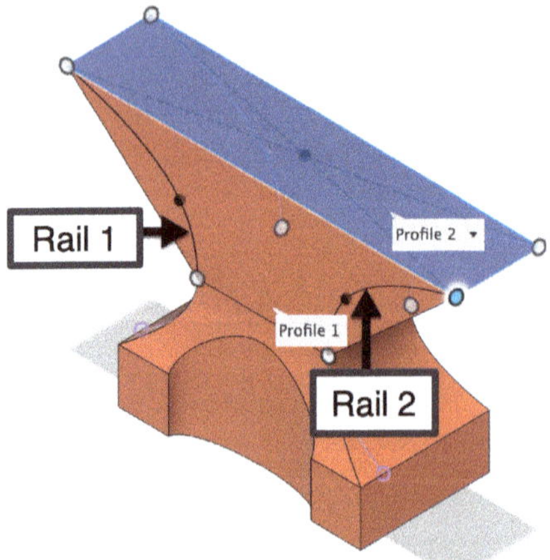

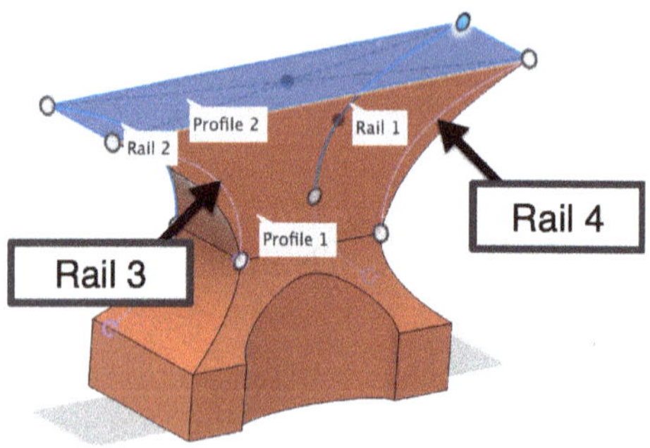

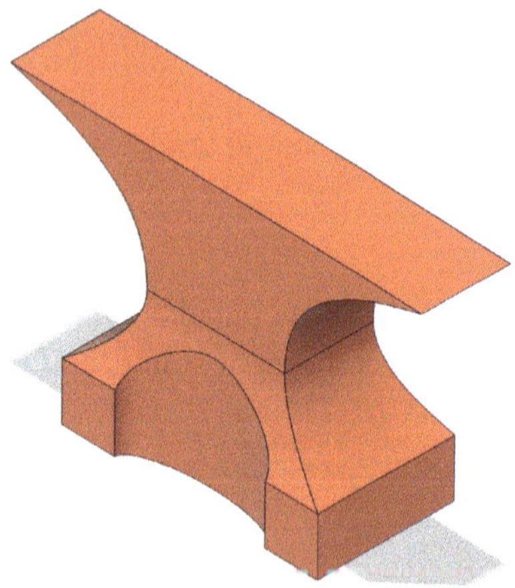

Creating the Extruded Cut Feature

1. Click **Create** panel > **Create Sketch** on the toolbar and click on the top face of the second loft feature.
2. Click **Create** panel **> Rectangle** on the **Sketch** contextual tab of the toolbar.
3. Draw the rectangle and apply dimension and constraints to it, as shown. Press **Esc** to deactivate the **Sketch Dimension** command.

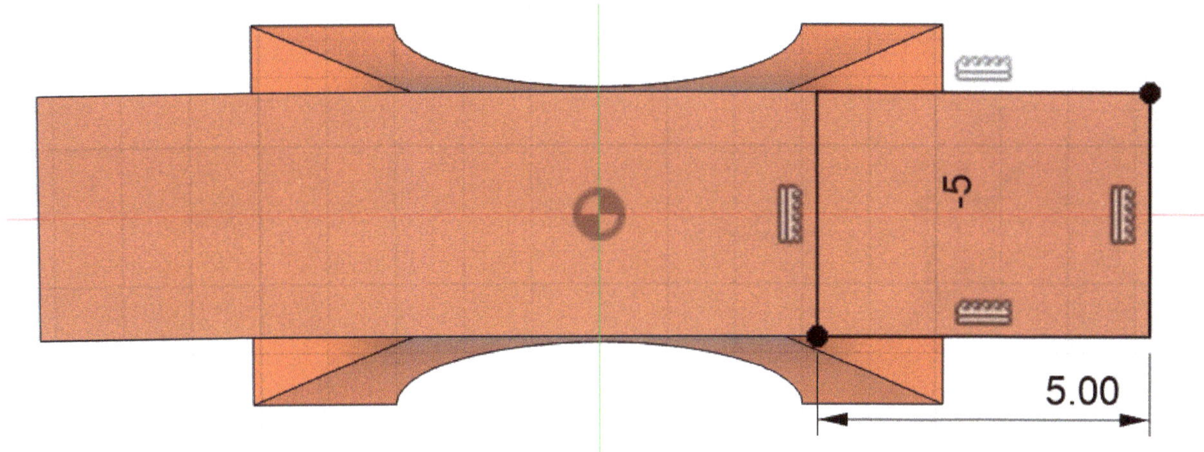

4. Click **Finish Sketch** on the toolbar.
5. Activate the **Extrude** command and select the sketch.
6. On the **Extrude** dialog, click **Extent Type > To Object**.
7. Select the curved face of the model, as shown.
8. Click **Operation > Cut** and click **OK** to create the extrude cut feature.

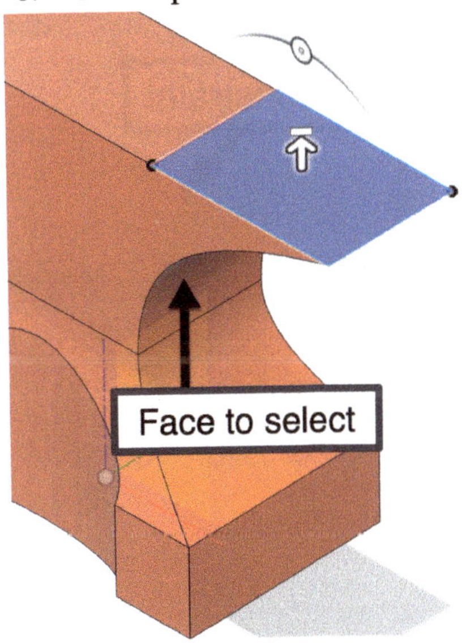

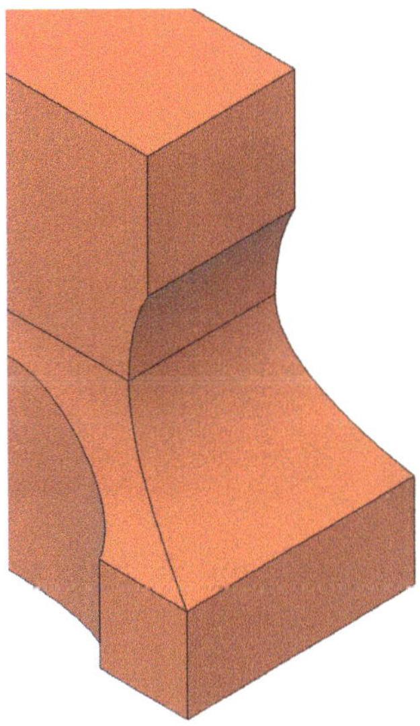

Creating the third Loft feature

1. Click **Create** panel **> Create Sketch** on the toolbar and click on the right face, as shown.

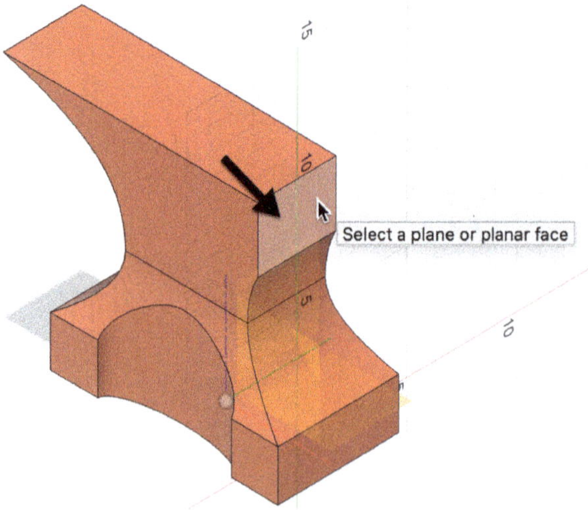

2. On the **Sketch** contextual tab of the toolbar, click **Create** panel > **Ellipse** .
3. Specify the three points of the ellipse, as shown.
4. Click **Constraints** panel > **MidPoint** on the **Sketch** contextual tab of the toolbar.
5. Select the top horizontal edge of the flat face and the top quadrant point of the ellipse.

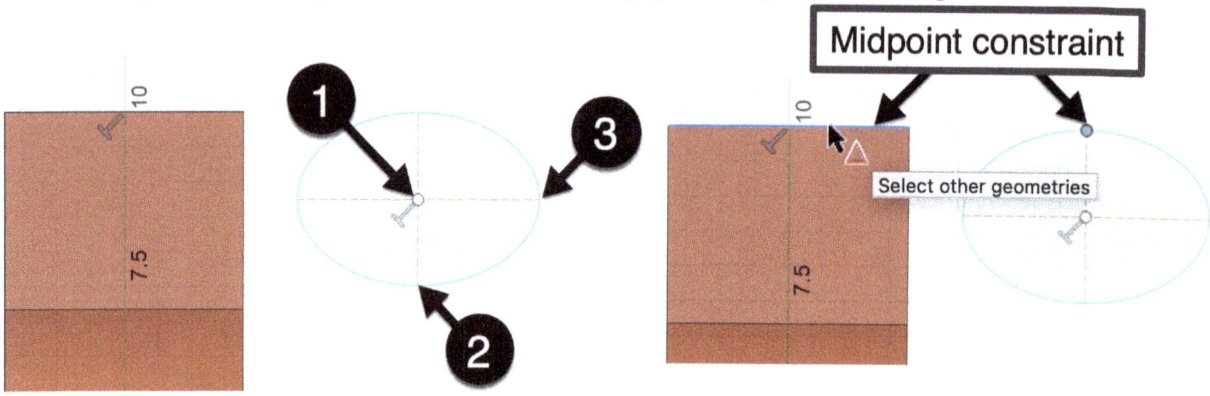

6. Likewise, select the right vertical edge of the flat face and the right quadrant point of the ellipse.

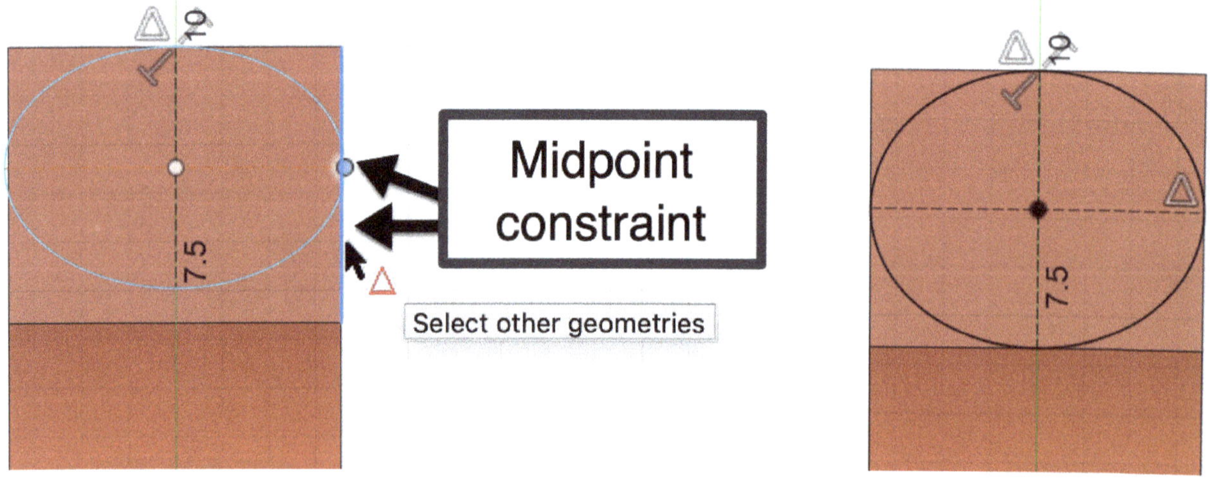

7. Click **Finish Sketch** on the toolbar.
8. Create a new offset plane to the right flat face. The Offset distance is 8.22.

9. Click **Create** panel > **Create Sketch** on the toolbar and select the newly created plane.

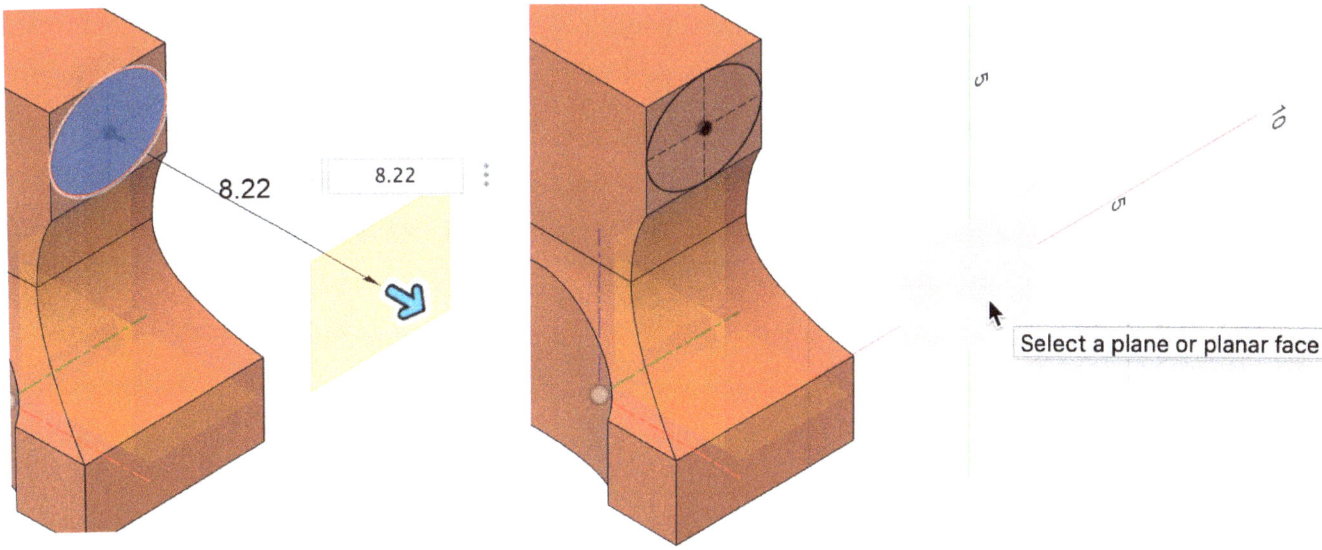

10. Click **Create** panel **> Point** on the **Sketch** contextual tab of the toolbar.
11. Click to specify the location of the point, as shown.
12. Click **Constraints** panel > **Coincident** on the **Sketch** contextual tab of the toolbar.
13. Select the sketch point and the top quadrant point of the ellipse, as shown.

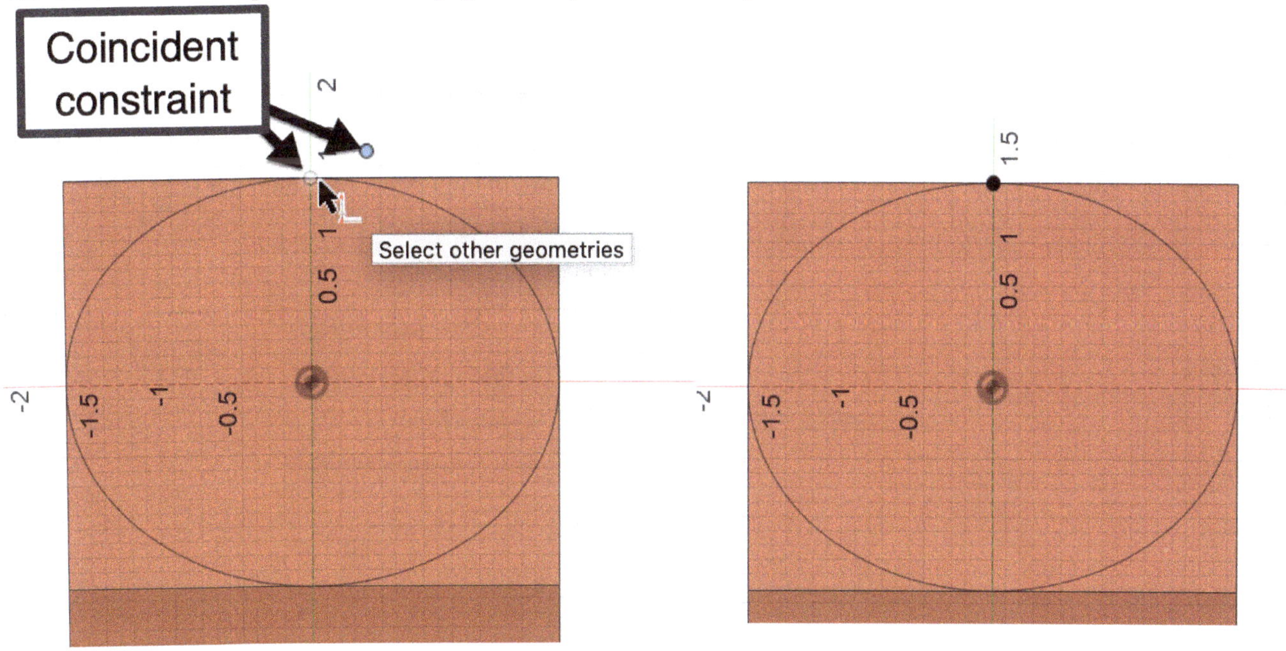

14. Click **Finish Sketch** on the toolbar.
15. Click the **Home** icon located at the bottom left corner of the ViewCube.
16. Click **Create** panel **> Create Sketch** on the toolbar and place the pointer on the XZ plane, as shown.
17. Click **Create** panel **> Fit Point Spline** on the **Sketch** contextual tab of the toolbar.
18. Specify the first two points of the spline, as shown. Next, select the sketch point displayed on the plane to specify the third point. Right-click and select **OK** to create the spline.

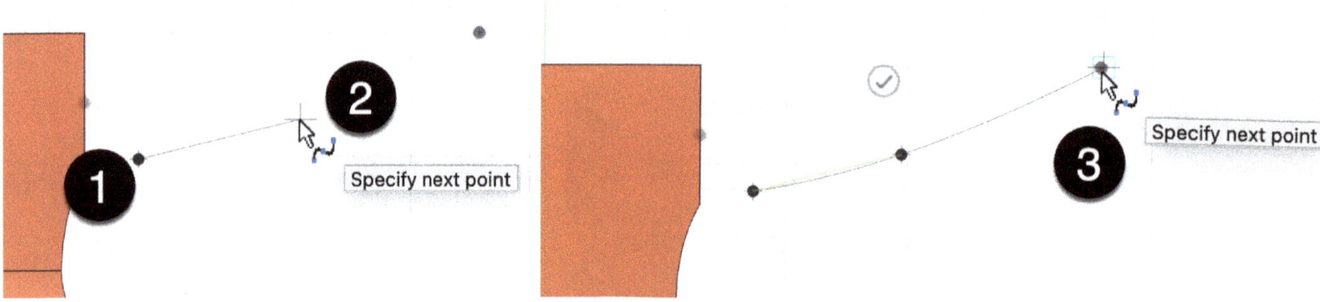

19. Click **Constraints** panel > **Coincident** on the **Sketch** contextual tab of the toolbar and select the start point of the spline. Next, select the bottom quadrant point of the ellipse, as shown.

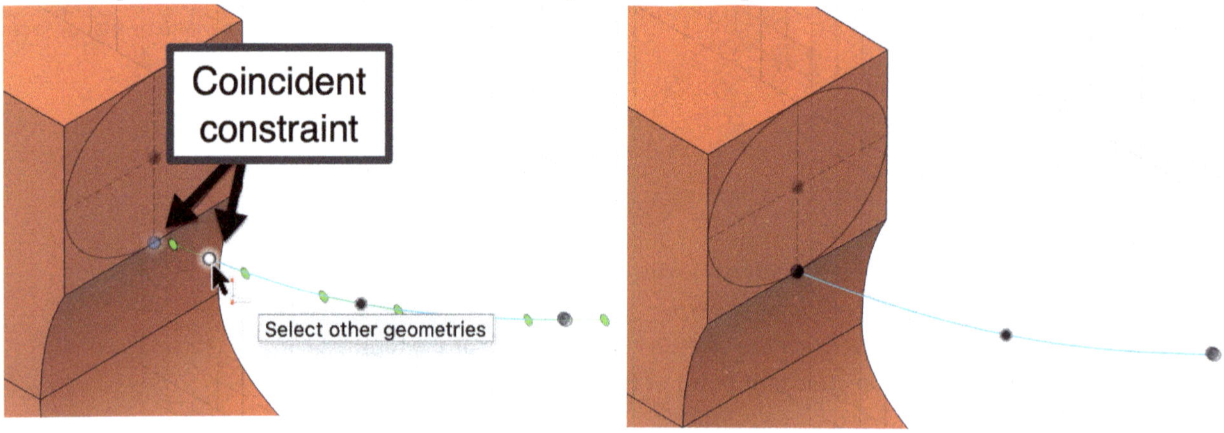

20. Activate the **Sketch Dimension** command (click **Create** panel > **Sketch Dimension** on the **Sketch** contextual tab of the toolbar) and apply dimensions to the midpoint of the spline, as shown.
21. Make sure that the Coincident Constraint is created between the sketch point and the endpoint of the spline.

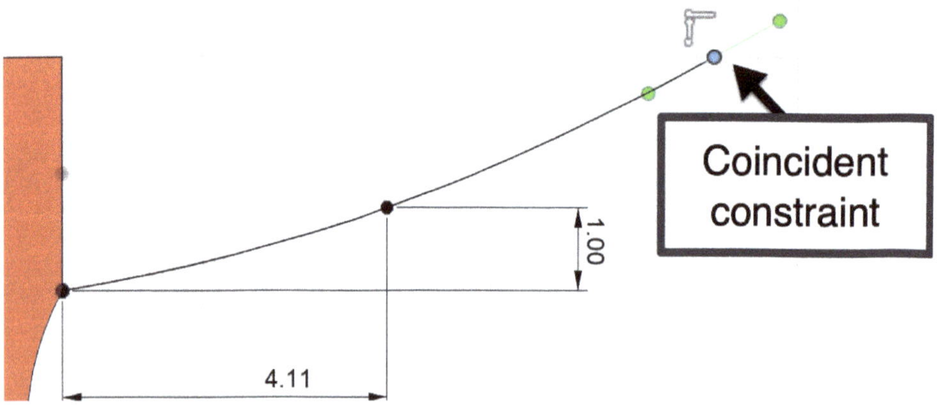

22. Click **Finish Sketch** on the toolbar.
23. Click the **Home** icon located at the top left corner of the ViewCube.
24. Click **Create** panel > **Create Sketch** on the toolbar and place the pointer on the XZ plane.
25. Click **Create** panel **> Line** on the toolbar on the **Sketch** contextual tab of the toolbar.
26. Create a line connecting the top quadrant point of the ellipse and the sketch point.

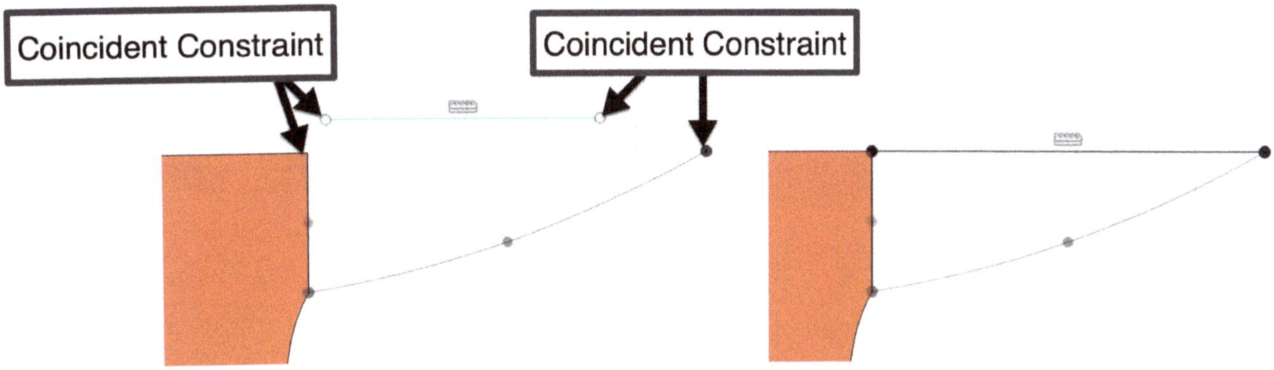

27. Click **Finish Sketch** on the toolbar.
28. Click **Create** panel > **Loft** on the **Solid** tab of the toolbar. Select the ellipse and the sketch point.
29. On the **Loft** dialog, click the **Rails** selection button.
30. Select the spline (Rail 1) and line (Rail 2), as shown.
31. Select **Operation > Join** and then click **OK** to create the loft feature.

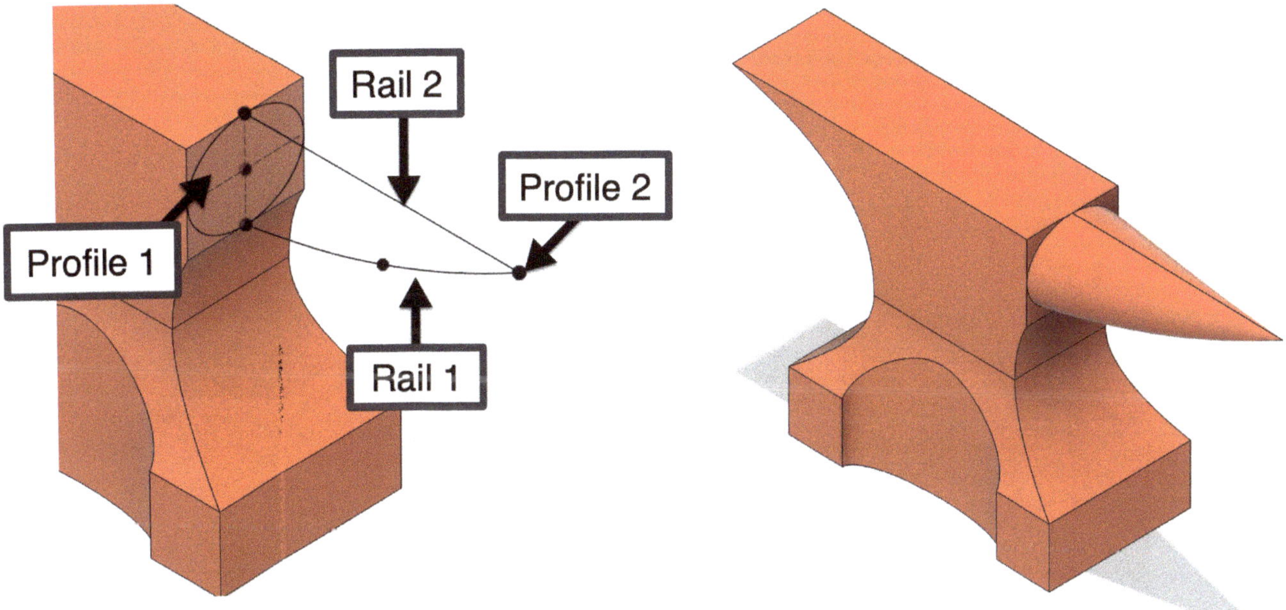

Creating the remaining Extruded Features

1. Click **Create** panel **> Extrude** on the toolbar, and then click on the top face of the model.
2. Click the arrow that appears on the selected face, and then drag the pointer upward. Next, type 1 and press Enter.

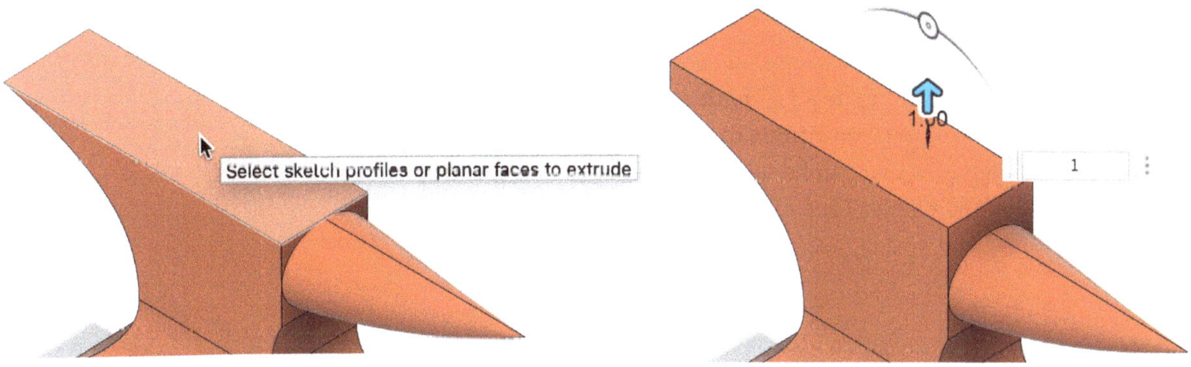

3. Create an extrude cut feature on the side face, as shown.

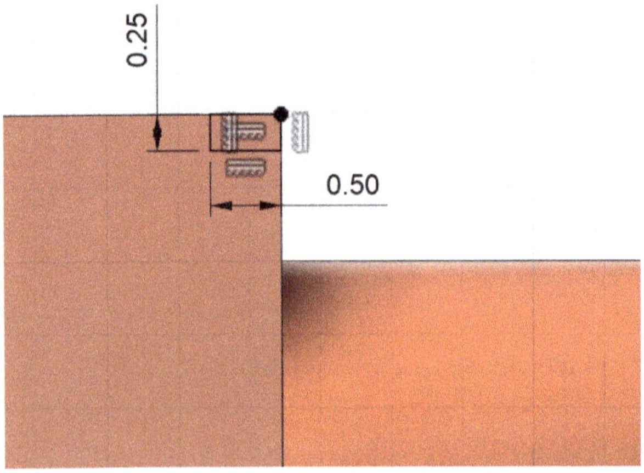

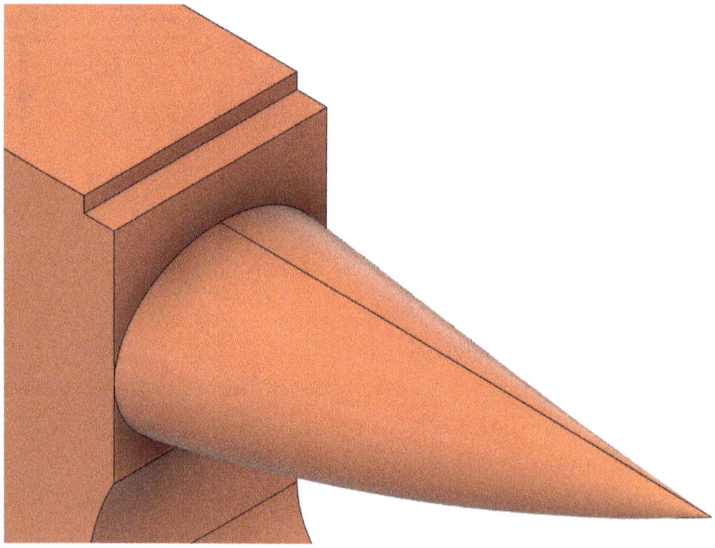

4. Create the extrude cut features for the circle and the square on the top face, as shown.

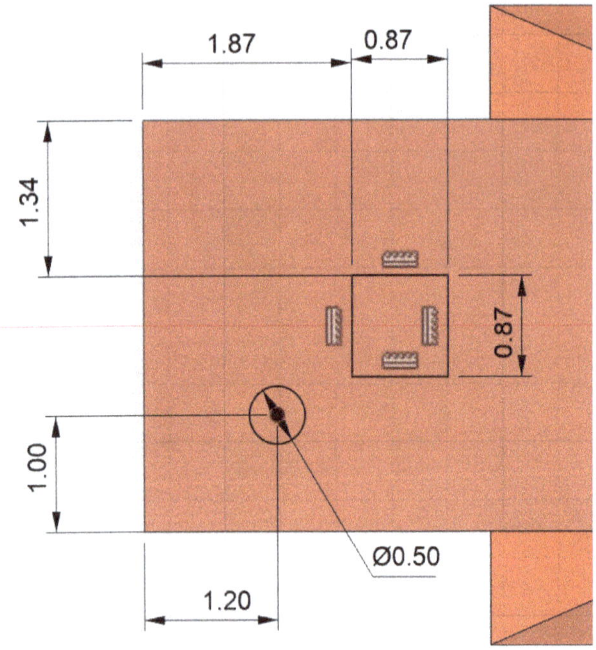

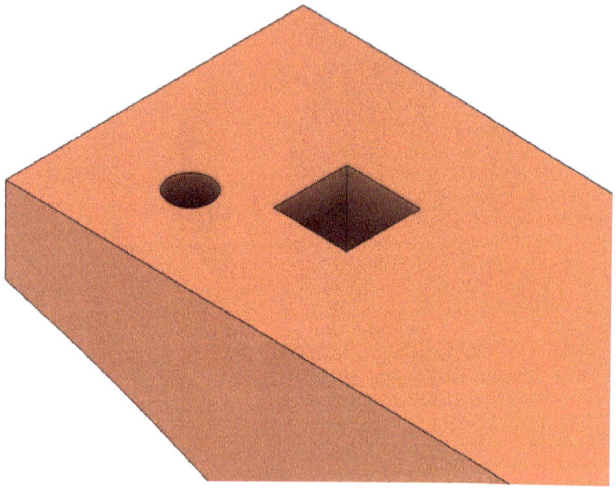

5. Save and close the file.

Questions

1. Describe the procedure to create a *Loft* feature.
2. List any two options in the **Conditions** drop-down.
3. List the type of elements that can be selected to create a *Loft* feature.
4. What is the use of the **Center Line** option?

Exercises

Exercise 1

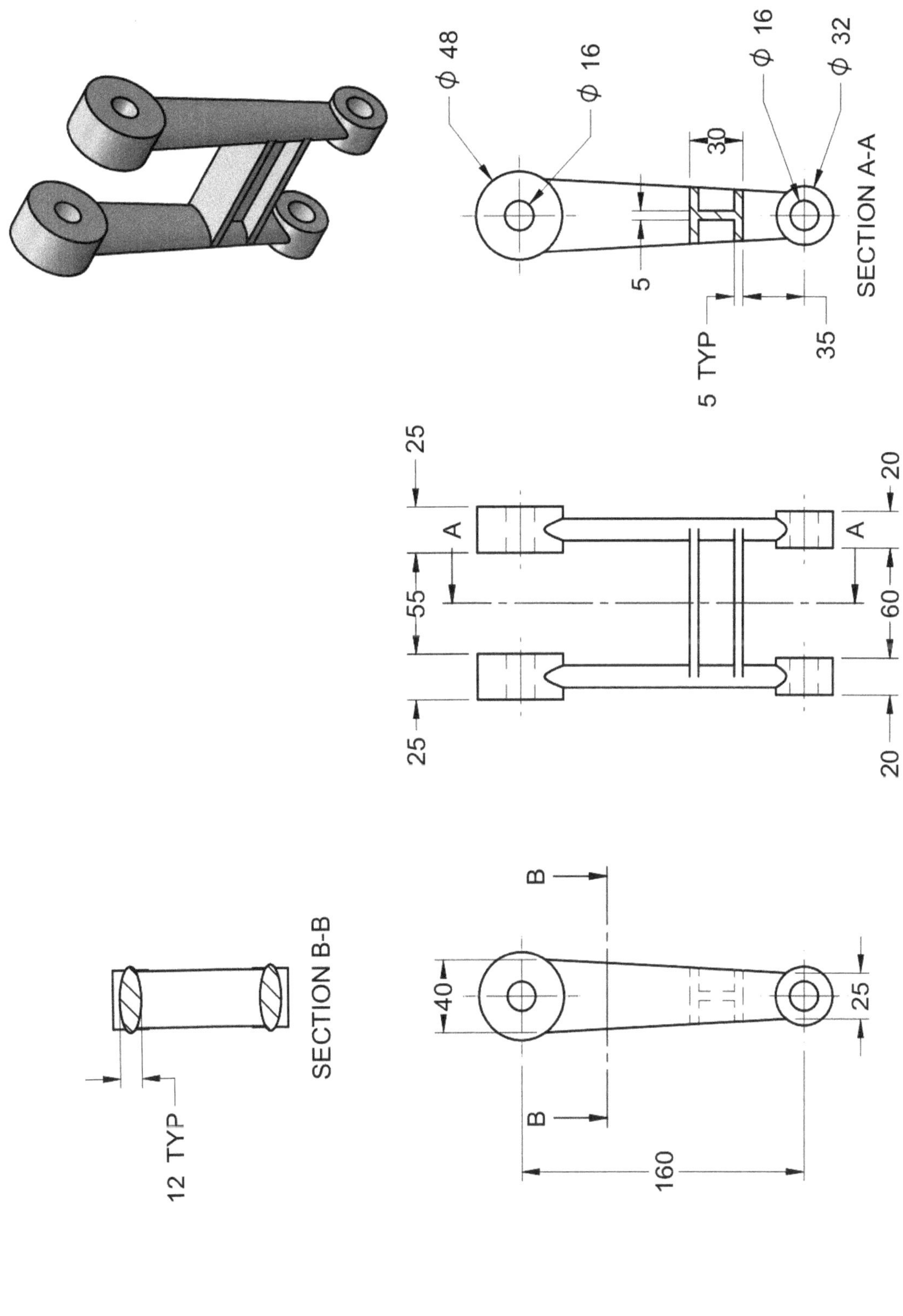

Chapter 8: Additional Features and Multibody Parts

Autodesk Fusion 360 offers you some additional commands and features which will help you to create complex models. These commands are explained in this chapter.

The topics covered in this chapter are:

- *Ribs*
- *Web*
- *Multi-body parts*
- *Split bodies*
- *Combine bodies*
- *Emboss*

Rib

This command creates rib features to add structural stability, strength, and support to your designs. Just like any other sketch-based feature, a rib requires a two-dimensional sketch. Create a sketch, as shown in the figure, and activate the **Rib** command (click **Create** panel **> Rib** on the **Solid** tab of the toolbar). Next, select the sketch and type-in a value in the **Thickness** box; the preview of the geometry appears. Use the **Flip Direction** icon to reverse the rib direction.

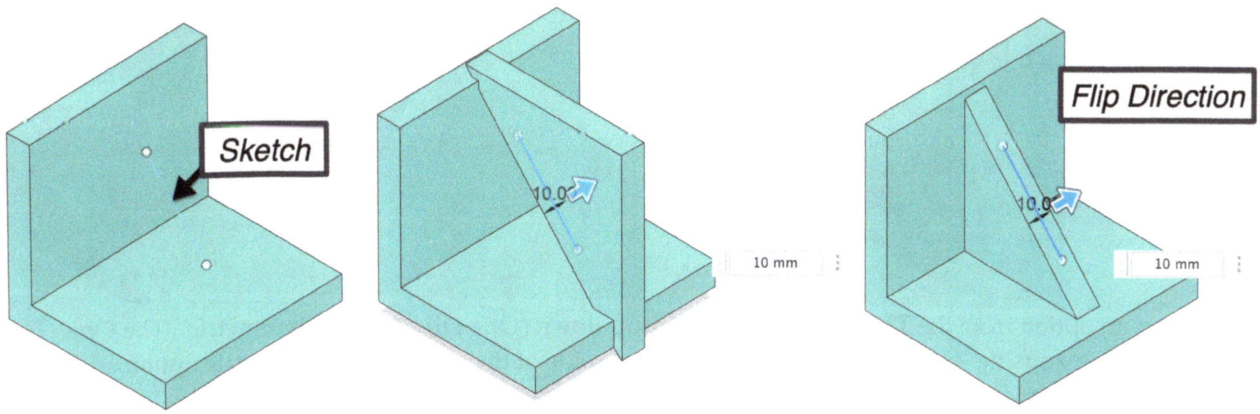

You can add the rib thickness to either side of the sketch line or evenly to both sides. Select **Thickness Direction > Symmetric** to add material in both directions of the sketch line. You can also set the depth of the rib using the **Extent Type: To Next** and **Distance**. The **To Next** option terminates the rib on the next face, and the **Distance** option creates the rib up to the specified depth.

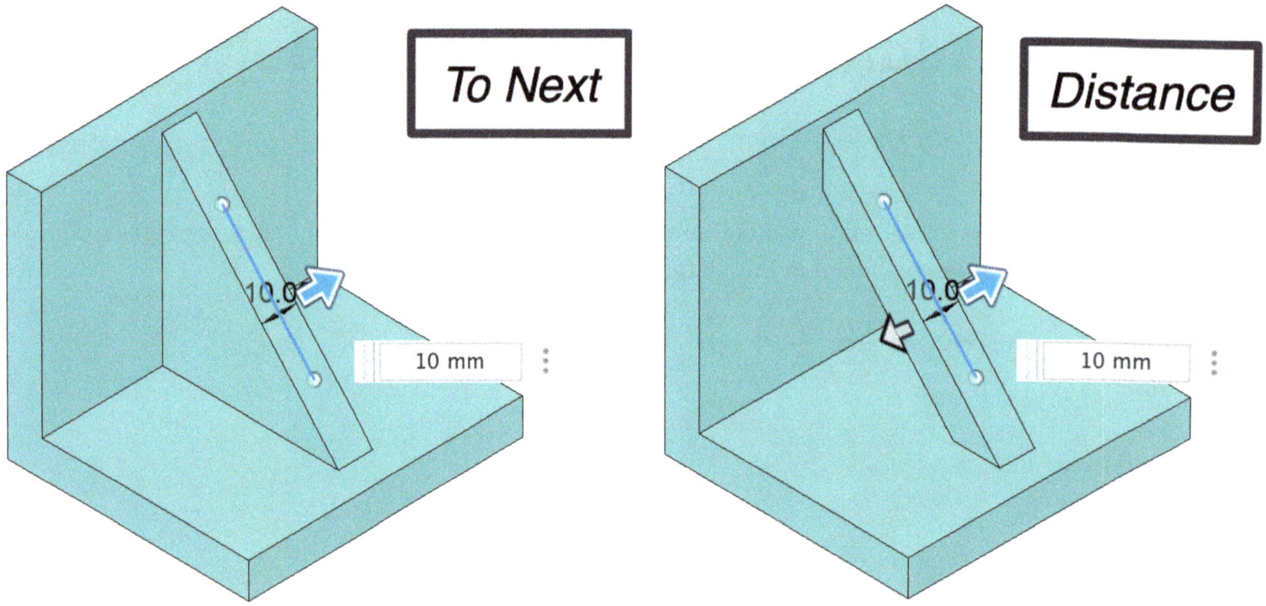

Web

This command is similar to the **Rib** command but creates multiple ribs at a time forming a network. Create a two-dimensional sketch, as shown in the figure, and activate the **Web** command (Click **Create** panel **> Web** on the **Solid** tab of the toolbar). Select the sketch elements one-by-one. Next, type-in a value in the **Thickness** box; the preview of the geometry appears.

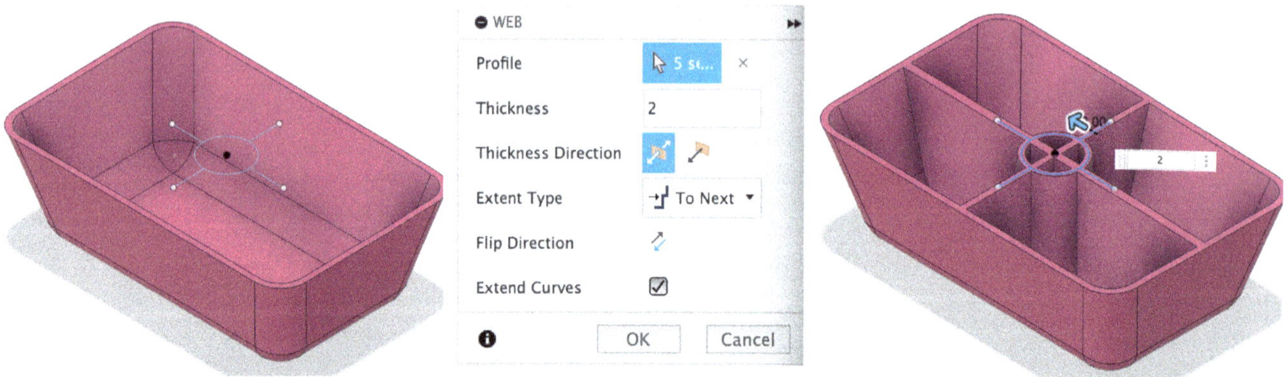

Next, select an option from the **Thickness Direction** drop-down (**One Direction** or **Symmetric**). The **One Direction** option adds the specified thickness value on one side of the sketch. The **Symmetric** option adds the thickness value symmetrically on both sides of the sketch.

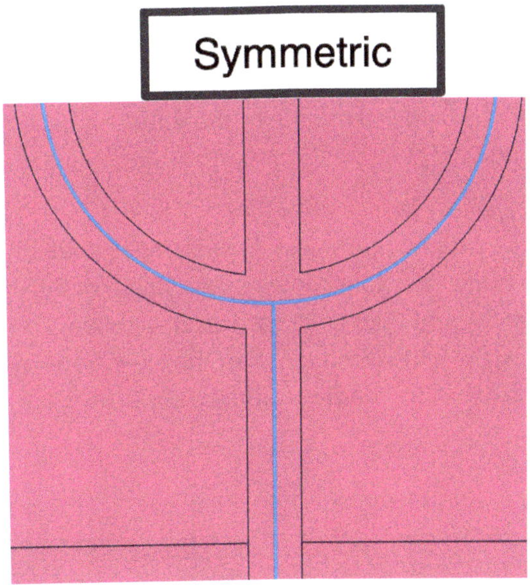

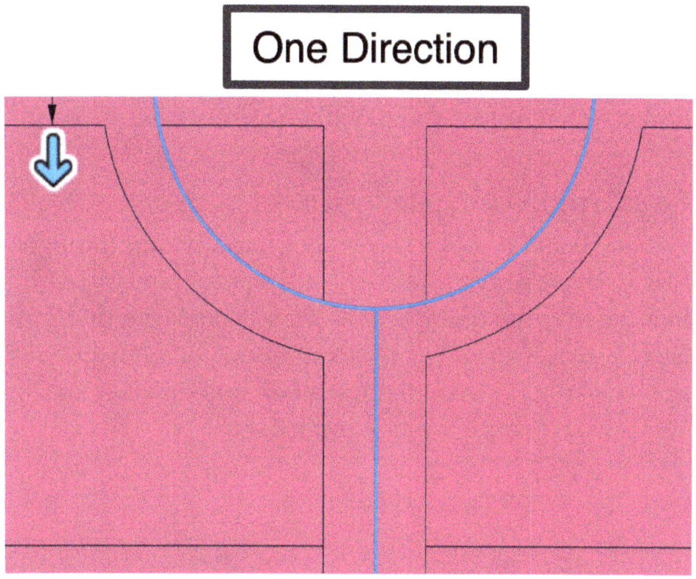

Next, select an option from the **Extent Type** drop-down (**To Next** or **Depth**). The **To Next** option creates the web up to the next surface. Whereas, the **Depth** option creates the web up to the value specified in the **Depth** box. Use the **Flip Direction** icon to reverse the web direction.

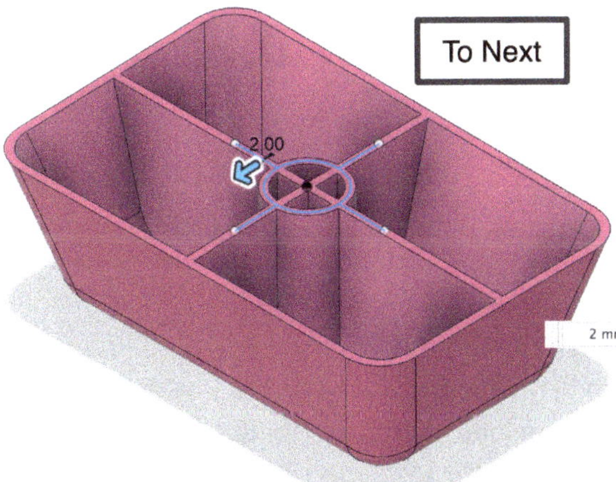

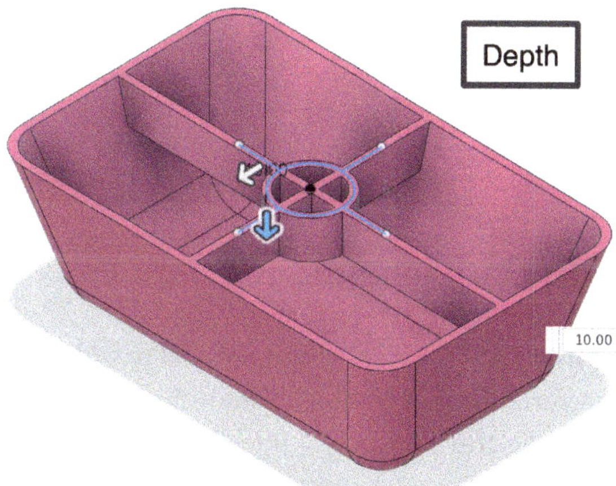

Check the **Extend Curves** option to extend the web up to the model boundaries.

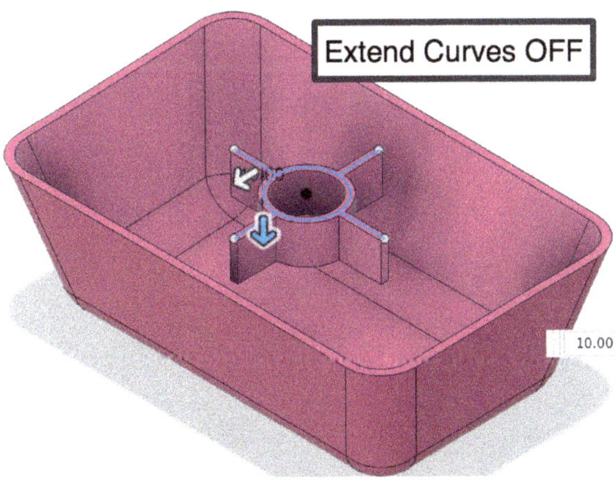

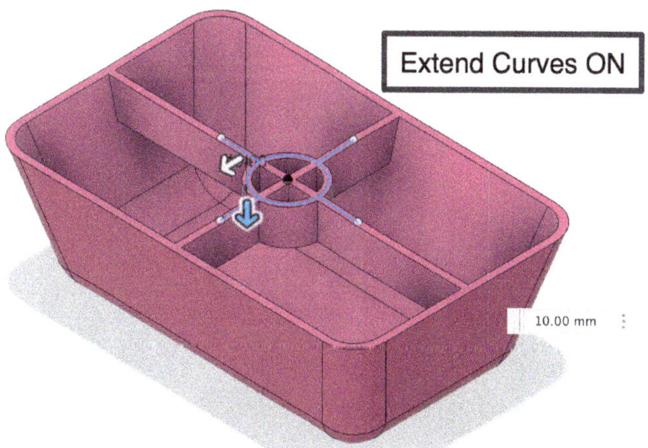

Next, click **OK** to complete the feature.

Multi-body Parts

Autodesk Fusion 360 allows the use of multiple bodies when designing parts. This opens the door to several design techniques that would otherwise not be possible. In this section, you will learn some of these techniques.

Creating Multiple bodies

The number of bodies in a component can change throughout the design process. Autodesk Fusion 360 makes it easy to create separate bodies inside a part geometry. Also, you can combine multiple bodies into a single body. In order to create multiple bodies in a component, first, create a solid body, and then create any sketch-based feature such as extruded, revolved, swept, or loft feature. While creating the feature, ensure that the **New Body** option is selected from the **Operation** drop-down on the dialog. Next, expand the **Bodies** folder in the **Browser** Window and notice the multiple bodies.

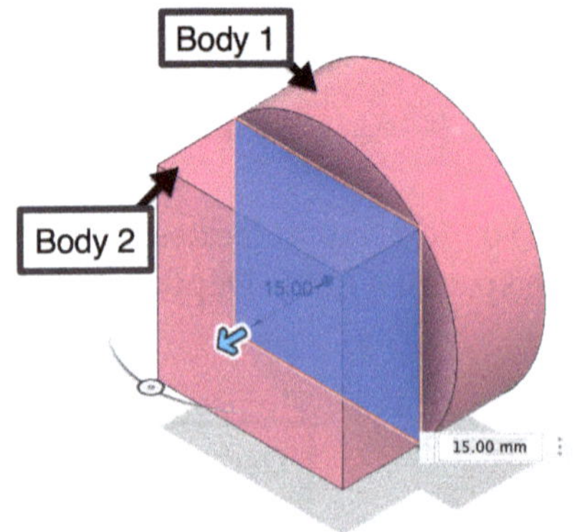

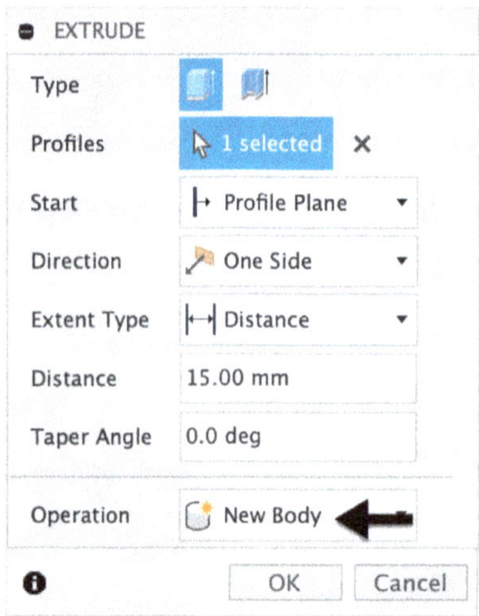

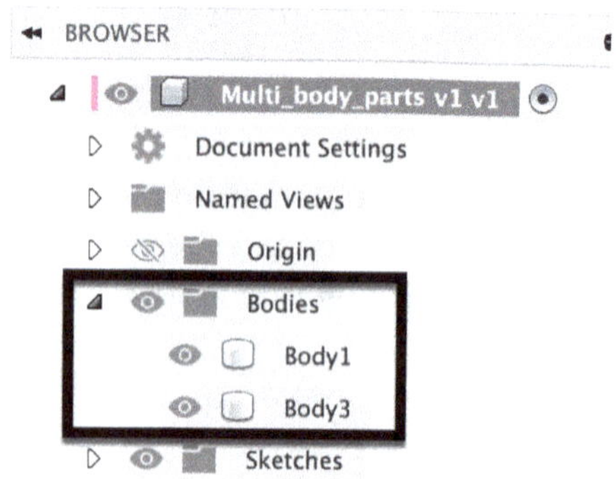

The Split Body command

The **Split Body**  command can be used to separate single bodies into multiple bodies. This command can be used to perform local operations. For example, if you apply the shell feature to the front portion of the model shown in the figure, the whole model will be shelled. To solve this problem, you must split the solid body into multiple bodies (In this case, separate the front portion of the model from the rest).

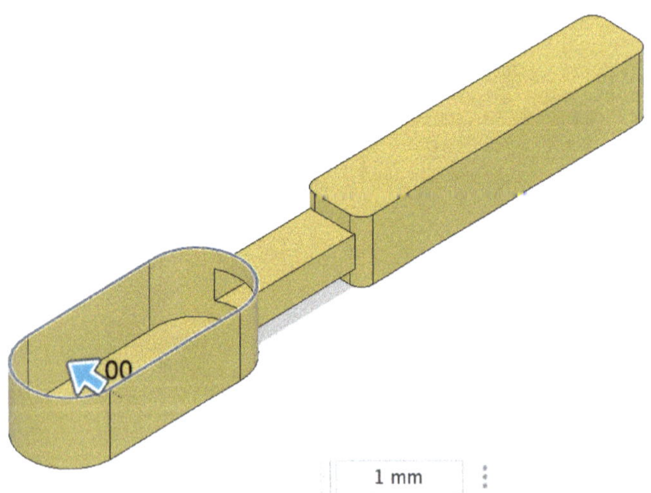

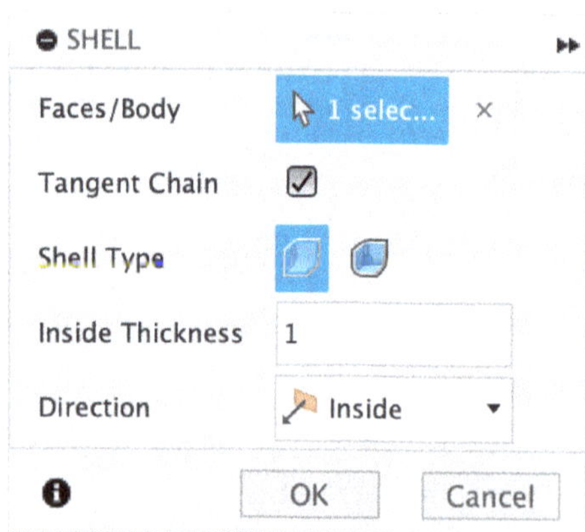

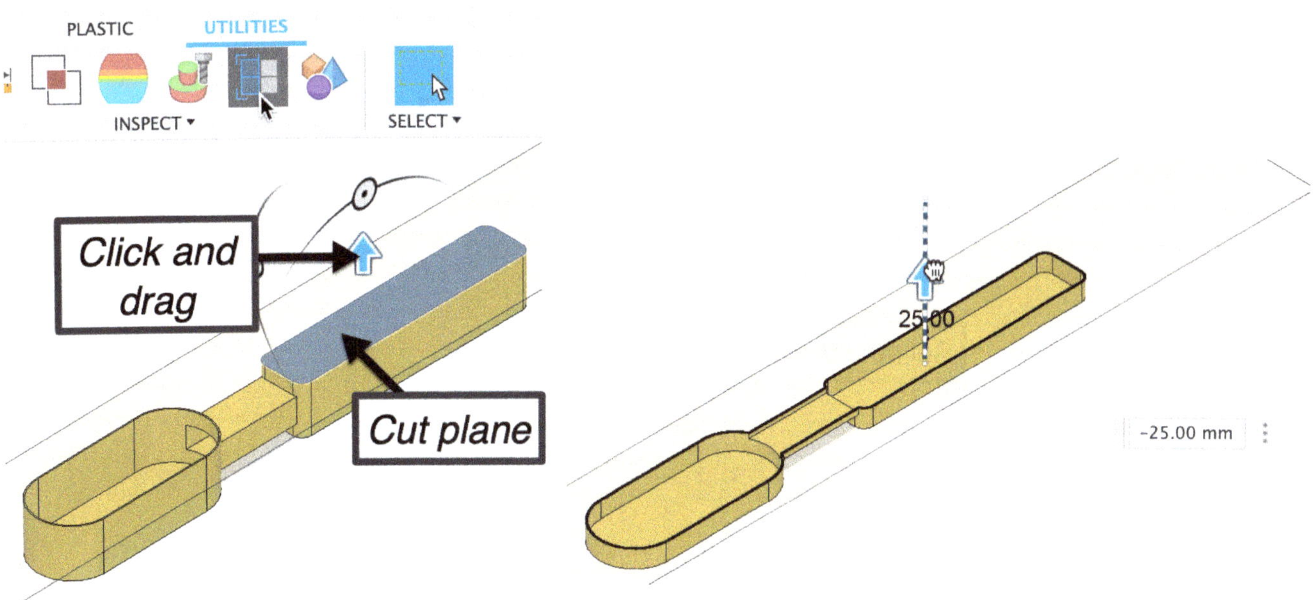

To split a body, you must have a splitting tool such as planes, sketch elements, surfaces, or bodies. In this case, a surface can be used as a splitting tool. To create a surface, click the **Surface** tab on the toolbar and click **Create** panel **> Patch** on the toolbar; the **Patch** dialog pops-up on the screen. Uncheck the **Enable Chaining** option on the **Patch** dialog. Next, select the edges of the curved face, as shown. Click **OK** to create the surface. You can use this surface as a split tool to split the solid body.

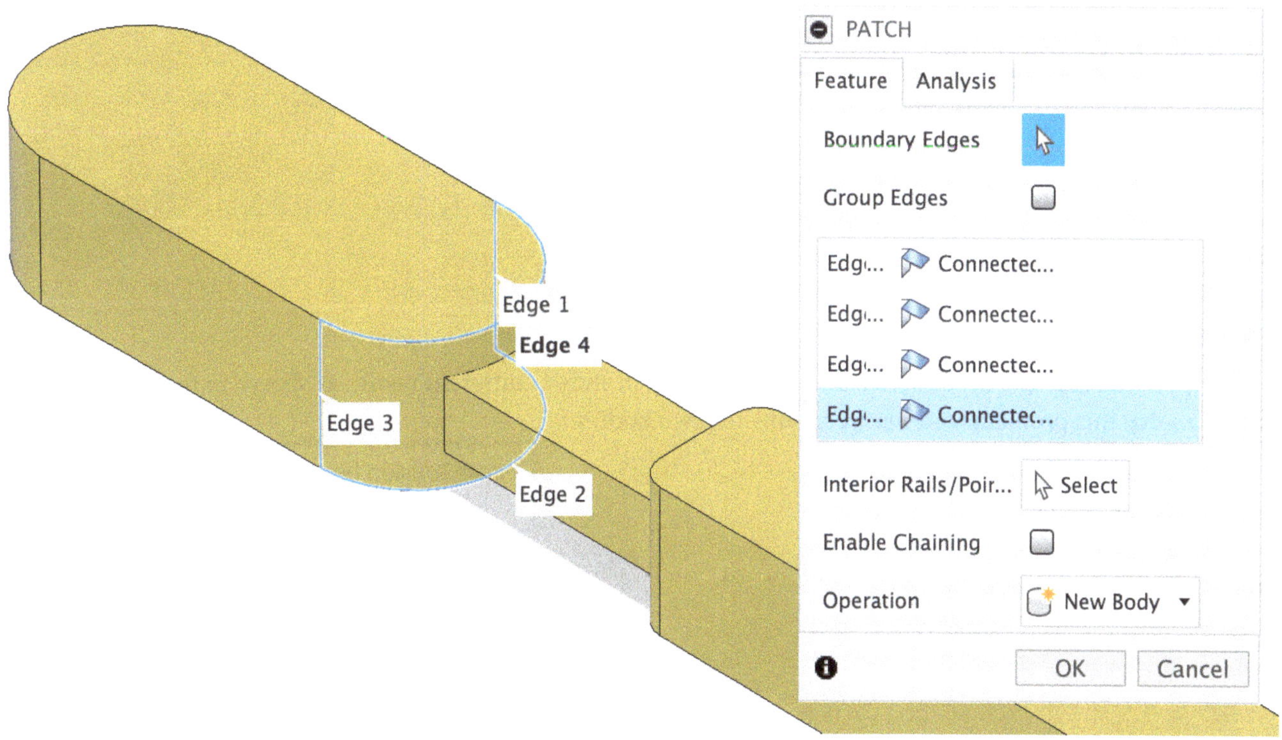

Activate the **Split Body** command (click **Modify** panel **> Split Body** on the **Solid** tab of the toolbar). On the **Split Body** dialog, select the solid body from the graphics window. Click the **Splitting Tool(s)** selection button and select the surface from the graphics window. Uncheck the **Extend Splitting Tool(s)** option and click **OK** to split the solid body. The solid is split into two separate bodies.

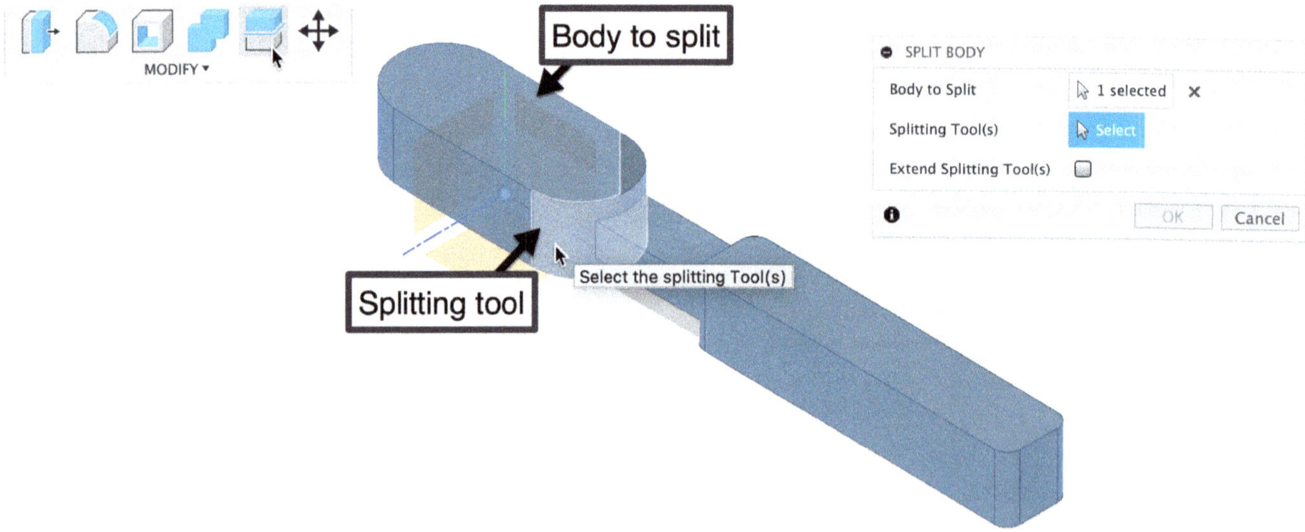

Now, create the shell feature on the split body.

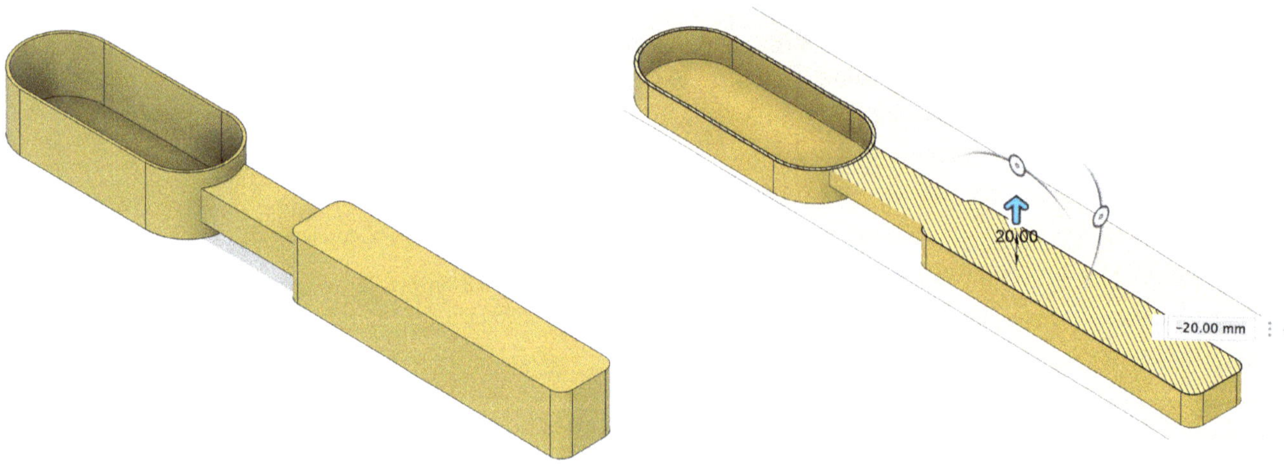

Combine

If you apply fillets to the edges between two bodies, it will show a different result, as shown in the figure. In order to solve this problem, you must combine the two bodies.

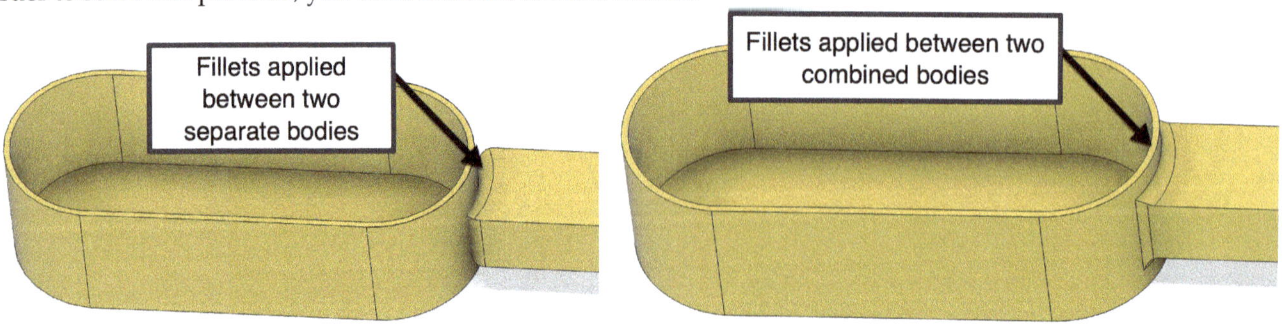

Activate the **Combine** command (on the **Solid** tab of the toolbar, click **Modify** panel **>** **Combine**), and select **Operation > Join** on the **Combine** dialog. Next, select the two bodies. Click **OK** on the dialog to join the bodies. Next, apply fillets to the edges.

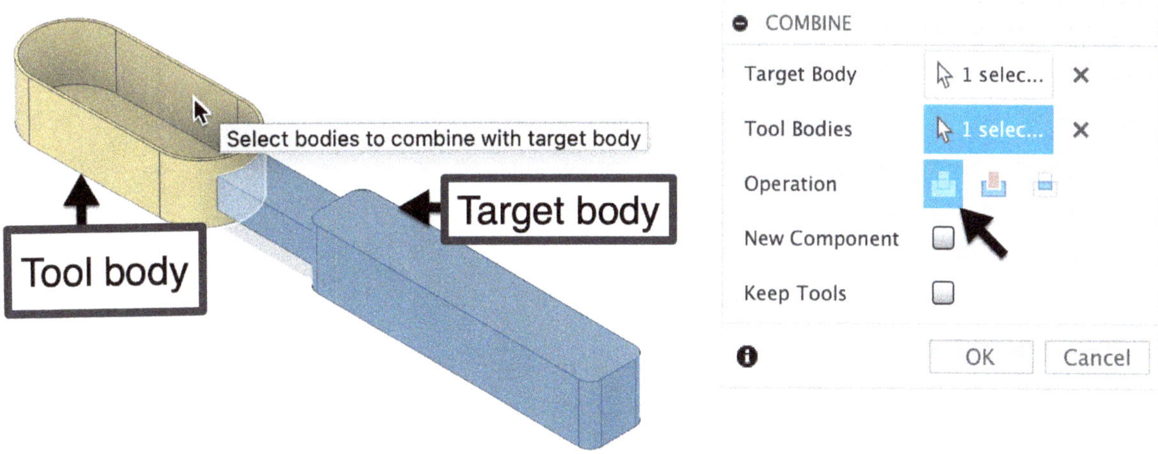

Intersect

By using the **Intersect** option, you can generate bodies defined by the intersecting volume of two bodies. Activate **Combine** command (click **Modify** panel **>** **Combine** on the **Solid** tab of the toolbar). On the **Combine** dialog, select **Operation** > **Intersect** and select two bodies. Click **OK** to see the resultant single solid body.

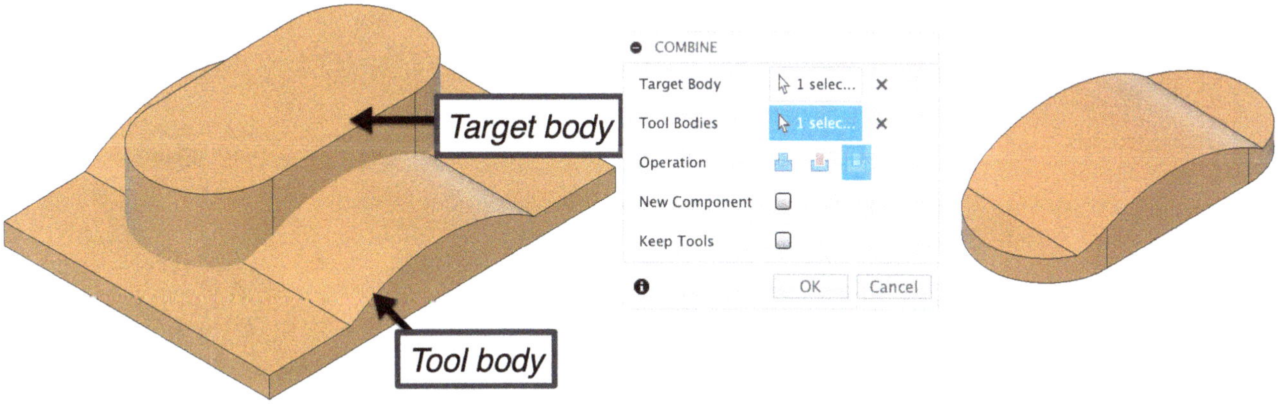

Cut

This option performs the function of subtracting one solid body from another. Activate the **Combine** command (click **Modify** panel **>** **Combine** on the **Solid** tab of the toolbar) and select **Operation > Cut** from the **Combine** dialog. Next, select the target and tool body. Click **OK** to subtract the tool body from the target.

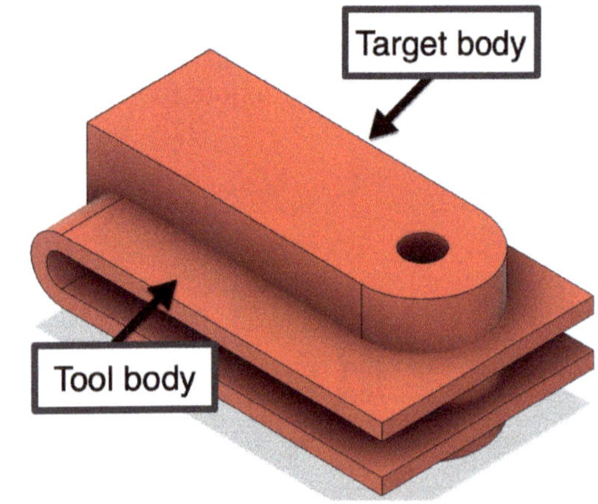

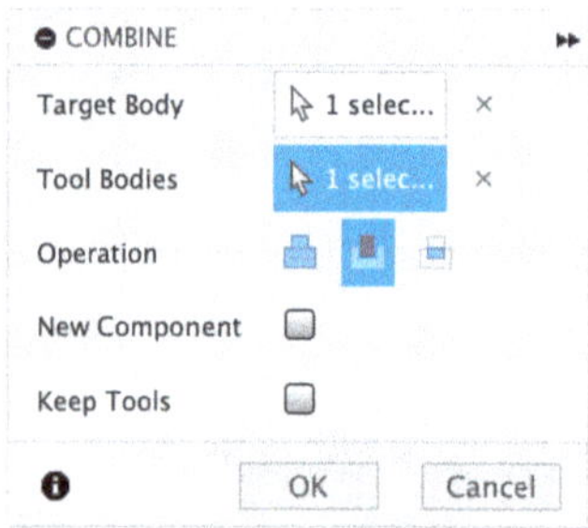

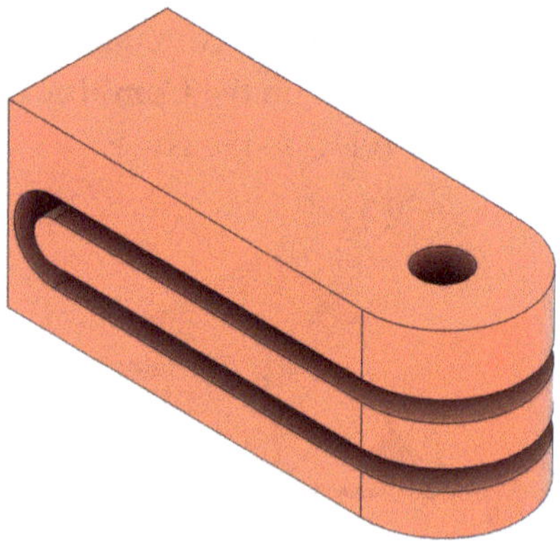

Emboss

This command embosses or engraves a text or shape on to the model geometry. For example, to engrave or emboss a sketch on to the cylindrical face of the model, create a cylindrical feature and plane offset from the XY Plane. Next, start a sketch on the offset plane. Next, click **Create** panel > **Text** on the **Sketch** tab of the toolbar. Specify the first and second corner of the text box. Next, enter the text in the **Text** box available on the **Text** dialog. Specify the **Font**, **Height**, and **Alignment** on the **Text** dialog and click **OK**. Click **Finish Sketch** on the toolbar.

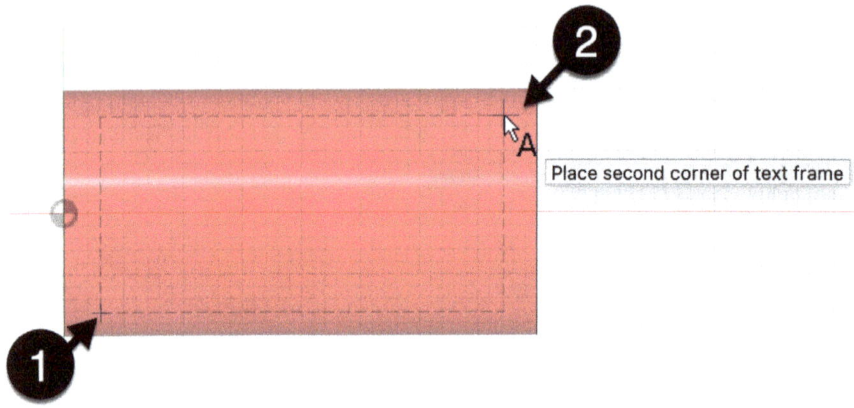

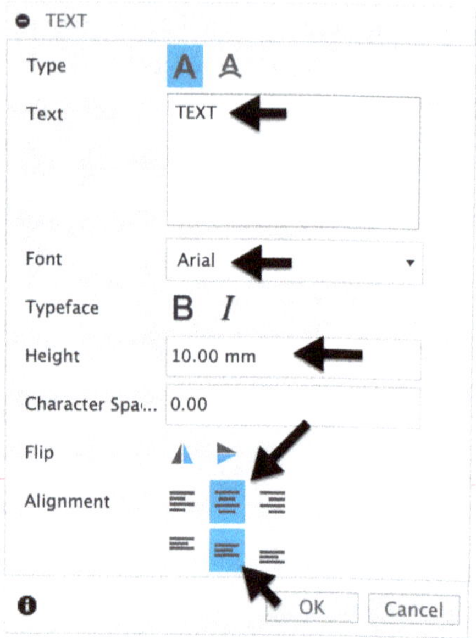

Activate the **Emboss** command (click **Solid > Create > Emboss** on the ribbon) and select the sketch. Click the **Faces** selection button on the **Emboss** dialog. Next, type a value in the **Depth** box, and then click the **Top Face Appearance** swatch located below the **Depth** box. Click **Effect** > **Emboss** to emboss the text. If you want to engrave the text, click **Effect** > **Engrave**, specify the **Depth** value.

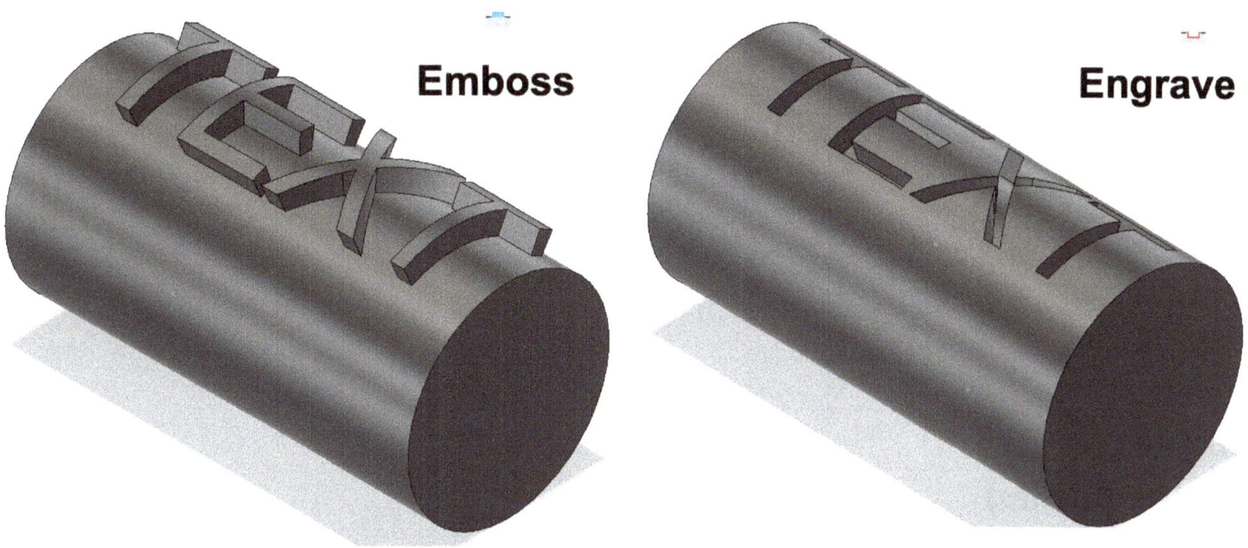

You can enter values in the **Horizontal Distance, Vertical Distance,** or **Rotation Angle** boxes available in the **Alignment** section to move the emboss/engrave in the horizontal/vertical direction or rotate it.

The Emboss moved in the Horizontal direction

The Emboss moved in the Vertical direction

The Emboss rotated about an angle

Solid Sweep

The **Solid Sweep** option in the **Sweep** command creates a solid by sweeping the volume of a solid body along a curve. To sweep a volume, first, create the target body and the tool path, and then create the tool body. Note that you should create the target and tool bodies as separate bodies (Set the **Operation** option to **New Body**). The tool path should be created on the target face. The target face can be planar or non-planar.

Activate the **Sweep** command (on the toolbar, click **Solid > Create > Sweep**). Next, select **Type > Solid Sweep** from the **Sweep** dialog and select the tool body. Click the **Path** selection button and select the planar tool path. On the **Sweep** dialog, select an option from the **Orientation** drop-down. Select **Operation > Cut** to remove material from the target body. Click **OK** to create the solid sweep.

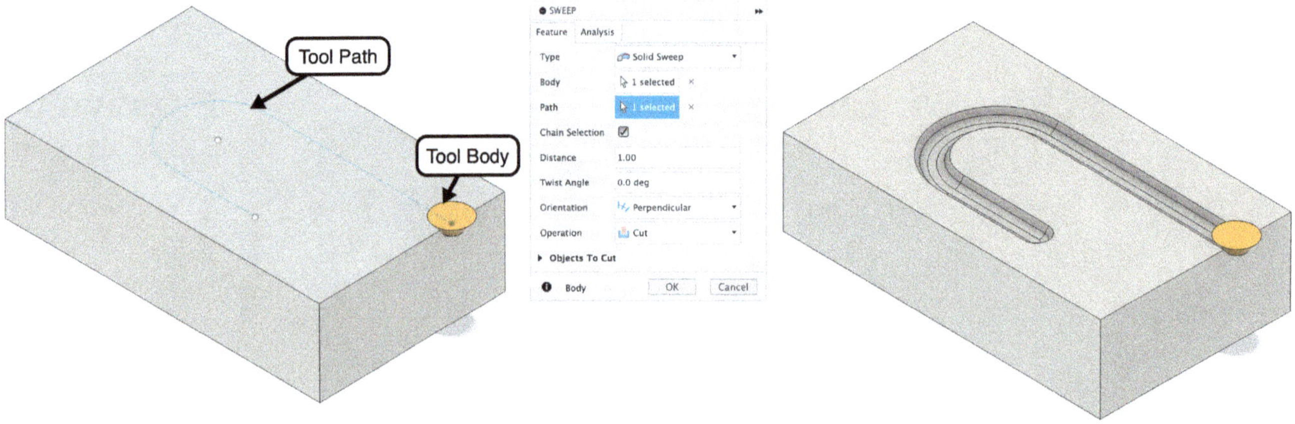

Examples

Example 1 (Inches)

In this example, you will create the part shown next.

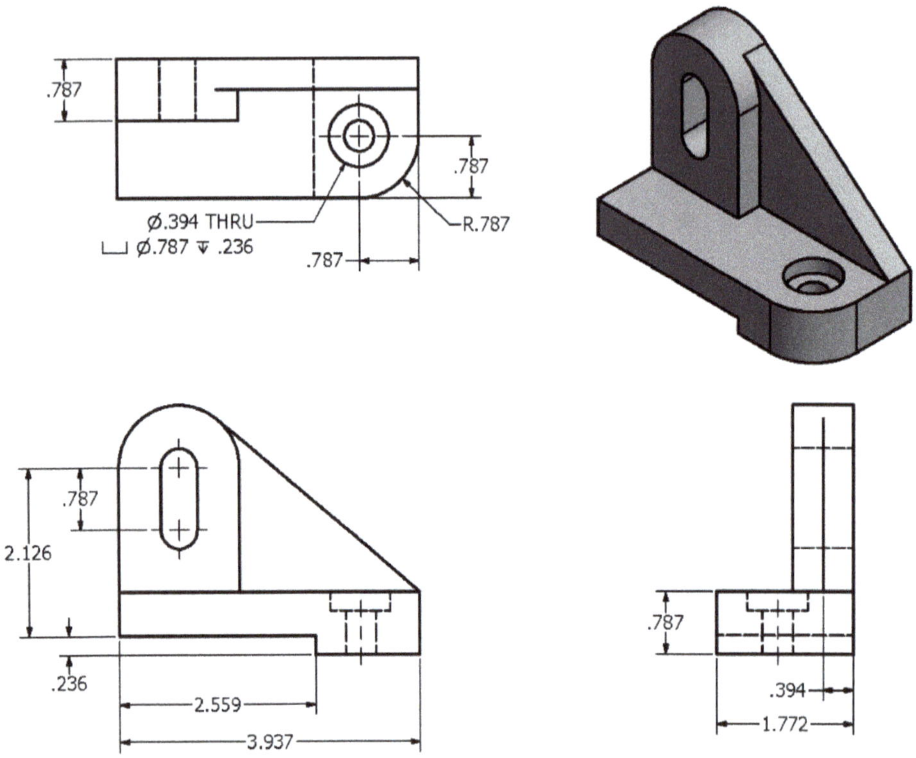

1. Start **Autodesk Fusion 360.**
2. On the **Application bar**, click **File > New Design**.
3. In the Browser window, expand **Document Settings** and place the cursor on **Units**. Next, click the **Change Active Units** icon.
4. On the **Change Active Units** dialog, select **Unit Type** drop-down > **inch (in), ouncemass** and click **OK**.
5. On the toolbar, click **Create** panel > **Create Sketch** and draw the sketch on the XY plane. Next, click **Finish Sketch** on the toolbar.
6. On the **Solid** tab of the toolbar, click **Create** panel **> Extrude**.
7. On the **Extrude** dialog, select **Extents > Distance** and enter 0.787 in the **Distance** box. Click the **Direction > One Side** and click **OK** to create the *Extrude* feature.

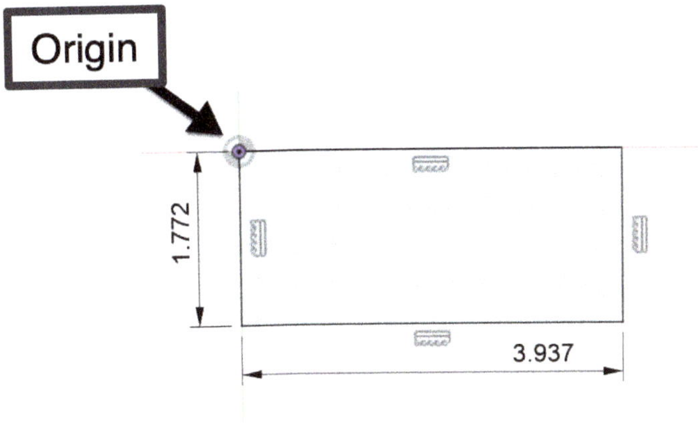

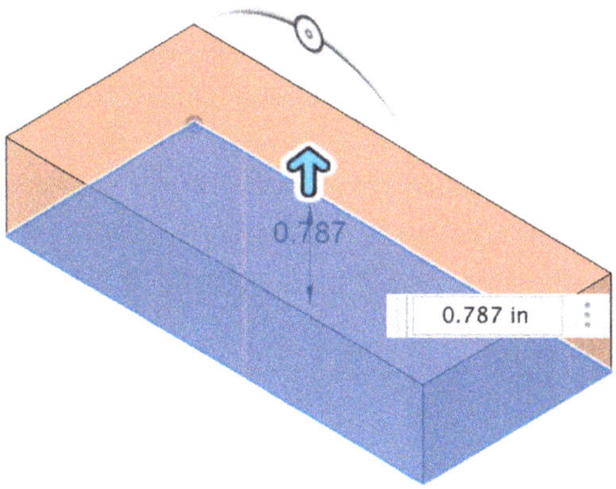

8. Activate the **Create Sketch** command and select the **XZ** plane.
9. Draw the sketch and add dimensions to it, as shown. Click **Finish Sketch** on the toolbar.

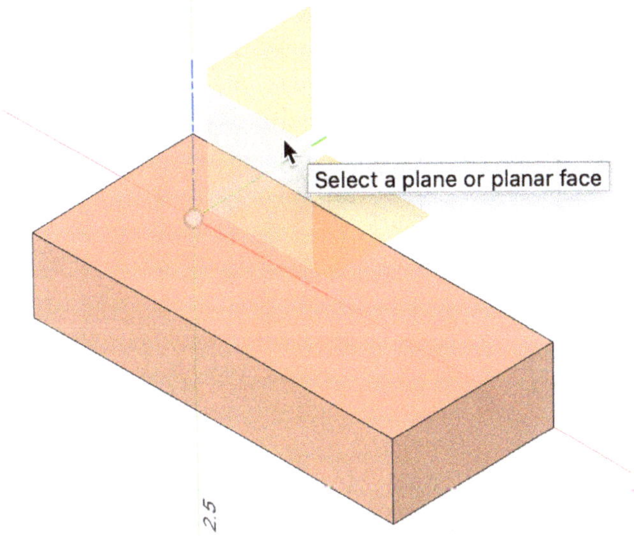

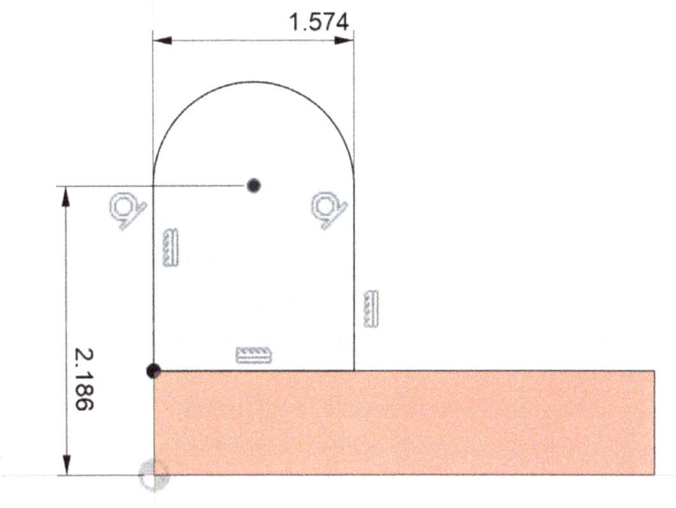

10. Activate the **Extrude** command and select the sketch. On the **Extrude** dialog, select **Extents > Distance** and enter -0.787 in the **Distance** box. Click **OK** to complete the Extrude feature.

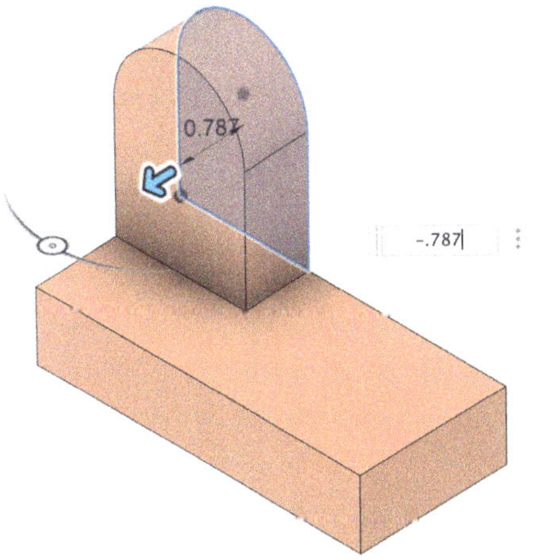

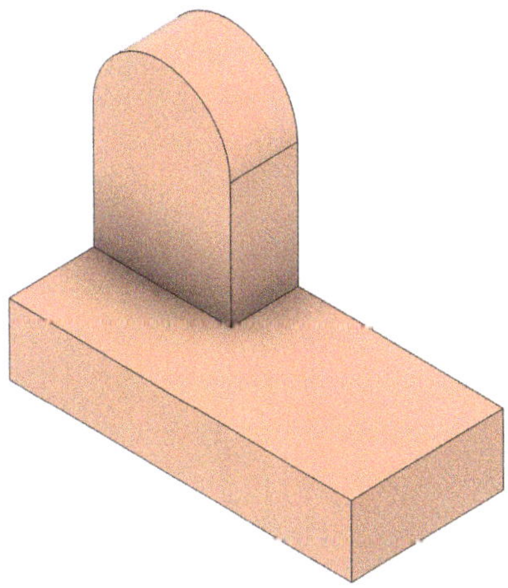

11. Activate the **Create Sketch** command and select the **XZ** plane. Draw an inclined line, as shown.

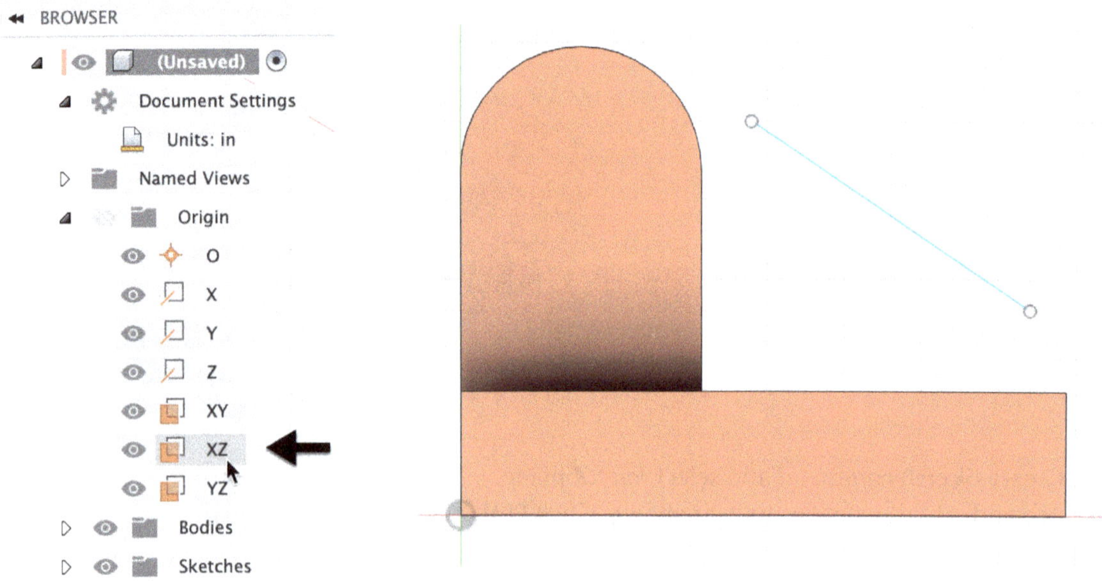

12. On the **Sketch** contextual tab of the toolbar, click **Constraints** panel **> Tangent**, and then select the inclined line and the curved edge; the line is made tangent to the edge.
13. On the **Sketch** contextual tab of the toolbar, click **Constraints** panel **> Coincident**, and then select the endpoint of the inclined line and the curved edge; the endpoint of the line is made coincident to the edge.
14. Likewise, make the other endpoint of the line coincident with the vertex point, as shown. Click **Finish Sketch** on the toolbar.

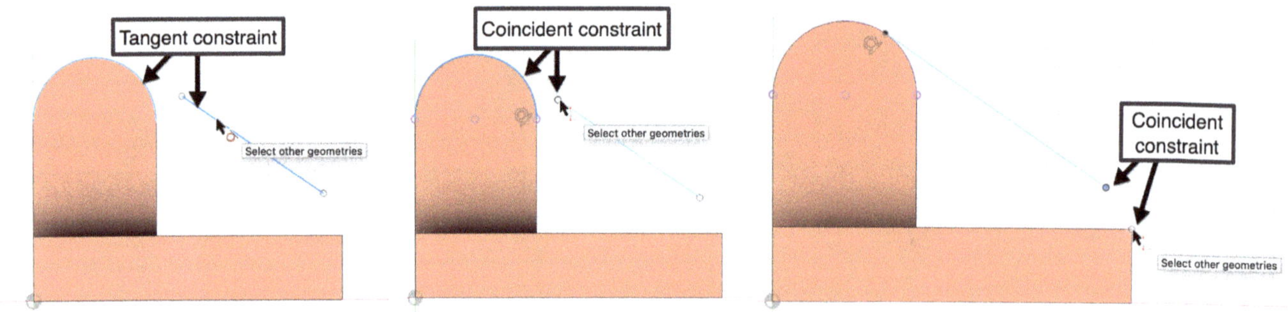

15. Click **Create** panel > **Rib** on the **Solid** tab of the toolbar. Next, select the sketch.
16. On the **Rib** dialog, select **Thickness Options > One Direction**.
17. Select **Depth Options > To Next** and type-in -0.394 in the **Thickness** box.
18. Click the **Flip Direction** icon. Next, click **OK** to create the *Rib* feature.

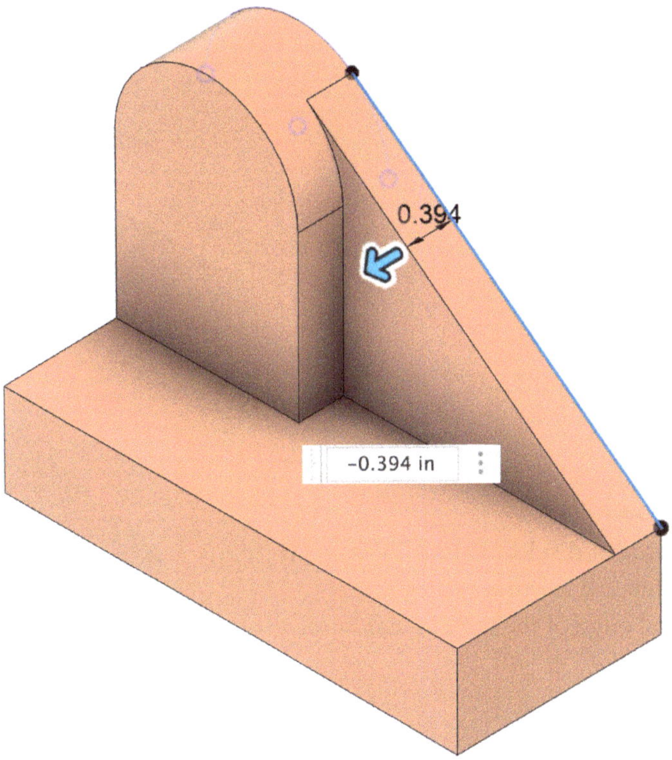

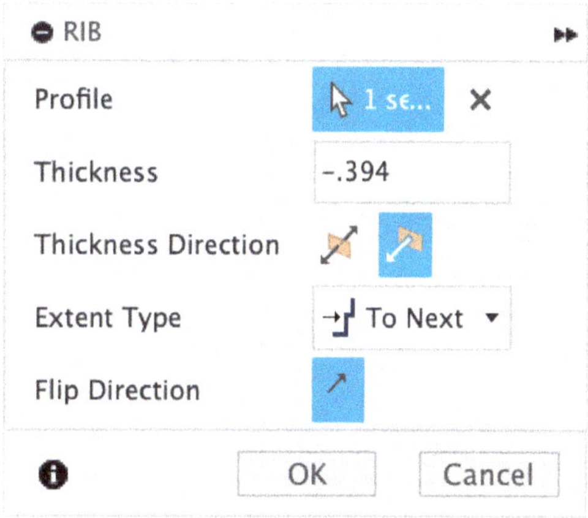

19. Activate the **Create Sketch** command and click on the front face of the second feature, as shown.
20. On the **Sketch** contextual tab of the toolbar, click **Create** panel **> Slot > Center to Center Slot**.
21. Place the pointer near the centerpoint of the curved edge; the centerpoint is highlighted in blue.
22. Click to select the centerpoint of the curved edge. Next, move the pointer downward and click to specify the second center of the slot.
23. Move the pointer outward and click to create the slot.

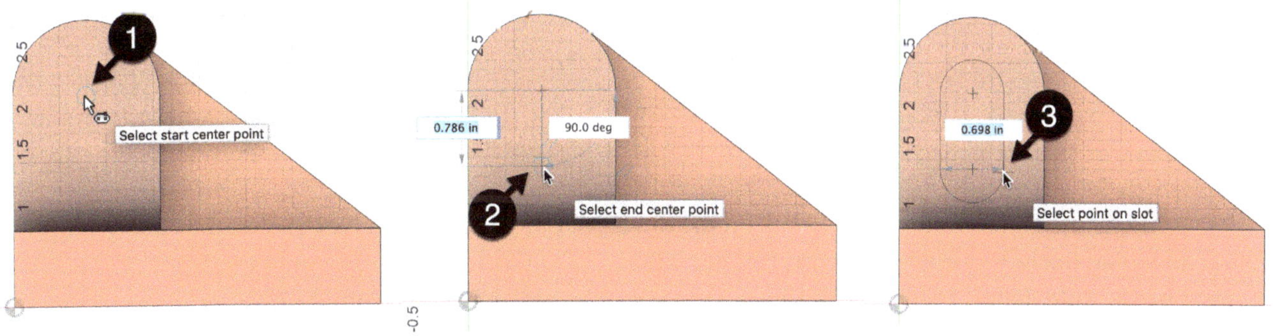

24. Add dimensions to the slot the click **Finish Sketch** on the toolbar.

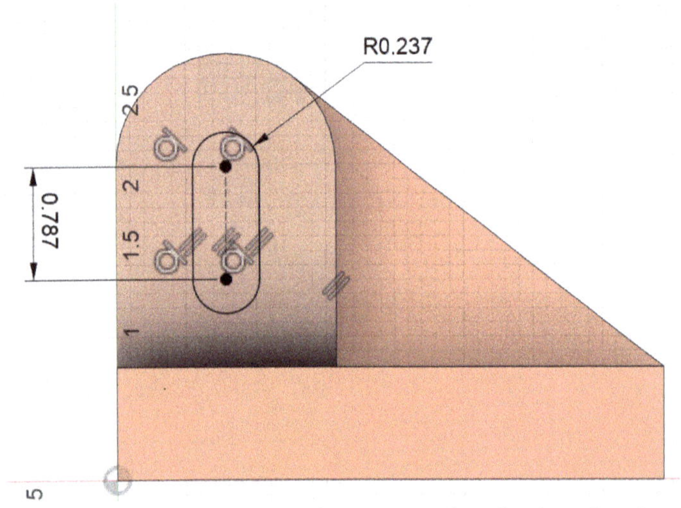

25. Activate the **Extrude** command and select the sketch.
26. On the **Extrude** dialog, click **Direction > One Side** and select **Extent Type > All**.
27. Select **Operation > Cut** and click **OK** to create the *Cut* feature.
28. Add a fillet of 0.787 in radius to the right vertical edge of the rectangular base.

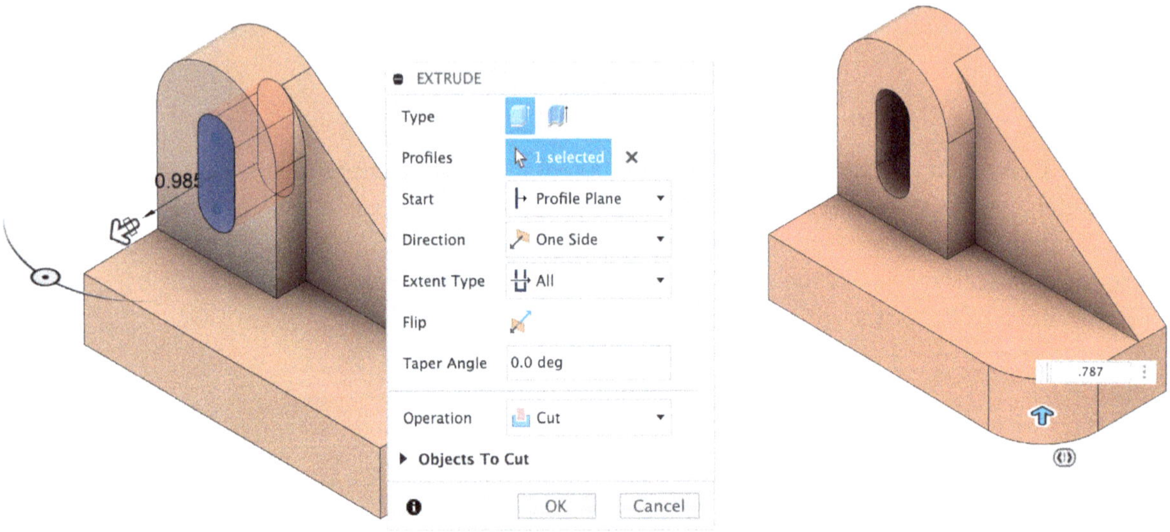

29. Activate the **Hole** command and click on the top face of the first feature. Next, select the curved edge of the fillet; the hole is made concentric to the fillet.
30. On the **Hole** dialog, specify the settings, as shown. Next, click **OK** to create the hole.

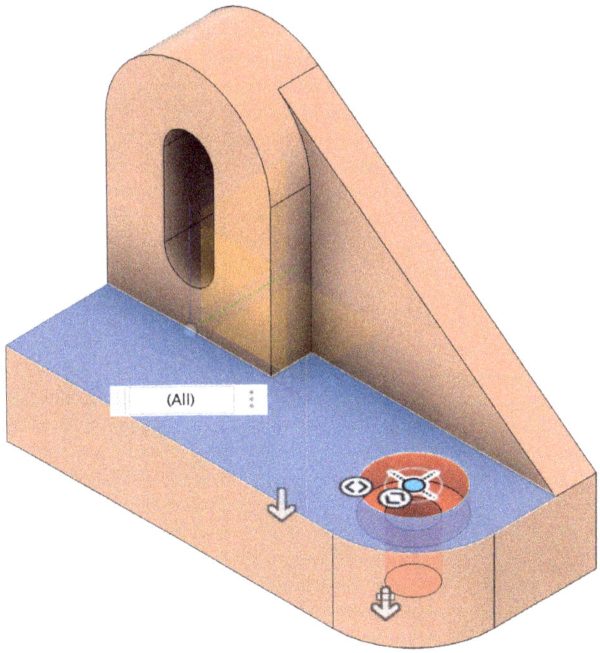

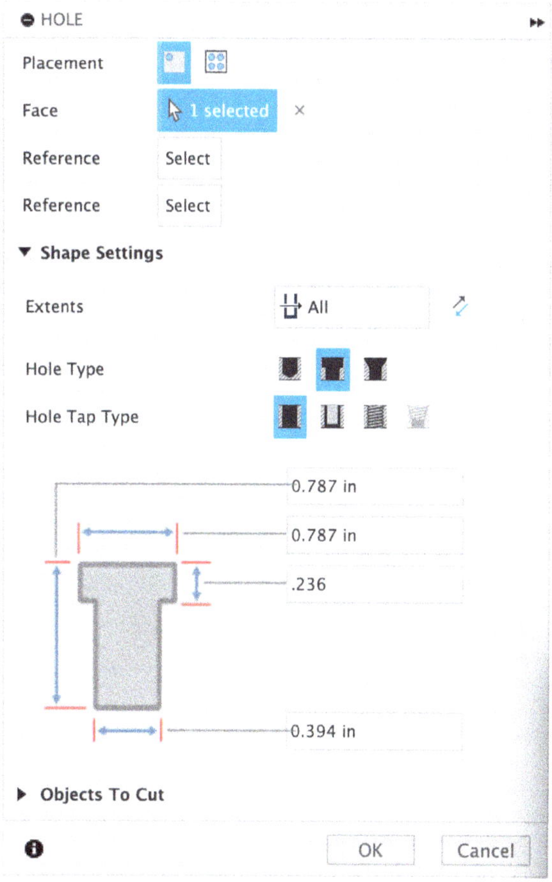

31. Activate the **Create Sketch** command and select the front face of the rectangular base.
32. Draw a sketch and add dimensions to it. Click **Finish Sketch** on the toolbar.
33. Create an *Extruded Cut* feature using the sketch.

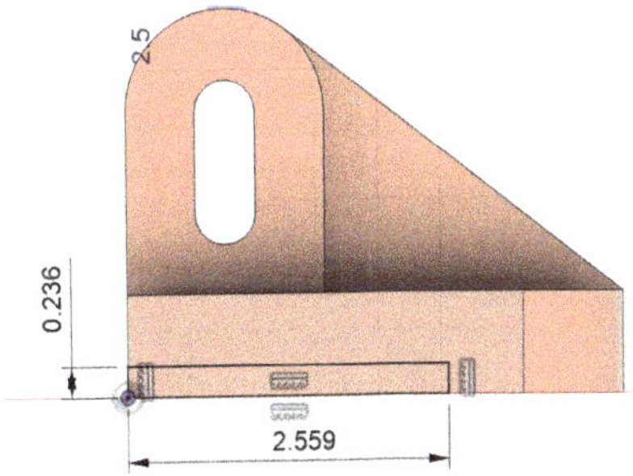

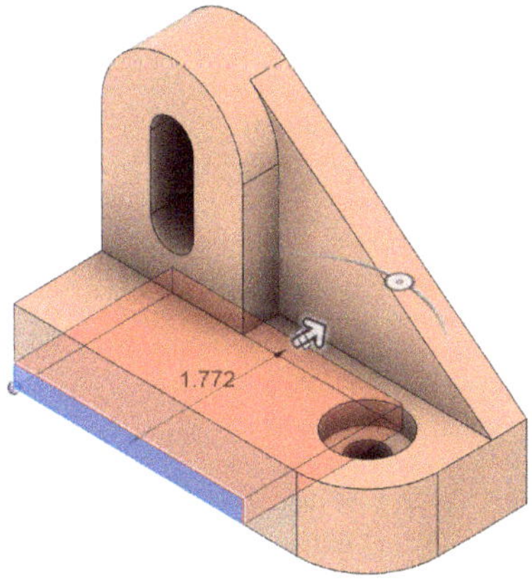

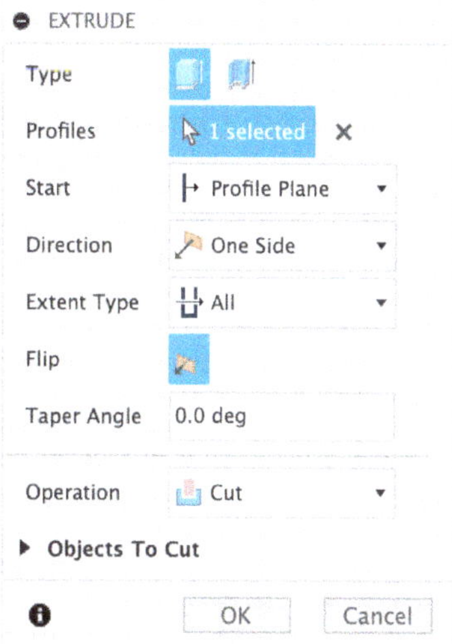

34. Save and close the part file.

Example 2 (Millimetres)

In this example, you will create the part shown next.

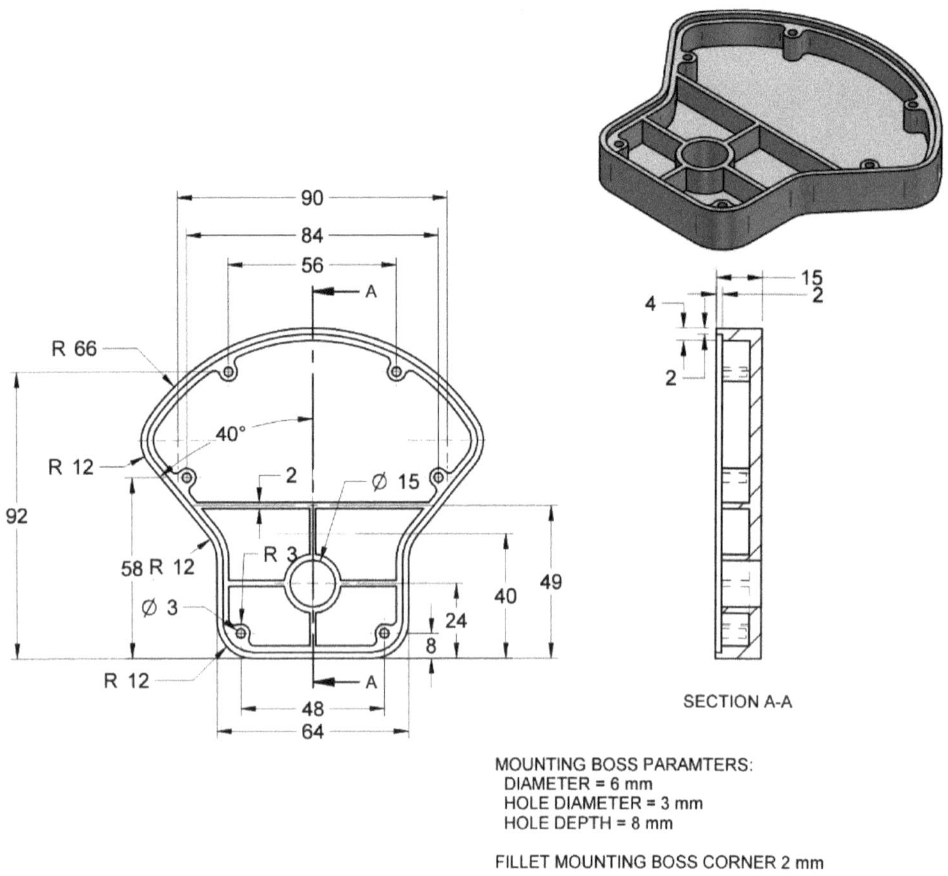

1. Start **Autodesk Fusion 360**.
2. On the Application bar, click **File > New Design.**
3. On the Browser window, expand the **Document Settings** node and place the pointer on the **Units** icon. Next, click the **Change Active Units** icon to open **Change Active Units** dialog.
4. Click **Unit Type > millimeter (mm), gram (g)** and click **OK**
5. To start a new sketch, click **Create** panel **> Create Sketch** on the **Sketch** contextual tab of the toolbar, and then select the **XY** Plane.
6. On the **Sketch** contextual tab of the toolbar, click **Create** panel **> Line**. Next, draw the sketch, as shown in the figure below.
7. Click **Linetype > Construction** on the **Sketch Palette**. Next, activate the **Line** command and create a vertical construction line passing through the origin.
8. On the **Sketch** contextual tab of the toolbar, click **Create** panel > **Mirror**, and then select the lines, as shown. Next, click the **Mirror** selection button and select the construction line.

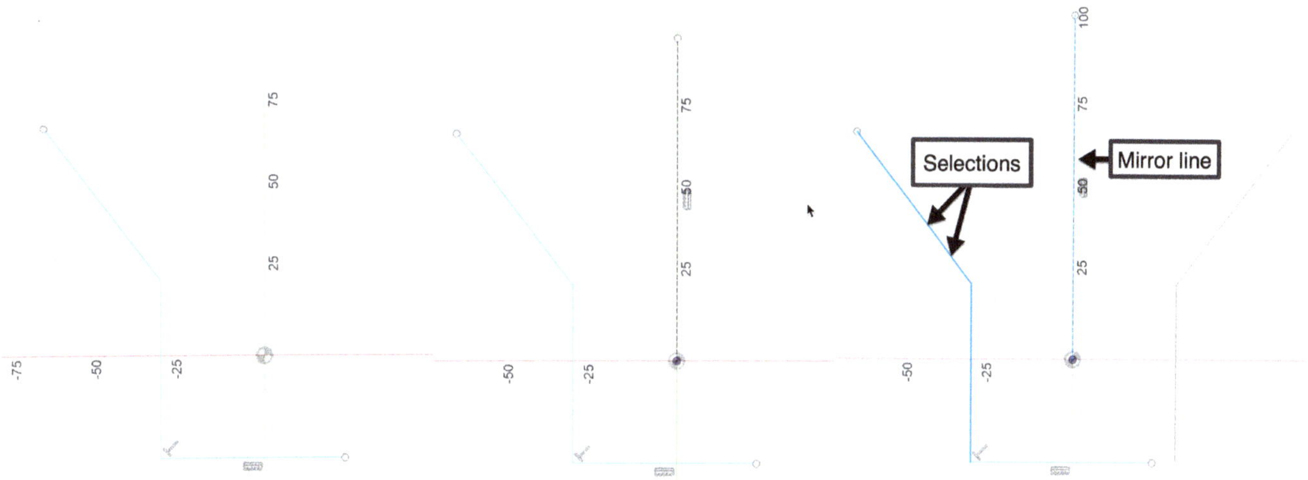

9. Click **Linetype > Construction** on the **Sketch Palette.**
10. On the **Sketch** contextual tab of the toolbar, click **Create** panel **> Arc > 3-Point Arc**, and then create an arc by specifying the points in the sequence, as shown.
11. On the **Sketch** contextual tab of the toolbar, click **Constraints** panel > **Coincident Constraint**. Next, select the endpoints of the lines at the bottom right corner of the sketch.

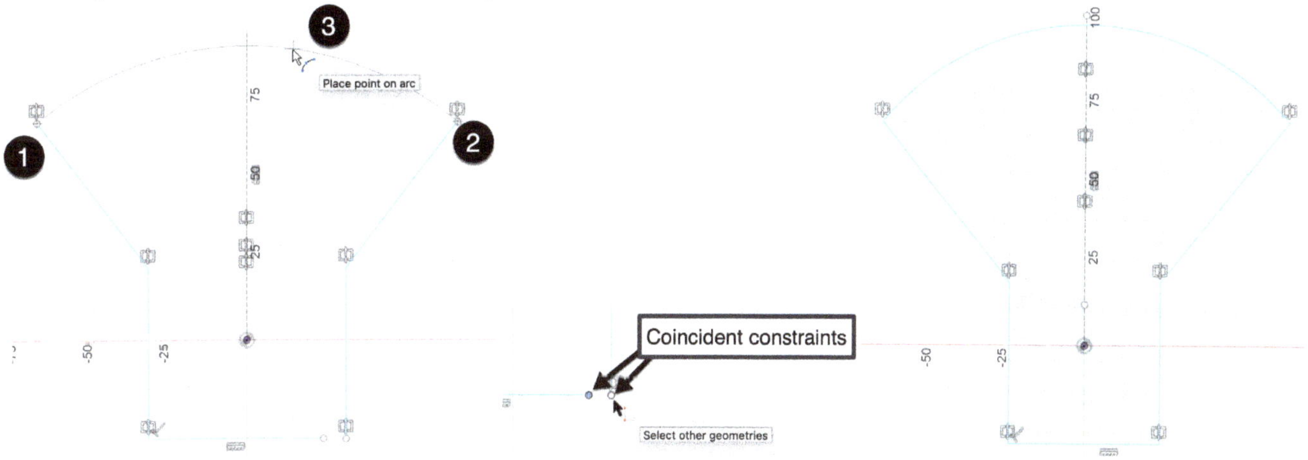

12. Apply dimensions to the sketch. Also, apply the **Coincident Constraint** between the center point of the arc and the sketch origin.

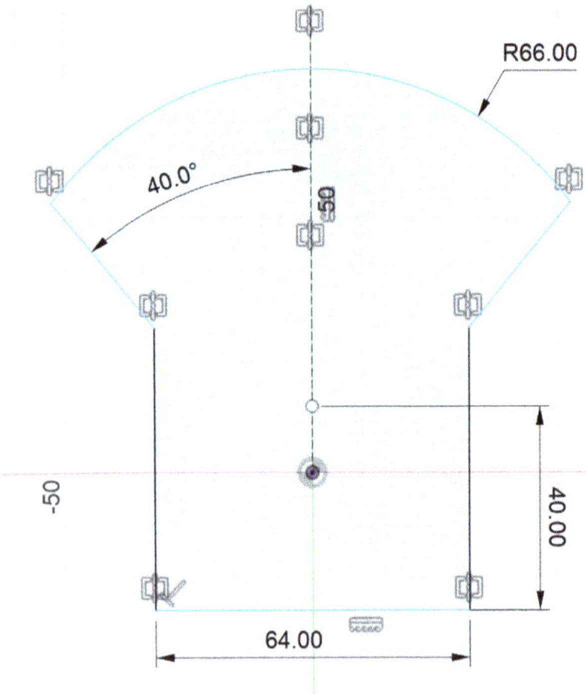

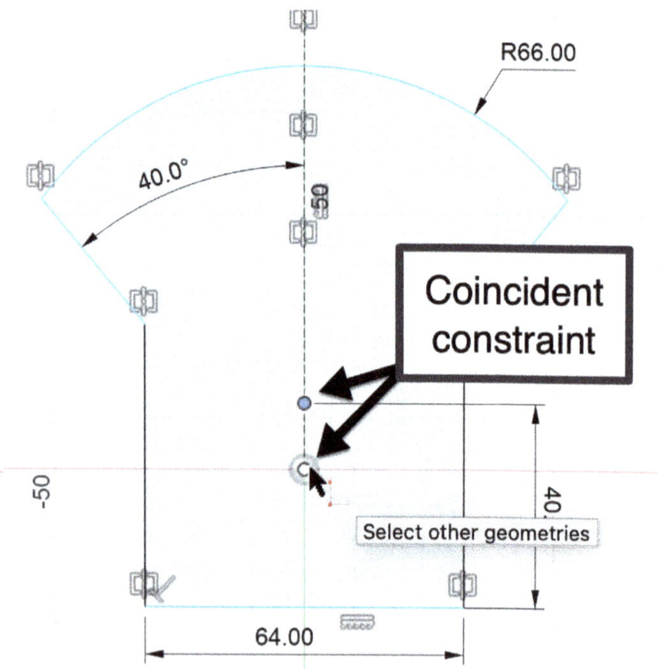

13. On the **Sketch** contextual tab of the toolbar, click **Constraints** panel > **Horizontal/Vertical**, and then select any one of the sharp corners, as shown. Next, select the sketch origin; the two selected points are made horizontal.

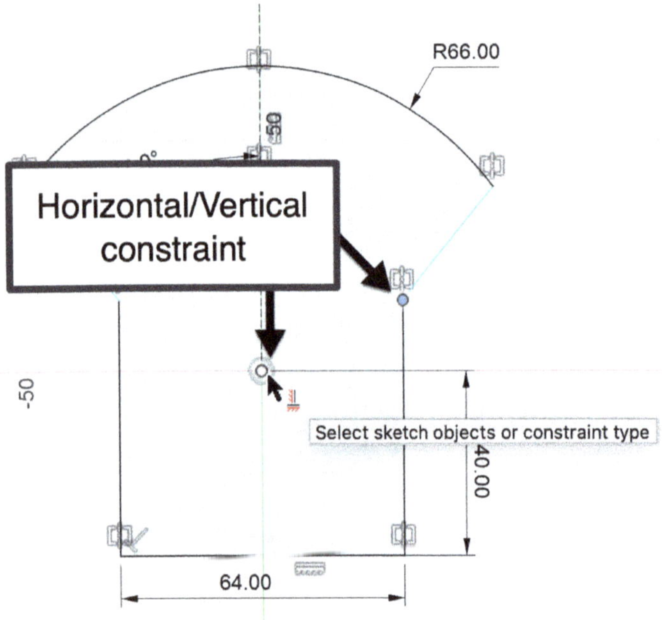

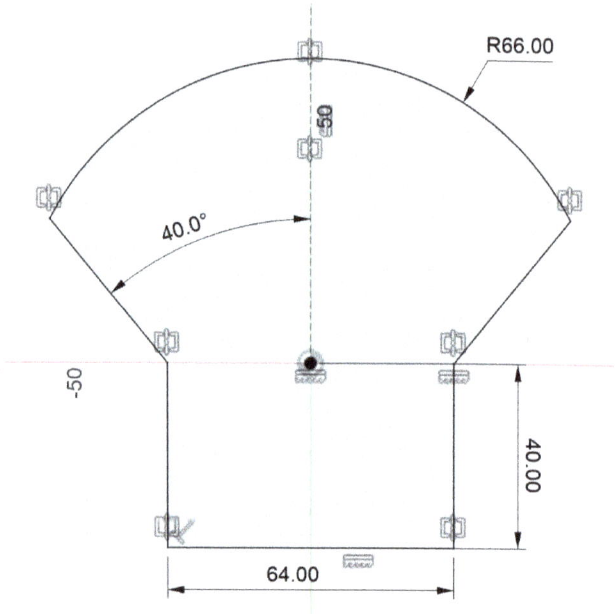

14. Click **Finish Sketch** on the toolbar and click the **Home** button on the Viewcube to change the view orientation.
15. Create the *Extrude* feature of 15 mm depth. Next, fillet the sharp corners of the model. The fillet radius is 12 mm.

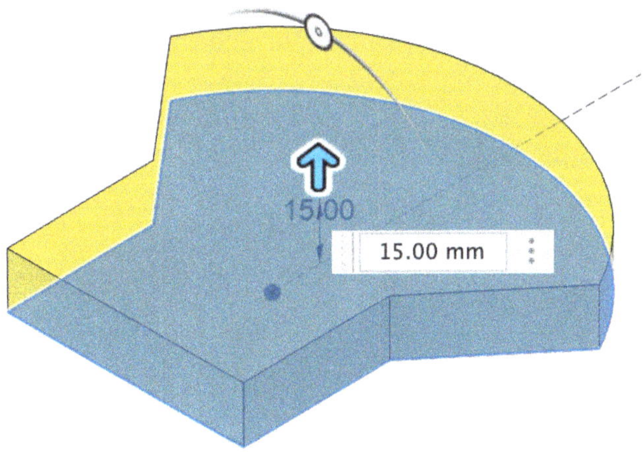

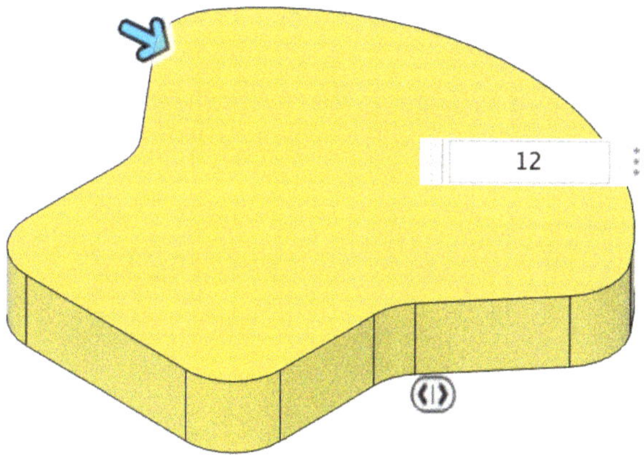

16. Create the *Shell* feature of 4 mm Inside Thickness.

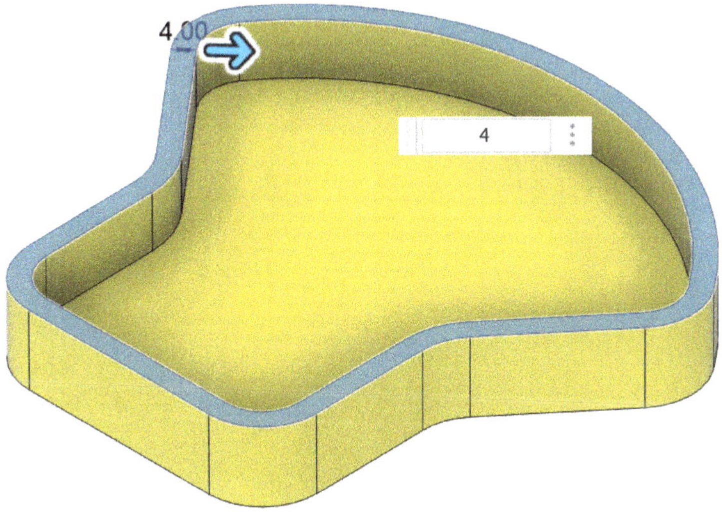

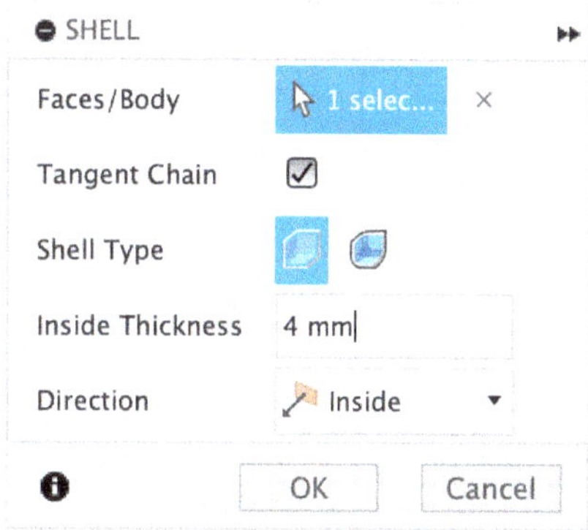

17. On the toolbar, click **Create** panel **>** **Create Sketch**. Select the top face of the shell feature, as shown.
18. On the **Sketch** contextual tab of the toolbar, click **Modify** panel > **Offset**.
19. Select the inner edge of the model.
20. On the **Offset** dialog, enter 2 in the **Offset position** box and click **Flip** icon to reverse the direction.

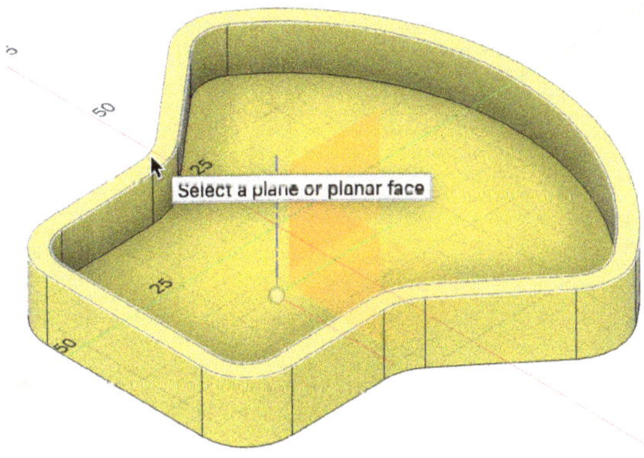

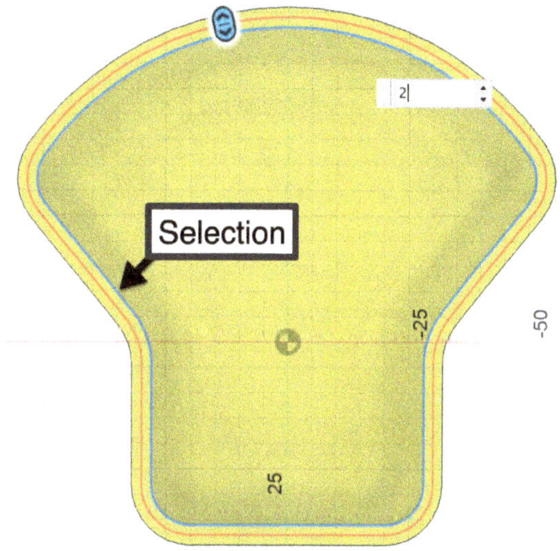

21. Click **OK** to create the offset. Next, click **Finish Sketch** on the toolbar.
22. Activate the **Extrude** command and click on the region enclosed by the sketch and inner edge of the shell feature.
23. Click **Extent Type > Distance** and enter **-2 mm** in the **Distance** box.
24. Click **Operation > Cut** and click **OK** to create the groove feature.

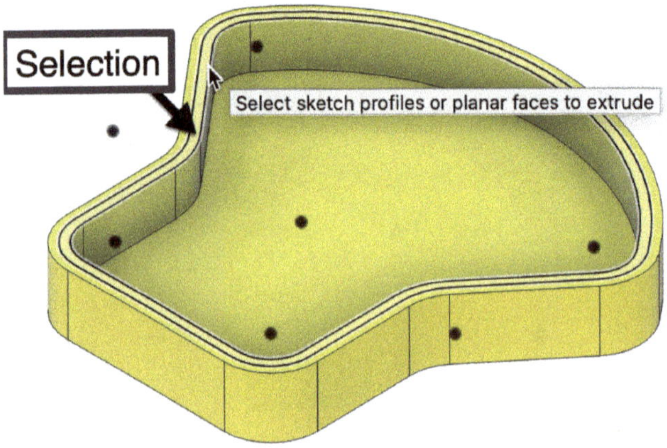

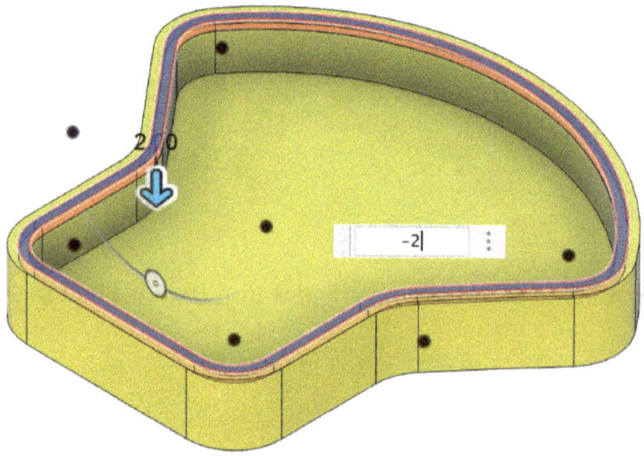

25. On the toolbar, click **Create** panel > **Create Sketch**, and then click on the bottom face of the groove feature.
26. Draw the circles and add dimensions to them, as shown. Click **Finish Sketch** on the toolbar.

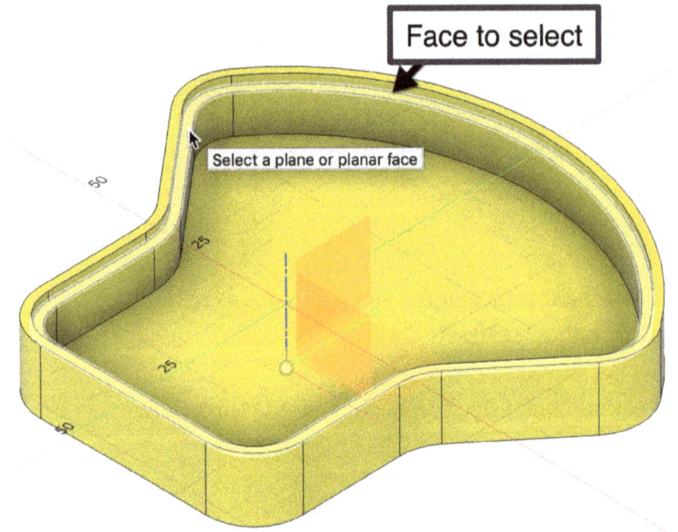

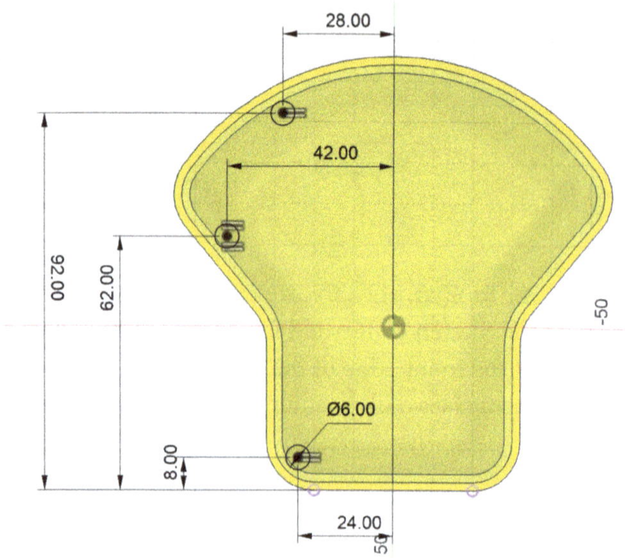

27. On the **Solid** tab of the toolbar, click **Create** panel **> Extrude**. Click inside the circles.
28. On the **Extrude** dialog, click **Extent Type > To Object** and select the bottom surface of the *Shell* feature, as shown.
29. Type-in **1** in the **Taper Angle** and select **Operation > Join**.
30. Click **OK** to create the *Extrude* feature.

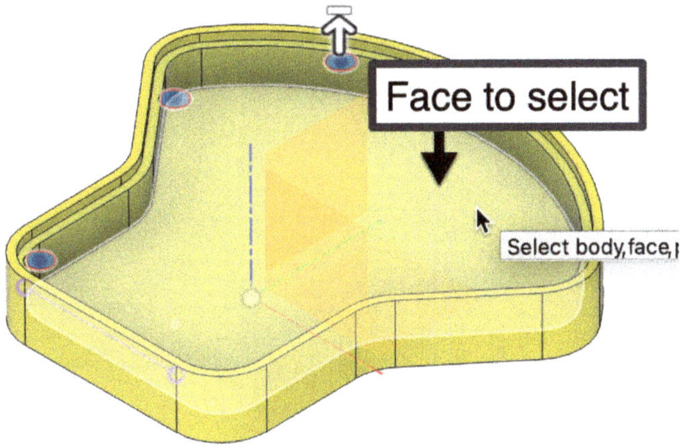

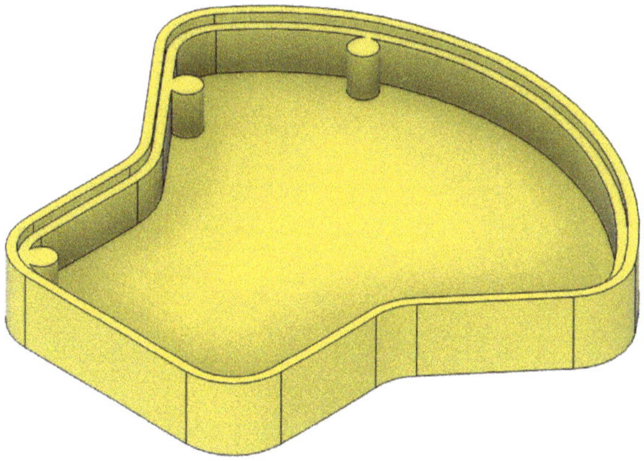

31. Click **Create** panel **> Create Sketch** and select the bottom face of the groove feature, as shown.
32. Create circles and apply the **Equal** constraint between them. Also, apply the **Concentric** constraint between the circles and circular edges of the extruded features.
33. Click **Finish Sketch** on the toolbar.

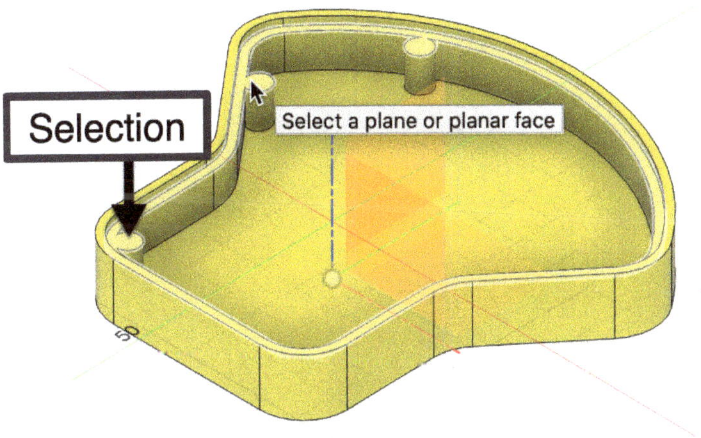

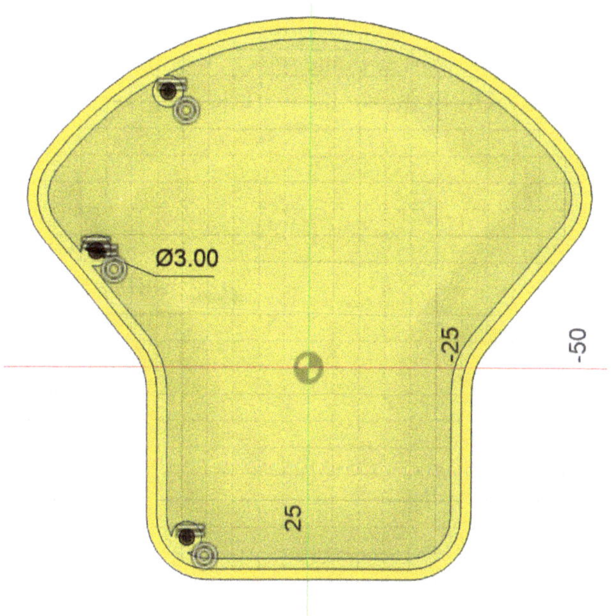

34. Click **Create > Extrude** on the **Solid** tab of the toolbar and select the newly created circles.
35. Click **Extent Type > Distance** and type-in -8 in the **Distance** box.
36. Type-in -1 in the **Taper Angle** and click **Operation > Cut**.

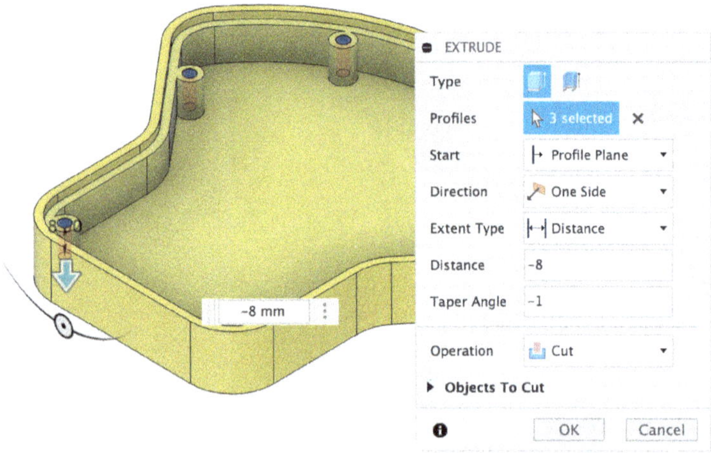

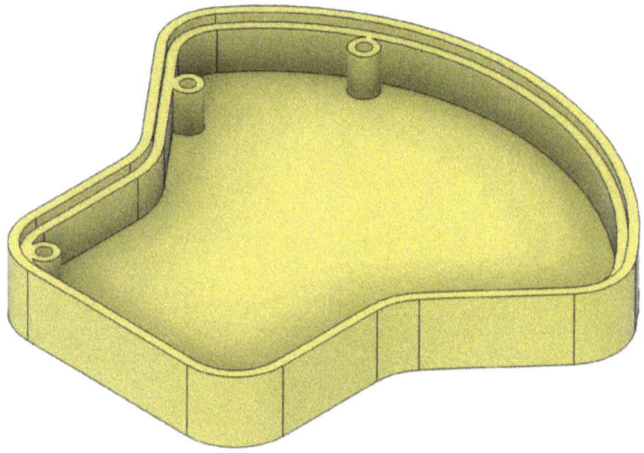

37. Click **OK** to create the *Extruded Cut* feature.
38. On the **Solid** tab of the toolbar, click **Create** panel **> Mirror**. Next, select **Type > Features** on the **Mirror** dialog.
39. Click the **Objects** selection button and select the *Extrude* and *Cut* features on the Timeline.
40. Click the **Mirror Plane** selection button and click the **YZ** plane on the coordinate system.
41. Click **OK** to mirror the extrude features.

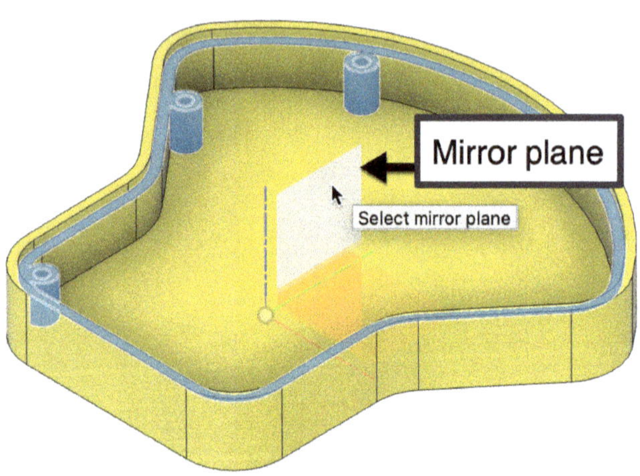

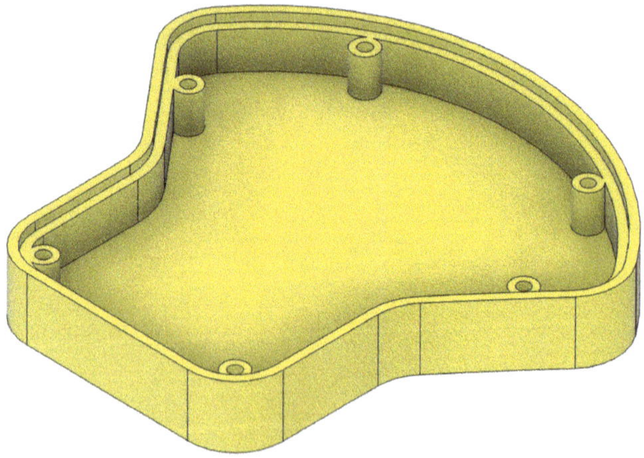

42. On the **Solid** tab of the toolbar, click **Modify** panel **> Fillet** and select the edges where the extruded features meet the walls of the geometry.
43. Type **2** in the **Radius** box. Click the **OK** button to fillet the selected edges.

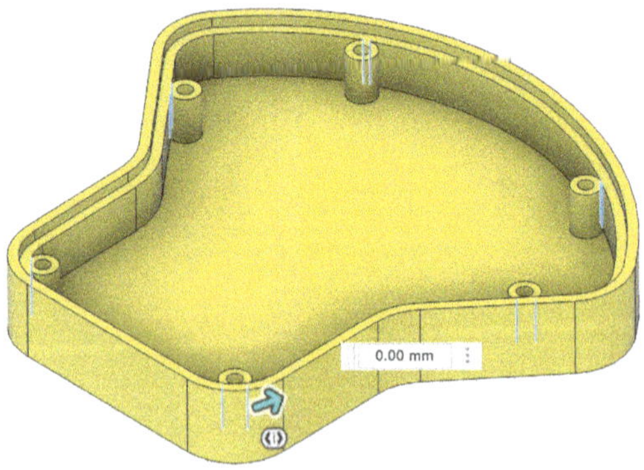

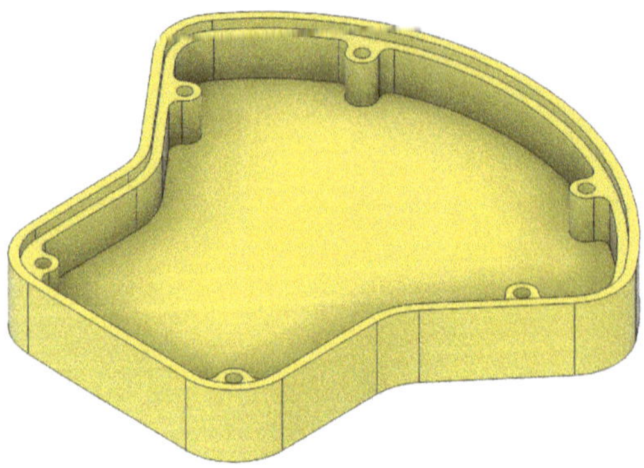

44. On the toolbar, click **Create** panel **> Create Sketch** and select the bottom face of the groove.
45. Create a sketch using the **Line** and **Center Diameter Circle** commands.
46. Apply the constraints and add dimensions to it, as shown.
47. Click **Finish Sketch** on the toolbar.

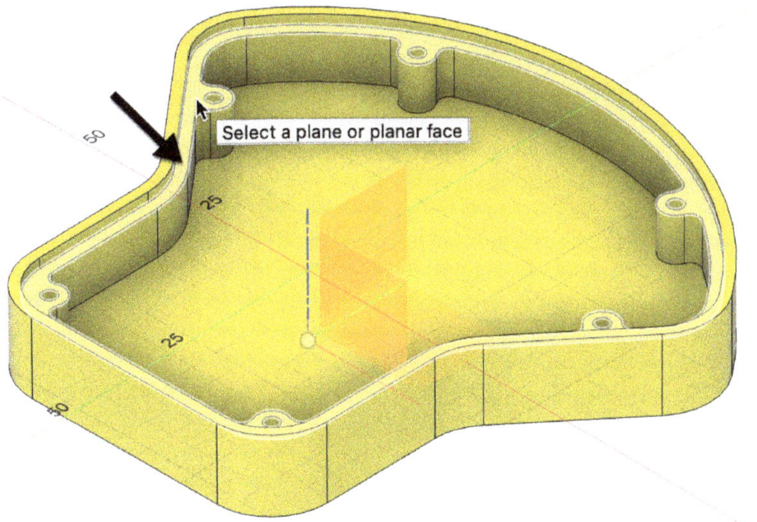

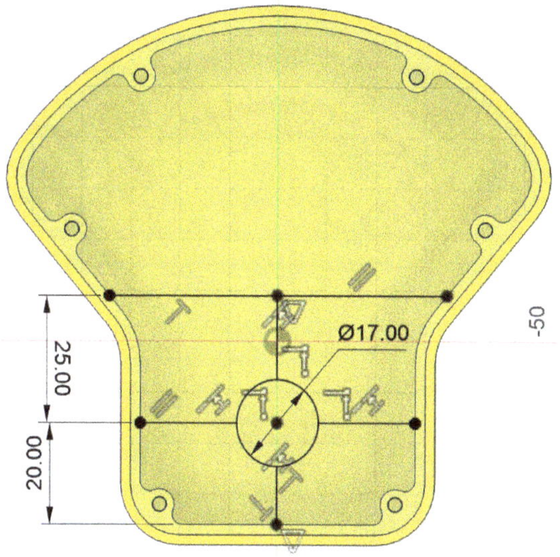

48. On the **Solid** tab of the toolbar, click **Create** panel **> Web** and select the entities of the sketch.
49. On the **Web** dialog, select **Thickness Options > Symmetric**.
50. Select **Depth Options > To Next** and type **1** in the **Thickness** box.
51. Uncheck the **Extended Curves** option and click **OK** to create the *Web* networks feature.

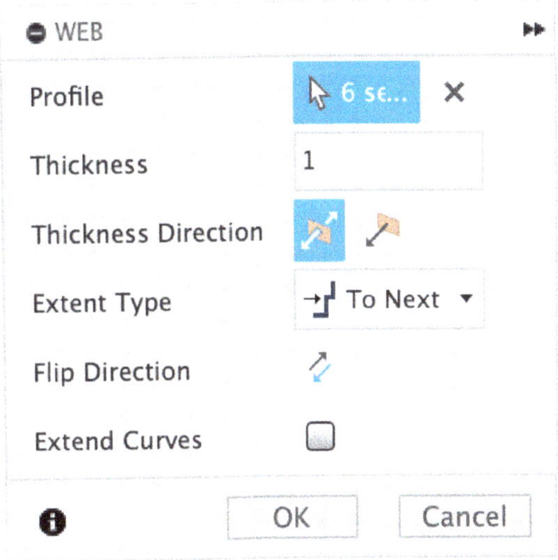

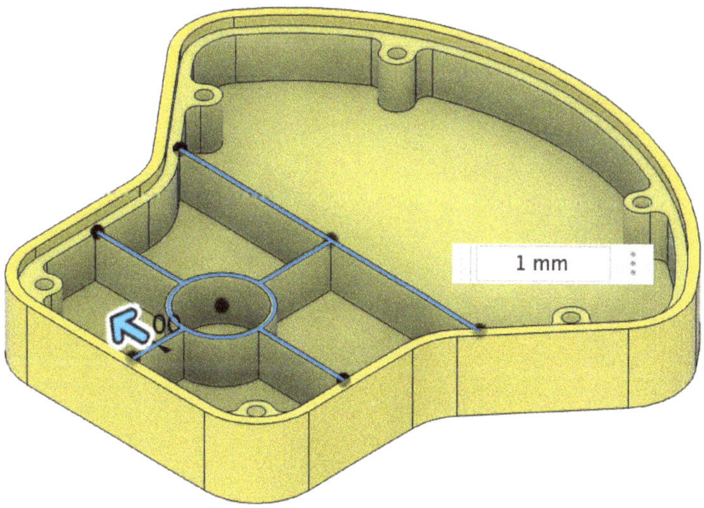

52. Save and close the file.

Example 3 (Inches)

In this example, you will create the part shown below.

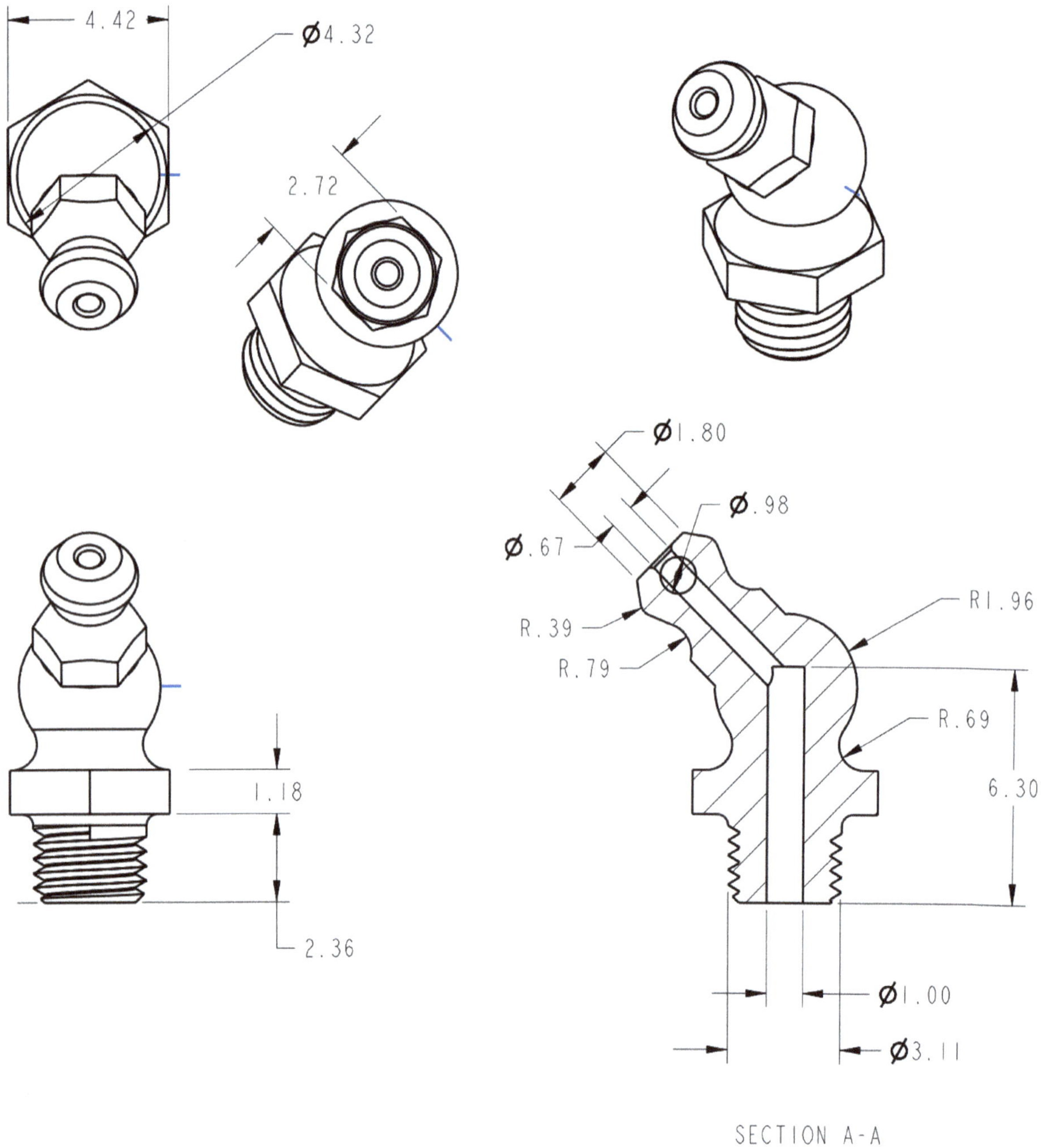
4.42
Ø4.32
2.72
1.18
2.36
Ø1.80
Ø.98
Ø.67
R.39
R.79
R1.96
R.69
6.30
Ø1.00
Ø3.11
SECTION A-A

Creating the First Feature

1. Start **Autodesk Fusion 360** by double-clicking the **Autodesk Fusion 360** icon on your desktop.
2. On the **Browser window**, expand **Document Settings** and place the cursor on **Units**; the **Change Active Units** icon appears.
3. Click on the **Change Active Units** icon to change the units; the **Change Active Units** dialog appears.
4. On this dialog, select **Unit Type** drop-down > **inch (in), ouncemass** from the drop-down and click **OK**.
5. To start a sketch, click **Create > Create Sketch** on the toolbar. Click on the XZ plane. The sketch starts.
6. On the toolbar, click **Sketch** tab > **Create** panel > **Line**.
7. Specify the start point of the line on the vertical reference.
8. Click on the origin point to define the second point.
9. Move the pointer horizontally toward right and click on the horizontal reference.
10. Move the pointer vertically up to a small distance and click.
11. Move the pointer horizontally toward right up to a small distance and click.
12. Move the pointer vertically up to a small distance and click.
13. Move the pointer horizontally toward left up to a small distance and click.

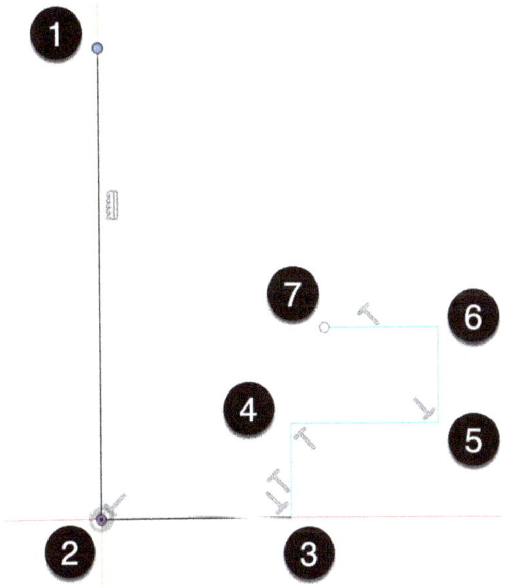

14. Add dimensions to the lines, as shown.

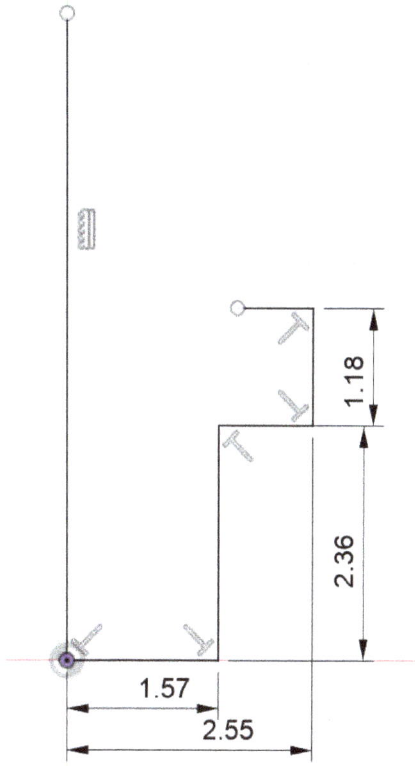

15. On the toolbar, click **Sketch** tab > **Create** panel > **Arc** drop-down > **3-Point Arc**.
16. Select the endpoint of the horizontal line.
17. Select the end point of the left vertical line.
18. Move the pointer toward right and click.

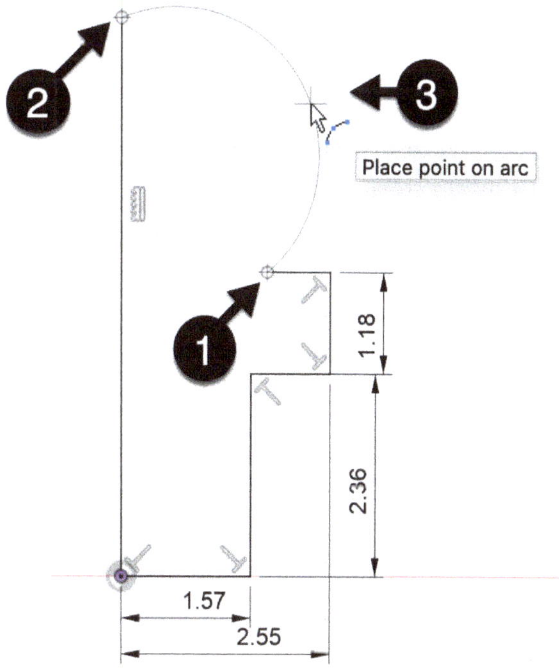

19. Apply the **Coincident** constraint between the centerpoint of the second arc and the vertical line, as shown.

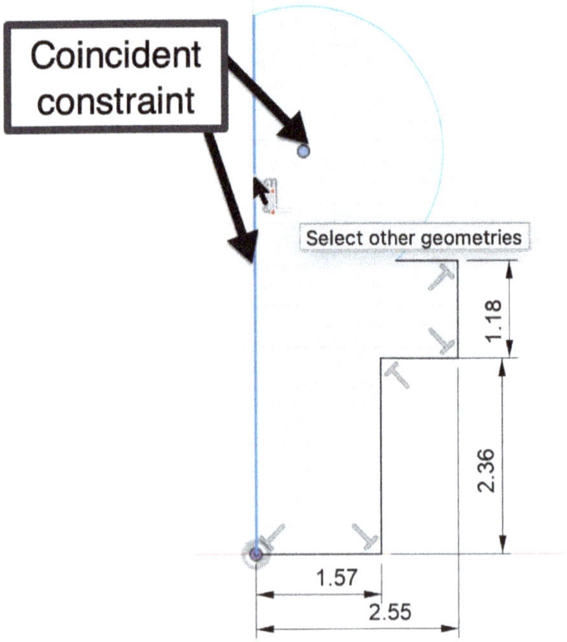

20. On the toolbar, click **Sketch** tab > **Modify** panel > **Fillet**.
21. Select the arc and the horizontal line.

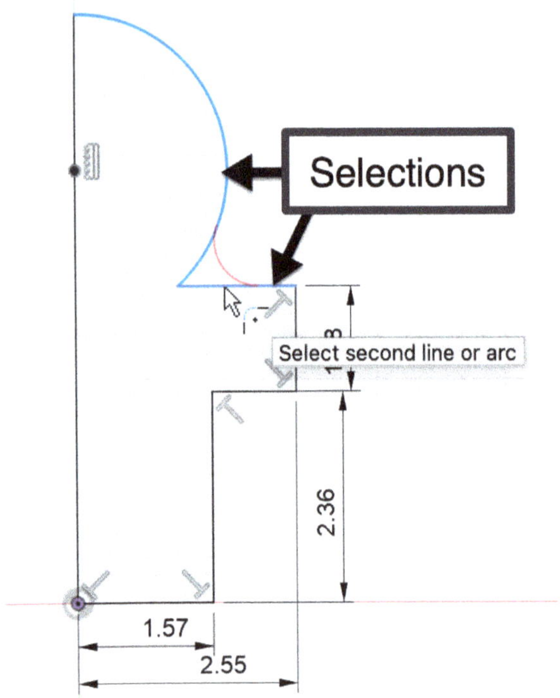

22. Right-click and select **OK**.

23. Add dimensions to the sketch, as shown.

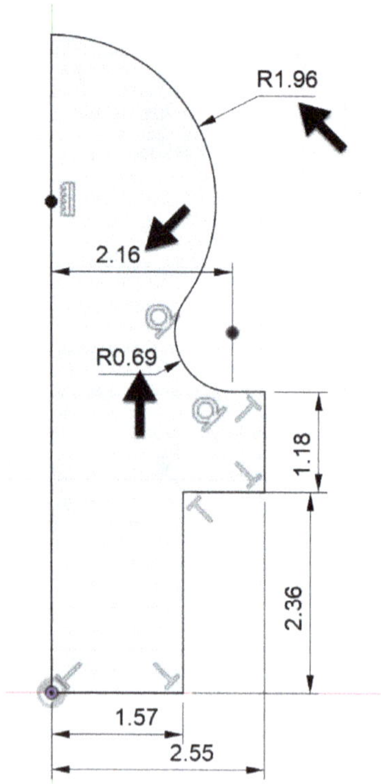

24. Click **OK** on the toolbar.
25. On the toolbar, click **Solid** tab > **Create** panel > **Revolve**.
26. Select the vertical line passing through the origin to define the axis of revolution.
27. Click the **OK** to create the *Revolved* feature.

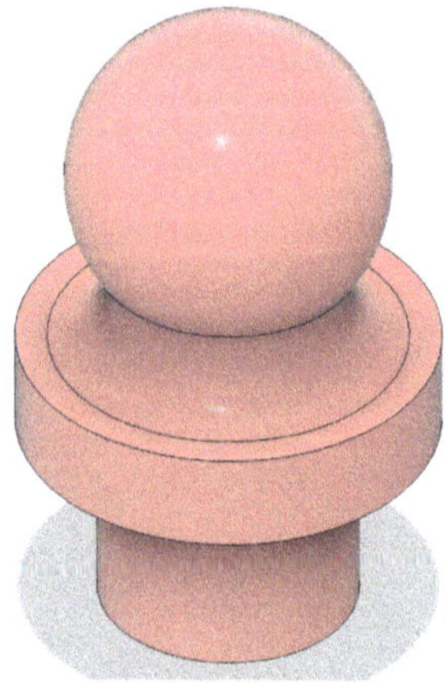

Creating the Extruded Cut Features

1. On the toolbar, click **Solid** tab > **Create** panel > **Create Sketch**.
2. Click on the flat face of the model, as shown.

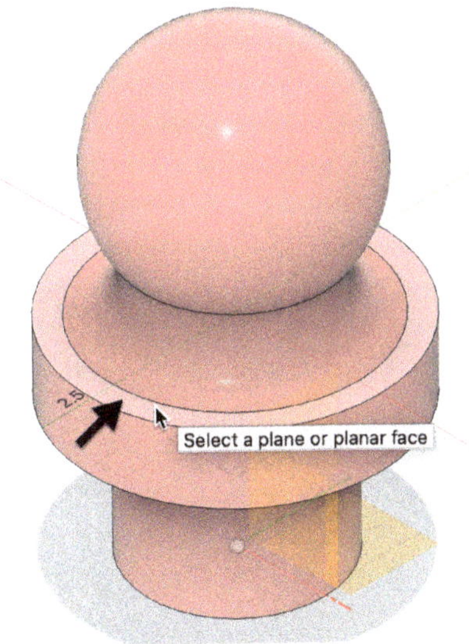

3. On the toolbar, click **Sketch** tab > **Create** panel > **Polygon** drop-down > **Inscribed Circle**.
4. Select the sketch origin.
5. Move the pointer outward and click on the circular edge of the model.

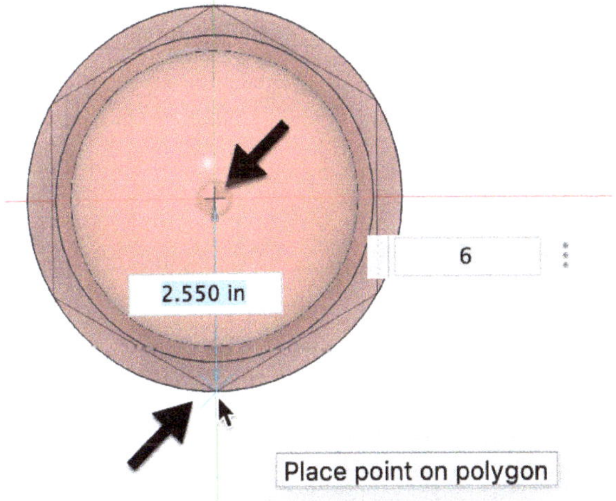

6. Move the pointer outward and click.
7. On the toolbar, click **Sketch** tab > **Constraints** panel > **Horizontal/Vertical**.
8. Select the sketch origin and the vertex point of the polygon, as shown.

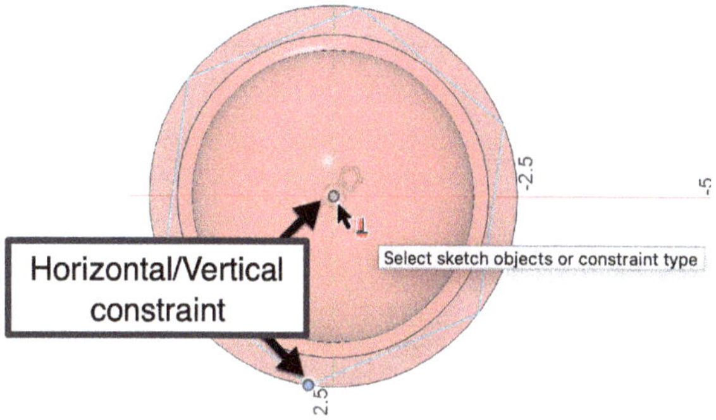

9. Click **Finish Sketch** on the toolbar.
10. On the toolbar, click **Solid** tab > **Create** panel > **Extrude**.
11. Click in the regions between the polygon and the circular edge, as shown.

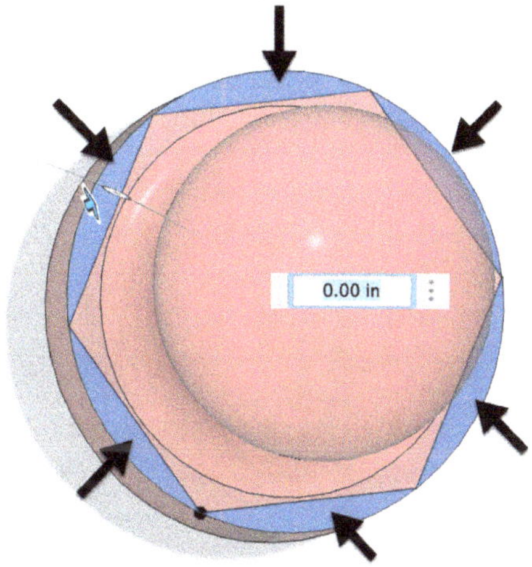

12. On the **Extrude** dialog, select **Operation > Cut**.
13. Select the **All** option from the **Extent Type** drop-down.
14. Click the **Flip** button.
15. Click **OK**.

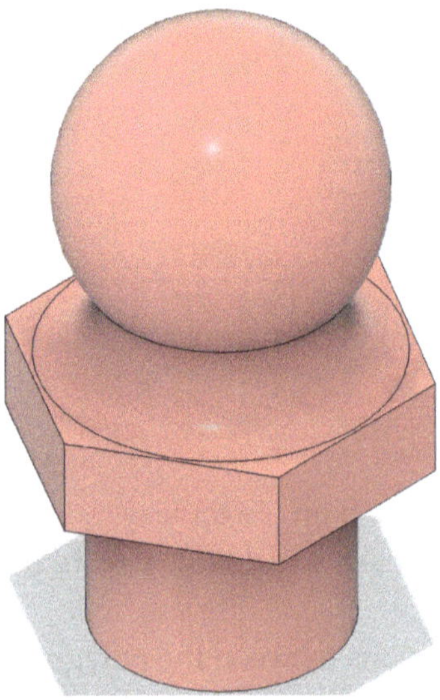

16. On the toolbar, click **Solid** tab > **Create** panel > **Hole**.
17. Click on the bottom face of the model, as shown.

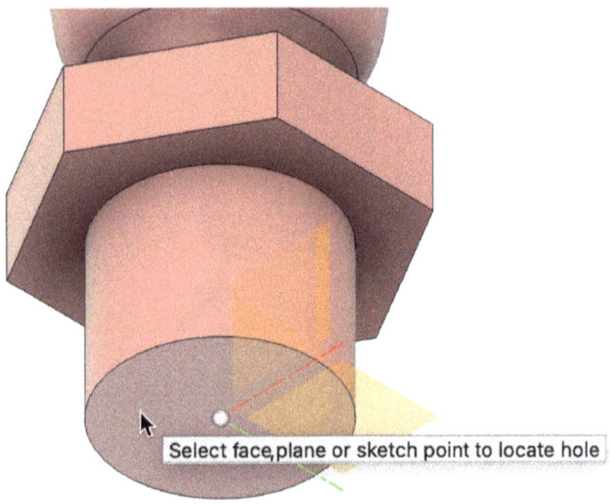

18. Select the circular edge.

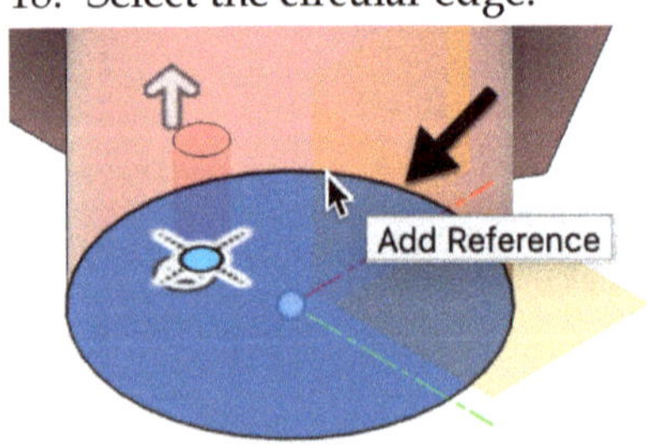

19. On the **Hole** dialog, set the **Diameter** value to **1**.
20. Type **6.3** in the **Depth** box.
21. Click **Drill Point > Flat**.
22. Click **OK**.

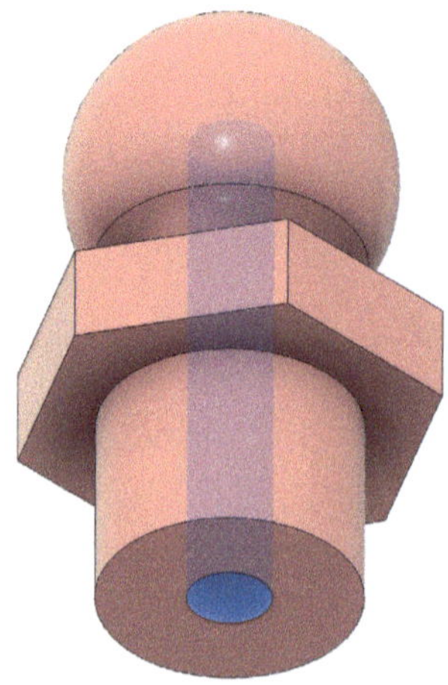

23. On the toolbar, click **Solid** tab > **Create** panel > **Create Sketch**.
24. Click on the XZ plane.
25. On the toolbar, click **Sketch > Project/Include > Intersect**.
26. Click the silhouette edge of the sphere and click **OK**.

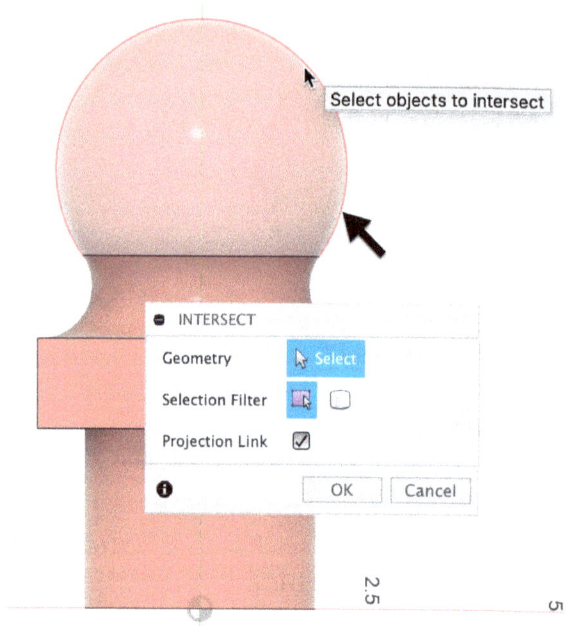

27. On the toolbar, click **Sketch** tab > **Create** panel > **Line**.
28. Select the centerpoint of the circular reference edge.
29. Move the pointer horizontally toward right and click.

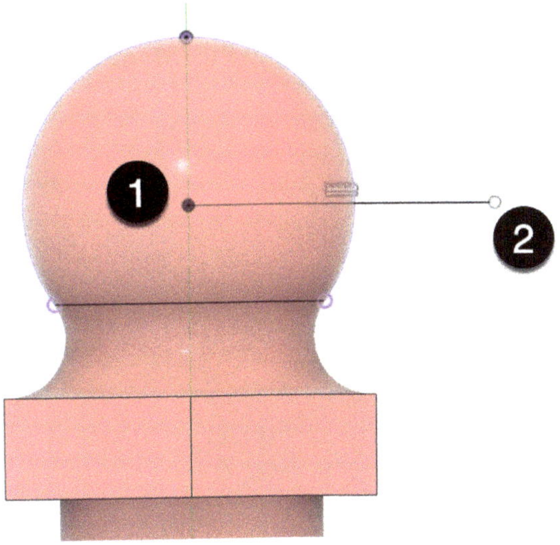

30. Press ESC.
31. Click **Finish Sketch** on the toolbar.
32. On the toolbar, click **Solid** tab > **Construct** panel > **Plane at angle**.
33. Select the newly created line.
34. Type 45 in the **Angle** box and click **OK**.

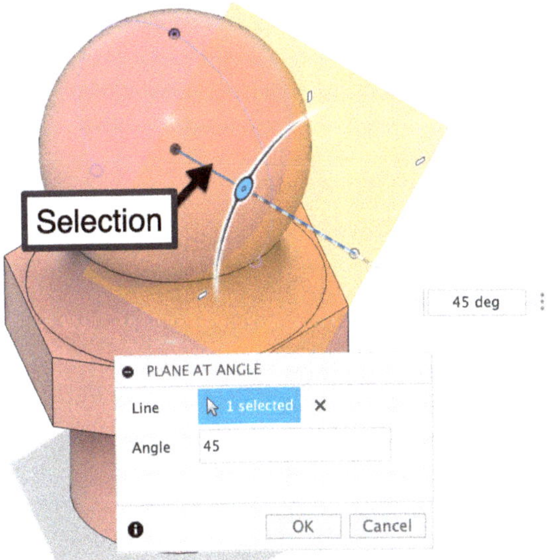

35. On the toolbar, click **Solid** tab > **Construct** panel > **Offset Plane**.
36. Select the newly created plane.
37. Type **1.37** in the **Distance** box.
38. Click **OK**.

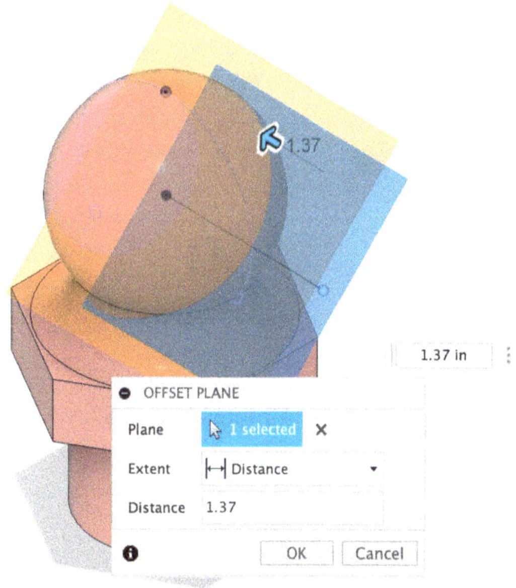

39. On the toolbar, click **Solid** tab > **Construct** panel > **Create Sketch**.
40. Select the newly created plane.
41. On the toolbar, click **Sketch** tab > **Create** panel > **Project/Include** > **Intersect**.
42. Select the sphere and click **OK**.

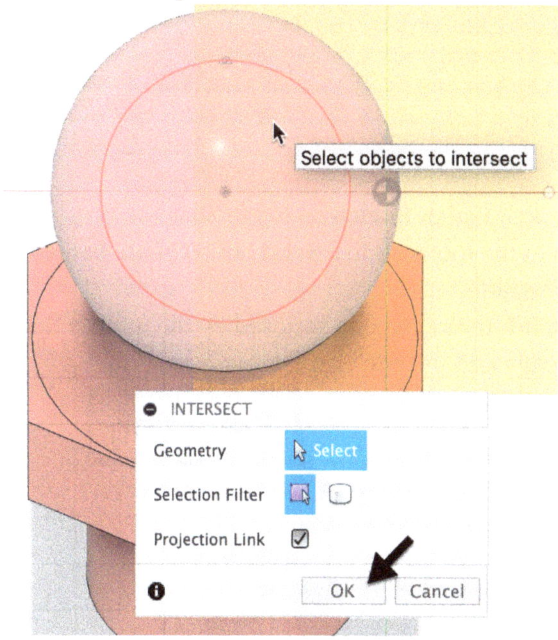

43. On the toolbar, click **Sketch** tab > **Create** panel > **Center Diameter Circle**.
44. Select the centerpoint of the intersection edge.
45. Move the pointer outward and click.

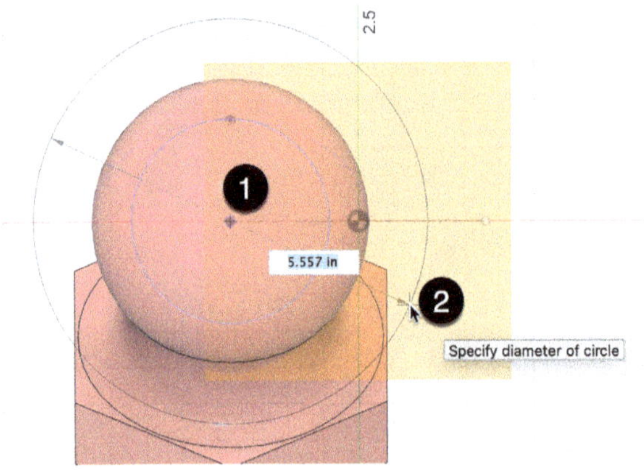

46. Change the diameter dimension to **3.5**.

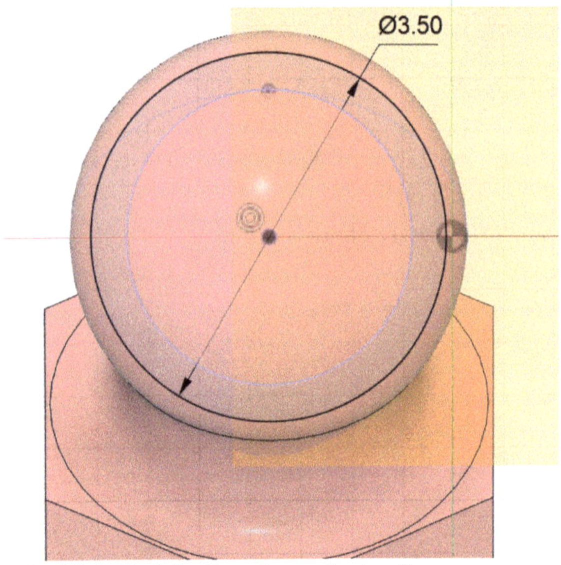

47. Click **Finish Sketch** on the toolbar.
48. On the toolbar, click **Solid** tab > **Create** panel > **Extrude**.
49. Click in the regions enclosed by the intersection edge and the circle.

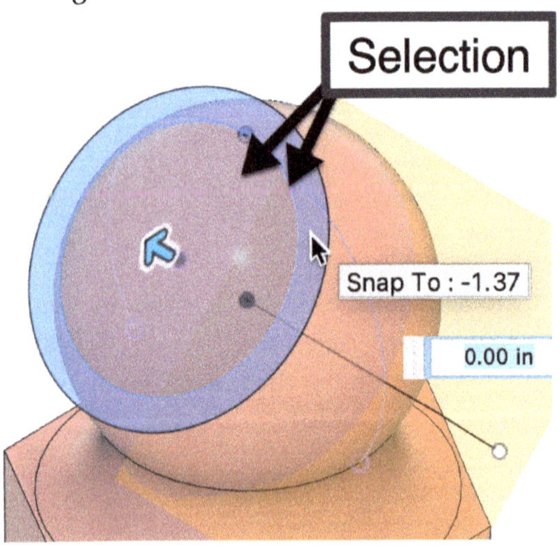

50. On the **Extrude** dialog, select **Operation > Cut**.
51. Select the **All** option from the **Extents Type** drop-down.
52. Click **OK**.

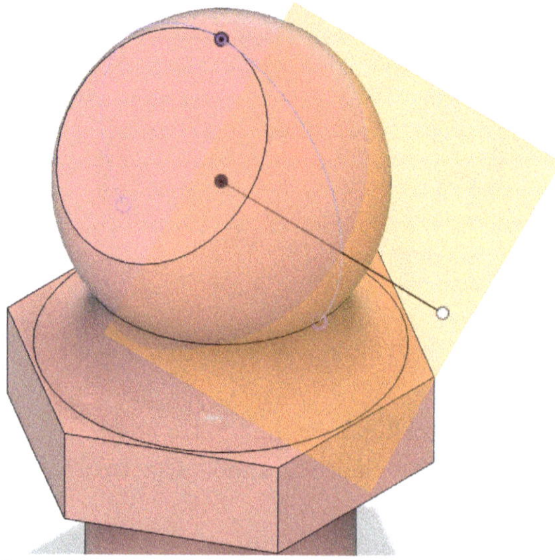

Creating the Revolved Feature

1. On the toolbar, click **Solid** tab > **Create** panel > **Create Sketch**.
2. Select the YZ plane.

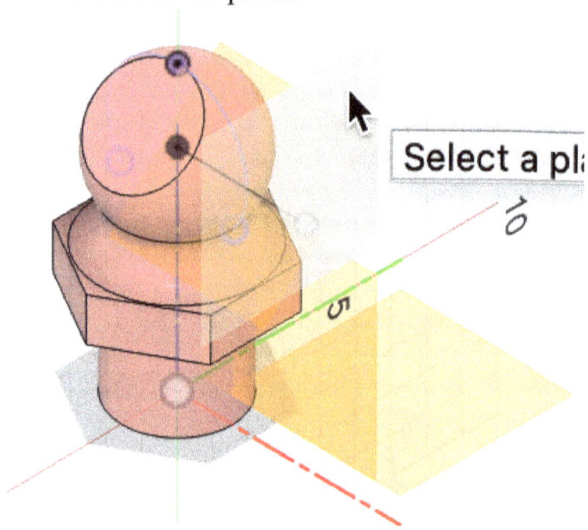

3. Create the sketch, as shown.

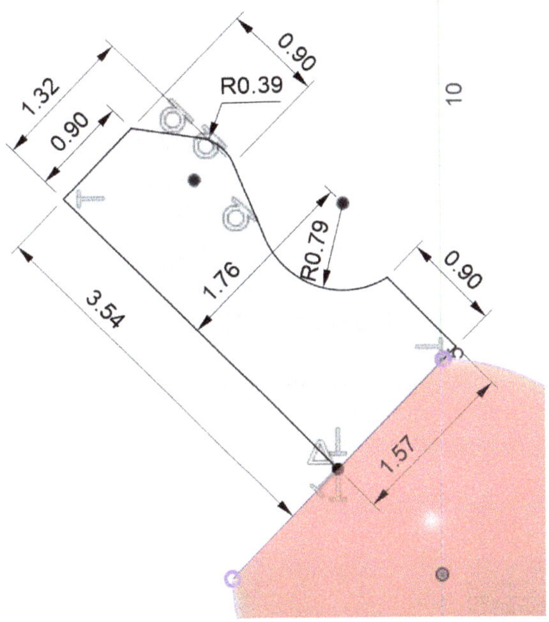

4. Click **Finish Sketch** on the toolbar.
5. Select the axis of revolution, as shown.

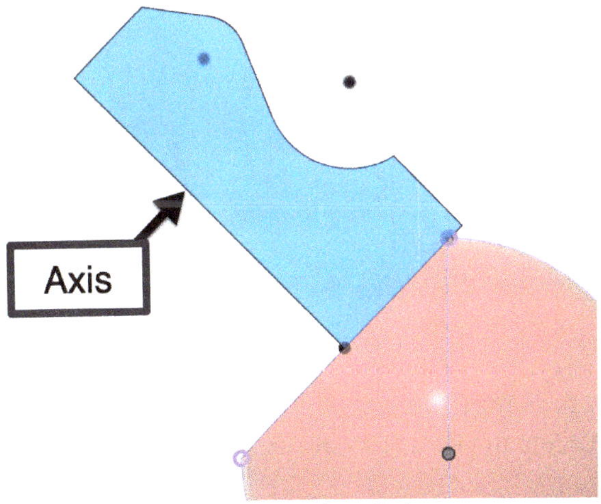

6. Click **OK** on the **Revolve** dialog.

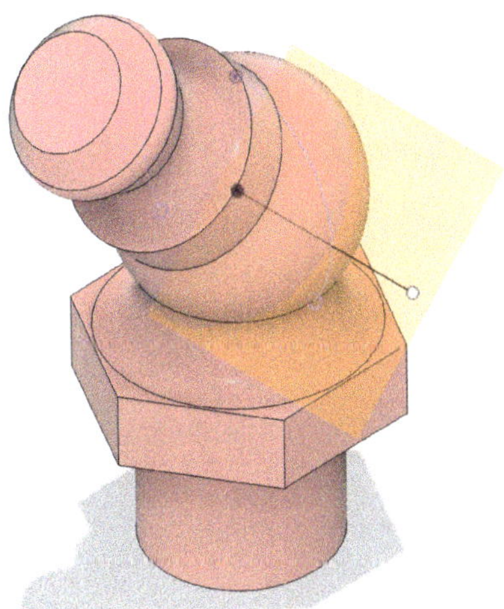

Creating the Extruded Cut Features

1. On the toolbar, click **Solid** tab > **Create** panel > **Create Sketch**.
2. Rotate the model and click on the flat face of the revolved feature, as shown.

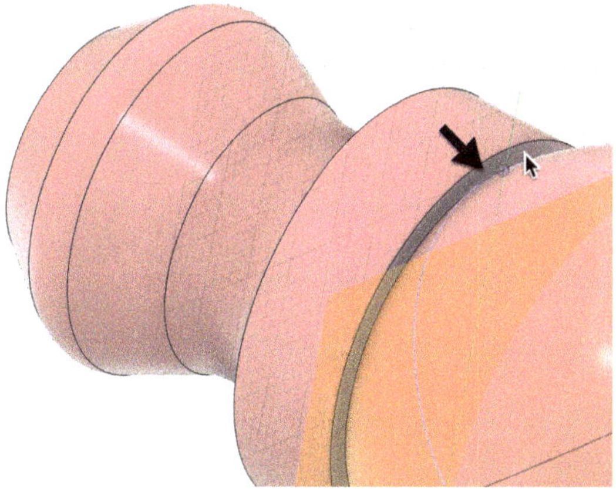

3. Check the **Slice** option on the **Sketch Palette**.
4. Create the sketch, as shown.

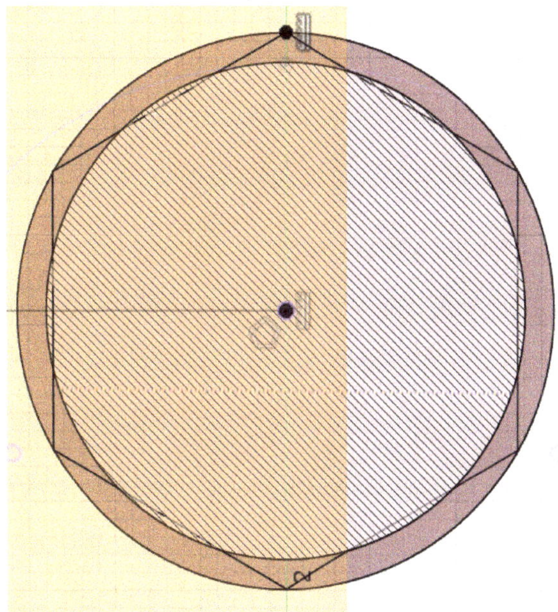

5. Click **Finish Sketch** on the toolbar.
6. On the toolbar, click **Solid** tab > **Create** panel > **Extrude**.
7. Click in the regions between the polygon and the circular edge.

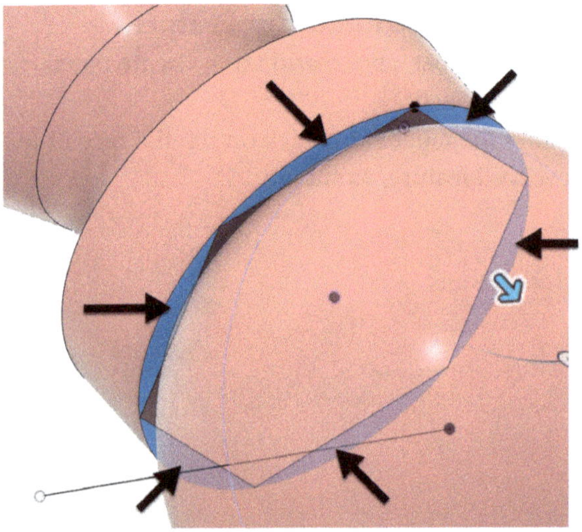

8. On the **Extrude** Dialog, select **Operation > Cut**.
9. Select the **All** option from the **Extents Type** drop-down.
10. Click the **Flip** button.
11. Click **OK**.

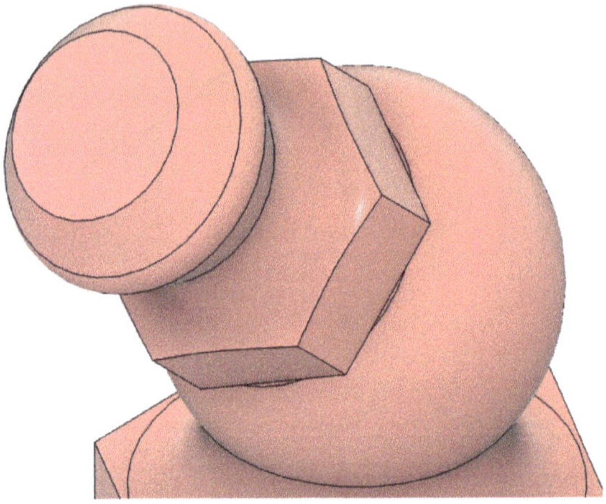

12. On the toolbar, click **Solid** tab > **Create** panel > **Hole**
13. Select the flat face of the revolved feature, as shown.

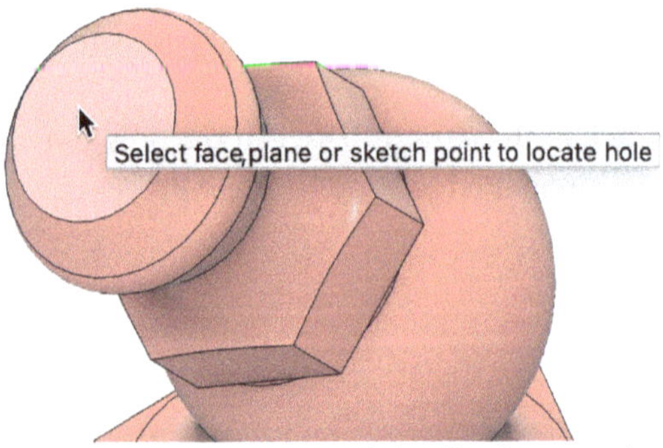

14. Select the circular edge of the flat face, as shown.

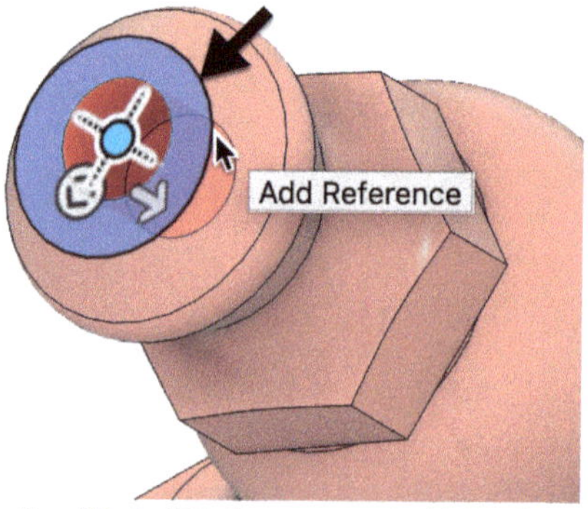

15. On the **Hole** Dialog, type **5.11** in the **Depth** box.
16. Type **0.67** in the **Diameter** box.
17. Click **OK**.

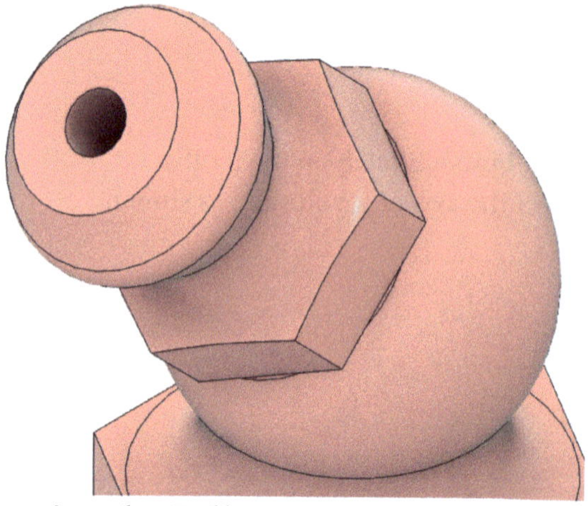

Creating the Ball

1. On the toolbar, click **Solid** tab > **Create** panel > **Create Sketch**.
2. Select the YZ plane.
3. Check the **Slice** option on the Sketch Palette.
4. Create the sketch, as shown.

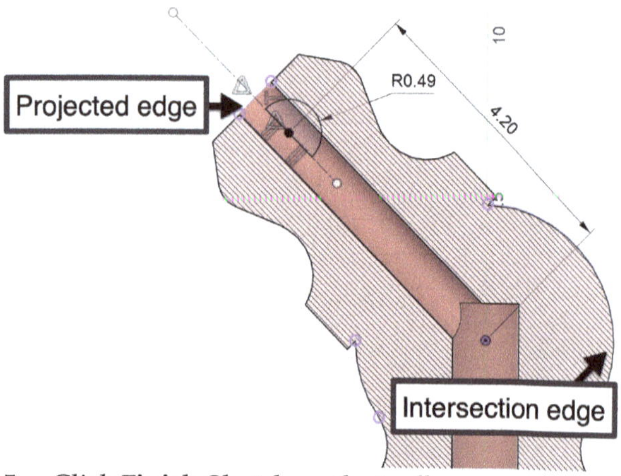

5. Click **Finish Sketch** on the toolbar.

6. On the toolbar, click **Solid** tab > **Create** panel > **Revolve**.
7. Select **Operation > New Body**.
8. Click **OK** on the **Revolve** dialog.

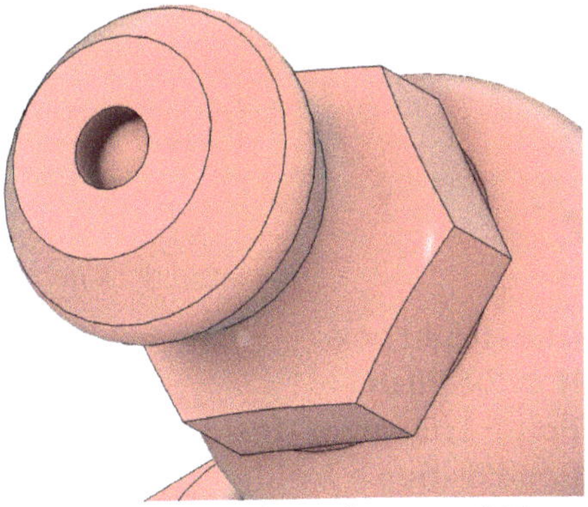

Creating the Chamfers and Rounds

1. On the toolbar, click **Solid** tab > **Modify** panel > **Chamfer**.
2. On the **Chamfer** dialog, select **Equal Distance** from the drop-down.
3. Select the circular edge, as shown.

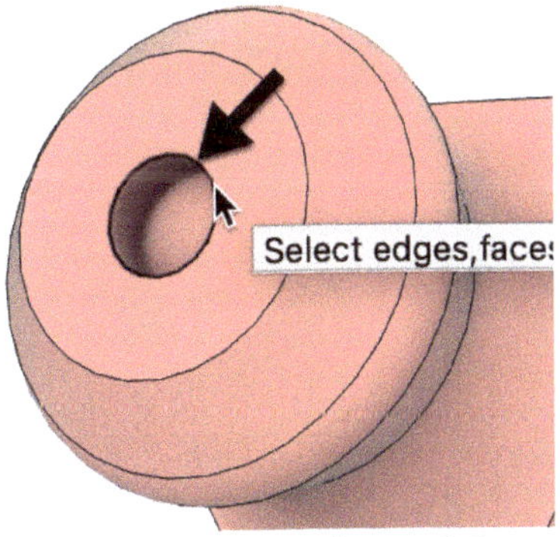

4. Set the **Distance** value to **0.1**.

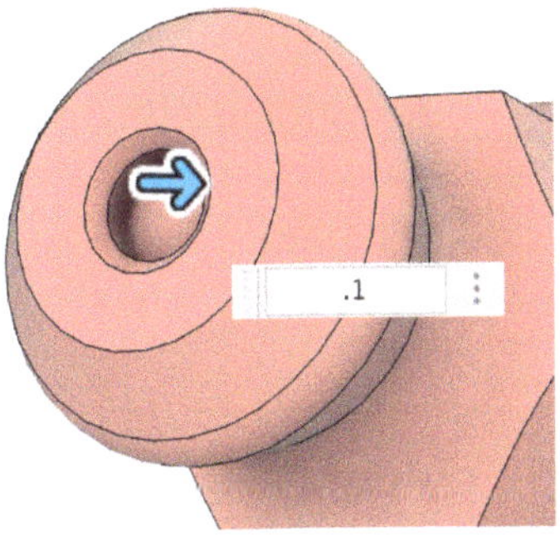

5. Click **OK**.
6. Likewise, chamfer the circular edge of the bottom face, as shown. The chamfer distance is **0.3**.

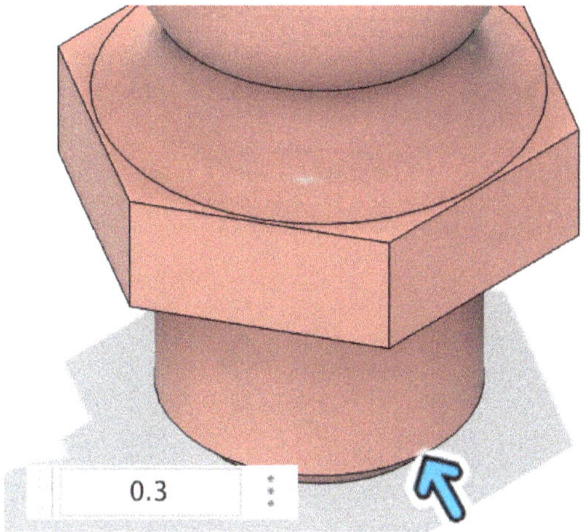

7. On the toolbar, click **Solid** tab > **Modify** panel > **Fillet**.
8. Select the circular edge, as shown.
9. Type **0.3** in the **Radius** box on the **Fillet** dialog.
10. Click **OK**.

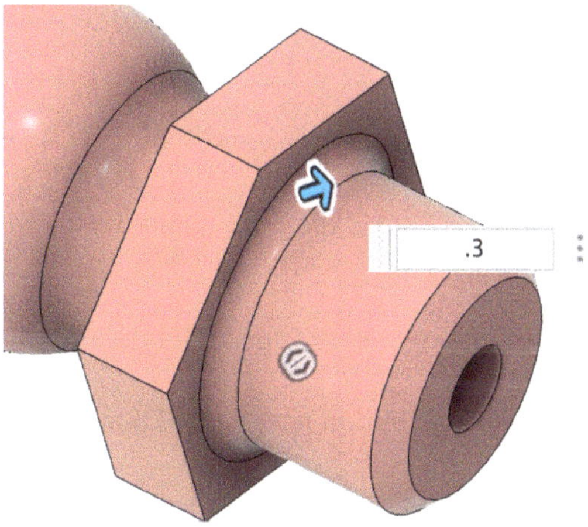

Creating the Helical Swept Cut

1. Create a plane offset from the XY plane. The offset distance is **1.85** inches.

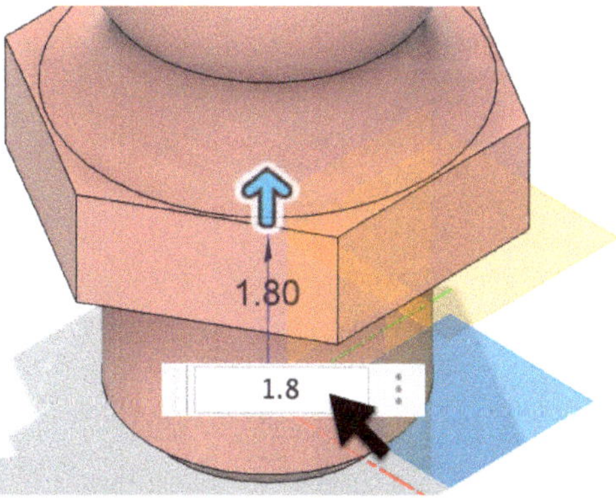

2. On the toolbar, click **Solid** tab > **Create** panel > **Coil** .
3. Select the newly created offset plane.

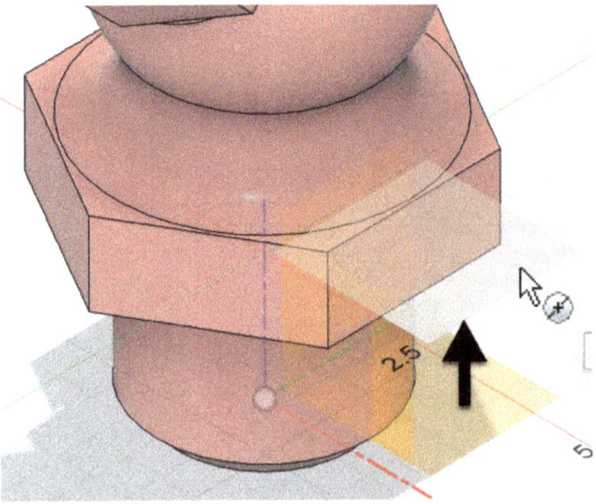

4. Select the sketch origin.
5. Move the pointer outward and click.

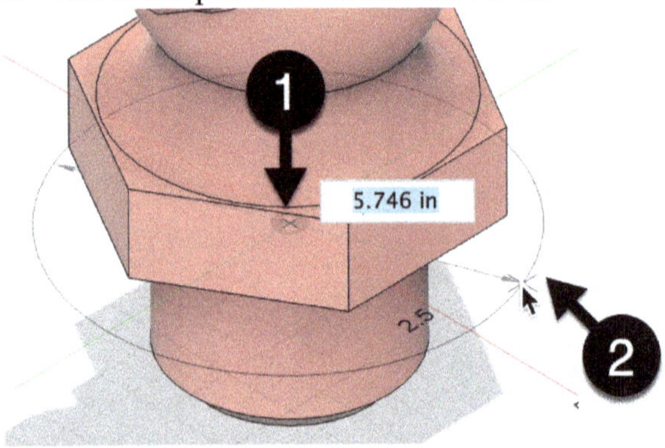

6. On the **Coil** dialog, select **Type > Height and Pitch**.
7. Click the **Options** button next to the **Diameter** box.
8. Select the **Measure** option and click on the circular edge, as shown.

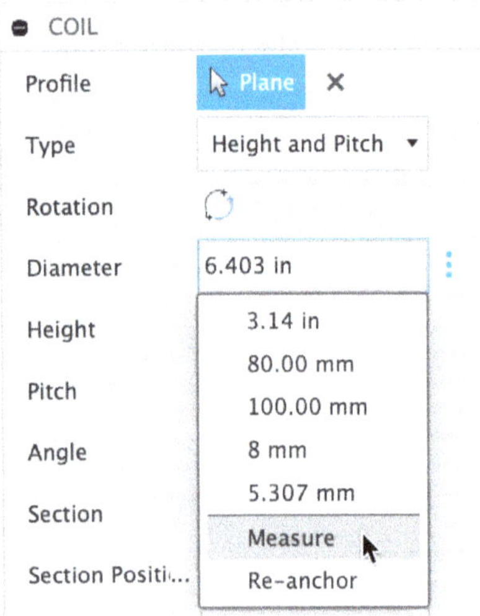

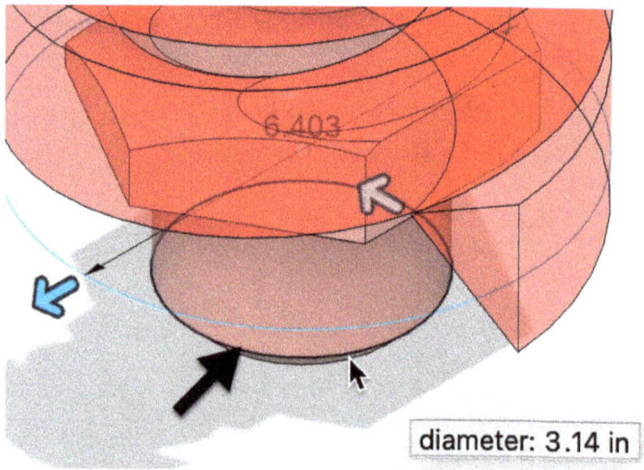

9. Type **-3** in the **Height** box.
10. Type **-0.394** in the **Pitch** box.
11. Select **Section > Triangular (Inside)**.
12. Select **Section Position > Inside**.
13. Type **0.394** in the **Section Size** box.
14. Select **Operation > Cut**.

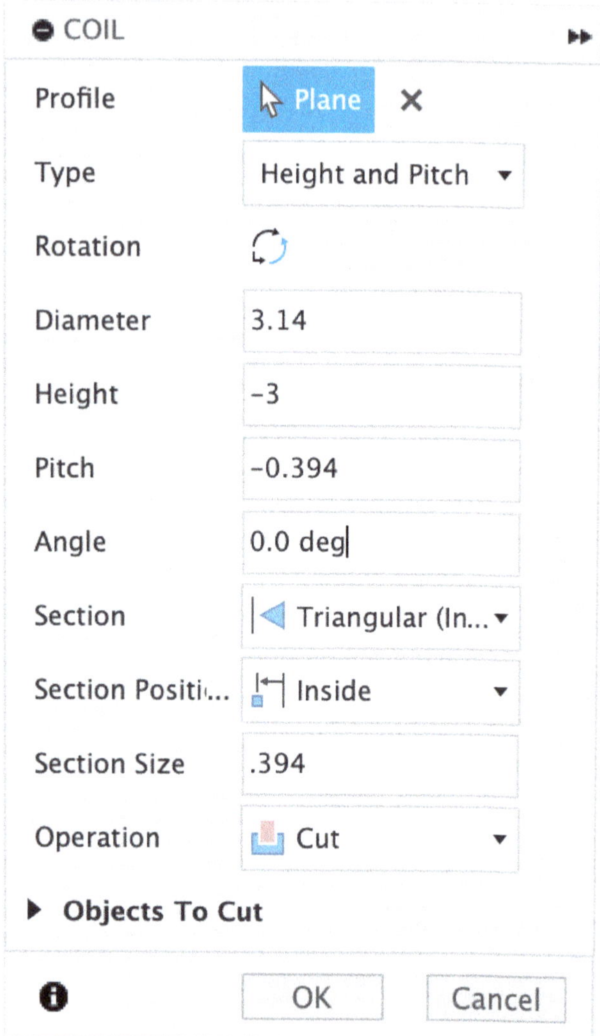

15. Click **OK** to create the coil.

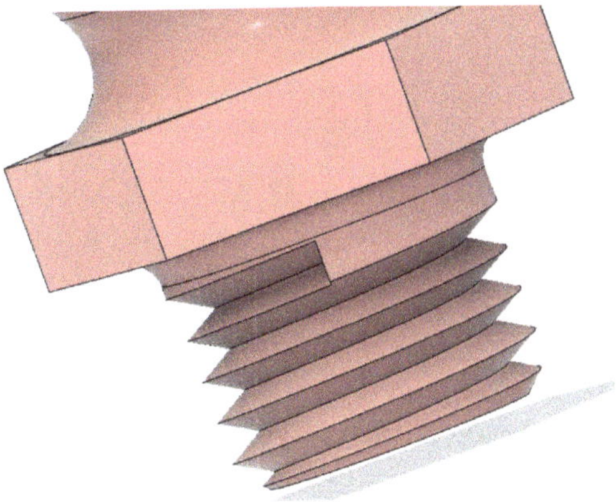

16. Apply fillet of 0.02 inch to the inner edge of the coil.

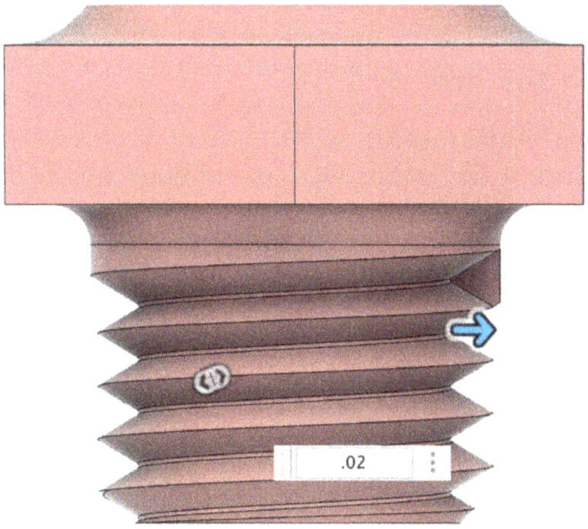

17. Save and close the design file.

Example 4 (Millimeters)

In this example, you will create the part shown below.

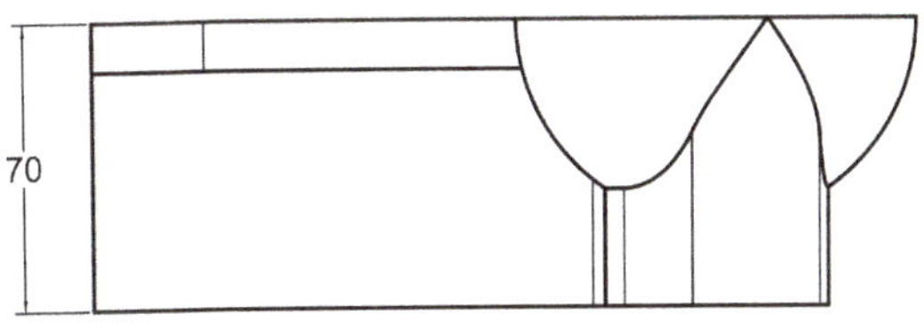

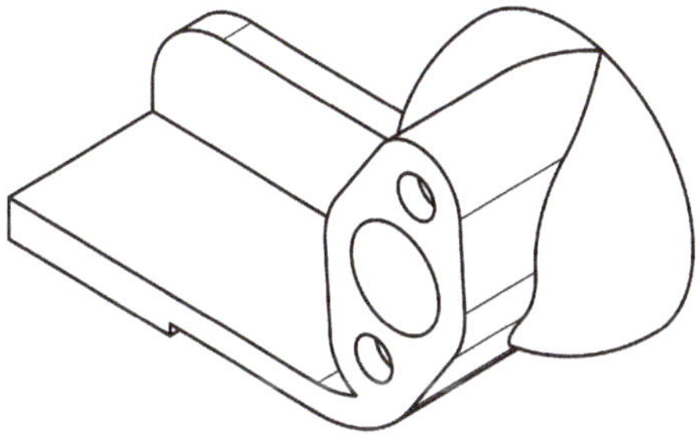

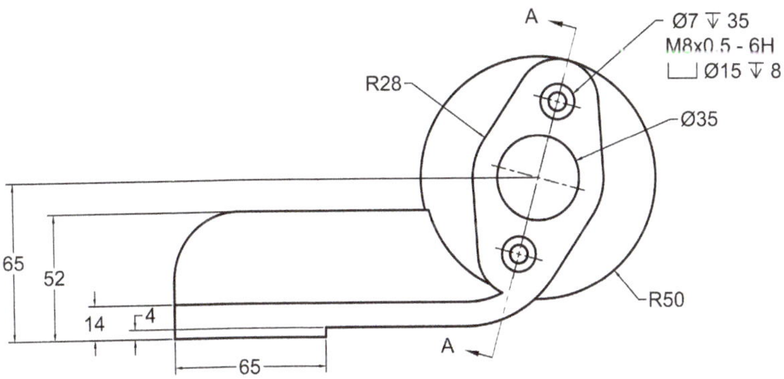

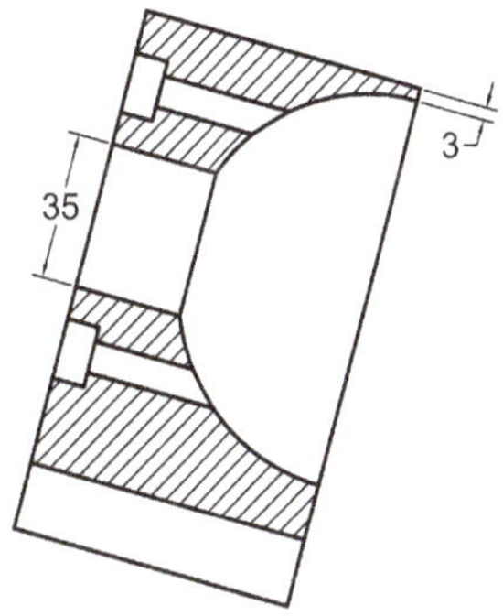

SECTION A-A
SCALE 1:1

Creating the First Feature

1. Start **Autodesk Fusion 360** by double-clicking the **Autodesk Fusion 360** icon on your desktop.
2. On the **Browser window**, expand **Document Settings** and place the cursor on **Units**; the **Change Active Units** icon appears.
3. Click on the **Change Active Units** icon to change the units; the **Change Active Units** dialog appears.
4. On this dialog, select **Unit Type > millimeter (mm), gram (g)** from the drop-down and click **OK**.
5. To start a sketch, click **Create > Create Sketch** on the toolbar. Click on the XZ plane. The sketch starts.
6. On the toolbar, click **Sketch** tab > **Create** panel > **Center Diameter Circle**.
7. Click on the origin point to define the centerpoint.
8. Move the pointer outward and click.
9. On the toolbar, click **Sketch** tab > **Create** panel > **Line**.
10. Select the top and bottom quadrant points of the circle.

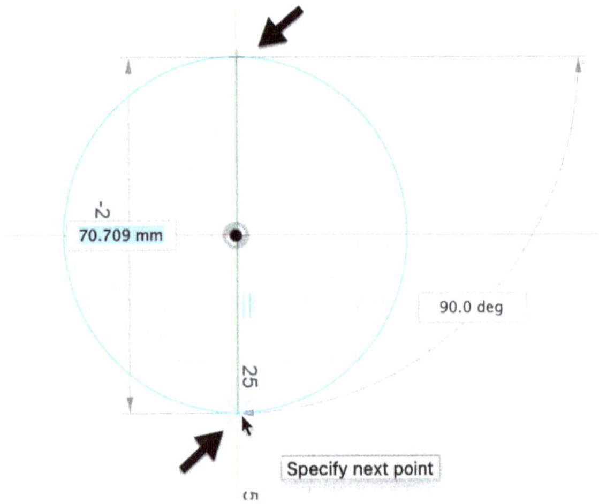

11. On the toolbar, click **Sketch** tab > **Modify** panel > **Trim**.
12. Click on the element to trim, as shown.

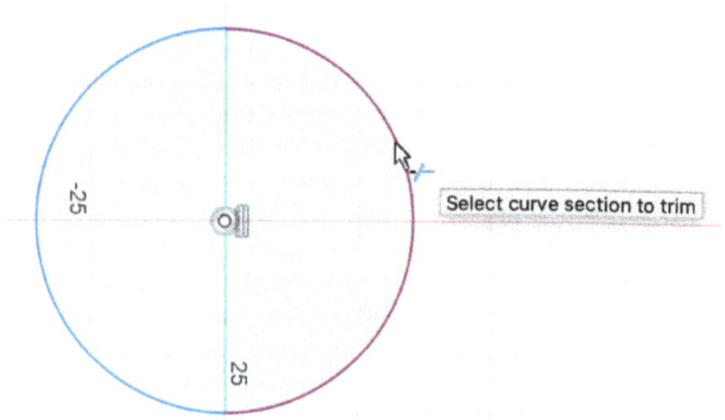

13. Add dimension to the vertical line, as shown.

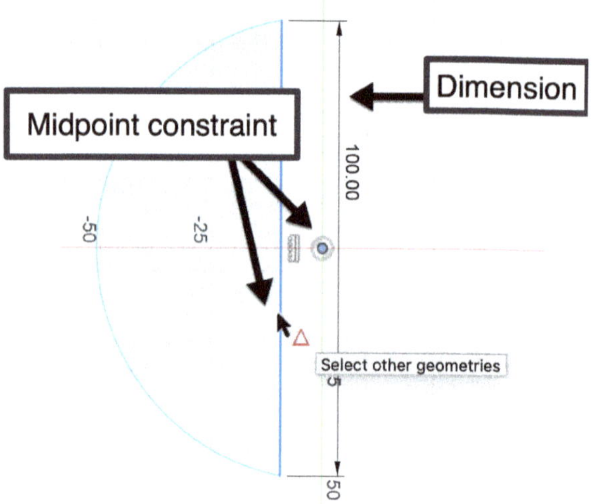

14. Click **Finish Sketch**.
15. On the toolbar, click **Solid** tab > **Create** panel > **Revolve**.
16. Select the sketch.
17. Click on the line passing through the origin.
18. On the **Revolve** dialog, type-in 180 in the **Angle** box and press ENTER.

Creating the Extruded Features

1. On the toolbar, click **Solid** tab > **Create** panel > **Create Sketch**.

2. Click on the XZ plane.
3. Create three circles, as shown.
4. Apply the **Equal** constraint between the two circles, as shown.

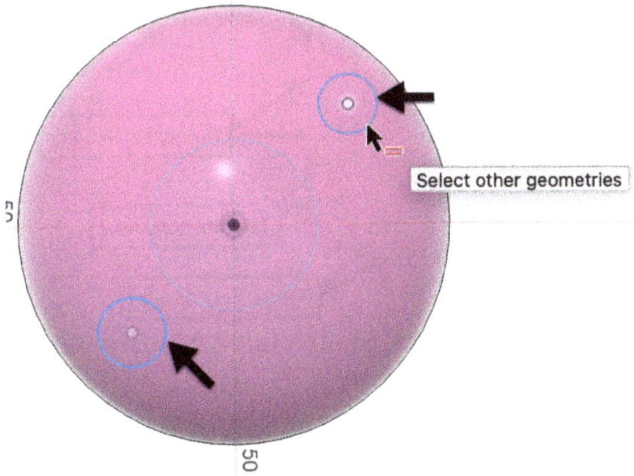

5. On the Sketch Palette, click **Options** > **Linetype** > **Construction**.
6. On the toolbar, click **Sketch** tab > **Create** panel > **Line**.
7. Select the centerpoints of the two circles, as shown.

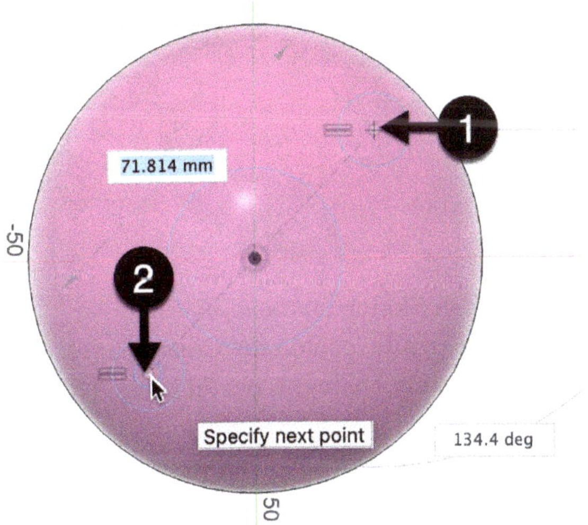

8. Press ESC.
9. On the toolbar, click **Sketch** tab > **Constraints** panel > **MidPoint**.
10. Select the centerpoint of the large circle.
11. Select the construction line.

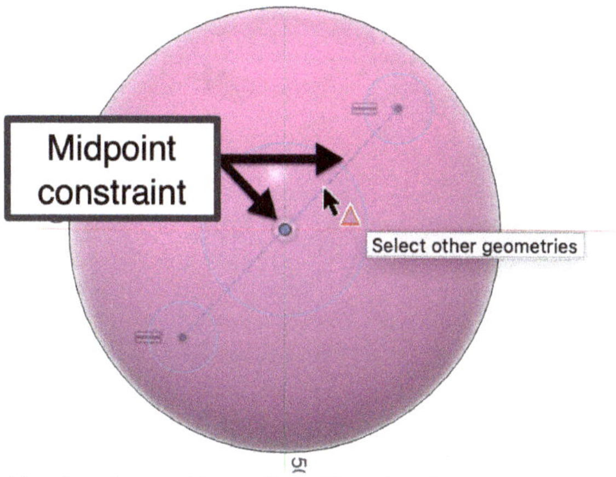

12. On the toolbar, click **Sketch** tab > **Constraints** panel > **Tangent**.
13. Select the small circle and the circular edge; the two entities are made tangent to each other.

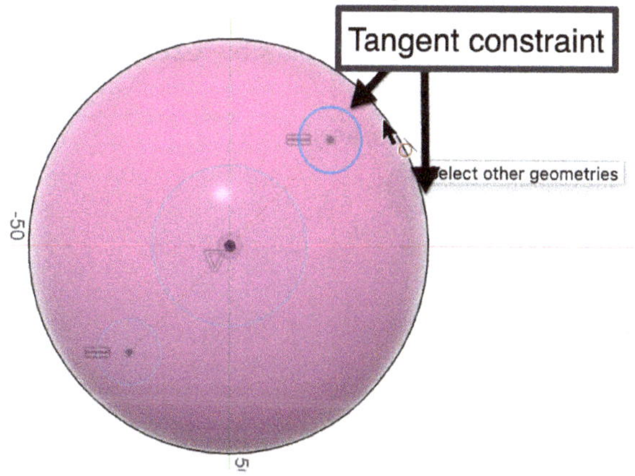

14. Create a vertical construction line, as shown.

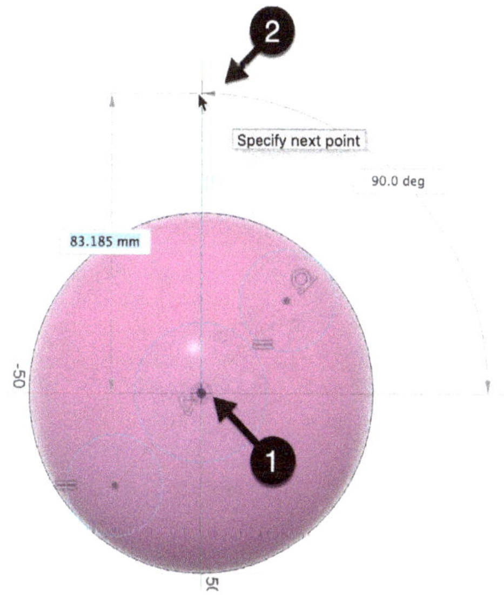

15. On the toolbar, click **Sketch** tab > **Create** panel > **Dimension**.
16. Create the dimensions, as shown.

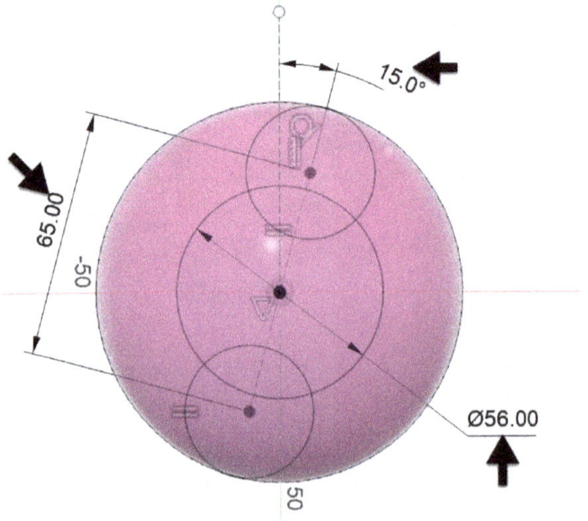

17. Deactivate the **Construction** icon on the **Sketch Palette**.
18. On the toolbar, click **Sketch** tab > **Create** panel > **Line**.
19. Select the two circles, as shown.

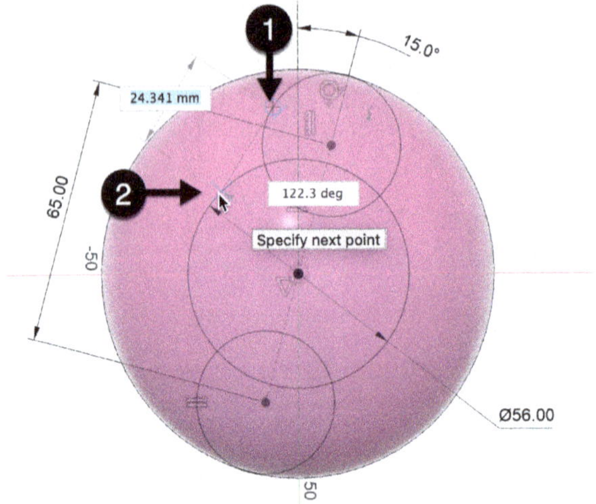

20. Likewise, create three more tangent lines, as shown.

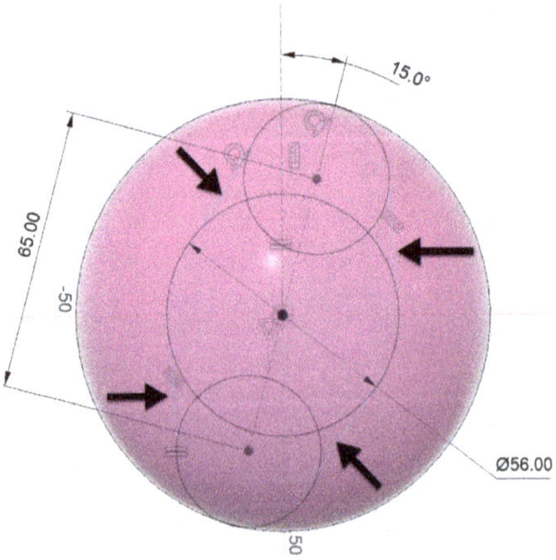

21. Apply the **Tangent** constraints between the lines and the circles.

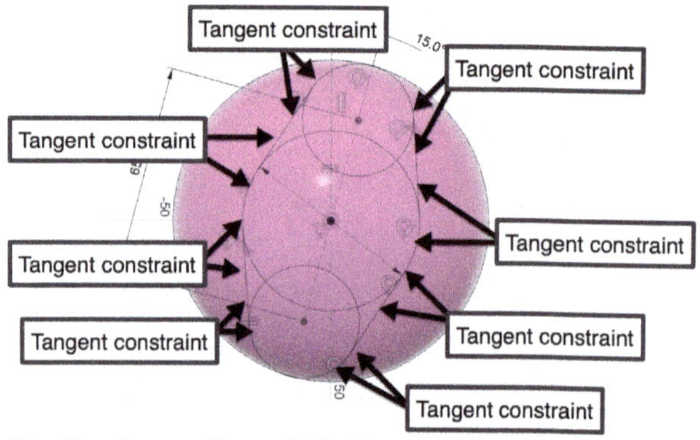

22. On the toolbar, click **Sketch** tab > **Modify** panel > **Trim**.
23. Select the inner segments of the circles, as shown.

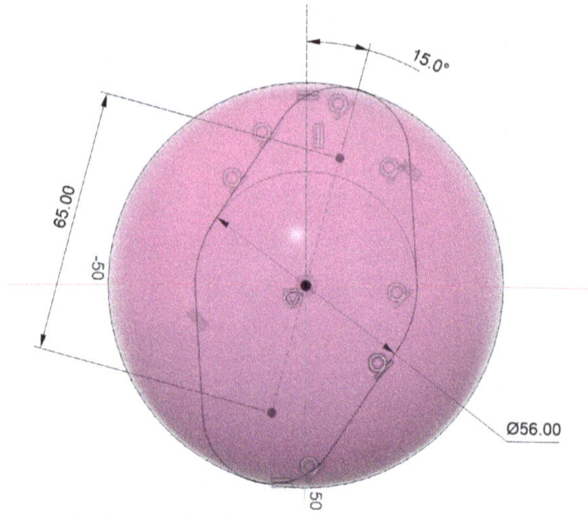

24. Click **Finish Sketch** on the toolbar.
25. Click the **Extrude** icon on the **Create** panel.
26. On the **Extrude** Dialog, type **-70** in the **Distance** box.
27. Click **OK** on the **Extrude** Dialog.

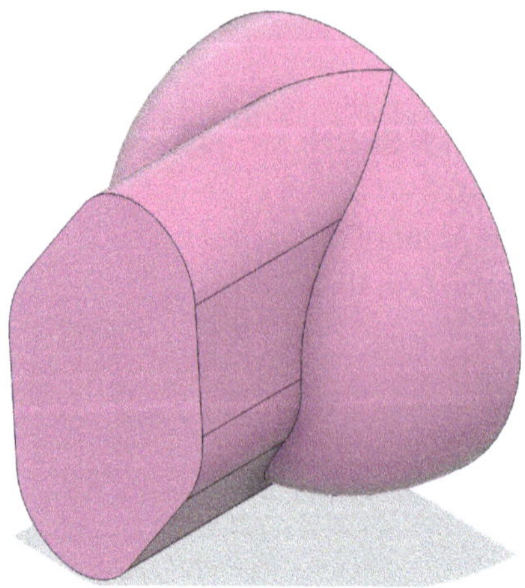

28. On the toolbar, click **Solid** tab > **Create** panel > **Create Sketch**.
29. Click on the XZ plane.
30. On the toolbar, click **Sketch** tab > **Create** panel > **Line**.
31. Create four lines, as shown.

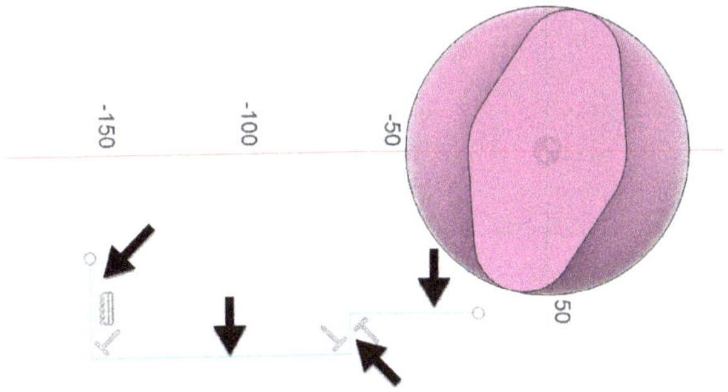

32. On the toolbar, click **Sketch** tab > **Create** panel > **Arc** drop-down > **Tangent Arc**.
33. Select the end point of the right horizontal line.
34. Move the pointer toward right and click, as shown.

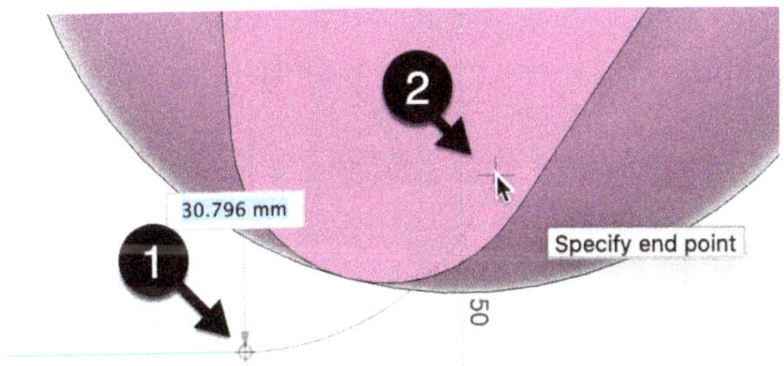

35. On the toolbar, click **Sketch** tab > **Constraints** panel > **Tangent**.
36. Select the newly created arc and the circular edge.

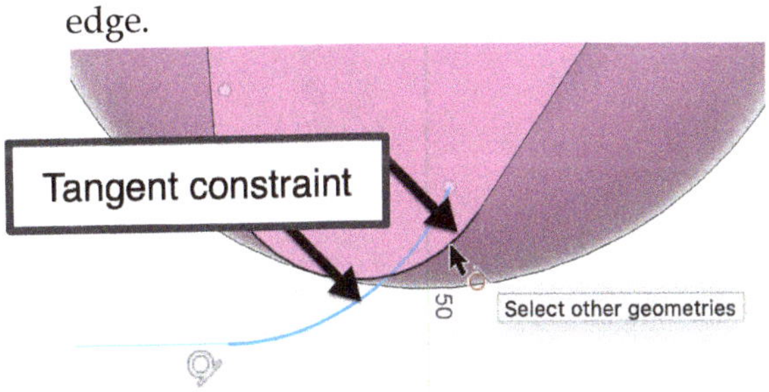

37. On the toolbar, click **Sketch** tab > **Constraints** panel > **Coincident**.
38. Select the endpoint of the newly created arc and the circular edge.

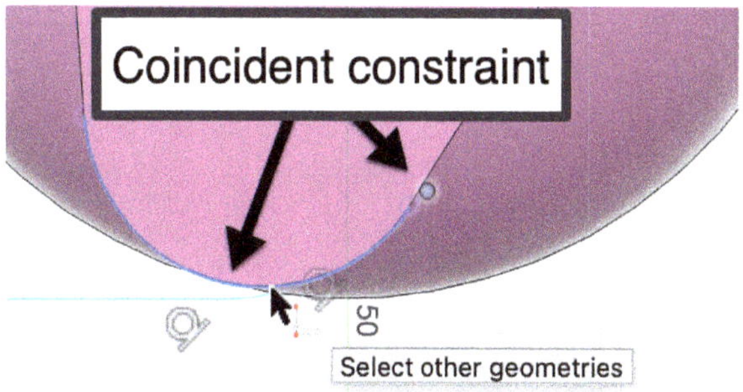

39. On the toolbar, click **Sketch** tab > **Modify** panel > **Offset**.
40. Deselect the **Chain Selection** option from the **Offset** dialog.
41. Select the arc and horizontal line, as shown.

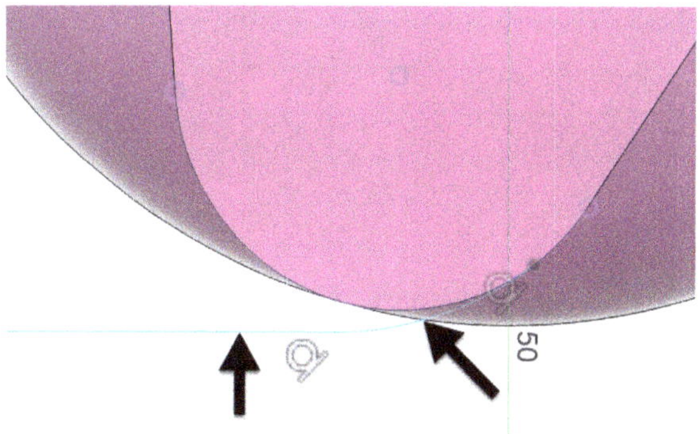

42. Type-in the **Offset position** value and click **OK**.

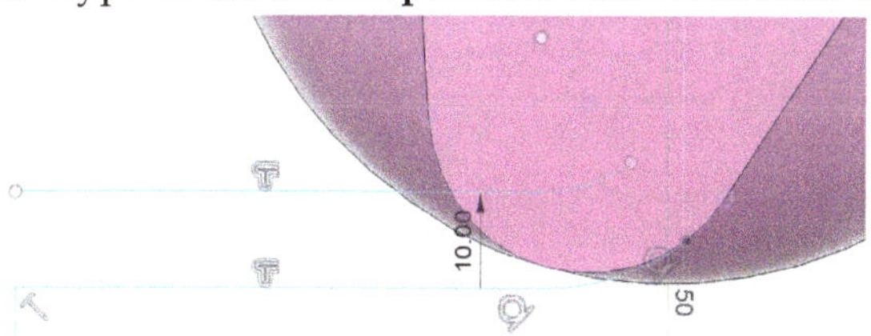

43. On the toolbar, click **Sketch** tab > **Modify** panel > **Extend**.
44. Select horizontal line, as shown.

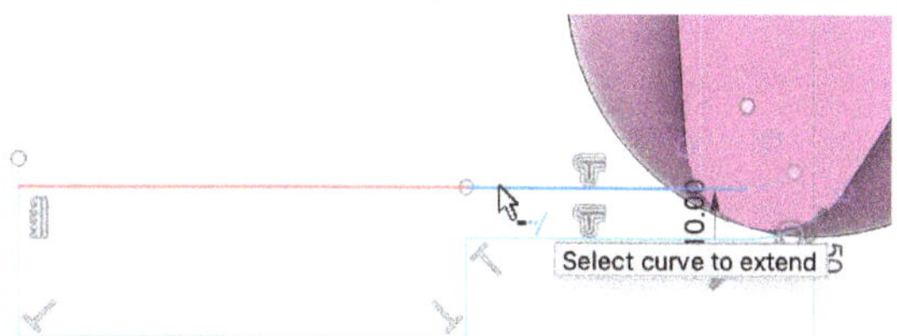

45. On the toolbar, click **Sketch** tab > **Modify** panel > **Trim**.
46. Select the unwanted portion of the vertical line, as shown.

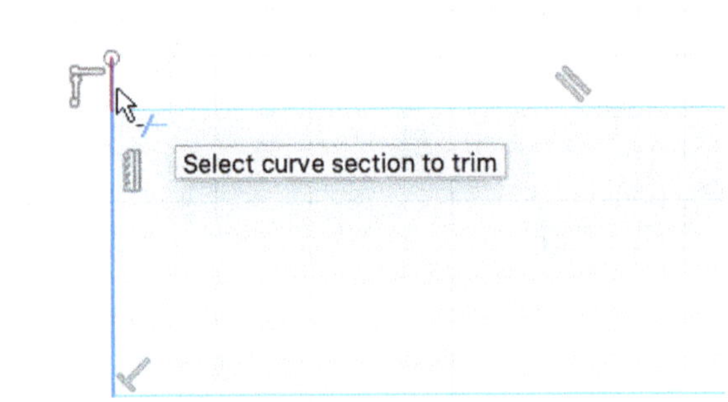

47. Create a line connecting the end points of the arcs, as shown.

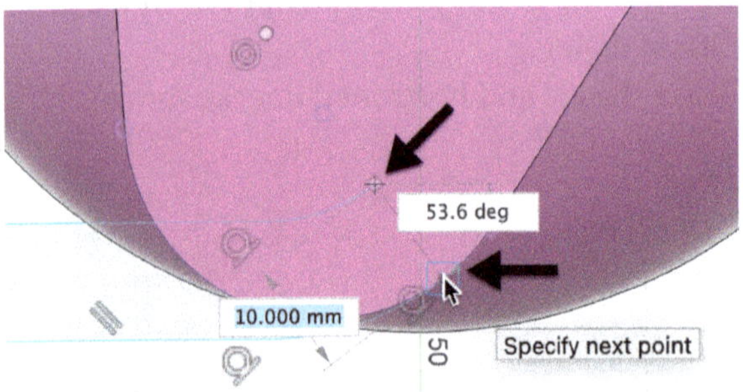

48. On the toolbar, click **Sketch** tab > **Constraints** panel > **Coincident**.
49. Select the endpoint of the arc and the quadrant point of the circular edge.

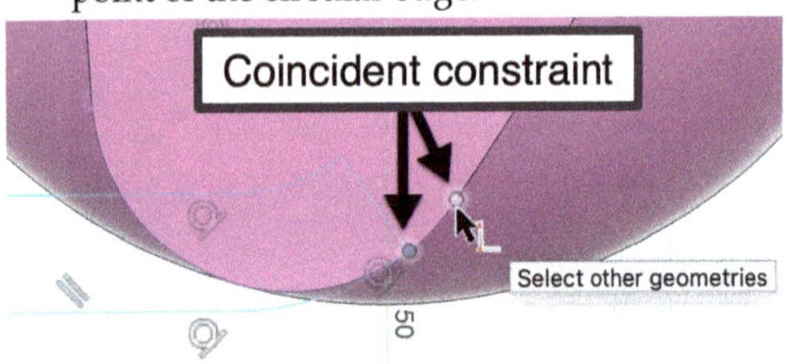

50. Add dimensions to the sketch, as shown.

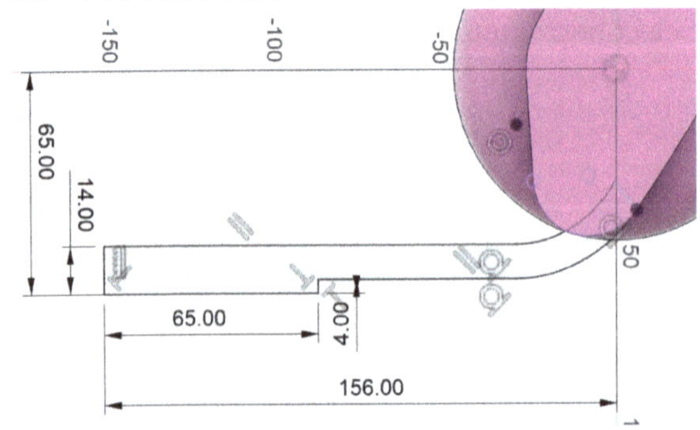

51. On the toolbar, click **Sketch** tab > **Constraints** panel > **Perpendicular**.
52. Select the line and linear edge, as shown.

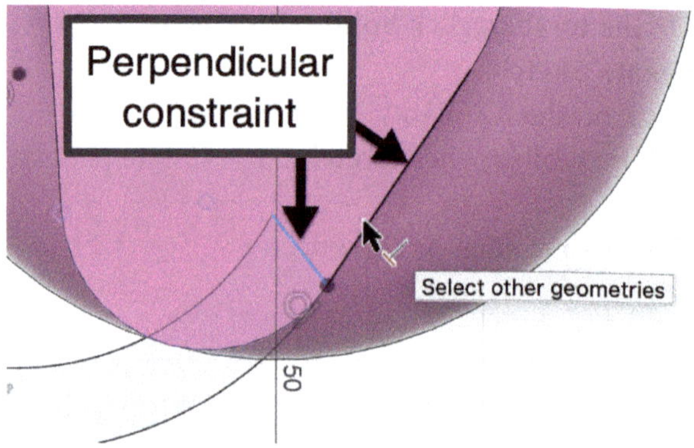

53. Click **Finish Sketch** on the toolbar.
54. Click the **Extrude** icon on the **Create** panel.
55. Click in the region enclosed by the sketch.
56. On the **Extrude** dialog, select **To Object** from the **Extent Type** drop-down.
57. Select the flat end face of the extruded feature, as shown.

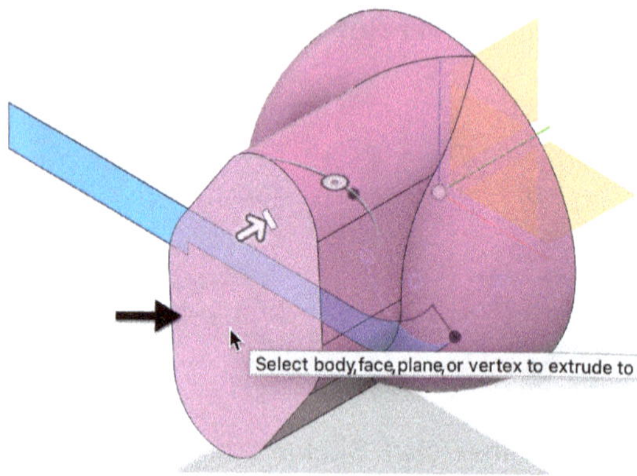

58. Select **Join** from the **Operation** drop-down.
59. Click **OK** on the **Extrude** Dialog.

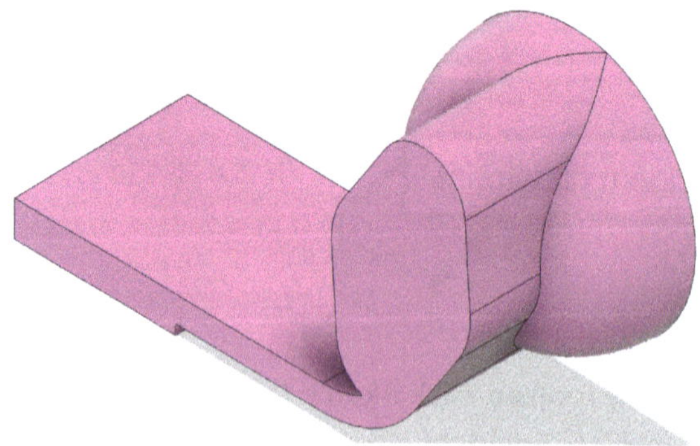

60. On the toolbar, click **Solid** tab > **Create** panel > **Create Sketch**.
61. Click on the XZ plane.
62. On the toolbar, click **Sketch** tab > **Create** panel > **Project/Include** > **Project**.
63. Select the horizontal and curved edges, as shown.

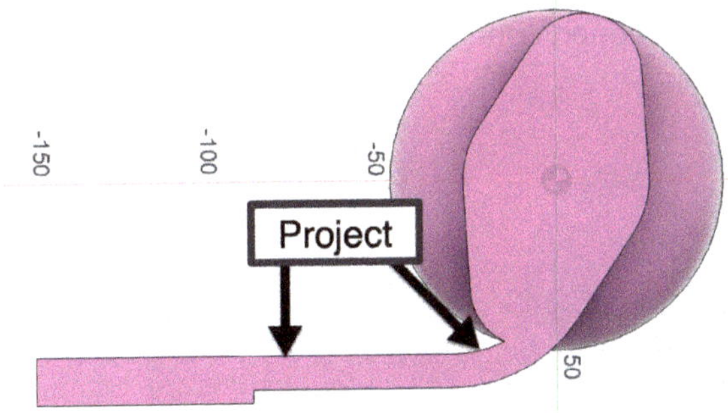

64. Click **OK** on the **Project** dialog.
65. On the toolbar, click **Sketch** tab > **Create** panel > **Line**.
66. Create two lines, as shown.

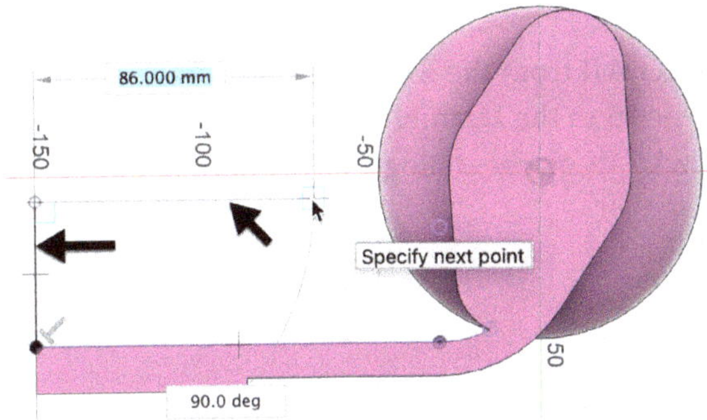

67. Add a fillet and dimensions to the sketch, as shown.

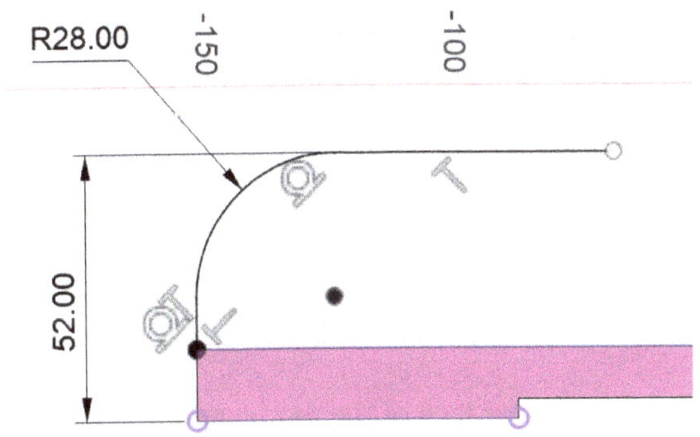

68. Click **Finish Sketch** on the toolbar.
69. On the toolbar, click **Solid** tab > **Create** panel > **Rib**.
70. Select the newly created sketch,
71. On the **Rib** dialog, select **Thickness Options > One Direction**.
72. Select **Depth Options > To Next**.
73. Type **-12** in the **Thickness** box.
74. Click the **Flip** icon.

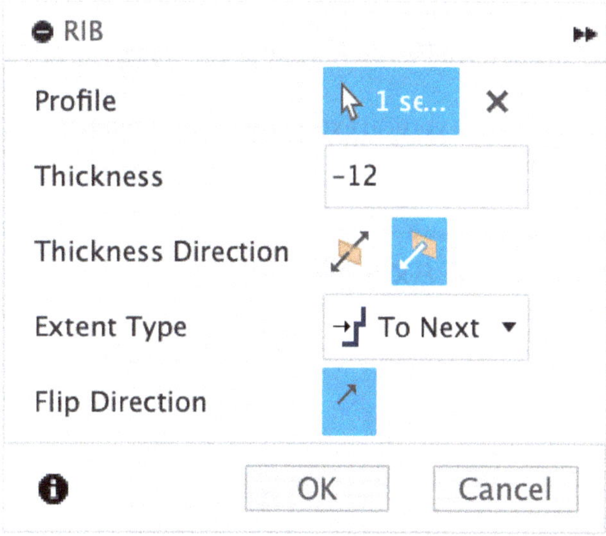

75. Click **OK** on the **Rib** dialog.

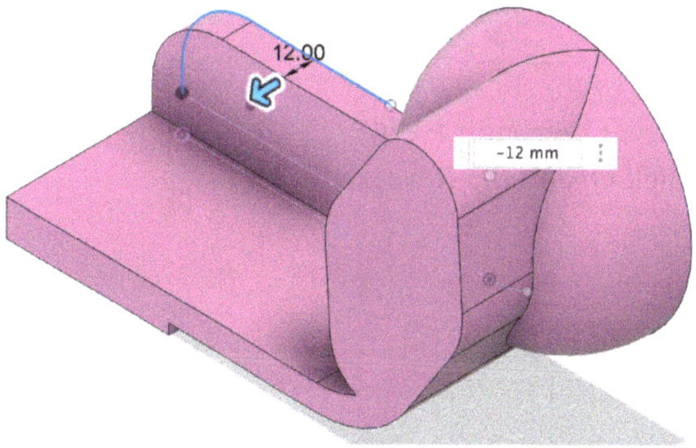

Creating the Revolved Cut Feature

1. On the toolbar, click **Solid** tab > **Create** panel > **Create Sketch**.
2. Select the XZ plane.
3. Create an arc and line, as shown.

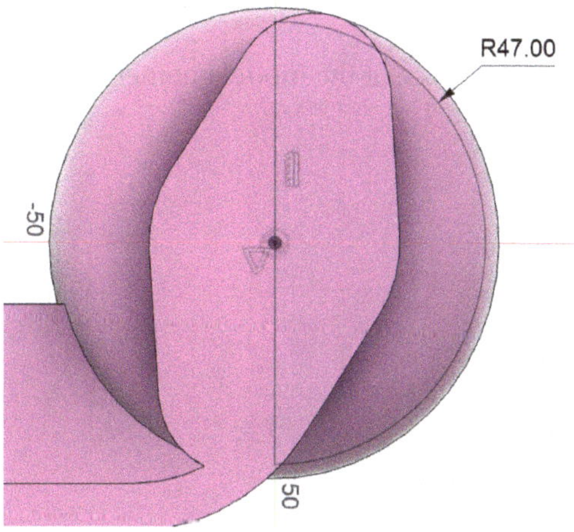

4. Click **Finish Sketch** on the toolbar.
5. On the toolbar, click **Solid** tab > **Create** panel > **Revolve**.
6. Select the vertical axis to define the revolution axis.

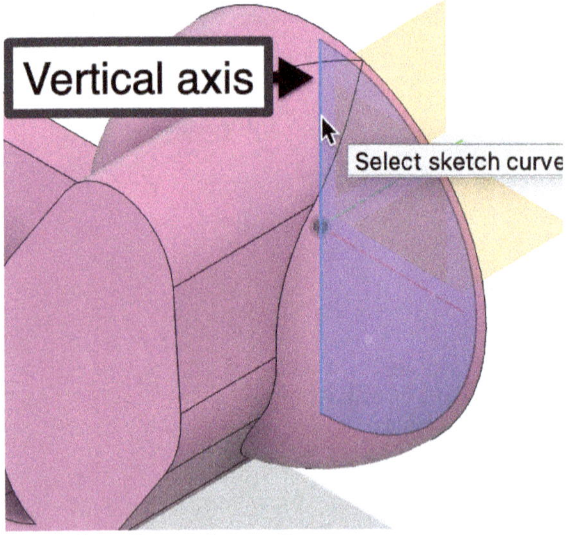

7. Select **Operation > Cut**.
8. Click **OK** on the **Revolve** dialog.

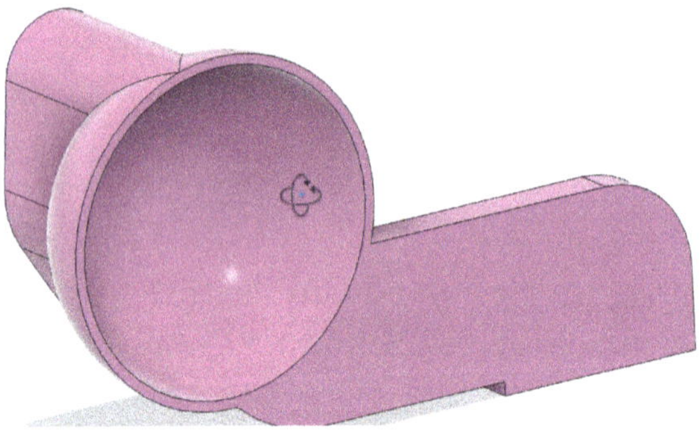

Creating the Hole Features

1. On the toolbar, click **Solid** tab > **Create** panel > **Hole**.
2. Select the front face of the model geometry.

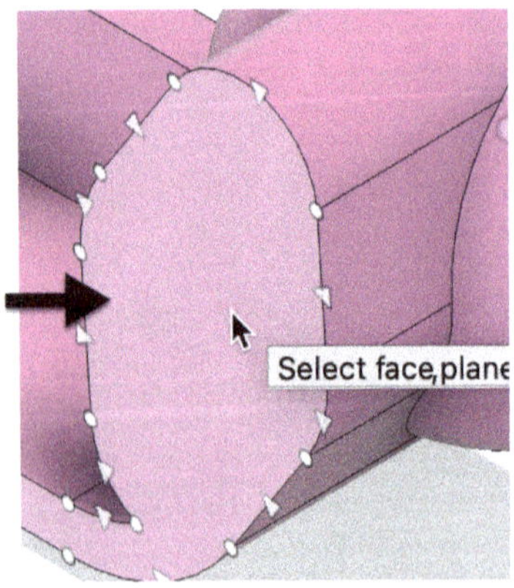

3. Select the curved edge of the front face; the hole is positioned concentric to the curved edge.

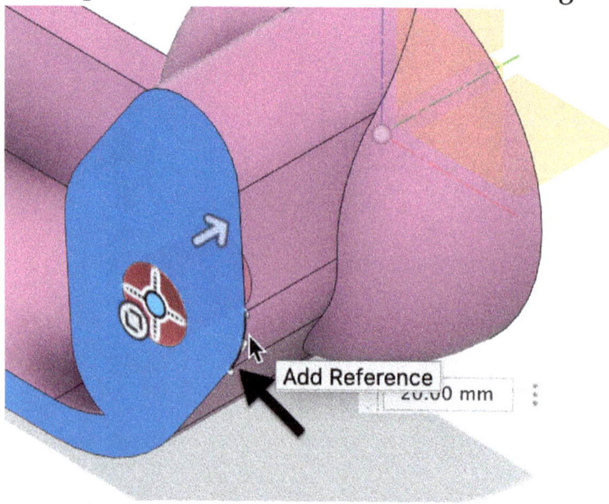

9. Select **All** from the **Extents** drop-down.
10. Type **35** in the **Diameter** box.
11. Click **OK** on the dialog.

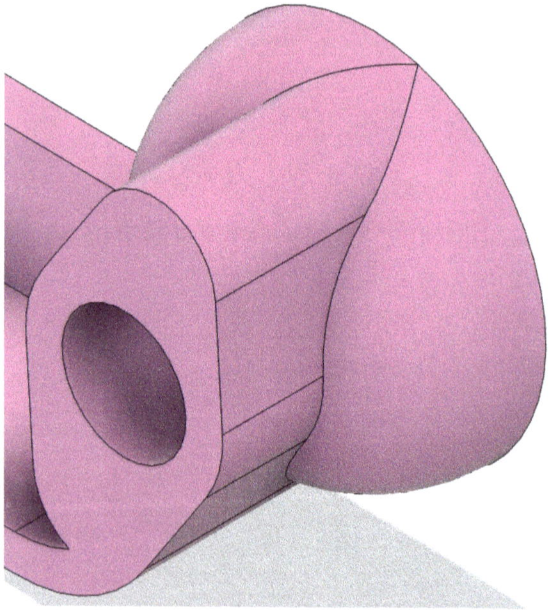

12. Select the front face of the model geometry.

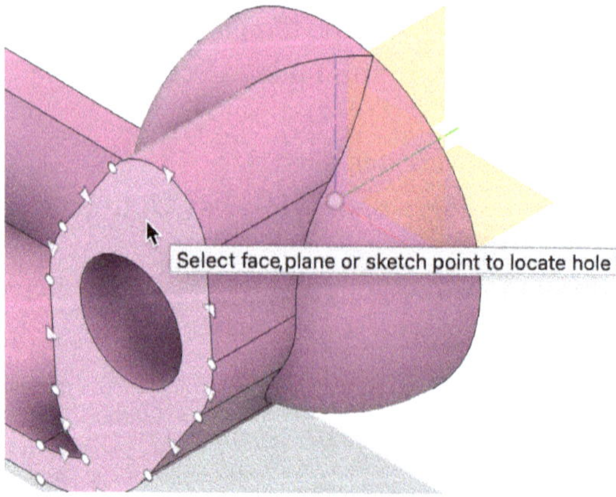

13. Select the curved edge of the model, as shown.

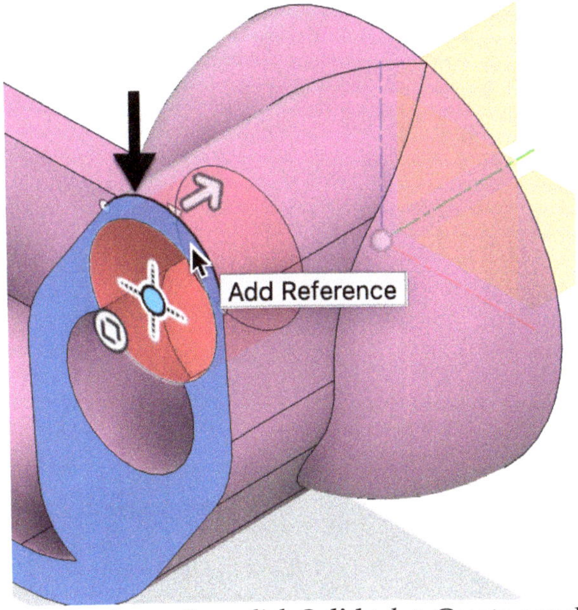

14. On the toolbar, click **Solid** tab > **Create** panel > **Hole**.
15. Select **Extents > All**.
16. On the **Hole** dialog, select **Hole Type > Counterbore**.
17. Select **Hole Tap Type > Tapped**.
18. Set the **Thread Type** to **ISO Metric Profile**.
19. Select 8 mm from the Size drop-down.
20. Select **M8X.5** from the **Designation** drop-down.
21. Type **14.5** in the **Counterbore Diameter** box.
22. Type **8** in the **Counterbore Depth** box.
23. Click **OK**.

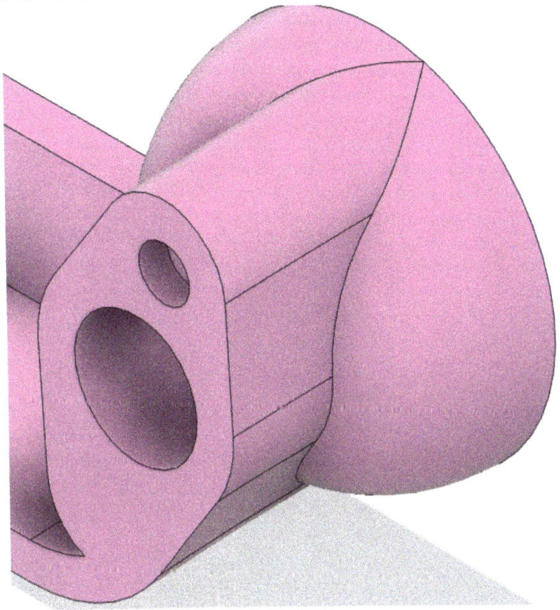

24. Likewise, create another hole, as shown.

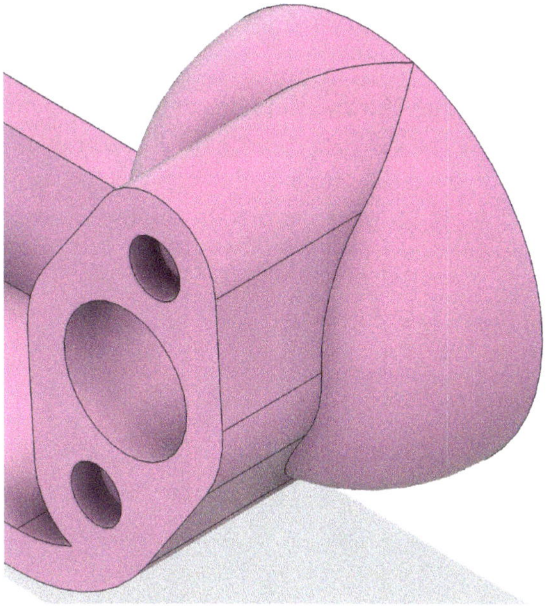

Creating the Rounds

1. On the toolbar, click **Solid > Modify > Fillet**.
2. Select the edges in the sequence, as shown.

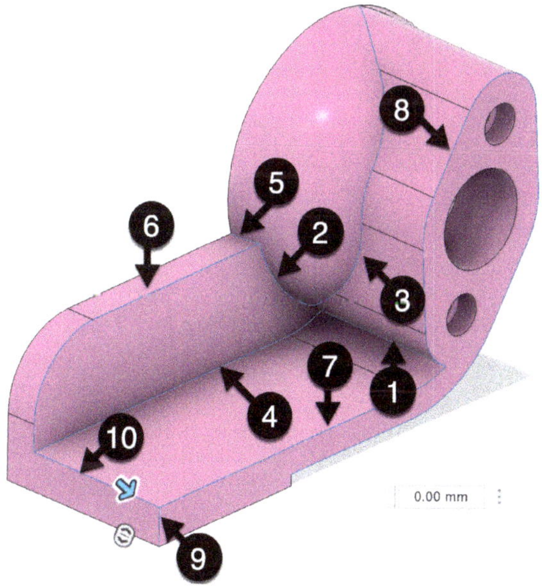

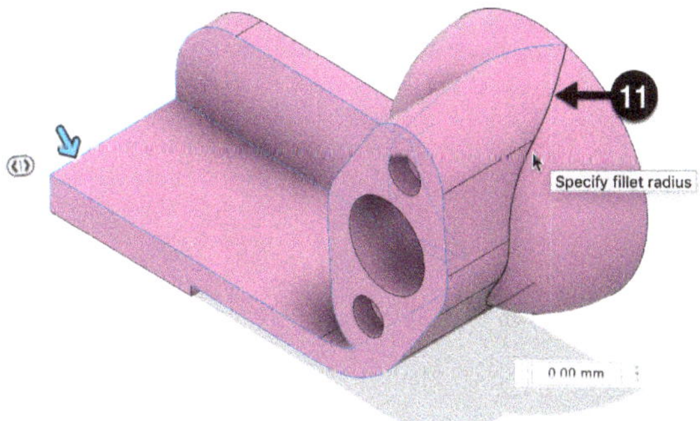

3. Type **4** in the **Radius** box and click **OK**.
4. Save and close the file.

Questions

1. What are the Thickness options of the **Web** command?
2. What are the Depth options in the **Rib** command?
3. Why do we create multi-body parts?
4. What are the commands used to emboss a text on a model?

Exercises

Exercise 1 (Millimeters)

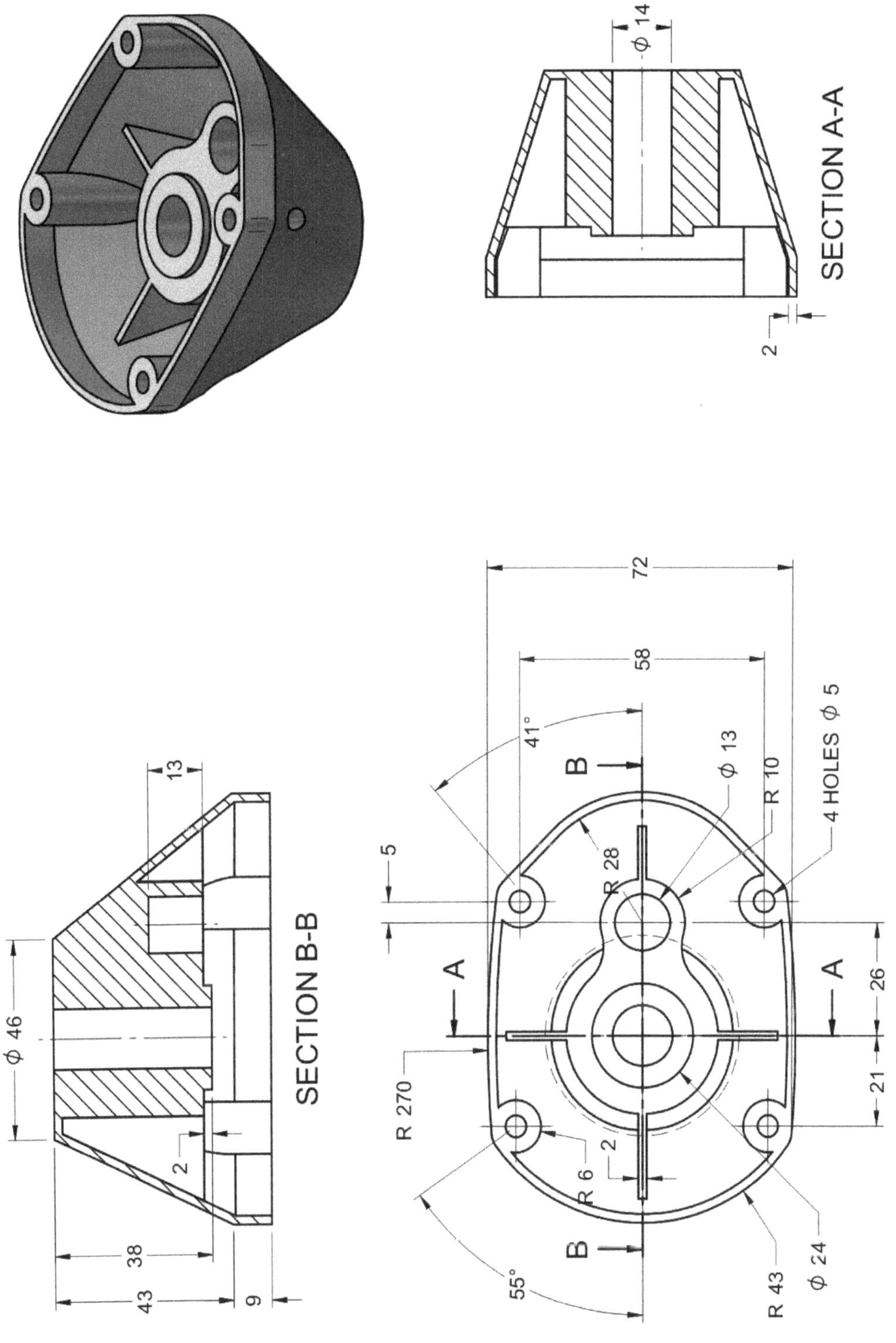

Exercise 2 (Millimeters)

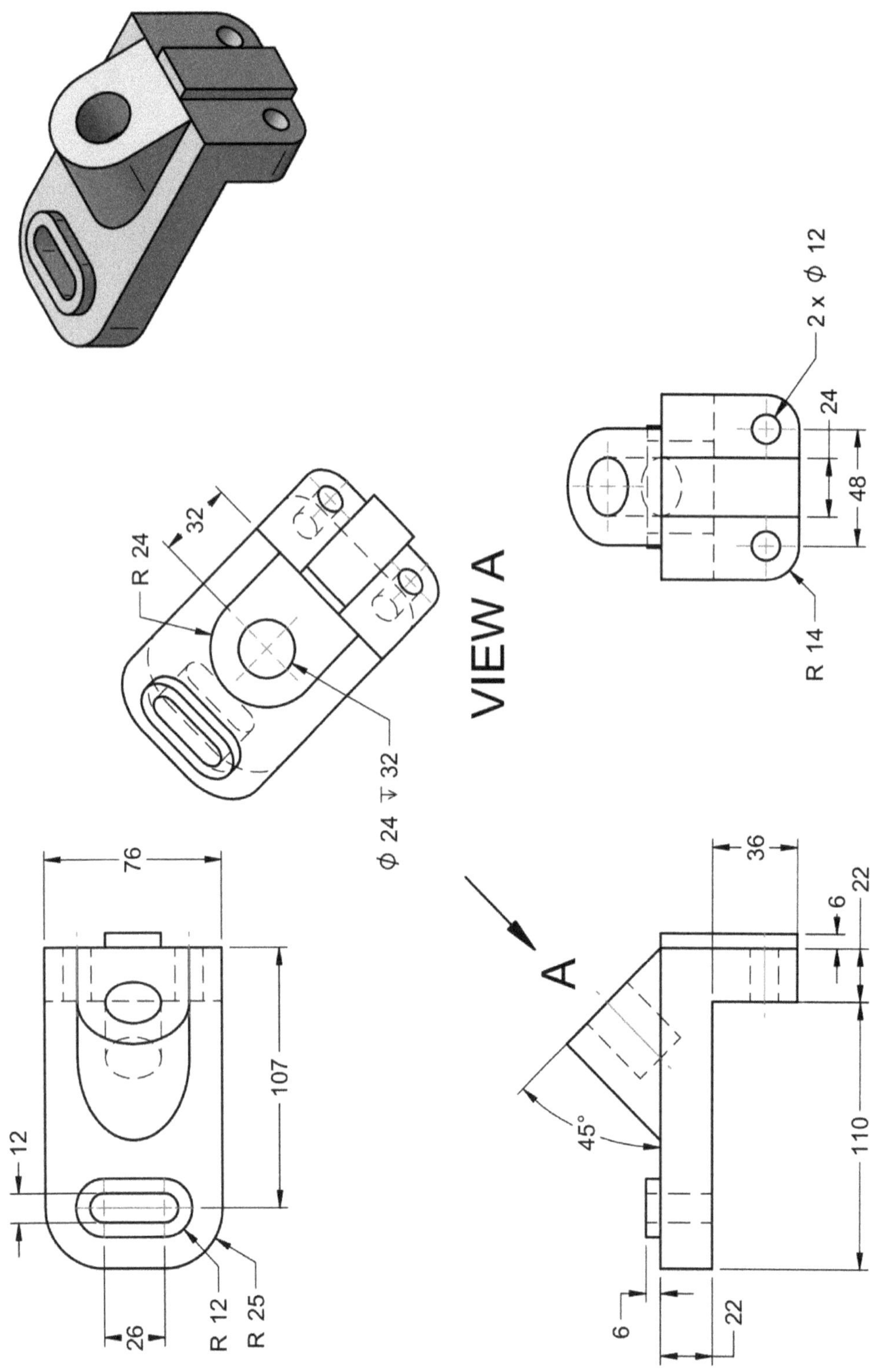

Exercise 3 (Inches)

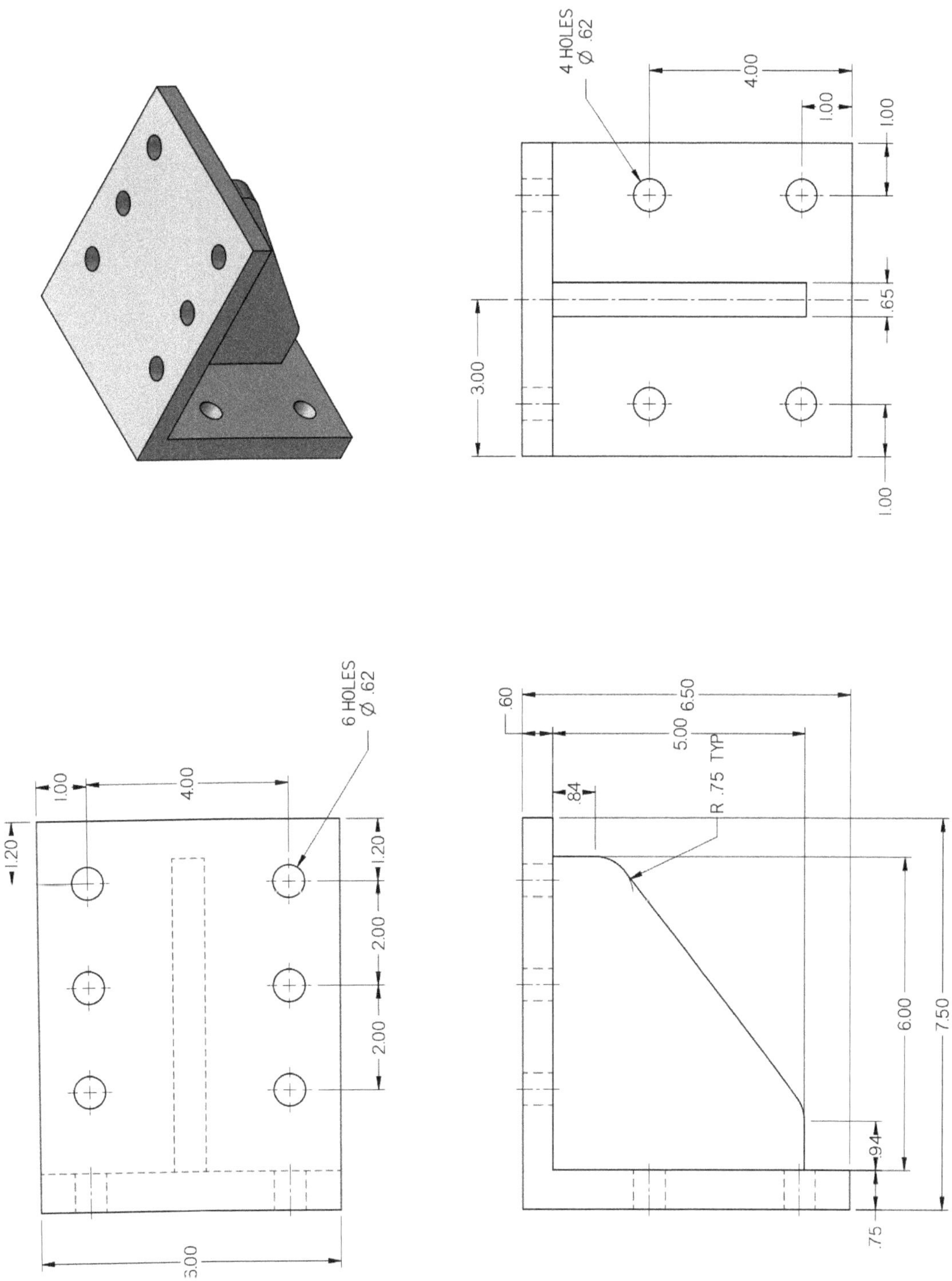

Chapter 9: Modifying Parts

In the design process, it is not required to achieve the final model in the first attempt. There is always a need to modify the existing parts to get the desired part geometry. In this chapter, you will learn various commands and techniques to make changes to a part.

The topics covered in this chapter are:

- *Edit Sketches*
- *Edit Features*
- *Suppress Features*

Edit Sketches

Sketches form the base of a 3D geometry. They control the size and shape of the geometry. If you want to modify the 3D geometry, most of the time, you are required to edit sketches. To do this, right click on the feature and select **Edit Profile Sketch**. Now, modify the sketch and click **Finish Sketch** on the toolbar. You will notice that the part geometry updates immediately.

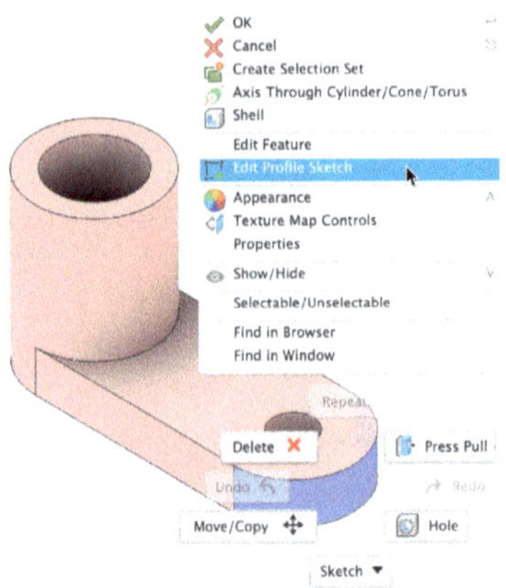

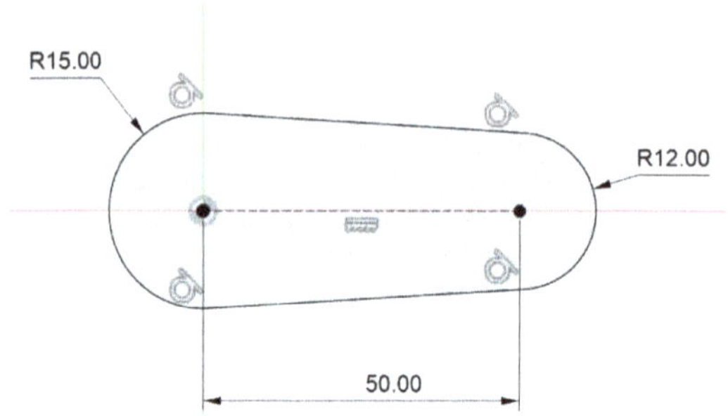

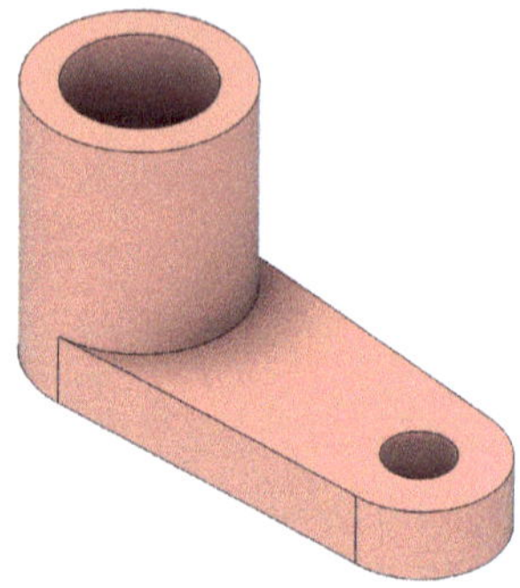

Edit Feature

Features are the building blocks of model geometry. To modify a feature, click the right mouse button on it and select **Edit Feature**. The dialog related to the feature appears. On this dialog, modify the parameters of the feature and click **OK**. The changes take place immediately.

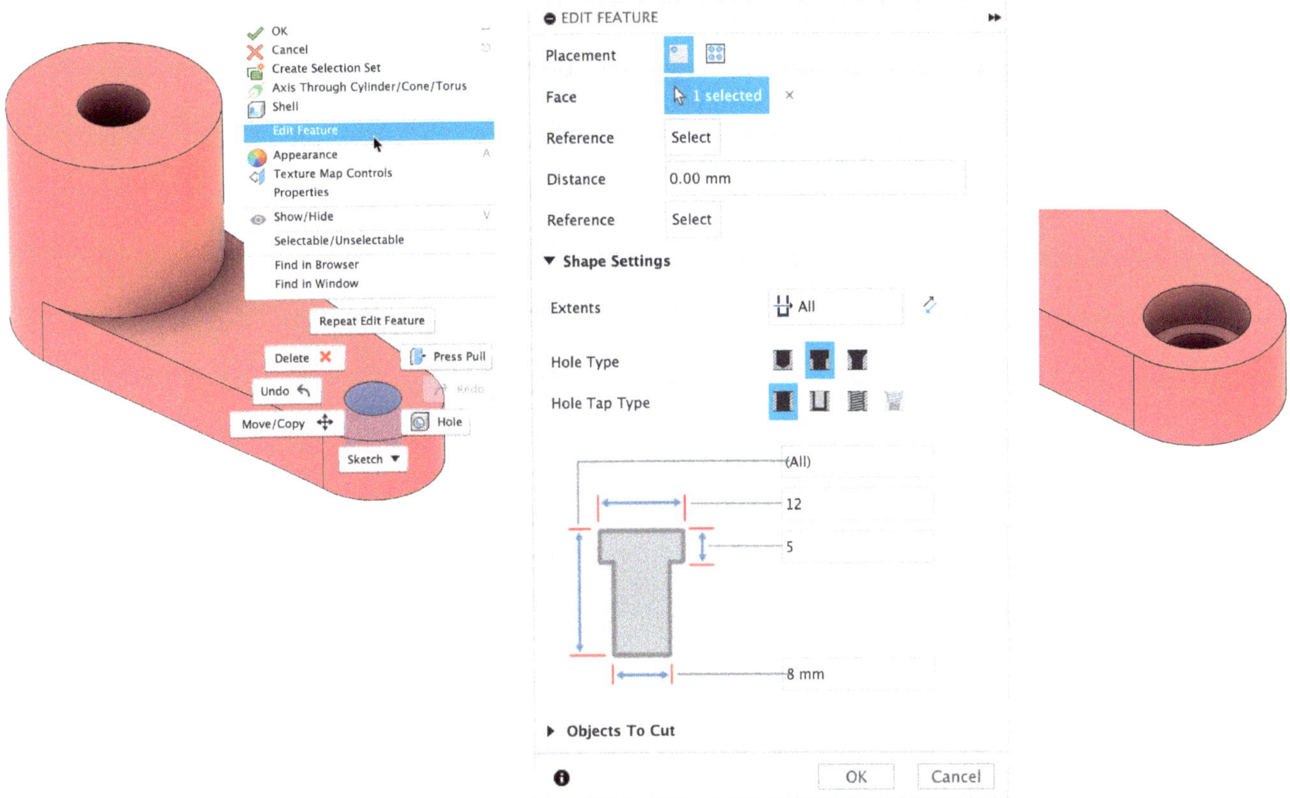

Suppress Features

Sometimes you may need to suppress some features of model geometry. In the Timeline, right-click on the feature to suppress, and then select **Suppress Features**.

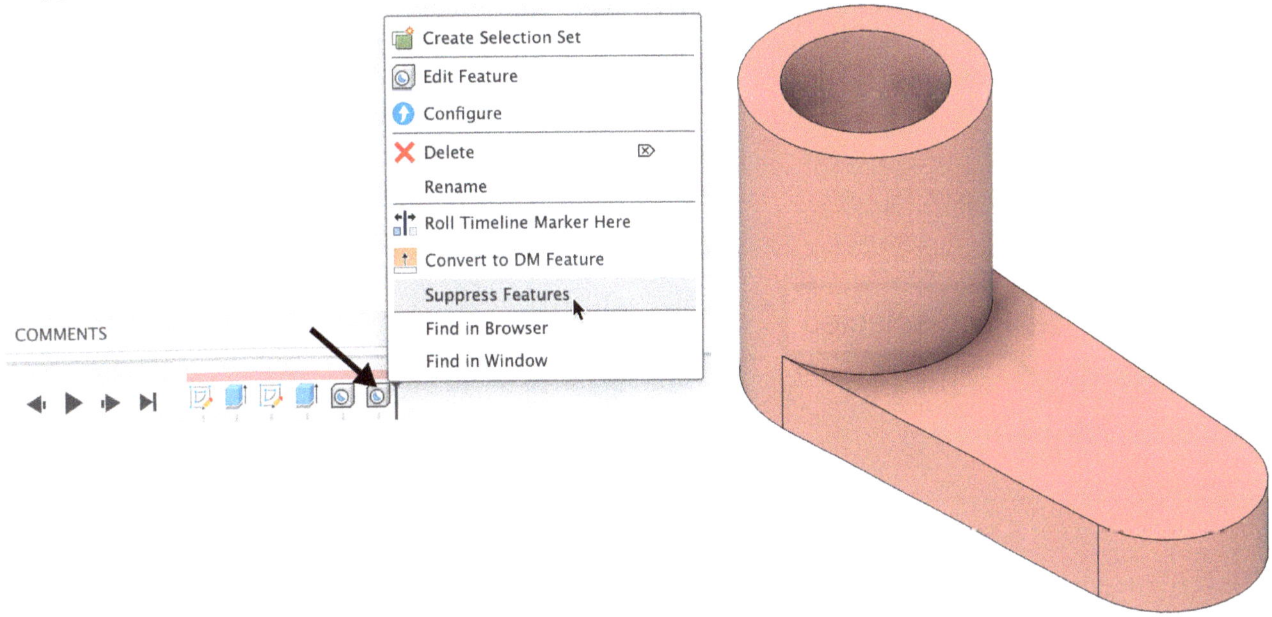

Resume Suppressed Features

If you want to resume the suppressed features, then right click on the suppressed feature in the Timeline and select **Unsuppress Features**; the feature is resumed.

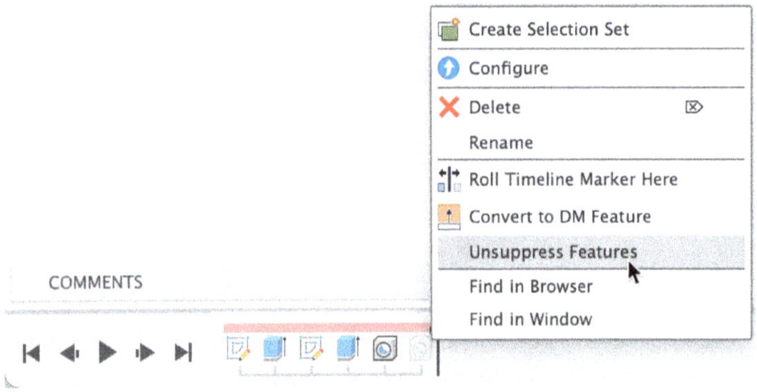

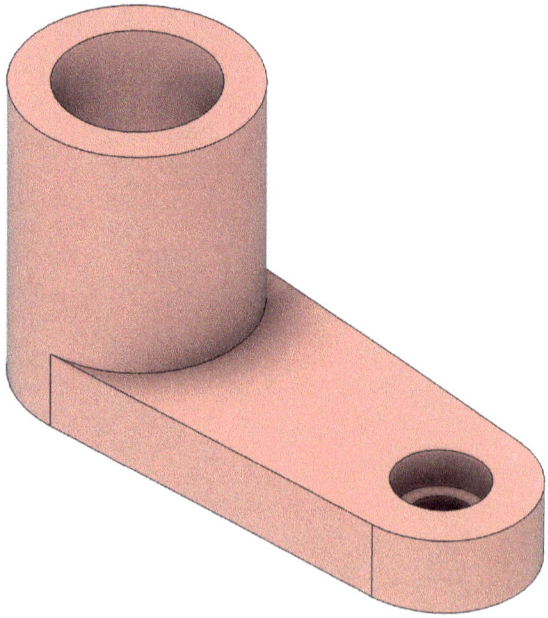

The Move/Copy command

This command moves the selected faces, bodies, components, or sketch objects. In this section, you will learn to move faces. Activate the **Move/Copy** command (on the **Solid** tab of the toolbar, click **Modify** panel > **Move/Copy**), and select **Move Object > Faces**. Next, select **Move Type > Free Move** and select a face. Drag the arrow that appears perpendicular to the selected face, and then release the pointer to define the distance. You can also type-in a value in the **Distance** box.

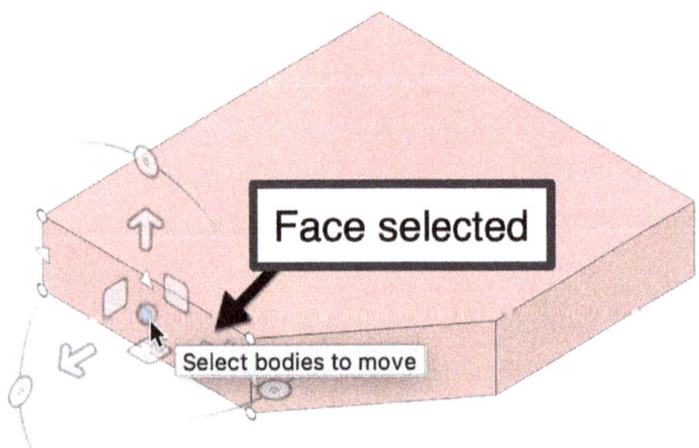

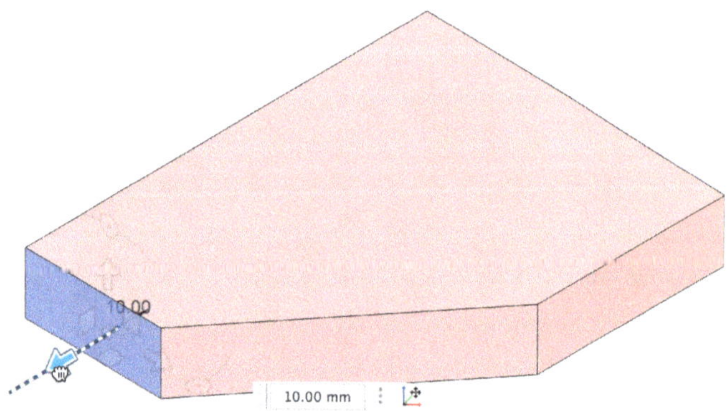

To rotate a face, select **Move Object > Faces** and **Move Type > Rotate** on the **Move/Copy** dialog. Next, select the face to rotate. Click the **Axis** selection button and select an edge to define the axis of rotation. Next, click and drag the angle handle (or) enter a value in the **Angle** box.

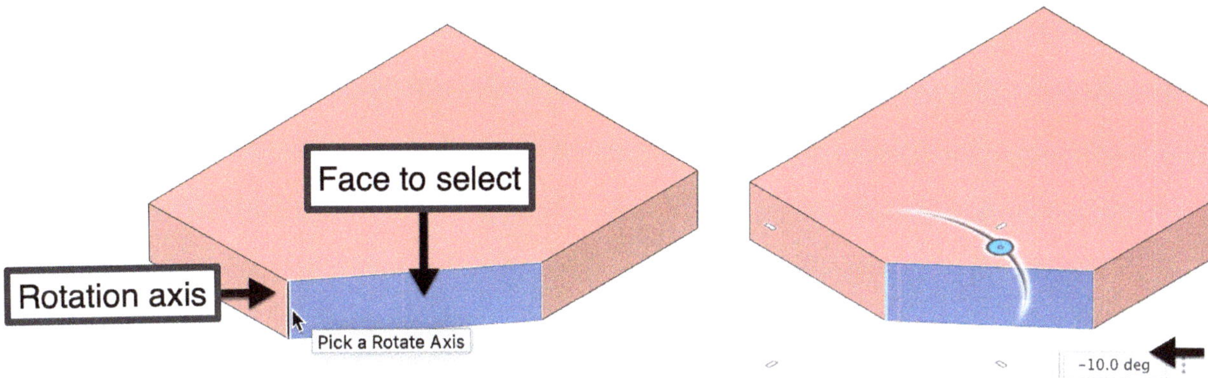

Press Pull

Use the **Press Pull** command (on the **Solid** tab of the toolbar, click **Modify** panel > **Press Pull**) to move faces in the direction perpendicular to them. Activate this command and select the faces to move. Next, click and drag the arrow that appears on the selected face.

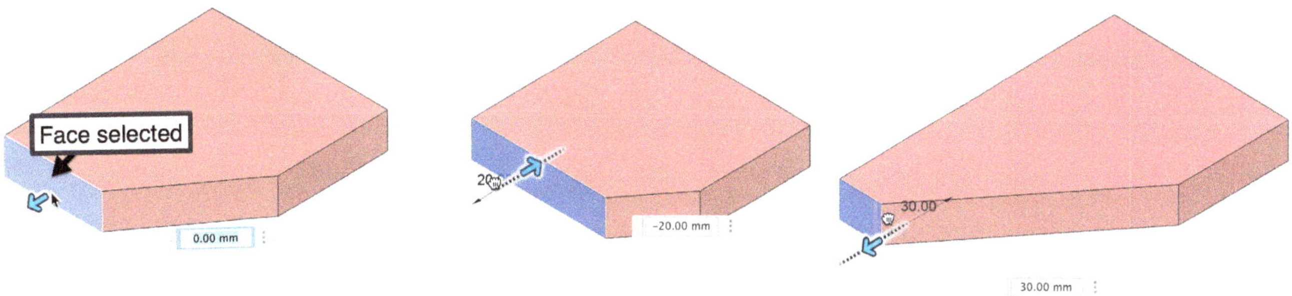

In addition to that, you can use the **Press Pull** command to edit the features of the model. For example, you can edit the Extrude feature of the model, as shown. To do this, activate the **Press Pull** command and select any one of the model faces. Next, select **Offset Type > Modify Existing Feature** and select the top face of the Extrude feature. Click and drag the arrow that appears on the selected face (or) enter a value in the **Distance** box. Click **OK**. Next, right-click on the Extrude feature in the Timeline and select **Edit Feature**; the **Distance** value of the Extrude feature is changed.

Modifying Parts

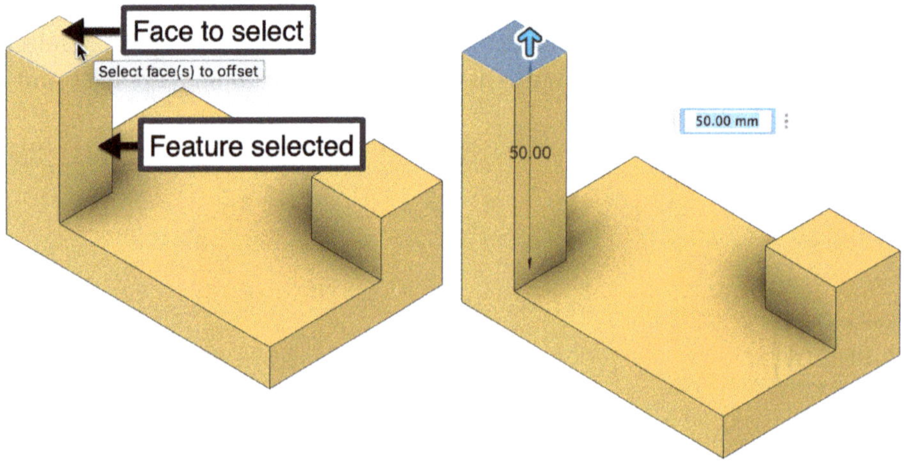

Examples

Example 1 (Inches)

In this example, you will create the part shown below and then modify it.

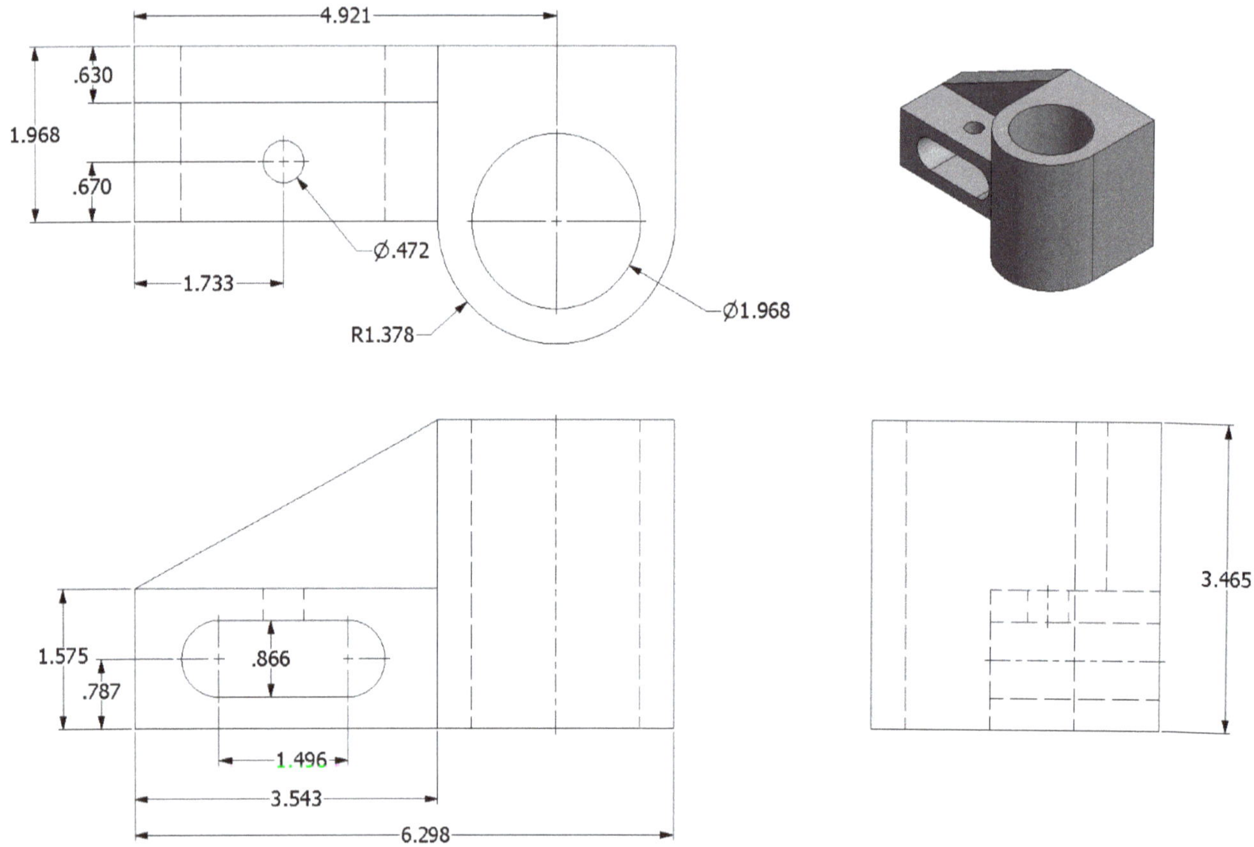

1. Start **Autodesk Fusion 360** and start a new design file and create the part using the tools and commands available in Fusion 360.

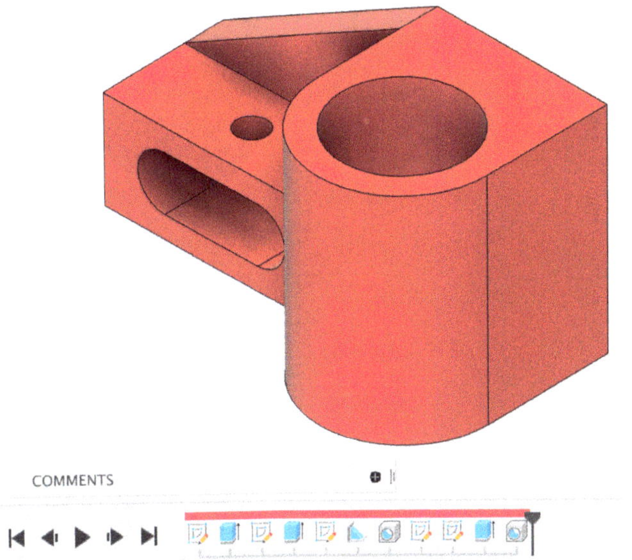

2. Right-click on the large hole and select **Edit Feature**; the **Edit Feature** dialog appears. On the **Edit Feature** dialog, select **Hole Type > Counterbore**.
3. Enter **1.378**, **1.968**, and **0.787** in the **Diameter**, **Counterbore Diameter**, and **Counterbore Depth** boxes, respectively. Click **OK**.

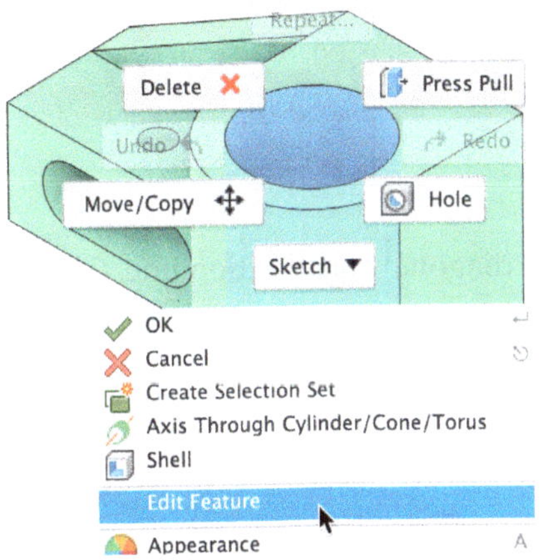

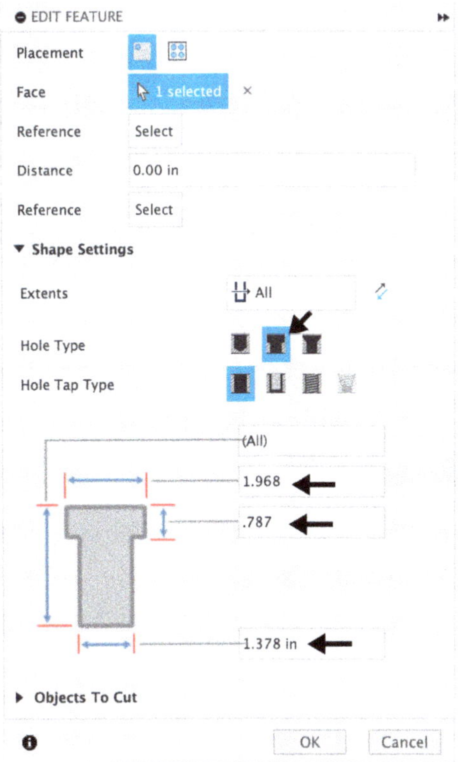

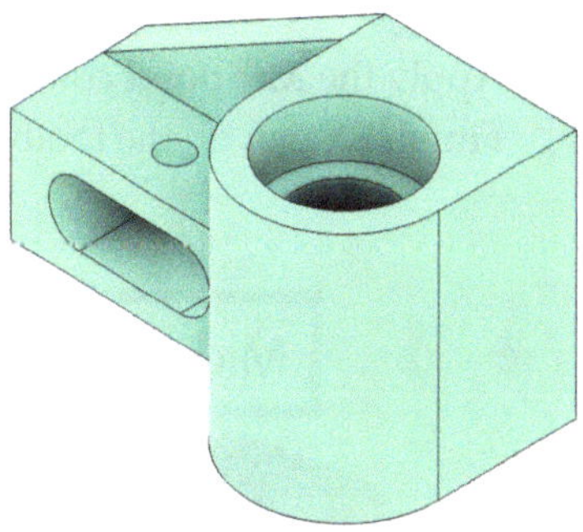

4. Right click on the rectangular *Extrude* feature and select **Edit Profile Sketch**. Modify the sketch, as shown. Click **Finish Sketch**.

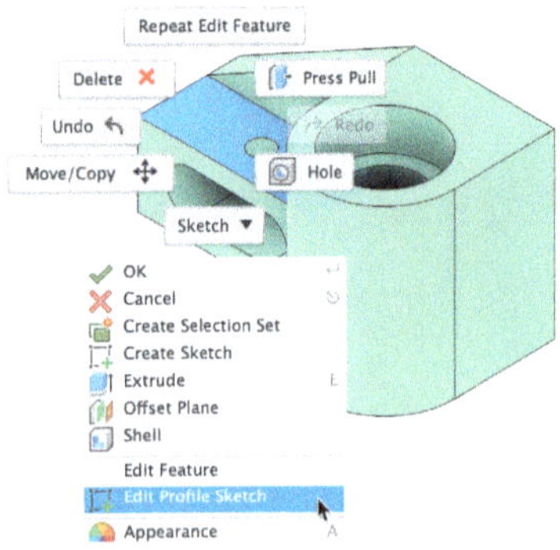

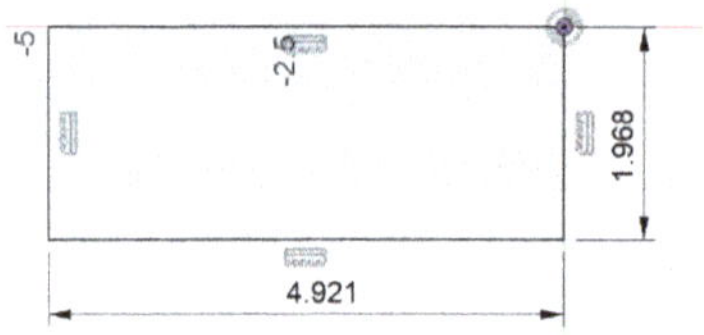

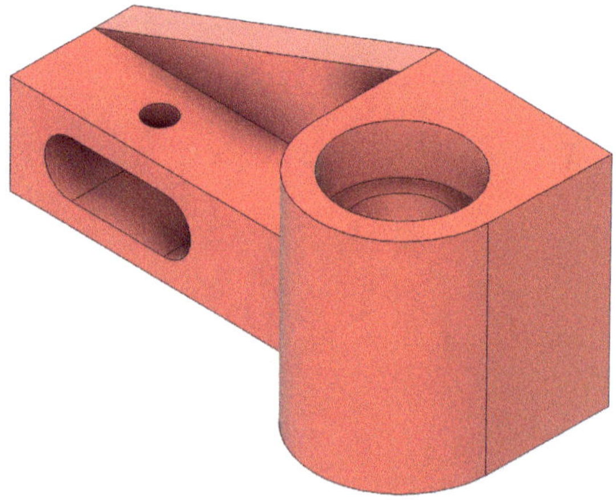

5. Right click on the slot and select **Edit Profile Sketch**.
6. Delete the dimensions of the sketch, as shown.
7. Create a diagonal construction line connecting the lower-left vertex and the upper right vertex of the extruded feature, as shown.

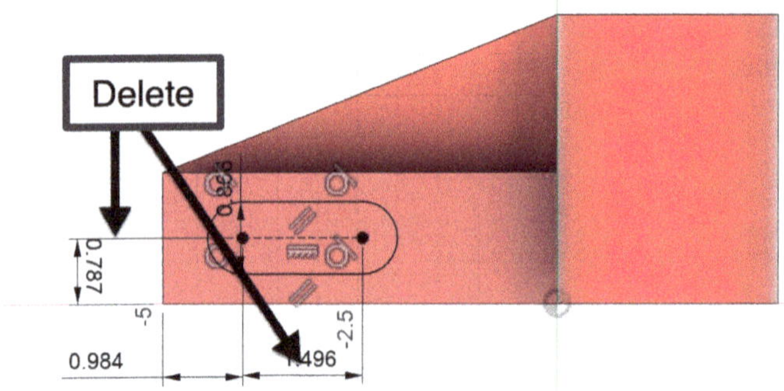

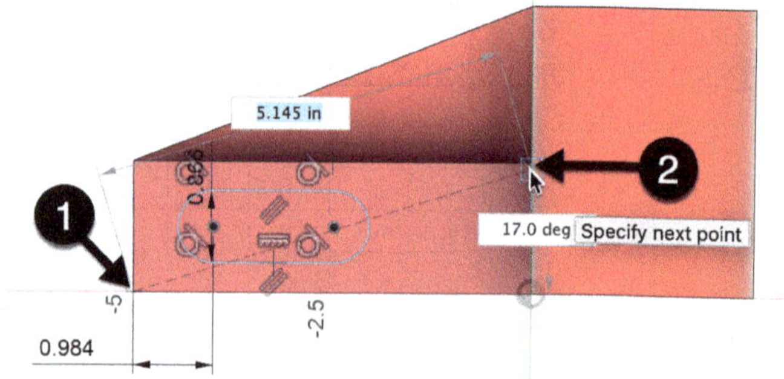

8. Apply the **Midpoint** constraint between the centerline of the slot and the diagonal construction line. Click **Finish Sketch** on the toolbar.

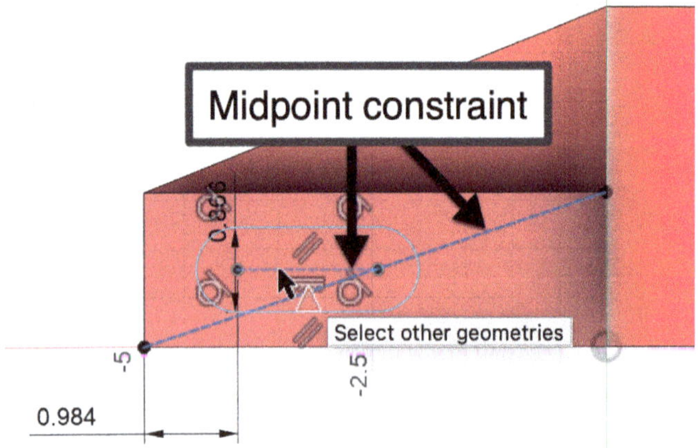

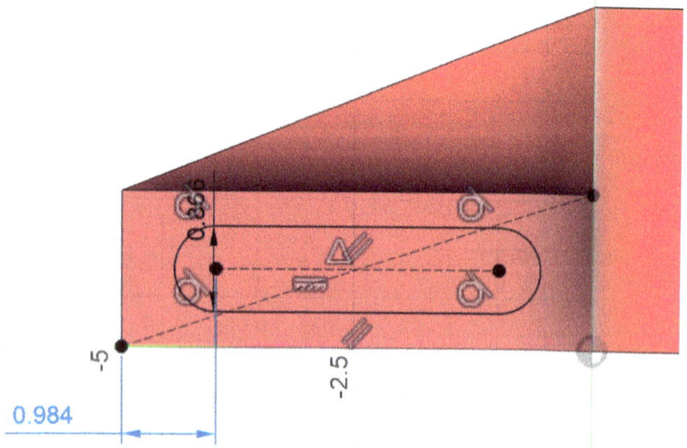

9. Right click on the sketch of the small hole, and then right-click and click **Edit sketch**. Next, delete the positioning dimensions.

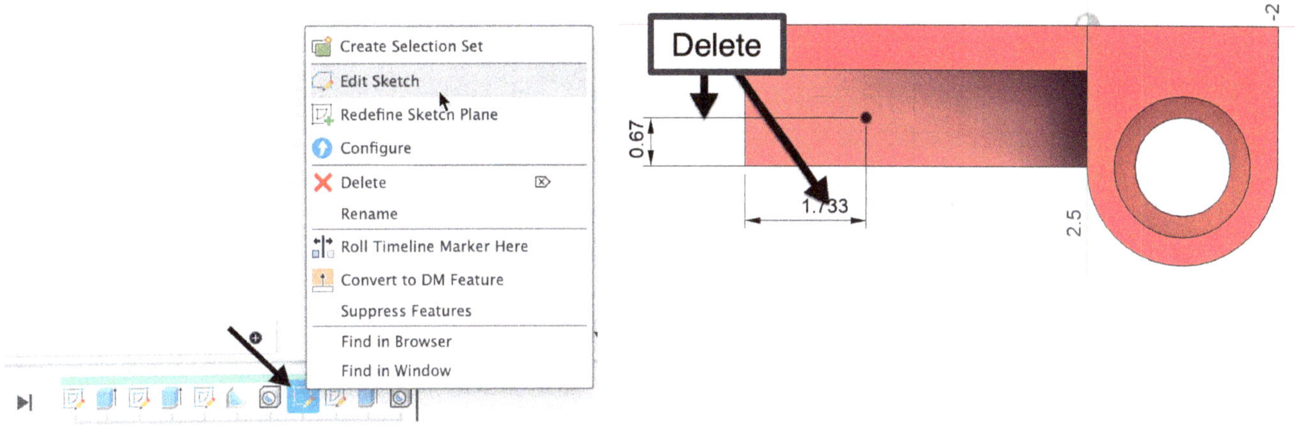

10. Create a construction line and make its ends coincident with the corners, as shown below.
11. On the **Sketch** contextual tab of the toolbar, click **Constraints** panel > **Midpoint**. Next, select the sketch point and the construction line; the point is positioned on the midpoint of the construction line.
12. Click **Finish Sketch** on the toolbar.

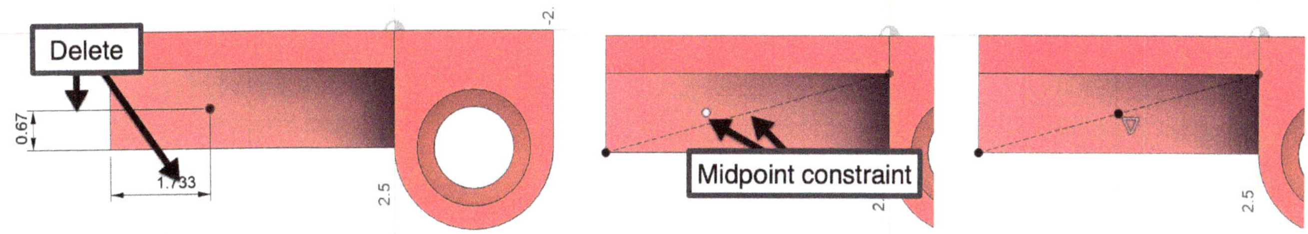

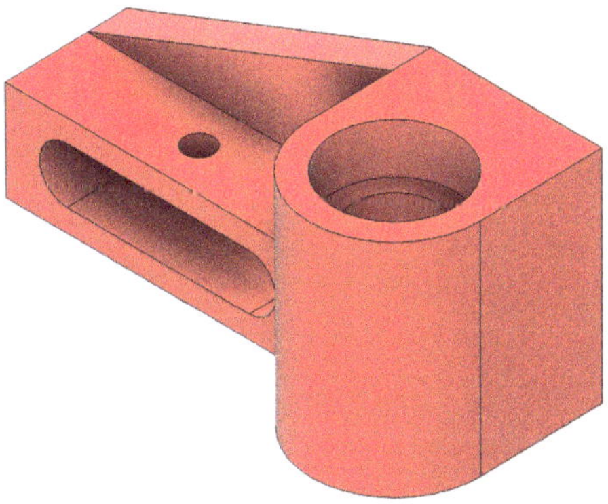

13. Now, change the size of the rectangular extrude feature. You will notice that the slot and hole are adjusted automatically.

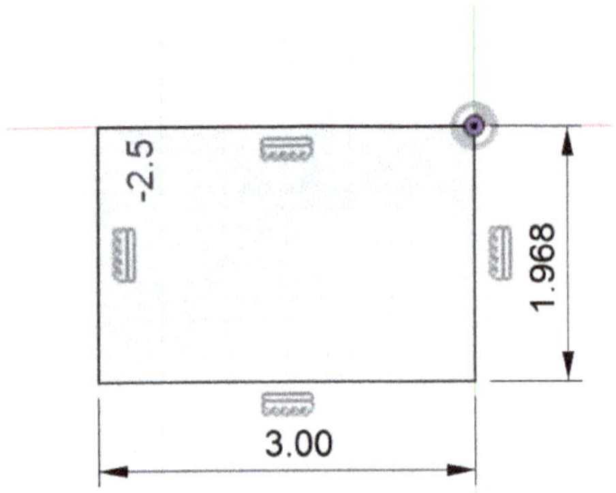

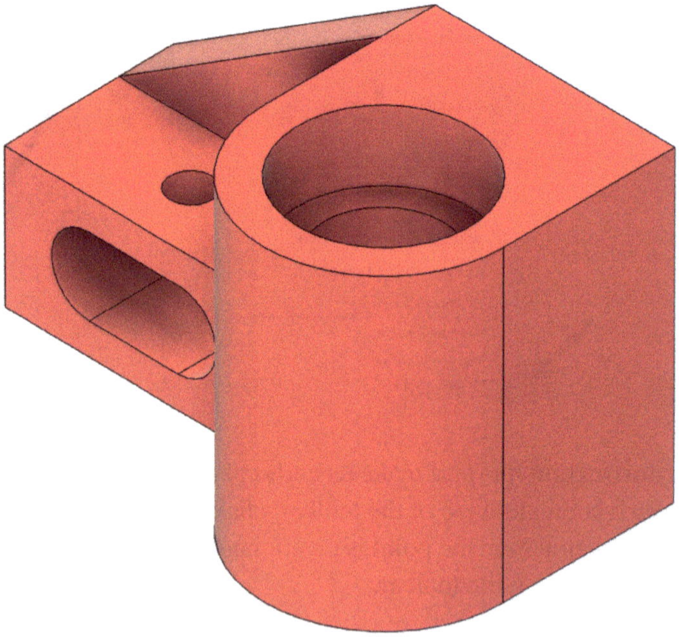

14. Save and close the file.

Example 2 (Millimetres)

In this example, you will create the part shown below, and then modify it using the editing tools.

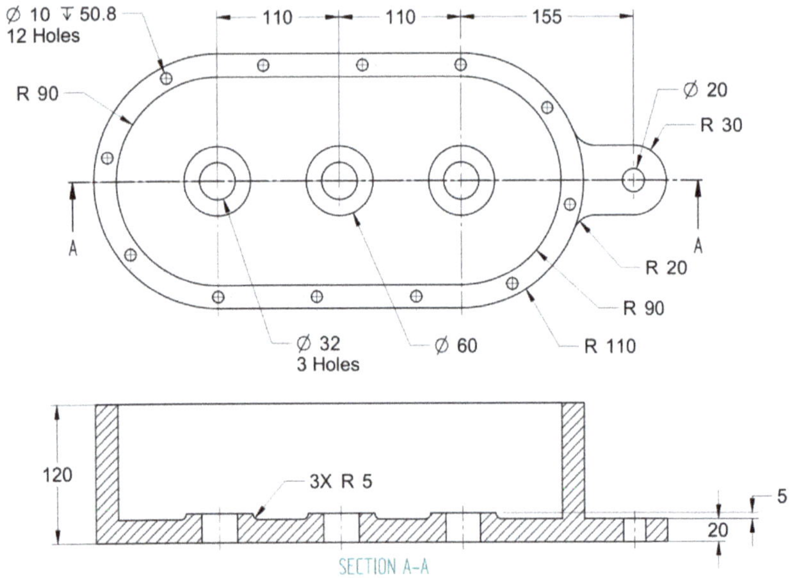

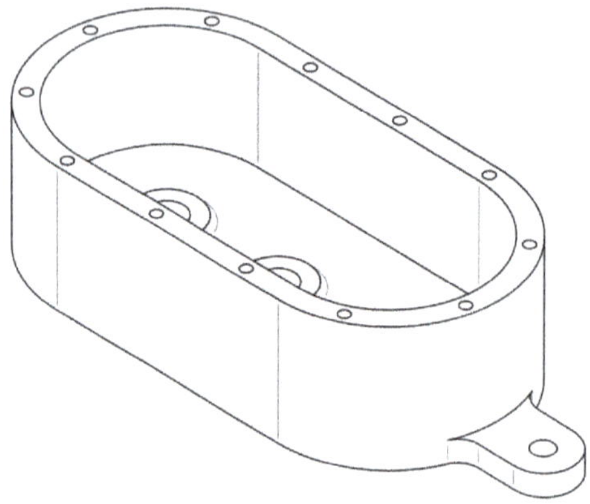

1. Start **Autodesk Fusion 360**.
2. On the **Application bar**, click **File > New Design**.
3. In the Browser window, expand **Document Settings** and place the cursor on **Units**. Next, click the **Change Active Units** icon.
4. On the **Change Active Units** dialog, click **Unit Type > millimeter (mm), gram (g)** and click **OK**.
5. Create the model using the tools and commands in **Autodesk Fusion 360**.

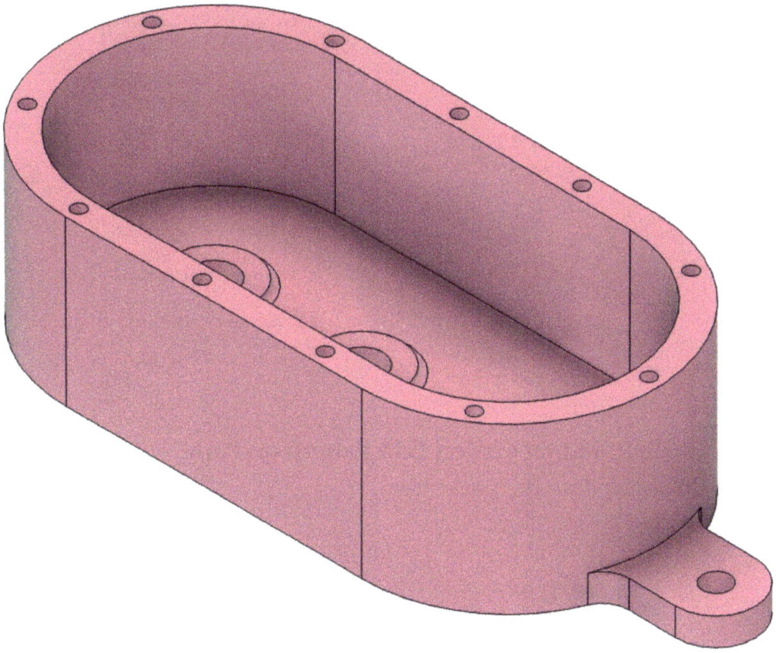

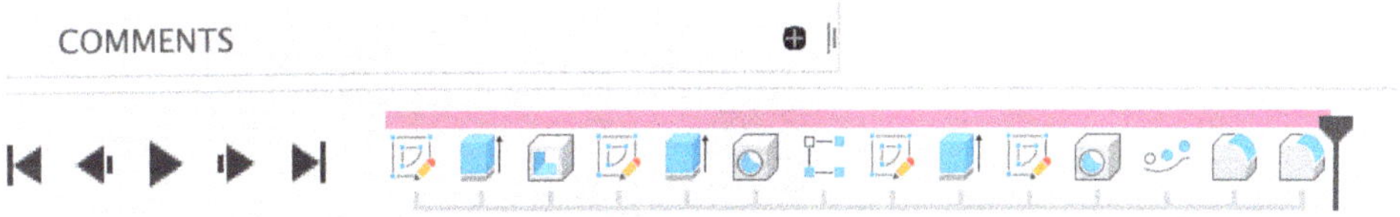

6. Right click on the 20 mm diameter hole, and then click **Edit Feature**; the **Edit Feature** dialog appears.
7. On the **Edit Feature** dialog, select **Hole Type > Counterbore**.
8. Set the **Counterbore Diameter** to 30 and **Counterbore Depth** to 10. Click **OK** to close the panel.

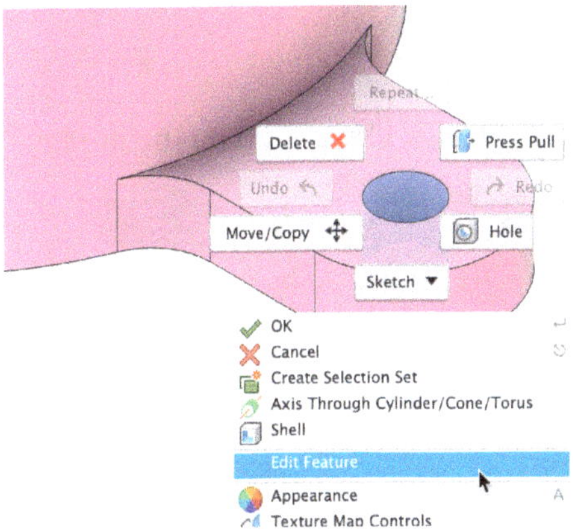

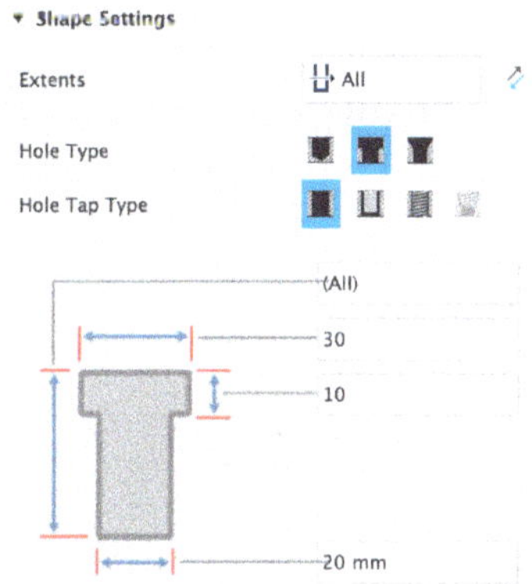

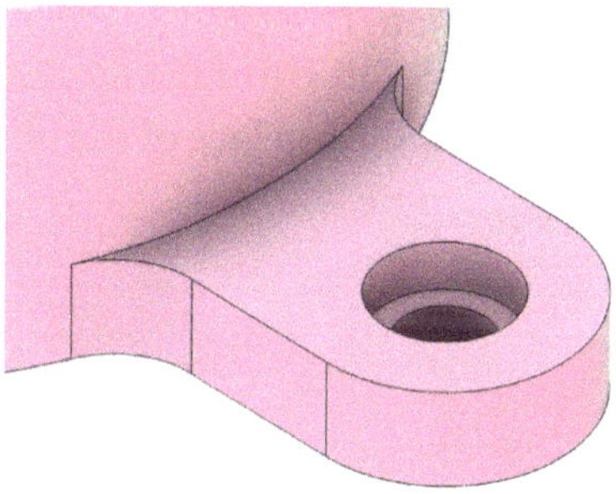

9. On the **Solid** tab of the toolbar, click **Modify** panel > **Move/Copy**, and then select **Move Object > Faces** on the **Move/Copy** dialog.
10. Select the faces of the counterbore hole, and then cylindrical face concentric to it.
11. Click **Move Type > Translate** on the **Move/Copy** dialog. Next, select the arrow pointing toward the right.
12. Type **20** in the **X Distance** box on the **Move/Copy** dialog, and click **OK**.

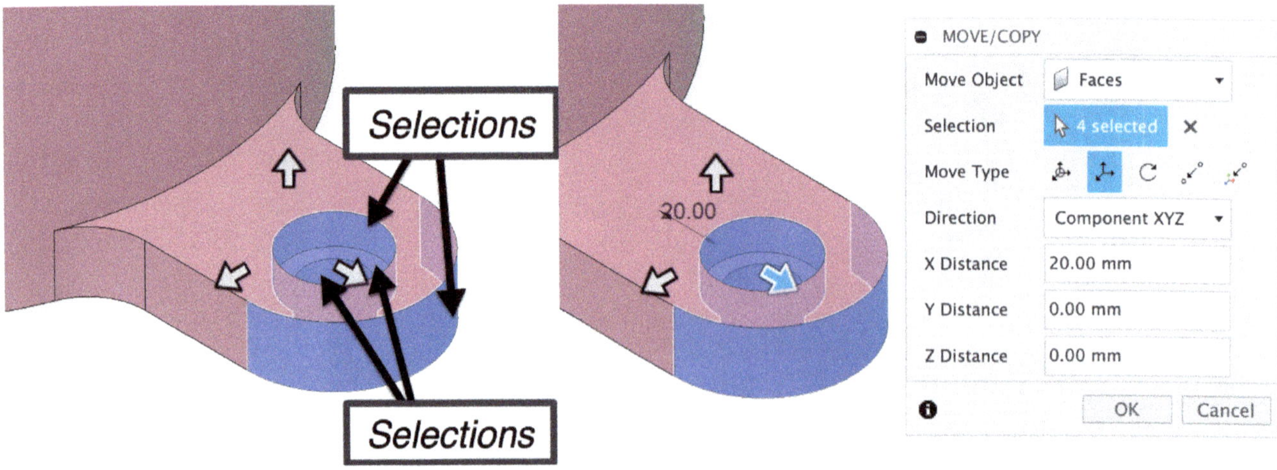

13. Right click on the Path pattern in the Timeline, and then select **Edit Pattern on Path**.
14. Type 14 in the **Quantity** box and click **OK** to update the pattern.

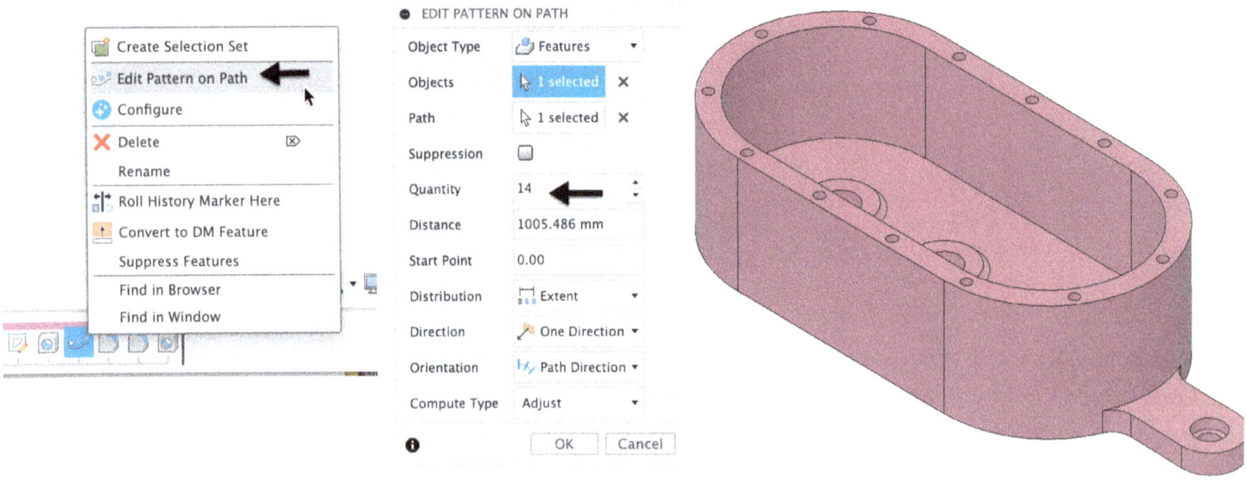

15. On the **Solid** tab of the toolbar, click **Modify** panel > **Press pull** .
16. Click on the top face of the geometry and type **80** in the **Distance** box and click **OK** to update the model.

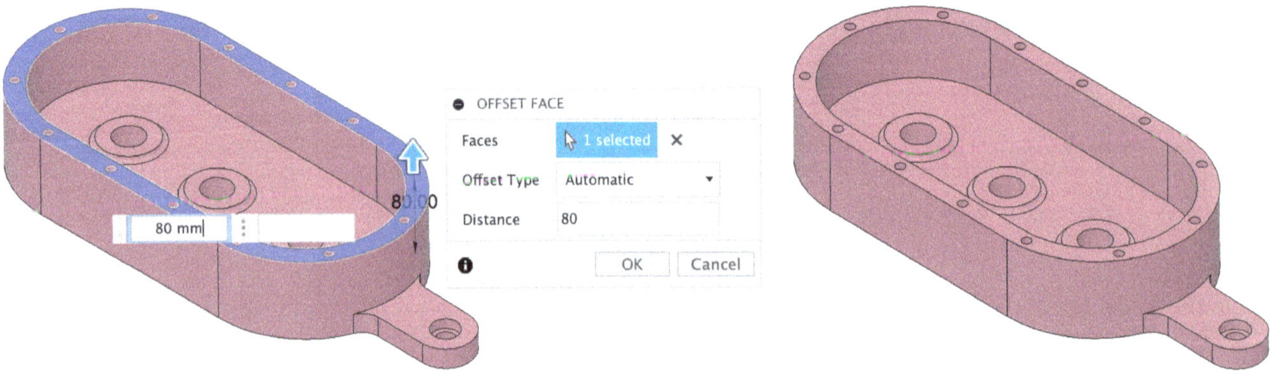

17. Save and close the file.

Questions

1. How to modify the sketch of a feature?
2. How to modify a feature using the **Press Pull** command?
3. How to suppress a feature?

Exercises

Exercise 1

Initial Part

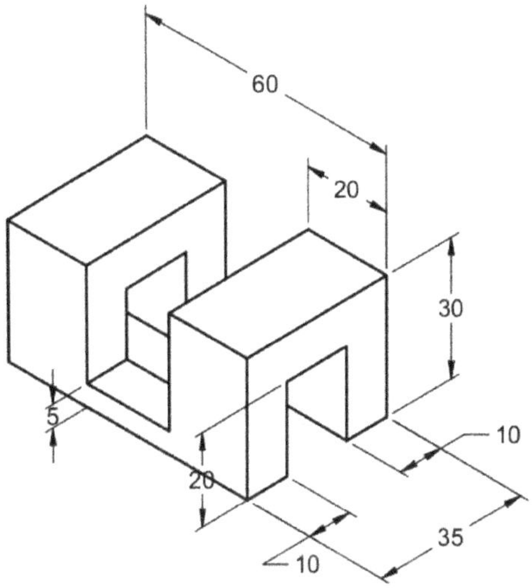

Modified Part

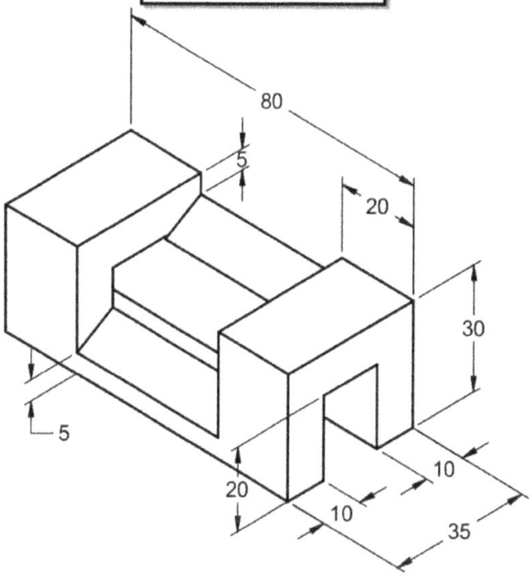

Chapter 10: Assemblies

After creating individual components, you can bring them together into an assembly. By doing so, it is possible to identify incorrect design problems that may not have been noticeable at the component level. In this chapter, you will learn how to bring components together and create real-life movements between them.

The topics covered in this chapter are:

- *Starting an assembly*
- *Inserting Components*
- *Adding Joints*
- *Check Interference*
- *Joint Origins*
- *Rigid Groups*
- *Locking/Unlocking Joints*
- *Editing Joint Limits*
- *Drive Joints*
- *Motion Link*
- *Motion Study*
- *Contact Sets*
- *Top-down Assembly Design*
- *As-built Joint*
- *Create Animations*

Starting an Assembly

In Autodesk Fusion 360, there is no separate environment to create an assembly. You can directly insert components into a design file (or) create new components in it. However, you need to save the design file before inserting any component into it.

Inserting Components

To insert components into a design file, first, you need to save it. Next, click the **Show Data Panel** icon located at the top left corner of the window. On the Data Panel, go to the folder in which the components are located. Click the right mouse button on the component to be inserted in the design, and then select **Insert into Current Design**.

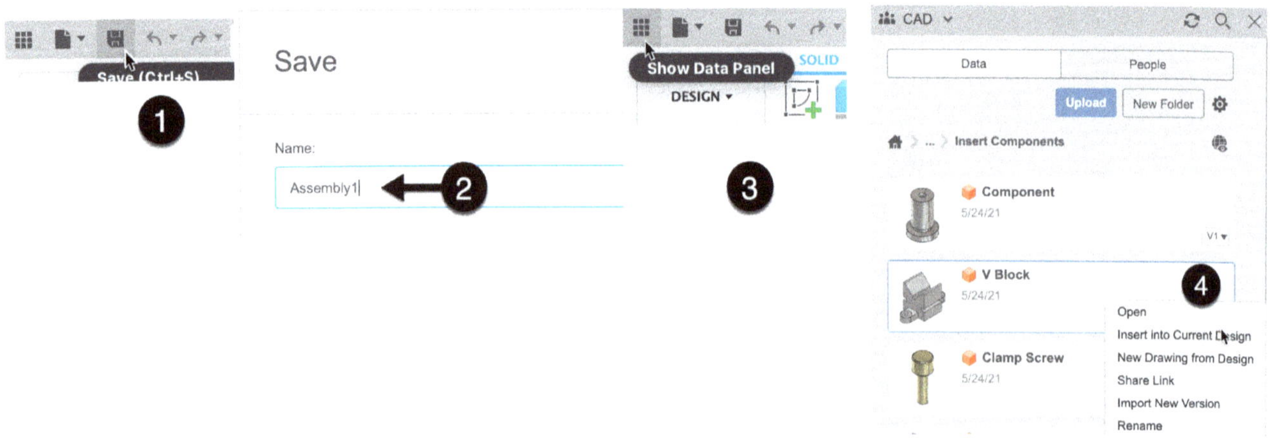

You can also insert a component into a design file using the **Insert Component** command. To do this, click **Solid** tab > **Assemble** panel > **Insert Component** on the toolbar. Next, browse to the required project and folder location on the **Insert Component** dialog. Next, select the component to be inserted and click the **Insert** button.

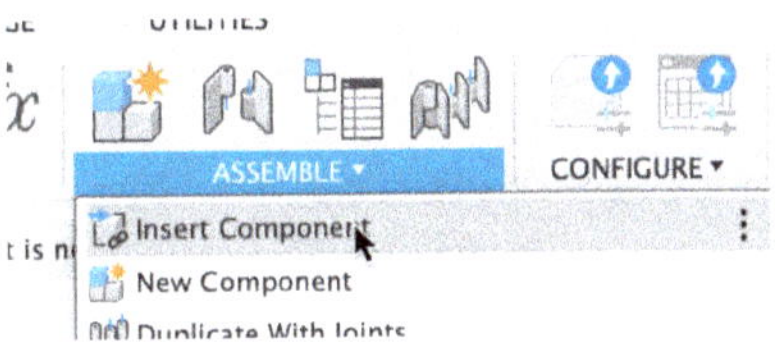

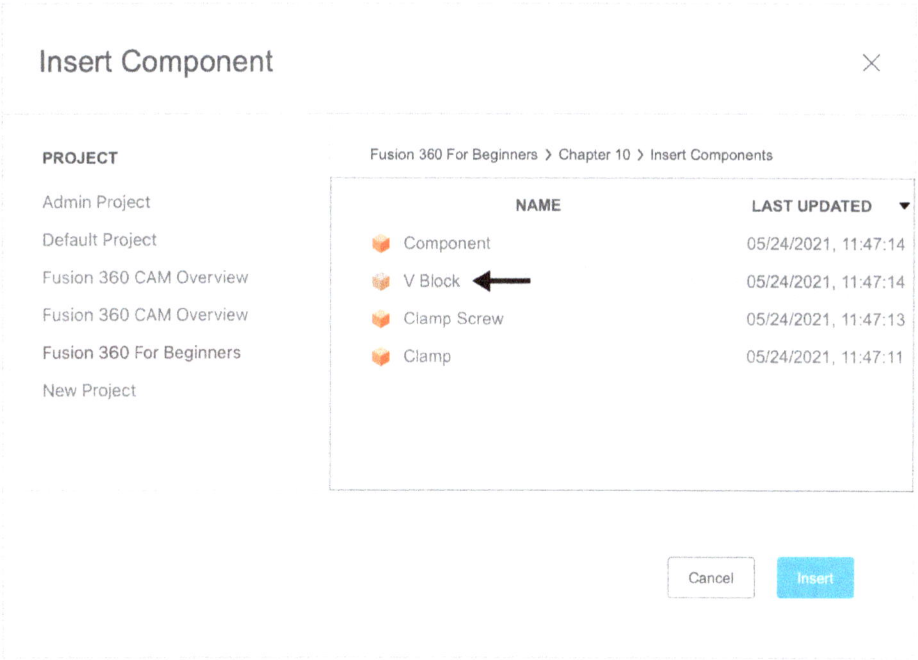

The selected component is inserted into the design, and the **Initial Position** dialog is displayed. Here, you can move or rotate the component as needed. To fix the component's position immediately, select the **Ground To Parent** checkbox directly within this dialog. After clicking **OK**, the component will be fixed at its location, eliminating all degrees of freedom.

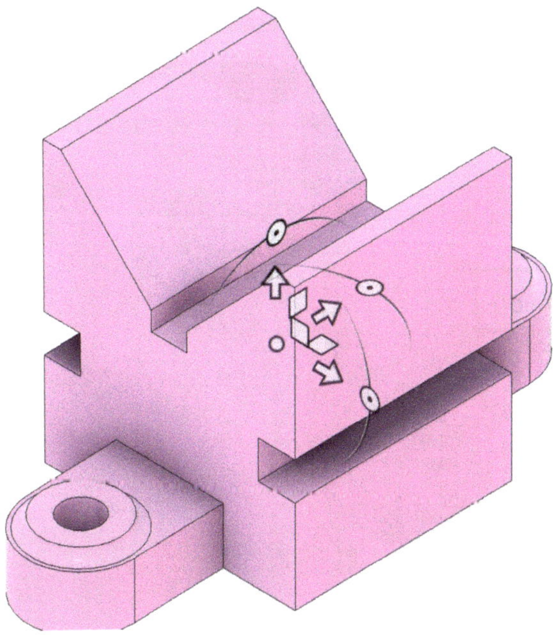

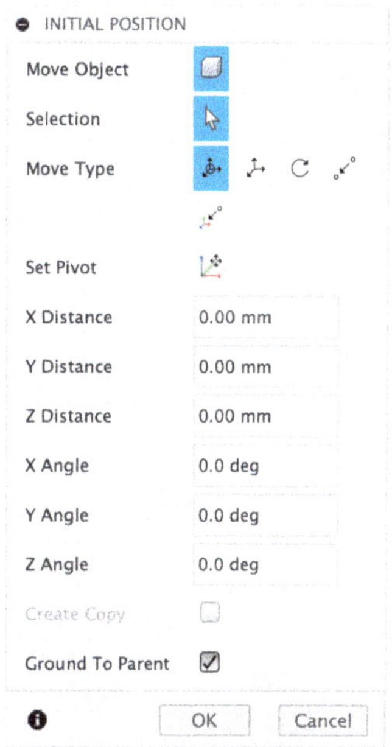

Likewise, insert the second component into the design. Next, click and drag any one of the rotate handles that appear on the component; the component is rotated.

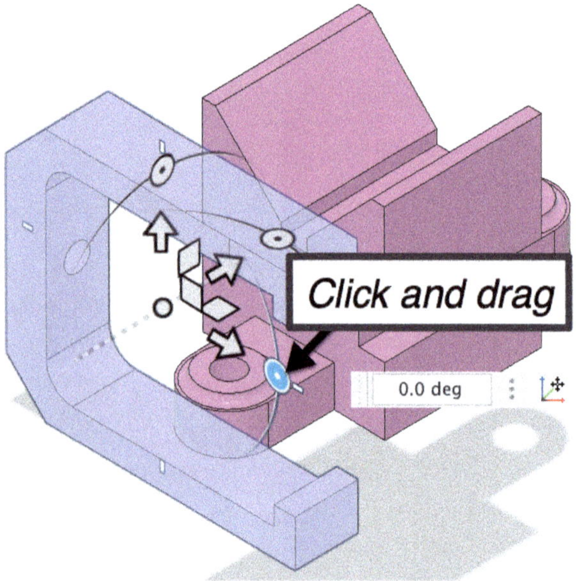

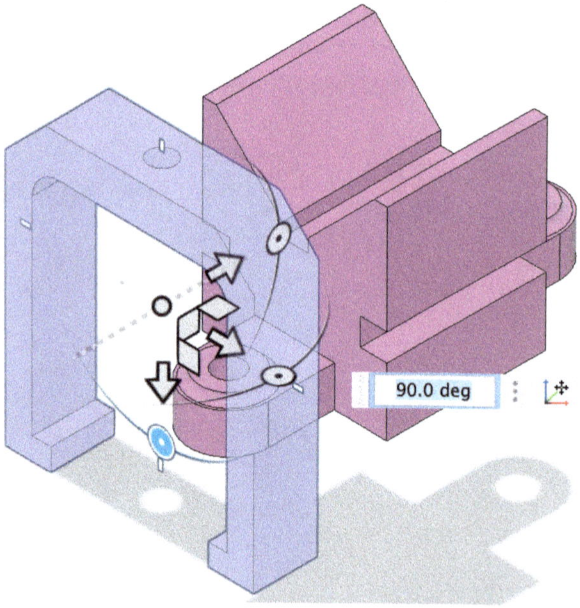

Click and drag the arrow handles to move the component along the X, Y, or Z axes. Next, click **OK** on the **Move/Copy** dialog.

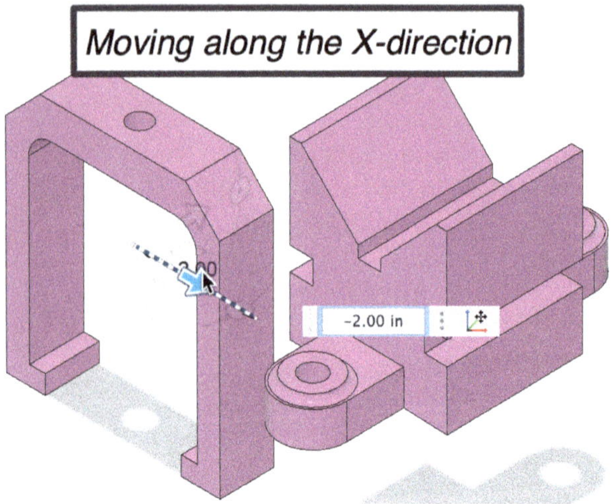

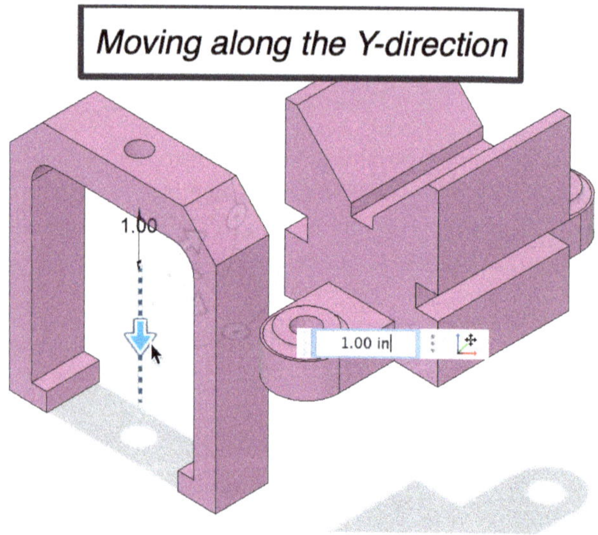

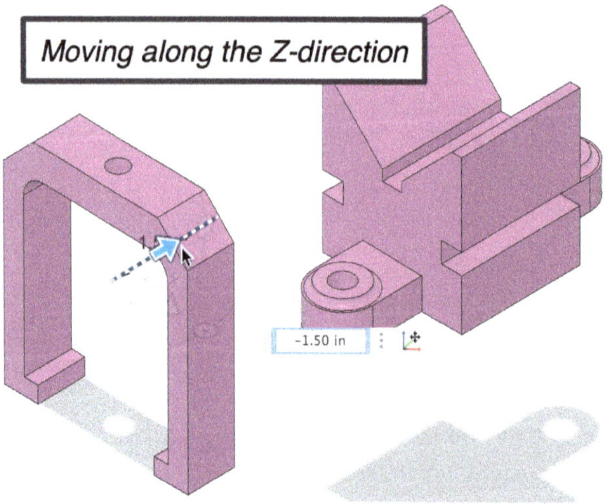

Component Color Cycling

The **Component Color Cycling Toggle** option (on the toolbar, click **Utilities > Inspect > Component Color Cycling Toggle**) helps you to add different colors to the components of the assembly. In doing so, you can differentiate between the components of the assembly easily.

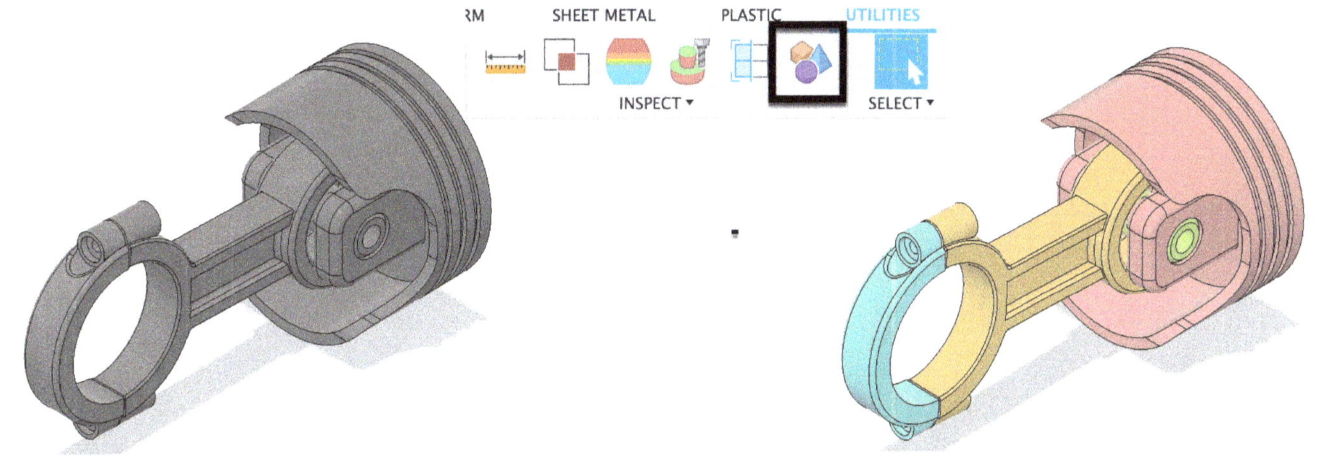

Joints

The **Joint** command is used to create the joints between the components to control the position and movement. You can select Midpoints, Center points, or Endpoints of the components to create the joint between them. To create a joint, click **Assemble > Joint** on the toolbar. On the **Joint** dialog, the **Motion** tab has many types of joints such as **Rigid**, **Revolute**, **Slider**, **Cylindrical**, **Planar**, **Pin-slot**, and **Ball**. These joints are explained next.

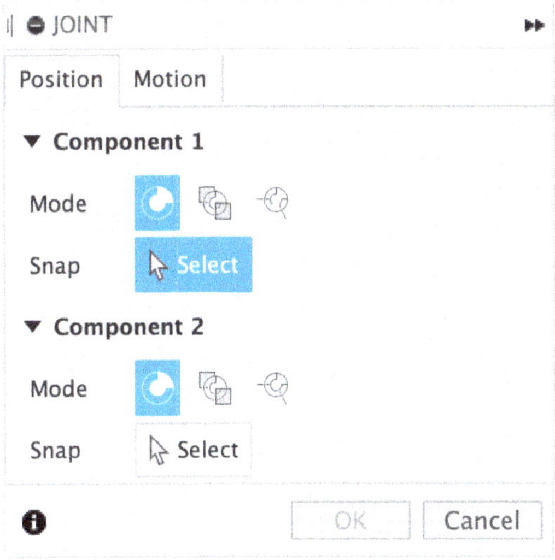

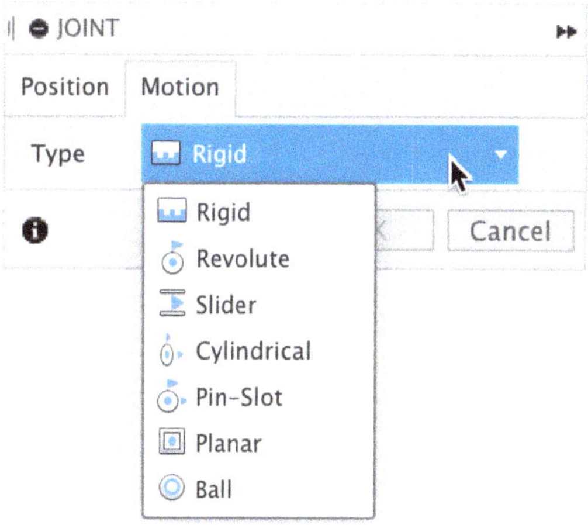

Ball Joint

The **Ball** option creates a ball joint between two spherical faces. Activate the **Joint** command and select a snap point on the spherical face of the first component. Select a snap point on the spherical face of the second component. The components will snap together. Click the **Motion** tab and select **Type > Ball**; the ball joint is created between the two components. Click the **Animate** icon on the **Joint** dialog to view the animation of the ball joint.

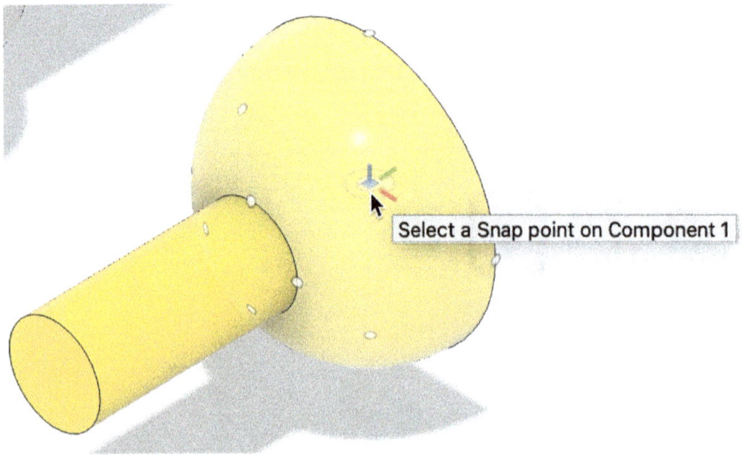

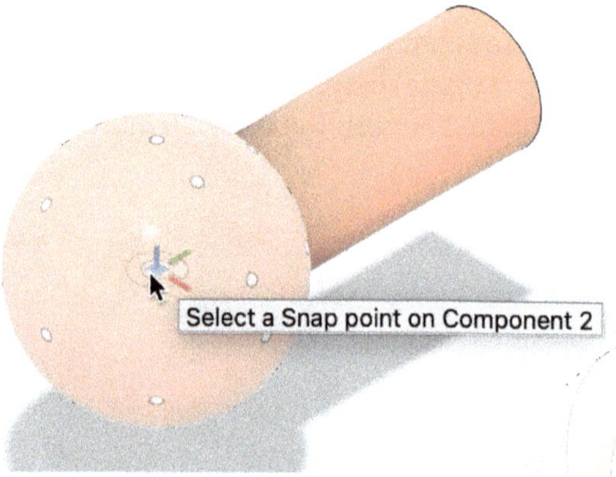

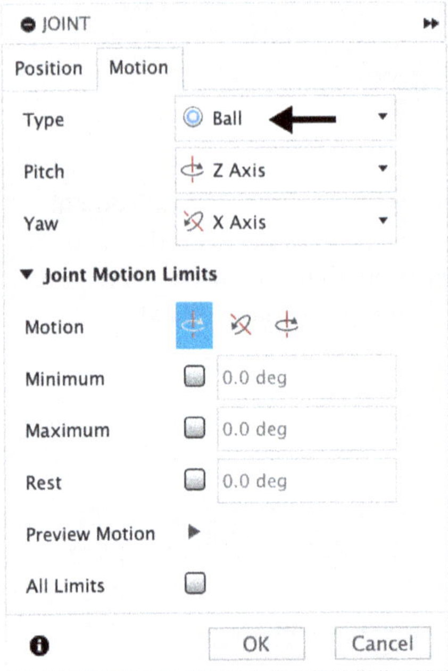

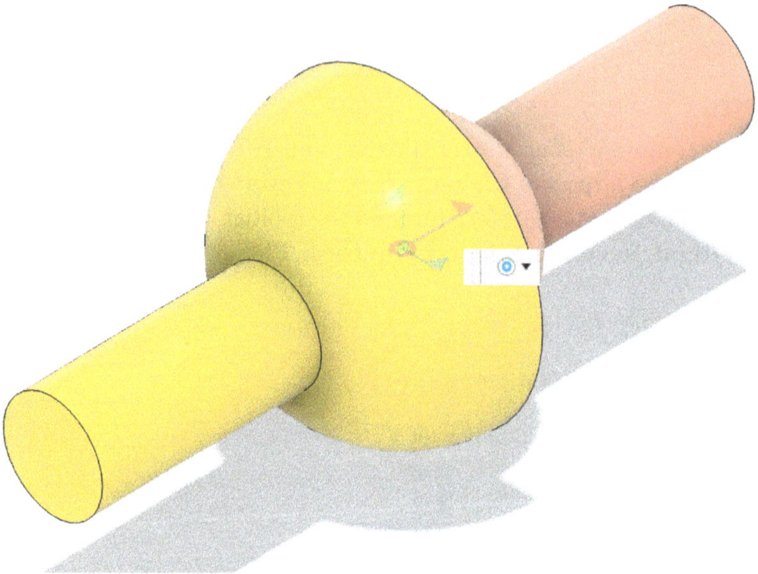

In the **Joint Motion Limits** section, click the **Motion** > **Pitch** icon, and then click the **Preview Motion** icon; the assembled component is rotated about the Z-axis.

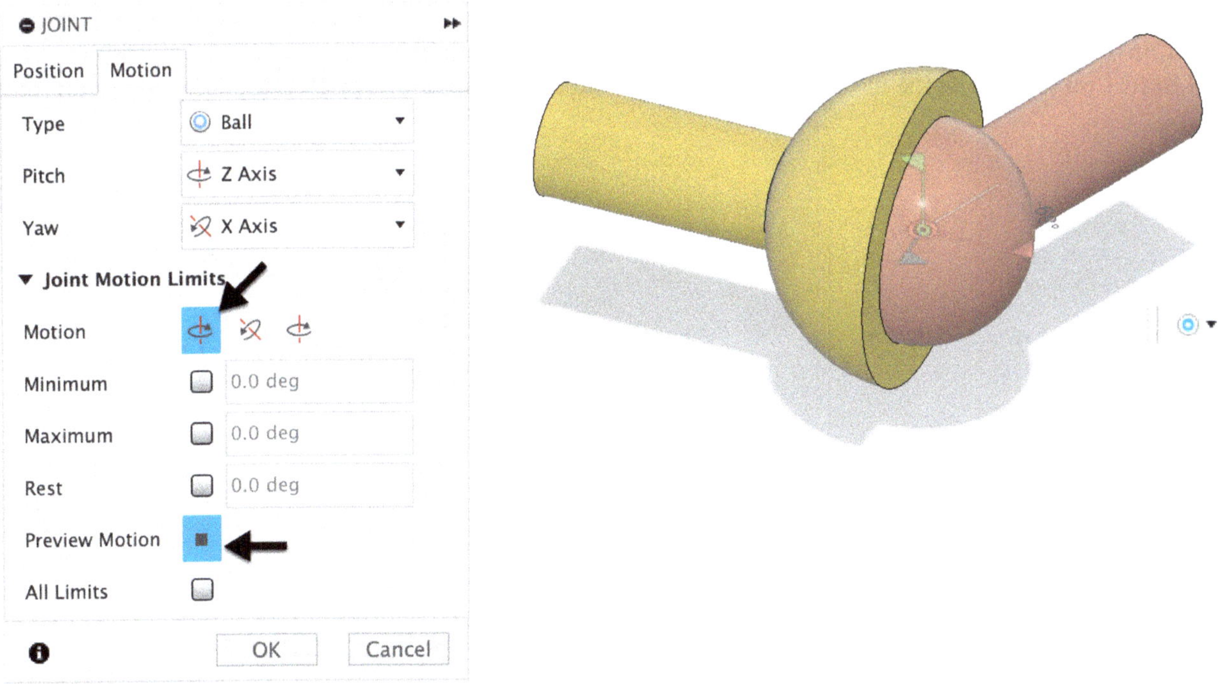

Click **Motion > Yaw**, and then click the **Preview Motion** icon; the component is rotated about the X-axis. Again, click the **Preview Motion** icon to stop the animation.

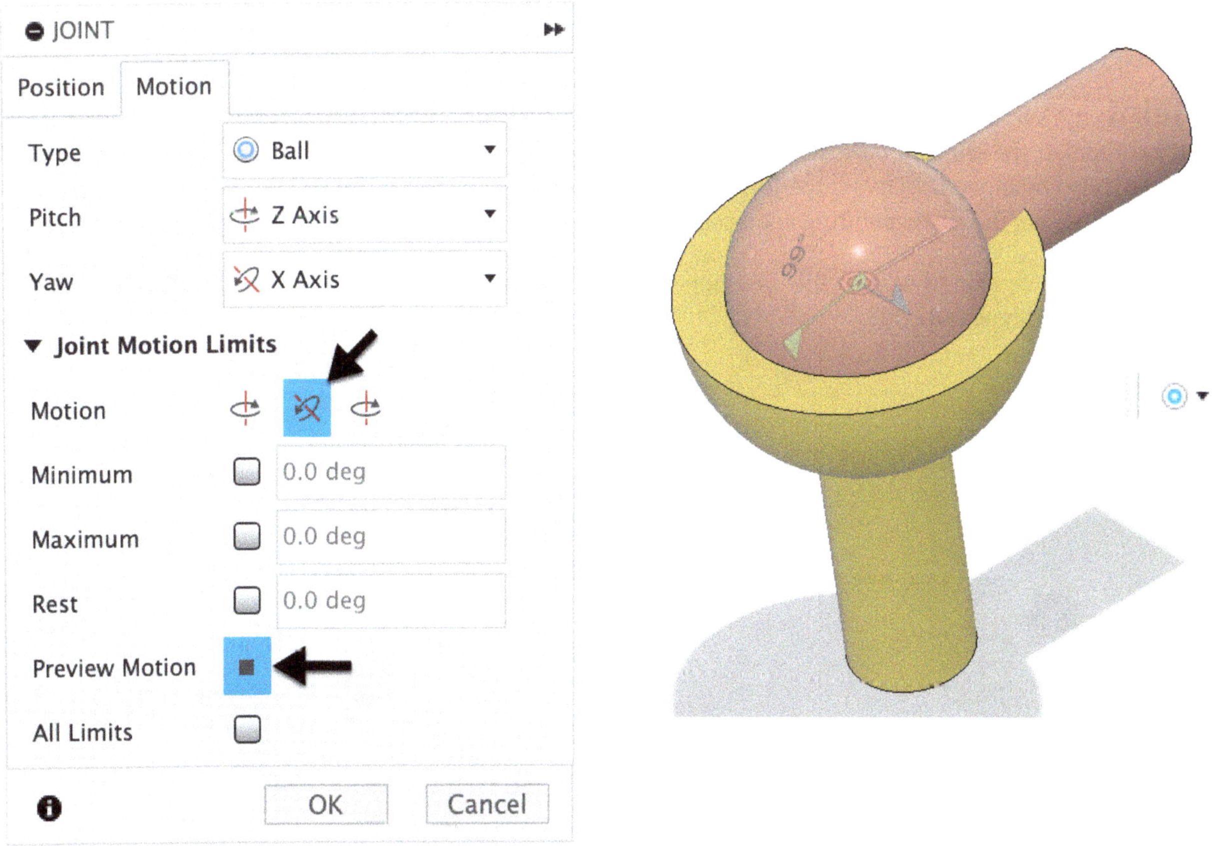

Click the **Motion > Pitch** under the **Joint Motion Limits** section and check the **Maximum** option; the **Maximum** and **Minimum** are enabled. Type **60** and **-60** in the **Maximum** and **Minimum** boxes, respectively. Click the **Preview Limits** icon to animate the motion with maximum and minimum limits. Click **OK** to create the ball Joint.

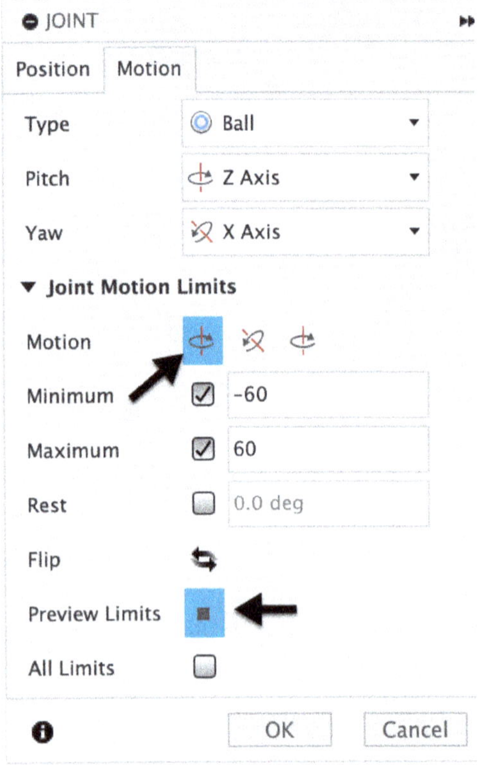

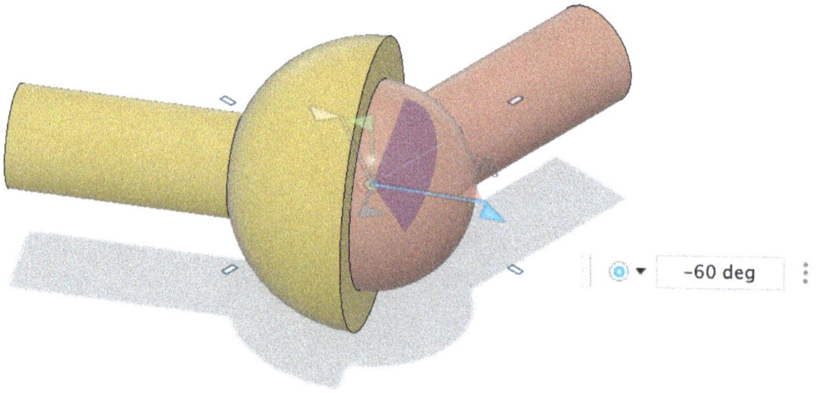

Rigid Joint

The **Rigid** joint makes the selected parts to form a rigid set. As you move a component of a rigid joint, the other component will also be moved. Activate the **Joint** command and select a snap point or joint origin on the first component. Next, select the corresponding snap point or joint origin on the second component. The parts will align. Click the **Flip** icon to reverse the direction of the component if required. On the **Joint** dialog, click the **Motion** tab and select **Type > Rigid**.

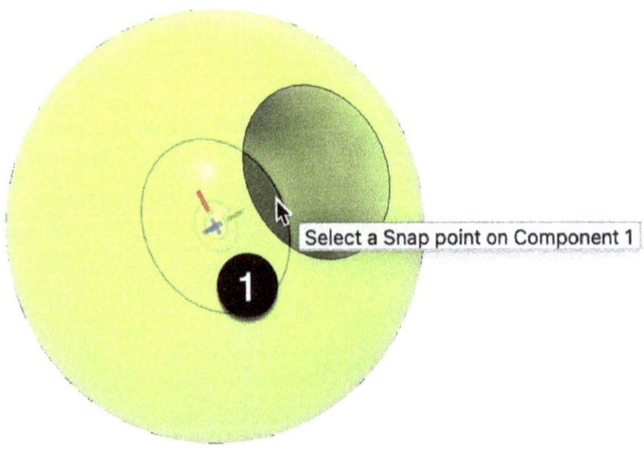

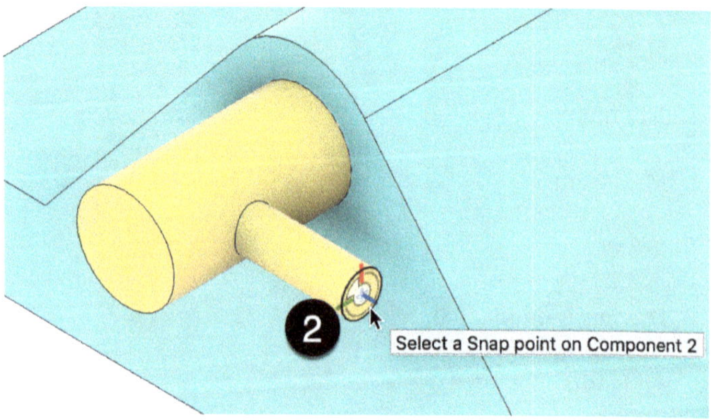

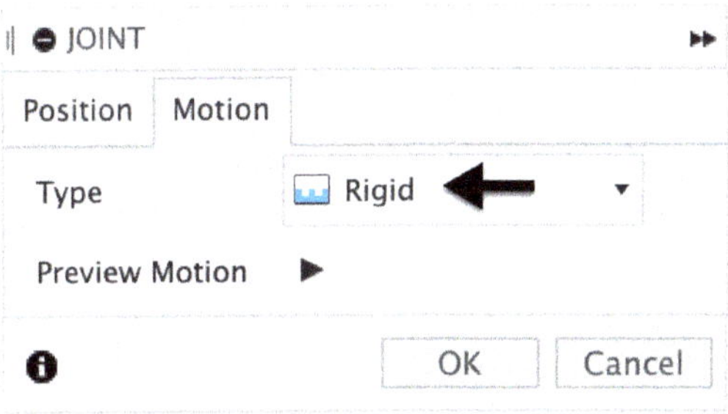

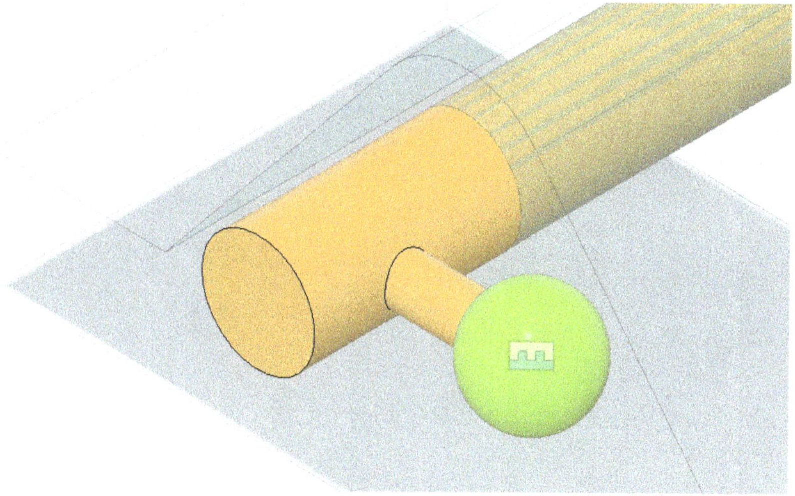

Click **OK** to create the rigid joint. Now, if you change the position or orientation of one component, then the other component of the rigid joint will also be affected.

Revolute Joint

The **Revolute** option creates a joint with a rotational degree of freedom. Activate the **Joint** command. Next, place the pointer on the cylindrical face of the first component; you can notice the three joint origins on the cylindrical face. Click the joint origin at the center of the end face of the cylinder to define the rotation axis.

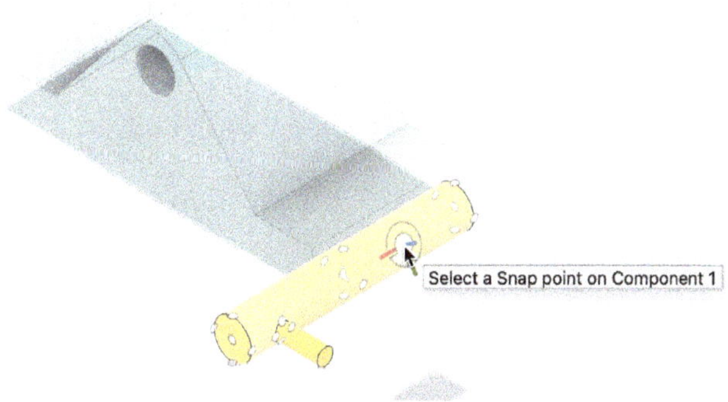

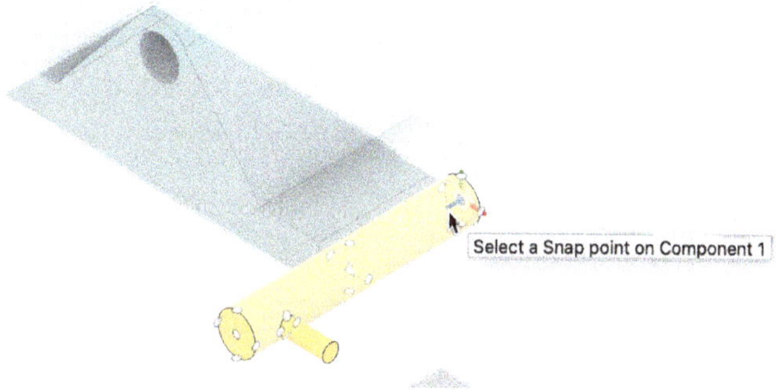

Likewise, select the joint origin on the end face of the second cylindrical feature. On the **Joints** dialog, click the **Motion** tab and select **Type > Revolute**; the two selected joint origins are aligned, and a revolute joint is created between the cylindrical faces.

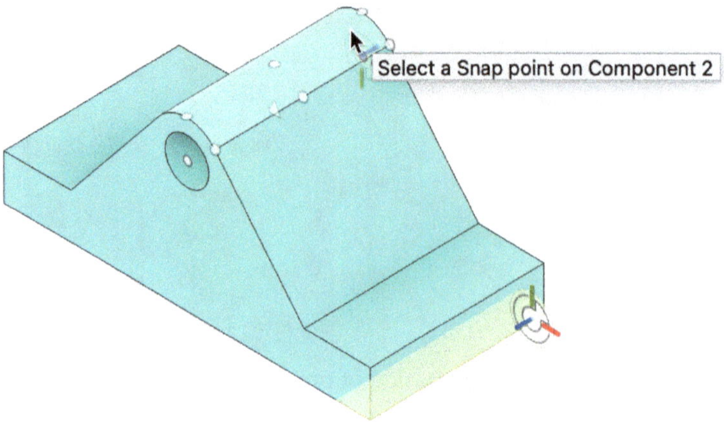

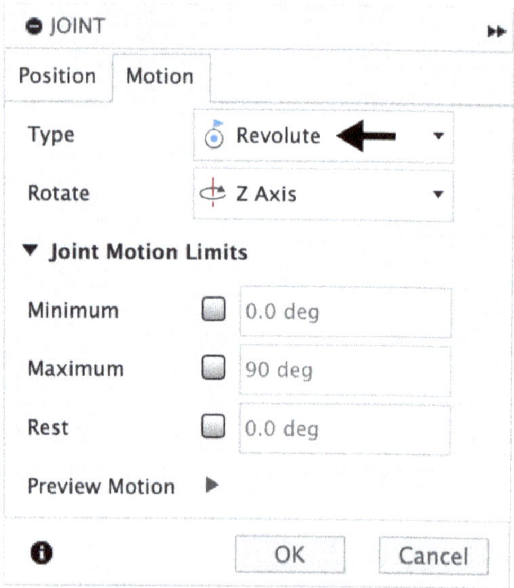

Check the **Maximum** option and type-in an angle value in the **Maximum** box. Next, type-in an angle value in the **Minimum** box. Click the **Preview Limits** icon to view the joint animation. Click the **Flip** icon to reverse the direction of the revolution. Next, click **OK** on the **Joint** dialog.

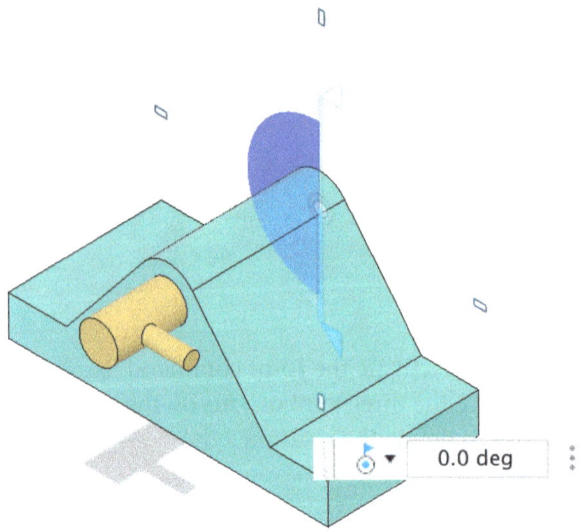

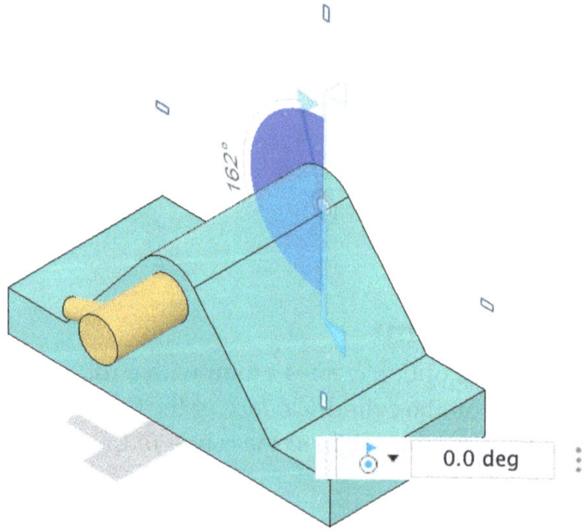

Cylindrical Joint

The **Cylindrical** joint has two degrees of freedom: translational and rotational. Activate the **Joint** command and select a joint origin on the cylindrical face of the first component. Next, select a joint origin on the cylindrical face of the target part. Click **Flip** to reverse the direction of the component, if required. Click the **Motion** tab and select **Type > Cylindrical**.

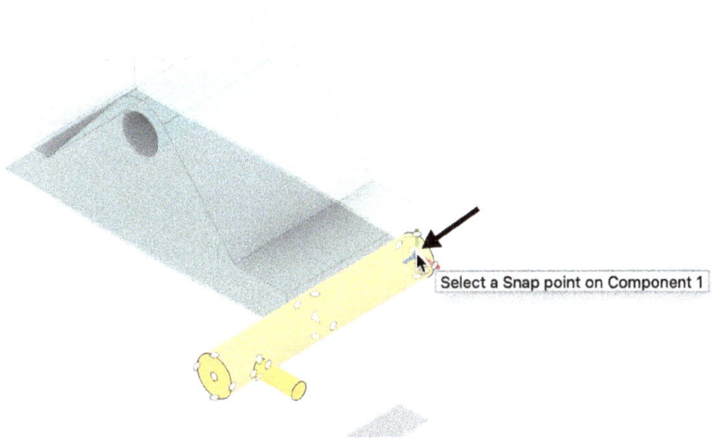

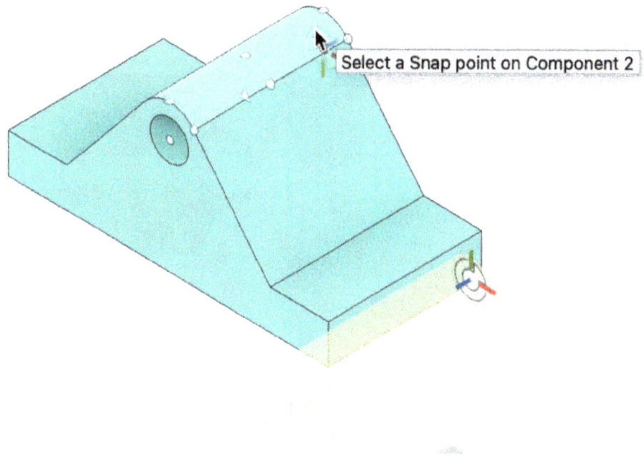

Select the **Z Axis** option from the **Axis** drop-down. You can also select the **Y Axis**, **X Axis** or **Custom** options. If you select the **Custom** option, you need to select an edge, line, or axis to define the axis of the cylindrical joint; the preview motion of the cylindrical joint appears. Next, click **Motion > Rotate** and check the **Maximum** option. Type-in values in the **Maximum** and **Minimum** boxes and click the **Preview Limits** icon; the rotation of the cylindrical joint is animated.

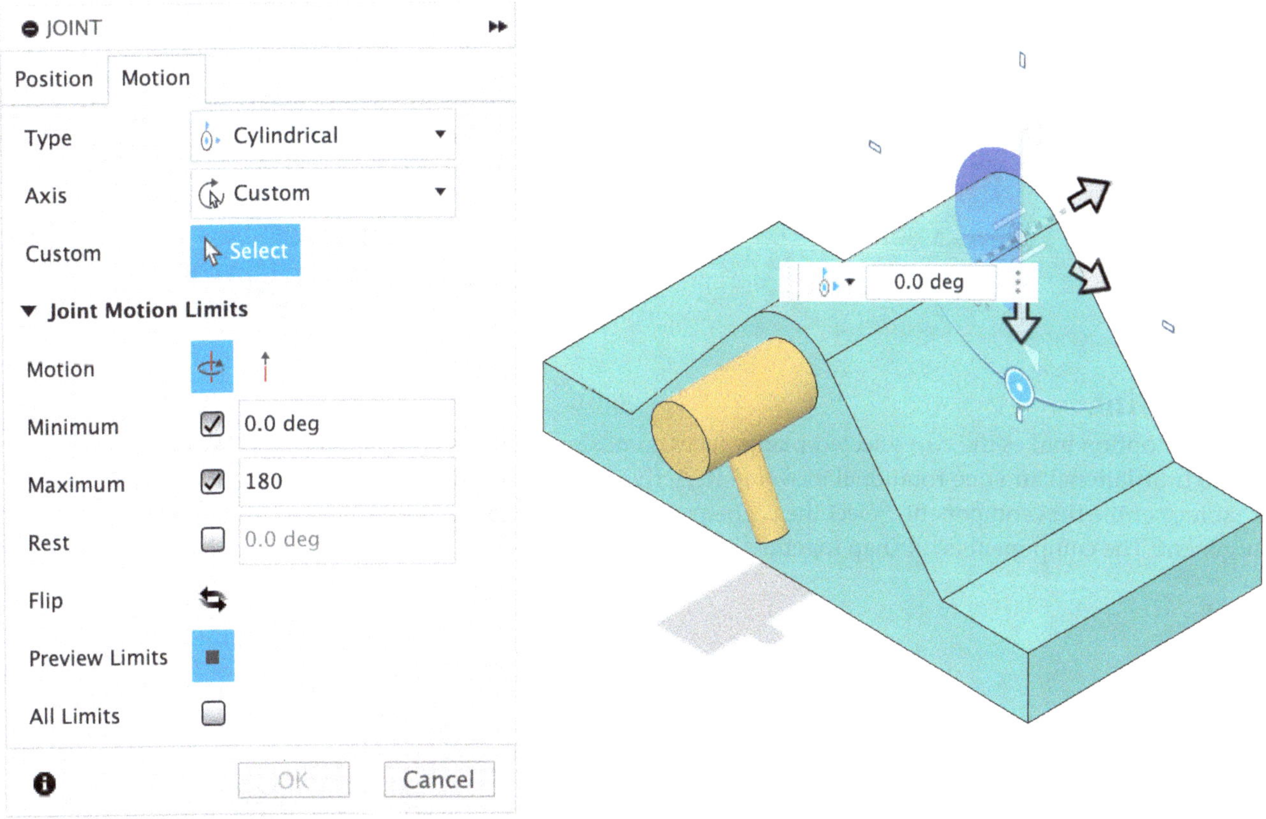

Click the **Motion > Slide** and check the **Maximum** and **Minimum** options. Next, type-in the **Maximum** and **Minimum** values and click the **Preview Limits** option. Check the **Rest** option and type in a value in the **Rest** box to define the initial position of the component.

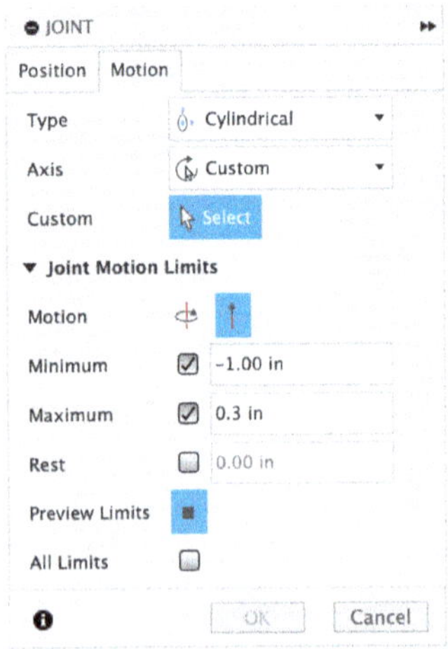

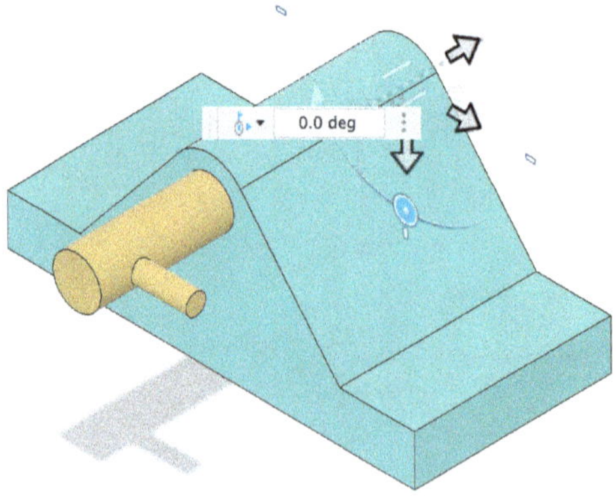

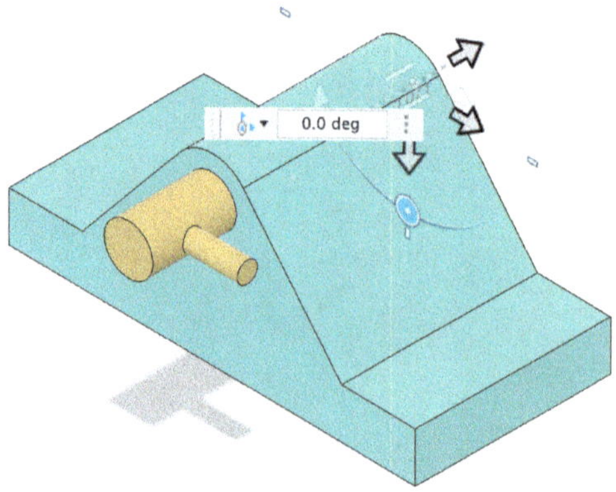

Check the **All Limits** option on the Joint dialog to animate the Cylindrical joint with all the rotational and slide motion limits. Click **OK** to create the cylindrical joint.

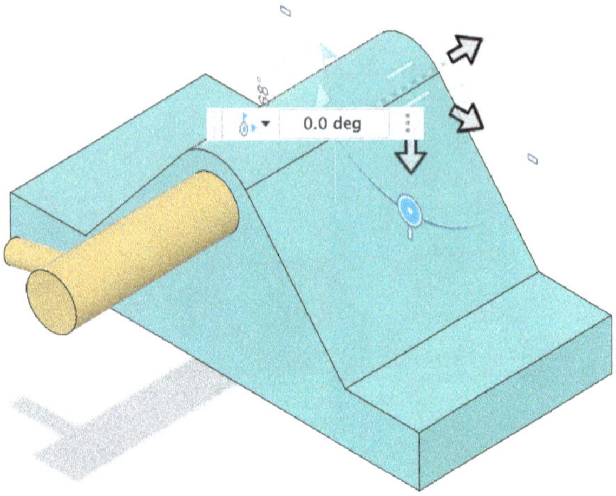

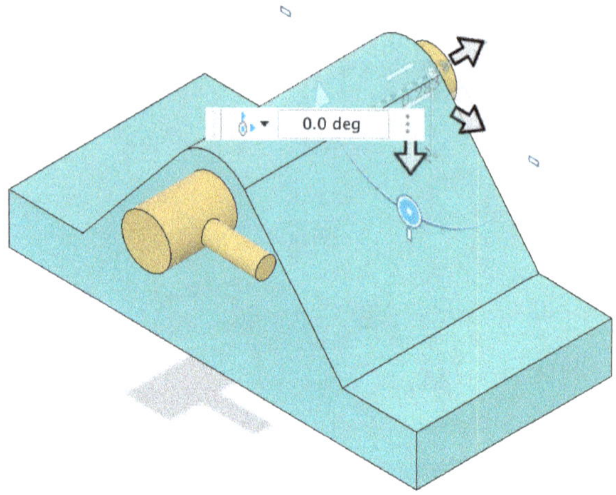

Planar Joint

The **Planar** option makes the two selected planar faces coincident with each other. Also, the placed component has two translational and one rotational movement. Activate the **Joint** command and select a joint origin on the planar face of the first component. Select the corresponding joint origin on the planar face of the second component. The components will snap together.

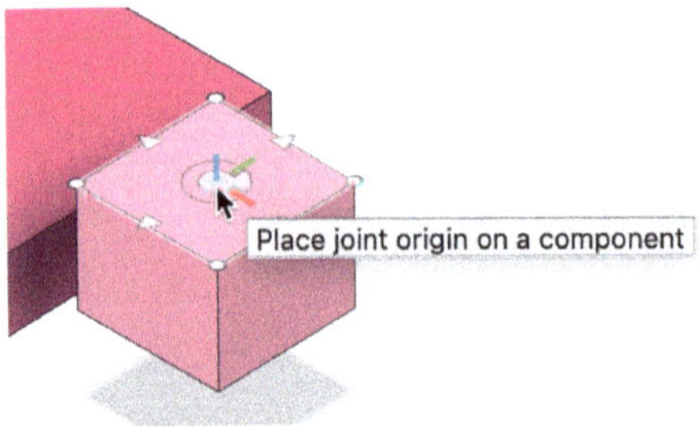

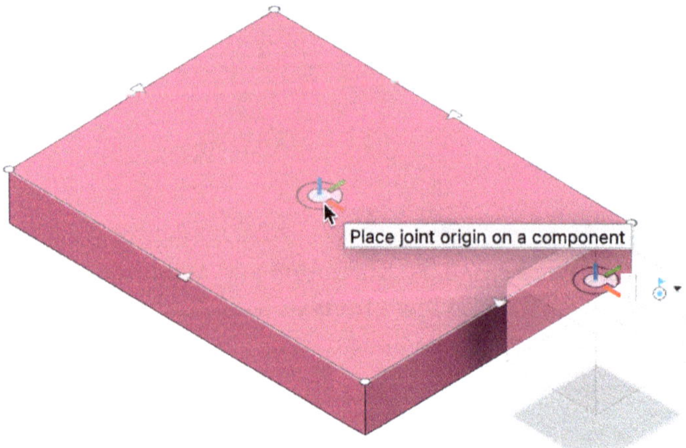

On the **Joint** dialog, click the **Motion** tab, and then select **Type > Planar**. Select the rotation axis from the **Normal** drop-down (in this example, select **Z Axis**). Next, select the axis from the **Slide** drop-down, and then click **OK** to create the planar joint.

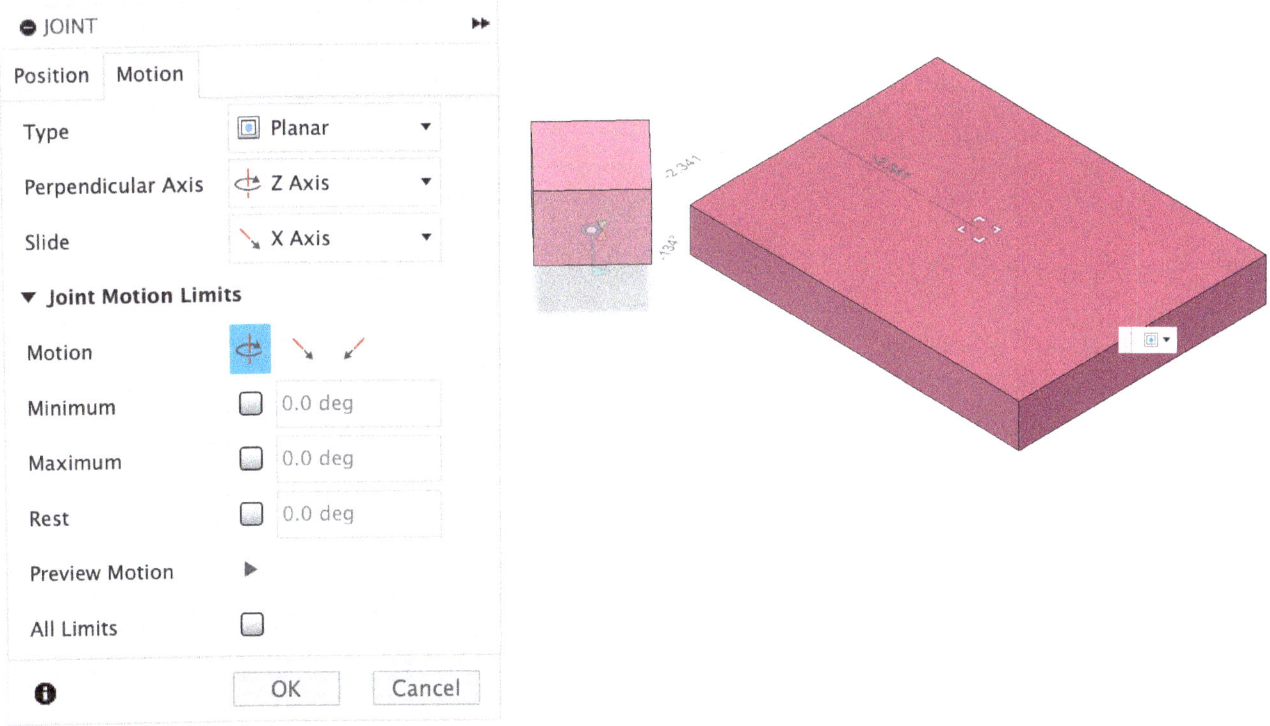

Click **Motion > Rotate** and check the **Minimum** and **Maximum** boxes. Next, type-in desired starting and ending angle values in the **Minimum** and **Maximum** boxes. To visualize the constrained movement, you can click the **Preview Limits** button, which will play an animation showing the component moving only within the specified rotational range.

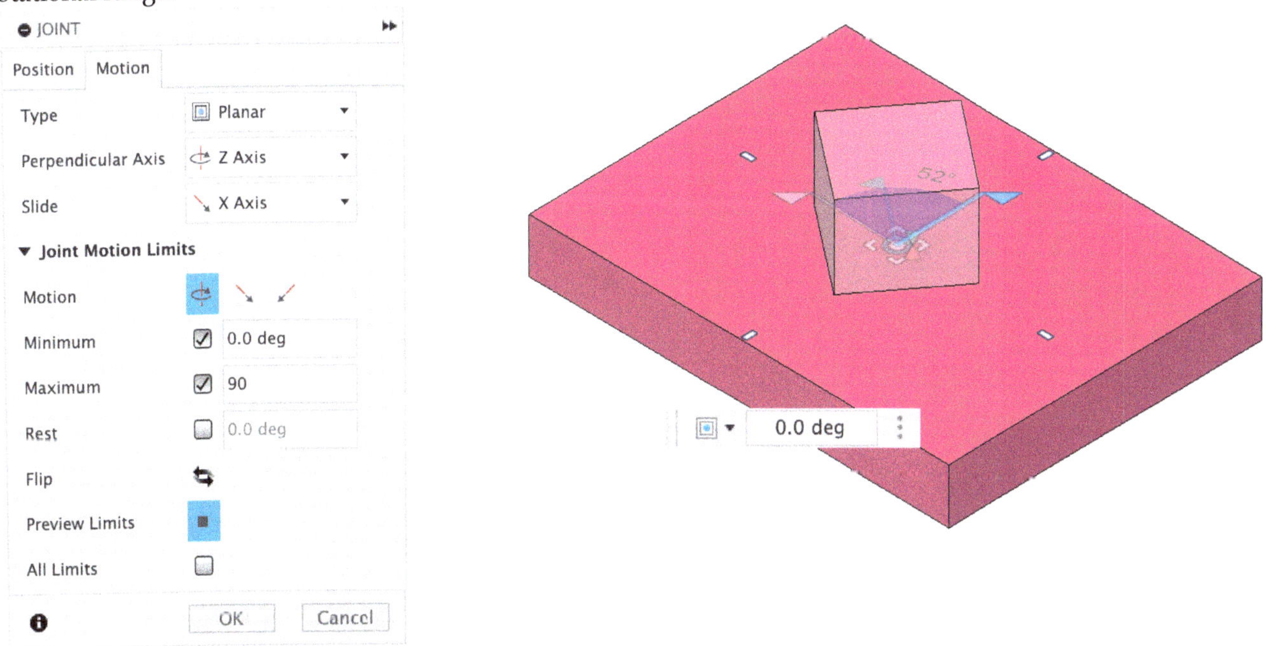

Click **Motion > Slide** and check the **Maximum**, **Minimum**, and **Rest** boxes. Next, enter values in the **Minimum**, **Maximum**, and **Rest** boxes, respectively. Likewise, select the second **Slide** icon and specify the **Minimum**, **Maximum**, and **Rest** values. Check the **All Limits** option and click the **Preview Limits** icon. Click **OK** to create the **Planar** joint.

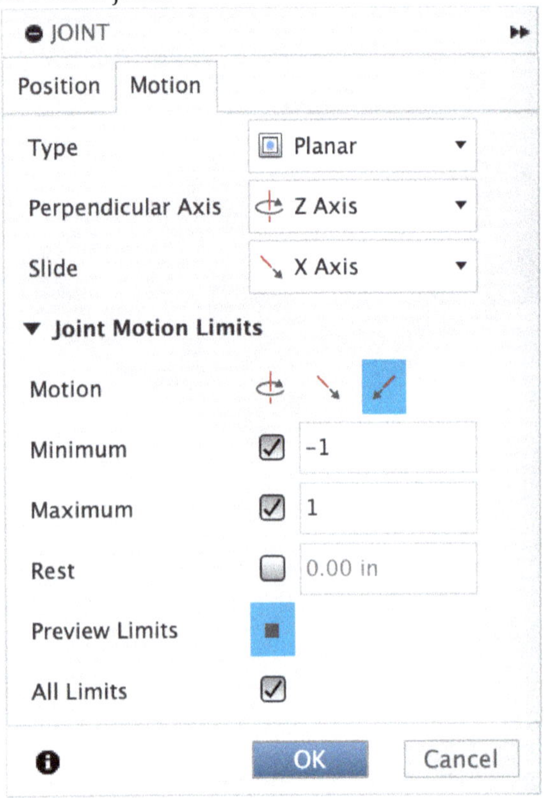

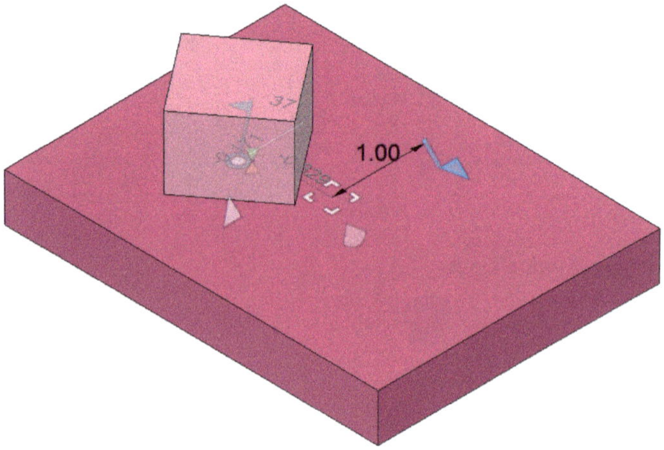

Slider Joint

The **Slider** option creates a slider joint between two components. The inserted component will slide on the target part. The sliding direction can be specified using the **Slide** drop-down. To create this joint, activate the **Joint** command and specify the joint origins on the placement and target parts, as shown.

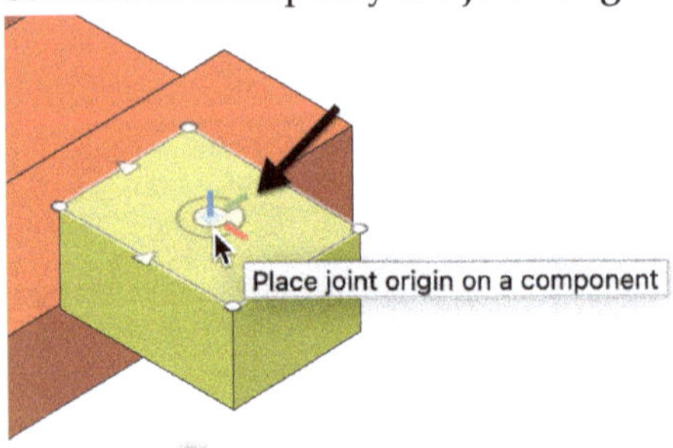

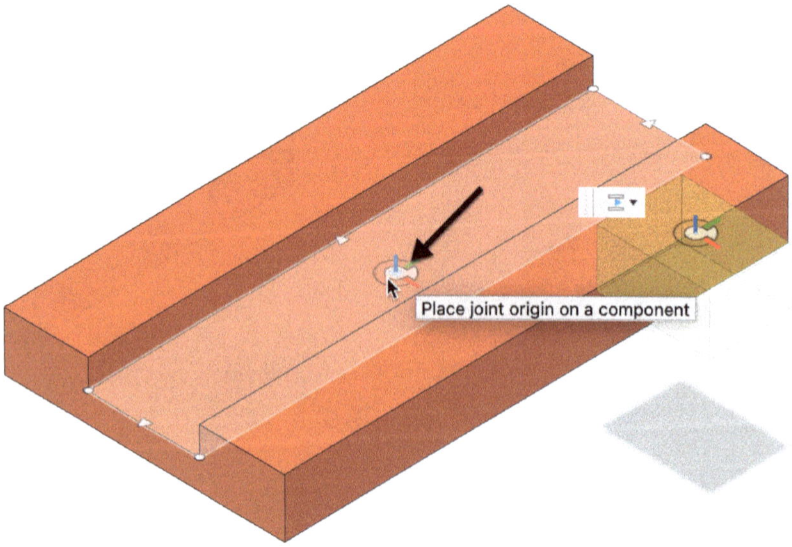

On the **Joint** dialog, click the **Motion** tab and select **Type > Slider**. Next, select the required axis from the **Slide** drop-down. You can also select the **Custom** option from the **Slide** drop-down and select and edge from the component.

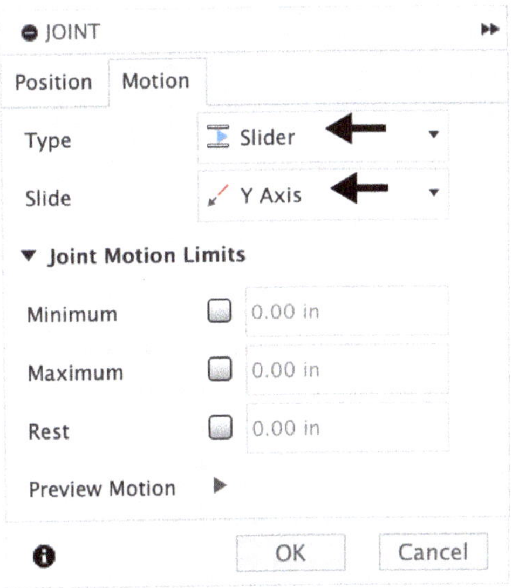

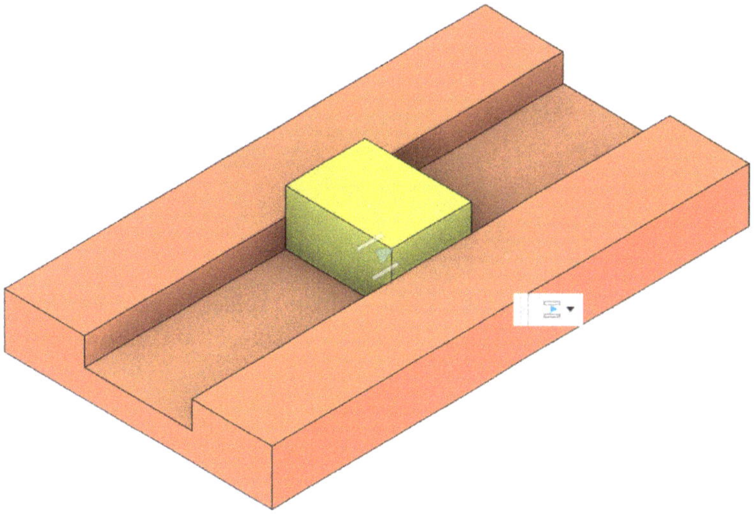

Next, check the **Minimum** and **Maximum** options and enter values in the **Maximum** and **Minimum** boxes. You can also use the **Measure** option to specify the **Maximum** and **Minimum** values. To do this, hover the pointer on the **Maximum** box and click the **Menu** option. Next, select the **Measure** option from the menu. Next, select an edge. The length of the selected edge is entered in the **Maximum** box. Likewise, specify the **Minimum** value and click **OK** on the **Joint** dialog.

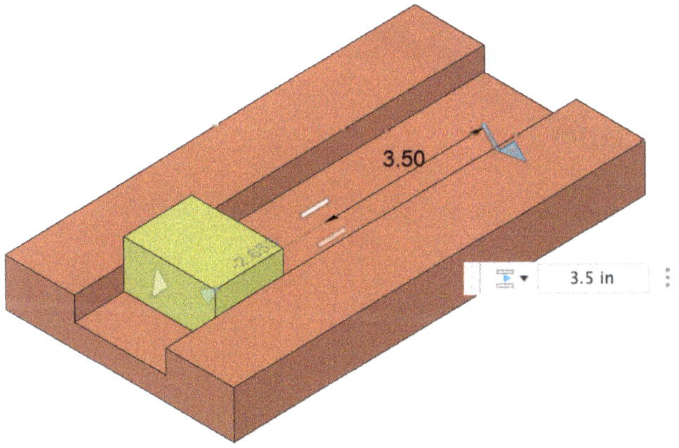

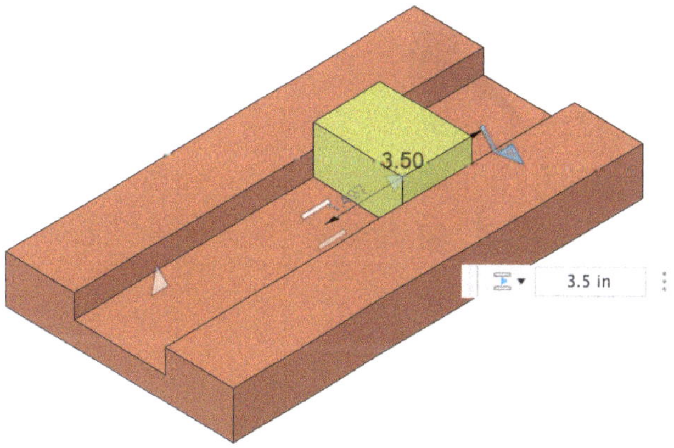

Pin-Slot Joint

The **Pin-Slot** option helps you to insert a cylindrical component into the slot. The cylindrical component will be able to translate along with the slot. In addition to that, it can rotate about its own axis. To create this joint, activate the **Joint** command and select a joint origin of the cylindrical component. Also, select the joint origin of the slot face of the second component.

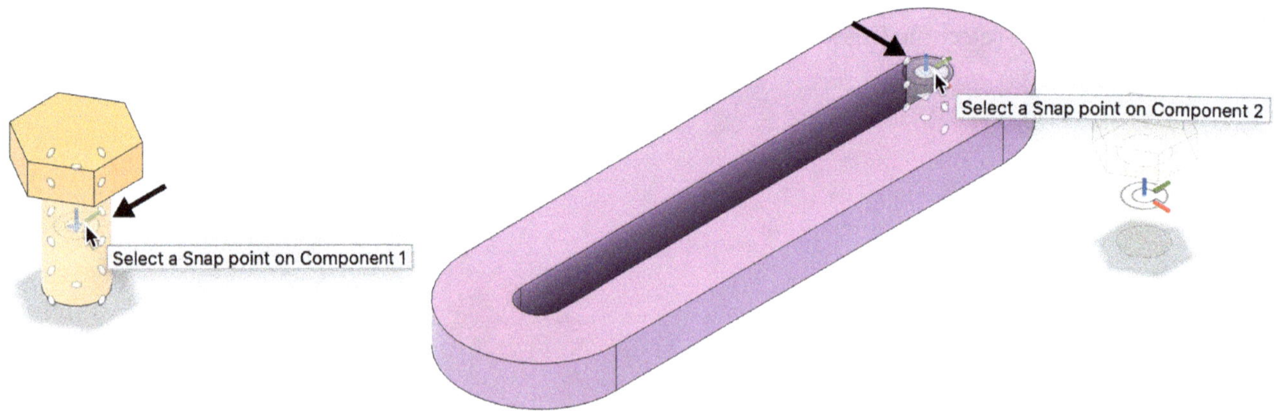

On the **Joint** dialog, click the **Motion** tab and select **Type > Pin-Slot**. Select the rotation axis from the **Rotate** drop-down (in this example, select **Z Axis**). Next, select the **Custom** option from the **Slide** drop-down, and then select the slot edge, as shown.

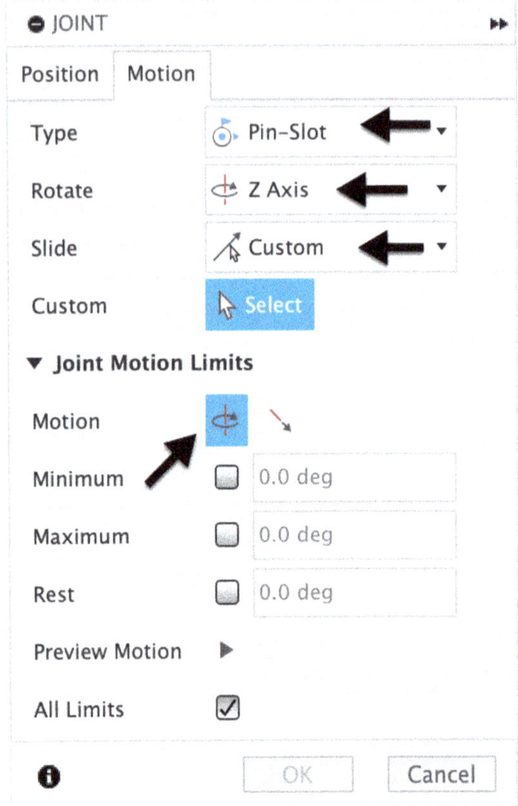

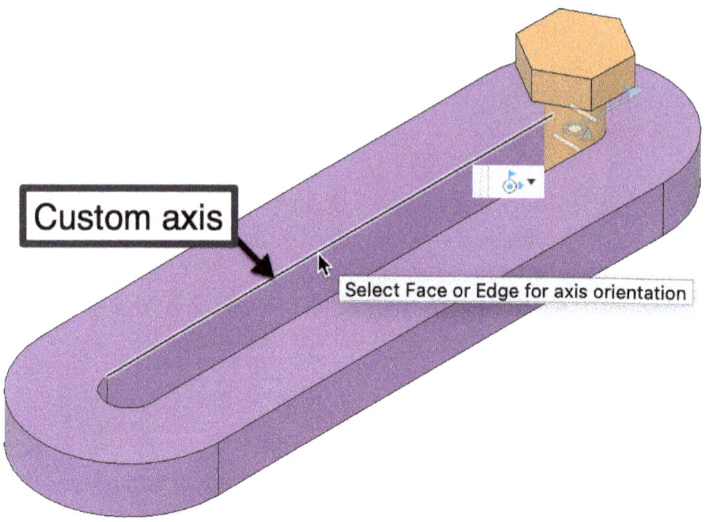

Select **Motion > Rotate** and specify the **Minimum** and **Maximum** values. Next, select **Motion > Slide** and specify the **Minimum** and **Maximum** values. Next, click the **Preview Motion** icon to view the animation of the Pin-Slot joint. Click **OK** to create the Pin-slot joint.

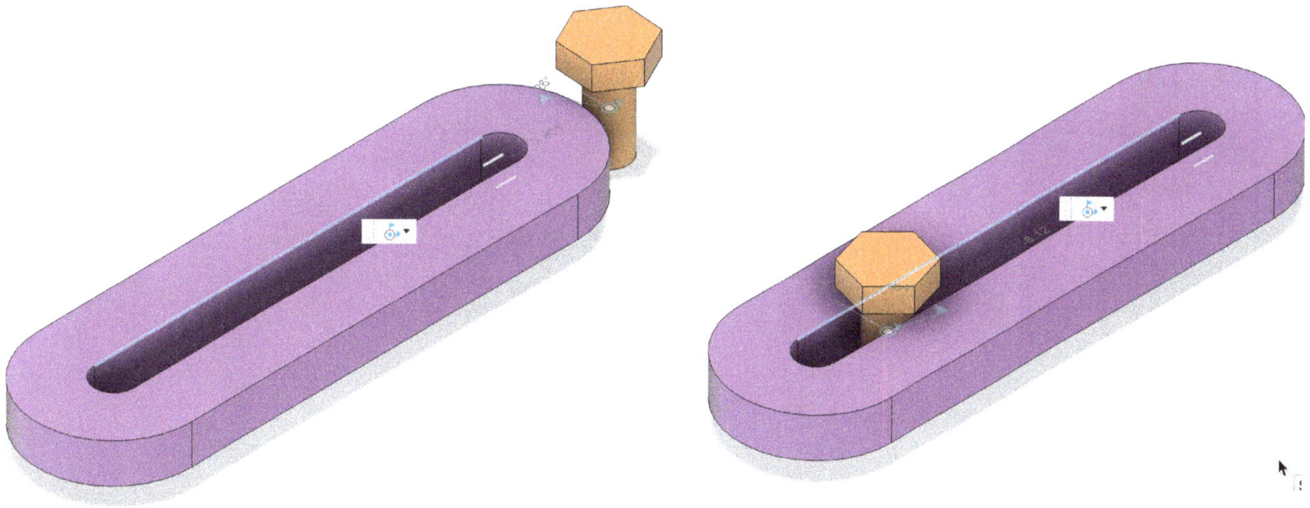

Joint Origins

Joint origins are snapping points on the components that are used to create a joint between two components. For example, activate the **Joint** command and place the pointer on the cylindrical face of the shaft, as shown. You can notice the snap points on the component at both the ends and middle. Select the joint origin displayed at the bottom end. Next, place the pointer on the hole; the joint origins appear. You can press and hold the Ctrl key (or command key on your Macbook) to select the joint origins located inside the hole.

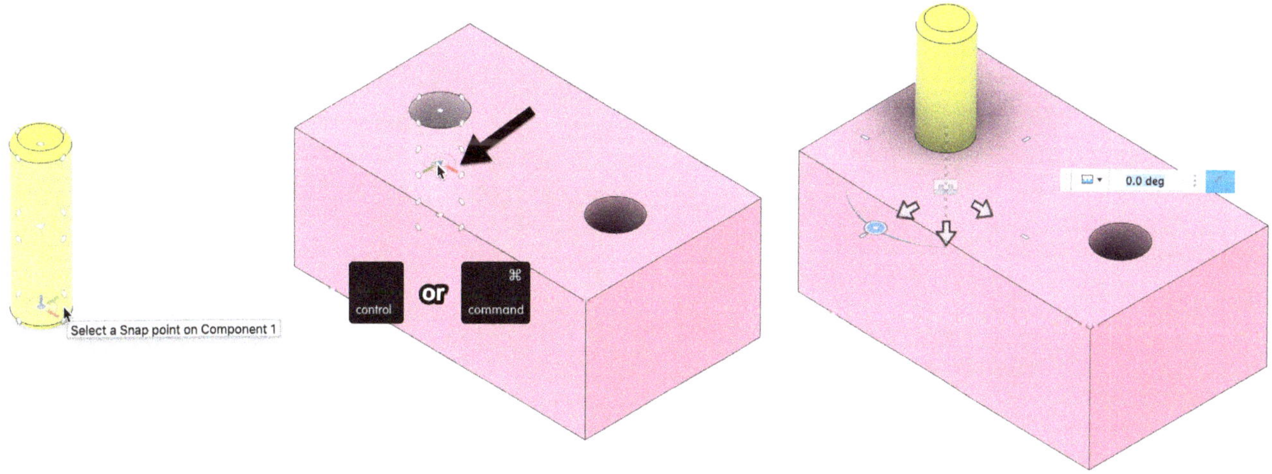

You have noticed that the joint origins are displayed at the ends and middle of the component. However, you can create a joint origin at the location other than the end and middle of the component. To do this, open the component in a separate tab. Next, click **Solid > Assemble > Joint Origin** on the toolbar.

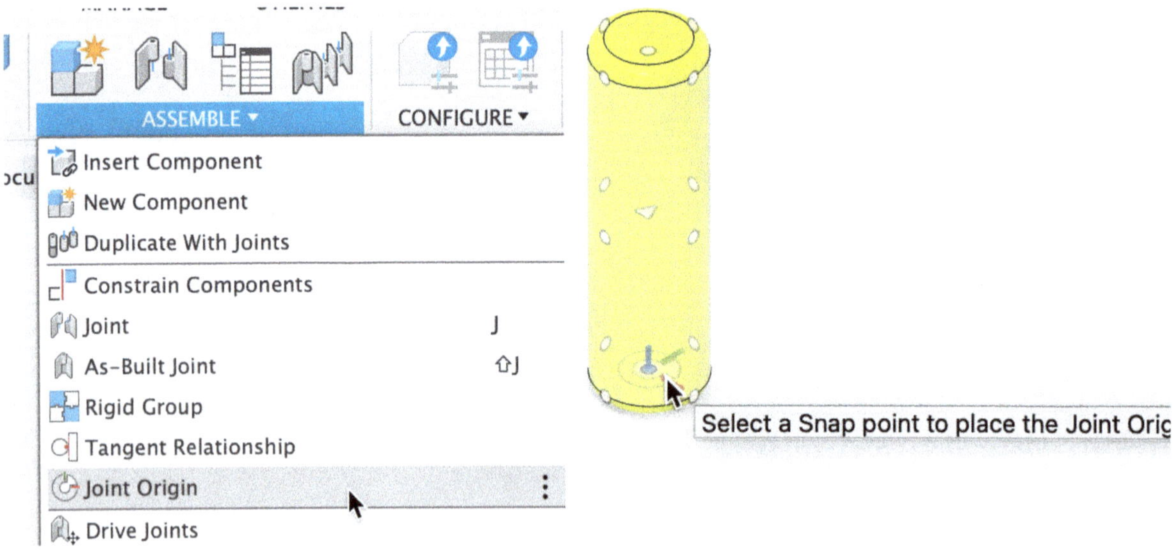

Next, select **Mode > Simple** from the **Joint Origin** dialog. Select the joint origin on the bottom end face of the component, as shown. On the **Joint Origin** dialog, type-in a value in the **Z Offset** box, and then click **OK**. Next, save and close the component.

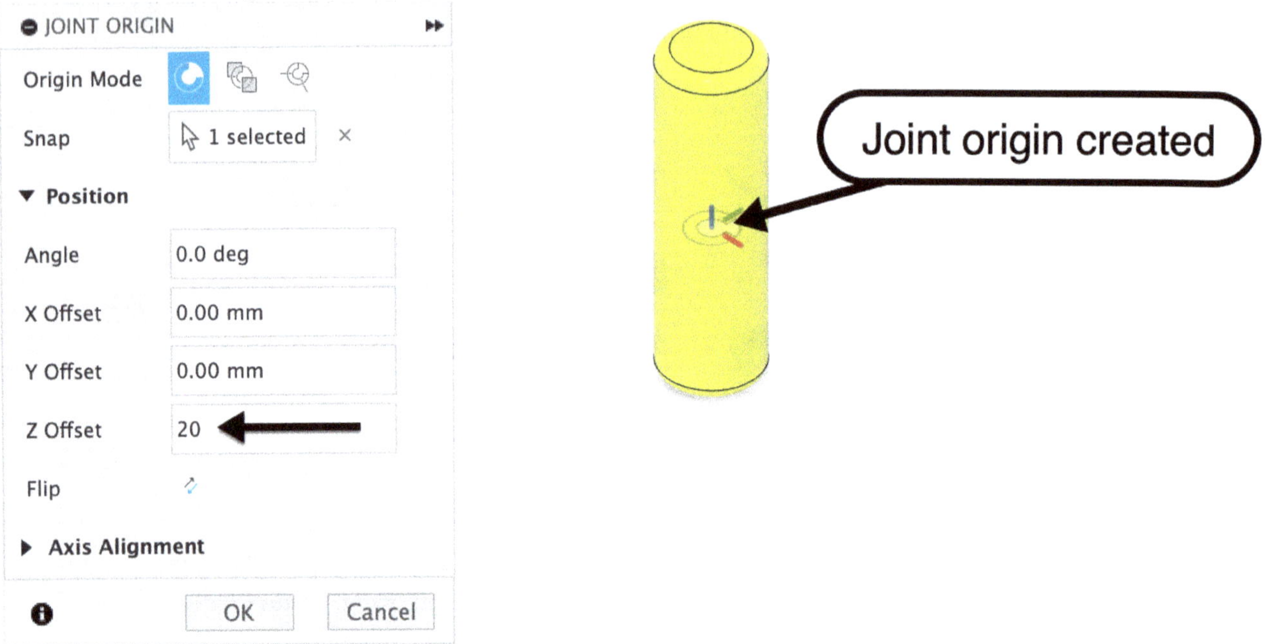

Open the assembly file and insert the component with a new joint origin. Next, activate the **Joints** command and select the newly created joint origin. Next, select the joint origin on the top end of the hole, as shown. Click **OK** to create the joint between the two joint origins. Now, change the **Visual Style** to **Wireframe** and notice that the component is placed in the hole without any intersection.

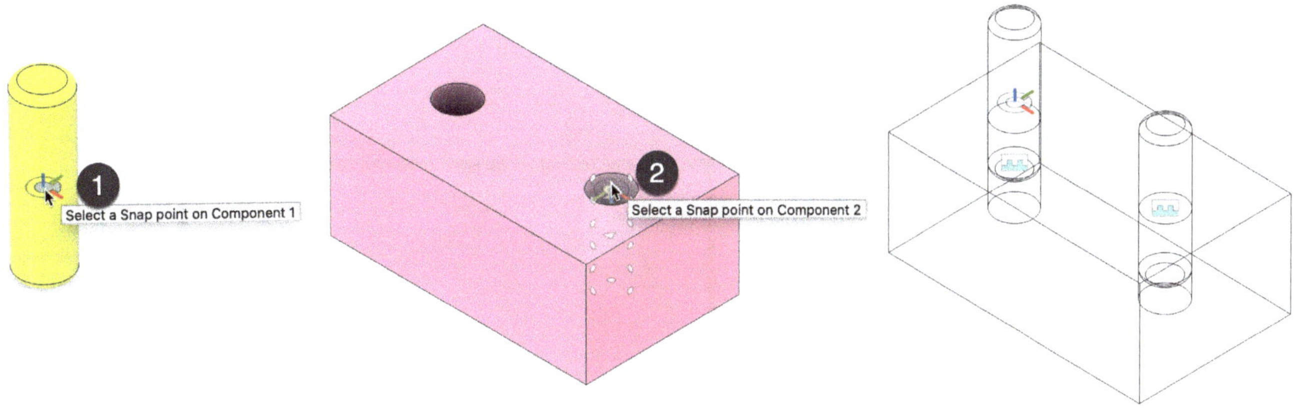

Tangent Relationship

The **Tangent** relationship makes a face of the component tangent to the set of connected faces of another component. Activate this command (click **Solid > Assemble > Tangent Relationship** on the toolbar). After activating this command, click on the face to be made tangent. Next, click on the tangent face on the target part. Click **OK** on the **Tangent Relationship** dialog; the first part will be made tangent to the target part.

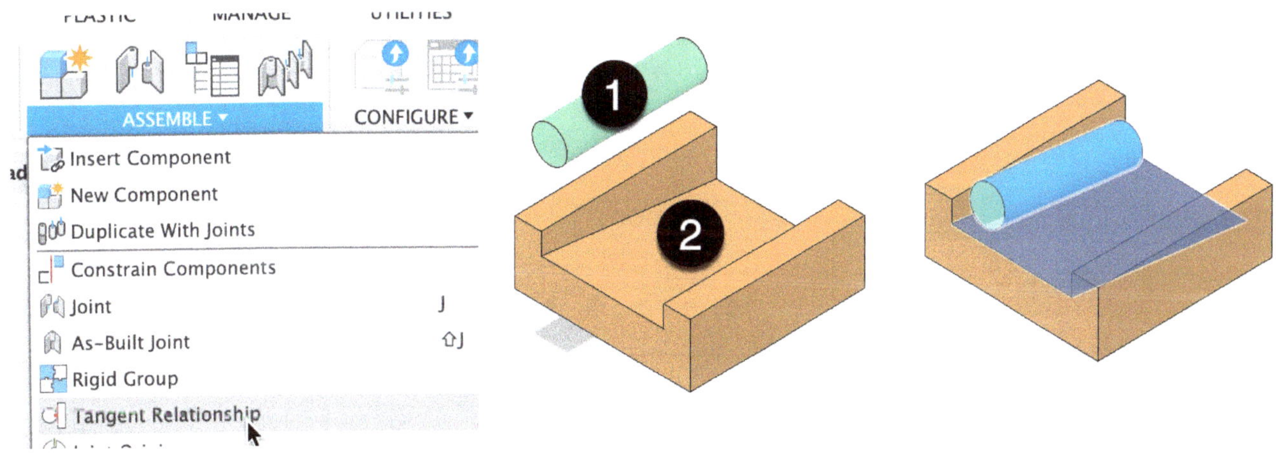

Click and drag the component; the tangent relationship maintained between the face of the first part and the connected set of faces of the second part.

Rigid Group

Earlier, you have learned about the **Rigid** joint, which is used to make two components as a rigid set. The **Rigid Group** command is similar to the **Rigid** joint except that it is used to combine multiple components as a rigid set.

To do this, click **Solid > Assemble > Rigid Group** on the toolbar, and then select the components to be combined. Click **OK** on the **Rigid Group** dialog.

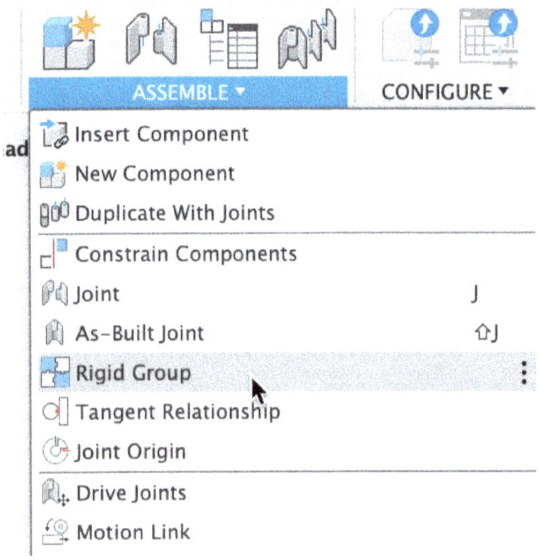

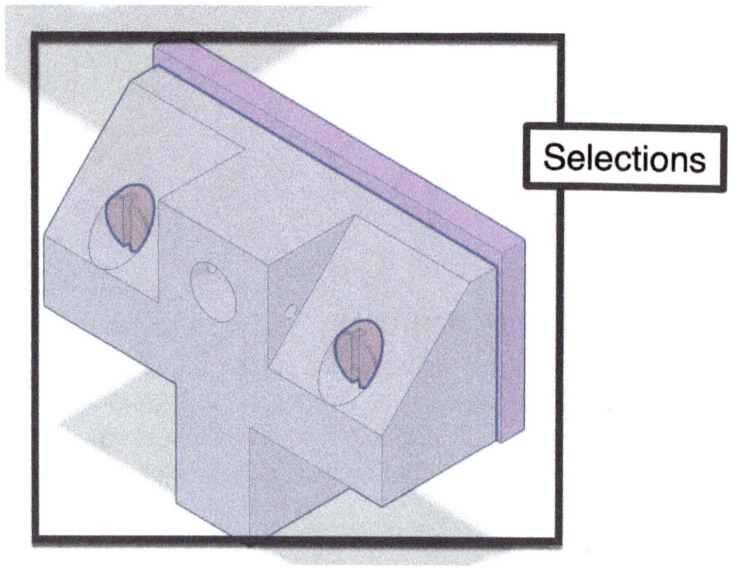

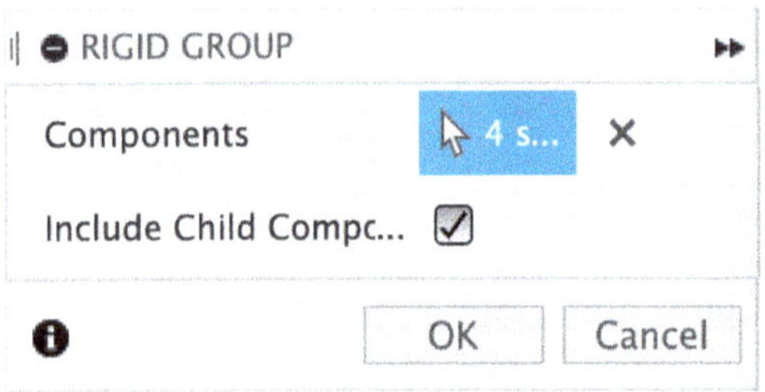

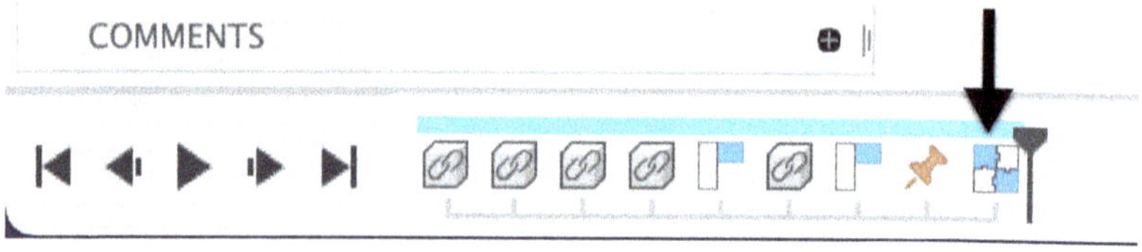

Now, create a joint between any one of the components of the rigid group and the remaining component of the assembly. The entire rigid group is constrained.

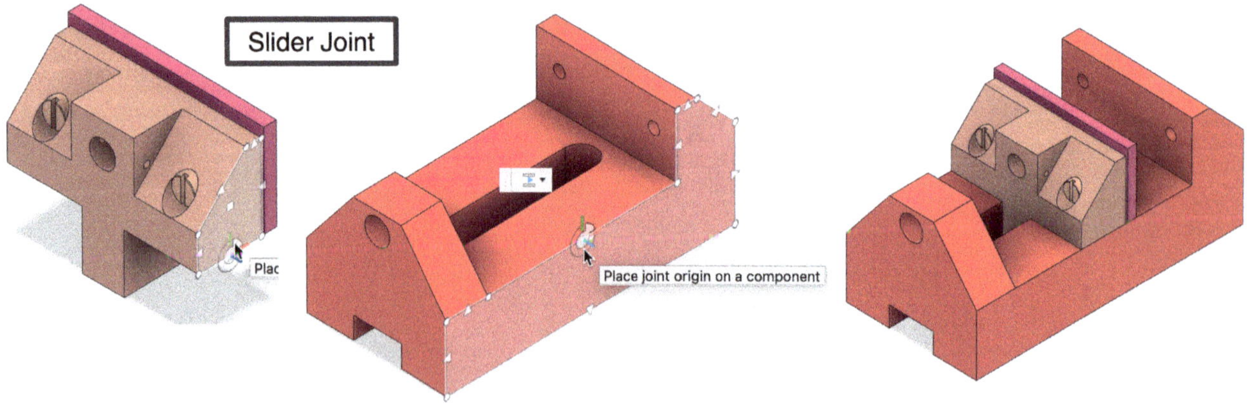

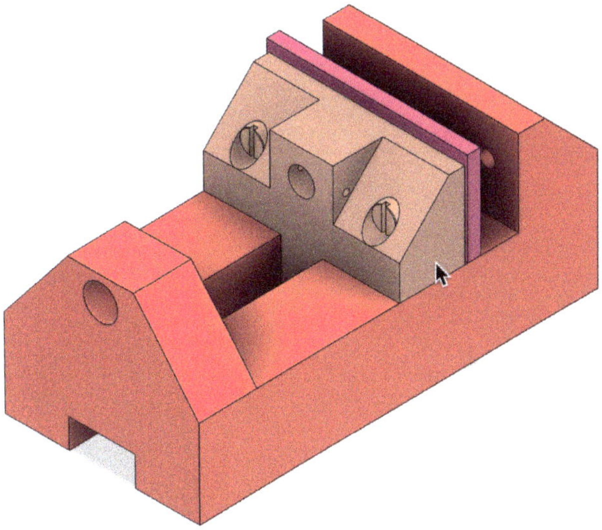

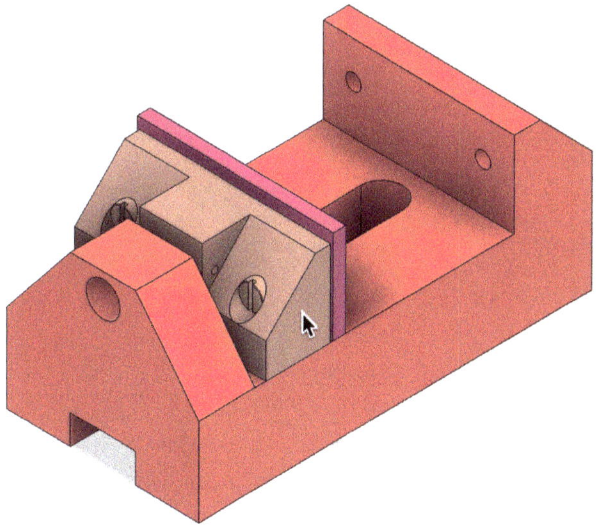

Locking/Unlocking Joints

Autodesk Fusion 360 allows you to lock a joint at a particular position. For example, the assembly with a slider joint is shown in the figure. In this assembly, the movable jaw is free to slide on the horizontal face of the base. You can lock the movable jaw at a particular location. To do this, click and drag the movable jaw to the desired position. Next, expand the **Joints** folder in the **Browser**. Click the right mouse button on the movable jaw in the graphics window, and then select **Find in Browser**; the movable jaw is highlighted in the Browser. Click the right mouse button on the movable jaw in the **Browser** and select the **Select Referencing joints** option; the joints referencing the movable jaw are highlighted in the **Joints** folder.

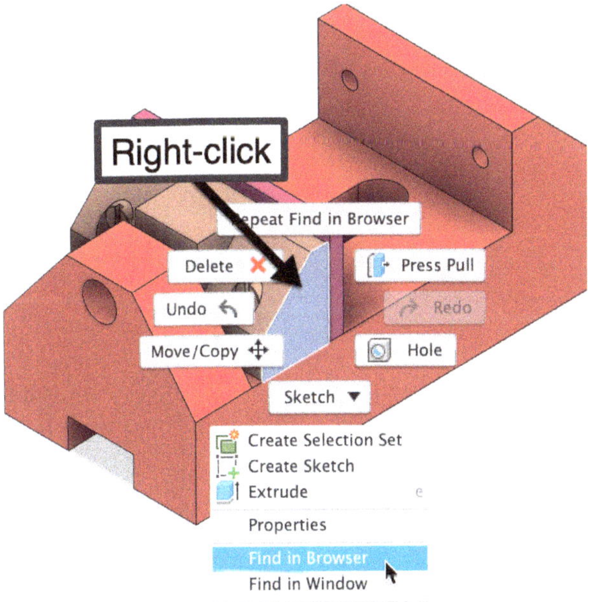

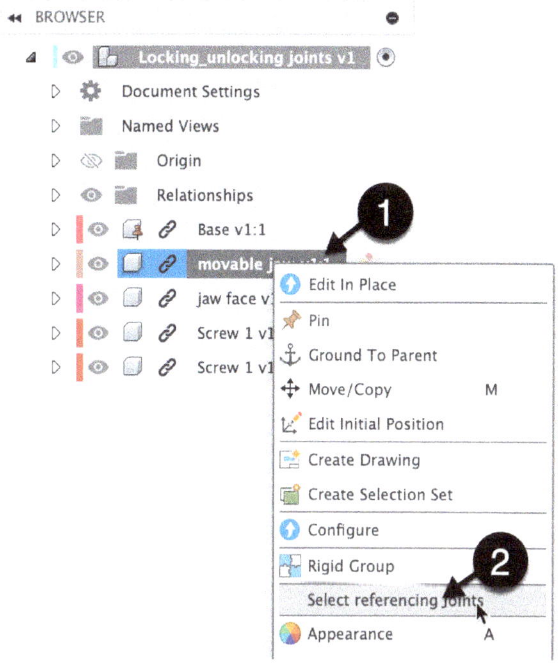

Now, right click on the highlighted **Slider** joint and select the **Lock Motion** option; the movable jaw is locked at its current position. Click and drag the movable jaw and notice that it is unmovable. To move the movable jaw, right click on the **Slider** joint in the **Joints** folder, and then select the **Unlock Motion** option.

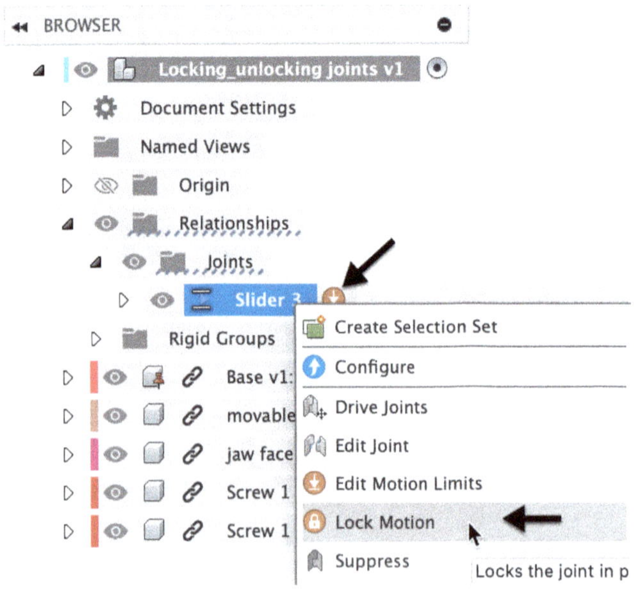

Editing Motion Limits

The **Edit Motion Limits** option allows you to specify limits for the movable component of a joint. For example, the movable jaw in the **Slider** joint is free to slide without any restriction.

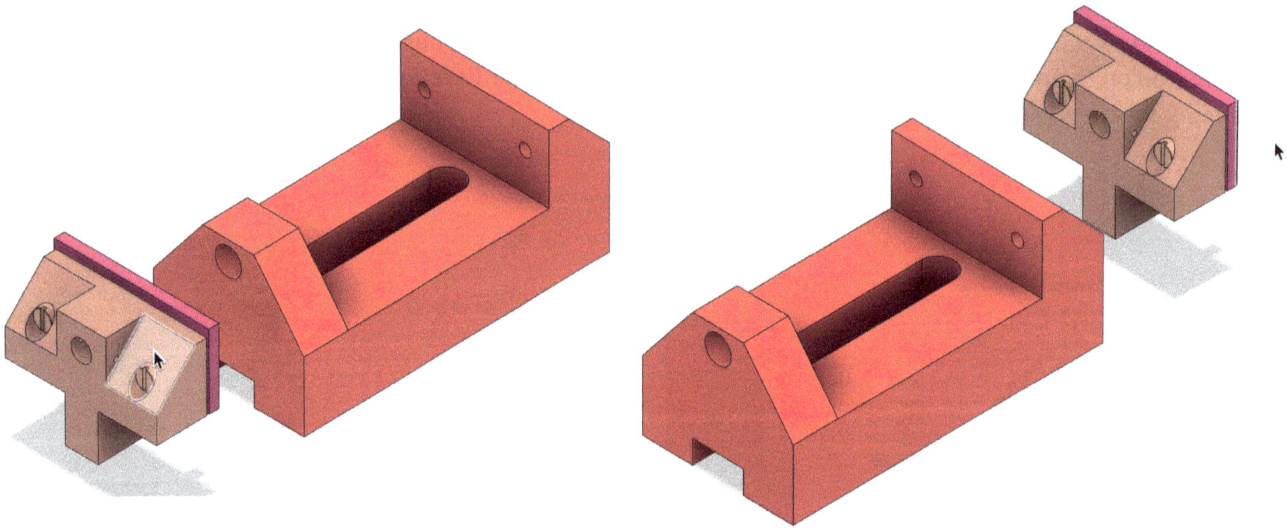

You can restrict the movement between the vertical faces of the Base. To do this, click the right mouse button on the **Slider** joint of the movable jaw, and then select **Go to Home Position**; the component is restored to its home position. Again, right click on the **Slider** joint and select **Edit Motion Limits**.

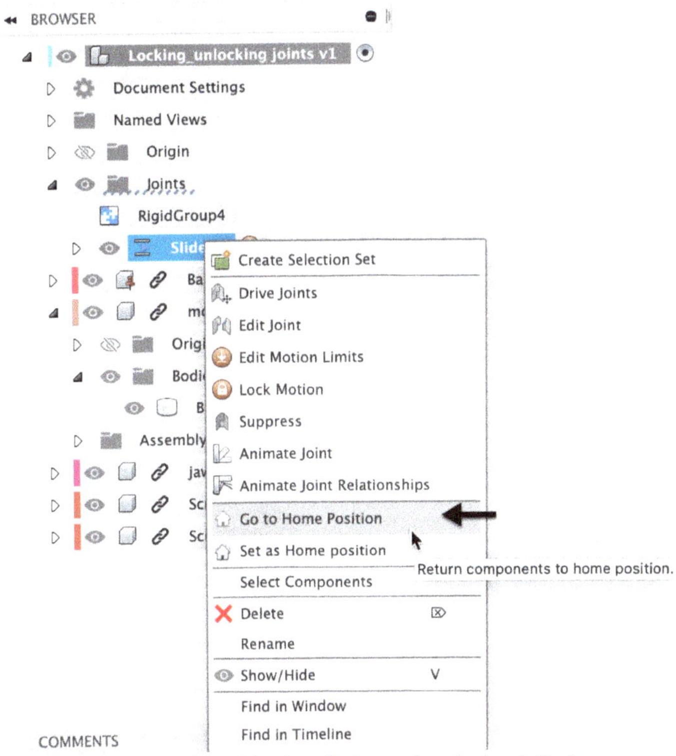

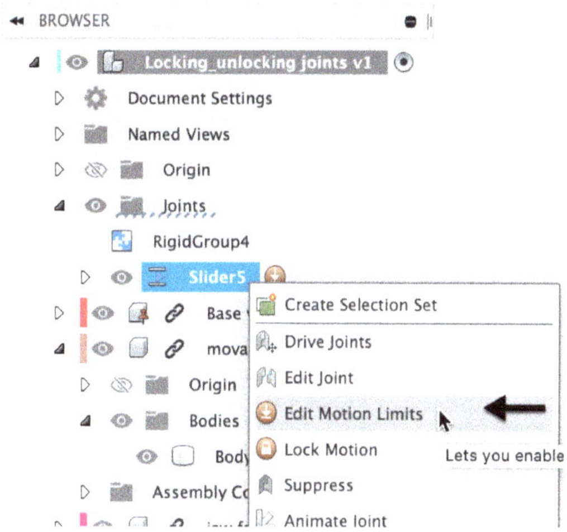

On the **Edit Motion Limits** dialog, check the **Minimum** option and click the menu button next to the value box located below it. Next, select the **Measure** option and click on the graphics window. Select the vertical faces of the two components, as shown; the distance between the selected faces is displayed in the value box. Click before the distance value and type -.

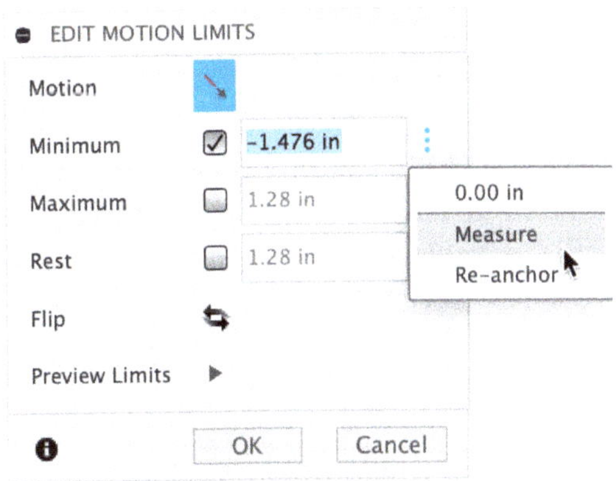

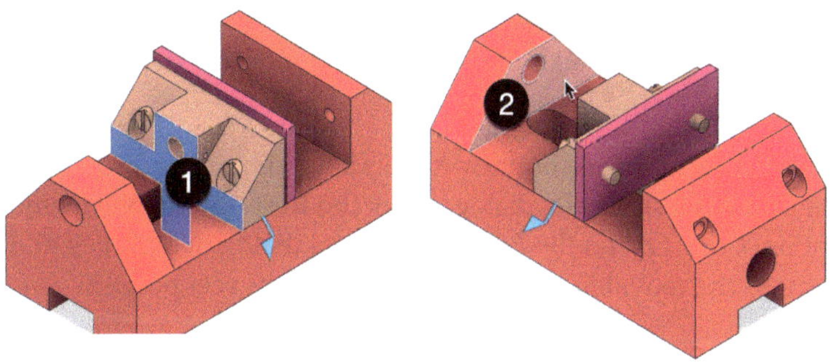

Next, check the **Maximum** option and click the menu button next to the value box displayed below the **Maximum** option. Select the **Measure** option and click on the graphics window. Next, select the two vertical faces of the assembly, as shown in the figure; the distance between the two faces will be entered in the value box. Click **OK** to apply the joint limits.

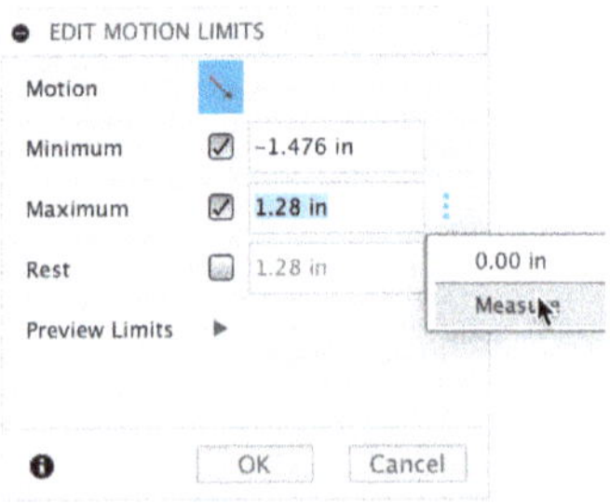

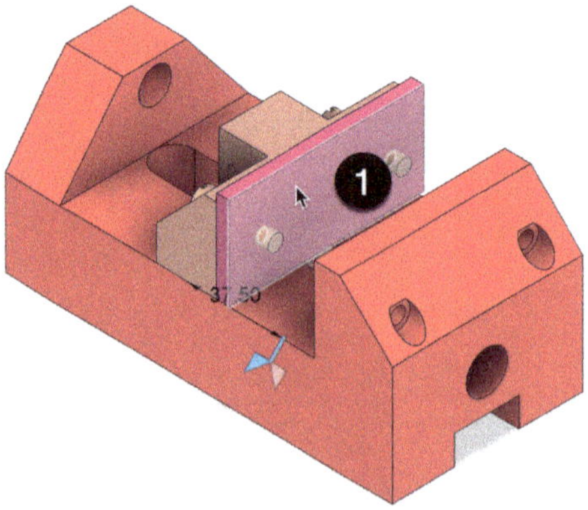

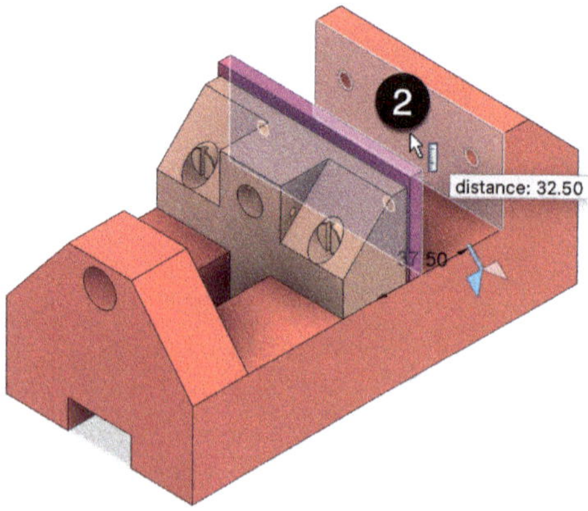

Click and drag the movable jaw and notice that the movement is constrained between the vertical faces of the Base. However, the movable jaw does not return to its initial position.

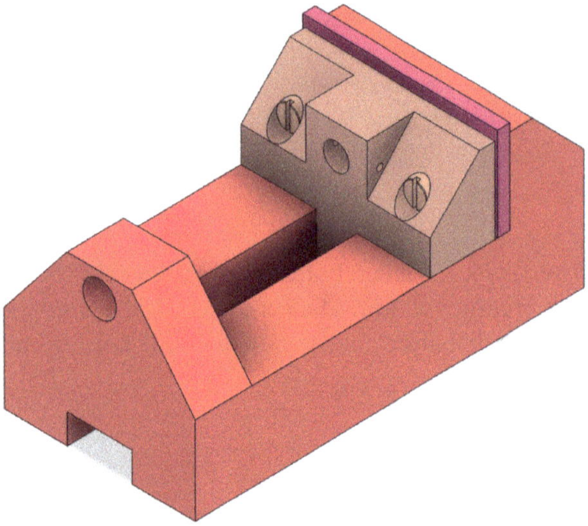

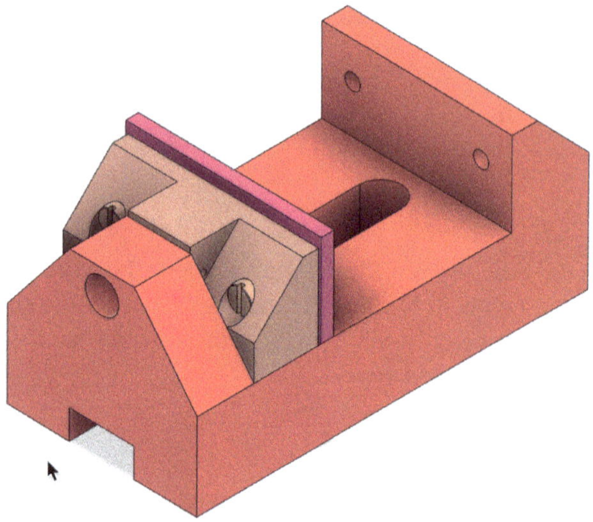

Click the right mouse button on the **Slider** joint in the Browser. Next, select the **Edit Motion Limits** option. On the **Edit Motion Limits** dialog, check the **Rest** option. Next, enter 0 in the value box displayed below the **Rest** option. Click **OK** on the **Edit Joint Limits** dialog. Next, click and drag the movable jaw. Release the mouse pointer; the movable jaw will be restored to its rest position.

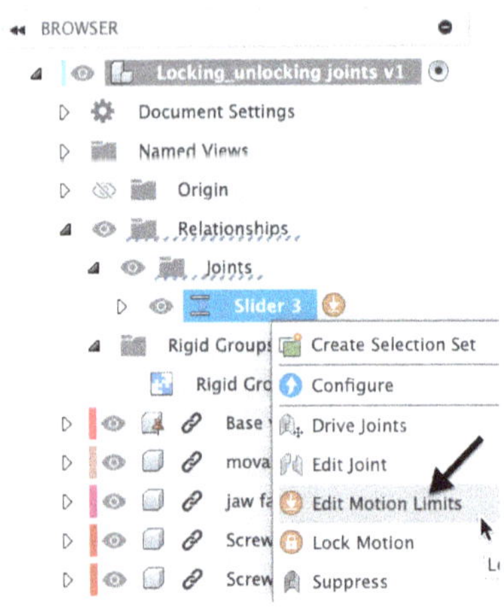

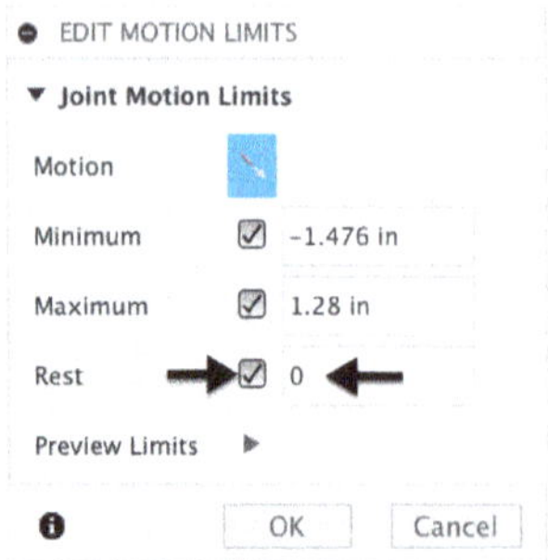

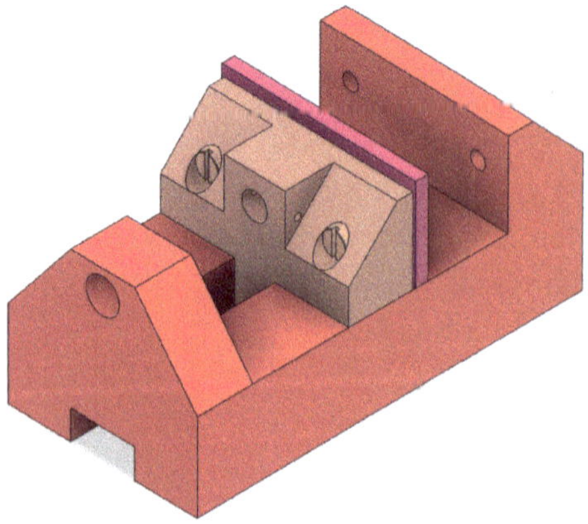

Edit Components Inside the Assembly

During the design process, the correct design is not achieved on the first attempt. There is always a need to go back and make modifications. Fusion 360 allows you to accomplish this process very easy. To modify a component in an assembly, select the component from the Browser; the selected component is highlighted in the graphics window. Next, click the **Edit in Place** icon displayed next to the selected component in the Browser; the **Associative Edit in Place** message box appears. It displays that the references to the other components will be captured in an assembly context. Click **OK** on the **Associative Edit in Place** message box; the component is activated in the assembly window.

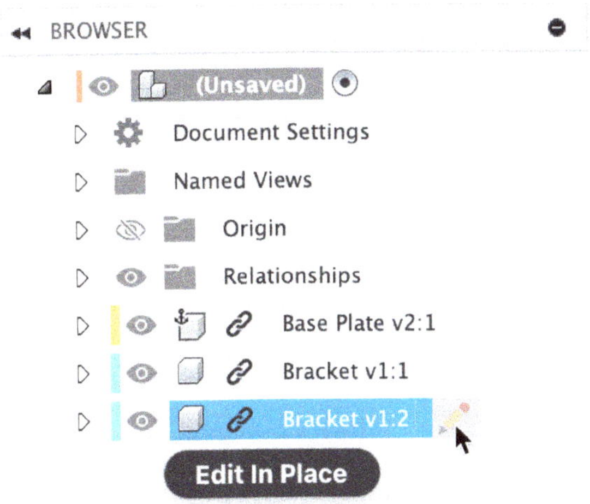

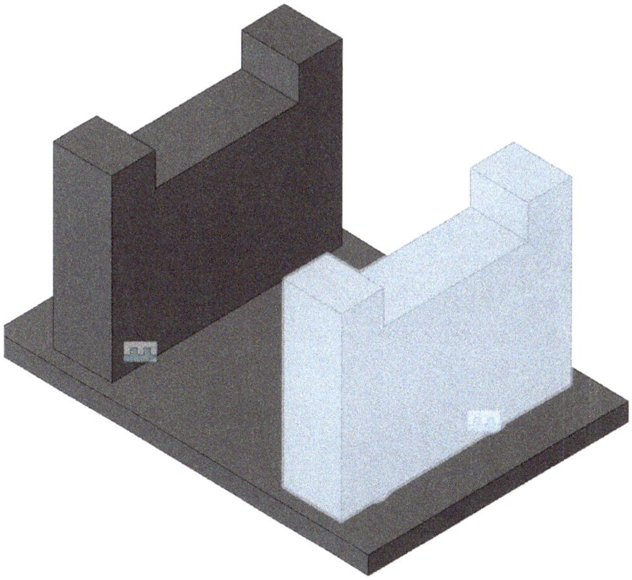

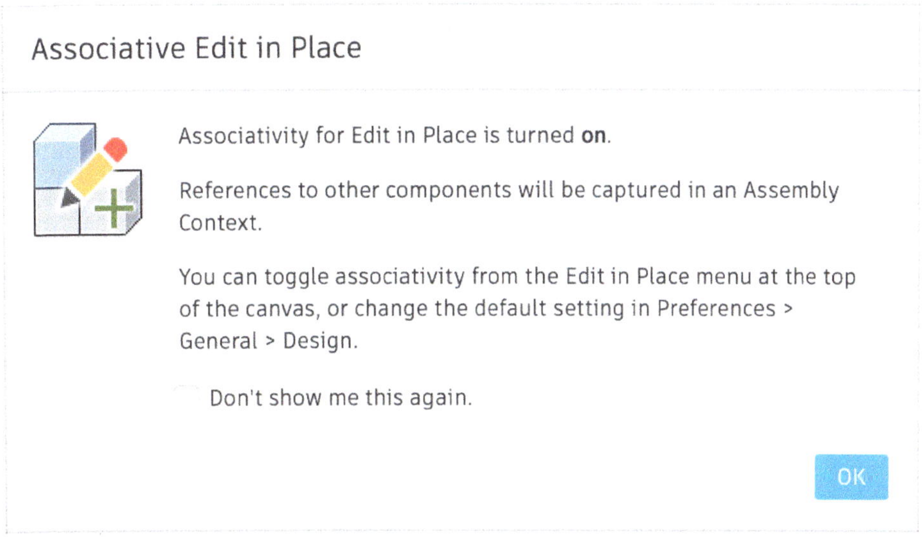

Make changes to the component and click the **Finish Edit in Place** icon the toolbar displayed in the graphics window. The assembly mode is activated.

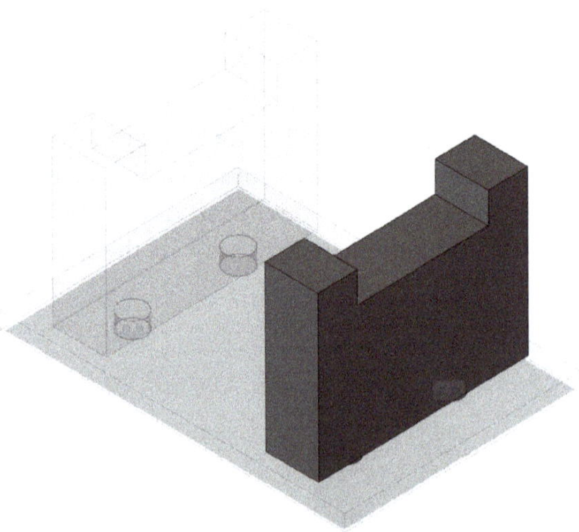

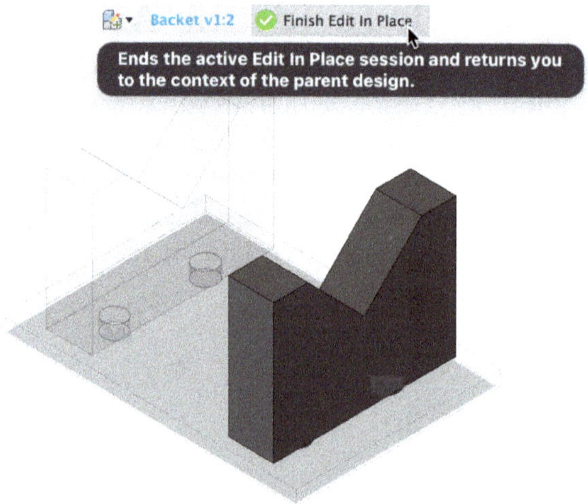

Drive Joints

The **Drive Joint** option helps you to position the components of a joint at the exact location by entering a value. To do this, locate the joint in the **Browser** and click the right mouse button on it. Next, select **Drive Joints** from the shortcut menu. Enter a value in the **Rotation** box (in case of a Revolute Joint) and click the **OK** button.

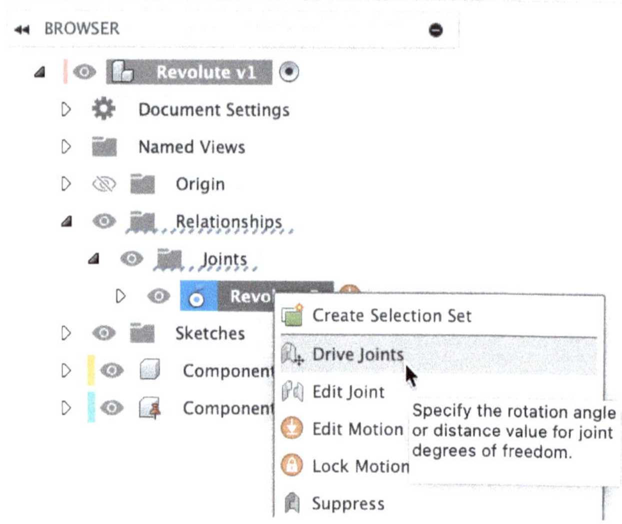

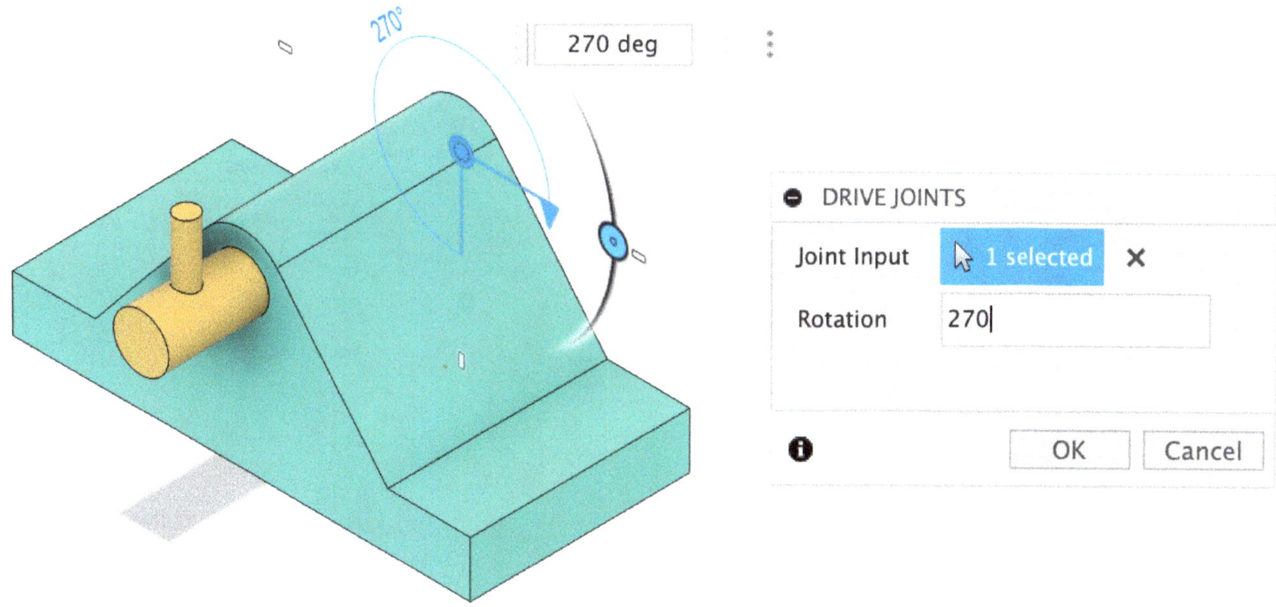

The options on the **Drive Joints** dialog change depending on the joint. For example, the **Pin-slot** joint has the **Distance** and **Rotation** boxes.

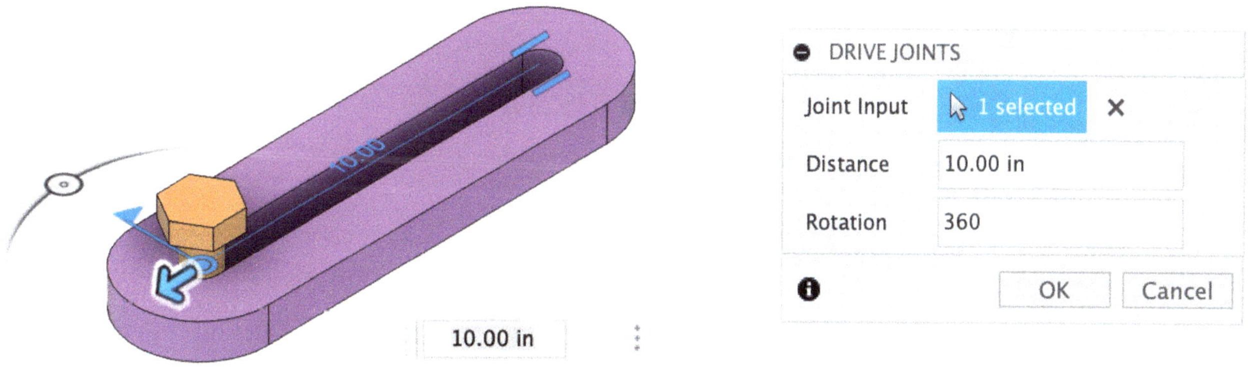

Planar Joint

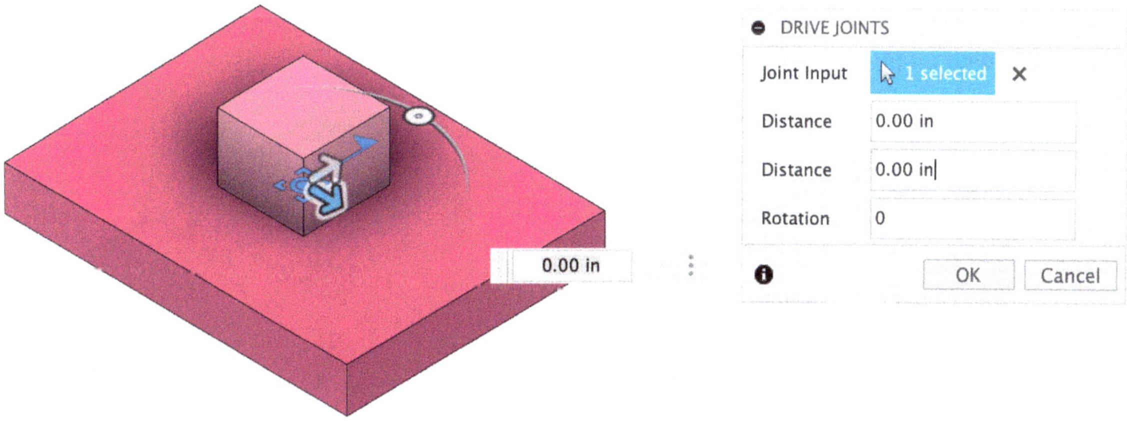

Slider Joint

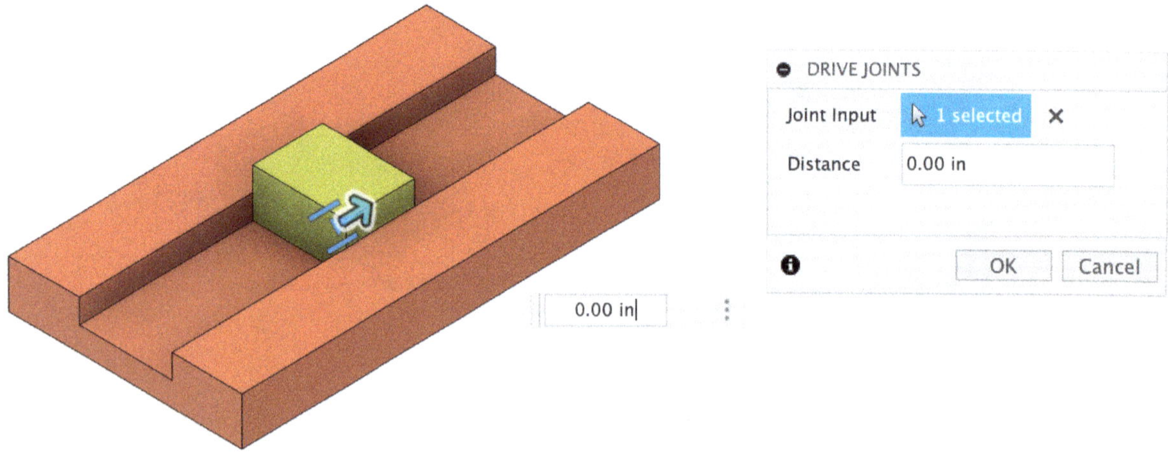

Cylindrical Joint

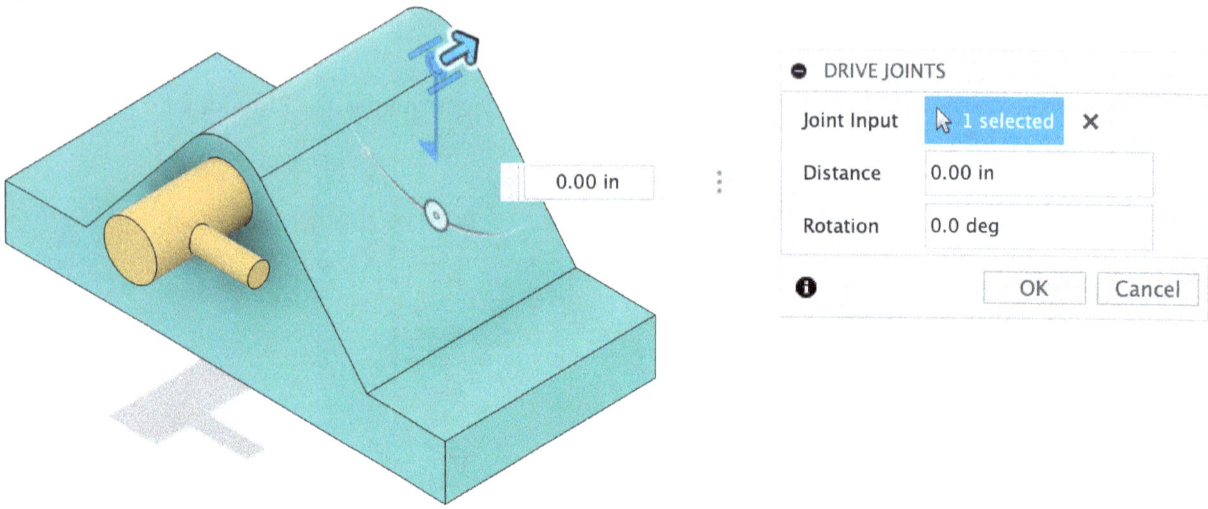

Duplicate with Joints

If you have an assembly where you need to assemble the same part multiple times, it would be a tedious process. In such cases, the **Duplicate with Joints** command will drastically reduce or even eliminate the time used to assemble commonly used parts. To use this command, first, you need to define a joint between two parts. For example, define the **Rigid** joint between the bolt and the hole.

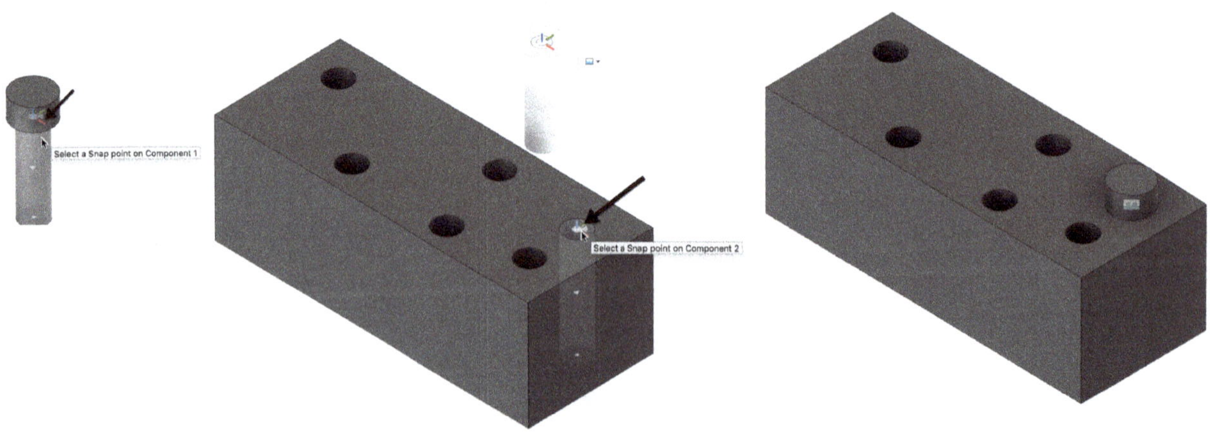

Activate the **Duplicate with Joints** command (click **Solid > Assemble > Duplicate with Joints** 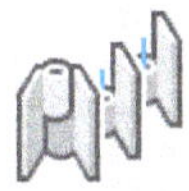 on the toolbar); the **Duplicate with Joints** dialog pops up on the screen. Select the component to be duplicated; the **Duplicate with Joints** dialog shows the list of Joints that can be duplicated.

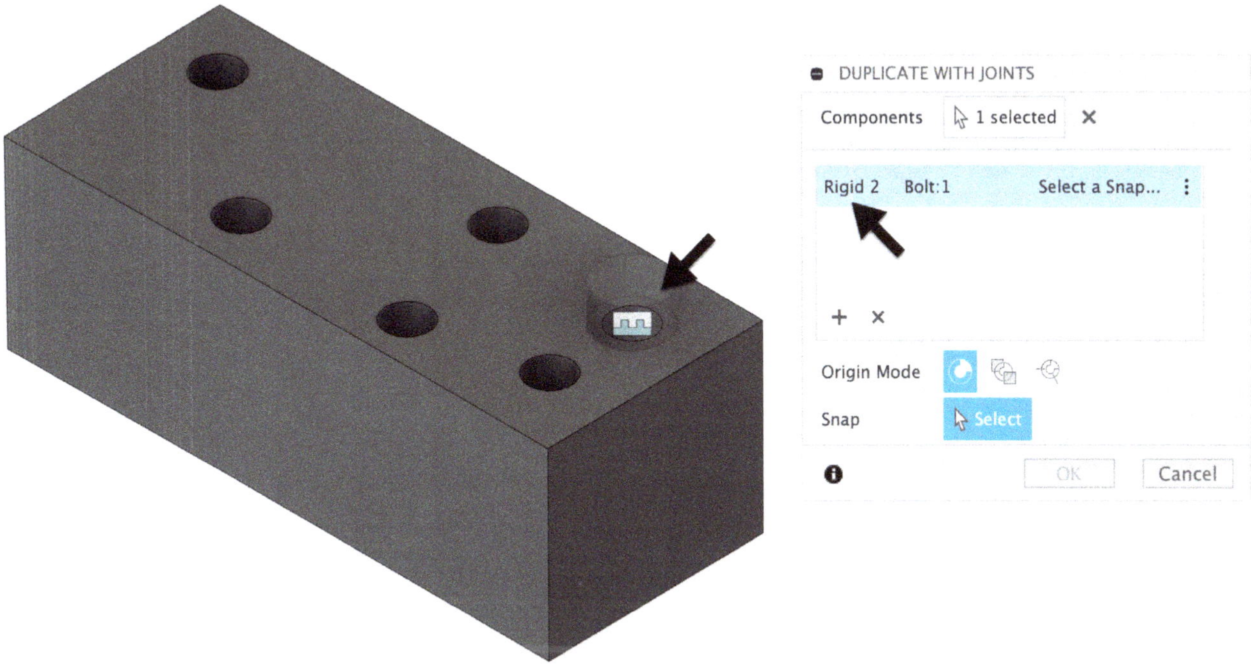

Now, select a snap point from the hole; the screw is inserted into the hole.

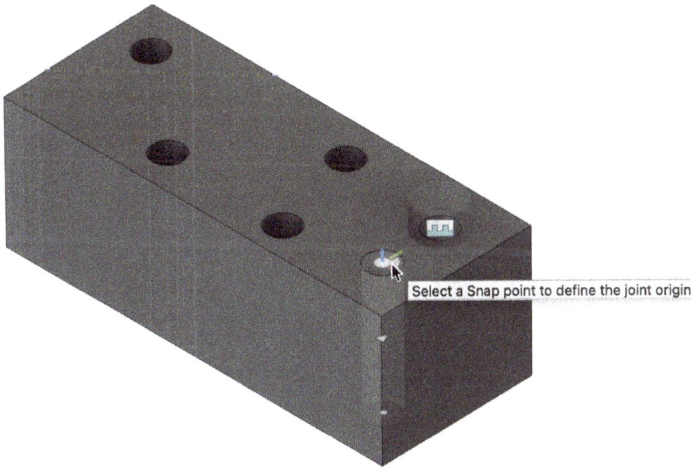

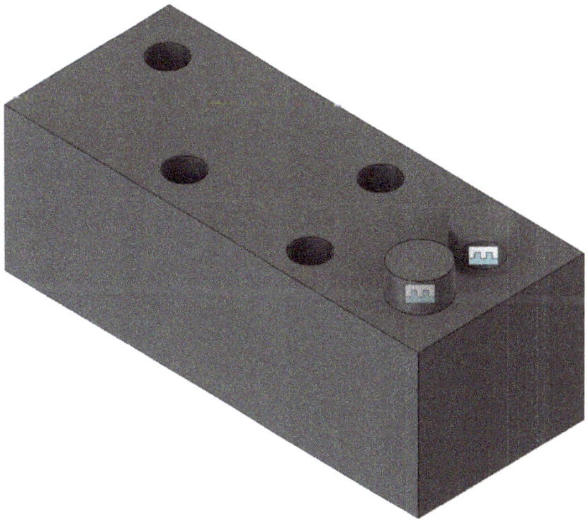

If you accidentally position the joint origin in the wrong direction, you can easily fix it by following a few simple steps. First, click on the **More** option located next to the instances in the **Duplicate With Joints** dialog box. This will display all of the duplicated instances. Next, move your cursor over the instances until you highlight the one that is positioned in the opposite direction. Once you have highlighted the incorrect instance, click the "**Flip**" button located next to it. This will reverse the direction of the selected instance, correcting the mistake.

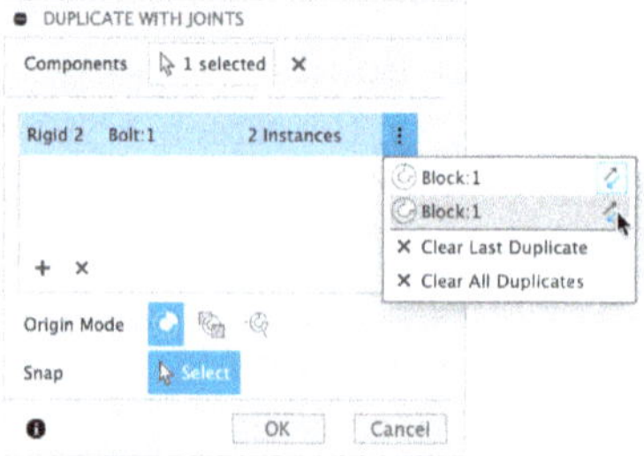

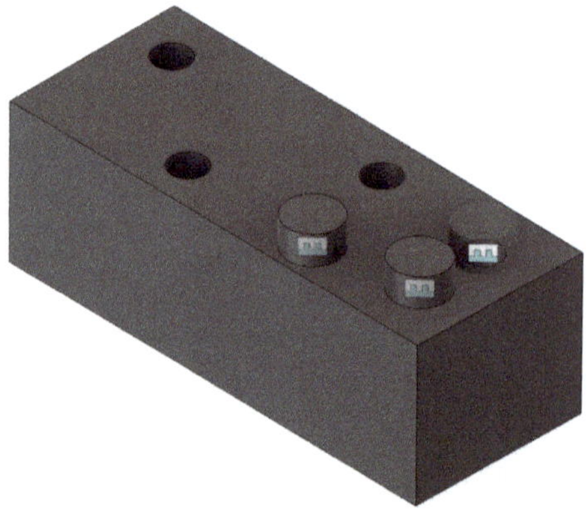

Motion Link

The **Motion Link** command is used to create a link between the joints. For example, you can link the revolute and slider joints such that the movable jaw slides when you rotate the screw.

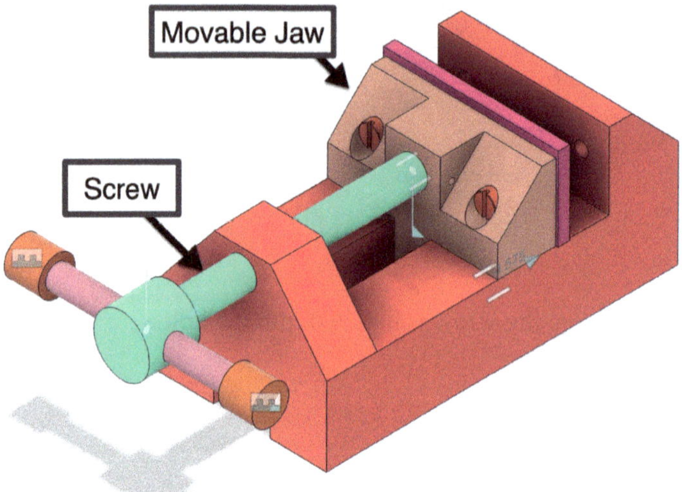

Activate this command (on the toolbar, click **Solid > Assembly > Motion Link**) and select the **Slider** and **Revolute** joints from the assembly. On the **Motion Link** dialog, type in values in the **Distance** and **Rotation** boxes, and then click **OK**.

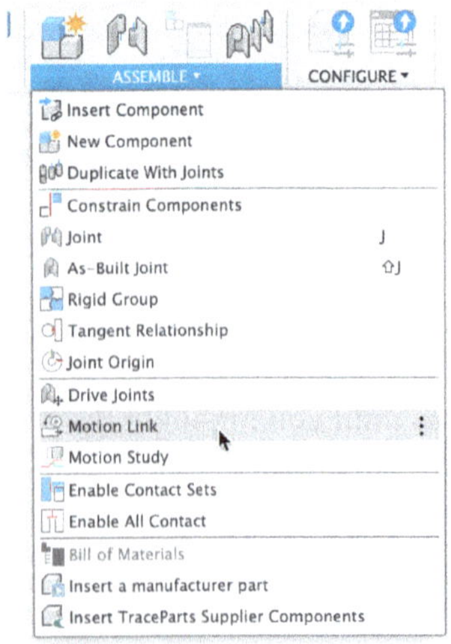

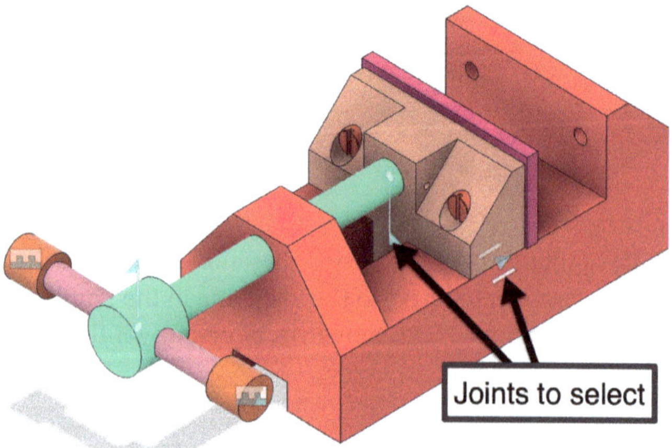

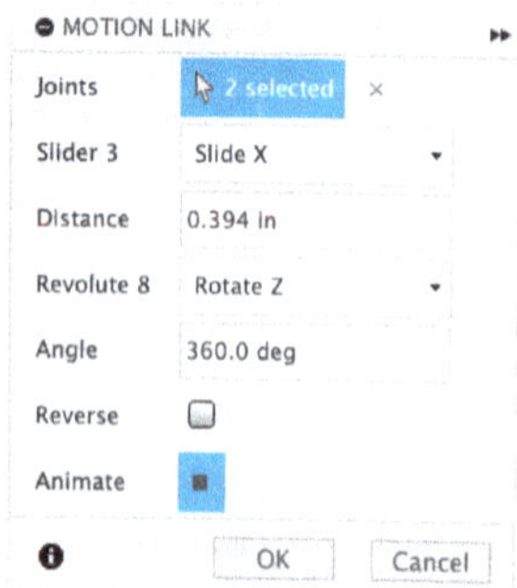

Motion Study

The **Motion Study** command helps you to do a motion study or motion analysis. You can define the movements of the assembly components by establishing a relation between the joints. On the toolbar, click **Solid > Assemble > Motion Study**; the **Motion Study** dialog appears. Next, select the first joint from the assembly or Browser; the selected joint is listed in the **Motion Study** dialog.

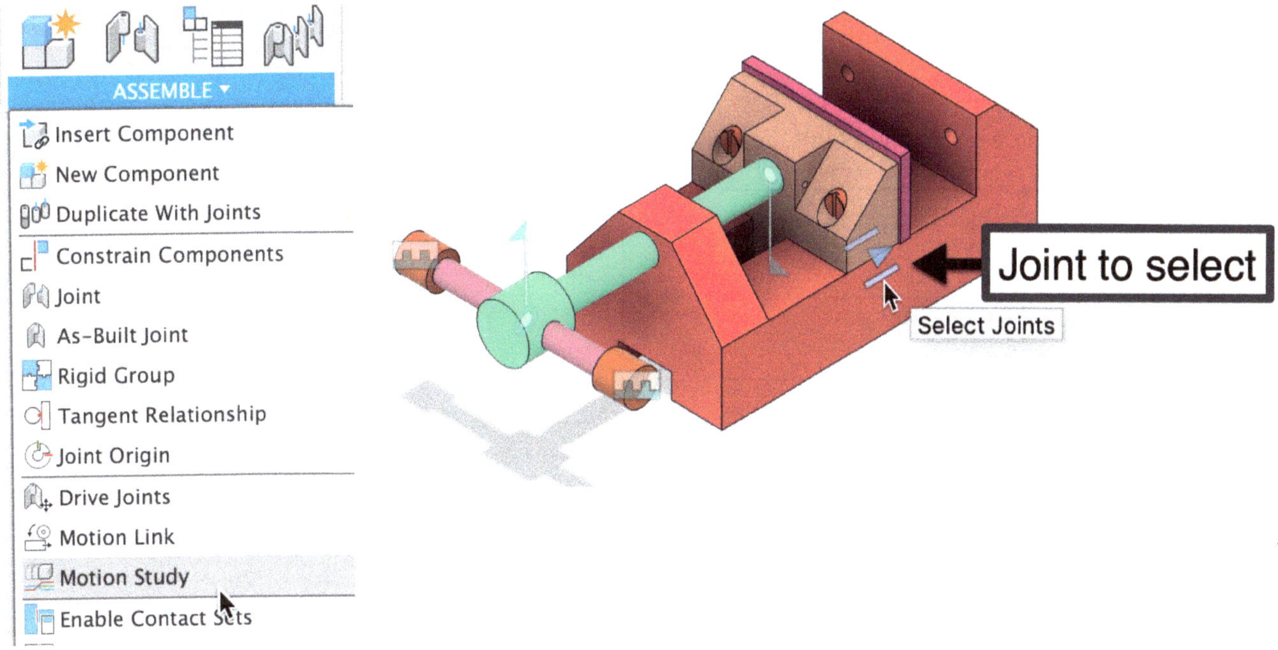

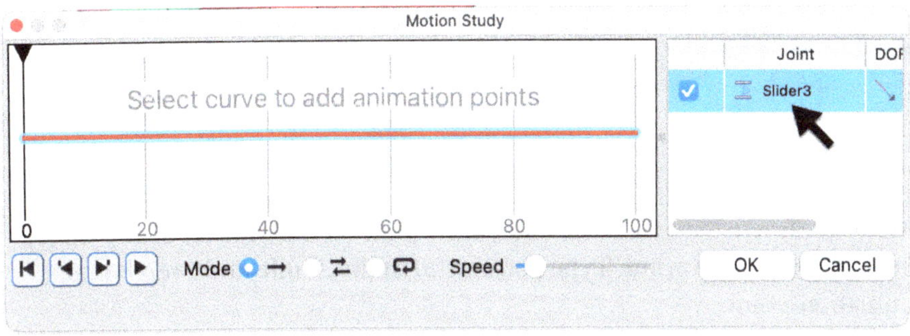

On the **Motion Study** dialog, click on the curve to add an animation point. Next, type 0.39 and 20 in the **Distance** and **Step** boxes, respectively. Press Enter to create the animation point.

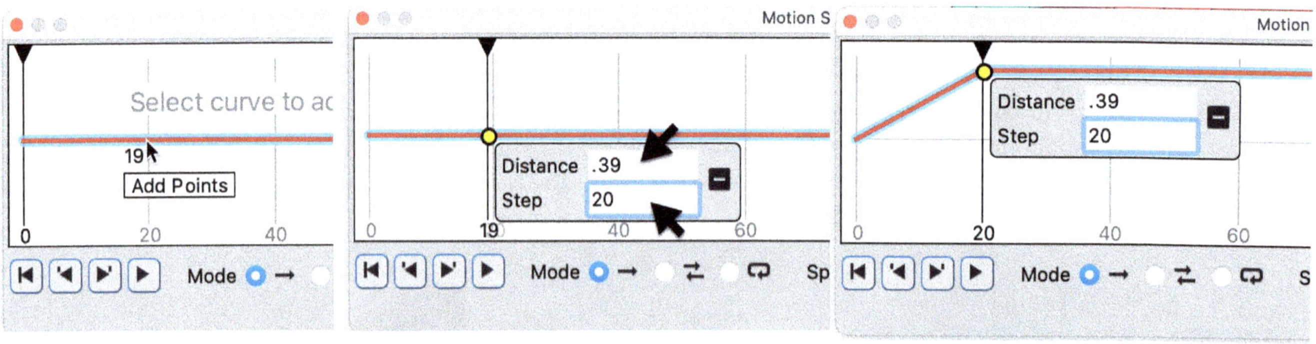

Likewise, create few more animation points, as shown.

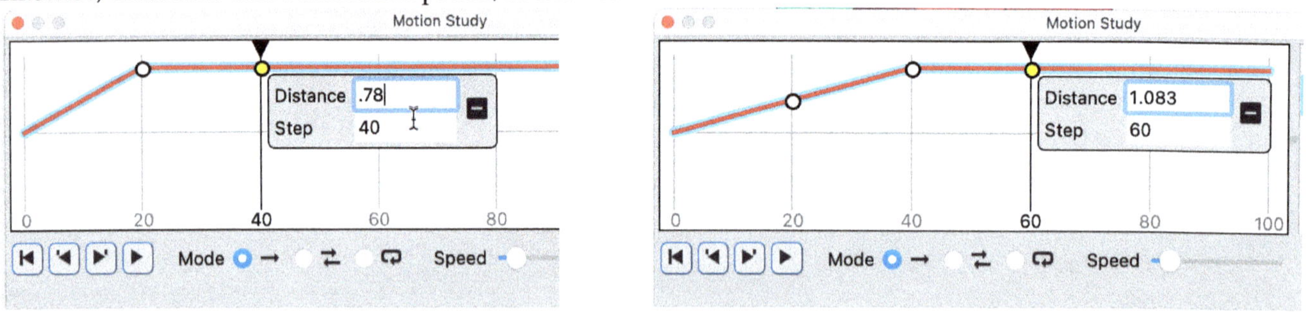

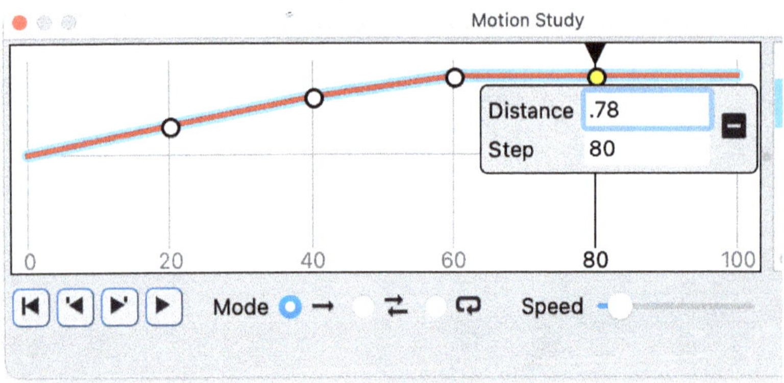

Select the **Revolute** joint from the assembly, as shown. Next, click the Revolute joint on the **Motion Study** dialog. Click on the highlighted curve to add the first animation point. Type 360 and 20 in the **Angle** and **Step** boxes, respectively. Press Enter to create the animation point.

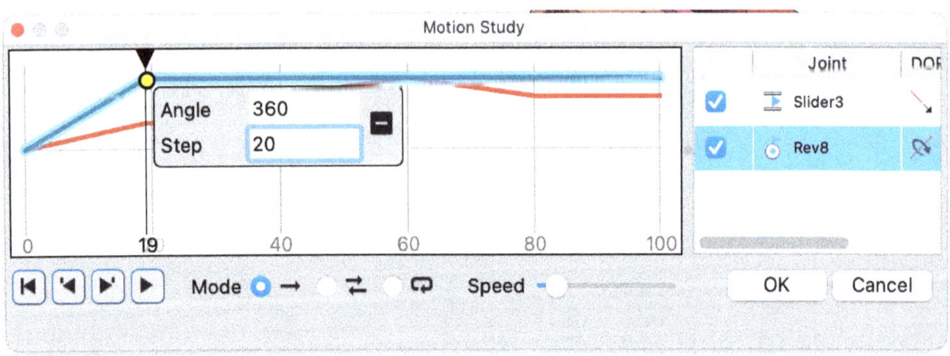

Likewise, create other animation points, as shown. Next, click the **Play** button on the **Motion Study** dialog, and then click **OK**.

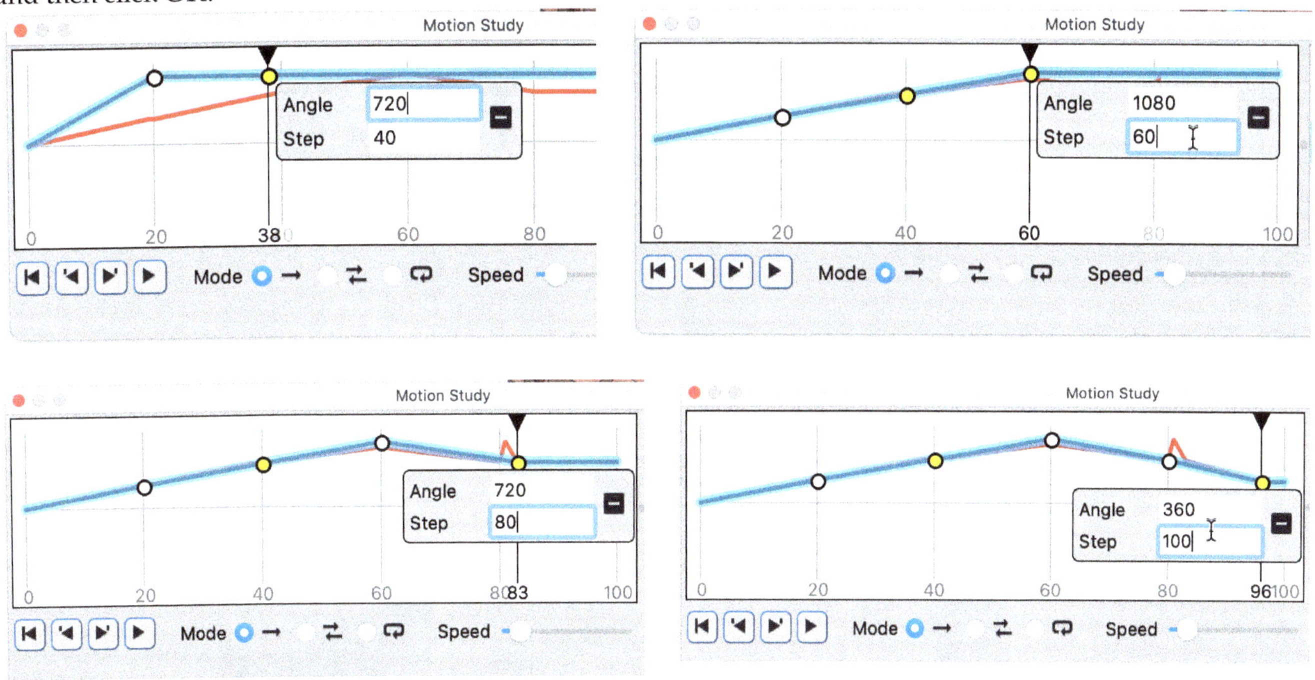

Check Interference

In an assembly, two or more parts can overlap or occupy the same space. However, this would be physically impossible in the real world. When you create joints between parts, Autodesk Fusion 360 develops real-world contacts and movements between them. However, sometimes, interferences can occur. To check such errors, Autodesk Fusion 360 provides you with a command called **Interference**. Activate this command (click **Utilities > Inspect > Interference** on the toolbar) and select all the components of the assembly. You can also create a selection window across the entire assembly. On the **Interference** dialog, check the **Include Coincident Faces** option to check for the faces that are coincident to each other. Click the **Compute** icon to show the interference. The **Interference results** dialog appears showing the number of interferences detected. Check the **Show all interferences** option on the **Interference results** dialog to highlight all the results in the graphics window. Next, click **OK** on the **Interference results** dialog.

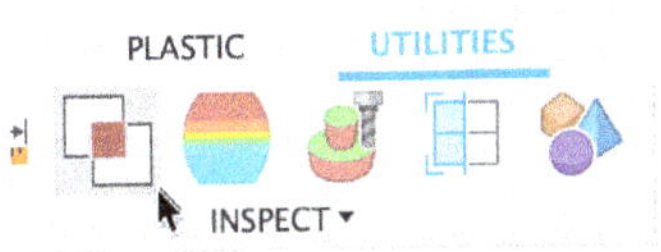

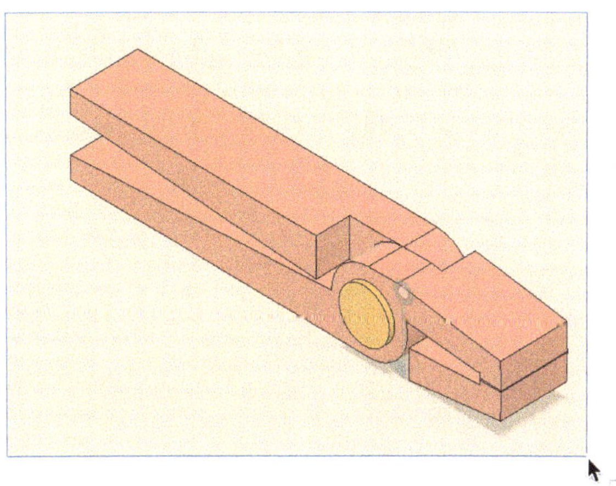

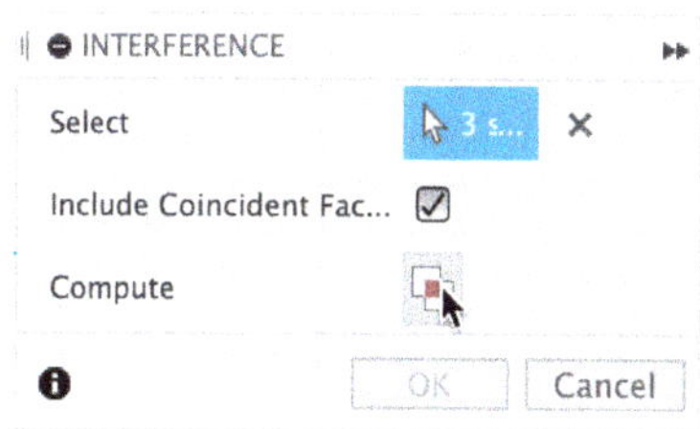

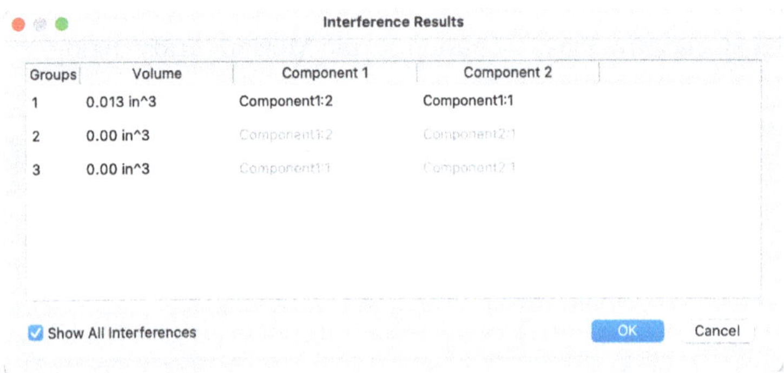

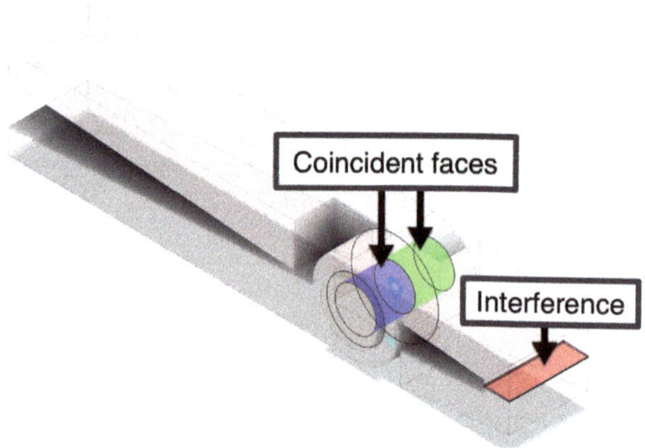

Contact Sets

Autodesk Fusion 360 allows you to create contact sets such that the components will stop when they touch each other. As a result, the intersection between the components is avoided. For example, click and drag the shaft in the assembly, as shown in the figure. You can notice that it intersects with the block.

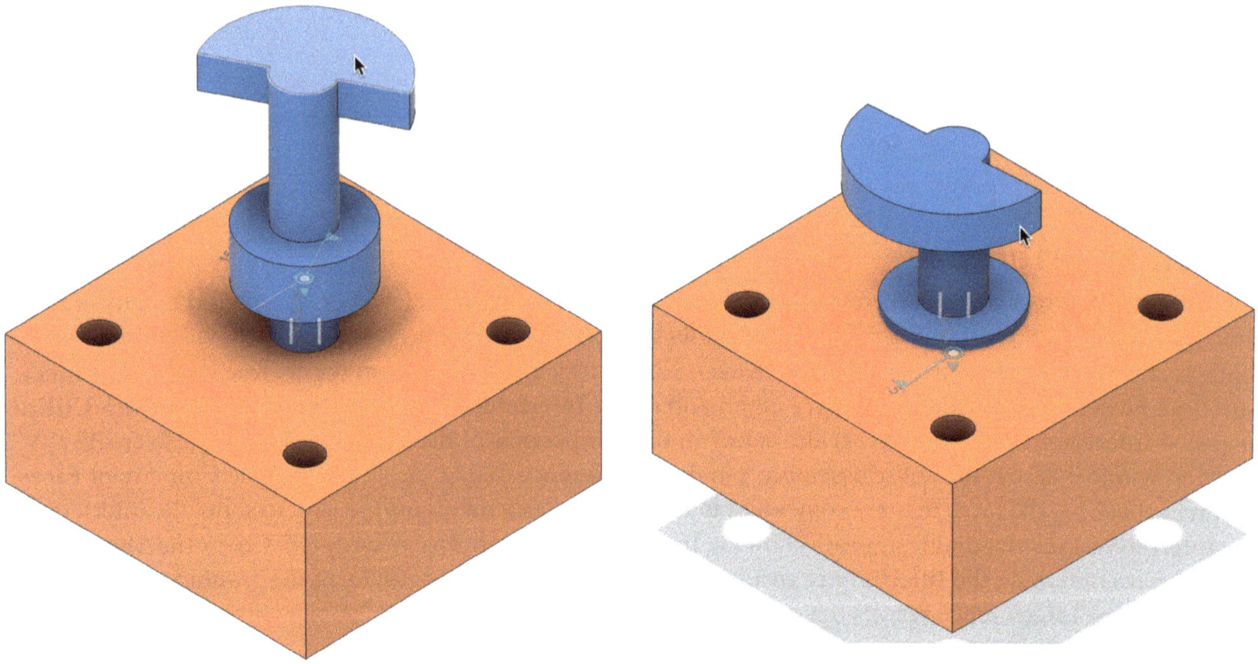

To avoid this, you need to create a contact set between the two components. To do this, click **Solid > Assemble > Enable Contact Sets** on the toolbar. Next, click **Solid > Assemble > New Contact Set** on the toolbar. Select the components to be included in the contact set, and then click **OK** on the **New Contact Set** dialog.

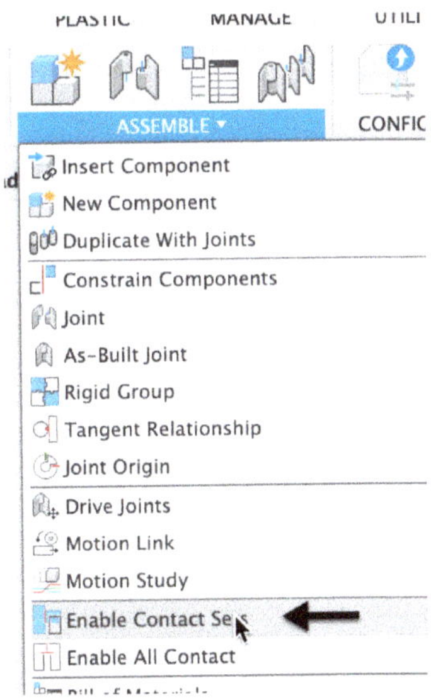

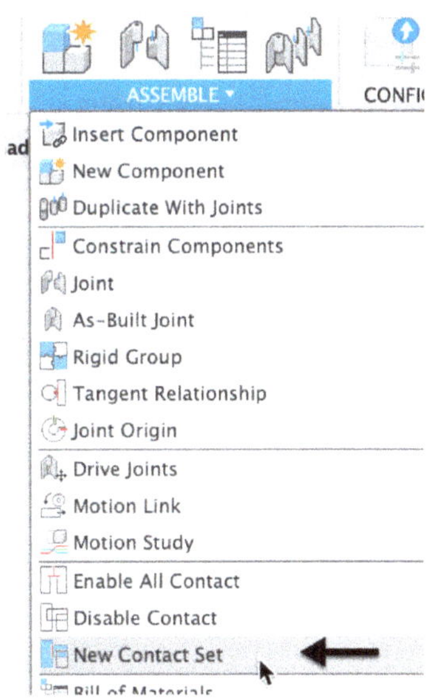

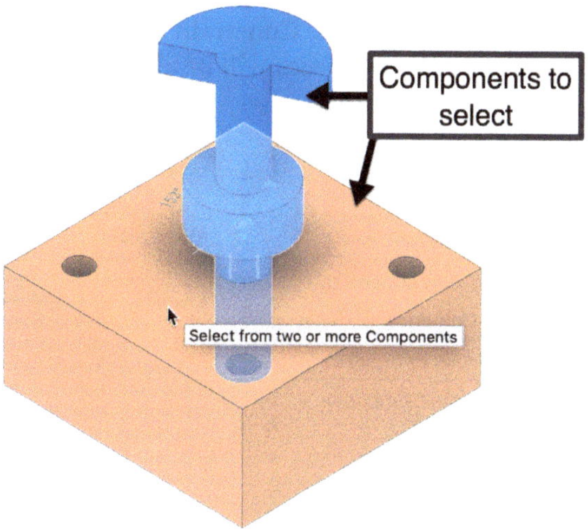

Click and drag the shaft and notice that it stops on touching the block. You can disable the contact sets by clicking **Solid > Assemble > Disable Contact** on the toolbar.

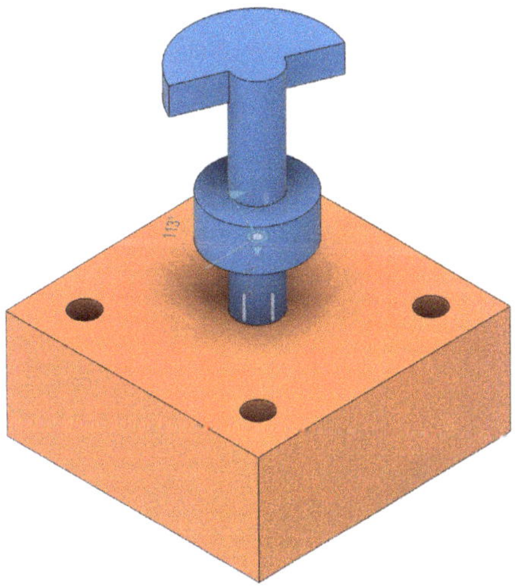

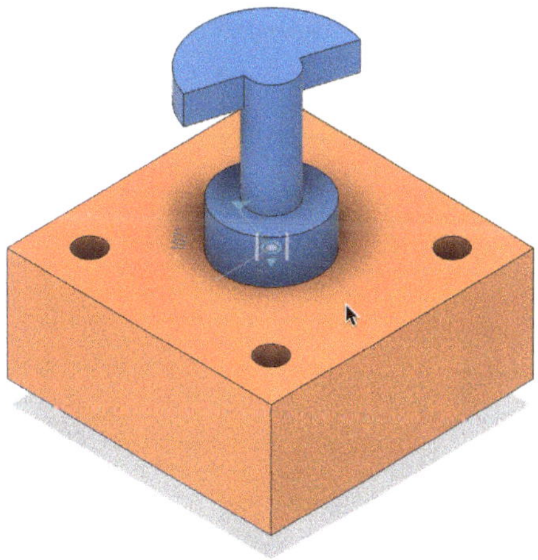

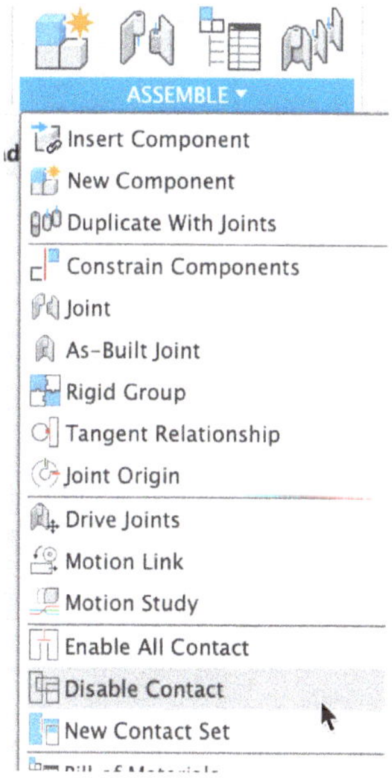

Applying Constraints

After inserting parts into an assembly, you have to apply constraints between them. By applying constraints, you can make parts to flush with each other or make two round faces concentric with each other. As you add constraints between parts, the degrees of freedom will be removed from them. By default, there are six degrees of freedom for a part (three linear and three rotational). Eliminating the degrees of freedom will make parts attached and interact with each other as in real life. Now, you will learn to add constraints between parts.

Align Constraint

The **Align** constraint makes two planar faces on separate components coplanar. The orientation of the two mated faces depends on whether they are set to be opposite or aligned, which can be toggled using the **Flip** button. To apply this constraint, click **Solid** tab > **Assemble** panel > **Constrain Components** on the toolbar. Next, select **Type > Align** from the **Constrain Components** dialog and select the face on the first part. Select a face on the target part. The two faces will be aligned in the same direction.

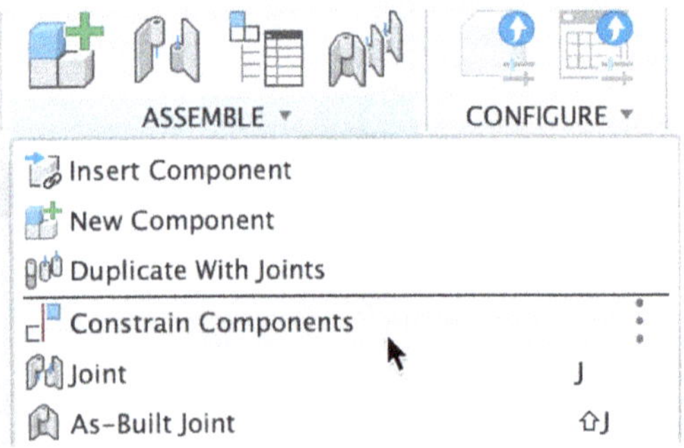

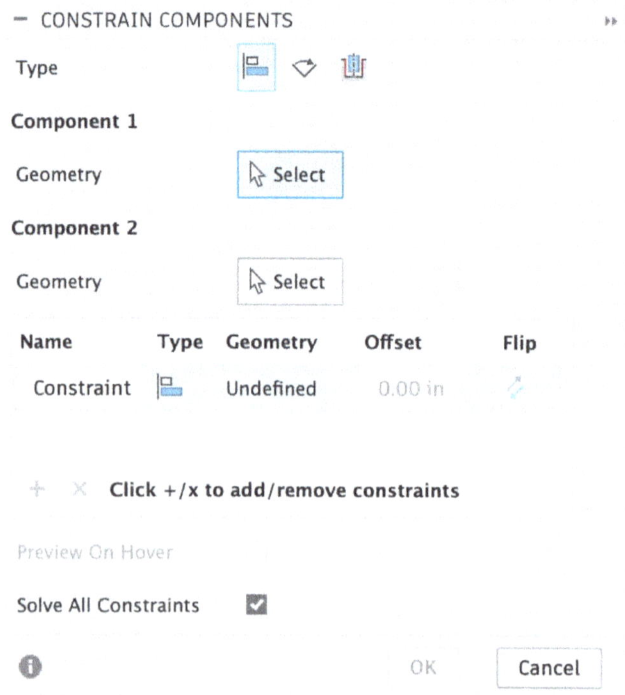

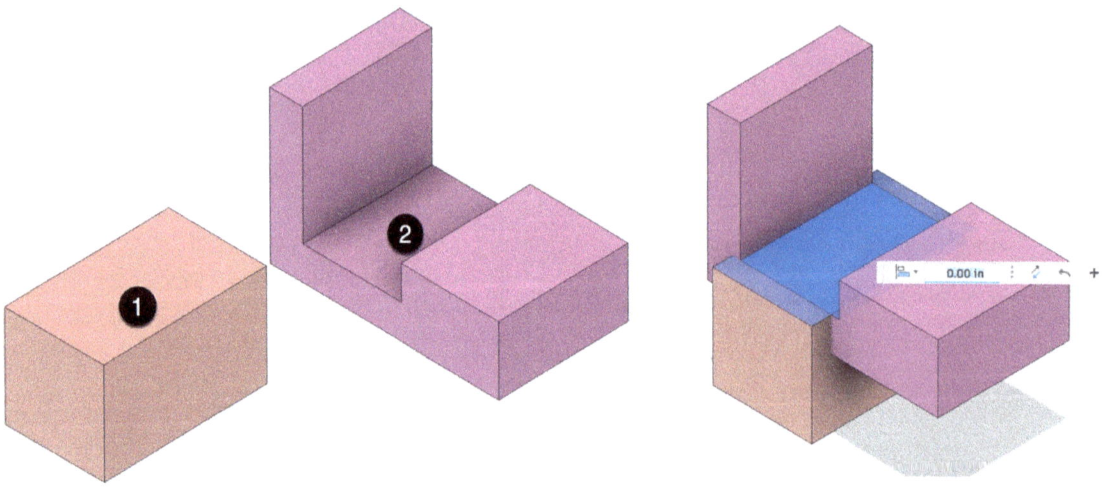

Click the **Flip** button to make the two selected faces aligned opposite to each other.

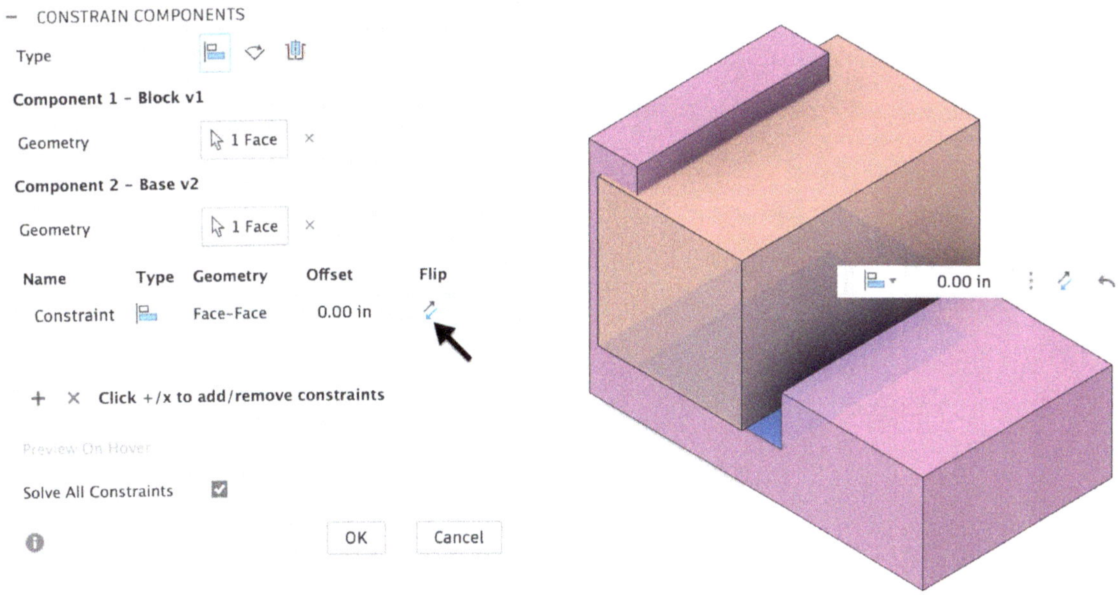

You can also enter an offset value in the **Offset** box on the **Constraint Components** dialog. The constrained components are offset from each other.

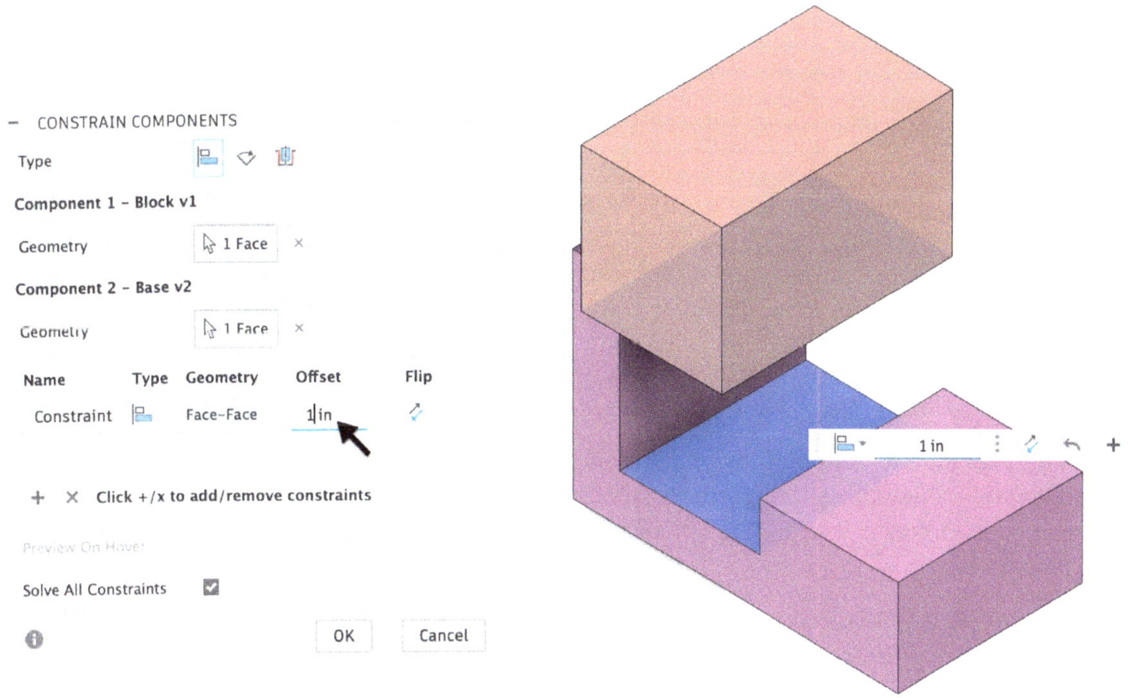

Aligning Axes or Edges using the Align Constraint

By using the **Align** constraint, you can make the axes of two cylindrical faces coincide with each other. Activate the **Constraint Components** command and click **Type > Align** icon on the **Constraint Components** dialog. Next, click on the round faces of the placement and target parts; the two cylindrical axes will coincide with each other. Click the **Flip** icon to position the two selected axes or edges in the direction opposite to each other.

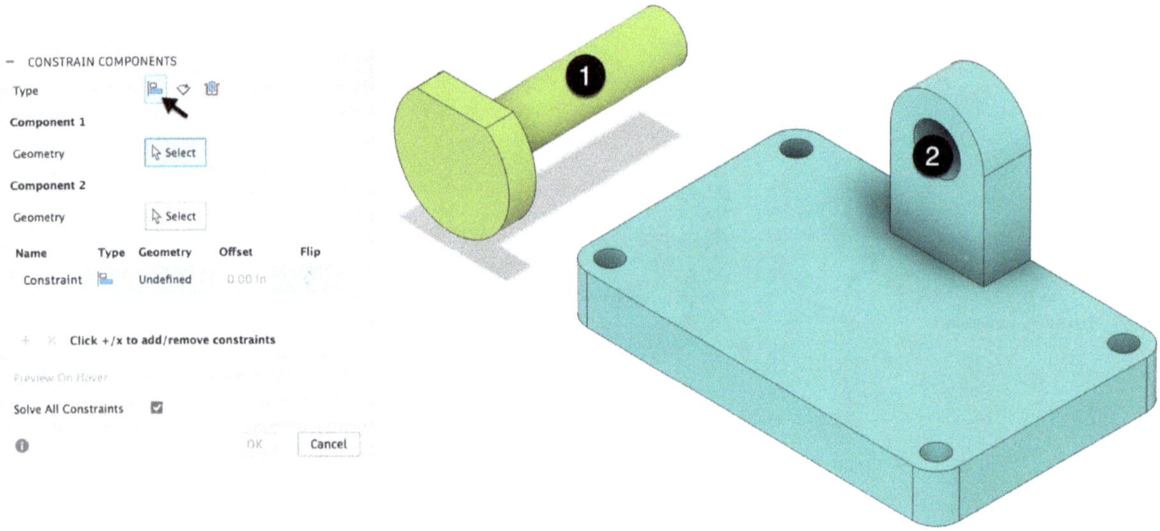

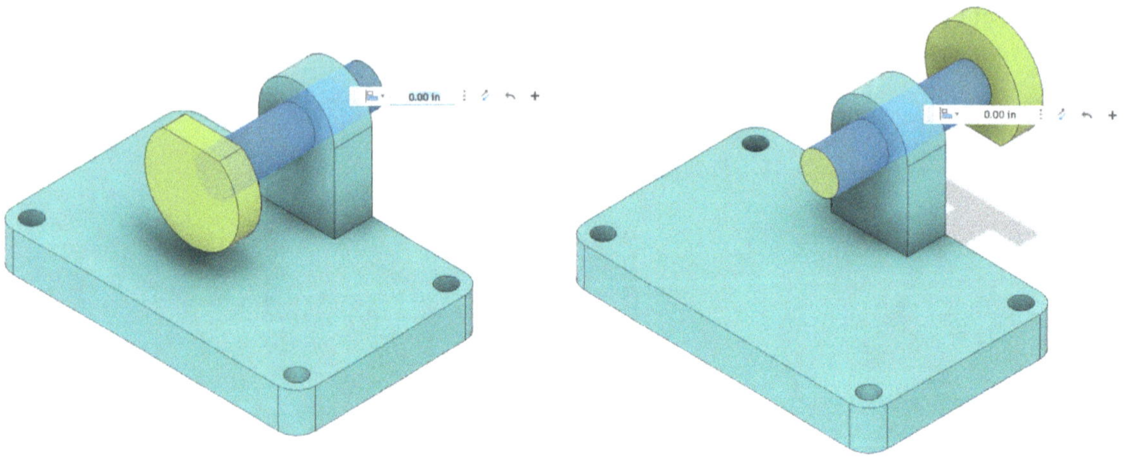

Angle Constraint

The **Angle** constraint is used to position faces at a specified angle. Activate the **Constrain Components** command (click **Solid > Assemble > Constrain Components**). On the **Constrain Components** dialog, click the **Angle** icon under the **Type** section. Next, click on a plane or linear element of the first part. Next, click on a plane or linear element of the second part.

Type in an angle value in the **Offset** box on the dialog. The first part will be positioned at the specified angle. Click the **Flip** button to reverse the orientation of the first part.

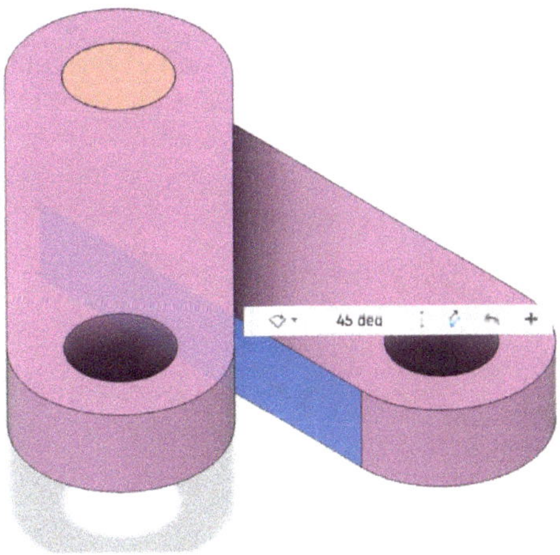

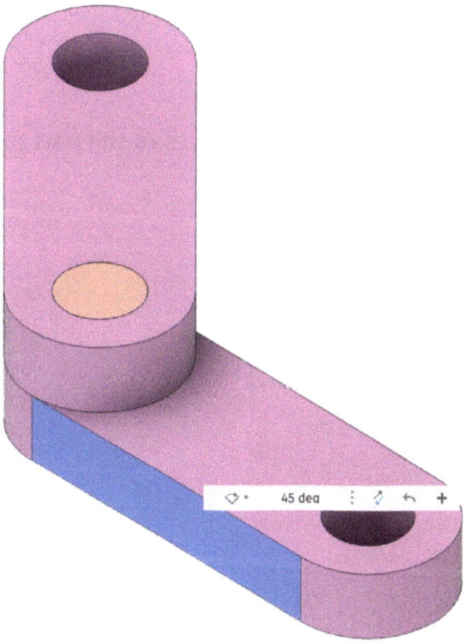

Center Constraint

The **Center** constraint allows you to place a part between two faces. Click **Solid > Assemble > Constrain Components** on the toolbar. On the **Constrain Components dialog**, click the **Type > Center** icon. Next, select the

Position Mode > Between Two Faces. Select the faces between which the part will be positioned. These faces are called width faces.

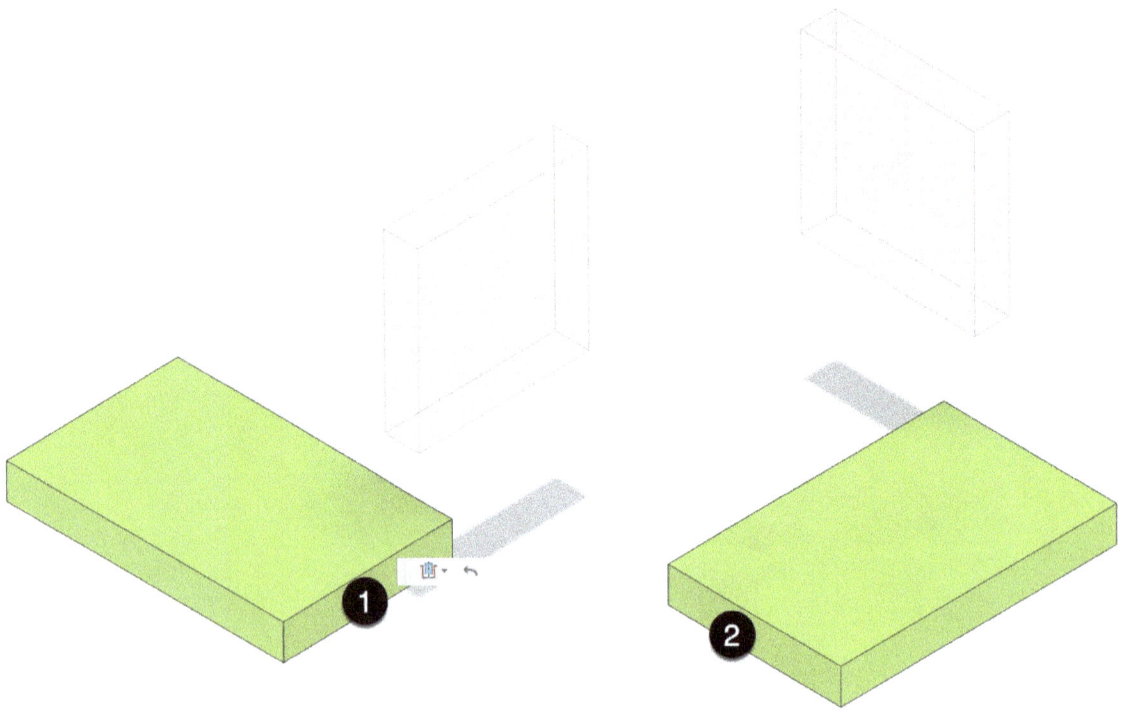

After selecting the width faces, select the faces of the part to be positioned; the part will be positioned at the center location between the width faces.

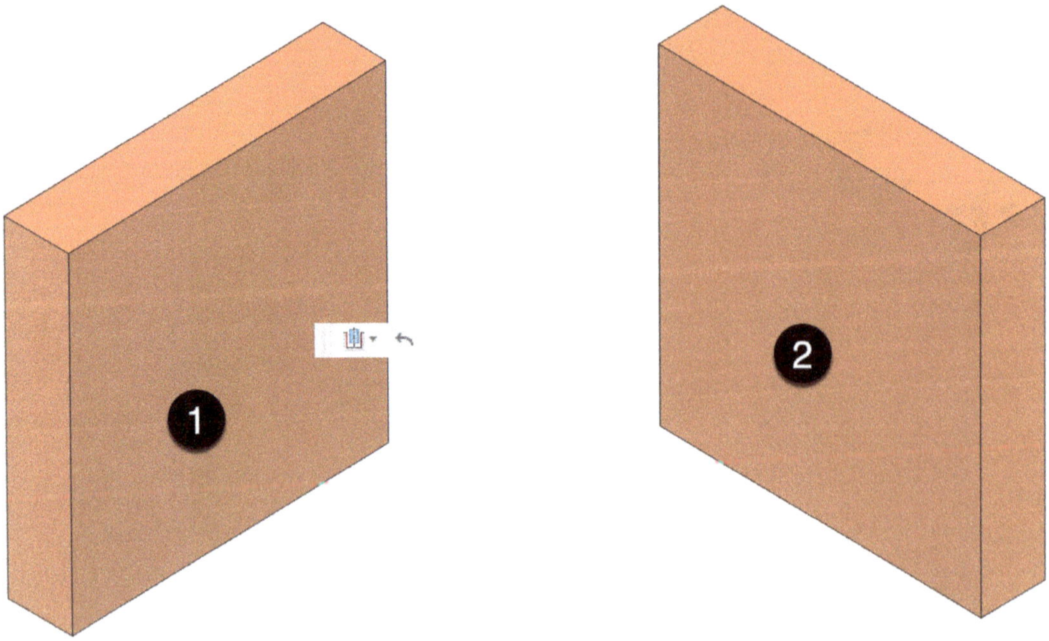

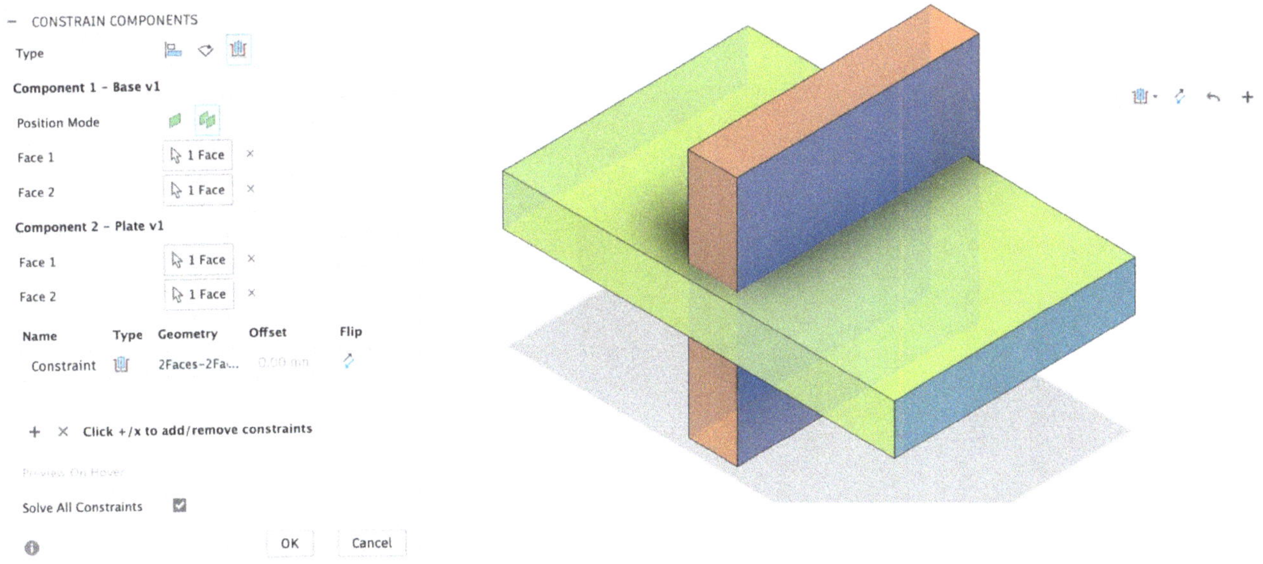

The **Simple** option in the **Position Mode** section allows you to constrain one face of a component midway between two faces of a second component. To do this, click **Solid > Assemble > Constrain Components** on the toolbar. On the **Constrain Components** dialog, click **Position Mode > Simple** and select the symmetric plane first component. Next, select the faces from the second component between which the first component is to be positioned.

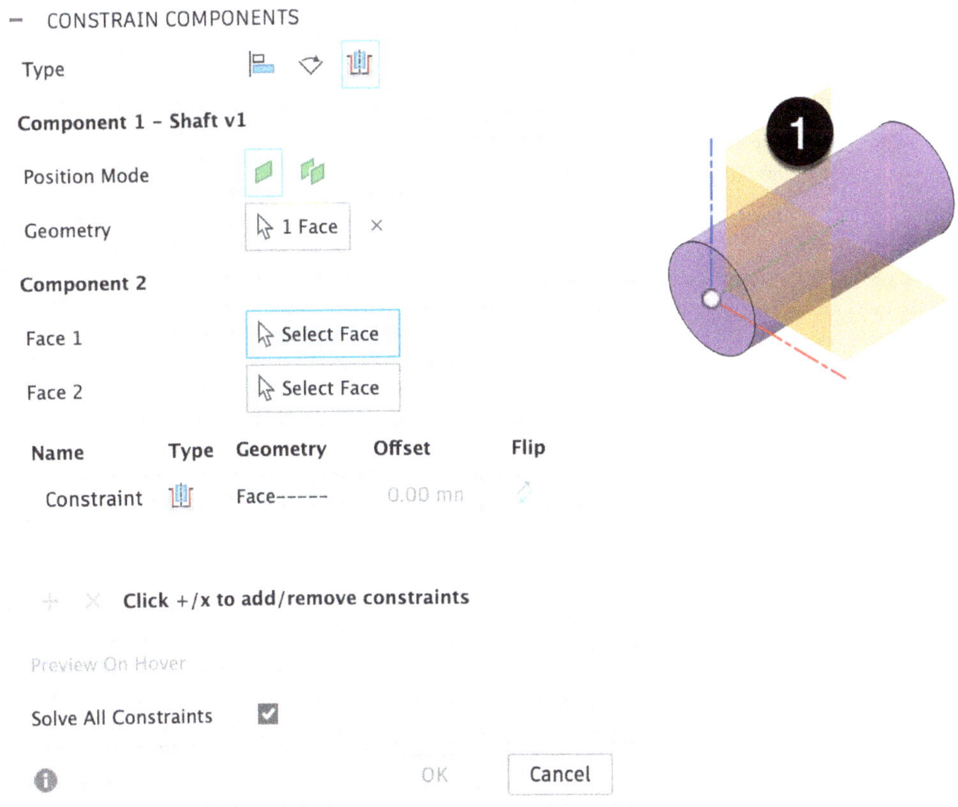

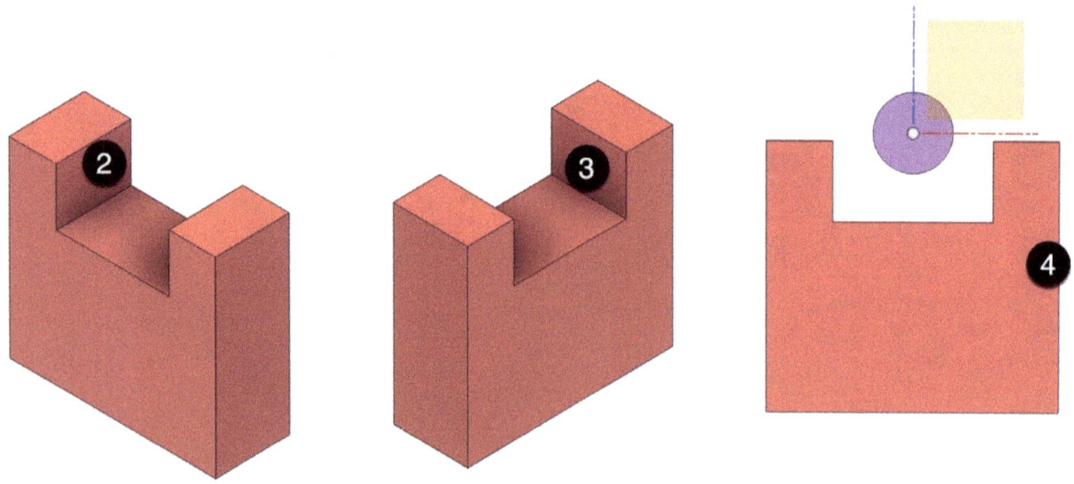

Sub-assemblies

The use of sub-assemblies has many advantages in Autodesk Fusion 360. Sub-assemblies make large assemblies easier to manage. They make it easy for multiple users to collaborate on a single large assembly design. They can also affect the way you document a large assembly design in 2D drawings. For these reasons, it is important for you to create sub-assemblies in a variety of ways. The easiest way to create a sub-assembly is to insert an existing assembly into another assembly. You need to simply right click on the sub-assembly in the Data Panel and select **Insert into current design**; the subassembly is inserted into the design. Next, create joints in the assembly. The process of creating joints is very simple. You are required to create a joint between only one component of a sub-assembly and a part of the main assembly. In addition to that, you can easily hide or suppress a group of components with the help of sub-assemblies.

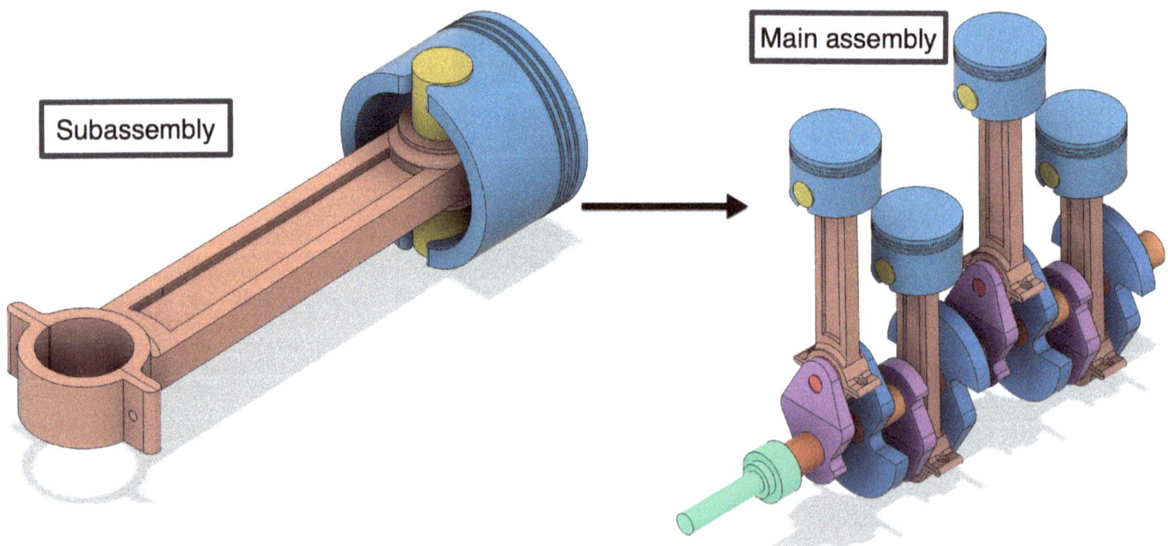

Top-Down Assembly Design

In Autodesk Fusion 360, there are two methods to create an assembly. The first method is to create individual components and then insert them into an assembly. This method is known as Bottom-Up Assembly Design. The second method is called Top-Down Assembly Design. In this method, you will create individual components within the assembly environment. This allows you to design an individual component while considering how it will interact with other components in an assembly. There are several advantages to Top-Down Assembly

Design. As you design a component within the assembly, you can be sure that it will fit properly. You can also use the edges from the other components as a reference.

New Component

Top-down assembly design can be used to add new components to an already existing assembly. You can also use it to create assemblies that are entirely new. To create a component using the Top-Down Design approach, activate the **New Component** command (click **Solid > Assemble > New Component** on the toolbar); the **New Component** dialog pops up on the screen. Next, you need to define the component location. You can select whether to create an **Internal** or **External** component. Select the **Internal** option to create the component within the assembly. Enter the name in the **Name** box. Select **Type > Standard** option to create a standard part. Select **Type > Sheet Metal** option, if you want to create a sheet metal component. Next, check the **Activate** option, and then click **OK**.

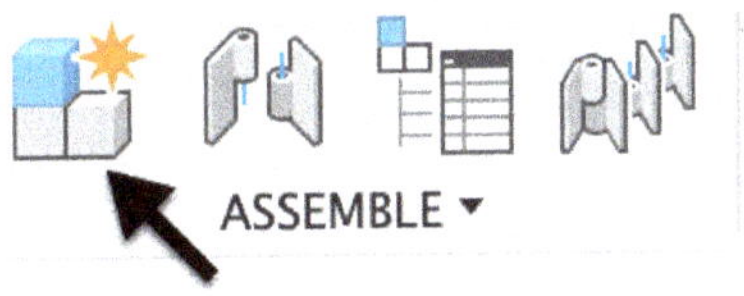

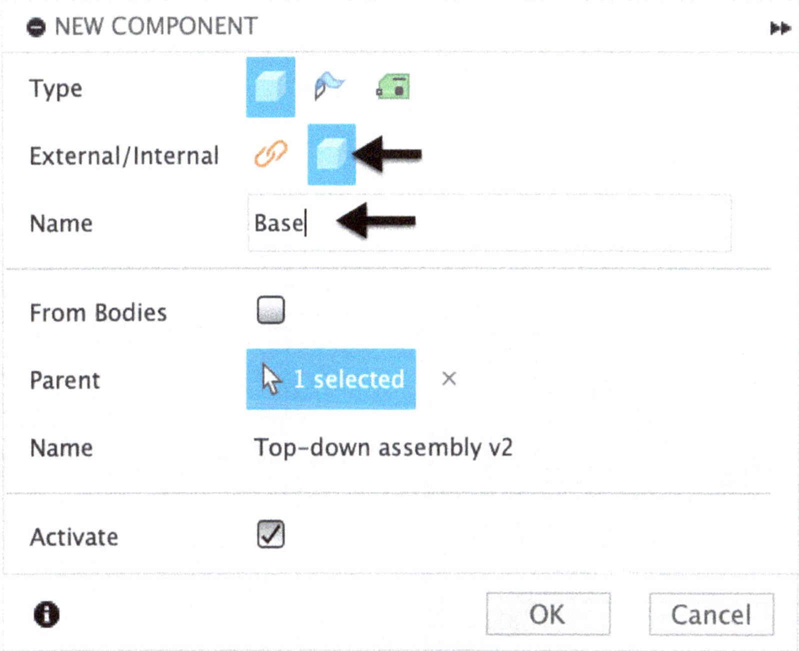

Create the component features. In the Browser, click the right mouse button on the assembly, and then select **Activate**; the assembly is activated.

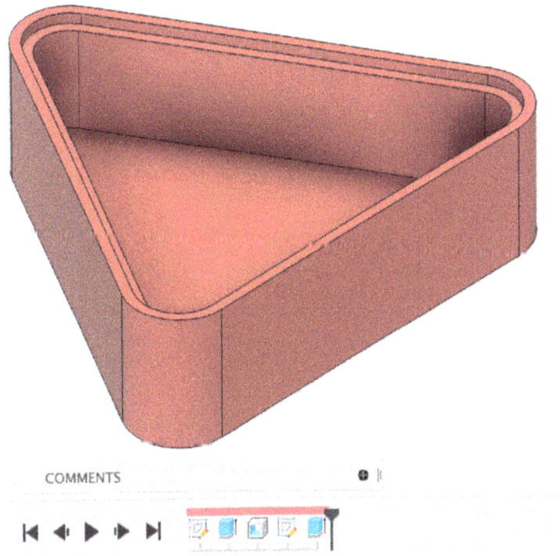

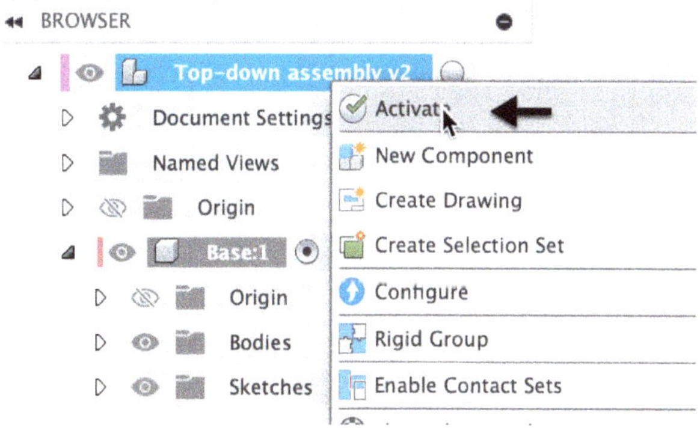

Again, activate the **New Component** command and enter the name of the component in the **Name** box. Next, click **OK** to create a new component. Click **Solid > Create > Create Sketch** on the toolbar and select the face on the first component, as shown. Next, click **Sketch > Create > Project / Include > Project** on the toolbar, and select the inner edges, as shown. Click **OK** on the **Project** dialog.

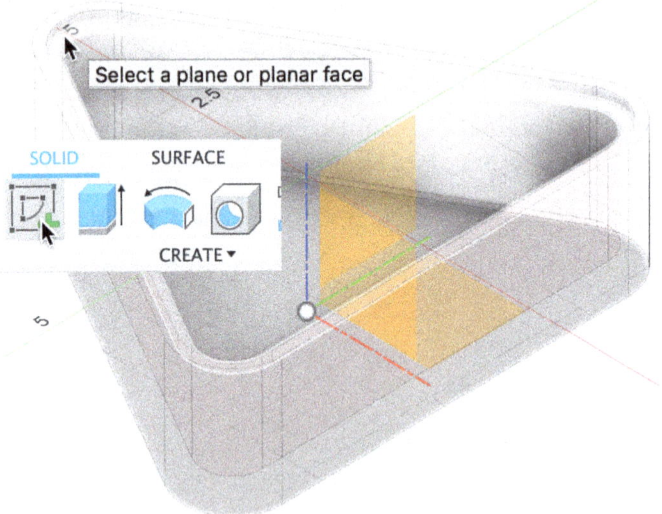

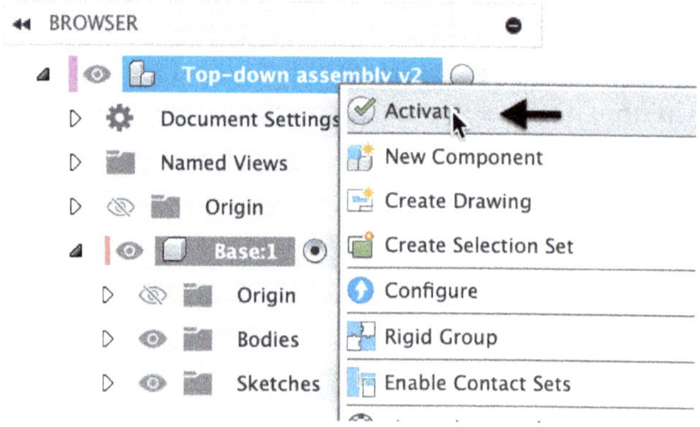

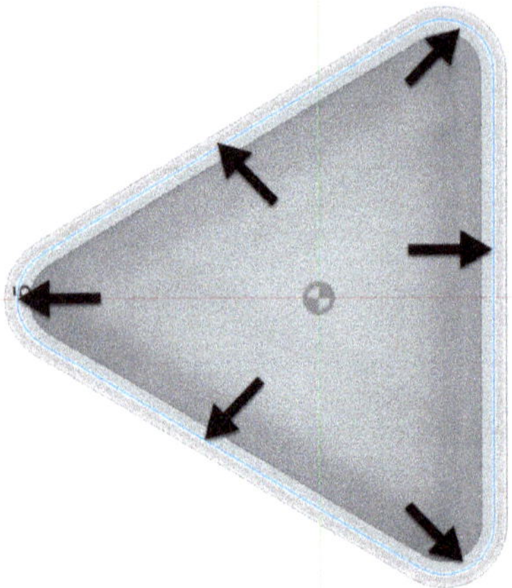

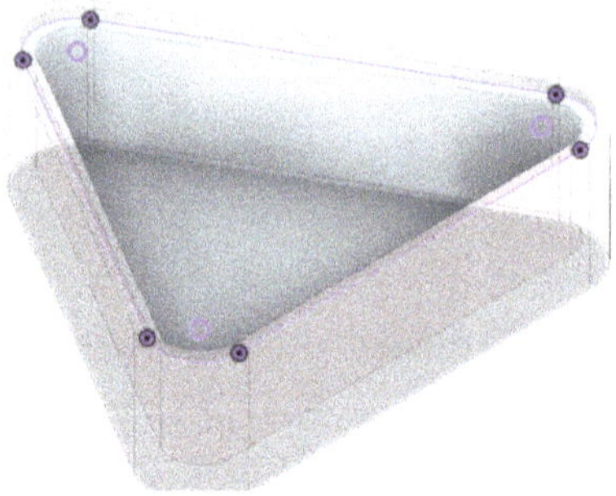

Click **Finish Sketch** on the toolbar. Next, activate the **Extrude** command and extrude the sketch. This makes it easy to create a component using the edges of the existing component.

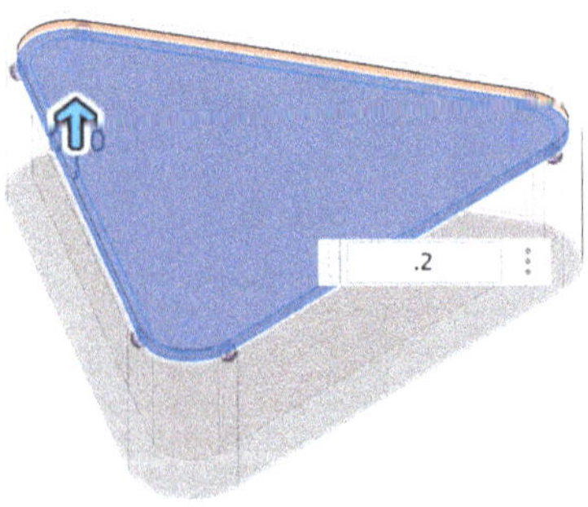

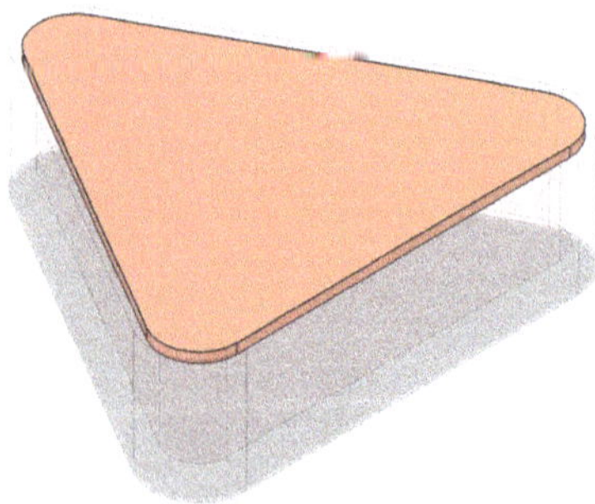

Place the pointer on the first component in the Browser. Next, click on the circular dot that appears next to the component; the component is activated. Now, modify the sketch on the first component; the linked component will also change automatically.

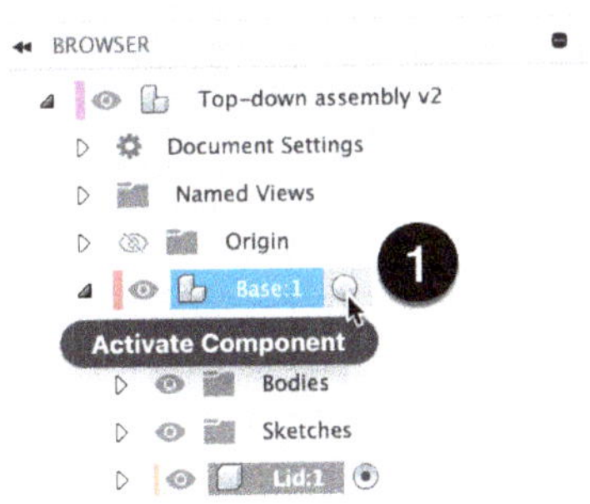

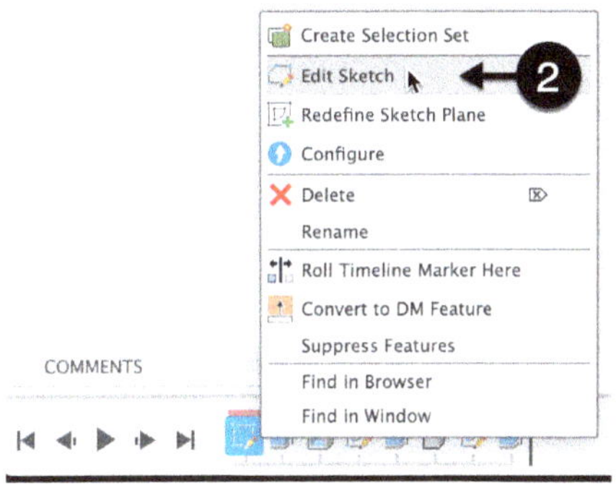

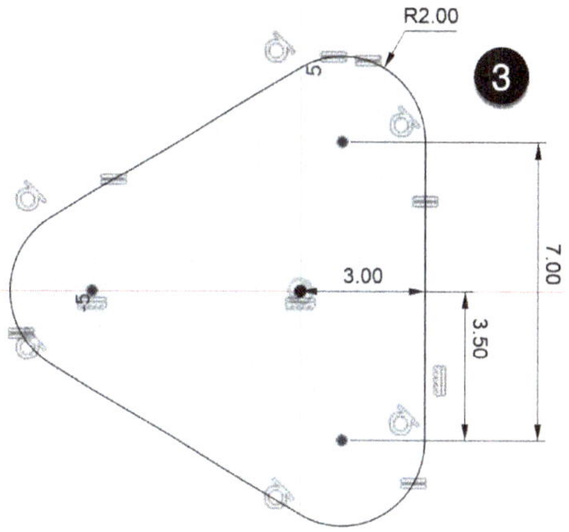

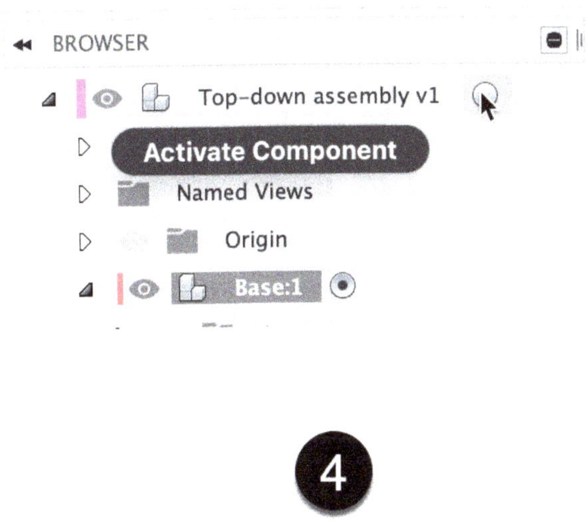

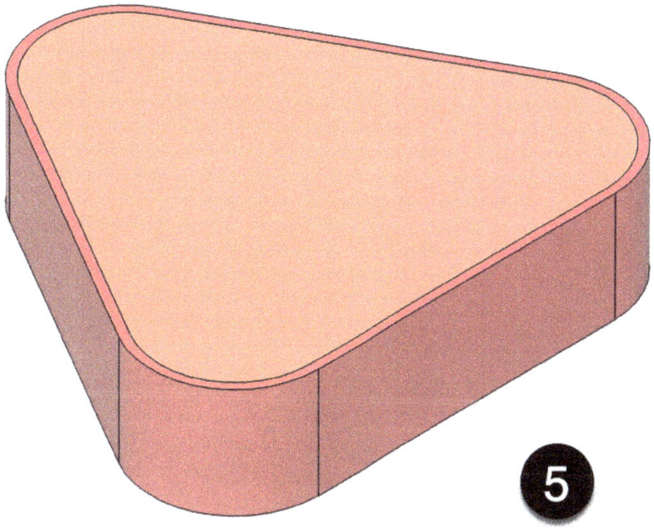

As-built Joint

The **As-built Joint** command helps you to create joints between the components that are positioned appropriately to each other. For example, you can use this command to create joints between the components of an imported assembly. In addition to that, you can create joints between the components that were created using the Top-down assembly design approach (using the **New Component** command).

Download the Piston assembly, and then click **File > Upload** on the Application Bar. Next, click the **Select Files** button and double click on the piston assembly. Click **Upload** to upload the file to the project folder. Next, double-click on the uploaded file in the **Data** panel; the file is opened.

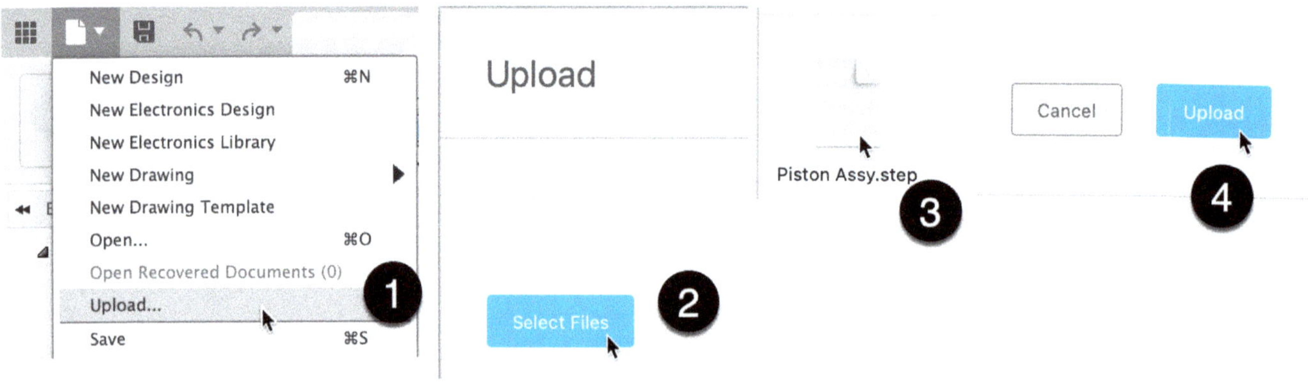

Click **Solid > Assemble > As-built Joint** on the toolbar. Select the Piston Rod and Piston Rod Cap from the graphics window. On the **As-Built Joint** dialog, select **Joint type > Rigid**, and then click **OK**.

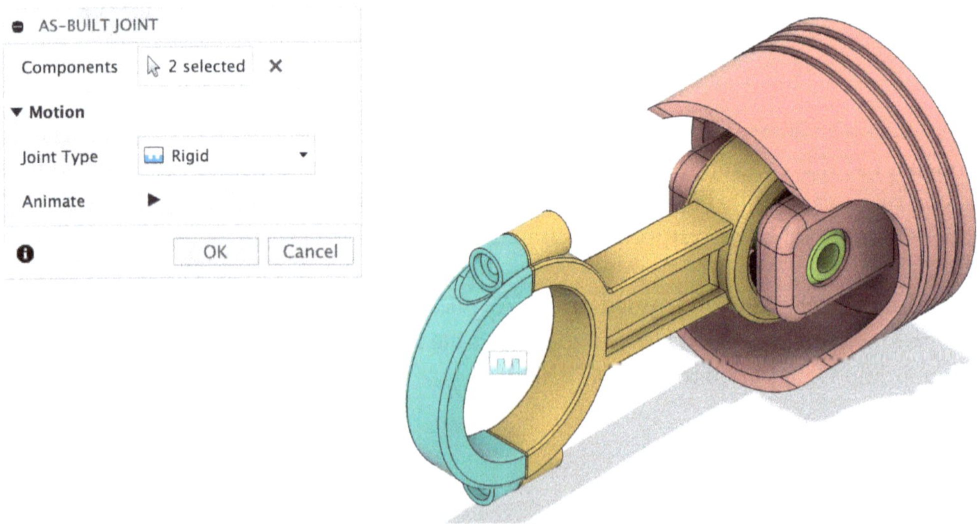

Again, activate the **As-built Joint** command and select the Piston rod and the Shaft. On the **As-built joint** dialog, select **Joint type > Revolute**. Next, place the pointer on the cylindrical face of the shaft, as shown. Press and hold the Ctrl key and select the joint origin located at the midpoint of the cylindrical face.

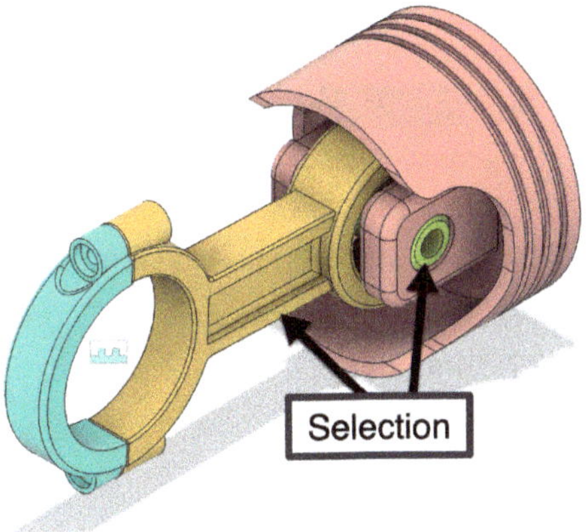

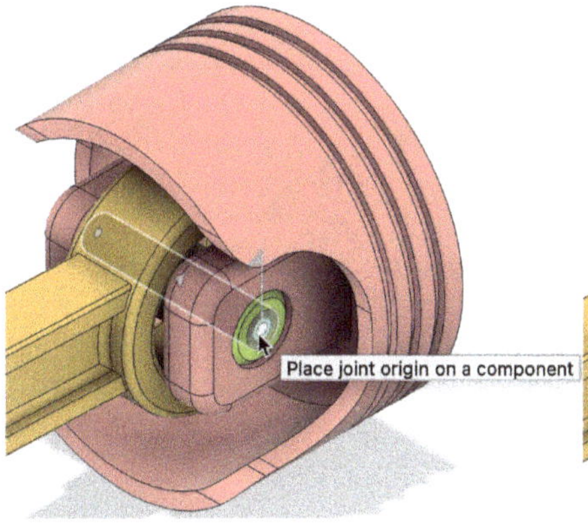

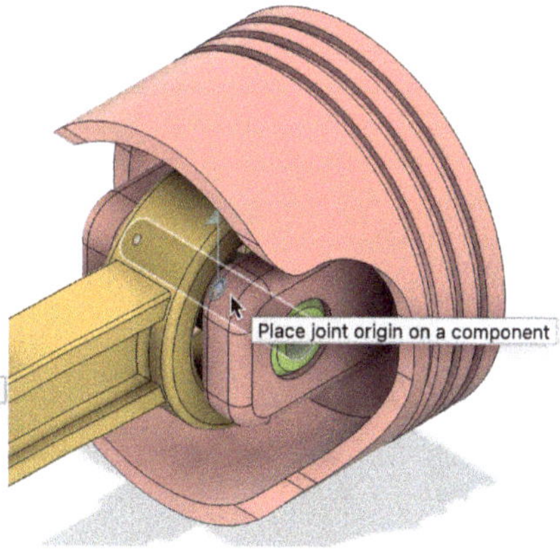

On the **As-built Joint** dialog, select **Rotate > Z Axis**, and then click the **Preview Motion** icon; the Shaft rotates. Next, click **OK** to create the Revolute joint.

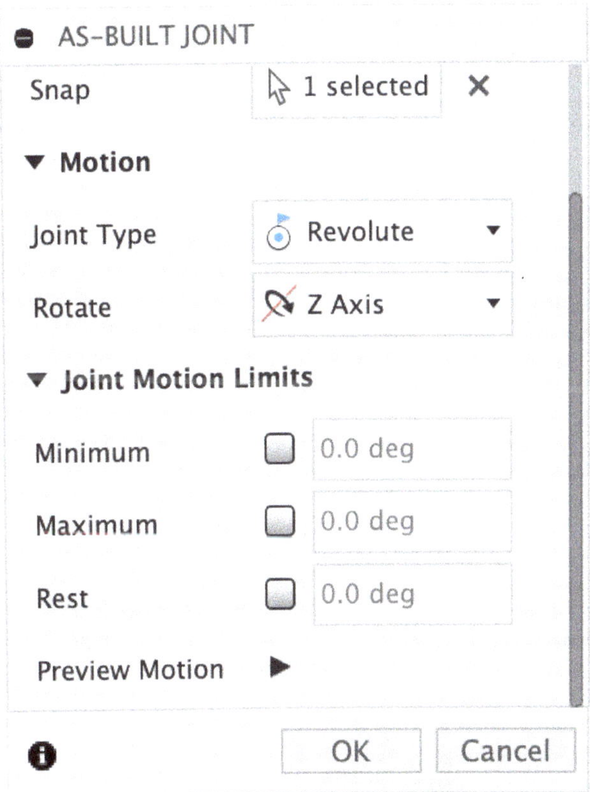

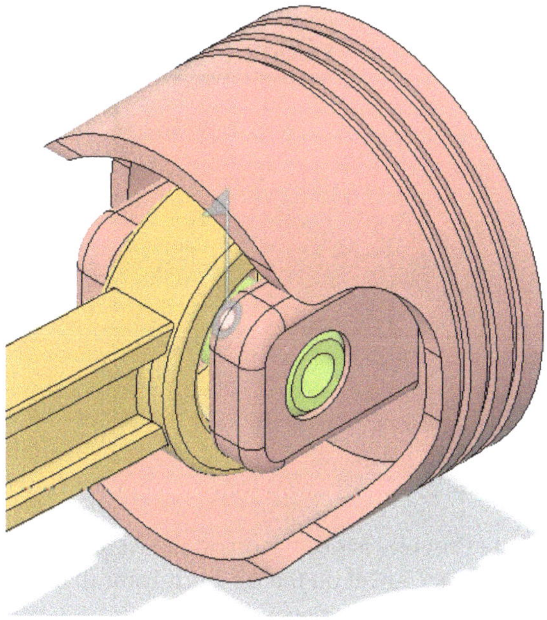

The **As-built Joint** command should be used when the components are already in the assembled state. It should not be used when the components are far away from each other. For example, click and drag the Piston head and place it at the location, as shown. Next, activate the **As-built Joint** command and click the **Capture Position** button on the **Fusion 360** message box. Select the Piston Head and Shaft from the graphics window.

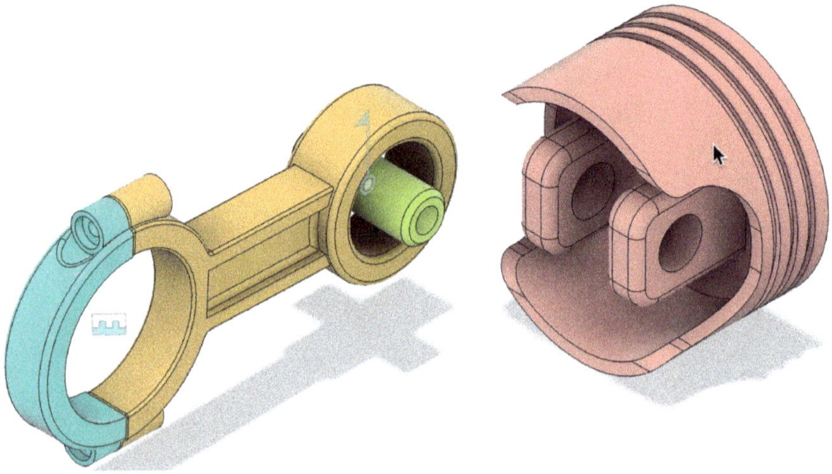

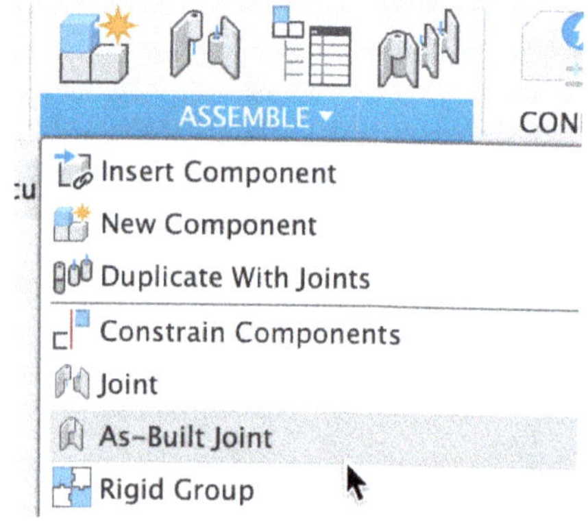

On the **As-built Joint** dialog, select **Type > Revolute**. Next, place the pointer on the cylindrical face of the Shaft and select the Joint Origin located at the Midpoint of the cylindrical face.

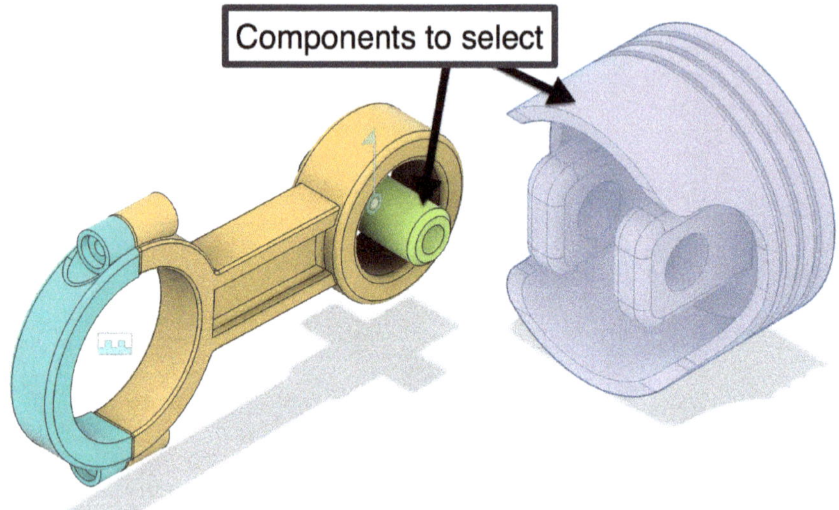

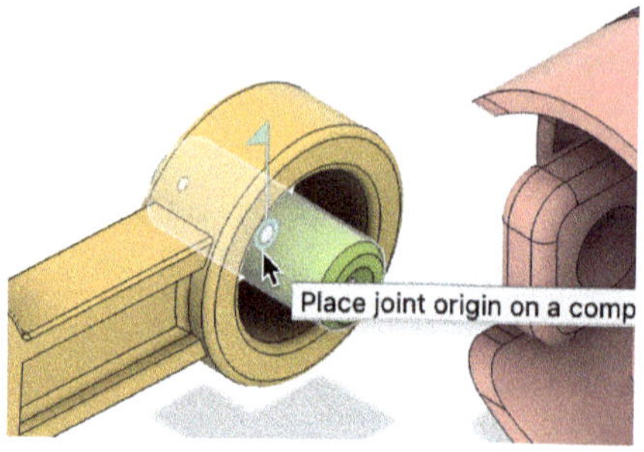

Click the **Preview Motion** icon on the **As-built Joint** dialog; the Piston Head rotates about the axis of the Shaft, as shown. Click **Cancel** on the **As-built Joint** dialog to cancel the Joint creation. Press Ctrl+Z to restore the Piston Head to its initial position.

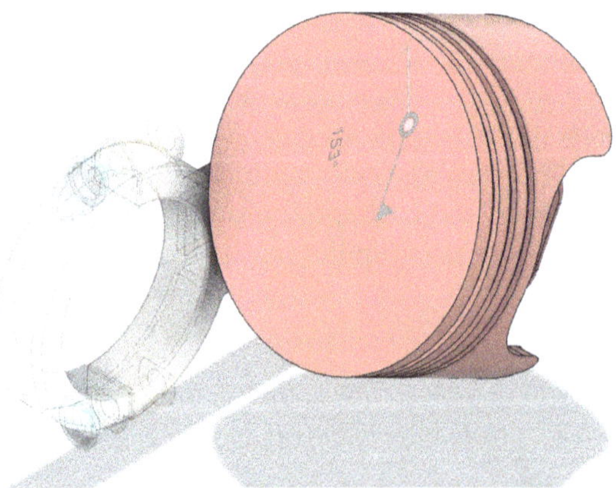

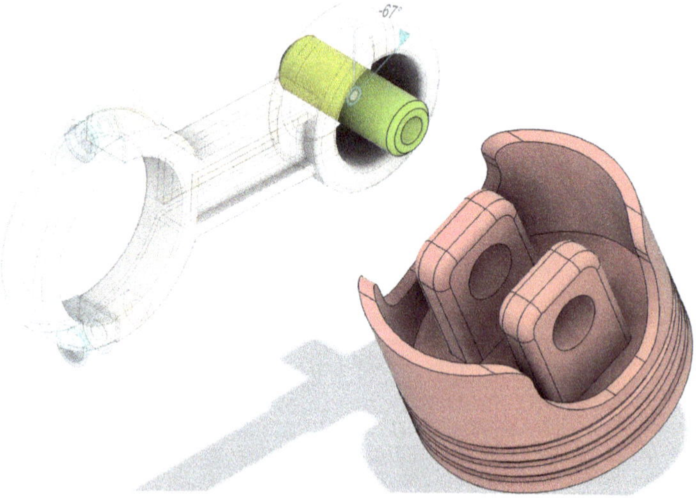

Insert Fastener

The **Insert Fastener** command places standards-based hardware into the assembly automatically. To insert hardware automatically, click **Solid > Insert > Insert Fastener** on the toolbar to open the **Insert Fastener** dialog with standard bolts, screws, washers, and nuts. From the **Standard** drop-down, choose a standard such as ISO, DIN, or ANSI, then expand the **Bolts and Screws** category and navigate through the subfolders until the required fastener appears. Use the search bar at any time to locate a specific family or size and select the desired bolt or screw.

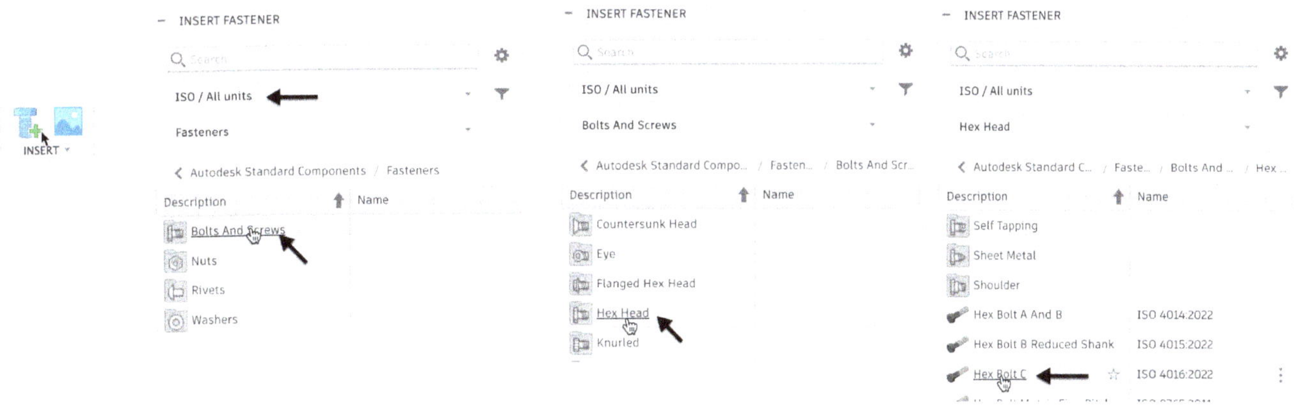

Hover over a hole to preview the fit, then click the hole to place the fastener with automatic sizing inferred from the hole geometry. Next, select the planar face that contains the selected hole to define the secondary geometry required for proper placement and alignment.

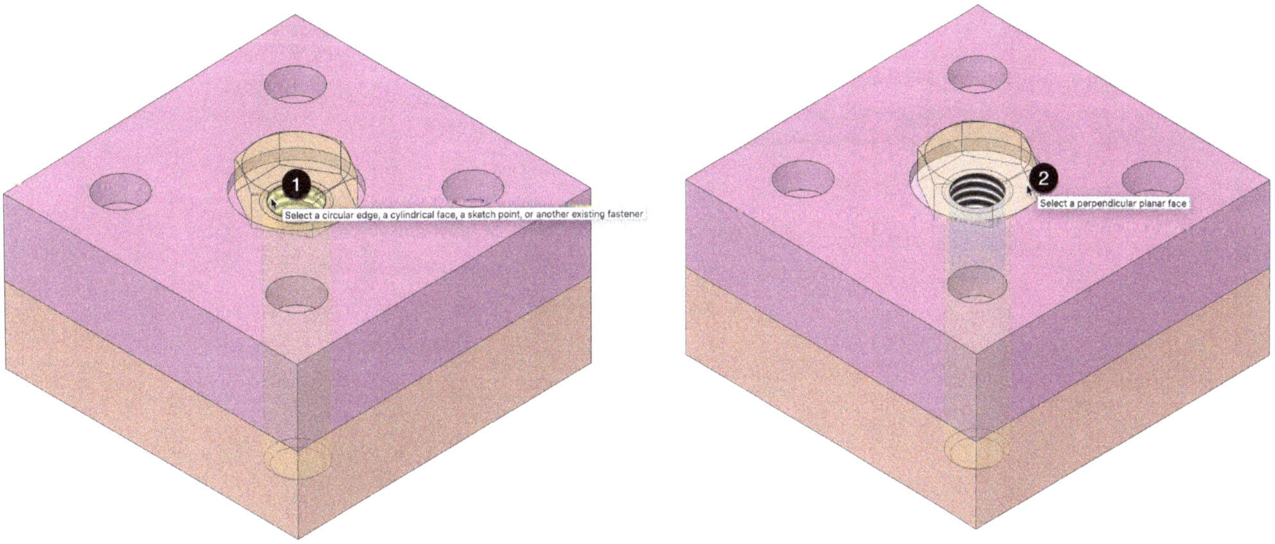

Drag the Length control to adjust the fastener length at the bottom of the inserted bolt or screw, or choose a value from the **Nominal length** drop-down in the dialog. Likewise, specify the **Material**, and **Finish**, and then click **Create and continue** to insert the fastener.

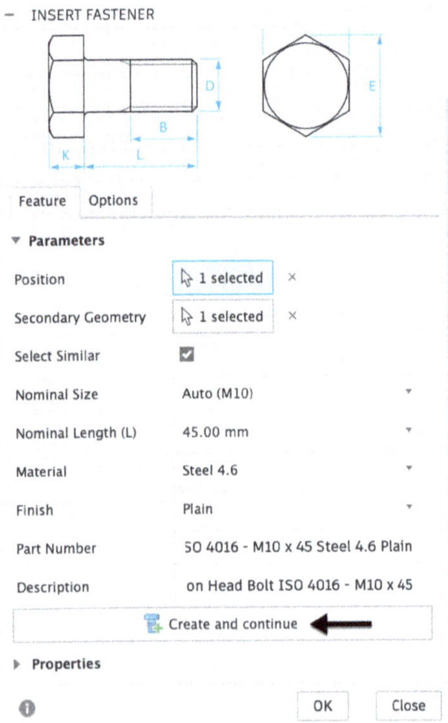

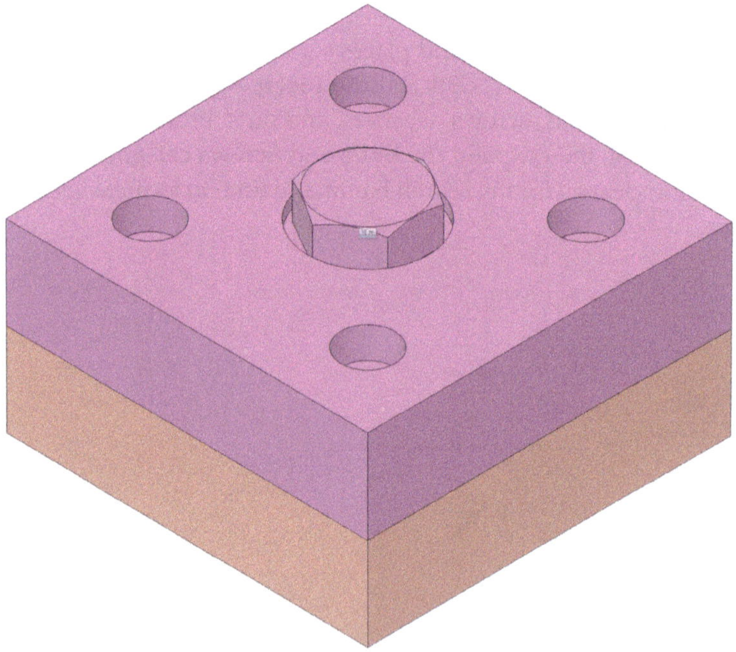

Click the Back icon located at the top of the **Insert Fastener** dialog. Next, select **Fasteners > Washers > Plain** from the **Public Libraries** drop-down.

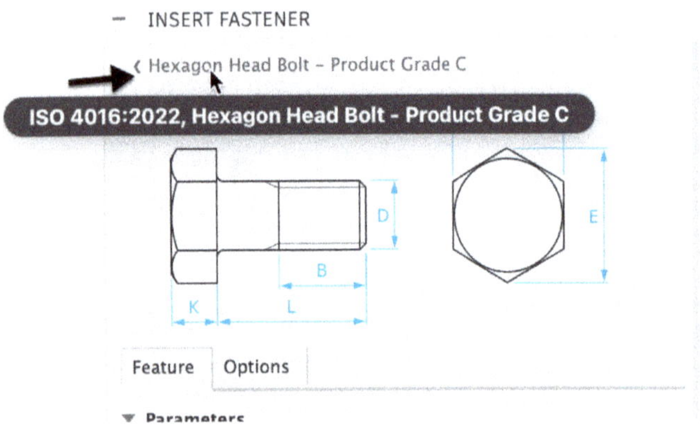

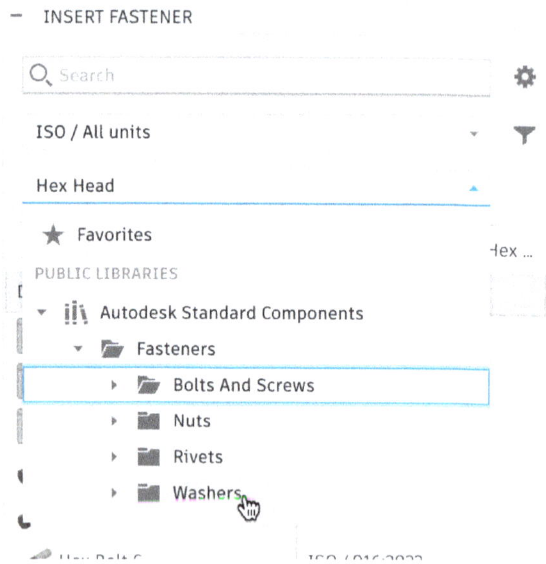

Select the desired washer type, then hover over the hole edge to preview the washer sized automatically from the hole geometry. Click **Create and continue** to place the washer and keep the dialog open for additional placements.

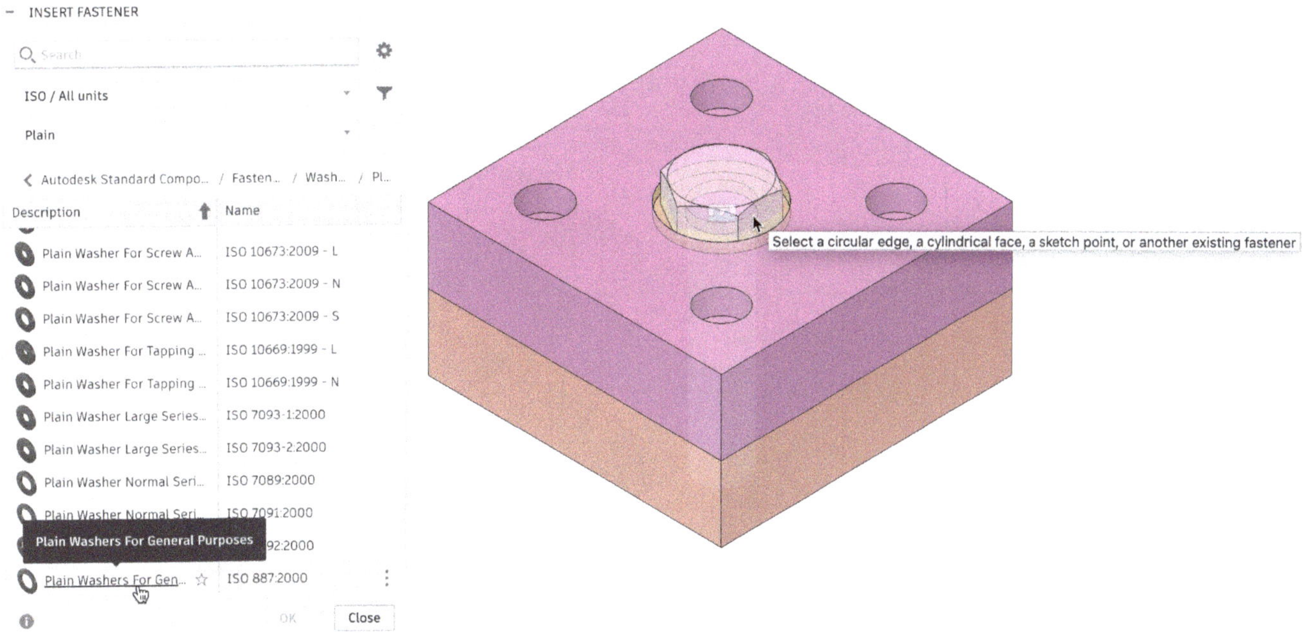

Click **Back**, then choose **Fasteners > Nuts > Hex** from the **Public Libraries** drop-down. Rotate the model to view the underside. Select the bolt to place a hex nut on its exposed end. Click **OK** to confirm, creating the required joints and BOM-ready components in the assembly.

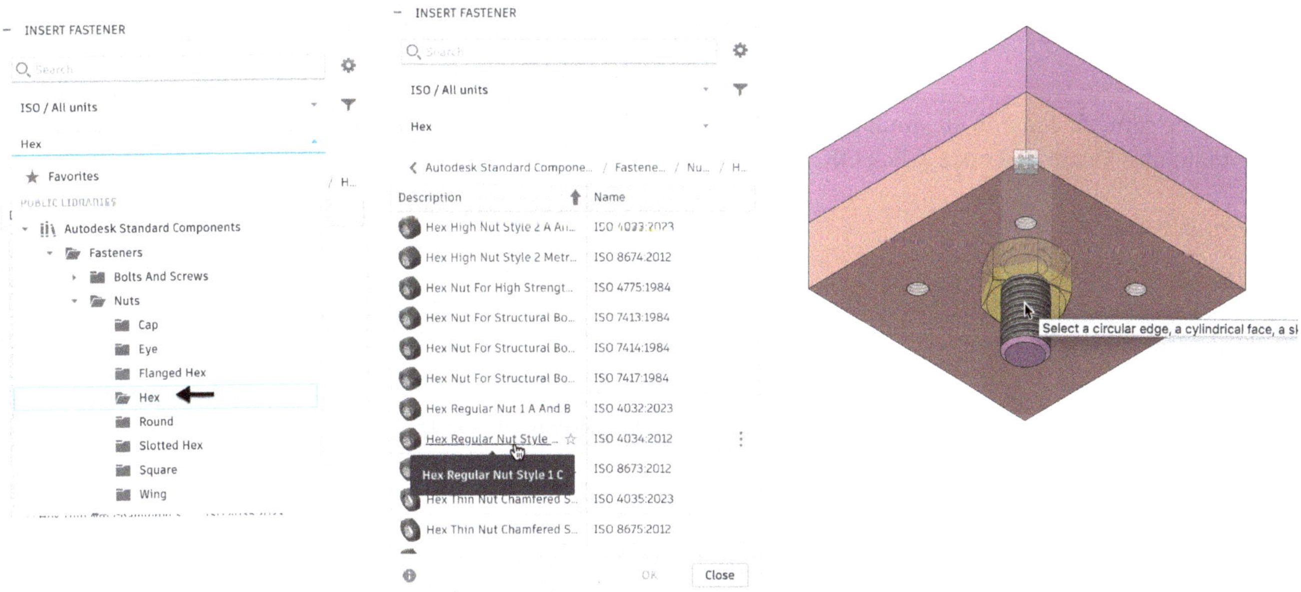

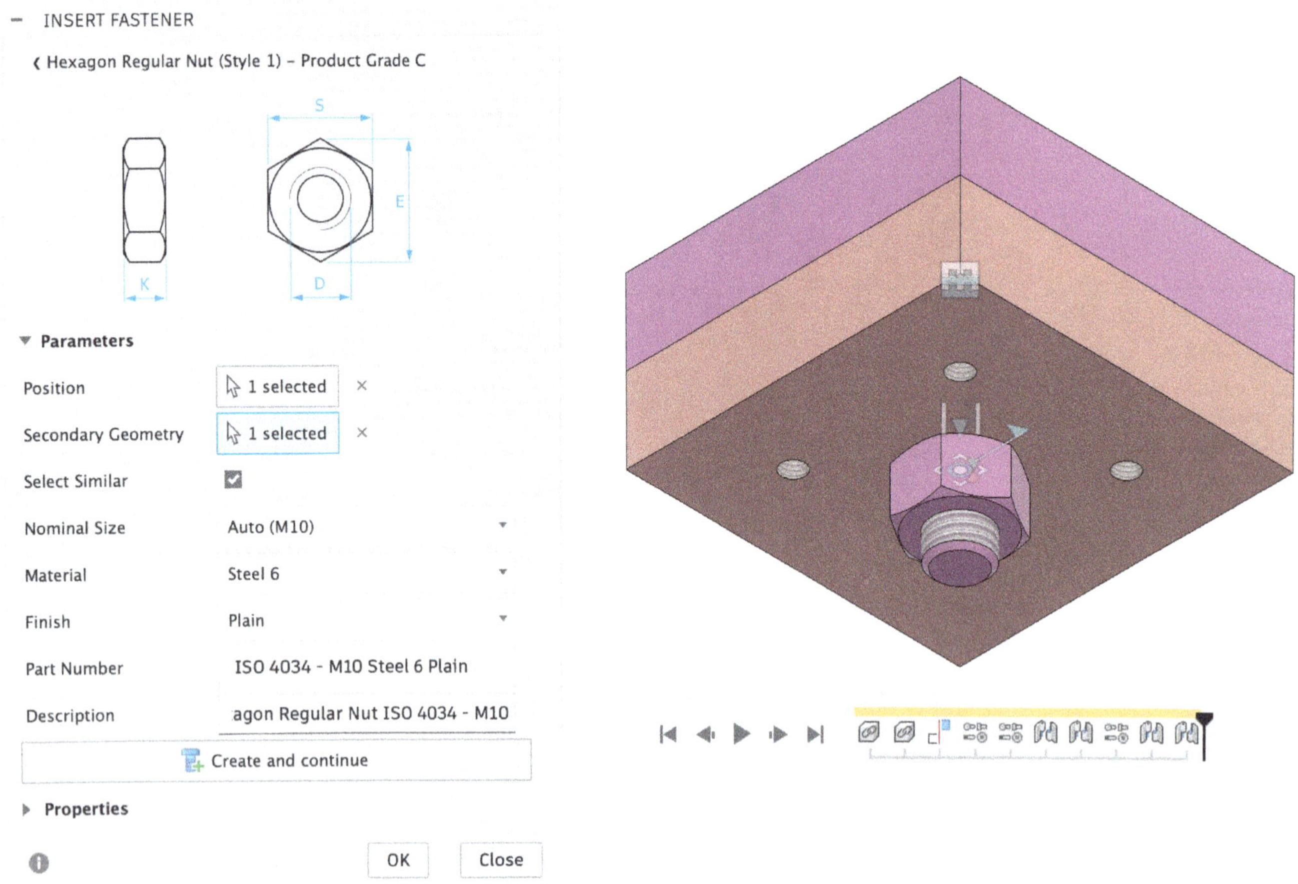

To place the same fastener in all similar holes, check the **Select similar** option and click a hole edge to populate every matching location at once. Click **OK**.

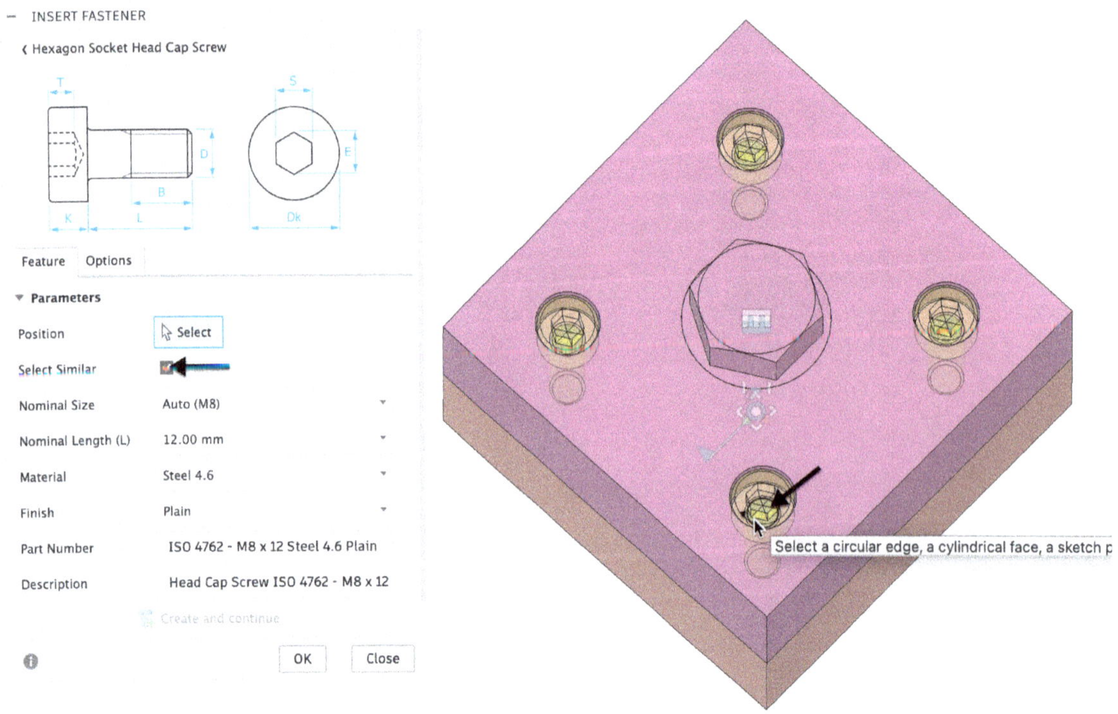

In the timeline, right-click the placed fastener and choose **Edit Fastener** to change size or length and Fusion updates the stack and placements accordingly.

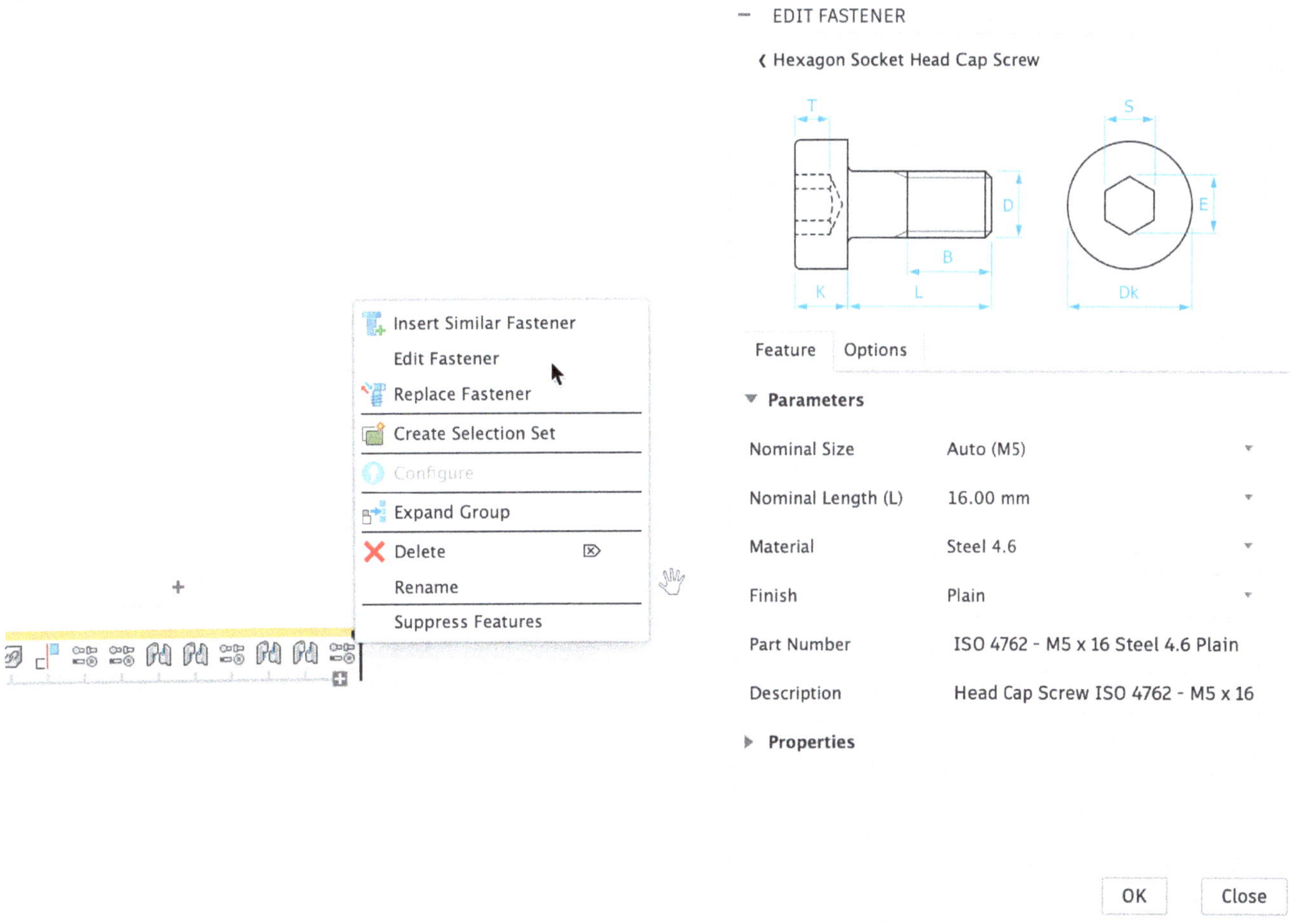

Creating Bill of Materials

The **Bill of Materials** command lists all parts and quantities in your design, lets you manage and export the list (for example, to Excel), and centralizes product data so teams can quickly buy, build, and maintain the product.

Open the main assembly for the full product. On the toolbar, click **Solid > Assemble > Bill of Materials** . On the **Bill Of Materials** dialog, expand or collapse levels to view components, subassemblies, part numbers, quantities, and descriptions from your design data. Next, click the **Column Settings** icon at the top-right of the Bill of Materials window, then check or uncheck the columns you want to see, such as **Part Number**, **Description**, **Quantity**, **Material**, **Revision**, or any custom fields needed for purchasing or production.

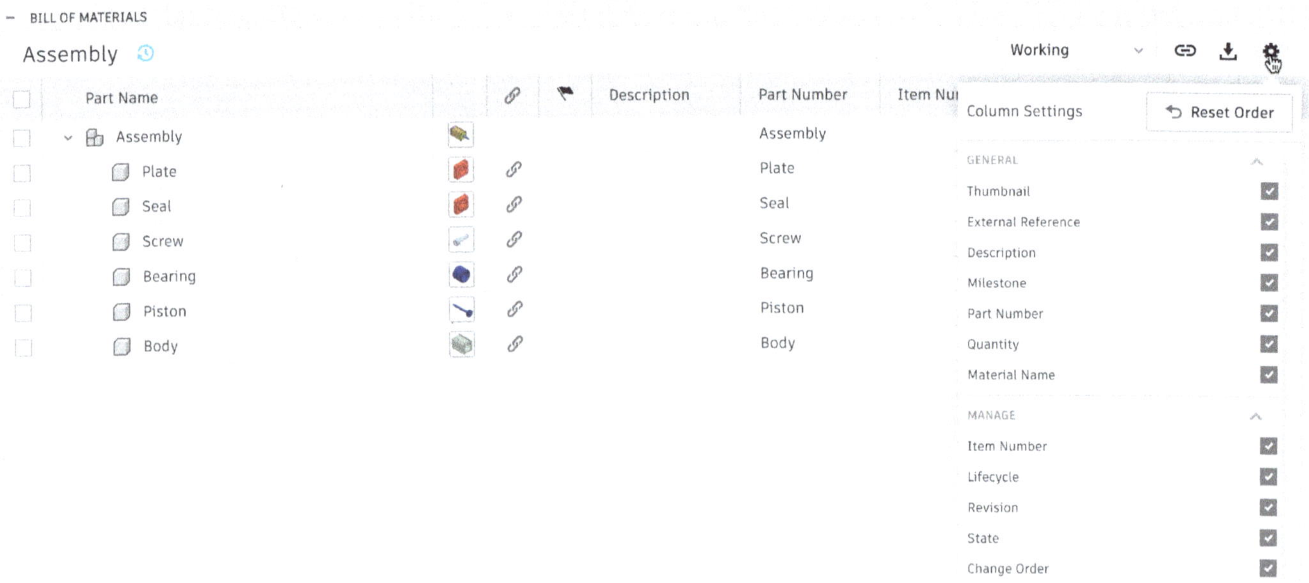

Click the **Export BOM** icon, then choose **Excel (.xlsx)** or **CSV (.csv)** to export the bill of materials. Click the **Download File** notification to save the file to your computer. Open the file in Excel or any spreadsheet application.

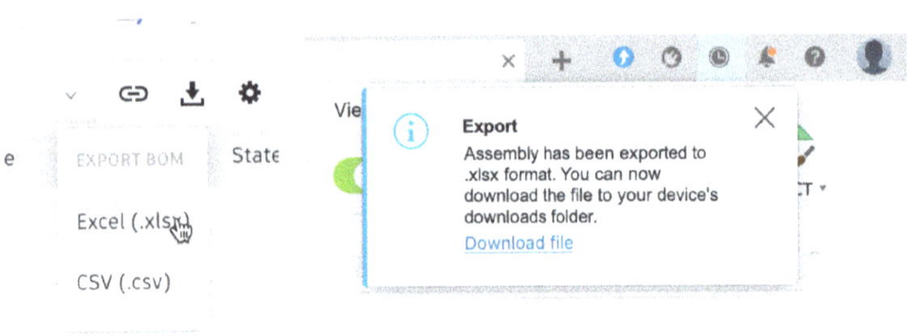

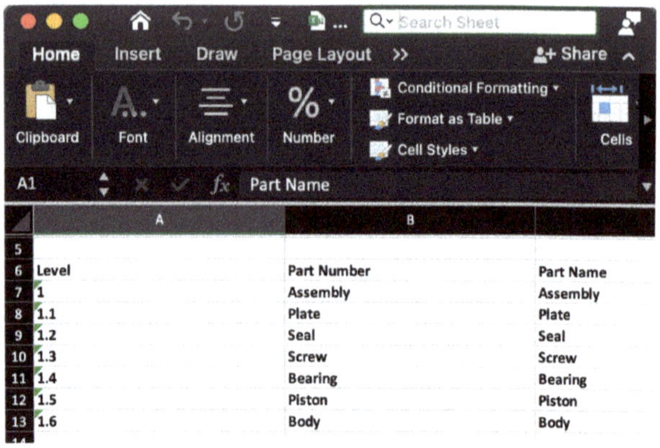

Creating Animations

Autodesk Fusion 360 provides you a separate workspace called **Animation** to create animations of the assembly. In this workspace, you can create exploded animations or display the functioning of the assembly. To create an animation, open the assembly design file and switch to **Animation** workspace. To do this, click the **Change Workspace** drop-down located at the left of the toolbar, and then select the **Animation** option.

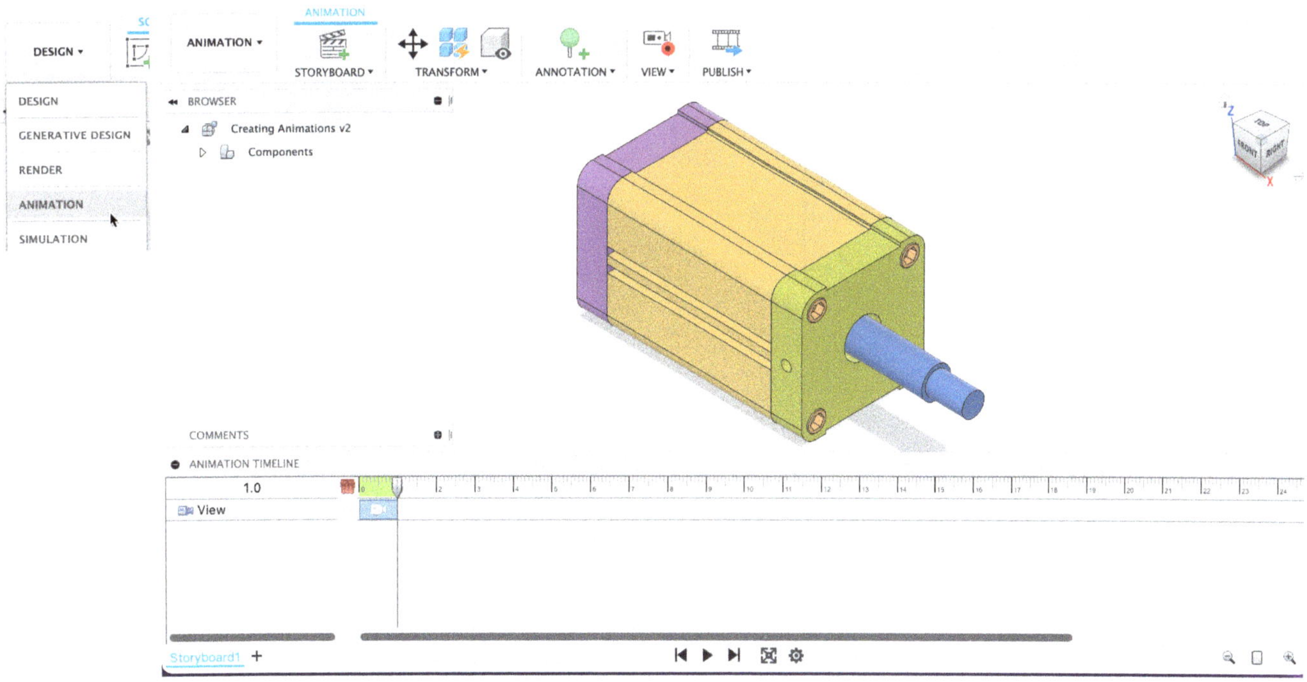

Creating a Storyboard

The Storyboard is displayed at the bottom of the window. It records the actions performed in the **Animation** workspace. By default, a storyboard is created when you activate the **Animation** workspace. You can rename the storyboard by double-clicking on its name and entering a new name.

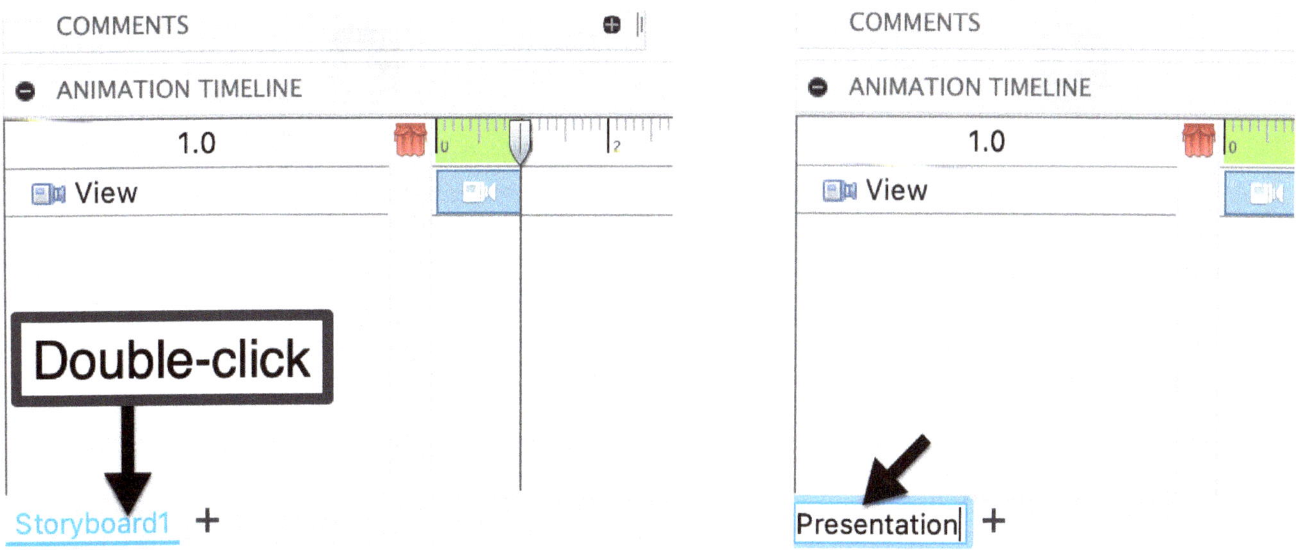

In addition to that, you can create a new storyboard by clicking the **New Storyboard** icon located next to the existing storyboard name (or) clicking the **New Storyboard**  command on the **Storyboard** panel of the toolbar. In doing so, the **New Storyboard** dialog appears. On this dialog, select an option (**Clean** or **Start from end of previous**) from the **Storyboard type** drop-down and click **OK**. Next, rename the newly created storyboard by right-clicking on it and selecting **Rename**.

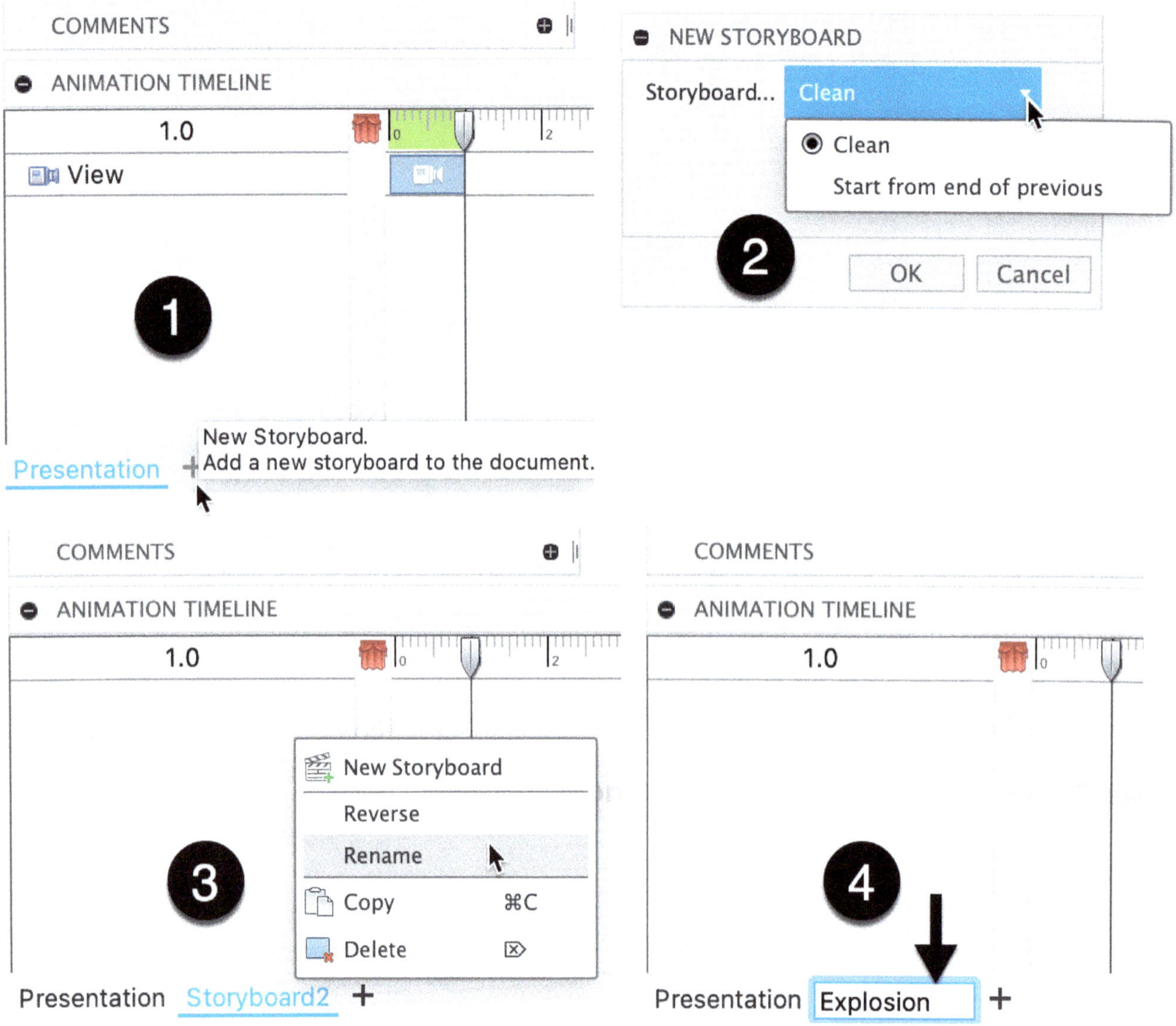

Auto-Exploding Components

The **Auto-Explode: All Levels** command explodes all the levels of the assembly, automatically. To explode the components automatically, select the **Components** node from the Browser, and then click the **Auto-Explode: All Levels** command on the **Transform** panel on the toolbar. Click and drag the **Explosion scale** slider to adjust space between the components. Next, click the **Trail Line Visibility** icon to turn on the trail lines between the components. Click the green check to explode the components.

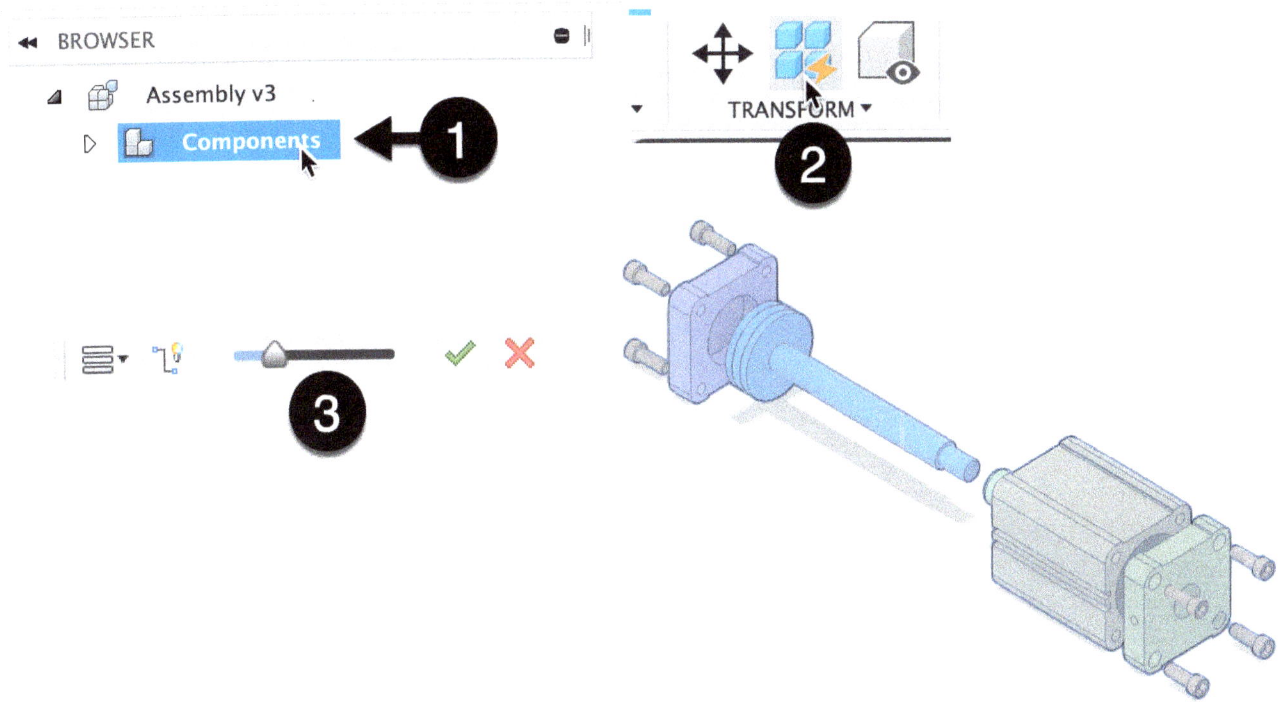

On the Storyboard, click the **Back to Storyboard beginning** icon to move the Playhead to the zero position. Next, click the **Play Current Storyboard** icon to play the explosion.

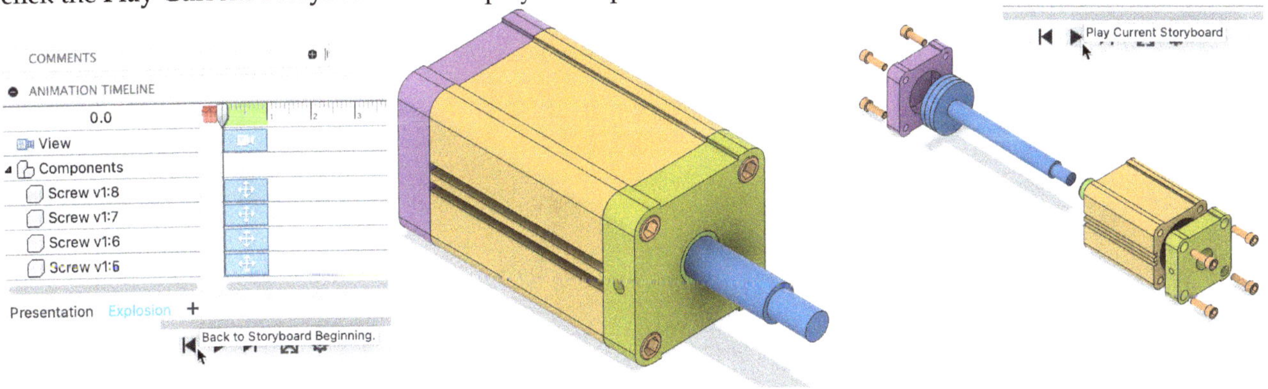

Turning ON/OFF the view recording

By default, the view recording is turned ON in the **Animation** workspace. The red dot on the **View** command on the toolbar indicates that. You can turn OFF the view recording by clicking the **View** command; the pause symbol appears on the **View** command. Also, the **View is not recording** message appears in the graphics window.

Animating the Camera

Click the **Presentation** tab on the Storyboard. Next, click and drag the playhead on the storyboard, and then release it on 2 seconds. Next, place the pointer on the model and move the scroll wheel in the forward direction; the model is zoomed-out, and the action is recorded in the timeline.

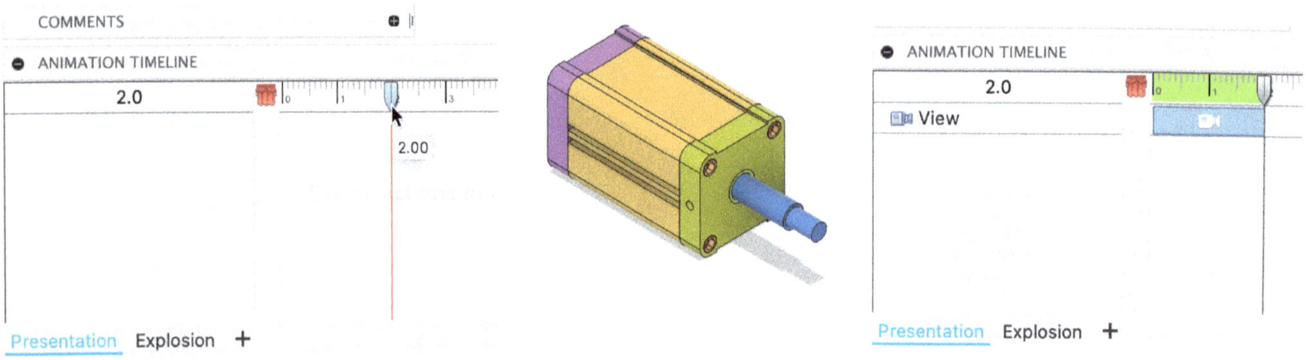

Drag the Playhead to 4 seconds and rotate the model slightly, as shown in the figure. The action is recorded in the timeline.

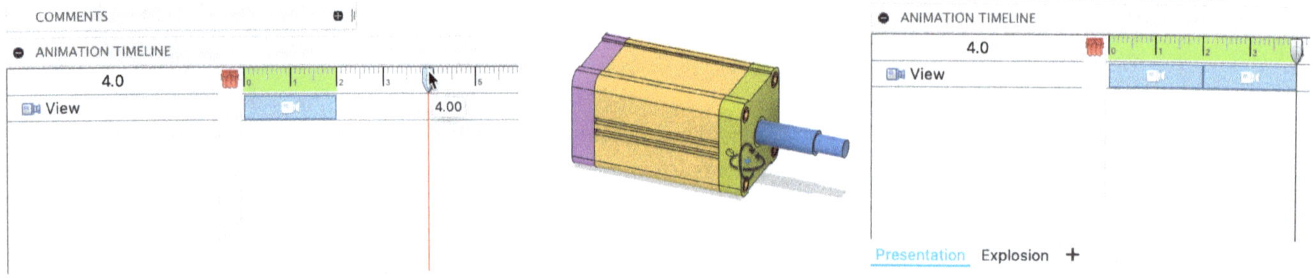

Drag the Playhead to 8 seconds and pan the model backward, as shown.

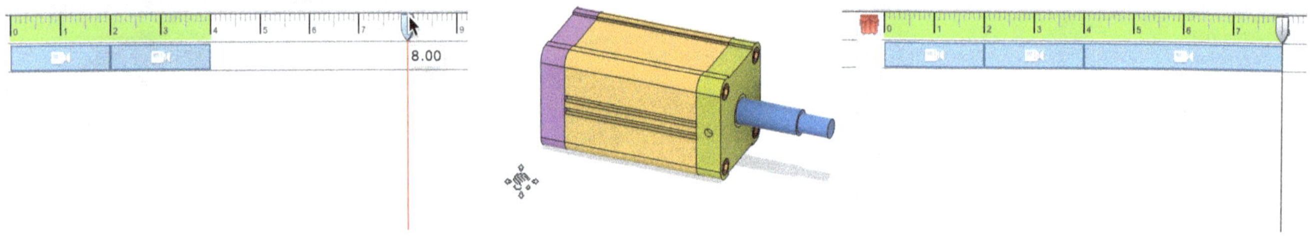

Drag the Playhead to 18 seconds and click the **Home** icon on the top left corner of the ViewCube.

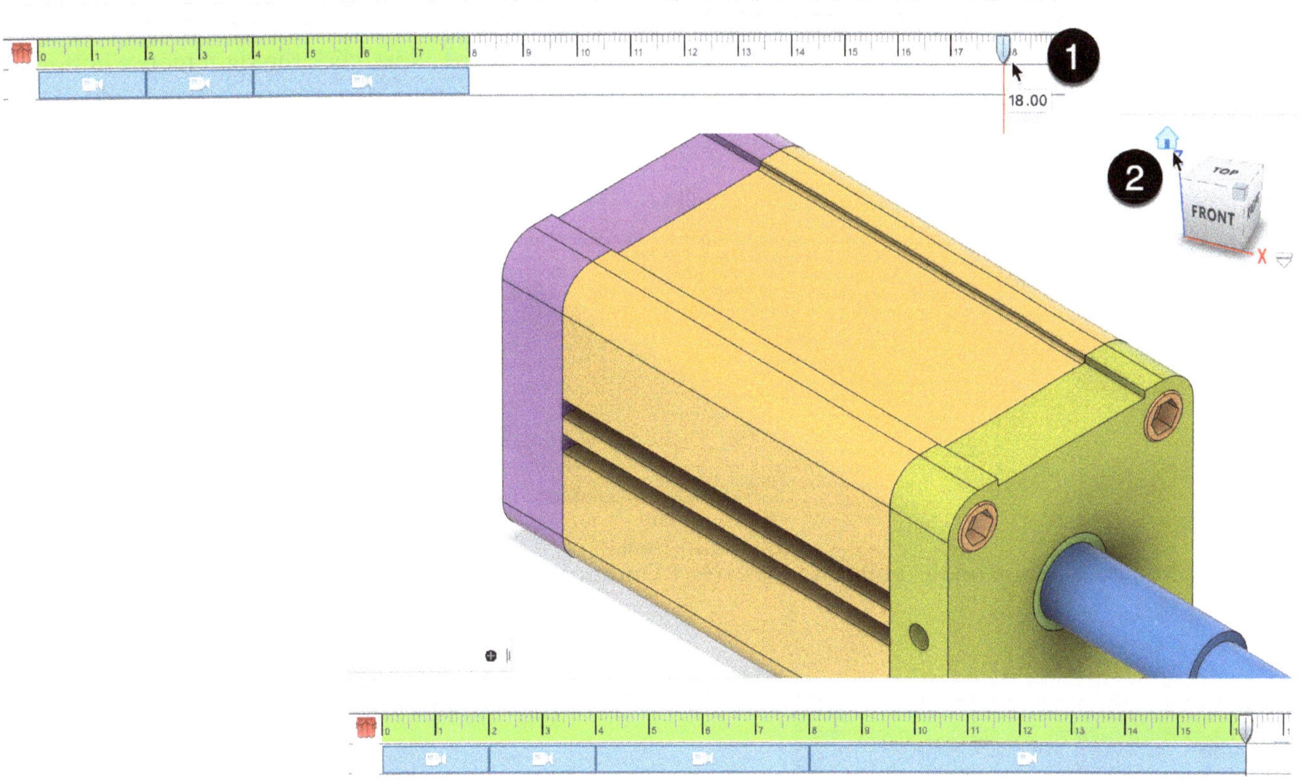

Click the **Back to Storyboard Beginning** icon, then click the **Play Current Storyboard** icon; the animation of the camera is played.

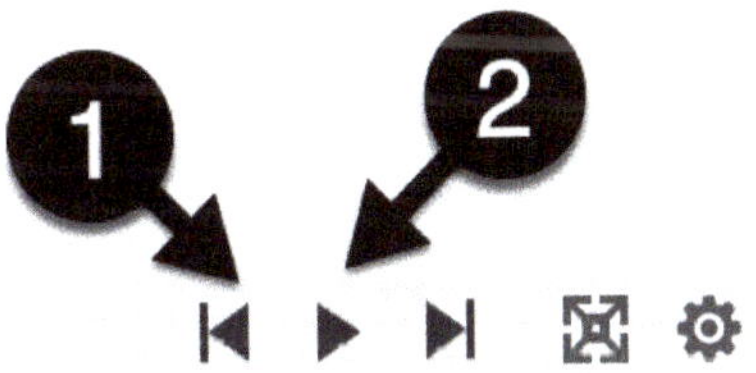

In the ANIMATION TIMELINE, click on the starting position of the last camera view. Next, press and hold the left mouse button and drag the pointer toward the right. Release the pointer on 10 seconds; a gap is created between the third and fourth camera views.

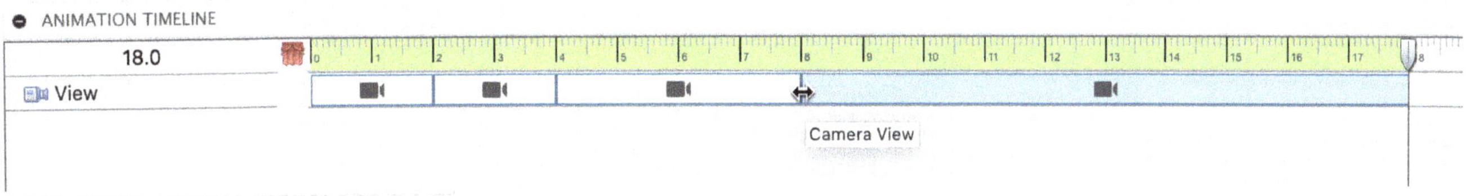

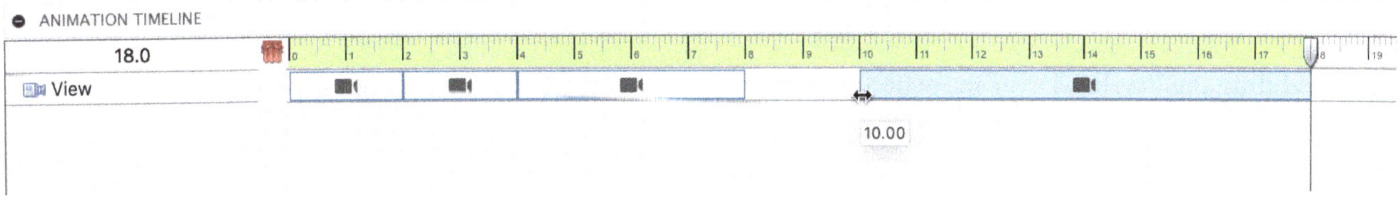

Click the **Back to Storyboard Beginning** icon, then click the **Play Current Storyboard** icon; notice that the camera pauses between the pan and home view.

Adding an Action to the Storyboard

Drag the Playhead and release it between 1 and 2 seconds on the storyboard. Next, click the right mouse button on the Body of the Cylinder assembly and then select **Show/Hide**; the body is hidden, and the action is added to the storyboard.

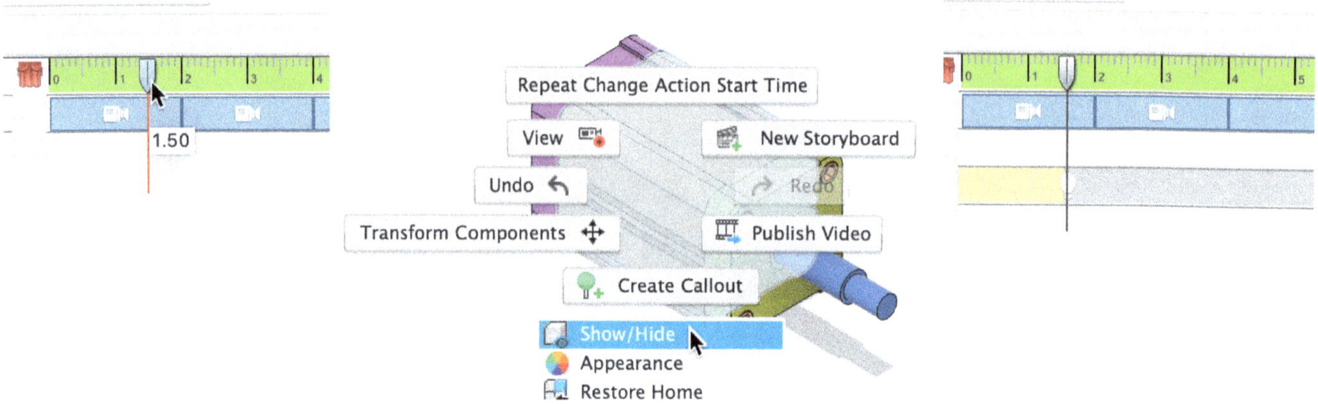

Click the right mouse button on the bulb, and then select **Duration**. Type 4 in the **Duration** box, and then click the green check.

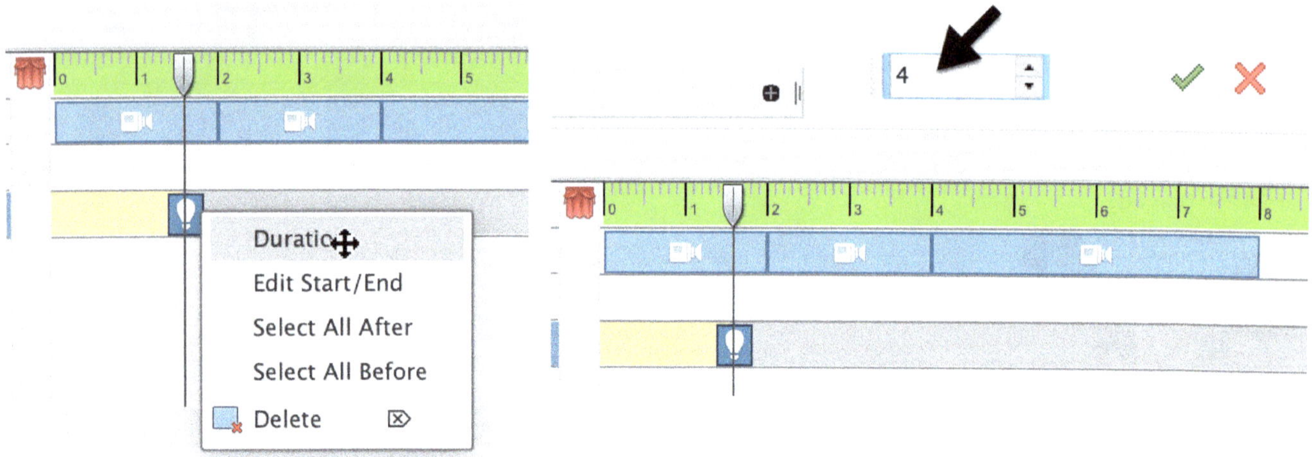

Select the action from the storyboard, press and hold the left mouse button, and then drag it toward left. Next, release it at 1 second.

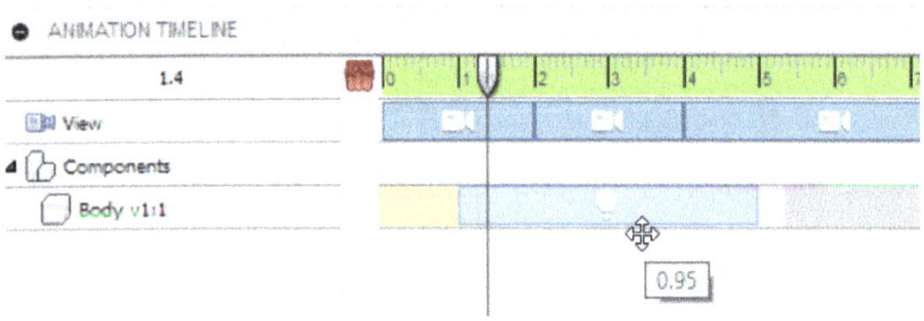

Click and drag the Playhead over the action, and then notice that the body is faded out slowly.

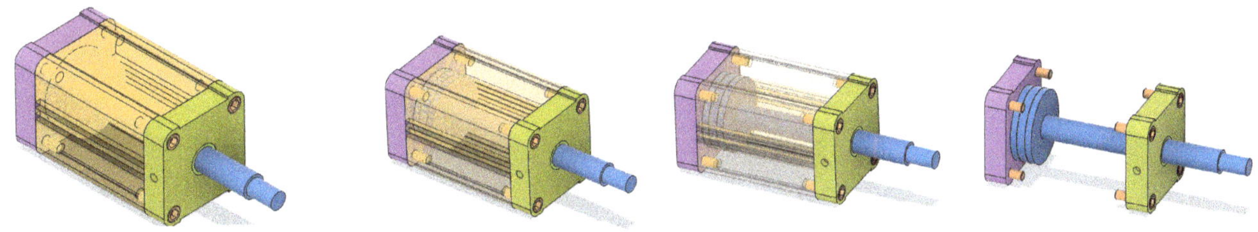

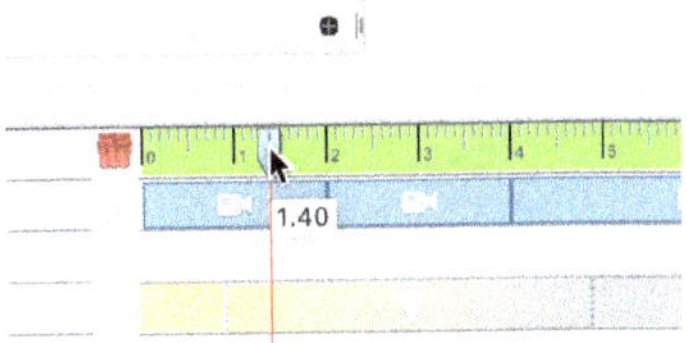

Transform Components

Click and drag the Playhead to 8 seconds. Next, expand the **Components** node in the Browser and turn ON the Body.

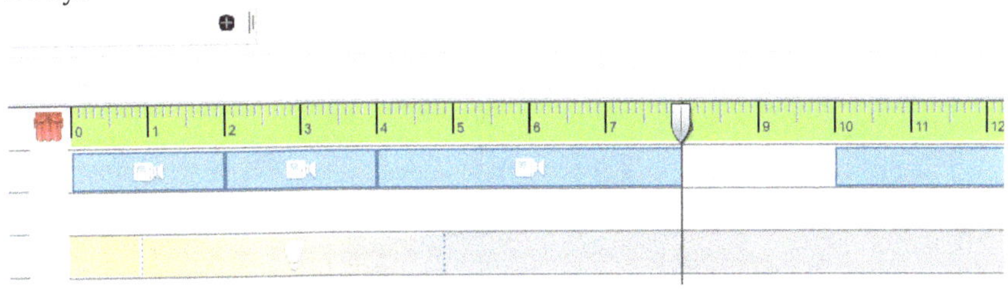

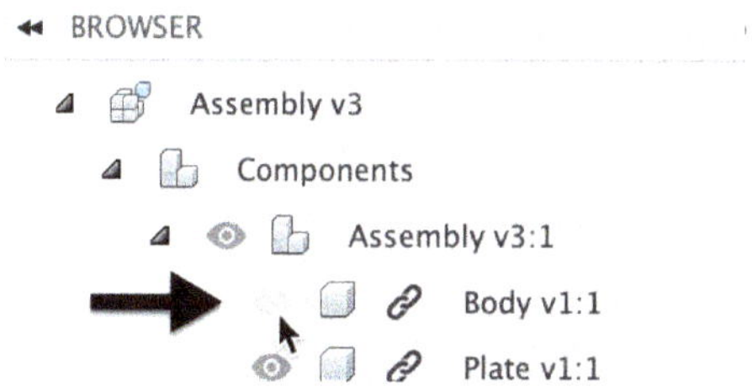

On the toolbar, click **Animation > Transform > Transform Components**. Next, press and hold the CTRL key and select the four screws on the front side. Click the **Trace Line Visibility** icon on the **Transform Components** dialog. Click and drag the arrow pointing in the Y direction. Type **-125** in the **Distance** box, and then click **OK** on the **Transform Components** dialog. Notice the **Move** actions recorded in the Storyboard.

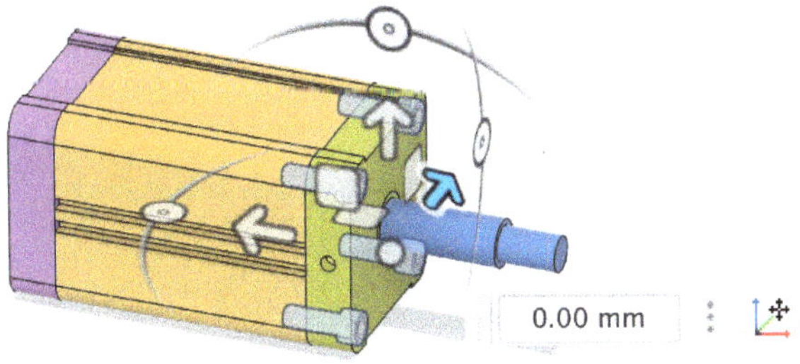

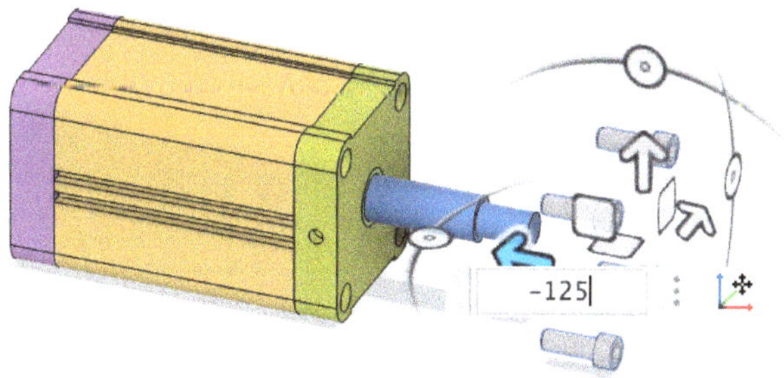

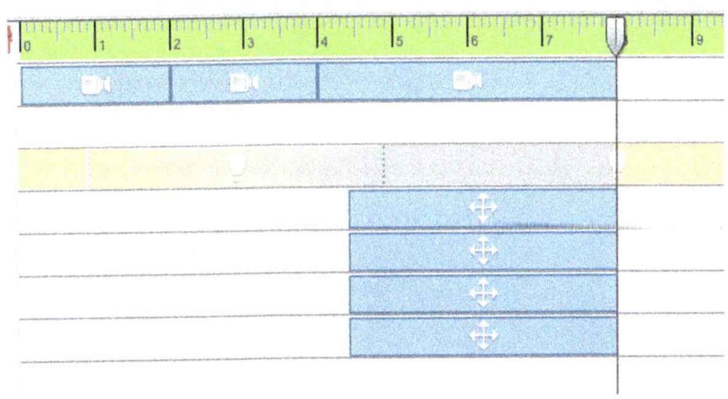

Click and drag the topmost Move action, and then release it at 8 seconds. Next, press and hold the CTRL key and select all the Move actions from the storyboard. Click the right mouse button and select **Align end time** from the menu.

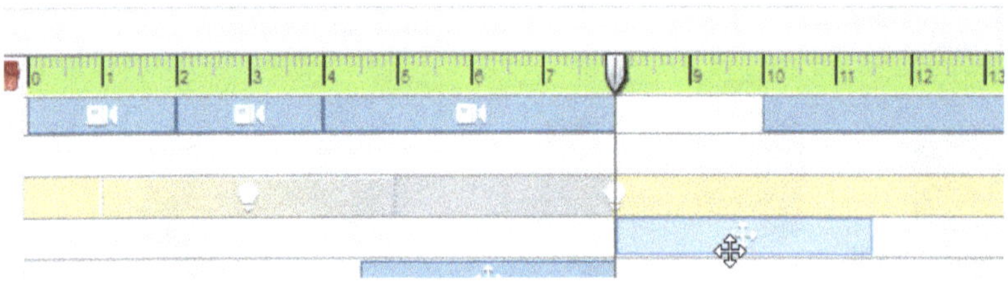

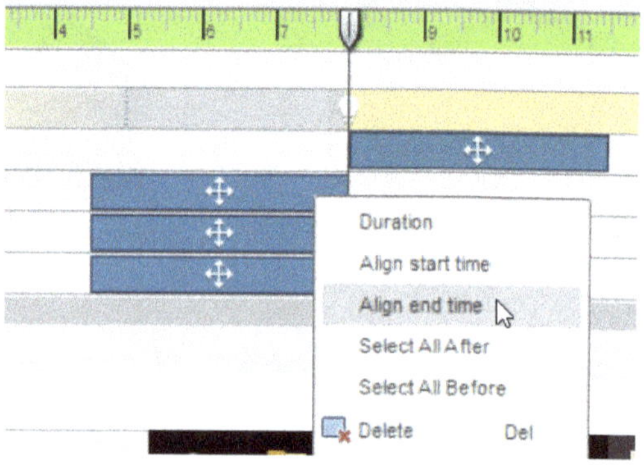

Adding Callouts

Use the **Create Callout** command to add callouts to the components in the **ANIMATION** workspace. On the toolbar, click **Annotation > Create Callout** and select a component from the assembly. Next, enter the callout text and click the green check to create the callout.

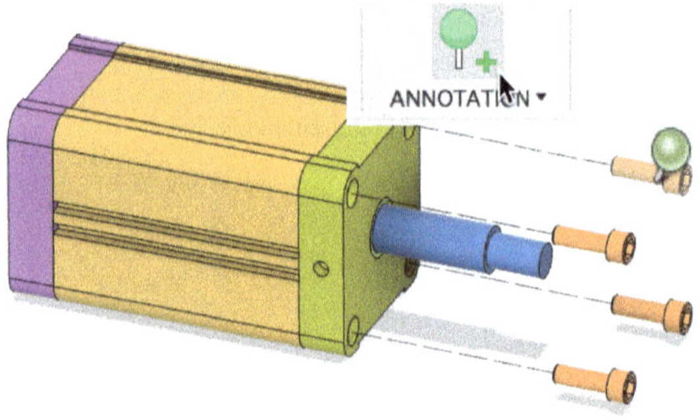

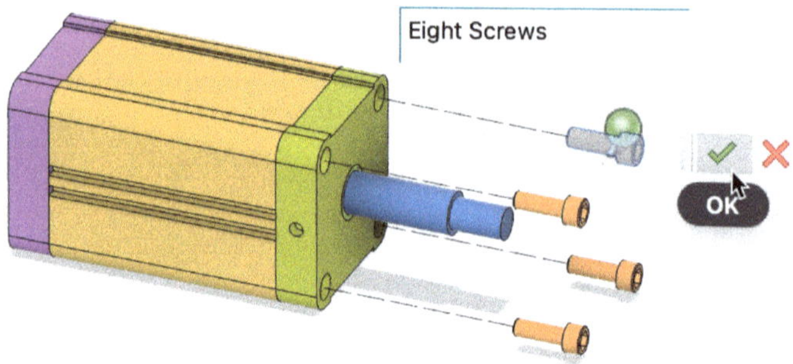

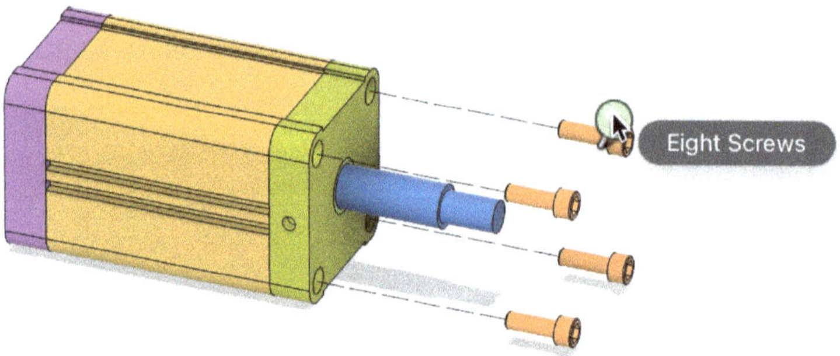

Exploding Components Manually

Autodesk Fusion 360 provides you the **Manual Explode** command to explode the components manually. Click the **Jump to Storyboard end** icon on the timeline. On the toolbar, click **Transform > Manual Explode** and select the component to be exploded. Next, click on any one of the arrows that appear on the selected component; the explosion direction is defined. Click and drag the **Explosion Scale** to define the explosion distance. Click the **Trail Line Visibility** icon, and then click the green check.

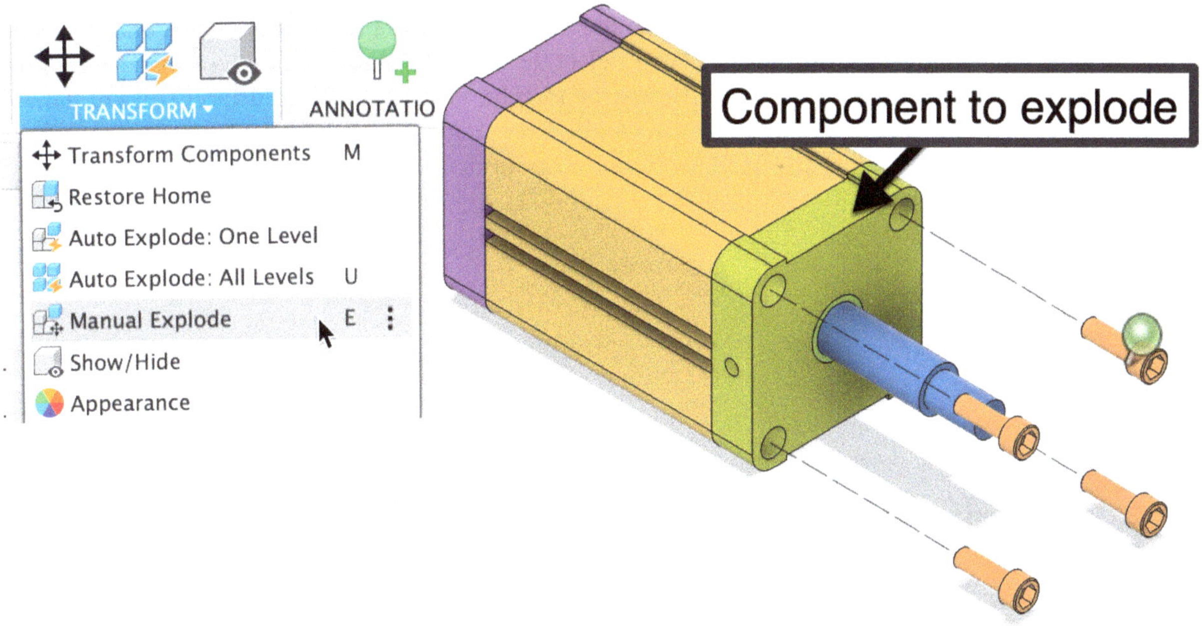
TRANSFORM
ANNOTATIO
Transform Components M
Restore Home
Auto Explode: One Level
Auto Explode: All Levels U
Manual Explode E
Show/Hide
Appearance
Component to explode

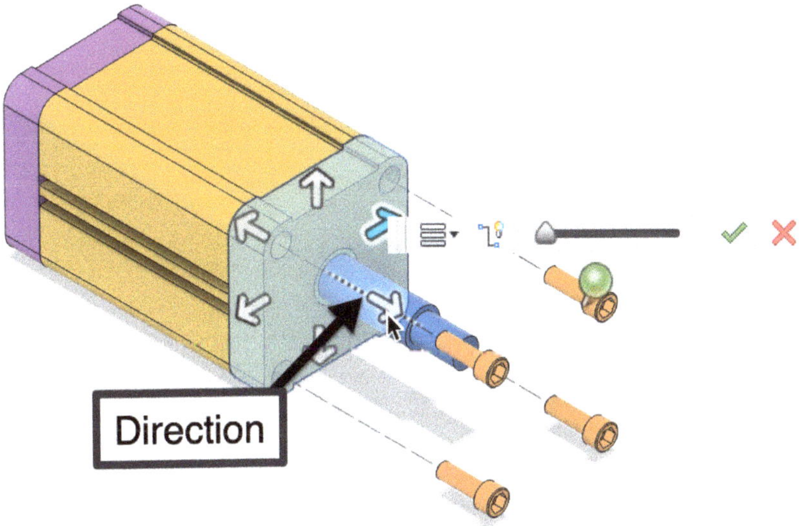
Direction

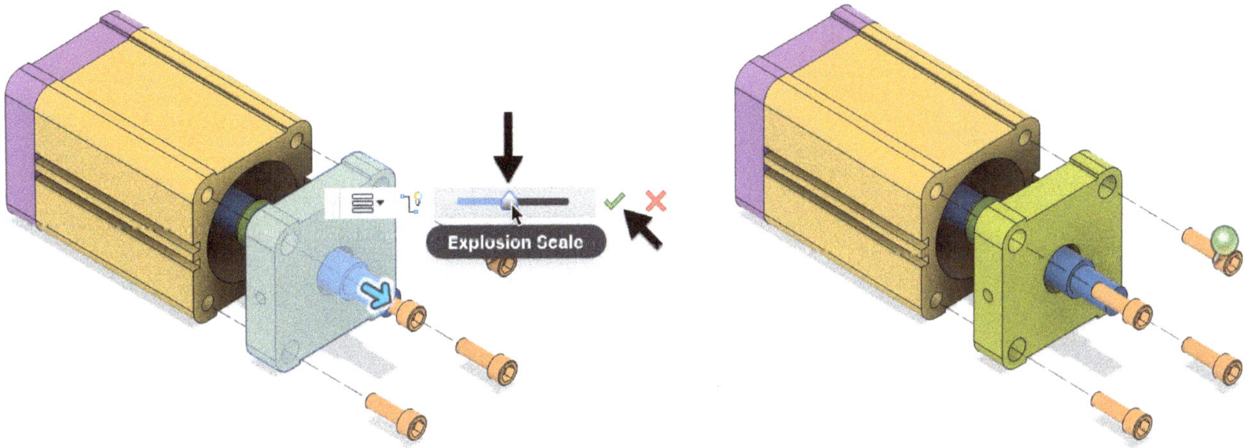
Explosion Scale

Publishing the Animation

To publish the animation, click **Publish > Publish Video** on the toolbar and select the **Current Storyboard** or **All Storyboard** option from the **Video Scope** drop-down. Next, select the video resolution from the Video Resolution drop-down. You can also select the **Custom** option and enter the **Height**, **Width**, and **Resolution** values of the video. Next, click **OK** and enter the name of the video file. On the **Save As** dialog, specify the location of the file on the cloud. In addition to that, you can check the **Save to computer** option to save the published file on your computer. Next, click the **Save** button.

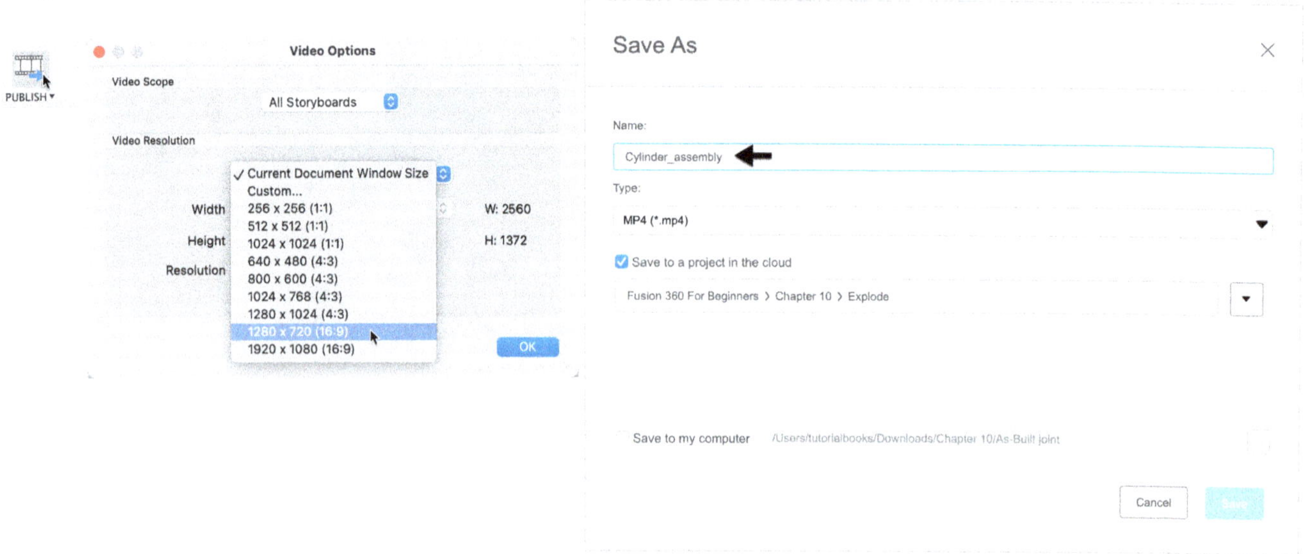

Examples

Example 1 (Bottom-Up Assembly)

In this example, you will create the assembly shown below.

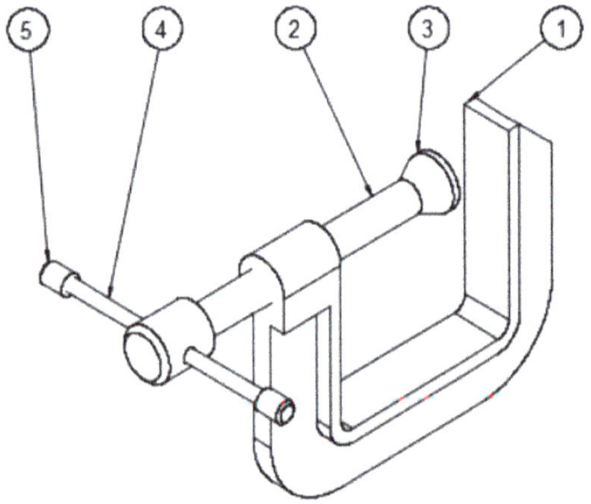

Parts List			
Item	Qty	Part Number	Material
1	1	Clamp Jaw	Steel
2	1	Spindle	Steel
3	1	Spindle Cap	Steel
4	1	Handle	Steel
5	2	Handle Cap	Steel

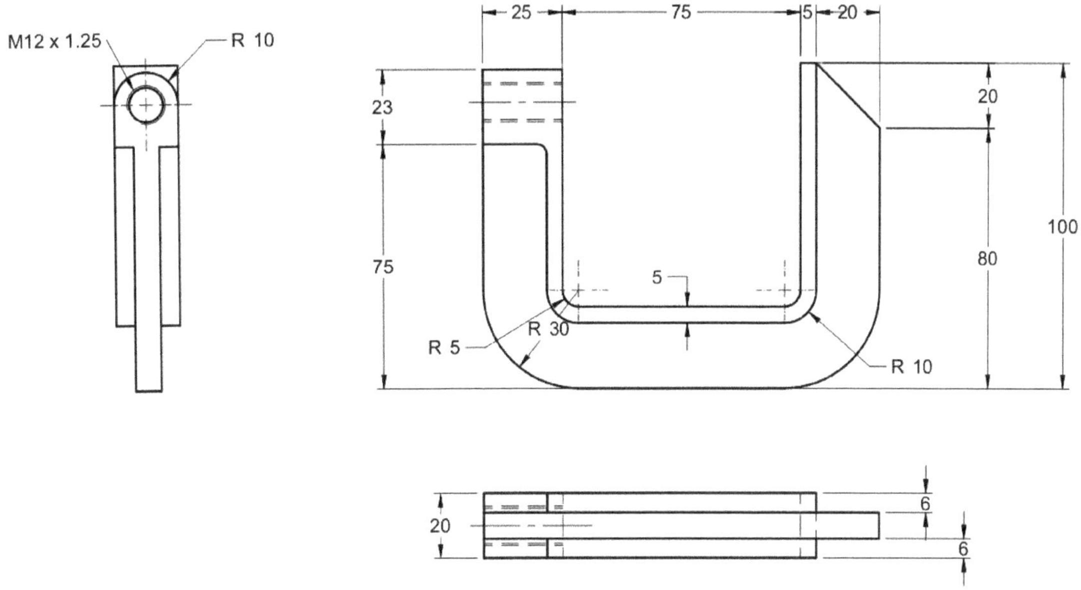

CLAMP JAW

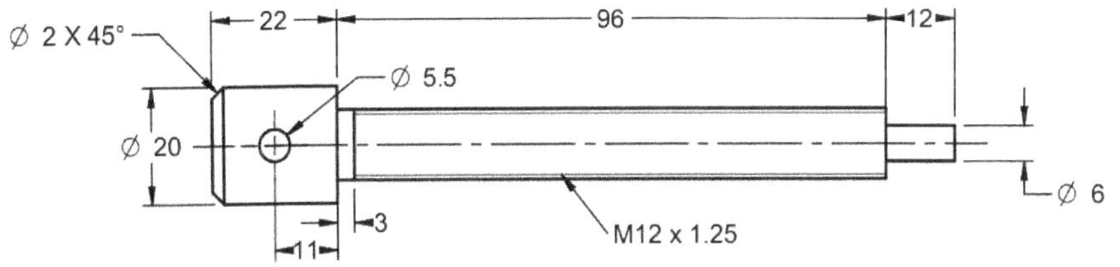

SPINDLE

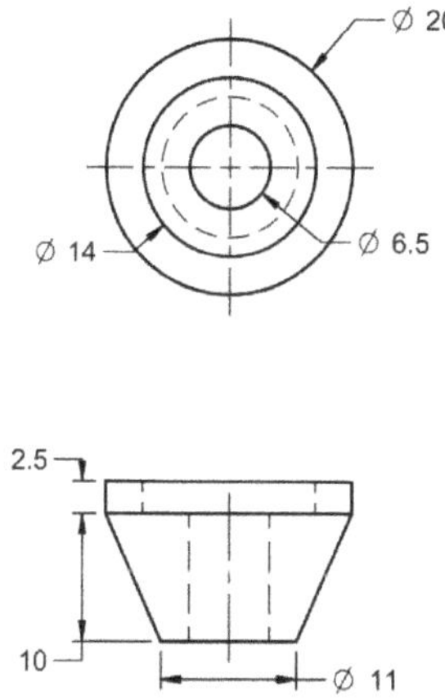

SPINDLE CAP

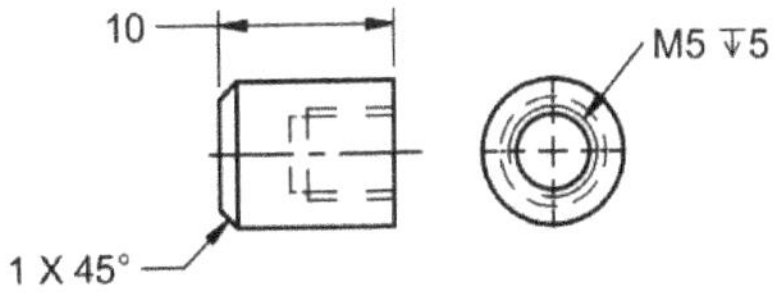

HANDLE CAP

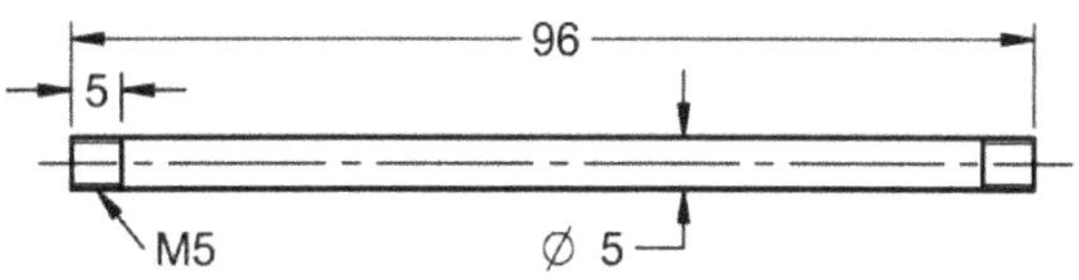

HANDLE

1. Start **Autodesk Fusion 360**.
2. Open the Fusion 360 For Beginners project in the **Data** panel.
3. Click the **New Folder** button and type G-Clamp, and then press Enter. Double-click on the folder to open it.
4. Create and save all the design files of the assembly. You can also get the part files by sending us an email to online.books999@gmail.com.

5. On the **Application bar**, click **File > New Design**.
6. In the Browser, expand the **Document Settings** node and place the pointer on the **Units** option. Next, click the **Change Active Units** icon.
7. On the **Change Active Units** dialog, select **Unit Type > millimeter (mm), gram (g)**. Next, click **OK**.
8. Click **Save** on the **Application bar** and enter **Example 1** in the **Name** box and click **Save**.
9. On the **Application bar**, click on the **Show Data Panel** icon.
10. Right-click on the **Clamp Jaw** file and click the **Insert into Current Design** option.

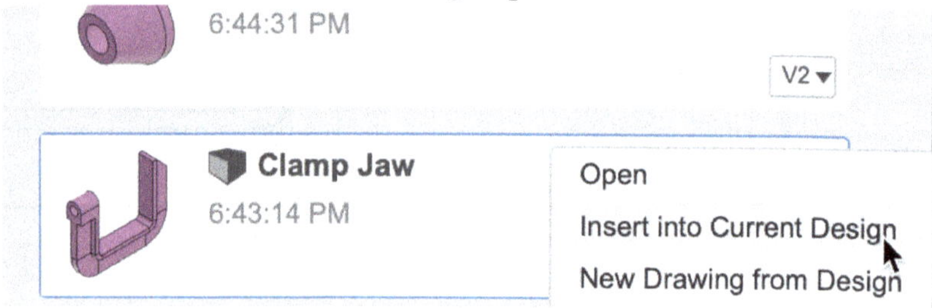

11. On the **Initial Position** dialog, check the **Ground To Parent** option and click **OK** to insert the design file and fix it at the origin.

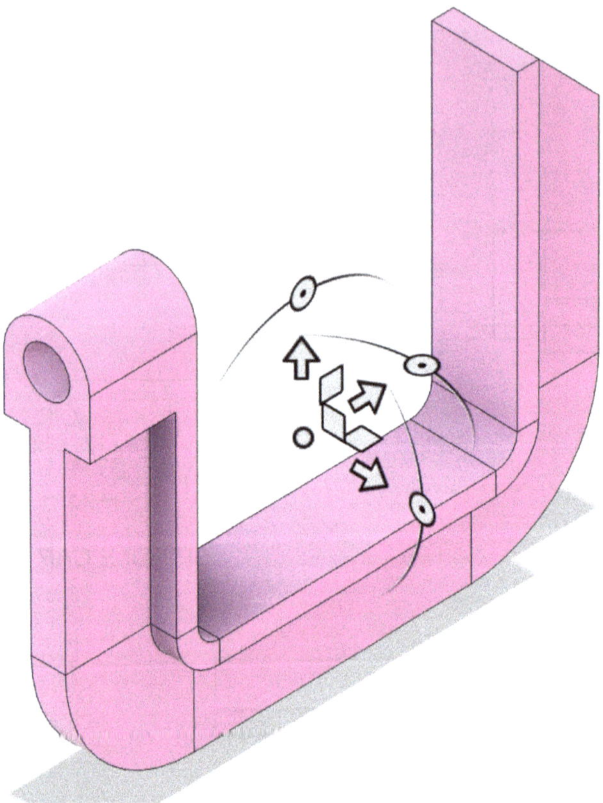

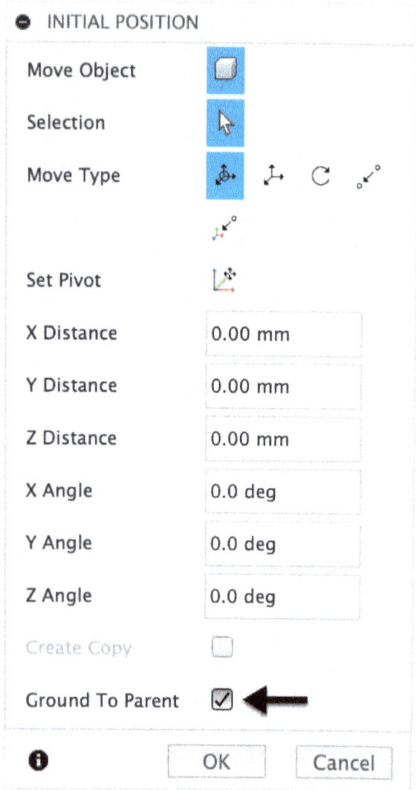

12. In the **Data** panel, right-click on the Spindle file and then select **Insert into Current Design**.
13. Click **OK** on the **Initial Position** dialog.

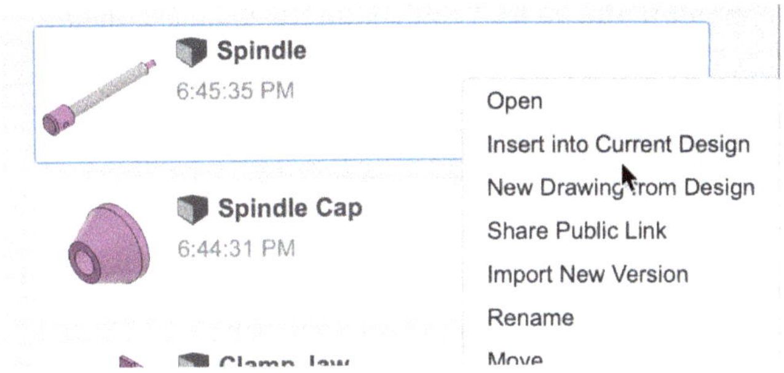

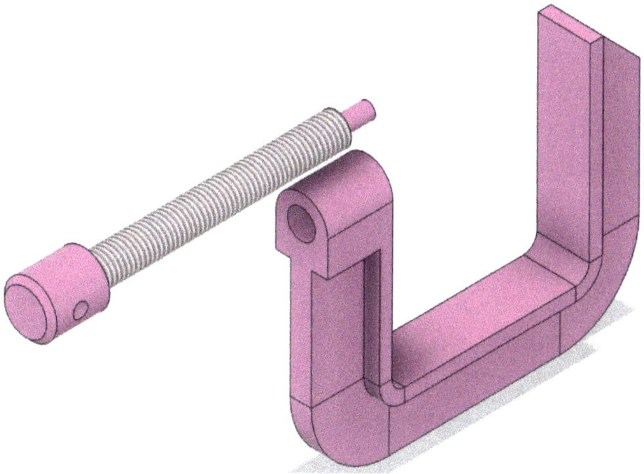

14. On the toolbar, click **Assemble > Joint** .
15. Select the circular edges of the *Spindle* and the *Clamp Jaw*, as shown.

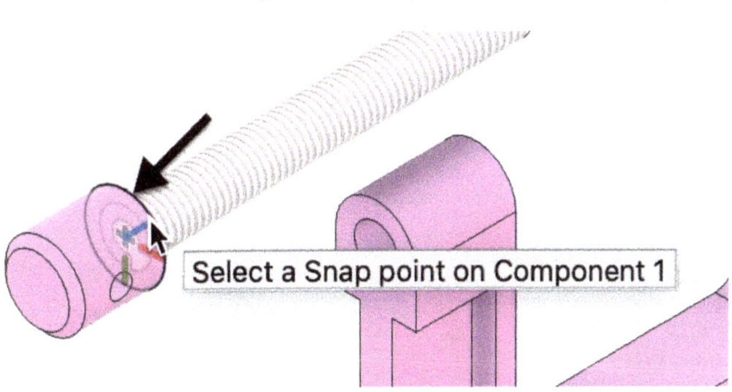

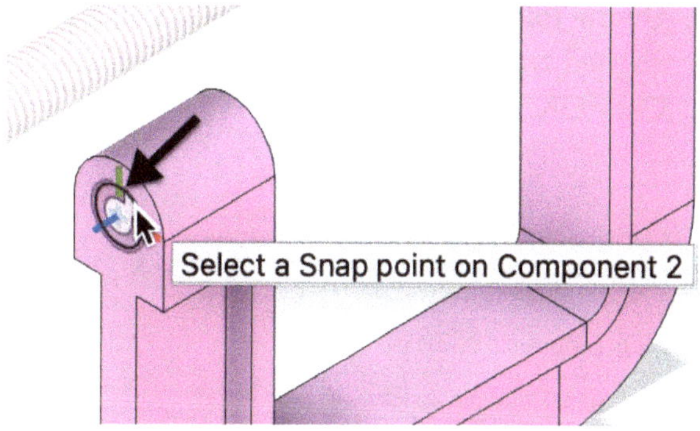

16. On the **Joint** dialog, click the **Motion** tab and select **Type > Cylindrical**.
17. On the **Joint** dialog, click the **Position** tab and type-in **31** in the **Offset Z** box under the **Joint Alignment** section. Next, click **OK**.

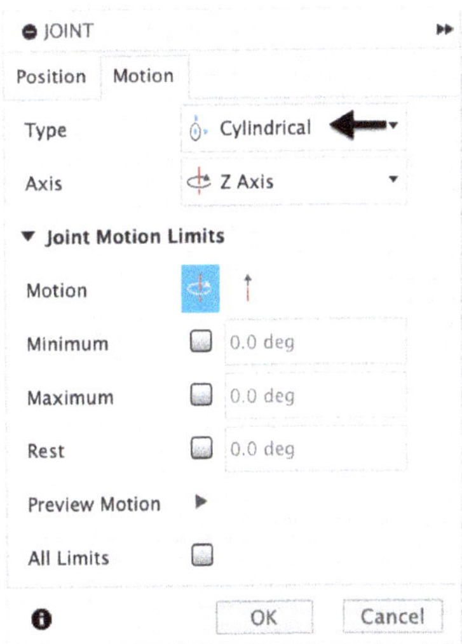

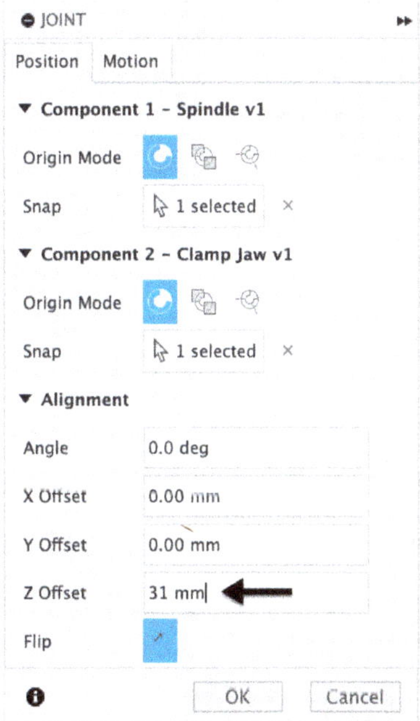

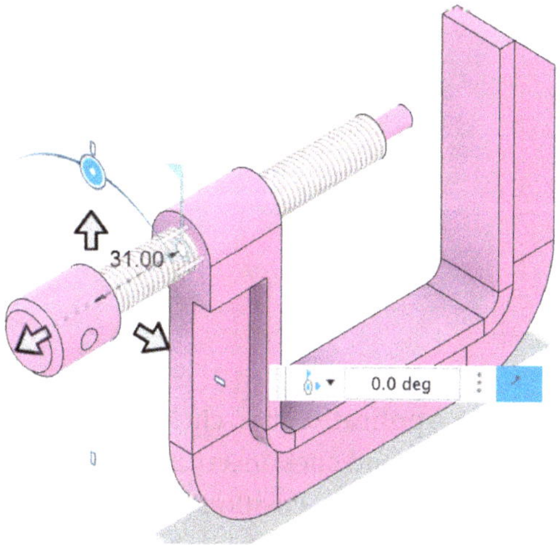

18. Click **Show Data Panel** and select *Spindle Cap*.

19. Right-click and click **Insert into Current Design**. Use the manipulator to move or rotate the *Spindle Cap* and click **OK** on the **Initial Position** dialog.
20. Next, click **Assemble > Joint** on the toolbar.
21. Click on the circular edge of the *Spindle Cap* hole, as shown.
22. Click on the circular edge of the *Spindle*, as shown.

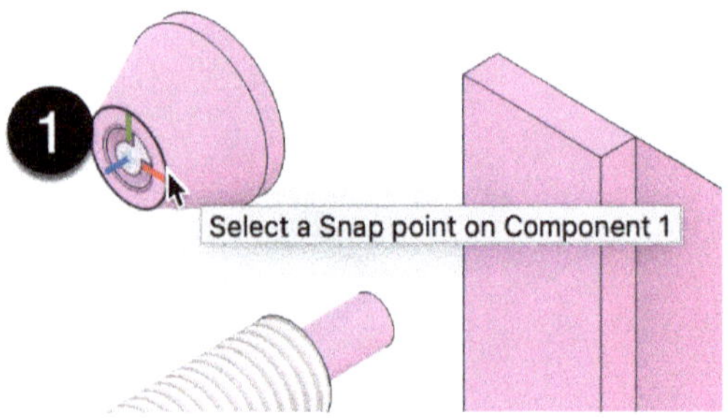

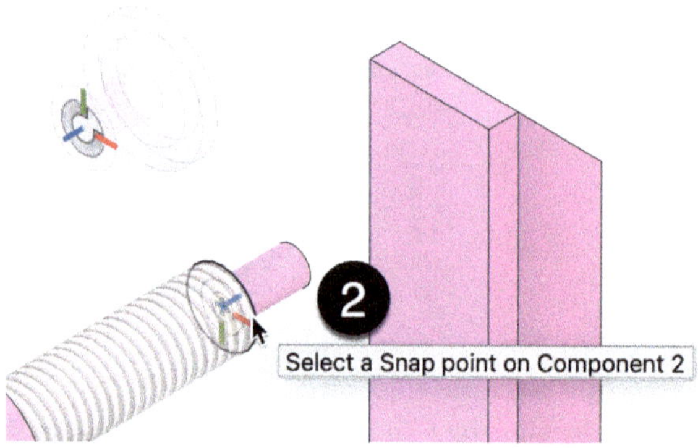

23. On the **Joint** dialog, click the **Motion** tab. Next, click **Type > Rigid**; the *Spindle* and *Spindle Cap* are axially aligned and positioned opposite to each other.
24. Click **OK**.

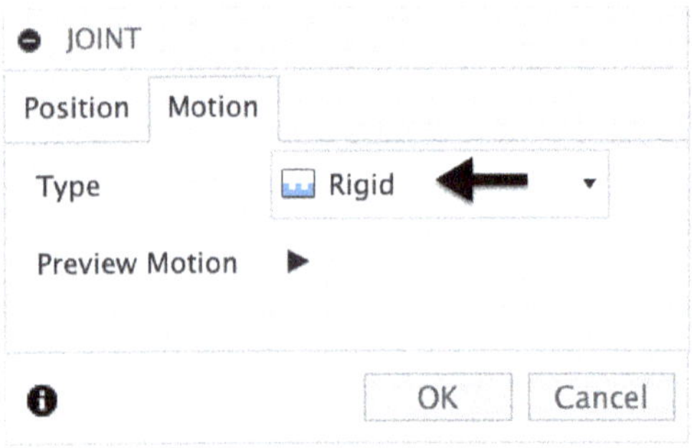

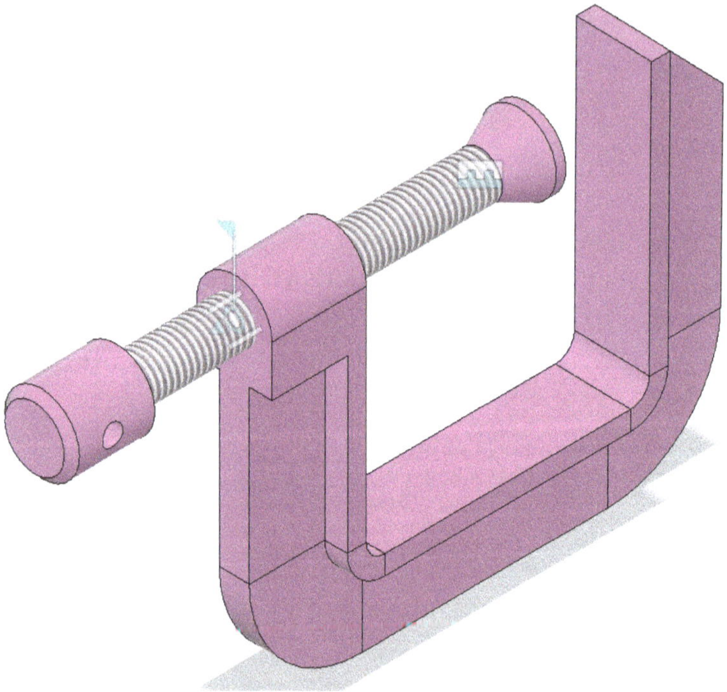

25. On the **Application bar**, click **Show Data Panel** and select the *Handle* design file.
26. Right-click and click **Insert into Current Design**. Use the manipulator to move or rotate the *Handle* and click **OK** on the **Initial Position** dialog.
27. On the toolbar, click **Assemble > Joint.**
28. Place the pointer on the cylindrical face of the handle and select the joint origin located at the midpoint.
29. Place the pointer on the cylindrical face of the Spindle hole. Next, press and hold the CTRL key and select the joint origin located at the midpoint.

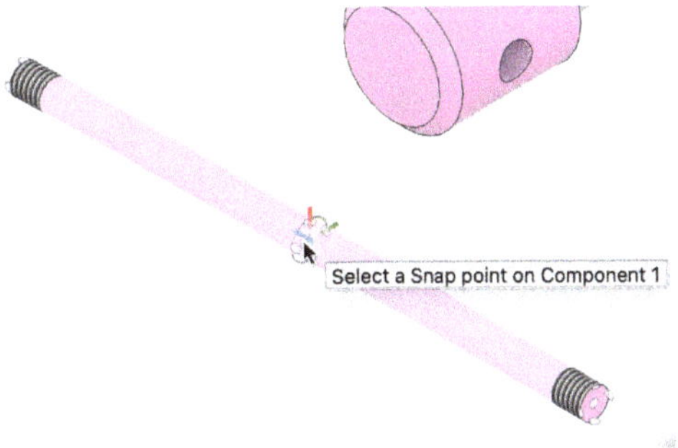

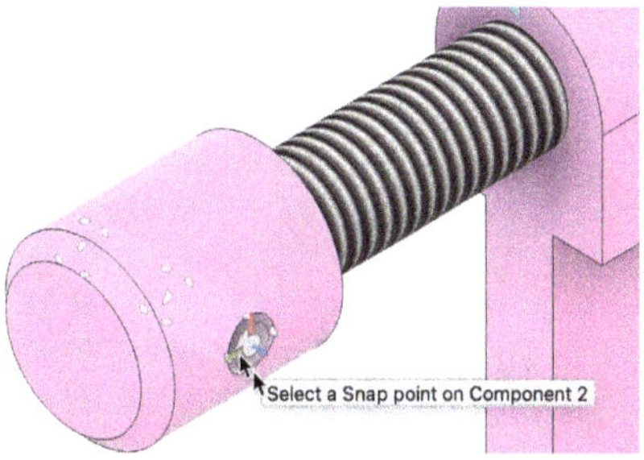

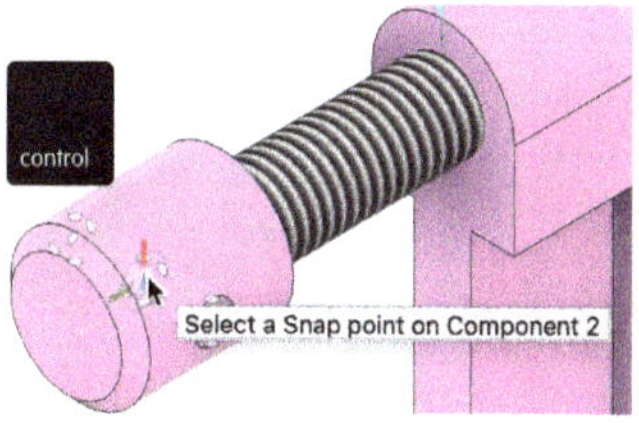

30. On the **Joint** dialog, click the **Motion** tab and click **Type > Cylindrical**.
31. Make sure that the **Axis** is set to the **Z Axis.** Next, click **OK** to create the joint.

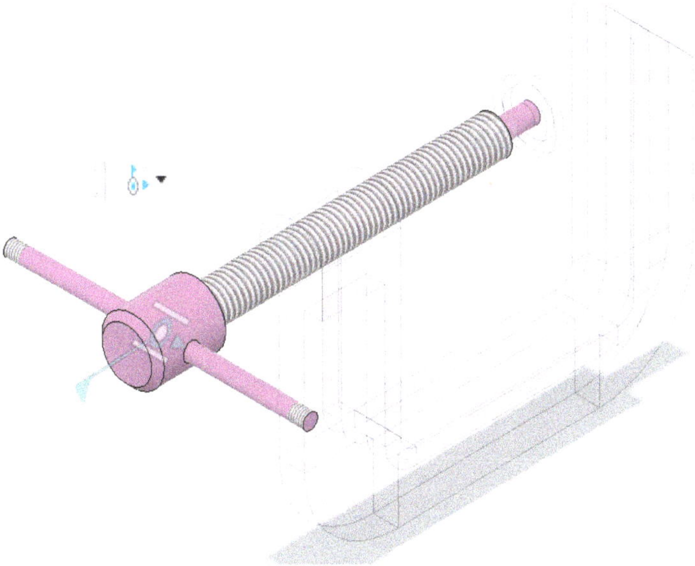

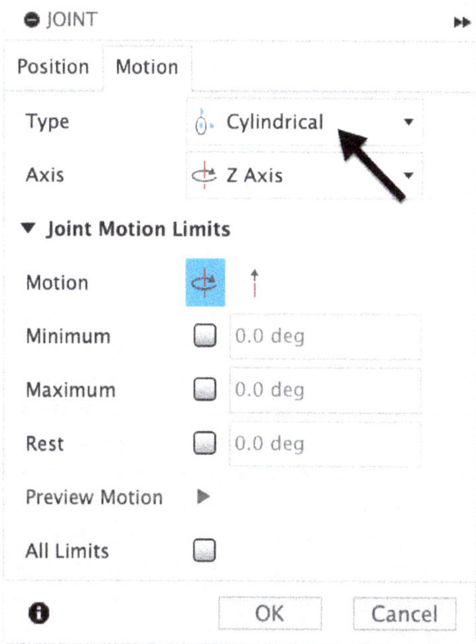

32. On the Solid toolbar, click **Assemble > Insert Component**. Next, browse to the location of the design file of the Example 1 and select the *Handle Cap*. Click the **Insert** button.
33. Use the manipulator to move or rotate the *Handle Cap* and click **OK** on the **Initial Position** dialog.

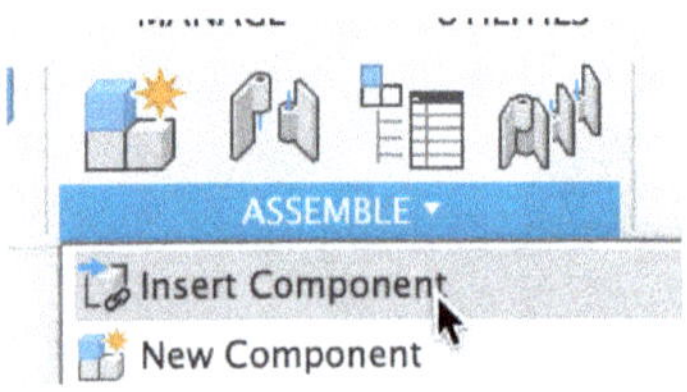

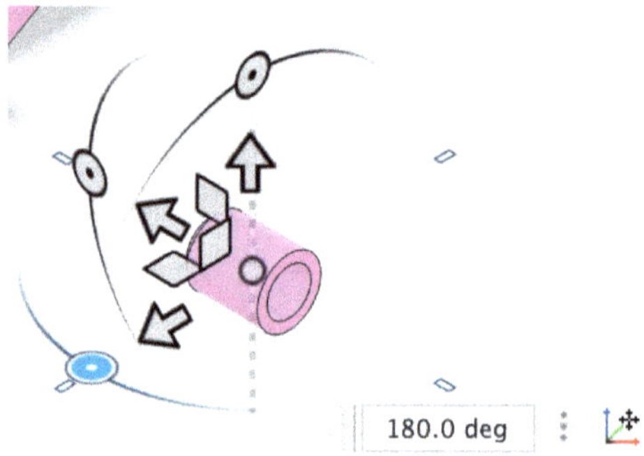

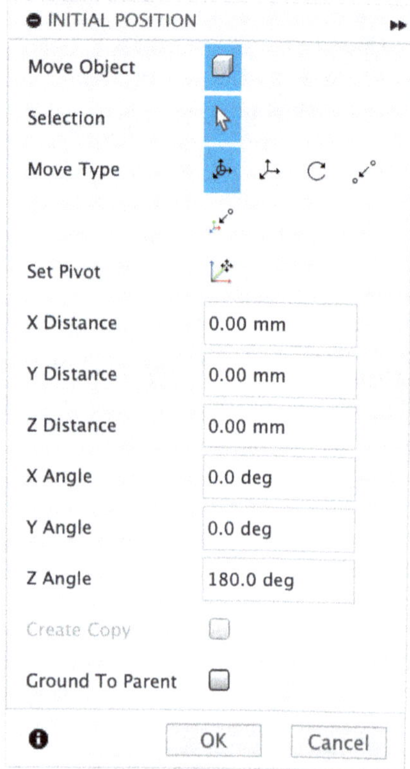

34. On the toolbar, click **Assemble > Joint**.
35. Place the pointer on the hole of the *Handle Cap*. Next, press and hold the Ctrl key and select Joint origin located at the inner end of the hole, as shown.
36. Select the circular edge of the *Handle*, as shown.
37. Click the **Flip** icon on the **Joints** dialog.

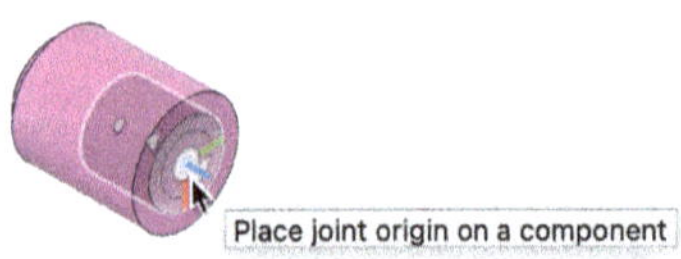

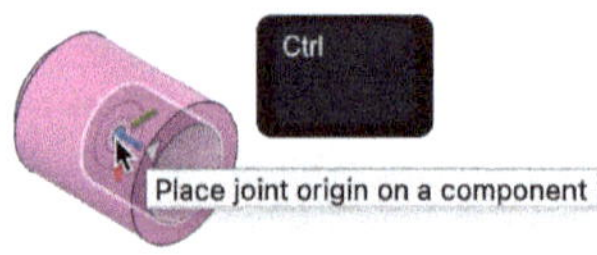

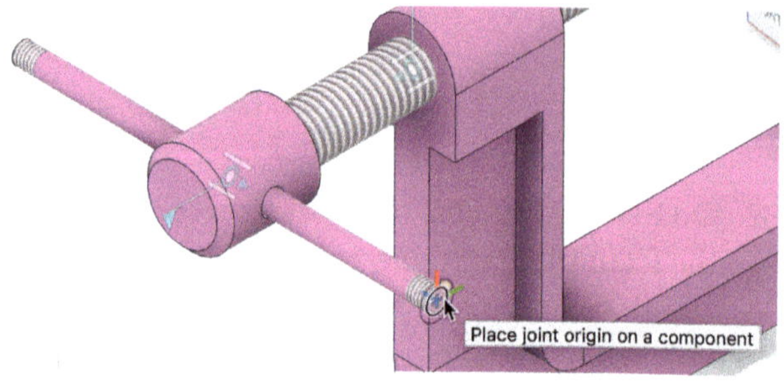

38. On the **Motion** tab, select **Type > Rigid**.

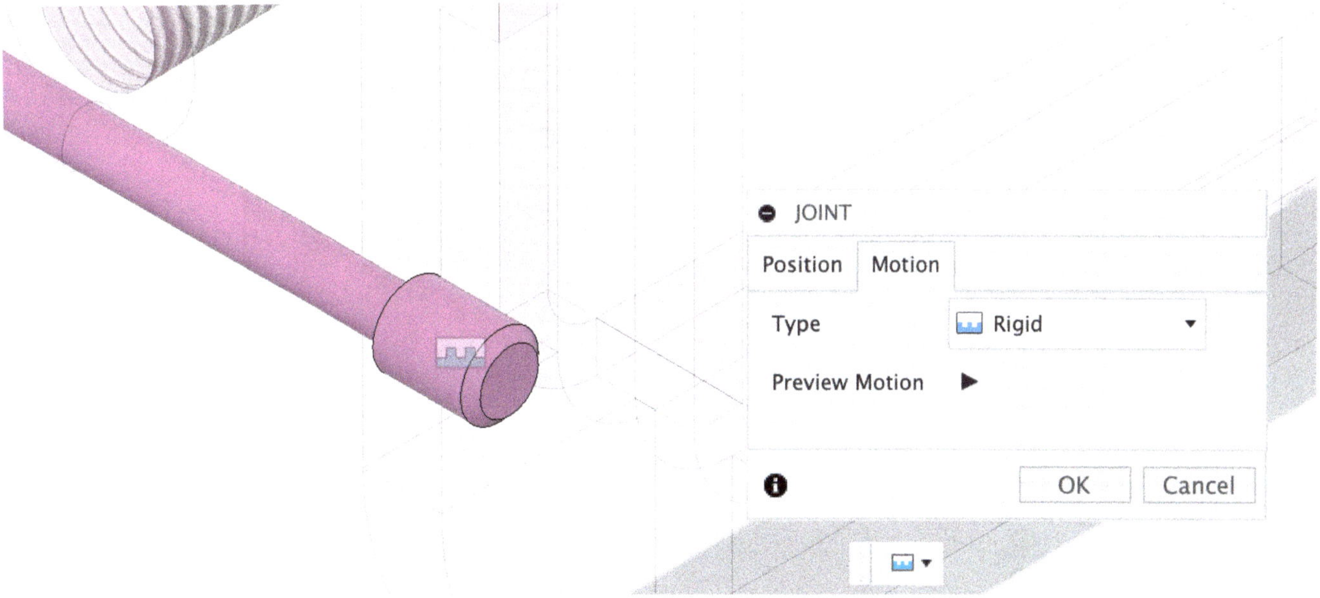

39. Likewise, insert another instance of the *Handle Cap*. Next, create the Rigid joint between the Handle Cap and the other end of the *Handle*.

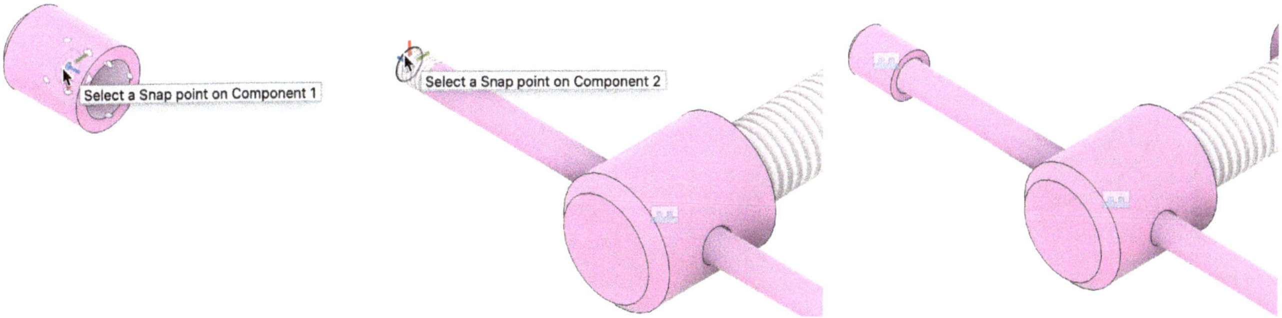

40. Save and close the assembly file.

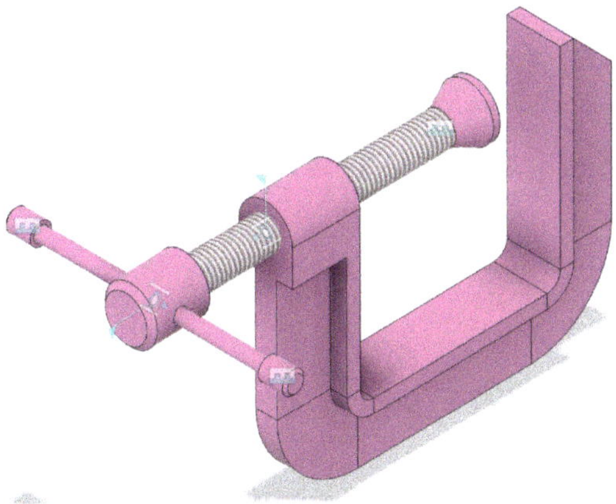

Example 2 (Top-Down Assembly)

In this example, you will create the assembly shown below.

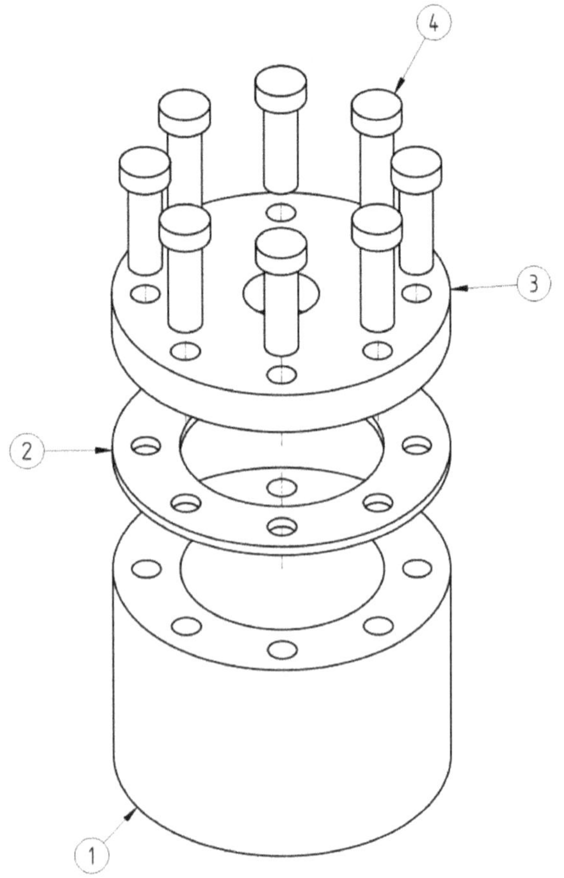

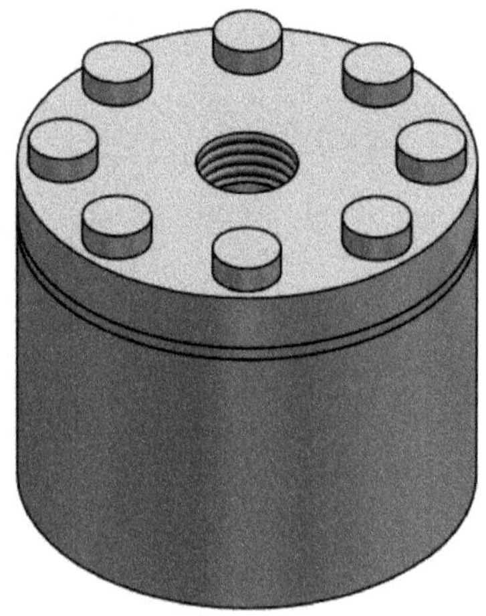

Item Number	File Name (no extension)	Quantity
1	Cylinder base	1
2	Gasket	1
3	Cover plate	1
4	Screw	8

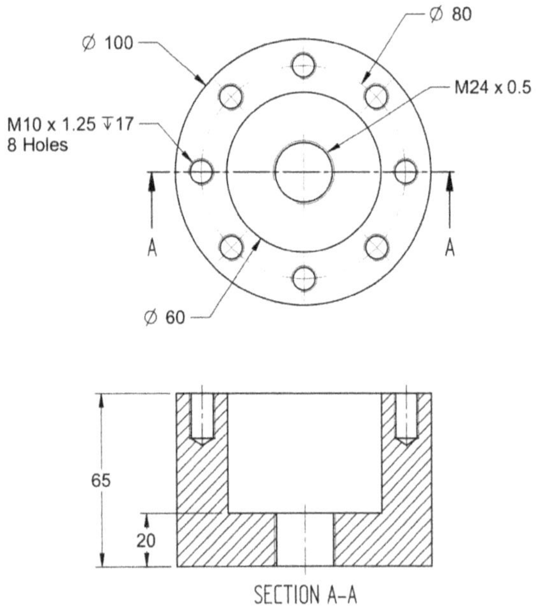

Cylinder Base

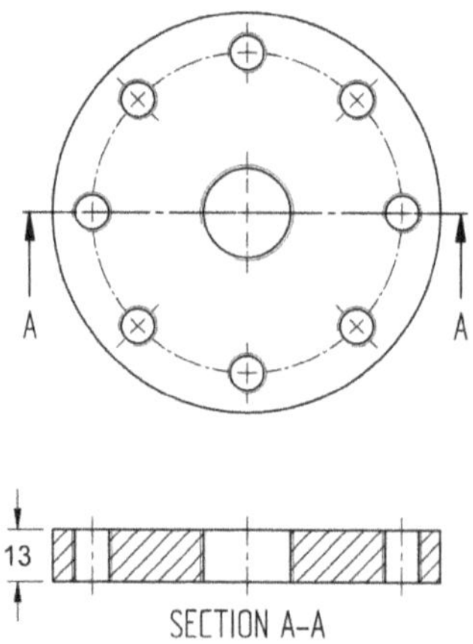

Cover Plate

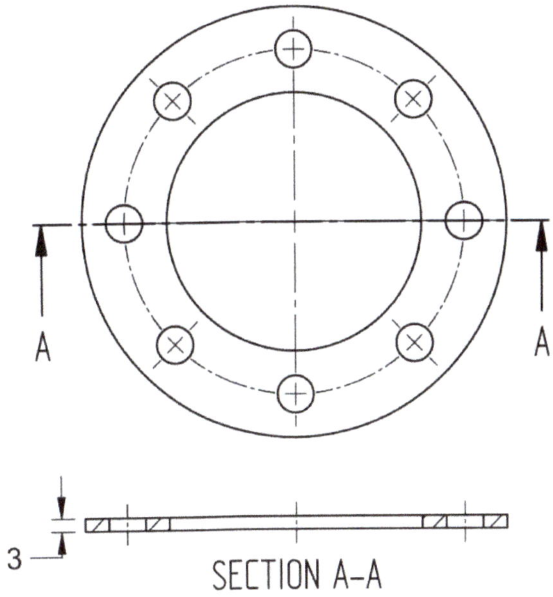

Gasket

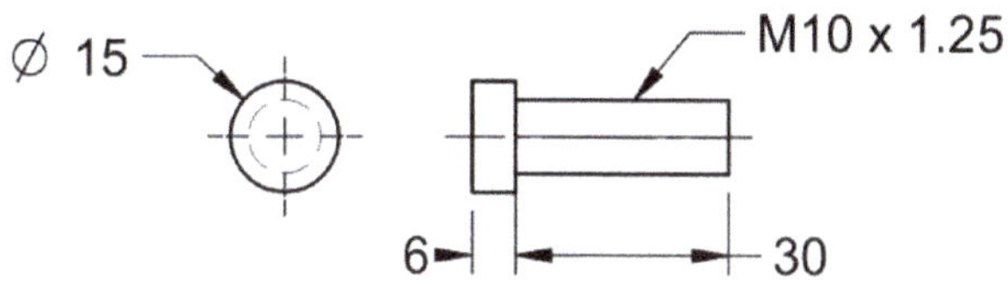

Screw

1. Start **Autodesk Fusion 360.**
2. Start a new design file and create the revolved feature, as shown.

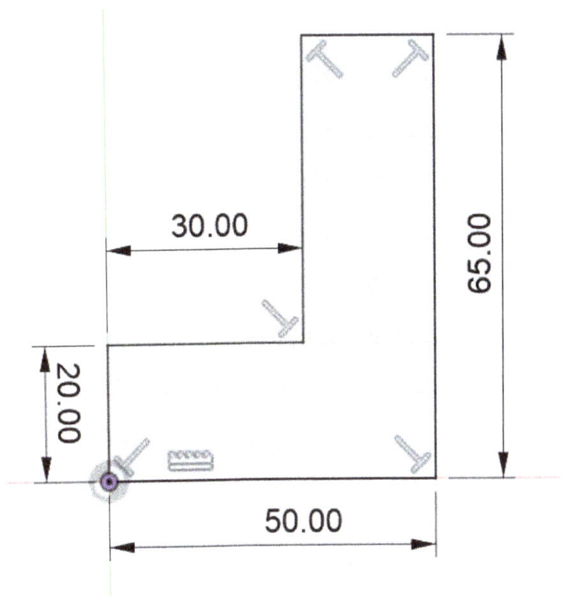

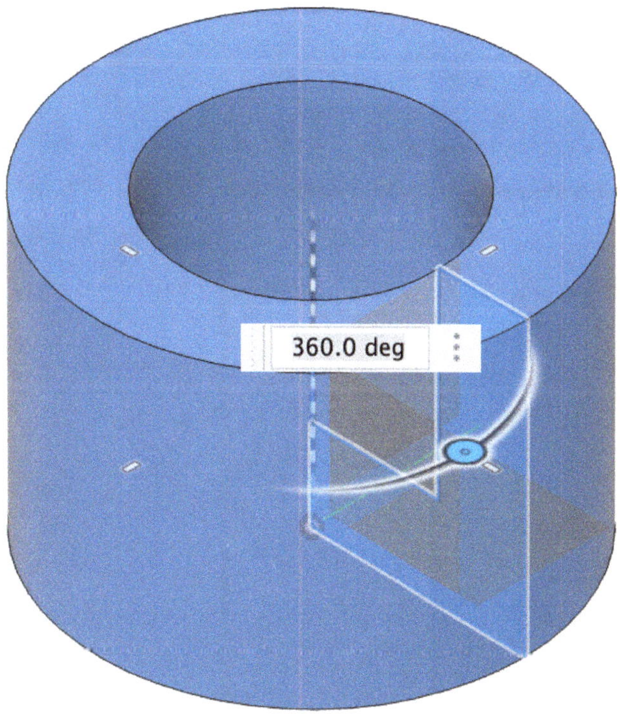

3. Click **Solid** > **Create > Create Sketch** on the toolbar and click on the top face of the cylinder base, as shown.
4. On the toolbar, click **Sketch** > **Create > Point** , and then click on the sketch plane.

5. On the toolbar, click **Sketch > Constraints > Horizontal/Vertical**. Next, select the origin and the sketch point, as shown.
6. Add a dimension of 40 mm between the sketch point and the origin. Next, click **Finish Sketch** on the toolbar.

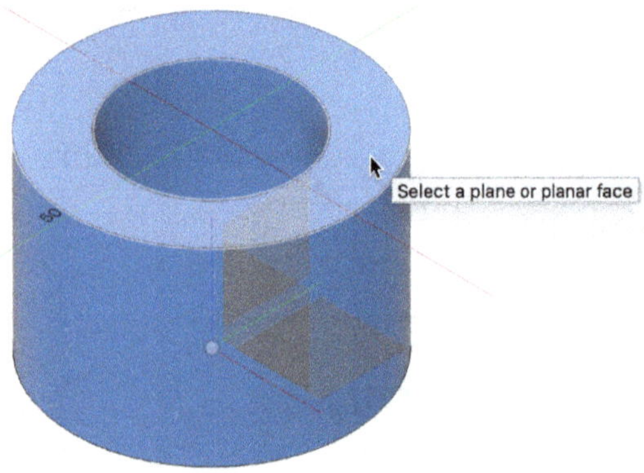

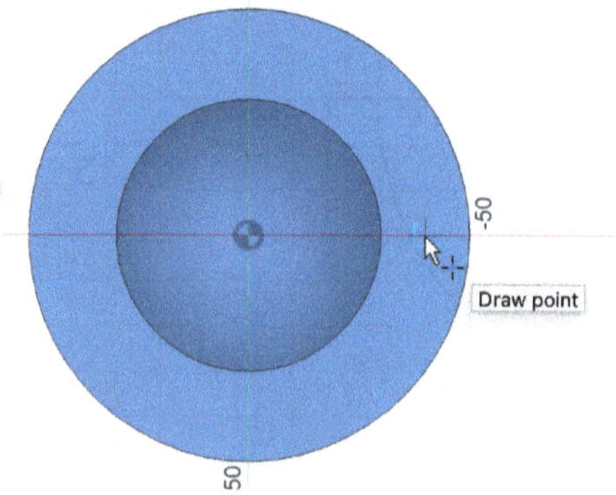

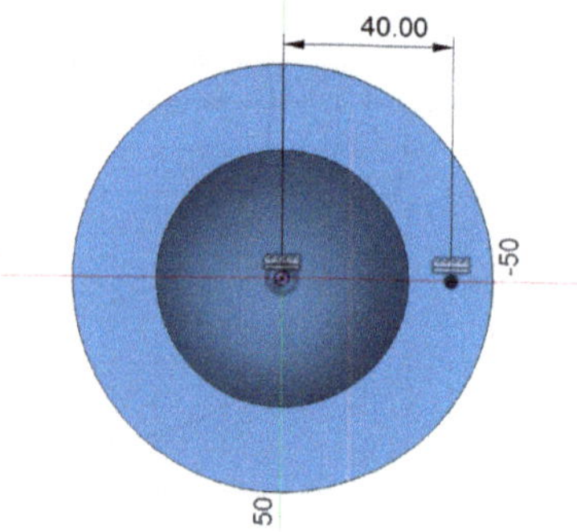

7. Click **Solid > Create > Hole** on the toolbar and select the sketch point.
8. On the **Hole** dialog, click **Hole Tap Type > Tapped** and **Drill Point > Angle**.
9. Specify the other parameters of the hole, as shown and click **OK**.

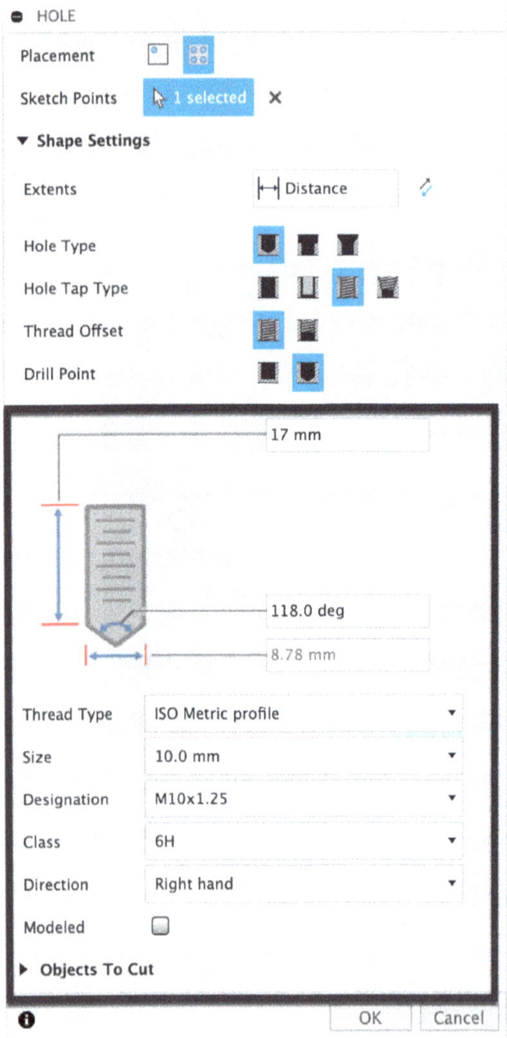

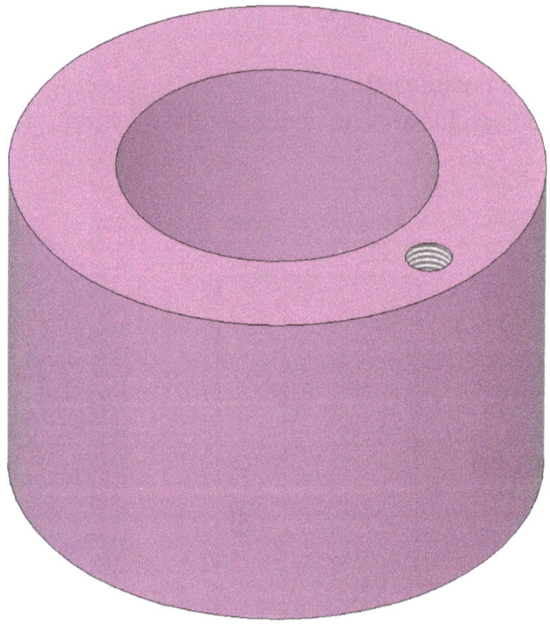

10. Click **Solid** > **Create > Pattern > Circular Pattern** on the toolbar.
11. On the **Circular Pattern** dialog, click **Pattern Type > Features**.
12. Click the **Objects** selection button and select the **Hole** feature.
13. Click the **Axis** selection button and select the outer most face of the *Cylinder Base*.
14. Select **Angular Spacing > Full**.
15. Type-in **8** in the **Quantity** box and select **Compute Option > Optimized**. Click **OK** to pattern the hole feature.

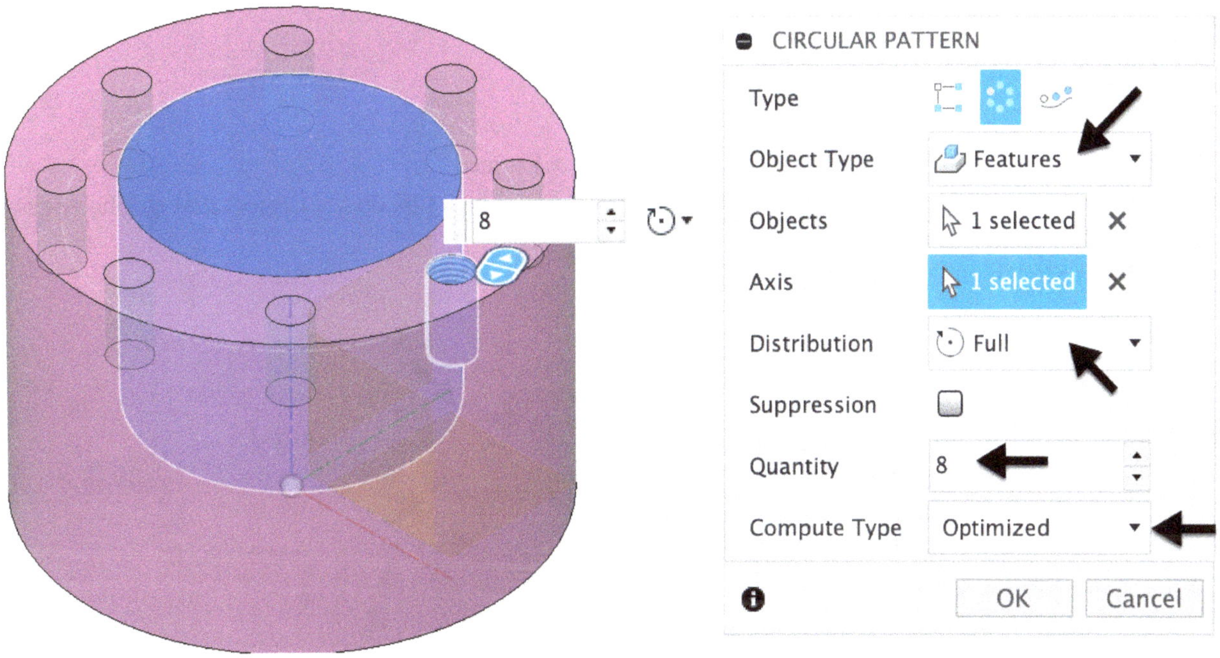

16. In the Browser, expand the **Bodies** folder and click the right mouse button on Body1. Next, select **Create Components from Bodies**; the body is converted into a component.
17. Double-click on the name of the Component1 and type Cylinder Base.

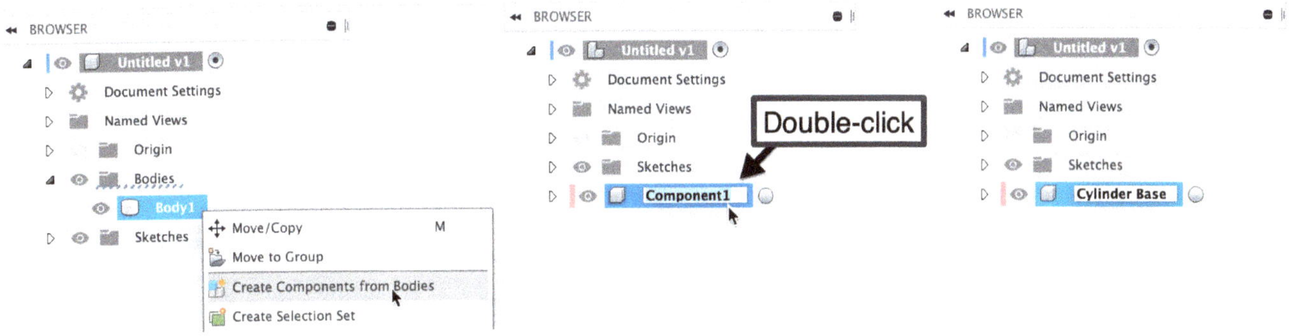

18. On the **Browser**, right-click on the *Cylinder Base* and select **Ground**.
19. On the toolbar, click **Solid** > **Assemble > New Component** ; the **New Component** dialog pops up on the screen. Select **Type > Standard** from the dialog. Next, select **External/Internal > Internal** .
20. On the dialog, type-in **Gasket** in the **Name** box. Next, check the **Activate** option and click **OK**.
21. Click **Solid > Create > Create Sketch** on the toolbar. Next, select the top face of the *Cylinder Base*.

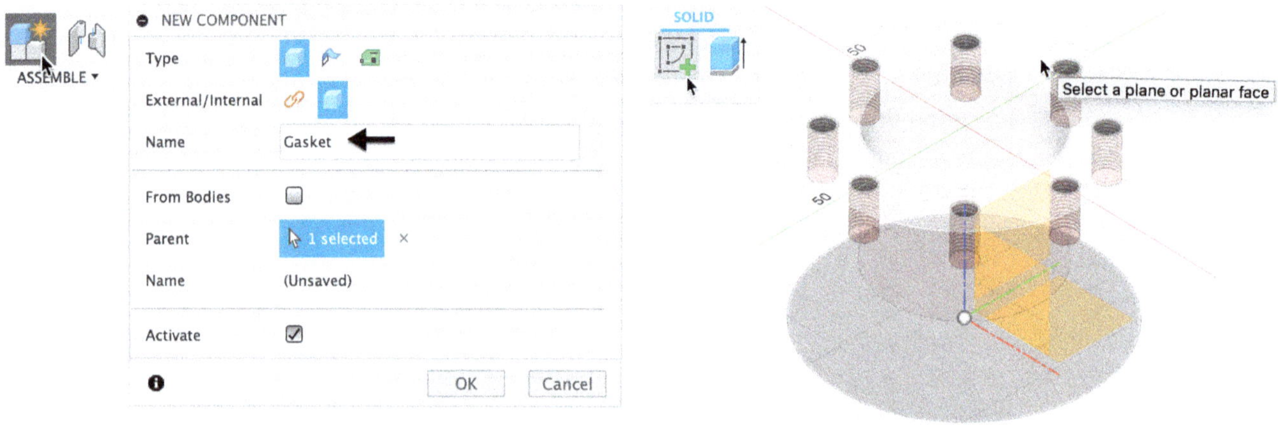

22. On the toolbar, click **Sketch > Create > Project / Include > Project**.
23. Click on the circular edges on the top face of the *Cylinder Base*. Click **OK** on the **Project** dialog. The edges are projected to the sketch plane.
24. Click **Finish Sketch** on the toolbar.

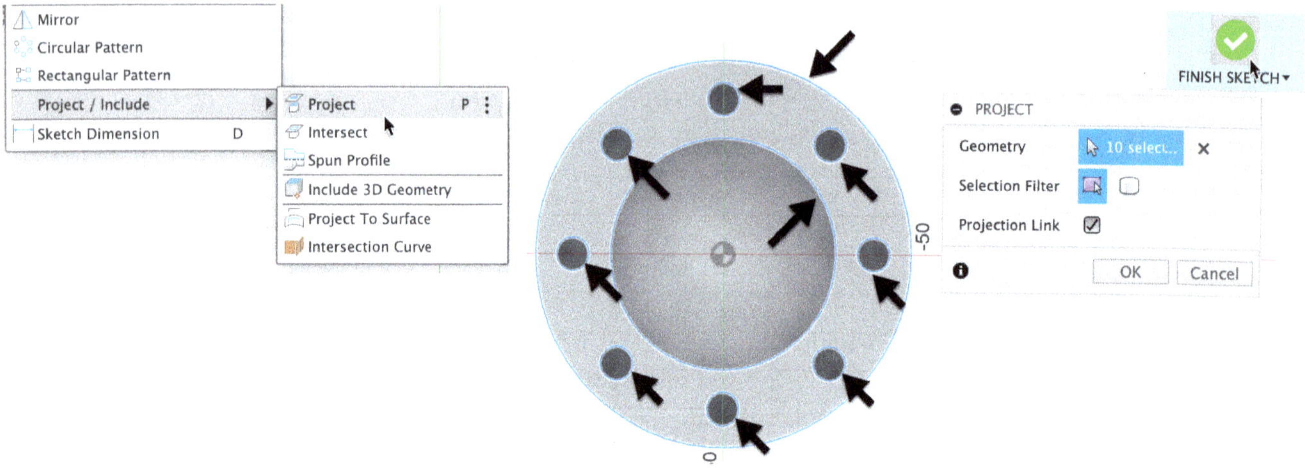

25. Activate the **Extrude** command and click on the region enclosed by the sketch, as shown.
26. On the **Extrude** dialog, select **Direction > One Side**.
27. Select **Distance** from the **Extent Type** drop-down and type 3 in the **Distance** box. Next, click **OK** to create the *Extrude* feature.

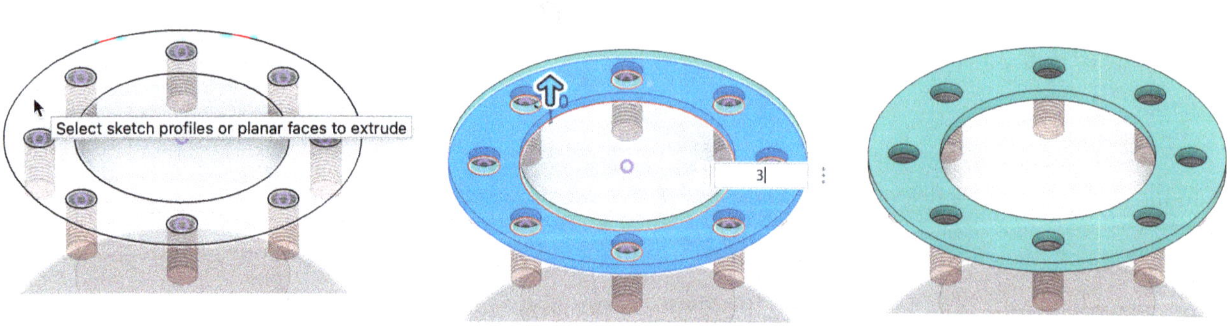

28. In the **Browser**, right-click on the assembly node located at the top, and then select **Activate** to return to the assembly session.

29. On the toolbar, click **Utilities > Inspect > Component Color Cycling Toggle**.

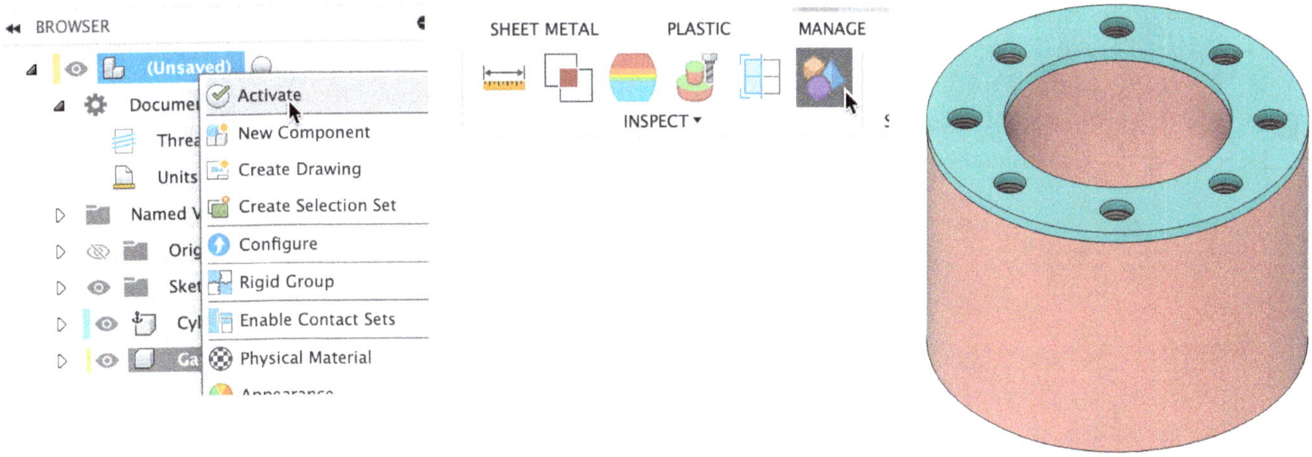

30. On the toolbar, click **Assemble > New Component** . The **New Component** dialog pops up on the screen.
31. On the dialog, type-in *Cover Plate* in the **Name** box and click **OK**.
32. Click **Solid > Create > Create Sketch** on the toolbar and click on the top face of the *Gasket*.
33. On the toolbar, click **Sketch > Create > Project / Include > Project** .
34. Select the outer and small circular edges of the *Gasket* and click **OK** on the **Project** dialog.

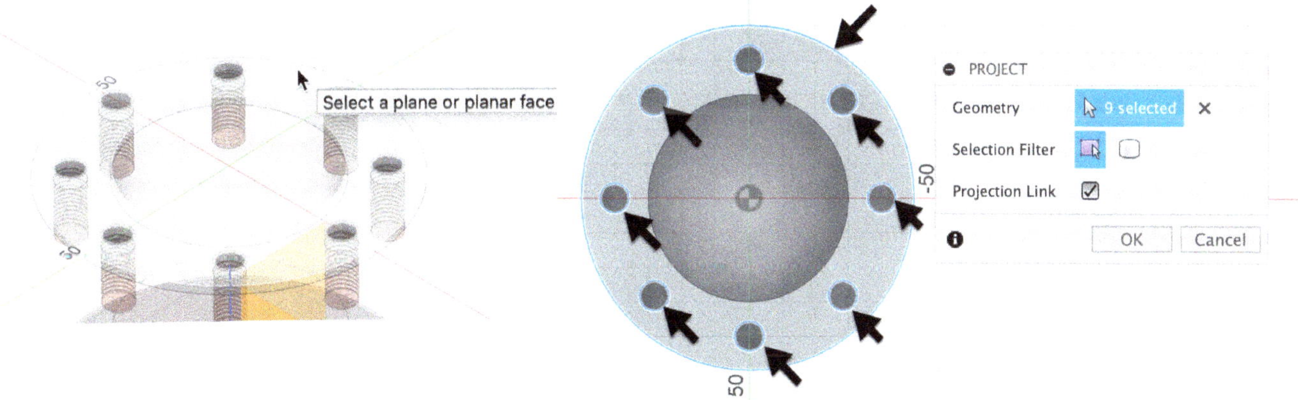

35. Click **Finish Sketch** on the toolbar.
36. Activate the **Extrude** command and click in the regions of the sketch, as shown. Type 13 in the **Distance** box and click **OK**.

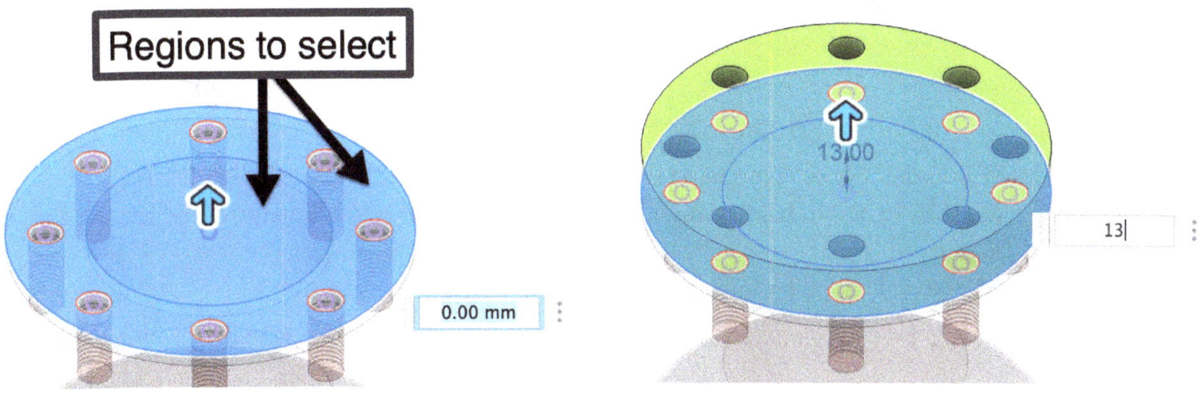

37. Activate the **Thread** command (click **Solid > Create > Thread** on the toolbar). Next, select any one of the holes from the graphics window.
38. On the **Thread** dialog, check the **Full Length** option.
39. Select **ISO Metric Profile** from the **Thread Type** drop-down.
40. Select **Size > 10** and **Designation > M10x1.25** on the **Thread** dialog. Next, click **OK** to create the thread.
41. Likewise, create threads on the remaining holes.

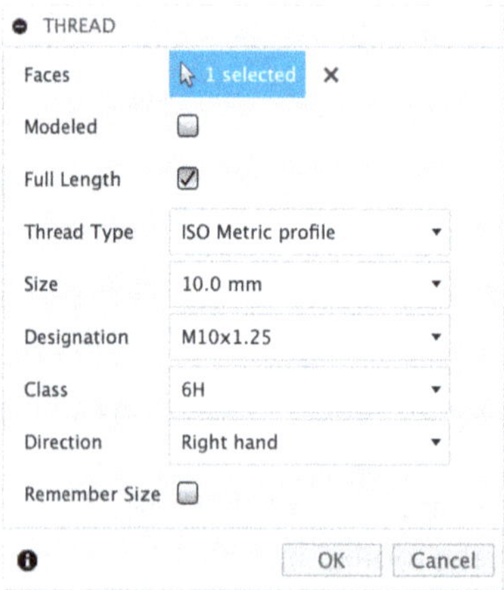

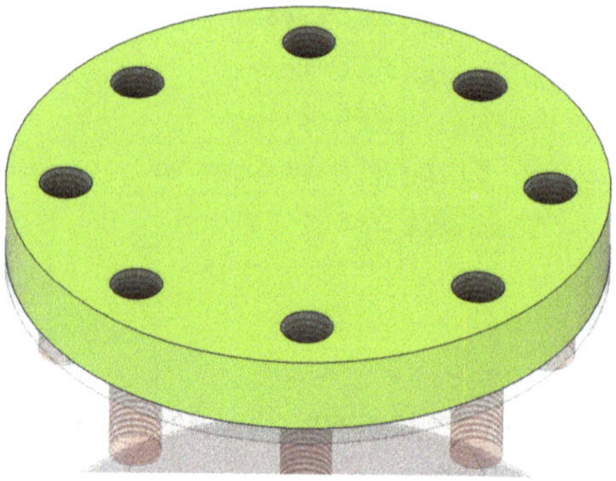

42. In the **Browser**, right-click on the assembly node located at the top, and then select **Activate** to return to the assembly session.

43. Activate the **New Component**  command and create the *Screw* file.
44. Click **Solid > Create > Create Sketch** on the toolbar and select the top face of the *Cover Plate*.
45. Activate the **Project** command and select any one of the circular edges of the holes. Click **OK** on the **Project** dialog box, and then click **Finish Sketch**.
46. Use the sketch and create an *Extrude* feature of -30 mm distance.

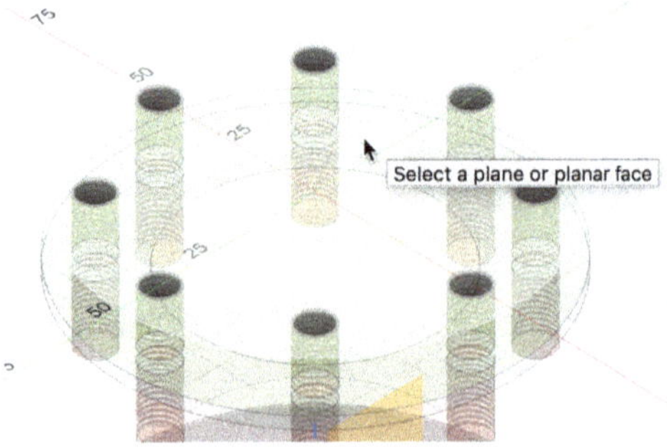

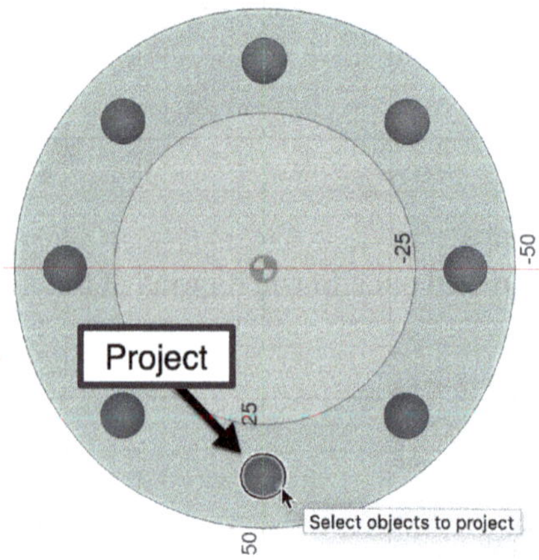

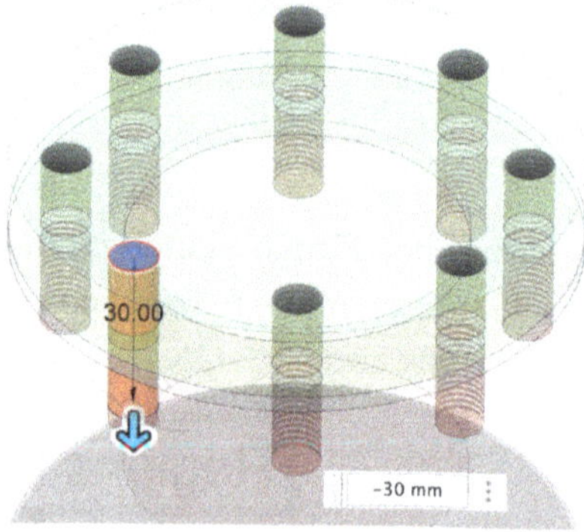

47. Activate the **Create Sketch** command and select the top face of the last *Extrude* feature.
48. Draw a circle of 15 mm diameter and make it concentric to the circular edge of the *Extrude* feature. Click **Finish Sketch**.
49. Extrude the circle in the upward direction. The extrude distance is 6 mm.

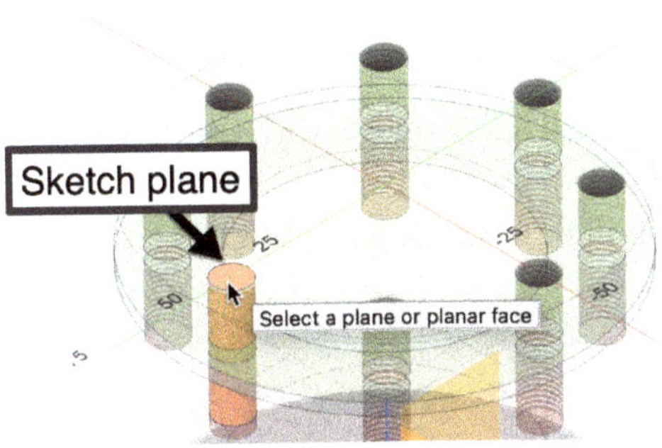

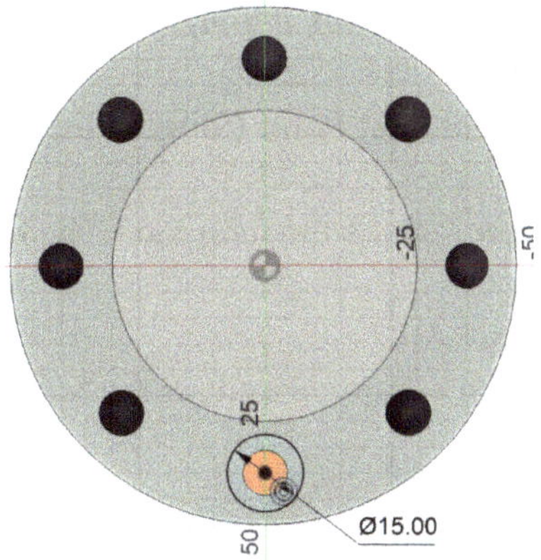

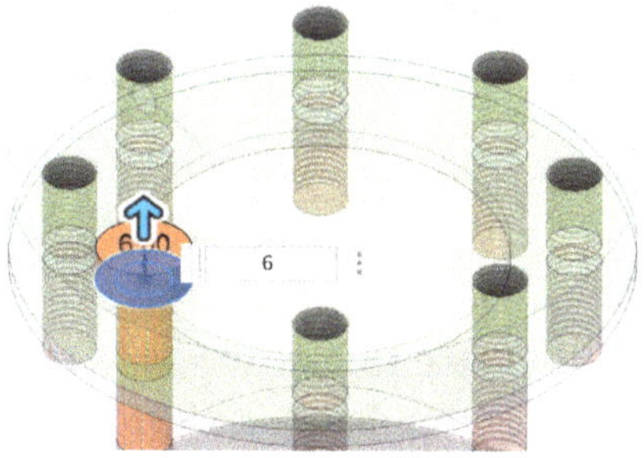

50. Activate the **Thread** command (click **Create > Thread** on the toolbar) and add a thread to the lower cylindrical face of the component. The thread size is M10 x 1.25; Make sure that the **Full Length** option is selected on the **Thread** dialog.

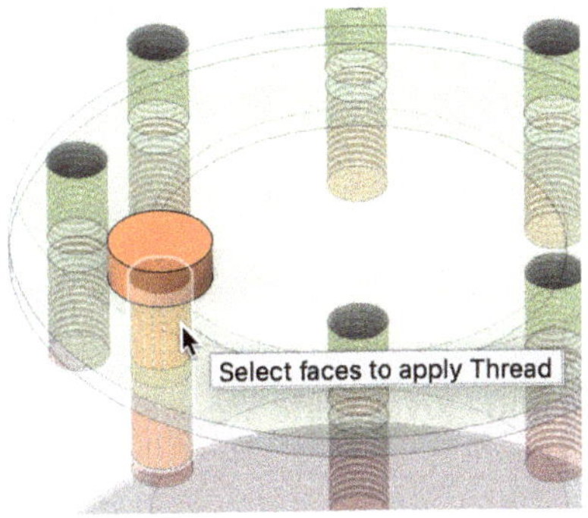

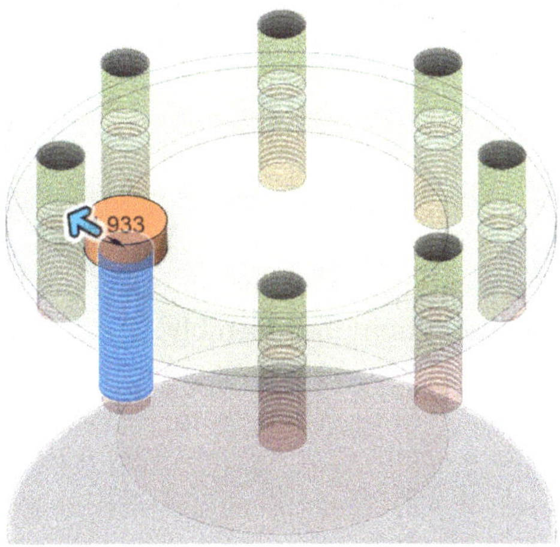

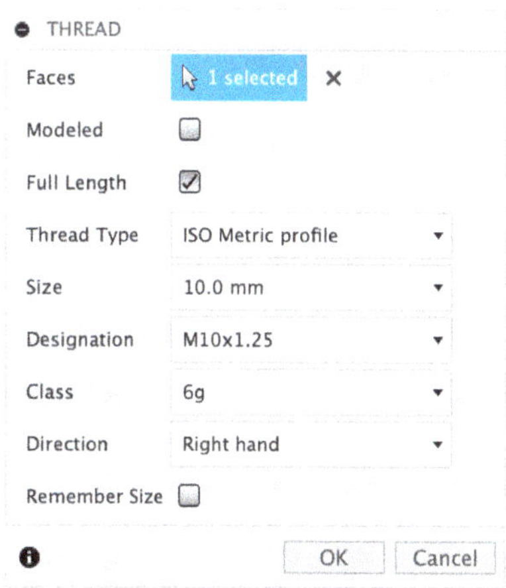

51. In the **Browser**, right-click on the assembly node located at the top and select **Activate** to return to the assembly session.
52. On the toolbar, click **Sketch > Pattern > Circular Pattern**; the **Circular Pattern** dialog pops up on the screen.
53. On this dialog, click **Pattern Type > Components** and select the Screw.
54. On the **Circular Pattern** dialog, click the **Axis** selection button and select the outermost face of the *Cylinder Base*.
55. Type-in **8** in the **Quantity** box and click **OK** to create a circular pattern of the Screws.

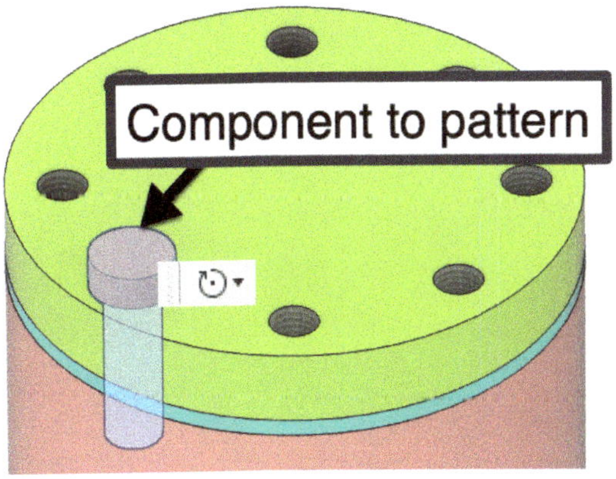

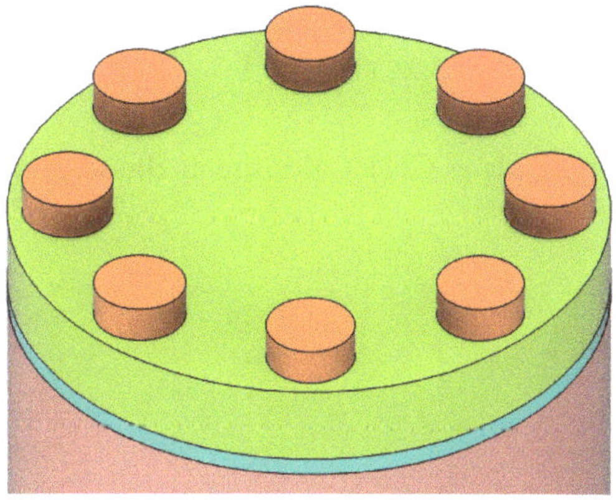

56. On the toolbar, click **Create > Hole**. The **Hole** dialog pops up on the screen.

57. On the **Hole** dialog, select **Placement > At Point (Single Hole)**  . Next, click on the top face of the *Cover Plate*.

58. Select the circular edge of the *Cover Plate* as the reference. The hole will be concentric to the circular edge of the *Cover Plate*.

59. On the **Hole** dialog, select **Extents > All**.

60. On this dialog, click **Hole Tap Type > Tapped** and set the hole options, as shown below.

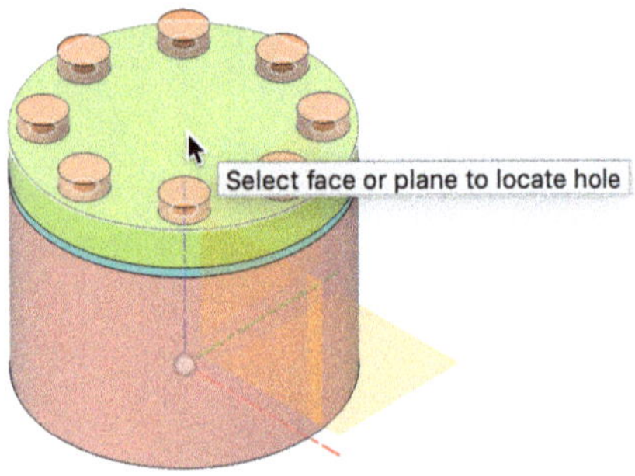

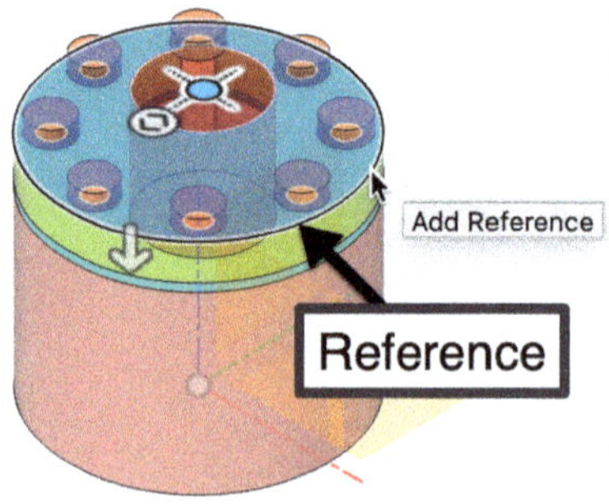

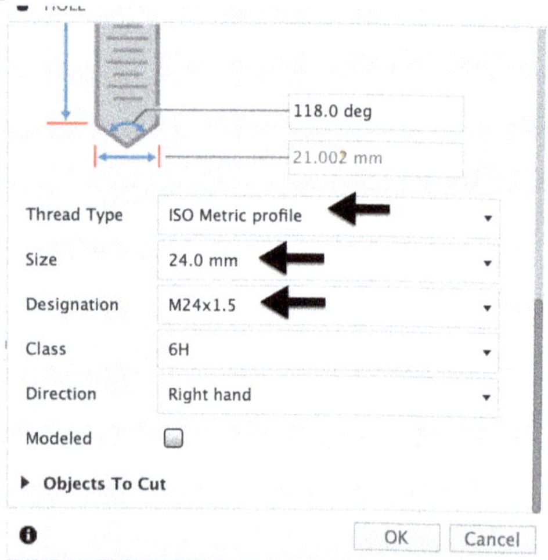

61. Expand the **Objects to Cut** section and make sure that the Cylinder Base and Cover Plate are selected. Next, click **OK** to create the hole throughout the assembly.

62. On the toolbar, click **Utilities > Inspect > Section Analysis**.

63. Select the YZ plane. Click **OK** to create the section.

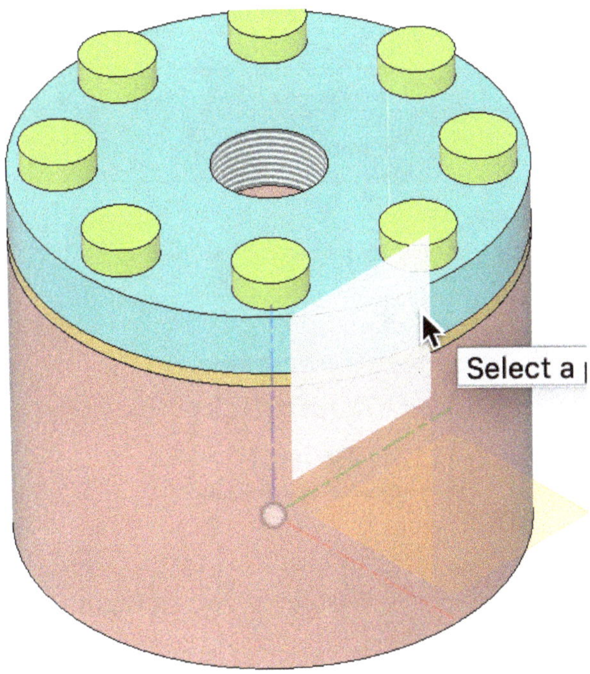

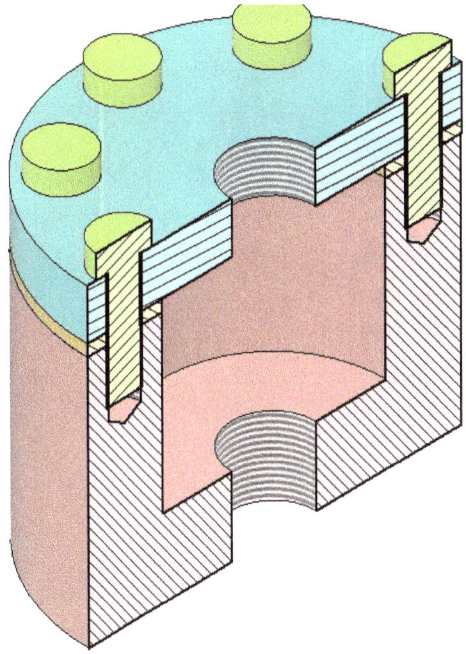

64. In the Browser, expand the **Analysis** folder and click the eye icon next to **Section1**. The section is hidden, and the complete assembly is displayed.

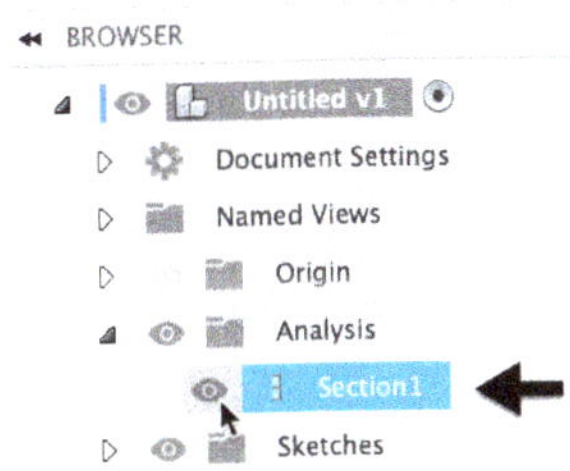

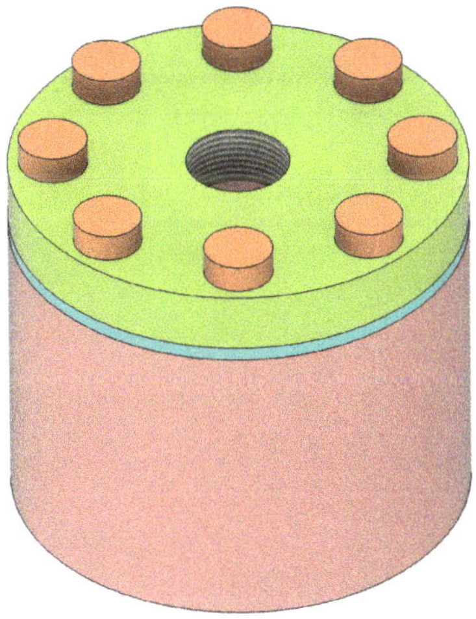

65. On the toolbar, click **Assemble > As-built Joint**. Next, select the *Cylinder Base* and the *Gasket*.
66. On the **As-built Joint** dialog, select **Type > Rigid**. Next, click **OK** to create the Rigid joint between the two selected components.

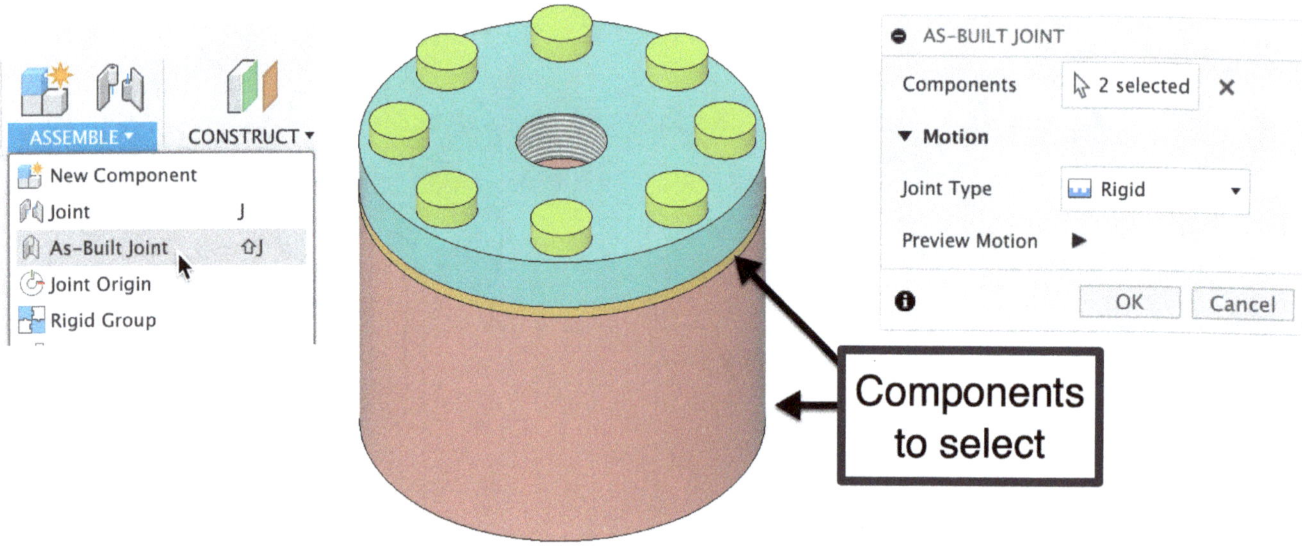

67. Activate the **As-built Joint** command and select the *Gasket* and the *Cover Plate*. Select **Type > Rigid** and click **OK** to create the Rigid joint.

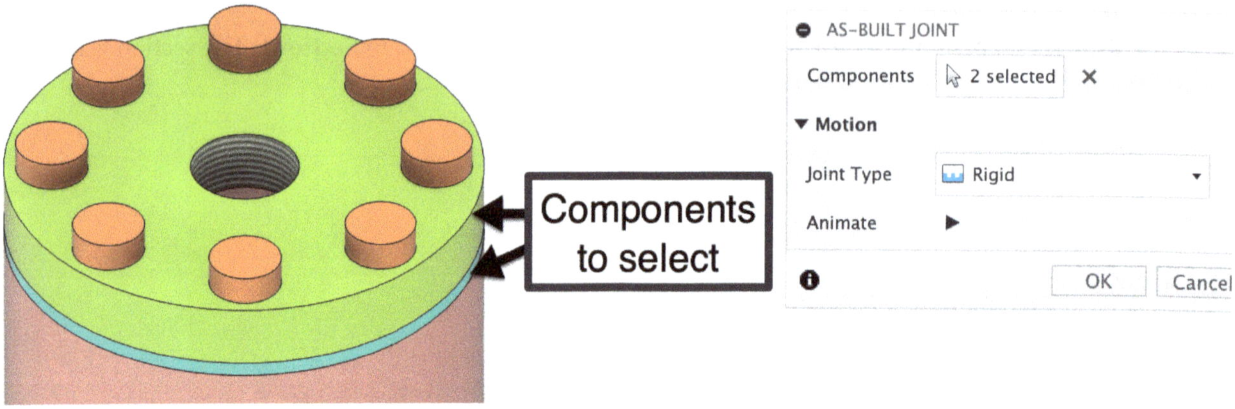

68. Likewise, create the Rigid joints between the Screws and the Cover Plate.
69. Save the design file as Pressure Cylinder and close it.

Example 3 (Animations)

In this example, you will create the animation of the assembly created in Example 2.

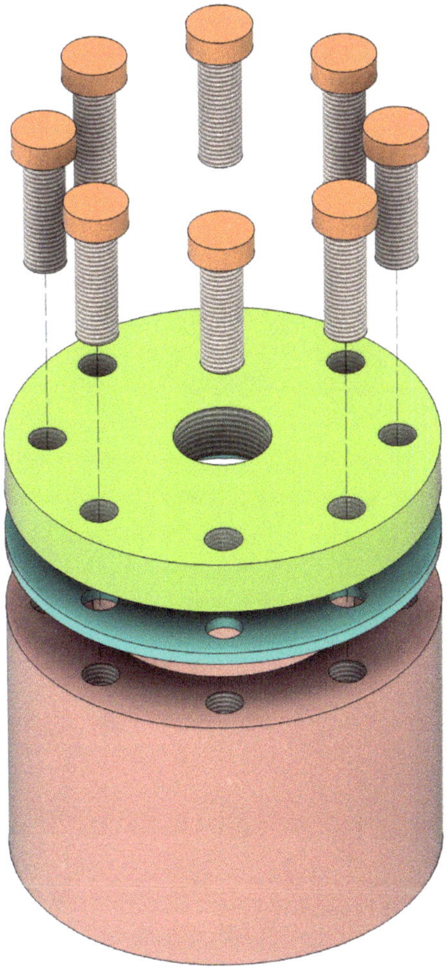

Starting the Animation

1. Open the **Pressure Cylinder** design file created in the previous tutorial.
2. On the toolbar, select **Workspace** drop-down > **Animation**; the animation workspace is loaded.
3. In the **Animation Timeline**, double-click on **Storyboard1** and type **Explosion**.
4. In the Browser, select the **Components** node.
5. On the toolbar, click **Transform > Auto Explode: All Levels**.

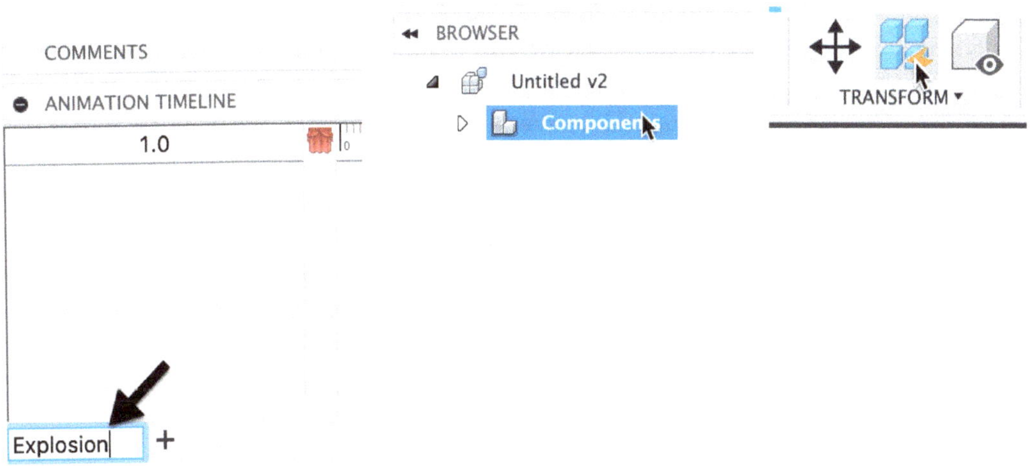

6. Click the **Trace Line Visibility** icon on the Explode toolbar. Next, click and drag the **Explosion Scale** slider to adjust the explosion distance.
7. Click **OK** to create the explosion. Next, click the middle mouse button; the exploded assembly is fitted on the screen.

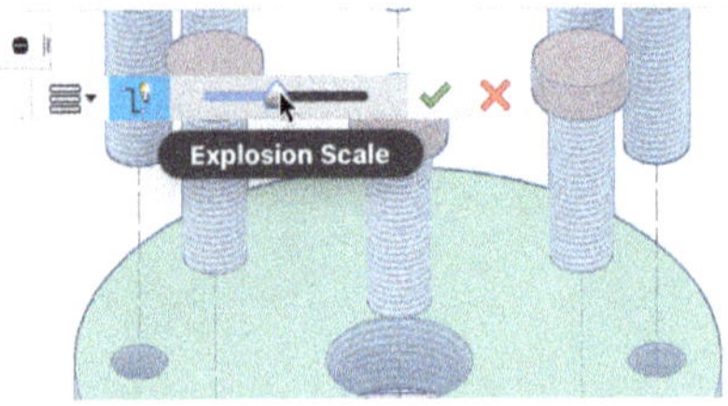

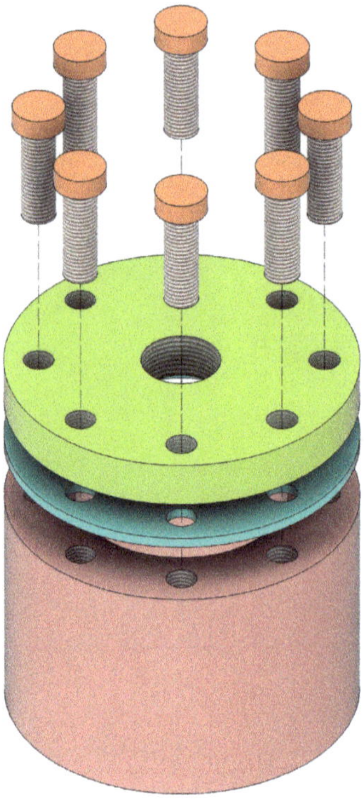

8. Click the **Play Current Storyboard** icon on the Storyboard to play the explosion.

Publishing the Explosion

1. On the toolbar, click **Publish > Publish Video**.
2. On the **Video Options** dialog, select **Video Scope > Current Storyboard.**
3. Select **1024 x 1024(1:1)** from the **Video Resolution** drop-down, and then click **OK.**
4. Type Example 3 in the **Name** box. Next, check the **Save to my computer** option and click the **Browse** button next to the file path.
5. Browse to the desired location on your computer and click **Save**. Again, click **Save** on the **Save As** dialog.
6. On the Application Bar, click **File > Save As**. Next, type Example 3 in the **Name** box and click **Save**.

Questions

1. How to convert a Body into a component?
2. What is the use of the **As-Built Joint** command?
3. List the advantages of Top-down assembly approach.
4. What is a grounded component?
5. What is the use of the **Joint Origin** command?

6. How do you create a sub-assembly in the assembly environment?
7. Briefly explain the **Contact Sets** command.
8. Why do we prefer the **Manual Explode** command to the **Auto Explode: All Levels** command?
9. What is the difference between the Rigid joint and the **Rigid Group** command?
10. How to perform a motion study?

Exercise 1

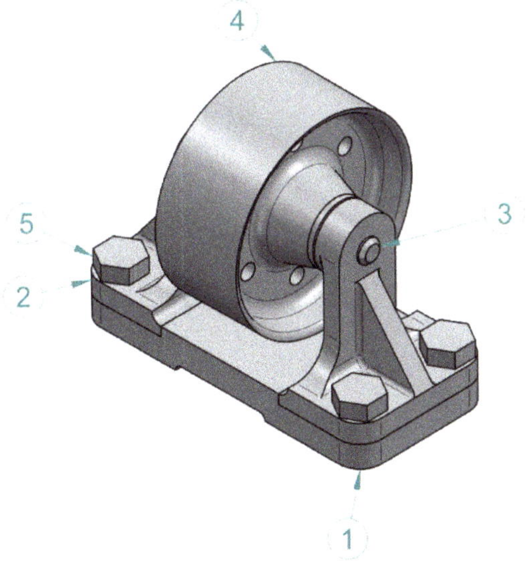

Item Number	File Name (no extension)	Quantity
1	Base	1
2	Bracket	2
3	Spindle	1
4	Roller-Bush assembly	1
5	Bolt	4

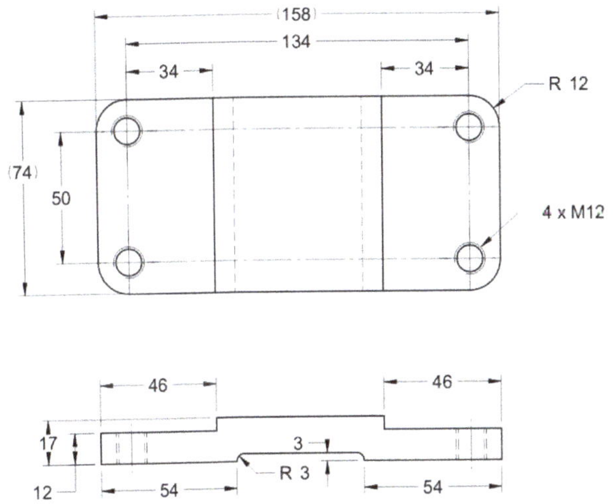

Base

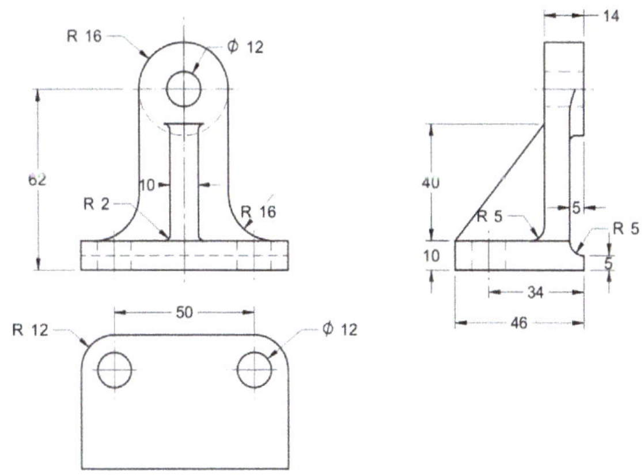

Bracket

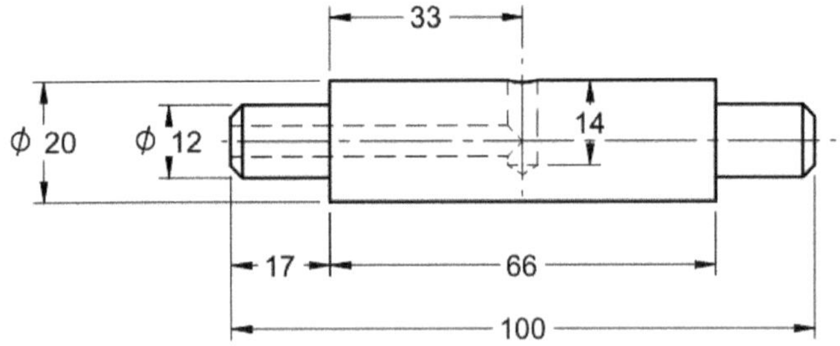

SPINDLE

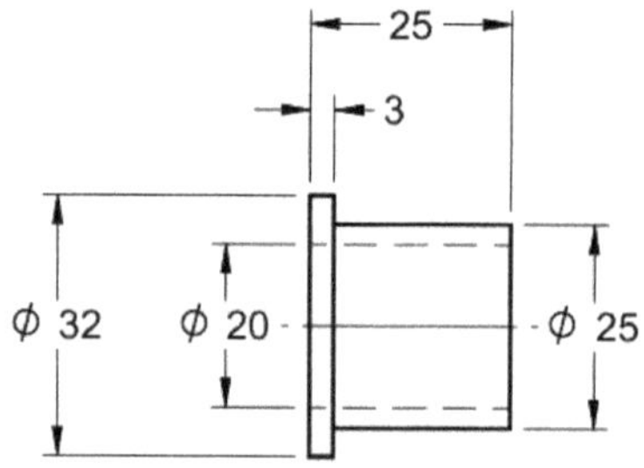

BUSH

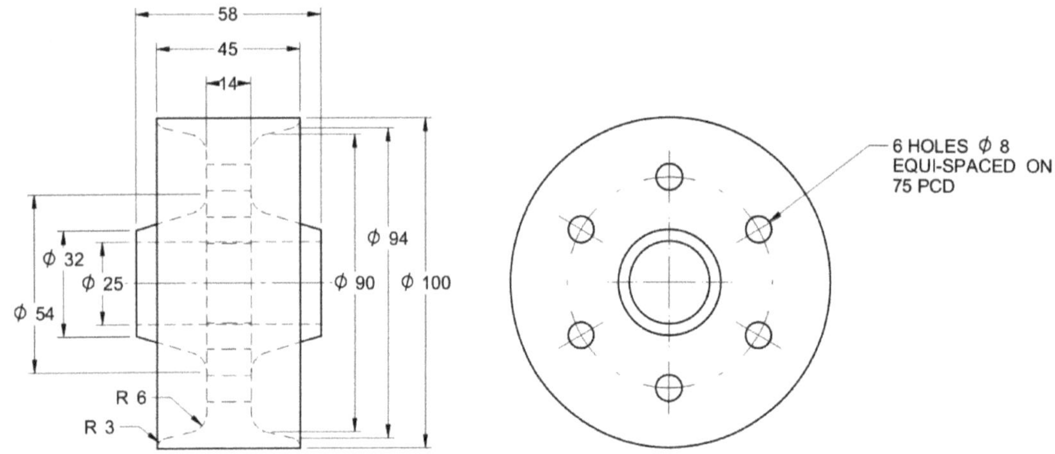

Roller

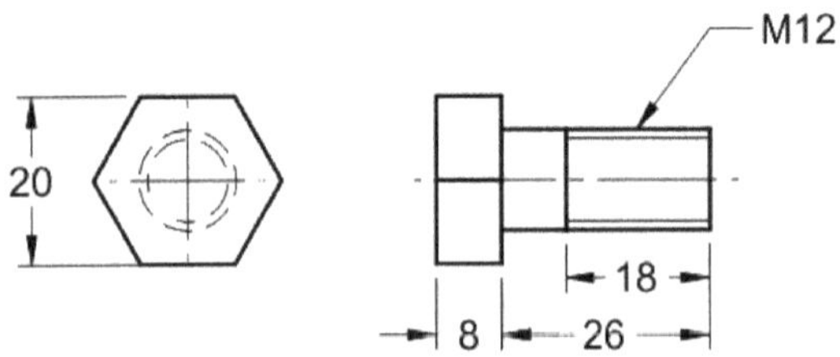

Bolt

Chapter 11: Drawings

Drawings are used to document your 3D models in the traditional 2D format, including dimensions and other instructions useful for manufacturing purposes. In Autodesk Fusion 360, you first create 3D models and assemblies and then use them to generate drawings. There is a direct association between the 3D model and the drawing. When changes are made to the model, every view in the drawing will be updated. This relationship between the 3D model and the drawing makes the drawing process fast and accurate. Because the 2D drawings are widely used in the mechanical industry, drawings are one of the three main file types you can create in Autodesk Fusion 360.

The topics covered in this chapter are:

- *Base Views*
- *Projected views*
- *Section views*
- *Detail views*
- *View Style*
- *Break Lines*
- *Exploded view*
- *Bill of Materials and Balloons*
- *Center Marks*
- *Centerlines*
- *Center Mark Pattern*
- *Dimensions*
- *Baseline Dimensions*
- *Chain Dimensions*
- *Ordinate Dimensions*
- *Hole callouts*
- *Text*

Starting a Drawing

To start a new drawing, first, open the design file of which you want to create the drawing. Next, click **File** drop-down > **New Drawing > From Design** on the Application Bar. On the **Create Drawing** dialog, select **Contents > Full Assembly** option, if you want to create the drawing of the entire assembly. If you want to create a drawing of a component of the assembly, then **Contents > Select** and select the components from the graphics window. Select the **From Scratch** option from the **Template** drop-down. Next, select the **Standard**, **Units**, and **Sheet Size**, and then click **OK**.

Drawings

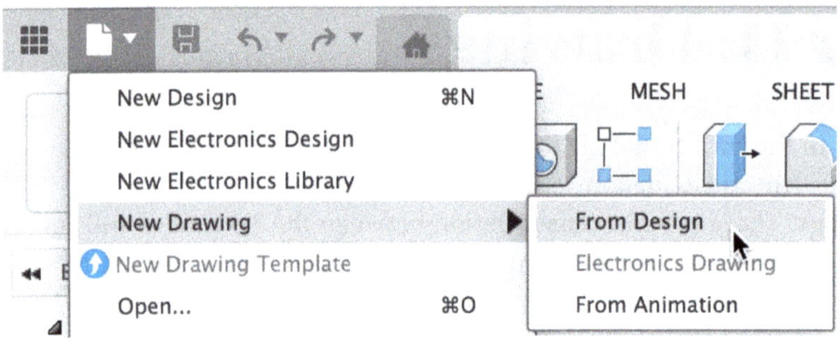

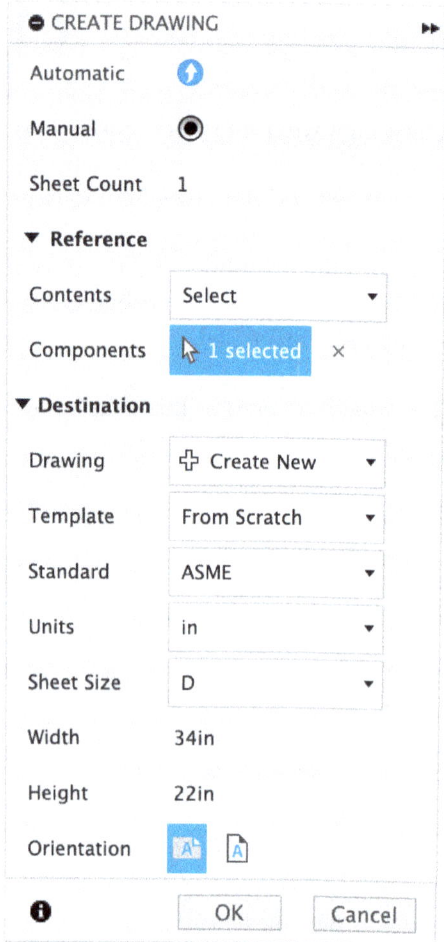

You can also create a drawing of part from the data panel. To do this, click the **Data panel** button on the top-left corner. Next, right-click on a part and select **New Drawing from Design.** Next, specify the options on the **Create Drawing** dialog and click **OK**; a drawing sheet is displayed along with the **Drawing View** dialog.

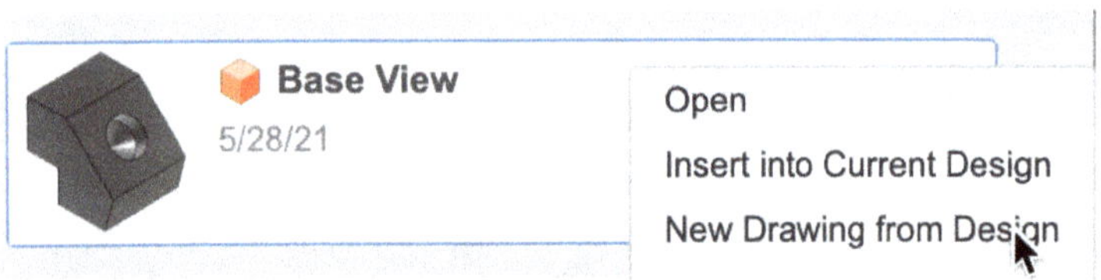

Creating Orthographic Views

Orthographic Views are standard representations of an object on a sheet. These views are created by projecting an object onto three different planes (top, front, and side planes). You can project an object by using two different methods: **First Angle Projection** and **Third Angle Projection**. The following figure shows the orthographic views that will be created when an object is projected using the **First Angle Projection** method.

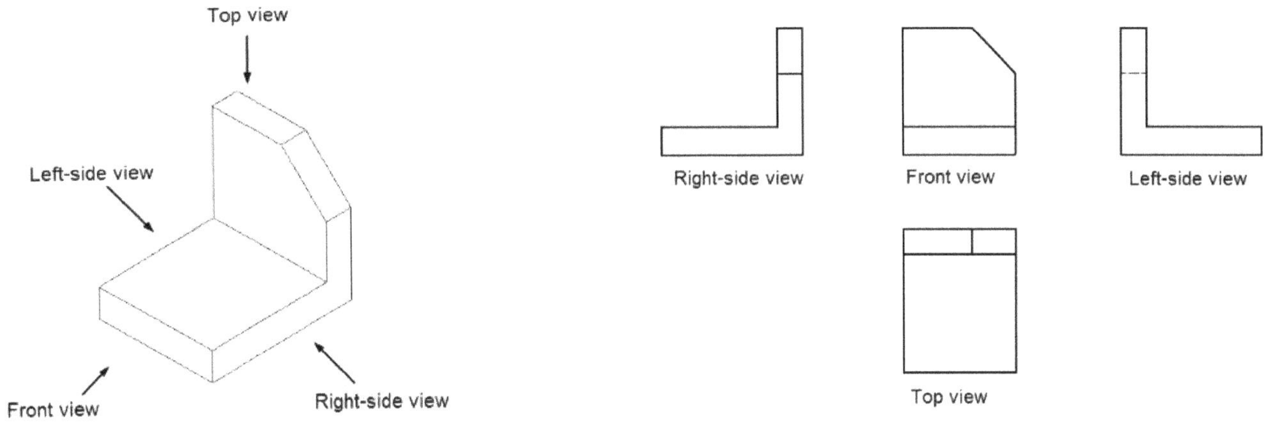

The following figure shows the orthographic views that will be created when an object is projected using the **Third Angle Projection** method.

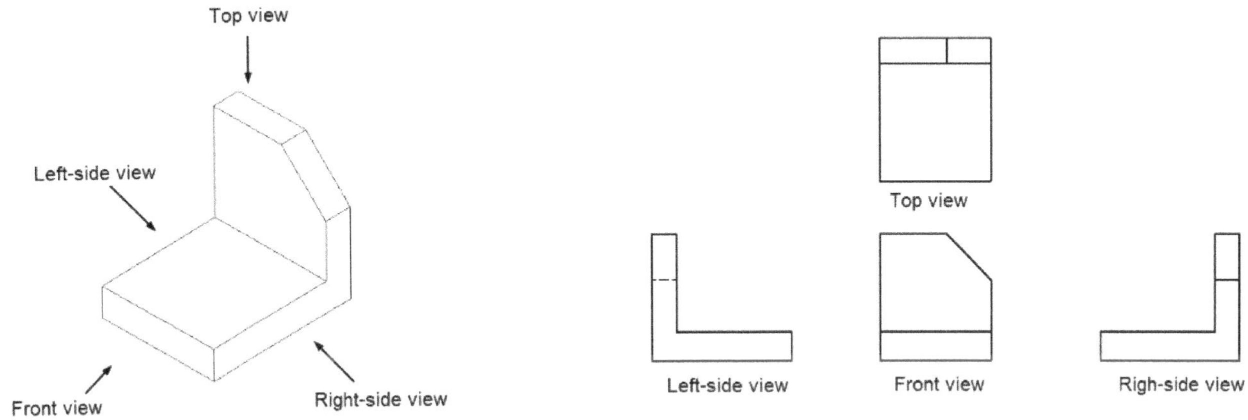

By default, the projection method is selected based on the standard selected from the **Create Drawing** dialog while creating a new drawing. However, you can override the projection method using the **Preferences** dialog. Click on your profile picture located at the top-right corner of the window, and then select the **Preferences** option; the **Preferences** dialog appears. Next, select **General > Drawing** from the tree view; the drawing settings are displayed. Notice that the **Standard** and **Units** are set as **Inherit From Design**, by default. Select an option from the **Standard** drop-down, and then check the **Override or Restore Format Defaults Below** option. Next, select the **First Angle** or **Third Angle** option from **Projection Angle** drop-down. Click **Apply** and **OK**.

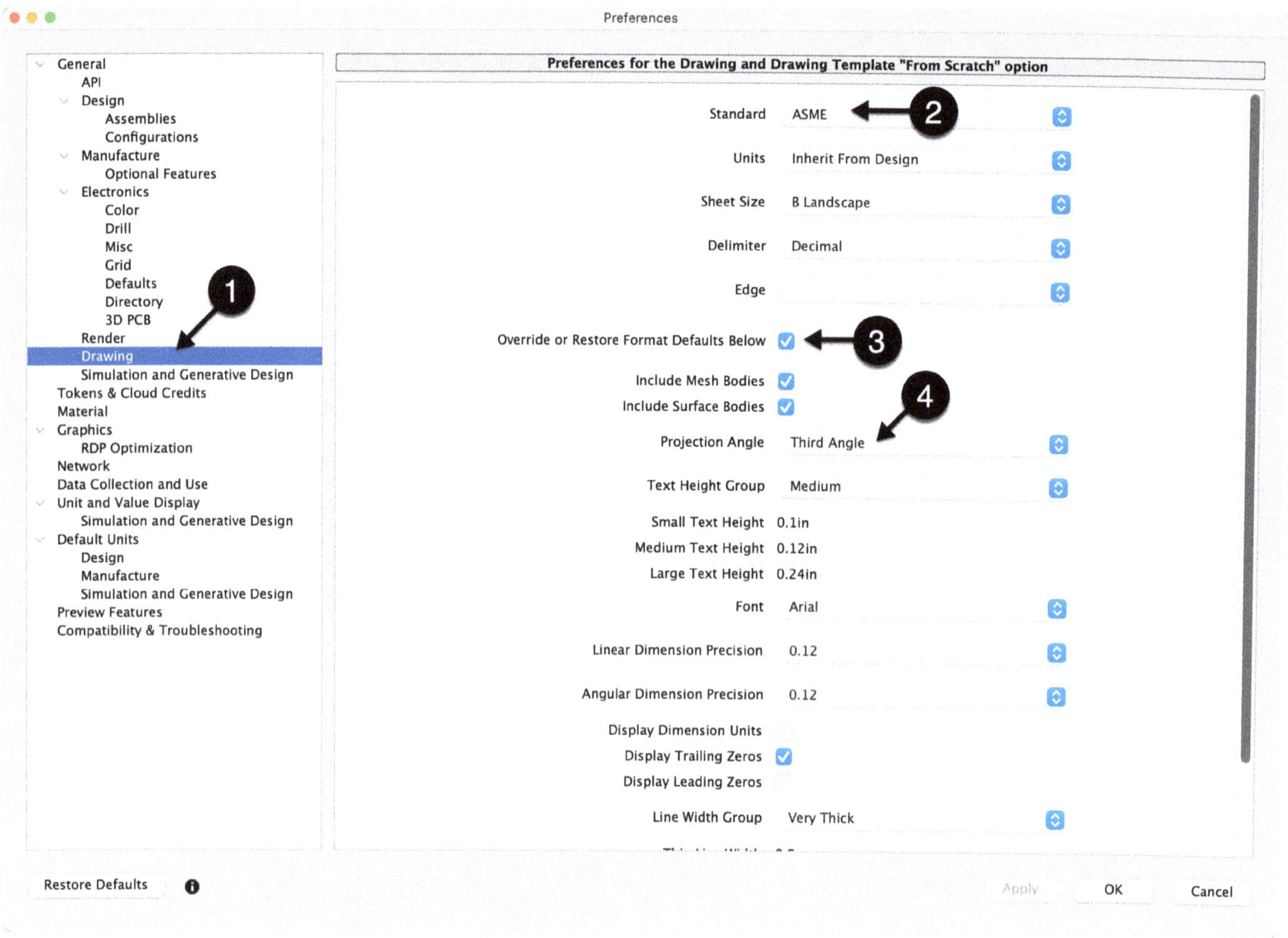

Creating a Base View

There are different standard views available in a 3D component, such as front, right, top, and isometric. In Autodesk Fusion 360, you can create these views using the **Base View** command. This command is activated if you have created a drawing from an already opened component. If it is not activated, click **Drawing > Create > Base View** on the toolbar; the **Drawing View** dialog appears, and a model view will be displayed on the sheet.

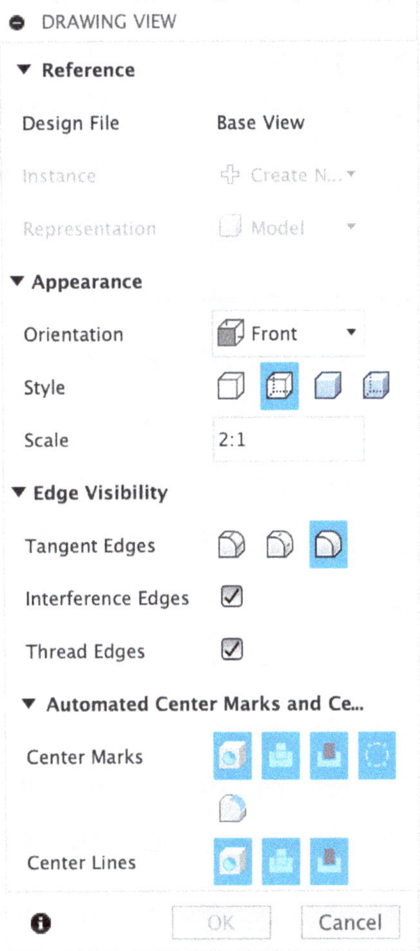

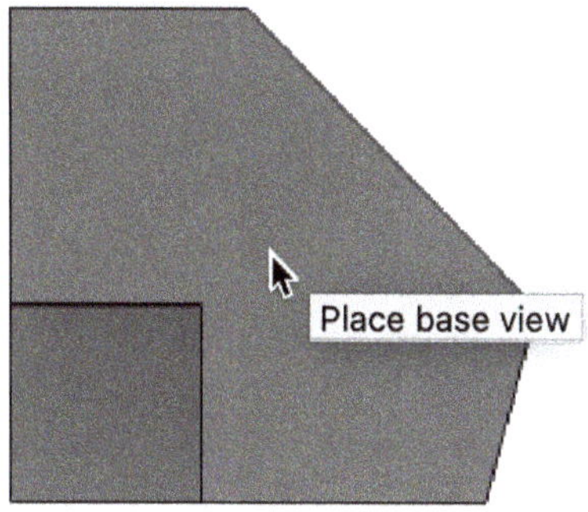

Use the **Orientation** drop-down on the **Drawing View** dialog to change the orientation of the view.

Change the scale factor in the **Scale** drop-down to adjust the size of the view to sheet size.

Next, move the pointer to the desired location. Now, you can create other views by projecting the base view. Click **OK** on the **Drawing View** dialog.

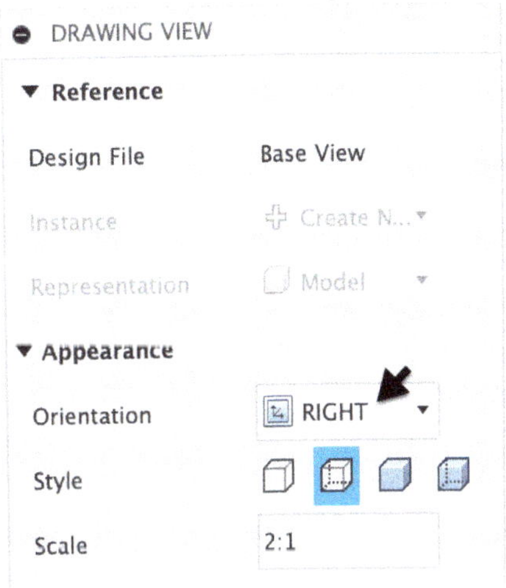

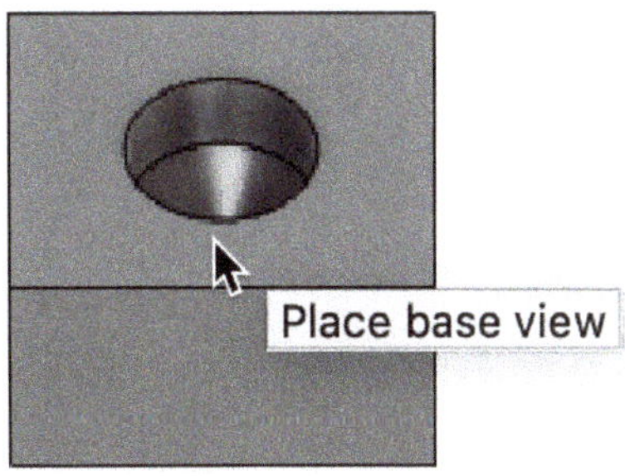

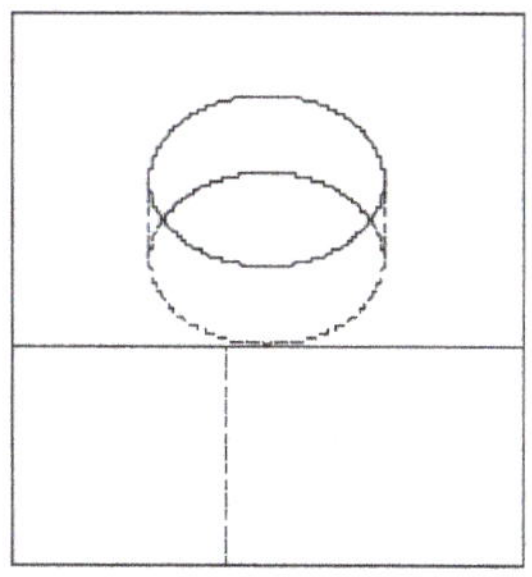

Projected View

After you have created the first view in your drawing, a projected view is one of the simplest views to create. Activate the **Projected View** command (click **Drawing > Create > Projected View** on the toolbar). After activating the command, select a view you wish to project from. Next, move the pointer in the direction you wish to have the view to be projected. Next, click on the sheet to specify the location. Click the **Create and continue** icon displayed on the view; the projected view will be created.

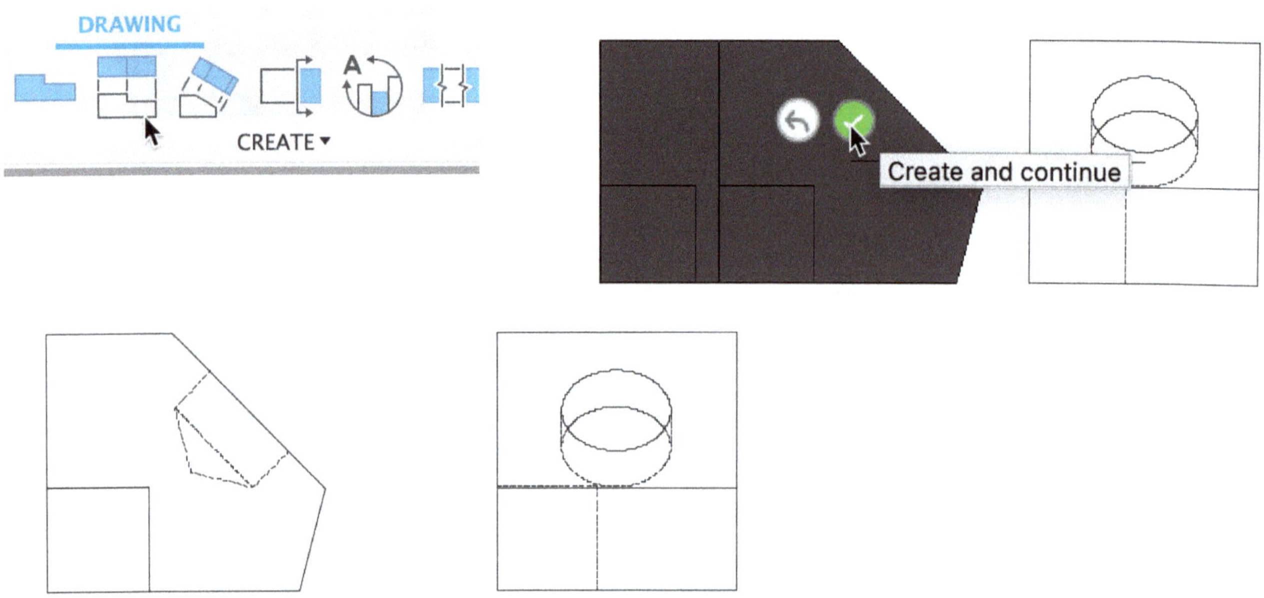

Auxiliary View

Most of the parts are represented using orthographic views (front, top and/or side views). However, many parts have features located on inclined faces. You cannot get the true shape and size for these features by using the orthographic views. To see an accurate size and shape of the inclined features, you need to create an auxiliary view. An auxiliary view is created by projecting the part onto a plane other than horizontal, front or side planes. To create an auxiliary view, activate the **Auxiliary View** command (click **Drawing > Create > Auxiliary View** on the toolbar). Click the angled edge of the model to establish the direction of the auxiliary view. Next, move the pointer to the desired location and click to locate the view. Click **OK** on the **Auxiliary View** dialog.

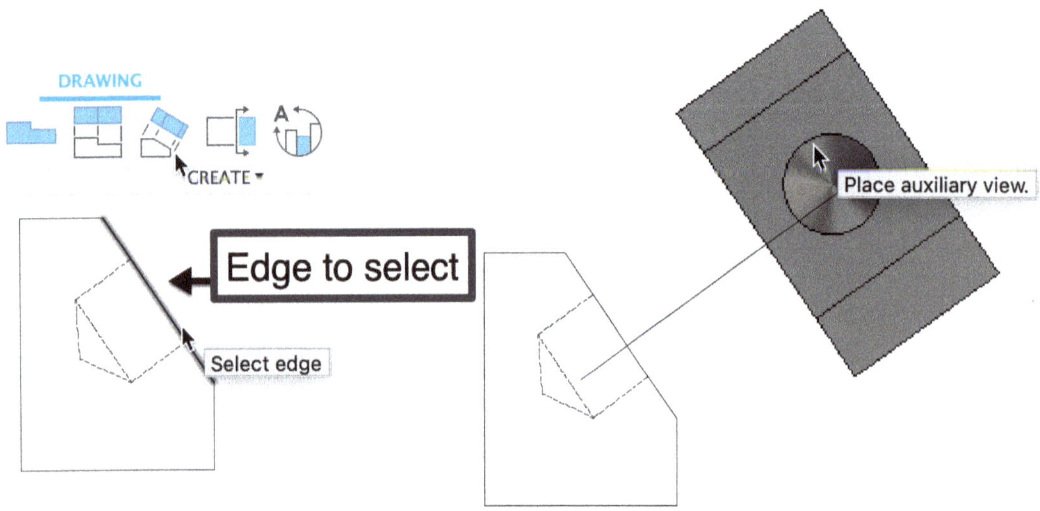

Section View

One of the most common views used in 2D drawings is the section view. Creating a section view in Autodesk Fusion 360 is very simple. Once a view is placed on the drawing sheet, you need to draw a line where you want to section the drawing view. Activate the **Section View** command (click **Drawing > Create > Section View** 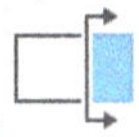 on the toolbar) and click on a drawing view. Now, you have to draw a line to define the section line. Place the pointer on the center point of the drawing view, and then move it upwards; a trace line appears. Click to specify the first point of the section line. Next, move the pointer downward and click outside the drawing view. After drawing a line, Click the **Create and Continue** icon.

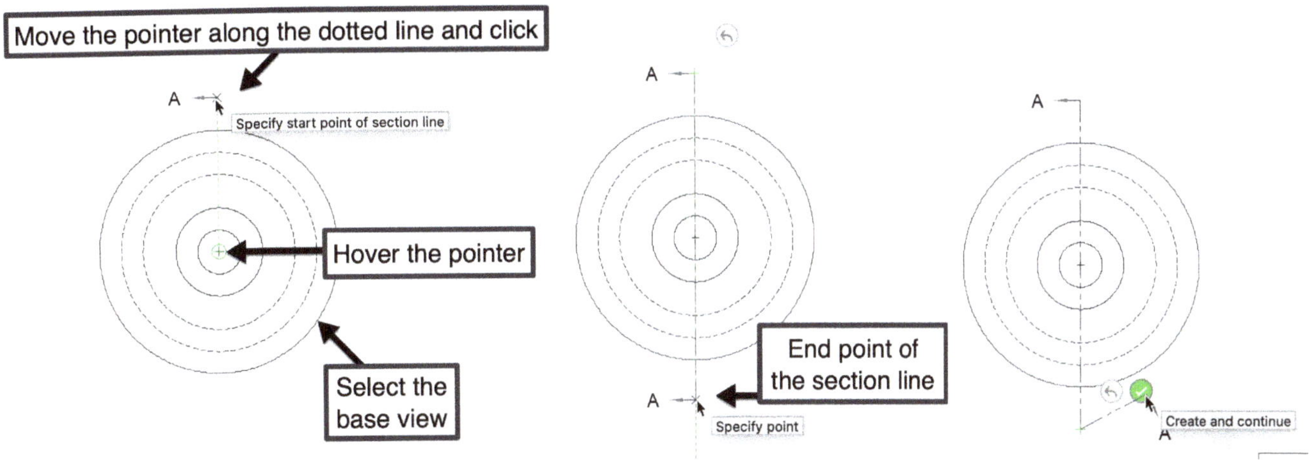

Move the pointer on either side of the cutting plane to indicate the view direction. Next, click to position the section view. Click **OK** on the **Drawing View** dialog to create the section view.

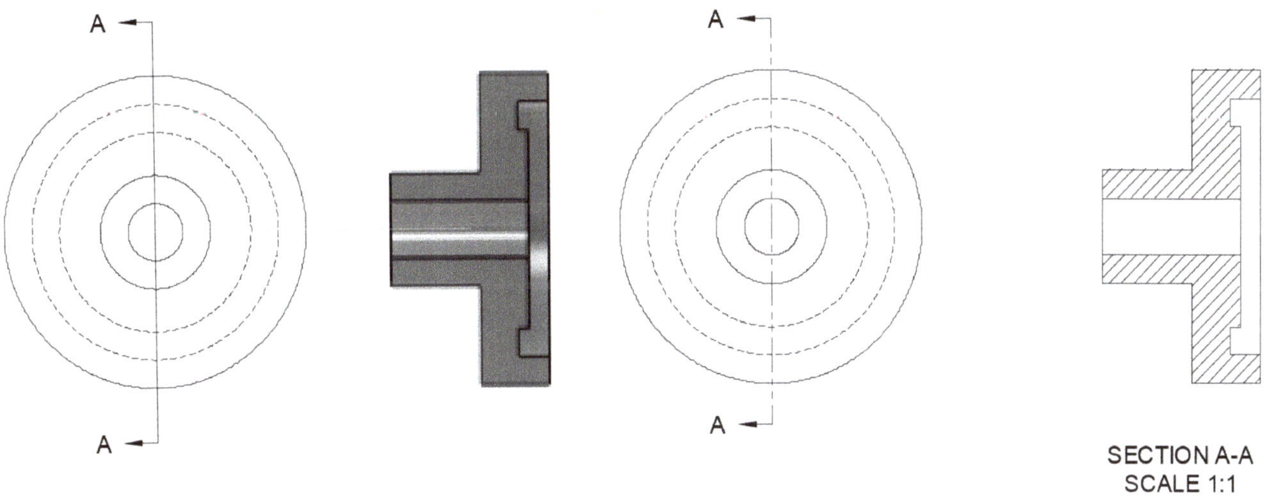

You can also use a multi-segment cutting line to create a section view.

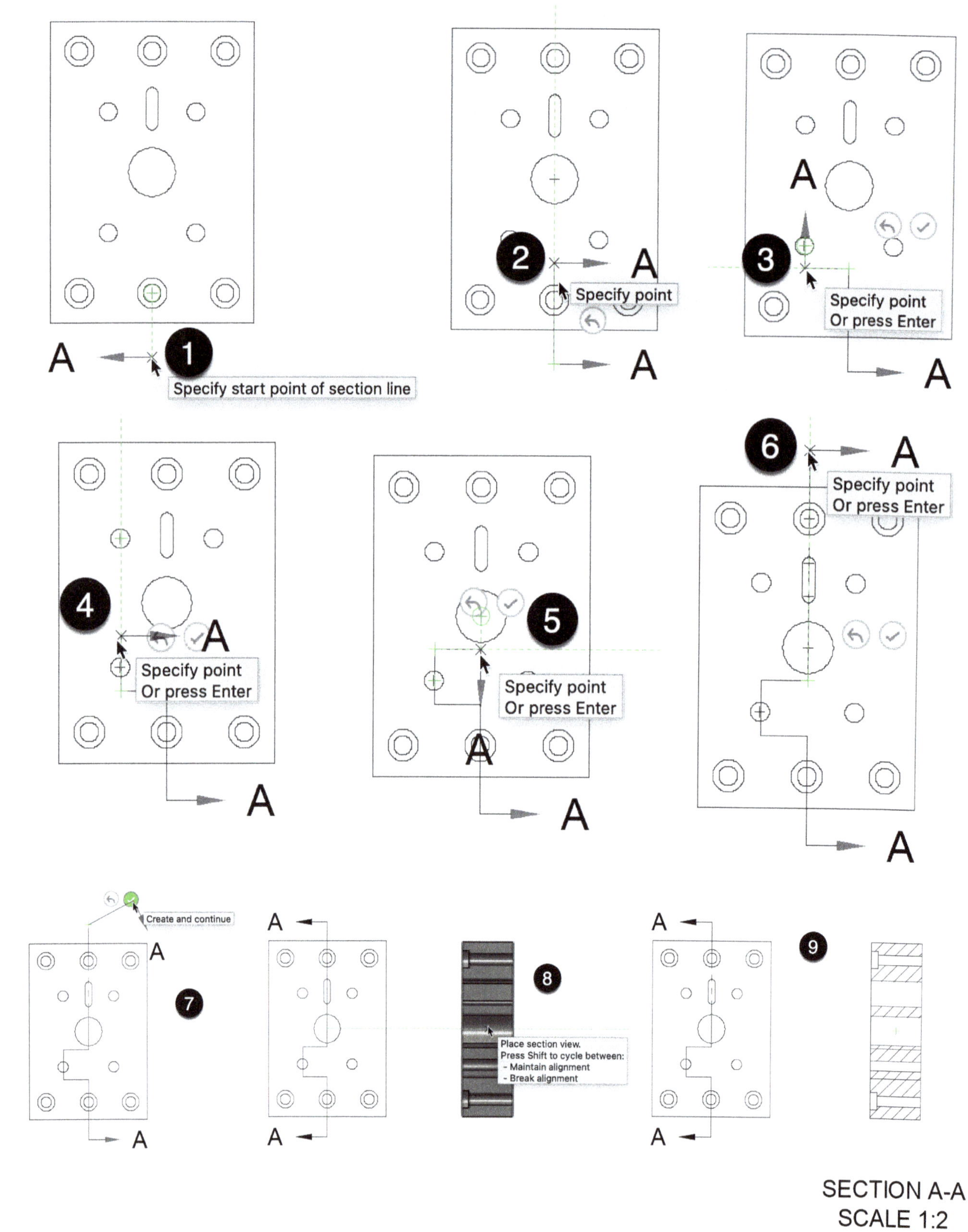

You can also create an aligned section view using the **Section View** command. Activate the **Section View** command and select the parent view. Next, specify the first point of the section plane. Select the center of the view; the second segment of the section line is attached to the pointer. Use a key point on the drawing view and specify the endpoint of the section line. Next, click **Create and Continue** .

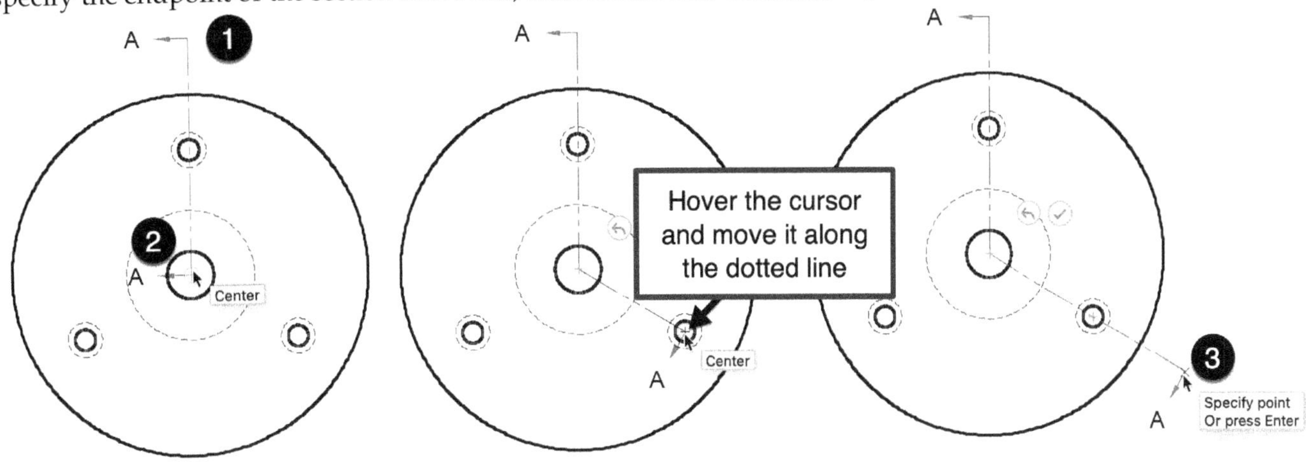

Move the pointer in the direction perpendicular to any one of the line segments of the section view. Next, click to position the aligned section view. Click **OK** on the **Section View** dialog.

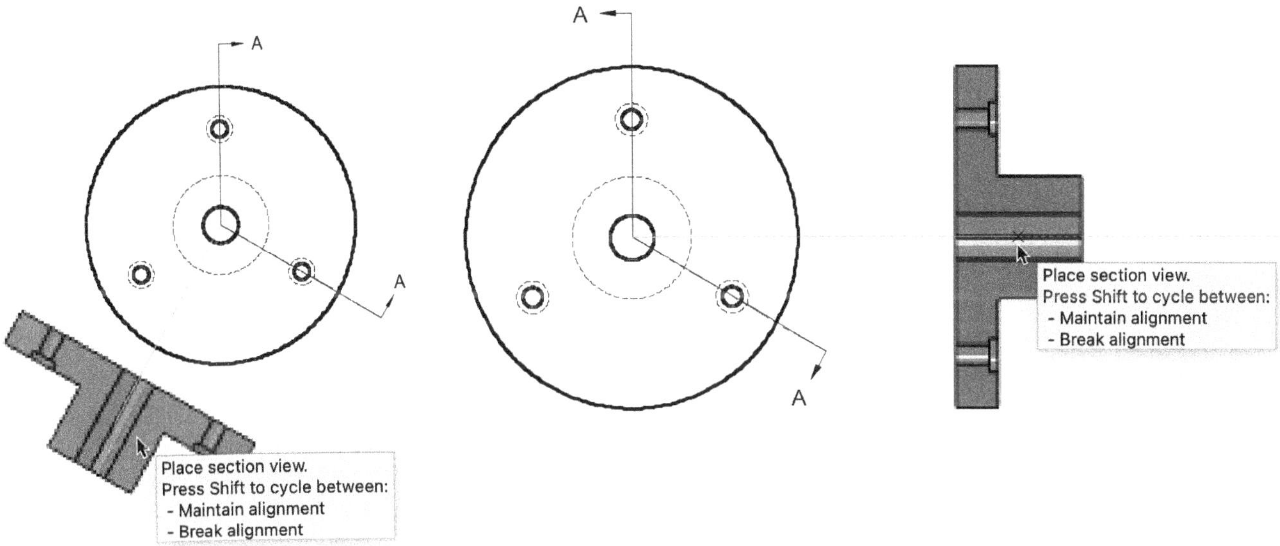

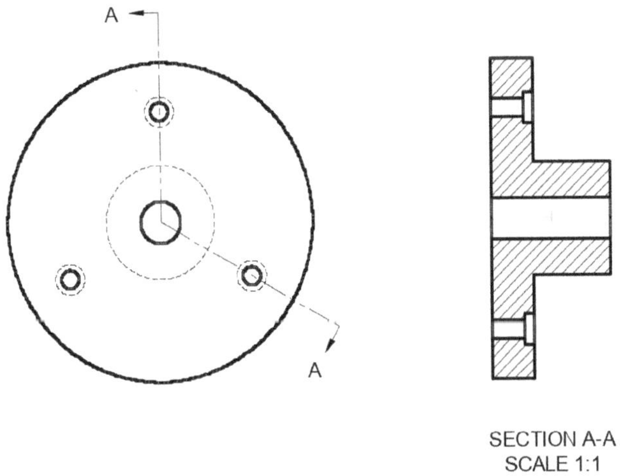

When creating a section view of an assembly, you can choose to exclude one or more components from the section view. For example, to exclude the piston of a pneumatic cylinder, first, activate the **Section view**

command. Next, create the section line on the base view; the **Drawing View** dialog appears. On this dialog, uncheck the checkbox next to the **Piston** body in the **Objects to cut** list. Next, move the pointer and click to specify the location of the section view. Click **OK** on the **Drawing View** dialog; you will notice that the piston is not cut.

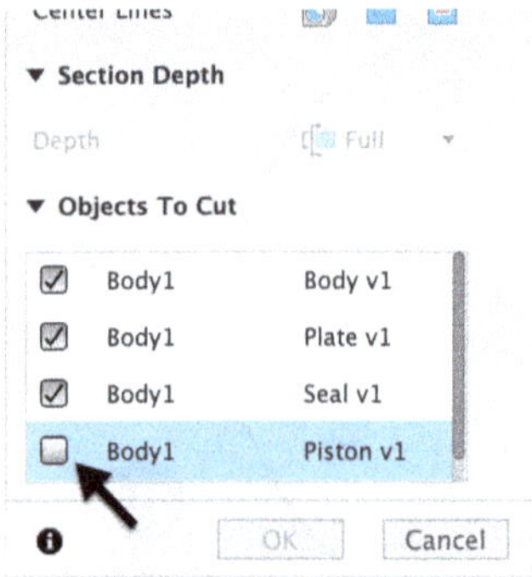

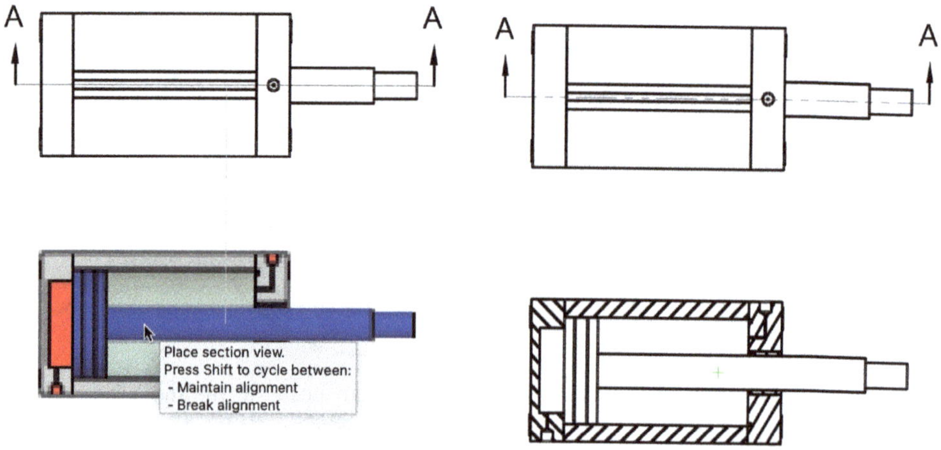

SECTION A-A
SCALE 1:2

Section Depth

The **Depth** drop-down in the **Section Depth** section has three options: **Full**, **Slice**, and **Distance**. The **Full** option displays the full depth of the sectioned part. The **Slice** option displays only the section of the part at the location of the selection plane.

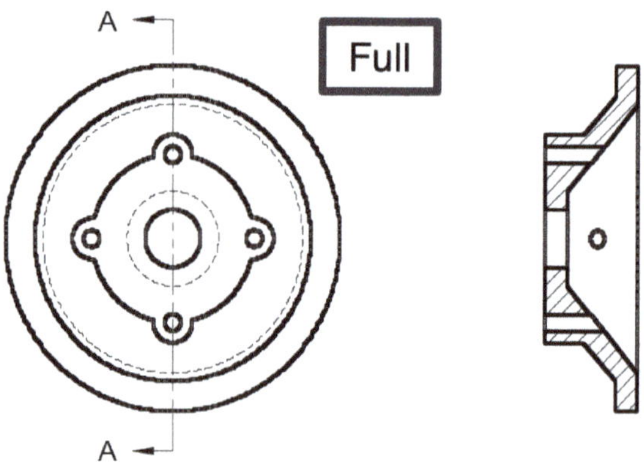

SECTION A-A
SCALE 1:1

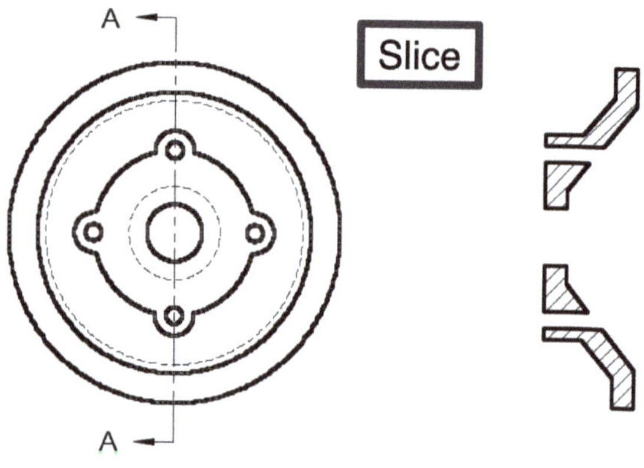

SECTION A-A
SCALE 1:1

The **Distance** option displays the material inside the part up to the specified distance. Select this option from the **Depth** drop-down and specify the depth point on the base view. You can also enter a value in the **Distance** box.

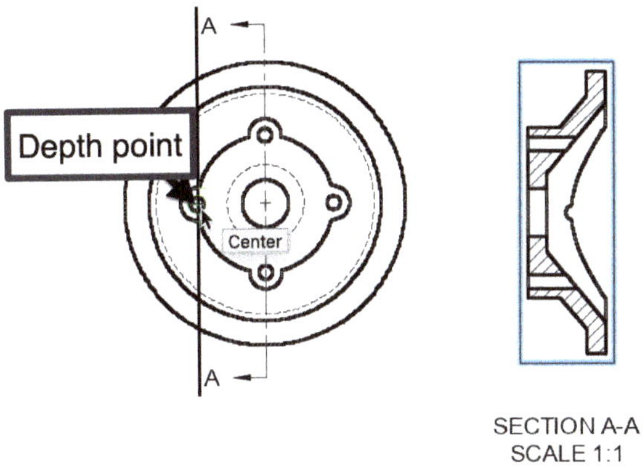

Editing the Hatch pattern of the Section View

To edit the hatch pattern of section view, double-click on it; the Hatch dialog appears.

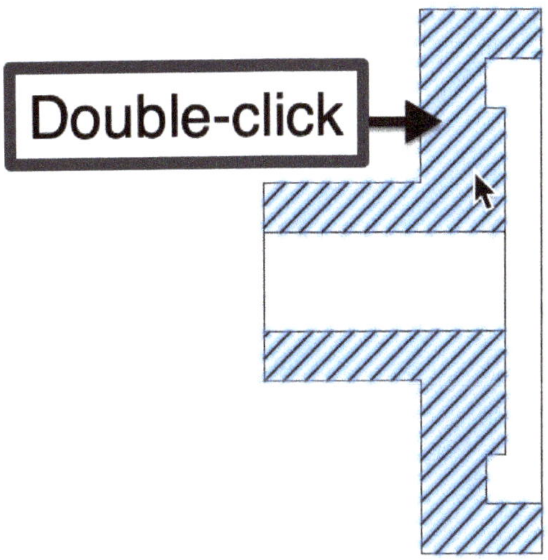

The **Pattern** drop-down has many standard hatch patterns.

The **Scale Factor** box has a default value of 1. Increase the **Scale Factor** value and notice that the spacing between the hatch lines increasing.

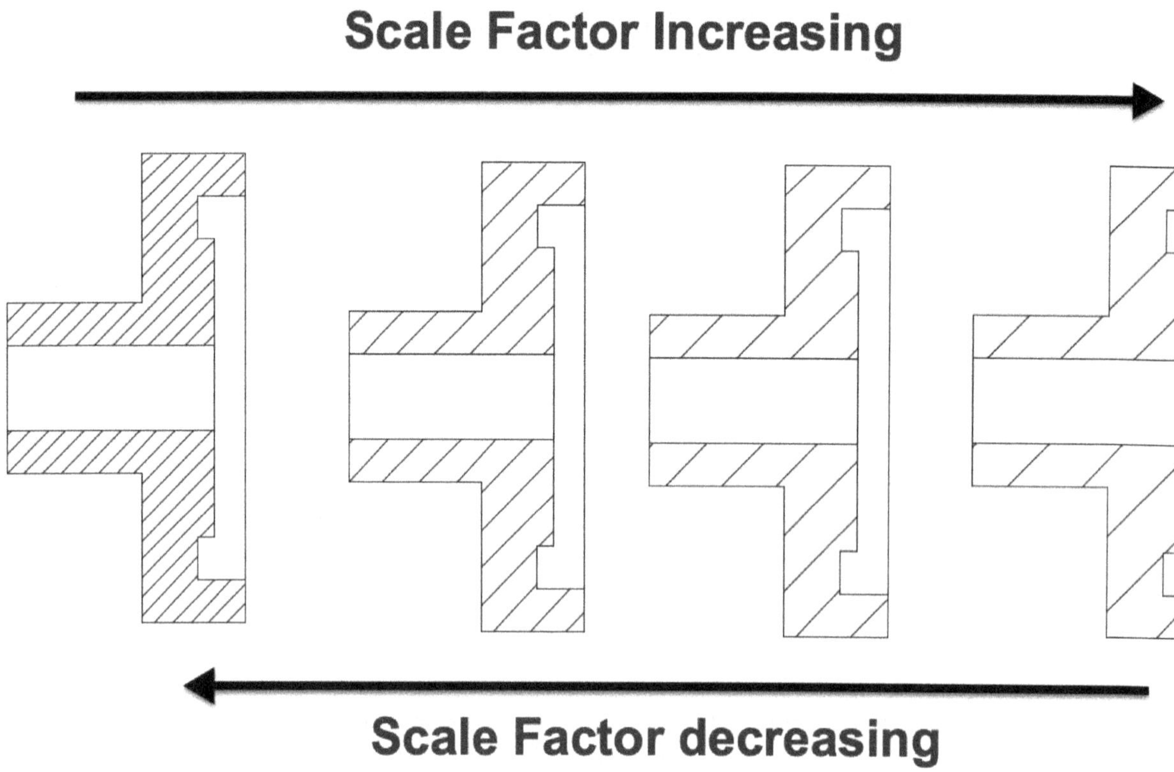

The **Angle** box has a default value of 0. Enter a new value in the **Angle** box and notice that the hatch lines rotated in the counter clockwise direction. Next, click **Close** on the **Hatch** dialog.

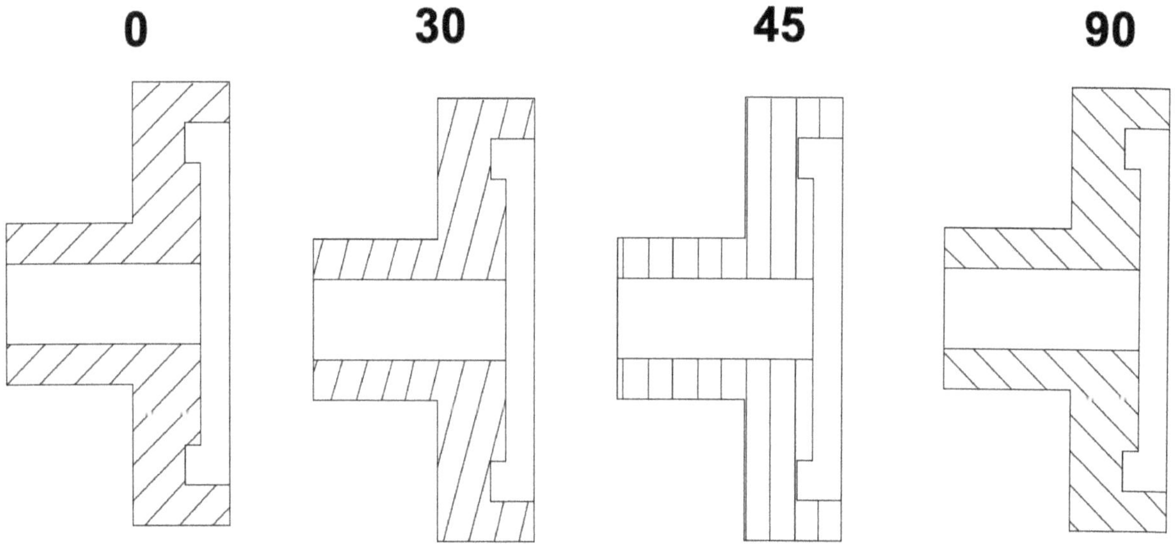

Click on the color swatch next to **Color**. This action opens the **Colours** dialog, where you can select a new color for the hatch pattern. The **Colours** dialog provides several ways to choose a color, including a color wheel, sliders for different color models, predefined color palettes, a color spectrum, and even a set of colored pencils. After selecting the desired color, click **OK** to apply the change.

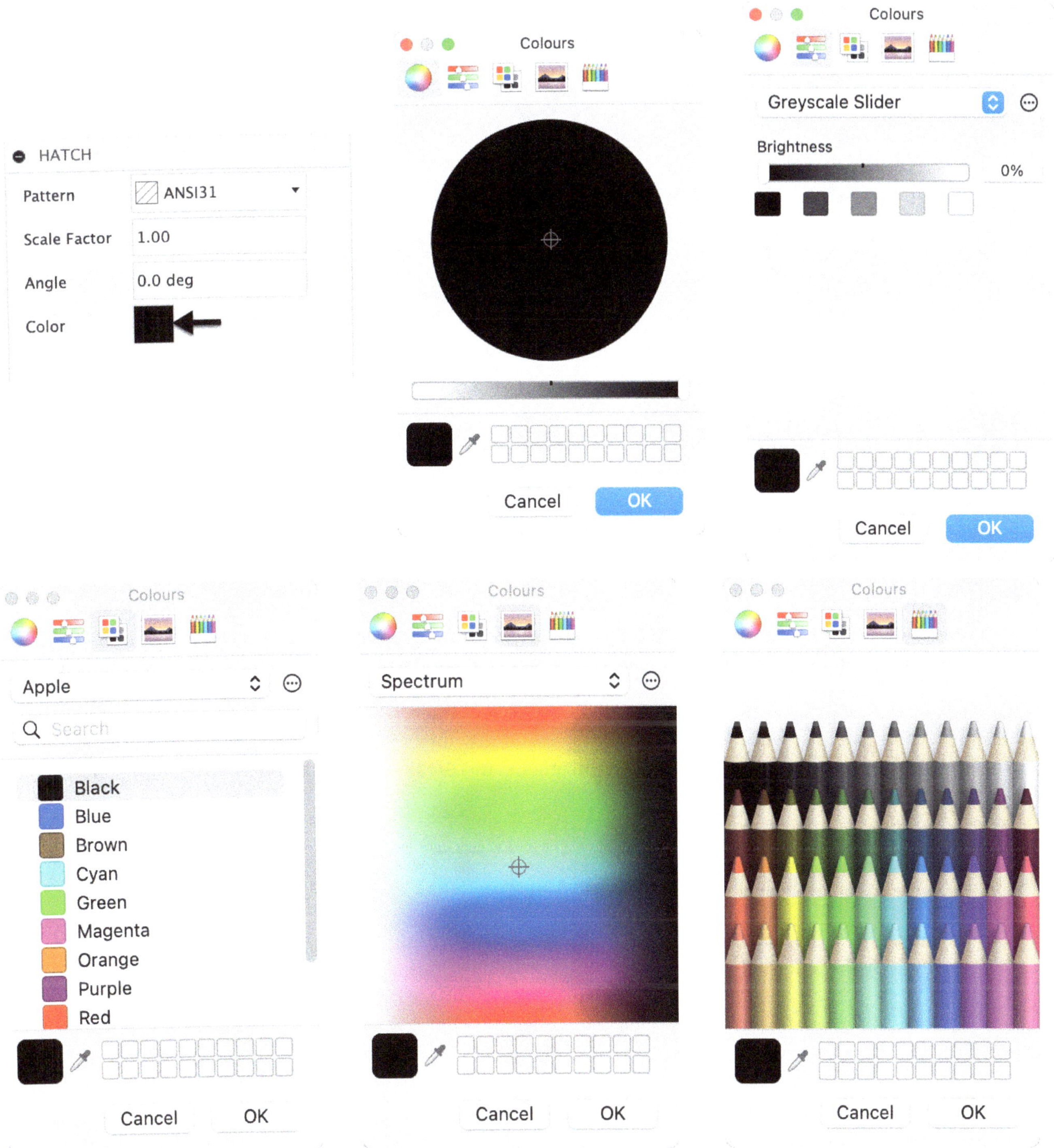

Detail View

If a drawing view contains small features that are difficult to see, a detailed view can be used to zoom in and make things clear. To create a detailed view, activate the **Detail View** command (click **Drawing > Create > Detail View** on the toolbar). Next, select the base view; this automatically activates the circle tool. Draw a circle to identify the area that you wish to zoom into. Once the fence shape is drawn, enter a value in the **Scale** box available on the **Drawing View** dialog; the detail view is scaled by the scale factor.

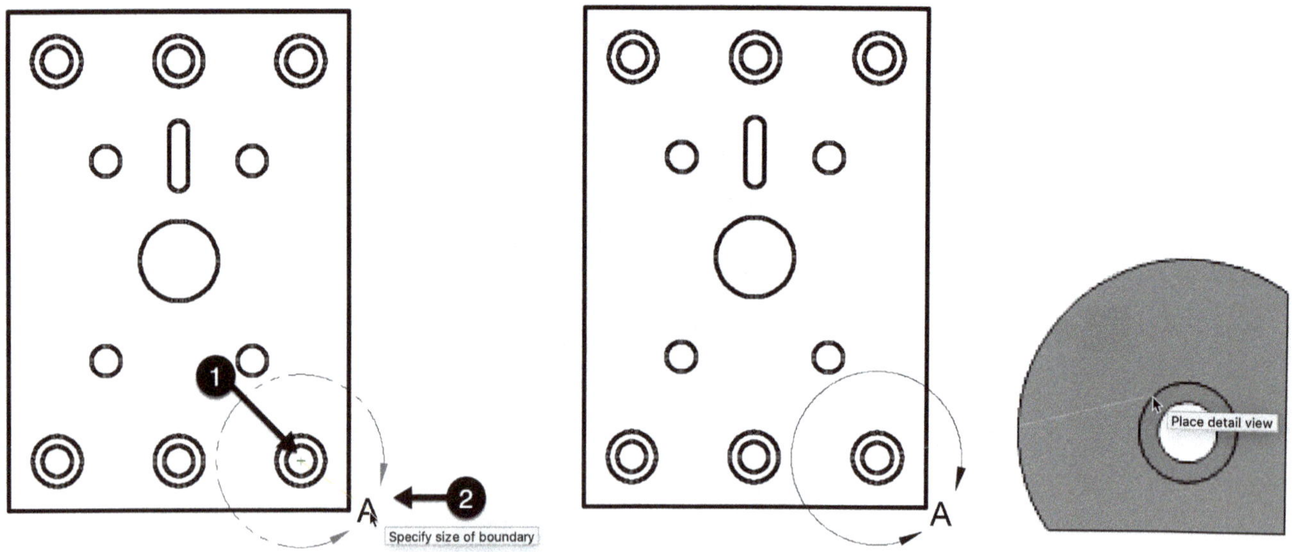

Click anywhere on the drawing sheet to place the detail view. Next, click **OK** to complete the detail view.

Break View

You can break a drawing view, which is too large to fit on the drawing sheet. You may need to break the view so that only important details are shown. To break a view, activate the **Break View** command (on the **Drawing** toolbar, click **Create > Break View**) and select the view. On the **Break View** dialog, set the **Orientation** to **Horizontal** or **Vertical**. Click once on the drawing view to locate the beginning of the break. Next, select another point on the drawing view to locate the end of the break. On the **Break View** dialog, type-in a value in the **Gap** box. Click **OK** to break the view.

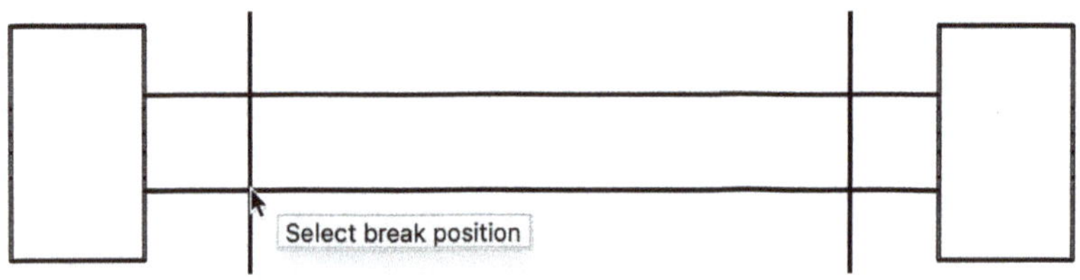

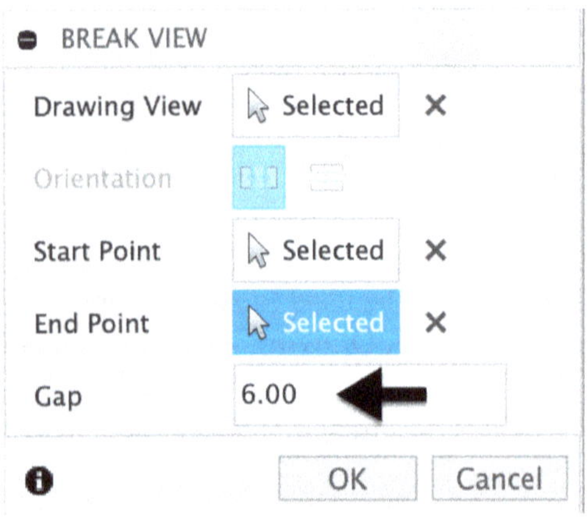

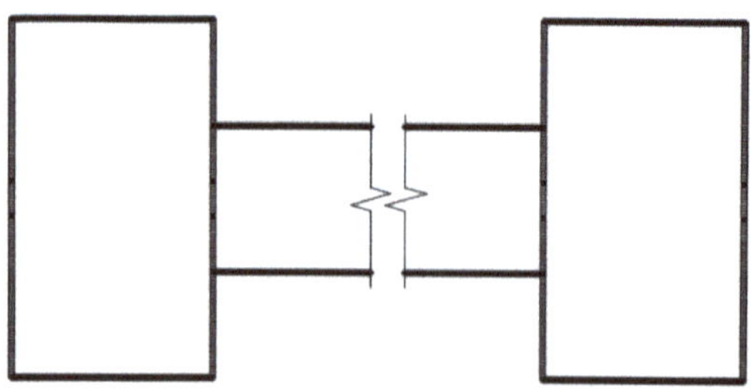

View Style

When working with Autodesk Fusion 360 drawings, you can control the way a model view is displayed by using the **Style** options. Select a view from the drawing sheet, and then right-click and select the **Edit View** option; the **Drawing View** appears. On this dialog, select the desired **Style** (**Visible Edges**, **Visible and Hidden Edges**, **Shaded**, **Shaded with Hidden Edges**) and click **Close**. The style of the view will be changed.

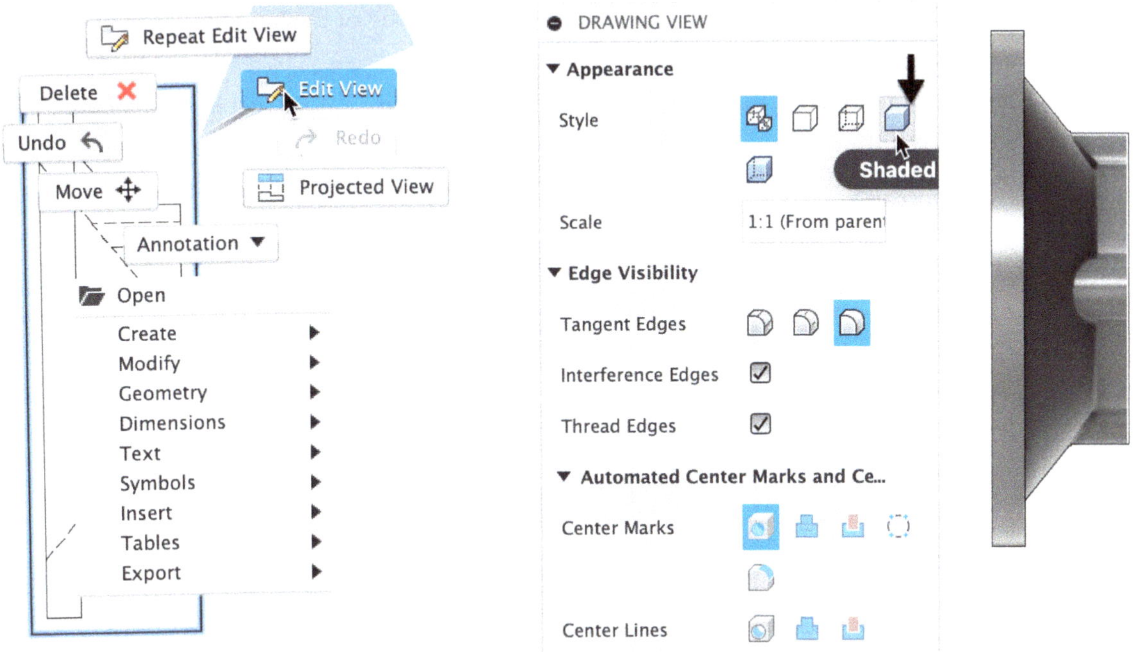

The following illustration shows the other Style options available in the **Appearance** section of the **Drawing View** dialog.

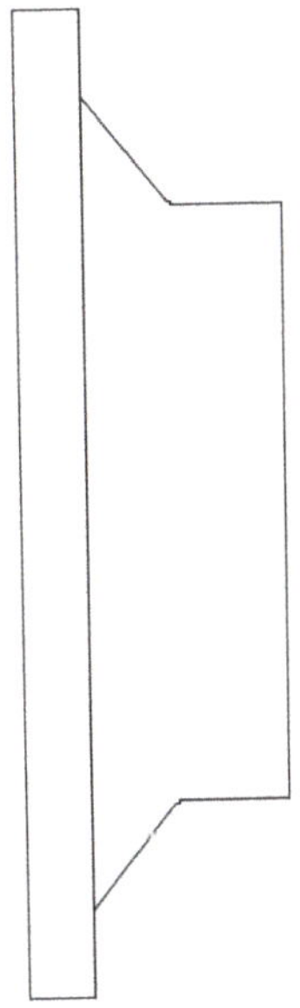

Visible Edges

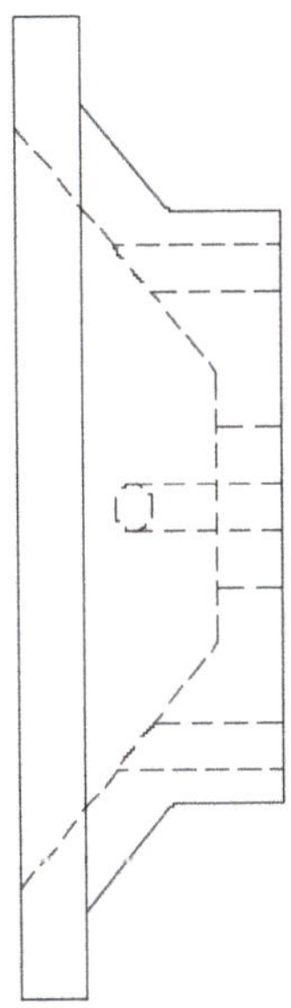

Visible and Hidden Edges

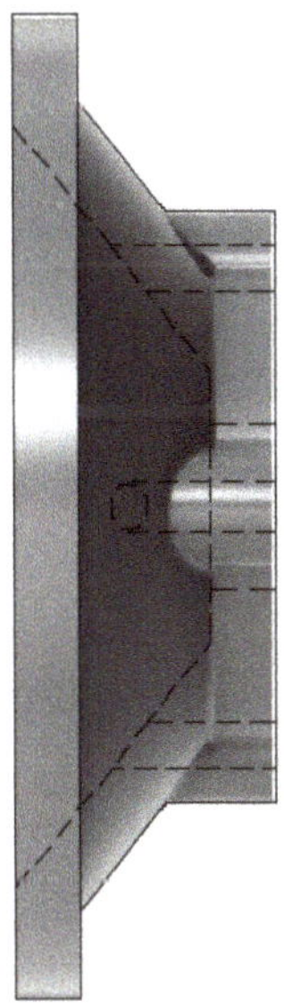

Shaded with Hidden edges

Edge Visibility

There are three set of options in the **Edge Visibility** section of the **Drawing View** dialog: **Tangent Edges**, **Interference Edges**, and **Thread edges**.

Tangent Edges

The tangent edges are edges of faces that have a common point of tangency and are topologically connected. Edge fillets are most commonly seen tangent edges. You can change the display of the tangent edges using three options: **Full Length**, **Shortened**, and **Off**. Select **Tangent Edges > Full Length**  to display the tangent edges well connected to each other. Select **Tangent Edges > Shortened**  to shorten the tangent edges where two of them are intersecting. Select **Tangent Edges > Off**  to hide the tangent edges in the drawing view.

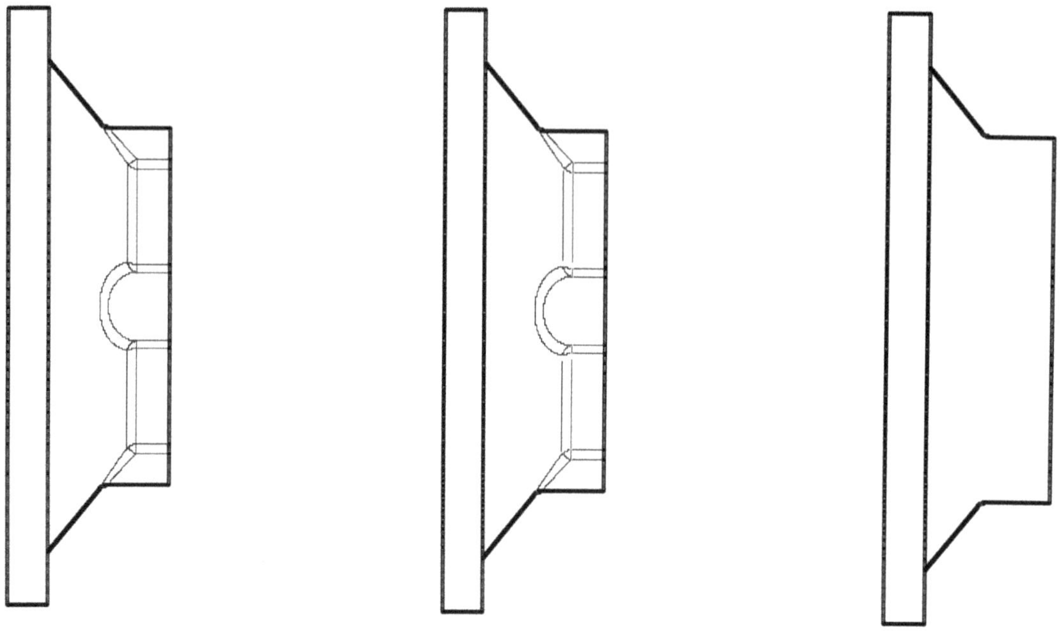

Full Length Shortened Off

Interferance Edges

The **Interference Edges** option displays the edges where two or more solid bodies interfere with each other.

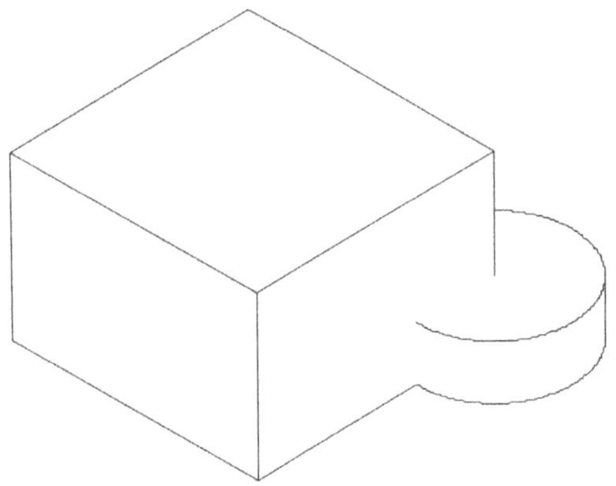

Interference Edge OFF

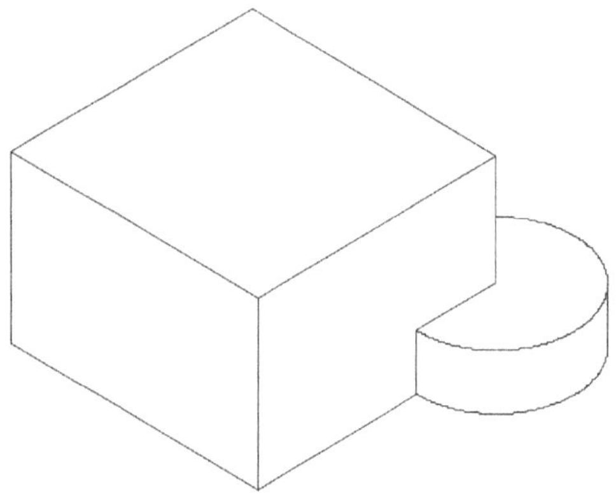

Interference Edges ON

Thread Edges

The **Thread Edges** option is checked by default. As a result, the thread edges are visible in the drawing view. Uncheck this option to hide the thread edges.

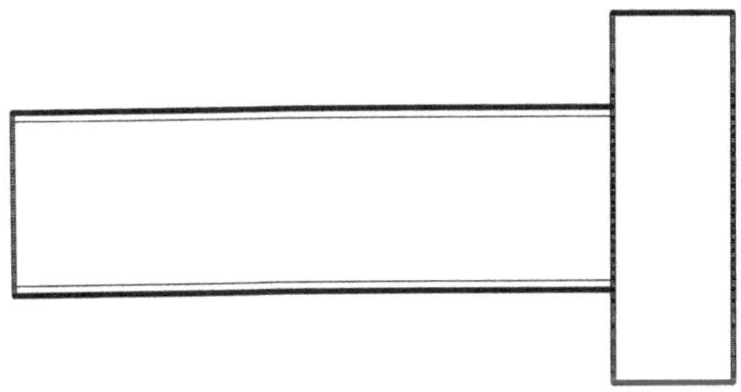

Thread Edges ON

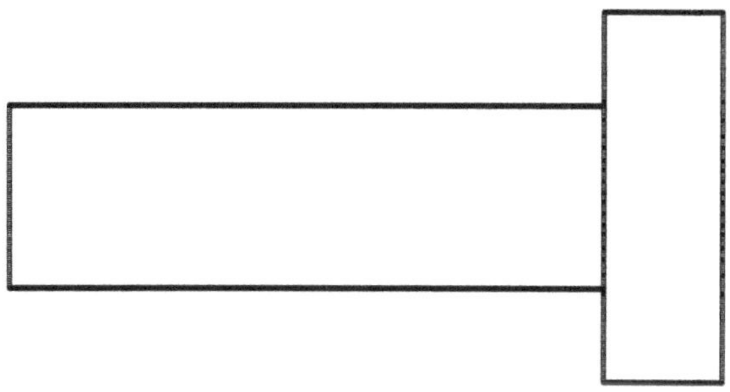

Thread Edge OFF

Exploded View

You can display an assembly in an exploded state as long as the assembly already has an exploded view defined in the animation workspace. If you want to add an exploded view to the drawing, open the assembly file containing the exploded view. Next, click **New > New Drawing > From Animation** on the Application Bar. Next, select the storyboard from the **Storyboard** drop-down, specify the other settings on the **Create Drawing** dialog, and then click **OK**; a drawing sheet appears.

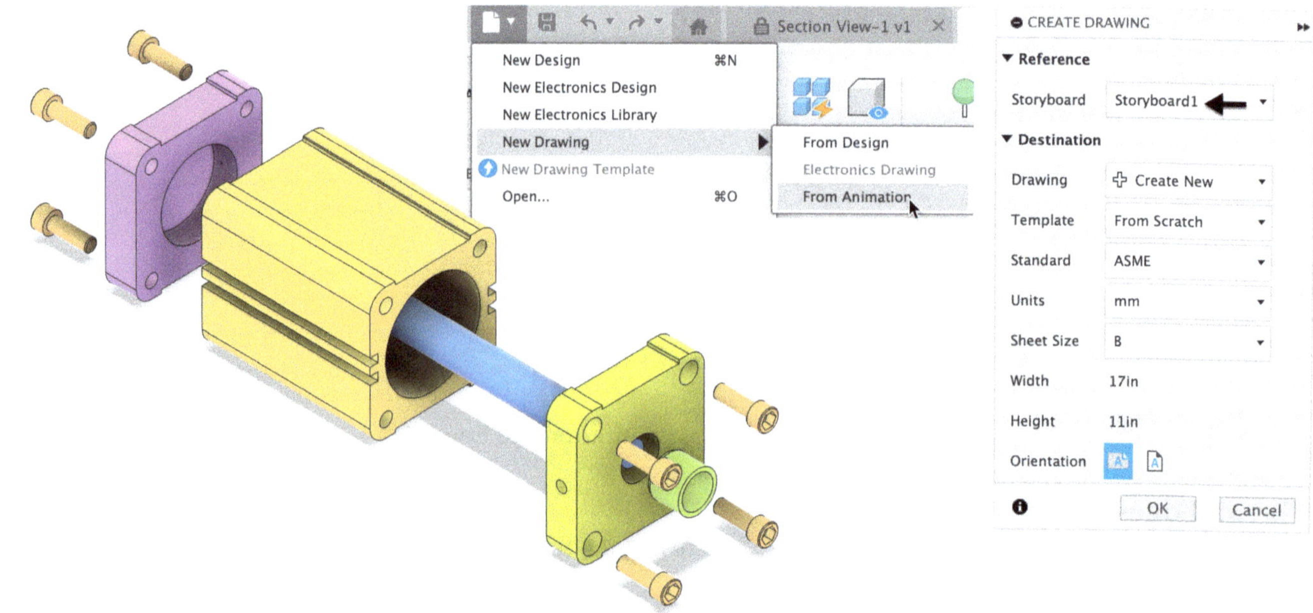

On the **Drawing View** dialog, specify the orientation, scale, and then click on the drawing sheet to place the exploded view. Next, click **OK** on the **Drawing View** dialog.

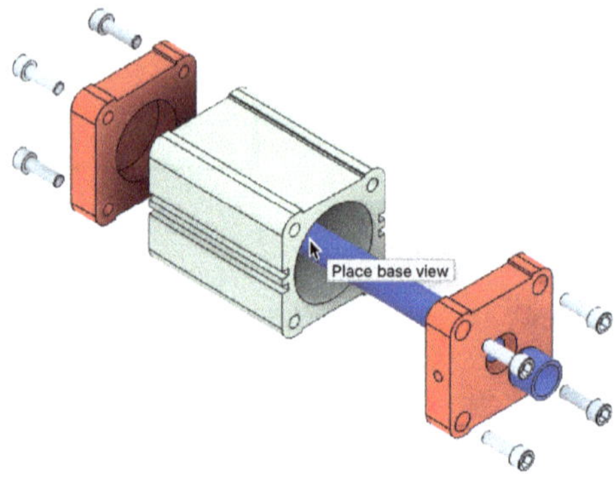

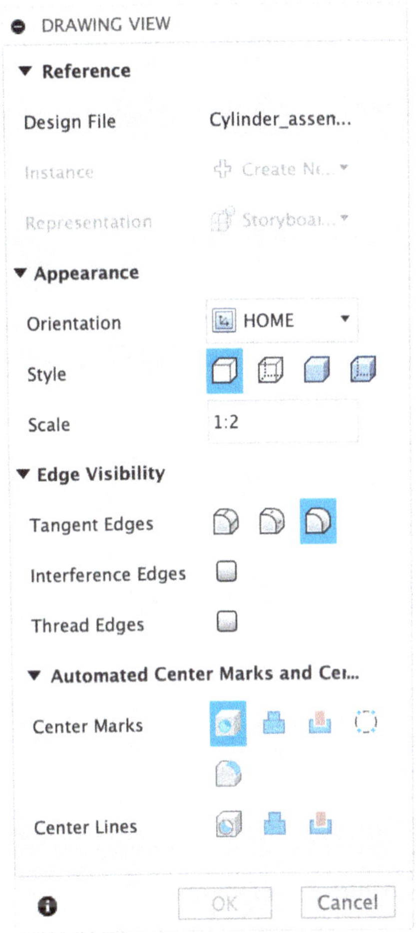

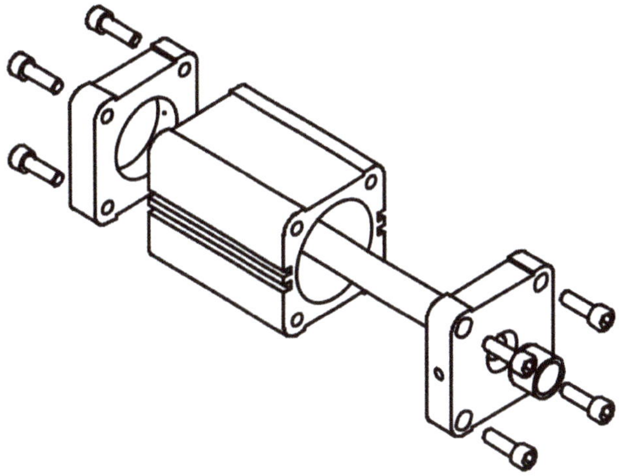

Bill of Materials and Balloons

Creating an assembly drawing is very similar to creating a component drawing. However, there are few things unique in an assembly drawing. One of them is creating a parts list. A parts list identifies the different components in an assembly. Generating a parts list is very easy in Autodesk Fusion 360. First, you need to have a view of the assembly. Next, click **Tables > Table** on the **Drawing** toolbar and then select **Type > Parts List** from the **Table** dialog. Next, select an option from the **Structure** drop-down. The **First Level** option displays the parts in the first level of the assembly. If an assembly has a subassembly, then it displays only the subassembly in the parts list. The parts inside the subassembly are not displayed. The **All Levels** option displays the subassembly and the parts inside it. Enter the title in the Title box and click on the drawing sheet; the parts list table is placed on the drawing sheet. Also, the balloons are added to the drawing view, if the **Auto Balloon** option is checked.

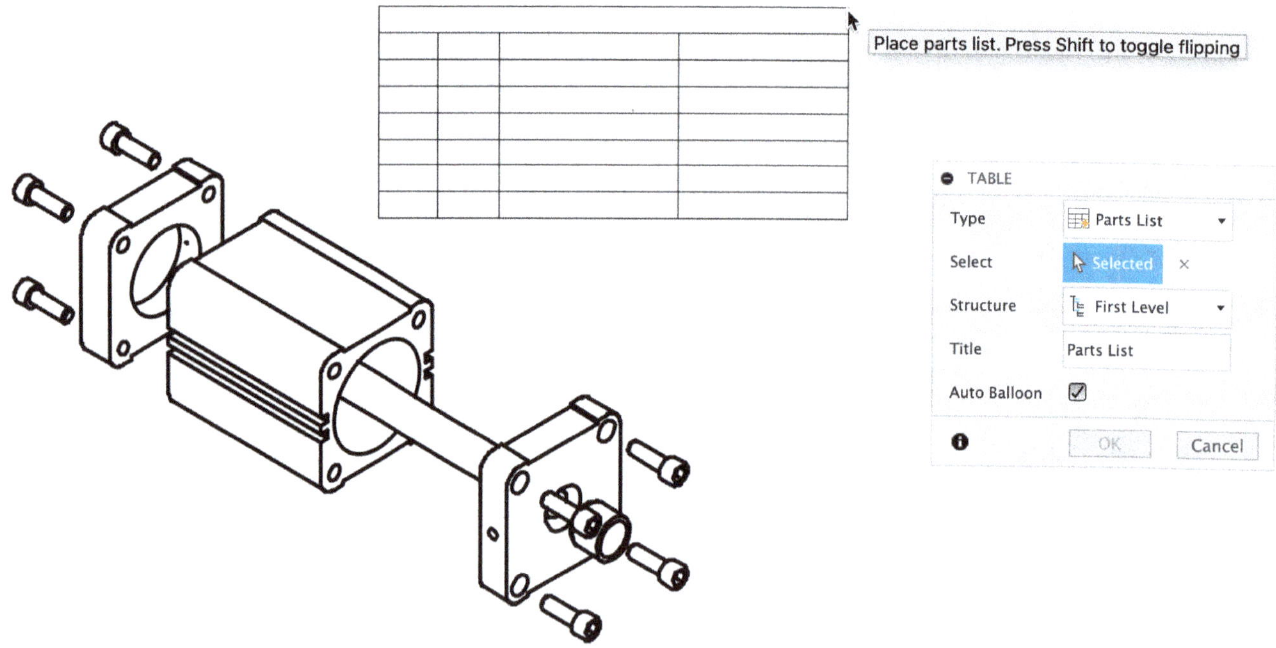

PARTS LIST			
ITEM	QTY	PART NUMBER	MATERIAL
1	1	BODY	GENERIC
2	1	PLATE	GENERIC
3	1	SEAL	GENERIC
4	1	PISTON	GENERIC
5	8	SCREW	GENERIC
6	1	BEARING	GENERIC

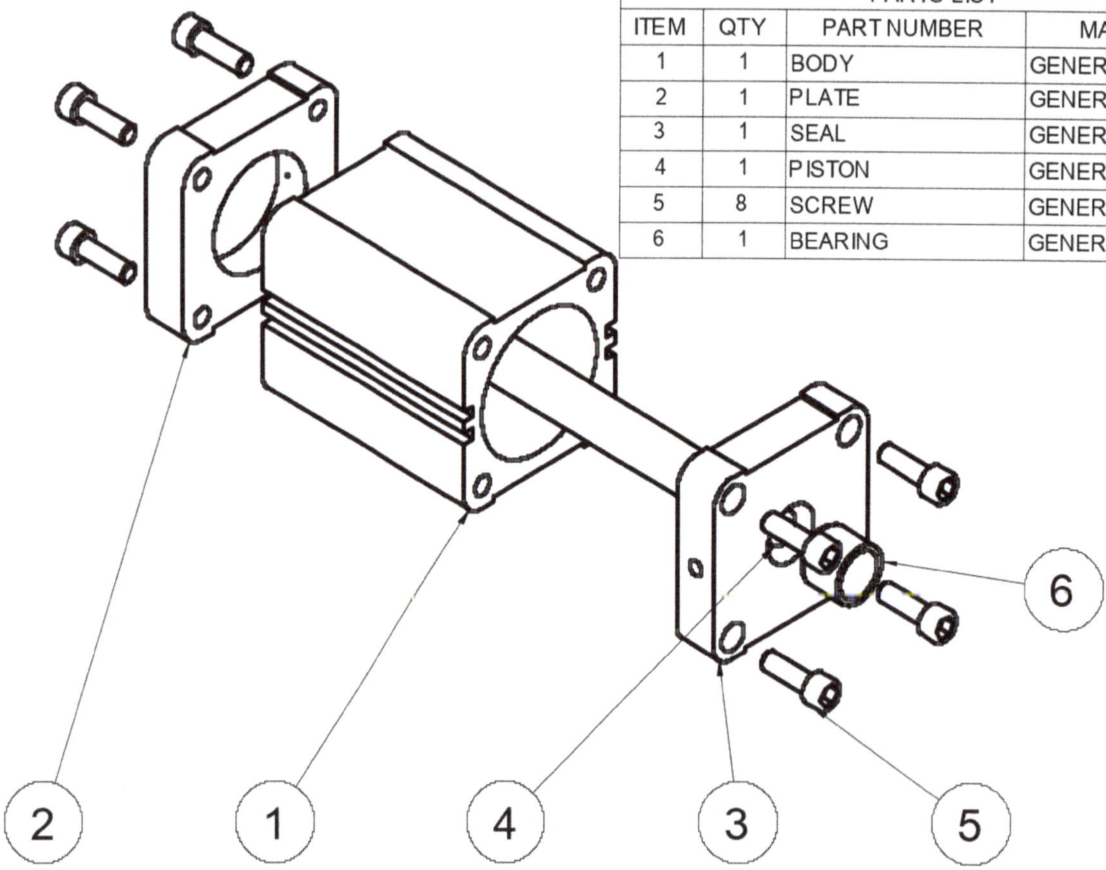

Double-click on the parts list table; the **Parts List** dialog appears. On this dialog, select the column names from the **Columns** list and arrange them using the **Move Up** and **Move Down** buttons. Click **Close** to apply the changes.

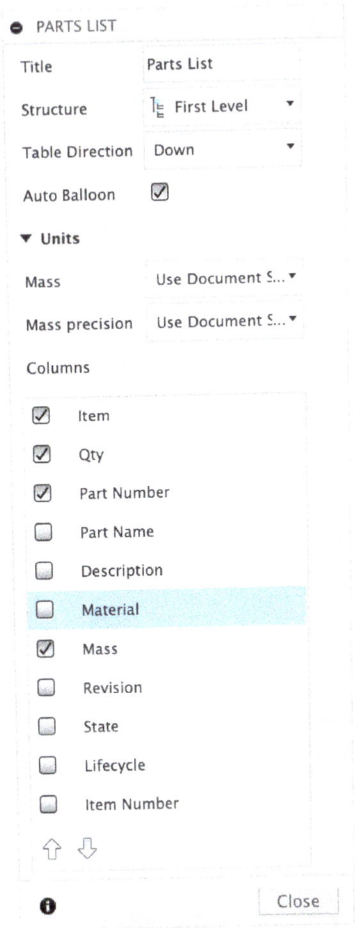

PARTS LIST			
ITEM	QTY	PART NUMBER	MASS
1	1	BODY	365.933 G
2	1	PLATE	95.335 G
3	1	SEAL	114.009 G
4	1	PISTON	116.636 G
5	8	SCREW	2.035 G
6	1	BEARING	3.383 G

Renumber

The **Renumber** command is used to rearrange the balloon or bend identifier numbering. On the **Drawing** toolbar, click **Tables > Renumber**. Next, select the balloon to be renumbered from the drawing sheet. Click **OK** to change the balloon number.

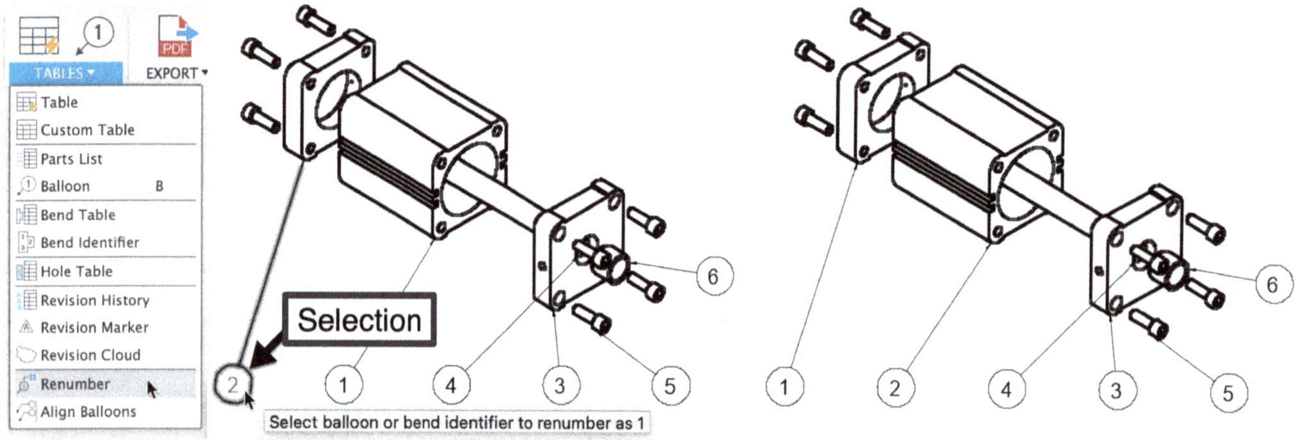

Align Balloons

This command is used to align the balloons along a straight line. On the **Drawing** toolbar, click **Tables > Align Balloons**. Next, select the balloons to be aligned. You can select all balloons by dragging a selection window across them. Next, press ENTER to accept the selection. Specify the start point of the alignment line. Move the pointer and notice that the spacing between the balloons is modified. Click to specify the end point of the alignment line.

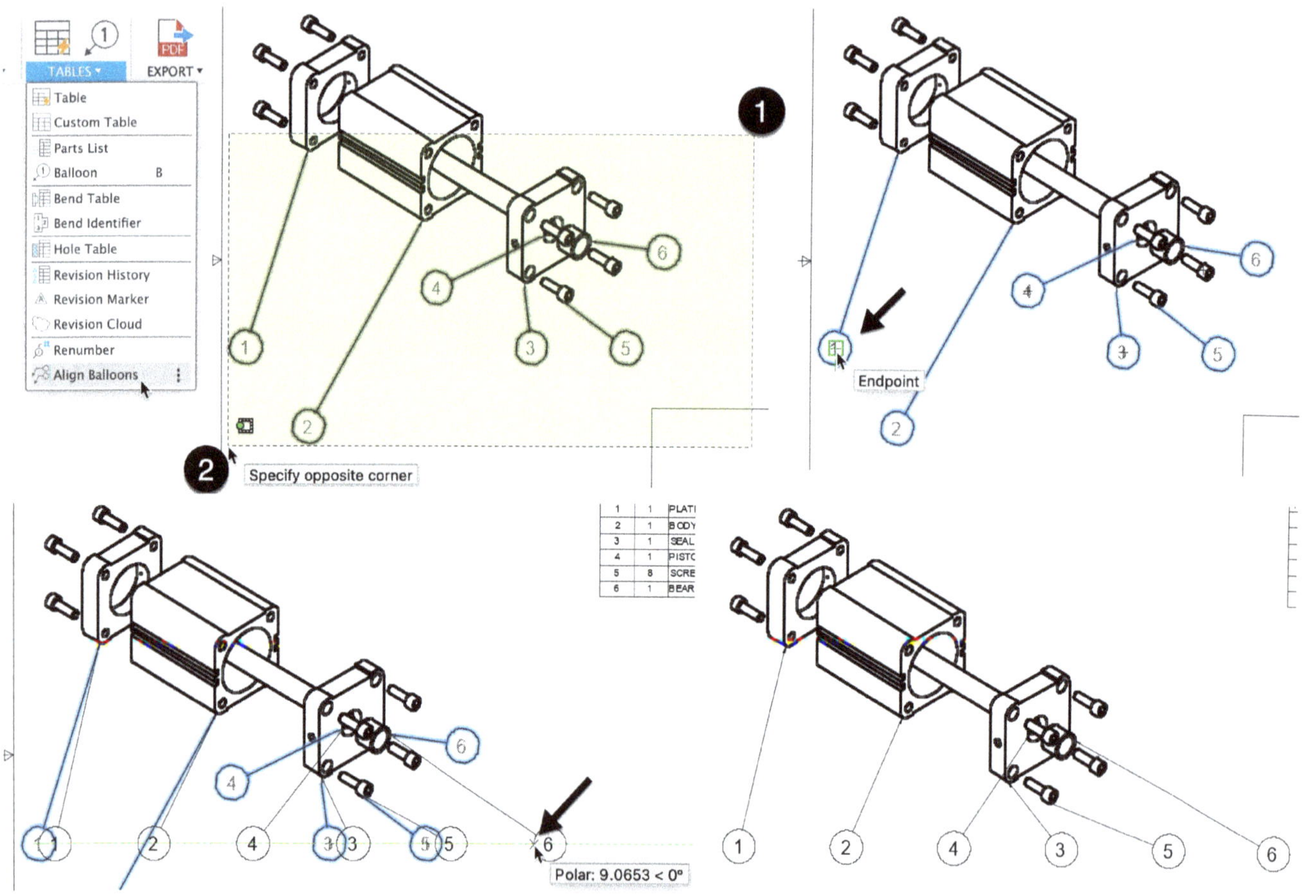

Center Marks and Centerlines

Centerlines and Centermarks are used in engineering drawings to denote hole centers and lines. To add center marks to the drawing, activate the **Center Mark** command (click **Geometry > Center Mark** on the **Drawing** toolbar) and click on the hole circles. Right click and select **OK**.

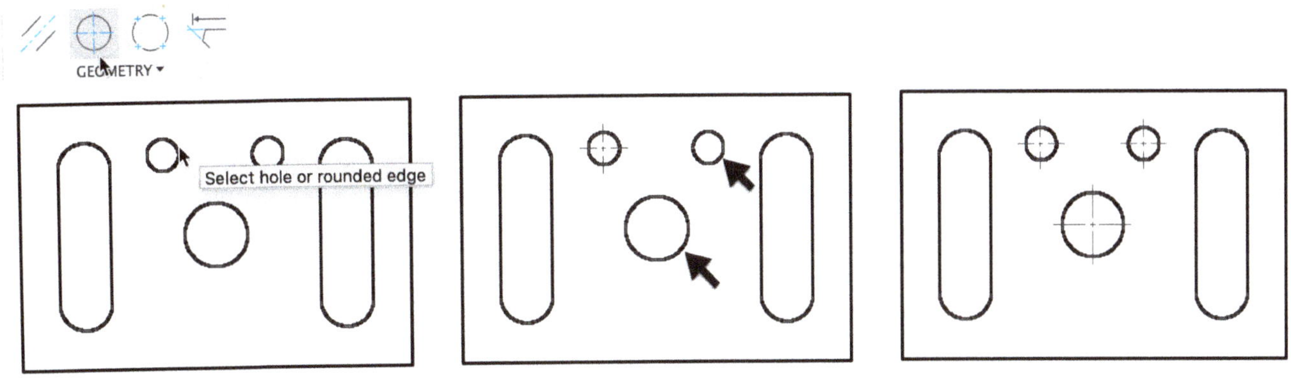

Centerline

The **Centerline** command is used to create a centerline bisecting two lines. This command is very helpful while creating a centerline on the section view or projected views. On the **Drawing** toolbar, click **Geometry > Centerline**, and then click on two edges of the drawing view. A centerline will be created between the two lines.

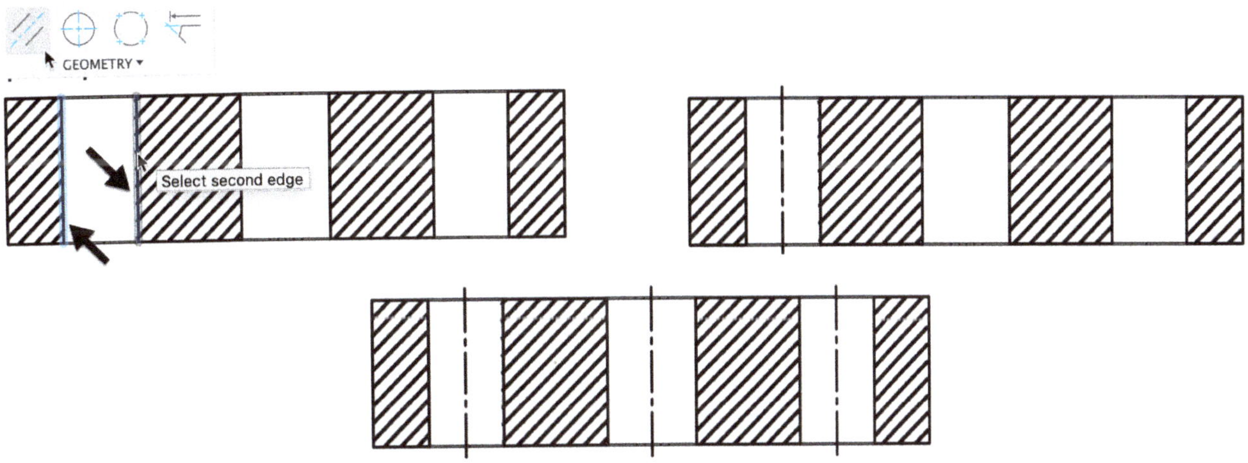

Center Mark Pattern

The **Center Mark Pattern** command (click **Geometry > Center Mark Pattern** on the **Drawing** toolbar) allows you to add center marks to the holes arranged in a circular fashion. Activate this command and select any one of the holes of the circular pattern. Check the **Auto-complete** option on the **Center Mark Pattern** dialog; a center mark pattern is created passing through the selected holes. Uncheck the **Full PCD** option if you want to create a partial center mark pattern. Check the **Center Mark** option if there is a circle at the center of the circular pattern. Next, click **OK** on the **Center Mark Pattern** dialog to complete the center mark pattern.

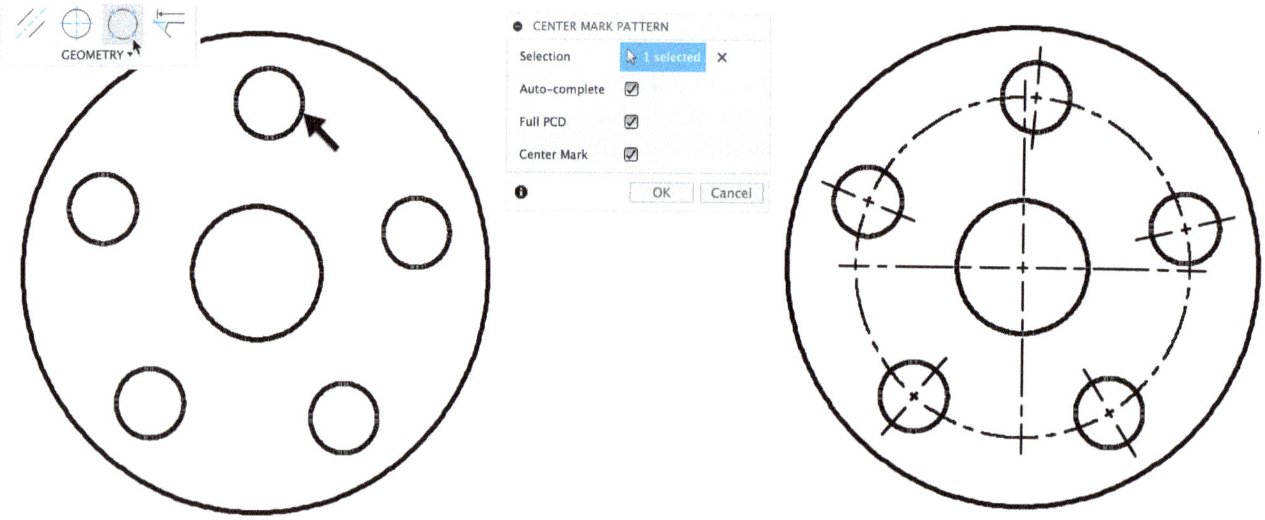

You can also use the **Center Mark Pattern** command to create centrelines for slots. To do this, uncheck the **Auto Complete** option, and then select the end caps of the slots. Next, click **OK** on the **Center Mark Pattern** dialog.

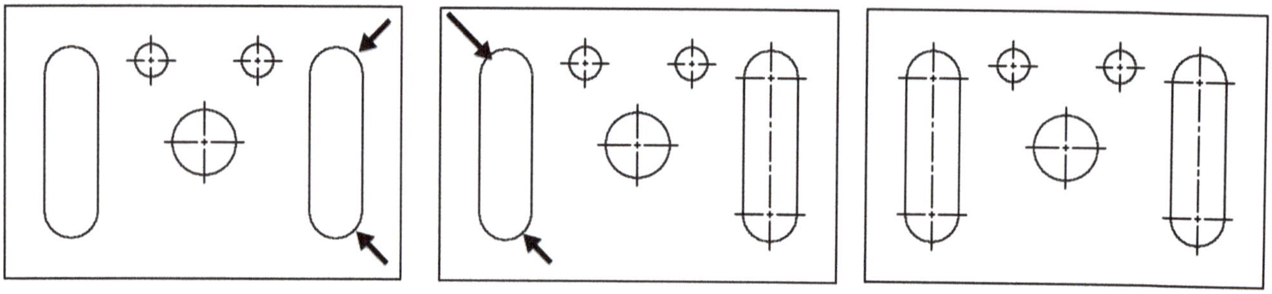

Dimensions

If you want to add dimensions, which are necessary to manufacture a part, activate the **Dimension** command and add them to the view (Learn about the **Dimension** command in **Chapter 2: Sketch Techniques**).

Baseline Dimension

The **Baseline Dimension** command allows you to create and arrange a dimension very quickly. Activate this command (on the **Drawing** toolbar, click **Dimension > Baseline Dimension** ), and then select the first extension line of a dimension from the drawing sheet; the origin of the baseline dimension is defined. Next, select a point from the drawing view; a new dimension is created between the origin and the selected point. Likewise, select the other points from the drawing view. Next, right click and select **OK**.

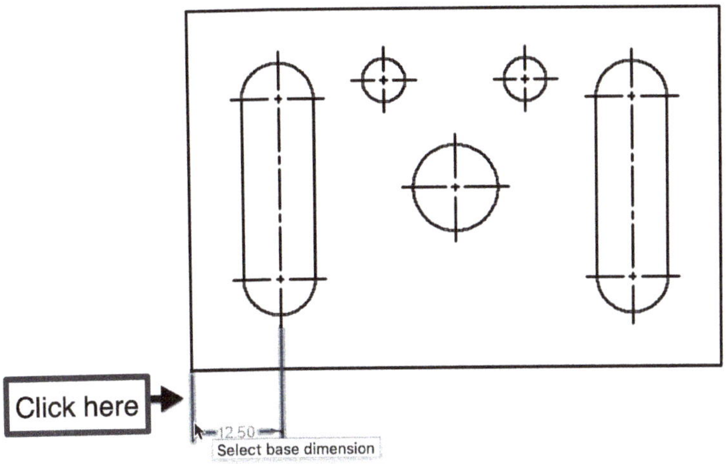

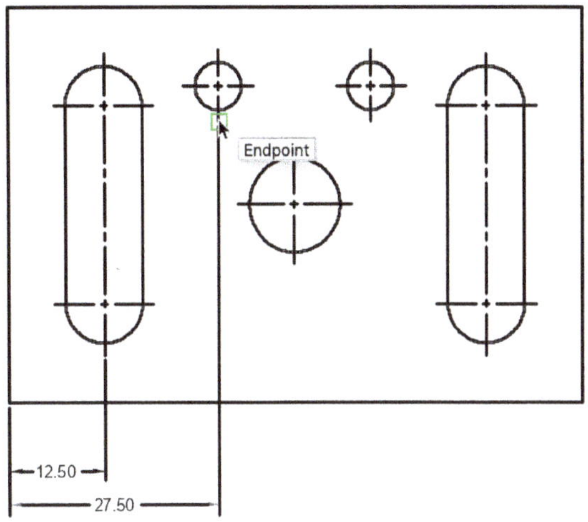

Chain Dimensions

This command creates chained dimensions. On the toolbar, click **Dimensions > Chain Dimension**. Next, select the extension line of the base dimension; a chained dimension is attached to the pointer. Move the pointer and specify the endpoint of the dimension; another dimension is attached to the pointer. Specify the endpoint of the dimension. Next, right click and select **OK** to complete the chain of dimensions.

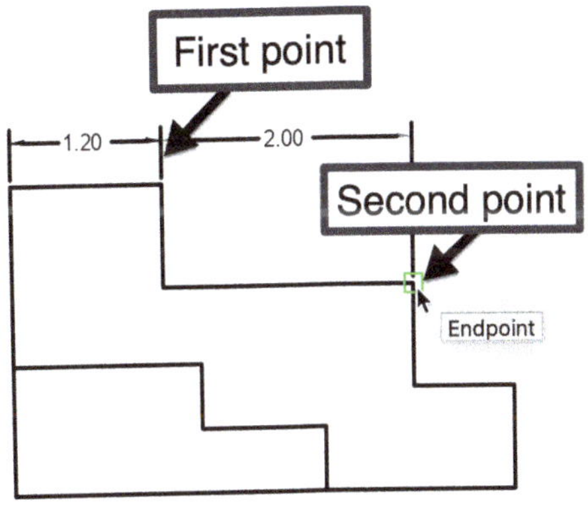

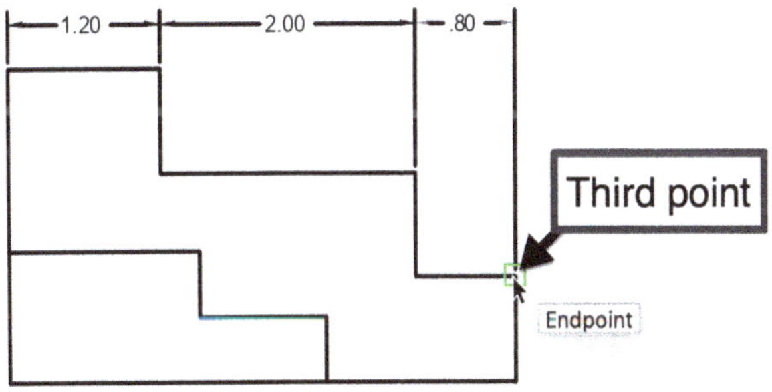

Ordinate Dimensions

Ordinate dimensions are another type of dimension that can be added to a drawing. To create them, activate the **Ordinate Dimension** command (click **Dimensions > Ordinate Dimensions** on the toolbar), and then select a point from the drawing view. Next, move the pointer in the horizontal or vertical direction and click to specify the location of the zero reference.

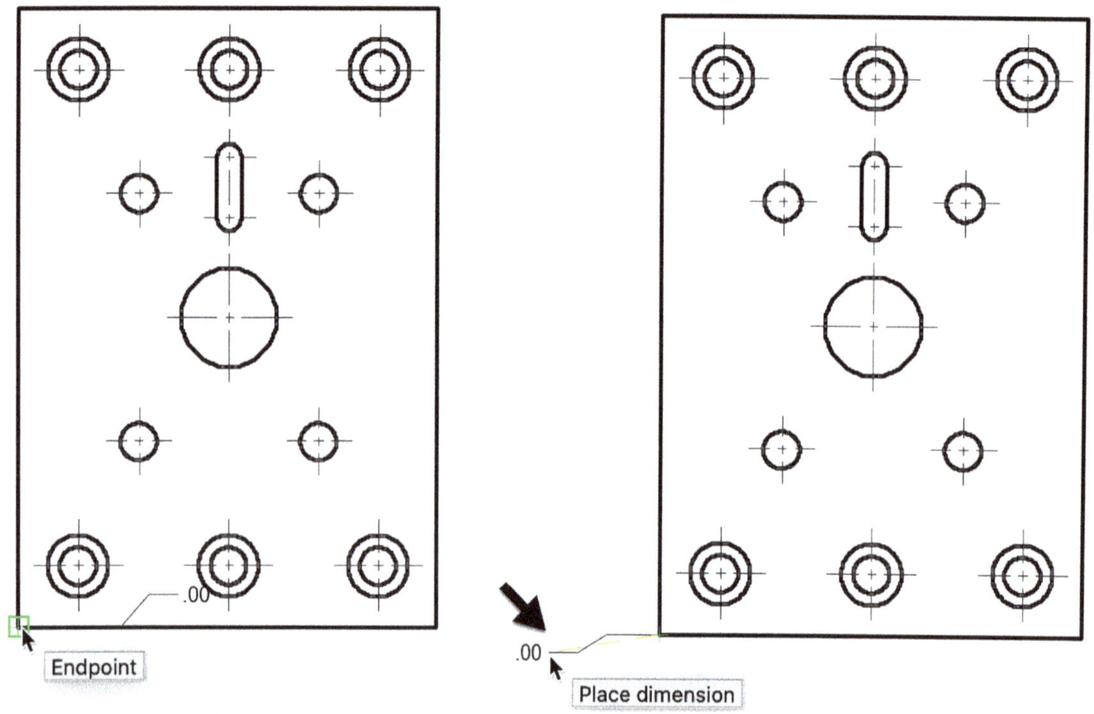

Select the point to be dimensioned, move the pointer in the direction of the zero reference, and then click to create the ordinate dimension. Likewise, add ordinate dimensions to other points. Next, right click and select **OK** after you have finished creating the ordinate dimensions.

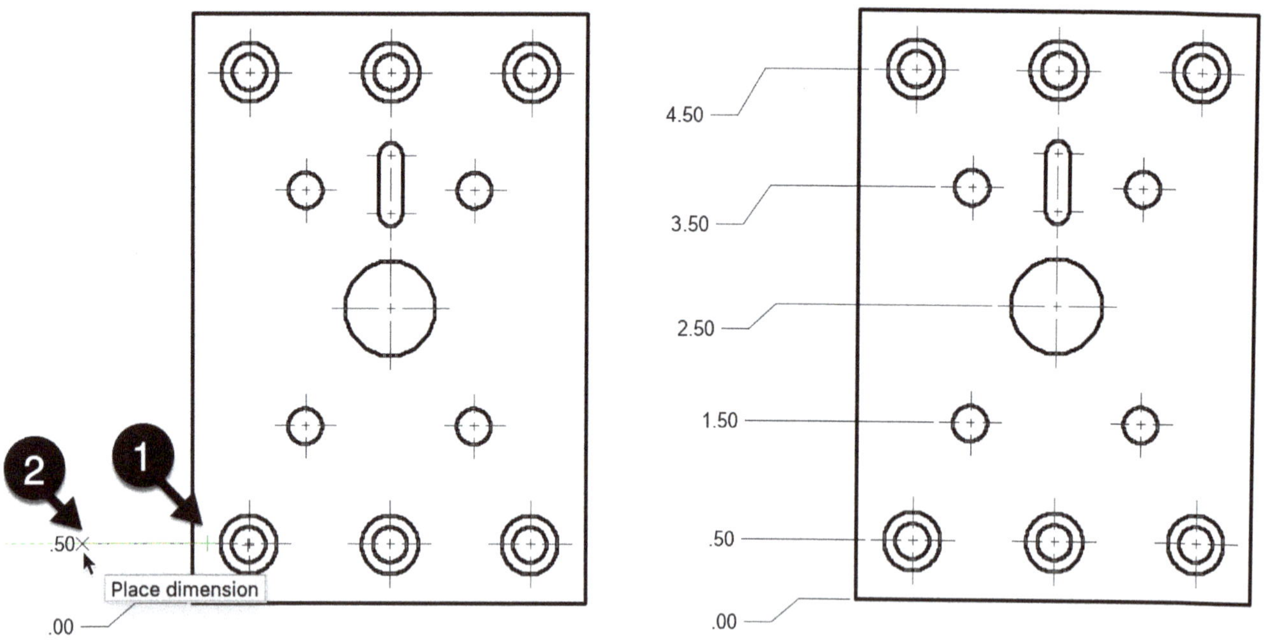

Changing the Origin

You can change the origin of the ordinate dimensions even after creating it. To do this, click on the origin of the ordinate dimension. Next, select the start point of the origin, move the pointer, and select the new origin point.

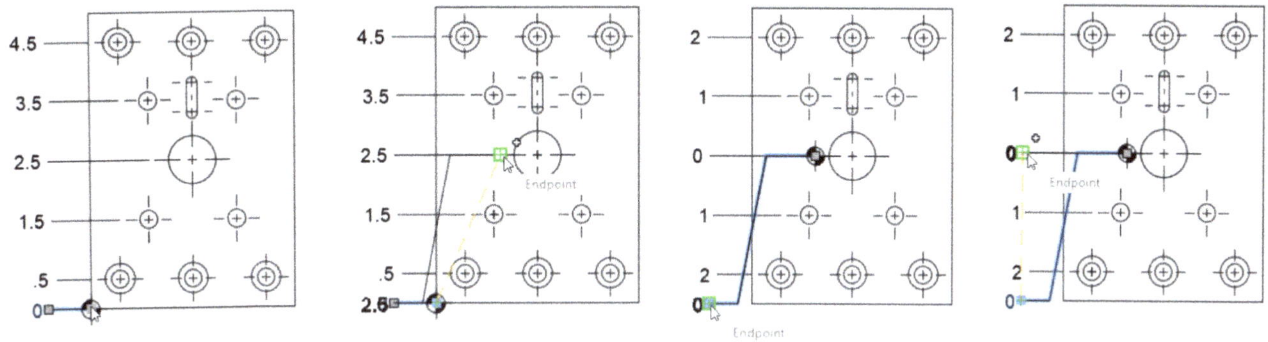

Arrange Dimensions

The **Arrange Dimensions** command is used to adjust the space between the dimensions. Click **Drawing > Dimensions > Arrange Dimensions** on the toolbar and select the **Type > Stack** from the **Arrange Dimensions** dialog. Next, select the base dimension from the drawing view. Select the dimensions to move from the base dimension. Type-in a value in the **Spacing** box and click **OK**; the dimensions will be adjusted with respect to the base dimension.

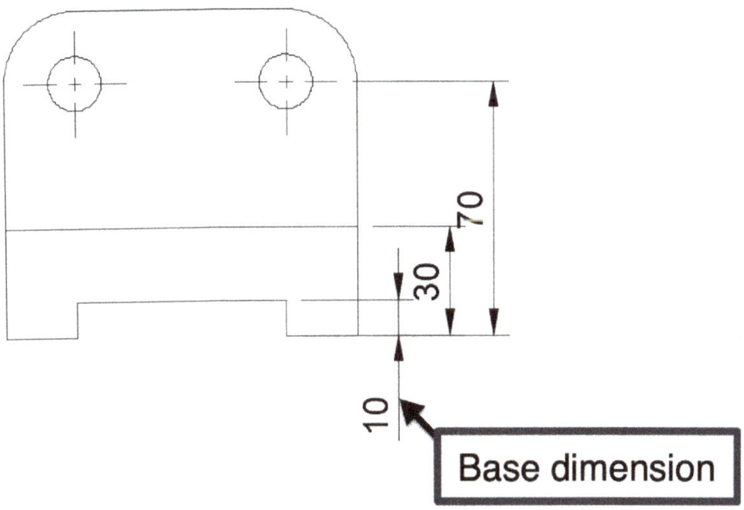

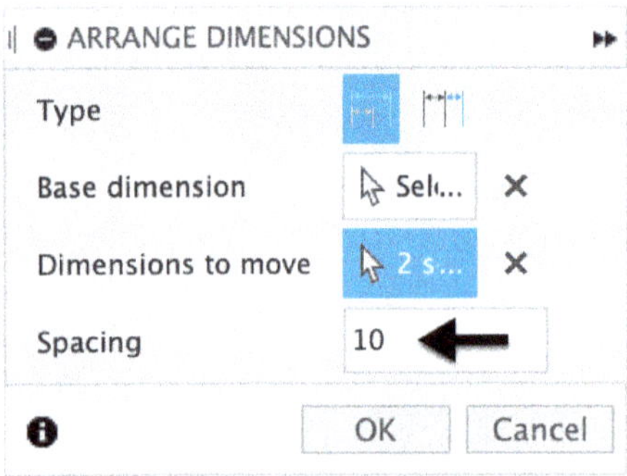

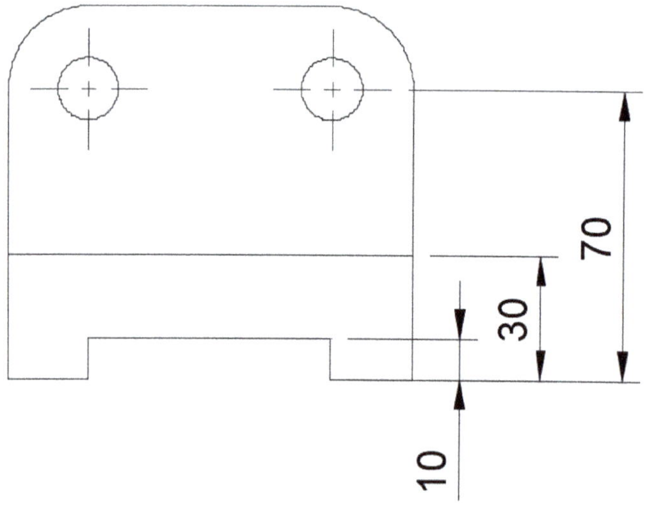

Activate the **Arrange Dimensions** command and select **Type > Aligned** . Next, select the base dimension from the drawing view. Select the dimensions to move from the drawing view and click **OK**; the dimensions are aligned to the base dimension.

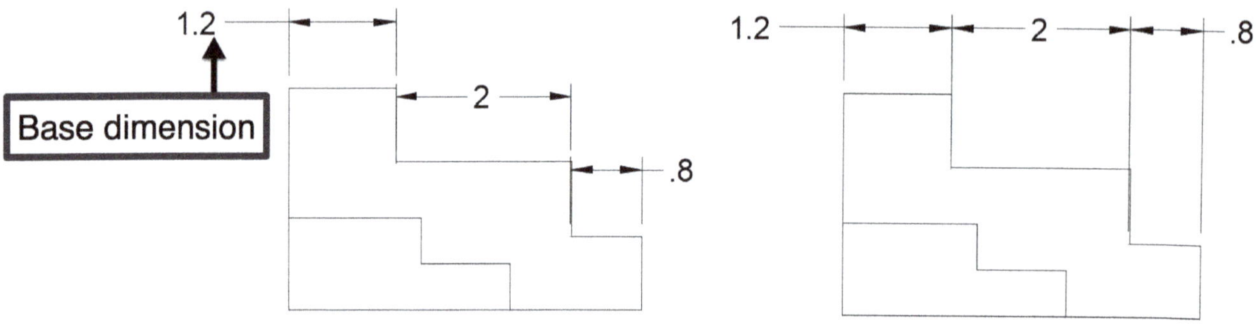

Dimension Break

This command adds or removes break from a dimension, extension, and leader lines. Click **Drawing > Dimensions > Dimension Break** 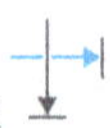 on the toolbar. Select the dimension intersecting with another object or dimension. Next, select **Operation > Add break** from the **Dimension Break** dialog. Click **OK** to add break to the dimension.

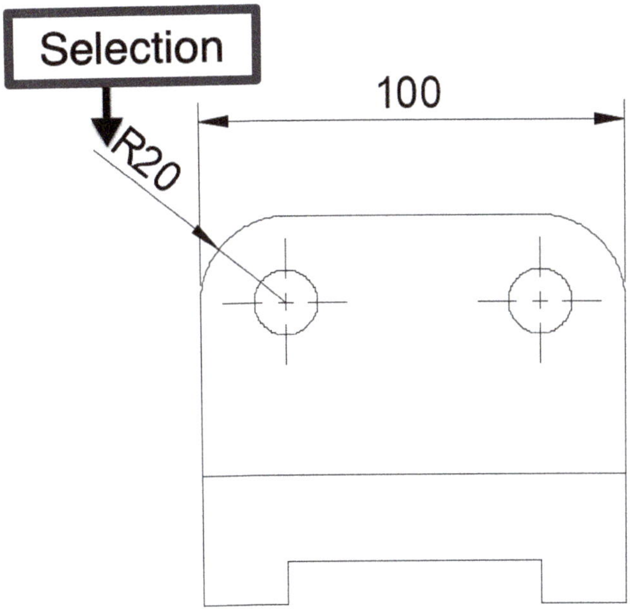

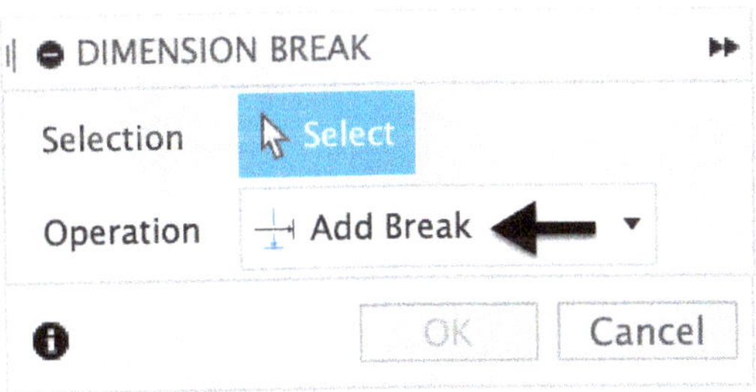

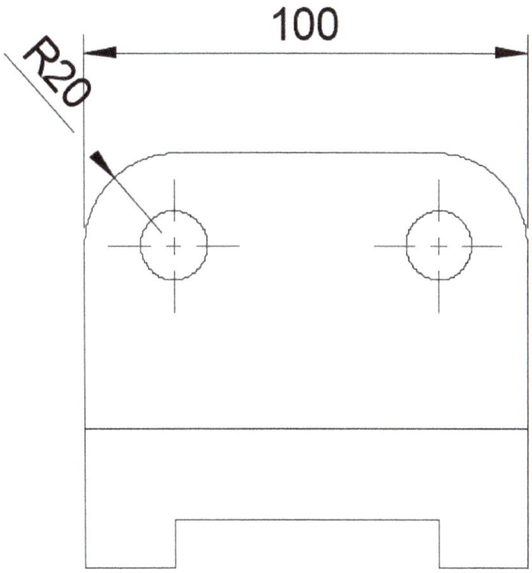

To remove a break from a dimension, activate the **Dimension Break** command and select the dimension from which the break is to be removed. Next, select **Operation > Remove Break** from the **Dimension Break** dialog and click **OK**.

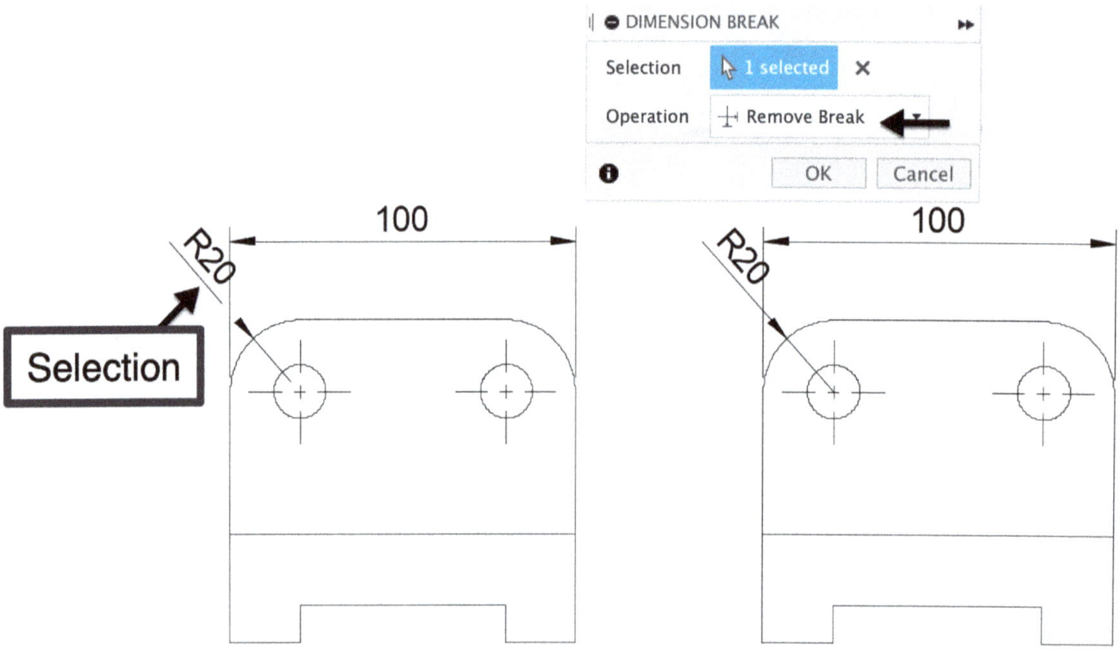

Flip Arrows

To flip arrows, use the **Flip Arrows** command. It lets you change the direction of arrowheads in dimensions. Simply select a dimension object and switch the arrowhead to the other side of the dimension line. This ensures clear and professional-looking drawings.

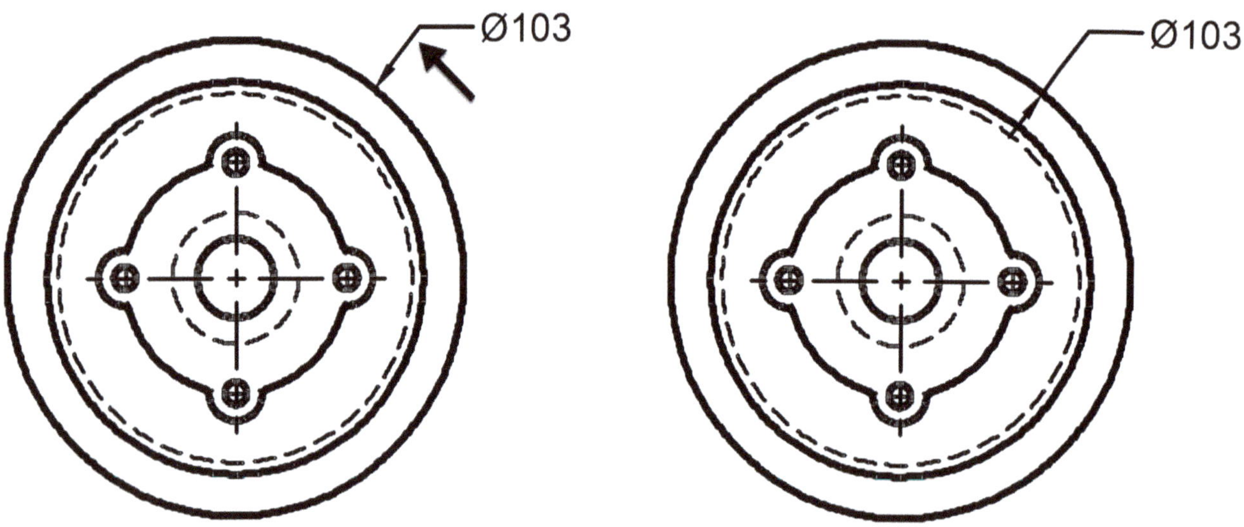

Arc Length Dimension

This command dimensions the total or partial length of an arc. Click **Drawing > Dimensions > Arc Length Dimension** on the ribbon. Select an arc from the drawing.

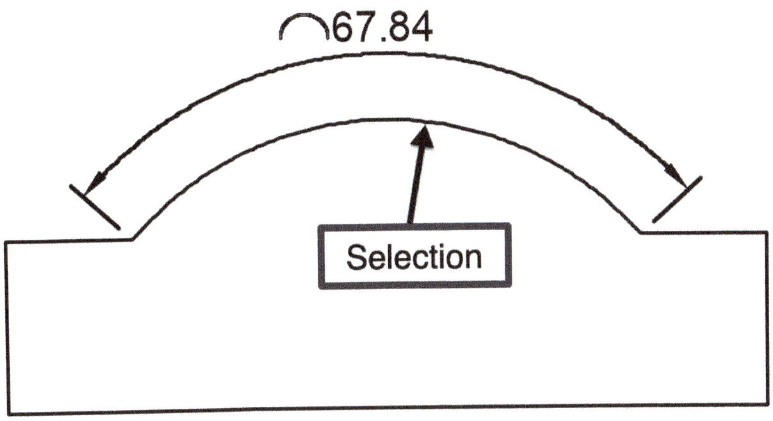

If you want to dimension only a partial length of an arc, then activate the **Arc Length Dimension** and select the arc to be dimension. Next, right click and select **Partial** option from the Marking menu. Select the two points on the arc. Move the pointer and click to position the dimension.

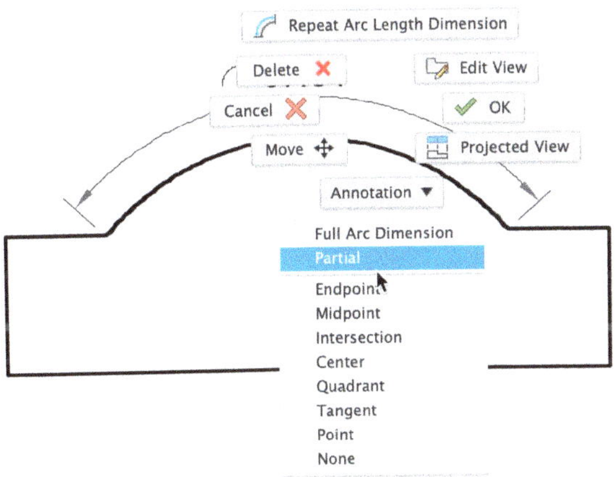

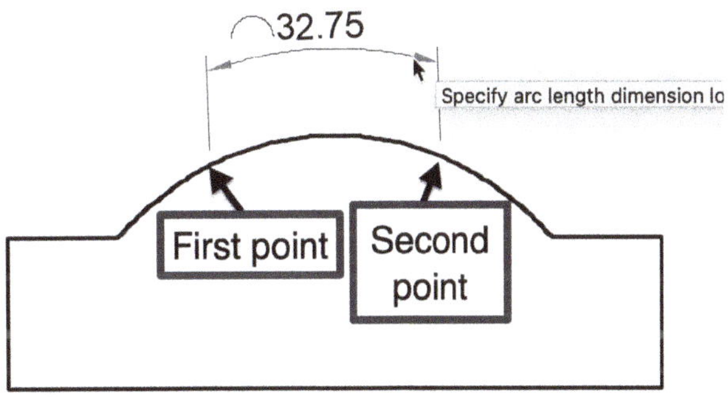

Jogged Radial Dimension

This command creates a jogged radial dimensions. A jogged radial dimension is created when it is not possible to show the center of an arc or circle. To add a jogged radial dimension, click **Drawing > Dimensions > Jogged Radial Dimension** on the toolbar. First, click on the arc or circle you want to dimension. Then, specify a new center point and place the dimension and jog line in your drawing.

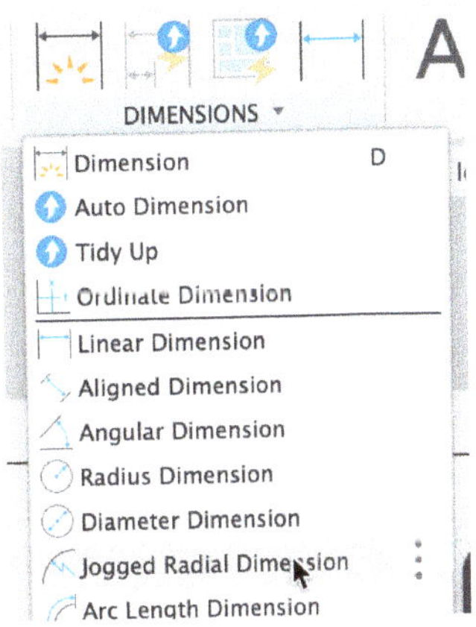

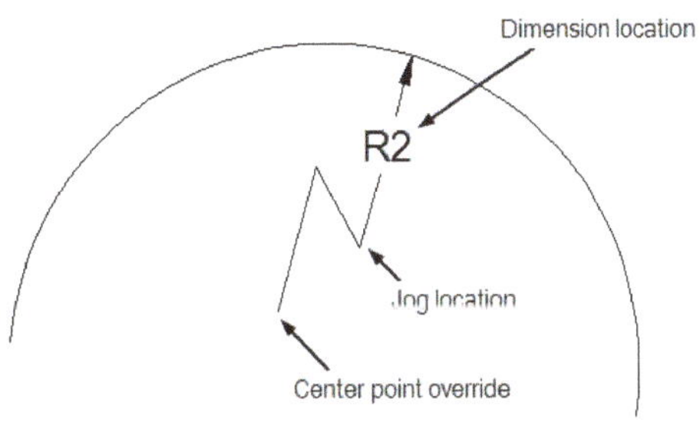

Adding Inspection Dimension

Autodesk Fusion 360 allows you to add an inspection dimension. The inspection dimension describes how frequently the dimension should be checked during the inspection process to ensure the quality of the component. Click **Drawing > Dimensions > Dimension** on the toolbar and add a dimension to the drawing view. Next, double-click on the newly added dimension; the **Dimension** dialog appears. Check the **Inspection** option on the **Dimension** dialog. Next, select the shape of the frame from the **Frame** drop-down. Enter the inspection rate in the **Rate** box. 100 means that the value will be checked every time during the inspection process. 50 means half the time. If required, enter the inspection label in the **Label** box. Next, click **Close**.

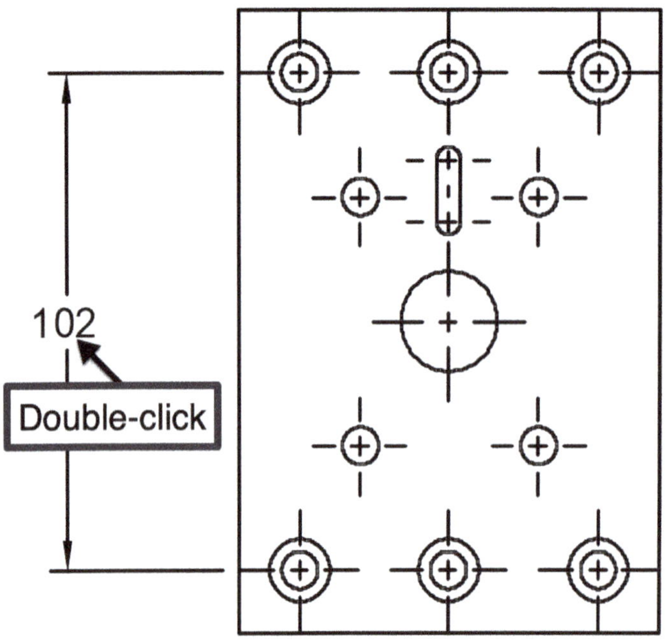

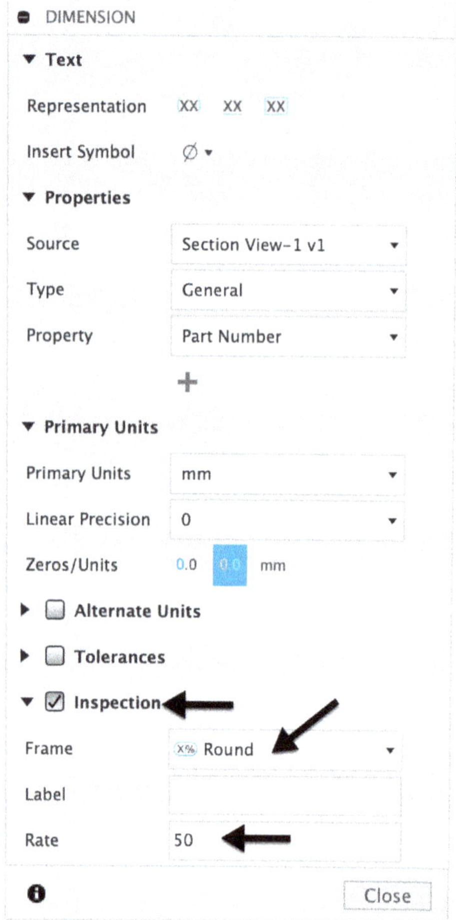

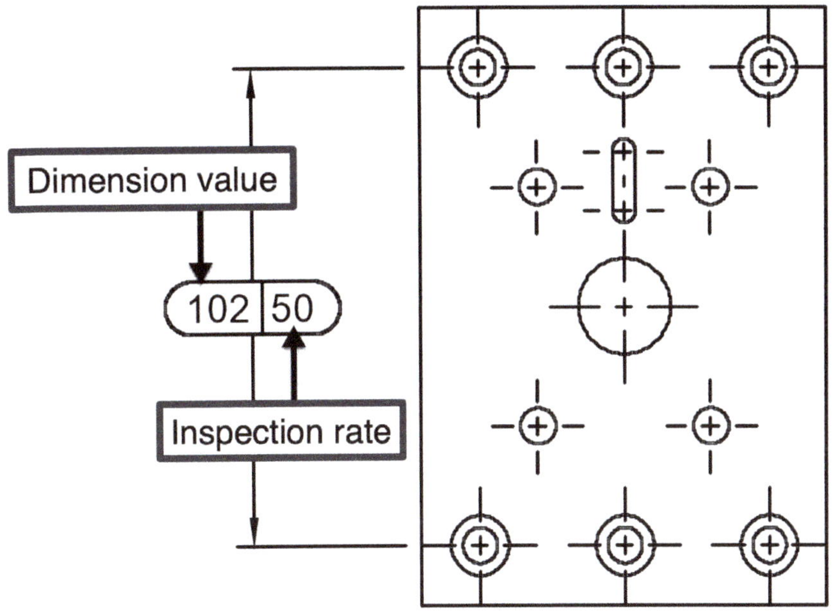

Edge Extension

The **Edge Extension** command allows you to create an associative geometry to locate the apparent intersection of two non-parallel edges. On the **Drawing** toolbar, click **Geometry > Edge Extension**. Next, select two non-parallel edges from the drawing view; the edge extension is added to the view. Next, activate the **Dimension** command and select the intersection point of the edge extension. Select the left corner point of the drawing view. Move the pointer downward and click to position the dimension.

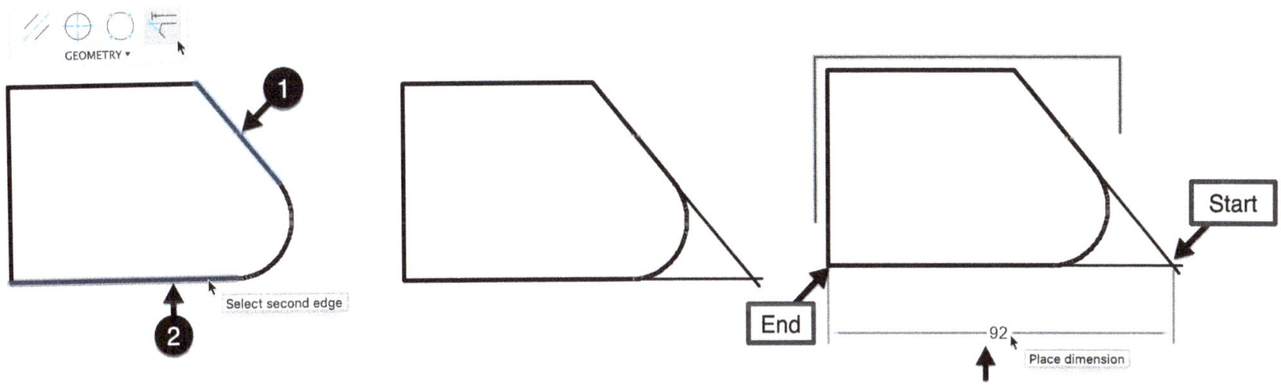

In the Browser window, right-click on the component used for creating the drawing view, and then select **Open**. Next, right-click on the sketch used to create the geometry, and then select **Edit Sketch**. Change the angle between the two non-parallel edges, and then click **Finish Sketch**. Click **Save** on the Application Bar.

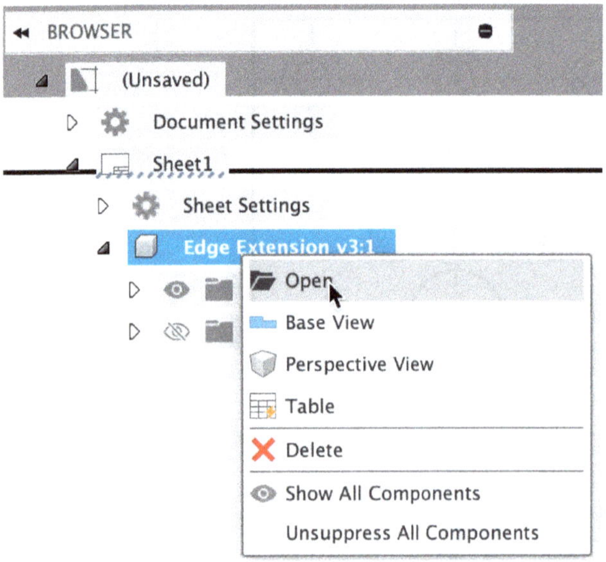

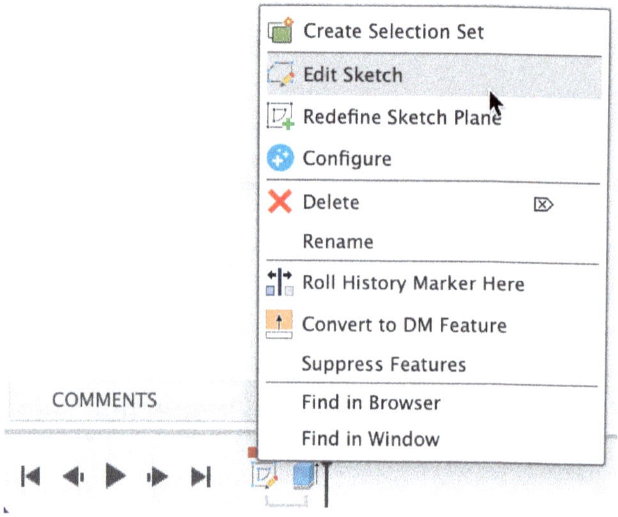

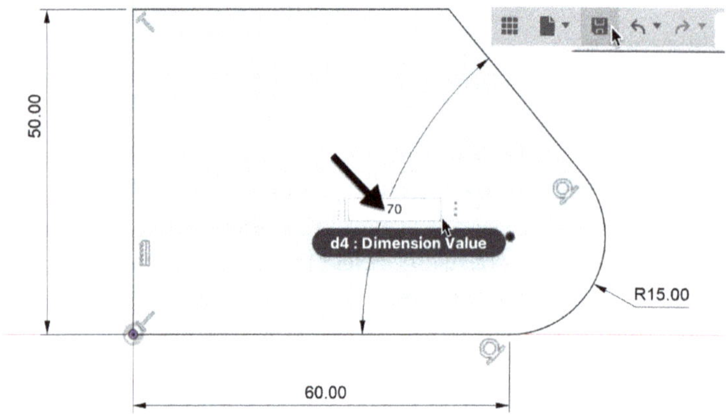

Click the **Reference** icon on the Application Bar; the drawing view and dimension between the apparent intersection and the corner point is updated.

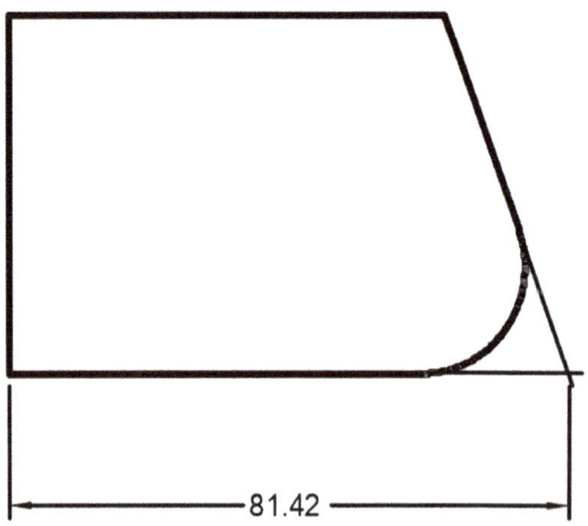

Adding Hole callouts

If you want to add a hole callout, then activate the **Hole and Thread Callout** command (on the toolbar, click **Text > Hole and Thread Callout**) and select the hole. Next, move the pointer diagonally and click to specify the location of the hole callout. Click **OK** on the **Note** dialog.

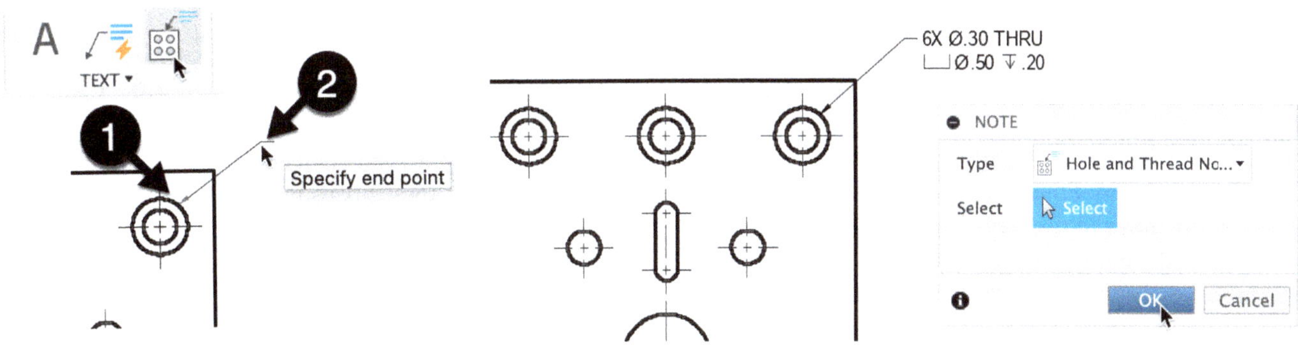

Text

Text is an important part of a drawing. You add text to provide additional details, which cannot be done using dimensions and annotations. To add a text, activate the **Text** command (click **Text > Text** on the toolbar). Next, specify the corners of the text box; the Text dialog appears. On the **Text** dialog, select the font and height. Type text in the text box.

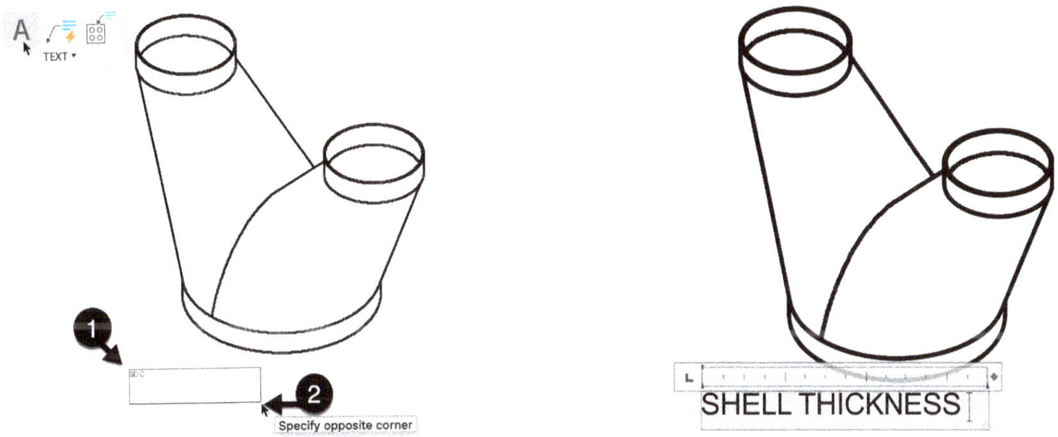

You can also insert a property into the text box. To do this, select the type of property (**General**, **Physical**, or **Parameter**) from the **Type** drop-down. Next, select the property to be inserted from the **Property** drop-down. Click the **Insert Property** icon and click the **Close** button.

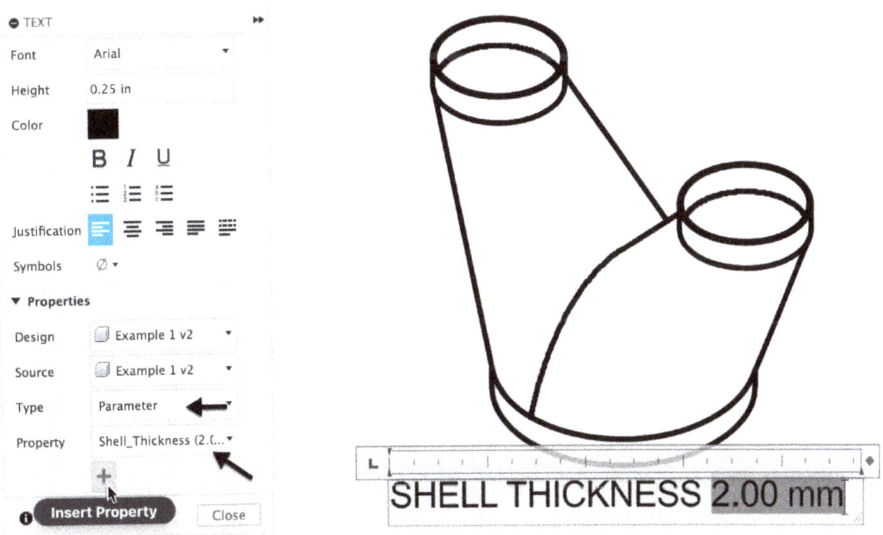

Hole Table

The **Hole Table** command creates a table showing the X, Y, and Z coordinates of the hole, sizes, and other properties. Activate the **Hole Table** command (on the toolbar, click **Drawing** tab > **Tables** panel > **Hole Table** ). On the **Table** dialog, type the title of the hole table in the **Title** box. Next, select an option from the **Arrange** drop-down. The **by Position** option arranges the holes in the table based on their position. The **by Size** option arranges the holes in the table based on their size. Next, specify the style of the origin point, and then click on the point of the drawing view to define the origin of the coordinate system. Click on the drawing sheet to place the hole table.

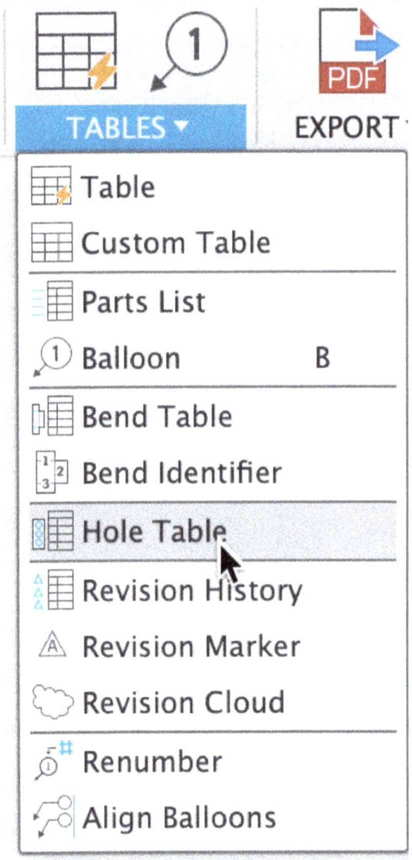

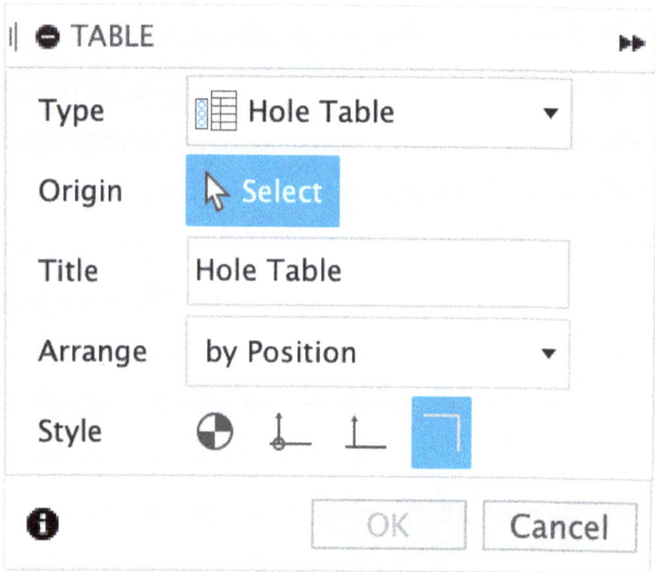

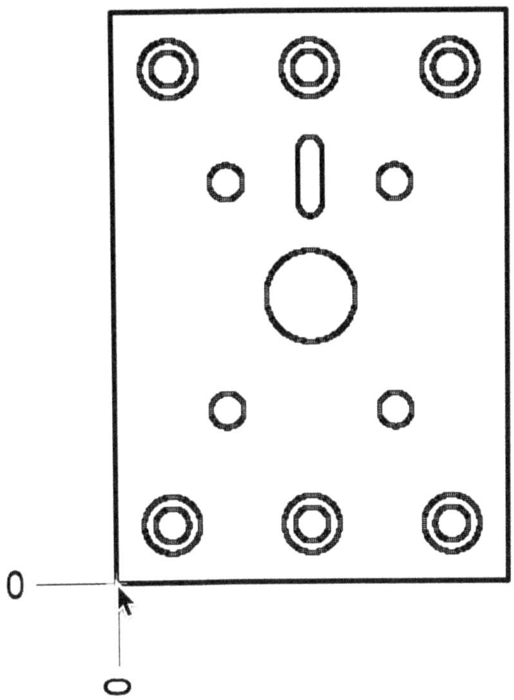

HOLE TABLE			
HOLE	X DIM	Y DIM	DESCRIPTION
A1	.5	.5	Ø.3 THRU ⌴Ø.5 ↧.2
A2	.5	4.5	Ø.3 THRU ⌴Ø.5 ↧.2
A3	1.75	.5	Ø.3 THRU ⌴Ø.5 ↧.2
A4	1.75	4.5	Ø.3 THRU ⌴Ø.5 ↧.2
A5	3	.5	Ø.3 THRU ⌴Ø.5 ↧.2
A6	3	4.5	Ø.3 THRU ⌴Ø.5 ↧.2
B1	1	1.5	Ø.3 THRU
B2	1	3.5	Ø.3 THRU
B3	2.5	1.5	Ø.3 THRU
B4	2.5	3.5	Ø.3 THRU
C1	1.75	2.5	Ø.8 THRU

Adding Dimensional Tolerances

During the manufacturing process, the accuracy of a part is an important factor. However, it is impossible to manufacture a part with the exact dimensions. Therefore, while applying dimensions to a drawing, we provide some dimensional tolerances, which lie within acceptable limits. The following example shows you to add dimensional tolerances in Fusion 360. Create a drawing view and add a dimension to it, as shown. Next, double-click on the dimension; the Dimension dialog appears. Check the **Tolerances** option on the **Dimension** and select **Type > Deviation.** Next, type 0.05 in the **Upper Tolerance** and **Lower Tolerance** boxes, respectively. Click **Close** on the **Dimension** dialog; the tolerances are added to the dimension.

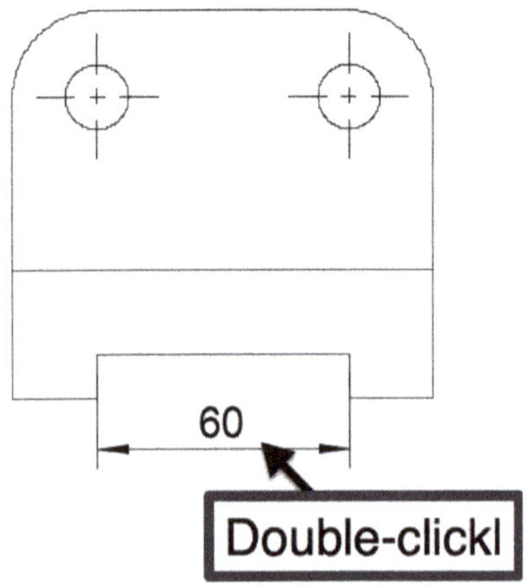

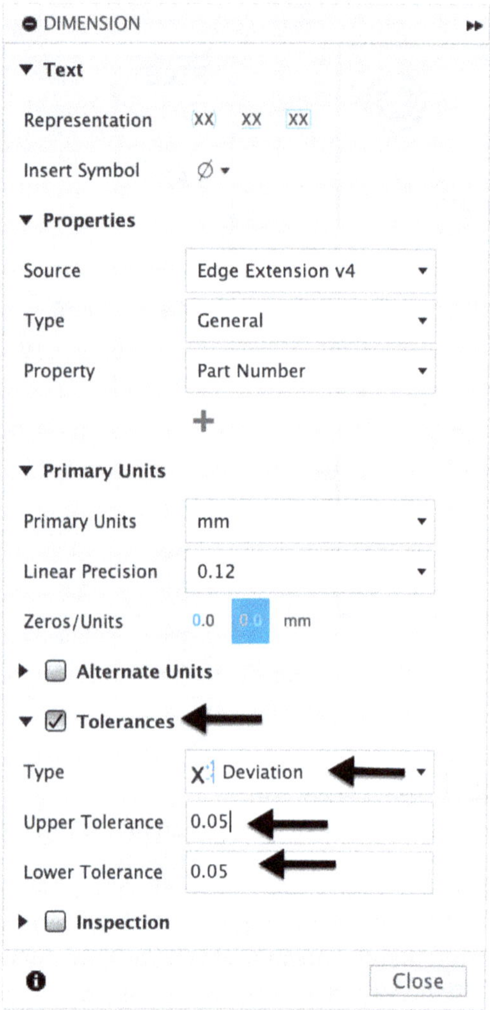

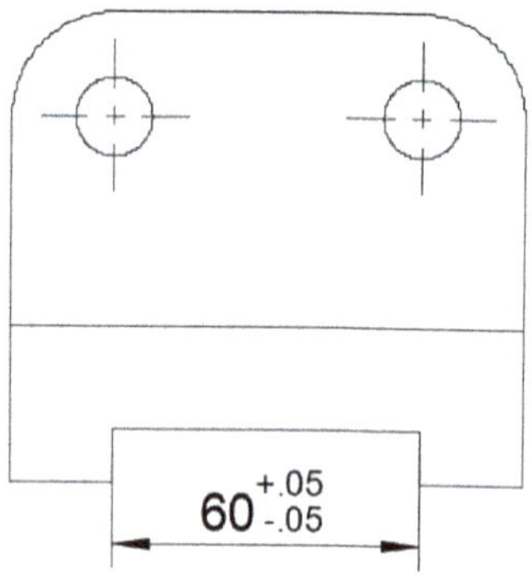

Geometric Dimensioning and Tolerancing

Earlier, you have learned how to apply tolerance to the size (dimensions) of a component. However, the dimensional tolerances are not sufficient for manufacturing a component. You must give tolerance values to its shape, orientation, and position as well. The following figure shows a note which is used to explain the tolerance value given to the shape of the object.

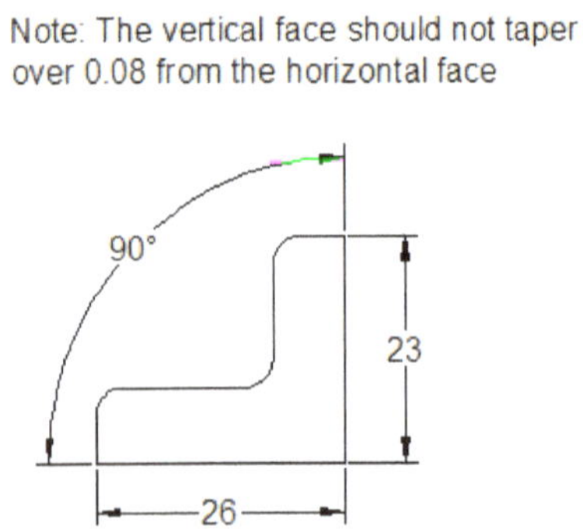

Drawings

Providing a note in a drawing may be confusing. To avoid this, we use Geometric Dimensioning and Tolerancing (GD&T) symbols to specify the tolerance values to shape, orientation, and position of a component. The following figure shows the same example represented by using the GD&T symbols. In this figure, the vertical face to which the tolerance frame is connected must be within two parallel planes 0.08 apart and perpendicular to the datum reference (horizontal plane).

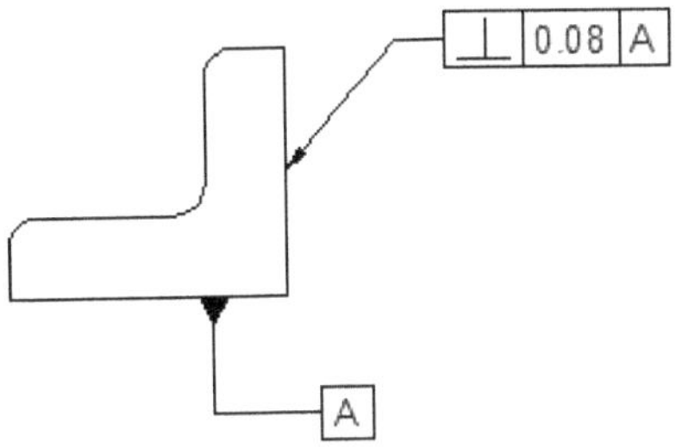

The Geometric Tolerancing symbols that can be used to interpret the geometric conditions are given in the table below.

Purpose		**Symbol**
To represent the shape of a single feature.	Straightness	⏤
	Flatness	⏥
	Cylindricity	⌭
	Circularity	○
	Profile of a surface	⌓
	Profile of a line	⌒
To represent the orientation of a feature with respect to another feature.	Parallelism	//
	Perpendicularity	⊥

	Angularity	∠
To represent the position of a feature with respect to another feature.	Position	⌖
	Concentricity and coaxiality	◎
	Run-out	↗
	Total Run-out	⌰
	Symmetry	⌯

Create the drawing view and add dimensions to it, as shown below. Next, click **Drawing > Symbols > Datum Identifier**  on the toolbar.

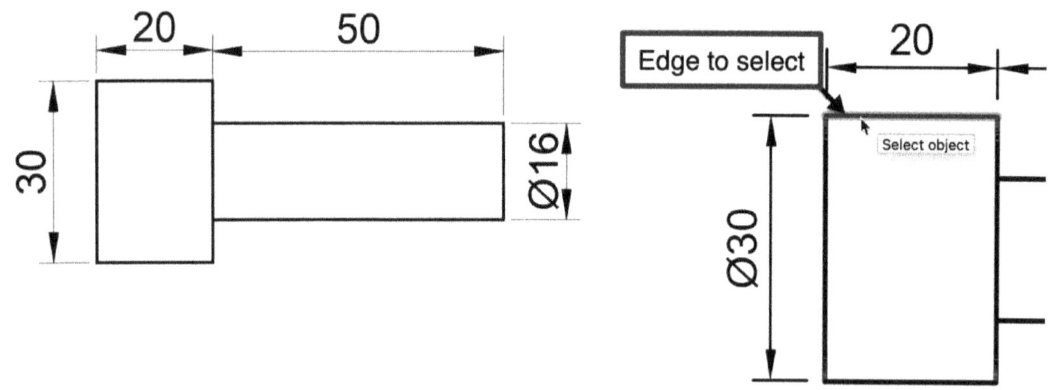

Move the pointer toward left and click. Next, move the pointer toward right and click. Move the pointer upward and click the green check. Type **A** in the **Identifier** box and click **OK**.

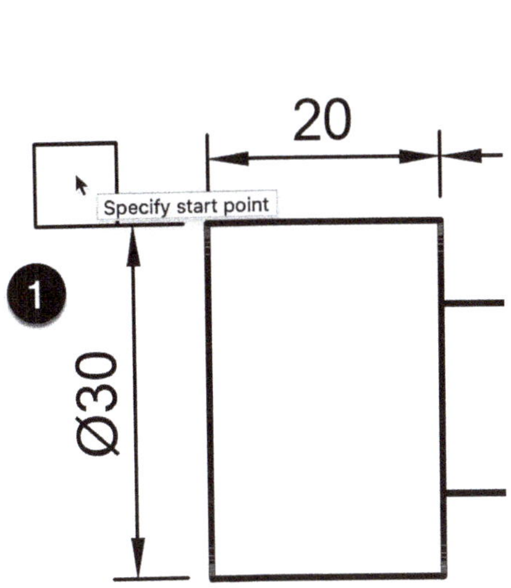

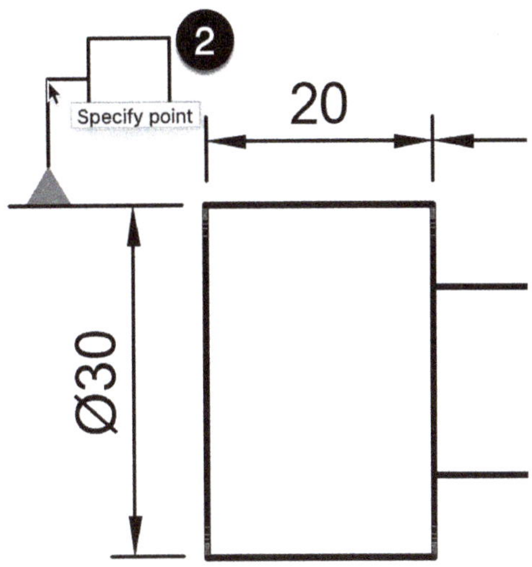

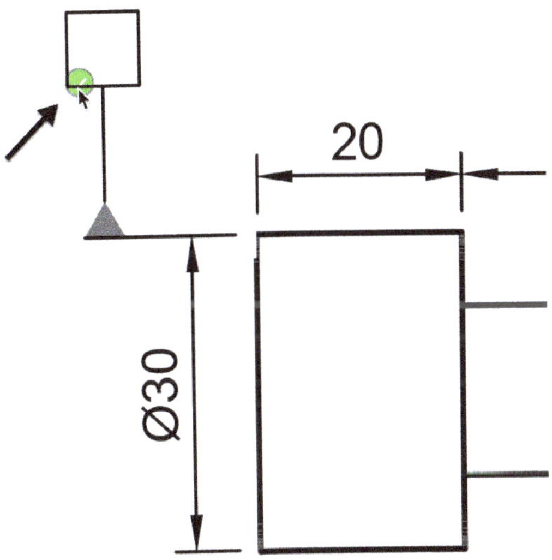

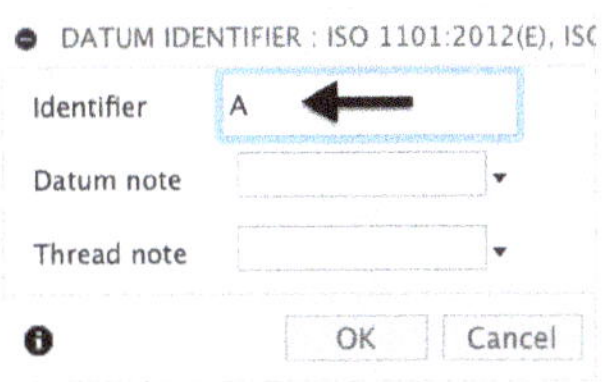

Click **Drawing > Symbols > Feature Control Frame** 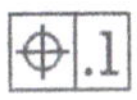 on the toolbar. Select the bottom horizontal edge of the drawing view, as shown. Move the pointer toward left and click. Next, move the pointer downward and click. Click the green check to create the feature control frame.

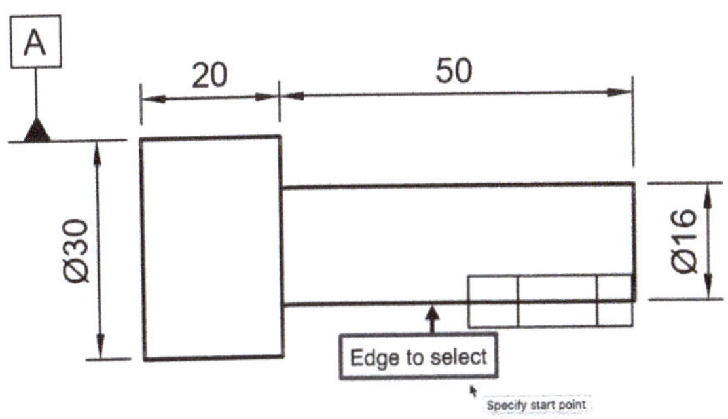

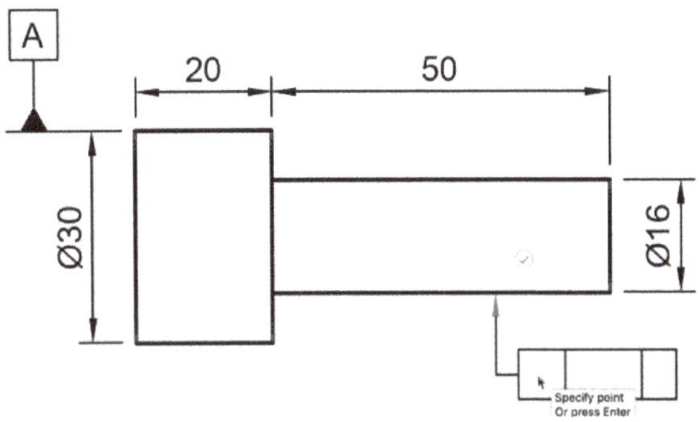

In the **Feature Control Frame** dialog, select **Characteristic > Concentricity**. Click the downward next to the **First tolerance** drop-down and select the Diameter symbol. Next, type **0.1** in the **First tolerance** box. Type **A** in the **First datum** box and click **OK**.

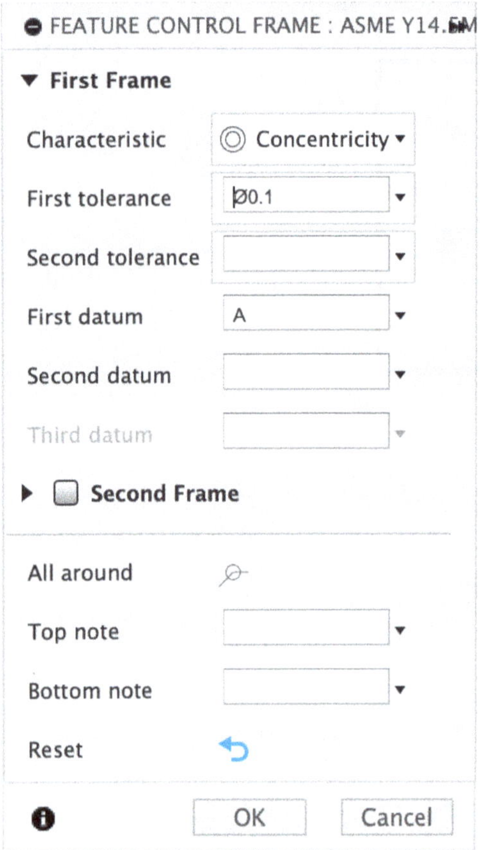

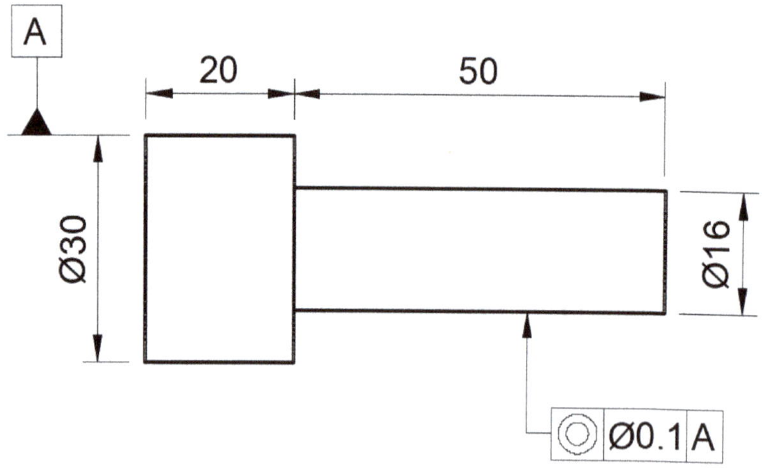

Surface Texture

The **Surface Texture** command allows you to specify the surface texture of a part face. Activate the **Surface Texture** command (on the toolbar, click **Drawing** tab > **Symbols** panel > **Surface Texture**). Next, select a model surface, move the pointer and click to specify the location of the surface texture symbol. Click the green check; the **Surface Texture** dialog appears. Note that the the Surface Texture Symbol aligns itself according to the angle of the attachment edge.

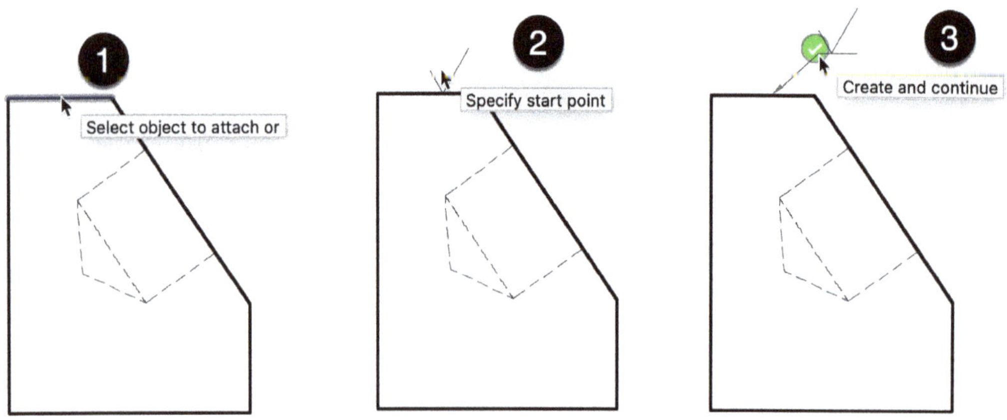

On the **Surface Texture** dialog, specify the **Symbol Type**. There symbol types: **Basic, Material removal required, Material removal prohibited.** Next, specify the **Direction of lay**. There are seven options available in the **Direction of lay** drop-down: **Parallel, Perpendicular, Crossed, Multi-directional, Circular, Radial**, and **Particular** or **Non-directional**.

The **Parallel** = symbol specifies that the surface texture is approximately parallel to the line indicating the surface where the symbol is placed.

The **Perpendicular** ⊥ symbol specifies that the surface texture is approximately perpendicular to the line indicating the surface where the symbol is placed.

The **Crossed** X symbol specifies that the surface texture is angular in both directions to the line indicating the surface where the symbol is placed.

The **Multi-directional** M symbol specifies that the surface texture is in multiple directions.

The **Circular** C symbol specifies that the surface texture approximately circular in relation to the center of the surface where the symbol is placed.

The **Radial** R symbol specifies that the surface texture is approximately radial in relation to the center of the surface where the symbol is placed.

The **Particulate or Non-directional** P symbol specifies that the surface texture is positioned in a particulate, non-directional, or protruding manner.

The illustration below displays three types of symbols for surface finish.

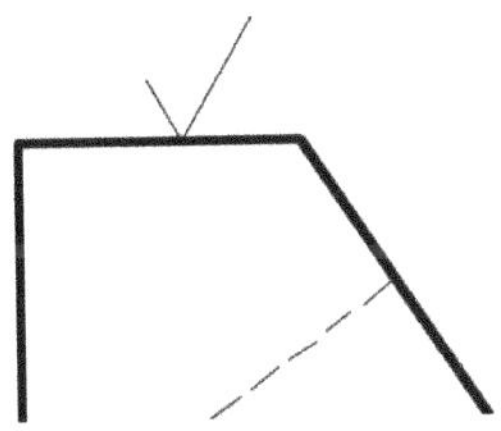

Basic with **None** Direction of lay

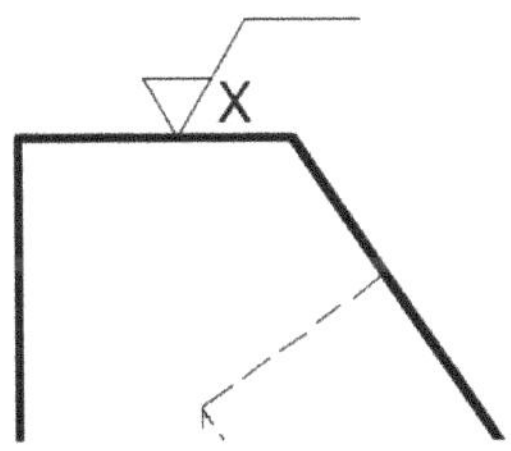

Material removal required with **Crossed** Direction of lay

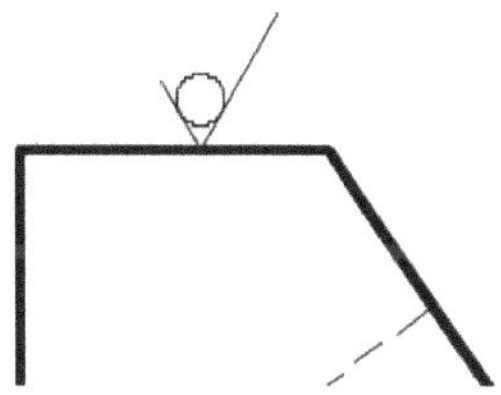

Material removal prohibited

Specify the **Roughness max, Roughness min**, and **Machining allowance** values.

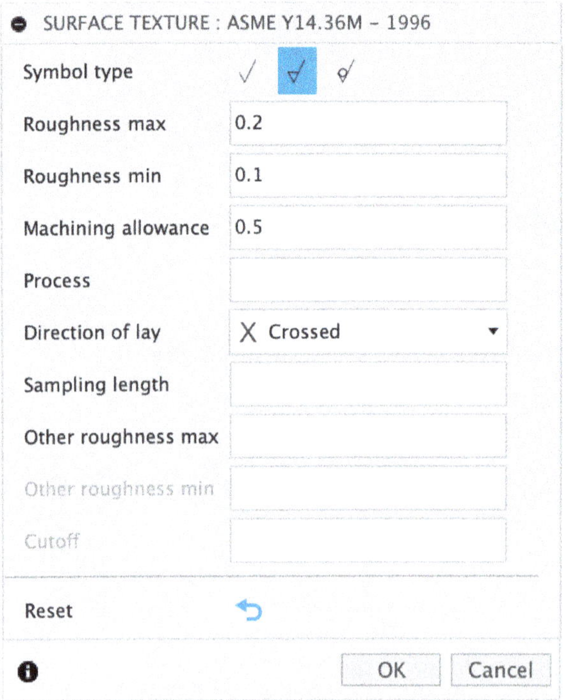

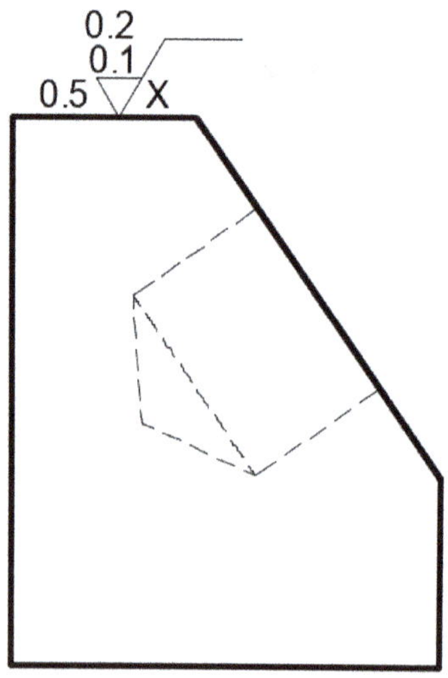

Likewise, specify the **Sampling length**, **Other roughness max**, and **Other roughness min** values. You can also specify the **Cutoff** value, if required. It is sampling length used while measuring the surface roughness. Next, click **OK** on the **Surface Texture** dialog.

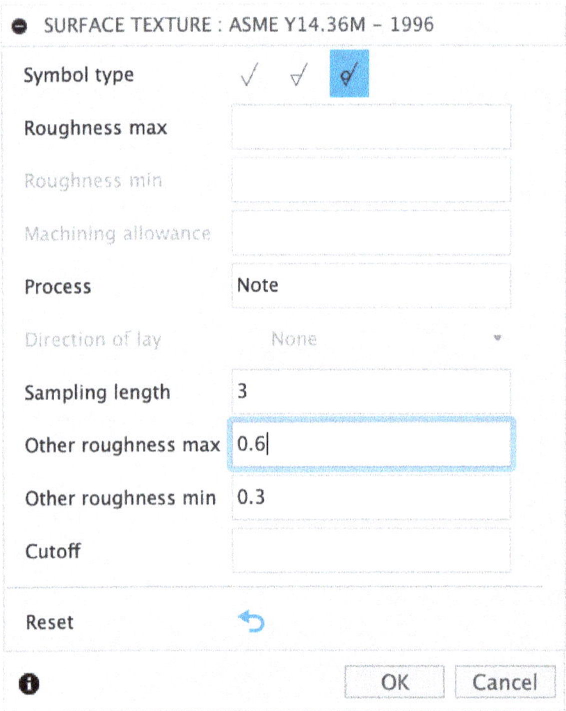

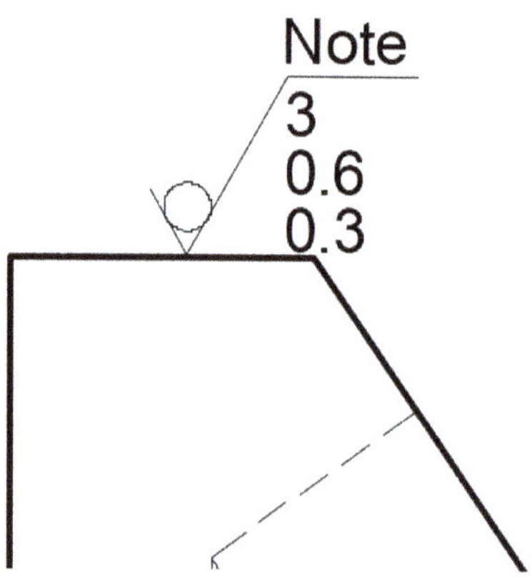

Examples

Example 1

In this example, you will create the 2D drawing of the part shown below.

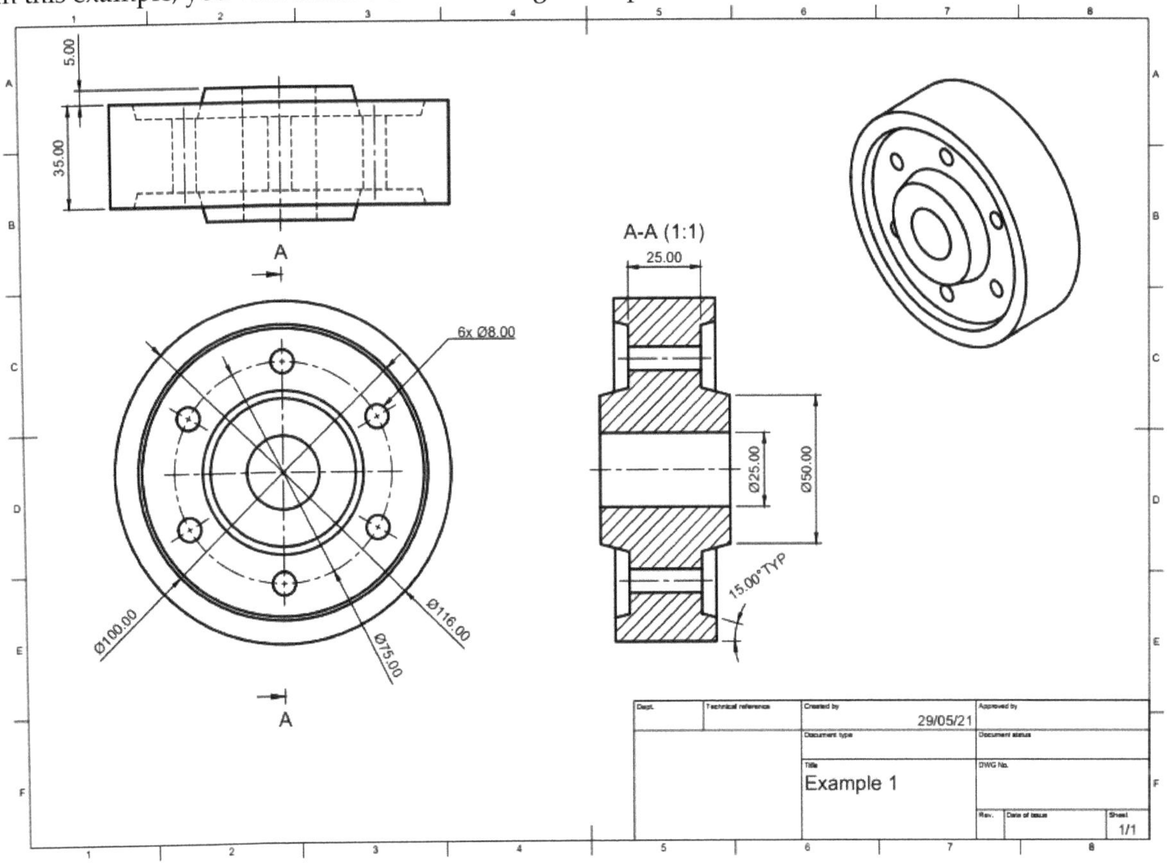

Starting a New Drawing File

1. To open the design file, browse to the location of Exercise 1 of Chapter 5 and double-click on the design file. (You can get the design file by sending us an email to online.books999@gmail.com).
2. On the toolbar, click **Model > Drawing > From Design**. The **Create Drawing** dialog pops up on the screen.
3. On the **Create Drawing** dialog, select **Drawing > Create New** and **Template > From Scratch**.
4. Select **Standard > ISO** and **Units > mm**. Next, set the **Sheet Size** to **A3**.
5. Select **Orientation > Landscape**. Click **OK** to start a new drawing file.

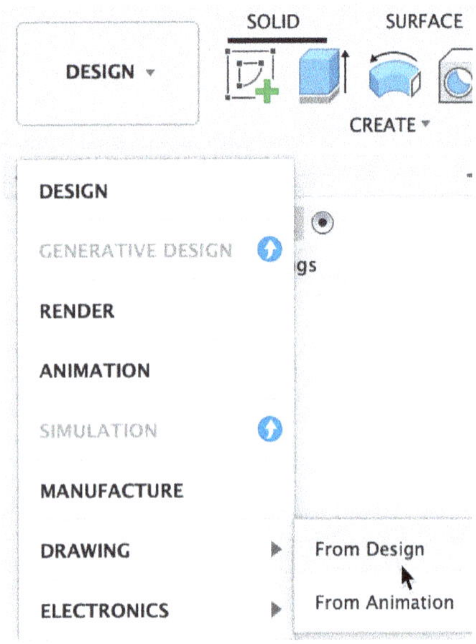

6. On the **Drawing View** dialog, select **Front** from the **Orientation** drop-down.
7. Set the **Style** to **Visible and Hidden Edges** and **Scale** to **1:1**.
8. Make sure that you select all the options in the **Automated Center Marks and Center Lines** section.
9. Move the pointer to the left portion of the sheet and click to place the base view.

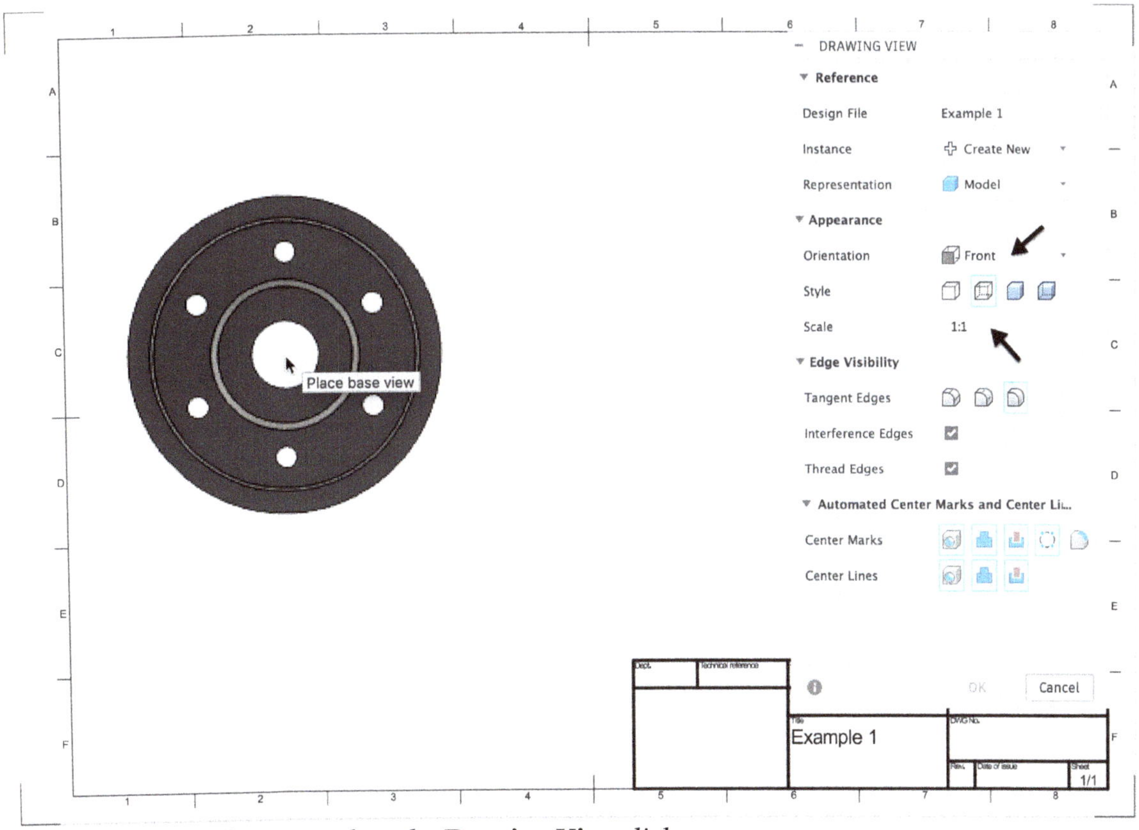

10. Click the **OK** button to close the **Drawing View** dialog.

11. On the toolbar, click **Drawing > Create > Projected View** and select the base view.

12. Move the pointer upward and click to place the projected view. Click the **Create and Continue** icon.

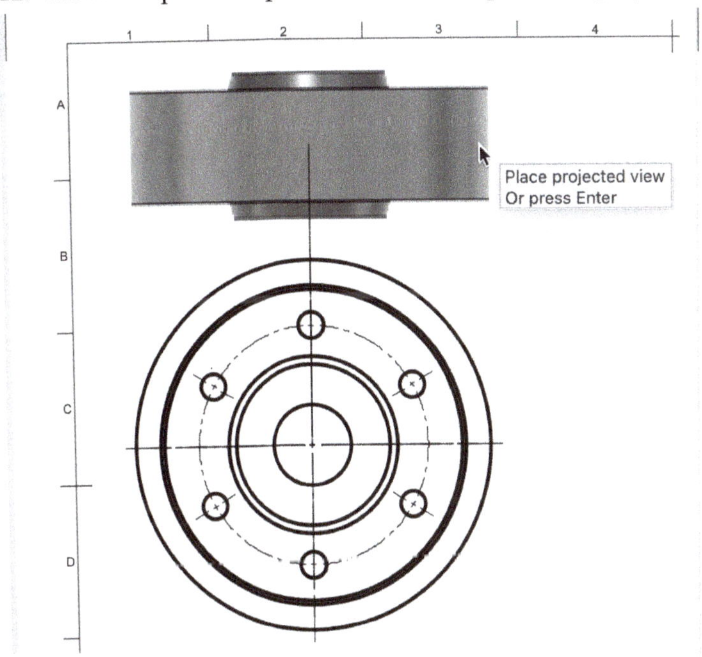

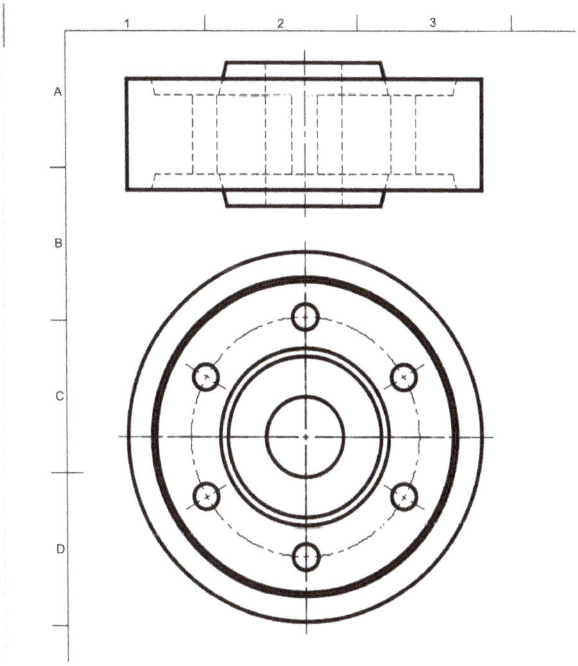

13. On the toolbar, click **Drawing > Create > Base View**.

14. On the **Drawing View** dialog, click **Appearance > Orientation > NE Isometric**.

15. Select **Style > Visible Edges** and select **Scale > 1:1**.
16. Move the pointer to the top right corner and click to position the isometric view.

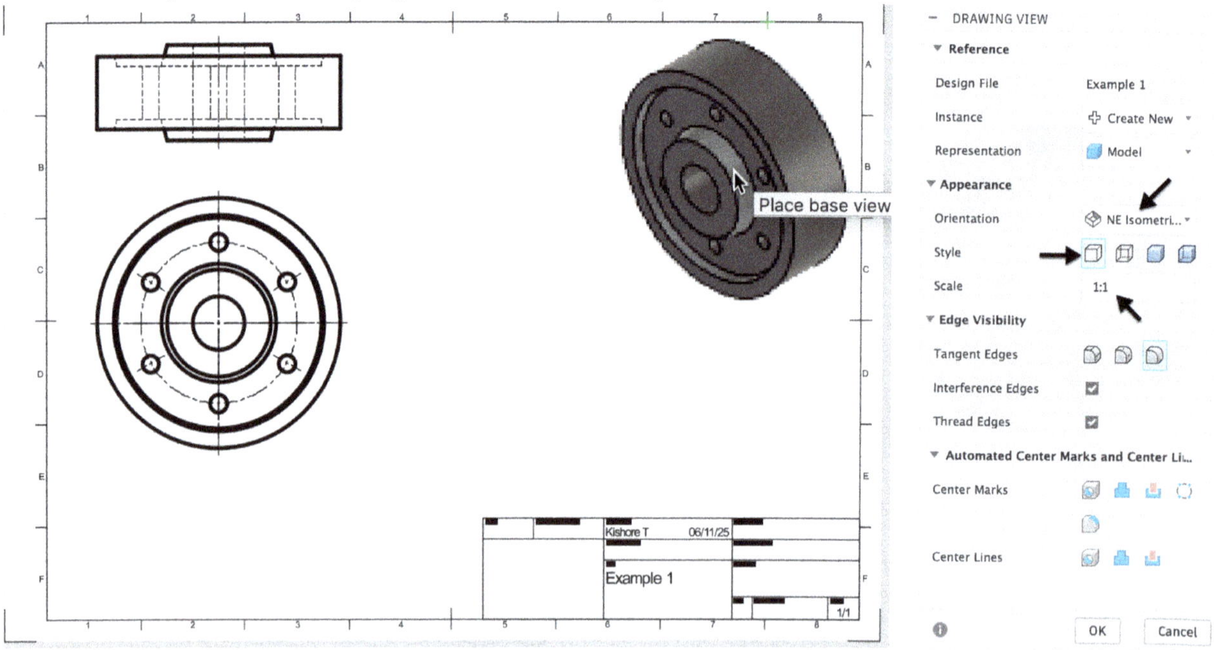

17. Click **OK** to close the **Drawing View** dialog.
18. Select the isometric view, right-click, and then select **Edit View**. On the **Drawing View** dialog, type-in **3:4** in the **Scale** box and press Enter. Next, click **Close** on the dialog.

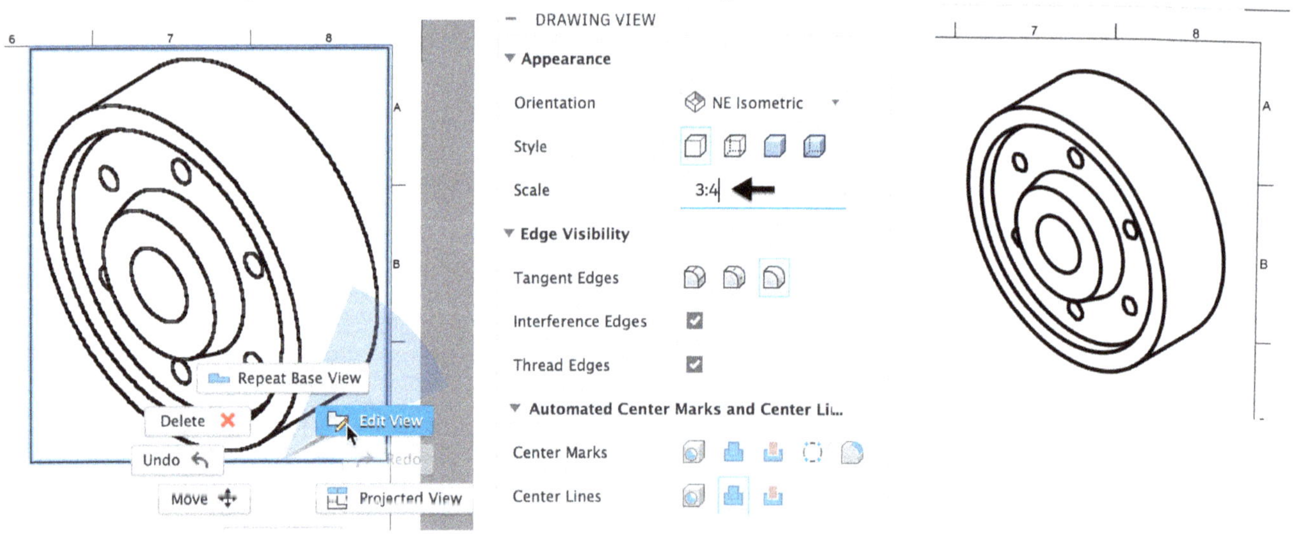

19. Activate the **Section View** command (click **Drawing > Create > Section View** on the toolbar) and select the front view.
20. Place the pointer on the center of view, and then move it vertically upward; a trace line appears between the cursor and the centerpoint.
21. Click to specify the start point of the cutting plane. Next, move the pointer vertically downward and click.
22. Right click and select **Continue**.

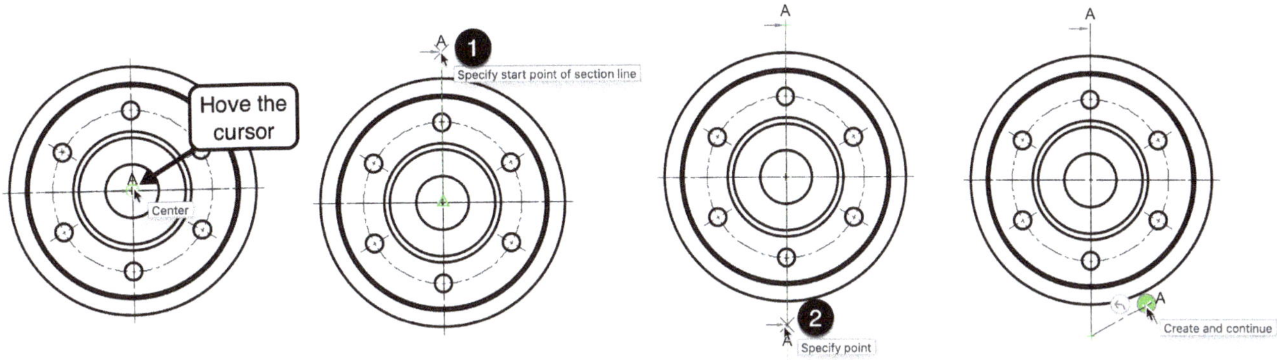

23. On the **Section View** dialog, click the **Style > Visible Edges** icon under the **Appearance** section.

24. Select the **Hole**  an **Round Cuts**  icons in **Center Marks** sub-section under the **Automated Center Marks and Center Lines** section. Deselect all the other options in this section.

25. Move the mouse pointer toward the right and click to position the view. Click **OK**.

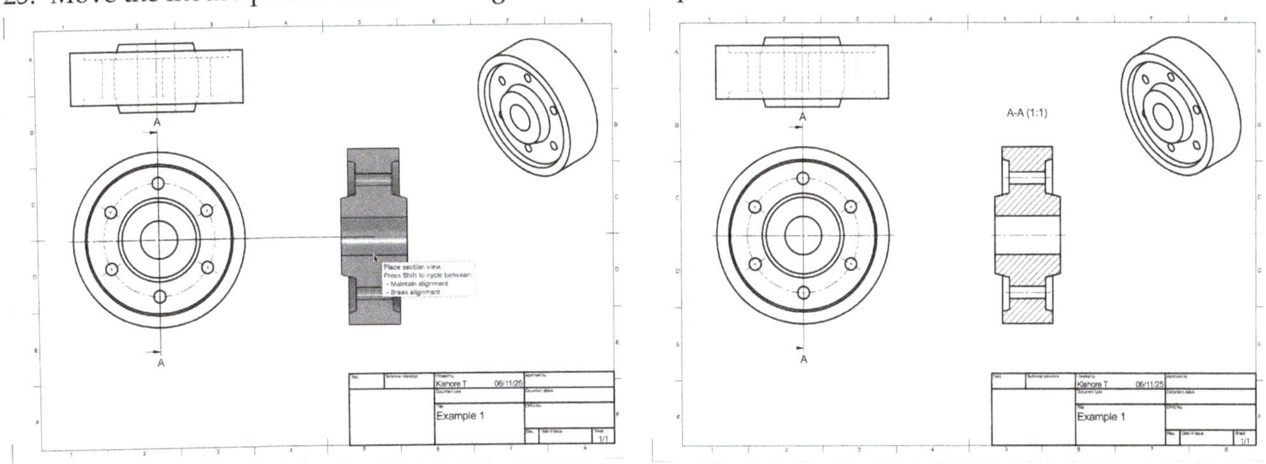

26. Activate the **Centerline** command (click **Geometry > Centerline**  on the toolbar). Click on the hidden hole edges of the top view.

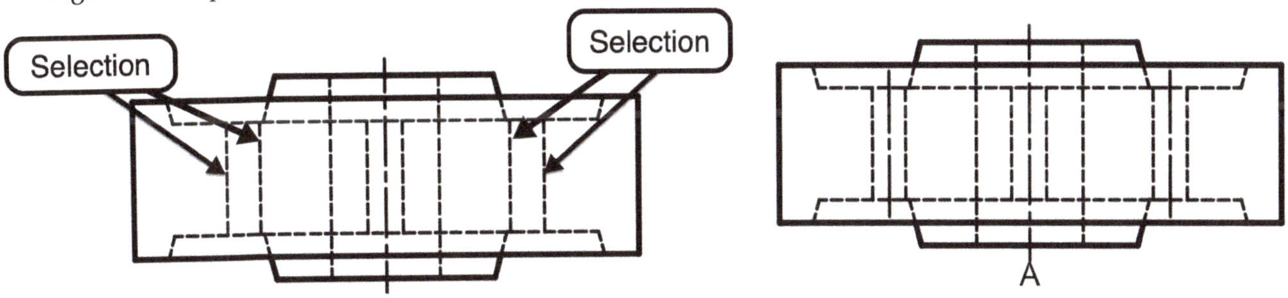

27. Activate the **Dimension** command (click **Dimensions > Dimension** 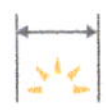 on the toolbar) and select the left vertical edge of the top view, as shown. Next, move the pointer toward the left and click to position the dimension.

28. Select the endpoints of the top view, as shown. Next, move the pointer toward the left and click to place the dimension.

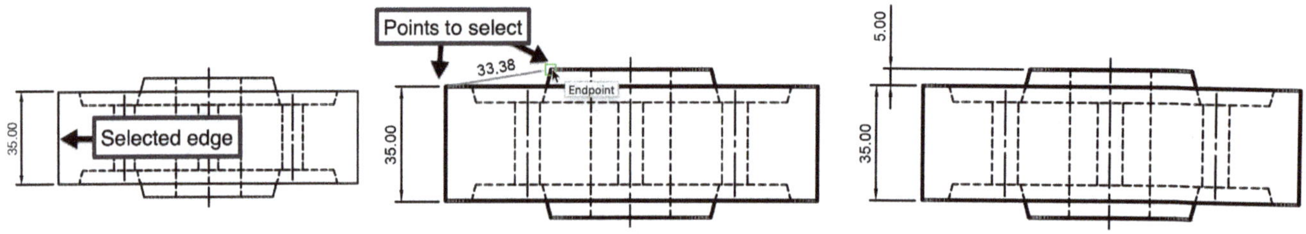

29. Click **Dimensions** drop-down > **Linear dimension** on the toolbar.
30. Select the endpoints of the two parallel edges of the section view, as shown. Next, move the pointer upward and click to position the dimension.

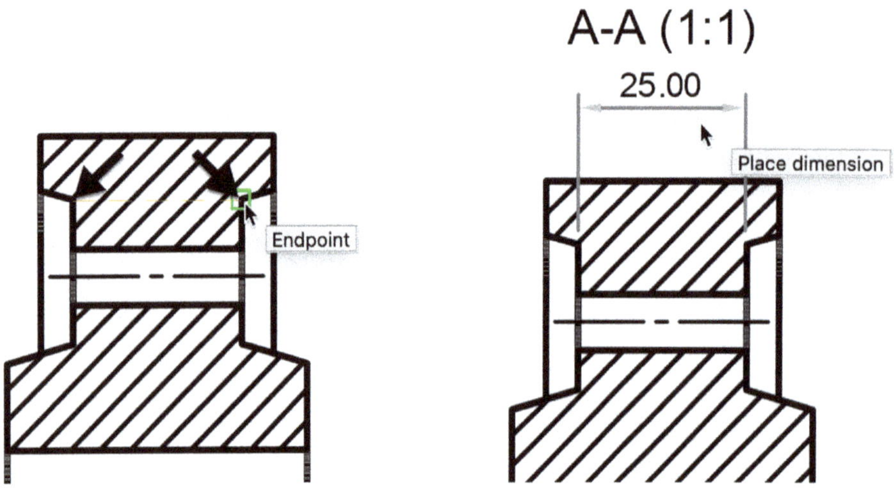

11. Click the **Dimension** command on the toolbar and select the two horizontal edges of the section view, as shown.
12. Move the pointer toward the right and click to position the dimension. Next, press Esc to deactivate the **Dimension** command.
13. Double-click on the **Dimension** value. Next, click before the dimension value.
14. On the **Dimension** dialog, click the **Insert Symbol** drop-down and select the diameter symbol. Next, click **Close** on the **Dimension** dialog.

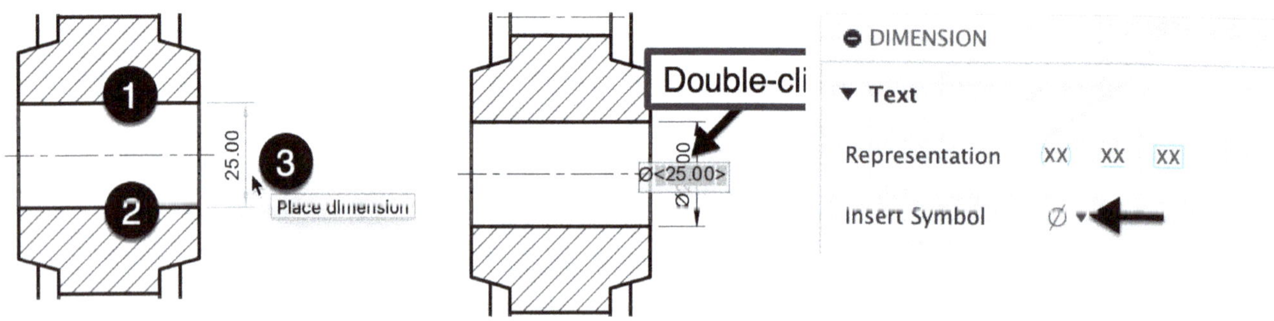

15. Likewise, add another dimension to the section view, as shown.

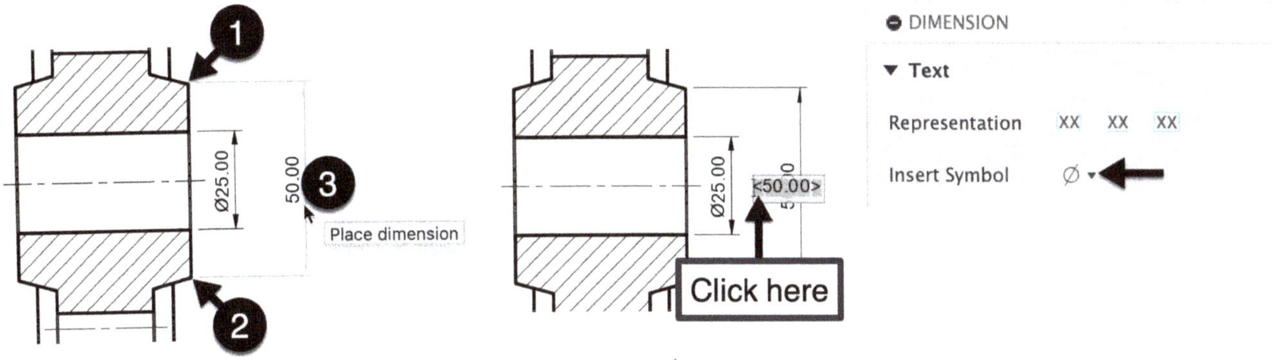

16. Click **Dimensions** drop-down > **Angular Dimension** on the toolbar. Next, select the two edges of the section view, as shown.
17. Move the pointer toward the right and click to position the angular dimension. Next, press Esc and double-click on the angular dimension.

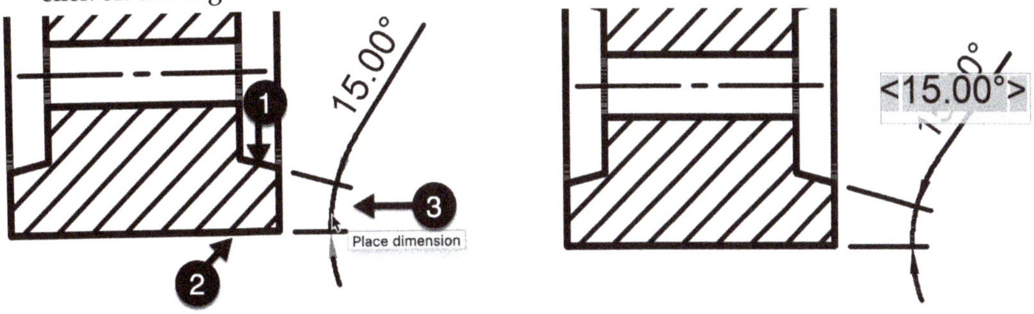

18. Type **TYP** and click **Close**.

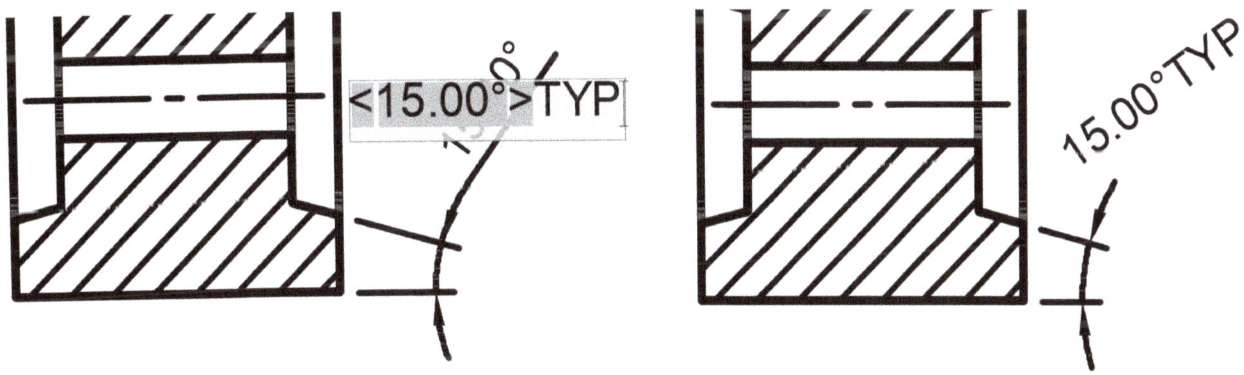

19. Click **Dimensions** drop-down > **Diameter dimension** on the toolbar. Next, select the outer circular edge of the front view, as shown.
20. Move the pointer and click to position the dimension at the location, as shown.
21. Likewise, create another diameter dimension, as shown.

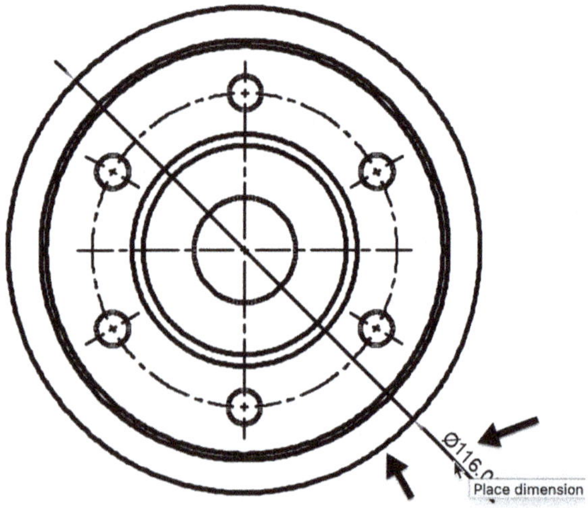

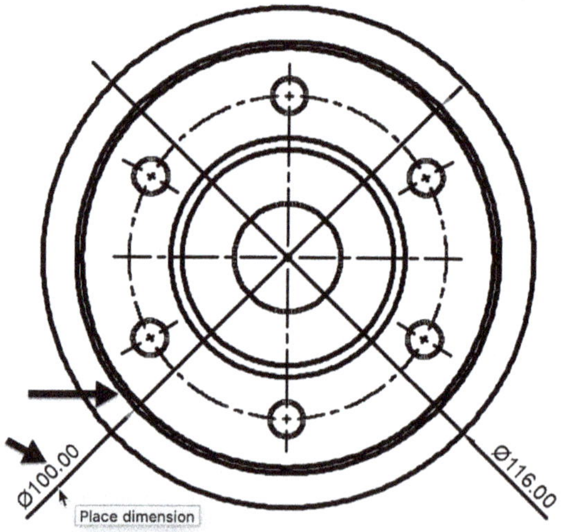

22. Activate the **Dimension** command (click the **Dimension** icon on the toolbar) and apply the diameter dimension to the centerline passing through the small holes, as shown.

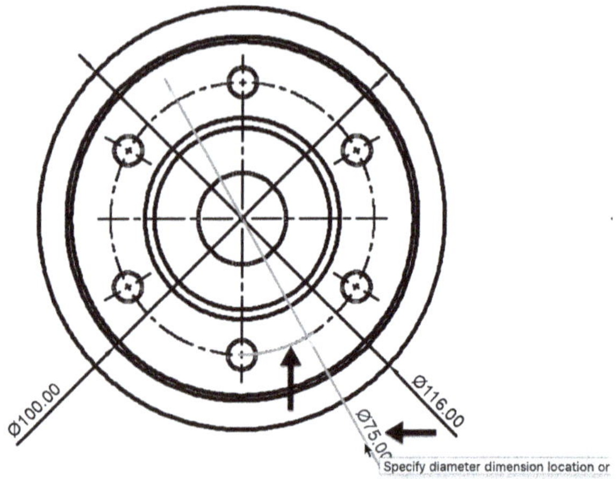

23. On the **Drawing** toolbar, click **Text > Note** . Next, select the small circle from the circular pattern.
24. Move the pointer diagonally and click to place the diameter dimension. Click **OK**.

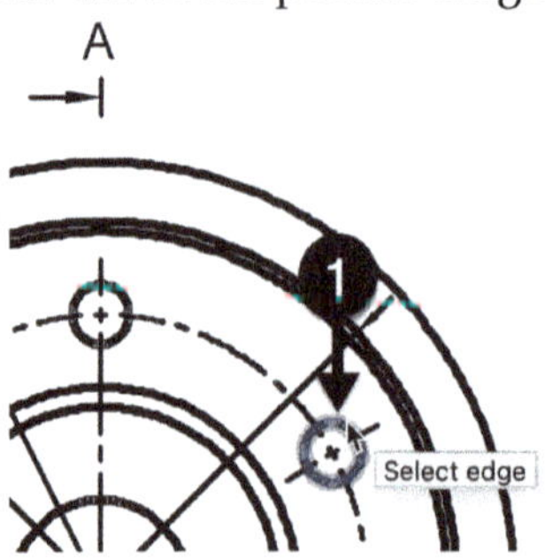

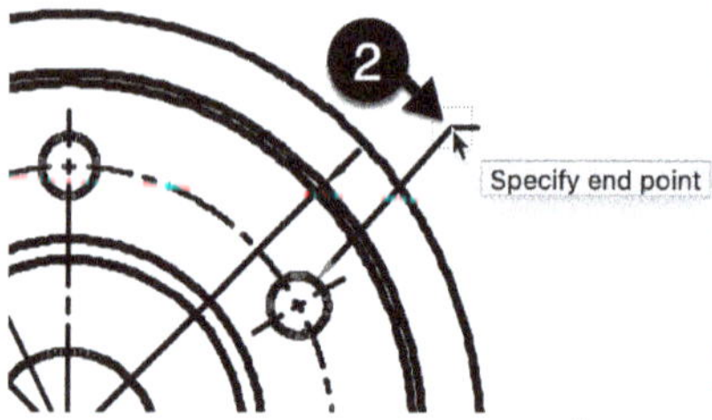

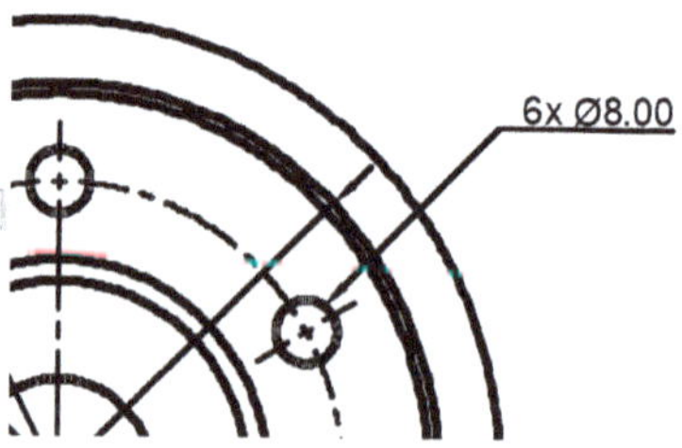

25. Click **Dimensions** drop-down > **Angular dimension** on the toolbar.
26. Select the centerlines of the two circles, as shown. Next, move the pointer outward and click to position the angular dimension.

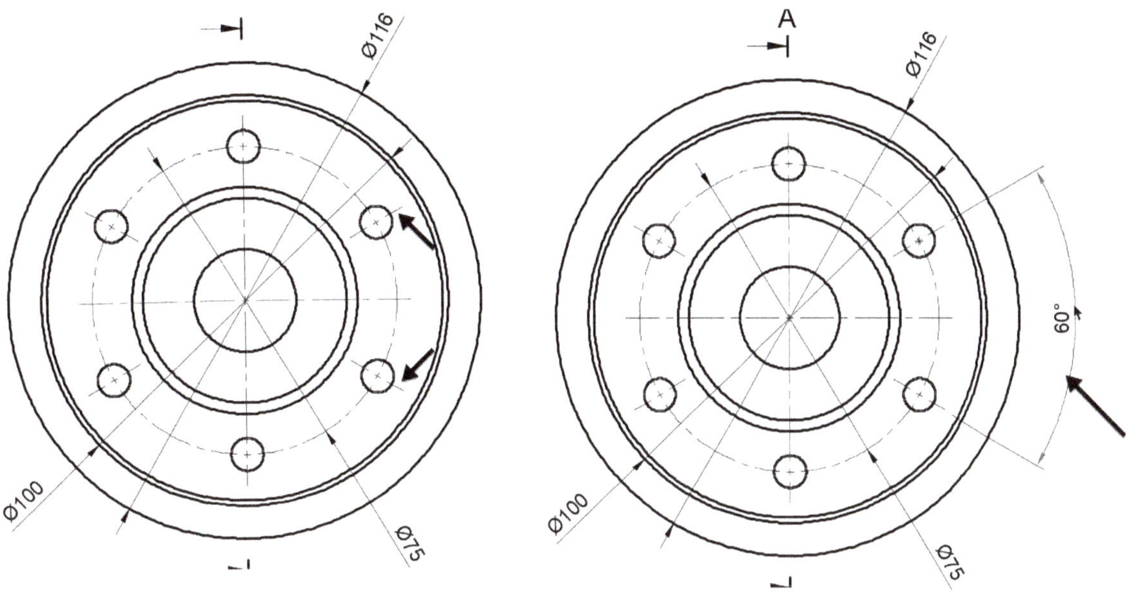

27. In the Browser, expand the **Document Settings** node and hove the pointer on the **Dimension Units: mm**. Next, click the **Change Dimension Units** icon.
28. On the **Document Settings** dialog, change the **Linear Precision** and **Angular Precision** values to **0**.
29. Click **OK** on the **Document Settings** dialog.

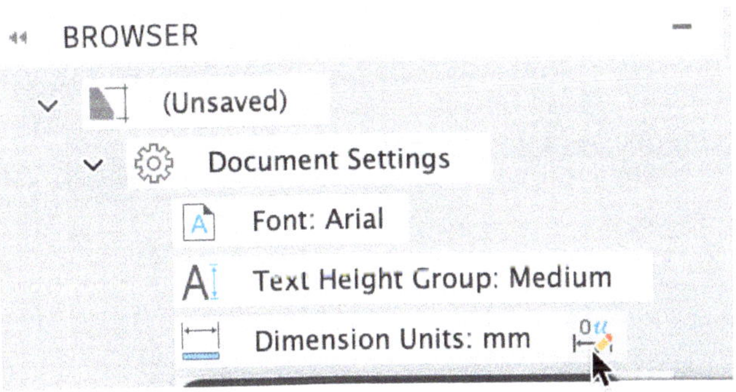

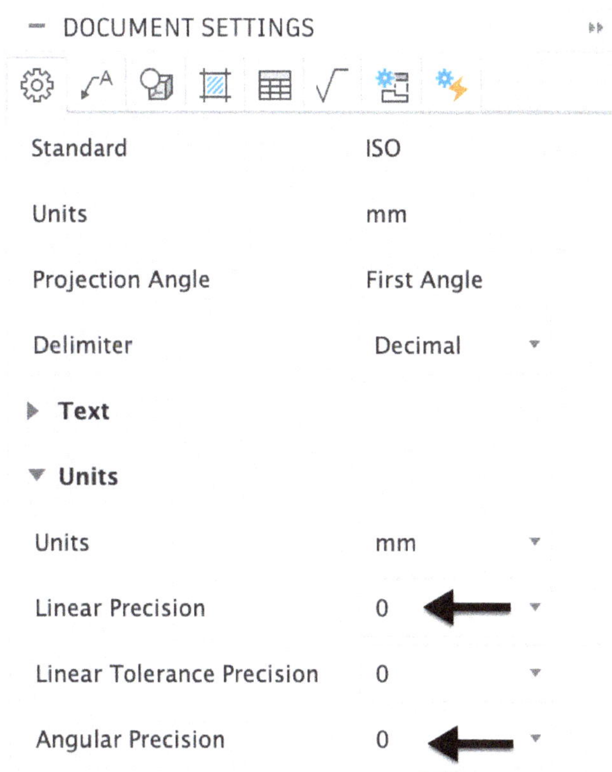

30. Click the **Save** icon located on the **Application Bar** and type Example 1 in the **Name** box. Next, click **Save**.
31. Save and close the drawing.

Example 2

In this example, you will create an assembly drawing shown below.

Drawings

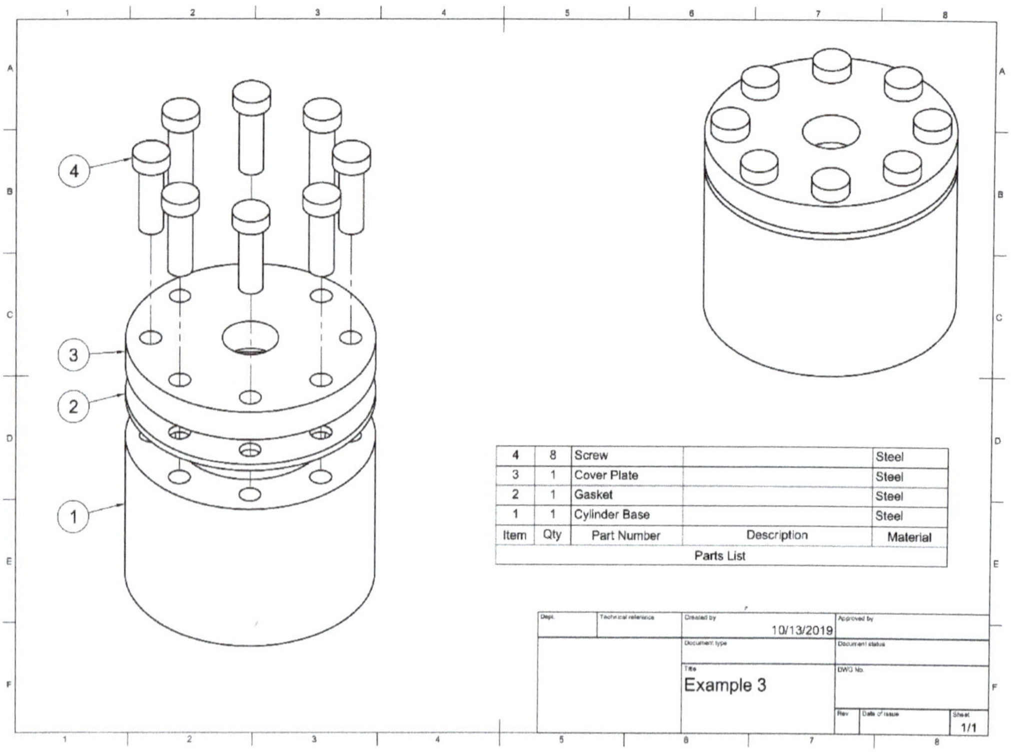

1. Start **Autodesk Fusion 360.**
2. Click the **Show Data Panel** icon located at the top left corner. Next, browse to the Chapter 10 folder and double click on the *Pressure Cylinder* design file. (You can get the design file by sending us an email to online.books999@gmail.com).
3. On the toolbar, click **Workspace** drop-down > **Drawing > From Design**. The **Create Drawing** dialog pops up on the screen.
4. On the **Create Drawing** dialog, check the **Full Assembly** option and select **Drawing > Create New.**

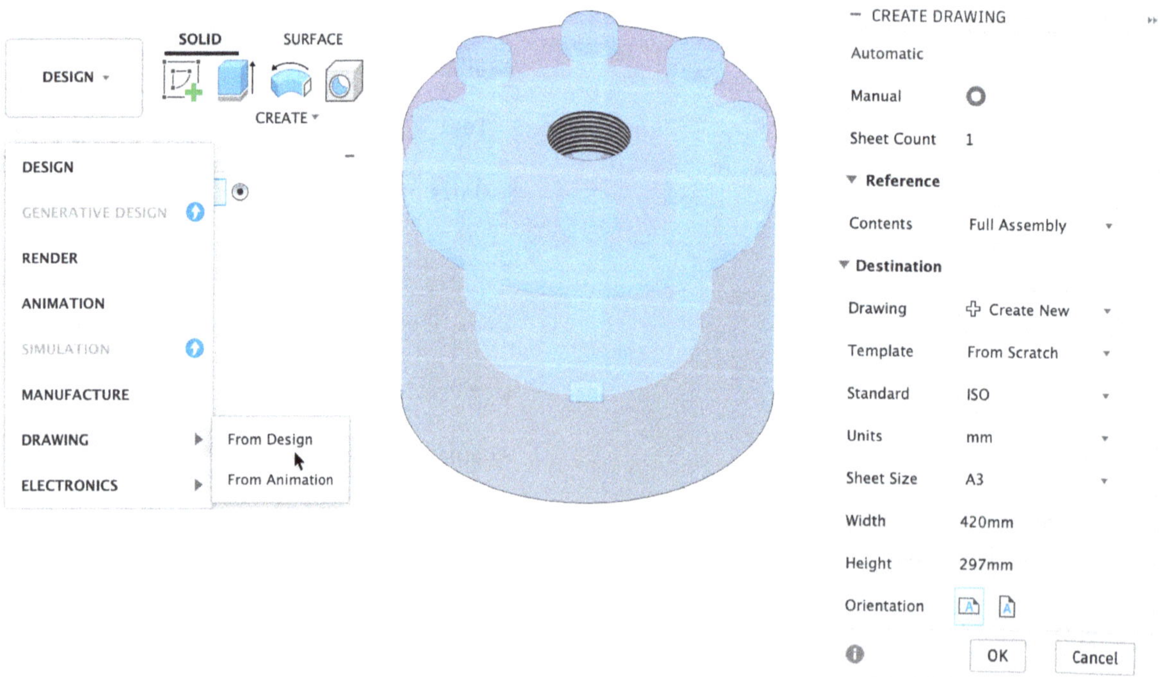

5. Leave the other default options and click **OK** to start a new drawing file.

6. On the **Drawing View** dialog, select **Home** from the **Orientation** drop-down.
7. Type **1:1** in the **Scale** box. Next, place the drawing view at the top right corner of the drawing sheet. Click **OK** to create the Isometric view.

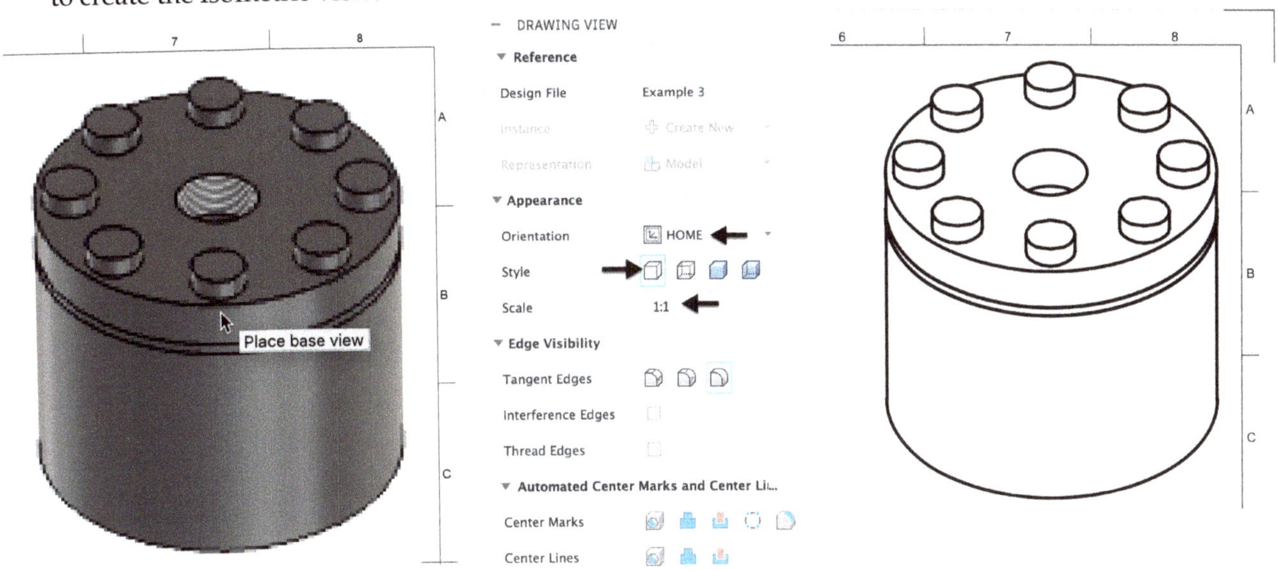

8. Activate the **Base View** command. On the **Drawing View** dialog, select **Representation > Storyboard1**.
9. On the **Drawing View** dialog, set the **Scale** value to 1:1. Position the exploded view at the location, as shown. Next, click **OK**.

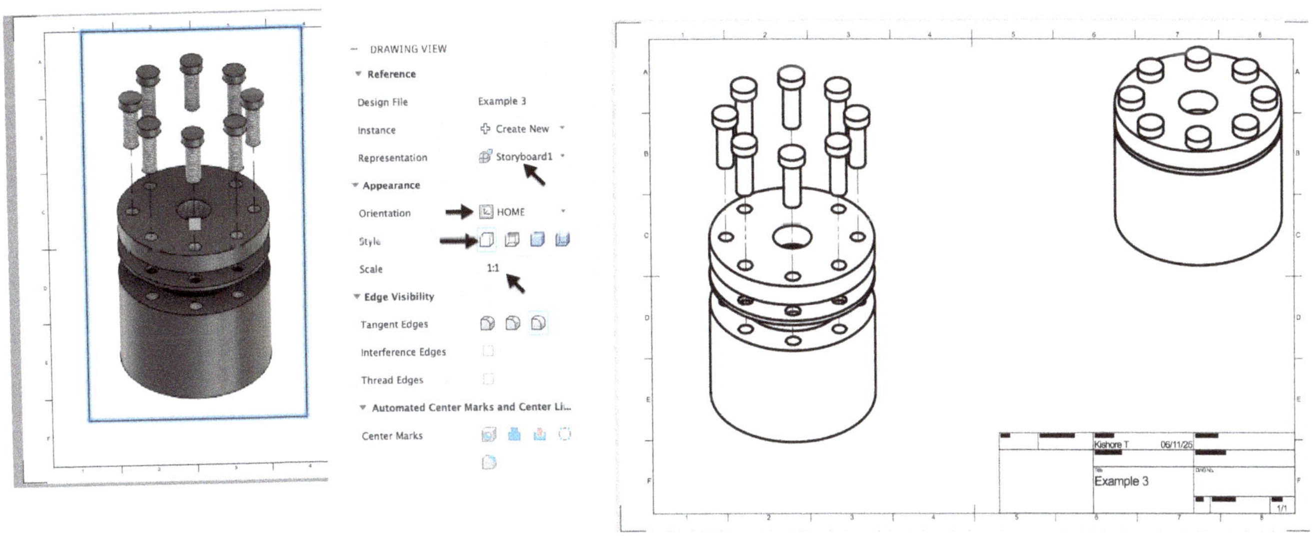

10. On the toolbar, click **Tables > Table**.
11. Select the exploded view and place the table list above the title block.

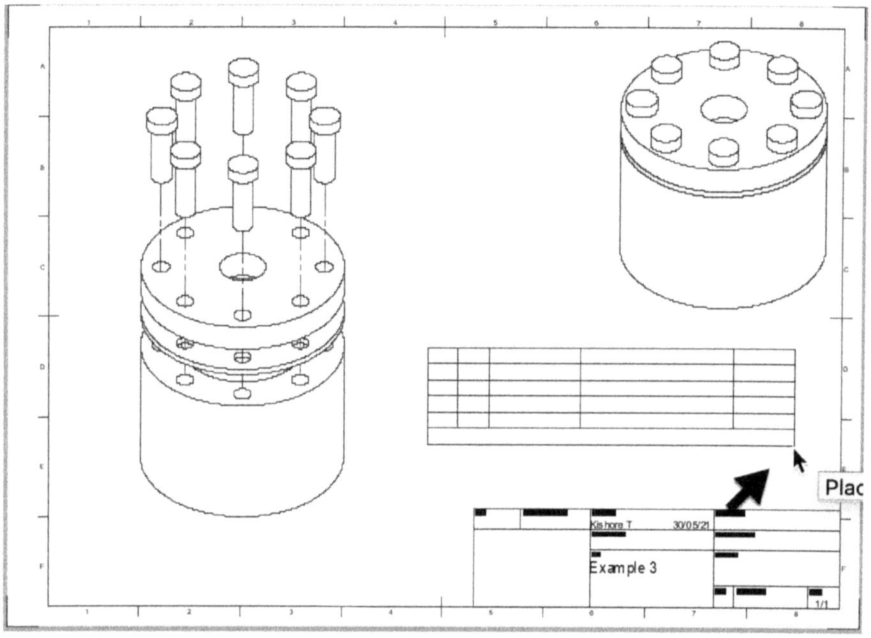

The balloons will be placed automatically.

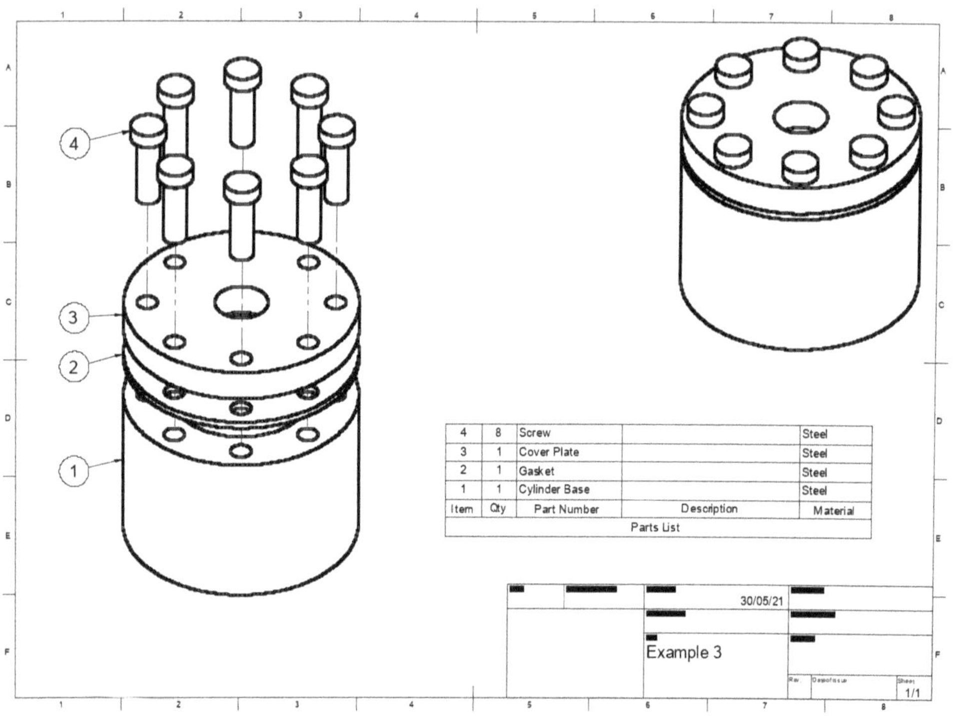

12. Save and close the drawing.

Questions

1. How to create drawing views using the **Base View** command?
2. How to change the View style of a drawing view?
3. How to update the drawing views when the part is edited?
4. List the commands used to create centerlines and center marks.
5. How to add symbols and texts to a dimension?

6. How to create aligned section views?
7. How to create an exploded view of an assembly?

Exercises

Exercise 1

Create orthographic views of the part model shown below. Add dimensions and annotations to the drawing.

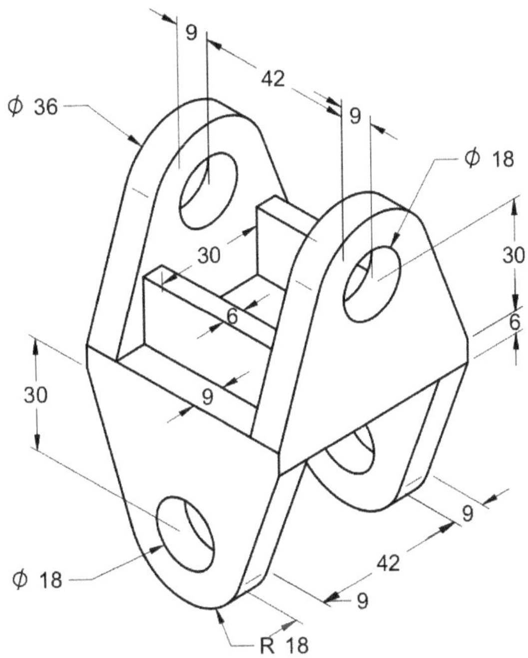

Exercise 2

Create orthographic views of the part model shown below. Add dimensions and annotations to the drawing.

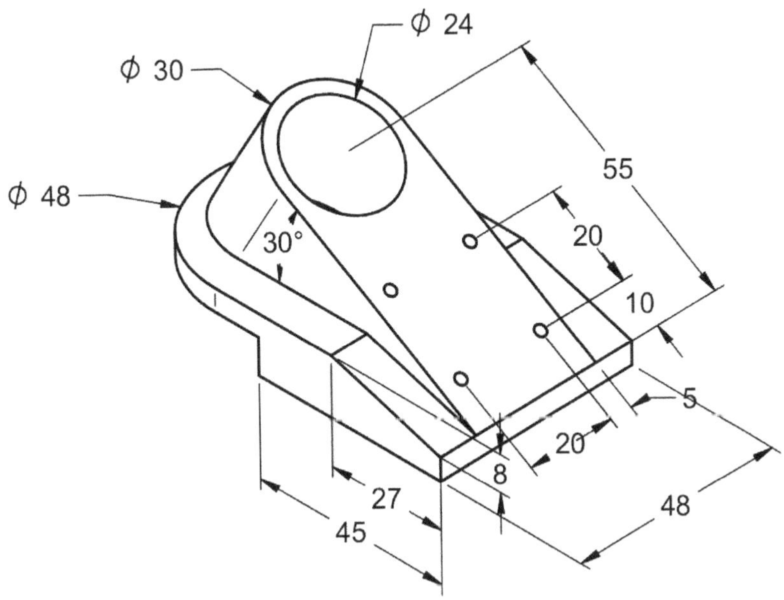

Index

www.ingramcontent.com/pod-product-compliance
Lightning Source LLC
Chambersburg PA
CBHW061152240926
51846CB00006B/988
9788199428959